Instructors:
Your time is valuable.
We're here for you!

SAGE
Premium Video

SAGE Publishing:
Our Story

Founded in 1965 by 24-year-old entrepreneur Sara Miller McCune, SAGE continues its legacy of making research accessible and fostering **CREATIVITY** and **INNOVATION**. We believe in creating fresh, cutting-edge content to help you prepare your students to thrive in the modern world and be **TOMORROW'S LEADING SOCIOLOGISTS**.

- By partnering with **TOP SOCIOLOGY AUTHORS** with just the right balance of research, teaching, and industry experience, we bring you the most current and applied content.

- As a **STUDENT-FRIENDLY PUBLISHER**, we keep our prices affordable and provide multiple formats of our textbooks so your students can choose the option that works best for them.

- Being permanently **INDEPENDENT** means we are fiercely committed to publishing the highest-quality resources for you and your students.

Sara Miller McCune founded SAGE Publishing in 1965 to support the dissemination of usable knowledge and educate a global community. SAGE publishes more than 1000 journals and over 800 new books each year, spanning a wide range of subject areas. Our growing selection of library products includes archives, data, case studies and video. SAGE remains majority owned by our founder and after her lifetime will become owned by a charitable trust that secures the company's continued independence.

Los Angeles | London | New Delhi | Singapore | Washington DC | Melbourne

Discover Sociology

Fourth Edition

The fourth edition of *Discover Sociology* is dedicated to the brave and relentless activists in this country and around the globe who speak out for truth, decency, and democracy. I am genuinely inspired by the many young people who are raising their voices to try to make our world kinder, greener, safer, and more equitable. As Nelson Mandela said, "A good head and good heart are always a formidable combination. But when you add to that a literate tongue or pen, then you have something very special."

—DSE

Discover Sociology

Fourth Edition

William J. Chambliss

Daina S. Eglitis
George Washington University

Los Angeles | London | New Delhi
Singapore | Washington DC | Melbourne

FOR INFORMATION:

SAGE Publications, Inc.
2455 Teller Road
Thousand Oaks, California 91320
E-mail: order@sagepub.com

SAGE Publications Ltd.
1 Oliver's Yard
55 City Road
London, EC1Y 1SP
United Kingdom

SAGE Publications India Pvt. Ltd.
B 1/I 1 Mohan Cooperative Industrial Area
Mathura Road, New Delhi 110 044
India

SAGE Publications Asia-Pacific Pte. Ltd.
18 Cross Street #10-10/11/12
China Square Central
Singapore 048423

Printed in Canada

Library of Congress Cataloging-in-Publication Data

Names: Chambliss, William J., author. | Eglitis, Daina Stukuls, author.

Title: Discover sociology / William J. Chambliss, Daina S. Eglitis, George Washington University.

Description: Fourth Edition. | Thousand Oaks : SAGE Publications, [2020] | Revised edition of the authors' Discover sociology, [2018] | Includes bibliographical references and index.

Identifiers: LCCN 2018042833 | ISBN 9781544333434 (pbk. : alk. paper)

Subjects: LCSH: Sociology.

Classification: LCC HM585 .C4473 2020 | DDC 301—dc23 LC record available at https://lccn.loc.gov/2018042833

Acquisitions Editor: Jeff Lasser
Content Development Editor: Liza Neustaetter
Editorial Assistant: Tiara Beatty
Production Editor: Andrew Olson
Copy Editor: Erin Livingston
Typesetter: Hurix Digital
Proofreader: Laura Webb
Indexer: Amy Murphy
Cover Designer: Scott Van Atta
Marketing Manager: Kara Kindstrom

This book is printed on acid-free paper.

18 19 20 21 22 10 9 8 7 6 5 4 3 2 1

About the Authors

William J. Chambliss (PhD, Indiana University) was a professor of sociology at The George Washington University from 1986 to 2014. During his long and distinguished career, he wrote and edited close to two dozen books and produced numerous articles for professional journals in sociology, criminology, and law. The integration of the study of crime with the creation and implementation of criminal law was a central theme in his writings and research. His articles on the historical development of vagrancy laws, the legal process as it affects different social classes and racial groups, and his efforts to introduce the study of state-organized crimes into the mainstream of social science research are among the most recognized achievements of his career. Dr. Chambliss was the recipient of numerous awards and honors, including a doctorate of laws *honoris causa*, University of Guelph, Guelph, Ontario, Canada, 1999; the 2009 Lifetime Achievement Award, Sociology of Law, American Sociological Association; the 2009 Lifetime Achievement Award, Law and Society, Society for the Study of Social Problems; the 2001 Edwin H. Sutherland Award, American Society of Criminology; the 1995 Major Achievement Award, American Society of Criminology; the 1986 Distinguished Leadership in Criminal Justice, Bruce Smith Sr. Award, Academy of Criminal Justice Sciences; and the 1985 Lifetime Achievement Award, Criminology, American Sociological Association. Professor Chambliss also served as president of the American Society of Criminology and the Society for the Study of Social Problems.

Daina S. Eglitis (PhD, University of Michigan–Ann Arbor) is an associate professor of sociology and international affairs and the director of undergraduate studies in the department of sociology at The George Washington University (GWU). Her scholarly interests include class and social stratification, historical sociology, contemporary theory, gender, and culture. She is the author of *Imagining the Nation: History, Modernity, and Revolution in Latvia* (Penn State Press, 2002), as well as numerous articles on social life and social change in postcommunist Latvia. She has held two Fulbright awards in Latvia and is a past recipient of research fellowships and awards from the U.S. Holocaust Memorial Museum, the American Council of Learned Societies, the National Council for Eurasian and East European Research, the International Research and Exchanges Board, and the Woodrow Wilson International Center for Scholars. Dr. Eglitis is the author of "The Uses of Global Poverty: How Economic Inequality Benefits the West," an article widely used by undergraduate students. At GWU, she teaches courses in contemporary sociological theory, class and inequality, and introduction to sociology, among others. She presents and writes on the topic of teaching and learning and is the author of the *Teaching Sociology* articles "Performing Theory: Dramatic Learning in the Theory Classroom" (2010) and "Social Issues and Problem-Based Learning in Sociology: Opportunities and Challenges in the Undergraduate Classroom" (2016). Outside the classroom, Dr. Eglitis is an avid reader of fiction (recent discoveries include *Annihilation*, *Exit West*, and *News of the World*) and loves to travel to new places (especially if they include an opportunity to paddleboard).

Brief Contents

Detailed Contents

©Seksan
Srikasemsuntorn/
Moment/Getty Images

©iStockphoto.com/
choness

©In Pictures Ltd./Corbis
via Getty Images

©Klaus Vedfelt/ DigitalVision/Getty Images

©AP Photo/Emilio Morenatti

Chapter 6 • Deviance and Social Control 139

©Peter Titmuss/Alamy
Stock Photo

Chapter 7 • Social Class and Inequality in the United States   169

©iStockphoto.com/
peeterv

Chapter 8 • Global Wealth, Poverty, and Inequality   197

©Bartosz Hadyniak/E+/
Getty Images

©John Moore/Getty
Images

Chapter 9 • Race and Ethnicity 223

Chapter 10 • Gender and Society 257

©ozgurdonmaz/E+/
Getty Images

Chapter 11 • Families and Society 293

©SAID KHATIB/AFP/
Getty Images

Chapter 12 • Education and Society — 325

©iStockphoto.com/
PeopleImages

©Chris Martin/Alamy
Stock Photo

©REUTERS/Omar
Sanadiki

Chapter 15 • Work, Consumption, and the Economy   417

©Artyom Geodakyan\
TASS via Getty Images

Chapter 16 • Health and Medicine 449

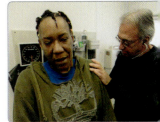

©Andy Cross/The Denver Post via Getty Images

©CHANDAN KHANNA/
AFP/Getty Images

©Mostafa Bassim/
Anadolu Agency/
Getty Images

Preface

The German physicist Albert Einstein wrote that "the important thing is not to stop questioning. Curiosity has its own reason for existing." Indeed, *curiosity* is the bedrock of all scientific inquiry because curiosity underlies the motivation and passion to seek answers to challenging questions. But curiosity is not enough. To be a component of good sociology, curiosity must be disciplined: Answers must be sought within the scientific tradition of gathering data through systematic observations and then shared with careful empirical and theoretical explanation of the findings. In this text, our goal is to pique students' curiosity about the social world—and then give them the academic tools to study that world, analyze it, and maybe even change it.

There are many introductory sociology textbooks, some of which are very good. We believe that our contribution to the marketplace of sociological texts and ideas is a book that engages the sociology student's curious mind—and then offers him or her the theoretical, conceptual, and empirical tools to analyze and understand the issues that affect our world, both local and global. We have written this book in a way that we hope will encourage students to keep reading, not only because of assigned pages but also because, with the encouragement of the instructor and the text, they have a desire to know more! We also endeavor to show the discipline of sociology as a source of critical skills valued in the job market and in graduate and professional education. We are delighted that previous editions of *Discover Sociology* have been well received, and it is our goal in the fourth edition to keep the best of those editions while integrating new ideas and research, as well as contemporary societal events and issues, to keep the book fresh and interesting. Below, we review some of the key features in this new edition.

Chapter Openers That Speak to Students

In this book, you will find chapters that begin with openers drawn from contemporary issues and events and that endeavor to speak to readers and to the kinds of experiences or concerns they have as students, as well as in other roles in the family or at work. The beginning of each chapter also features "What do you think?" questions intended to engage students' curiosity and give a preview of interesting issues that will be covered in the chapter.

Sociology Is a Scientific Discipline

Every chapter in the book integrates empirical research from sociology, highlighting the point that sociology is about the *scientific understanding* of the social world—rigorous research can illuminate the sociological roots of diverse phenomena and institutions, ranging from poverty and deviance to capitalism and the nuclear family. Research may also result in conflicting or ambiguous conclusions. Students learn that social life is complex and that sociological research is an ongoing effort to explain why things are as they are—and how they might change.

Key Themes and Boxed Features

Each chapter has a mix of boxed features that highlight key themes in this book.

- The sociological imagination, of course, is a foundational concept in the discipline. It is important throughout the book, and we also feature *Private Lives, Public Issues* boxes that illustrate the relationship between our individual lives and the social forces that shape them.

- Second, power is a key theme in sociology—and in this text. Sociologists want to know how power is distributed, how it is reproduced, and how it is exercised in social relationships and institutions. The unequal distribution of power is one important topic of sociological inquiry, and this text offers *Inequality Matters* boxes that probe manifestations of and explanations for power and resource disparities.

- Third, we emphasize the importance of being a critical consumer of information. We are surrounded by sources of data that stream into our lives from the Internet, newspapers, peers and colleagues, friends and family, and academic studies. Sociology asks us to look carefully at information and to understand its sources and assumptions in order to ascertain what it illuminates and what it obscures. To this end, we include *Behind the Numbers* boxes to give students the opportunity to look critically and carefully at statistical information on social problems such as unemployment and poverty, among others.

- Fourth, contemporary life, from politics to popular culture to personal interactions, is increasingly structured and influenced by social media. Social science is only beginning to grasp the significance of these dramatic developments. The book's *Social Life, Social Media* boxes endeavor to provide a sociological perspective on social media's functions, contributions, and consequences.

- Finally, the book highlights globalization and global perspectives in an effort to help students develop a fuller understanding of the place of their lives, their communities, and their country in an interconnected, interdependent, and multicultural international environment—and to enable them to see how other countries around the world are experiencing societal changes and challenges. The book's *Global Issues* boxes are part of this effort.

All of the boxed features include questions for students to help them reflect on the material and link it back to the chapter's larger themes.

New in This Edition

An important goal of the fourth edition of *Discover Sociology* is to retain the most effective features of prior editions while responding to the ideas and requests of reviewers and faculty for new or expanded coverage of issues such as intersectionality, student activism, and labor market changes that will affect today's college students. This edition features updated social indicators, bringing in the latest data available from the U.S. Census Bureau, the Bureau of Labor Statistics, the Centers for Disease Control and Prevention, and the Pew Research Center, among others, as well as many new openers and essay boxes that show the sociological significance of interesting contemporary issues and controversies.

A New Feature: Discover Intersections

We are excited to introduce a new feature in the fourth edition of the book: *Discover Intersections*. In recent decades, sociologists have increasingly sought to identify ways in which achieved and ascribed characteristics such as gender, race, ethnicity, class, religion, sexual orientation, and others intersect with one another in social practices and institutions and, significantly, how these intersections affect access to, for instance, education, occupational status, and political voice. Put another way,

> When it comes to social inequality, people's lives and the organization of power in a given society are better understood as being shaped not by a single axis of social division, be it race or gender or class, but by many axes that work together and influence each other. (Hill Collins & Bilge, 2016, p. 2)

Each chapter in the book offers students an opportunity to consider intersections between the key sociological topic covered in the chapter and issues covered in other parts of the book, drawing their attention to, for instance, relationships between school disciplinary measures (Chapter 6) and student race (Chapter 9); the nexus between race and ethnicity (Chapter 9) and the gender wage gap (Chapter 10); and the correlation between poverty (Chapter 7) and health challenges such as obesity (Chapter 14). The goal of this feature is to encourage broad, analytical thinking about complex issues of inequality by drawing attention to specific relationships between topics covered across the text. We hope that you will find this feature useful.

An Expanded *Discover & Debate* Feature

In the Core Concepts edition of *Discover Sociology*, we introduced a new feature, *Discover & Debate*. With this feature, we sought to go beyond discussion questions and pro/con approaches to contemporary issues and controversies, instead opting to provide an effective discussion model for instructors and students that takes the form of a debate. We believe that a basic understanding of debate and, in particular, the construction and evaluation of reasoned arguments, is vital to civic life, civil interaction, and even social change. In a society that often addresses vital issues in soundbites and tweets, it is particularly challenging but important to develop the skills and knowledge to evaluate positions on issues critically and to construct evidence-based arguments. Beginning with Chapter 2, every chapter includes a *Discover & Debate* essay that presents a motion for debate, basic background on the issue under discussion, and an introduction to arguments on both sides of the issue. It also includes questions to consider when evaluating each position and a debate tip to help students build their knowledge and skills in debating issues. This edition of *Discover Sociology* features some new topics of debate, including state-funded tuition-free higher education (Chapter 12), taxpayer funding of religious education (Chapter 13), the election of the U.S. president through a popular vote (Chapter 14), and the application of uniform environmental protection standards for developing and economically advanced countries (Chapter 17). We hope you will find this to be a valuable addition to the full-length edition of this text.

Updated Openers and Boxes

This edition features a significant number of new chapter openers and essay boxes that draw from events of contemporary interest and concern. In this edition, we feature new opening stories on a wide range of topics that include the problem of food insecurity on U.S. college campuses (Chapter 12), questions about humans' future emotional relationships with robot companions (Chapter 4), contemporary recognition and remembrance of lynching in the U.S. (Chapter 9), controversies in international athletics over who will (or won't) be categorized as a woman (Chapter 10), and the growth of Jediism as a new global religion (Chapter 13). New box essays include a sociological consideration of proxemics, the human use of physical space, and cultural differences in personal space (Chapter 4); the birth of the U.S. war on drugs (Chapter 6); the rise of the "three comma club" (the billionaire class) and how their wealth is counted or concealed (Chapter 8); and the persistent problem of racial discrimination in everyday life that has been documented in social media with the hashtag #livingwhileblack (Chapter 9).

Connecting Sociology and Career Success

As an instructor of introductory sociology, you are probably frequently asked by students, "What can I do with a sociology degree?" This is an important question for students (and, often, their parents) and instructors. This book offers instructors and students a unique feature that speaks directly and specifically to this question.

In the fourth edition of *Discover Sociology*, all of the chapters beginning with Chapter 2 feature an essay that accomplishes two major tasks. First, every essay highlights specific skills students learn as sociology majors and describes those skills in ways that provide students a vocabulary that they can use in the job market. Second, each essay profiles a graduate with a degree in sociology who is putting his or her skills to work in an interesting occupation or workplace. Graduates share in their own words what they learned from sociology and how it has contributed to their skills, knowledge, and career.

This feature helps students make a link between sociological skills and future careers in a wide array of occupational fields. It is important to note that this feature is not only for sociology majors! Sociology is often among the general education courses completed by students across a variety of disciplines, and it can help all students develop important skills—such as critical thinking, data literacy, and written communication—that they will need in the workplace. A *Washington Post* report on technology jobs, for instance, notes,

> As tech jobs evolve at the pace of light through fiber-optic cable, . . . leaders of tech firms such as Mozilla, Reddit and Tumblr say students should consider schools that not only will teach them traditional skills like coding, but also the softer skills that aren't listed in the course guide but are essential to the 21st-century workplace: working with others, problem-solving, the ability to pick up enough from disciplines other than their own to create products users believe are indispensable to their lives. (Lednicer, 2014)

Clearly, for students across disciplines, there is value in understanding and naming the skills that they gain when they study sociology. We encourage all students to take advantage of this valuable feature.

Photos and Graphics

The photographs in this edition have been carefully selected to help students put images together with ideas, events, and phenomena. A good photo can engage a student's curiosity and give him or her a visual vehicle for remembering the material under discussion. This has been our goal in choosing the photos included here. We have also carefully prepared visually appealing graphics, including tables, figures, and maps, to attract students' attention and enhance learning.

Glossaries for Learning

This book features marginal glossaries, offering students easy access to definitions of key concepts, phenomena, and institutions. Additionally, key terms are bolded in the text, and a comprehensive glossary is available at the end of the book.

Chapter Review

Every chapter ends with a summary of key learning points and a set of discussion questions to review what students have learned and to foster critical thinking about the materials.

Digital Resources

Discover Sociology includes a comprehensive ancillary package that utilizes new media and a wide range of instructional technologies designed to support instructor course preparation and student learning.

Student Study Site

An open-access student study site, available at edge.sagepub.com/chambliss4e, provides a variety of additional resources to build students' understanding of the book content and extend their learning beyond the classroom. Students will have access to the following features for each chapter:

- **eFlashcards and Web Quizzes:** These mobile-friendly resources reinforce understanding of key terms and concepts that have been outlined in the chapters.
- **SAGE Journal Articles:** Exclusive full-text journal articles have been carefully selected for each chapter. Each article supports and expands on the concepts presented in the chapter.
- **Video, Audio, and Web Links:** These carefully selected, Web-based resources feature relevant articles, interviews, lectures, personal stories, inquiries, and other content for use in independent or classroom-based explorations of key topics.
- **MCAT Guide:** This guide summarizes the content in each chapter, highlighting the relevant topics tested on the MCAT (Medical College Admission Test). Each chapter entry also contains links to resources that allow students to understand and explore specific topic areas in more detail.

And much more!

Instructor Teaching Site

A password-protected instructor teaching site, available at edge.sagepub.com/chambliss4e, provides integrated sources for all instructor materials, including the following key components for each chapter:

- The test bank, available in Word and ExamView, contains multiple-choice, true/false, short-answer, and essay questions for each chapter. The test bank provides you with a diverse range of prewritten options as well as the opportunity to edit any question and/or insert your own personalized questions to assess students' progress and understanding effectively.
- Editable, chapter-specific Microsoft PowerPoint slides offer you complete flexibility in easily creating a multimedia presentation for your course. Highlight essential content, features, and artwork from the book.
- Lecture notes summarize key concepts on a chapter-by-chapter basis to help with preparation for lectures and class discussions.
- Sample course syllabi for semester and quarter courses provide suggested models for use in the creation of syllabi for your courses.
- Chapter-specific discussion questions can help you launch classroom interaction by prompting students to engage with the material and by reinforcing important content.

- Lively and stimulating ideas for class activities can be used to reinforce active learning. The activities apply to individual or group projects.

And much more!

Interactive E-book

Discover Sociology is also available as an interactive e-book, which can be packaged with the text for $5 or purchased separately. This interactive e-book includes premium video resources.

SAGE Coursepacks

SAGE coursepacks makes it easy to import our quality instructor and student resource content into your school's learning management system with minimal effort. Intuitive and simple to use, SAGE coursepacks gives you the control to focus on what really matters: customizing course content to meet your students' needs. The SAGE coursepacks, created specifically for this book, are customized and curated for use in Blackboard, Canvas, Desire2Learn (D2L), and Moodle.

In addition to the content available on the SAGE edge site, the coursepacks include the following:

- Pedagogically robust assessment tools that foster review, practice, and critical thinking and offer a better, more complete way to measure student engagement. These include the following:
  - Diagnostic chapter pretests and posttests that identify opportunities for student improvement, track student progress, and ensure mastery of key learning objectives.
  - Assignable premium video and SAGE Stats data activities bring concepts to life, increasing student engagement and appealing to different learning styles. The activities feed to your gradebook.
  - Integrated links to the eBook version that make it easy to access the mobile-friendly version of the text, which can be read anywhere, anytime.

Acknowledgments

I am grateful to the terrific editors and staff at SAGE, including Jeff Lasser, Liza Neustaetter, Kara Kindstrom, Sarah Dillard, Gabrielle Piccininni, Scott Van Atta, Andrew Olson, Diane Wainwright, Erin Livingston, and Tiara Beatty. It is a privilege to work with this creative, smart, and supportive group. Thank you as well to SAGE's amazing and hardworking sales staff.

I am also indebted to colleagues and graduate students who have helped over four editions with the materials that went into the book. Among those who contributed ideas and assistance are the Department of Sociology at GWU's Michelle Kelso, Steven Tuch, Greg Squires, Ivy Ken, Antwan Jones, Ronald Weitzer, Fran Buntman, Hiromi Ishizawa, Emily Morrison, Michael Wenger, and Richard Zamoff. In addition, I owe a debt of gratitude to Ann Scammon of the GWU Career Center for her contributions to the materials on career development in the first and second editions and to Carolyn Vasques Scalera for her terrific work on "What Can I Do with a Sociology Degree?" in the third edition. I would like to extend special thanks to the excellent research assistants who have supported this book: for this edition, Ertrell Harris; for the Core Concepts edition, Srushti Upadhyay; for the third edition, Marwa Moaz, and on Chapter 6, Anna Eglitis; for the second edition, Ann Horwitz and Chris Moloney; for the first edition, Chris Moloney, Jee Jee Kim, Claire Cook, Scott Grether, Ken Leon, Ceylan Engin, and Adam Bethke. Finally, for their patience and support, I also thank the sociology department office staff, Octavia Kelsey and Kate D'Amica. This project could not have been brought to completion without the valuable help and skills of all of the people named.

I am so grateful to my family, particularly my husband, Joseph Burke and my children, Niklavs and Anna. They continue to be an important source of inspiration, ideas, and information for this ever-evolving project. Their influence is present throughout the book and they are, as always, the shining center of my little universe.

Finally, I thank all of the reviewers listed below, who contributed to *Discover Sociology* with excellent suggestions, creative insights, and helpful critiques.

Reviewers for the Fourth Edition

Jessica Bishop-Royse, DePaul University
Scott Coahran, Merced College
Heather Downs, Jacksonville University
Candan Duran-Aydintug, University of Colorado Denver
M. Faye Hanson-Evans, University of Texas Arlington
Kia Heise, California State University–Los Angeles
Ting Jiang, Metropolitan State University of Denver

Robert S. Mackin, Texas A&M University
Brian Monahan, Baldwin Wallace University
Naghme Morlock, Gonzaga University
Marvin Pippert, Young Harris College
Milanika Tuner, independent researcher
Alicia M. Walker, Missouri State University
Kristi D. Wood-Turner, West Virginia University

Reviewers for the Third Edition

Laura Chambers Atkins, Jacksonville University
Marian Colello, Strayer University
Leslie Elrod, University of Cincinnati
Matthew Green, College of DuPage
Othello Harris, Miami University
Belinda Hartnett, Strayer University
Rick Jones, Marquette University
Lauren Kempton, University of New Haven
Veena S. Kulkarni, Arkansas State University
Elaine Leeder, Sonoma State University
Olena Leipnik, Sam Houston State University

Peter LeNeyee, Strayer University
Robert Sean Mackin, Texas A&M University
Aurelien Mauxion, Columbia College
Debra M. McCoy, Strayer University
Virginia Merlini, Strayer University
Allan Mooney, Strayer University
Andrew J. Prelong, University of Northern Colorado
Angela Primm-Bethea, Strayer University
Terri Slonaker, San Antonio College
Lia Chervenak Wiley, The University of Akron
Susan L. Wortmann, Nebraska Wesleyan University

Reviewers for the Second Edition

Dianne Berger-Hill, Old Dominion University

Alison J. Bianchi, University of Iowa

Michael Bourgoin, Queens College, The City University of New York

Paul E. Calarco Jr., Hudson Valley Community College

Nicolette Caperello, Sierra College

Susan E. Claxton, Georgia Highlands College

Sonya R. De Lisle, Tacoma Community College

Heather A. Downs, Jacksonville University

Leslie Elrod, University of Cincinnati

S. Michael Gaddis, University of Michigan

Cherly Gary-Furdge, North Central Texas College

Louis Gesualdi, St. John's University

Todd Goodsell, University of Utah

Matthew Green, College of DuPage

Ashley N. Hadden, Western Kentucky University

Othello Harris, Miami University

Michael M. Harrod, Central Washington University

Sarah Jacobson, Harrisburg Area Community College

Kimberly Lancaster, Coastal Carolina Community College

Katherine Lawson, Chaffey Community College

Jason J. Leiker, Utah State University

Kim MacInnis, Bridgewater State University

Barret Michalec, University of Delaware

Amanda Miller, University of Indianapolis

Christine Mowery, Virginia Commonwealth University

Scott M. Myers, Montana State University

Frank A. Salamone, Iona College

Bonita A. Sessing-Matcha, Hudson Valley Community College

Richard States, Allegany College of Maryland

Myron T. Strong, Community College of Baltimore County

Heather Laine Talley, Western Carolina University

P.J. Verrecchia, York College of Pennsylvania

Jerrol David Weatherly, Coastal Carolina Community College

Debra L. Welkley, California State University, Sacramento

Luis Zanartu, Sacramento City College

Reviewers for the First Edition

Kristian P. Alexander, Zayed University

Lori J. Anderson, Tarleton State University

Shannon Kay Andrews, University of Tennessee at Chattanooga

Joyce Apsel, New York University

Gabriel Aquino, Westfield State College

Janet Armitage, St. Mary's University

Dionne Mathis Banks, University of Florida

Michael S. Barton, University at Albany

Jeffrey W. Basham, College of the Sequoias

Paul J. Becker, University of Dayton

Alison J. Bianchi, University of Iowa

Kimberly Boyd, Piedmont Virginia Community College

Mariana Branda, College of the Canyons

Jennifer Brennom, Kirkwood Community College

Denise Bump, Keystone College

Nicolette Caperello, Sierra College

Michael J. Carter, California State University, Northridge

Vivian L. Carter, Tuskegee University

Shaheen A. Chowdhury, College of DuPage

Jacqueline Clark, Ripon College

Susan Eidson Claxton, Georgia Highlands College

Debbie Coats, Maryville University

Angela M. Collins, Ozarks Technical Community College

Scott N. Contor, Idaho State University

Denise A. Copelton, The College at Brockport, State University of New York

Carol J. Corkern, Franklin University

Jennifer Crew Solomon, Winthrop University

William F. Daddio, Georgetown University

Jeffrey S. Debies-Carl, University of New Haven

Melanie Deffendall, Delgado Community College

Marc Jung-Whan de Jong, State University of New York, Fashion Institute of Technology

David R. Dickens, University of Nevada, Las Vegas

Keri Diggins, Scottsdale Community College

Amy M. Donley, University of Central Florida

Amanda Donovan, Bristol Community College

Heather A. Downs, Jacksonville University

Daniel D. Doyle, Bay College

Dorothy E. Everts, University of Arkansas–Monticello

Gary Feinberg, St. Thomas University

Bernie Fitzpatrick, Western Connecticut State University

Tonya K. Frevert, University of North Carolina at Charlotte

Cherly Furdge, North Central Texas College

S. Michael Gaddis, University of North Carolina at Chapel Hill

Robert Garot, John Jay College of Criminal Justice

Todd A. Garrard, University of Texas at San Antonio

Cherly Gary-Furdge, North Central Texas College

Marci Gerulis-Darcy, Metropolitan State University

Louis Gesualdi, St. John's University

Jennifer E. Givens, University of Utah

John Glass, Collin College

Malcolm Gold, Malone University

Thomas B. Gold, University of California, Berkeley

Matthew Green, College of DuPage

Johnnie M. Griffin, Jackson State University

Randolph M. Grinc, Caldwell College

Greg Haase, Western State College of Colorado

Dean H. Harper, University of Rochester

Anne S. Hastings, University of North Carolina at Chapel Hill

Anthony L. Haynor, Seton Hall University

Roneiko Henderson-Beasley, Tidewater Community College

Marta T. Henriksen, Central New Mexico Community College

Klaus Heyer, Nunez Community College

Jeremy D. Hickman, University of Kentucky

Bonniejean Alford Hinde, College of DuPage

Joy Crissey Honea, Montana State University Billings

Caazena P. Hunter, University of North Texas

John Iceland, Pennsylvania State University

Robert B. Jenkot, Coastal Carolina University

Wesley G. Jennings, University of South Florida

Audra Kallimanis, Wake Technical Community College

Ali Kamali, Missouri Western State University

Leona Kanter, Mercer University

Earl A. Kennedy, North Carolina State University

Lloyd Klein, York College, The City University of New York

Julie A. Kmec, Washington State University

Todd M. Krohn, University of Georgia

Veena S. Kulkarni, Arkansas State University

Karen F. Lahm, Wright State University

Amy G. Langenkamp, Georgia State University

Barbara LaPilusa, Montgomery College

Jason LaTouche, Tarleton State University

Ke Liang, Baruch College, The City University of New York

Carol S. Lindquist, Bemidji State University

Travis Linnemann, Kansas State University

Stephen Lippmann, Miami University

David G. LoConto, Jacksonville State University

Rebecca M. Loew, Middlesex Community College

Jeanne M. Lorentzen, Northern Michigan University

Betsy Lucal, Indiana University South Bend

George N. Lundskow, Grand Valley State University

Crystal V. Lupo, Auburn University

Brian M. Lynch, Quinebaug Valley Community College

Kim A. MacInnis, Bridgewater State University

Mahgoub El-Tigani Mahmoud, Tennessee State University

Lori Maida, The State University of New York

Hosik Min, Norwich University

Madeline H. Moran, Lehman College, The City University of New York

Amanda Moras, Sacred Heart University

Rebecca Nees, Middle Georgia College

Christopher Oliver, University of Kentucky

Sophia M. Ortiz, San Antonio College

Kathleen N. Overmiller, Marshall University

Josh Packard, Midwestern State University

Marla A. Perry, Nashville State Community College

Daniel Poole, Salt Lake Community College

Shana L. Porteen, Finlandia University

Eric Primm, University of Pikeville

Jeffrey Ratcliffe, Drexel University

Jo Reger, Oakland University

Daniel Roddick, Rio Hondo College

David Rohall, Western Illinois University

Olga I. Rowe, Oregon State University

Josephine A. Ruggiero, Providence College

Frank A. Salamone, Iona College;

Stephen J. Scanlan, Ohio University

Michael D. Schulman, North Carolina State University

Maren T. Scull, University of Colorado Denver

Shane Sharp, Northern Illinois University

Mark Sherry, The University of Toledo

Amber M. Shimel, Liberty University

Vicki Smith, University of California, Davis

Dan Steward, University of Illinois at Urbana–Champaign

Myron T. Strong, Community College of Baltimore County

Richard Sullivan, Illinois State University

Sara C. Sutler-Cohen, Bellevue College

Joyce Tang, Queens College, The City University of New York

Debra K. Taylor, Metropolitan Community College–Maple Woods

Richard Tewksbury, University of Louisville

Kevin A. Tholin, Indiana University–South Bend

Brian Thomas, Saginaw Valley State University

Lorna Timmerman, Indiana University East

Cynthia Tooley-Heddlesten, Metropolitan Community Colleges–Blue River

Okori Uneke, Winston-Salem State University

Paula Barfield Unger, McLennan Community College

P.J. Verrecchia, York College of Pennsylvania

Joseph M. Verschaeve, Grand Valley State University

Edward Walker, University of California, Los Angeles

Tom Ward, New Mexico Highlands University

Lisa Munson Weinberg, Florida State University

Casey Welch, Flagler College

Shonda Whetstone, Blinn College

S. Rowan Wolf, Portland Community College

Loreen Wolfer, University of Scranton

Jason Wollschleger, Whitworth University

Kassia R. Wosick, New Mexico State University

Discover Sociology

1

WHAT DO YOU THINK?

1. Can societies be studied scientifically? What does the scientific study of societies entail?

2. What is a theory? What role do theories play in sociology?

3. In your opinion, what social issues or problems are most interesting or important today? What questions about those issues or problems would you like to study?

LEARNING OBJECTIVES

1.1 Describe the sociological imagination.

1.2 Understand the significance of critical thinking in the study of sociology.

1.3 Trace the historical development of sociological thought.

1.4 Identify key theoretical paradigms in the discipline of sociology.

1.5 Identify the three main themes of this book.

A CURIOUS MIND

A goal of this book is to take you on a sociological journey. But let's begin with a basic question: *What is sociology?* First of all, sociology is a discipline of and for curious minds. Sociologists are deeply committed to answering the question, "Why?" Why are some people desperately poor and others fabulously wealthy? Why does racial segregation in housing and public education exist, and why does it persist more than half a century after civil rights laws were enacted in the United States? What accounts for the decline of marriage among the poor and the working class—as well as among the millennial generation? Why is the proportion of women entering and completing college rising while men's enrollment has fallen? Why, despite this, do men as a group still earn higher incomes than do women as a group? And how is it that social media is simultaneously praised as a vehicle of transformational activism

©Westend61/Getty Images

Sociology seeks to construct a body of scientific and rigorous knowledge about social relations, groups, and societies. A new area of interest is the way social media is changing the way we interact with our social environment and with one another.

and criticized as a cause of social alienation and civic disengagement? Take a moment to think about some *why* questions you have about society and social life: As you look around you, hear the news, and interact with other people, what strikes you as fascinating but perhaps difficult to understand? What are you curious about?

Sociology is an academic discipline that takes a scientific approach to answering the kinds of questions our curious minds imagine. When we say that sociology is **scientific**, we mean that it is *a way of learning about the world that combines logically constructed theory and systematic observation*. The goal of sociological study and research is to base answers to questions like those above on careful examination of the roots of social phenomena such as poverty, segregation, and the wage gap. Sociologists do this with *research methods*—surveys, interviews, observations, and archival research, among others—which yield data that can be tested, challenged, and revised. In this text, you will see how sociology is done—and you will learn how to do sociology yourself.

Concisely stated, **sociology** is *the scientific study of human social relations, groups, and societies*. Unlike *natural sciences* such as physics, chemistry, and biology, sociology is one of several *social sciences* engaged in the scientific study of human beings and the social worlds they consciously create and inhabit. The purpose of sociology is to understand and generate new knowledge about human behavior, social relations, and social institutions on a larger scale. The sociologist adheres to the principle of **social embeddedness**: *the idea that economic, political, and other forms of human behavior are fundamentally shaped by social relations*. Thus, sociologists pursue studies on a wide range of issues occurring within, between, and among families, communities, states, nations, and the world. Other social sciences, some of which you may be studying, include anthropology, economics, political science, and psychology.

Sociology is a field in which students have the opportunity to build strong core knowledge about the social world with a broad spectrum of important skills, ranging from gathering and analyzing information to identifying and addressing social problems to effective written and oral communication. Throughout this book, we draw your attention to important skills you can gain through the study of sociology and the kinds of jobs and fields in which these skills can be put to work.

Doing sociology requires that you build a foundation for your knowledge and understanding of the social world. Some key foundations of sociology are the *sociological imagination* and *critical thinking*. We turn to these below.

Scientific: A way of learning about the world that combines logically constructed theory and systematic observation.

Sociology: The scientific study of human social relations, groups, and societies.

Social embeddedness: The idea that economic, political, and other forms of human behavior are fundamentally shaped by social relations.

The Sociological Imagination

As we go about our daily lives, it is easy to overlook the fact that large-scale economic, political, and cultural forces shape even the most personal aspects of our lives. When parents divorce, for example, we tend to focus on individual explanations: A father was devoted more to his work than to his family; a mother may have felt trapped in an unhappy marriage but stuck with it for the sake of young children. Yet while personal issues are inevitable parts of a breakup, they can't tell the whole story. When many U.S. marriages end in divorce, forces larger than incompatible personalities or marital discord are at play. But what are those greater social forces, exactly?

As sociologist C. Wright Mills (1916–1962) suggested half a century ago, uncovering the relationship between what he called *personal troubles* and *public issues* calls for a **sociological imagination** (1959/2000b). The sociological imagination is *the ability to grasp the relationship between individual lives and the larger social forces that shape them—* that is, to see where biography and history intersect.

In a country such as the United States, where individualism is part of the national heritage, people tend to believe that each person creates his or her life's path and largely disregards the social context in which this happens. When we cannot get a job, fail to earn enough to support a family, or experience marital separation, for example, we tend to see it as a personal trouble. We do not necessarily see it as a public issue. The sociological imagination, however, invites us to make the connection and to step away from the vantage point of a single life experience to see how powerful social forces—for instance, changes in social norms, racial or gender discrimination, large shifts in the economy, or the beginning or end of a military conflict—shape the obstacles and opportunities that contribute to the unfolding of our life's story. Among Mills's (1959/2000b) most often cited examples is the following:

> When, in a city of 100,000, only one man is unemployed, that is his personal trouble, and for its relief we properly look to the character of the man, his skills, and his immediate opportunities. But when in a nation of 50 million employees, 15 million men are unemployed, that is an issue, and we may not hope to find its solution within the range of opportunities open to any one individual. The very structure of opportunities has collapsed. Both the correct statement of the problem and the range of possible solutions require us to consider the economic and political institutions of the society, and not merely the personal situation and character of a scatter of individuals. (p. 9)

Sociological imagination: The ability to grasp the relationship between individual lives and the larger social forces that help to shape them.

To apply the idea to contemporary economic conditions, we might look at recent college graduates. If many of the young adults graduating from college today are finding employment in fields of interest to them, they may account for their success by citing personal effort and solid academic qualifications. These are, of course, very important! The sociological imagination, however, suggests that there are also larger social forces at work. The recent economic recovery in the United States has manifested in the form of growing job creation and more hiring: The official unemployment rate for all college graduates with a bachelor's degree in 2017 was 2.5% (U.S. Bureau of Labor Statistics, 2018). Early 2018 figures show that the rate of unemployment of young college graduates (ages 21–24) was higher, at about 6.4% for men and 4.7% for women, although this represents a significant drop after the postrecession high of nearly 10% (Figure 1.1). If your friends or relatives who graduated during the economic recession of 2007 to 2009, or even the first years following that period, encountered challenges securing a job after graduation, this suggests that personal effort and qualifications are only part of the explanation for the success of one class of college completers and the frustration of another.

Understanding this relationship is particularly critical for people in the United States, who often regard individuals as fully responsible for their social, educational, and economic successes and failures. For instance, it is easy to fault the poor for their poverty, assuming they only need to work harder and pull themselves up by their bootstraps. We may neglect the powerful role of social forces such as racial or ethnic discrimination, the outsourcing or automation of manufacturing jobs that used to employ those with less education, or the dire state of public education in many economically distressed rural and urban areas. The sociological imagination implores us to seek the intersection between private troubles, such as a family's poverty, and public issues, such as lack of access to good schooling and jobs paying a living wage, to develop a more informed and comprehensive understanding of the social world and social issues.

It is useful, when we talk about the sociological imagination, to bring in the concepts of *agency* and *structure*. Sociologists often talk about social actions—individual and group behavior—in these terms. **Agency** can be understood as *the ability of individuals and groups to exercise free will and to make social changes on a small or large scale.* **Structure** is a complex term but may be defined as *patterned social arrangements that have effects on agency and are, in turn, affected by agency.* Structure may enable or constrain social

Agency: The ability of individuals and groups to exercise free will and to make social changes on a small or large scale.

Structure: Patterned social arrangements that have effects on agency and are, in turn, affected by agency.

■ FIGURE 1.1 Unemployment Rate of Young College Graduates (Ages 21–24), by Gender and Race/Ethnicity, 2000 and 2018

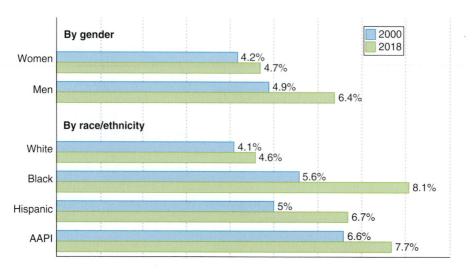

Source: "The Class of 2018," by Elise Gould, Zane Mokhiber, and Julia Wolfe. May 10, 2018. Washington, DC: Economic Policy Institute. https://www.epi.org/publication/class-of-2018-college-edition/. Reprinted with permission.

Notes: AAPI stands for Asian American/Pacific Islander. Data for 2000 and 2018 use an average of January 1998–December 2000 and March 2015–February 2018, respectively.

C. Wright Mills highlighted the use of the sociological imagination in studying social issues. When 16% of urban residents are poor by the government's official measure, we cannot assume that the sole cause is personal failings; we must ask how large-scale social and economic forces are implicated in widespread socioeconomic disadvantage experienced in many communities.

action. For example, sociologists talk about the class structure, which is composed of social groups who hold varying amounts of resources such as money, political voice, and social status. They also identify normative structures—for instance, they might analyze patterns of social norms regarding "appropriate" gender behaviors in different cultural contexts.

Sociologists take a strong interest in the relationship between structure and agency. Consider that, on one hand, we all have the ability to make choices—we have free will and we can opt for one path over another. On the other hand, the structures that surround us impose obstacles on us or afford us opportunities to exercise agency: We can make choices, but they may be enabled or constrained by structure. For instance, in the early 1900s, we could surely have found bright young women in the U.S. middle class who wanted to study law or medicine. The social norms of the time, however, held that young women of this status were better off marrying and caring for a husband, home, and children. There were also legal constraints to women's entry into higher education and the paid labor force. So, although the women in our example might have individually argued and pushed to get an education and have professional careers, the dreams of this group were constrained by powerful normative and legal structures that identified women's place as being in the home.

Consider also the relationship between the class structure and individual agency as a way of thinking about social mobility in U.S. society. If, for instance, a young man today whose parents are well educated and whose family is economically prosperous wishes to go to college and study to be an architect, engineer, or college professor, his position in the class structure (or the position of his family) is *enabling*—that is, it raises the probability that he will be able to make this choice and realize it. If, however, a young man from a poor family with no college background embraces these same dreams, his position in the class structure is likely to be *constraining*: Not only does his family have insufficient economic means to pay for college, but he may also be studying in an underfunded or underperforming high school that cannot provide the advanced courses and other resources he needs to prepare for college. A lack of college role models may also be a factor. This does not mean that the first young man will inevitably go to college and realize his hopes and the second will not; it does, however, suggest that structural conditions favor the first college aspirant over the second.

To understand why some students go to college and others do not, sociologists would say that we cannot rely on individual choice or will (agency) alone—structures, whether subtly or quite obviously, exercise an influence on social behavior and outcomes. At the same time, we should not see structures as telling the whole story of social behavior because history shows the power of human agency in making change, even in the face of obstacles. Agency itself can transform structures (for example, think about the ways women's historical activism has helped to transform limiting gender norms for women today). Sociologists weigh both agency and structure and study how the two intersect and interact. For the most part, sociologists understand the relationship as *reciprocal*—that is, it goes in both directions, as structure affects agency and agency, in turn, can change the dimensions of a structure (Figure 1.2).

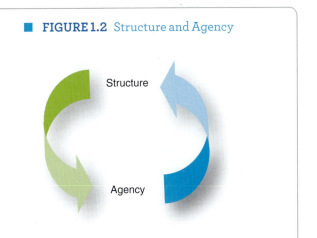

■ FIGURE 1.2 Structure and Agency

Structure

Agency

DISCOVER INTERSECTIONS
An Introduction

In this book, you will find short features titled *Discover Intersections*. In recent decades, sociologists have increasingly endeavored to identify ways in which achieved and ascribed characteristics, such as gender, race, ethnicity, class, religion, sexual orientation, and others, overlap with one another in social practices and institutions and, importantly, how these overlapping characteristics affect access to resources such as power and political voice. Put another way, "When it comes to social inequality, people's lives and the organization of power in a given society are better understood as being shaped not by a single axis of social division, be it race or gender or class, but by many axes that work together and influence each other" (Hill Collins & Bilge, 2016, p. 2). For example, when looking at inequalities of gender, it behooves us to recognize particular ways in which race and class, practices that disadvantage women in corporate workplaces, or stereotypes affect how women are perceived and received when seeking a job or a raise. Each chapter provides an opportunity to consider intersections that exist between the sociological topics that we cover separately in the chapters, but are deeply linked in the foundations of social life.

Critical Thinking

Taking a sociological perspective requires more than an ability to use the sociological imagination. It also entails **critical thinking**, *the ability to evaluate claims about truth by using reason and evidence.* In everyday life, we often accept things as true because they are familiar, feel right, or are consistent with our beliefs. Critical thinking takes a different approach—recognizing weak arguments, rejecting statements not supported by empirical evidence, and questioning our assumptions. One of the founders of modern sociology, Max Weber, captured the spirit of critical thinking in two words when he said that a key task of sociological inquiry is to acknowledge "inconvenient facts."

Critical thinking requires us to be open-minded, but it does not mean that we must accept all arguments as equally valid. Those supported by logic and backed by evidence are clearly preferable to those that are not. For instance, we may

---

Critical thinking: The ability to evaluate claims about truth by using reason and evidence.

passionately agree with Thomas Jefferson's famous statement, "That government is best that governs least." Nevertheless, as sociologists we must also ask, "What evidence backs up the claim that less government is better under all circumstances?"

To think critically, it is useful to follow six simple rules (adapted from Wade & Tavris, 1997):

1. **Be willing to ask any question, no matter how difficult.** The belief in small government is a cherished U.S. ideal. But sociologists who study the role of government in modern society must be willing to ask whether there are circumstances under which more—not less—government is better. Government's role in areas such as homeland security, education, and health care has grown in recent decades—what are the positive and negative aspects of this growth?

2. **Think logically and be clear.** Logic and clarity require us to define concepts in a way that allows us to study them. "Big government" is a vague concept that must be made more precise and measurable before it provides for useful research. Are we speaking of federal, state, or local government, or all of these? Is "big" measured by the cost of government services, the number of agencies or offices within the government, the number of people working for it, or something else? What did Jefferson mean by "best," and what would that "best" government look like? Who would have the power to define this notion?

3. **Back up your arguments with evidence.** Founding Father Thomas Jefferson is a formidable person to quote, but quoting him does not prove that smaller government is better in the 21st century. To find evidence, we need to seek out studies of contemporary societies to see whether there is a relationship between a population's well-being and the size of government or the breadth of services it provides. Because studies may offer contradictory evidence, we also need to be able to assess the strengths and weaknesses of arguments on different sides of the issue.

4. **Think about the assumptions and biases—including your own—that underlie all studies.** You may insist that government has a key role to play in modern society. On the other hand, you may believe with equal passion that big government is one root of the problems in the United States. Critical thinking requires that we recognize our beliefs and biases. Otherwise, we might unconsciously seek out only evidence that supports our argument, ignoring evidence to the contrary. Passion has a role to play in research: It can motivate us to devote long hours to studying an issue. But passion should not play a role when we are weighing evidence and drawing conclusions.

5. **Avoid anecdotal evidence.** It is tempting to draw a general conclusion from a single experience or anecdote, but that experience may illustrate the exception rather than the rule. For example, you may know someone who just yesterday received a letter mailed two years ago, but that is not evidence that the U.S. Postal Service is inefficient or does not fulfill its mandates. To determine whether this government agency is working well, you would have to study its entire mail delivery system and its record of work over time.

6. **Be willing to admit when you are wrong or uncertain about your results.** Sometimes we expect to find support for an argument only to find that things are not so clear. For example, consider the position of a sociologist who advocates small government and learns that Japan and Singapore initially became economic powerhouses because their governments played leading roles in promoting growth or a sociologist who champions an expanded role for government but learns from the downturn of the 1990s in the Asian economies that some societal needs can be better met by private enterprise. Empirical evidence may contradict our beliefs: We learn from recognizing erroneous assumptions and having a mind open to new information.

©iStockphoto.com/BrianPIrwin

Another well-known quote from Thomas Jefferson is, "The tree of liberty must be refreshed from time to time with the blood of patriots and tyrants." Taking a critical perspective, how might we evaluate the meaning and applicability of the quote to the U.S. today?

Discover & Debate

WHAT IS DISCOVER & DEBATE?

In the fourth edition of *Discover Sociology*, we are pleased to expand our recently introduced feature, *Discover & Debate*. These essays, which appear in every chapter, offer more than discussion questions for the classroom. Rather, they provide a robust discussion model for instructors and students that takes the form of debate. A basic understanding of debating and, in particular, of the construction and evaluation of reasoned arguments is vital to civic life, civil interaction, and even social change. In a society that often addresses vital issues in sound bites and tweets, it is particularly challenging but important to develop the skills and knowledge to evaluate issues critically and to build evidence-based arguments.

What Is a Debate?

According to the *Oxford English Dictionary*, debate is a "formal discussion on a particular matter in a public meeting or legislative assembly, in which opposing arguments are put forward and which usually ends with a vote" (2010). Although most commonly associated with electoral politics, debates are also used in high schools and colleges to help students learn to gather and evaluate information and to build strong evidence-based positions on issues of social, political, economic, and cultural importance.

Debate is a form of public speaking; it is a formal, oral contest between teams or individuals on an assigned proposition or "motion." It is an idea, statement, or policy that teams formally argue. A typical debate comprises two teams—the affirmative side and the opposition side. The affirmative side speaks *for* the motion, meaning they advocate and speak in favor of it, whereas the opposition speaks *against* the motion.

What is the difference between a debate and an argument? Debates are structured arguments, where each participant is given a specific amount of time to present and defend his or her arguments. The motion is announced prior to the debate, and each team is randomly assigned a side. This aspect of academic debate is notable because it underscores the importance of understanding and recognizing the strengths and weaknesses of both sides of an issue. Debaters are given preparation time to develop arguments using empirical data. The first speakers on each team introduce their side of the argument and present the order in which team members will discuss the motion. The opening opposition speaker rebuts the argument presented by the opening affirmative speaker. This format continues throughout the debate.

The affirmative side presents its argument, whereas the opposition side following them rebuts it and presents its side.

In competitive debating, a panel of judges evaluates speakers on the substantive content of arguments, time management, style, and delivery and determines a winner. The judges' goal is not to label one side as right or wrong—assigned issues are normally too complex to categorize with such simple labels. This is important because it highlights the point that on a significant number of controversial and frequently debated issues, a strong supporting argument can be made for all sides of an issue. Being a good debater does not mean choosing a "right" side and labeling the opposing side as "wrong." Rather, it means constructing a well-reasoned argument based on empirical evidence and an understanding of the strengths and weaknesses of all sides of the debate.

A serious debate is fundamentally about presenting, defending, and challenging ideas with reasoned arguments. Constructing a strong argument is dependent on information literacy and on the ability to discern facts from opinions and evidence from ideology—skills from which we as engaged citizens and sociologists benefit. Being a competent debater entails understanding all sides of an issue. Our goal with this feature is to help you develop skills to engage in well-informed and well-reasoned debate, whether that debate takes place in an academic or a political setting or in a less-formal setting.

Each chapter offers a *Discover & Debate* feature that presents a motion for debate, basic background on a current social issue, and an introduction to key arguments from two sides. It also includes questions to consider when evaluating each position and a debate tip to help you build debate skills and develop a winning argument.

What Are Sociological Debates?

Sociology is a discipline with a broad reach. Sociologists may debate issues related to media and violence, the labor market and economy, gender roles and status, crime and punishment, and many others. In the chapters that follow, we will introduce motions for debate on contemporary social issues and provide you with a basic discussion model to build strong arguments and counterarguments. The next time you see or hear these issues discussed, you will be better prepared to evaluate the positions presented and form your own arguments.

Critical thinking also means becoming critical consumers of the information that surrounds us—news, social media, surveys, texts, magazines, and scientific studies. To be a good sociologist, it is important to look beyond the commonsense understanding of social life and develop a critical perspective. Being critical consumers of information entails paying attention to the sources of information we encounter and asking questions about how data were gathered. In this text, *Behind the Numbers* boxes will look critically at data on issues such as unemployment, poverty, and high school dropouts, helping us to understand what is illuminated and what is obscured by these commonly cited social indicators.

The Development of Sociological Thinking

Humans have been asking questions about the nature of social life as long as people have lived in societies. Aristotle and Plato wrote extensively about social relationships more than 2,000 years ago. Ibn Khaldun, an Arab scholar writing in the 14th century, advanced several sociological concepts we recognize today, including ideas about social conflict and cohesion. Yet modern sociological concepts and research methods did not emerge until the 19th century, after the Industrial Revolution, and then largely in those European nations undergoing dramatic societal changes such as industrialization and urbanization.

The Birth of Sociology: Science, Progress, Industrialization, and Urbanization

We can trace sociology's roots to four interrelated historical developments that gave birth to the modern world: *the scientific revolution, the Enlightenment, industrialization, and urbanization*. Since these developments initially occurred in Europe, it is not surprising that sociological perspectives and ideas evolved there during the 19th century. By the end of the 19th century, sociology had taken root in North America as well; somewhat later, it gained a foothold in Central and South America, Africa, and Asia. Sociology throughout the world initially bore the stamp of its European and North American origins, although recent decades have brought a greater diversity of perspectives to the discipline.

The Scientific Revolution

The rise of modern natural and physical sciences, beginning in Europe in the 16th century, offered scholars a more advanced understanding of the physical world. The success of natural science contributed to the belief that science could be fruitfully applied to human affairs, thereby enabling people to improve society or even perfect it. Auguste Comte (1798–1857) coined the term *sociology* to characterize what he believed would be a new "social physics"—that is, the scientific study of society.

The Enlightenment

Inspired in part by the success of the physical sciences, French philosophers in the 18th century such as Voltaire (1694–1778), Montesquieu (1689–1755), Diderot (1719–1784), and Rousseau (1712–1778) promised that humankind could attain lofty heights by applying scientific understanding to human affairs. Enlightenment ideals such as equality, liberty, and fundamental human rights found a home in the emerging social sciences, particularly sociology. Émile Durkheim (1858–1917), considered by many to be the first modern sociologist, argued that sociological understanding would create a more egalitarian, peaceful society, in which individuals would be free to realize their full potential. Many of sociology's founders shared the hope that a fairer and more just society would be achieved through the scientific understanding of society.

The Industrial Revolution

The Industrial Revolution, which began in England in the mid- to late 18th century and soon spread to other countries, dramatically changed European societies. Traditional agricultural economies and the small-scale production of handicrafts in the home gave way to more efficient, profit-driven manufacturing based in factories. For instance, in 1801 in the English city of Leeds, there were about 20 factories manufacturing a variety of goods. By 1838, Leeds was home to 106 woolen mills alone, employing 10,000 people.

Small towns, including Leeds, were transformed into bustling cities, showcasing extremes of wealth and poverty as well as opportunity and struggle. In the face of rapid social change and growing inequality, sociologists sought to gain a social scientific perspective on what was happening and how it had come about. German theorist and revolutionary Karl Marx (1818–1883), who had an important impact on later sociological theory concerning modern societies and economies, predicted that industrialization would make life increasingly intolerable for the masses. He believed that private property ownership by the wealthy allowed for the exploitation of working people and that its elimination would bring about a utopia of equality for all.

Urbanization: The Population Shift toward Cities

Industrialization fostered the growth of cities as people streamed from rural fields to urban factories in search of work. By the end of the 19th century, more than 20 million people lived in English cities. The population of London alone exceeded 7 million by 1910.

Early industrial cities were often fetid places, characterized by pollution and dirt, crime, and crowded housing tenements. In Europe, sociologists lamented the passing of communal village life and its replacement by a savage and alienating urban existence. Durkheim, for example, worried about the potential breakdown of stabilizing beliefs and values in modern urban society. He argued that

Industrialization brought new workers to cities, and urban populations grew dramatically in a short period of time. Sociologists such as Émile Durkheim theorized the normative effects of moving from small, traditional communities to diverse, unfamiliar, populous cities.

Interestingly, Harriet Martineau translated into English the work of Auguste Comte, who dismissed women's intellect, saying, "Biological philosophy teaches us that . . . radical differences, physical and moral, distinguish the sexes . . . biological analysis presents the female sex . . . as constitutionally in a state of perpetual infancy, in comparison with the other" (Kandal, 1988, p. 75).

whereas traditional communities were held together by shared culture and **norms,** or *accepted social behaviors and beliefs,* modern industrial communities were threatened by **anomie,** or a *state of normlessness that occurs when people lose sight of the shared rules and values that give order and meaning to their lives.* In a state of anomie, individuals often feel confused and anxious because they do not know how to interact with each other and their environment. Durkheim raised the question of what would hold societies and communities together as they shifted from homogeneity and shared cultures and values to heterogeneous masses of diverse cultures, norms, and occupations.

Nineteenth-Century Founders

Despite its largely European origins, early sociology sought to develop universal understandings that would apply to other peoples, times, and places. The discipline's principal acknowledged founders—Auguste Comte, Harriet Martineau, Émile Durkheim, Karl Marx, and Max Weber— left their marks on sociology in different ways.

Auguste Comte

Auguste Comte (1798–1857), a French social theorist, is credited with founding modern sociology, naming it, and establishing it as the scientific study of social relationships. The twin pillars of Comte's sociology were the study of **social statics**, *the way society is held together,* and the analysis of **social dynamics**, *the laws that govern social change.* Comte believed that social science could be used effectively to manage the social change resulting from modern industrial society but always with a strong respect for traditions and history.

Comte proclaimed that his new science of society was **positivist.** This meant that it was to be *based on facts alone,* which should be determined scientifically and allowed to speak for themselves. Comte argued that this purely factual approach was the proper method for sociology. He argued that all sciences—and all societies—go through three stages. The first stage is a theological one, in which key ways of understanding the world are framed in terms of superstition, imagination, and religion. The second stage is a metaphysical one, characterized by abstract speculation but framed by the basic belief that society is the product of natural rather than of supernatural forces. The third and last stage is one in which knowledge is based on scientific reasoning from the "facts." Comte saw himself as leading sociology toward its final positivist stage.

Comte left a lasting mark on modern sociology. The scientific study of social life continues to be the goal of sociological research. His belief that social institutions have a strong impact on individual behavior—that is, that our

---

Norms: Accepted social behaviors and beliefs.

Anomie: A state of normlessness that occurs when people lose touch with the shared rules and values that give order and meaning to their lives.

Social statics: The way society is held together.

Social dynamics: The laws that govern social change.

Positivist: Science that is based on facts alone.

As a founding figure in the social sciences, Auguste Comte is associated with *positivism,* the belief that the study of society must be anchored in facts and the scientific method.

Émile Durkheim pioneered some of sociology's early research on such topics as social solidarity and suicide. His work continues to inform sociological study and understanding of social bonds and the consequences of their unraveling.

actions are the products of personal choices and the surrounding social context—remains at the heart of sociology.

Harriet Martineau

Harriet Martineau (1802–1876) was an English sociologist who, despite deafness and other physical challenges, became a prominent social and historical writer. Her greatest handicap was being a woman in male-dominated intellectual circles that failed to value female voices. Today, she is frequently recognized as the first major woman sociologist.

Deeply influenced by Comte's work, Martineau translated his six-volume treatise on politics into English. Her editing helped make Comte's esoteric prose accessible to the English-speaking world, ensuring his standing as a leading figure in sociology. Martineau was also a distinguished scholar in her own right. She wrote dozens of books, more than 1,000 newspaper columns, and 25 novels, including a three-volume study, *Society in America* (1837), based on observations of the United States that she made during a tour of the country.

Martineau, like Comte, sought to identify basic laws that govern society. She derived three of her four laws from other theorists. The fourth law, however, was her own and reflected her progressive (today we might say *feminist*) principles: For a society to evolve, it must ensure social justice for women and other oppressed groups. In her study of U.S. society, Martineau treated slavery and women's experience of dependence in marriage as indicators of the limits of the moral development of the United States. In her view, the United States was unable to achieve its full social potential while it was morally stunted by persistent injustices such as slavery and women's inequality. The question of whether the provision of social justice is critical to societal development remains a relevant and compelling one today.

Émile Durkheim

Auguste Comte founded and named the discipline of sociology, but French scholar Émile Durkheim (1858–1917) set the field on its present course. Durkheim established the early subject matter of sociology, laid out rules for conducting research, and developed an important theory of social change.

For Durkheim, sociology's subject matter was **social facts**, *qualities of groups that are external to individual members yet constrain their thinking and behavior.* Durkheim argued that such social facts as religious beliefs and social duties are external—that is, they are part of the social

Social facts: Qualities of groups that are external to individual members yet constrain their thinking and behavior.

context and are larger than our individual lives. They also have the power to shape our behavior. You may feel compelled to act in certain ways in different contexts—in the classroom, on a date, at a religious ceremony—even if you are not always aware of such social pressures.

Durkheim also argued that only social facts can explain other social facts. For example, there is no scientific evidence that men have an innate knack for business compared with women, but in 2012, women headed only 18 of the *Fortune* 500 companies. A Durkheimian approach would highlight women's experience in society—where historically they have been socialized into more domestic values or restricted to certain noncommercial professions—and the fact that the social networks that foster mobility in the corporate world today are still primarily male to help explain why men dominate the upper ranks of the business world.

Durkheim's principal concern was explaining the impact of modern society on **social solidarity**, *the bonds that unite the members of a social group.* In his view, in traditional society, these bonds are based on similarity—people speak the same language, share the same customs and beliefs, and do similar work tasks. He called this *mechanical solidarity.* In modern industrial society, however, bonds based on similarity break down. Everyone has a different job to perform in the industrial division of labor, and modern societies are more likely to be socially diverse. Nevertheless, workers in different occupational positions are dependent on one another for things such as safety, education, and the provision of food and other goods essential to survival. The people filling these positions may not be alike in culture, beliefs, or language, but their dependence on one another contributes to social cohesion. Borrowing from biology, Durkheim called this *organic solidarity*, suggesting that modern society functions as an interdependent organic whole, like a human body.

Yet organic solidarity, Durkheim argued, is not as strong as mechanical solidarity. People no longer necessarily share the same norms and values. The consequence, according to Durkheim, is anomie. In this weakened condition, the social order disintegrates and pathological behavior increases (Durkheim, 1922/1973a).

Consider whether the United States, a modern and diverse society, is held together primarily by organic solidarity or whether the hallmark of mechanical solidarity, a **collective conscience**—*the common beliefs and values that bind a society together*—is in evidence. Do public demonstrations of patriotism on nationally significant anniversaries such as September 11 and July 4 indicate mechanical solidarity built on a collective sense of shared values, norms, and practices? Or do the deeply divisive politics of recent years suggest that social bonds are based more fully on practical interdependence?

Karl Marx

The extensive writings of Karl Marx (1818–1883) influenced the development of economics and political science as well as sociology. They also shaped world politics and inspired communist revolutions in Russia (later the Soviet Union), China, and Cuba, among others.

Marx's central idea was deceptively simple: Almost all societies throughout history have been divided into economic classes, with one class prospering at the expense of others. All human history, Marx believed, should be understood as the product of **class conflict**, *competition between social classes over the distribution of wealth, power, and other valued resources in society* (Marx & Engels, 1848/1998).

In the period of early industrialization in which he lived, Marx condemned capitalism's exploitation of *working people*, the **proletariat**, by the *ownership class*, the **bourgeoisie**. As we will see in later chapters, Marx's views on conflict and inequality are still influential in contemporary sociological thinking, even among sociologists who do not share his views on society.

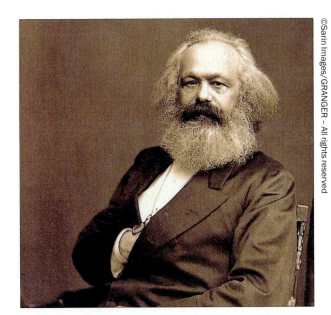

Karl Marx was a scholar and critic of early capitalism. His work has been thoroughly studied and critiqued around the world.

Social solidarity: The bonds that unite the members of a social group.

Collective conscience: The common beliefs and values that bind a society together.

Class conflict: Competition between social classes over the distribution of wealth, power, and other valued resources in society.

Proletariat: The working class; wage workers.

Bourgeoisie: The capitalist (or property-owning) class.

Private Lives, Public Issues

WHY DO COUPLES GET DIVORCED?

Until about the middle of the 20th century, most marriages were "'til death do us part." In 1940, the rate of divorce in the United States was 2.0 per 1,000 population. In 1960, it was still 2.2 per 1,000, but it rose consistently through the 1970s, peaking in 1981 at 5.3 per 1,000 before dropping back to 3.2 per 1,000 in 2016 (Figure 1.3). What accounts for the shifting landscape of marital breakup in the United States?

The sociological imagination suggests to us that marriage and divorce, seemingly the most private of matters, are public issues as well as personal ones. Certainly, the end of a marriage is a profoundly personal experience and rooted in disagreements, conflicts, or crisis faced by a couple. At the same time, researchers recognize that there are structural and normative shifts that are important for understanding the context in which marriages are made, experienced, and ended.

Consider the fact that when wages for the working class began to stagnate in the mid-1970s, growing numbers of women went to work to help their families make ends meet. More women also went to college and pursued careers as a path to financial stability and personal fulfillment, a path enabled in part by the 1972 passage of Title IX, a federal law prohibiting discrimination on the basis of sex in any educational program receiving federal financial

support. In fact, today more women than men finish undergraduate degrees (a topic we cover in depth in Chapter 10), and women have a higher measure of economic independence than ever before. The combination of educational attainment and satisfying careers reinforces women's autonomy, making it easier for those who are in unhappy marriages to leave them. Greater social acceptance of divorce has also removed much of the stigma once associated with a failed marriage.

After rising to its peak in 1981, the divorce rate in the United States began to decline again, falling to and staying below 4.0 per 1,000 in 2000. Can we find the roots of this shift in sociological phenomena as well? Arguably, several more recent societal changes could be implicated in a dropping divorce rate. For example, as we will see in Chapter 11, fewer people today are marrying at all: The decline has been particularly notable among millennials as well as among the poor and the working class, shrinking the pool from which divorced couples could emerge. More couples today are also cohabiting: Some break up before marriage, whereas others may discover compatibility that translates into a durable marriage. Furthermore, a trend toward later marriage, when careers have already been established, may mean that couples are likely to marry for love rather than for economic

■ **FIGURE 1.3**   144 Years of Marriage and Divorce in the United States

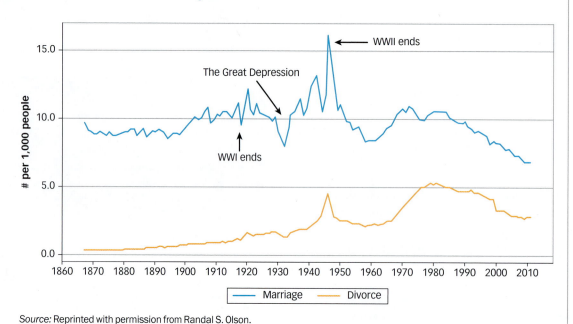

Source: Reprinted with permission from Randal S. Olson.

©Charles Gullung/Photonica/Getty Images

stability and are more likely to stay together. Economic stability, in fact, continues to be an important variable in the sociological picture: One demographic category where divorce remains high is among less-educated, low-income couples.

Societal changes can be implicated in the rise—and decline—of divorce in the United States. The sociological imagination helps us to see that this private trouble is, in many respects, influenced by public issues, including women's growing economic independence, the dynamism of cultural norms related to marriage and divorce, and financial stresses experienced by less-educated and lower-income couples. Social research methods, which we will discuss in the next chapter, can help us learn to ask and study the kinds of sociological questions that will help us understand these trends more fully.

Think It Through

- What other private troubles might sociologists identify as public issues? Can you use the sociological imagination to discuss any of the social issues and problems of interest to you?

Marx focused his attention on the emerging capitalist industrial society (Marx, 1867/1992a, 1885/1992b, 1894/1992c). Unlike his contemporaries in sociology, however, Marx saw capitalism as a transitional stage to a final period in human history in which economic classes and the unequal distribution of rewards and opportunities linked to class inequality would disappear and be replaced by a utopia of equality.

Although many of Marx's predictions have not proved to be correct, his critical analysis of the dynamics of capitalism proved insightful. Among other things, Marx argued that capitalism would lead to accelerating technological change, the replacement of workers by machines, and the growth of monopoly capitalism.

Marx also presciently predicted that ownership of the **means of production**, *the sites and technology that produce the goods* (and sometimes services) *we need and use*, would come to be concentrated in fewer and fewer hands. As a result, he believed, a growing wave of people would be thrust down into the proletariat, which owns only its own labor power. In modern society, large corporations have progressively swallowed up or pushed out smaller businesses; where small lumberyards and pharmacies used to serve many communities, corporate giants such as Home Depot, CVS, and Best Buy have moved in, putting locally owned establishments out of business.

In many U.S. towns, small business owners have joined forces to protest the construction of "big box" stores such as Walmart (now the largest private employer in the United States), arguing that these enormous establishments,

although they offer cheap goods, wreak havoc on local retailers and bring only the meager economic benefit of masses of entry-level, low-wage jobs. From a Marxist perspective, we might say that the local retailers, in resisting the incursion of the big box stores into their communities, are fighting their own proletarianization. Even physicians, many of whom used to own their own means of production in the form of private medical practices, have increasingly been driven by economic necessity into working for large health maintenance organizations (HMOs), where they are salaried employees.

Unlike Comte and Durkheim, Marx thought social change would be revolutionary, not evolutionary, and would be the product of oppressed workers rising up against a capitalist system that exploits the many to benefit the few.

Max Weber

Max Weber (1864–1920), a German sociologist who wrote at the beginning of the 20th century, left a substantial academic legacy. Among his contributions are an analysis of how Protestantism fostered the rise of capitalism in Europe (Weber, 1904–1905/2002) and insights into the emergence of modern bureaucracy (Weber, 1919/1946). Weber, like other founders of sociology, took up various political causes, condemning injustice wherever he found it. Although pessimistic about capitalism, he did not believe, as did Marx, that some alternative utopian form of society would arise. Nor did he see sociologists enjoying privileged insights into the social world that would qualify them to wisely counsel rulers and industrialists, as Comte (and, to some extent, Durkheim) had envisioned.

Weber believed that an adequate explanation of the social world begins with the individual and takes into account the meaning of what people say and do. Although

---

Means of production: The sites and technology that produce the goods we need and use.

he argued that research should be scientific and value free, Weber also believed that to explain what people do, we must use a method he termed **Verstehen**, *the German word for interpretive understanding. This methodology*, rarely used by sociologists today, *sought to explain social relationships by having the sociologist/observer imagine how the subjects being studied might have perceived and interpreted the situation.* Studying social life, Weber felt, is not the same as studying plants or chemical reactions because human beings act on the basis of meanings and motives.

Weber's theories of social and economic organization have also been highly influential (Weber, 1921/2012). Weber argued that the modern Western world showed an ever-increasing reliance on logic, efficiency, rules, and reason. According to him, modern societies are characterized by the development and growing influence of **formal rationality**, a context in which people's pursuit of goals is increasingly shaped by rules, regulations, and larger social structures. One of Weber's most widely known

illustrations of formal rationality comes from his study of **bureaucracies**, *formal organizations characterized by written rules, hierarchical authority, and paid staff, intended to promote organizational efficiency.* Bureaucracies, for Weber, epitomized formally rational systems: On the one hand, they offer clear, knowable rules and regulations for the efficient pursuit of particular ends, such as obtaining a passport or getting financial aid for higher education. On the other hand, he feared, the bureaucratization of modern society would also progressively strip people of their humanity and creativity and result in an iron cage of rationalized structures with irrational consequences.

Weber's ideas about bureaucracy were remarkably prescient in their characterization of our bureaucratic (and formally rationalized) modern world. Today, we are also confronted regularly with both the incredible efficiency and the baffling irrationality of modern bureaucratic structures. Within moments of entering into an efficiently concluded contract with a wireless phone service provider, we can become consumers of a cornucopia of technological opportunities, with the ability to chat on the phone or

W. E. B. Du Bois, the first African American to receive a PhD from Harvard, wrote 20 books and more than 100 scholarly articles on race and race relations. Today, many of his works are classics in the study of African American lives and race relations in the United States.

Max Weber made significant contributions to the understanding of how capitalism developed in Western countries and its relationship to religious beliefs. His work on formal rationality and bureaucracy continues to influence sociologists' study of modern society.

Verstehen: The German word for interpretive understanding; Weber's proposed methodology for explaining social relationships by having the sociologist imagine how subjects might perceive a situation.

Formal rationality: A context in which people's pursuit of goals is shaped by rules, regulations, and larger social structures.

Bureaucracies: Formal organizations characterized by written rules, hierarchical authority, and paid staff, intended to promote organizational efficiency.

receive text messages from almost anywhere, post photographs or watch videos online, and pass the time on social media platforms. Should we later be confused by a bill and need to speak to a company representative, however, we may be shuttled through endless repetitions of an automated response system that never seems to offer us the option of speaking with another human being. Today, Weber's presciently predicted irrationality of rationality is alive and well.

Significant Founding Ideas in U.S. Sociology

Sociology was born in Europe, but it took firm root in U.S. soil, where it was influenced by turn-of-the-century industrialization and urbanization as well as by racial strife and discrimination. Strikes by organized labor, corruption in government, an explosion of European immigration, racial segregation, and the growth of city slums all helped mold early sociological thought in the United States. By the late 1800s, numerous universities in the United States were offering sociology courses. The first faculties of sociology were established at the University of Kansas (1889), the University of Chicago (1892), and Atlanta University (1897). Below, we look at a handful of sociologists who have had an important influence on modern sociological thinking in the United States. Throughout the book, we will learn about more U.S. sociologists who have shaped our perspectives today.

 # Social Life, Social Media

CAPTURING THE WORLD IN 280 CHARACTERS

What is Twitter? Just over a decade ago, no such question could have been asked. *To twitter* meant only to chatter (or to impart a "short burst of inconsequential information;" Johnson, 2013), and *tweeting* was for the birds. Today, the social media platform Twitter is a significant and ubiquitous form of communication used by social activists, politicians, celebrities and fans, the news media, sports teams, advertisers, and friend groups. Social media reaches across the globe: According to a recent analysis, of the world's 7.3 billion inhabitants, about 3.4 billion are Internet users and 2.3 billion are active social media users. Both figures rose by 10% in the last year alone and are expected to grow (Chaffey, 2016). The rise of users in the United States has been dramatic. According to the Pew Research Center, in 2005, about 7% of the U.S. population used social media. In 2017, it had reached 69% (Pew Research Center, 2018). Globally, Twitter is the third most popular social media platform on the planet (Figure 1.4), finding its most avid users in Indonesia, Turkey, Saudi Arabia, India, and the Philippines (Chaffey, 2015).

The Twitter social media site (https://about .twitter.com/company) was created by Jack Dorsey, Evan Williams, and Biz Stone. On March 21, 2006, Jack Dorsey (@Jack) sent out the first tweet. It said, "just setting up my twttr." Today, Twitter has over 310 million "monthly active users," tweeting in over 40 languages. A company that had eight employees in 2008 has grown to 3,800 employees worldwide. At this point, then, we can return to our opening question:

What is Twitter? Novelist David Foster Wallace has been quoted as saying that Twitter is "the bathroom wall of the American psyche." The magazine *The New Yorker* responded to Wallace's characterization by asking its readers to use their own tweets to define Twitter. Among their entries:

- "Alone Together" (@dnahinga)
- "Communicative disease" (@Wodespain)
- "the carrier pigeon of the 21st century" (@Rajiv_Narayan)
- "Twitter is the dimestore in the marketplace of ideas" (@anglescott)
- "an infinite orchestra hall, where everyone has a kazoo solo anytime they want for 140 seconds" (@Shan19the6man6). ("Questioningly winner," 2012, para. 2–4)

Are you a Twitter user or follower? How would you define it in 280 characters or less?

From a sociological perspective, the key question that follows is this: What is the sociological significance of Twitter? The social media platform has been credited with contributing to scientific and medical knowledge as well as to investment wisdom. *Social Media Today* points out that the U.S. Geological Survey has used tweets to track earthquakes: "The USGS had found that by tracking mentions of the term 'earthquake', within specific parameters which they'd defined, they could better track seismic activity across the globe than they'd been able to via their previous measurement systems" (Hutchinson, 2016,

(Continued)

(Continued)

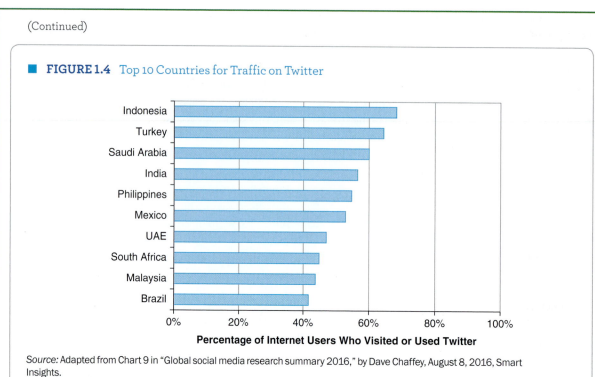

■ **FIGURE 1.4**   Top 10 Countries for Traffic on Twitter

Source: Adapted from Chart 9 in "Global social media research summary 2016," by Dave Chaffey, August 8, 2016, Smart Insights.

"Health and Safety," para. 1). It has also been used to track influenza outbreaks. The same article notes that a small number of financial services companies "are using Twitter data to deliver better predictive results" with monitoring of information and conversations available on the site (Hutchinson, 2016, "Off to Market," para. 2). The sociological significance is more challenging to assess. Twitter has been at the forefront of social protest organizing across the globe. It has been used by politicians and celebrities to share news and to energize supporters and fans. It has also been used as a platform to spread rumors, conspiracy theories, and fear. Pressing social and political issues can't be debated in 280 characters without missing important complexities. In this book's *Social Life, Social Media* boxes, we look at the spectrum of ways Twitter—and other key social media platforms—reflects, affects, and shapes our social world in positive and problematic ways.

Think It Through

- To what extent do social media platforms such as Twitter simply provide a medium for sharing opinions, ideas, and information? To what extent are they also powerful media for shaping people's perspectives and practices?

Follow us on Twitter to keep up with current sociological stories and research! We're at **@DiscoverSoc1**.

Share your own ideas at **#DiscoverSociology**.

Robert Ezra Park

The sociology department at the University of Chicago, which gave us what is often known as the "Chicago School" of sociology, dominated the new discipline in the United States at the start of the 20th century. Chicago sociologist Robert Ezra Park (1864–1944) pioneered the study of urban sociology and race relations. Once a muckraking journalist, Park was an equally colorful academic, reportedly coming to class in disheveled clothes and with shaving soap still in his ears. But his students were devoted to him, and his work was widely recognized. His 1921 textbook, *An Introduction to the Science of Sociology,* coauthored with his Chicago colleague Ernest Burgess, helped shape the discipline. The Chicago School studied a broad spectrum of social phenomena, from hoboes and flophouses (inexpensive dormitory-style housing) to movie houses, dance halls, and slums, and from youth gangs and mobs to residents of Chicago's ritzy Gold Coast.

Park was a champion of racial integration, having once served as personal secretary to the African American educator Booker T. Washington. Yet racial discrimination was evident in the treatment of Black sociologists, including

W. E. B. Du Bois, a contemporary of many of the sociologists working in the Chicago School.

W. E. B. Du Bois

A prominent Black sociologist and civil rights leader at the African American Atlanta University, W. E. B. Du Bois (1868–1963) developed ideas that were considered too radical to find broad acceptance in the sociological community. At a time when the U.S. Supreme Court had ruled that segregated "separate but equal" facilities for Blacks and Whites were constitutional and when lynching of Black Americans had reached an all-time high, Du Bois condemned the deep-seated racism of White society. Today, his writings on race relations and the lives of U.S. Blacks are classics in the field.

Du Bois sought to show that racism was widespread in U.S. society. He was also critical of Blacks who had "made it" and then turned their backs on those who had not. One of his most enduring ideas is that in U.S. society, African Americans are never able to escape a fundamental awareness of race. They experience a **double consciousness**, as he called it—*an awareness of themselves as both Americans and Black, never free of racial stigma*. He wrote, "The Negro is sort of a seventh son . . . gifted with second-sight . . . this sense of always looking at one's self through the eyes of others" (Du Bois, 1903/2008, p. 12). Today, as in Du Bois's time, physical traits such as skin color may shape people's perceptions and interactions in significant and complex ways.

Charlotte Perkins Gilman

Charlotte Perkins Gilman (1860–1935) was a well-known novelist, feminist, and sociologist of her time. Because of her family's early personal and economic struggles, she had only a few years of formal schooling in childhood, although she would later enroll at the Rhode Island School of Design. She read widely, however, and she was influenced by her paternal aunts, who included suffragist Isabella Beecher Stowe and writer Harriet Beecher Stowe, author of *Uncle Tom's Cabin* (1852), an anti-slavery novel.

Gilman's most prominent publication was her semiautobiographical short story, *The Yellow Wallpaper* (1892), which follows the decline of a married woman shut away in a room (with repellent yellow wallpaper) by her husband, ostensibly for the sake of her health. Gilman used the story to highlight the consequences of women's lack of autonomy in marriage. She continued to build this early feminist thesis in the book *Women and Economics: A Study of the Economic Relation Between Men and Women as a Factor in Social Evolution* (1898/2006), which includes this memorable quote:

The labor of women in the house, certainly, enables men to produce more wealth than they otherwise could; and in this way women are economic factors in society. But so are horses. The labor of horses enables men to produce more wealth than they otherwise could. The horse is an economic factor in society. But the horse is not economically independent, nor is the woman. (p. 7)

Gilman's work represents an early and notable effort to look at sex roles in the family not as natural and inevitable, as many saw them at the time, but as social constructions that had the potential to change and to bring greater autonomy to women in the home and society.

Robert K. Merton

After World War II, sociology began to apply sophisticated quantitative models to the study of social processes. There was also a growing interest in the grand theories of the European founders. At Columbia University, Robert K. Merton (1910–2003) undertook wide-ranging studies that helped further establish sociology as a scientific discipline. Merton is best known for his theory of deviance (Merton, 1938), his work on the sociology of science (Merton, 1996), and his iteration of the distinction between manifest and latent functions as a means for more fully understanding the relationships between and roles of sociological phenomena and institutions in communities and society (Merton, 1968). He emphasized the development of theories in what he called the *middle range*—midway between the grand theories of Weber, Marx, and Durkheim and quantitative studies of specific social problems.

C. Wright Mills

Columbia University sociologist C. Wright Mills (1916–1962) is best known in the discipline for describing the *sociological imagination*, the imperative in sociology to seek the nexus between private troubles and public issues. In his short career, Mills was prolific. He renewed interest in Max Weber by translating many of his works into English and applying his ideas to the contemporary United States. But Mills, who also drew on Marx, identified himself as a "plain Marxist." His concept of the sociological imagination can be traced in part to Marx's famous statement that "man makes history, but not under circumstances of his own choosing," meaning that even though we are agents of free will, the social context has a profound impact on the obstacles or opportunities in our lives.

Mills synthesized Weberian and Marxian traditions, applying sociological thinking to the most pressing problems of the day, particularly inequality. He advocated an activist sociology with a sense of social responsibility. Like many sociologists, he was willing to turn a critical eye on

---

Double consciousness: Among African Americans, an awareness of themselves as both American and Black, never free of racial stigma.

"common knowledge," including the belief that the United States is a democracy that represents the interests of all people. In a provocative study, he examined the workings of the "power elite," a small group of wealthy businessmen, military leaders, and politicians who Mills believed ran the country largely in their own interests (Mills, 1956/2000a).

Women in Early Sociology

Why did so few women social scientists find a place among sociology's founders? After all, the American (1776) and French (1789) revolutions elevated such lofty ideals as freedom, liberty, and equality. Yet long after these historical events, women and minorities were still excluded from public life in Europe and North America. Democracy—which gives people the right to participate in their governance—was firmly established as a principle for nearly a century and a half in the United States before women achieved the right to vote in 1920. In France, it took even longer—until 1945.

Sociology as a discipline emerged during the first modern flourishing of feminism in the 19th century. Yet women and people of non-European heritage were systematically excluded from influential positions in the European universities where sociology and other modern social sciences originated. When women did pursue lives as scholars, the men who dominated the social sciences largely ignored

their writings. Feminist scholar Julie Daubié won a prize from the Lyon Academy for her essay "Poor Women in the Nineteenth Century," yet France's public education minister denied her a diploma on the grounds that he would be "forever holding up his ministry to ridicule" (Kandal, 1988, pp. 57–58). Between 1840 and 1960, almost no women held senior academic positions in the sociology departments of any European or U.S. universities, with the exception of exclusively women's colleges.

Several woman scholars managed to overcome these obstacles to make significant contributions to sociological inquiry. For example, in 1792, the British scholar Mary Wollstonecraft published *A Vindication of the Rights of Women*, arguing that scientific progress could not occur unless women were allowed to become men's equals by means of universal education. In France in 1843, Flora Tristan called for equal rights for women workers, "the last remaining slaves in France." Also in France, Aline Valette published *Socialism and Sexualism* in 1893, nearly three quarters of a century before the term *sexism* found its way into spoken English (Kandal, 1988).

An important figure in early U.S. sociology is Jane Addams (1860–1935). Addams is best known as the founder of Hull House, a settlement house for the poor, sick, and aged that became a center for political activists and social reformers. Less well known is the fact that under

The *sociological imagination* involves viewing seemingly personal issues through a sociological lens. C. Wright Mills is best known for coining this catchy and popular term.

Underappreciated during her time, Jane Addams was a prominent scholar and early contributor to sociology. She is also known for her political activism and commitment to social reform.

Addams's guidance, the residents of Hull House engaged in important research on social problems in Chicago. *Hull-House Maps and Papers*, published in 1895, pioneered the study of Chicago neighborhoods, helping to shape the research direction of the Chicago School of sociology. Following Addams's lead, Chicago sociologists mapped the city's neighborhoods, studied their residents, and helped create the field of community studies. Despite her prolific work—she authored 11 books and hundreds of articles and received the Nobel Peace Prize for her dedication to social reform in 1931—she never secured a full-time position at the University of Chicago, and the school refused to award her an honorary degree.

As Harriet Martineau, Jane Addams, Julie Daubié, and others experienced, early female sociologists were not accorded the same status as their male counterparts. Only recently have many of their writings been rediscovered and their contributions acknowledged in sociology.

What Is Sociological Theory?

Often, multiple sociologists look at the same events, phenomena, or institutions and draw different conclusions. How can this be? One reason is that they may approach their analyses from different theoretical perspectives. In this section, we explore the key theoretical paradigms in sociology and look at how they are used as tools for the analysis of society.

Sociological theories are *logical, rigorous frameworks for the interpretation of social life that make particular*

assumptions and ask particular questions about the social world. The word *theory* is rooted in the Greek word *theoria*, which means "a viewing." An apt metaphor for a theory is a pair of glasses. You can view a social phenomenon such as socioeconomic inequality; poverty, deviance, or consumer culture; or an institution such as capitalism or the family by using different theories as lenses.

As you will see in the next section, in the discipline of sociology, several major categories of theories seek to examine and explain social phenomena and institutions. Imagine the various sociological theories as different pairs of glasses, each with colored lenses that change the way you see an image: You may look at the same institution or phenomenon as you put on each pair, but it will appear differently, depending on the glasses you are wearing. Keep in mind that sociological theories are not "truths" about the social world. They are logical, rigorous analytical tools that we can use to inquire about, interpret, and make educated predictions about the world around us. From the vantage point of any sociological theory, some aspects of a phenomenon or an institution are illuminated while others are obscured. In the end, theories are more or less useful depending on how well *empirical data*—that is, knowledge gathered by researchers through scientific methods—support their analytical conclusions. Below, we outline the basic theoretical perspectives that we will be using in this text.

> **Sociological theories:** Logical, rigorous frameworks for the interpretation of social life that make particular assumptions and ask particular questions about the social world.

TABLE 1.1   The Three Principal Sociological Paradigms

THEORETICAL PERSPECTIVE AND FOUNDING THEORIST(S)	STRUCTURAL FUNCTIONALISM (ÉMILE DURKHEIM)	SOCIAL CONFLICT (KARL MARX)	SYMBOLIC INTERACTIONISM (MAX WEBER, GEORGE HERBERT MEAD)
Assumptions about self and society	Society is a system of interdependent, interrelated parts, like an organism, with groups and institutions contributing to the stability and equilibrium of the whole social system.	Society consists of conflicting interests, but only some groups have the power and resources to realize their interests. Some groups benefit from the social order at the expense of other groups.	The self is a social creation; social interaction occurs by means of symbols such as words, gestures, and adornments; shared meanings are important to successful social interactions.
Key focus and questions	Macrosociology: What keeps society operating smoothly? What functions do different societal institutions and phenomena serve for society as a whole?	Macrosociology: What are the sources of conflict in society? Who benefits and who loses from the existing social order? How can inequalities be overcome?	Microsociology: How do individuals experience themselves, one another, and society as a whole? How do they interpret the meanings of particular social interactions?

The three dominant theoretical perspectives in sociology are *structural functionalism*, *social conflict theory*, and *symbolic interactionism*. We outline their basic characteristics below and will revisit them again throughout the book. Symbolic interactionism shares with the functionalist and social conflict paradigms an interest in interpreting and understanding social life. Nevertheless, the first two are **macro-level paradigms**, *concerned with large-scale patterns and institutions*. Symbolic interactionism is a **micro-level paradigm**—it is *concerned with small-group social relations and interactions*.

Structural functionalism, social conflict theory, and symbolic interactionism form the basic foundation of contemporary sociological theorizing (Table 1.1). Throughout this book, we will introduce variations on these theories as well as new and evolving theoretical ideas in sociology.

The Functionalist Paradigm

Structural functionalism (or *functionalism*—the term we use in this book) *seeks to explain social organization and change in terms of the roles performed by different social structures, phenomena, and institutions*. Functionalism characterizes society as made up of many interdependent parts—an analogy often cited is the human body. Each part serves a different function, but all parts work together to ensure the equilibrium and health of the entity as a whole. Society, too, is composed of a spectrum of different parts with a variety of different functions, such as the government, the family, religious and educational institutions, and the media. According to the theory, together, these parts contribute to the smooth functioning and equilibrium of society.

The key question posed by the functionalist perspective is, "What function does a particular institution, phenomenon, or social group serve for the maintenance of society?" That is, what contribution does a given institution, phenomenon, or social group make to the equilibrium, stability, and functioning of the whole? Note the underlying assumption of functionalism: Any existing institution or phenomenon does serve a function; if it served no function, it would evolve out of existence. Consequently, the central task of the functionalist sociologist is to discover what function an institution or a phenomenon—for instance, the traditional family, capitalism, social stratification, or deviance—serves in the maintenance of the social order.

Émile Durkheim is credited with developing the early foundations of functionalism. Among other ideas,

Durkheim observed that all known societies have some degree of deviant behavior, such as crime. The notion that deviance is functional for societies may seem counterintuitive: Ordinarily, we do not think of deviance as beneficial or necessary to society. Durkheim, however, reasoned that since deviance is universal, it must serve a social function—if it did not serve a function, it would cease to exist. Durkheim concluded that one function of deviance—specifically, of society's labeling of some acts as deviant—is to remind members of society what is considered normal or moral; when a society punishes deviant behavior, it reaffirms people's beliefs in what is right and good.

Talcott Parsons (1902–1979) expanded functionalist analysis by looking at whole social systems, such as government, the economy, and the family, and how they contribute to the functioning of the whole social system (Parsons, 1964/2007, 1967). For example, he wrote that traditional sex roles for men and women contribute to stability on both the micro familial level and the macro societal level. Parsons argued that traditional socialization produces instrumental or rational and work-oriented males and expressive or sensitive, nurturing, and emotional females. Instrumental males, he reasoned, are well suited for the competitive world of work, whereas their expressive female counterparts are appropriately prepared to care for the family. According to Parsons, these roles are complementary and positively functional, leading men and women to inhabit different spheres of the social world. Complementary rather than competing roles contribute to solidarity in a marriage by reducing competition between husband and wife. Critics have rejected this idea as a justification of inequality.

As this example suggests, functionalism is conservative in that it tends to accept rather than question the status quo; it holds that any given institution or phenomenon exists because it is functional for society, rather than asking whether it might benefit one group to the detriment of others, as critics say Parsons's position on gender roles does. One of functionalism's long-standing weaknesses is a failure to recognize inequalities in the distribution of power and resources and how those affect social relationships.

Merton attempted to refine the functionalist paradigm by demonstrating that not all social structures work to maintain or strengthen the social organism, as Durkheim and other early functionalists seemed to suggest. According to Merton, a social institution or phenomenon can have both positive functions and problematic dysfunctions. Merton broadened the functionalist idea by suggesting that **manifest functions** are the *obvious and intended functions of a phenomenon or institution*. **Latent functions**, by

---

Macro-level paradigms: Theories of the social world that are concerned with large-scale patterns and institutions.

Micro-level paradigm: A theory of the social world that is concerned with small-group social relations and interactions.

Structural functionalism: A theory that seeks to explain social organization and change in terms of the roles performed by different social structures, phenomena, and institutions; also known as *functionalism*.

Manifest functions: The obvious and intended functions of a phenomenon or institution.

Latent functions: Functions of a phenomenon or institution that are not recognized or expected.

Inequality Matters

WHY ARE SOME PEOPLE POOR AND OTHERS RICH?

The concentration of wealth at the top of the economic ladder and the widespread struggle of millions of others to make do with scant resources are critical issues on both the domestic and global levels. One common explanation of the stark economic disparities in the United States is that they are the outcome of individual differences in talent, ambition, and work ethic. Although personal effort is very important, the fact that more than 12.7% of the population lives below the official poverty line, including disproportionate numbers of Blacks (21.2%), Hispanics (18.3%), and children 18 and under (17.5%; Fontenot, Semenga, & Kollar, 2018), should lead our sociological imaginations to recognize social and economic forces that underlie what we see in the data—and around us.

What are some of the sociological factors we might study to understand the existence and persistence of poverty in a wealthy country (Figure 1.5)? Consider the argument that educational opportunity is not equally distributed: In most of the United States,

schools are still funded primarily by local property taxes. Consequently, school districts in areas with high property values have more assets to tax than low-value areas. This means more money to spend on teachers, textbooks, and technology as well as on the maintenance of schools, playgrounds, and athletic facilities. Even within districts, individual schools in wealthier neighborhoods benefit from greater parental resources, such as donated funds and volunteer hours. Without a strong educational foundation that prepares them for a competitive economy, already-poor children are at greater risk of remaining poor as adults, a topic we take up in Chapter 12. Recent social mobility research, in fact, suggests that there is a good probability that a family's economic status is reproduced in the next generation.

Macro-level economic changes affecting the U.S. labor market have also had a significant effect on many families and communities, a subject we'll explore in both Chapters 7 and 15. Automation and

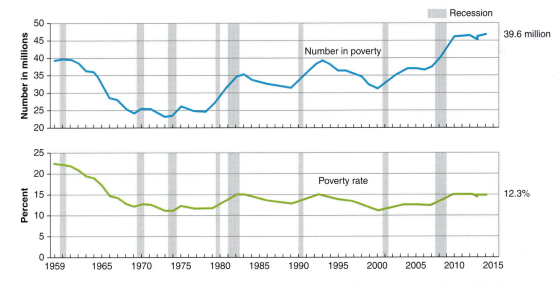

■ **FIGURE 1.5** Number in Poverty and Poverty Rate: 1959 to 2017

Source: Kayla Fontenot, Jessica Semenga, & Melissa Kollar. (2018). Income and Poverty in the United States: 2017. Washington, DC: U.S. Bureau of the Census. Retrieved from https://www.census.gov/library/publications/2018/demo/P60–263.html.

Note: The 2013 data reflect the implementation of the redesigned income questions. The data points are placed at the midpoints of the respective years. For information on confidentiality protection, sampling error, nonsampling error, and definitions, see <ftp://ftp2.census.gov/programs-surveys/cps/techodocs/cpsmar15.pdf>

(Continued)

(Continued)

Why are children of poor parents more likely to be poor as adults? This is a question of fundamental interest to sociologists.

Service jobs, including restaurant and retail work, have expanded as the manufacturing sector has contracted, but these positions are less secure and more poorly paid—they are far less likely to give workers a lift into the middle class. This makes a solid education more critical than ever, but as we noted above, young people growing up in low-income areas have fewer opportunities to access such an education.

Wealth, poverty, and inequality are complex sociological phenomena. In these boxes, and throughout the book, we seek to help you more fully understand their roots, manifestations, and consequences.

Think It Through

- If, as our sociological imaginations suggest, poverty is both a private trouble and a public issue, what are public issues other than those identified in this essay that may contribute to the existence and persistence of poverty in some families, communities, and regions?

the movement abroad of manufacturing jobs since the 1970s have reduced the availability of jobs for less-educated workers that pay a middle-class wage.

contrast, are *functions that are not recognized or expected.* He used the famous example of the Hopi rain dance, positing that although the manifest function of the dance was to bring rain, a no less important latent function was to reaffirm social bonds in the community through a shared ritual. Consider another example: A manifest function of war is usually to vanquish an enemy, perhaps to defend a territory or to claim it. Latent functions of war—those that are not the overt purpose but may still have powerful effects—may include increased patriotism in countries engaged in the war, a rise in the profits of companies manufacturing military equipment or contracting workers to the military, and changes in national budgetary priorities.

The Social Conflict Paradigm

In contrast to functionalism, the **social conflict paradigm** (which we refer to in this book as *conflict theory*) *seeks to explain social organization and change in terms of the conflict that is built into social relationships.* Conflict theory

is rooted in the ideas about class and power put forth by Marx. Although Durkheim's structural functionalist lens asked how different parts of society contribute to stability, Marx asked about the roots of conflict. Conflict theorists pose the questions, "Who benefits from the way social institutions and relationships are structured? Who loses?" The social conflict paradigm focuses on what divides people rather than on what unites them. It presumes that

The manifest function of a vehicle is to transport a person efficiently from Point A to Point B. One latent function is to say something about the status of the driver.

Social conflict paradigm: A theory that seeks to explain social organization and change in terms of the conflict that is built into social relations; also known as *conflict theory.*

group interests drive relationships, and that various groups in society (for instance, social classes, ethnic and racial groups, women and men) will act in their own interests. Conflict theory thus assumes not that interests are shared but that they may be different and irreconcilable and, importantly, that only some groups have the power and resources to realize their interests. As a result, conflict is—sooner or later—inevitable.

From Marx's perspective, the bourgeoisie benefits directly from the capitalist social order. If, as Marx suggests, the capitalist class has an interest in maximizing productivity and profit and minimizing costs (including the cost of labor in the form of workers' wages) and the working class has an interest in earning more and working less, then the interests of the two classes are difficult to reconcile. The more powerful group in society generally has the upper hand in furthering its interests.

After Marx, the body of conflict theory expanded tremendously. In the 20th century and today, theorists have extended the reach of the perspective to consider how control of culture and the rise of technology (rather than just control of the means of production) underpins class domination (Adorno, 1975; Horkheimer, 1947) as well as how the expanded middle class can be accommodated in a Marxist perspective (Wright, 1998). Many key ideas in feminist theory take a conflict-oriented perspective, although the focus shifts from social class to gender power and conflict (Connell, 2005) as well as ways in which race is implicated in relations of power (Collins, 1990).

Recall Durkheim's functionalist analysis of crime and deviance. According to this perspective, society defines crime to reaffirm people's beliefs about what is right and dissuade them from deviating. A conflict theorist might argue that dominant groups in society define the behaviors labeled *criminal* or *deviant* because they have the power to do so. For example, street crimes such as robbery and carjacking are defined and punished as criminal behavior. They are also represented in reality television programs, movies, and other cultural products as images of criminal deviance. On the other hand, corporate or white-collar crime, which may cause the loss of money or even lives, is less likely to be clearly defined, represented, and punished as criminal. From a conflict perspective, white-collar crime is more likely to be committed by members of the upper class (for instance, business or political leaders or financiers) and is less likely to be punished harshly compared with street crime, which is associated with the lower-income classes, although white-collar crime may have even greater economic and health consequences. A social conflict theorist would draw our attention to the fact that the decision makers who pass our laws are mostly members of the upper class and govern in the interests of capitalism and their own socioeconomic peers.

A key weakness of the social conflict paradigm is that it overlooks the forces of stability, equilibrium, and consensus in society. The assumption that groups have conflicting (even irreconcilable) interests and that those interests are realized by those with power at the expense of those with less power fails to account for forces of cohesion and stability in societies.

Symbolic Interactionism

Symbolic interactionism argues that *both the individual self and society as a whole are the products of social interactions based on language and other symbols*. The term *symbolic interactionism* was coined by U.S. sociologist Herbert Blumer (1900–1987) in 1937, but the approach originated in the lectures of George Herbert Mead (1863–1931), a University of Chicago philosopher allied with the Chicago School of sociology. The symbolic interactionist paradigm argues that people acquire their sense of who they are only through interaction with others. They do this by means of **symbols**, *representations of things that are not immediately present to our senses*. Symbols include such things as words, gestures, emoticons, and tattoos, among others.

Recall our earlier discussions of the theoretical interpretations of deviance and crime. A symbolic interactionist might focus on the ways in which people label one another as *deviant* (a symbolic act that uses language), the factors that make such a label stick, and the meanings underlying such a label. If you are accused of committing a crime you did not commit, how will the label of *criminal* affect the way others see you? How will it affect the way you see yourself, and will you begin to act differently as a result? Can being labeled *deviant* be a self-fulfilling prophecy? For the symbolic interactionist, sociological inquiry is the study of how people interact and how they create and interpret symbols in the social world.

Although symbolic interactionist perspectives draw our attention to important micro-level processes in society, they may miss the larger structural context of those processes, such as discovering who has the power to make laws defining what or who is deviant. For this reason, many sociologists seek to use both macro- and micro-level perspectives when analyzing social phenomena such as deviance.

The three paradigms described above lead to diverse images of society, research questions, and conclusions about the patterns and nature of social life. Each "pair of glasses" can provide a different perspective on the social

Symbolic interactionism: A microsociological perspective that posits that both the individual self and society as a whole are the products of social interactions based on language and other symbols.

Symbols: Representations of things that are not immediately present to our senses.

world. Throughout this text, the three major theoretical paradigms—and some new ones we will encounter in later chapters—will help us understand key issues and themes of sociology.

Principal Themes in This Book

We began this chapter with a list of *why* questions with which sociologists are concerned and about which any one of us might be curious. Behind these questions, we find several major themes, which are also some of the main themes in this book. Three important focal points for sociology—and for us—are (1) power and inequality and the ways in which the unequal distribution of social, economic, and political resources shape opportunities, obstacles, and relationships; (2) the societal changes occurring as a result of globalization and the growing social diversity of modern communities and societies; and (3) the powerful impact of technological change on modern lives, institutions, and states.

Power and Inequality

As we consider broad social topics such as gender, race, social class, and sexual orientation and their effects on social relationships and resources, we will be asking who has **power**—*the ability to mobilize resources and achieve goals despite the resistance of others*—and who does not. We will also ask about variables that influence the uneven distribution of power and how some groups use power to create advantages for themselves (and disadvantages for others) and how disadvantaged groups mobilize to challenge the powerful.

Power is often distributed unequally and can be used by those who possess it to marginalize other social groups. **Inequality** refers to *differences in wealth, power, political voice, educational opportunities, and other valued resources.* The existence of inequality not only raises moral and ethical questions about fairness, but it can also tear at the very fabric of societies, fostering social alienation and instability. Furthermore, it may have negative effects on local and national economies. Notably, economic inequality is increasing both within and between many countries around the globe, a fact that makes understanding the roots and consequences of this phenomenon—that is, asking the *why* questions—ever more important.

Globalization and Diversity

Globalization is *the process by which people all over the planet become increasingly interconnected economically, politically, culturally, and environmentally.* Globalization is not new. It began nearly 200,000 years ago, when humans first spread from their African cradle into Europe and Asia. For thousands of years, humans have traveled, traded goods, and exchanged ideas over much of the globe, using seaways or land routes such as the famed Silk Road, a stretch of land that links China and Europe. But the rate of globalization took a giant leap forward with the Industrial Revolution, which accelerated the growth of global trade. It made another dramatic jump with the advent of the Information Age, drawing together individuals, cultures, and countries into a common global web of information exchange. In this book, we consider a spectrum of manifestations, functions, and consequences of globalization in areas such as the economy, culture, and the environment.

Growing contacts between people and cultures have made us increasingly aware of social diversity as a feature of modern societies. **Social diversity** is *the social and cultural mixture of different groups in society and the societal recognition of difference as significant.* The spread of culture through the globalization of media and the rise of migration has created a world in which almost no place is isolated. As a result, many nations today, including the United States, are characterized by a high degree of social diversity.

Social diversity brings a unique set of sociological challenges. People everywhere have a tendency toward **ethnocentrism**, a *worldview whereby one judges other cultures by the standards of one's own culture and regards one's own way of life as normal—and often superior to others.* From a sociological perspective, no group can be said to be more human than any other. Yet history abounds with examples of people lashing out at others whose religion, language, customs, race, or sexual orientation differed from their own.

Technology and Society

Technology is the practical application of knowledge to transform natural resources for human use. The first human technology was probably the use of rocks and other blunt instruments as weapons, enabling humans to hunt large

---

Power: The ability to mobilize resources and achieve goals despite the resistance of others.

Inequality: Differences in wealth, power, political voice, educational opportunities, and other valued resources.

Globalization: The process by which people all over the planet become increasingly interconnected economically, politically, culturally, and environmentally.

Social diversity: The social and cultural mixture of different groups in society and the societal recognition of difference as significant.

Ethnocentrism: A worldview whereby one judges other cultures by the standards of one's own culture and regards one's own way of life as normal and often superior to others.

Global Issues

LOCAL CONSUMPTION, GLOBAL PRODUCTION

Try this at home: Walk through your dorm room, apartment, or house and make a list of the places the products you find were manufactured. Be sure to check electronic equipment such as your laptop and smartphone. Open your closets and drawers and look at some labels on your clothing and footwear. Can you locate where other household items such as your microwave oven or coffeemaker were manufactured? Take a look at your list: What countries do you find there? It is likely that you will find that people who live outside the U.S. produced most of the necessities and luxuries of your everyday life. Even a car manufactured in the U.S. is likely to have parts that have passed through the hands of workers abroad.

When you checked your closet, did you find any clothing made in the U.S.? If not, you are not alone. In 1950, about 95% of clothing purchased in this country was made domestically. By 1980, the share fell to 70%. Today, an estimated 2% of our clothing is manufactured in the U.S. (Vatz, 2013). The rest is manufactured in factories around the globe: Just after the turn of the millennium, the clothing chain The Gap was ordering its goods from about 1,200 factories across 42 countries (Cline, 2013). What are some of the sociological effects of this shift?

U.S. consumption of goods grew in the latter half of the 20th century. This came about as appetites were whetted by new advertising campaigns and credit options increased, even as wages stagnated in the mid-1970s. Notably as well, as more goods were manufactured abroad, they also became less expensive: "In 1960, an average American household spent over 10 percent of its income on clothing and shoes—equivalent to roughly $4,000 today. The average person bought fewer than 25 garments each year (Vatz, 2013, para. 1). By contrast, in 2016, U.S. households spent roughly $1,800 annually on clothes, accounting for 3.1% of total expenses (Bureau of Labor Statistics, 2018). But less money can buy more goods: In 2015, the average U.S. female consumer owned 30 outfits, compared to 9 in 1930 (Johnson, 2015).

The falling costs of goods for consumers have come at a price. As clothing and other manufacturers have shifted production abroad, there have been dramatic disruptions in the labor market. As we will see in Chapter 15, outsourcing abroad as well as increased automation of production have contributed to declining wages and lost jobs for manufacturing workers in the U.S. Furthermore, millions of workers around the world are today employed in factories that are poorly regulated and operate largely outside the view of the consumers who buy their products. These poor conditions were highlighted in 2013, when 1,135 garment workers producing high-end clothing in a factory in Dhaka, Bangladesh, were killed when their building collapsed; despite a building evacuation conducted after cracks were detected in the building on the previous day, workers were ordered to come to work ("Rana Plaza collapse," 2016). Just two years later, in 2015, at the Kentex factory in the Philippines, which manufactured cheap rubber shoes and flipflops for the global market, 74 workers lost their lives when sparks from a welder's tool started a fire. Employees were trapped in the blaze without access to fire escapes. It was also revealed that the factory was without an alarm or sprinkler system to protect their workers (van der Zee, 2015).

On the one hand, even with these risks, many workers in developing countries leave their rural homes to seek out opportunities to earn and learn in new urban factories, just as they did in the early decades of the Industrial Revolution in Western Europe. On the other hand, the world's low-wage workers, many of whom are women, are vulnerable to exploitation, and their hours are long and their work sites can be unpleasant or, as the incidents in Bangladesh and the Philippines have demonstrated, even deadly. The conditions under which some workers toil today cause us to recall the 19th-century English factories that inspired Marx to write his powerful critique of capitalism's darker sides.

Can the needs and desires of consumers and workers around the globe be reconciled? What do you think?

Think It Through

- The cheap and ample fashion options that fill U.S. malls are often made by poorly compensated female labor abroad. Do labor conditions matter to U.S. consumers? Should they matter?

---

animals for food. Agriculture—planting crops such as rice or corn in hopes of reaping a yearly harvest—represents another technological advance, one superior to simple foraging in the wild for nuts and berries. The use of modern machinery, which ushered in the Industrial Revolution, represents still another technological leap, multiplying the productivity of human efforts. Today, we are in the midst of another revolutionary period of technological change:

the information revolution. Thanks to the microchip, the Internet, and mobile technology, an increasing number of people around the world now have instant access to a mass of information that was unimaginable 10 or 20 years ago. The information revolution is creating postindustrial economies based far more heavily on the production of knowledge than on the production of goods, as well as new ways of communicating that have the potential to draw people around the world together—or tear them apart. No less importantly, revolutions in robotics and artificial intelligence promise to alter the world of work in ways that we are only beginning to recognize.

Together, these three themes provide the foundation for this text. Our goal is to develop a rigorous sociological examination of power and inequality, globalization and diversity, and technology and society to help you better understand the social world from its roots to its contemporary manifestations to its possible futures.

Why Study Sociology?

A sociological perspective highlights the many ways that we both influence and are powerfully influenced by the social world around us: Society shapes us, and we, in turn, shape society. A sociological perspective enables us to see the social world through a variety of different lenses (recall the glasses metaphor we used when talking about theory): Sociologists might explain class differences and why they persist, for instance, in many different ways. Different theories illuminate different aspects of a sociological phenomenon or institution, enabling us to assemble a fuller, more rigorous perspective on social life.

Why are the issues and questions posed by sociology incredibly compelling for all of us to understand? One reason is that, as we will see throughout this book, many of the social issues sociologists study—marriage, fertility, poverty, unemployment, consumption, discrimination, and many others—are related to one another in ways we may not immediately see. A sociological perspective helps us to make connections between diverse social phenomena. When we understand these connections, we are better able to understand social issues, to address social problems, and to make (or vote for) policy choices that benefit society.

For example, a phenomenon such as the decline of marriage among the working class, which we mentioned at the start of the chapter, is related to growing globalization, declining employment in the manufacturing sector, and the persistently high rate of poverty among single mothers. Consider these social phenomena as pieces of a puzzle. One of the defining characteristics of economic globalization is the movement of manufacturing industries away from the United States to lower-wage countries. As a result, jobs in U.S. manufacturing, an economic sector dominated by men, have been declining since the 1970s. The decreasing number of less-educated men able to earn a wage high enough to support a family in turn is related to a decline in marriage among the working class. Even as marriage rates fall, however, many women still desire

---

 ## What Can I Do with a Sociology Degree?

AN INTRODUCTION

Have you ever wondered what you could do with a sociology degree, or how you can take the skills you'll learn in this major and use them in your career? This book can help you answer that question: Near the end of each chapter, we feature a short essay that links your study of sociology to potential career fields. In the *What Can I Do with a Sociology Degree?* feature, we highlight the professional skills and core knowledge that the study of sociology helps you develop. This set of skills and competencies, which range from critical thinking and written communication skills to aptitude in qualitative and quantitative research to the understanding of diversity, prepares you for the workforce as well as for graduate and professional school.

In every chapter that follows, this feature describes a specific skill that you can develop through the study of sociology. Each chapter also profiles a sociology graduate who shares what he or she learned through the study of sociology and how that particular skill has been valuable in his or her job. A short U.S. Bureau of Labor Statistics overview of the occupational field in which the graduate is working, its educational requirements, median income, and expected growth potential is also included to provide key information on each occupation.

Although this feature highlights sociology majors and graduates, it also speaks to students taking sociology who are majoring in other disciplines—being aware of your skills and able to articulate them precisely and clearly is important, no matter your chosen field of study or career path.

to have families, so the proportion of nonmarital births rises. Single mothers with children are among the demographic groups in the United States most likely to be poor, and their poverty rate has remained high even in periods of economic prosperity.

Although the relationships between sociological factors are complex and sometimes indirect, when sociology helps us fit them together, we gain a better picture of the issues confronting all of us—as well as of U.S. society and the larger world. Let's begin our journey.

SUMMARY

- **Sociology** is the **scientific** study of human social relationships, groups, and societies. Its central task is to ask what the dimensions of the social world are, how they influence our behavior, and how we, in turn, shape and change them.

- Sociology adheres to the principle of **social embeddedness**, the idea that economic, political, and other forms of human behavior are fundamentally shaped by social relationships. Sociologists seek to study through scientific means the social worlds that human beings consciously create.

- The **sociological imagination** is the ability to grasp the relationship between our individual lives and the larger social forces that help to shape them. It helps us see the connections between our private lives and public issues.

- **Critical thinking** is the ability to evaluate claims about truth by using reason and evidence. Often, we accept things as true because they are familiar, seem to mesh with our own experiences, and sound right. Critical thinking instead asks us to recognize poor arguments, reject statements not supported by evidence, and even question our own assumptions.

- Sociology's roots can be traced to the scientific revolution, the Enlightenment, industrialization and the birth of modern capitalism, and the urbanization of populations. Sociology emerged in part as a tool to enable people to understand the dramatic changes taking place in modern societies.

- Sociology generally traces its classical roots to Auguste Comte, Émile Durkheim, Max Weber, and Karl Marx. Early work in sociology reflected the concerns of the men who founded the discipline.

- In the United States, scholars at the University of Chicago focused on reforming social problems stemming from industrialization and urbanization. Women and people of color worked on the margins of the discipline because of persistent discrimination.

- Sociologists base their study of the social world on different theoretical perspectives that shape theory and guide research, often resulting in different conclusions. The major sociological paradigms are **structural functionalism**, the **social conflict paradigm**, and **symbolic interactionism**.

- Major themes in sociology include the distribution of **power** and growing inequality, **globalization** and its accompanying social changes, the growth of **social diversity**, and the way advances in technology have changed communication, commerce, and communities.

- The early founders of sociology believed that scientific knowledge could lead to shared social progress. Some modern sociologists question whether such shared scientific understanding is indeed possible.

KEY TERMS

DISCUSSION QUESTIONS

1. Think about Mills's concept of the sociological imagination and its ambition to draw together what Mills called *private troubles* and *public issues*. Think of a private trouble that sociologists might classify as also being a public issue. Share your example with your classmates.

2. What is critical thinking? What does it mean to be a critical thinker in our approach to understanding society and social issues or problems?

3. In the chapter, we asked why women's voices were marginal in early sociological thought. What factors explain the dearth of women's voices? What about the lack of minority voices? What effects do you think these factors may have had on the development of the discipline?

4. What is *theory*? What is its function in the discipline of sociology?

5. Recall the three key theoretical paradigms discussed in this chapter—structural functionalism, conflict theory, and symbolic interactionism. Discuss the ways these diverse "glasses" analyze deviance, its labeling, and its punishment in society. Try applying a similar analysis to another social phenomenon, such as class inequality or traditional gender roles.

Want a better grade?

Get the tools you need to sharpen your study skills. Access practice quizzes, eFlashcards, videos, and multimedia at **https://edge.sagepub.com/chambliss4e**.

Discover Sociological Research

2

WHAT DO YOU THINK?

1. What kinds of research questions could one pose to guide studies of sociological phenomena such as long-term poverty, cyberbullying, teen pregnancy, family homelessness, millennial consumption habits, or the high dropout rate in some high schools?

2. What factors might affect the honesty of people's responses to survey or interview questions?

3. What makes a sociological research project ethical or unethical?

LEARNING OBJECTIVES

2.1 Describe the scientific method and distinguish between qualitative and quantitative research.

2.2 Describe the components of a scientific theory and how a scientific theory is tested.

2.3 Identify key methods of sociological research and explain when it is appropriate to use them.

2.4 Understand the steps in a sociological research project.

2.5 Summarize the importance of learning to do sociological research.

NO ROOF OVERHEAD: RESEARCHING EVICTION IN AMERICA

In *Evicted: Poverty and Profit in the American City,* sociologist Matthew Desmond (2016a) writes that

> millions of Americans are evicted every year because they can't make rent.... In 2013, 1 in 8 poor renting families nationwide were unable to pay all of their rent, and a similar number thought it would be likely they would be evicted soon. (pp. 4–5)

Desmond argues that eviction is not only a consequence of poverty but also a cause because the lack of a stable home undermines the ability of the poor to get and keep a job and to establish children in good schools, and it can lead to stress, depression, and even suicide. As a *New York Times* book review of *Evicted*

©Andrew Lichtenstein/Corbis via Getty Images

poignantly notes, "Living in extreme poverty in the United States means waging an almost gladiatorial battle for creature comforts that luckier people take for granted. And of all those comforts, perhaps the most important is a stable, dignified home" (Senior, 2016, para. 4).

Desmond builds his research around a powerful, on-the-ground ethnographic account of the lives of eight Milwaukee families caught in a web of destitution and despair as they try to navigate the private rental market in that city. They include Arleen and her two young sons, fighting to find safe haven as Arleen struggles with money, depression, and the behavioral troubles of her boys. He also offers an account of the multigenerational Hinkston family, including young teenager Ruby, whose efforts at the public library to construct a bright, pleasant virtual home with a free online computer game are a grim contrast to her own living conditions in low-rent housing, which are characterized by instability, cockroaches, and chronically clogged plumbing.

Desmond points out that their stories are not isolated accounts; rather, in 2013, 67% of poor renting families received no housing assistance—the demand for housing help far outpaces the availability of subsidized apartments and housing vouchers. This leaves families to seek what they hope will be permanent shelter in a private low-rent housing market that is rife with dismal, dirty, and even dangerous living conditions. Significantly, even the worst housing may stretch the resources of many families beyond their means: The majority of poor families today spend over half their income on rent, whereas about one quarter spend over 70% (Desmond, 2016a, p. 4). An unanticipated expense, a dispute with a landlord, or the loss of a job can easily put families on the street. The lack of resources and an eviction record can keep them there for a significant period of time.

Desmond's work is a good example of qualitative sociological research, and he recognizes its significance to academic and policy debates. By using a scientific approach and rigorous field research, Desmond casts light on the little-examined but significant problem of evictions. He recognizes the struggles of those who are most at risk of eviction—low-income minority women: "Women living in black neighborhoods in Milwaukee represent 9.6% of the population, but 30% of evictions" (Desmond, 2015, pp. 3–4). Importantly, he also sees that there is profit to be made from the misery of others, and he documents the multitude of ways in which landlords exploit the low-end market for their benefit, skimping on repairs, failing to provide even basic appliances (apparently a legal action), and keeping even low rents high enough that if tenants fail to pay, the landlord can evict them, keep the deposit, and move on to a new renter (Desmond, 2016a). As a sociologist, Desmond has described and defined his problem, examined its causes and consequences, and provided policy prescriptions to address it.

In this chapter, we examine the ways sociologists like Matthew Desmond study the social world. First, we distinguish between sociological understanding and common sense. Then we discuss the key steps in the research process itself. We examine how sociologists test their theories using a variety of research methods, and finally, we consider the ethical implications of doing research on human subjects.

Sociology and Common Sense

Using science means using a unique way of seeing to investigate the world around us. The essence of the **scientific method** is straightforward: It is *a process of gathering empirical (scientific and specific) data, creating theories, and rigorously testing theories.* In sociological research, theories and empirical data exist in a dynamic relationship (Figure 2.1). Some sociological research begins from general theories, which offer "big picture" ideas: **Deductive reasoning** *starts from broad theories about the social world but proceeds to break them down into more specific and testable hypotheses.* Sociological **hypotheses** are *ideas about the world, derived from theories, that describe possible relationships between social phenomena.* Some research begins from the ground up: **Inductive reasoning** *starts from specific data, such as interviews, observations, or field notes, that may focus on a single community or event and endeavors to identify larger patterns from which to derive more general theories.*

Sociologists employ the scientific method in both quantitative and qualitative research. **Quantitative research**, which is often done through methods such as large-scale surveys, *gathers data that can be quantified and offers insight into broad patterns of social behavior* (for example, the percentage of U.S. adults who use corporal punishment such as spanking with their children) *and social attitudes* (for example, the percentage of U.S. adults who approve of corporal punishment) without necessarily delving into the meaning of or reasons for the identified phenomena. **Qualitative research**, such as that conducted by Matthew Desmond, *is characterized by data that cannot be quantified (or converted into numbers), focusing instead on generating in-depth knowledge of social life, institutions, and processes* (for example, why parents in particular demographic groups are more or less likely to use spanking as a method of punishment). It relies on the gathering of data through methods such as focus groups, participant and nonparticipant observation,

---

Scientific method: A process of gathering empirical (scientific and specific) data, creating theories, and rigorously testing theories.

Deductive reasoning: Starts from broad theories about the social world but proceeds to break them down into more specific and testable hypotheses.

Hypotheses: Ideas about the world, derived from theories, that describe possible relationships between social phenomena.

Inductive reasoning: Starts from specific data, such as interviews, observations, or field notes, that may focus on a single community or event and endeavors to identify larger patterns from which to derive more general theories.

Quantitative research: Research that gathers data that can be quantified and offers insight into broad patterns of social behavior and social attitudes.

Qualitative research: Research that is characterized by data that cannot be quantified (or converted into numbers), focusing instead on generating in-depth knowledge of social life, institutions, and processes.

■ **FIGURE 2.1** The Relationship Between Theory and Research

Theory

Research

TABLE 2.1 Annual Prevalence Rate of Drug Use by 12th Graders, 2014

	MARIJUANA	COCAINE	CRACK	LSD	ECSTASY
White	35.1	2.3	0.8	2.4	3.9
Black	35.9	1.6	1.3	1.1	1.7
Hispanic	37.1	3.6	1.7	2.0	3.9

Johnston, L. D., O'Malley, P. M., Bachman, J. G., Schulenberg, J. E., & Miech, R.A. (2014). Demographic subgroup trends among adolescents in the use of various licit and illicit drugs, 1975–2014. *Monitoring the Future Occasional Paper No. 83.* Ann Arbor, MI: Institute for Social Research.

---

interviews, content analysis, and archival research. Generally, population samples in qualitative research are small because they focus on in-depth understanding.

Personal experience and common sense about the world are often fine starting points for sociological research. They can, however, mislead us. In the 14th century, common sense suggested to people that the earth was flat; after all, it *looks* flat. Today, influenced by stereotypes and media portrayals of criminal behaviors, many people believe Black high school and college students are more likely than their White counterparts to use illegal drugs such as marijuana, cocaine, crack, and heroin. But common sense misleads on both counts. The earth is not flat (as you know!), and Black high school and college students are slightly *less* likely than White students to use illegal drugs (Table 2.1).

Consider the following ideas, which many believe to be true, although all are false:

Common Wisdom

I know women who earn more than their husbands or boyfriends. The gender wage gap is no longer an issue in the United States.

Sociological Research

Data show that men as a group earn more than women as a group. For example, in 2017, men had a weekly median income of $941 compared with $770 for women for all full-time occupations (U.S. Bureau of Labor Statistics, 2018, Table 39). There is some statistical variation, but data suggest that women as a group earn between 79 and 83 cents to a dollar that men earn (American Association of University Women [AAUW], 2016). These figures compare all men and all women who work full time and year-round. Reasons for the gap include worker characteristics (such as experience, education, and ability to negotiate salary), job characteristics (such as hours required), devaluation of women's work by society, and pay discrimination against female workers (AAUW, 2016; Cabeza, Johnson, & Tyner, 2011; Reskin & Padavic, 2002). Although some women, of course, earn more than some men, the overall pattern of men outearning women remains in place today. This topic is discussed in greater detail in Chapter 10.

Common Wisdom

Homeless people lack adequate shelter because they do not work.

Sociological Research

Finding safe permanent housing is a challenge for many U.S. residents, even those who work for pay. Low wages and poor benefits in the service industry, where many less-educated people work, as well as a shortage of adequate housing options for low-income families, can make finding permanent shelter a challenge. As we saw in the opening story, many poor families are subject to the vagaries of a rental market that prices low-wage workers out: When tenants fail to make the rent, they can be put out on the street (Desmond, 2016a). Some homeless, particularly those who are part of the small population of the long-term homeless, do not work: "Nearly all of the long-term homeless have tenuous family ties and some kind of disability, whether it is a drug or alcohol addiction, a mental illness, or a physical handicap" (Culhane, 2010, para. 4). Alas, this is a group that would benefit from housing in facilities that can treat their ailments so they can attain self-sufficiency. The important sociological subjects of poverty and access (or lack thereof) to resources are discussed more fully in Chapter 7.

Common Wisdom

Education is the great equalizer. All children in the United States have the opportunity to get a good education. Low academic achievement is a personal failure.

Sociological Research

Public education is free and available to all in the U.S., but the quality of education can vary dramatically. Consider the fact that in many states and localities, a major source of public school funding is local property taxes, which constitute an average of about 45% of funding (state and federal allocations make up the rest; National Public Radio, 2016). As such, communities with high property values have richer sources of funding from which to draw educational resources, whereas poor communities—even those with high tax rates—have more limited pools. As well, high levels of racial segregation persist in U.S. schools. A U.S. Government Accountability Office report found that the proportion of schools that are highly segregated by race and class—that is, where more than 75% of children get free or reduced-price lunch and more than 75% are Black or Hispanic—is rising, climbing from 9% to 16% of schools between 2001 and 2014. It is also significant that students in the high-poverty and majority-Black or Hispanic schools were less likely to have access to the range of math and science courses available to their peers in better-off schools and to be subject to harsher disciplinary measures (U.S. Government Accountability Office, 2016). Research also shows a relationship between academic performance and class and racial segregation: Students who are not isolated in poor, racially segregated schools perform better on a variety of academic measures than those who are (Condron, 2009; Logan, Minca, & Adar, 2012). The problem of low academic achievement is complex, and no single variable can explain it. At the same time, the magnitude and persistence of this problem suggests that we are looking at a phenomenon that is a public issue rather than a personal trouble. We discuss issues of class, race, and educational attainment further in Chapter 12.

Even deeply held and widely shared beliefs about society and social groups may be inaccurate—or more nuanced and complex than they appear on the surface. Until it is tested, common sense is merely conjecture. Careful research allows us to test our beliefs to gauge whether they are valid or merely anecdotal. From a sociological standpoint, empirical evidence is granted greater weight than common sense. By basing their decisions on scientific evidence rather than on personal beliefs or common wisdom, researchers and students can draw informed conclusions and policy makers can ensure that policies and programs are data driven and maximally effective.

Research and the Scientific Method

Scientific theories are *explanations of how and why scientific observations are as they are.* A good scientific theory has the following characteristics:

- *It is logically consistent.* One part of the theory does not contradict another part.

- *It can be disproved.* If the findings contradict the theory, then we can deduce that the theory is wrong. Although we can say that testing has failed to

Scientific theories: Explanations of how and why scientific observations are as they are.

disprove the theory, we cannot assume the theory is true if testing confirms it. Theories are always subject to further testing, which may point to needed revisions, highlight limitations, or strengthen conclusions.

Theories are made up of **concepts**, *ideas that summarize a set of phenomena.* Concepts are the building blocks of research and prepare a solid foundation for sociological work. Some key concepts in sociology are *social stratification, social class, power, inequality,* and *diversity,* which we introduced in the opening chapter.

To gather data and create viable theories, we need to define concepts in ways that are precise and measurable. A study of social class, for example, would need to begin with a working definition of that term. An **operational definition** of a concept *describes the concept in such a way that it can be observed and measured.* Many sociologists define *social class* in terms of dimensions such as income, wealth, education, occupation, and consumption patterns. Each of these aspects of class has the potential to be measurable. We may construct operational definitions in terms of *qualities* or *quantities* (Babbie, 1998; Neuman, 2000). In terms of qualities, we might say that the *upper-middle class* is composed of working professionals who have completed advanced degrees, even though there may be a broad income spread between those with a master's degree in fine arts and those with a master's degree in business administration. This definition is based on an assumption of *class* as a social position that derives from educational attainment. Alternatively, by using quantity as a key measure, we might operationally define *upper class* as households with an annual income greater than $150,000 and *lower class* as households with an annual income of less than $20,000. This definition takes income as the preeminent determinant of class position, irrespective of education or other variables.

Consider a social issue of contemporary interest— bullying. Imagine that you want to conduct a research study of bullying to determine how many female middle schoolers have experienced bullying in the past academic year. You would need to begin with a clear definition of *bullying* that operationalizes the term. That is, to measure how many girls have experienced bullying, you would need to articulate what constitutes bullying. Would you include physical bullying? If so, how many instances of being pushed or punched would constitute bullying? What kinds of verbal behaviors be considered bullying? Would you include cyberbullying? To study a phenomenon such as bullying, it is not enough to assume

Some research on bullying relies on self-reports, whereas other data come from peer reports. Research (Branson & Cornell, 2009) suggests that more than twice as many students (11%) were labeled bullies in peer reports than in self-reports (5%), highlighting the fact that definitions of what constitutes bullying may differ, and any method of data collection has limitations.

that we know it when we see it. Empirical research relies on the careful and specific definition of terms and the recognition of how definitions and methods affect research outcomes.

Relationships between Variables

In studying social relationships, sociologists also need *variables.* A **variable** is *a concept that can take on two or more possible values.* For instance, sex can be male or female, work status can be employed or unemployed, and geographic location can be inner-city, suburbs, or rural area. We can measure variables both *quantitatively* and *qualitatively.* **Quantitative variables** include *factors that can be counted,* such as unemployment rates, victimization rates, and drug use frequency. **Qualitative variables** are *variables that express qualities and do not have numerical values.* Qualitative variables might include physical characteristics such as gender or eye color or attitudinal characteristics such as a parent's preference for a private or public school or a commuter's preference for riding public transportation or driving to work.

Sociological research often tries to establish a relationship between two or more variables. Suppose you want to find out whether more education is associated with higher earnings. After asking people about their years of schooling and their annual incomes, both of which are quantitative variables, you could estimate the degree of *correlation* between the two. **Correlation**—literally,

Concepts: Ideas that summarize a set of phenomena.

Operational definition: Describes the concept in such a way that it can be observed and measured.

Variable: A concept or its empirical measure that can take on two or more possible values.

Quantitative variables: Factors that can be counted.

Qualitative variables: Variables that express qualities and do not have numerical values.

Correlation: The degree to which two or more variables are associated with one another.

"co-relationship"—is *the degree to which two or more variables are associated with one another.* Correlating the two variables *years of education* and *annual income* demonstrates that the greater the education, the higher the income (Figure 2.2). Do you see the exception to that relationship? How might you explain it?

When two variables are correlated, we are often tempted to infer a **causal relationship**, *a relationship between two variables in which one variable is the cause of the other.* Nevertheless, even though two variables are correlated, we cannot assume that one causes the other. For example, ice cream sales rise during the summer, as does the homicide rate. These two events are correlated in the sense that both increase during the hottest months. Yet, because the sharp rise in ice cream sales does not *cause* rates of homicide to increase (nor, clearly, does the rise in homicide rates cause a spike in ice cream consumption), these two phenomena do not have a causal relationship. Correlation does not equal causation.

Sometimes an observed correlation between two variables is the result of a **spurious relationship**—a *correlation between two or more variables caused by another factor that*

is not being measured rather than a causal link between the variables themselves.* In the example above, the common factor missed in the relationship is the temperature. When it's hot, more people want to eat ice cream. Studies also show that rising temperatures are linked to an increase in violent crimes—although after a certain temperature threshold (about 90 degrees), crimes wane again (Gamble & Hess, 2012). Among the reasons more violent crimes are committed in the warm summer months is the fact that people spend more time outdoors in social interactions, which can lead to confrontations.

Let's take a look at another example: Imagine that your school newspaper publishes a study concluding that coffee drinking causes poor test grades. The story is based on a survey of students that found those who reported drinking a lot of coffee the night before an exam scored lower than did their peers who had consumed little or no coffee. Having studied sociology, you wonder whether this relationship might be spurious. What is the "something else" that is not being measured here? Could it be that students who did not study in the days and weeks prior to the test and stayed up late the night before cramming—probably consuming a lot of coffee as they fought sleep—earned lower test grades than did peers who studied earlier and got adequate sleep the night before the test? The overlooked variable, then, is the amount of studying students did in the weeks preceding the exam, and we are likely to

---

Causal relationship: A relationship between two variables in which one variable is the cause of the other.

Spurious relationship: A correlation between two or more variables caused by another factor that is not being measured rather than a causal link between the variables themselves.

■ **FIGURE 2.2** Correlation Between Education and Median Weekly Earnings in the United States, 2017

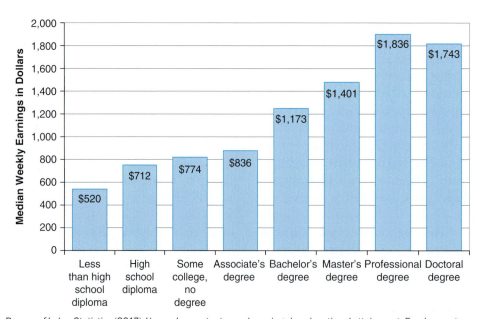

Source: Bureau of Labor Statistics (2017). Unemployment rates and earnings by educational attainment. *Employment projections.* Washington DC: U.S. Government Printing Office.

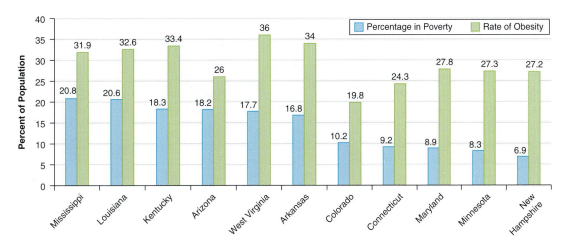

■ **FIGURE 2.3** Correlation Between Percentage in Poverty and Self-Reported Rates of Obesity, 2017

Source: Centers for Disease Control and Prevention, (2017). Prevalence of Self-Reported Obesity among U.S. Adults by Race/ Ethnicity, State and Territory, BRFSS, 2014–2016. Retrieved from https://www.cdc.gov/obesity/data/prevalence-maps.html.

find a positive correlation and evidence of causation in looking at time spent studying and grade outcomes.

Sociologists attempt to develop theories systematically by offering clear operational definitions, collecting unbiased data, and identifying evidence-based relationships between variables. Sociological research methods usually yield credible and useful data, but we must always critically analyze the results to ensure their validity and reliability and to check that hypothesized relationships are not spurious.

Testing Theories and Hypotheses

Once we have defined concepts and variables with which to work, we can endeavor to test a theory by positing a hypothesis. Hypotheses enable scientists to check the accuracy of their theories. For example, data show that some positive correlation exists between obesity and poverty rates at the state level: Mississippi, West Virginia, Kentucky, and Louisiana, which are among the poorest states in the country, are also among the states with the highest obesity rates (Figure 2.3). As well, four of the ten wealthiest states in the U.S. are among those with the lowest obesity rates. A **positive correlation** is *a relationship showing that as one variable rises or falls, the other does as well.* As we noted above, sociologists are quick to point out that correlation does not equal causation. Researchers are interested in creating and testing hypotheses to explain cases of positive correlation—they are also interested in explaining exceptions to the pattern of correlation between two (or more) variables.

In fact, researchers have explored and hypothesized the relationship between poverty and obesity. Among the conclusions they have drawn is that living in poverty—and living in poor neighborhoods—puts people at higher risk of obesity, although the risk is pronounced for women and far less clear for men (Hedwig, 2011; Smith, 2009). Factors that researchers have identified as contributing to a causal path between poverty and obesity include a lack of access to healthy food choices and safe, accessible spaces for physical exercise; a deficit of time to cook healthy foods and to exercise; and lack of funds to purchase high-quality foods. They have also cited the stress induced by poverty. Although the data cannot lead us to conclude decisively that poverty is a cause of obesity, research can help us to gather evidence that supports or refutes a hypothesis about the relationship between these two variables.

In the case of a **negative correlation**, *one variable increases as the other decreases.* As we discuss later in Chapter 11, which focuses on the family and society, researchers have found a negative correlation between male unemployment and rates of marriage. That is, as rates of male unemployment in a community rise, rates of marriage in the community fall. Observing this relationship, sociologists have conducted research to test explanations for this relationship (Edin & Kefalas, 2005; Wilson, 2010).

Keep in mind that we can never prove theories to be decisively right—we can only prove them wrong.

Positive correlation: A relationship showing that as one variable rises or falls, the other does as well.

Negative correlation: A relationship showing that as one variable increases, the other decreases.

Proving a theory right would require the scientific testing of absolutely every possible hypothesis based on that theory—a fundamental impossibility. In fact, good theories are constructed in a way that makes it logically possible to prove them wrong. This is Karl Popper's (1959) famous **principle of falsification**, or **falsifiability**, which holds that *to be scientific, a theory must lead to testable hypotheses that can be disproved if they are wrong.*

Validity and Reliability

For theories and hypotheses to be testable, both the concepts used to construct them and the measurements used to test them must be accurate. When our observations adequately reflect the real world, our findings have **validity**—that is, *the degree to which concepts and their measurements accurately represent what they claim to represent.* For example, suppose you want to know whether the crime rate in the United States has gone up or down. For years, sociologists depended on police reports to measure crime. Nevertheless, researchers could assess the validity of these tallies only if subsequent surveys were administered nationally to victims of crime. If the victim tallies matched those of the police reports, then researchers could say the police reports were a valid measure of crime in the United States. The National Crime Victimization Survey enables researchers to assess validity because it offers data on victimization, even for crimes that have not been reported to authorities.

Sociologists are also concerned with the reliability of their findings. **Reliability** is *the extent to which researchers' findings are consistent with the findings of different studies of the same thing or with the findings of the same study over time.* Sociological research may suffer from problems of validity and reliability because of **bias**, *a characteristic of results that systematically misrepresent the true nature of what is being studied.* Bias can creep into research as a result of the use of inappropriate measurement instruments.

©BRENDAN SMIALOWSKI/AFP/Getty Images

The Metropolitan Washington Council of Governments distinguishes between the *permanently supported homeless*, who have housing but are at risk as a result of extreme poverty and/or disability, and the *chronically homeless*, who are continually homeless for a year or more than four times in three years. Do you think that these categories fully encompass the homeless population?

TABLE 2.2 How Truthful Are Survey Respondents? (in Percentages)

Survey Question	THREAT OF VALIDATION		NO THREAT OF VALIDATION	
	Anonymous	*Named*	*Anonymous*	*Named*
Ever smoked?	63.5	72.9	60.5	67.8
Smoked in the last month?	34.5	39.5	25.9	21.8
Smoked in the last week?	26.0	25.5	14.4	17.6

Source: Adams, J., Parkinson, L., Sanson-Fisher, R. W., & Walsh, R. A. (2008). Enhancing self-report of adolescent smoking: The effects of bogus pipeline and anonymity. *Addictive Behaviors, 33*(10), 1291–1296.

Principle of falsification (or falsifiability): The principle, advanced by philosopher Karl Popper, that to be scientific, a theory must lead to testable hypotheses that can be disproved if they are wrong.

Validity: The degree to which concepts and their measurements accurately represent what they claim to represent.

Reliability: The extent to which researchers' findings are consistent with the findings of different studies of the same thing or with the findings of the same study over time.

Bias: A characteristic of results that systematically misrepresent the true nature of what is being studied.

For example, suppose the administrator of a city wants to know whether homelessness has risen in recent years. She operationally defines *the homeless* as those who sleep in the street or in shelters and dispatches her team of researchers to city shelters to count the number of people occupying shelter beds or sleeping on street corners or park benches. A sociologist reviewing the research team's results might question the administrator's operational definition of what it means to be homeless and, by extension, her findings. Are the homeless solely those spending nights in shelters or on the streets? What about those who stay with friends after eviction or camp out in their cars? In this instance, a sociologist might suggest that the city's measure is biased because it misrepresents (and undercounts) the homeless population by failing to define the concept in a way that captures the broad manifestations of homelessness.

Bias can also occur in research when respondents do not tell the truth (see Table 2.2). An example of this is a study in which respondents were asked whether they used illegal drugs or had driven while impaired. All were asked the same questions, but some were wired to a machine they were told was a lie detector. The subjects who thought their truthfulness was being monitored by a lie detector reported higher rates of illegal drug use than did subjects who did not. Based on the assumption that actual drug use would be about the same for both groups, the researchers concluded that the subjects who were not connected to the device were underreporting their actual illegal drug use and that simply asking people about drug use would lead to biased findings because respondents would not tell the truth.

The reticence to truthfully self-report drug use and impaired driving may also be related to a phenomenon that researchers call **social desirability bias,** which is *a response bias based on the tendency of respondents to answer a question in way that they perceive will be favorably received.* That is, many respondents want to present themselves positively to the interviewer. Social desirability bias is most likely to be a problem in studies that examine, for instance, participation in elections (Holbrooke & Krosnick, 2009), engaging in physical exercise (Brenner & Delamater, 2014), or "cyberloafing" at work (Akbulut, Donmez, & Dursun, 2017). Because exercising, voting, and being productive at work are widely perceived as positive activities, there is greater reticence to report behavior that does not adhere to the perceived norm.

Objectivity in Scientific Research

Even if sociologists develop theories based on good operational definitions and collect valid and reliable data, like all human beings, they have passions and biases that may color their research. For example, criminologists long ignored the criminality of women because they assumed that women were not disposed toward criminal behavior. Researchers therefore did not have an accurate picture of women and crime until this bias was recognized and rectified.

Personal values and beliefs may affect a researcher's **objectivity** or *ability to represent the object of study accurately.* In the 19th century, sociologist Max Weber argued that for scientific research to be objective, it has to have **value neutrality**—*the characteristic of being free of the influence of* *personal beliefs and opinions that would influence the course of research.* The sociologist should acknowledge personal biases and assumptions, make them explicit, and prevent them from getting in the way of observation and reporting.

How can we best achieve objectivity? First, recall Karl Popper's principle of falsification, which proposes that the goal of research is not to prove our ideas correct but to find out whether they are wrong. To accomplish this, researchers must be willing to accept that the data they collect might contradict their most passionate convictions. Research should deepen human understanding, not prove a particular point of view.

A second way we can ensure objectivity is to invite others to draw their own conclusions about the validity of our data through **replication**, *the repetition of a previous study using a different sample or population to verify or refute the original findings.* For research to be replicated, the original study must spell out in detail the research methods employed. If potential replicators cannot conduct their studies exactly as the original study was performed, they might accidentally introduce unwanted variables. To ensure the most accurate replication of their work, researchers should archive original materials such as questionnaires and field notes and allow replicators access to them.

Popper (1959) describes scientific discovery as an ongoing process of confrontation and refutation. Sociologists usually subject their work to this process by publishing their results in scholarly journals. Submitted research undergoes a rigorous process of peer review, in which other experts in the field of study examine the work before the results are finalized and published. Once research has been published in a reputable journal such as the *American Sociological Review* or the *Journal of Health and Social Behavior,* other scholars read it with a critical eye. The study may then be replicated in different settings.

Doing Sociological Research

Sociological research requires careful preparation and a clear plan that guides the work. The purpose of a sociological research project may be to obtain preliminary knowledge that will help formulate a theory or to evaluate an existing theory about society and social life. As part of the strategy, the researcher selects from a variety of **research methods**—*specific techniques for systematically*

Social desirability bias: A response bias based on the tendency of respondents to answer a question in way that they perceive will be favorably received.

Objectivity: The ability to represent the object of study accurately.

Value neutrality: The characteristic of being free of personal beliefs and opinions that would influence the course of research.

Replication: The repetition of a previous study using a different sample or population to verify or refute the original findings.

Research methods: Specific techniques for systematically gathering data.

gathering data. In the following sections, we look at a range of research methods and examine their advantages and disadvantages. We also discuss how you might prepare a sociological research project of your own.

Sociological Research Methods

Sociologists employ a variety of methods to learn about the social world (Table 2.3). Since each has strengths and weaknesses, a good research strategy may be to use several different methods. If they all yield similar findings, the researcher is more likely to have confidence in the results. The principal methods are the survey, fieldwork (either participant observation or detached observation), experimentation, working with existing information, and participatory research.

Survey Research

A **survey** uses *a questionnaire or interviews administered to a group of people in person or by telephone or e-mail to determine their characteristics, opinions, and behaviors.* Surveys are versatile, and sociologists often use them to test theories or to gather data. Some survey instruments, such as National Opinion Research Center questionnaires, consist of closed-ended questions that respondents answer by choosing from among the responses presented. Others, such as the University of Chicago's Social Opportunity Survey, consist of open-ended questions that permit respondents to answer in their own words.

An example of survey research conducted for data collection is the largest survey in the nation, the U.S. Census, which is conducted every 10 years. The census is not designed to test any particular theory. Rather, it gathers voluminous data about U.S. residents that researchers, including sociologists, use to test and develop a variety of theories. In this text, you will find U.S. Census data in many chapters.

Usually, a survey is conducted on *a small number of people,* a **sample**, selected to represent a **population**, *the whole group of people to be studied.* The first step in designing a survey is to identify the population of interest. Imagine that you are doing a study of sociological factors that affect grades in college. Who would you survey? Members of a certain age group only? People in the

airline industry? Pet owners? To conduct a study well, we need to identify clearly the survey population that will most effectively help us answer the research question. In your study, you would most likely choose to survey students now in college because they offer the best opportunity to correlate grades with circumstances and behaviors.

Once we have identified a population of interest, we need to select a sample, as we are unlikely to have the time or money to talk to all the members of a given population, especially if it is a large one. Other things being equal, larger samples better represent the population than do smaller ones. Nevertheless, with proper sampling techniques, sociologists can use small (and therefore inexpensive) samples to represent large populations. For instance, a well-chosen sample of 1,000 U.S. consumers can be used to represent 100,000 U.S. consumers with a fair degree of accuracy, enabling surveys to make predictions about economic behavior with reasonable confidence. Sampling is also used for looking at social phenomena such as marriages and online dating in a population: A recent paper, based on a sample of 4,200 U.S. adults, suggests that those with Internet access at home are more likely to have partners, even controlling for other factors (Rosenfeld & Thomas, 2012).

Ideally, a sample should reflect the composition of the population we are studying. For instance, if you want to be able to use your research data about college students to generalize about the entire college student population of the United States, you would need to collect proportional samples from two-year colleges, four-year colleges, large universities, community colleges, online schools, and so on. It would not be adequate to survey only students at online colleges or only female students at private four-year schools.

To avoid bias in surveys, sociologists may use **random sampling**, whereby *everyone in the population of interest has an equal chance of being chosen for the study.* Typically, they make or obtain a list of everyone in the population of interest. Then they draw names or phone numbers, for instance, by chance until the desired sample size is reached (today, such work can be done by computers). Large-scale random sample surveys permit researchers to draw conclusions about large numbers of people on the basis of small numbers of respondents. For our survey of college students, we could (theoretically) take all U.S. college students as our starting point and sample randomly from that group. We might also choose to use a stratified

---

Survey: A research method that uses a questionnaire or interviews administered to a group of people in person or by telephone or e-mail to determine their characteristics, opinions, and behaviors.

Sample: A small number of people; a portion of the larger population selected to represent the whole.

Population: The whole group of people studied.

Random sampling: Sampling in which everyone in the population of interest has an equal chance of being chosen for the study.

TABLE 2.3   Key Sociological Research Methods

RESEARCH METHOD	APPROPRIATE CIRCUMSTANCES
Survey research	When basic information about a large population is desired. Sociologists usually conduct survey research by selecting samples that are representative of the entire populations of interest.
Fieldwork	When detailed information is sought, and when surveys are impractical for getting the information desired (for example, in studying youth gangs or gamblers). Fieldwork usually relies on small samples, especially compared to surveys.
Detached observation	When researchers desire to stay removed from the people being studied and must gather data in a way that minimizes impact on the subjects. Detached observations are often supplemented with face-to-face interviews.
Participant observation	When firsthand knowledge of the subjects' direct experience is desired, including a deeper understanding of their lives
Experimentation	When it is possible to create experimental and control groups that are matched on relevant variables but provided with different experiences in the experiment
Use of existing information	When direct acquisition of data is either not feasible or not desirable because the event studied occurred in the past or because gathering the data would be too costly or too difficult
Participatory research	When a primary goal is training people to gain political or economic power and acquire the necessary skills to do the research themselves

sample: In **stratified sampling**, *researchers divide a population into a series of subgroups* (for instance, students at four-year public universities, students at two-year colleges, students at online schools, etc.) *and take random samples from within each group.* This can be used to ensure representation from all subgroups (such as college students at different types of schools) in the final research sample.

Researchers may assemble survey respondents through other sampling means. For example, they may use convenience sampling or snowball sampling. Imagine you are doing a survey of college students to learn what factors students consider when they choose a major. You may opt for a *convenience sample* of students at your school: This could include students in your classes, friends from clubs or organizations on campus, or if you live on campus, people in your dormitory. The term *convenience sample* suggests that the selection is driven by convenience rather than by systematic sampling.

You might use *snowball sampling* if you know a lot of students in your major but not in other majors. In such a case, if you wanted a wider sample, you could ask a few people you do know in other majors to refer classmates from those majors. From those classmates, you could expand your reach still further into other majors. Your sample then expands like a snowball, building from a core group outward through recruitment. Researchers sometimes rely on snowball sampling when they are trying to access a group that is insular or difficult to reach, such as sex workers or drug addicts.

Nonrandom samples such as those gathered through convenience or snowball sampling can be suggestive of findings, but they are rarely generalizable by themselves and must be used with care.

In constructing surveys, sociologists are also concerned with ensuring that the questions and their possible responses will capture the respondents' points of view. The wording of questions is an important factor; poor wording can produce misleading results, as the following example illustrates. In 1993, an American Jewish Committee/Roper poll was taken to examine public attitudes and beliefs about the Holocaust. To the astonishment of many, the results indicated that fully 22% of survey respondents expressed a belief the Holocaust had never happened. Not immediately noticed was the fact that the survey contained some very awkward wording, including the question "Does it seem possible or does it seem impossible to you that the Nazi extermination of the Jews never happened?" Can you see why such a question might produce a questionable result? The question's compound structure and double-negative wording almost certainly confused many respondents.

The American Jewish Committee released a second survey with different wording: "Does it seem possible to you that the Nazi extermination of the Jews never happened, or do you feel certain that it happened?" The results of the second poll were quite different. Only about 1% of respondents thought it was possible the Holocaust never happened, while 8% were unsure (Kagay, 1994). Despite the follow-up poll that corrected the mistaken perception of the previous poll's results, the new poll was not as methodologically rigorous as it could have been; a single survey question

Stratified sampling: Dividing a population into a series of subgroups and taking random samples from within each group.

should ask for only one type of response. The American Jewish Committee's second survey contained a question that attempted to gauge two different responses simultaneously.

A weakness of surveys is that they may reveal what people say rather than what they do. Responses are sometimes self-serving, intended to make the interviewee look good in the eyes of the researcher. As we saw in an earlier example, a respondent may not wish to reveal his or her drinking or drug habits. A well-constructed survey, however, can overcome these problems. Assuring the respondent of anonymity, assigning interviewers with whom respondents feel comfortable, and building in questions that ask for the same information in different ways can reduce self-serving bias in survey research.

The 2016 presidential election—and the polls leading up to the election that predicted a win for Democratic candidate Hillary Clinton—have raised some questions about survey research and decisions made by professional pollsters regarding sample selection as well as respondent behavior (see the *Behind the Numbers* box in this chapter for more on this topic). Since the election, researchers and pollsters have looked at what pre-election polls got right and what they got wrong. Studies suggest that many polls underestimated the number of undecided voters who chose to vote for Trump either right before the election or in the voting booth (Cohn,

2017; Kennedy et al., 2017). Though national polls correctly predicted Clinton winning the popular vote by a few percentage points, state polls understated Trump's support, particularly in the so-called Rust Belt states of the Midwest (Cohn, 2017; Kennedy et al., 2017). In the six presidential elections prior, three states in this region (Pennsylvania, Michigan, and Wisconsin) voted Democratic and the 2016 polls showed Clinton winning there as well. Trump, however, claimed narrow victories in all three states (Kennedy et al., 2017).

In contrast to previous elections, educational attainment of the electorate also played a role in the gap between predicted outcome and actual outcome. That is, because well-educated voters have historically been more likely to participate in polls, they were overrepresented in pre-election surveys. In the election, however, actual voter turnout was more educationally diverse (Cohn, 2017; Kennedy et al., 2017).

Finally, some researchers have hypothesized a "shy Trump" effect, which is based on social desirability bias. This analysis suggests that voters who took part in telephone polls were uncomfortable telling pollsters that they were voting for a widely unpopular candidate, Trump. However, there is limited evidence to support this idea, especially because support for Trump was similarly reflected in online polls, which were anonymous (Cohn, 2017; Kennedy et al., 2017).

Behind the Numbers
WHAT FACTORS AFFECT SURVEY RESPONSES?

If you are a follower of the news—whether on television, in newspapers, or online—you know that survey results are a popular media topic. We commonly hear about surveys asking respondents to indicate their support or rejection of particular public policies that seek to determine whether people believe in climate change or support same-sex marriage or limitations on gun ownership or that are gathering information on health behaviors such as exercise and diet. During election seasons, we read nearly every day about polling on the popularity (or lack thereof) of current officeholders and their challengers.

Survey research is an important part of learning more about societal attitudes, ideologies, and behaviors. It is useful, for this reason, to understand some of its strengths and limitations. Research about survey research suggests that factors we might not consider can affect responses. In this essay, we discuss two such factors: *question order effects* and *social desirability bias*.

Question order can affect survey findings in part because respondents have a desire to be consistent in their responses (a "consistency effect"; Schuman & Presser, 1981). A study (Wilson, Moore, McKay, & Avery , 2008) on the issue of question order noted that "public opinion polls show that the public expresses greater support for gender-targeted AA [affirmative action] than race-targeted AA, but no research has addressed the extent to which expressed support for one group influences expressed support toward the other" (p. 514). The authors set out to determine if asking respondents about one or the other affirmative-action target group would affect their stated attitudes about the other. In fact, they found that question order affected responses. Specifically, respondents who were asked about affirmative action for women *first* were more likely to favor it than to oppose it: That is, about 63% supported affirmative action for women and 29% rejected it. When respondents were asked about affirmative action for women *after* being asked about such programs for racial minorities, support dropped: 57% supported affirmative action for women and 34% rejected it. Similarly, a greater percentage of respondents expressed support for racially targeted affirmative action when the question was asked after a question about affirmative action for women (57%) than when it was asked first (50%). The authors write that "results suggest that for the American public as a whole, support for one type of AA program is indeed affected by whether that program is considered by itself or in the context of both types of AA programs" (p. 518).

A second factor that may affect survey responses is *social desirability bias*, "the tendency of respondents to give answers they perceive to be socially desirable regardless of their own true positions" (Powell, 2013, p. 1054). An example of this can be found in measures on voter turnout. Because voting is a socially desirable behavior, research suggests that self-reported voting behavior may not match up with actual voter turnout: That is, there is a tendency for people to say they voted in an election even if they did not (Presser, 1990). The respondent's bias toward choosing a response that he or she believes will be perceived as socially acceptable by the interviewer may also affect survey findings on political candidates or social issues. For example, as racism has become socially unacceptable in the U.S., some polls on Black candidates in political races have shown evidence of social desirability bias: "Some individuals who favor the White candidate will actually express support for the Black candidate in an apparent attempt to appear racially tolerant to the interviewer" (Powell, 2013, p. 1055).

Recent research has shown declining effects of social desirability bias on mixed-race election polling (Hopkins, 2009), but other work finds a continued effect on some social issues, including same-sex marriage. In research conducted before the U.S. Supreme Court legalized same-sex marriage nationally, Powell (2013) found that there was a gap between public support expressed in pre-election surveys for local or state ballot initiatives legalizing

same-sex marriage and actual voting-day support. He determined that "other things equal, election day opposition to same-sex marriage is between 5% and 7% greater than found in pre-election polls" (p. 1065). The wish to avoid stigma by voicing a position perceived to be socially acceptable to the interviewer may, thus, have an effect on survey responses to socially sensitive issues.

©iStockphoto.com/izusek

Think It Through

- Survey researchers seek to gather accurate and unbiased data on attitudes and actions, but responses can be affected by a variety of factors, including question order and social desirability bias. Can you think of other factors—perhaps mentioned in the body of the chapter—that could affect survey outcomes? How can these problems in survey research be addressed?

Fieldwork

Fieldwork is *a research method that uses in-depth and often extended study to describe and analyze a group or community.* Sometimes called *ethnography,* it takes the researcher into the field, where he or she directly observes—and sometimes interacts with—subjects in their social environment.

Social scientists, including sociologists and anthropologists, have employed fieldwork to study everything from hoboes and working-class gangs in the 1930s (Anderson, 1940; Whyte, 1943) to prostitution and drug use among inner-city women (Maher, 1997) and Vietnam veterans motorcycling across the country to the Vietnam Veterans Memorial in Washington, DC (Michalowski & Dubisch, 2001). Matthew Desmond's (2016a) work on poor families experiencing eviction is another example of the use of fieldwork in sociological research.

Fieldwork: A research method that uses in-depth and often extended study to describe and analyze a group or community; also called *ethnography.*

Sociologists may use snowball sampling in their research. Snowball sampling involves using a core group of known respondents as sources to contact new respondents, expanding the core group outward like a snowball.

Most fieldwork combines several different methods of gathering information. These include interviews, detached observation, and participant observation.

An **interview** is *a detailed conversation designed to obtain in-depth information about a person and his or her activities.* When used in surveys, interview questions may be either open-ended or closed-ended. They may also be formal or informal. In fieldwork, the questions are usually open-ended to allow respondents to answer in their own words. Sometimes the interviewer prepares a detailed set of questions; at other times, the best approach is simply to have a list of relevant topics to cover.

Good researchers guard against influencing respondents' answers. In particular, they avoid the use of **leading questions**—*questions that tend to elicit particular responses.* Imagine a question on attitudes toward the marine environment that reads "Do you believe tuna fishing with broad nets, which leads to the violent deaths of dolphins, should be regulated?" The bias in this question is obvious—the stated association of broad nets with violent dolphin deaths creates a bias in favor of a *yes* answer. Accurate data depend on good questions that do not lead respondents to answer in particular ways.

Sometimes a study requires that researchers in the field keep a distance from the people they are studying and simply observe without getting involved. The people being observed may or may not know they are being observed. This approach is called *detached observation.* In his study of two delinquent gangs (the Saints and the Roughnecks), William J. Chambliss, coauthor of this text, spent many hours observing gang members without being involved in what they were doing. With the gang members' permission, he sat in his car with the window rolled down so he could hear them talk and watch their behavior while they hung out on a street corner. At other times, he would observe them playing pool while he played at a nearby table. Chambliss sometimes followed gang members in his car as they drove around in theirs and sat near enough to them in bars and cafés to hear their conversations. Through his observations at a distance, he was able to gather detailed information on the kinds of delinquencies the gang members engaged in. He was also able to unravel some of the social processes that led to their behavior and observe other people's reactions to it.

Detached observation is particularly useful when the researcher has reason to believe other forms of fieldwork might influence the behavior of the people to be observed. It is also helpful for checking the validity of what the researcher has been told in interviews. A great deal of sociological information about illegal behavior has been gathered through detached observation.

One problem with detached observation is that the information gathered is likely to be incomplete. Without talking to people, we are unable to check our impressions against their experiences. For this reason, detached observation is usually supplemented by in-depth interviews. In his study of the delinquent gang members, Chambliss (1973, 2001) periodically interviewed them to complement his findings and check the accuracy of his detached observations.

Another type of fieldwork is *participant observation,* a mixture of active participation and detached observation.

Interview: A detailed conversation designed to obtain in-depth information about a person and his or her activities.

Leading questions: Questions that tend to elicit particular responses.

When looking at the relationship between violent video games and violent behavior, researchers must account for many variables. What variables would you choose to study and why?

Participant observation can sometimes be dangerous. Chambliss's (1988b) research on organized crime and police corruption in Seattle, Washington, exposed him to threats from the police and organized crime network members who feared he would reveal their criminal activities. Desmond's (2016a) work also included participant observation; he spent significant amounts of time with the Milwaukee residents he studied, seeking to carefully document their voices and experiences.

Experimentation

Experiments are *research techniques for investigating cause and effect under controlled conditions.* We construct experiments to measure the effects of **independent or experimental variables** (*variables the researcher changes intentionally*) on **dependent variables** (*variables that change as a result of changes in other variables*). To put it another way, researchers modify one controllable variable (such as diet or exposure to violent movie scenes) to see what happens to another variable (such as willingness to socialize or the display of aggression). Some variables, such as sex, ethnicity, and height, do not change in response to stimuli and thus do not make useful dependent variables.

In a typical experiment, researchers select participants who share characteristics such as age, education, social class, or experiences that are relevant to the experiment. The participants are then randomly assigned to two groups. The first, called the *experimental group,* is exposed to the independent variable—the variable the researchers hypothesize will affect the subjects' behavior. The second group is assigned to the *control group.* These subjects are not exposed to the independent variable—they receive no special attention. The researchers then measure both groups for the dependent variable. For example, if a neuroscientist wanted to conduct an experiment on whether listening to classical music affects performance on a math exam, he or she might have an experimental group listen to Mozart, Bach, or Chopin for an hour before taking a test. The control group would take the same test but would not listen to any music beforehand. In this example, exposure to classical music is the independent variable, and the quantifiable results of the math test are the dependent variable.

To study the relationship between violent video game play and aggression, researchers took a longitudinal approach by examining the sustained violent video game play and aggressive behavior of 1,492 adolescents in Grades 9 through 12 (Willoughby, Adachi, & Good, 2012). Their results showed a strong correlation between playing violent video games and being more likely to engage in or approve of violence. This body of literature represents another example of the importance of research methodology; the same researchers, in a separate study, found that the level of competitiveness in a video game, and not the violence itself, had the greatest influence on aggressive behavior (Adachi & Willoughby, 2011). More research on this topic may help differentiate between the effects of variables and avoid conclusions based on spurious relationships.

Working with Existing Information

Sociologists frequently work with existing information and data gathered by other researchers. Why would researchers choose to reinterpret existing data? Perhaps they want to do a secondary analysis of statistical data collected by an agency such as the U.S. Census Bureau, which makes its materials available to researchers studying issues ranging broadly from education to poverty to racial residential segregation. Or they may want to work with archival data to examine the cultural products—posters, films, pamphlets, and such—used by an authoritarian regime in a given period to legitimate its power or disseminated by a social movement such as the civil rights movement to spread its message to the masses.

Statistical data include *quantitative information obtained from government agencies, businesses, research studies, and other entities that collect data for their own or others' use.* The U.S. Bureau of Justice Statistics, for example, maintains a rich storehouse of information on several criminal justice social indicators, such as prison populations, incidents of crime, and criminal justice expenditures. Many other government agencies routinely conduct surveys of commerce, manufacturing, agriculture, labor, and housing. International organizations such as the United Nations and the World Bank collect annual data on the health, education, population, and economies of nearly all countries in the world. Many businesses publish annual reports that yield basic statistical information about their financial performance.

Document analysis is *the examination of written materials or cultural products: previous studies, newspaper reports, court records, campaign posters, digital reports, films, pamphlets, and other forms of text or images produced by individuals, government agencies, private organizations, and others.* Nevertheless, because such documents are not always compiled with accuracy in mind, good researchers exercise caution in using them. People who keep records are often aware that others will see the records and take pains to avoid including anything unflattering. The diaries and

---

Experiments: Research techniques for investigating cause and effect under controlled conditions.

Independent or experimental variables: Variables the researcher changes intentionally.

Dependent variables: Variables that change as a result of changes in other variables.

Statistical data: Quantitative information obtained from government agencies, businesses, research studies, and other entities that collect data for their own or others' use.

Document analysis: The examination of written materials or cultural products: previous studies, newspaper reports, court records, campaign posters, digital reports, films, pamphlets, and other forms of text or images produced by individuals, government agencies, private organizations, or others.

memoirs of politicians are good examples of documents that are invaluable sources of data but that must be interpreted with great caution. The expert researcher looks at such materials with a critical eye, double-checking with other sources for accuracy where possible.

This type of research may include historical research, which entails the analysis of historical documents. Often, such research is comparative, examining historical events in several different countries for similarities and differences. Unlike historians, sociologists usually identify patterns common to different times and places; historians tend to focus on particular times and places and are less likely to draw broad generalizations from their research. An early master of the sociological approach to historical research was Max Weber (1919/1946, 1921/1979), who contributed to our understanding of (among many other things) the differences between religious traditions in the West and those in East Asia.

Content analysis is the systematic examination of forms of documented communication. A researcher can take a content analysis approach by coding and analyzing patterns in cultural products such as music, laws, tweets, blogs, and works of art. An exciting aspect of social science research is that your object of curiosity can become a research question. In 2009, sociologists conducted a content analysis of 403 gangsta rap songs to assess whether rap's reputation of being misogynistic (hostile to women) was justified (Weitzer & Kubrin, 2009). The analysis found that although only about a fifth of the songs in the sample contained lyrics that were notable for their "objectification, exploitation, and victimization" of women (p. 25), most portrayals of women were still gender stereotypical and disempowering.

Participatory Research

Although sociologists usually try to avoid having an impact on the people they study, one research method is employed specifically to foster change. *Participatory research* supports an organization or community trying to improve its situation when it lacks the necessary economic or political power to do so by itself. The researcher fully participates by training the members to conduct research on their own while working with them to enhance their power (Freire, 1972; Whyte, 1991). Such research might be part of, for instance, empowering a community to act against the threat of HIV/AIDS, as has been done in places such as San Francisco, California and Nairobi, Kenya. Participatory research is an effective way of conducting an empirical study while also furthering a community or organizational goal that will benefit from the results of the study.

 ## Social Life, Social Media

DOES TECHNOLOGY AFFECT STUDYING?

In 2011, the National Survey of Student Engagement (NSSE) surveyed about 416,000 U.S. students at 673 institutions of higher education, asking about student relationships with faculty, engagement in class and on campus, and access to support. It also asked about a new topic—hours spent studying by major. Consistent with the results of other recent surveys, the NSSE found that students are spending fewer hours studying than did their counterparts in previous decades. If the average student reported studying about 24 hours per week in 1961, by 2011, the average student reported about 14 hours of study time (Babcock & Marks, 2010; NSSE, 2012). Within this figure are variations by major, ranging from about 24 hours per week for architecture majors to 10 for speech majors. Sociology majors reported studying an average of 13.8 hours per week (de Vise, 2012). A 2016 study by the Heritage Foundation concluded that, overall, college students are spending about 8 hours per week in class and 11 hours studying (Burke, Amselem, & Hall, 2016). These findings invite the question of what factors might be behind the decline in self-reported hours spent studying.

Some hypotheses on the decline implicate modern technology for at least two reasons. First, it has been suggested that students study less because they are spending substantial time engaged with social media. One pilot study at Ohio State University concluded that students who used Facebook had poorer grades than those who did not, though the question of time spent studying was not asked (Karpinski & Duberstein, 2009). Another study found that even though Facebook use had a negatively predictive impact on students' grade point average, the effect was slight, unless students were heavy users (Junco, 2012). More recently, researchers determined that students who use social media while studying and those who use social media very frequently perform slightly worse academically than their peers. Interestingly, however, the study did not find that students who are active on social media spend less time studying (Marker, Gnambs, & Appel, 2017).

Second, students may be reporting less study time because technology has cut the hours of work needed for some tasks. Although preparing a research paper in the past may have demanded hours in the library stacks or in pursuit of an expert to interview, today, an online search engine can bring up a wealth of data earlier generations could not have imagined. Far fewer students consult research librarians or use library databases than in the past. Notably, however, a recent study suggests that the quality of data students have the skills to find in their searches is mixed and often low (Kolowich, 2011).

Technology is only one possible factor in the decline in the time U.S. students spend studying. One study posits, for instance, that study time has decreased as achievement standards have fallen (Babcock & Marks, 2010). There is no denying that one of the most dramatic differences between the 1960s and today is the proliferation of social media and technology, which suggests that an explanatory relationship may exist.

Think It Through

- Imagine that your final paper for this semester involves answering the research question, "What is the impact of social media on students' studying habits in college?" How would you go

about answering this question? How would you collect data for your project?

Follow us on Twitter to keep up with current sociological stories and research! We're at **@DiscoverSoc1.**

Share your own ideas at **#DiscoverSociology.**

©iStockphoto.com/alejandrophotography

Has technology helped or hindered your studying in college? Does it mostly offer research help—or additional distractions?

arise during research and adapting new methods to fit the circumstances. Thus, the stages of research can vary, even when sociologists agree about the basic sequence. At the same time, for student sociologists, it is useful to understand the key building blocks of good sociological research. As you read through the following descriptions of the stages (Figure 2.4), think about a topic of interest to you and how you might use that as the basis for an original research project.

Frame Your Research Question

"Good research," Thomas Dewey observed, "scratches where it itches." Sociological research begins with the formulation of a question or questions to be answered. Society offers an endless spectrum of compelling issues to study: Does exposure to violent video games affect the incidence of aggressive behavior in adolescents? Does religious faith affect voting behavior? Is family income a good predictor of performance on standardized college entrance tests such as the ACT or SAT? Beyond the descriptive aspects of social phenomena, sociologists are also interested in how relationships between the variables they examine can be explained.

Formulating a research question precisely and carefully is one of the most important steps toward ensuring a successful research project. Research questions come from

Doing Sociology: A Student's Guide to Research

Sociological research seldom follows a formula that indicates exactly how to proceed. Sociologists often have to feel their way as they go, responding to the challenges that

■ **FIGURE 2.4** Sociological Research Formula

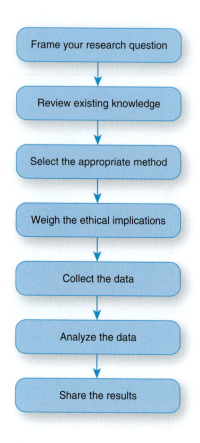

is usually published and peer-reviewed research studies. Your purpose in conducting the literature review is to learn about studies that have already been done on your topic of interest so that you can set your research in the context of existing studies. You will also use the literature review to highlight how your research will contribute to this body of knowledge.

Select the Appropriate Method

Now you are ready to think about how your research question can best be answered. Which of the research methods described earlier will give the best results for the project and is most feasible for your research circumstances, experience, and budget?

If you wish to obtain basic information from a relatively large population in a short period of time, then a survey is the best method to use. If you want to obtain detailed information about a smaller group of people, then interviews might be most beneficial. Participant observation and detached observation are ideal research methods for verifying data obtained through interviews or, for the latter, when the presence of a researcher might alter the research results. Document analysis and historical research are good choices for projects focused on inaccessible subjects and historical sociology. Remember, sociological researchers often use multiple methods.

Weigh the Ethical Implications

Research conducted on other human beings—as much of sociological research is—poses certain ethical problems. An outpouring of outrage after the discovery of gruesome experiments conducted by the Nazis during World War II prompted the adoption of the Nuremberg Code, a collection of ethical research guidelines developed to help prevent such atrocities from ever happening again (Table 2.4). In addition to these basic guidelines, scientific societies throughout the world have adopted their own codes of ethics to safeguard against the misuse and abuse of human subjects.

Before you begin your research, it is important that you familiarize yourself with the American Sociological Association's code of ethics (www.asanet.org/about/ethics.cfm) as well as with the standards of your school, and carefully follow both. Ask yourself whether your research will cause the subjects any emotional or physical harm. How will you guarantee their anonymity? Does the research violate any of your own ethical principles?

Most universities and research institutes require researchers to complete particular forms before undertaking experiments using human subjects, describing the research methods to be used and the groups of subjects who will take part. Depending on the type of research, a researcher may need to obtain written agreement from the

many sources. Some arise from problems that form the foundation of sociology, including an interest in socioeconomic inequalities and their causes and effects or the desire to understand how power is exercised in social relationships. Sociologists are also mindful that solid empirical data are important to public policies on issues of concern such as poverty, occupational mobility, and domestic violence.

Keep in mind that you also need to define your terms. Recall our discussion of operationalizing concepts. For example, if you are studying middle school bullying, you need to make explicit your definition of bullying and how that will be measured. The same holds true if you are studying a topic such as illiteracy or aggressive behavior.

Review Existing Knowledge

Once you identify the question you want to ask, you need to conduct a review of the existing literature on your topic. The literature may include published studies, unpublished papers, books, dissertations, government documents, newspapers and other periodicals, and increasingly, data disseminated on the Internet. The key focus of the literature review, however,

TABLE 2.4   The Nuremberg Code

	DIRECTIVES FOR HUMAN EXPERIMENTATION
1.	The voluntary consent of the human subject is absolutely essential.
2.	The experiment should be such as to yield fruitful results for the good of society.
3.	The experiment should be so designed and based on the results of animal experimentation and a knowledge of the natural history of the disease.
4.	The experiment should be so conducted as to avoid all unnecessary physical and mental suffering and injury.
5.	No experiment should be conducted where there is an *a priori* reason to believe that death or disabling injury will occur.
6.	The degree of risk to be taken should never exceed that determined by the humanitarian importance of the problem to be solved by the experiment.
7.	Proper preparations should be made and adequate facilities provided to protect the experimental subject against even remote possibilities of injury, disability, or death.
8.	The experiment should be conducted only by scientifically qualified persons.
9.	During the course of the experiment, the human subject should be at liberty to bring the experiment to an end.
10.	During the course of the experiment, the scientist in charge must be prepared to terminate the experiment at any stage if he has probable cause to believe, in the exercise of the good faith, superior skill, and careful judgment required of him, that a continuation of the experiment is likely to result in injury, disability, or death to the experimental subject.

Source: The Nuremberg Code, United States Holocaust Memorial Museum, https://www.ushmm.org/information/exhibitions/online-exhibitions/special-focus/doctors-trial/nuremberg-code.

Discover & Debate

PUBLIC OPINION RESEARCH

Motion: Polling is an accurate way of gauging public attitudes about politics and society.

Background: In a democracy, the public's voice matters. President Abraham Lincoln said, "What I want to get done is what the people desire to have done, and the question for me is how to find that out exactly." But how do we know what "the people" are thinking, how they are voting, and how they assess the direction of politics, the economy, and social life? Survey research, specifically public opinion polling, offers a means of peering into the public mind. Large-scale scientifically based polling began in the United States early in the 20th century. Near the end of the 1948 presidential race, the *Chicago Tribune* famously published the headline, "Dewey Defeats Truman," when, in fact, Harry S. Truman had defeated Thomas Dewey to win the election; this represents a well-known failure of political polling, although later presidential polls have been largely accurate in predicting winners. The 2016 presidential contest, however, in which most polls predicted a win for Hillary Clinton over Donald Trump, has raised new questions about polling approaches and accuracy.

Questions for Consideration

- How should pollsters address the problem of declining response rates in political polling?

- What kinds of messages about polling are present in the U.S. political environment? How might these affect participation rates?

- Are polls of people's attitudes toward issues other than politics, such as education funding, same-sex marriage, U.S. military involvement abroad, or how to address the opioid epidemic, important? If yes, why are they important?

Debate Tip

- Follow the model used by academic debaters, which foresees the development of a debate position in five steps.

(Continued)

(Continued)

1. Introduce your debate topic. Explain why it is important to you and to the audience.

2. State your main argument about the topic. You may break down the thesis of the argument into smaller parts.

3. Support your points with credible evidence.

4. Recognize and acknowledge a possible challenge to your argument, and briefly address it.

5. Finish with a statement that wraps up your argument and guides your audience to a conclusion.

AFFIRMATIVE ARGUMENTS	OPPOSITION ARGUMENTS
Reputable polling organizations use scientifically selected samples to represent a population of interest as closely as possible. This enables them to learn about the attitudes and practices of a large population with a small number of respondents.	Bias can be introduced into surveys by factors such as interviewer effects, question order effects, and social desirability bias, which may cause respondents to give answers that do not correspond to their actual beliefs or actions.
Historically, political polling, particularly for presidential contests, has a strong record of accuracy.	Shifts in technology use may affect participation and representativeness of samples. For example, as fewer people use landline phones and more exclusively use mobile phones, survey organizations may have difficulty reaching prospective respondents and, hence, assembling a representative population sample.
Because they try to maintain reputations for accuracy, scientific polling organizations recognize errors and adjust for them in future polls. For example, in the 2016 presidential election, assumptions about who were "likely voters" did not correspond fully with actual voters: Because educated voters were more likely to respond to polls, the preferences of less-educated voters were only partially captured in polls, particularly in the Midwestern states that played a decisive role in the election.	A lack of trust in media and polling organizations may affect the willingness of some people to participate in polls, potentially skewing the sample.

subjects for their participation. Today, a study similar to that conducted by Philip Zimbardo in the 1970s at Stanford University (described in the *Private Lives, Public Issues* box) would be unlikely to be approved because of the stress put on the experiment's subjects in the course of the research. Approval of research involving human subjects is granted with an eye to both fostering good research and protecting the interests of those partaking in the study.

Collect and Analyze the Data

Collecting data is the heart of research. It is time consuming but exciting. During this phase, you will gather the information that will allow you to make a contribution to the sociological understanding of your topic. If your data set is qualitative (for example, open-ended responses to interview questions or observations of people), you will proceed by carefully reviewing and organizing your field notes, documents, and other sources of information. If your data set is quantitative (for example, completed closed-ended surveys), you will proceed by entering data into spreadsheets, comparing results, and analyzing your findings using statistical software.

Your analysis should offer answers to the research questions with which you began the study. Be mindful in interpreting your data, and avoid conclusions that are speculative or not warranted by the actual research results. Do your data support or contradict your initial hypothesis? Or are they simply inconclusive? Report *all* of your results. Do your findings have implications for larger theories in the discipline? Do they suggest the need for further study of another dimension of the issue at hand? Good research need not have results that unequivocally support your hypothesis. A finding that refutes the hypothesis can be instructive as well.

Share the Results

However fascinating your research may be to you, its benefits are amplified when you take advantage of opportunities to share it with others. You can share your findings with the sociological community by publishing the results in academic journals. Before submitting research for publication,

During the Nuremberg Trials, which brought key figures of the Nazi Party of Germany to justice, the practices of some Nazi medical personnel were found to be unethical and even criminal. The Nuremberg Code, which emerged from these trials, established principles for any type of human experimentation.

you must learn which journals cover your topic areas and review those journals' standards for publication. Some colleges and universities sponsor undergraduate journals that offer opportunities for students to publish original research.

Other outlets for publication include books, popular magazines, newspapers, video documentaries, and websites. Another way to communicate your findings is to give a presentation at a professional meeting. Many professional meetings are held each year; at least one will offer a panel suited to your topic. In some cases, high-quality undergraduate papers are selected for presentation. If your paper is one, relevant experts at the meeting will likely help you interpret your findings further.

Why Learn to Do Sociological Research?

The news media provides us with an immense amount of round-the-clock information. Some of it is very good; some of it is misleading. Reported "facts" may come from sources that have agendas or are motivated by self-interest, such as political interest groups, lobbying groups, media outlets, and even government agencies. Perhaps the most problematic are "scientific" findings that are agenda driven, not scientifically unbiased. In particular, because we live in a time of information saturation, it is important that we learn to be

---

 ## Private Lives, Public Issues

WHY DO HUMANS COMMIT ATROCITIES?

In the early 1970s, social psychologist Philip Zimbardo (1974; Haney, Banks, & Zimbardo, 1973) set out to investigate how role expectations shape behavior: That is, he wanted to see how individual actions were, to a significant degree, products of a social environment rather than a particular personality. Specifically, he was intrigued by the possibility that the frequently observed cruelty of prison guards was a consequence of the institutional setting and role, not of the guards' personalities.

In an experiment that is still widely cited and discussed, Zimbardo converted the basement of a Stanford University building into a makeshift prison. A newspaper ad seeking young men to take part in the experiment for pay drew 70 subject candidates, who were given a battery of physical and psychological tests to assess their emotional stability and maturity. The most mature 24 were selected for the experiment and randomly assigned

Despite questions about the ethics of Philip Zimbardo's experiment, sociologists still study his work. Is it wrong to use research data gathered by means we now consider unethical? Do the results of research ever justify subjecting human beings to physical or psychological discomfort, invasion of privacy, or deception?

(Continued)

(Continued)

to roles as guards or prisoners. Those assigned to be prisoners were "arrested," handcuffed, and taken to the makeshift prison by the Palo Alto police. The behavior of the guards and the prisoners was filmed.

Within a week, the prison setting took on many of the characteristics of actual prisons. The guards were often aggressive and seemed to take pleasure in being cruel. The prisoners began planning escapes and expressed hostility and bitterness toward the guards. The subjects in the experiment so identified with their respective roles that many of them displayed signs of depression and anxiety. As a result, some were released early, and the experiment was canceled before the first week was over.

Since the participants had been screened for psychological and physical problems, Zimbardo concluded that the results could not be attributed to their personalities. Instead, the prison setting itself (the *independent variable*) appeared to be at the root of the guards' brutal behavior and the prisoners' hostility and rebelliousness (the *dependent variables*). Zimbardo's research shows how profoundly private lives are shaped by the behavioral expectations of the roles we occupy in social institutions.

Think It Through

- Zimbardo's experiment could not be repeated today, as it would violate guidelines for ethical research with human subjects. How might a researcher design an ethical experiment to test the question of the circumstances under which apparently normal individuals will engage in violent or cruel acts?

---

critical consumers of information and to ask questions about the quality of the data presented to us. Carefully gathered and precise data are important not only as sources of information but also as the basis of informed decision making on the part of elected officials and others in positions of power.

Because you now understand how valid and reliable data are gathered, you can better question the veracity and reliability of others' claims. For example, when a pollster announces that 80% of the American people favor Joe Conman for Congress, you can ask, "What was the size of the sample? How representative is it of the population? How was the survey questionnaire prepared? Exactly what questions were asked?" If it turns out that the data are based on the responses of 25 residents of a gated Colorado community or that a random sample was used but the survey included leading questions, you know the results do not give an accurate picture.

Similarly, your grasp of the research process allows you to have greater confidence in research that was conducted properly. You should put more stock in the results of a nationwide Centers for Disease Control and Prevention survey of college students' drug use or safe-sex choices that used carefully prepared questionnaires tested for their validity and reliability and less stock in data gathered by a reporter untrained in scientific methods who interviewed a small, nonrandom sample of students on a single college campus.

You have also taken the first step in learning how to gather and evaluate data yourself. Realizing the value of theories that can be tested and proved false if they are wrong is the first step in developing your own theories and hypotheses. By using the concepts, processes, and definitions introduced in this chapter, you can conduct research that is valid, appropriate, and even publishable.

In short, these research tools will help you be a more critical consumer of information and enhance your understanding of the social world around you. Other benefits of learning sociology will become apparent throughout the following chapters as you discover how the research process is applied to cultures, societies, and the institutions that shape your life.

 ## What Can I Do with a Sociology Degree?

QUANTITATIVE RESEARCH SKILLS

Sociologists use quantitative research skills to conduct systematic empirical investigations of social phenomena using statistical methods. Quantitative research encompasses those studies in which data are expressed in terms of numbers. Important sources of quantitative data include surveys and observations. The objective of quantitative research in sociology is to gather rigorous data and to use numerical data to characterize the dimensions of an issue or the extent of a problem (this could include, for instance, the collection of statistical data on rates of obesity and poverty in neighborhoods or states and the calculation of the correlation of the two phenomena). Data may be used to develop or test hypotheses about the roots of a sociological phenomenon or problem.

Knowledge of quantitative methods is a valuable skill in today's job market. Learning to collect and analyze quantitative data, which is an important part of a sociological education, prepares you to do a wide variety of job tasks, including survey development, questionnaire design, market research, brand health tracking, and financial quantitative modeling and analysis.

Amber Henderson, Survey Statistician, U.S. Census Bureau

The George Washington University, MA in Sociology

I work in the Center for Survey Measurement as a statistician at the U.S. Census Bureau. The goal of the Census Bureau is to provide timely, accurate, and quality data while minimizing the various sources of survey error. When fielding a survey, it must go through all of the phases of what we call the survey life cycle. *This includes tasks such as project planning, data collection, data analyses, and reporting. During my first year at Census, I*

used statistical software packages to manipulate, edit, and analyze data for surveys on education. Statistical software is a valuable tool for those who work with data. I used it frequently to run basic descriptive statistics and to check the data for error. For example, if a respondent gave a date of birth that indicated they were 12 years of age and listed his or her marital status as married, *I would flag these data points for potential inconsistencies.*

In my current role at Census, I do a lot more survey research where I specialize in structured cognitive interviewing and develop survey questions. The core sociology courses I took both during undergraduate and graduate school prepared me for my career at Census. I use a lot of what I learned in my courses on sociological research methods and data analysis to choose the best research method and work effectively and accurately with the Census Bureau's survey data. People often look puzzled when they learn you want to study sociology, but what they do not realize is that it's a multidimensional field. Sociology and my professors taught me both the qualitative and quantitative skills I needed to land my dream job. I wouldn't change a thing!

Career Data: Statisticians

- 2017 Median Pay: $84,760 per year
- $40.75 per hour
- Typical Entry-Level Education: Master's degree
- Job Growth, 2016–2026: 33% (Much faster than average)

Source: Bureau of Labor Statistics, *Occupational Outlook Handbook*, 2017.

SUMMARY

- Unlike commonsense beliefs, sociological understanding puts our biases, assumptions, and conclusions to the test.

- As a science, sociology combines logically constructed theory and systematic observation to explain human social relations.

- **Inductive reasoning** generalizes from specific observations; **deductive reasoning** consists of logically deducing the empirical implications of a particular theory or set of ideas.

- A good theory is logically consistent, testable, and valid. The **principle of falsification** holds that if theories are to

be scientific, they must be formulated in such a way that they can be disproved if wrong.

- Sociological **concepts** must be operationally defined to yield measurable or observable variables. Often, sociologists operationally define **variables** so they can measure these in quantifiable values and assess **validity** and **reliability** to eliminate **bias** in their research.

- Quantitative analysis permits us to measure correlations between variables and identify **causal relationships**. Researchers must be careful not to infer causation from correlation.

- Qualitative analysis is often better suited than **quantitative research** to producing a deep understanding of how the people being studied view the social world. On the other hand, it is sometimes difficult to measure the reliability and validity of **qualitative research**.

- Sociologists seek **objectivity** when conducting their research. One way to help ensure objectivity is through the **replication** of research.

- Research strategies are carefully thought-out plans that guide the gathering of information about the social world. They also suggest the choice of appropriate **research methods**.

- Research methods in sociology include **survey** research (which often relies on random sampling), **fieldwork** (including participant observation and detached observation), **experiments**, working with existing information, and participatory research.

- Sociological research typically follows seven steps: framing the research question, reviewing the existing knowledge, selecting appropriate methods, weighing the ethical implications of the research, collecting data, analyzing data, and sharing the results.

- To be ethical, researchers must be sure their research protects the privacy of subjects and does not cause them unwarranted stress. Scientific societies throughout the world have adopted codes of ethics to safeguard against the misuse and abuse of human subjects.

KEY TERMS

scientific method, 33
deductive reasoning, 33
hypotheses, 33
inductive reasoning, 33
quantitative research, 33
qualitative research, 33
scientific theories, 34
concepts, 35
operational definition, 35
variable, 35
quantitative variables, 35
qualitative variables, 35
correlation, 35
causal relationship, 36

spurious relationship, 36
positive correlation, 37
negative correlation, 37
principle of falsification
    (or falsifiability), 38
validity, 38
reliability, 38
bias, 38
social desirability bias, 39
objectivity, 39
value neutrality, 39
replication, 39
research methods, 39
survey, 40

sample, 40
population, 40
random sampling, 40
stratified sampling, 41
fieldwork, 43
interview, 44
leading questions, 44
experiments, 45
independent or experimental
    variables, 45
dependent variables, 45
statistical data, 45
document analysis, 45

DISCUSSION QUESTIONS

1. Think about a topic of contemporary relevance in which you may be interested (for example, poverty, juvenile delinquency, teen births, or racial neighborhood segregation). Using what you learned in this chapter, create a simple research question about the topic. Match your research question to an appropriate research method. Share your ideas with classmates.

2. What is the difference between quantitative and qualitative research? Give an example of each from the chapter. In what kinds of cases might one choose one or the other research method to effectively address an issue of interest?

3. Sociologists often use interviews and surveys as methods for collecting data. What are potential problems with these methods of which researchers need to be aware? What steps can researchers take to ensure that the data they are collecting are of good quality?

4. Imagine that your school has recently documented a dramatic rise in plagiarism reported by teachers. Your sociology class has been invited to study this issue. Consider what you learned in this chapter about survey research and design a project to assess the problem.

5. In this chapter, you learned about the issue of ethics in research and read about the Zimbardo prison experiment. How should knowledge collected under unethical conditions (whether it is sociological, medical, psychological, or other scientific knowledge) be treated? Should it be used in the same way as data collected under ethically rigorous conditions?

Want a Better Grade?

Get the tools you need to sharpen your study skills. Access practice quizzes, eFlashcards, video, and multimedia at **https://edge.sagepub.com/chambliss4e**.

©In Pictures Ltd./Corbis via Getty Images

Culture and Mass Media

3

WHAT DO YOU THINK?

1. What is the relationship between popular culture and public attitudes about social issues such as same-sex marriage? Do changes in popular culture help drive changes in public attitudes, or are shifting societal attitudes reflected in popular culture?

2. Do graphic representations of violence in films, television, music, and video games have an effect on the attitudes and behaviors of children? What about adults?

3. Does a shared global culture exist? What are its key characteristics?

LEARNING OBJECTIVES

3.1 Define the component parts of culture, including values, norms, and taboos.

3.2 Recognize the significance of language in representing culture.

3.3 Discuss the relationship between culture and mass media and the debate over mass culture and violence.

3.4 Explain how sociologists theorize the relationship between culture and social class.

3.5 Apply functionalist and conflict perspectives to the phenomenon of global culture.

POPULAR CULTURE AND THE UNDEAD

In late 2018, the television series *The Walking Dead* debuted its ninth season. The long-running program follows a small band of survivors trying to evade flesh-eating zombies who have overtaken human society. The main character, Rick, and his compatriots have spent nearly a decade on television fighting for survival against the fearsome "walkers," who relentlessly hunt human and beast. The undead have not only overrun the planet, however, but they have also assumed a dominating role in popular culture. Along with following the adventures of *The Walking Dead*, consumers of horror can read zombie books (such as *World War Z*, which was also made into a movie, and *The Zombie Survival Guide*), play zombie video games (for instance,

©Album/Alamy Stock Photo

Resident Evil and *House of the Dead*), and watch zombie films (such as *Maze Runner: The Scorch Trials, I Am Legend, 28 Days Later,* and the upcoming *The Dead Don't Die*). In 2014, the Centers for Disease Control and Prevention even used public interest in zombies to launch a disaster preparedness campaign, offering the public tips for surviving an onslaught of the undead. According to Dr. Ali Khan, the architect of the campaign, "If you are generally well equipped to deal with a zombie apocalypse, you will be prepared for a hurricane, pandemic, earthquake, or terrorist attack" (http://www.cdc.gov/phpr/zombies.htm).

Why are zombies a cultural phenomenon in the 21st-century United States? Some writers suggest that films, television, and other cultural forms reflect social anxieties: As sociologist Robert Wuthnow (1989) wrote, "If cultural products do not articulate closely enough with their social settings, they are likely to be regarded . . . as irrelevant, unrealistic, artificial, and overly abstract" (p. 3). In the post–World War II period of the 1940s and 1950s, Americans were dogged by fears of technology run amok (particularly nuclear fears after the first use of an atomic weapon) and the threat of communist infiltration or invasion (Booker, 2001). Popular science fiction films such as *The Day the Earth Stood Still* (1951) and *Invasion of the Body Snatchers* (1956) captured paranoia about alien beings who possessed powerful weapons and could arrive at any moment to destroy society and the state. The fear of communism and the concern about proliferation of destructive technology were embodied in otherworldly creatures who could enter a community undetected and crush resistance with deadly force.

Is the cultural proliferation of zombies a window into contemporary fears? Kyle W. Bishop (2010) writes that the rise of zombie popularity after traumatic societal events such as the terrorist attacks on New York City and Washington, DC, on September 11, 2001; the disease fears generated by deadly outbreaks of viruses such as SARS; and even Hurricane Katrina is not a coincidence. Rather, zombie stories resonate with a public that is anxious about the threat of societal calamity, whether natural or human made. Zombies evoke, Bishop (2009) suggests, a fear response, although the object of fear is not necessarily the zombie itself: "Because the aftereffects of war, terrorism, and natural disasters so closely resemble the scenarios of zombie cinema . . . [these films have] all the more power to shock and terrify a population that has become otherwise jaded by more traditional horror films" (p. 18).

In an entertainment publication article on *The Walking Dead*, the author observed,

> There's a fascinating question [that] critics should be answering: What is it about a show that is so relentlessly bleak that allows it to still resonate at such [an] unexpected scale? What does it say about America? . . . It's the polar opposite of the escapist fare that typically serves as popular entertainment, a dystopian nightmare if there ever was one. (Wallenstein, 2014, para. 18)

If critics don't have an answer, then sociologists might: Cultural products are more than entertainment—they are a mirror of society. Popular culture in the form of films or television may capture our utopian dreams, but it is also a net that catches and reflects pervasive societal fears and anxieties.

In this chapter, we will consider the multitude of functions of culture and media (which is a key vehicle of culture) and we will seek to understand how culture both constructs and reflects society in the United States and around the globe. We begin our discussion with an examination of the basic concept of *culture*, taking a look at material and nonmaterial culture as well as ideal and real culture in the United States. We then explore contemporary issues of language and its social functions in a changing world. The chapter also addresses issues of culture and media, asking how media messages may reflect and affect behaviors and attitudes. We then turn to the topic of culture and class and the sociological question of whether culture and taste are linked to class identity and social reproduction. Finally, we examine the evolving relationship between global and local cultures, in particular, the influence of U.S. mass media on the world.

Culture: Concepts and Applications

What is culture? The word *culture* might evoke images of song, dance, and literature—the beat of Latin salsa, Polish folk dances performed by girls with red ribbons braided into their hair, or the latest in a popular series of fantasy novels. It might remind you of a dish from the Old Country made by a beloved grandparent or a spicy Indian meal you ate with friends from New Delhi.

Culture, from a sociological perspective, comprises *the beliefs, norms, behaviors, and products common to the members of a particular group.* Culture is integral to our social experience of the world. It offers diversion and entertainment, but it also helps form our identities and gives meaning to the artifacts and experiences of our lives. Culture shapes and permeates material objects such as folk costumes, rituals such as nuptial and burial ceremonies, and language as expressed in conversation, poetry, stories, and music. As social beings, we make culture, but culture also makes us in ways that are both apparent and subtle.

Material and Nonmaterial Culture

Every culture has both material and nonmaterial aspects. We can broadly define **material culture** as *the physical objects that are created, embraced, or consumed by society that help shape people's lives.* Material culture includes television programs, computer games, software, and other artifacts of human creation. It also emerges from the physical environment inhabited by the community. For example, in the countries surrounding the Baltic Sea, including Poland, Latvia, and Lithuania, amber (a substance created when the resin of fallen seaside pines is hardened and smoothed by decades or centuries in the salty waters) is an important part of local cultures. It is valued both for its decorative properties in jewelry and for its therapeutic properties; it is said to relieve pain. Amber has become a part of the material culture in these countries rather than

elsewhere because it is a product of the physical environment in which these communities dwell.

Material culture also includes the types of shelters that characterize a community. For instance, in seaside communities, homes are often built on stilts to protect against flooding. The materials used to construct homes have historically been those available in the immediate environment—wood, thatch, or mud, for instance—although the global trade in timber, marble, granite, and other components of modern housing has transformed the relationship between place and shelter in many countries.

Nonmaterial culture is composed of *the abstract creations of human cultures, including ideas about behavior, language, and social practices.* Nonmaterial culture encompasses aspects of the social experience, such as behavioral norms, values, language, family forms, and institutions. It also reflects the natural environment in which a culture has evolved.

Although material culture is concrete and nonmaterial culture is abstract, the two are intertwined: Nonmaterial culture may attach particular meanings to the objects of material culture. For example, people will go to great lengths to protect an object of material culture such as a national flag, not because of what it is—imprinted cloth—but because of the nonmaterial culture it represents, including ideals about freedom and patriotic pride. To grasp the full extent of nonmaterial culture, you must first understand three of the sociological concepts that shape it: *beliefs, norms,* and *values* (Table 3.1).

Beliefs

We broadly define **beliefs** as *particular ideas that people accept as true.* We can believe based on faith, superstition, science, tradition, or experience. To paraphrase the words of sociologists W. I. Thomas and D. S. Thomas (1928), beliefs may be understood as real when they are real in their consequences. They need not be objectively true. For example, during the witch hunts in early colonial America, rituals of accusation, persecution, and execution could be sustained in communities such as Salem, Massachusetts, because there was a shared

---

Culture: The beliefs, norms, behaviors, and products common to the members of a particular group.

Material culture: The physical objects that are created, embraced, or consumed by society that help shape people's lives.

Nonmaterial culture: The abstract creations of human cultures, including ideas about behavior, language, and social practices.

Beliefs: Particular ideas that people accept as true.

TABLE 3.1   Cultural Concepts and Characteristics

CONCEPT	CHARACTERISTICS
Values	General ideas about what is good, right, or just in a culture
Norms	Culturally shared rules governing social behavior (*oughts* and *shoulds*)
Folkways	Conventions (or weak norms), the violation of which is not very serious
Mores	Strongly held norms, the violation of which is very offensive
Taboos	Very strongly held norms, the violation of which is highly offensive and even unthinkable
Laws	Norms that have been codified
Beliefs	Particular ideas that people accept as true

Many people find flag burning offensive because the flag, an object of material culture, is a symbol of the country and its ideals. The Supreme Court, however, has held in a series of cases that symbolic expression is protected by the First Amendment, which explicitly protects free speech.

belief in the existence of witches and diabolical power. From 1692 through 1693, more than 200 people were accused of practicing witchcraft; of these, 20 were executed, 19 by hanging and 1 by being pressed to death between heavy stones. Beliefs, similar to other aspects of culture, are dynamic rather than static: When belief in the existence of witchcraft waned, so did the witch hunts. In 1711, a bill was passed that restored "the rights and good names" of those who had been accused, and in 1957, the state of Massachusetts issued a formal apology for the events of the past (Blumberg, 2007).

Norms

In any culture, a set of ideas exists about what is right, just, and good as well as about what is wrong and unjust. Norms, as we noted in Chapter 1, are *accepted social behaviors and beliefs,* the common rules of a culture that govern the behavior of people belonging to that culture.

The marriage of Prince Harry and Meghan Markle in May of 2018 captured worldwide attention. Celebrity weddings—as well as royal weddings—are often an object of intense public interest.

Sociologist Robert Nisbet (1970) writes, "The moral order of society is a kind of tissue of 'oughts': negative ones which forbid certain actions and positive ones which [require certain] actions" (p. 226). We can think of norms as representing a set of *oughts* and *ought nots* that guide behavioral choices such as where to stand relative to others in an elevator, how long to hold someone's gaze in conversation, how to conduct the rites of passage that mark different stages of life, and how to resolve disagreements or conflicts. Some norms are enshrined in legal statutes; others are inscribed in our psyches and consciences. Weddings bring together elements of both.

The wedding ceremony is a central ritual of adult life with powerful social, legal, and cultural implications. It is also significant economically: The term *wedding industrial complex* (Ingraham, 1999) has been used to describe a massive industry that generates over $72 billion in revenue and employs over a million people (Schmidt, 2017). This comes as little surprise when we consider that in 2016, the estimated average amount spent on a wedding was just over $35,000 (Vasel, 2017). The wedding as a key cultural image and icon is cultivated in families, religions, and the media. Wedding images are used to sell products ranging from cosmetics to furniture, and weddings constitute an important theme in popular movies, including *My Big Fat Greek Wedding* (2002) and *My Big Fat Greek Wedding 2* (2016), *The Wedding Crashers* (2005), *Bridesmaids* (2011), and *Mike and Dave Need Wedding Dates* (2016). Popular television series such as *The Office, Sex and the City,* and *Nashville* have used weddings as narratives for highly anticipated season finales or premiers. The reality program *Say Yes to the Dress* enthralls viewers with the drama of choosing a wedding gown and *Four Weddings* pits four brides against one another to pull off the "perfect wedding," while *90 Day Fiancé* follows long-distance couples who must decide whether or not to wed before the foreign partner's visa expires. The wedding ritual is a powerful artifact of our culture. In light of this, a sociologist might ask, "What are the

In the years before the U.S. Supreme Court legalized same-sex marriage, public attitudes about marriage were shifting. According to one poll, watching television programs such as *Modern Family*, which prominently features a same-sex couple, made some viewers more likely to support same-sex marriage (Appelo, 2012).

cultural components of the ritual of entering matrimony, the wedding ceremony?"

Sociologist William Graham Sumner (1906–1959) distinguished among several different kinds of norms, each of which can be applied to weddings. **Folkways** are *fairly weak norms that are passed down from the past, the violation of which is generally not considered serious within a particular culture.* A folkway that has been part of many U.S. wedding rituals is the "giving away" of the bride: The father of the bride symbolically "gives" his daughter to the groom, signaling a change in the woman's identity from daughter to wife. Some couples today reject this ritual as patriarchal because it recalls earlier historical periods when a woman was treated as chattel given—literally—to her new husband by her previous keeper, her father.

Some modern couples are choosing to walk down the aisle together to signal an equality of roles and positions. Although the sight of a couple going to the altar together might raise a few eyebrows among more traditional guests, this violation of the "normal" way of doing things does not constitute a serious cultural transgression and, because culture is dynamic, may in time become a folkway itself.

Mores (pronounced "MOR-ays") are *strongly held norms, the violation of which seriously offends the standards of acceptable conduct of most people within a particular culture.* In a typical American wedding, the person conducting the ceremony plays an important role in directing the events, and the parties enacting the ritual are expected to respond in conventional ways. For instance, when the officiant asks the guests whether anyone objects to the union, the convention is for no one to object. When an objector surfaces (more often in television programs and films than in real life), the response of the guests is shock and dismay: The ritual has been disrupted and the scene violated.

Taboos are *powerful mores, the violation of which is considered serious and even unthinkable within a particular culture.* The label of taboo is commonly reserved for behavior that is extremely offensive: Incest, for example, is a nearly universal taboo. There may not be any taboos associated with the wedding ritual itself in the United States, but there are some relating to marital relationships. For instance, while in some U.S. states it is not illegal to marry a first cousin, in most modern communities, doing so violates a taboo against intermarriage in families.

Laws are *codified norms or rules of behavior.* Laws formalize and institutionalize society's norms. There are laws that govern marriage: For instance, until very recently, in many states, marriage was legally open only to heterosexual adults who are not already married to other people. In many respects, this was consistent with long-standing societal norms. Over time, however, the normative climate shifted, and a majority of Americans expressed support for same-sex marriage. In June 2015, the Supreme Court of the United States ruled in *Obergefell v. Hodges* that state-level bans on same-sex marriage are not constitutional. Today, marriage is legally open to both heterosexual and homosexual couples, although there have been instances of county clerks in some states refusing to grant marriage licenses to same-sex couples because they claim it violates their beliefs.

Values

Similar to norms, values are components of nonmaterial culture in every society. **Values** are *the abstract and general standards in society that define ideal principles, such as those governing notions of right and wrong.* Sets of values attach to the institutions of society at multiple levels. You may have heard about national or patriotic values, community values, and family values. These can all coexist harmoniously within a single society. Because we use values to legitimate and justify our behavior as members of a country or community or as individuals, we tend to staunchly defend the values we embrace (Kluckhohn & Strodtbeck, 1961).

Folkways: Fairly weak norms that are passed down from the past, the violation of which is generally not considered serious within a particular culture.

Mores: Strongly held norms, the violation of which seriously offends the standards of acceptable conduct of most people within a particular culture.

Taboos: Powerful mores, the violation of which is considered serious and even unthinkable within a particular culture.

Laws: Codified norms or rules of behavior.

Values: The abstract and general standards in society that define ideal principles, such as those governing notions of right and wrong.

©AF archive/Alamy Stock Photo

Is there a specific set of values we can define as *American*? According to a classic study by Robin M. Williams Jr. (1970), "American values" include personal achievement, hard work, material comfort, and individuality. U.S. adults value science and technology, efficiency and practicality, morality and humanitarianism, equality, and "the American way of life." A recent Pew Research Center examined the question of what respondents value as part of the American Dream: Interestingly, an "essential" part of the American Dream cited by 77% of respondents was "freedom of choice in how to live" (Figure 3.1; Smith, 2017).

Researchers have identified a widening split in political values in the U.S. population, most acutely along partisan lines: That is, there are growing differences in expressed attitudes about issues ranging from social welfare to traditional family values. Although there are many shared values across race, gender, class, and other demographic characteristics, there are stark and growing differences along party lines. According to Parker (2012), between 1987 and 2012, there was a dramatic split in the share of Republicans, Democrats, and independents who agreed that "the government should take care of people who can't take care of themselves" (see Figure 3.2). A more recent study suggests one possible explanation for this split: Republican respondents are likely to attribute poverty to a lack of effort, while their Democratic counterparts are more likely to attribute it to circumstances beyond a person's control (see Figure 3.3; Smith, 2017).

The 2012 Pew survey also asked respondents about values they attribute to others: Respondents were asked

■ **FIGURE 3.1** Views About the American Dream

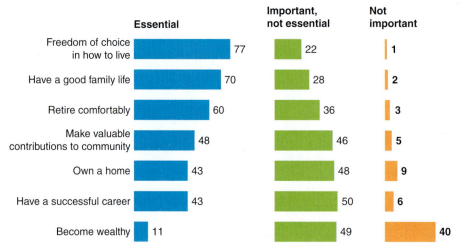

Source: "Most think the 'American dream' is within reach for them." Pew Research Center, Washington, D.C. (October 31, 2017) http://www.pewresearch.org/fact-tank/2017/10/31/most-think-the-american-dream-is-within-reach-for-them/ft_17-10-31_americandream_definitions/ Pew Research Center, Washington, D.C. (October 31, 2017)

■ **FIGURE 3.2** Political Party Affiliation and Support for Social Welfare

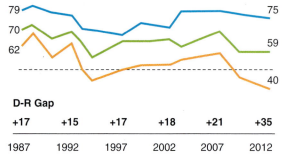

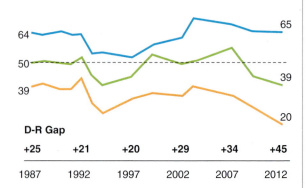

Source: Pew Research Center, 2012.

■ **FIGURE 3.3** Political Party Affiliation and Attitude toward Wealth and Poverty

Source: "Widening Gap Between Republicans and Democrats on Why People Are Rich and Poor," by the Pew Research Center, May 2, 2017 (www.pewresearch.org/fact-tank/2017/05/02/why-people-are-rich-and-poor-republicans-and-democrats-have-very-different-views/ft_17-05-02_richpoor_2/).

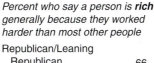

Percent who say a person is **rich** generally because they worked harder than most other people

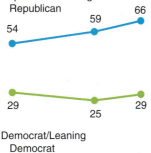

Republican/Leaning Republican
54   59   66

29   25   29

Democrat/Leaning Democrat
2014   2015   2016   2017

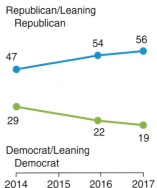

Percent who say a person is **poor** generally because of a lack of effort on their part

Republican/Leaning Republican
47   54   56

29   22   19

Democrat/Leaning Democrat
2014   2015   2016   2017

The ugly step-sisters, Anastasia and Drizella, from the story of Cinderella are only two of many children's story characters who combine an unattractive appearance with flawed personalities. How do we reconcile the idea that "beauty is only skin deep" with the images of popular culture?

to indicate whether they believed that "in the last 10 years, values held by the middle class and poor people have gotten more similar, more different, or have had no change." About 47% of respondents said that they believed values between the social classes had gotten "more similar," while 41% suggested they had gotten "more different" (the remaining respondents indicated "no change" or "don't know"). Pew did not specify particular values. Hence, respondents were left to interpret the meaning of the question. How would you interpret this question on shifting values? How would you respond? How might we explain Pew's results?

Structural functionalists including Talcott Parsons (1951) have proposed that values play a critical role in the social integration of a society. Nevertheless, values do not play this role by themselves. They are abstract—vessels into which any generation or era pours its meanings in a process that can be both dynamic and contentious. For instance, equality is a value that has been strongly supported in the

United States since the country's founding. The pursuit of equality was a powerful force in the American Revolution, and the Declaration of Independence declares that "all men are created equal" (Wood, 1993). Yet, equality has been defined differently across various eras of U.S. history. In the first half of the country's existence, *equality* did not include women or African Americans, who were by law excluded from its benefits. Over the course of the 20th century, equality became *more* equal as the rights of all citizens of the United States, regardless of race, gender, or class status, were formally recognized as equal before the law.

Ideal and Real Culture in U.S. Society

Beauty is only skin deep. Don't judge a book by its cover. All that glitters is not gold. These bits of common wisdom are part of U.S. culture. We rarely recall where we first heard them; we simply know them because they are part of the cultural framework of our lives. These three statements represent a commitment of sorts that society will value our inner qualities more than our outward appearances. They are also examples of **ideal culture**, *the values, norms, and behaviors that people in a given society profess to embrace,* even though the actions of the society may often contradict them.

Real culture consists of *the values, norms, and behaviors that people in a given society actually embrace and exhibit.* In the United States, for instance, empirical research shows that conventional attractiveness offers consistent advantages (Hamermesh, 2011). From childhood onward, the stories our parents, teachers, and the media tell us seem to sell the importance of beauty. Stories such as *Snow White, Cinderella,* and *Sleeping Beauty* connect beauty with morality

Ideal culture: The values, norms, and behaviors that people in a given society profess to embrace.

Real culture: The values, norms, and behaviors that people in a given society actually embrace and exhibit.

©Entertainment Pictures/Alamy Stock Photo

Overweight characters in film and television are often featured in the role of a fat, funny sidekick. Less frequently do they occupy the most visible role in mainstream movies and programs. In the *Pitch Perfect* films, Fat Amy, played by Rebel Wilson, is a comedic, eccentric foil to Beca, played by Anna Kendrick, who is stylish, ambitious, and serious.

and goodness and unattractiveness with malice, jealousy, and other negative traits. The link between unattractive (or unconventional) appearance and unattractive behavior is unmistakable, especially in female figures. Consider other characters many American children are exposed to early in life, such as nasty Cruella de Vil in *101 Dalmatians,* the dastardly Queen of Hearts of *Alice in Wonderland,* and the angry octopod Ursula in *The Little Mermaid.*

On television (another medium that disseminates important cultural stories), physical beauty and social status are powerfully linked. Overweight or average-looking characters populate television shows featuring working- or lower middle-class people, for example, *Family Guy* and *The Office.* Programs such as *Modern Family* and *Mike & Molly* offer leading characters who are pleasant and attractive—and often overweight. In the latter, for instance, Mike is a police officer and Molly is an elementary school teacher (she later becomes an author). They are also commonly featured in the role of the fat, funny sidekick, who can be seen in films such as *Bridesmaids, Pitch Perfect,* and *Lady Bird.* Typically, they have not broken the glass ceiling of high-status jobs that remain largely reserved for their thinner prime-time peers. Characters such as those we encounter on *Scandal, Mad Men, Empire, Gossip Girls,* and *Sex and the City* are almost invariably svelte and stylish—and occupy higher rungs on the status hierarchy.

There is a clear **cultural inconsistency**, *a contradiction between the goals of ideal culture and the practices of real culture,* in our society's treatment of conventional attractiveness. Do we "judge a book by its cover"? Studies suggest this is precisely what many of us do in a variety of social settings:

- In the workplace, conventionally attractive job applicants appear to have an advantage in securing

jobs (Hamermesh, 2011; Marlowe, Schneider, & Nelson, 1996; Shahani-Denning, 2003; Tews, Stafford, & Zhu, 2009). Women in one study who were an average of 65 pounds heavier than the norm of the study group earned about 7% less than their slimmer counterparts did, an effect equivalent to losing about one year of education or two years of experience. The link between obesity and a "pay penalty" has been confirmed by other studies (Harper, 2000; Lempert, 2007). Interestingly, some research has not found strong evidence that weight affects the wages of African American or Hispanic female workers (Cawley, 2001; DeBeaumont, 2009).

- In the courtroom, some defendants who do not meet conventional standards of attractiveness are disadvantaged (DeSantis & Kayson, 1997; Gunnell & Ceci, 2010; Taylor & Butcher, 2007). Mazzella and Feingold (1994) note that defendants charged with certain crimes, such as rape and robbery, benefit from being attractive. This is consistent with the "beautiful is good" hypothesis (Dion, Berscheid, & Walster, 1972), which attributes a tendency toward leniency to the belief that attractive people have more socially desirable characteristics. Ahola, Christianson, and Hellstrom (2009) suggest that female defendants in particular are advantaged by attractive appearance.

- Studies of college students have found that they are likely to perceive attractive people as more intelligent than unattractive people (Chia, Allred, Grossnickle, & Lee, 1998; Poteet, 2007). This bias has also been detected in students' evaluations of their instructors: A pair of economists found that the independent influence of attractiveness gives some instructors an advantage on undergraduate teaching evaluations (Hamermesh & Parker, 2005).

- Social media is routinely used to shame both public and private figures who do not fit the mold of conventional body acceptability. For example, after hosting a 2012 presidential debate on television, veteran CNN correspondent Candy Crowley was mocked on Twitter with comments about her weight. In 2013, Buzzfeed reported that a blog called Return of Kings sponsored a "fat shaming week" on Twitter (Okun, 2013). In 2016, Facebook rejected an ad featuring plus-size model Tess Holliday wearing a modest bikini, arguing that it violated the company's "health and fitness policy" for ads. Facebook later apologized (Hillin, 2016).

Another example of cultural inconsistency can be seen in our purported commitment to the ideal that "honesty is the best policy." We find an unambiguous embrace of

Cultural inconsistency: A contradiction between the goals of ideal culture and the practices of real culture.

honesty in the stories of our childhood. Think of *Pinocchio*: Were you warned as a child not to lie because it might cause your nose to grow? Did you ever promise a friend that you would not reveal his or her secret with a pinky swear and the words "Cross my heart and hope to die; stick a needle in my eye"? Yet most people do lie.

Why is this so? We may lie to protect or project a certain image of ourselves. Sociologist Erving Goffman (1959), a symbolic interactionist, called this *misrepresentation*. Goffman argued that all of us, as social actors, engage in this practice because we are concerned with defining a situation—whether it be a date or a job interview or a meeting with a professor or boss—in a manner favorable to ourselves. It is not uncommon for job seekers to pad their résumés, for instance, to leave the impression on potential employers that they are qualified or worthy. A CareerBuilder survey recently found that about 56% of employers had detected lying on a résumé. Common lies included misrepresentations of educational credentials, skill sets, dates of employment, and prior job responsibilities. According to the same survey, about 70% of employers spend under five minutes reviewing a résumé and half spend less than two minutes (CareerBuilder, 2015), suggesting that some dishonesty probably goes unnoticed.

Studies suggest that cheating and plagiarism are common among high school students (Table 3.2) and college students. In one study of 23,000 high school students, about half reported that they had cheated on a test in the past year. Just under a third also responded that they had used the Internet to plagiarize assigned work (Josephson Institute Center for Youth Ethics, 2012). Notably, a 2009 study suggests that about half of teens age 17 and younger believe cheating is necessary for success (Josephson Institute of Ethics, 2009). A recent *Atlantic Monthly* article on academic dishonesty suggests that

cheating is omnipresent in American higher education. In 2015, Dartmouth College suspended 64 students

©Image Source/Getty Images

Is academic integrity the norm in higher education today? Or do you think that many students engage in activities such as cheating on tests or plagiarizing papers? How would you design a study to examine these questions at your own school?

TABLE 3.2   Ethical and Unethical Behavior among High School Students in 2012 (in Percentages)

	NEVER	ONCE	TWO OR MORE TIMES
Copied an Internet document for a class assignment	45	26	29
Cheated on a test	49	24	28
Lied to a teacher about something significant	45	26	29

Source: Josephson Institute Center for Youth Ethics. (2012). *2012 Report Card on the Ethics of American Youth.*

suspected of cheating in—irony of ironies—an ethics class in the fall term. The previous school year, University of Georgia administrators reported investigating 603 possible cheating incidents; nearly 70 percent of the cases concluded with a student confession. In 2012, Harvard had its turn, investigating 125 students accused of improper collaboration on a final exam in a government class. (Barthel, 2016, para. 1)

Much contemporary cheating takes place with the help of technology: That may include practices such as plagiarizing a term paper from the Internet or using a mobile phone to look up answers during class. In fact, reports of academic dishonesty have risen with the advent of the Internet, though a leading researcher in the field suggests that it has turned down again recently. Are high levels of plagiarism and cheating a product primarily of access to opportunities enabled by the Internet—or are they a product of trends in the culture that diminish the importance of integrity? What do you think?

Why do you think there is such a big gap between what we say and what we do? Do you think most people are culturally inconsistent? What about you?

Ethnocentrism

Much of the time, a community's or society's cultural norms, values, and practices are internalized to the point that they become part of the natural order. Sociologist Pierre Bourdieu (1977) describes these internalized beliefs as **doxic**: those beliefs that are *taken for granted as natural*

Doxic: Taken for granted as natural or normal in society.

Private Lives, Public Issues
IDEAL CULTURE AND ITS CONSEQUENCES

Whether you are male or female, you may sometimes experience feelings of inadequacy as you follow your favorite celebrities on Instagram, watch popular series on television or Netflix, or leaf through ads in magazines like *Vogue, Cosmopolitan,* or *GQ*. You may get a sense that, in this market- and media-constructed universe, your face, hair, body, and clothing do not fit the ideal. You may wish that you had the "right look" or that you were leaner, thinner, or more muscular. You would not be alone.

One survey of college-age women found that 83% desired to lose weight. Among these, 44% of women of normal weight intentionally ate less than they wanted, and most of the women did not have healthy dieting habits (Malinauskas, Raedeke, Aeby, Smith, & Dallas, 2006). Another study examining body weight perceptions among college students found that women with exaggerated body weight perceptions were more likely to engage in unhealthy weight management strategies and were more depressed than those women with accurate perceptions of their weight (Harring, Montgomery, & Hardin, 2011).

Using our sociological imagination, we can deduce that the weight concerns many people—particularly women—experience as personal troubles are in fact linked to public issues. Worrying about (and even obsessing over) weight is a widely shared phenomenon. Millions of women diet regularly, and some manifest extreme attention to weight in the form of eating disorders (National Institute of Mental Health, 2017).

In addition to dieting, one way many people try to combat a negative body image is through posts on social media. With the growth of social media outlets such as Facebook and Instagram, photo editing applications, and capturing the perfect

angle, individuals have the opportunity to alter their image to fit society's body ideal in only a few clicks, something that used to take professionals hours to do—or that could not be done at all (Cosslett, 2016). Whether it is through a simple filter or extensive alterations, people can digitally rid themselves of insecurities and present their ideal image to the world. According to one report, up to 90% of teen girls have edited pictures to appear thinner or even to avoid cyberbullying (Bingham, 2015). One researcher also found that some girls had images of Victoria's Secret models as their phone screensaver as "thinspirations," a motivational term often used in pro-anorexia/bulimia circles that promotes thinness and glorifies certain aspects of thinness, such has visible ribs and thigh gaps (Cosslett, 2014, 2016).

As individuals, we experience the consequences of an artificially created ideal as a personal trouble—unhappiness about our appearance—but the deliberate construction and dissemination of an unattainable ideal for the purpose of generating profits is surely a public issue. Reflecting a conflict perspective, psychologist Sharlene Hesse-Biber (1997) has suggested that to understand the eating disorders and disordered eating so common among U.S. women, we ought to ask not "'What can women do to meet the ideal?' but 'Who benefits from women's excessive concern with thinness?'" (p. 32). This is the sociological imagination at work.

Think It Through

- How would you summarize key factors that explain the broad gap between ideal culture, which entreats us not to judge a book by its cover, and real culture, which pushes women and men to pursue unattainable physical perfection?

---

or normal in society. But the social organization of our lives is not natural, although it appears that way. Instead, norms, values, and practices are *socially constructed.* That is, they are the products of decisions and directions chosen by groups and individuals (often, a conflict theorist would argue, those with the most power). And although all human societies share certain similarities, different societies construct different norms, values, and practices and then embrace them as "just the way things are."

Because we tend to perceive our own culture as natural and normal, it emerges as the standard by which we tend to judge everything else. This is indicative of ethnocentrism, which, as noted in Chapter 1, is *a worldview whereby we judge other cultures by the standards of our own and regard our own way of life as normal and better than others.* That which deviates from our own normal social order can appear exotic, even shocking. Other societies' rituals of death, for example, can look astonishingly different from those to which we are accustomed. This description of an ancient burial practice from the North Caucasus provides an illustration:

> Scythian-Sarmatian burials were horrible but spectacular. A royal would be buried in a *kurgan* [burial mound] alongside piles of gold, weapons, horses, and, Herodotus writes, "various members of his household: one of his concubines, his butler, his cook, his groom, his steward, and his chamberlain—all of them strangled." A year later, 50 fine horses and 50 young men would be strangled, gutted, stuffed with chaff, sewn up, then impaled and stuck around the *kurgan* to mount a ghoulish guard for their departed king. (Smith, 2001, pp. 33–34)

Let's interpret this historical fragment using two different cultural perspectives. From an **etic perspective**—that is, *the perspective of the outside observer*—the burial ritual looks bizarre and shockingly cruel. Nevertheless, to understand it fully and avoid a potentially ethnocentric perspective, we need to call on an **emic perspective**, *the perspective of the insider,* and ask, "What did people in this period believe about the royals? What did they believe about the departed and the experience of death itself? What did they believe about the utility of material riches in the afterlife and the rewards the afterlife would confer on the royals and those loyal to them?" Are there death rituals in the U.S. cultural repertoire that might appear exotic or strange to outsiders even though we see them as normal?

Putting aside the ethnocentric perspective allows us to embrace **cultural relativism**, *a worldview whereby we understand the practices of another society sociologically, in terms of that society's norms and values and not our own.* In this way, we can come closer to an understanding of cultural beliefs and practices such as those that surround the end of life. Whether the body of the departed is viewed or hidden, buried or burned, feasted with or feasted for, danced around or sung about, a culturally relativist perspective allows the sociologist to conduct his or her examination of the roots of these practices most rigorously.

We may also call on cultural relativism to help us understand the rituals of another people, the Nacirema, described here by anthropologist Herbert Miner (1956):

> Nacirema culture is characterized by a highly developed market economy which has evolved in a rich natural habitat. Although much of the people's time is devoted to economic pursuits, a large part of the fruits of these labors and a considerable portion of the day are spent in ritual activity. The focus of this activity is the human body, the appearance and health of which loom as a dominant concern in the ethos of the people. . . .
>
> The fundamental belief underlying the whole system appears to be that the human body is ugly and that its tendency is to debility and disease. Incarcerated in such a body, man's only hope is to avert these characteristics through the use of powerful influences of ritual and ceremony. Every household has one or more shrines devoted to this purpose. The more powerful individuals in this society have several shrines in their houses. . . .
>
> The focal point of the shrine is a box or chest which is built into the wall. In this chest are kept many charms and magical potions without which no native believes he could live. These preparations are secured from a variety of specialized practitioners. . . . However, the medicine men do not provide the curative potions for their clients, but decide what the ingredients should be and then write them down in an ancient and secret language. This writing is understood only by the medicine men and by the herbalists who, for another gift, provide the required charm. (pp. 503–504)

What looks strange here, and why? Did you already figure out that *Nacirema* is *American* spelled backward? Miner invites his readers to see American rituals linked to the body and health not as natural but as *part of a culture.* Can you think of other norms or practices in the United States that we could view from this perspective? What about the all-American game of baseball, the high school graduation ceremony, the language of texting, or the cultural obsession with celebrities or automobiles?

Subcultures

When sociologists study culture, they do not presume that in any given country—or even community—there is a single culture. They may identify a dominant culture within any group, but significant cultural identities exist in addition to, or sometimes in opposition to, the dominant one. These are **subcultures**, *cultures that exist together with a dominant culture but differ from it in some important respects.*

Etic perspective: The perspective of the outside observer.

Emic perspective: The perspective of the insider, the one belonging to the cultural group in question.

Cultural relativism: A worldview whereby the practices of a society are understood sociologically in terms of that society's norms and values, and not the norms and values of another society.

Subcultures: Cultures that exist together with a dominant culture but differ from it in some important respects.

In the Tibetan sky burial, the body is left on a mountaintop exposed to the elements. This once-common practice of "giving alms to the birds" represented belief in rebirth and the idea that the body is an unneeded empty shell. In Indonesia, mass cremations take place where bodies are placed in sarcophagi of various sizes with animal representations. In New Orleans, a casket is paraded through the street. Death and burial rituals are components of culture.

Some subcultures, including ethnic subcultures, may embrace most of the values and norms of the dominant culture while simultaneously choosing to preserve the values, rituals, and languages of their (or their parents' or grandparents') cultures of origin. Members of ethnic subcultures such as Armenian Americans and Cuban Americans may follow political events in their heritage countries or prefer their children to marry within their groups. It is comfort in the subculture rather than rejection of the dominant culture that supports the vitality of many ethnic subcultures.

In a few cases, however, ethnic and other subcultures do reject the dominant culture surrounding them. The Amish choose to elevate tradition over modernity in areas such as transportation (many still use horse-drawn buggies), occupations (they rely on simple farming), and family life (women are seen as subordinate to men), and they lead a retreatist lifestyle in which their community is intentionally separated from the dominant culture.

Sociologists sometimes also use the term *counterculture* to designate subcultural groups whose norms, values, and practices deviate from those of the dominant culture. The hippies of the 1960s, for example, are commonly cited as a counterculture to mainstream middle America, although many of those who participated in hippie culture aged into fairly conventional middle-class lives.

Even though there are exceptions, most subcultures in the United States are permeated by the dominant culture, and the influence runs both ways. What, for example, is an "all-American" meal? Your answer may be a hamburger and fries. But what about other U.S. staples, such as Chinese takeout and Mexican burritos? Mainstream culture has also absorbed the influence of the United States' multicultural heritage: Salsa music, created by Cuban and Puerto Rican American musicians in 1960s New York, is widely popular, and world music, a genre that reflects a range of influences from the African continent to Brazil, has a broad United States following. Some contemporary pop music, as performed by artists such as Lady Gaga, incorporates elements of British glam, U.S. hip-hop, and central European dance. The influence is apparent in sports as well: Soccer, now often the youth game of choice in U.S. suburbs, was popularized by players and fans from South America and Europe. Mixed martial arts, a combat sport popularized by the U.S. organization Ultimate Fighting Championship, incorporates elements of Greco-Roman wrestling, Japanese karate, Brazilian jujitsu, and Muay Thai (from Thailand).

Culture and Language

Well over a billion people on our planet speak a dialect of Chinese as their first language. English and Spanish are the first languages of another 300 million people each. More than 182 million people speak Hindi, the primary official language of India, as a first language. In contrast, the world's 3,500 least widely spoken languages share 8.25 million speakers. Aka, another language of India, has between 1,000 and 2,000 native speakers. The Mexican language of Seri has between 650 and 1,000 speakers. Euchee, a Native American language, has four fluent speakers left. According to an article in *National Geographic,* "one language dies every 14 days," and we can expect to lose about half the 7,000 languages spoken around the world by the end of the 21st century (Rymer, 2012). What is the significance of language loss for human culture?

Symbols, like the names we assign to the objects around us, are cultural representations of social realities or, as we put it in Chapter 1, representations of things that are not immediately present to our senses. They may take the form of letters or words, images, rituals, or actions. When we use language, we imbue these symbols with meaning. **Language** is *a symbolic system composed of verbal, nonverbal, and written representations that are vehicles for conveying meaning.*

Language: A symbolic system composed of verbal, nonverbal, and written representations that are vehicles for conveying meaning.

In the 1930s, Edward Sapir and Benjamin Whorf developed the *Sapir–Whorf hypothesis,* which posits that our understandings and actions emerge from language—that is, the words and concepts of our own languages structure our perceptions of the social world. Language is also closely tied to cultural objects and practices. Consider that the Aka language has more than 26 words to describe beads, a rich vocabulary suited for a culture in which beads not only are decorative objects but also convey status and facilitate market transactions. In the Seri language, to inquire where someone is from you ask, "Where is your placenta buried?" This question references a historical cultural practice of burying a newborn's afterbirth by covering it with sand, rocks, and ashes (Rymer, 2012).

As languages like Aka and Seri die out, usually replaced by dominant tongues such as Spanish, English, Chinese, Arabic, and Russian, we lose the opportunity to more fully understand the historical and contemporary human experience and the natural world (see Figure 3.4). For instance, the fact that some small languages have no words linked to specific numbers and instead use only relative designations such as *few* or *many* opens the possibility that our number system may be a product of culture rather than of innate cognition, as many believe. Or consider that the Seri culture, based in the Sonoran Desert, has names for animal species that describe behaviors that natural scientists are only beginning to document (Rymer, 2012). Language is a cultural vehicle that enables communication, illuminates

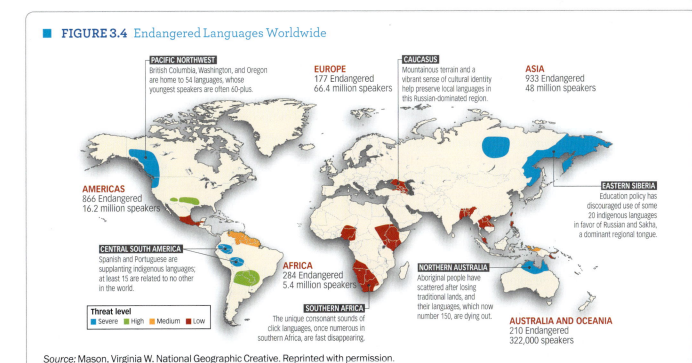

■ **FIGURE 3.4** Endangered Languages Worldwide

PACIFIC NORTHWEST
British Columbia, Washington, and Oregon are home to 54 languages, whose youngest speakers are often 60-plus.

EUROPE
177 Endangered
66.4 million speakers

CAUCASUS
Mountainous terrain and a vibrant sense of cultural identity help preserve local languages in this Russian-dominated region.

ASIA
933 Endangered
48 million speakers

AMERICAS
866 Endangered
16.2 million speakers

EASTERN SIBERIA
Education policy has discouraged use of some 20 indigenous languages in favor of Russian and Sakha, a dominant regional tongue.

CENTRAL SOUTH AMERICA
Spanish and Portuguese are supplanting indigenous languages; at least 15 are related to no other in the world.

AFRICA
284 Endangered
5.4 million speakers

NORTHERN AUSTRALIA
Aboriginal people have scattered after losing traditional lands, and their languages, which now number 150, are dying out.

Threat level
■ Severe ■ High ■ Medium ■ Low

SOUTHERN AFRICA
The unique consonant sounds of click languages, once numerous in southern Africa, are fast disappearing.

AUSTRALIA AND OCEANIA
210 Endangered
322,000 speakers

Source: Mason, Virginia W. National Geographic Creative. Reprinted with permission.

beliefs and practices, roots a community in its environment, and contributes to the cultural richness of our world. Each language lost represents the erasure of cultural history, knowledge, and human diversity (Living Tongues Institute for Endangered Languages, n.d.).

Language and Social Integration

Conflict theorists focus on disintegrative forces in society, while functionalists study integrative forces. Where social conflict theorists see culture as serving the interests of the elite, functionalists argue that shared values and norms maintain social bonds both between individuals and between people and society (Parsons & Smelser, 1956). By serving as a vehicle for the dissemination of these values and norms, culture functions to keep society stable and harmonious and gives people a sense of belonging in a complex, even alienating, social world (Smelser, 1962). To illustrate, consider the issue of language use in the United States.

In part as a response to the increased use of Spanish and other languages spoken by members of the nation's large immigrant population, an English-only movement has arisen that supports the passage of legislation to make English the only official language of the United States and its government. Proponents argue that they want to "restore the great American melting pot," although the movement has roots in the early 20th century, when President Theodore Roosevelt wrote,

> We have room for but one language in this country, and that is the English language, for we intend to see that the crucible turns our people out as Americans . . . and not as dwellers in a polyglot boarding house.

Like today, Roosevelt's era was characterized by high rates of immigration to the United States.

How would a functionalist analyze the English-only movement? He or she might highlight language as a vehicle of social integration and a form of social glue. Indeed, the English-only movement focuses on the function of language as an integrative mechanism. For example, the organization ProEnglish states on its website (http://www.proenglish.org), "We work through the courts and in the court of public opinion to defend English's historic role as America's common, unifying language, and to persuade lawmakers to adopt English as the official language at all levels of government." From this perspective, the use of different primary languages in a single country is dysfunctional to the extent that it undermines the common socialization that comes from a shared language and culture.

A substantial proportion of U.S. residents support legislation making English the official language: A 2014 Huffington Post/YouGov survey found that 70% of respondents agreed with this position (Swanson, 2014). A year later, in 2015, some members of Congress introduced a bill that would have declared English as the official language and would have required that all new citizens show English proficiency. While that bill did not pass, 31 states have adopted English as the official language (Govtrack, 2016).

At the same time, most homes and residents are already active users of English, even if one fifth also use another home language. Interestingly, a 2013 Gallup poll found that about half of respondents agreed that it is "essential" (20%) or "important" (50%) for Americans to learn a second language, although only about a third are conversant in a second language (Jones, 2013).

Many people embrace cultural diversity and emphasize the value of **multiculturalism**, *a commitment to respecting cultural differences rather than trying to submerge them into a larger, dominant culture.* Multiculturalism recognizes that the country is as likely to be enriched by its differences as it is to be divided by them. In a globalizing world, knowledge of other cultures and proficiency in languages other than English is important. In fact, a functionalist might also regard the U.S. Census data cited above as indicative of *both* the common language that proponents of official English see as crucial to national unity and the cultural diversity that enriches the country and allows it to incorporate a variety of languages in its national and global political, cultural, and economic dealings—which is also positively functional for the country (Figure 3.5).

Culture and Mass Media

From a sociological perspective, we are all *cultured* because we all participate in and identify with a culture or cultures. In one conventional use of the term, however, some classes of people are considered *more cultured* than others. We refer to people who attend the symphony, are knowledgeable about classic literature and fine wines, and possess a set of distinctive manners as cultured, and we often assume a value judgment in believing that being cultured is better than being uncultured.

We commonly distinguish between high culture and popular culture. **High culture** consists of *music, theater, literature, and other cultural products that are held in particularly high esteem in society.* It can also encompass a particular body of literature or a set of distinctive tastes. High culture is usually associated with the wealthier, more-educated classes in society, but this association can shift over time. William Shakespeare's plays were popular with the English masses

---

Multiculturalism: A commitment to respecting cultural differences rather than trying to submerge them into a larger, dominant culture.

High culture: Music, theater, literature, and other cultural products that are held in particularly high esteem in society.

■ FIGURE 3.5 Percentage of U.S. Population Speaking a Language Other Than English at Home, 2010*

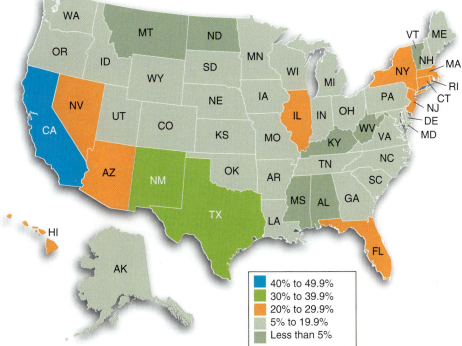

Legend:
- 40% to 49.9%
- 30% to 39.9%
- 20% to 29.9%
- 5% to 19.9%
- Less than 5%

Source: U.S. Census Bureau. (2010). "Population 5 Years and Older Who Spoke a Language Other Than English at Home by Hispanic Origin and Race: 2009." *American Community Survey Briefs.*

Most recent data available.

when they were staged in open public theaters during his lifetime. Lobster was a meal of the poor in colonial America. This suggests that high culture's association with educated and upper income elites may be more a function of accessibility—the prohibitive cost of theater tickets and lobster meat today, for instance—than with "good taste" as such.

Popular culture encompasses *the entertainment, culinary, and athletic tastes shared by the masses.* It is more accessible than high culture because it is widely available and less costly to consume. Popular culture can include music that gets broad airplay on the radio, television shows and characters that draw masses of viewers (for example, *The Walking Dead, Stranger Things, The Crown,* and *Homeland*), blockbuster films and series (such as the *Black Panther, Star Wars,* or *Wonder Woman*), Oprah's Book Club, and spectator sports (such as professional wrestling and baseball). Because it is an object of mass consumption, popular culture plays a key role in shaping values, attitudes, and consumption in society. It is an optimal topic of sociological study because,

as we noted in our opening story, it not only *shapes* but also *is shaped by* society.

Mass media is *media of public communication intended to reach and influence a mass audience.* The mass media constitutes a vehicle that brings us culture, in particular—although certainly not exclusively—popular culture. Although mass media permeates our lives today, its rise is more recent than we may realize. Theorist Jürgen Habermas (1962/1989) points out that the *public sphere* as a fundamental part of social life emerged only with the rise of industrial society; that is, prior to the development of printing presses and the spread of literacy, most communication was oral and local. The appearance of mass-circulation newspapers in the 1700s and the growth of literate populations spurred the growth of a public sphere in which information could be widely circulated and, as Habermas points out, public attitudes shaped. In the 20th century, mass media gained influence through the adoption of electronic means of communication ranging from the radio to television to the Internet.

Popular culture: The entertainment, culinary, and athletic tastes shared by the masses.

Mass media: Media of public communication intended to reach and influence a mass audience.

Global Issues

LANGUAGE, RESISTANCE, AND POWER IN NORTHERN IRELAND

This chapter raises the problem of language loss—that is, the persistent and expanding extinction of small languages across our planet. In a few places, however, little-used languages are being revived for reasons that range from cultural to economic to political. In some instances, as in the case of Northern Ireland, language revival fits into all three categories.

©Paul White/Alamy Stock Photo

The dominant language in the country of Northern Ireland has long been English, but there is a growing campaign to revive the Irish language, a tongue with little in common with English (consider the Irish word for independence: *neamhspleáchas*). The Irish language (also known as Irish Gaelic or *Gaeilge*) is a minority language in Northern Ireland. As of the country's 2001 census, 167,487 people (10.4% of the population) had "some knowledge of Irish" (Zenker, 2010). The use of Irish in Northern Ireland had nearly died out by the middle of the 20th century, but today, efforts are under way to bring the language back to education, commerce, and political life ("In the Trenches," 2013).

Northern Ireland has a history of violent conflict with its British neighbor. Early in the 20th century, Ireland was shaken by conflict between the Irish Catholic majority and the Protestant minority, who supported British rule and feared the rule of the Catholic majority. In 1920, the British Parliament passed the Government of Ireland Act, which sought to pacify the parties with the separation of Ireland into a free state of southern counties. In 1922, the larger part of Ireland seceded from the United Kingdom to become the independent Irish Free State (after 1937, this became the current state of Ireland). The six northeastern counties, together known as Northern Ireland, remained within the United Kingdom. Northern Ireland has since been the site of sporadic conflict between (mainly Catholic) nationalists and (mainly Protestant) unionists (Kennedy-Pipe, 1997).

The area remained largely peaceful until the late 1960s, when violence broke out in Londonderry and Belfast, foreshadowing three decades of armed conflict between British troops stationed in Northern Ireland and the rebellious Irish Republican Army (IRA), which represented primarily the interests of the Irish Catholic population. The violent conflicts over home versus British rule, which included terrorism committed by the IRA against British interests and populations, resulted in more than 3,000 deaths in this period (BBC, 2014b). A U.S.-brokered agreement helped to quell the violence in 1998, though sporadic problems remained. Nearly a decade later, in 2007, key parties to the conflict, including leaders of the Catholic and Protestant factions, took the reins of the country in a power-sharing agreement.

The interest in revival of the language dates back to the period of conflict, known locally as "the Troubles." In the 1960s, a small number of language enthusiasts set up a tiny Irish-speaking community in a Belfast neighborhood. By the 1970s, with the conflict in progress, Irish nationalist prisoners being held by the British in Maze Prison also began learning Irish, calling out words between cells and scrawling their words on the prison walls (Feldman, 1991). The effort spread to neighborhoods where families of the prisoners resided and, according to author Feargal Mac Ionnrachtaigh (2013), it became part of an "anti-colonial struggle."

Today, Irish nationalists, some of them veterans of the war against British rule, have taken up the mantle of Irish language revival, and the language is now the medium of instruction for about 5,000 schoolchildren in the country. Although this is only a tiny fraction of the total school population, supporters of language revival occupy some key governmental positions in Northern Ireland, and there has been an effort to enact the Irish Language Act, which would establish new rights to the use of the language in official business, thus creating new job opportunities for fluent speakers ("In the Trenches," 2013).

Today, Northern Ireland is peaceful. The Irish language, a part of the local heritage, is being revived. It remains to be seen, however, whether this will serve to draw together two communities with a long history of conflict (the country is

about evenly split between the Catholic and Protestant communities) or will deepen the divide as the nationalist Catholic population embraces Irish while the pro-British Protestants resist.

Think It Through

- Why does language matter to communities large and small? What does the Irish language revival movement share with movements such as the official English movement in the United States, which supports a powerful and widespread language? How is it different?

Marshall McLuhan (1964) sought to understand the influence of mass media on society, suggesting that "the medium is the message"— the medium itself has an influence on how the message is received and perceived. Television, for instance, is fundamentally different from print in how it communicates information. In other words, in looking at only a particular message, we may miss the power of the messenger itself and how that transforms social life. McLuhan also asserted that electronic media such as television constructed a *global village* in which people around the world, who did not and never would know one another, could be engaged with the same news event. For example, it was reported by FIFA, the world's governing body of soccer, that in the summer of 2014, more than a billion people (about a seventh of the world's population) tuned in for the final game between Germany and Argentina (Associated Press, 2015).

From a sociological perspective, the function of the mass media can be paradoxical. On the one hand, mass media is a powerful and effective means for conveying information and contributing to the development of an informed citizenry: Mass-circulation newspapers, television networks such as CNN and BBC, and radio news programs inform us about and help us understand important issues. On the other hand, some sociologists argue that mass media promotes not active engagement in society but rather disengagement and distraction. Habermas (1962/1989), for instance, writes of the salons and coffeehouses of major European cities, where the exchange of informed opinions formed a foundation for later public political debates. He suggests, however, that the potential for the development of an active public sphere has been largely quashed by the rise of media that have substituted mass entertainment for meaningful debate, elevating sound bites over sound arguments.

Douglas Kellner (1990) has written that modern technology and media—and television in particular—constitute a threat to human freedom of thought and action in the realm of social change. Kellner suggests that the television

industry "has the crucial ideological functions of legitimating the capitalist mode of production and delegitimating its opponents" (p. 9). That is, mainstream television appears to offer a broad spectrum of opinions, but in fact, it systematically excludes opinions that seem to question the fundamental values of capitalism (for example, the right to accumulate unlimited wealth and power) or to critique not individual politicians, parties, and policies but the system within which they operate. Because television is such a pervasive force in our lives, the boundaries it draws around debates on capitalism, social change, and genuine democracy are significant.

Karl Marx wrote that the ruling ideas of any society are those of the ruling class. Arguably, many of those ideas are conveyed through television. Does television, which delivers images and messages to our homes as we watch for an average of seven hours a day, foster passivity and make us vulnerable to manipulation? What about the Internet? How does it expand human creativity, freedom, and action? How does it limit them?

The mass media brings us the key forms of modern entertainment that constitute popular culture. Although some researchers theorize the effects of mass media on the public sphere, others look at how these media shape attitudes and practices—sometimes in negative ways. In the section that follows, we turn our attention to another dimension of culture: the controversial relationship between culture, mass media, and the negative but pervasive phenomenon of sexual violence against women.

Culture, Media, and Violence

Statistics suggest that rape and sexual assault devastate the lives of thousands of U.S. women every year. According to the National Crime Victimization Survey, in 2016, there were 323,450 rapes, attempted rapes, or sexual assaults in the United States (Morgan & Kena, 2017). Men and boys also fall prey to these crimes, though in smaller numbers.

Social Life, Social Media

MUSIC, MONEY, AND MARKETING

©Kevin Winter/Getty Images for iHeartMedia

William Shakespeare famously wrote that "if music be the food of love, play on." Bono, the lead singer of the globally recognized pop group U2, has said that "music can change the world because it can change people," a sentiment echoed by renowned guitarist Jimi Hendrix, who asserted that "music doesn't lie. If there is something to be changed in this world, then it can only happen through music." Indeed, music is widely seen as a salve for emotional wounds (Michael Jackson called it "a mantra that soothes the soul"), a soundtrack for real-life romance and heartbreak, a vehicle of release from stress, and a carrier of powerful messages of societal transformation.

But music today is also a significant marketing tool. A report in *The Atlantic Monthly* points out that more brands are paying for product placement in pop songs. The article quotes Adam Kluger, chief executive officer (CEO) of the Kluger Agency, which specializes in "lyrical product placements," as saying that a brand placement in a hit single "can easily offset the entire production and marketing budget" for the song (Brennan, 2015, p. 40). Brand references in music are growing. According to William Brennan's calculation, these references appeared 109 times in the top 30 *Billboard* songs in 2012 compared with 47 times in 2002—and zero times in 1962. The popular song "I Am the One" by DJ Khalid featuring Justin Bieber, Chance the Rapper, Lil Wayne, and Quavo references two fashion brands (Chanel and Gucci). The song also talks about Netflix. Similarly, in "Closer," the Chainsmokers (a DJ duo) sing to their love interest, asking her to meet "in the backseat of (her) Rover." Product placement is also present in music videos. For example, Ariana Grande's 2016 "Focus on Me" video features the young singer with her Samsung Galaxy Note phone dancing in a galaxy-themed background.

The appearance of brand name goods and companies in popular music, whether purchased by an advertiser or not, is common. A National Public Radio report noted that an examination of the top 20 songs of the three years up to 2017 determined that about 212 different brands had been mentioned in songs. The recent rap song, "Bad and Boujee," by Migos and Lil Uzi Vert features 19 brand names (Lonsdorf, 2017).

The melding of advertising and culture is a topic in which sociologists have taken an interest. Critical theorists Theodor Adorno and Max Horkheimer (Horkheimer, 1947; Horkheimer & Adorno, 1944/2007) write of the "culture industry." They distinguish between *culture*, which, they suggest, retains the potential to be a vehicle for creativity, critique, and social change, and the *culture industry*. By contrast to culture, the culture industry engages in a mass deception by manufacturing homogenized, predictable, and banal cultural products that function to pacify and sell rather than inform and provoke. Indeed, the two theorists judge the culture industry to be one that promises an "escape from reality but it really offers an escape from the last thought of resisting that reality" (Horkheimer & Adorno, 1944/2007, p. 116). The road to happiness, as told by the culture industry, is through consumption and conformity. The magic (or deception) of the culture industry is rendered all the more powerful for the fact that its coercion and "unfreedom" are pleasant to the masses (Marcuse, 1964).

From the perspective of the critical theorists, the marriage of music and marketing is predictable, the outcome of a process of consumerization of culture that characterizes modern capitalism. Can music be independent of the market? Should it strive to be? What do you think?

Think It Through

- Can popular music play a role as both a progressive force and a marketing tool? Can you think of examples of artists or songs that occupy one or both roles?

Follow us on Twitter to keep up with current sociological stories and research! We're at **@DiscoverSoc1**.

Share your own ideas at **#DiscoverSociology**.

One explanation for this number might be that these sexual assaults are perpetrated by thousands of deviant individuals and are the outcomes of particular and individual circumstances. Applying the sociological imagination, however, means recognizing the magnitude of the problem and considering the idea that examination of individual cases alone, while important, is inadequate for fully understanding the phenomenon of rape and sexual assault in the United States. To paraphrase C. Wright Mills, it is a personal trouble *and* a public issue.

Some researchers have posited the existence of a **rape culture**, *a social culture that provides an environment conducive to rape* (Boswell & Spade, 1996; Buchwald, Fletcher, & Roth, 2005; Sanday, 1990). According to some scholars, rape culture has been pervasive in the U.S. legal system. Feminist theorist and legal scholar Catharine MacKinnon (1989) argues that legislative and judicial processes regarding rape utilize a male viewpoint. Consider, for instance, that until the late 1970s, most states did not treat spousal rape as a crime. This conclusion was based, at least in part, on the notion that a woman could not be raped by her husband because sexual consent was taken as implied in the marital contract.

Some researchers argue that the legal culture takes rape less seriously than other crimes of violence (Taslitz, 1999). Legal scholar Stephen J. Schulhofer (2000) has written that the law

> punishes takings by force (robbery), by coercive threats (extortion), by stealth (larceny), by breach of trust (embezzlement), and by deception (fraud and false pretenses). . . . Yet sexual autonomy, almost alone among our important personal rights, is not fully protected. The law of rape, as if it were only a law against the "robbery" of sex, remains focused almost exclusively on preventing interference by force. (pp. 100–101)

Schulhofer notes that this problem is linked to a culture that treats male sexual aggression as natural. Taslitz (1999) asserts that the cultural stories brought into courtrooms render proceedings around rape problematic by situating them in myths, such as the idea that a female victim was "asking for it."

Some research in the fields of sociology and communications suggests that popular culture promotes rape culture by normalizing violence. This is not to argue that culture is a direct cause of sexual violence (or other kinds of violence) but rather to suggest that popular culture renders violence part of the social scenery by making its appearance so common in films, video games, and music videos that it evolves from being shocking to being utterly ordinary (Katz & Jhally, 2000a, 2000b). How does this process occur?

Some scholars argue that popular media embraces *violent masculinity,* a form of masculinity that associates *being a man* with being aggressive and merciless. Popular action films often highlight violent male protagonists, as in *X-Men: Apocalypse* (2016), *Logan* (2017), and *Deadpool 2* (2018). Outside of the realm of fiction, dominant male sports such as football and hockey elevate physical violence as entertainment and venerate the toughest players on the field or the ice.

While popular culture features many images of male violence against other men, violent images may also normalize violence against women. Hip-hop has long been associated with misogynistic lyrics and videos, although it is hardly alone in its objectification of women (Morgan, 1999; Pough, 2004; Weitzer & Kubrin, 2009). Many commercial films also feature rough—even violent—treatment of women, offered as entertainment. The most gratuitous violence in films such as *Hush* (2016), *The Cutting Room* (2015), *The Girl with the Dragon Tattoo* (2011), and *The Killer Inside Me* (2010) is reserved for female victims. Popular culture's most predictable normalization of violence against women occurs in pornography, a multibillion-dollar-a-year industry in the United States. Fictionalized portrayals of sexual activity range from coercion of a compliant and always-willing female to violent rape simulations in which consent is clearly refused.

Although researchers do not propose that lyrics or images disseminated by mass media cause sexual violence *directly,* some suggest that popular culture's persistent use of sex-starved, compliant, and easily victimized female characters sends messages that forced sex is no big deal, that women really want to be raped, and that some invite rape by their appearance. In a study of 400 male and female high school students, Cassidy and Hurrell (1995, cited in Workman & Freeburg, 1999) determined that respondents who heard a vignette about a rape scenario and then viewed a picture of the victim (in reality, a model for the research) dressed in provocative clothing were more likely than those who saw her dressed in conservative clothing, or who saw no picture at all, to judge her responsible for her assailant's behavior and to say his behavior was justified and not really rape. More recent studies have reproduced findings that rape myths are widely used to explain and even justify sexual violence (Hammond, Berry, & Rodriguez, 2011).

A 2003 study found that victims' attire is not a significant factor in sexual assault. Instead, rapists look for signs of passivity and submissiveness (Beiner, 2007). Why, with evidence to the contrary, do such rape myths (common but rarely true beliefs about rapists and rape victims) exist? Studies link regular exposure to popular print, television, film, and Internet media with acceptance of rape myths among college-age men and women (Kahlor & Morrison, 2007; Katz, 2006, cited in Lonsway et al., 2009; Reinders, 2006), although female undergraduates in a comparative study were less likely to believe rape myths and more likely to believe victims than their male peers (Stephens et al., 2016).

Rape culture: A social culture that provides an environment conducive to rape.

Many popular sports, including hockey, football, and boxing, feature violence as a key component of the entertainment. What makes the physical violence of these sports enthralling for audiences?

Is culture, particularly culture that includes music and movies that normalize violence, a sociological antecedent of real violence? How does this affect men? How does it affect women?

Culture, Class, and Inequality

In their studies of culture and class, sociologists consider whether the musical and artistic tastes of different socioeconomic classes vary and, if so, why. Although the answer may be interesting in itself, researchers are also likely to go a step farther and examine the links among culture, power, and class inequality. Particularly when using a social conflict lens, sociologists have long sought to show how elites use culture to gain or maintain power over other groups.

Sociologist Pierre Bourdieu has used culture to help explain the phenomenon of **social class reproduction**, *the way in which class status is reproduced from generation to generation.* Bourdieu (1984) discusses the concept of **cultural capital**, *wealth in the form of knowledge, ideas, verbal skills, and ways of thinking and behaving.* Karl Marx argued that the key to power in a capitalist system is economic capital, particularly possession of the means of production. Bourdieu extends this idea by suggesting that cultural capital can also be a source of power. Children from privileged backgrounds have access to markedly different stores of cultural capital than do children from working-class backgrounds.

Children of the upper and middle classes come into the education system—the key path to success in modern industrial societies—with a set of language and academic skills, beliefs, and models of success and failure that fit into and are validated by mainstream schools. Children from less-privileged backgrounds enter with a smaller amount of validated cultural capital; their skills, knowledge base, and styles of speaking are not those that schools conventionally recognize and reward. For example, while a child from a working-class immigrant family may know how to care for her younger siblings, prepare a good meal, and translate for non–English-fluent parents, her parents (similar to many first-generation immigrants) may have worked multiple jobs and may not have had the skills to read to her or the time or money to expose her to enriching activities. By contrast, her middle-class peers are more likely to have grown up with parents who regularly read to them, took them to shows and museums, and quizzed them on multiplication problems. Although both children come to school with knowledge and skills, the cultural capital of the middle-class child can be more readily "traded" for academic success—and eventual economic gains.

In short, schools serve as locations where the cultural capital of the better-off classes is exchanged for educational success and credentials. This difference in scholastic achievement then translates into economic capital as high achievers assume prestigious, well-paid positions in the workplace. Those who do not have the cultural capital to trade for academic success are often tracked into jobs in society's lower tiers. Class is reproduced as cultural capital begets academic achievement, which begets economic capital, which again begets cultural capital for the next generation.

Clearly, however, the structure of institutional opportunities, while unequal, cannot alone account for broad reproduction of social class across generations. Individuals, after all, make choices about education, occupations, and the like. They have free will—or, as sociologists put it, *agency,* which is understood as the capacity of individuals to make choices and to act independently. Bourdieu (1977) argues that agency must be understood in the context of structure. To this end, he introduces the concept of **habitus**, *the internalization of objective probabilities and the subsequent expression of those probabilities as choice.* Put another way, people come to want that which their own experiences and those of the people who surround them suggest they can realistically have—and they act accordingly.

Consider the following hypothetical example of habitus in practice. In a poor rural community where few people go to college, fewer can afford it, and the payoff of higher education is not obvious because there are few immediate role models with such experience, Bourdieu would argue that an individual's choice not to prioritize getting into college reflects

---

Social class reproduction: The way in which class status is reproduced from generation to generation, with parents passing on a class position to their offspring.

Cultural capital: Wealth in the form of knowledge, ideas, verbal skills, and ways of thinking and behaving.

Habitus: The internalization of objective probabilities and subsequent expression of those probabilities as choice.

DISCOVER INTERSECTIONS
Habitus and the Social Reproduction of Inequalities

In the section above, you learned about the concept of *habitus*, which is sometimes characterized as the process of people coming to want what they can (structurally) have. As you read about, for example, roots of the gender wage gap in Chapter 10, or differences in educational attainment by race or ethnicity or family income in Chapter 12, consider whether—or how—habitus may play a role in helping us to understand the existence and persistence of inequalities.

Many U.S. films earn more money abroad than they do in the United States. Action films such as *Avengers: Infinity War* are particularly popular with moviegoers around the globe. What makes these films appealing to a global audience?

both agency *and* structure. That is, she makes the choice not to prepare herself for college or to apply to college, but going to college would likely not have been possible for her anyway as a result of her economic circumstances and perhaps as a result of an inadequate education in an underfunded school. By contrast, the habitus of a young upper-middle-class person makes the choice of going to college almost unquestionable. Nearly everyone around her has gone or is going to college, the benefits of a college education are broadly discussed, and she is socialized from her early years to understand that college will follow high school—alternatives are rarely considered. Furthermore, a college education is accessible—she is prepared for college work in a well-funded public school or a private school, and family income, loans, or scholarships will contribute to making higher education a reality. Bourdieu thus suggests that social class reproduction appears on its face to be grounded in individual choices and merit, but fundamental structural inequalities that underlie class reproduction often go unrecognized (or, as Bourdieu puts it, "misrecognized"), a fact that benefits the well-off.

Culture and Globalization

There is a pervasive sense around the world that globalization is creating a homogenized culture—a landscape dotted in every corner of the globe with the Golden Arches and the face of Colonel Sanders beckoning the masses to consume hamburgers and fried chicken. The familiar songs of Beyoncé, Ed Sheeran, and Drake are broadcast on radio stations from Bangladesh to Bulgaria to Belize, while rebroadcasts of such popular U.S. soap operas as *The Bold and the Beautiful* provide a picture of ostensibly "average" U.S. lives on the world's television screens. In fact, about 70% of studio revenue in Hollywood is generated in overseas markets; that is, many films make far more money abroad than in the United States. Action-oriented films in particular garner large audiences in markets such as China and Russia (Brook, 2014): For example, within weeks of its release, *The Fate of the Furious* (2017),

had earned $1 billion, with over 80% of that earned overseas. More recently, *Wonder Woman* took in about $411 million in the United States and another $819 million worldwide (Mendelson, 2017).

We see the effects of globalization—and of Americanization in particular—in cultural representations such as McDonald's restaurants, U.S. pop music and videos, and bottles of Coca-Cola spreading around the world. According to press reports, even in the Taliban era in Afghanistan, a time when a deeply conservative Islamist ideology was enforced throughout society, the culture of global Hollywood seeped in through the cracks of fundamentalism's wall. In January of 2001, the Taliban rounded up dozens of barbers in the capital city of Kabul because they had been cutting men's hair in a style known locally as the "Titanic":

> At the time, Kabul's cooler young men wanted that Leonardo DiCaprio look, the one he sported in the movie. It was an interesting moment because under the Taliban's moral regime, movies were illegal. . . . Yet thanks to enterprising video smugglers who dragged cassettes over mountain trails by mule, urban Afghans knew perfectly well who DiCaprio was and what he looked like. (Freund, 2002, p. 24)

How should a sociologist evaluate the spread of a globalized culture? Is globalization, on balance, positive or negative for countries, communities, and corporate entities? Is it only about business, or does it also have political implications? The conflict and functionalist perspectives offer us different ways of seeing contemporary **global culture**, *a type of culture—some would say U.S. culture—that has spread across*

Global culture: A type of culture—some would say U.S. culture—that has spread across the world in the form of Hollywood films, fast-food restaurants, and popular music heard in virtually every country

the world in the form of Hollywood films, fast-food restaurants, and popular music heard in virtually every country. This is a culture that draws heavily, though by no means exclusively, on U.S. trends and tastes.

A functionalist examining the development and spread of a broad global culture might begin by asking, "What is its function?" He or she could deduce that globalization spreads not only material culture in the form of food and music but also nonmaterial culture in the form of values and norms. Globalized norms and values can strengthen social solidarity and consequently serve to reduce conflict between states and societies. Therefore, globalization serves the integrative function of creating some semblance of a common culture that can foster mutual understanding and a foundation for dialogue.

Recall from Chapter 1 that functionalism assumes that the social world's many parts are interdependent. Indeed, globalization highlights both the cultural and the economic interdependence of countries and communities. The book *Global Hollywood* (Miller, Govil, McMurria, & Maxwell, 2002) describes what its authors call a *new international division of cultural labor,* a system of cultural production that crosses the globe, making the creation of culture an international rather than a national phenomenon (though profits still flow primarily into the core of the filmmaking industry in Hollywood).

The blockbuster film *Slumdog Millionaire* (2008) offers an example of the international division of cultural labor. The film, about a poor 18-year-old orphan who finds himself on the cusp of winning India's "Who Wants to Be A Millionaire?" quiz show, was directed by Englishman Danny Boyle and codirected by New Delhi native Loveleen Tandan from a screenplay by Boyle's countryman Simon Beaufoy that was based on the 2005 novel *Q & A* by Indian writer Vikas Swarup. In 2009, the film, distributed in the United States by Warner Independent Pictures but shown internationally, received nine Academy Awards, including Best Picture. The Indian cast of *Slumdog Millionaire* includes both established local actors and young Mumbai slum dwellers, some of whom were later found to have earned very little from their efforts. Boyle has argued, however, that the filmmakers worked to ensure future educational opportunities and shelter for the young actors. The film's global appeal was huge, and it generated almost $378 million in box office returns, leading the *Wall Street Journal* to label it "the film world's first globalized masterpiece" (Morgenstern, 2008).

From the social conflict perspective, we can view the globalization of culture as a force with the potential to perpetuate economic inequality—particularly because globalization is a product of the developed world. Although a

Not all of the actors who were part of *Slumdog Millionaire*, a blockbuster film, benefited from its success. The local extras—as well as some of the central characters—took away little financial gain from the film.

©SAJAD HUSSAIN/AFP/Getty Images

In its more than half-century of operation, McDonald's has become one of the most recognized icons of U.S. life and culture; Ronald McDonald is said to be the most recognized figure in the world after Santa Claus. McDonald's serves 68 million customers every day in over 36,000 restaurants in 120 countries around the globe.

©iStockphoto.com/paulprescott72

functionalist would highlight the creative global collaboration and productive interdependence of a film such as *Slumdog Millionaire,* a conflict theorist would ask, "Who benefits from such a production?" Although Western film companies, producers, and directors walk away with huge profits, the slum dwellers used as actors or extras garner far less sustained global interest or financial gain.

A conflict theorist might also describe how the globalization of cheap fast food can cripple small independent eateries that serve indigenous (and arguably healthier) cuisine. An influx of global corporations inhibits some local people from owning their own means of production and providing employment to others. The demise of local restaurants, cafés, and food stalls represents a loss of the cuisines and thus the unique cultures of indigenous peoples. It also forces working people to depend on large corporations for their livelihoods, depriving them of economic independence.

Discover & Debate

VIOLENCE IN MEDIA

Motion: Exposure to violence in films, television programs, music, and video games is harmful to children. It has negative individual and societal effects.

Background: Media is an important part of everyone's life, particularly in the age of smartphones and other technologies that bring us near-constant access to news, entertainment, and social interaction. Violent content is common in the media to which we are exposed: According to one study, about 90% of movies, 68% of video games, and 60% of TV shows include some depictions of violence (Wilson, 2008). The rate of gun violence in PG-13 rated films, especially comic book inspired, exceeds that of R-rated films and has done so since 2012 (Romer, Jamieson, & Jamieson, 2017). Research also shows that young people age 8 to 12 spend, on average, six hours per day engaged with media, while teenagers age 13 to 18 spend about nine hours per day (Common Sense Media, 2015). More than 20 hours per week are spent playing video games, and some males are exposed to video games for 40 hours or more per week (Bailey, West, & Anderson, 2011). Popular examples of violence in media include movies such as the *Avengers* and *X Men* series; television programs such as *Game of Thrones*, *The Walking Dead*, and *Power Rangers*; and video games such as *Call of Duty* and *Grand Theft Auto*. The question of whether children's exposure to violence is causally related to increased aggressive behavior, desensitization to violence, and fear of being harmed is one that evokes significant debate.

Questions for Consideration

- If research shows a relationship between exposure to violence in media and real-life consequences such as aggression and desensitization to violence, whose responsibility is it to respond? How should the government, parents, and the producers of cultural products respond?

- Is the inclusion of violence in films, television, and other media an issue of free speech? Can it be legally controlled? Should it be legally controlled?

- Should adult exposure to violent media be a concern for society?

Debate Tip

- It is important to have strong opening and concluding statements. Direct quotations, facts and figures, and thought-provoking questions help in making a strong opening for a debate. Finish with a statement that wraps up your argument and guides your audience to a conclusion.

AFFIRMATIVE ARGUMENTS	OPPOSITION ARGUMENTS
Media is an important agent of socialization, so we would expect exposure to violence in media to affect children and young people. Exposure to violence in films, television programs, and videos is associated in numerous research studies with greater propensity for aggressive behavior in children and adolescents.	Correlation is not causation: A correlation between the presence of violence in media and violence in real life does not establish a direct causal relationship between the two.
Violence in media rarely depicts consequences. Especially in video games and action films, harming or killing someone is often an action that is rewarded. This sends confusing messages to children.	Violent crime rates in the United States have declined in recent years. The experience of some other countries also challenges this argument. For example, Japan has high levels of media violence in popular films and video games, but the incidence of serious crimes committed by young people is falling.
Research shows that children, particularly very young children, cannot distinguish reality from fiction.	It is challenging to isolate triggers for real-life violence: In addition to media, violent behavior may be linked to mental health issues, exposure to interpersonal threats or violence, economic deprivation, and access to weapons, among others.

Although functionalism and conflict theory offer different interpretations of globalization, both offer valuable insights. Globalization may bring people together through common entertainment, eating experiences, and communication technologies, and, at the same time, it may represent a threat—real or perceived—to local cultures and economies as indigenous producers are marginalized and the sounds and styles of different cultures are replaced by a single mold set by Western entertainment marketers.

Journalist Thomas Friedman has suggested that although most countries cannot resist the forces of globalization, it is not inevitably homogenizing. In *The Lexus and the Olive Tree: Understanding Globalization*, Friedman (2000) writes that

> the most important filter is the ability to "glocalize." I define healthy glocalization as the ability of a culture, when it encounters other strong cultures, to absorb influences that naturally fit into and can enrich that culture, to resist those things that are truly alien and to compartmentalize those things that, while different, can nevertheless be enjoyed and celebrated as different. (p. 295)

The concept of *glocalization* highlights the idea of cultural hybrids born of a pastiche of both local and global influences.

In *The Globalization of Nothing*, sociologist George Ritzer (2007) proposes a view of globalization that integrates what he calls *grobalization*, the product of "the imperialistic ambitions of nations, corporations, organizations, and the like and their desire . . . to impose themselves on various geographic areas" (p. 15). Ritzer adds that the "main interest of the entities involved in grobalization is in seeing their power, influence, and in many cases, profits grow (hence the term *grobalization*) throughout the world" (p. 16). The concept of *grobalization* draws from classical sociological theorists such as Karl Marx and Max Weber. For instance, where Marx theorized capitalism's imperative of economic imperialism, Ritzer offers contemporary examples of grobalization's economic and cultural imperialism, exporting not only brand-name products but also the values of consumerism and the practical vehicles of mass consumption, such as credit cards.

How will the world's cultures shift in the decades to come? Will they globalize or remain localized? Will they glocalize or grobalize? Clearly, the material culture of the West, particularly of the United States, is powerful: It is pushed into other parts of the world by markets and merchants, but it is also pulled in by people eager to hitch their stars to the modern Western world. Local identities and cultures continue to shape people's views and actions, but there is little reason to believe that McDonald's, KFC, and Coca-Cola will drop out of the global marketplace. The dominance of U.S. films, music, and other cultural products is also likely to remain a feature of the world cultural stage.

Why Study Culture and Media through a Sociological Lens?

Culture is a vital component of a community's identity—through language, objects, and practices, culture embodies a community and its environment. Culture is powerful and complex. As we have seen in this chapter, cultural products, including those disseminated by the mass media, both reflect and shape our societal hopes and fears, norms and beliefs, and rituals and practices. From flesh-eating zombies and classical music to folk dances and folkways, culture is

 What Can I Do with a Sociology Degree?

CRITICAL THINKING

Critical thinking entails the evaluation of claims about society, politics, the economy, culture, the environment, or any other area of knowledge with the application of reason and evidence. *Critical thinking skills* are very broad, but they have several key elements, including the ability to rigorously evaluate data, carefully and systematically analyze a problem or situation, and draw conclusions that recognize strengths and weaknesses of an argument or position. They also include the inclination and knowledge needed to be a critical consumer of information, thoughtfully questioning rather than simply accepting arguments or solutions at face value.

Critical thinking in sociology is not about *criticizing* but about developing a nuanced understanding of phenomena, institutions, and practices. Every chapter in this book seeks to help you sharpen your critical thinking by enabling you to see more deeply into the social processes and structures that affect our lives and society and to raise questions about social phenomena we may take for granted. As a sociologist in training, you will develop a more comprehensive understanding of your social world and will learn to ask critical questions about why things are as they are and to seek out and find evidence-based answers to those questions.

Aniqa Anwar, Senior Analyst at R/GA

Brown University, AB in Sociology (Honors)

I currently work as a senior analyst at an advertising agency. My role consists of analyzing data across several marketing channels, interpreting and evaluating the information, coming up with actionable solutions to improve campaign/brand performance and strategy, and distilling the information into easily digestible presentations for our clients. My day to day consists of working with varying data sets and gleaning meaningful information from them and presenting insights and solutions effectively. The theoretical foundation for this was built through a lot of my sociology classes and the papers and studies I had to read for them, and the practical foundation was built through assisting on research studies as well as conducting and working through my own data-heavy senior thesis.

One of the best skills one can learn from studying sociology is the ability to think critically and find meaningful patterns in data and interpret them effectively. Sociology provided a framework to help me understand and process quantitative and qualitative information and present them in a way that is impactful and evidence based. Critical thinking, while key in any job, is especially valuable in data-heavy roles like mine, as companies will always want to hire analytical thinkers who are data savvy.

Career Data: Market Research Analysts

- 2017 Median Pay: $63,230 per year
- $30.40 per hour
- Typical Entry-Level Education: Bachelor's degree
- Job Outlook, 2016–2026: 23% (Much faster than average)

Source: Bureau of Labor Statistics, *Occupational Outlook Handbook*, 2017.

at the core of the human experience. We are all profoundly "cultured."

Culture can be a source of integration and harmony, as functionalists assert, or it can be a vehicle of manipulation and oppression, as conflict theorists often see it. There is compelling evidence for both perspectives, and context is critical for recognizing which perspective better captures the character of a given cultural scenario.

The study of culture is much more than an intellectual exercise. In this chapter, you encountered several key cultural questions that are important objects of public discussion today. Does mass media foster viewer engagement in public life, or does it distract and disengage us from the pressing problems of our times? Is violence in the media just entertainment, or does it contribute, even indirectly, to violence in relationships and society? Will the evolution of a more global culture play an integrative role between societies, or will smaller cultures resist homogenization and assert their own power, bringing about conflict rather than harmony? These are questions of profound importance in a media-saturated and multicultural world—a sociological perspective can help us to make sense of them.

SUMMARY

- **Culture** consists of the beliefs, norms, behaviors, and products common to members of a particular social group. **Language** is an important component of cultures. The Sapir–Whorf hypothesis points to language's role in structuring perceptions and actions. Culture is a key topic of sociological study because, as human beings, we have the capacity to develop it through the creation of artifacts such as songs, foods, and values. Culture also influences our social development: We are products of our cultural beliefs, behaviors, and biases.

- Sociologists and others who study culture generally distinguish between material and nonmaterial culture.

Material culture encompasses physical artifacts—the objects created, embraced, and consumed by a given society. **Nonmaterial culture** is generally abstract and includes culturally accepted ideas about living and behaving. The two are intertwined because nonmaterial culture often gives particular meanings to the objects of material culture.

- Norms are the common rules of a culture that govern people's actions. **Folkways** are fairly weak norms, the violation of which is tolerable. **Mores** are strongly held norms; violating them is subject to social or legal sanction. **Taboos** are the most closely held mores;

violating them is socially unthinkable. **Laws** codify some, although not all, of society's norms.

- **Beliefs** are particular ideas that people accept as true, although they need not be objectively true. Beliefs can be based on faith, superstition, science, tradition, or experience.

- **Values** are the general, abstract standards of a society and define basic, often idealized principles. We identify national values, community values, institutional values, and individual values. Values may be sources of cohesion or of conflict.

- **Ideal culture** consists of the norms and values that the people of a society profess to embrace. **Real culture** consists of the real values, norms, and practices of people in a society.

- Ethnocentrism is the habit of judging other cultures by the standards of one's own.

- Sociologists entreat us to embrace **cultural relativism**, a perspective that allows us to understand the practices of other societies in terms of those societies' norms and values rather than our own.

- Multiple cultures may exist and thrive within any country or community. Some of these are **subcultures**, which exist together with the dominant culture but differ in some important respects from it.

- **High culture** is an exclusive culture often limited in its accessibility and audience. High culture is widely associated with the upper class, which both defines and embraces its content. **Popular culture** encompasses entertainment, culinary, and athletic tastes that are broadly shared. As mass culture, popular culture is more fully associated with the middle and working classes.

- **Rape culture** is a social culture that provides an environment conducive to rape. Some sociologists argue that we can best understand the high number of rapes and attempted rapes in the United States by considering both individual circumstances and the larger social context, which contains messages that marginalize and normalize the problem of sexual assault.

- **Global culture**—some would say U.S. culture—has spread across the world in the form of Hollywood films, fast-food restaurants, and popular music heard in almost every country.

KEY TERMS

culture, 59	ideal culture, 63	multiculturalism, 70
material culture, 59	real culture, 63	high culture, 70
nonmaterial culture, 59	cultural inconsistency, 64	popular culture, 71
beliefs, 59	doxic, 65	mass media, 71
folkways, 61	etic perspective, 67	rape culture, 75
mores, 61	emic perspective, 67	social class reproduction, 76
taboos, 61	cultural relativism, 67	cultural capital, 76
laws, 61	subcultures, 67	habitus, 76
values, 61	language, 69	global culture, 77

DISCUSSION QUESTIONS

1. This chapter discusses tensions between ideal and real culture in attitudes and practices linked to conventional attractiveness and honesty. Can you think of other cases where ideal and real cultures collide?

2. Following the ideas of the critical theorists in sociology, this chapter suggests that mass media may play a paradoxical role in society, offering both the information needed to bring about an informed citizenry and disseminating mass entertainment that distracts and disengages individuals from debates of importance. Which of these functions do you think is more powerful?

3. What is cultural capital? What, according to Bourdieu, is its significance in society? How does one acquire valued cultural capital, and how is it linked to the reproduction of social class?

4. The chapter presents an argument on the relationships among culture, social and mass media, and sexual violence with a discussion of the concept of a rape culture. Describe the argument. Do you agree or disagree with the argument? Explain your position.

5. Sociologist George Ritzer sees within globalization two processes—"glocalization" and "grobalization." What is the difference between the two? Which is, in your opinion, the more powerful process, and why do you believe this? Support your point with evidence.

Want a better grade?

Get the tools you need to sharpen your study skills. Access practice quizzes, eFlashcards, video, and multimedia at **https://edge.sagepub.com/chambliss4e**.

©Klaus Vedfelt/DigitalVision/Getty Images

Socialization and Social Interaction

4

WHAT DO YOU THINK?

1. Is the personality of an individual determined at birth?

2. Has social media become a key agent of socialization of children and teens? Does its influence outweigh that of the other agents of socialization, such as family and schools?

3. Do people adjust their self-presentation in interactions to leave particular impressions? Might we say that we have different "social selves" that we present in different settings?

LEARNING OBJECTIVES

4.1 Describe how sociologists theorize the birth of the social self.

4.2 Explain the significance of agents of socialization in the development of the self.

4.3 Discuss socialization across the life course.

4.4 Define the concept of *total institutions*.

4.5 Theorize social interaction from a sociological perspective.

MY ROBOT, MY FRIEND

Is it odd for human beings to have emotional relationships with robots? In popular culture, humans have long engaged in friendly, professional, or practical interactions with robots. Consider the long-running *Star Wars* franchise: Among the central relationships in the now four-decade-old original film are the bonds between Luke Skywalker and his robotic sidekicks, C3PO and R2-D2. The most recent film in the franchise, *Solo: A Star Wars Story* (2018), continues the trend, highlighting a strong emotional connection between the space pirate Lando Calrissian and his spunky female companion and copilot, a robot named L3-37. When L3-37 is destroyed in a shootout, Lando is visibly shaken and mourns the loss of his friend. Today, back in the real world, humanoid robots are making their debut in both work places and social spaces. What will this mean for social interaction in the future? What are the risks and benefits of human relationships with robots?

©Andia/UIG via Getty Images

A writer for the *Atlantic Monthly* muses that "self-operating machines are permeating every dimension of society, so that humans find themselves interacting more frequently with robots than ever before—often without even realizing it. The human–machine relationship is rapidly evolving as a result. Humanity, and what it means to be a human, will be defined in part by the machines people design" (LaFrance, 2016, para. 4). Indeed, as robots become a more ubiquitous part of human environments, some researchers are cautioning that the overattribution of human qualities and intentions to robots holds some dangers. The author notes what some scientists have dubbed "the android fallacy": That is, the computer scientists who coined that term have suggested that, "it's essential for humans to think of robots as tools, not companions—a tendency they say is 'seductive but dangerous'" (Ibid., para. 38). The threat, they suggest, lies in the possibility that a programmer's intention (which could be benign, but could also be selfish, greedy, or dangerous) may be interpreted by a human as a robot's "free will" and the balance of control in the relationship between human and robot may shift as the human cedes power to the machine. Indeed, they say, consider the power that technology already holds in determining choices we make about where to eat, where to shop, and whom to date.

On the other hand, robots with human qualities may provide opportunities for interaction to people who are frail, disabled, or lonely—and they can be a lot of fun. Some companies are already marketing "companion robots" that can do tasks such as remind an older adult to take his or her medications, play music and record video, and interact on a rudimentary level. Researchers say that it will not be long before these same robots can perform meaningful care functions such as lifting and dressing humans, which will move them into even more intimate spaces with humans. As the population ages, shifting some of these tasks to robotic companions may be beneficial, though, again, some researchers urge caution, arguing that there is danger in emotional attachments to machines that cannot reciprocate but may be able to manipulate:

> As AI gets smarter and smarter, it will be easier to trick people—especially children and the elderly—into thinking the relationship is reciprocal. And such a bond is a powerful thing. Imagine an unscrupulous toy maker inventing a doll so sophisticated that it appears animate to a kid. Now imagine the toy maker exploiting that bond by having the doll tell the kid to buy a personality upgrade for $50. (Simon, 2017, para. 15)

What will be the significance of this introduction of robots into our personal lives to the formation of social bonds and practice of social interaction? Do potential benefits outweigh costs? Can robots be our friends, companions, and colleagues? What do you think?

In this chapter, we examine the process of socialization and the array of agents that help shape our social selves and our behavioral choices. We begin by looking into the "nature versus nurture" debate and what sociology says about that debate. We then discuss key agents of socialization as well as the ways in which socialization may differ in total institutions and across the life course. We then examine theoretical perspectives on socialization. Finally, we look at social interaction and ways in which sociologists conceptualize our presentation of self and our group interactions, something that future sociologists may be rewriting as we increasingly interact not only with other humans but with robots and other technologies.

The Birth of the Social Self

Socialization is *the process by which people learn the culture of their society.* It is a lifelong and active process in which individuals construct their sense of who they are, how to think, and how to act as members of their culture. Socialization is our primary way of reproducing culture, including norms and values and the belief that our culture represents "normal" social practices and perceptions.

The principal agents of socialization (including parents, teachers, religious institutions, peers, television, and social media) exert enormous influence on us. Socialization takes place every day, usually without our thinking about it: when we speak, when others react to us, when we observe others' behavior—whether in person or on a screen—and in almost every other human interaction.

Debate has raged in the social sciences over the relative influence of genetic inheritance ("nature") and cultural and social experiences ("nurture") in shaping people's lives (Coleman & Hong, 2008; Ridgeway & Correll, 2004). If inborn biological predispositions explain differences in behaviors and interests between, say, sixth-grade boys and girls or between a professional thief and the police officer who apprehends him, then understanding socialization will do little to help us understand those differences. On the other hand, if biology cannot adequately explain differences in attitudes, characters, and behaviors, then it becomes imperative that we examine the effects of socialization.

Almost no one today argues that behavior is entirely determined by either socialization or biology. There is doubtless an interaction between the two. What social scientists disagree about, however, is which is more important in shaping a person's personality, philosophy of life, and social actions. In this text, we lean toward socialization because we believe the evidence points in that direction.

Social scientists have found little support for the idea that personalities and behaviors are rooted exclusively in human nature. Indeed, little human behavior is purely natural. For example, humans have a biological capacity for language, but language is learned and develops only through interaction. The weight of socialization in the development of language, reasoning, and social skills is dramatically illustrated in cases of children raised in isolation. If a biologically inherited mechanism alone triggered language, it would do so even in people who grow up deprived of contact with other human beings. If socialization plays a key role, however, then such people would not only have difficulty learning to use language, but they would also lack a capacity to play the social roles to which most of us are accustomed.

One of the most extensively documented cases of social isolation occurred more than 200 years ago. In 1800, a "wild boy," later named Victor, was seen by hunters in the forests of Aveyron, a rural area of France (Shattuck, 1980). Victor had been living alone in the woods for most of his 12 or so years and could not speak, and although he stood erect, he ran using both arms and legs like an animal. Victor was taken into the home of Jean-Marc-Gaspard Itard, a young medical doctor who, for the next 10 years, tried to teach him the social and intellectual skills expected of a child his age. According to Itard's careful records, Victor managed to learn a few words, but he never spoke in complete sentences. Although he eventually learned to use the toilet, he continued to evidence "wild" behavior, including public masturbation. Despite the efforts of Itard and others, Victor was incapable of learning more than rudimentary social and intellectual skills; he died in Paris in 1828.

Other studies of the effects of isolation have centered on children raised by their parents, but in nearly total isolation. For 12 years, from the time she was one and a half years old, "Genie" (a pseudonym) saw only her father, mother, and brother, and only when one of them came to feed her. Genie's father did not allow his wife or Genie to leave the house or have any visitors. Genie was either strapped to a child's potty-chair or placed in a sleeping bag that limited her movements. Genie rarely heard any conversation. If she made noises, her father beat her (Curtiss, 1977; Rymer, 1993).

When Genie was 13, her mother took her and fled the house. Genie was unable to cry, control her bowels, eat solid food, or talk. Because of her tight confinement, she had not even learned to focus her eyes beyond 12 feet. She was constantly salivating and spitting, and she had little controlled use of her arms or legs (Rymer, 1993). Gradually, Genie learned some of the social behavior expected of a child. For example, she learned to wear clothing and use the toilet. Nevertheless, although intelligence tests did not indicate reasoning disability, even after five years of concentrated effort on the part of a foster mother, social workers, and medical doctors, Genie never learned to speak beyond the level of a four-year-old, and she did not interact with others. Although she responded positively to those who treated her with sympathy, Genie's social behavior remained severely underdeveloped for the rest of her life (Rymer, 1993).

Genie's and Victor's experiences underscore the significance of socialization, especially during childhood. Their cases show that even biologically rooted capacities do not develop into recognizable human ways of acting and thinking, unless the individual interacts with other humans in a social environment. Children raised in isolation fail to develop complex language, abstract thinking, notions of cooperation and sharing, or even a sense of themselves as

---

Socialization: The process by which people learn the culture of their society.

social beings. In other words, they do not develop the hallmarks of what we know as humanity (Ridley, 1998).

Sociologists and other social scientists have developed theories to explain the role of socialization in the development of social selves. What these theories recognize is that whatever the contribution of biology, ultimately, people as social beings are made, not born. Below, we explore four approaches to understanding socialization: behaviorism, symbolic interactionism, developmental stage theories, and psychoanalytic theories.

Behaviorism and Social Learning Theory

Behaviorism is *a psychological perspective that emphasizes the effect of rewards and punishments on human behavior.* It arose during the late 19th century to challenge the then-popular belief that human behavior results primarily from biological instincts and drives (Baldwin & Baldwin, 1986, 1988; Dishion, McCord, & Poulin, 1999). Early behaviorist researchers, such as Ivan Pavlov (1849–1936) and John Watson (1878–1958) and, later, B. F. Skinner (1904–1990), demonstrated that even behavior thought to be purely instinctual (such as a dog salivating when it sees food) may be produced or extinguished through the application of rewards and punishments. Thus, a pigeon will learn to press a bar if that triggers the release of food (Skinner, 1938, 1953; Watson, 1924). Behaviorists concluded that both animal and human behavior can be learned, and neither is purely instinctive.

When they turned to human beings, behaviorists focused on **social learning**, *the way people adapt their behavior in response to social rewards and punishments* (Baldwin & Baldwin, 1986; Bandura, 1977; Bandura & Walters, 1963). Of particular interest was the satisfaction people get from imitating others. Social learning theory thus combines the reward-and-punishment effects identified by behaviorists with the idea that we model the behavior of others; that is, we observe the way people respond to others' behavior.

Social learning theory would predict, for example, that if a boy gets high fives from his friends for talking back to his teacher—a form of encouragement rather than of punishment—he is likely to repeat this behavior. What's more, other boys may imitate it. Social learning researchers have developed formulas for predicting how rewards and punishments affect behavior. For instance, rewards given repeatedly may become less effective when the individual becomes satiated: If you have just eaten a huge piece of cake, you are less likely to feel rewarded by the prospect of another.

Social behaviorism is not widely embraced today as a rigorous perspective on human behavior. One reason is that only in carefully controlled laboratory environments is it easy to demonstrate the power of rewards and punishments. In real social situations, the theory is of limited value as a predictor. For example, whether a girl who is teased ("punished") for engaging in a "masculine" pursuit such as football or wrestling will lose interest in the sport depends on many other variables, such as the support of family and friends and her own enjoyment of the activity. The simple application of rewards and punishments is hardly sufficient to explain why people repeat some behaviors and not others.

In addition, behaviorist theories violate Popper's principle of falsification (discussed in Chapter 2). Since what was previously rewarding may lose effectiveness if the person is satiated, if a reward does not work, we can always attribute its failure to satiation. Therefore, no matter the outcome of the experiment, the theory has to be true; it cannot be proved false. For these reasons, sociologists find behaviorism an inadequate theory of socialization. To explain how people become socialized, they highlight theories that emphasize symbolic interaction.

Socialization as Symbolic Interaction

Recall from the introductory chapter that *symbolic interactionism* views the self and society as resulting from social interaction based on language and other symbols. Symbolic interactionism has been especially fruitful in explaining how individuals develop a social identity and a capacity for social interaction (Blumer, 1969, 1970; Hutcheon, 1999; Mead, 1934, 1938).

An early contribution to symbolic interactionism was Charles Horton Cooley's (1864–1929) concept of the **looking-glass self**, the *self-image that results from our interpretation of other people's views of us.* For example, children who are frequently told they are capable and bright will tend to see themselves as such and act accordingly. On the other hand, children who are repeatedly told they lack intelligence or are slow will lose pride in themselves and act the part. According to Cooley (1902/1964), we are constantly forming ideas about how others perceive and judge us, and the resulting *self-image*—the way we view ourselves—is, in turn, the basis of our social interaction with others.

Cooley recognized that not everyone we encounter is equally important in shaping our self-image. **Primary groups** are *small groups characterized by intense emotional*

Behaviorism: A psychological perspective that emphasizes the effect of rewards and punishments on human behavior.

Social learning: The way people adapt their behavior in response to social rewards and punishments.

Looking-glass self: The concept developed by Charles Horton Cooley that our self-image results from how we interpret other people's views of us.

Primary groups: Small groups characterized by intense emotional ties, face-to-face interaction, intimacy, and a strong, enduring sense of commitment.

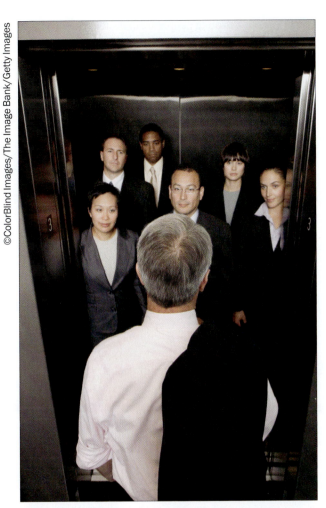

Society has unwritten but widely understood rules for standing with strangers in an elevator. We learn these conventional practices from interactions and observations. Can you identify these unwritten rules? What constitutes a violation, and how are these rules enforced?

ties, face-to-face interaction, intimacy, and a strong, enduring sense of commitment. Families, close friends, and lovers are all examples of primary groups likely to shape our self-image. **Secondary groups**, on the other hand, come together for reasons that *are functional or fleeting rather than emotional or enduring.* These groups may be based on interests or economic exchange: They could include a workplace, a running club, or even a military field exercise. Today, they may even include the "friends" that one acquires on social media platforms such as Facebook: According to the Pew Research Center (2014c), the average number of such friends for millennials is 250, while for Generation X, it averages 200. Younger baby boomers average 98 friends. Secondary groups typically have less influence in forming our self-image than do primary groups, although, arguably, social media has unleashed the modern power of "likes" that can

have a profound effect on one's self-image. Both kinds of groups act on us throughout our lives; the self-image is not set at some early stage but continues to develop throughout adulthood (Barber, 1992; Berns, 1989).

Both primary and secondary groups also serve as **reference groups**, *groups that provide standards for judging our attitudes or behaviors.* When you consider your friends' reactions to your dress or hairstyle or new smartphone, you are using your peers as a reference in shaping your decisions.

George Herbert Mead (1863–1931), widely regarded as the founder of symbolic interactionism, explored the ways in which self and society shape one another. Mead proposed that the self comprises two parts: the "I" and the "me." The **I** is *the impulse to act; it is creative, innovative, unthinking, and largely unpredictable.* The **me** is *the part of the self through which we see ourselves as others see us.* (Note the similarity between Mead's *me* and Cooley's *looking-glass self.*) The *I* represents innovation and the me represents social convention and conformity. In the tension between them, the me is often capable of controlling the I. When the *I* initiates a spontaneous act, the me raises society's response: *How will others regard me if I act this way?*

Mead further argued that people develop a sense of self through **role-taking**, *the ability to take the roles of others in interaction.* For example, a young girl playing soccer may pretend to be a coach; in the process, she learns to see herself (as well as other players) from a coach's perspective. Mead proposed that childhood socialization relies on an expanding ability to take on such roles, moving from the extreme self-centeredness of the infant to an adult ability to take the standpoint of society as a whole. He outlined four principal stages in socialization that reflect this progression: the preparatory, play, game, and adult stages. The attainment of each stage results in an increasingly mature social self.

1. During the *preparatory stage,* children younger than 3 years old relate to the world as though they are the center of the universe. They do not engage in true role-taking but respond primarily to things in their immediate environments, such as their mothers' breasts, the colors of toys, or the sounds of voices.

2. Children 3 or 4 years of age enter the *play stage,* during which they learn to take the attitudes and

Secondary groups: Groups that are impersonal and characterized by functional or fleeting relationships.

Reference groups: Groups that provide standards for judging our attitudes or behaviors.

I: According to George Herbert Mead, the part of the self that is the impulse to act; it is creative, innovative, unthinking, and largely unpredictable.

Me: According to George Herbert Mead, the part of the self through which we see ourselves as others see us.

Role-taking: The ability to take the roles of others in interaction.

Young children learn to see the world from the perspective of others in part through play, which allows them to take the role of another person.

roles of the people with whom they interact. **Significant others** are *specific people important in children's lives whose views have the greatest impact on the children's self-evaluations.* By role-playing at being mothers or fathers, for example, children come to see themselves as their parents see them. Nevertheless, according to Mead, they have not yet acquired the complex sense of self that lets them see themselves through the eyes of *many* different people or society.

3. The *game* stage begins when children are about 5 and learn to take the roles of multiple others. The game is an effective analogy for this stage. For example, to be an effective basketball player, an individual must have the ability to see himself or herself from the perspective of teammates, the other team, and the coach and must play accordingly. He or she must know the rules of the game. Successful negotiation of the social world also requires that people gain the ability to see themselves as others see them, to understand societal "rules," and to act accordingly. This stage signals the development of a self that is aware of societal positions and perspectives.

4. Game playing takes the child to the final *adult stage.* At this stage, young people begin to internalize the **generalized other**, *the abstract sense of society's norms and values by which people evaluate themselves.* They act on a set of socially normative principles that may or may not serve their self-interest—for example, voluntarily joining the military to fight in a war that might injure or kill them because

patriotic young people are expected to defend their country or choosing to return a wallet full of cash to its owner because taking something that belongs to someone else is wrong. By the adult stage, a person is capable of understanding abstract and complex cultural symbols, such as love and hate, success and failure, friendship, patriotism, and morality.

Mead also had a vision that in the future, people would be able to assimilate a multitude of generalized others, adapting their behavior in terms of their own as well as other people's cultures. Mead's dream of a highly multicultural world may someday be a reality as globalization makes more people aware of the value of other cultures.

Stages of Development: Piaget and Kohlberg

Like Mead and Cooley, the Swiss social psychologist Jean Piaget (1896–1980) believed humans are socialized in stages. Piaget devoted a lifetime to researching how young children develop the ability to think abstractly and make moral judgments (Piaget, 1926, 1928, 1930, 1932). His theory of **cognitive development**, based largely on studies of Swiss children at play (including his own), argues that *an individual's ability to make logical decisions increases as the person grows older.* Piaget noted that infants are highly **egocentric**, *experiencing the world as if it were centered entirely on them.* In stages over time, socialization lets children learn to use language and symbols, to think abstractly and logically, and to see things from different perspectives.

Piaget also developed a theory of moral development, which holds that as they grow, people learn to act according to abstract ideas about justice or fairness. This theory parallels his idea of cognitive development, since both describe overcoming egocentrism and acquiring the ability to take other points of view. Eventually, children come to develop abstract notions of fairness, learning that rules should be judged relative to the circumstances. For example, even if the rules say "three strikes and you're out," an exception might be made for a child who has never played the game or who is physically challenged.

Lawrence Kohlberg (1927–1987) extended Piaget's ideas about moral development. In his best-known study, subjects were told the story of the fictitious "Heinz," who was unable to afford a drug that might prevent his wife from dying of cancer. As the story unfolds, Heinz breaks into the druggist's shop and steals the medication. Kohlberg asked

---

Significant others: According to George Herbert Mead, the specific people who are important in children's lives and whose views have the greatest impact on the children's self-evaluations.

Generalized other: The abstract sense of society's norms and values by which people evaluate themselves.

Cognitive development: The theory, developed by Jean Piaget, that an individual's ability to make logical decisions increases as the person grows older.

Egocentric: Experiencing the world as if it were centered entirely on oneself.

his subjects what they would have done, emphasizing that there is no right or wrong answer. Using experiments such as this, Kohlberg (1969, 1983, 1984) proposed three principal stages (and several substages) of moral development:

1. The *preconventional stage,* during which people seek simply to achieve personal gain or avoid punishment. A person might support Heinz's decision to steal on the grounds that it would be too difficult to get the medicine by other means or oppose it on the grounds that Heinz might get caught and go to jail. Children are typically socialized into this rudimentary form of morality between ages 7 and 10.

2. The *conventional stage,* during which the individual is socialized into society's norms and values and would feel shame or guilt about violating them. The person might support Heinz's decision to steal on the grounds that society would judge him callous if he let his wife die or oppose it because people would call Heinz a thief if he were caught. Children are socialized into this more developed form of morality at about age 10, and most people remain in this stage throughout their adult lives.

3. The *postconventional stage,* during which the individual invokes general, abstract notions of right and wrong. Even though Heinz has broken the law, his transgression has to be weighed against the moral cost of sacrificing his wife's life. People at the highest levels of postconventional morality will go beyond social convention entirely, appealing to a higher set of abstract principles.

Some scholars have argued that Kohlberg's theory reflects a strong male bias because it derives from male rather than from female experience. Foremost among Kohlberg's critics is Carol Gilligan (1982; Gilligan, Ward, & Taylor, 1989), who argues that men may be socialized to base moral judgment on abstract principles of fairness and justice, but women are socialized to base theirs on compassion and caring. She showed that women scored lower on Kohlberg's measure of moral development because they valued how other family members were affected by Heinz's decision more than abstract considerations of justice. Because it assumes that abstract thinking represents a higher stage of development, Gilligan suggests, Kohlberg's measure is biased in favor of male socialization.

Research testing Gilligan's ideas has found that men and women alike adhere to *both* care-based and justice-based forms of moral reasoning (Gump, Baker, & Roll, 2000; Jaffee & Hyde, 2000). Differences between the sexes in these kinds of reasoning are, in fact, small

or nonexistent. Studies of federal employees (Peek, 1999), a sample of men and women using the Internet (Anderson, 2000), and a sample of Mexican American and Anglo-American students (Gump et al., 2000) have all found no significant difference between men and women in the degree to which they employ care-based and justice-based styles of moral reasoning. Might there be cases in which men and women as groups exercise moral reasoning differently? Does gender affect moral reasoning? What do you think?

Biological Needs versus Social Constraints: Freud

Sigmund Freud (1856–1939), an Austrian psychiatrist, had a major impact on the study of socialization as well as on the disciplines of psychology and psychiatry. Freud (1905, 1929, 1933) founded the field of **psychoanalysis**, *a psychological perspective that emphasizes the complex reasoning processes of the conscious and unconscious mind.* He stressed the role of the unconscious mind in shaping human behavior and theorized that early childhood socialization is essential in molding the adult personality by age 5 or 6. In addition, Freud sought to demonstrate that in order to thrive, a society must socialize its members to curb their instinctive needs and desires.

■ **FIGURE 4.1** The Id, Ego, and Superego, as Conceived by Freud

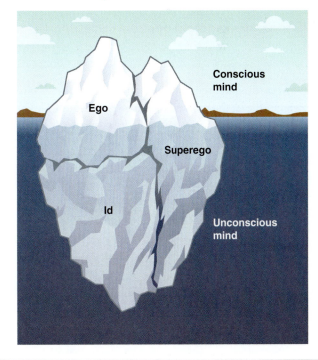

Psychoanalysis: A psychological perspective that emphasizes the complex reasoning processes of the conscious and unconscious mind.

TABLE 4.1   Comparison of Mead's and Freud's Theories of Socialization

MEAD'S STAGES	FREUD'S PSYCHOANALYTIC THEORY
Preparatory: Highly limited role-taking in which the individual views the world through his or her own eyes.	**Id:** The repository of basic biological drives and needs, which seeks instant gratification.
Play: The individual takes on the roles of significant others, one at a time.	**Ego:** The self that, once developed, balances the forces of the id and superego. The ego is necessary in the socialization process for the individual to become a well-adjusted adult.
Game: The individual is able to view the world through the eyes of multiple others, simultaneously.	**Superego:** The values and norms of society. May conflict with the id.
Maturity: The individual is able to take the attitude of the generalized other and can view the world through the eyes of society as a whole.	

Source: Adapted from Mead, G. H. (1934). *Mind, self, and society.* Chicago: University of Chicago Press.

According to Freud, the human mind has three components: the id, the ego, and the superego (Figure 4.1). The **id** is *the repository of basic biological drives and needs,* which Freud believed to be primarily bound up in sexual energy. (*Id* is Latin for "it," reflecting Freud's belief that this aspect of the human personality is not even truly human.) The **ego** (Latin for "I") is *the "self," the core of what we regard as a person's unique personality.* The **superego** *consists of the values and norms of society insofar as they are internalized, or taken in, by the individual.* The concept of the superego is similar to the notion of a conscience.

Id: According to Sigmund Freud, the part of the mind that is the repository of basic biological drives and needs.

Ego: According to Sigmund Freud, the part of the mind that is the "self," the core of what is regarded as a person's unique personality.

Superego: According to Sigmund Freud, the part of the mind that consists of the values and norms of society insofar as they are internalized, or taken in, by the individual.

Freud believed that babies are all id. Left to their own devices, they will seek instant gratification of their biological needs for food, physical contact, and nurturing. Therefore, according to Freud, to be socialized, they must eventually learn to suppress such gratification. The child's superego, consisting of cultural *should*s and *should not*s, struggles constantly with the biological impulses of the id. Serving as mediator between id and superego is the child's emerging ego. In Freud's view, the child will grow up to be a well-socialized adult to the extent that the ego succeeds in bending the biological desires of the id to meet the social demands of the superego.

Since Freud claimed that personality is set early in life, he viewed change as difficult for adults, especially if psychological troubles originate in experiences too painful to face or remember. Individuals must become fully aware of their repressed or unconscious memories and unacceptable impulses if they ever hope to change (Freud, 1933). Freud's psychoanalytic therapy focused on accessing deeply buried feelings to help patients alter current behaviors and feelings. Whereas Mead saw socialization as a lifelong process relying on many socialization agents, for Freud, it stopped at a young age. Table 4.1 compares Mead's and Freud's views point by point.

Agents of Socialization

Among primary groups, the family is, for most people, the most critical agent of socialization. Other significant agents are school, peer groups, work, religion, and technology and mass media, including the Internet and social media (Figure 4.2).

Child-rearing practices within families can vary along many dimensions—ethnic background, religious affiliation, even social class. Because U.S. culture is ethnically diverse, it is difficult to describe a "typical" American family (Glazer, 1997; Stokes & Chevan, 1996). Among Latinos, for example, the family often includes grandparents, aunts, uncles, cousins, and in-laws, who share child-rearing responsibilities. Among Latino youth, scholars have identified the family, especially mothers, as a central force that informs the ethnic identity development process (Supple, Ghazarian, Frabutt, Plunkett, & Sands, 2006).

The Family

The family is a primary group in which children, especially during the earliest years of their lives, are physically and emotionally dependent on adult members. It plays a key role in transmitting norms, values, and culture across generations, and as a result, it is the first and usually the foremost source of socialization in all societies.

Children usually first encounter their society in the family, learning socially defined roles such as father, mother, sister, brother, uncle, aunt, and grandparent and the expected behaviors attached to them. Parents often hold stereotypical notions of how boys and girls should be, and they reinforce gender behaviors in countless subtle and not-so-subtle ways. A father may be responsible for grilling and yard work while a mother cooks dinner and cleans the house. On the other hand, some families embrace egalitarian or nonconventional gender roles. Although same-sex couple families are more likely than families headed by opposite-sex couples to challenge gender-normative roles and behaviors, they sometimes still enforce or support more traditional gender roles for their children (Ackbar, 2011; Bos & Sandfort, 2010).

The way parents relate to their child affects almost every aspect of the child's behavior, including the ability to resolve conflicts through the use of reason instead of violence and the propensity for emotional stability or distress. The likelihood that young people will be victims of homicide, commit suicide, engage in acts of aggression against other people, use drugs, complete their secondary education, or have an unwanted pregnancy also is greatly influenced by childhood experiences in the family (Campbell & Muncer, 1998; McLoyd & Smith, 2002; Muncer & Campbell, 2000). For example, children who are regularly spanked or otherwise physically punished internalize the idea that violence is an acceptable means of achieving goals and are more likely than peers who are not spanked to engage in aggressive delinquent behavior. They are also more likely to have low self-esteem, suffer depression, and do poorly in school (Straus, Sugarman, & Giles-Sims, 1997). (See the *Private Lives, Public Issues* box on pages 95–96.)

Research suggests that child-rearing practices may vary somewhat by social class. Parents whose jobs require them to be subservient to authority and to follow orders without raising questions typically stress obedience and respect for authority at home, while parents whose work gives them freedom to make their own decisions and be creative are likely to socialize their children into norms of creativity and spontaneity. Since many working-class jobs demand conformity while middle- and upper-middle-class jobs are more likely to offer independence, social class may be a key factor in explaining differences in family socialization of children (Kohn, 1989; Lareau, 2002).

■ **FIGURE 4.2** Agents of Socialization

Source: Supple et al., 2006; Umaña-Taylor et al., 2011.

Family patterns are changing rapidly in the United States, partly because of declining marriage rates and low overall fertility rates. Such changes can affect socialization. For example, children raised by a single parent may not be actively exposed to a male or a female role model in the home or may experience economic hardship that determines where they go to school or with whom they socialize outside the home. Being an only child is also a different experience from being raised in a family of multiple children, where both attention and roles may differ. Children raised in blended families (the result of remarriage) may have stepparents and stepsiblings whose norms, values, and behaviors are unfamiliar. Same-sex couple families may both challenge and, as noted earlier, reinforce conventional modes of socialization, particularly with respect to gender socialization. Although families are changing, their influence as agents of socialization remains powerful.

Teachers and School

Children in the United States often begin schooling when they enter day care or preschool as infants or toddlers, and they spend more hours each day and more days each year in school than was the case a hundred years ago (although they spend less time in school than

Inequality Matters

GENDER AND SOCIALIZATION IN CHILDREN'S BOOKS

©iStockphoto.com/davidf

As a foundational part of early childhood socialization, books matter. But how do they matter? In the world of children's literature, there has been a lot of discussion of the gender of characters, whether human or nonhuman, and the significance of the gender of main characters for very young book consumers. In this essay, we look at contemporary research on gender diversity in children's books and consider why it matters in the socialization process.

Children's books have long been a source of interest to researchers (Crisp & Hiller, 2011; Gooden & Gooden, 2001). Melanie Koss (2015), who notes that "Picture books are educational tools and most children come into contact with them; consequently, the content of picture books matters" (p. 32), posits that diversity matters in books. To underscore her point, she quotes the work of R. S. Bishop: "Children need to see themselves reflected in literature (i.e., look into a mirror), to see the lives of others (i.e., look into a window), and to see themselves as able to transverse between groups and worlds (i.e., pass through a sliding glass door)" (Bishop, 1990, quoted in Koss, 2015, p. 32).

A recent review of popular children's literature of the 20th century offered some compelling findings that reiterate and expand upon what existing research has suggested about gender parity in books. The study, which covered the period from 1900 to 2000, examined about 6,000 children's books. Among the

authors' conclusions were the following: Male characters constituted about 57% of central characters in any given year, while female main characters were present in about 31% of books. In all books, some adult male or male animal characters were present; this was not true of females. Over a third of books in any year featured a male character in the title; just over 17% had a female character in the title. Interestingly, gender parity among animal characters was less common than gender parity among human characters. Notably, gender representation did not follow a linear pattern of progress: that is, parity did not grow steadily through the 20th century. Rather, gender representation was most unequal in the middle of the century, with the greatest proportion of male characters appearing in books published between 1930 and 1969. It was most equal at the end of the century, in the period following the women's activist movements of the 1960s and 1970s (McCabe et al., 2011).

What is the sociological significance of these findings? Does gender representation matter? Sociologist Janice McCabe, one of the coauthors of the 2011 study, suggests that it matters because "the widespread pattern of underrepresentation of females that we find supports the belief that female characters are less important and interesting than male characters. . . . This may contribute to a sense of unimportance among girls and privilege among boys," particularly in a context where this message is also reiterated in other popular media such as cartoons, children's films, and video games (Florida State News, 2011).

Think It Through

- Think back to the favorite books of your childhood. What do you remember about them? Who were the main characters? How do your recollections of the characters and stories align with or challenge research findings about gender and children's books?

their peers in Europe and Asia). Indeed, education has taken on a large role in helping young people prepare for adult society. In addition to reading, writing, math,

and other academic subjects, schools are expected to teach values and norms such as patriotism, competitiveness, morality, and respect for authority, as well as basic social skills. Some sociologists call this the **hidden curriculum**, *the unspoken classroom socialization into the norms, values, and roles of a society that* schools provide along with the *"official"* curriculum. The hidden curriculum may include "lessons" in gender roles taught through teachers' differing expectations of boys and girls, with, for instance, boys pushed to pursue higher math courses while girls are encouraged to embrace language and literature (Sadker, Zittleman, & Sadker, 2003). It may entail "lessons" that reinforce

Hidden curriculum: The unspoken classroom socialization into the norms, values, and roles of a society that schools provide along with the "official" curriculum.

Private Lives, Public Issues
CHILD-REARING AND PUNISHMENT IN U.S. FAMILIES

Although many people still believe in the adage "Spare the rod and spoil the child," the use of physical punishment in the United States has declined over time, although studies on the issue produce mixed results, depending on whether respondents are queried about attitudes or practices. On the one hand, a large Child Trends study found high levels of support for the statement that children sometimes need a "good, hard spanking," although the response differed somewhat by gender: About 76% of men and 65% of women agreed with the assertion (Child Trends, 2014). On the other hand, a survey conducted by the Pew Research Center (2015b) reports that 53% of respondents "never spank" their child or children (Figure 4.3). By contrast, 17% answered that they

■ **FIGURE 4.3** Use of Spanking by Racial and Educational Groups

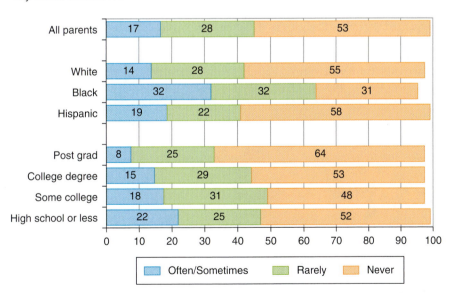

% saying they use spanking as a form of discipline with any of their children . . .

	Often/Sometimes	Rarely	Never
All parents	17	28	53
White	14	28	55
Black	32	32	31
Hispanic	19	22	58
Post grad	8	25	64
College degree	15	29	53
Some college	18	31	48
High school or less	22	25	52

Source: "Parenting in America," Pew Research Center, Washington, DC (December 2015b). http://www.pewsocialtrends.org/2015/12/17/parenting-in-america/.

Note: Voluntary responses of "Child is too young/old" and "Don't know/Refused" not shown. Whites and Blacks include only those who are not Hispanic. Hispanics are of any race.

(Continued)

(Continued)

spank "often" or "sometimes," and 28% said they spank "rarely." Interestingly, the study found that proportions of parents indicating that they spank varied by race and education. Even though, overall, the use of corporal punishment is low, just 8% of parents with graduate-level education reported that they spanked often or sometimes, compared with 22% for those with a high school education or less. There were also differences by race, with Hispanic parents most likely to indicate they "never spank" (58%) and Black parents more likely to say they spank sometimes or often (32%).

Spanking is of interest to sociologists because it highlights the nexus between private lives and public issues. On the one hand, it is a personal decision made by parents in the home; on the other hand, research suggests that it may have social consequences that are borne more widely. For example, a study on young children found that when boys and girls 6 to 9 years old were spanked, they became more antisocial—more likely to cheat, tell lies, act cruelly to others, break things deliberately, and get into trouble at school (Straus et al., 1997). Another study concluded that corporal punishment, and even some lesser forms of parental punishment, could have a strong effect on a child's ability to cope later in life (Welsh, 1998). More recently, a meta-analysis of spanking that covered five decades of research and included studies of over 160,000 children concluded that children who were spanked were more likely to have mental health problems and to be antisocial than their peers who were not spanked. In addition, being spanked also correlated with higher risks of depression, anxiety, and paranoia—and even a lower tested IQ (Gershoff & Grogan-Kaylor, 2016).

There has been research that suggests less malign effects. For example, research by psychologist Marjorie Lindner Gunnoe (1997), which tracked more than 1,100 children over a five-year period, found that although some 8- to 11-year-old boys, but not girls, who had been spanked regularly got into more fights at school, children of both sexes ages 4 to 7 who had been spanked regularly got into fewer fights than children who were not spanked. As well, children who were spanked were found in some studies to be more compliant, though the effects were limited to the short term—in the long term, many children were more defiant. Significantly, there is also the question of whether correlation adds up to causation, and some researchers caution that it is possible that some children with a predisposition to aggressive behavior may elicit harsher punishments, thus throwing into question whether more aggressive behavior is a cause or consequence of spanking (Gershoff & Grogan-Kaylor, 2016).

Although the research findings on the effects of physical punishment differ somewhat, a significant proportion of the evidence suggests that spanking may result in detrimental outcomes for children and even society—suggesting that this private trouble can indeed be a public issue.

Think It Through

- Using the knowledge you have gained through the study of socialization, and knowing the results of research on the effects of physical punishment on children's behavior, could you design a social policy or program to reduce the use of physical punishment in the home?

Follow us on Twitter to keep up with current sociological stories and research! We're at **@DiscoverSoc1**.

Share your own ideas at **#DiscoverSociology**.

---

class status, with middle- and upper-class children having access to classes and schools with advanced subjects, advanced technology, and outstanding teachers, and poor children provided a smaller selection of less academically challenging or vocational classes and limited access to advanced teaching technologies and highly trained educators (Bowles & Gintis, 1976; Kozol, 2005). At the same time, the hidden curriculum may also include what is not taught: For example, if an English class typically relies on reading material with White main characters, this may teach students of color that their cultures are not appreciated or that people of their ethnic group cannot be heroes.

Peers

Peers are people of the same age and, often, of the same social standing. Peer socialization begins when a child starts to play with other children outside the family, usually during the first year of life, and grows more intense in

Schools are an important agent of socialization. Students learn academic skills and knowledge, but they also gain social skills, acquire dominant values of citizenship, and practice obedience to authority.

©Ronnie Kaufman/Larry Hirshowitz/Blend Images/Getty Images

school. Conformity to the norms and values of friends is especially compelling during adolescence and continues into adulthood (Harris, 2009; Ponton, 2000; Sebald, 2000). In U.S. society, most adolescents spend more time with their peers than with their families as a result of school, athletic activities, and other social and academic commitments. Sociological theories thus often focus on young people's peer groups to account for a wide variety of adult behavioral patterns, including the development of self-esteem and self-image, career choices, ambition, and deviant behavior (Cohen, 1955; Hine, 2000; Sebald, 2000).

Judith Rich Harris (2009) argues that after the first few years of life, a child's friends' opinions outweigh the opinions of parents. To manage these predominant peer group influences, she suggests, parents must try to ensure that their children have the "right" friends. But this is an increasingly complex problem when "friends" may be Internet acquaintances who are difficult to monitor and of whom parents may be unaware.

The adolescent subculture plays an extremely important part in the socialization of adolescents in the modern world. Researchers have described the following characteristics of this subculture (Hine, 2000; Sebald, 2000):

1. A set of norms not shared with the adult or childhood cultures and governing interaction, statuses, and roles.

2. An *argot* (the special vocabulary of a particular group) that is not shared with nonadolescents and is often frowned upon by adults and school officials. Think about the jargon used by young people who text—many adults can read it only with difficulty!

3. Various underground media and preferred media programs, music, and Internet sites.

4. Unique fads and fashions in dress and hairstyles that often lead to conflict with parents and other adult authorities over their appropriateness.

5. A set of "heroes, villains, and fools." Sometimes adults are the "villains and fools," while the adults' "villains and fools" are heroes in the adolescent subculture.

6. A more open attitude than that found in the general culture toward experimentation with drugs and, at times, violence (fighting, for example).

Teenagers differ in the degree to which they are caught up in, and therefore socialized by, the adolescent subculture. Harris's (2009) claim that parents are largely irrelevant is no doubt an overstatement, yet in Western cultures, peer socialization does play a crucial part in shaping many of the ideas, self-images, and attitudes that will persist throughout individuals' lives.

Sociologists use the term **anticipatory socialization** to describe the process of *adopting the behaviors or standards of a group one emulates or hopes to join.* For example, teen girls who seek to be part of a fashionable, popular clique may adopt the dress and behavioral norms of the young women in the group the want to enter. Similarly, college students with political aspirations may seek out internships with political leaders, where they can practice dressing and acting out the part. Anticipatory socialization looks to future expectations rather than to only the present experience.

Organized Sports

Organized sports are a fundamental part of the lives of millions of children in the United States: By one estimate, 21.5 million children and teens ages 6 to 17 participate in at

DISCOVER INTERSECTIONS

Peers, Media, and Violence in Society

In the section above, you read about research that shows the influence of peers on young people's socialization. In our chapter on culture and mass media (Chapter 3), you learned about studies that suggest that media has an influence on violent behavior. How would you combine these two bodies of information to create a hypothesis about possible roots of violent behavior among young people? How might you research and test your hypothesis?

Anticipatory socialization: Adoption of the behaviors or standards of a group one emulates or hopes to join.

least one organized sport (Kelley & Carchia, 2013). About 40% of kids between 6 and 12 are involved in a team sport (Rosenwald, 2016). If it is the case, as psychologist Erik Erikson (1950) posited, that in middle childhood children develop a sense of "industry or inferiority," then it is surely the case that in a sports-obsessed country such as the United States, one avenue for generating this sense of self is through participation in sports.

Being part of a sports team and mastering skills associated with sports are activities that are widely recognized as valuable; they are presumed to build character and to contribute to hard work, competitiveness, and the ability to perform in stressful situations and under the gaze of others (Friedman, 2013), all of which are positively evaluated. In fact, research suggests that there are particular benefits of sports for girls, including lower rates of teen sexual activity and pregnancy (Sabo, Miller, Farrell, Melnick, & Barnes, 1999) and higher rates of college attendance, labor force participation, and entry into male-dominated occupations (Stevenson, 2010). Some studies have also found improved academic performance relative to nonparticipants for all athletes, although they have shown some variation in this effect by race and gender (Eccles & Barber, 1999; Miller, Melnick, Barnes, Farrell, & Sabo, 2005).

At the same time, sports participation has been associated in some research literature with the reinforcement of gender stereotypes (Jakubowska & Byczkowska-Owczarek, 2018) and socialization into negative attitudes, including homophobia. In a study of more than 1,400 teenagers, Osborne and Wagner (2007) found that boys who participated in "core" sports (football, basketball, baseball, and/or soccer) were three times more likely than their nonparticipant peers to express homophobic attitudes. In a country in which sports and sports figures are widely venerated and participation (particularly for boys) is labeled as "masculine," there may also be negative effects for boys who are not athletic or who do not enjoy sports.

Religion

Religion is a central part of the lives of many people around the world. Although the United States has a notable proportion of inhabitants who identify as atheists, about 76% of U.S. adults indicate they are members of a religion, and nearly 36% attend religious services once a week. Even among the one fifth of the population who declare themselves unaffiliated with any particular religion, 61% believe in God and more than 20% say that they pray every day (Pew Forum on Religion and Public Life, 2015). Beginning with Émile Durkheim, sociologists have noted the role of religion in fostering social solidarity. Talcott Parsons (1970) pointed out that religion also acts as an agent of

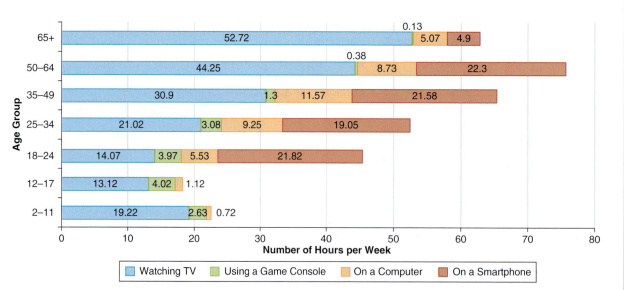

FIGURE 4.4 Average Number of Hours per Week of Screen Time

Source: "The Nielsen Total Audience Report Q2 2017." Nielsen.com.

Note: Data not available for smartphone usage for 2- to 17-year-olds, but some studies have estimated that children 2 to 11 years old may spend as much as 14 hours a week on smartphones, and teens 12 to 17 may spend nearly 27 hours per week on their smartphones (Houghton et al., 2015).

socialization, teaching fundamental values and beliefs that contribute to a shared normative culture.

Different religions function in similar ways, giving their followers a sense of what is right and wrong, how to conduct themselves in society, and how to organize their lives. Some socialize their followers with abstract teachings about morality, service, or self-discipline, directing believers to, for example, serve their fellow human beings or to avoid the sin of vanity. Others contain abstract teachings but specific rules about dress and hairstyles. The Amish faith entreats young men to remain clean-shaven prior to marriage, but married men must grow beards. Sikh men of India wear turbans that cover their hair, which they do not cut.

Like other agents of socialization and social control, religion directs its followers to choose certain paths and behaviors and not others. This is not to say that we are compelled to behave a certain way but rather that socialization often leads us to control our own behavior because we fear social ostracism or other negative consequences.

Mass Media and Social Media

Among the most influential agents of socialization in modern societies are technology and the mass media. Newspapers, magazines, movies, radio, and television are all forms of mass media. Television has long been an influential agent of socialization: According to Nielsen ratings, the typical American spends 4 hours and 27 minutes in front of a TV screen per day; this includes regularly broadcast television programs and DVR/time-shifted TV viewing (Nielsen, 2017). The overall numbers are down from previous years; however, with the increase in technology, more households (58.7%) are adapting to new ways of receiving content by streaming through smart TVs, multimedia devices, and/or game consoles (Nielsen, 2017; Figure 4.4). When we add time spent watching streaming content from Netflix, HBO, or other services—as well as time spent on social media—it's clear that overall, screen time is rising in the United States (Nielsen, 2017). Americans now own four digital devices on average, and the typical U.S. consumer spends 75 hours a week consuming content across devices (Nielsen, 2018).

Child psychologists, sociologists, and parents' groups pay special attention to the impact of TV and other media violence on children and young adults. Media studies during the past 20 years have largely come to a common conclusion: Media violence has the clear potential to socialize children, teenagers, and even adults into a greater acceptance of real-life violence. This is true for males and females, Whites and nonwhites. Much media violence is directed against women, and a large body of research supports the conclusion that media violence promotes tolerance among men for sexual violence, including rape (Rodenhizer &

A key component of contemporary young adult communication on social media—and a centerpiece of platforms such as Snapchat and Instagram—is the "selfie," a term that made its debut in the Merriam-Webster dictionary in 2014 (Webster, 2014).

Edwards, 2017; Ward, 2016; Ybarra, Strasburger, & Mitchell, 2014). The argument is not that viewing violent shows is a direct cause of violence; rather, viewers may become immunized to the sight of violence. Still, given that most people who are exposed to violence in the media do not become violent, the part played by the media as an agent of socialization is probably less important than the contribution made by other agents, such as family and peers.

The media plays a role in socialization by creating fads and fashions for how people should look, what they should wear, and what kinds of friendships they should have. These influences, and accompanying gender stereotypes, are particularly strong during adolescence. Children's cartoons, prime-time television, TV advertisements, and popular cable networks often depict males and females (as well as people of different races and ethnicities) in stereotyped ways. Teenage girls, for example, are likely to be depicted as boy crazy and obsessed with their looks; teenage boys are shown as active, independent, and sexually and physically aggressive (Kahlenberg & Hein, 2010; Maher, Herbst, Childs, & Finn, 2008; Ward & Aubrey, 2017). Females' roles also portray mostly familial or romantic ideals, whereas males fulfill work-related roles (Lauzen, Dozier, & Horan, 2008). These stereotypes have been found to influence children's gender perceptions (Aubrey & Harrison, 2004; Gerding & Signorielli, 2014). Additionally, gender stereotypes influence beliefs across the spectrum of sexual orientation, with gay teens embracing stereotypes in ways comparable to their heterosexual peers (Bishop, Kiss, Morrison, Rushe, & Specht, 2014).

Social media is among the newest agents of socialization, but its rise and reach have been spectacular. Consider recent research that shows how many hours per day teens

Television offers a variety of female images ranging from independent working women to "fashionistas." From the *Mary Tyler Moore Show* (1970–1977) to *Sex in the City* (1998–2004) to *Scandal* (2012–2018), images can both reflect and construct ideas about femininity.

are spending on the Internet: A Pew survey found that 45% of teen respondents indicated that they are online "almost constantly" and 44% are online "several times a day." In 2014–2015, the figures were 24% and 56%, respectively. While not all of this online time is spent on social media, the platforms Snapchat and Instagram have continued to gain young followers (Anderson & Jiang, 2018).

When online interactions are mixed with off-line face-to-face interactions, Internet use can foster new personal relationships and build stronger communities (Valentine, 2006; Wellman & Hampton, 1999). The types of friendships adolescents create and maintain through social media reflect the friendships they have off-line (Mazur & Richards, 2011). Since online interaction is often anonymous and occurs from the safety of familiar places, people with characteristics society tends to stigmatize, such as obesity or a stutter, can enter virtual communities where such differences are not perceived or punished (McKenna & Bargh, 1998) and interests such as chess or movies can be shared. Finally, the moderate use of e-mail and the Internet can help children and teens maintain and strengthen interpersonal relationships (Subrahmanyam & Lin, 2007).

The Internet can have negative social consequences, too. As we discuss elsewhere in the text, researchers have linked high levels of use with declines in communication within households, shrinking social circles, and increased depression and loneliness (Dokoupil, 2012a, 2012b; Kraut et al., 1998; Yen, Yen, & Ko, 2010). Extreme cases can develop into Internet addiction, a relatively recent phenomenon characterized by a search for social stimulation and escape from real-life problems (Armstrong, Phillips, & Saling, 2000; Block, 2008). Although the Internet can be a valuable learning tool for children, it can also damage their development by decreasing the time they spend in face-to-face interactions and exposing them to inappropriate information and images (Bremer & Rauch, 1998; Lewin, 2011b; Livingstone & Brake, 2010).

Another form of negative socialization is *cyberbullying*—taunting, teasing, or verbal attacks through e-mail, text, or social networking sites with the intent to hurt the victim (Van DeBosch & Van Cleemput, 2008). Cyberbullying is a problem of acute concern to social workers, child psychologists, and school administrators (Slovak & Singer, 2011). Children and adolescents who are bullied in real life are sometimes both cyberbullies and victims of cyberbullying (Dilmac, 2009; Smith et al., 2008; Tyman, Saylor, Taylor, & Comeaux, 2010). Victims take to the Internet to get revenge, often through anonymous attacks, but this perpetuates the bullying cycle online and in real life. One study found that hurtful cyber-teasing between adolescents in romantic relationships can escalate into real-life shouting, throwing of objects, or hitting (Madlock & Westerman, 2011).

Interestingly, teens, who are the most avid users of social media, are not in agreement on its larger effects. A recent study found that while 45% of teens indicated that the effects of social media were neither positive nor negative, 31% responded that the effects were mostly positive, citing connections with family and friends as the most positive aspect. At the same time, 24% categorized effects as mostly negative, citing bullying and rumor spreading as the worst aspect (Anderson & Jiang, 2018). How would you characterize the effects of social media on society? On your own life?

Work

For most adults in the United States, postadolescent socialization begins with entry into the workforce. Although workplace norms calling for conformity or individuality are frequently taught by parents in the home, expectations at work can differ from those we experience in primary groups such as the family and peer groups.

Arguably, workplace socialization has had a particular influence on women, dramatically changing gender roles in many countries, including the United States. Beginning in the 1960s, paid work afforded women increased financial independence, allowing them to marry later—or not at all—and bringing them new opportunities for social interaction and new social roles.

Employment also often socializes us into both the job role and our broader role as a member of a collective (sharing the same employer). Becoming a teacher, chef, factory worker, lawyer, or retail salesperson, for instance, requires learning specific skills and the norms, values, and practices associated with that position. In that role, the employee may also internalize the values and norms of the employer and may even come to identify with the employer: Notice that employees who are speaking about their workplaces will often refer to them rather intimately, saying, for instance, not that "*Company X* is hiring a new sales manager" but rather that "*we* are hiring a new sales manager."

Even "occupations" outside the bounds of legality are governed by rules and roles learned through socialization. Harry King, a professional thief studied by William J. Chambliss, learned not only how to break into buildings and open safes but also how to conform to the culture of the professional thief. A professional thief never "rats" on a partner, for example, or steals from mom-and-pop stores. In addition, King acquired a unique language that enabled him to talk to other thieves while in the company of nonthieves ("Square Johns"), police officers, and prison guards (King & Chambliss, 1984).

Socialization and Aging

Most theories of socialization focus on infancy, childhood, and adolescence, but people do not stop changing once they become adults. Work, social relationships, and the media, for example, shape socialization over the life course.

Some processes of life course socialization remain steady into older age. For example, today, as younger adults enter the workforce later, older adults are staying in the workforce longer. According to Pew Research, nearly 27% of U.S. adults ages 65 to 74 are in the workforce, a figure that is projected to rise to 32% by 2022 (Drake, 2014). This upward trend is driven by a variety of factors that include economic pressures to continue working for pay, the larger number of women in the workforce who are choosing to stay longer, and improving health in the senior population.

Other processes of life course socialization shift as adults get older. As people approach retirement, for instance, anticipatory socialization kicks in to help them envision their futures. Seniors may pay more attention to how friends react to retirement, whether they are treated differently as they age, and how older people are portrayed in the media. Notably, in U.S. media programming and advertisements, seniors are seriously underrepresented relative to their numbers in the nation's population. When they are presented, older characters are often shown positively, although they are also likely to be gender stereotyped and wealthier than in the real world (Kessler, Racoczy, & Staudinger, 2004; Lee, Carpenter, & Meyers, 2007). As well, there has been a pattern in Hollywood films of ignoring or mocking seniors' sexuality: An article in *The Atlantic* on this topic pointed out that

©Vincent Sandoval/WireImage/Getty Images

Meyrowitz (1985) writes that "old people are respected [in media portrayals] to the extent that they can behave like young people" (p. 153). Betty White is a highly recognized actress whose roles are often humorous and appealing to younger crowds. Think about portrayals of older persons you have seen recently in movies or on television. Do you agree with this assessment?

aging male actors are often relegated to "dirty old men" roles—but compared to older actresses, they have more opportunities to play people with active sex lives. It's just that they're usually having sex with younger women. The options for aging actresses are largely roles that in no way recognize their sexuality except as something that has faded, or those that depict them as deluded, wannabe sex kittens, fooling themselves about the extent of their sexual attractiveness. (Kelly, 2012, para. 6)

This observation underscores an earlier point that portrayals of seniors are often saturated with gender stereotypes but also that stereotypes about age (and youth bias) permeate mass media images of older adults.

There is a perception that seniors are more likely than younger adults to disengage from society, moving away from relationships, activities, and institutions that previously played key roles in their lives. Although this is the case for some seniors, research suggests that most remain active as long as they are healthy (Rubin, 2006). In fact, the notion that seniors are disengaged is belied by the fact that many adults become more politically active in their older years. Consider the fact that Americans 65 and older are more likely than any other age group to vote (Figure 4.5; Taylor & Lopez, 2013).

Older adults are also increasingly likely to be engaged in the digital world. Recent research shows that about 56% of adults 65 and older who go online use Facebook, a figure that represents nearly a third of seniors (Duggan, Ellison, Lampe, Lenhart, & Madden, 2015). Technology offers seniors a spectrum of ways to stay connected to family and friends and to meet new friends: Some research suggests that adults older than 60 are the fastest-growing segment of the online dating market. Accordingly, the Internet offers a variety of dating sites targeted specifically to older Americans who, according to researchers Wendy K. Watson and Claude Stelle,

appear to market themselves differently on online dating sites than younger adults. Gone is the focus on appearance and status . . . the senior population appears to be more interested in honest self-representation and being compatible rather than discussing areas such as sexual prowess and nightlife. (Bowling Green State University, 2012, para. 4)

Interestingly, age is not the only factor that influences technology use: Although younger seniors are more likely to use technology, use is also significantly affected by income and education. Overall, seniors with higher incomes and levels of education use technology more. For example, 81% of seniors whose household income is above $75,000 own smartphones, compared to 27% of those with earnings less than $30,000 (Anderson & Perrin, 2017).

As people age, health and dying also become increasingly important and influential in structuring their perceptions and interactions. Married couples face the prospect of losing a spouse, and all seniors may begin to lose close friends. The question of what it might be like to live alone is more urgent for women than for men since men, on average, die several years younger than women do. Very old people in particular are likely to spend time in the hospital or in a nursing home, which requires being socialized into a total institution (discussed below). Growing older is thus influenced by socialization as significant and challenging as in earlier life stages.

Clearly, socialization is a lifelong process. Our early primary socialization lays a foundation for our social selves, which continue to develop through processes of secondary socialization, including our interactions with technology, media, education, and work. But can we be resocialized? That is, can our social selves be torn down and reconstituted in new forms that conform to the norms, roles, and rules of entirely different social settings? We explore this question in the following section.

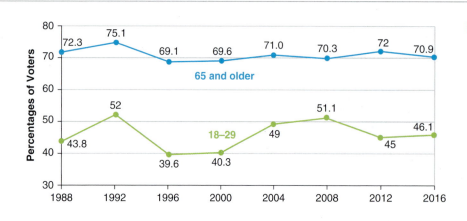

■ **FIGURE 4.5** Reported Voting Rates, 1988–2016

Source: File, Thom. "Voting in America: A Look at the 2016 Presidential Election." *United States Census Bureau.* n.p., 10 May 2017. Web. 22 May 2017. https://www.census.gov/newsroom/blogs/random-samplings/2017/05/voting_in_america.html.

Total Institutions and Resocialization

Although individuals typically play an active role in their own socialization, in one setting—the total institution—they experience little choice. **Total institutions** are *institutions that isolate individuals from the rest of society to achieve administrative control over most aspects of their lives.* Examples include prisons, the military, hospitals (especially mental hospitals), and live-in drug and alcohol treatment centers. Administrative control is achieved through rules that govern all aspects of daily life, from dress to schedules to interpersonal interactions. The residents of total institutions are subject to inflexible routines rigidly enforced by staff supervision (Goffman, 1961; Malacrida, 2005).

A major purpose of total institutions is **resocialization**, *the process of altering an individual's behavior through control of his or her environment.* Goffman (1961) referred to this as the "mortification of self," or the process of degrading and, over time, transforming the self of the individual subject to the discipline of the total institution. The first step is to break down the sense of self. In a total institution, every aspect of life is managed and monitored. The individual is stripped of identification with the outside world. Institutional haircuts, uniforms, round-the-clock

These marines are part of a total institution in which they are subject to regimentation and control of their daily activities by an authoritative body. They are expected to exhibit obedience to authority and to elevate the collective over the individual good.

inspections, and abuse, such as the harassment of new recruits to a military school, contribute to breaking down the individual's sense of self. In extreme situations, such as in concentration camps, psychological and even physical torture may also be used.

Once the institutionalized person is "broken," the institution begins rebuilding the personality. Desirable behaviors are rewarded with small privileges, such as choice of work duty in prisons. Undesirable behaviors are severely punished, such as by the assignment of humiliating or painful work chores. Since the goal of the total institution is to change attitudes as well as behaviors, even a hint that the resident continues to harbor undesirable ideas may provoke disciplinary action.

How effective are total institutions in resocializing individuals? The answer depends partly on the methods used, partly on the individual, and partly on peer pressure.

Total institutions: Institutions that isolate individuals from the rest of society to achieve administrative control over most aspects of their lives.

Resocialization: The process of altering an individual's behavior through control of his or her environment, for example, within a total institution.

Global Issues

PROXEMICS AND THE CULTURAL DIMENSIONS OF PERSONAL SPACE

How do you know how close or far to stand from someone when meeting for the first time? When initiating a conversation? When trying to win affection or trust? When conducting business?

The proximity that we choose, consciously or even unconsciously, is not necessarily natural or instinctive. Rather, it may be a product of our socialization. American anthropologist

(Continued)

(Continued)

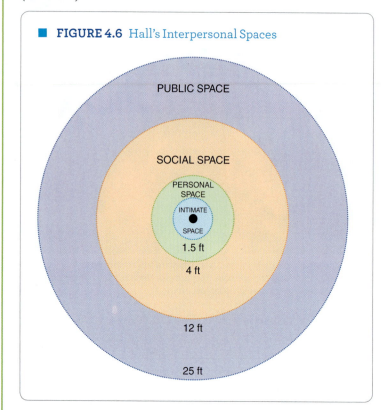

■ **FIGURE 4.6** Hall's Interpersonal Spaces

that aligns with hypotheses about "contact cultures" (South America, the Middle East, Southern Europe) and "noncontact cultures" (Northern Europe, North America, Asia) (Hall, 1966). At the same time, there were some interesting variations within the "contact" or "noncontact" cultures: For instance, while Romanians preferred significant distance from strangers, friends were welcome to move close, but their neighbors the Hungarians wanted to keep both strangers and friends at some distance. Argentinians and other South Americans needed less personal space than those from several other cultures, including those of Asian countries and the Middle Eastern country of Saudi Arabia (Sorokowska, et al., 2017).

It is not uncommon for businesses, agencies, or organizations that send representatives overseas to tutor them in the arts of nonverbal communication. For instance, while most Western cultures use a nod of the head to indicate "yes" and a shake of the head to indicate "no," a few European cultures, including Bulgarian, attribute opposite meanings to these nonverbal gestures. The recognition of personal space boundaries is among the topics in which would-be travelers are schooled: One consulting firm cautions that, "Violations of cultural preferences for personal space can be discomforting. If you are allowed more actual personal space than your cultural preference demands, you might regard your partner as being cold, shy, or unfriendly. If [your] personal [space] is too small, you might think that your partner is intrusive, rude, or even aggressive" (https://cultureplusconsulting .com/2015/06/15/cultural-differences-in-non-verbal-communication/). Learning—and sometimes relearning—the "rules" of social and spatial interaction is clearly part of our lifelong socialization in modern societies.

Think It Through

- Think about experiences you have had meeting people in or from other countries or even other regions of the country. Did you detect any differences in preferences of personal space?

Edward T. Hall studied *the human use of space*, a field he termed proxemics. Hall described four distinct zones of space (Figure 4.6) and hypothesized who is (and is not) permitted to enter the zones: for instance, the "intimate zone" is only for one's close friends, relatives, and significant others, while the next zone, "personal space," could be used by friends, colleagues, or classmates. Violations of space, he suggested, could lead to anger, discomfort, or anxiety (Hall, 1966).

Hall posited that distances of comfort could vary by culture and country, and a recent study underscores this observation. In the study, researchers asked 8,943 respondents in 42 countries to indicate on a graph showing two figures how they identified appropriate personal distances between themselves, their intimates, and strangers. Across cultures, some commonalties emerged: For instance, in nearly all countries, women preferred more distance from strangers than men. Older respondents wanted more space than younger respondents. But there were also important differences: They found, for instance, that respondents from countries with warmer climates were more tolerant of close proximity than those from colder climates, a determination

In the most extreme total institutions, Nazi concentration camps, some inmates came to identify with their guards and torturers, even helping them keep other prisoners under control. Most, however, resisted resocialization until their death or release (Bettelheim, 1979).

Prisons often fail at resocialization because inmates identify more with their fellow prisoners than with the administration's agenda. Inmates in U.S. prisons may well be resocialized, but it is not likely to be to the norms of prison officials or the wider society. Rather, prisoners learn the norms of other prisoners, and as a result, many come out of prison more hardened in their criminal behavior than before.

Even when an institution is initially successful at resocialization, individuals who return to their original social environments often revert to earlier behavior. This reversal confirms that socialization is an ongoing process, continuing throughout a person's lifetime as a result of changing patterns of social interaction.

Social Interaction

Socialization at every stage of life occurs primarily through *social interaction*—interaction guided by the ordinary, taken-for-granted rules that enable people to live, work, and socialize together (Ridgeway & Smith-Lovin, 1999). Spoken words, gestures, body language, and other symbols and cues come together in complex ways to enable human communication. The sociologist must look behind the everyday aspects of social interaction to identify how it unfolds and how social norms and language make it possible.

Social interaction usually requires conformity to social conventions. According to Scheff (1966), violation of the norms of interaction is generally interpreted as a sign that the person is abnormal, perhaps even dangerous. A person in a crowded elevator who persists in engaging strangers in loud conversations, for example, and disheveled homeless people who shuffle down the street muttering to themselves evoke anxiety if not repugnance.

Norms govern a wide range of interactive behaviors. For example, making eye contact when speaking to someone is valued in mainstream U.S. culture; people who don't make eye contact are considered dishonest and shifty. By contrast, among the Navajo and the Australian Aborigines, as well as in many East Asian cultures, direct eye contact is considered disrespectful, especially with a person of greater authority. Norms also govern how close we stand to friends and strangers in making conversation. In North American and Northern European cultures, people avoid standing closer than a couple of feet from one another unless they are on intimate terms (Hall, 1973). Men in the United States are socialized to avoid displays of intimacy with other men, such as walking arm in arm. In Nigeria, however, men who are close friends or relatives hold hands when walking together, while in Italy, Spain, Greece, and some Middle Eastern countries, men commonly throw their arms around each other's shoulders, hug, and even kiss.

Two different approaches to studying social interaction are Erving Goffman's metaphor of interaction as theater and conversation analysts' efforts to study the way people manage routine talk. We discuss these approaches later, but first we look briefly at some sociologists' studies of social interaction.

Studies of Social Interaction

Studies of social interaction have frequently drawn on the symbolic interactionist perspective. They illuminate nearly every form and aspect of social interaction. For example, research on battered women shows how victims of domestic violence redefine their situations to come to grips with abusive relationships (Hattery, 2001). One strategy is to deny the partner's violent behavior altogether, whereas another is to minimize the partner's responsibility, attributing it to external factors such as unemployment, alcoholism, or mental illness. Or the victim will define her own role as caretaker and assume responsibility for "saving" the abusive partner. A woman who eventually decides to leave an abusive relationship must, some research suggests, redefine her situation so as to change her self-image. She must come to see herself as a victim of abuse who is capable of ending the abusive relationship, rather than as someone responsible for "solving" her mate's "problem" (Johnson & Ferraro, 1984).

Recent studies of social interaction have covered many topics, including the following:

- The way online gamers coordinate their individual actions with one another and through the user interface to succeed at games such as World of Warcraft (Williams & Kirschner, 2012)

- The strategies homeless youth use to manage and alleviate stigma, including creating friendships or attempting to pass as nonhomeless, as well as acting aggressive and fighting back (Roschelle & Kaufman, 2004)

- The ways in which a sense of "corporate social responsibility" is promoted and learned by corporate executives in the work environment (Shamir, 2011)

Discover & Debate

HOW MUCH HOMEWORK?

Motion: Students in Grades K–12 have too much homework. Homework should be banned.

Background: Since the beginning of formal mass schooling in the United States, the use of homework as a key educational tool has been alternately embraced and frowned on by educators and parents as well as by students. In the mid-1950s, the launch of the Sputnik satellite by the Soviet Union raised concerns about U.S. competitiveness, spurring efforts to bring greater academic rigor into the education system. On the other hand, the late 1960s brought rising parental concern that homework was crowding out children's outdoor recreation and creative activities. In the 1980s, the National Commission on Excellence in Education's report, *A Nation at Risk* (1983), spurred new concerns and a renewed belief in the value of homework. By the end of the century, there was a push for more homework. By the end of the century, there was again a backlash against high levels of homework, particularly in the lower grades. The debate over homework and how much is too much continues to invite discussion and disagreement.

Questions for Consideration

- Are widely available Internet offerings such as term paper writing services affecting the effectiveness of homework assignments?

- Does homework create opportunities for cooperative interaction when students ask for help or advice from friends, siblings, or parents? Or does it isolate busy students from family and social activities?

- How does the U.S. experience compare with that of other countries? What are standard homework practices in other countries, and how does student academic performance in those countries compare to that in the United States?

Debate Tip

- It is important to know your argument but be flexible with it. Be a good listener, and take note of the arguments presented by the other team that you did not consider. Flexibility enhances the ability to respond to new ideas being brought up during the debate while linking them to your original argument.

AFFIRMATIVE ARGUMENTS	OPPOSITION ARGUMENTS
Students spend about 7 hours a day at school during the school year. Many students also participate in after-school activities such as sports, clubs, or jobs and want to spend time with their families. Homework adds to young people's stress and time burdens.	Students learn through practice and repetition. Homework is an opportunity to review materials and to improve retention of materials.
In the younger grades, homework often requires parental supervision and support, creating a burden for parents, who may be busy with work or other obligations.	Homework is needed, beginning in the early grades, to establish good study and time management habits that students will need in higher grades and in college.
Homework can dull rather than encourage student enthusiasm for learning, particularly if tasks are rote rather than creative.	Homework gives parents an opportunity to play a role in a child's education and helps them to evaluate a child's progress.

The Dramaturgical Approach: Erving Goffman

Erving Goffman (1959, 1961, 1963a, 1967, 1972), a major figure in the study of social interaction, developed a set of theoretical ideas that make it possible to observe and describe social interaction. Goffman used what he termed the **dramaturgical approach**, *the study of social interaction as if it were governed by the practices of theatrical performance.*

According to Goffman, people in their everyday lives are concerned, similar to actors on a stage, with the

Dramaturgical approach: Developed by Erving Goffman, the study of social interaction as if it were governed by the practices of theatrical performance.

presentation of self, *the creation of impressions in the minds of others to define and control social situations.* For instance, to serve many customers simultaneously, a waiter must take charge with a "presentation of self" that is polite but firm and does not allow customers to usurp control by taking too much time ordering. After only a short time, the waiter asserts control by saying, "I'll give you a few minutes to decide what you want" and walks away.

As people interact, they monitor themselves and each other, looking for clues that reveal the impressions they are making on others. This ongoing effort at impression management results in a continual realignment of the individuals' "performances" as the "actors" refit their roles using dress, objects, voice, and gestures in a joint enterprise.

Continuing the metaphor of a theatrical performance, Goffman divides spheres of interaction into two stages. In the *front stage,* we are social actors engaged in a process of impression management through the use of props, costumes, gestures, and language. A professor lecturing to her class, a young couple on their first date, and a job applicant in an interview all are governed by existing social norms, so the professor will not arrive in her nightgown, nor will the prospective employee greet his interviewer with a high-five rather than with a handshake. Just as actors in a play must stick to their scripts, so too, suggests Goffman, do we as social actors risk consequences (such as failed interactions) if we diverge from the normative script.

Goffman offers insights into the techniques we as social actors have in our repertoire. Among them are the following:

- *Dramatic realization* is the actor's effort to mobilize his or her behavior to draw attention to a particular characteristic of the role he or she is assuming. What impression does a baseball umpire strive to leave on his audience (the teams and fans)? Arguably, he would like to embody authority, so he makes his calls loudly and with bold gestures.

- *Idealization* is an actor's effort to embody in his or her behaviors the officially accredited norms and values of a community or society. Those with fewer economic resources might purchase faux designer bags or watches to conform to perceived societal expectations of material wealth.

- *Misrepresentation* is part of every actor's repertoire, ranging from kind deception (telling a friend she looks great when she doesn't) to self-interested untruth (telling a professor a paper was lost in a computer crash when it was never written) to bald-faced prevarication (lying to conceal an affair). The actor wants to maintain a desired impression in the eyes of the audience: The friend would like to be perceived as kind and supportive, the student as conscientious and hardworking, and the spouse as loyal and loving.

- *Mystification* is largely reserved for those with status and power and serves to maintain distance from the audience to keep people in awe. Corporate leaders keep their offices on a separate floor and don't mix with employees, while celebrities may avoid interviews and allow their on-screen roles to define them as savvy and smart.

We may also engage in impression management as a team. A team consists of two or more actors cooperating to create a definition of the situation favorable to them. For example, members of a sports team work together, although some may be more skilled than others, to convey a definition of themselves as a highly competent and competitive group. Or the members of a family may work together to convey to their dinner guests that they are content and happy by acting cooperatively and smiling at one another during the group interaction.

The example of the family gives us an opportunity to explore Goffman's concept of the *back stage,* where actors let down their masks and relax or even practice their impression management. Before the dinner party, the home is a back stage. One parent is angry at the other for getting cheap rather than expensive wine; one sibling refuses to speak to the parent who grounded her; and the other won't stop texting long enough to set the table. Then the doorbell rings. Like magic, the home becomes the front stage as the adults smilingly welcome their guests and the kids begin to carry out trays of snacks and drinks. The guests may or may not sense some tension in the home, but they play along with the scenario so as not to create discomfort. When the party ends, the home reverts to the back stage, and each actor can relax his or her performance.

Goffman's work, similar to Mead's and the work of other sociologists focusing on socialization, sees the social self as an outcome of society and social interactions. Goffman, however, characterizes the social self not as a *possession*—a dynamic but still essentially real self—but rather as a *product* of a given social interaction, which can change as we seek to manage impressions for different audiences. Would you say that Mead or Goffman offers a better characterization of us as social actors?

Presentation of self: The creation of impressions in the minds of others to define and control social situations.

Ethnomethodology and Conversation Analysis

Routine, day-to-day social interactions are the building blocks of social institutions and ultimately of society itself. **Ethnomethodology** is used to study *the body of commonsense knowledge and procedures by which ordinary members of a society make sense of their social circumstances and interactions. Ethno* refers to "folk" or ordinary people; *methodology* refers to the methods they use to govern interaction—which are as distinct as the methods used by sociologists to study them. Ethnomethodology was created through Harold Garfinkel's

The film *The Wizard of Oz* offers a good example of mystification. Although the wizard is really, in his own words, "just a man," he maintains his status in Oz by hiding behind a curtain and using a booming voice and fiery mask to convey the impression of awesome power.

work in the early 1960s. Garfinkel (1963, 1985) sought to understand exactly what goes on in social interactions after observing that our interpretation of social interaction depends on the context. For example, if a child on a playground grabs another child's ball and runs with it, the teacher may see this as a sign of the child's aggressiveness, while fellow students see it as a display of courage. Social interaction and communication are not possible unless most people have learned to assign similar meanings to the same interactions. By studying the specific contexts of concrete social interactions, Garfinkel sought to understand how people come to share the same interpretations of social interactions.

Garfinkel also believed that in all cultures, people expect others to talk in a way that is coherent and understandable and become anxious and upset when this does not happen. Making sense of one another's conversations is even more fundamental to social life than cultural norms, Garfinkel argued, since without ways of arriving at meaningful understandings, communication, and hence culture, is not possible. Because the procedures that determine how we make sense of conversations are so important to social interaction, another field developed from ethnomethodology that focuses on talk itself: conversation analysis.

Conversation analysis investigates *the way participants in social interaction recognize and produce coherent conversation* (Schegloff, 1990, 1991). In this context, *conversation*

includes about any form of verbal communication, from routine small talk to emergency phone calls to congressional hearings and court proceedings (Heritage & Greatbatch, 1991; Hopper, 1991; Whalen & Zimmerman, 1987, 1990; Zimmerman, 1984, 1992).

Conversation analysis research suggests that social interaction is not simply a random succession of events. Rather, people construct conversations through a reciprocal process that makes the interaction coherent. One way in which we sequentially organize conversations is *turn taking,* a strategy that allows us to understand an utterance as a response to an earlier one and a cue to take our turn in the conversation. A person's turn ends once the other conversants indicate they have understood the message. For example, by answering "Fine" to the question "How are you?" you show that you have understood the question and are ready to move ahead.

On the other hand, answering "What do you mean?" or "Green" to the question "How are you?" is likely to lead to conversational breakdown. Conversational analysts have identified several techniques commonly used to repair such breakdowns. For example, if you begin speaking but realize midsentence that the other person is already speaking, you can repair this awkward situation by pausing until the original speaker finishes his or her turn and then restarting your turn.

Later research emphasized the impact of the larger social structure on conversations (Wilson, 1991). Sociologists looked at the use of power in conversations, including the power of the dispatcher over the caller in emergency phone calls (Whalen, Zimmerman, & Whalen, 1990; Zimmerman, 1984, 1992), of the questioner over the testifier

---

Ethnomethodology: A sociological method used to study the body of commonsense knowledge and procedures by which ordinary members of a society make sense of their social circumstances and interaction.

Conversation analysis: The study of how participants in social interaction recognize and produce coherent conversation.

in governmental hearings (Molotch & Boden, 1985), and of men over women in male–female interactions (Campbell, Klein, & Olson, 1992; Fishman, 1978; West, 1979; West & Zimmerman, 1977, 1983; Zimmerman & West, 1975, 1980). The last instance, in particular, illustrates how the larger social structure—in this case, gender structure—affects conversation. Even at the most basic and personal level—a private conversation between two people—social structures exercise a potentially powerful influence.

Why Study Socialization and Social Interaction?

Have you ever wondered why you and some of your classmates or neighbors differ in worldviews, coping strategies for stress, or values concerning right and wrong? Understanding socialization and social interaction sheds light on such differences and what they mean to us in everyday life. For example, if you travel abroad, you will have a sense of how cultural differences come to be and appreciate

that no culture is more "normal" than another—each has its own norms, values, and roles taught from earliest childhood.

By studying socialization, you also come to understand the critical socializing roles that peers, schools, and work environments play in the lives of children, adolescents, and young adults. The growing influence of the mass media, including the Internet and other technological innovations in communication, means we must pay close attention to these sources of socialization and social interaction as well. As people spend more time on the Internet talking to friends and strangers, experimenting with new identities, and seeking new forms of and forums for social interaction, sociologists may need to rethink some of their ideas about the influence of agents such as parents and schools; perhaps these may recede in importance—or grow. Sociologists also ask how our presentation of self is transformed when we create social selves in the anonymous space of social media. What kinds of research could you imagine conducting to learn more about the digital world as an agent of socialization and a site of modern social interaction?

 # What Can I Do with a Sociology Degree?

INTERPERSONAL SKILLS

Interpersonal skills are those that allow for constructive, effective communication and relationships between two or more people. The development of interpersonal skills may seem increasingly irrelevant in a world of telework and where more and more of our interactions occur via impersonal devices and even anonymous social media posts. But unless you are a lone worker in a remote outpost, your job will inevitably require some amount of interpersonal interaction. Sociology not only provides a conceptual framework for understanding the nature of social interactions (Chapters 4 and 5), but it also nurtures the development of important interpersonal skills essential to the workplace. The sociological imagination (Chapter 1) gives us perspective—on ourselves and others. Understanding that our locations in the social structure impact who we are, what we have, and how we think is an important step in building more effective relationships with individuals, groups, and communities. It helps to clarify our own biases and assumptions.

The study of sociology also increases *perspective taking*, or the ability to put yourself in someone

else's shoes. Sociology can help illuminate cultural differences in communication and interaction, the understanding of which can prevent misunderstandings or misconceptions. For example, rather than assuming that a quiet student is unengaged or a parent who doesn't come to Parent-Teacher Association meetings is uninvolved, a teacher may question whether cultural differences regarding the teacher-student role or access to transportation or translation services is preventing involvement. This can help increase empathy and cultural competence and decrease prejudice, stereotyping, and discrimination. Sociology seeks to ask questions rather than make assumptions about people's motivations and behaviors. Understanding diverse perspectives is the first step in being able to work effectively across differences. By helping to illuminate sources of difference and conflict, and encouraging dialogue across those differences (of race, class, religion, age, gender, and sexuality), sociology can foster important communication and conflict resolution skills that facilitate not just interpersonal but also intergroup relationships. These are all essential skills when working with others to accomplish a task and build community in the workplace.

(Continued)

(Continued)

Devin Frawley, Social Services Assistant at Consulate Health Care

Florida Gulf Coast University, BA in Sociology

My sister was diagnosed with bipolar depression at the age of 16. At that time, I was studying at Florida Gulf Coast University in Fort Myers, Florida. I spent most of my freshman year of college driving to and from Orlando (where my family lived) to visit my sister in numerous hospitalizations. I watched as my sister's mental illness consumed the lives of each and every one of my family members, and I watched as my sister fell further and further into a place so dark we didn't know if light could be reached. My parents finally admitted her to a rehabilitation center, which saved my sister's life and ignited my passion. I was taking introduction to sociology classes at the time, as an undeclared major, and started connecting themes within the courses to issues involving mental illness, which is a widespread problem in our country. I wrote a couple of papers on the subject and even did my course project on social issues related to mental illness, using my sociological imagination to make the connection between private troubles and public issues. By the end of the semester, my sister was healing rapidly, and I had officially declared myself a sociology major.

I now hold the position of social services assistant at a subacute rehabilitation center. My job duties include attaining resources for residents as well as residents' family members. I was asked a question during my interview: "Why a career in social services at a rehabilitation center?" I answered the question honestly, telling my supervisor this story and how, ultimately, I felt I could better benefit the lives of others due to my experience as one of those "others" myself. I used my interpersonal skills to acquire the position by explaining that my sense of place, location, and life experiences have prepared me for this role. My supervisor later told me I had an outstanding interview and that although I didn't have as much experience as the other candidates, she could tell I was more driven and motivated by this field of work than the other candidates. I credit landing the position to an important aspect of my degree in sociology: the acquisition of interpersonal skills.

Career Data: Social and Human Service Assistant

- 2017 Median Pay: $33,120 per year
- $15.92 per hour
- Typical Entry-Level Education: High School degree or equivalent
- Job Outlook: 16% (Much faster than average)

Source: Bureau of Labor Statistics, *Occupational Outlook Handbook*, 2017.

SUMMARY

- **Socialization** is a lifelong, active process by which people learn the cultures of their societies and construct a sense of who they are.

- What we often think of as "human nature" is, in fact, learned through socialization. Sociologists argue that human behavior is not determined biologically, although biology plays some role; rather, human behavior develops primarily through social interaction.

- Although some theories emphasize the early years, sociologists generally argue that socialization takes place throughout the life course. The theories of Sigmund Freud and Jean Piaget emphasize the early years, while those of George Herbert Mead, Lawrence Kohlberg, and Judith Harris give more consideration to the whole life course (although Mead's **role-taking** theory focuses on the earlier stages of the life course). According to Mead,

children acquire a sense of self through symbolic interaction, including the role-taking that eventually enables the adult to take the standpoint of society as a whole.

- Kohlberg built on Piaget's ideas to argue that a person's sense of morality develops through different stages, from that in which people strictly seek personal gain or seek to avoid punishment to the stage in which they base moral decisions on abstract principles.

- The immediate family provides the earliest and typically foremost source of socialization, but school, work, peers, religion, sports, and mass media, including the Internet, all play a significant role.

- Socialization may differ by social class. Middle-class families place a somewhat greater emphasis on creativity and independence, while working-class families often stress obedience to authority. These differences, in turn, reflect the corresponding workplace differences associated with social class.

- In **total institutions**, such as prisons, the military, and hospitals, individuals are isolated so that society can achieve administrative control over their lives. By enforcing rules that govern all aspects of daily life, from dress to schedules to interpersonal interactions, total institutions can open the way to **resocialization**, which is the breaking down of the person's sense of self and the rebuilding of the personality.

- According to Erving Goffman's **dramaturgical approach**, we are all actors concerned with the **presentation of self**

in social interaction. People perform their social roles on the "front stage" and are able to avoid performing on the "back stage."

- **Ethnomethodology** is a method of analysis that examines the body of commonsense knowledge and procedures by which ordinary members of a society make sense of their social circumstances and interaction.

- **Conversation analysis**, which builds on ethnomethodology, is the study of the way participants in social interaction recognize and produce coherent conversation.

KEY TERMS

socialization, 87	role-taking, 89	hidden curriculum, 95
behaviorism, 88	significant others, 90	anticipatory socialization, 97
social learning, 88	generalized other, 90	total institutions, 103
looking-glass self, 88	cognitive development, 90	resocialization, 103
primary groups, 88	egocentric, 90	dramaturgical approach, 106
secondary groups, 89	psychoanalysis, 91	presentation of self, 107
reference groups, 89	id, 92	ethnomethodology, 108
I, 89	ego, 92	conversation analysis, 108
me, 89	superego, 92	

DISCUSSION QUESTIONS

1. What are agents of socialization? What agents of socialization do sociologists identify as particularly important? Which of these would you say have the most profound effects on the construction of our social selves? Make a case to support your choices.

2. The United States is a country where sports are an important part of many people's lives—many Americans enjoy playing sports, while others follow their favorite sports teams closely in the media. How are sports an agent of socialization? What roles, norms, or values are conveyed through this agent of socialization? Does this vary by sport?

3. What role does the way people react to you play in the development of your personality and your self-image?

How can the reactions of others influence whether or not you develop skills as an athlete or a student or a musician, for example?

4. Recall Goffman's ideas about social interaction and the presentation of self. How have social media sites such as Facebook, Snapchat, and Instagram affected the presentation of self? Have there been changes to what Goffman saw as our front and back stages?

5. What are the key characteristics of total institutions such as prisons and mental institutions? How does socialization in a total institution differ from ordinary socialization?

Want a better grade?

Get the tools you need to sharpen your study skills. Access practice quizzes, eFlashcards, videos, and multimedia at **https://edge.sagepub.com/chambliss4e**.

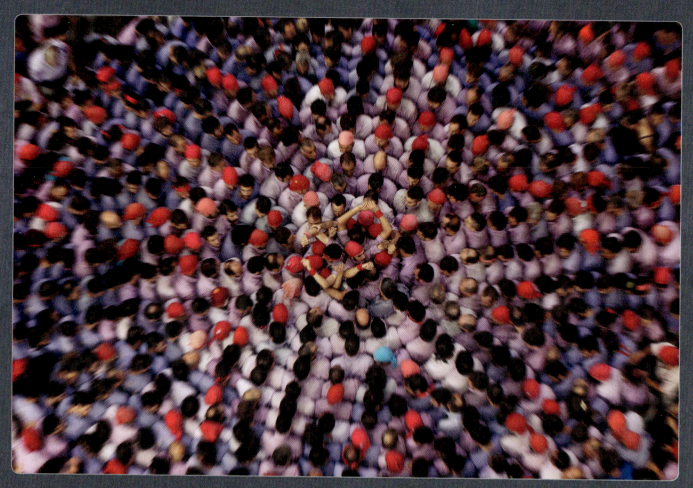

Groups, Organizations, and Bureaucracies

5

WHAT DO YOU THINK?

1. Do most people conform to the expectations of the groups to which they belong? What explains conformity? What explains dissent?

2. Why do many people think of bureaucracies as inefficient and annoying? What would be the alternative?

3. Could a group of college students working together on a societal issue such as rising student debt, child hunger, or veteran homelessness bring about significant social change?

LEARNING OBJECTIVES

5.1 Describe primary and secondary groups and their effects.

5.2 Discuss the power of groups in terms of their composition, leadership, and conformity.

5.3 Explain the sociological concepts of economic, cultural, and social capital.

5.4 Describe three types of formal organizations.

5.5 Apply a sociological lens to modern bureaucracies.

GROUPTHINK: A CASE OF DEADLY CONSEQUENCES

If a friend, classmate, or member of your club or team was seriously injured, what would you do? It is likely that most people would respond by calling for emergency assistance. Under some circumstances, however, this fails to happen. Consider the case of Penn State University student Timothy Piazza. In 2017, Timothy was a sophomore student pledging the Beta Theta Psi fraternity. After a night of heavy drinking with his fraternity brothers, the young man tumbled down the steps of the frat house, resulting in a traumatic brain injury. According to a news account of the incident, "as he drifted in and out of consciousness, about 20 brothers failed to dial 911 or get outside help from the Penn State University campus—waiting 12 harrowing hours before one of them finally called emergency responders" (Ortiz & Lubell, 2017, para. 2). Two days later, Timothy was dead. Why did no one call for help sooner when immediate medical intervention might have saved him?

©AP Photo/Gene J. Puskar

The case is complex, and a spectrum of answers to these questions may be offered. One possibility, however, is that *groupthink* played a role. The term was coined in the 1950s and highlights the idea that members of a group choose to elevate consensus and conformity—and preservation of the group—above other values. According to Professor Alan Reifman of Texas Tech University,

> Leaders of a group become committed to a course of action—in this case, making feckless attempts to revive Mr. Piazza without calling the authorities—and follow through on it with great single-mindedness. . . . In groupthink, many of the group members appear to be on the "same page" in executing the plan, but if there is any dissent, it is suppressed. (Ortiz & Lubell, 2017, para. 9)

Indeed, in this instance, one young man entreated the others to allow him to take Timothy to the hospital, but he was dismissed.

When decisions are based primarily on how other group members will react, rather than on ethical, professional, legal, or medical considerations, groupthink can—as this case shows—lead to devastating outcomes. The influence of the group can foster deviance—but at the same time, group bonds are fundamental to our lives and a key part of socialization and social integration. The roles that groups play in society are clearly complex, and they are a key focus of sociological study.

We begin this chapter with an overview of the nature of social groups, looking at primary and secondary groups and their effects on our lives. We also examine the power of groups in fostering integration and enforcing conformity, among other key functions. We then turn to a discussion of the importance of capital in social group formation and action, followed by an exploration of the place of organizations in society. Next, we address a topic about which sociologist Max Weber wrote extensively and with which we all have some experience—bureaucracies. We end the chapter with a consideration of the modern roles of governmental and nongovernmental organizations in the pursuit of social change.

The Nature of Groups

The male elephant is a solitary creature, spending much of its life wandering alone, interacting with other elephants only when it is time to mate or if another male intrudes on its territory. Female elephants, by contrast, live their lives in groups. Both male and female human beings are similar to the female elephant: We are social animals who live our entire lives in the company of others. Our lives are social, and we can better understand them by looking at the types of groups with which we are associated. Each of us is born into an emotionally and biologically connected group we know as *the family*. As we mature, we become increasingly interconnected with other people, some our own age and others not, at school, on sports teams, and through various

Secondary groups may evolve into primary groups for some members. For example, when young people who play together on a sports team begin to socialize away from the field or court, they may form bonds of friendship that come to constitute a primary group.

TABLE 5.1   The Characteristics of Primary and Secondary Groups

CHARACTERISTIC	PRIMARY GROUP	SECONDARY GROUP
Social distance of relationships	Low: face-to-face	High: indirect, remote
Intimacy	High: "fusion of personalities"	Low: relatively impersonal
Importance in forming the social self	Fundamental: earliest complete experience of social unity	Secondary: occurs later in life, no all-embracing experience of social unity
Degree of mutual identification with others	High: "we"	Low: "they"
Degree of permanence	High: change but slowly over time	Low: likely to change over time
Examples	Family; children's playgroups; neighborhood and community groups; clubs, fraternities, and sororities	Secondary schools, colleges, and universities; businesses and other workplaces; government agencies; bureaucracies of all sorts

other social interactions and increasingly via the Internet and social media. We consolidate and accumulate friends, teammates, and classmates—different groups with whom we interact on a regular basis. Eventually, we get jobs and engage with coworkers and other people we encounter in the course of our work. Along the way, we may form and maintain friendship groups, either in person or virtually, that share our interests in particular activities or lifestyles, such as poker, model airplanes, or music. Sometimes we are part of groups that gather for special events, such as watching a college football game or attending a presidential inauguration or political demonstration.

A moment's reflection on these types of groups reveals that they differ in many important ways, particularly in the degree of intimacy and social support their members experience. Sociologists distinguish between *primary* and *secondary* groups. *Primary groups* are characterized by intense emotional ties, intimacy, and identification with membership in the group. *Secondary groups* are large, impersonal groups with minimal emotional and intimate ties (Cooley, 1909). Interestingly, the Internet is increasingly blurring the boundary distinctions between primary and secondary groups—very large, ostensibly impersonal groups can take on an intimate feeling thanks to the power of virtual communication and information sharing.

Primary groups are of significance because they exert a long-lasting influence on the development of our social selves (Cooley, 1902/1964). Charles Horton Cooley (1864–1929), who first introduced the distinction between primary and secondary groups, argued that people belong to primary groups mainly because these groups satisfy personal needs of belonging and fulfillment. People become part of secondary groups such as business organizations, schools, work groups, athletic clubs, and governmental

bodies to achieve specific goals: to earn a living, to get a college degree, to compete in sports, and so on. (For a summary of the characteristics of primary and secondary groups, see Table 5.1.)

The Power of Groups

As you learned in Chapter 4, we often judge ourselves by how we think we appear to others, which Cooley termed the *looking-glass self*. Groups as well as individuals provide the standards by which we make these self-evaluations. Robert K. Merton (1968), following Herbert Hyman (1942), elaborated on the concept of the *reference group* as a measure by which we evaluate ourselves. Importantly, a reference group provides a standard for judging our own attitudes or behaviors.

For most of us, the family is the reference group with the greatest impact in shaping our early view of ourselves. As we mature, and particularly during adolescence, peers replace or at least compete with the family as the reference group through which we define ourselves. Today, thanks to the growth of social media, many people establish virtual reference groups and intimate primary groups with people they have never seen face-to-face.

Reference groups may be primary, such as the family, or secondary, such as a group of soldiers in the same branch of service in the military. They may even be fictional. One of the chief functions of advertising, for example, is to create sets of imaginary reference groups that will influence consumers' buying habits. We are invited to purchase a particular vehicle or fragrance, for instance, in order to join an ostensibly exclusive group of sophisticated, sexy consumers of that item. Reference groups can have powerful effects on our purchasing as well as on our other social actions.

Does Size Matter?

Another significant way in which groups differ has to do with their size. The German sociologist Georg Simmel (1858–1918) was one of the first to call attention to the influence of group size on people's behavior. Since Simmel's time, small-group researchers have conducted a number of laboratory experiments to discover how group size affects both the quality of interaction in the group and the group's effectiveness in accomplishing certain tasks (Levine & Crowther, 2008; Lucas & Lovaglia, 1998).

The simplest group, which Simmel (1955) called a **dyad**, *consists of two persons.* Simmel reasoned that dyads, which offer both intimacy and conflict, are likely to be simultaneously intense and unstable. To survive, they require the full attention and cooperation of both parties. Dyads are typically the sources of our most elementary social bonds, often constituting the groups in which we are most likely to share our deepest secrets. The commitment two people make through marriage is one way to form a dyadic group. But dyads can also be very fragile. If one person withdraws from the dyad, it vanishes. That is why, as Simmel believed, a variety of cultural and legal norms arise to support dyadic groups, including marriage, in societies where such groups are regarded as an important source of social stability.

Adding one other person to a dyad changes the group relationship considerably, making what Simmel termed a **triad**. Triads are apt to be more stable than dyads, since the presence of a third person relieves some of the pressure on the other two members to always get along and maintain the energy of the relationship. One person can temporarily withdraw his or her attention from the relationship without necessarily threatening it. In addition, if two members have a disagreement, the third can play the role of mediator, as when you try to patch up a falling-out between two friends or coworkers (see Figure 5.1).

On the other hand, however, an **alliance (or coalition)** *may form between two members of a triad, enabling them to "gang up" on the third member, thereby destabilizing the group.* Alliances are most likely to form when no member is clearly dominant and all three are competing for the same thing—for example, when three friends are given a pair of tickets to a concert and have to decide which two will go. Larger groups share some of the characteristics of triads. For instance, on *Lost* or in *Lord of the Flies,* alliances form within the group of survivors as individuals forge special

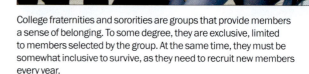

College fraternities and sororities are groups that provide members a sense of belonging. To some degree, they are exclusive, limited to members selected by the group. At the same time, they must be somewhat inclusive to survive, as they need to recruit new members every year.

©Steve Skjold/Alamy Stock Photo

relationships with one another to get access to greater power or resources for survival.

Theoretically, in forming an alliance, a triad member is most likely to choose the weaker of the two other members, if there is one. But why would this be the case if picking a stronger member would strengthen the alliance? Choosing a weaker member enables the member seeking to form the alliance to exercise more power and control within the alliance. However, in some revolutionary coalitions, the two weaker members form an alliance to overthrow the stronger one (Goldstone, 2001; Grusky, Bonacich, & Webster, 1995).

Going from a dyad to a triad illustrates an important sociological principle first identified by Simmel: *As group size increases, the intensity of relationships within the group decreases while overall group stability increases.* There are exceptions to every principle, however. Intensity of interaction among individuals within a group decreases as the size of the group increases because, for instance, a larger number of outlets or alternative arenas for interaction exist for individuals who are not getting along (Figure 5.2). In a dyad, only a single relationship is possible; however, in a triad, three different two-person relationships can occur. Adding a fourth person leads to six possible two-person relationships, not counting subgroups that may form. In a 10-person group, the number of possible two-person relationships increases to 45! When one relationship doesn't work out to your liking, you can easily move on to another, as you sometimes may do at large parties.

Larger groups tend to be more stable than smaller ones because the withdrawal of some members does not threaten the survival of the entire group. For example, sports teams do not cease to exist simply because of the loss of one player, even though that player might have been important to the team's overall success. Beyond a certain size, perhaps a dozen

---

Dyad: A group consisting of two persons.

Triad: A group consisting of three persons.

Alliance (or coalition): A subgroup that forms between group members, enabling them to dominate the group in their own interest.

■ **FIGURE 5.1** A Dyad and a Triad

Dyad Relationship

Triad Relationship

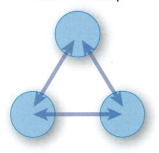

■ **FIGURE 5.2** A Complex Network of Relationships

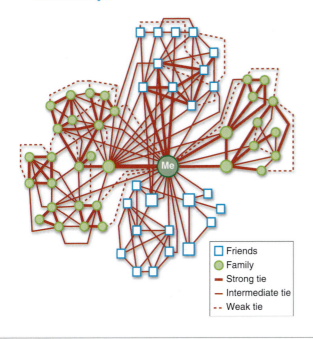

Friends
Family
— Strong tie
— Intermediate tie
--- Weak tie

This sense of being part of an in-group or clique is often what unites the members of fraternities, sororities, and other campus organizations. Cliquishness is especially likely to occur when a group consists of members who are similar to one another in such social characteristics as age, gender, class, race, or ethnicity. Members of rich families, for example, may sometimes be reluctant to fraternize with people from the working class; men may prefer to play basketball only with other men; and students who belong to a particular ethnic group may seek out each other's company in the dormitory or cafeteria. The concept of **social closure**, originally developed by Max Weber, is especially relevant here, insofar as it speaks to the *ability of a group to strategically and consciously exclude outsiders or those deemed "undesirable" from participating in the group or enjoying the group's resources* (Murphy, 1988; Parkin, 1979).

Groups don't always exclude outsiders, however (Blau, 1977; Stolle, 1998). For example, if your social group or club is made up of members from different social classes or ethnic groups, you are more likely to appreciate diversity thanks to your firsthand experience. This experience with difference may perhaps lead you to be more inclusive of others not like yourself in other aspects of your life; for example, in bringing together a group to work on a project. This, of course, is an optimistic outlook and one that we embrace and hope holds true in practice.

At the same time, researchers have found that exposure to differences of race, ethnicity, religion, social class, and other characteristics may in fact lead to negative consequences and exclusion—thus highlighting that there are two sides to every coin. The idea here is that exposure to different people or things may heighten the threat level that people feel and associate with differences, causing them to want to exclude those people or things from their lives (Blalock, 1967; Markert, 2010).

Types of Group Leadership

A leader is a person able to influence the behavior of other members of a group. All groups tend to have leaders, even if the leaders do not have formal titles. Leaders come in a variety of forms: autocratic, charismatic, democratic, laissez-faire, bureaucratic, and so on. Some leaders are especially effective in motivating members of their groups or organizations, inspiring them to achievements they might not ordinarily accomplish. Such a **transformational leader**

Social closure: The ability of a group to strategically and consciously exclude outsiders or those deemed "undesirable" from participating in the group or enjoying the group's resources.

Transformational leader: A leader who is able to instill in group members a sense of mission or higher purpose, thereby changing (transforming) the nature of the group itself.

people, groups may also develop a formal structure. Formal leadership roles may arise, such as president or secretary, and official rules may develop to govern what the group does. We discuss formal organizations later in this chapter.

Larger groups can sometimes be exclusive, since it is easier for their members to limit their social relationships to the group itself, avoiding relationships with nonmembers.

Private Lives, Public Issues
WHAT CAN FICTIONAL STORIES TEACH US ABOUT GROUPS?

Under the leadership of Bellamy and Clarke, the 100 attempt to survive the harsh surface conditions, battle hostile Grounders, and establish communication with the Ark.

In 2014, CW premiered a new drama series, *The 100*, that follows the adventures of one hundred teenage delinquents living in a space "Ark" after a nuclear apocalypse on Earth. After concerns arise about the safety of the ship, the group is sent back to the planet to test if it is habitable. The series, which is based on a book of the same name by Kass Morgan, begins with the group landing on the wrong part of Earth and needing to explore the area in order to find the supplies they were promised. Clarke and Bellamy emerge as the two principle leaders, but with shifting alliances, survival becomes a challenge. There is conflict within the group, as the teens struggle to agree on how to communicate with the Ark, which still remains in space, and how to protect themselves from the Grounders, an unpredictable and dangerous group of survivors who inhabit the planet. Although they are all working toward the same goal—survival—their interpersonal conflicts and their first taste of freedom after imprisonment get in the way of realizing their collective well-being. The group's survival depends on cooperation, but shifting alliances, contests for power, and individual interests challenge the pursuit of a collective good.

Fully 60 years earlier, in 1954, British author William Golding published the novel *Lord of the Flies*, the story of 30 boys marooned on a Pacific island as the world around them erupts into war. The group

of boys is initially led by Jack and Ralph, and the survivors cooperate to construct shelters, gather and hunt food, and maintain a smoking fire to draw the attention of passing ships. Over time, however, the pursuit of the collective good frays, as many of the boys shirk their tasks and develop a fear of a supernatural force, "the beast," on the island. A struggle for leadership emerges, impulses and forces for civility dissolve, and the group descends into deadly savagery, leaving two of the key characters dead before the group is finally rescued.

Though fictional and separated by over half a century, *The 100* and *Lord of the Flies* are interesting (if somewhat hyperbolic) microcosms of the challenges of groups. Even where surviving or thriving depends on participation from all parties, shared interests do not ensure cooperation. Competition over power and resources, individual interests that may conflict with the group interest, and interpersonal tensions can undermine a group's achievement of a goal.

Consider some real-life issues where group cooperation (though on a massive scale) would help to ensure that global society can survive and thrive: the challenges of climate change and its threat to island and shoreline communities; the danger of antibiotic overuse in medicine and industrial agriculture, which is leading to the development of dangerous "superbugs" that cannot be treated with existing medicines; or the danger to all of humankind of nuclear weapons. To some degree, in each of these cases, the inhabitants of our planet have worked or are working together toward positive collective outcomes. At the same time, many problems remain unresolved, and efforts to work together may be undermined by struggles over power, leadership, ideology, and profit.

Think It Through

- Group cooperation is vital to community survival, but individual interests may be in conflict with the collective good. Is this conflict inevitable?

goes beyond the merely routine, *instilling in group members a sense of mission or higher purpose and thereby changing (transforming) the nature of the group itself* (Burns, 1978; Kanter, 1983; Mehra, Dixon, Brass, & Robertson, 2006).

Transformational leaders leave their marks on their organizations and can be vital inspirations for social change in the world. Nelson Mandela, the first Black African president of postapartheid South Africa, had spent 27 years in prison,

©AF archive/Alamy Stock Photo

having been convicted of treason against the White-dominated government. Nonetheless, his moral and political position was so strong that upon his release, he immediately assumed leadership of the African National Congress (ANC), leading that political group to the pinnacle of power in South Africa and then assuming the office of president of the country.

Most leaders are not as visionary as Mandela, however. A leader who simply "gets the job done" is a **transactional leader**, *concerned with accomplishing the group's tasks, getting group members to do their jobs, and making certain the group achieves its goals.* Transactional leadership is routine leadership. For example, the teacher who effectively gets through the lesson plan each day but does not necessarily transform the classroom into a place where students explore new ways of thinking and behaving that change their educational lives is exercising transactional leadership.

For leaders to be effective, they must somehow get others to follow them. How do they do that? At one end of the spectrum, a leader might coerce people into compliance and subordination; at the other end, people may willingly comply with and subordinate themselves to a leader. The basic sociological notion of *power,* the ability to mobilize resources and achieve a goal despite the resistance of others, captures the first point (Emerson, 1962; Hall, 2003; Weber, 1921/2012). The related notion of **legitimate authority**, *power exercised over those who recognize it as deserved or earned,* captures the second (Blau, 1964). For example, prison guards often rely on the use of force to ensure compliance with their orders, whereas professors must depend on their legitimate authority if they hope to keep their students attentive and orderly.

Sociologists have typically found authority to be more interesting than the exercise of raw force. After all, it is not surprising that people will follow orders when someone holds a gun to their heads. But why do they go along with authority when they are *not* overtly compelled to do so?

Part of the answer is that people often regard authority as legitimate when it seems to accompany the leadership

Nelson Mandela played an influential role in leading South Africa out of apartheid in the late 1980s and early 1990s. Prior to assuming the presidency of the postapartheid South African government, Mandela, writing from a prison cell, inspired many South Africans, as well as people in other parts of the world, to form anti-apartheid coalitions and groups.

position. A teacher, for example, would appear to possess the right to expect students to listen attentively and behave respectfully. Power stemming from an official leadership position is termed **positional power**; that *power depends on the leader's role in the group* (Chiang, 2009; Hersey, Blanchard, & Natemeyer, 1987; Raven & Kruglianski, 1975). At the same time, some leaders derive their power from their unique ability to inspire others. Power that derives from the leader's personality is termed **personal power**; *it depends on the ability to persuade rather than the ability to command* (van Dijke & Poppe, 2006).

In most situations, the effective exercise of personal power, rather than positional power, is more likely to result in highly motivated and satisfied group members. When group members are confused or ill prepared to undertake a particular task, however, they seem to prefer the more command-oriented style associated with positional leadership (Hersey et al., 1987; Mizruchi & Potts, 1998; Patterson, 1989; Podsakoff & Schriesheim, 1985; Schaefer, 2011).

Conformity to Groups

Following group norms such as getting tattoos or piercings or wearing the trendiest brand of jeans seems relatively harmless. At the same time, conformity to group pressure can lead to destructive behavior such as drug abuse or

---

Transactional leader: A leader who is concerned with accomplishing the group's tasks, getting group members to do their jobs, and making certain that the group achieves its goals.

Legitimate authority: A type of power that is recognized as deserved or earned.

Positional power: Power that depends on the leader's role in the group.

Personal power: Power that depends on the ability to persuade rather than the ability to command.

■ **FIGURE 5.3** The Asch Experiments: A Study in Conformity

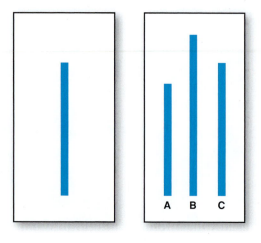

serious crimes against others. For this reason, sociologists and social psychologists have long sought to understand why most people tend to go along with others—and under what circumstances they do not.

Some of the earliest studies of conformity to group pressures were conducted by psychologist Solomon Asch more than 60 years ago. In one of his classic experiments, Asch (1952) told the group of young male undergraduates in the study that they were taking a "vision test." Subjects were instructed to identify which of three lines of different length most closely matched a fourth (Figure 5.3). The differences between the line lengths were obvious; subjects had no difficulty making the correct match. Asch then arranged a version of the experiment in which the lines to be matched were presented in a group setting, with each person calling out the answer one at a time.

In the second version of the experiment, all but one of the subjects were accomplices of Asch's, who intentionally attempted to deceive the outsider in the group by saying that two lines that were clearly unequal in length were identical. The experiment was conducted with 18 trials, 12 of which were "clinical"—that is, in a dozen of the trials, Asch's accomplices called out the incorrect answer to determine if the subject would follow. Asch's experiment found that about 32% of subjects conformed on the experimental trials; across 12 trials, 75% of subjects conformed at least once. In the experiments where no intentionally misleading answers were given, the subjects offered incorrect responses less than 1% of the time. Asch's experiments demonstrated that many people are willing to discount their own perceptions rather than contradict group consensus.

Interestingly, while Asch showed the power of conformity, his experiment also recognized the potential power of

dissent. When even one of the experimenter's seven confederates "dissented" from the group consensus, the subject was far more likely to assert that the line lengths were unequal. A later study (Allen & Levine, 1968) affirmed this point, showing that the presence of even a single dissenter could dramatically reduce conformity.

How do you think you would respond if you were the subject in an experiment similar to that conducted by Solomon Asch (and had not read this account first)? Would you conform or dissent?

Obedience to Authority

Another classic study of conformity was conducted by Stanley Milgram (1963). One of his specific research questions concerned what allowed ordinary German citizens to go along with and even participate in the mass killing of Jews, Romani (also known as *Gypsies*), homosexuals, the disabled, and others who were judged socially undesirable by the Nazis during World War II. Obedience is a kind of conformity. Milgram thus desired to find the boundaries of obedience, to identify how far a person would be willing to go if an authority figure encouraged him or her to complete a given task. His study produced some chilling answers.

In Milgram's experiment male volunteers were told by an actor dressed in a white lab coat (an authoritative prop) to read aloud pairs of words from a list someone in another room was to memorize and repeat. Whenever the "learner" (an accomplice in the research) made a mistake, the subject was instructed to give the learner an electric shock by flipping a switch on an official-looking machine (which was actually fake). With each mistake, the voltage (intensity) of the purported shock was to be increased, until it eventually reached the highest levels, visibly labeled on the machine "450 volts—danger, severe shock."

In reality, the learner never received any electric shocks, but he reacted audibly and physically as if he had, emitting cries that grew louder and more pained, pounding on the table, and moving about in his chair (the cries were prerecorded and played back). Meanwhile, the "scientist" ordered the subject to proceed with the experiment and continue administering shocks, saying things such as, "The experiment requires that you continue" even when the learner expressed concern about his "bad heart."

More than half the participants in the study obeyed the commands to keep going, administering what they believed to be electric shocks up to the maximum voltage until nothing but an eerie silence came from the other room. What happened here? How could ordinary, basically good people so easily conform to orders that turned them into potential accomplices to injury or death?

Most people would say that they are not capable of committing horrendous acts, yet Stanley Milgram's famous experiment illustrated how obedience to authority can lead people to commit actions that result in harm to others.

The answer, Milgram found, was deceptively simple: Ordinary people will conform to orders given by someone in a position of power or authority, particularly when the authority is understood to take responsibility for the action. They will do so even when those orders result in harm to other human beings. Many ordinary Germans who participated in the mass execution of Jews in Nazi concentration camps allegedly did so on the ground that they were "just following orders." Milgram's research, though ethically questionable, produced sobering findings for those who believe that only "other people" would bow to authority.

The 2012 film *Compliance,* which is based on real-life incidents, depicts the events that unfold when a prank phone caller, an unidentified male, calls a fast-food establishment and, pretending to be a police officer, enlists the aid of the store manager to help him crack an ostensibly important case. Once the manager agrees to help the "officer," the prankster tells the manager to perform increasingly invasive acts against a female employee. Obeying a figure believed to be a legitimate (though unseen) authority, in several of the incidents on which the movie is based, restaurant managers actually strip-searched female employees (Kavner, 2012; Wolfson, 2005).

Another example of obedience to authority even in the face of dangerous consequences took place at the Edgewood Arsenal in Maryland, the site of top-secret military experiments involving more than 7,000 U.S. soldiers from the 1950s through the 1970s. Many soldiers volunteered for duty at Edgewood unaware of, or even deceived about, exactly what would be asked of them. Once at Edgewood, they were informed that if they refused to participate in any required duties, they could face jail time for insubordination or receive an unsatisfactory review in their personnel files, and during the Vietnam era, some were reportedly threatened with being sent to war. The soldiers were experimented on repeatedly, often exposed

to a variety of dangerous chemical and biological toxins, including sarin gas, VX gas, LSD, tranquilizers, and barbiturates, some of which produced extended and untreated hallucinations (Martin, 2012; Young & Martin, 2012). The Edgewood Arsenal experiments highlight the point that individuals are likely to comply with any demands made by persons in positions of authority out of fear of the repercussions associated with failure to comply, even if what they are asked to do seems dangerous or even potentially lethal to others—or to themselves.

Groupthink

Common wisdom may suggest that we put our heads together to solve a problem, but pressures to go along with the crowd sometimes result in poor decisions rather than creative new solutions to problems. You have probably had the experience of feeling uneasy about voicing your opinion while in a group struggling with a difficult decision. Irving L. Janis (1972, 1989; Janis & Mann, 1977) coined the term **groupthink** to describe *what happens when members of a group ignore ways of thinking and plans of action that go against the group consensus.* Not only does groupthink frequently embarrass potential dissenters into conforming, but it can also produce a shift in perceptions so that group members rule out alternative possibilities without seriously considering them. Groupthink may facilitate a group's reaching a quick consensus, but the consensus may also be ill chosen, as we saw in our opening story.

Janis undertook historical research to see whether groupthink had characterized U.S. foreign policy decisions, including the infamous Bay of Pigs invasion of Cuba in 1961. Newly elected president John F. Kennedy inherited from the preceding administration a plan to provide U.S. supplies and air cover while an invasion force of exiled Cubans parachuted into Cuba's Bay of Pigs to liberate the country from Fidel Castro's communist government. A number of Kennedy's top advisers were certain the plan was fatally flawed but refrained from countering the emerging consensus. As it happened, the invasion was a disaster. The ill-prepared exiles were immediately defeated, Kennedy suffered public embarrassment, and the Cold War standoff between the Soviet Union and the United States deepened.

How could Kennedy's advisers, people of strong will and independent judgment educated at elite universities, have failed to voice their concerns adequately? Janis identified a number of possible reasons. For one, they were hesitant to disagree with the president, lest they lose his favor. Nor did they want to diminish group harmony in a crisis

Groupthink: A process by which the members of a group ignore ways of thinking and plans of action that go against the group consensus.

Discover & Debate

THE PROBLEM OF CYBERBULLYING

Motion: Schools should regulate and punish cyberbullying committed by their students against other students.

Background: Bullying in schools is not a new phenomenon. The story of a young victim and an aggressive classroom bully has been part of the educational landscape and even popular culture for decades. Cyberbullying, however, is a relatively new development, as the problem of threats, shaming, and ostracism have moved from the school yard to cyberspace. Policy makers, school administrators, teachers, and parents are confronting a problem that occupies a legal gray area and demands a balance between free speech, rights, privacy protections, institutional authority, and student safety.

Questions for Consideration

- Who should have a say in determining what behaviors constitute cyberbullying?

- Do the characteristics of a school matter in this debate? Should one differentiate between private and public schools? Should students at colleges and universities be treated differently than students in elementary, junior high school, and high school when it comes to cyberbullying?

- If students create negative posts about teachers on social media, is this cyberbullying? Should this be treated the same as cyberbullying of other students?

Debate Tip

- Practice gathering data from academic sources, such as peer-reviewed journals. When seeking academic sources in a library database, try various combinations of key words to find the most effective and applicable search items.

AFFIRMATIVE ARGUMENTS	OPPOSITION ARGUMENTS
Schools should actively police bullying by checking students' social media accounts for evidence when bullying is suspected or reported, for example. This contributes to the safety and psychological and physical well-being of all students.	Schools should strive to make the school environment safe, but they should not seek to regulate student behavior outside of school, including on social media. Schools should endeavor to educate students about the civil use of social media, but they should not be responsible for policing their use of social media outside of school.
Most schools have an enumerated code of student conduct that includes prohibitions against bullying. The school's code of conduct should be applicable to students both at school and outside of school.	The regulation of student speech on social media, even if it is offensive, may constitute a violation of free speech rights guaranteed by the First Amendment.
The First Amendment free speech rights of a student are not limitless. The goal of protecting a student from bullying may trump the right to free speech.	Parents, rather than schools, should be the primary regulators of young people's social media conduct. The problem of cyberbullying is one that parents should manage.

situation where teamwork was important. The cohesion of the group was of key concern. In addition, there was little time for them to consult outside experts who might have offered radically different perspectives. All these circumstances contributed to a single-minded pursuit of the president's initial ideas rather than an effort to generate effective alternatives.

Think about your own experiences working with groups, whether at work, on a class project, or in a campus organization. Have you ever "gone along to get along" or felt pressured to choose a particular path of action in spite of your own reservations? Or, conversely, have you ever chosen to refuse to conform in spite of the pressure? What factors affected your decision in either case?

Economic, Cultural, and Social Capital

One of the most important additions to the sociological study of groups is the contribution of the French school of thought known as **structuralism**, or *the idea that an*

Structuralism: The idea that an overarching structure exists within which culture and other aspects of society must be understood.

overarching structure exists within which culture and other aspects of society must be understood. A leading proponent, the French sociologist Pierre Bourdieu, provides an analytical framework that extends our understanding of the way group relationships and memberships shape our lives. Bourdieu argues that several forms of *capital*—that is, social currency—stem from our association with different groups. These forms of capital are of importance in the reproduction of socioeconomic status in society.

Economic capital, the most basic form, consists of *money and material that can be used to access valued goods and services.* Depending on the social class you are born into and the progress of your education and career, you will have more or less access to economic capital and more or less ability to take advantage of this form of capital. Another form is *cultural capital,* or your interpersonal skills, habits, manners, linguistic styles, tastes, and lifestyles. For instance, in some social circles, having refined table manners and speaking with a distinctive accent place a person in a social class that enhances his or her access to jobs, social activities, and friendship groups.

Friendship groups and other social contacts also provide **social capital**, *the personal connections and networks that enable people to accomplish their goals and extend their influence* (Bourdieu, 1984; Coleman, 1990; Putnam, 2000). College students who join fraternities and sororities expect that their "brothers" or "sisters" will help them get through the often challenging social and academic experiences of college. Other political, cultural, or social groups on campus offer comparable connections and opportunities. Many new (as well as more seasoned) employees and prospective employees join LinkedIn, a social media site that offers possibilities for people to expand their professional social networks, a key part of nurturing social capital.

While social capital is strongly influenced by socioeconomic class status, it may also be related to gender, to race, and intersectionally to both gender and race (McDonald & Day, 2010; McDonald, Lin, & Ao, 2009). In a study of social networks and their relationship to people's information about job leads, sociologists Matt Huffman and Lisa Torres (2002) found that women benefited from being part of networks that included more men than women; those who had more women in their social networks had a diminished probability of hearing about good job leads. Interestingly, the predominance of men or women in a man's social network made no discernible difference. The researchers

suggested that perhaps the women were less likely to learn about job leads, and, notably, when they knew of leads, they were more likely to pass them along to men than to other women. Similarly, McDonald and Mair (2010) and Trimble and Kmec (2011) explored issues of networking in relation to women's career opportunities over their lifetimes and also the extent to which networks aid women in attaining jobs. Both teams of researchers found that social capital in the form of networks of relations has very distinct and important effects for women. The advent of professional networking sites online offers sociologists the opportunity to expand this research to see if and how gender affects social networks and their professional benefits, as research from the field of psychology suggests that job networking sites (including LinkedIn) play an important role in the job acquisition process (Bohnert & Ross, 2010).

We often hear the phrase, "It's not what you know; it's who you know." Indeed, history shows that social networks are important. The Bush family has had a disproportionate impact on American political life. Members of the Bush family have twice been elected to the presidency and have held the governorships of Florida and Texas. Members of the family continue to be prominent in public life.

DISCOVER INTERSECTIONS

Capital and Social Stratification

In our chapter on social class and inequality in the United States (Chapter 7), you will be exploring the phenomenon of socioeconomic stratification. We will be discussing how modern socioeconomic hierarchies come to exist and persist. What role do you see economic, social, and cultural capital, which were discussed in the section above, playing in the creation and reproduction of class status? Can you think of ways in which other variables like gender, race, or sexual orientation might affect the acquisition of capital?

Economic capital: Money and material that can be used to access valued goods and services.

Social capital: The personal connections and networks that enable people to accomplish their goals and extend their influence.

Economic, cultural, and social capital confer benefits on individuals, at least in part through membership in particular social groups. Characteristics such as class, race, ethnicity, and gender, among others, can have effects on the capital one has. Membership in organizations such as fraternities, exclusive golf clubs, or college alumni associations can offer important network access. These are some examples of the kinds of organizations that shape our lives and society, sometimes to our benefit, sometimes to our disadvantage. Below, we look at organizations and their societal functions through the sociological lens.

Organizations

People frequently band together to pursue activities they could not readily accomplish by themselves. A principal means for accomplishing such cooperative actions is the **organization**, *a group with an identifiable membership that engages in concerted collective actions to achieve a common purpose* (Aldrich & Marsden, 1988). An organization can be a small primary group, but it is more likely to be a larger, secondary one: Universities, churches, armies, and business corporations are all examples of organizations. Organizations are a central feature of all societies, and their study is a core concern of sociology today.

Organizations tend to be highly formal in modern industrial and postindustrial societies. A **formal organization** is *rationally designed to achieve particular objectives, often by means of explicit rules, regulations, and procedures.* Examples include a state or county's department of motor vehicles or the federal Internal Revenue Service. As Max Weber (1919/1946) first recognized almost 100 years ago, modern societies are increasingly dependent on formal organizations. One reason is that formality is often a requirement for legal standing. For a college or university to be legally accredited, for example, it must satisfy explicit written standards governing everything from faculty hiring to fire safety. Today, formal organizations are the dominant form of organization across the globe.

Types of Formal Organizations

Thousands of different kinds of formal organizations serve every imaginable purpose. Sociology seeks to simplify this diversity by identifying the principal types. Amitai Etzioni

(1975) grouped organizations into three main types, based on the reasons people join them: utilitarian, coercive, and normative. In practice, of course, many organizations, especially utilitarian and normative organizations, include elements of more than one type.

Utilitarian organizations are *those that people join primarily because of some material benefit they expect to receive in return for membership.* For example, you probably enrolled in college not only because you want to expand your knowledge and skills but also because you know that a college degree will help you get a better job and earn more money later in life. In exchange, you have paid tuition and fees, devoted countless hours to studying, and agreed to submit to the rules that govern your school, your major, and your courses. Many of the organizations people join are utilitarian, particularly those in which they earn a living, such as corporations, factories, and banks.

Coercive organizations are *those in which members are forced to give unquestioned obedience to authority.* People are often forced to join coercive organizations because they have been either sentenced to punishment (prisons) or remanded for mandatory treatment (mental hospitals or drug treatment centers). Coercive organizations may use force or the threat of force, and sometimes confinement, to ensure compliance with rules and regulations. Guards, locked doors, barred windows, and monitoring are all features of jails, prisons, and mental hospitals. Sometimes people join coercive organizations voluntarily, but once they are members, they may not have the option of leaving as they desire. An example of such an organization is the military: While enlisting is voluntary in the United States, once a person joins, he or she is subject to discipline and the demand for submission to authority in a rigidly hierarchical structure. Coercive organizations are examples of total institutions, which you read about in Chapter 4. By encompassing all aspects of people's lives, total institutions can radically alter people's thinking and behavior.

Normative organizations, or **voluntary associations**, are those *that people join of their own will to pursue morally worthwhile goals without expectation of material reward.* Belonging to such organizations may offer social prestige or moral or personal satisfaction. (Of course, such organizations may also serve utilitarian purposes, such as a

---

Organization: A group with an identifiable membership that engages in concerted collective actions to achieve a common purpose.

Formal organization: An organization that is rationally designed to achieve particular objectives, often by means of explicit rules, regulations, and procedures.

Utilitarian organizations: Organizations that people join primarily because of some material benefit they expect to receive in return for membership.

Coercive organizations: Organizations in which members are forced to give unquestioned obedience to authority.

Normative organizations (or voluntary associations): Organizations that people join of their own will to pursue morally worthwhile goals without expectation of material reward.

charitable group you join partly to hand out your business card and boost your chances for monetary gain.)

The United States is a nation of normative organization joiners. Individuals affiliate with volunteer faith-related groups such as the YMCA, Hillel, and the Women's Missionary Society of the African Methodist Episcopal Church; charitable organizations such as the Red Cross; social clubs and professional organizations; politically oriented groups such as the National Association for the Advancement of Colored People (NAACP); and self-help groups such as Alcoholics Anonymous and Overeaters Anonymous. According to the National Center for Charitable Statistics (2016), there are more than a million public charities; 105,000 private foundations; and 368,000 other types of nonprofit organizations, such as fraternal organizations and civic leagues. Many of these organizations provide their members with a sense of connectedness while enabling them to accomplish personal and moral goals.

Normative organizations may also erect barriers based on social class, race, ethnicity, and gender. Those traditionally excluded from such organizations, including women, Latinos, Native Americans, African Americans, and other people of color, have, in response, formed their own voluntary associations. Although it may seem that these, too, are exclusionary, such groups have a different basis for their creation—the effort to remedy social inequality. Social justice, as a result, is often their primary concern.

Below, we shift our gaze from voluntary and coercive organizations to a phenomenon that is familiar to most of us—the bureaucracy. While we have some control over our membership in many organizations, we are all—as U.S. residents, taxpayers, students, or recipients of mortgage or college loans, among others—subject to the reach of modern bureaucracy.

Bureaucracies

The authority structure of most large organizations today is bureaucratic. In this section, we will look at the modern bureaucracy—the way it operates and some of its shortcomings. We will also see how bureaucratic structures have been modified or reformed to offer an alternative type of organization.

Max Weber (1919/1946) was the first sociologist to examine the characteristics of bureaucracy in detail. As noted in Chapter 1, Weber defined a *bureaucracy* as a type of formal organization based on written procedural rules, arranged into a clear hierarchy of authority, and staffed by full-time paid officials. Although Weber showed that bureaucracies could be found in many different societies throughout history, he argued that they became a dominant

form of social organization only in modern society, where they came to touch key aspects of our daily lives. In particular, Weber suggested that bureaucracies are a highly rational form of organization because they were devised to achieve organizational goals with the greatest degree of efficiency—that is, to optimize the achievement of a task.

Note that when Weber characterized bureaucracies as *rational*, he did not assume that they would always be *reasonable*. By *rational*, he meant that they were organized based on knowable rules and regulations that laid out a particular path to a goal rather than on general or abstract principles or ideologies. As we know from our own contacts with bureaucratic structures—whether they involve long waits on the phone to speak to a human being rather than a computer or the confusing pursuit of the correct person to whom one must turn in a critical student loan application—they are not, in fact, always reasonable.

To better understand the modern bureaucracy, Weber (1919/1946) identified what he referred to as the *ideal type* of this form of organization, describing the characteristics that would be found if the quintessential bureaucracy existed (Figure 5.4). While Weber recognized that no actual bureaucracy necessarily possesses all of the characteristics he identifies, he argued that, by clearly articulating them, he was describing a standard against which actual bureaucracies could be judged and understood.

■ **FIGURE 5.4** The Ideal Typical Bureaucracy

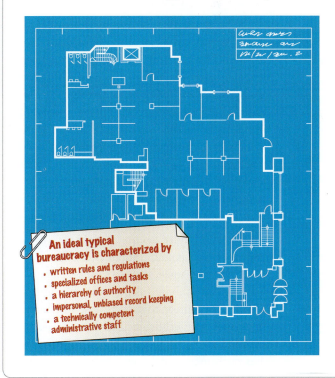

An ideal typical bureaucracy is characterized by

- written rules and regulations
- specialized offices and tasks
- a hierarchy of authority
- impersonal, unbiased record keeping
- a technically competent administrative staff

Written Rules and Regulations

The routine operation of the bureaucracy is governed by written rules and regulations, the purpose of which is to ensure that universal standards govern all aspects of bureaucratic behavior. Typically, rules govern everything from the hiring of employees to the reporting of an absence due to illness. They are usually spelled out in an organizational manual or handbook, now often available to employees on a human resources website, that describes in detail the requirements of each organizational position. While these rules and regulations can be lengthy and complex, they are—in theory—knowable, and the expectation is that those who work in and seek the services of a given organization will adhere to them—sometimes even if they don't seem to make sense!

- **Specialized offices:** Positions in a bureaucracy are organized into "offices" that create a division of labor within the organization. The duties of each office, such as bookkeeping or paying invoices, are described in the organizational manual. Each office specializes in one particular bureaucratic function to the exclusion of all others. Such specialization is one of the reasons that bureaucratic organization is said to be efficient; bureaucratic officials are supposed to become experts at their particular tasks, efficient cogs in a vast machine. The efficiency is, ideally, beneficial for the organization and its clients. If you are seeking to clear up a problem with your tuition bill, you will not visit the admissions office because you know the expert advice you seek is to be found in the student accounts office.

- **Hierarchy:** A bureaucracy is organized according to the vertical principle of hierarchy, so that each office has authority over one or more lower-level offices, and each in turn is responsible to a higher-level office. At the top, the leader of the organization stands alone; in the well-known words of then–U.S. president Harry S. Truman, "The buck stops here." The organizational chart of a bureaucracy therefore generally looks similar to a pyramid. Again, efficiency is achieved through the knowable hierarchy of power that governs the organization.

- **Impersonality in record keeping:** Within a bureaucracy, communications are likely to be formal and impersonal. Written forms—paperwork or the electronic equivalent—substitute for more personalized human contact, because bureaucracies must maintain written records or databases of all important actions. Modern computer technology has vastly increased the ability of organizations to maintain and access records. In some ways, this is an advantage—for example, when it allows you to register for classes via smartphone instead of standing in line for hours waiting to fill out forms. On the other hand, you may regret the loss of human contact and the inflexibility of the process, however efficient it may be. This impersonality also, ideally, has the effect of ensuring that all clients are treated equally and efficiently rather than capriciously; in reality, however, people with substantial economic, social, or cultural capital often have the easiest time navigating bureaucracies.

- **Technically competent administrative staff:** A bureaucracy generally seeks to employ a qualified professional staff. Anyone who by training and expertise is able to perform the duties of a particular position in an office of the organization is deemed eligible to fill the position. Work in the bureaucracy is a full-time job, ideally providing a career path for the bureaucrat, who must demonstrate the training and expertise necessary to fill each successive position. In its ideal form, the system is a meritocracy—that is, positions are filled on the basis of merit or qualifications, typically demonstrated by performance on competitive exams, rather than on applicants' knowing the "right" people. In practice, however—as is true of the other characteristics listed above—an actual bureaucracy is unlikely to meet this standard fully. In fact, getting hired into the organization and advancing in it are likely to be influenced not strictly by objective criteria such as education and experience but also by such social variables as age, gender, race, and social connections.

A Critical Evaluation

Bureaucracies popularly evoke images of paper pushers and annoying red tape. In their studies of bureaucracy, sociologists, too, have had much to say about this form of organization, with mixed conclusions. Max Weber recognized that bureaucracies can, indeed, provide organizational efficiency in getting the job done. In contrast to earlier organizational forms, many of which filled positions through nepotism, bribes, or other non–merit-based forms of promotion and were founded to serve the needs of their leaders or small elite groups, modern bureaucracies have many redeeming qualities in spite of the frustrations they cause.

At the same time, Weber argued that a bureaucracy may create what he termed an *iron cage*—a prison of rules and regulations from which there is little escape (DiMaggio & Powell, 1983; Weber, 1904–1905/2002). The iron cage,

©Myung J. Chun/Los Angeles Times via Getty Images

What would you say are the ideal–typical characteristics of a bureaucracy? Does your description comport with that put forth by Max Weber?

which Weber memorably described as having the potential to be a "polar night of icy darkness," is a metaphor. We become "caged" in bureaucratic structures when we build them to serve us (as rules and regulations would ideally do) but they ultimately come to trap us by denying our humanity, creativity, and autonomy.

As you think about this metaphor of the iron cage, consider encounters with bureaucratic structures that you have had: If you've ever had the feeling that solving a personal or family problem concerning tuition, taxes, or immigration would require speaking to a human being with the power to make a decision or to see that your case is an exception in some way—but no such human was available!—then you can see what Weber meant. We make rules and regulations to keep order and to have a set of knowable guidelines for action and decisions, but what happens when the rules and regulations and their enforcement become the *ends* of an organization rather than a *means* to an end? Then we are in the iron cage.

Sociologists have identified a number of specific problems that plague bureaucracies, many of which may be familiar and could be thought of as representing *irrationalities of rationality*:

- **Waste and incompetence:** As long as administrators appear to be doing their jobs—filing forms, keeping records, responding to memos, and otherwise keeping busy—nobody really wants to question whether the organization as a whole is performing effectively or efficiently. Secure in their positions, bureaucrats may become inefficient, incompetent, and often indifferent to the clients they are supposed to serve.

- **Trained incapacity:** We have all seen bureaucrats who "go by the book," even when a situation clearly

calls for fresh thinking. Thorstein Veblen (1899), a U.S. sociologist and contemporary of Weber's, termed this tendency *trained incapacity,* a learned inability to exercise independent thought. However intelligent they may otherwise be, such bureaucrats make poor judgments when it comes to decisions not covered by the rule book. They become so obsessed with following the rules and regulations that they lose the ability and flexibility to respond to new situations.

- **Goal displacement:** Bureaucracies may lose sight of the original goals they were created to accomplish. Large corporations such as General Motors and Hewlett-Packard and government organizations such as the Department of Homeland Security employ thousands of middle-level employees whose job it is to handle the paperwork required in manufacturing automobiles or computers or in protecting the country. Perhaps understandably, such people may, over time, become preoccupied with getting their own jobs done and, driven by the need to ensure the continuation of particular practices or programs linked to their positions, eventually lose touch with the larger goals of the organization. This shift in focus adds to costs, lowers efficiency, and may prove detrimental to corporations that compete in a global economy and governments seeking to accomplish goals and stay within tight budgets.

Although Weber presented a sometimes-chilling picture of bureaucracies operating as vast, inhuman machines, we all recognize that, in practice, there is often a human face behind the counter. In fact, much important work done in bureaucratic organizations is achieved through informal channels and personal ties and connections rather than through official channels, as sociologist Peter Blau showed in his research (Blau & Meyer, 1987). For example, a student who wishes to register late for a class may avoid having to get half a dozen signatures if he or she knows the professor or a staff person in the registrar's office. However, because of the shortcomings of bureaucratic forms of organization, some theorists have argued for the development of alternative organizational forms. We discuss some of these after looking at the relationship between bureaucracy and democracy.

Bureaucracy and Democracy

Max Weber argued that bureaucracies were an inevitable outgrowth of modern society, with its large-scale organizations, complex institutional structure, and concern with rationality and efficiency. Yet many observers have viewed bureaucracy as a stifling, irrational force that dominates our lives and threatens representative government. In *Les Employés*

(1841/1985), French novelist Honoré de Balzac, who popularized the term *bureaucracy,* called it "the giant power wielded by pigmies" and a "fussy and meddlesome" government. Do bureaucracies inevitably lead to a loss of freedom and erosion of democracy? Are there more humanistic alternatives to bureaucracies that allow freer, more fulfilling participation in the organization? Let's look briefly at the views of sociologist Robert Michels on the incompatibility between democracy and bureaucracy, then see what some people have done to try to reform this organizational structure.

Michels (1876–1936), another contemporary of Weber's, argued that bureaucracy and democracy are fundamentally at odds. He observed that the Socialist Party in Germany, originally created to democratically represent the interests of workers, had become an oligarchy, a form of organization in which a small number of people exert great power. For him, this was an example of what he termed the **iron law of oligarchy**, *an inevitable tendency for a large-scale bureaucratic organization to become ruled undemocratically by a handful of people.* (*Oligarchy* means the rule of a small group over many people.)

Following Weber, Michels argued that in a large-scale bureaucratic organization, the closer you are to the top, the greater the concentration of power. People typically get to the top because they are ambitious, hard-driving, and effective in managing the people below or because they have economic and social capital to trade for proximity to power. Once there, leaders increase their social capital through specialized access to information, resources, and influential people—access that reinforces their power. They also often appoint subordinates who are loyal supporters and thus further enhance their position. Such leaders may come to regard the bureaucracy as a means to meet their own needs or those of their social group. The democratic purposes of an organization may become subordinate to the needs of the dominating group.

Since all modern societies require large-scale organizations to survive, Michels believed that democracies—or, in some cases, organizations—may sow the seeds of their own destruction by breeding bureaucracies that eventually grow into undemocratic oligarchies. While there are few signs that, for instance, the United States (which has many large-scale bureaucracies) is drifting from democracy, one could make a case that institutions such as the U.S. Congress show some tendencies to act in the interests of political parties or powerful members rather than the interests of constituents. For example, a bill on disaster relief or unemployment insurance may be held up when a party leader feels that stalling the bill might confer political advantage on his or her party.

In response to what they feel is the stifling effect of bureaucratic organizations, some people have sought alternative forms of organizations designed to allow greater freedom and more fulfilling participation. For example, as part of the sweeping countercultural spirit of the late 1960s and early 1970s, many youthful activists joined collectives, small organizations that operate by cooperation and consensus. Food cooperatives, employee-run newspapers and health clinics, and "free schools" sprang up as organizations that sought to operate by consensus rather than by bureaucracy. Members of these organizations shunned hierarchy, avoided a division of labor based on expertise, and happily sacrificed efficiency in favor of more humanistic relationships.

The founders of these organizations believed they were reviving more personal organizational arrangements that could better enable society to reach certain goals. Although these organizations initially met with some success and left a legacy, they also confronted a larger society in which more conventional forms of organization effectively shut them out.

Members of such organizations as the food cooperatives and employee-run newspapers and health clinics of the 1960s and 1970s favored the values of cooperation and service over the more competitive and materialistic values of the larger society. In the exuberance of that period, members of collectives believed they were forging a radically new kind of antibureaucratic organization.

In her examination of early collectives, sociologist Joyce Rothschild-Whitt (1979) studied several that self-consciously rejected bureaucracy in favor of more cooperative forms. In one health clinic, for example, all jobs were shared (to the extent legally possible) by all members: Doctors would periodically answer telephones and clean the facility, while nurses and paramedical staff would conduct examinations and interview patients. While the doctors were paid somewhat more than the other staff members, the differences were not large and were the subject of negotiation by everyone who worked at the clinic.

As long as the collectives remained small, they were able to maintain their founders' values. On the other hand, vastly reduced pay differentials between professional and nonprofessional staff, job sharing, and collective decision making often made it difficult for the collectives to compete for employees with organizations that shared none of these values (Rothschild-Whitt, 1979). Doctors, for example, could make much more money in conventional medical practice, without being expected to answer telephones or sweep the floor. Over time, the original cooperative values tended to erode, and many of the new organizations came to resemble conventional organizations in the larger society. Still, more than three decades after Rothschild-Whitt studied them, a number of these original groups still exist. Although they may have lost some of their collective zeal, they still operate more cooperatively than most traditional organizations.

Iron law of oligarchy: Robert Michels's theory that there is an inevitable tendency for a large-scale bureaucratic organization to become ruled undemocratically by a handful of people.

Inequality Matters

LAW, BUREAUCRACY, AND THE POVERTY PENALTY

Does the law penalize people for being poor? In theory, U.S. law is blind to color, creed, economic status, and other personal characteristics, as is the administrative application of the law. In practice, however, the poor are often subject to consequences for minor infractions that are not visited upon those who are better off. Consider the following cases, documented by the *Washington Post*:

Damian Stinnie, a 24-year-old lymphoma patient, was forced into homelessness because he could not pay his traffic fines. A Ferguson, Missouri, woman ended up spending six days in jail and owing more than $1,000 because she could not pay a $151 parking ticket. A Tennessee man with liver disease failed to get treatment after he lost his driver's license for nonpayment of traffic tickets ("Obey the judge, lose your job," 2018, para. 1).

The *Post's* editorial describes local and state legal systems that impose severe penalties for administrative violations, such as the failure to pay a parking ticket,

and that, in the words of the writer, "seem geared toward squeezing revenue from desperate people rather than ensuring public safety" (Ibid., para. 3). William Moyer (2018) reports that over 7 million people may have lost their licenses due to unpaid court or administrative debt resulting from the failure to pay traffic tickets or appear in court to contest the tickets. Moyer writes, "Suspensions can keep unsafe drivers off the road but also can prevent people who haven't committed serious crimes from working, getting their children to school and getting out of debt, according to advocates for the poor" (para. 3).

Those who object to the practice of license revocation for nonpayment of traffic fines question whether it is appropriate and fair to build a web of penalties that create significant legal and financial jeopardy for the poor. While a middle-class motorist incurring a speeding or parking violation is unlikely to find the financial or personal costs of the ticket onerous, a poor driver who is unable to pay may be setting himself or herself up for a multitude of punishments and penalties.

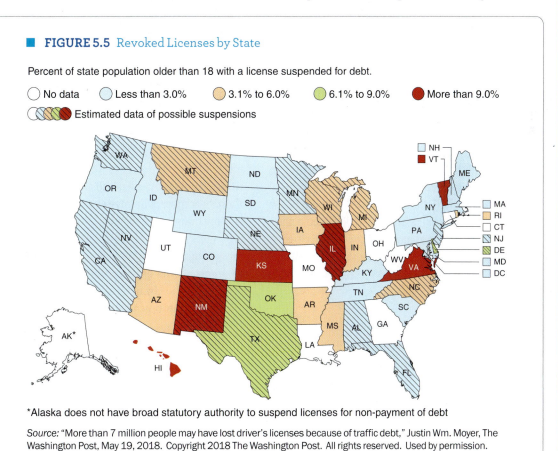

■ **FIGURE 5.5** Revoked Licenses by State

Percent of state population older than 18 with a license suspended for debt.

◯ No data   ◯ Less than 3.0%   ◯ 3.1% to 6.0%   ◯ 6.1% to 9.0%   ● More than 9.0%

◯◯◯◯● Estimated data of possible suspensions

*Alaska does not have broad statutory authority to suspend licenses for non-payment of debt

Source: "More than 7 million people may have lost driver's licenses because of traffic debt," Justin Wm. Moyer, The Washington Post, May 19, 2018. Copyright 2018 The Washington Post. All rights reserved. Used by permission.

(Continued)

(Continued)

The loss of a license can exact a significant cost when one needs to drive to a job, medical appointments, or school. In a handful of states, more than 6% of the driving population has had a license revoked for nonpayment of fines (Figure 5.5; Moyer, 2018).

In a recent case in Tennessee, a judge restored the driving rights of a young mother who had lost her license after failing to pay $477.50 for speeding and failure to provide proof of insurance. Without her license, she had lost her job as a waitress (Moyer, 2018). A few states are moving toward broader efforts to provide relief for those who lose their license for failure to pay. For instance, in 2017, California passed a bill ending the practice of suspending driver's licenses

for unpaid court debt. Instead, drivers will be offered options such as a payment plan, a reduced payment, or community service. Michigan, too, has taken steps to help those with lost driving privileges gain them back (Schwartzapfel, 2017).

Think It Through

- It has been suggested by some observers that penalties for minor infractions could be assessed on a sliding scale: Those who are well off would pay more while those who are poor would pay less, but both groups would pay a fine proportional to what they earn. Would this be fair? Why or why not?

A more recent foray away from hierarchically and bureaucratically organized entities has been made by the online retailer Zappos. In early 2014, the company announced that it planned to introduce a "holacracy," replacing traditional management structures with "self-governing 'circles.'" The goal of holacracy, according to a media account of the practice, is to "organize a company around the work that needs to be done instead of around the people who do it." Hence, a holacracy is devoid of job titles; instead, employees are integrated into multiple circles of cooperative workers. A few other companies are experimenting with holacracy as well (McGregor, 2014). Do workers perform well in contexts of dispersed or ambiguous authority? Results at Zappos, according to *Fortune* magazine, have been mixed, and after three years of the new management style, the company fell off the 100 Best Companies to Work For list, where it had occupied a place for the past eight years. The change has been described as fostering both chaos and new ideas and is slated to continue (Reingold, 2016).

The Global Organization

Organizations from multinational corporations to charitable foundations span the globe and increasingly contribute to what some sociologists believe is a "homogenization" of the world's countries (McNeely, 1995; Neyazi, 2010; Scott & Meyer, 1994; Thomas, Meyer, Ramirez, & Boli, 1987). You can listen to the same music, employ the same Internet search engine, see the same films, and eat the same meals (if you wish) in Bangalore and Baku as you do in Berlin and Boston.

Global organizations are not new. The Hanseatic League, a business alliance between German merchants and cities, dominated trade in the North and Baltic Seas from the mid-12th to the mid-18th centuries. The British East India Company virtually owned India and controlled the vast bulk of trade throughout the Far East for several centuries. In 1919, following World War I, the League of Nations was formed, uniting the most economically and militarily powerful nations of the world in an effort to ensure peace and put an end to war. When Germany withdrew and began expanding its borders throughout Europe, however, the League dissolved.

After World War II, a new effort at international governance was made in the form of the United Nations (UN), begun in 1945. The United Nations is still important and active today: Its power is limited, but its influence has grown. It not only mediates disputes between nations, but it is also ever present in international activities ranging from fighting hunger and HIV/AIDS to mobilizing peacekeeping troops and intervening to address conflicts and their consequences.

International organizations exist in two major forms: those established by national governments and those established by private organizations. We consider each separately below.

International Governmental Organizations

The first type of global organization is the **international governmental organization (IGO)** *established by treaties between governments to facilitate and regulate trade between the member countries, promote national security*

International governmental organization (IGO): An international organization established by treaties between governments to facilitate and regulate trade between the member countries, promote national security, protect social welfare and human rights, or ensure environmental protection.

Médecins sans Frontières (MSF or Doctors without Borders) works around the world to serve underserved or conflict-torn countries and communities. In this photo, a doctor from MSF examines children suffering from malnutrition in a hospital in Bambari, Central African Republic.

(both the League of Nations and the United Nations were created after highly destructive world wars), *protect social welfare or human rights, or ensure environmental protection.*

Some of the most powerful IGOs today were created to unify national economies into large trading blocs. One of the most complex IGOs is the European Union (EU), whose rules now govern 28 countries in Europe; five additional countries have applied for EU entry. The European Union was formed to create a single European economy in which businesses could operate freely across borders in search of markets and labor and workers could move freely in search of jobs without having to go through customs or show passports at border crossings. EU member states have common economic policies, and 18 of them share a single currency (the euro). Not all Europeans welcome economic unity, however, since it means their countries must surrender some of their economic power to the EU as a whole. Being economically united by a single currency also means the economic problems felt by one country are distributed among all the other countries to some degree. Thus, when economic crisis hit Europe in 2008, the severe economic woes of Greece, Portugal, and Spain (among others) caused serious problems for stronger EU economies, like that of Germany.

IGOs can also wield considerable military power, provided that their member countries are willing to do so. The North Atlantic Treaty Organization (NATO) and the United Nations, for example, have sent troops from some of their participating nations into war zones in Iraq and Afghanistan in recent years. Yet, because nations ultimately control the use of their own military forces, there are limits

to the authority of even the most powerful military IGOs, whose strength derives from the voluntary participation of their member nations.

IGOs often reflect inequalities in power among their members. For example, the UN Security Council is responsible for maintaining international peace and security and is therefore the most powerful organization within the United Nations. Its five permanent members include the United Kingdom, the United States, China, France, and Russia, which gives these countries significant clout over the Security Council's actions. The remaining 10 Security Council member countries are elected by the UN General Assembly for two-year terms and therefore have less lasting power than the permanent members.

At the beginning of the 20th century, there were only about three dozen IGOs in the world, although data for that time are incomplete. By 1981, when consistent reporting criteria were adopted, there were 1,039; by 2011, the most recent year for which data are available, there were 7,608 (Union of International Associations, 2011).

International Nongovernmental Organizations

The second type of global organization is the **international nongovernmental organization (INGO)**, *established by agreements between the individuals or private organizations making up the membership and existing to fulfill an explicit mission.* Examples include Doctors without Borders (Médecins sans Frontiers), the International Sociological Association, the World Wildlife Federation, and the International Red Cross. Global business organizations (GBOs) represent a subtype within the broader category of INGOs. The concept of the GBO captures the fluid and highly interconnected nature of our modern globalized labor market in which employees often interact and communicate with people from other nations and cultures, facilitated by technology and online networks. Similar to the number of IGOs, the number of INGOs (including GBOs) has increased exponentially in recent years—from fewer than 200 near the beginning of the 20th century to more than 20,000 by 1985 and up to 56,834 in 2011 (Union of International Associations, 2011).

International nongovernmental organization (INGO): An international organization established by agreements between the individuals or private organizations making up the membership and existing to fulfill an explicit mission.

Global Issues

AMNESTY INTERNATIONAL AND THE GLOBAL CAMPAIGN FOR HUMAN RIGHTS

Azza Soliman is a human rights activist and lawyer in Egypt, where her work has included defending victims of torture, arbitrary detention, domestic abuse, and rape. She is the co-founder of the Centre for Egyptian Women's Legal Assistance and Lawyers for Justice and Peace, organizations that provide legal assistance and support to women in poverty. Because of their work, Soliman and many of her colleagues in the human rights community have been labelled spies and threats to national security. They have been placed under state surveillance and endured harassment by security forces and pro-government media. In 2016, Soliman was arrested and interrogated by Egyptian police, and now faces charges for tax evasion, operating a civil society organization without proper registration, and slandering Egypt's image by claiming that Egyptian women are at risk of rape. Her assets have been frozen, she has been banned from travelling, and could face time in prison. Amnesty International, an advocacy organization for global human rights, calls for its members and supporters to "stand with the brave" and to free imprisoned human rights defenders in Egypt and elsewhere.

Imprisonment is not the only threat to many around the world who challenge their governments. According to Amnesty International (2016), governments in more than 25 countries executed 1,634 prisoners in 2015—but the actual total is likely much higher. Amnesty International also reports that at least 20,292 people were on death row at the end of 2015, and people continued to be sentenced and executed, even for offenses that do not meet the "most serious crimes" threshold of intentional killing, as set in international law and standards.

Amnesty International is an INGO comprised of over 7 million people, including 2 million

members and more than 5 million activists and supporters across more than 150 countries and territories, including over a million in the United States (Amnesty International, n.d.). One of its goals is to help secure the freedom of people imprisoned because of their political beliefs or actions, especially those in immediate danger of torture or execution. Amnesty International has helped thousands of individual prisoners since it was founded in Britain in 1961. It functions as a global pressure group made up of ordinary citizens. Anyone can join, pay nominal annual dues, and become part of a global "urgent action network" that is regularly mobilized to send government officials faxes, letters, and e-mail and social media entreaties on behalf of prisoners. Amnesty International also sends delegations to countries where government abuses are rampant. The reports these delegations write draw worldwide media attention to the world's prisons and political prisoners.

NGOs such as Amnesty International highlight the power that ordinary citizens have when they band together toward the achievement of a defined goal. If you could create an NGO or INGO to draw attention to a social or political issue, what issue would you choose? How would you persuade others to support your cause?

Think It Through

- In cases of groups such as Amnesty International, does size matter? Is a larger group more effective than a smaller collective of activists? Does the use of Internet platforms such as Facebook, Twitter, and YouTube in social action campaigns make the size of the group of supporters more or less important?

INGOs are primarily concerned with promoting the global interests of their members, largely through influencing the United Nations, other IGOs, or individual governments. They also engage in research, education, and the spread of information by means of international conferences, meetings, and journals. INGOs have succeeded in shaping the policies of powerful nations. One prominent INGO is Islamic Relief Worldwide (IRW). The organization, founded in the United Kingdom, conducts projects in

over 30 countries. IRW has affiliated partners in countries such as Chechnya, India, Kenya, and Pakistan. One of its most prominent branches, Islamic Relief USA (IRUSA), is based in Alexandria, Virginia. IRUSA has many domestic programs, such as the annual Day of Dignity ("Faiths Unite," 2015), when volunteers distribute food, medical care, hygiene kits, blankets, clothing, and more to homeless and needy persons. IRUSA has also been active during natural disasters such as Hurricane Katrina and Hurricane Sandy.

Staying true to the mission of IRW, IRUSA also works in 37 countries, including Bosnia, Ghana, Ecuador, Jordan, and the Philippines. In 2015, IRUSA was named a Top-Rated Nonprofit by Great Nonprofits (Great Nonprofits, 2016). In 2016, IRUSA was awarded four out of four stars by Charity Navigator (Charity Navigator, 2016). Although they are far more numerous than IGOs and have achieved some successes, INGOs have less power over state actions and policies, since legal power (including enforcement) ultimately lies with governmental organizations and treaties. At the same time, their influence in individual countries can be considerable, sometimes with very positive effects, and at other times, with more problematic outcomes, as our *Global Issues* box shows.

Why Study Groups and Organizations?

You now have a good idea of how the groups and organizations to which you belong exert influence over your life. They help to determine who you know and, in many ways, who you are. The primary groups of your earliest years were crucial in shaping your sense of self—a sense that will change only very slowly over the rest of your life. Throughout your life, groups are the wellspring of the norms and values that enable and enrich your social life. At the same time, they are the source of nonconforming behavior; the rebel is shaped by group membership as much as the more mainstream and conventional citizen.

Although groups remain central in our lives, group affiliation in the United States is rapidly changing. To some degree, long-standing conventional groups appear to be losing ground. For example, today's typical college students are less likely to join civic groups and organizations—or even to vote—than were their parents. At the same time, many are active "netizens," joining and creating groups for both amusement and civic or political causes through such vehicles as Facebook and Twitter.

The global economy and information technology are also redefining group life in ways we can already perceive. For instance, workers in earlier generations spent much of their careers in a relatively small number of long-lasting, bureaucratic organizations; younger workers today are much more likely to be part of a succession of networked, flexible, and even virtual organizations.

How will these trends affect the quality of our social relationships? Will the blurring between primary and secondary groups continue and expand? Will our growing reliance on social media as a key forum for interaction foster integration or alienation? In our changing social environment, these questions pose important frontiers for sociological analysis.

 ## What Can I Do with a Sociology Degree?

LEADERSHIP SKILLS AND TEAMWORK

Sociology students not only examine theories and research about groups and organizations (Chapter 5), they often have multiple opportunities both in and out of class to develop leadership and teamwork skills that are essential in the workplace. In fact, many of the skills discussed in other "Skills and Careers" sections in this book are essential to leadership and teamwork, especially problem solving (Chapter 6), understanding diversity (Chapter 10), interpersonal skills (Chapter 4), and community resource skills (Chapter 16).

Effective leaders must be able to harness organizational and community resources as well as human capital to meet goals. They must be able to identify and address challenging group dynamics to ensure that people work together effectively. Leadership of a team requires the ability to work with team members and stakeholders of diverse backgrounds. Sociology students gain a critical understanding of issues of power and inequality and intergroup relationships, especially the ways in which social identities of race, class, gender, sexual orientation, and so forth influence interaction and participation. Sociology students learn to ask critical questions about who is participating and who has the power to make decisions. The interpersonal competencies discussed elsewhere, particularly increased self-awareness and perspective taking and communication and conflict resolution skills, are essential to effective leadership and teamwork in diverse workplaces. Sociology students are increasingly exposed to experiential learning

(Continued)

(Continued)

opportunities that encourage the development of these skills firsthand through student leadership programs, internships, and service learning in various organizations.

Jillian Hubbard, Principal and Founder of Jillian Hubbard Consulting

The George Washington University, BA in Multicultural Studies

As a principal and founder of my own firm, I provide consulting services to organizations and individuals in the areas of organizational development, talent development, and diversity and inclusion to help organizations best achieve their identified steps for improvement. In my career, I've led and supported a variety of projects to assist individuals and organizations in initiatives such as volunteer recruitment, values development and implementation, staff management support, and workshop development and facilitation. Most recently, as a consultant with the American Conference on Diversity, I led the organization in the assessment of its program department and developed detailed plans to strengthen its intern, volunteer, and student alumni programs.

My long-standing passion for developing people, teams, and organizations stems from a series of formative educational and professional experiences, including my courses in sociology, which demonstrated to me how strong communication, shared understanding, team-oriented leadership, and thoughtful strategy can create lasting personal and professional transformation. Leadership and teamwork skills are important for all levels of organization leaders and supporters in a variety of environments, including corporate, government, and nonprofit.

Career Data: Training and Development Specialists

- 2017 Median Pay: $60,360 per year
- $29.02 per hour
- Typical Entry-Level Education: Bachelor's degree
- Job Outlook, 2016–2026: 11% (Faster than average)

Source: Bureau of Labor Statistics, *Occupational Outlook Handbook*, 2017.

SUMMARY

- The importance of social groups in our lives is one of the salient features of the modern world. Social groups are collections of people who share a sense of common identity and regularly interact with one another based on shared expectations. There are many conceptual ways to distinguish social groups sociologically in order to better understand them.

- Among the most important characteristics of a group is whether or not it serves as a reference group—that is, a group that provides standards by which we judge ourselves in terms of how we think we appear to others, what sociologist Charles Horton Cooley termed the *looking-glass self.*

- Group size is another variable that is an important factor in group dynamics. Although their intensity may diminish, larger groups tend to be more stable than smaller groups of two (**dyads**) or three (**triads**) people. While even small groups can develop a formal group structure, larger groups develop a formal structure.

- Formal structures include some people in leadership roles—that is, those group members who are able to influence the behavior of the other members. The most common form of leadership is **transactional**—that is, routine leadership concerned with getting the job done. Less common is **transformational leadership**, which is concerned with changing the very nature of the group itself.

- Leadership roles imply that the role occupant is accorded some power, the ability to mobilize resources and get things done despite resistance. Power derives from two principal sources: the personality of the leader (**personal power**) and the position that the leader occupies (**positional power**). Max Weber highlighted the importance of charisma as a source of leadership as well as leadership deriving from traditional authority (a queen inherits a throne, for example).

- In general, people are highly susceptible to group pressure. Many people will conform to group norms or obey orders from an authority figure, even when there are potentially negative consequences for others or even for themselves.

- Important aspects of groups are the networks that are formed between groups and among the people in them. Networks constitute broad sources of relationships, direct and indirect, including connections that may be extremely important in business and politics. Women, people of color, and lower-income people typically have less access to the most influential economic and political networks than do upper-class White males in U.S. society.

- As a consequence of unequal access to powerful social networks, there is an unequal division of social capital in society. **Social capital** is the knowledge and connections that enable people to cooperate with one another for mutual benefit and to extend their influence. Some social scientists have argued that social capital has declined in the United States during the last quarter century—a process they worry indicates a decline in Americans' commitment to civic engagement.

- **Formal organizations** are organizations that are rationally designed to achieve their objectives by means of rules, regulations, and procedures. They may be **utilitarian**, **coercive**, or **normative**, depending on the reasons for joining. One of the most common types of formal organizations in modern society is the bureaucracy. Bureaucracies are characterized by written rules and regulations, specialized offices, a hierarchical structure, impersonality in record keeping, and professional administrative staff.

- The **iron law of oligarchy** holds that large-scale organizations tend to concentrate power in the hands of a few people. As a result, even supposedly democratic organizations tend to become undemocratic when they become large.

- A number of organizational alternatives to bureaucracies exist. These include collectives, which emphasize cooperation, consensus, and humanistic relations. Networked organizations, which increase flexibility by reducing hierarchy, are similar to collectives in their organization.

- Two important forms of global organizations are **international governmental organizations (IGOs)** and **international nongovernmental organizations (INGOs)**. Both kinds of organizations play increasingly important roles in the world today, and IGOs—particularly the United Nations—may become key organizational actors as the pace of globalization increases.

KEY TERMS

dyad, 116	personal power, 119	coercive organizations, 124
triad, 116	groupthink, 121	normative organizations (or voluntary
alliance (or coalition), 116	structuralism, 122	associations), 124
social closure, 117	economic capital, 123	iron law of oligarchy, 128
transformational leader, 117	social capital, 123	international governmental
transactional leader, 119	organization, 124	organization (IGO), 130
legitimate authority, 119	formal organization, 124	international nongovernmental
positional power, 119	utilitarian organizations, 124	organization (INGO), 131

DISCUSSION QUESTIONS

1. Can you think of a time when a group to which you belonged was making a decision you thought was wrong—ethically, legally, or otherwise—but you went along anyway? How do your experiences confirm or refute Janis's characterization of groupthink and its effects?

2. List the primary and secondary groups of which you are a member, then make another list of the primary and secondary groups to which you belonged five years ago. Which groups in these two periods were most important for shaping (a) your view of yourself, (b) your political beliefs, (c) your goals in life, and (d) your friendships?

3. Think of a time when you chose to go along to get along with a group decision, even when you were inclined to think or behave differently. Think of a time when you opted to dissent, choosing a path different from that pursued by your group or organization. How would you account for the different decisions? How might sociologists explain them?

4. What did Stanley Milgram seek to test in his human experiments at Yale University? What did he find? Do you think that a similar study today would find the same results? Why or why not?

5. Max Weber suggested that bureaucracy, while intended to maximize efficiency in tasks and organizations, could also be highly irrational. He coined the term *the iron cage* to talk about the web of rules and regulations he feared would ensnare modern societies and individuals. On one hand, societies create organizations that impose rules and regulations to maintain social order and foster the smooth working of institutions such as the state and the economy. On the other hand, members of society may often feel trapped and dehumanized by these organizations. Explain this paradox using an example of your own encounters with the "iron cage" of bureaucracy.

Want a better grade?

Get the tools you need to sharpen your study skills. Access practice quizzes, eFlashcards, videos, and multimedia at **https://edge.sagepub.com/chambliss4e**.

Deviance and Social Control

WHAT DO YOU THINK?

1. Is everyone deviant at least some of the time? Does this make deviance normal?

2. Why did the rate of imprisonment rise dramatically in the U.S. beginning in the 1980s?

3. What methods of controlling deviance are available to countries and communities? What methods do you believe are more or less effective for controlling deviance?

LEARNING OBJECTIVES

6.1 Define *deviance* from a sociological perspective.

6.2 Describe key theories used in sociology to explain deviance.

6.3 Identify types of deviance studied by sociologists.

6.4 Discuss how deviance is controlled and punished in the U.S. today.

TO SOLVE A MURDER

A recent *Washington Post* investigation revealed that in 50 of the country's largest cities, about 49% of homicide investigations result in an arrest. In its analysis of 52,000 murders committed in the last the decade, the report found significant differences in cases where murders are solved by law enforcement and where, in the article's words, "murder is common but arrests are rare" (Lowery, Kelly, Mellnik, & Rich, 2018, para. 4). While the rate of violent crime in the U.S. has fallen significantly in recent years, the homicide arrest rate in 34 of the 50 cities examined has also declined. City-level data alone, however, fails to show an important aspect of the issues: specifically, in many cities, arrest rates for criminal homicide in some city neighborhoods diverge dramatically from the city's average.

In Omaha, Nebraska, for instance, police made arrests in about 60% of the city's homicide cases; in one particular 12-block neighborhood on the city's eastern side, however, the arrest rate was just 15%.

Maps highlight variations by city neighborhood (Figure 6.1). The article notes that "some cities, such as Baltimore and Chicago, solve so few homicides that vast areas stretching for miles experience hundreds of homicides with virtually no arrests" (Lowery, Kelly, Mellnik, & Rich, 2018, para. 6.). What explains the vast

©David McNew/Getty Images

■ **FIGURE 6.1**   Indianapolis Homicides

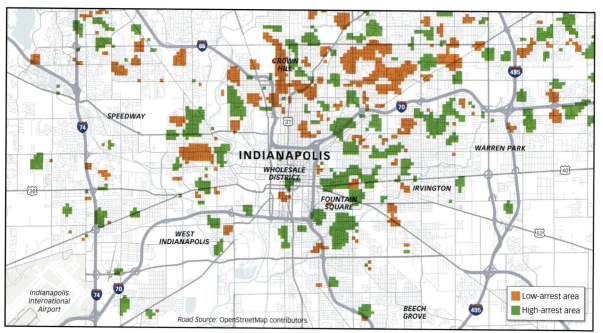

Source: Lowery, W., Kelly, K., Mellnik, T., & Rich, S. (2018, June 6). Where Killings Go Unsolved. *The Washington Post.*

differences in homicide arrest rates between neighborhoods in the same city? The issue is complex, but several factors stand out.

First, in neighborhoods with low arrest rates, relationships between police and residents are marked by low levels of confidence and trust (Tyler, 2005). Particularly in minority neighborhoods where residents may feel that they do not get adequate respect and protection from police officers, a sense that has been exacerbated by high-profile police shootings of unarmed Black men, low levels of trust translate into low levels of cooperation (Kochel, 2017). Paradoxically,

> detectives say they cannot solve homicides without community cooperation, which makes it almost impossible to close cases in areas where residents already distrust police. As a result, distrust deepens, and killers remain on the street with no deterrent (Lowery, Kelly, Mellnik, & Rich, 2018, para. 9).

Second, residents in high-crime neighborhoods may fear retaliation from killers if they cooperate with police (Riedel & Jarvis, 1999). In Indianapolis, Indiana, police point out that last year, a local gang posted a video on YouTube with the title, "Ain't no tellin." The video, which was filmed at a cemetery, featured gang members acting out a scene in which "a young man is bound, doused in gasoline and set on fire—presumably for cooperating with police" (Lowery, Kelly, Mellnik, & Rich, 2018, para. 24).

Third, the race and ethnicity of victims and police are relevant factors in this story. On the one hand, arrest rates vary significantly by the race of the victim: When the victim was White, an arrest was made in 63% of cases; when the victim was Hispanic, in 48% of cases;

and when the victim was Black, in 46% of cases. On the other hand, while most low-arrest zones are in minority-dominated neighborhoods, most police departments and homicide detectives are White. For instance, in Indianapolis, where just 64 of 155 homicides in 2017 resulted in an arrest, 69% of murder victims are Black and only six of 30 homicide detectives are nonwhite (Lowery, Kelly, Melnick, & Rich, 2018). A recent study in the United Kingdom found that "diversity can mitigate the institutionalized practice of officers acting on implicit assumptions about minorities being inherently more unlawful than whites." Increased diversity also correlated with lower rates of "stop and search" of minority residents, which had the effect of increasing trust between the police and community residents (Hong, 2015).

Research shows that homicide clearance rates are affected by a spectrum of factors, which are both in and outside of police control: whether a victim is a member of a gang, whether the killing was drug related, the number of detectives assigned to the case, and whether the police response was under 30 minutes, among others (Braga & Dusseault, 2018). As we saw at the beginning of this section, they are also affected by neighborhood: The risk of a crime going unsolved is significantly greater when the victim resides in a low-income and minority-dominated area.

Resolution of homicide cases contributes to justice and closure for victims' families and communities. Would greater clearance rates also contribute to a lowered incidence of crimes in low-arrest neighborhoods? What other effects might there be? What do you think?

Deviance is an expansive concept, encompassing an array of attitudes, behaviors, and conditions, of which only a small part fall under the category of crime, including homicides or robberies. We begin this chapter by looking at how *deviance* is defined. This is followed by an examination of different perspectives that sociologists employ to understand and explain deviant behavior. We then consider the spectrum of ways in which U.S. society exercises social control over groups and behaviors defined as deviant, including both criminal and noncriminal behavior.

What Is Deviant Behavior?

Deviance *is any attitude, behavior, or condition that violates cultural norms or societal laws and results in disapproval, hostility, or sanction if it becomes known.* By contrast, a **crime** *is any act defined in the law as punishable by fines, imprisonment, or both.*

Several important aspects of our definition of deviance deserve greater elaboration. First, *deviance* is a broad term that may encompass crimes but often refers to noncriminal attitudes, practices, and conditions. Second, deviance is not restricted to specific groups, genders, or generations. Third, what is considered deviant can include things that are not consciously chosen, such as medical conditions, mental or physical illnesses, and physical defects and abnormalities. Fourth, deviance is a relative, subjective concept. Definitions of deviance vary from place to place, across time, and among

©iStockphoto.com/Portra

Sociologists suggest that what is labeled *deviant* depends on cultural norms and changes over time and place. Tattoos, once limited to a few subcultures, are widely accepted in U.S. society, although individuals who change their appearance very dramatically may still be subject to this label.

Deviance: Any attitude, behavior, or condition that violates cultural norms or societal laws and results in disapproval, hostility, or sanction if it becomes known.

Crime: Any act defined in the law as punishable by fines, imprisonment, or both.

groups within society. Finally, our definition of deviance suggests that it is primarily a reaction against something. Therefore, deviance is best seen as a label applied to the attitudes, practices, or conditions of other people or groups. As such, moral, social, and legal judgments play a role in decisions regarding what is or is not deviant.

Is all deviance criminal? In fact, most of the attitudes, practices, and conditions considered deviant by society at any given time are not criminal. For example, while having extensive tattoos or piercings may be considered deviant, it is not criminal. The follow-up question—Are all criminal acts deviant?—has a more complicated answer. Although the label *crime* applies to acts that are widely agreed to be deviant in nature (for example, murder, robbery, rape, the sexual exploitation of children, and arson), such consensus is lacking regarding other kinds of crimes. Use of illicit drugs, some types of gambling, vagrancy, and adult prostitution are a few examples of crimes that lack societal consensus about their deviance. Once an act is labeled *criminal*, formal sanctions can be applied to control it and the people who engage in it. One should be cautious not to make the assumption that every act labeled a crime is considered deviant by all of society's members, or that every form of deviance is or should be criminalized.

The diversity of opinion surrounding deviance and criminality stems from the fact that most societies in the modern world are pluralistic. **Pluralistic societies** are *made up of many diverse groups with different norms and values,* which may or may not change over time. In a pluralistic society, what is deviant for one social group may be acceptable or normal in another, and even long-held beliefs and practices are sometimes subject to transformation over time. For example, in the 1800s, members of the Church of Jesus Christ of Latter-day Saints (Mormons) practiced polygamy—specifically, men could have multiple wives—but by the end of the 19th century, the church officially condemned that practice. Similarly, in 2005, after centuries of supporting the execution of juveniles for **capital offenses**, which are *crimes punishable by death,* the U.S. Supreme Court ruled that it is unconstitutional to execute anyone for a crime he or she committed before the age of 18. Prior to this ruling, 22 individuals had been executed for crimes they committed while younger than age 18 (Death Penalty Information Center, n.d.). The shifting legal status of marijuana, which is now legal to purchase and consume for medical purposes in several states and is legal for recreational use in Colorado, Washington State, Oregon, Alaska, and Washington, DC (Drug Policy Alliance, n.d.), is also

illustrative of dynamic definitions of deviance. In each case, norms pertaining to practices or punishment shifted over time, creating a new normal.

How Do Sociologists Explain Deviance?

What explains deviance? Below, we look at a spectrum of theoretical perspectives that seek to explain why people engage in deviance. We divide these theories broadly into explanatory and interactionist categories. Theories that try to explain *why* deviance does (or does not) occur, including biological, functionalist, and conflict perspectives, differ from interactionist theories, which seek to understand *how* deviance is defined, constructed, and enacted through social processes such as labeling.

Biological Perspectives

Early social scientists were convinced that deviant behavior—from alcoholism to theft to murder—was caused by biological or anatomical abnormalities (Hooton, 1939). For example, some early researchers claimed that *skull configurations of deviant individuals differed from those of nondeviants,* a theory known as **phrenology**. Other theorists claimed that deviants were **atavisms**, or *throwbacks to primitive early humans* (Lombroso, 1896), and that they also had body types that differed from those of noncriminals (Sheldon, 1949). These early biological theories have been disproved, but the search for biological causes of deviance continues, with some interesting findings in individual cases (Wright, Tibbetts, & Daigle, 2008). Advances in medical technology, especially increased use of magnetic resonance imaging (MRI and fMRI [functional MRI]), have enabled researchers to uncover patterns of brain function, physiology, and response unique to some deviant or criminal individuals (Giedd, 2004). Nevertheless, most modern biological theories do not attribute deviance to biology alone. Instead, they argue that some deviance may be the product of an interaction between biological and environmental factors (Denno, 1990; Kanazawa & Still, 2000; Mednick, Moffitt, & Stack, 1987).

One method for testing biological theories is to compare children with their parents to see whether children of parents with deviant lifestyles are more likely to recreate those lifestyles than are children whose parents are not deviant. Research has found that people who suffer from alcoholism and some forms of mental illness (particularly schizophrenia, chronic depression, and bipolar personality disorder) are indeed more likely to have parents with similar problems

---

Pluralistic societies: Societies made up of many diverse groups with different norms and values.

Capital offenses: Crimes punishable by death.

Phrenology: A theory that the skull configurations of deviant individuals differ from those of nondeviants.

Atavisms: Throwbacks to primitive early humans.

than are people who do not have these conditions (Dunner, Gershon, & Barrett, 1988; Scheff, 1988).

Nevertheless, studies comparing the frequency of deviance between generations do not always control for the possibility that children of alcoholic, schizophrenic, depressed, or bipolar parents may have learned coping strategies that show up as symptoms of these problems, rather than having inherited a biological predisposition. Children of farmers are more likely to be farmers than are children of urban office workers, but we would not argue that farming is a biologically determined trait. Furthermore, many children of parents who are deviant are not deviant themselves, and many people with deviant lifestyles come from mainstream families (Chambliss & Hass, 2011; Katz & Chambliss, 1995; Scheff, 1988).

Studies that have found similarities in patterns of deviant behavior between twins are often cited as evidence in support of biological theories of deviance. The Danish sociologist Karl Christiansen (1977) examined the life histories of 7,172 twins. Among these, 926 had been convicted of a crime. Christiansen found that 35% of the identical male twins who had been convicted of a crime had twin brothers who had also been convicted of a crime. Among male fraternal twins, 21% who had committed a crime had brothers who also had committed a crime (Christiansen, 1977). Biological theorists interpret these findings as support for the theory that biological factors contribute to deviant and criminal behavior (Mednick, Gabrielli, & Hutchings, 1987).

Interestingly, critics of biological theories see this evidence as *disproving* the influence of biology. Among both men and women, in most cases where one twin has committed a crime, the other twin has not. Moreover, if criminal behavior were genetically determined, we should expect that nearly all twin brothers or sisters of identical twins who are criminals should also be criminals (Katz & Chambliss, 1995).

Cesare Lombroso, an early criminologist, theorized that criminals were throwbacks to primitive humans. Although his theory has been disproved by research, the search for biological causes of criminality continues.

To the extent that identical twins do show similar patterns of deviance as adults, we can attribute these patterns to their common socialization: Identical twins are more likely than other siblings to be treated the same, dressed alike, and sometimes even confused with one another.

A more nuanced approach to biological explanations of deviance attempts to incorporate *both* sets of factors. The nature *versus* nurture paradigm is essentially converted to nature *and* nurture. Criminologist Kevin Beaver and a team of researchers took a more critical approach to this question by examining a general theory of crime posited by Gottfredson and Hirschi. A major tenet of this theory is that low self-control is largely a result of parental management influences and not of biogenetic factors. Beaver's study, which analyzed twin data drawn from the National Longitudinal Study of Adolescent Health, estimated that genetic factors accounted for 52% to 64% of the variance in low self-control, with twins' nonshared environments accounting for the remaining variance (Beaver, Wright, DeLisi, & Vaughn, 2008). As expansive genetic and biological data become increasingly accessible, a school of thought within criminology is pursuing the question of how biological factors may play a part in crime and deviance.

Functionalist Perspectives

Functionalist theories suggest that we must examine culture, especially shared norms and values, to understand why people behave the way they do. Recall that functionalist theory assumes society is characterized by a high degree of consensus on norms and values. It regards deviance as an abnormality that society seeks to eliminate, much as an organism seeks to rid itself of a parasite. At the same time, functionalist theory sees a certain amount of deviant behavior as useful—or functional—for society. It suggests that deviance—or the labeling of some behaviors as deviant—contributes to social solidarity by enhancing members' sense of the boundary between right and wrong (Durkheim, 1893/1997).

Deviance and Social Solidarity

Émile Durkheim (1858–1917), the father of functionalist theories of deviance, hypothesized that deviant behavior serves a positive function in society by drawing moral boundaries, delineating what behavior is acceptable and what is not within a community. Durkheim argued that we can describe a society lacking consensus on what is right and wrong as being in a state of *anomie,* a condition of confusion that occurs when people lose sight of the shared rules and values that give order and meaning to their lives. In one of his most famous studies, Durkheim sought to show that anomie is a principal cause of suicide, itself a deviant act.

Durkheim (1897/1951) gathered extensive data on suicide in France and Italy and found that these data supported the theory that societies characterized by high levels of anomie also have high levels of suicide. Moreover, he argued that his research demonstrated that suicide rates vary depending on the level of *social solidarity,* the social bonds that unite members of a group. Durkheim discovered, for example, that single men had higher rates of suicide than married men, Protestants a higher rate than Catholics, and men higher rates than women. Durkheim suggested that the higher rates were correlated with lower levels of social solidarity in the groups to which people were attached.

Durkheim's research methods—the statistics as well as the sampling procedures—were primitive, compared with modern-day methods. Since he first published his research, however, hundreds of studies have looked at suicide differences between men and women, between industrialized and developing countries, and even among the homeless. Most of these empirical studies have found considerable support for Durkheim's anomie theory (Cutright & Fernquist, 2000; Diaz, 1999; Kubrin, 2005; Lester, 2000; Simpson & Conklin, 1989; Wasserman, 1999). Durkheim's theory has spawned some of the most influential contemporary theories of deviance, including those of Robert K. Merton, Richard Cloward, and Lloyd Ohlin, which we discuss below.

Structural Strain Theory

In the 1930s, American sociologist Robert K. Merton (1968) adapted Durkheim's concept of anomie into a general theory of deviance. According to Merton's theory, **structural strain** is *a form of anomie that occurs when a gap exists between the culturally defined goals of a society and the means available in society to achieve those goals.*

Merton argued that most people in a society share a common understanding of the goals they should pursue as well as the legitimate means for achieving those goals. For example, success (as measured in terms of wealth, consumption, and prestige) is widely regarded as an important goal in U.S. society. Moreover, there appears to be widespread consensus on the legitimate means for achieving success—education, an enterprising spirit, and hard work, among others.

Most people pursue the goal of "success" by following established social norms. Merton referred to such behavior as *conformity.* Nevertheless, success is not always attainable through conventional means or conformity. When this occurs, Merton argued, the resulting contradiction between societal goals and the means of achieving them creates *strain,* which may result in four different types of deviant behavior. His **strain theory** suggests that *when there is a discrepancy between the cultural goals for success and the means available to achieve those goals, rates of deviance will be high.* Reactions to the discrepancy will lead to the types of deviance depicted in the first column in Table 6.1. Since Merton's original formulation of strain theory, other researchers have expanded on his work. For example, Kaufman (2009) explored the relation between general strains and gender, finding that serious strains may affect men and women differently and influence their inclination to engage in deviance. Women, Kaufman found, are especially likely to engage in deviance in response to depression.

Opportunity Theory

Although Merton's theory helps us understand the structural conditions leading to high rates of deviance, it neglects the fact that not everyone has the same access to deviant solutions. This is the point made by Richard Cloward and Lloyd Ohlin (1960), who developed **opportunity theory** as an extension of Merton's strain theory. According to Cloward and Ohlin, *people differ not only in their motivations to engage in deviant acts but also in their opportunities to do so.* For instance, only the presence of a demand for illicit drugs, plus access to supplies of those drugs through producers, offers opportunities for individuals to become drug dealers. Similarly, unless you have access to funds you can secretly convert to your own use, you are unlikely to consider embezzlement as an option, much less carry it out. Deviance, then, is more likely in a community when the opportunities for it exist.

TABLE 6.1 Merton's Typology of Deviance

TYPE OF RESPONSE	CULTURAL GOALS	LEGITIMACY OF MEANS
Conformity	Accept	Accept
Innovation	Accept	Reject
Ritualism	Reject	Accept
Retreatism	Reject	Reject
Rebellion	Reject/substitute	Reject/substitute

Source: Data from Merton, Robert K. (1968, orig. 1938). *Social theory and social structure.* NY: Free Press, pp. 230–246.

Structural strain: In Merton's reformulation of Durkheim's functionalist theory, a form of anomie that occurs when a gap exists between the culturally defined goals of a society and the means available in society to achieve those goals.

Strain theory: The theory that when there is a discrepancy between the cultural goals for success and the means available to achieve those goals, rates of deviance will be high.

Opportunity theory: The theory that people differ not only in their motivations to engage in deviant acts but also in their opportunities to do so.

Global Issues

GLOBALIZATION AND CRIMINAL OPPORTUNITIES

Globalization has increased the potential for crime networks to gain wealth and political power (Block & Weaver, 2004; Naylor, 2002). At the top of the list of crimes facilitated by processes linked to globalization are money laundering and the smuggling and illicit selling of drugs, weapons, and human beings. Digital networks have multiplied these opportunities, opening new doors to global criminality.

Some of the criminal behavior takes place within legitimate institutions. For example, nearly every major bank in Europe and the United States has been found guilty of laundering money or other significant fraud at some point. In December 2012, the British bank HSBC was fined $1.9 billion for laundering billions of dollars in drug profits and for allowing terrorist groups to launder money through its Mexican affiliate (Douglas, 2013). In 2011 and 2014, the Swiss bank UBS, the British bank Barclays, and the Royal Bank of Scotland were found guilty of international rigging of interest rates by fraudulently setting the rates established through the London Interbank Offered Rate, a benchmark for interest rates covering everything from home mortgages to student loans (BBC, 2014a; Douglas, 2013). There are no reliable data on how many of these crimes occur annually, in part because of the complexity of the transactions and the lack of transparency in many aspects of global banking.

Much global criminality, however, takes place in the shadowy corners of the global marketplace. One key site for the international trade in drugs, weapons, and other illicit goods is the "dark web," an encrypted network that is not easily accessed by users of the Internet. For example, the Silk Road, a site on the dark web, was estimated at its peak to be a $1.2 billion market; it traded in illegal drugs and guns, among others. Its operator, Ross Ulbricht, was sentenced to life in prison without parole in 2015 after being caught in a Federal Bureau of Investigation (FBI) sting and prosecuted. A year later, the FBI shut down a copycat site, Silk Road 2.0. Interestingly, one of the reasons the prosecution asked for such a harsh sentence was that they hoped it would send a message to other would-be dealers on the dark web. Alas, detection and prosecution of transactions on the dark web is challenging. An article in *Wired* notes that an independent researcher

has documented in an ongoing survey of more than 70 dark web drug markets created after Ulbricht founded the Silk Road, [that] only five of those sites' administrators have been arrested. For many of the others, the security model Ulbricht pioneered—using Tor and bitcoin to protect administrators, buyers and sellers—has successfully kept law enforcement fumbling in the shadows. (Greenberg, 2015, para. 2)

Trafficking in exotic and endangered plants and animals is yet another lucrative business. In recent years, smuggling of these products has increased in part due to the emergence of consumer markets for plant and animal products in rising economies such as China and Vietnam (Bremer, 2012). Goods ranging from traditional Asian medicines to carved ivory to high-priced furs to exotic pets are smuggled from their places of origin and sold clandestinely. By one estimate, the trade in illegal wildlife alone is a $19 billion a year global business. According to a recent article,

The black market in wildlife parts and products is the fourth-largest illegal industry worldwide, behind narcotics, counterfeiting and human trafficking, and it may well outstrip other illicit enterprises in terms of the variety of crimes and the complexities they pose for law enforcement. (Rosen, 2014, para. 11)

The smuggling of people has also become a major international criminal enterprise. People pay large sums of money to be smuggled from poorer countries into wealthier ones where they imagine exists an opportunity for a better life. Women and girls are

(Continued)

©Boris Roessler/dpa/picture-alliance/Newscom

(Continued)

smuggled across borders for prostitution, sometimes under false pretenses, such as promises of jobs as waitresses or nannies. The extent of trafficking in women and girls for prostitution can only be estimated, but law enforcement and international task forces point to an alarming increase in the smuggling of human beings (Polaris Project, n.d.).

Globalization has brought benefits to countries and communities, but it has also, as we have

seen, contributed to the expansion of criminal enterprises.

Think It Through

- Who is responsible for addressing the problem of globalized crime in the contemporary world? What sociological factors make the prevention and prosecution of globalized crime particularly challenging?

Control Theory

Agreeing with the functionalist claim that a society's norms and values are the starting point for understanding deviance, Gottfredson and Hirschi's (1990/2004) **control theory** *explains that the probability of delinquency or deviance among children and teenagers is rooted in social control.* Gottfredson and Hirschi differ from Durkheim and Merton, however, regarding the importance of a general state of anomie in creating deviance, arguing instead that a person's acceptance or rejection of societal norms depends on that individual's life experiences.

Gottfredson and Hirschi (1990/2004; also, Hirschi, 2004) assert that deviance arises from **social bonds**, or *individuals' connections to others,* especially institutions, rather than from anomie. Forming strong social bonds with people and institutions that disapprove of deviance, they argue, keeps people from engaging in deviant behaviors. Conversely, people who do not form strong social bonds will engage in deviant acts because they have nothing to lose by acting on their impulses and do not fear the consequences of their actions.

Furthermore, control theorists argue that most deviant acts are spontaneous. For example, a group of teenagers see a drunken homeless man sleeping on a bench and decide to take his backpack, or a man learns of a house whose owners are on vacation and decides to burglarize it. Some people will succumb to such temptations. Those who do not, according to Gottfredson and Hirschi, have a greater willingness to conform. This willingness, in turn, comes from associating with people who are committed to conventional roles and morality.

Some evidence supports this theory. For example, delinquency is somewhat less common among youth who have strong family attachments, perform well in school, and feel

©AP Photo/Louis Lanzano

Cloward and Ohlin (1960) argue that people are more likely to engage in deviance when the social context presents opportunities for it to occur. For instance, unless you have access to a significant amount of money at your workplace, you are unlikely to engage in embezzlement or fraud.

they have something to lose by appearing deviant in the eyes of others (Gottfredson & Hirschi, 1990/2004; Hirschi, 1969). On the other hand, we could scarcely argue that white-collar criminals such as Bernie Madoff, who pleaded guilty to massive financial fraud in 2009, do not have strong social bonds to society. The success of many white-collar criminals in business suggests that they have spent their lives conforming to societal norms, yet they also commit criminal acts that cost U.S. taxpayers, investors, and pension holders billions of dollars (McLean & Elkind, 2003). Thus, although control theory explanations of deviance may prove useful in certain instances, they have limitations.

Conflict Perspectives

Recall that the conflict perspective makes the assumption that groups in society have different interests and differential access to resources with which to realize those interests. In contrast to the functionalist perspective, the conflict perspective does not assume shared norms and values. Rather, it presumes that groups with power will use that power to

Control theory: The theory that explains that that probably of delinquency or deviance among children and teenagers is rooted in social control.

Social bonds: Individuals' connections to others (see also control theory).

maintain control in society and keep other groups at a disadvantage. As we will see below, conflict theory can be fruitfully used in the study of deviance.

Subcultures and Deviance

More than three quarters of a century ago, Thorsten Sellin (1938) pointed out that the cultural diversity of modern societies results in conflicts between social groups over what kinds of behavior are right and wrong. Sellin argued that deviance is best explained through **subcultural theories**, which *identify the conflicting interests of different segments of the population,* whether it be over culture (as in Sellin's case) or, more generally, over particular rituals or behaviors. For example, immigrants to the United States bring norms and values with them from their original cultures and, to the extent that these conflict with the norms and values of the adopted country, they may be perceived—and sometimes punished—as deviant by the dominant culture.

Some practices of migrant communities might breach U.S. conventions: For instance, some Southeast Asian families (among others) still choose to follow traditional customs of arranged marriages for adult children. Although this is clearly not the norm in the United States, it is not illegal. Other customary practices, however, violate U.S. criminal laws. For instance, the practice of female genital circumcision by some immigrants from North Africa and the Middle East is a violation of U.S. law. As well, even though physical violence against a woman is understood in some communities as a husband's prerogative in marriage, immigrants to the United States who practice domestic violence are subject to arrest and prosecution.

It is not only cultural differences between immigrants and the host country that create subcultures of perceived or real deviance. Sociologists also analyze juvenile gangs, professional thieves, White racist groups, and a host of other groups as subcultures in which deviance is the norm (Chambliss & King, 1984; Cohen, 1955; Etter, 1998; Hamm, 2002).

Class-Dominant Theory

Class-dominant theories *propose that what is labeled deviant or criminal—and therefore who gets punished—is determined by the interests of the dominant class* (Quinney, 1970). For example, since labor is central to the functioning of capitalism, those who do not work will be labeled as deviant in capitalist societies (Spitzer, 1975). In a similar vein, since private property is a key foundation of capitalism, those who engage in acts against property, such as stealing or vandalism, will be labeled as criminal. And because profits are realized through buying and selling things in the capitalist marketplace, unregulated market activities (such as selling drugs on the street, making alcohol without a license, or even operating a catering service out of one's home without proper licensing) will also be defined as deviant and criminal.

Critics of class-dominant theory point out that laws against the interests of the ruling class do get passed. Laws prohibiting insider trading on the stock market, governing the labor practices of corporations, and giving workers the right to strike and form trade unions were all signed over the strident opposition of big business interests (Chambliss, 2001). To incorporate these facts, criminologist William J. Chambliss (1988a) proposed a structural contradiction theory that takes into account the limitations of (as well as the power of) capitalists in a capitalist society.

Structural Contradiction Theory

Rather than seeing the ruling class as all-powerful in determining what is deviant or criminal, **structural contradiction theory** argues that *conflicts generated by fundamental contradictions in the structure of society produce laws defining certain acts as deviant or criminal* (Chambliss, 1988a; Chambliss & Hass, 2011; Chambliss & Zatz, 1994). For instance, there is a fundamental structural contradiction in capitalist economies between the need to maximize profits (which keeps wages down) and the need to maximize consumption (which requires high wages). Consider a U.S. business that, to maximize profits, keeps wages and salaries down, perhaps by moving its factories to a part of the world where wages are low. As jobs move overseas, the availability of jobs to unskilled and semiskilled workers in the United States declines. The loss of jobs produces downward pressure on wages and a loss of purchasing power. Yet capitalism depends on people buying the things that are produced—corporations cannot profit unless they sell their products.

Trapped in the contradiction between norms valuing consumerism and an economic system that can make consumption of desired material goods and services difficult or even impossible for many, some (but not all) people will resolve the conflict by resorting to deviant and criminal acts such as cheating on income taxes, writing bad checks, or profiting from illegal markets, by selling drugs or committing theft. Of course, it is not only lower-income people who deviate to increase their consumption of material goods. Everyone who wants to enjoy a higher standard of living is a candidate for deviant or criminal behavior, according to structural contradiction theory. The head of a giant

---

Subcultural theories: Theories that explain deviance in terms of the conflicting interests of different segments of the population.

Class-dominant theories: Theories that propose that what is labeled deviant or criminal—and therefore who gets punished—is determined by the interests of the dominant class.

Structural contradiction theory: The theory that conflicts generated by fundamental contradictions in the structure of society produce laws defining certain acts as deviant or criminal.

corporation may be as tempted to violate criminal laws to increase company profits (and personal income) as is the 13-year-old from a poor family who snatches a pair of sunglasses from the drugstore.

Structural contradiction theory holds that societies with the greatest gaps between what people earn and what they are normatively enticed to consume will have the highest levels of deviance. Since industrial societies differ substantially in this regard, we can compare them to test this theory. Societies such as Finland, Denmark, Sweden, and Norway, for instance, provide a "social safety net" that guarantees all citizens a basic standard of living. Therefore, poorer residents in Scandinavian countries are able to come much closer to what their societies have established as a "normal" standard of living. The fact that rates of assault, robbery, and homicide are anywhere from 3 to 35 times higher in the United States than in these countries (depending on which country is compared) is what structural contradiction theory would predict (Archer & Gartner, 1984).

Globalization is another example of the way structural contradictions lead to changes in deviant behavior. The ability to trade worldwide increases the wealth of populations and nations that are able to take advantage of global markets. Nevertheless, it also increases opportunities for criminal activities such as money laundering, stealing patents and copyrights, and trafficking in people, arms, and drugs.

Feminist Theory

The sociological study of deviance—as with most areas of academic study—has for centuries been dominated by men. As a result, most theories and research have reflected a male point of view. Recent years, however, have witnessed a sea change in the sociological perspective as women have become better represented in sociology and criminology.

In the 1980s, a **feminist perspective on deviance** emerged within the sociological tradition (Campbell, 1984; Chesney-Lind, 1989, 2004; Messerschmidt, 1986). The starting point of feminist explanations of deviance is the observation that *studies of deviance have been biased because*

Girls sometimes form gangs in neighborhoods where male street gangs are prevalent. These girl gangs are often auxiliaries of male gangs engaged in selling drugs and committing petty crimes. Joining a gang may require an initiation ritual that involves violence, including rape.

almost all the research has been done by, and about, males, largely ignoring female perspectives on deviant behavior as well as analyses of differences in the types and causes of female deviance (Messerschmidt, 1993). By ignoring the female population, deviance theory has avoided one of the most challenging issues in the field: Why do rates of deviance—and especially criminal deviance—vary by gender?

Early feminist theory argued that gender-specific cultural norms partly account for the different rates of deviance between men and women (Adler, 1975; Steffensmeier & Allen, 1998). For example, women traditionally have been socialized into the roles of wife and mother, where behavior is more tightly prescribed than it is for men. Moreover, women's deviant behavior is more likely to be subject to **stigmatization**—that is, to be *branded as highly disgraceful*—than is comparable male behavior. For example, a woman who has multiple sexual partners may be socially shamed as a "slut," while a sexually promiscuous man is not disdained and might even be praised and admired by peers.

Feminists have argued that an adequate theory of deviance must take into account the particular ways in which women are victimized by virtue of their gender (Chesney-Lind, 2004; Mann & Zatz, 1998; Sokoloff & Raffel, 1995). For example, studies show that before becoming involved in the juvenile justice system, many girls labeled delinquent were runaways escaping sexual and physical abuse. In a 2014 study, 31% of girls reported a personal experience of sexual violence in the home, 41% reported being physically abused, and 84% reported experiencing family violence.

Feminist perspective on deviance: A perspective that suggests that studies of deviance have been biased because almost all the research has been done by, and about, males, largely ignoring female perspectives on deviant behavior as well as analyses of differences in the types and causes of female deviance.

Stigmatization: The branding of behavior as highly disgraceful (see also labeling theory).

Girls reported having been sexually abused at a rate 4.4 times higher than boys (Levintova, 2015). This research supports the hypothesis that many girls labeled delinquent have been driven out of their homes by abusive parents or relatives.

Women also continue to be disproportionately represented in cases of inmate sexual assault and victimization. Although women constitute under 7% of the total inmate population in the United States, they make up one third of all prisoner sexual victimization cases (Guerino & Beck, 2011).

Interactionist Perspectives

Interactionist perspectives provide a language and framework for looking at how deviance is constructed, including how individuals are connected to the social structure. Interactionist approaches also explain why some people are labeled deviant and behave in deviant ways while others do not. A central tenet of many interactionist approaches is that we see ourselves through the eyes of others, and our resulting sense of ourselves conditions how we behave. This idea has been applied to the study of deviant behavior in the development of both labeling theory and differential association theory.

Labeling Theory

Labeling theory holds that *deviant behavior is a product of the labels people attach to certain types of behavior* (Asencio & Burke, 2011; Lemert, 1951; Tannenbaum, 1938). From this perspective, deviance is seen as socially constructed. That is, labeling theory holds that deviance is the product of interactions wherein the response of some people to certain types of behaviors produces a label of *deviant* or *not deviant*. In turn, these labels, which also end up being applied to people engaging in certain types of behavior, can influence how people conduct themselves. Thus, labeling theory is sometimes referred to as *societal reaction theory.*

One of the founders of labeling theory, Edwin Lemert (1951), argued that the labeling process has two steps: primary deviance and secondary deviance. **Primary deviance** occurs *at the moment an activity is labeled as deviant by others.* **Secondary deviance** occurs *when a person labeled deviant accepts the label as part of his or her identity and, as a result, begins to act in conformity with the label.* To illustrate his theory, Lemert reported on a group of people in the U.S. Northwest with an unusually high incidence of stuttering. Observing the interactions among people in this group, he concluded that stuttering was common in the group partly because the members were stigmatized and labeled as stutterers (primary deviance). These stutterers then began to view themselves through this label and increasingly acted in accordance with it—which included a greater amount of stuttering than otherwise would have been the case (secondary deviance).

Chambliss's (2001) observations of the Saints and the Roughnecks also support labeling theory. In spite of engaging in similar kinds of crime and mischief, the working-class teens (the "Roughnecks") he studied in one community were labeled deviant while the middle-class boys (the "Saints") he observed were not. Chambliss sought to understand this difference. He noted that, first, the actions of the Roughnecks were far more visible than those of the Saints. With their access to automobiles, the Saints were able to remove themselves from the sight of the community, but the Roughnecks congregated in a public area where they could be seen by teachers or the police. Second, the demeanors of the gang members differed. Although the Saints showed remorse and respect, the Roughnecks offered a barely veiled contempt for authority. This resulted in different responses to their misdeeds. Third, adults in the community showed bias toward the Saints, who were presumed to be "good boys sowing wild oats" rather than "bad boys." Chambliss concluded that labels matter. Those who were labeled as *bad* largely lived up (or down) to expectations. Those whose youthful transgressions were not transformed into labels lived up to more positive expectations and became successful adults. These self-fulfilling prophecies suggest that the ways in which we opt to label individuals and groups can have important effects on outcomes.

Differential Association Theory

Another interactionist approach to the study of deviance looks at how deviance is transmitted culturally and argues that we learn deviant behaviors through our social interactions. **Differential association theory** holds that *deviant and criminal behavior results from regular exposure to attitudes favorable to acting in ways that are deviant or criminal* (Burgess & Akers, 1966; Church, Jaggers, & Taylor, 2012; Sutherland, 1929). For example, the corporate executive who embezzles company funds may have learned the norms and values appropriate to this type of criminal activity by associating with others already engaged in it. Similarly, kids and teenagers living in areas where selling and using drugs are common practices will be more likely than their peers not exposed to that subculture to develop attitudes favorable toward using and selling drugs. Conversely, populations

---

Labeling theory (or societal reaction theory): A symbolic interactionist approach holding that deviant behavior is a product of the labels people attach to certain types of behavior.

Primary deviance: A term developed by Edwin Lemert; the first step in the labeling of deviance, it occurs at the moment an activity is labeled deviant (see also secondary deviance).

Secondary deviance: A term developed by Edwin Lemert; the second step in the labeling of deviance, it occurs when a person labeled deviant accepts the label as part of his or her identity and, as a result, begins to act in conformity with the label (see also primary deviance).

Differential association theory: The theory that deviant and criminal behavior results from regular exposure to attitudes favorable to acting in ways that are deviant or criminal.

Discover & Debate

DEVIANCE AND SOCIAL CONTROL

Motion: Mandatory minimum sentences for drug crimes are a good policy for deterring and punishing drug use and trafficking.

Background: Mandatory minimum sentencing practices have a long history in U.S. criminal justice. According to the U.S. Sentencing Commission, Congress put into place the first mandatory minimum sentences in the late 18th century. Mandatory minimum penalties have long been associated with the most serious criminal offenses, including murder and treason. The broad application of mandatory minimums to drug crimes is more recent: The Anti-Drug Abuse Act of 1986 set out many of the sentencing guidelines that are currently used or were recently used for drug crimes.

Questions for Consideration

- Under what circumstances should judges be granted discretion in handing down a sentence for a drug crime?

- Are there crimes for which mandatory minimum sentences are always appropriate?

- Is mass incarceration an inevitable outcome of mandatory minimum sentencing practices?

Debate Tip

- Conduct a mock debate with your team members. This will help you to practice your speech and present your arguments in a more articulate and composed manner.

AFFIRMATIVE ARGUMENTS	OPPOSITION ARGUMENTS
Mandatory minimum sentencing ensures that a standard of justice is uniformly applied.	Mandatory minimum sentencing does not ensure the uniform application of a standard of justice because bias may be introduced at other levels of the criminal justice system. For example, prosecutors choose what charges to file and police determine whom to surveille and arrest.
Mandatory minimum sentencing deters criminal behavior because consequences for that behavior are predictable and unambiguous.	The lack of discretion in sentencing can lead to sentences that are disproportionate to the seriousness of the crime (for instance, possession of a small quantity of a drug for personal use) or the circumstances of the crimes (for instance, a perpetrator may also be a victim of coercion).
Mandatory minimum sentencing encourages cooperation by lower-level defendants seeking to avoid harsh punishments and may thus help catch higher-level offenders.	Mandatory minimum sentencing practices have contributed to mass incarceration in the United States, which imprisons more Americans per capita than any other developed democratic country.

with different subcultures or attitudes toward particular forms of deviance (such as illicit drug usage) may not experience the same rates of crime.

According to Sutherland's (1929) differential association theory, the more we associate with people whose behavior is deviant, the greater the likelihood that our behavior will also be deviant. Sutherland, therefore, linked deviance with such factors as the frequency and intensity of our associations with other people, how long they last, and how early in our lives they occur. Much has changed since Sutherland developed his theory, and today, many of our interactions take place through technologies such as the Internet and smartphones. A modern adaptation of Sutherland's theory would certainly have to take into account the importance of the unique methods of interacting today in promoting both deviant and conforming behavior.

Symbolic interactionist theories, similar to functionalist and conflict theories, provide us with considerable insight into the social processes that lead to deviance and crime in society. We might come to the conclusion that each of the competing theories makes sense and has some empirical support yet also fails to explain all the behaviors we classify as deviant or criminal. This debate and interaction between theories is essential to the development of scientific knowledge (Popper, 1959). Thus, even though there are many unique ways to examine the same topic without necessarily reaching one perfect answer with any of them, we should be reassured that each theoretical orientation presented in this chapter can be useful in explaining certain facets of deviance and crime. It is up to the researcher to decide which theory to use and why, and for others to determine whether the use of the theory was a success or failure.

Types of Deviance

As noted in the opening to this chapter, deviance comes in many varieties, from the relatively benign to the extremely harmful. In this section, we explore some of the ways in which deviance can manifest in society.

Everyday Deviance

A broad spectrum of acts could fall under the label of *everyday deviance*, from plagiarism among high school or college students to shoplifting, underage alcohol consumption, using pornography, smoking, eating meat, or calling in sick to work or school when you actually feel fine. All of these are considered deviant behaviors, actions, or conditions by some individuals and/or groups, although they are also actions in which many people engage at some point—or regularly.

In the discussion of everyday deviance, we recognize the pluralistic nature of U.S. society. Taking a subcultural perspective, we may find that smoking is more acceptable among some societal subgroups (for instance, truck drivers) than it is among others (such as fitness instructors). So, too, with eating meat: The owner of a barbecue restaurant and a vegan are likely to hold starkly different views regarding the deviance of eating meat or subsisting on a vegan diet. In turn, these views are representative of the broader societal subcultures and groups to which these individuals belong.

Everyday deviance can be explained in a variety of ways. For instance, we might use labeling theory. Pornography represents an example in which both the behavior (using pornography) and the physical object (the pornographic movie or magazine) have been labeled as deviant. We could therefore make the argument that pornography is deviant simply because people have chosen to label it as such. Yet this explanation, as you might have sensed, is pretty basic.

We could strengthen our understanding of what makes pornography deviant by including a conflict perspective. Thus, we could look at who in society has the power to define pornography as deviant and what goals such a definition might serve for that particular group. The point is that deviance in its various forms has many potential explanations, which can be strengthened through the combination of different theoretical perspectives.

Sexual Deviance

Sex, sexual orientations, and sexual practices are diverse, as are the responses to them. We are currently witnessing a process of redefinition of what deviance means within the context of intimate relationships. Look no further than the popular novel *Fifty Shades of Grey,* and the book sequels and films that followed, which made headlines for the depiction of kinky sex and for being on the nightstands of many "ordinary" men and women. *The New York Times* recently published an article titled, "Is an Open Marriage a Happier Marriage?" (Dominus, 2017), a piece that spent several days atop the newspaper's "most popular" list online. As public interest in these cultural products grows, we might argue that some "traditional" notions regarding sex, sexual orientation, and sexual activities are themselves increasingly becoming deviant because they simply do not reflect the realities of modern intimate life.

Definitions of sexual deviance can include many things—from the choices we make in terms of those with whom we begin intimate relationships to how and where those relationships are carried out. Although we could use many explanations to examine sexual deviance, by looking at the continuing controversy over same-sex marriage from a conflict perspective, we see an ongoing struggle between those groups that have long determined what passes for acceptable sexual behavior (for instance, religious groups) and those that seek to redefine normal and acceptable sexual behavior to include things other than heterosexual sex and marriage.

Deviance of the Powerful

The crimes of the famous and powerful are ubiquitous and wide ranging, from the fraudulent reporting of corporate profits to the misleading of investors to bribery, corruption, misuse of public trust, and violence. The most powerful people in public life engage in many of the same types of deviance as ordinary men and women (McLean & Elkind, 2003; McLean & Nocera, 2010; Reiman & Leighton, 2012). Sociologically, what must be taken into account is that deviance knows no class bounds.

There is normally quite a bit of public and press interest in deviance committed by athletes, celebrities, and political figures. According to *Sports Illustrated*, between January 2012 and September 2014, 33 National Football League players were arrested on charges of domestic violence, battery, assault, and murder; nearly half of the charges involved violence against women (*Sports Illustrated*, 2014). Major League Baseball player Alex Rodriguez of the New York Yankees was suspended for the 2014 season for using banned substances and lying about it. In 2015, rapper Vanilla Ice was arrested for burglary and grand theft for stealing bicycles and a couch, among other items, from a foreclosed house. The same year, actor Bill Cosby, accused by more than 50 women of assault, was charged with aggravated indecent assault. In the spring of 2018, Cosby was convicted of three counts of sexual assault and sentenced to 3 to 10 years in prison (Seemayer & Chestang, 2015).

The response of the public to the deviance of political leaders is often particularly pointed, given the trust,

Behind the Numbers

COUNTING CRIME IN THE UNITED STATES

Measuring the incidence of crime is challenging. Consider what factors might stand in the way of achieving a rigorously accurate accounting of crimes that occur in the United States in any given year. Many crimes are never reported to the police: If you forget your textbook at the library and it's gone when you return, you may choose to report the theft to the authorities or you may decide it's too much of a bother, since you probably won't get the book back. In some communities, there is a high level of distrust in law enforcement officials, so even more serious crimes such as aggravated assault may go unreported. Violent crimes are more likely than property crimes to be reported to the police, although some property crimes, such as auto theft, will be reported in high numbers since insurance companies normally require a police report before compensating the victim. Notably, the percentage of crimes reported to police has risen steadily in the last 20 years (M. Schwartz, personal communication, June 28, 2016).

What we know quantitatively about crime in the United States is built on the foundations of two programs. First, many statistical reports on crime are based on the FBI's Uniform Crime Reporting (UCR) Program. The UCR counts as crime that has been brought to the attention of the police through reports or arrests. It gathers information for a limited set of crimes: murder and nonnegligent manslaughter, forcible rape, robbery, aggravated assault, burglary, larceny–theft, motor vehicle theft, and arson. (Data on other crimes are collected but based on arrest data only.) According to the FBI, "The UCR Program is a voluntary city, university and college, county, state, tribal, and federal law enforcement program that provides a nationwide view of crime based on the submission of statistics by law enforcement agencies throughout the country" (FBI, n.d., para. 1). The UCR is dependent on the "submission of statistics," so crimes that occur but are not reported do not appear in the data.

Second, data on the incidence of crime are also gathered through the National Crime Victimization Survey (NCVS). The NCVS, unlike the UCR, does not rely on police report or arrest data. Rather, it relies on a sample of the U.S. population: Every year, about 90,000 households composed of about 160,000 people are surveyed to learn about the "frequency, characteristics, and consequences of criminal victimization in the United States." Every household is interviewed twice during the year and asked about a spectrum of crimes: rape, sexual assault, robbery, aggravated and simple assault, theft, household burglary, and motor vehicle theft. Murder is not included in the victimization survey because it cannot be a self-reported crime. The NCVS sorts the information to learn about the victimization of particular demographic groups such as racial minorities, the elderly, the young, urban residents, and so forth (U.S. Bureau of Justice Statistics, Office of Justice Programs, n.d.). Because the NCVS is based on a sample rather than reported numbers like the UCR, the resulting figures are extrapolated to the U.S. population.

Because each of these reports uses a different methodology, the results can be quite different. For example, consider the following: You have gone out to a restaurant with a friend. You hang your leather jacket on a rack by the door rather than taking it to your table. As you prepare to leave after the meal, you realize that your jacket is gone. Do you report it to the restaurant management? Probably. Do you report it to the police? If you choose to report it, it is likely to become a part of the UCR, where it will be recorded as a larceny, whether or not the perpetrator is caught or you get your jacket back. If you choose not to report it, it will not appear in the UCR. If you happen to be a part of the national sample of the NCVS, it will be recorded as a theft in those figures. If you are not part of the sample, your loss will not be recognized in the figures.

How do larceny and theft figures compare in the UCR and NCVS? In 2013, the UCR reported that there were 1,899 larcenies per 100,000 people in the U.S. In the same year, the NCVS reported that there were 100.5 thefts per 1,000 people 12 years of age and older. If we multiply the NCVS figure by 100 to get comparable figures, we see that the NCVS figure of 10,050 per 100,000 population is about 5.3 times higher than the UCR figure of 1,899 per 100,000 population. Although the comparison is imperfect, it suggests that there is a gap between the incidence of crimes and their reporting to police. Both the UCR and the NCVS provide valuable information about crime in the U.S., but conclusive figures cannot be determined from either report.

Think It Through

- If you were to create a program with the goal of rigorously measuring crime on your campus, how would you structure the program? What lessons would you draw from the UCR and NCVS approaches?

©Andrew Harrer/Bloomberg via Getty Images

Scott Pruitt was the U.S. Environmental Protection Agency (EPA) head until recent public scandals and federal investigations of his abuse of power and misuse of taxpayer money forced him out of office.

responsibility, and power vested in those individuals. In 2016, former Speaker of the U.S. House of Representatives, Dennis Hastert, pled guilty for illegal actions linked to a $3.5 million payment to silence allegations of sexual misconduct with a student when he was a high school teacher and coach decades ago. Prosecutors say he molested at least four high-school-age boys (Davey & Smith, 2016). In March 2018, Representative Blake Farenthold, a Republican from Texas, resigned his seat in Congress, bowing to pressure put on him after an investigation revealed that he had used $84,000 in taxpayers' money to settle a sexual harassment claim with a former Congressional employee (Politico, 2018).

On the one hand, empirical data show that the powerful are more likely than those without power to escape punishment for deviance. On the other hand, public figures who are caught in acts of deviance are often subject to acute media attention and broad disdain, particularly when their acts violate public trust and waste public resources.

Crime

Our discussion thus far has been concerned primarily with deviance in a general sense—those attitudes, behaviors, and conditions that are widespread but generally not condemned by all or seen as especially serious. In this section, we discuss *crime*—acts that are sometimes considered deviant and are defined under the law as punishable by fines, imprisonment, or both. Law enforcement agencies across the United States take rigorous steps to record formally how much crime occurs, to prosecute criminal offenders, and to control and prevent crime.

Violent and Property Crimes

A great deal of effort is expended on the measurement of crime in U.S. society. This is accomplished through official,

limited records such as the FBI's Uniform Crime Reports (UCR) and the collection of survey data from individuals and households across the country via the National Crime Victimization Survey (NCVS). These measures of crime, especially the UCR, focus predominantly on violent and property crimes, serious forms of deviance that nearly every person in society agrees should be made illegal (see the *Behind the Numbers* box in this chapter).

According to the FBI UCR Program, **violent crimes** are composed of four offenses: *murder and negligent manslaughter, rape, robbery, and aggravated assault*. They are "those offenses that involve force or threat of force" (FBI, 2017a, para. 1). **Property crimes** in the UCR are *crimes that involve the violation of individuals' ownership rights, including burglary, larceny–theft, motor vehicle theft, and arson*. According to the FBI, "The object of the theft-type offenses is the taking of money or property, but there is no force or threat of force against the victims" (FBI, 2017b, para. 1). Property crimes are much more common in the United States than violent crimes, although their number, like the number of violent crimes (Figure 6.2), has been steadily declining (Figure 6.3). Recent data show that since 2008, violent crimes and property crimes have declined by 23% (Gelb & Denney, 2018). Variations of serious deviance, including violent and property crimes, can be analyzed from a variety of perspectives. For instance, violent crimes might be viewed from an opportunity theory perspective and property crimes in terms of societal strain. How might such analyses look?

Organized Crime

Sociologists define **organized crime** as *crime committed by criminal groups that provide illegal goods and services*. Gambling, prostitution, selling and trafficking in illegal drugs, black marketeering, loan sharking, and money laundering are some of the most prominent activities of organized crime (Block & Chambliss, 1981; Glenny, 2009; McCoy, 1991; Paoli, 2003).

White-Collar Crime

To meet the demand for illegal goods and services, criminal organizations have flourished in U.S. urban areas since the 1800s (Woodiwiss, 2000). Over the years, they have recruited members and leadership from more impoverished groups in society, such as new immigrants in big cities, who may have great aspirations but limited means of achieving

---

Violent crimes: Crimes that involve force or threat of force, including murder and negligent manslaughter, rape, robbery, and aggravated assault.

Property crimes: Crimes that involve the violation of individuals' ownership rights, including burglary, larceny/theft, motor vehicle theft, and arson.

Organized crime: Crime committed by criminal groups that provide illegal goods and services.

■ **FIGURE 6.2** Violent Crime Rate in the United States

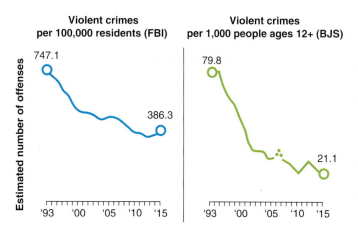

Source: Pew Research and Bureau of Justice Statistics and FBI.

Note: FBI figures include reported crimes only. Bureau of Justice Statistics (BJS) figures include unreported and reported crimes. 2006 and 2016 BJS estimates are not comparable with other years due to methodological changes.

■ **FIGURE 6.3** Property Crime Rate in the United States

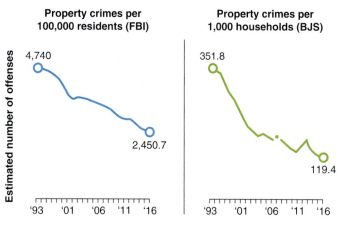

Sources: Pew Research and Bureau of Justice Statistics and FBI.

them (Block & Weaver, 2004). Consequently, organized crime has been dominated by the most recent arrivals to urban areas: Irish, Jewish, and Italian mobs in the past and Asian, African, South American, and Russian mobs today (Albanese, 1989; Finckenauer & Waring, 1996; Hess, 1973).

Depictions of organized crime in movies and television shows such as *The Sopranos, The Godfather, Scarface,* and *Goodfellas* have popularized the erroneous impression that there is an international organization of criminals (the Mafia) dominated by Italian Americans. The reality is that organized crime consists of thousands of different groups throughout the United States and the world. No single

ethnic group or organization has control over most or even a major share of these activities, which include human trafficking and weapons and drug smuggling (Block & Weaver, 2004; Chambliss, 1988a).

When most people think of crime, they think of the violent and property crimes discussed above—and they think of crimes committed by those in lower socioeconomic groups. But the forms of crime perpetrated by individuals and groups who possess great power, authority, and influence are also often deeply harmful to society.

White-collar crime is *crime committed by people of high social status in connection with their work* (Sutherland, 1949/1983). There are two principal types: crimes committed for the benefit of the individual who commits them and crimes committed for the benefit of the organization for which the individual works.

Among the many white-collar crimes that benefit the individual are the theft of money by accountants who alter their employers' or clients' books and the overcharging of clients by lawyers. More costly types of white-collar crime occur when corporations and their employees engage in criminal conduct either through *commission* (by doing something criminal) or *omission* (by failing to prevent something criminal or harmful from occurring).

White-collar crimes of all sorts receive considerable media attention. The following constitute a sample of white-collar criminal cases publicized over the past few years:

- In 2008, at the height of the U.S. recession, Bernard "Bernie" Madoff, a former Wall Street executive, was arrested and charged with managing an intricate criminal scheme that stole at least $50 billion from corporate and individual investors. Madoff pled guilty to 11 criminal counts in Manhattan's federal district courthouse and was sentenced to 150 years in prison (Rosoff, Pontell, & Tillman, 2010).

- In 2010, financial giant JPMorgan Chase was fined $48.6 million by British financial regulators for "failing to keep clients' funds separate from those of the firm." The error went undetected for more than seven years and placed billions of dollars of client funds at risk of being lost (Werdigier, 2010).

White-collar crime: Crime committed by people of high social status in connection with their work.

- General Motors Corporation, which received close to $50 billion in bailout funds from American taxpayers to stay financially solvent, was implicated in a scandal in early 2014 for failing to fix a defective ignition switch in its Chevrolet Cobalt line of vehicles (Isidore, 2012; Wald, 2014). The company allegedly chose not to make the fix, which caused vehicles to lose power while running and may have resulted in more than a dozen deaths, because doing so would have added to the cost of each car (Lienert & Thompson, 2014). The National Highway Transportation Safety Administration, which is charged with regulating and investigating complaints about motor vehicle safety, knew of the deaths linked to the vehicles with defective switches as early as 2007 but did not act (Wald, 2014).

- In 2014, JPMorgan was fined again, this time more than $461 million, by the Financial Crimes Enforcement Network (FinCEN) of the U.S. Department of the Treasury for violating the Bank Secrecy Act by failing to report the suspicious activities of Bernie Madoff (Financial Crimes Enforcement Network, 2014).

- In 2015, the Consumer Financial Protection Bureau (2015) fined Citibank $700 million for the deceptive marketing of credit card add-on products.

- In 2017, the car manufacturer Volkswagen AG (VW) agreed to plead guilty to three criminal felony counts and to pay a penalty of $2.8 billion for selling 590,000 diesel fuel vehicles in the United States that employed a "defeat device" to cheat on mandated emissions tests and then seeking to cover up the crime (U.S. Department of Justice Office of Public Affairs, 2017).

In April 2018, Facebook chief executive officer (CEO) Mark Zuckerberg testified in front of the U.S. Congress. Zuckerberg was grilled about the theft of Facebook user data. The sale, loss, and theft of private data stored by companies such as Facebook has come under increasing scrutiny in our digital age.

Police Corruption and Police Brutality

Policing is a job vested with trust, responsibility, and authority. Police officers are the frontline enforcers of laws that are expected to limit the amount of crime that occurs in society. When violent or property crimes are committed, we rely on the police for protection and investigation. Members of the law enforcement community, however, are not immune to deviance, including corruption. In 2016, for example, three New York Police Department commanders were arrested for taking extensive gifts (including hotel rooms, jewelry, and basketball tickets) from businessmen seeking "illicit favors from the police" (Rashbaum & Goldstein, 2016).

Police brutality is another form of deviance that has a long history in the U.S. The responses of Southern police officers and sheriffs, such as Bull Connor in Birmingham, Alabama, to the 1960s civil rights marches provide well-documented examples. Police brutality continues to occur, although it often escapes sanction. The videotaped beating of Rodney King in the 1990s by four White members of the Los Angeles Police Department was a vivid example of the treatment many minority city residents suffered at the hands, and batons, of the police. Violence committed by police officers has been in the headlines with much greater frequency in recent years, perhaps because it is more likely today that incidents of violence will be caught by someone's mobile phone camera or a police body camera. Public attention has been particularly focused on the killing of unarmed Black men by police: Of 987 police shootings documented in 2017, in 68 documented cases, the victim was unarmed (*The Washington Post*, "Fatal Force, 2017). According to a *Washington Post* analysis of 2016 data, "unarmed black men were seven times as likely as unarmed whites to die from police gunfire" (Somashekhar, Lowery, Alexander, Kindy, & Tate, 2015, para. 8). In one case, a University of Cincinnati police officer pulled a Black driver over for having no front license plate. The incident ended with the officer shooting Samuel Du Bose in the head. Because the killing was captured on a body camera, the officer was arrested and charged with murder (Blow, 2015), though in most recent cases, officers have not been charged with a crime. Policing is a dangerous profession, and officers need to protect themselves and their colleagues, but violence against civilians is a high-profile problem that cannot be ignored. In light of the multitude of killings of unarmed Black men, the question of how race affects officers' reaction to a suspect is also relevant to both understanding and addressing the problem.

Both corruption and brutality represent important forms of criminal deviance committed by representatives of state authority. How can we make sense of these forms of deviance?

In the case of both police corruption and the use of excessive force by law enforcement officers, Sutherland's differential association theory may provide insights. Some studies and first-person accounts demonstrate that police officers are often exposed to various forms of deviance once they become members of the force (Kappeler, Sluder, & Alpert, 1998; Maas, 1997). Exposure to attitudes favorable to the commission of deviance and crime, especially in light of the intensity and duration of the relationships police officers form with one another, may lead some to engage in those same types of deviant or criminal behaviors. We can also view the police as having a distinct culture and, thus, see police brutality and corruption in terms of the subcultural expectations that accompany police work. Some members of the police subculture may see certain behaviors, actions, and perspectives, especially regarding the use of force, as a necessary part of accomplishing the demands of police work.

State Crimes

Finally, we turn to perhaps the most harmful form of crime among the powerful: state crime. Although police brutality and corruption are especially egregious examples of crimes occurring among those with power, state crimes rank above even them in terms of the seriousness and potential harm that may result from their commission.

State crimes *consist of criminal or other harmful acts of commission or omission perpetrated by state officials in the pursuit of their jobs as representatives of the government.* Needless to say, governments do not normally keep statistics on their own criminal behavior. Nonetheless, we do know from various contemporary and historical examples that such crimes are not uncommon (Chambliss, Michalowski, & Kramer, 2010; Green & Ward, 2004; Moloney & Chambliss, 2014; Rothe, 2009). Contemporary examples of state crime cover a spectrum of deviance and take place across the globe. Some examples include the routine torture of detainees at the U.S. military prison in Guantánamo Bay, Cuba; the secret transportation and torture of battlefield detainees in foreign prisons; and even the violation of international laws leading up to the 2004 invasion of Iraq (Grey, 2006; Kramer & Michalowksi, 2005; Paglen & Thompson, 2006; Ratner & Ray, 2004). In one study, the Chinese government was found to have taken a role in the trafficking of human body parts. The study's author found that the organs of executed prisoners were harvested by government-approved doctors and were sold to corporations and other entities for use in organ transplantation and cosmetic surgery, often at substantial profits, without the consent of the prisoners' families (Lenning, 2007). In 2016, some members of Russia's Olympic Team and the entire Paralympic Team were barred from the Rio Olympic Games due to a far-reaching doping conspiracy. In the 2018 Winter Olympic Games, athletes from Russia were forced to complete as the Olympic Athletes from Russia (OAR) team and were barred from carrying or wearing their country's flag as punishment for the country's history of doping in athletics.

Social Control of Deviance

The persistence of deviant behavior in society leads inevitably to a variety of measures designed to control it. **Social control** is defined as the *attempts by certain people or groups in society to control the behaviors of other individuals and groups to increase the likelihood that they will conform to established norms or laws.* Thus, deviance, the definition of which tends to require some sort of moral judgment, also attracts attempts at social control, usually exercised by those people or groups who possess **social power**, or *the ability to exercise social control.*

©JOSH EDELSON/AFP/Getty Images

Protesters in many U.S. cities have sought to draw attention to the problem of police brutality. In this photo, marchers demonstrate after the shooting of Stephon Clark in Sacramento, California, in March 2018.

State crimes: Criminal or other harmful acts of commission or omission perpetrated by state officials in the pursuit of their jobs as representatives of the government.

Social control: The attempts by certain people or groups in society to control the behaviors of other individuals and groups to increase the likelihood that they will conform to established norms or laws.

Social power: The ability to exercise social control.

Informal social control is *the unofficial means through which deviance and deviant behaviors are discouraged in society; it most often occurs among ordinary people during their everyday interactions.* It ranges from frowning at someone's sexist assertion to threatening to take away a child's cell phone to coerce conformity to the parent's wishes. Informal social control mechanisms explain why people don't spit on the floor in a restaurant, do choose to pay back a friend who lent them $5, or say "thank you" in response to a favor. These behaviors and responses are governed not by formal laws but by informal expectations of which we are all aware and that lead us to make certain choices. Much of the time, these informal social controls lead us into conformity with societal or group norms and away from deviance. Informal controls are thus responsible for keeping most forms of non-criminal deviance in check.

Socialization, which we have discussed in earlier chapters, thus, plays a significant role in the success of informal social control. When parents seek to get their children to conform to the values and norms of their society, they teach them to do one thing and not another. Peer groups of workers, students, and friends also implement informal social control through means such as embarrassment and criticism that work to

Suspension and expulsion significantly reduce the chance that young people will finish high school. Importantly, those without a high school degree are at greater risk of imprisonment. More than two thirds of males in state and federal prison do not have a high school diploma.

©iStockphoto.com/zodebala

control behavior and thus deviance. Bonds to institutions and people enact various informal social controls on our behavior. Such bonds have been shown to be crucial in explaining why some people engage in deviance and others do not (Laub & Sampson, 2003; Sampson & Laub, 1990).

Formal social control is defined as *official attempts to discourage certain behaviors and visibly punish others.* In the

Informal social control: The unofficial means through which deviance and deviant behaviors are discouraged in society; most often occurs among ordinary people during their everyday interactions.

Formal social control: Official attempts to discourage certain behaviors and visibly punish others; most often exercised by the state.

 ## Inequality Matters

THE WAR ON DRUGS IS BORN

In 1986, Len Bias was a University of Maryland basketball phenomenon, known to fans of the game across the country. Just two days after being drafted by the Boston Celtics, a team coming off of yet another National Basketball Championship victory, Bias died of a cocaine overdose that sent him into cardiac arrest (Weinberg, 2004). Although Bias had been using powdered cocaine, the press largely blamed crack for Bias's death, a rumor that exacerbated the widespread social panic over crack's public consequences. Reflecting on the roots of modern mass imprisonment in the United States, Jon Schuppe (2016) writes,

> In life, Len Bias was basketball's next great hope, contender for a crown that went instead to Michael Jordan. In death, he became a trigger for the war on drugs. Bias' 1986 cocaine overdose helped sparked a panic, stoked by false rumors and a high-stakes political campaign, that culminated in a law that swept thousands of low-level drug offenders—most of them young and

black—into prison. Thirty years later, America is still reeling from the impact. (para. 1)

The death of Len Bias coincided with a hotly contested midterm congressional election campaign in which both parties were seeking an advantage. Eric Sterling, then a congressional aide, points out that House Speaker Thomas O'Neill, a Democrat from Boston, "realized that the national concern about this could be the basis for a comprehensive anti-drug, anti-crime bill," shifting some advantage to his party (quoted in National Public Radio [NPR], 2011). When congressional Republicans reviewed the proposal, they were not satisfied with sentencing provisions for some offenders: "In the final days before adjournment—without any hearings—a mandatory sentencing provision was added" (NPR, 2011, para. 6).

The mandatory minimum sentences that arose from that bill had several important consequences. First, they had a disproportionate impact on minority

(Continued)

(Continued)

■ **FIGURE 6.4** U.S. State and Federal Prison Population, 1925–2016

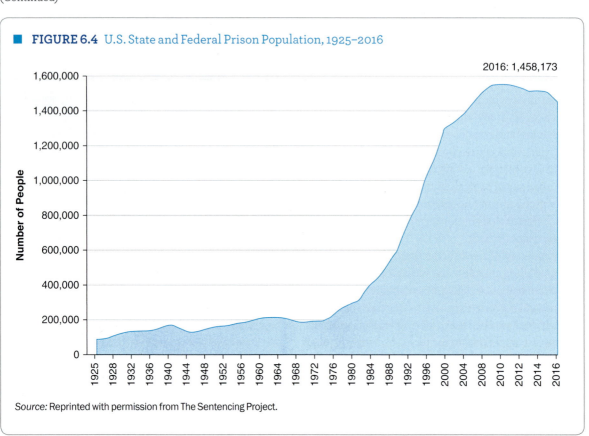

2016: 1,458,173

Source: Reprinted with permission from The Sentencing Project.

offenders, who were more likely to end up in prison for crimes (including possession of drugs) that previously would have earned a lesser sentence. The penalties for crack cocaine, widely associated with users and sellers in poor Black neighborhoods, were harsh: Laws "were weighted heavily against crack, requiring only 5 grams to trigger a five-year prison sentence, compared to 500 grams for powder cocaine. The sentences rose to 10 years with 50 grams of crack and 5,000 grams of powder" (Schuppe, 2016, "'Dark chapter,'" para. 1). Penalties for powdered cocaine, more costly and more likely to be the drug of choice for better-off White users, were dramatically lower.

Second, the laws had a deep impact on impoverished minority neighborhoods. Because males were most likely to be arrested, convicted, and imprisoned, many families were suddenly without sons, brothers, and fathers. As an article on the effects of mass incarceration on families notes, "By 2000, more than 1 million black children had a father in jail or prison—and roughly half of those fathers were living in the same household as their kids when they were locked up. Paternal incarceration is associated with behavior

problems and delinquency, especially among boys" (Coates, 2015, Part II, para. 8). The costs to families accrue even after release as ex-offenders may be excluded from public housing and have a difficult time finding employment.

Third, mandatory minimum sentences for drug crimes contributed to the dramatic rise of the prison population in the United States (Figure 6.4). In 2007, the rate of imprisonment in the United States peaked at 767 people per 100,000 (Coates, 2015). More recently, it has dropped to 450 per 100,000, although this continues to be far more than other modern democratic states around the globe (Carson, 2015, 2018).

Think It Through

- The U.S. has a significantly higher prison population than peer states around the world. Many inmates in the country's prisons and jails are serving time for drug crimes, including possession of drugs. In your opinion, how should drug crimes such as possession (for one's own use) be addressed?

modern world, formal social control is most often exercised by societal institutions associated with the state, including the police, prosecutors, courts, and prisons. The goal of all these institutions is to suppress, reduce, and punish those individuals or groups who engage in criminal forms of deviance. Theft, assault, vandalism, cheating on income taxes, fraudulent reporting of corporate earnings, and insider trading on the stock market—all have been deemed crimes and represent forms of criminal deviance. As such, they are subject to formal social control.

For an act to be criminal, several elements must be present. First, a specific law must prohibit the act and a punishment of either prison or a fine (or both) must be specified for violation of the law. Most important, the act must be intended, and the person committing the act must be capable of having the necessary intent. Someone judged to be mentally ill, which U.S. criminal law defines as the person "not knowing right from wrong" at the time of the act, cannot have the required legal intent and therefore cannot be held criminally liable for committing an illegal act. Nevertheless, the insanity defense is not accepted in all states: Idaho, Montana, Kansas, and Utah do not recognize insanity as a defense. In other state courts and federal courts, the burden of proof regarding a defendant's mental state is on the defendant. The U.S. Supreme Court refused to hear a case from Idaho in which a defendant claimed he had a constitutional right to claim insanity as a defense (Barnes, 2012).

In the sections that follow, we discuss some key issues associated with formal social control in U.S. society, including discipline in schools, the phenomenon of mass imprisonment, and the death penalty.

Schools and Discipline: Is There a School-to-Prison Pipeline?

As many U.S. public schools have tightened discipline in recent years, some observers suggest that children are diverging onto two roads: Some are tracked to careers and college, while others are tracked to prison. The **school-to-prison pipeline** refers to *the policies and practices that push schoolchildren, particularly at-risk youth, out of classrooms and into the juvenile and criminal justice systems* (American Civil Liberties Union, n.d.). Schools have made an attempt to ameliorate disciplinary problems and to promote safety in schools, but what effect has this had on children? This tightened discipline has not only affected high school students but has trickled down to preschools, increasing the probability of student infractions being harshly punished. What can a preschooler do to merit

suspension? Suspensions in preschool have resulted from such behaviors as the child kicking off his or her shoes and crying. Where this is categorized as a disturbance to the classroom, the child may be subject to disciplinary action.

What factors can help us understand the school-to-prison pipeline? First, following the 1999 Columbine shooting, when two high school students killed 13 and injured 24 students in a shooting rampage and then shot themselves, some schools enacted **zero-tolerance policies**, *school or district policy that sets predetermined punishments for certain misbehaviors and punishes the same way, no matter the severity or the context of the behavior*. This potentially helpful measure has also caused problems. The policy punishes children for a variety of infractions, including minor ones: Punishable offenses may range from carrying aspirin (which is considered a drug) to skipping class to threatening a teacher to concealing a weapon. Zero-tolerance policies have led to a rise in detentions, suspensions, and expulsions (U.S. Department of Education Office for Civil Rights, 2014).

Second, school officials have increased police presence in the schools with the intention of protecting students. This, however, has resulted in more student arrests for infractions that would have previously been handled by the school. Together with zero-tolerance policies, this has resulted in more severe punishment and more student contact with the justice system (American Civil Liberties Union, n.d.). Students as young as 10 have been treated like criminals for minor offenses such as talking back or cutting class. In a case in Queens, New York, a 12-year-old girl was taken away in handcuffs after doodling on her desk with an erasable marker (Herbert, 2010). In-school police presence increases the risk of students being pushed into the juvenile justice system, which in turn puts them at higher risk for dropping out as well as for future encounters with the criminal justice system.

Third, some observers have suggested that the increased emphasis on standardized testing results as a measure of school success may be introducing a perverse incentive to push out students who are less likely than their peers to perform well on these tests (Advancement Project, 2010). For example, a National Bureau of Economic Research paper used four years of data from Florida at the time that the state introduced a high-stakes testing regime. The author found that "while schools always tend to assign harsher punishments to low-performing students than high-performing students . . . this gap grows substantially throughout the testing window. Moreover, this testing window-related gap is only observed for students in testing grades" (Figlio, 2005, pp. 4–5).

School-to-prison pipeline: The policies and practices that push students, particularly at-risk youth, out of schools and into the juvenile and criminal justice system.

Zero-tolerance policies: School or district policy that sets predetermined punishments for certain misbehaviors and punishes the same way, no matter the severity or the context of the behavior.

Punishment and Race in the U.S.

Students of color, particularly boys, are more likely to receive punishment for disciplinary infractions in school. In this chapter, we see the longer-term consequences for this differential treatment. In the education and society chapter of this book (Chapter 12), you will see where these disparities begin: More punitive measures are taken against Black children and children with disabilities as early as preschool. Can addressing issues of inequality in disciplinary actions early in a child's education help address the problem of the school-to-prison pipeline? What other measures might be taken by the U.S. education system to both improve academic outcomes and reduce negative consequence for Black children?

Some policies that underpin the school-to-prison pipeline appear to be easing; for instance, the New York City Council, seeking greater transparency in the discipline process, now calls for detailed police reports on which students are arrested and why ("Criminalizing children at school," 2013). Nevertheless, the disproportionately high suspension and expulsion rate for students of color continues to be a key concern. Black students are three times more likely than White students to be both suspended and expelled. The police presence in schools has exacerbated the racial divide: Although Black students only represent 16% of student enrollment, they represent 31% of school-related arrests (U.S. Department of Education Office for Civil Rights, 2014). The divide has called into question the equality of the school system and the justice system. How can schools balance the need to ensure student safety while providing support for the success of all their students? What do you think?

■ **FIGURE 6.5** Incarceration Rates per 100,000 by Gender, Race, and Ethnicity in the United States, 2016

White women	49
Black women	96
Latina women	67
White men	400
Black men	2,415
Latino men	1,092

Source: Reprinted with permission from The Sentencing Project.

Imprisonment in the United States

Controlling serious, criminal forms of deviance typically includes the arrest and prosecution of individuals who have committed violent crimes or property crimes and, to a lesser extent, individuals engaged in police brutality or corruption, white-collar crime, organized crime, or state crime. Common sense would seem to indicate that most of the people subject to various formal social controls would be those implicated in some type of violent criminal deviance, such as murder, rape, or assault. Interestingly, however, of the roughly 11 million arrests in the United States in 2015, the highest number of arrests were for drug abuse violations (estimated at 1,488,707 arrests), larceny–theft (estimated at 1,160,390), and driving under the influence (estimated at 1,089,171) (FBI, 2015b). In 2016, about 47% of federal prisoners had been sentenced for drug offenses (Carson, 2018).

Another indication of the importance of formal social control in the modern world is the very high number of people imprisoned (Figure 6.5). Indeed, even though the U.S. prison population has declined in recent years, the United States still imprisons a vastly higher percentage of its population than does any other industrial society. In total, 6,613,500 or about 1 in 38 U.S. adults today is under some form of correctional system supervision, in either prison or jail, on probation, or on parole (Kaeble & Cowhig, 2018).

The large and sudden increase in the number of people in prison or under some form of correctional supervision that began around the 1980s is intriguing to sociologists, since it occurred during a period when both violent and property crime rates had been declining. What accounts for the unprecedented rise in imprisonment in the United States? Among the key reasons, researchers cite the following:

1. **Mandatory minimum sentences**: Federal and state legislators in the 1980s passed *legislation stipulating that a person found guilty of a particular crime must be sentenced to a minimum number of years in prison*. This reduced judges' ability to use their discretion in sentencing and led to a substantial increase in the average prison term.

2. **"Three strikes" laws**: Some *state and federal laws sentence an individual to life in prison who has been found guilty of committing three felonies or serious crimes punishable by a minimum*

Mandatory minimum sentences: Legislation stipulating that a person found guilty of a particular crime must be sentenced to set minimum numbers of years in prison.

"Three strikes" laws: State and federal laws that sentence an individual to life in prison who has been found guilty of committing three felonies or serious crimes punishable by a minimum of a year in prison.

of one year in prison. "Three strikes" laws became popular after several high-profile murders were committed by ex-felons, raising concerns that their release was leading to more crimes in the community. *The New York Times* reported in 2013 that 9,000 offenders were serving life in prison in California, comprising many whose third strike was a nonserious, nonviolent offense. In 2011, the U.S. Supreme Court ordered the state to reduce its prison population by 137.5% of capacity (*The New York Times*, 2013).

3. The **"war on drugs"**: As we saw in the Inequality Matters essay, mandatory minimums are intertwined with the "war on drugs," which was born in the 1980s. To some degree, panic over the dangers of crack cocaine fueled *efforts by the U.S. state and federal governments to curb the illegal drug trade and reduce drug use by punishing drug possession, use, and trafficking more harshly.* This led to a significant increase in the number of people in prison. For example, in 2015, there were about 11 million arrests in the United States, of which roughly 1.5 million were for minor drug law violations—not for serious trafficking or distribution offenses (FBI, 2015b). In late 2016, nearly half of the federal prisoners incarcerated were serving time for drug offenses (Carson, 2018).

Over the past several decades, changes in criminal laws and criminal sentencing have resulted in much stricter forms of social control in relationship to certain types of crime. In turn, this led to a huge increase in the U.S. prison population, although the imprisonment rate has turned downward in recent years: At year's end in 2016, the United States imprisoned 450 persons per 100,000 residents of all ages and 582 persons per 100,000 residents age 18 or older. Both statistics represent the lowest rate of imprisonment in more than a decade and continue decreases that began in 2007 and 2008 (Carson, 2018).

Formal mechanisms of social control administered through the criminal justice system have not been applied equally or proportionally to all groups in society. Those most likely to be imprisoned and punished for engaging in criminal deviance are disproportionately people of color. Blacks and Hispanics are arrested and imprisoned at much higher rates than Whites, despite the fact that Whites make up a much larger proportion of the total U.S. population (Glaze & Herberman, 2013). Statistics show that Black men have a 32% chance of

serving time in prison at some point during their lives; for Latino men, the chance is 17% and for White men, 6% (Sentencing Project, n.d.). Black men are incarcerated at a rate of about 1,824 per 100,000; for Hispanic men, the rate is more than 820 per 100,000. White men, by contrast, have an incarceration rate of 312 per 100,000 (Carson & Anderson, 2016). If current trends continue, Black males between the ages of 19 and 34 will experience an even greater overrepresentation in the prison population (Figure 6.5). Incarceration rates for women, although lower overall than those for men, exhibit a similar disproportionate racial trend, with Black women twice as likely as Hispanic women and three times more likely than White women to end up in jail or prison (Carson & Golinelli, 2014; Sipes, 2012).

People of color are more likely than Whites to be arrested and imprisoned for several reasons, all of which relate to the extension of formal social control over criminal deviance (Mann & Zatz, 1998). First, impoverished inner-city residents are disproportionately nonwhite, and the inner city is where the "war on drugs" has been most avidly waged (Anderson, 1999; Chambliss, 2001). As a consequence, drug-related arrests disproportionately affect people of color, who, despite constituting only 13% of the total U.S. population, represent more than 30% of people arrested for drug violations.

Second, the work of policing generally focuses on poor neighborhoods, where crowded living conditions force many activities onto the streets. Illegal activities are therefore much more likely to attract police attention in poor neighborhoods than in dispersed suburban neighborhoods.

Finally, racism in practices of prosecution and sentencing may also account for greater arrest and imprisonment rates of people of color. Even though many more Whites than nonwhites are arrested for crimes, people of color are more likely to be imprisoned for their offenses (Austin, Dimas, & Steinhart, 1992).

The Stigma of Imprisonment

We often refer to those leaving prison as people who have "done their time" or "paid their debt to society." Arguably, however, an array of laws and policies essentially ensure that ex-offenders continue to be punished by limiting their access to political voice, housing, and employment. According to the U.S. Department of Justice (n.d.), about 650,000 ex-offenders are released from prison every year. Notably, an estimated two thirds will reoffend within three years. A careful consideration of the roadblocks faced by former prisoners when they are released may, arguably, help society to understand and reduce the problem of recidivism.

"War on drugs": Actions taken by U.S. state and federal governments to curb the illegal drug trade and reduce drug use by punishing drug possession, use, and trafficking more harshly.

Notably, ex-offenders who have served time for a felony are denied a political voice in many states in this country. Although a poll released by YouGov showed that about 54% of Americans believe that ex-felons should have their right to vote restored once they have completed their sentences (Moore, 2016), only two states (Maine and Vermont) have laws that allow persons with felony convictions to never lose their right to vote and only 14 states have automatic restoration after release (National Conference of State Legislatures, 2016).

Many ex-offenders also face significant barriers to housing after release. Many people who are released from incarceration do not know where they are going to live. Approximately one third expect to go to homeless shelters upon release. Ex-offenders have been, in many areas, banned from public housing, although studies show that stable housing can reduce recidivism. Notably as well, in some instances, entire families have been evicted from their homes in public housing after taking in a family member returning from prison. In response, several cities have started to rethink their housing policies: Accordingly, "local public housing authorities can no longer use arrest records as 'the sole basis for denying admission, terminating assistance or evicting tenants'" (Carpenter, 2015, para. 3). In 2016, the U.S. Department of Housing and Urban Development released new guidelines that also make it more difficult for landlords and home sellers to discriminate against those with criminal backgrounds (Abdullah, 2016).

Most importantly, ex-offenders face the often-daunting challenge of finding a job. Data from the New York State Division of Parole show that only 36% of able-bodied parolees who had been out of prison for 30 days or more were employed in 2014. As an article on the problem notes,

> Former inmates often face enormous challenges finding work after they've been released: not only have many of them been out of the workforce for years, but often their criminal record prevents them from even getting their foot in the door in the first place. (Vega, 2015, para. 4)

A national "ban the box" movement has arisen in some areas with the goal of eliminating the box that job applicants are sometimes required to check on their applications if they have been convicted of a crime, most often a felony. Recently, 14 states and several dozen cities passed laws requiring employers to postpone background checks until the later stages of the hiring process to reduce discrimination against ex-offenders (Appelbaum, 2015). Ensuring access to job opportunities in the legal economy is a key way to reintegrate former prisoners into society.

The U.S. justice system releases several hundred thousand men and women from prisons and back into society every year. There are two paths that an ex-offender can follow: the road back to the criminal justice system or the road to reintegration. Arguably, laws and policies that erect obstacles to stable housing and employment, as well as participation in society through access to the ballot, play a role in determining the probability an ex-prisoner will follow one or the other path.

The Death Penalty in the United States

A **capital crime**, sometimes called a *capital offense*, is a *crime, such as murder, which is severe enough to merit the death penalty (capital punishment).* There are 41 offenses listed by the federal government as being punishable by death. Crimes that fall under this category include espionage, treason, and aircraft hijacking, as well as murder in particular circumstances.

In the United States, some states have and use the death penalty, others do not impose a death penalty, and still others have the death penalty but operate under a governor-imposed moratorium on the practice. Eighteen states use capital punishment; the most prominent are Texas and Georgia, although California has the most inmates on death row—741 at the end of 2016. In 2016, 20 people were executed in six states: seven of these were in Texas, and nine in Georgia. Nineteen states and the District of Columbia have abolished the death penalty. Four states have a governor-imposed moratorium; that is, the governor has the discretion to halt the use of the death penalty while in office (Figure 6.6; Death Penalty Information Center, 2016a).

The death penalty is a controversial practice in the United States. Few modern democratic states use it. Countries that practice it most frequently include China, Iran, North Korea, and Yemen. The United States is the fifth member of that group (Amnesty International, 2012). Those in favor of the death penalty argue that it is an appropriate punishment that may deter future crime and uphold a safe society by eliminating threats to the public. Beyond the argument of deterrence, they suggest that it is a form of retributive justice and provides closure for the families of the victims. Opponents of the death penalty challenge the idea that the death penalty is an effective deterrent: Consider that the South, which accounts for 80% of executions, has a higher murder rate than the Northeast, which accounts for just 1% of executions. They argue that erroneous punishments are irreversible: Indeed, since 1973, 160 people have been released from death row after it was found that they had been wrongfully convicted (Death Penalty Information Center, 2018). Furthermore, the cost of a death penalty case is usually greater than the cost of life in prison in part because the appeals process can stretch for years. Finally,

Capital crime: A crime, such as murder, which is severe enough to merit the death penalty (see capital punishment).

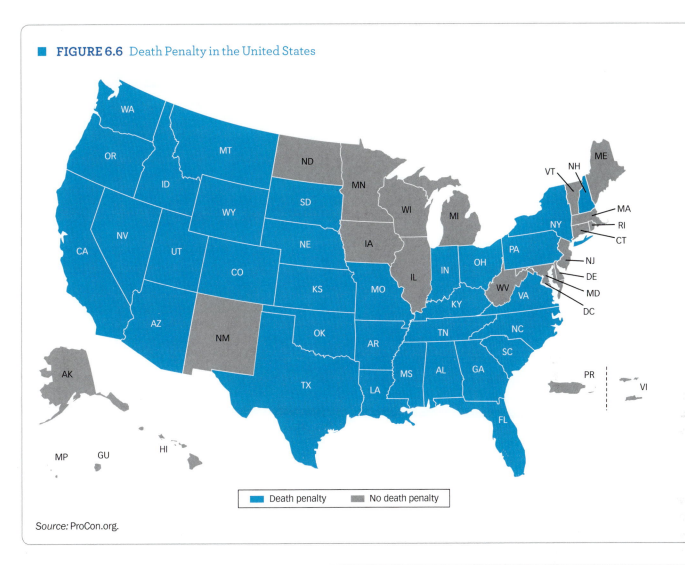

■ FIGURE 6.6 Death Penalty in the United States

Death penalty

No death penalty

Source: ProCon.org.

although more White prisoners were executed in the past year, the imposition of the death penalty has historically been biased against Black defendants, who are disproportionately found on death row (Figure 6.7). For example, a 2007 Yale University study found that African American defendants received the death penalty at three times the rate of White defendants when the victim was White (cited in Amnesty International, 2012).

In 2014, Maryland became the latest state to abolish the death penalty. Governor Martin O'Malley signed the ban into law and took the unusual step of emptying out death row, commuting the sentences of the four remaining prisoners (Berman, 2014). Efforts are underway in many other states to follow Maryland's lead, although the public and politicians continue to be divided on this controversial means of punishment.

Why Study Deviance?

The sociological perspective focuses the lens through which we view deviant behavior. It highlights the fact that

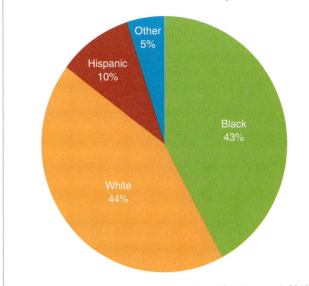

■ FIGURE 6.7 Death Row Inmates by Race, 2016

Other 5%

Hispanic 10%

Black 43%

White 44%

Source: NAACP Legal Defense Fund, "Death Row U.S.A.," January 1, 2016.

Note: Percentages may not equal 100% due to rounding.

the line between "deviant" and "normal" behavior is often arbitrary: What is deviant to one group is normal and even expected behavior to another.

Mainstream media and "official" depictions of deviance often overlook or ignore some of the more serious manifestations of deviance in the culture. So, too, do local communities. For example, in his research on the Saints and the Roughnecks, Chambliss (2001) found that middle-class boys were much more likely to have their deviant behavior written off as simply "sowing their wild oats," even though the behavior was dangerous and costly to society. On the other hand, the community was quick to judge, and apply deviant labels to, a lower-income group of boys. Such findings suggest a need for sociologists to delve more deeply into stereotypes of gangs and delinquency as phenomena associated almost exclusively with poor urban youth.

Similarly, sociological research and theory remind us that focusing on the deviance of the poor and minorities blinds us to an understanding of deviance among the rich and powerful. Criminal deviance, as discussed earlier in this chapter, is widespread throughout modern societies. Some of the most dangerous and costly patterns of deviant behavior are systematically practiced by corporate executives, politicians, and government officials. The sociological perspective demands that in such cases, we ask questions about power and who has the power to define deviance and to enforce their definitions.

©AP Photo/Sue Orocki, File

Since 1977, most executions in the United States have been done by lethal injection, a method that replaced the electric chair in many states. About 80% of executions are by lethal injection.

The findings of sociologists who study deviant behavior generally and criminal deviance in particular suggest that social control policies such as imprisonment have limited effects. Instead, these findings point to the need to change the social conditions that lead to criminality in the first place. The implications of most sociological studies of deviance are that street crime and gang activity in poor urban neighborhoods can best be controlled through the creation of jobs and other opportunities for those who otherwise cannot hope to succeed. In the case of white-collar, political, and governmental crimes, the organizational structures that make it rewarding to violate laws and social norms will have to change for there to be any hope of reducing deviance among the elite.

What Can I Do with a Sociology Degree?

CONFLICT DYNAMICS AND RESOLUTION SKILLS

Conflict resolution skills are of value when two or more entities—individuals, employees and employers, social groups, businesses, or countries, among others—engage in a process to resolve a disagreement that may be related to values or perceptions or to social, economic, environmental, or political interests. Sociological study offers students the opportunity to develop competencies in the analysis of conflict dynamics. Understanding the dynamics of conflict involves the ability to research and recognize the fundamental issues at the root of conflicts, to take the perspectives of different parties in a conflict, and to communicate effectively with groups in conflict. Understanding conflict dynamics and using this knowledge to resolve conflicts are related to sociology's general orientation toward problem analysis and problem solving.

It is in our interest as sociologists and citizens of the world to think in informed and creative ways about averting and addressing conflicts over resources as well as other sources of tension between states, societies, and groups. As a sociology student, you will have the opportunity to study different theoretical perspectives on conflict and its sources and to become familiar with research studies that delve into the roots of conflicts from the community to the global level. Understanding conflict dynamics and utilizing that knowledge to address and prevent or resolve conflicts are skills of great value in a heterogeneous and complex social and global environment.

Captain Jennifer Griffin, Patrol Troop Commander with the Delaware State Police

PhD in Sociology with a Concentration in Gender and Deviance

Captain Jennifer Griffin has been a trooper with the Delaware State Police for 16 years. She has had assignments as a patrol trooper, a school resource officer, and a grant manager and planner in the Planning Section; she has been the director of the Internal Affairs Unit, and she is currently a patrol troop commander. As a young woman, Captain Griffin says she always knew that her career calling was to be a police officer, and so she pursued her bachelor's degree in criminal justice. However, within one year of becoming a state trooper, she realized that she wanted to earn her master's degree. During that time, she says, "I realized how much I enjoyed school and research, and how much more the research and the lessons meant to me because I was studying the field in which I was working." After she completed her master's, she continued on and earned her doctorate in sociology with concentrations in gender and deviance.

Captain Griffin's doctoral studies included writing her dissertation, which was titled "Stress in the 21st Century: Are We Protecting Those Who Protect Others?" She says she chose a research topic based on her experience as a police officer and wanted to use her research abilities and training to gain information to help police officers deal with the stress and strains of policing. Through her research, she was able to open a dialogue between police officers and the Delaware State Police administration to discuss stress, burnout, work–family conflict, and the relationships among officers from different demographic groups.

Her advice to other students is this: "Find an area within the field that you are most interested in and focus on how you can make it meaningful to not only you but to the field, because you really never know the doors that will open for you in the process."

Career Data: Police and Detectives

- 2017 Median Pay: $62,960 per year
- $30.27 per hour
- Typical Entry-Level Education: High school diploma or equivalent
- Job Outlook, 2016–2026: 7% (As fast as average)

Source: Bureau of Labor Statistics, *Occupational Outlook Handbook*, 2017.

SUMMARY

- Notions of what constitutes **deviance** vary considerably and are relative to the norms and values of particular cultures as well as the labels applied by certain groups or individuals to specific behaviors, actions, practices, and conditions. Even **crimes**, which are particular forms of especially serious deviance, are defined differently from place to place and over time, and they depend on social and political processes.

- In **pluralistic societies** such as the United States, it is difficult to establish universally accepted notions of deviance.

- Most sociologists do not believe there is a direct causal link between biology and deviance. Whatever the role of biology, deviant behaviors are culturally defined and socially learned.

- Functionalist theorists explain deviance in terms of the functions it performs for society. Émile Durkheim argued that some degree of deviance serves to reaffirm society's normative boundaries. Robert K. Merton argued that deviance reflects **structural strain** between the culturally defined goals of a society and the means society provides for achieving those goals. **Opportunity theory** emphasizes access to deviance as a major source of deviance. **Control theory** focuses on the presence of interpersonal bonds as a means of keeping deviance in check.

- Conflict theories explain deviance in terms of the conflicts between different groups, classes, or subcultures in society. **Class-dominant theories** of deviance emphasize how wealthy and powerful groups are able to define as deviant any behavior that runs counter to their interests. **Structural contradiction theory** argues that conflicts are inherent in social structure; it sees the sorts of structural strains identified by Merton as being built into society itself. The **feminist perspective on deviance** reminds us that, until relatively recently, research on deviance was conducted almost exclusively by males. Recent feminist theories argue that many women labeled as deviant are themselves victims of deviant behavior, such as delinquent girls who are, in fact, runaways escaping sexual and physical abuse.

- Symbolic interactionist theorists argue that deviance, like all forms of human behavior, results from the ways in which we come to see ourselves through the eyes of others. One version of symbolic interactionism is **labeling theory**, which argues that deviance results mainly from the labels others attach to our behavior.

- **Violent crimes** are the most heavily publicized, but the most common are **property crimes** and victimless crimes. Although there is a public perception in the United States that crime is increasing, both of those crime rates have decreased.

- Although crime is often depicted as concentrated among poor racial minorities, crimes are committed by people from all walks of life. **White-collar crime** and **state crime** are two examples of crime committed by people in positions of wealth and power. They exact enormous financial and personal costs from society.

- Deviance and criminal deviance are both controlled socially through mechanisms of **informal social control**, such as socialization, and **formal social control**, such as arrests and imprisonment.

- Means of formal social control include the growth of **zero-tolerance policies** and policing in schools, **mandatory minimum sentences** for certain crimes and mass incarceration, and the use of the death penalty.

- A disproportionate number of people of color are arrested and incarcerated in the United States. This phenomenon is linked to a variety of factors that include the concentration of the **"war on drugs"** on poor, minority neighborhoods and racism in arrest, prosecution, and sentencing of those who engage in deviant behavior.

KEY TERMS

deviance, 141	class-dominant theories, 147	state crimes, 156
crime, 141	structural contradiction theory, 147	social control, 156
pluralistic societies, 142	feminist perspective on deviance, 148	social power, 156
capital offenses, 142	stigmatization, 148	informal social control, 157
phrenology, 142	labeling theory, 149	formal social control, 157
atavisms, 142	primary deviance, 149	school-to-prison pipeline, 159
structural strain, 144	secondary deviance, 149	zero-tolerance policies, 159
strain theory, 144	differential association theory, 149	mandatory minimum sentences, 160
opportunity theory, 144	violent crimes, 153	"three strikes" laws, 160
control theory, 146	property crimes, 153	"war on drugs", 161
social bonds, 146	organized crime, 153	capital crime, 162
subcultural theories, 147	white-collar crime, 154	

DISCUSSION QUESTIONS

1. As we saw in the *Behind the Numbers* box, measuring crime, including property crimes and violent crimes, can be challenging. Often, a single source is not enough to provide a comprehensive picture. What kinds of factors affect the accuracy of statistics on the incidence of crime? How can a researcher overcome such problems to gain an accurate picture?

2. Labeling theories in the area of criminology suggest that labeling particular groups as deviant can set in motion a self-fulfilling prophecy. That is, people may become that which is expected of them—including becoming deviant or even criminally deviant. Can you think of other social settings where labeling theory might be applied?

3. Think about some theoretical explanations for why people commit crime—differential association, social control, labeling, and so on. You might conclude that they all make sense on an intuitive level. Yet, there is contradictory evidence for each of these theories; that is, some data

support each theory and some data contradict it. What is the difference between seeing intuitive sense in a theory and testing it empirically?

4. Why, according to the chapter, did the rate of imprisonment rise in the United States in the 1980s? Why are a disproportionate number of prison inmates people of color?

5. Why, according to sociologists, are the crimes of the powerful (politicians, businesspeople, and other elites) less likely to be severely punished than those of the poor, even when those crimes have mortal consequences?

Want a better grade?

Get the tools you need to sharpen your study skills. Access practice quizzes, eFlashcards, videos, and multimedia at **https://edge.sagepub.com/chambliss4e**.

Social Class and Inequality in the United States

WHAT DO YOU THINK?

1. What is income? What is wealth? Why is it important to distinguish between the two when studying class status and inequality?

2. What factors explain rising income and wealth inequality in the U.S.?

3. What explains the existence and persistence of widespread poverty in the U.S.?

LEARNING OBJECTIVES

7.1 Identify characteristics of stratification in traditional and modern societies.

7.2 Describe components of social class, including income, wealth, occupation, status, and political voice.

7.3 Describe dimensions of socioeconomic inequality in the United States.

7.4 Discuss the problem of neighborhood poverty.

7.5 Analyze the existence and persistence of stratification and poverty from sociological perspectives.

POVERTY AND PROFIT

According to the U.S. Census, about 6% of the U.S. population resides in a trailer park. Mobile homes comprise the largest share of the nonsubsidized market for affordable housing in the U.S., providing about 8.5 million housing units to about 20 million residents at an average cost of just over $37,000 (Kirk, 2017). Up until the 1990s, many trailer parks were owned by local residents, some of whom lived on site and knew their tenants. The demand for affordable housing, which grew when hundreds of thousands of Americans lost their homes in the foreclosure crisis that peaked between about 2008 and 2010, however, has made the parks an attractive investment

©Mario Tama/Getty Images

opportunity and ownership has moved out of localities and into the domain of wealthy investors (Salamon & MacTavish, 2017).

Among those already earning significant returns on this demand are high-profile investors such as Sam Zell, whose controlling interest in about 140,000 parks earned him $777 million in revenue in 2014, and Warren Buffet, the second richest man in the U.S., who owns both the country's largest mobile home manufacturer and two biggest mobile home lenders. Investment in mobile home parks is an attractive proposition. In the words of one owner: "'Sell to the masses, eat with the classes.' There's a lot more poor people than there are rich people and they're not making any more trailer parks" (Neate, 2015).

An article in *Bloomberg Markets* profiled one such investor:

> When Dan Weissman worked at Goldman Sachs Group Inc. and, later, at a hedge fund, he didn't have to worry about methamphetamine addicts chasing his employees with metal pipes. Or SWAT teams barging into his workplace looking for arsonists.

> Both things have happened since he left Wall Street and bought five mobile home parks: four in Texas and one in Indiana. Yet he says he's never been so relaxed in his life. . . .

> [He] attributes his newfound calm to the supply–demand equation in the trailer park industry. With more of the U.S. middle class sliding into poverty and many towns banning new trailer parks, enterprising owners are getting rich renting the concrete pads and surrounding dirt on which residents park their homes.

> The greatest part of the business is that we go to sleep at night not ever worrying about demand for our product. . . . It's the best decision I've ever made. (Effinger & Burton, 2014)

For those interested in investment, millionaire Frank Rolfe offers Mobile Home University, a three-day, $200 boot camp to prepare them. Among the lessons for would-be landlords: "[The rents] do not go down, that's one thing that's a safe bet in the trailer park world" (Neate, 2015).

While profits for investors grow, the fortunes of those who inhabit the country's trailer parks may be sinking. Indeed, as rents rise, many trailer park residents are trapped in an economic conundrum: new options for parking the trailer are few and moving a trailer (which is not as mobile as the name would imply) is costly and difficult. Unlike a conventionally built residence, ownership of a mobile home rarely confers the benefits of rising value and home equity. Rather, a mobile home is similar to a vehicle, which loses value after its purchase, making it difficult to use the mobile home as a stepping stone to a standard home purchase (Salamon & MacTavish, 2017).

The decline of the U.S. middle class has wrought substantial consequences for millions of families. It has also, as the story above suggests, opened new economic opportunities for others, including members of the upper class. The economic security of the middle class, particularly its less educated fraction, has been declining since the late 1970s. At the top of the economic ladder, however, incomes have risen and fortunes expanded. These important changes in U.S. class structure are of great interest to sociologists. Helping you to understand them is a key goal of this chapter.

We begin this chapter with an examination of forms of stratification in traditional and modern societies, followed by a discussion of the characteristics of caste, social class, and stratification. Next, we look at important quantitative and qualitative dimensions of inequality and both household and neighborhood poverty in the United States. We then turn to a discussion of theoretical perspectives on class and inequality. Next, we shift our gaze to key dimensions of global inequality and ask why these deep global disparities exist and persist.

Stratification in Traditional and Modern Societies

In the United States today, there is substantial **social inequality**—a *high degree of disparity in income, wealth, power, prestige, and other resources.* Sociologists capture the disparities between social groups conceptually with an image from geology: They suggest that society, similar to the earth's surface, is made up of different layers. **Social stratification** is thus *the systematic ranking of different groups of people in a hierarchy of inequality.* Sociologists seek to outline the quantitative dimensions and the qualitative manifestations of social stratification in the United States and around the globe, but—even more important—they endeavor to identify the social roots of stratification.

Stratification systems are considered *closed* or *open,* depending on how much mobility between layers is available to groups and individuals within a society. Caste societies (closed) and class societies (open) represent two important examples of systems of stratification.

Caste Societies

In a **caste society**, *social positions are closed, so that all individuals remain at the social level of their birth throughout life.* Social status is based on personal characteristics—such as race or ethnicity, parental religion, or parental caste—that are present at birth, and social mobility is virtually impossible. Social status, then, is the outcome of ascribed rather than of achieved characteristics.

Historically, castes have been present in some agricultural societies, such as rural India and South Africa prior to the end of White rule in 1992. In the United States before the end of the Civil War in 1865, slavery imposed a racial caste system because enslavement was usually a permanent condition (except for those slaves who escaped or were freed by their owners). In the eyes of the law, the slave was a form of property without personal rights. Some argue that institutionalized racial inequality and limits on social mobility for African Americans remained fixtures of the U.S. landscape even after the end of slavery (Alexander, 2010; Dollard, 1957; Immerwahr, 2007). Indeed, enforced separation of Blacks and Whites was supported by federal, state, and local laws on education, family formation, public spaces, and housing as late as the 1960s.

Caste systems are far less common in countries and communities today than they were in centuries past. For example, India is now home to a rising middle class, but it has long been described as a caste-based society because of its historical categorization of the population into four basic castes (or *varnas*): priests, warriors, traders, and workmen. These categories, which can be further divided, are based on the country's majority religion, Hinduism. At the bottom of this caste hierarchy one finds the *Dalits* or *untouchables*, the lowest caste.

Since the 1950s, India has passed laws to integrate the lowest caste members into positions of greater economic and political power. Some norms have also changed, permitting members of different castes to intermarry. Although members of the lowest castes still lag in educational attainment compared with higher-caste groups, India today is moving closer to a class system.

Class Societies

In a **class society**, *social mobility allows an individual to change his or her socioeconomic position.* Class societies exist in modern economic systems and are defined by several characteristics. First, they are *economically based,* at least in theory—the hierarchy of social positions is determined largely by economic status (whether earned or inherited) rather than by religion or tradition. Second, class systems are *relatively fluid*: Boundaries between classes are violable and can be crossed. In fact, in contrast to caste systems, in class systems, social mobility is looked at favorably. It has long been an American aspiration for parents to hope that their children will live better than they do. Finally, class status is understood

---

Social inequality: A high degree of disparity in income, wealth, power, prestige, and other resources.

Social stratification: The systematic ranking of different groups of people in a hierarchy of inequality.

Caste society: A system in which social positions are closed, so that all individuals remain at the social level of their birth throughout life.

Class society: A system in which social mobility allows an individual to change his or her socioeconomic position.

to be *achieved rather than ascribed*: Status is, ideally, not related to a person's position at birth or religion or race or other inherited categories, but to the individual's merit and achievements in education, entrepreneurship, and work.

As we will see in this chapter, these ideal-typical characteristics of class societies do not necessarily correspond to historical or contemporary reality, and class status can be profoundly affected by factors such as race, gender, and class of birth.

Sociological Building Blocks of Social Class

Nearly all socially stratified systems share three characteristics. First, rankings apply to **social categories**—*categories of people who share common characteristics without necessarily interacting or identifying with one another.* In many societies, women may be ranked differently than men, wealthy people differently than the poor, and highly educated people differently than those with little schooling. Individuals may be able to change their rank (through education, for instance), but the categories themselves continue to exist as part of the social hierarchy.

Second, people's opportunities and experiences are shaped by how their social categories are ranked. Ranking may be linked to **achieved status**, *social position linked to a person's acquisition of socially valued credentials or skills,* or **ascribed status**, *social position linked to characteristics that are socially significant but cannot generally be altered (such as race or gender).* Although anyone can exercise individual agency, membership in a social category may influence whether an individual's path forward (and upward) is characterized by obstacles or opportunities.

The third characteristic of a socially stratified system is that the hierarchical positioning of social categories tends to change slowly over time. Members of groups that enjoy prestigious and preferential rankings in the social order tend to remain at the top, although the expansion of opportunities may change the composition of groups over time.

Societal stratification has evolved through historical stages. The earliest human societies, based on hunting and gathering, had little social stratification; there were few resources to divide, so differences within communities were

©John Moore/Getty Images

Across the United States, increases in rent have dramatically outpaced increases in wages, contributing to high rates of eviction in many poor neighborhoods. By one estimate, about a fifth of Black women renters have faced eviction, often more than once (Desmond, 2016a, 2016b).

not very pronounced, at least materially. Advances in agriculture produced considerably more wealth and a consequent rise in social stratification. The hierarchy in agricultural societies increasingly came to resemble a pyramid, with a large number of poor people at the bottom and successively smaller numbers in the upper tiers of better-off members.

Modern capitalist societies are, predictably, even more complex: Some sociologists suggest that the shape of class stratification resembles a teardrop (Figure 7.1), with a large number of people in the middle ranks, a slightly smaller number of people at the bottom, and very few people at the top.

Before we continue, let's look at what sociologists mean when they use the term *class*. **Class** refers to *a person's economic position in society, which is usually associated with income, wealth, and occupation (and sometimes associated with political voice).* Class position at birth strongly influences a person's **life chances**, *the opportunities and obstacles the person encounters in education, social life, work, and other areas critical to social mobility.* **Social mobility** is *the upward or downward status movement of individuals or groups over time.* Many middle-class Americans have experienced downward mobility in recent decades. Upward social mobility may be experienced by those who earn educational credentials or have social networks they can tap. A college degree is one important step toward upward mobility for many people.

The class system in the United States is complex, as class is composed of multiple variables. We may,

---

Social categories: Categories of people who share common characteristics without necessarily interacting or identifying with one another.

Achieved status: Social position linked to an individual's acquisition of socially valued credentials or skills.

Ascribed status: Social position linked to characteristics that are socially significant but cannot generally be altered (such as race or gender).

Class: A person's economic position in society, which is usually associated with income, wealth, and occupation (and sometimes associated with political voice).

Life chances: The opportunities and obstacles a person encounters in education, social life, work, and other areas critical to social mobility.

Social mobility: The upward or downward status movement of individuals or groups over time.

however, identify some general descriptive categories. Our descriptions follow the class categories used by Gilbert and Kahl, as shown in Figure 7.1 (Gilbert, 2011). At the bottom of the economic ladder, one finds what economist Gunnar Myrdal (1963), writing in the 1960s, called the *underclass*: "a class of unemployed, unemployables, and underemployed who are more and more hopelessly set apart from the nation at large" (p. 10). The term has been used by sociologists such as Erik Olin Wright (1994) and William Julius Wilson (1978), whose work on the "black underclass" described that group as "a massive population at the very bottom of the social ladder plagued by poor education and low-paying, unstable jobs" (p. 1).

People who perform manual labor or work in low-wage sectors such as food service and retail jobs are generally understood to be working class, although some sociologists distinguish those in the *working class* from the *working poor*. Households in both categories cluster below the median household income in the United States and are characterized by breadwinners whose education beyond high school is limited or nonexistent. People in both categories depend largely on hourly wages, even though the working poor have lower incomes and little or no wealth; although they are employed, their wages fail to lift them above the poverty line, and many struggle to meet even basic needs. Author David Shipler (2005) suggests that they are "invisible," as U.S. mainstream culture does not equate work with poverty.

Those who provide skilled services of some kind (whether legal advice, electrical wiring, nursing, or accounting services) and work for someone else are considered—and usually consider themselves—middle class. Lawyers, teachers, social workers, plumbers, auto sales representatives, and store managers are all widely considered to be middle class, although there may be significant income, wealth, and educational differences among them, leading some observers to distinguish between the (middle) *middle class* and the *upper middle class*. As most Americans describe themselves in surveys as "middle class," establishing quantitative categories is challenging. In fact, in 2010, the White House Task Force on the Middle Class, led by Vice President Joe Biden, opted for a descriptive rather than a statistical definition of the middle class, suggesting that its members are "defined by their aspirations more than their income. [It is assumed that] middle class families aspire to homeownership, a car, college education for their children,

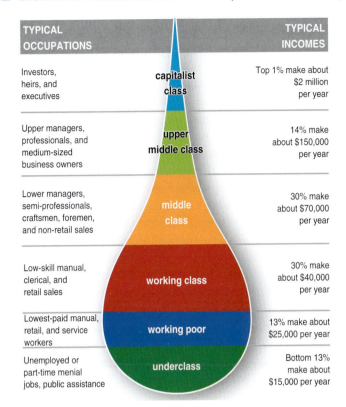

■ FIGURE 7.1 Class in the United States (Gilbert-Kahl Model)

TYPICAL OCCUPATIONS		TYPICAL INCOMES
Investors, heirs, and executives	**capitalist class**	Top 1% make about $2 million per year
Upper managers, professionals, and medium-sized business owners	**upper middle class**	14% make about $150,000 per year
Lower managers, semi-professionals, craftsmen, foremen, and non-retail sales	**middle class**	30% make about $70,000 per year
Low-skill manual, clerical, and retail sales	**working class**	30% make about $40,000 per year
Lowest-paid manual, retail, and service workers	**working poor**	13% make about $25,000 per year
Unemployed or part-time menial jobs, public assistance	**underclass**	Bottom 13% make about $15,000 per year

Source: Gilbert, D. L. (2015). *The American class structure in an age of growing inequality*. Thousand Oaks, CA: SAGE.

health and retirement security and occasional family vacations" (U.S. Department of Commerce, Economics and Statistics Administration, 2010).

Those who own or exercise substantial financial control over large businesses, financial institutions, or factories are generally considered to be part of the upper class, a category Gilbert and Kahl term the *capitalist class* (Gilbert, 2011). This is the smallest of the categories and consists of those whose wealth and income, whether gained through work, investment, or inheritance, are dramatically greater than those of the rest of the population.

Below, we look more closely at some key components of social class position: income, wealth, occupation, status, and political voice.

Income

Income is *the amount of money a person or household earns in a given period of time*. Income is earned most commonly at a job and less commonly through investments. Household

---

Income: The amount of money a person or household earns in a given period of time.

income also includes government transfers such as Social Security payments, veterans' benefits, or disability checks. Income typically goes to pay for food, clothing, shelter, health care, and other costs of daily living. It has a fluid quality in that it flows into a household in the form of pay-period checks and then flows out again as the mortgage or rent is paid, groceries are purchased, and other daily expenses are met.

U.S. household incomes have largely stagnated over the past decades, a topic we cover in detail later in the chapter. Effects of the recent economic crisis have not been felt evenly, but they have been experienced by all U.S. ethnic and racial groups (Figure 7.2). Income gains in the United States, however, have been disproportionately concentrated among top earners. According to a recent study by Glassdoor Economic Research, average chief executive officer (CEO) pay in S&P 500 companies is around $13.8 million per year; average median worker pay in those companies is about $77,800. Thus, the average ratio of CEO pay to median worker pay is 204 (meaning that CEOs earn 204 times more than their employees earn; Glassdoor, 2015). Starting in 2017, public companies will be required to share the ratio of CEO to worker salaries, providing even more transparency for inequalities in some of the world's biggest companies (U.S. Securities and Exchange Commission, 2015).

Wealth

Wealth (or net worth) differs from income in that it is *the value of everything a person owns minus the value of everything he or she owes.* Wealth becomes a more important source of status as people rise on the income ladder.

For most working- and middle-class Americans, home ownership is their primary source of wealth: about two thirds of the median household's wealth is comprised of housing equity. Changes in home values due to large-scale economic shifts can significantly affect household wealth.

For most people in the United States who possess any measurable wealth, the key source of wealth is home equity, which is essentially the difference between the market value of a home and what is owed on the mortgage. This form of wealth is *illiquid* (as opposed to *liquid*); illiquid assets are those that are logistically difficult to transform into cash because the process is lengthy and complicated. So, a family needing money to finance car repairs, meet educational expenses, or even ride out a period of unemployment cannot readily transform its illiquid wealth into cash.

Economists and sociologists treat **net financial assets** as *a measure of wealth that excludes illiquid personal assets, such as the home and vehicles.* Examples of net financial assets are stocks, bonds, cash, and other forms

---

Wealth (or net worth): The value of everything a person owns minus the value of everything he or she owes.

Net financial assets: A measure of wealth that excludes illiquid personal assets, such as the home and vehicles.

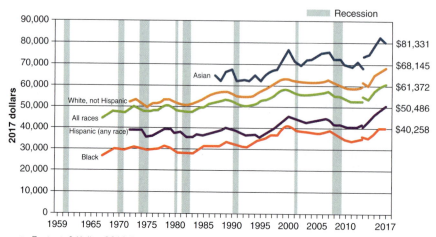

■ **FIGURE 7.2** U.S. Real Median Household Income by Racial and Ethnic Group, 1967–2017

Source: Table A-1. Semenga, Fontent, & Kollar. 2018. Income and poverty in the United States. https://www.census.gov/content/dam/Census/library/publications/2018/demo/p60-263.pdf.

©iStockphoto.com/andresr

How would you define the U.S. middle class? Should it be defined by income, wealth, or education? Should it be defined by aspirations and achievements?

of investment assets. These are the principal sources of wealth used by the rich to secure their position in the economic hierarchy and, through reinvestment and other financial vehicles, to accumulate still more wealth.

Wealth, unlike income, is built up over a lifetime and may be passed down to the next generation. It is used to create new opportunities rather than merely to cover routine expenditures. Income buys shoes, coffee, and car repairs; wealth buys a high-quality education, business ventures, and access to travel and leisure that are out of reach of most, as well as financial security and the creation of new wealth. Those who possess wealth have a decided edge at getting ahead in the stratification system. In the United States, wealth is largely concentrated at the very top of the economic ladder.

Occupation

An **occupation** is *a person's main vocation*. In the modern world, this generally refers to *paid employment*. Occupation is an important determinant of social class because it is the main source of income in modern societies. The U.S. Bureau of Labor Statistics tracks 840 detailed occupational categories in the United States. Sociologists have used various classifications to reduce these to a far smaller number of categories. For example, jobs are described as *blue collar* if they are based primarily on manual labor (factory workers, agricultural laborers, truck drivers, and miners) and *white collar* if they require mainly analytical skills or formal education (doctors, lawyers, and business managers). The term *pink collar* is sometimes used to describe semiskilled, low-paid service jobs that are primarily held by women (waitresses, salesclerks, and receptionists).

In the 1990s, some writers adopted the term *gold collar* to categorize the jobs of young professionals who commanded huge salaries and high occupational positions very early in their professional careers thanks to the technology bubble and economic boom of the 1990s (Wonacott, 2002). After the bubble burst, gold-collar workers were more often found in the financial sector, earning very substantial salaries and benefits. The economic recession that commenced in 2007 put a damper on growth in salaries and benefits of gold-collar workers, but they have risen again in recent years.

Status

Status refers to *the prestige associated with a social position*. It varies based on factors such as family background and occupation. A considerable amount of social science research has gone into classifying occupations according to the degrees of status or prestige they hold in public opinion.

We might expect white-collar jobs to rank more highly in prestige than blue-collar jobs, but do they? Doctors and scientists are indeed at the top of the prestige scale—but so are less highly paid professionals such as nurses and firefighters (who top the poll results discussed in this section, with 80% of respondents indicating that firefighters have "very great prestige"). Also in the top ranks are military officers and emergency medical technicians (with 78% and 72% conferring "very great prestige" on them, respectively). At the bottom are politicians, stockbrokers, accountants, and real estate agents (only 32% of respondents indicated "very great prestige" for real estate agents). It seems occupations that require working with ideas (scientist, engineer) or providing professional services that contribute to the public welfare (emergency medical technician, doctor, firefighter) have the highest prestige, and perhaps surprisingly, the U.S. public does not always link prestige to income (Mekouar, 2016).

Prestige rankings of specific occupations have been relatively stable over time, although changes do occur. For instance, since 1977, scientists have gained 16 points (after falling by 9 points in 2009) and journalists have increased by 30 points to 47%. What factors might explain these shifts? Have societal changes taken place that might contribute to our understanding of why occupations such as these rise and fall on the prestige scale?

Political Voice

Political power is *the ability to exercise influence on political institutions and/or political actors to realize personal or group interests*. It involves the mobilization of resources (such as money or technology or political support of a desired

---

Occupation: A person's main vocation or paid employment.

Status: The prestige associated with a social position.

In the 2016 Harris poll, emergency medical technicians/ paramedics were ranked among the top 10 most prestigious professions. According to the Bureau of Labor Statistics, in 2016, the average salary of these first responders was less than $33,000 annually. What explains the discrepancy between the social value and economic valuation of this occupation?

constituency) and the successful achievement of political goals (such as the passage of legislation favorable to a particular group).

Sociological analyses of power have revealed a pyramid-shaped stratification system in the United States as well as in most advanced industrial societies, including those of Western Europe. At the top are a handful of political figures, businesspeople, and other leaders with substantial power over political decision-making and the national economy. Moving down the pyramid, we encounter more people—and less power (Domhoff, 2009).

Sociologist C. Wright Mills began to write as early as the 1950s about the existence of a "power elite," which he defined as a group comprising elites from the executive branch of government, the military, and the corporate community who share social ties, a common worldview born of socialization in prestigious schools and clubs, and professional links that create revolving doors between positions in these three areas (Mills, 1956/2000a).

In contrast to the pluralist perspective on U.S. democracy, which suggests that political power is fluid and passes, over time, among a spectrum of groups and interests who compete in the political arena, Mills offered a critical perspective. He described a concentration of political power in the hands of a small elite. According to Mills, even though power over local issues remains largely in the hands of elected legislatures and interest groups, decision-making power over issues of war and peace, global economic interests, and other matters of international and national consequence remain with the power elite. The power of

Political power: The ability to exercise influence on political institutions and/or political actors to realize personal or group interests.

the masses is little more than an illusion in Mills's view; the masses are composed of "entirely private" individuals wrapped up in personal concerns and largely disconnected from the political process.

In recent elections, the U.S. middle class has been at the center of political discourse, but are decision makers addressing its fundamental economic concerns, including stagnating wages and challenges such as the steep cost of higher education? Or do the interests of the wealthy guide policy making? What do you think? In the following, we look more closely at trends in inequality in the United States.

Class and Inequality in the U.S.: Dimensions and Trends

The United States prides itself on being a nation of equals. Indeed, except for the period of the Great Depression of the 1930s, inequality declined throughout much of the 20th century, reaching its lowest levels during the 1960s and early 1970s. But during the past three decades, inequality has been on the rise again. The rich have gotten much richer, middle-class incomes have stagnated, and a growing number of poor are struggling to make ends meet.

Income Inequality

Sociologist Richard Sennett (1998) writes,

Europeans from [Alexis de] Tocqueville on have tended to take the face value for reality; some have deduced we Americans are indeed a classless society, at least in our manners and beliefs—a democracy of consumers; others, like Simone de Beauvoir, have maintained we are hopelessly confused about our real differences. (p. 64)

Was Tocqueville right or Beauvoir? Are we classless or confused? What are the dimensions of our differences? Let us look at what statistics tell us.

Every year, the U.S. Census Bureau calculates how income is distributed across the population of earners. All households are ranked by annual income and then categorized into *quintiles,* or fifths. The U.S. Census Bureau calculates how much of the *aggregate income,* or total income, generated in the United States each quintile gets. In other words, imagine all legally earned and reported income thrown into a big pot—that is, the aggregate income. The Census Bureau wants to know (and we do, too!) how much of this income goes to each quintile of earners. In a society with equal distribution across quintiles, each fifth of earners would get about one fifth of the income in the pot. Conversely, in a society with complete inequality across quintiles, the top would get everything, and the bottom quintiles would be left empty-handed. The United States, like all other countries, falls between these two hypothetical extremes.

In Figure 7.3, we see how aggregate income in the United States is divided among quintiles of earners. When we look at the pie, we see that income earners at different levels take in disparate proportions of the income total. Those in the bottom quintile take in just over 3% of the aggregate income, while those in the top quintile get more than half; that means the top 20% of earners bring in as much as all in the bottom 80% combined. No less significant is the fact that the top 5% take in more than 22% of the total income—more than the bottom 40% combined (DeNavas-Walt & Proctor, 2014).

Data compiled by economists Emmanuel Saez and Thomas Piketty, with a formula that uses pretax income (as do the census figures) but includes capital gains, suggest an even more stratified picture. According to Saez and Piketty's calculations, about 50% of pretax income goes to the top 10% of earners: Notably, the income is not composed primarily of wages but of capital income such as capital gains and dividends (Tankersley, 2016). Within this well-off decile (or tenth) of earners, there is a still more dramatic division of income, because the top 1% of earners takes about a fifth of the aggregate income (Saez, 2010). Clearly, gains have been concentrated at the top of the income ladder. As economist Joseph Stiglitz (2012) points out, the fraction of the aggregate income taken by the upper 1% has doubled since 1980, while the fraction that goes to the upper 0.1% has nearly tripled over that period.

When we study issues such as income inequality, we benefit from understanding the data we gather in their historical context. Figure 7.3 presents a snapshot of one moment in time, but what about decades past? The economic prosperity of the middle to late 1990s brought some benefit to most American workers: The median U.S. income rose faster at the end of the 1990s than it had since the period from the late 1940s to the middle 1950s. Saez (2010) calculates that the real annual growth of income among the bottom 99% of earners grew 2.7% in the period he terms the "Clinton Expansion" (1993–2000), but it dropped during the 2000–2002 recession (by 3.3%) and again during the 2007–2008 period (by 6.9%). On the whole, the period from 1993 to 2008 saw a real annual growth of only 0.75% for the incomes of the bottom 99%. Over the same period, the top 1% of earners experienced a real annual growth of almost 4% (although this group also experienced significant losses in the recessionary periods).

From about World War II until the middle 1970s, the top 10% earned less than a third of the national income pool

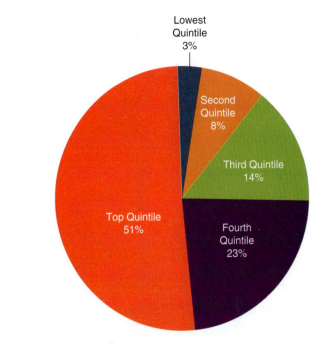

■ FIGURE 7.3 Shares of Aggregate U.S. Income by Quintile, 2018

Source: Table A-2. Semenga, Fotentot, & Kollar. 2018. Income and Poverty in the United States. https://www.census.gov/library/publications/2018/demo/p60-263.html.

Note: Values add up to 99%.

(Pearlstein, 2010). In the years since, however, the incomes of people at or near the top have risen far faster than those of earners at the bottom or middle of the income scale (Figure 7.4). The stagnation of wages is illustrated by the poor growth of average wages of young high school and college graduates (Figure 7.5). The economic position of college graduates is significantly better than that of high school graduates, but wage growth has been slow for both groups. For those with no college degree, lagging wage growth has contributed to economic struggles in recent decades (Kroeger & Gould, 2017).

Even for those with a college degree in hand, the labor market can be challenging: The Economic Policy Institute estimates that more than 12% of men and 11% of women graduates are **underemployed** (Gould, Mokhiber, & Wolfe, 2018). That is, they are *working in jobs that do not make full use of their skills* (for instance, a college graduate working in a job that does not require a college degree) *or working part time when they would like to be working full time*. Notably, Figure 7.6 shows only those graduates who are working part time when they would like to be working full time.

Underemployed: Working in jobs that do not make full use of one's skills or working part time when one would like to be working full time.

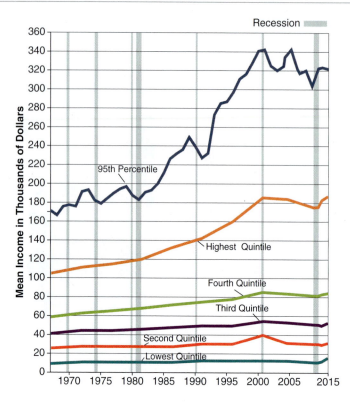

■ **FIGURE 7.4** Changes in Income Inequality in the United States, 1967–2015

Source: Table A-2. Semenga, Fontent, & Kollar. 2017. Income and poverty in the United States. https://www.census.gov/content/dam/Census/library/publications/2017/demo/P60–259.pdf.

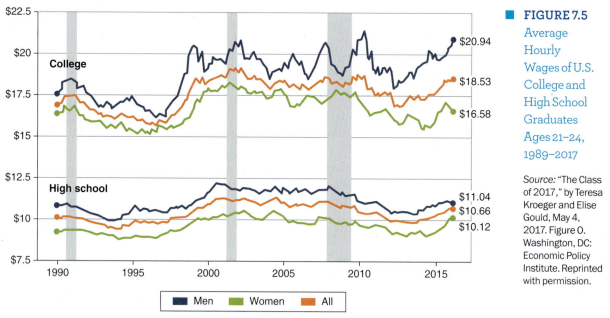

■ **FIGURE 7.5** Average Hourly Wages of U.S. College and High School Graduates Ages 21–24, 1989–2017

Source: "The Class of 2017," by Teresa Kroeger and Elise Gould, May 4, 2017. Figure O. Washington, DC: Economic Policy Institute. Reprinted with permission.

A recent publication by the Federal Reserve Bank of New York, estimates that in early 2018, 42% of young college graduates were working in jobs that did not require a college degree (Federal Reserve Bank of New York, 2018).

Wealth Inequality

We see the growth of inequality in the distribution of income, but what about the wealth gap? What are its dimensions? Is it growing or shrinking? Recall that even though income has a fluid quality—flowing into the household with a weekly or monthly check and flowing out again as bills are paid and other goods of daily life are purchased—wealth has a more solid quality. Wealth represents possessions that do not flow into and out of the household regularly but instead provide a set of assets that can buy security, educational opportunity, and comfortable retirement years. The distribution of wealth gives us another

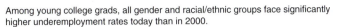

Among young college grads, all gender and racial/ethnic groups face significantly higher underemployment rates today than in 2000.

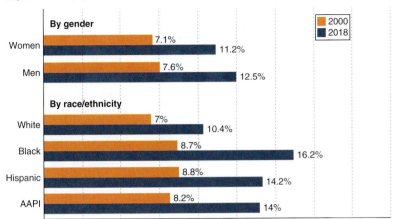

■ **FIGURE 7.6**

Underemployment by Gender and Race/ Ethnicity, 2000 and 2018

Source: "The Class of 2018," by Elise Gould, Zane Mokhiber, and Julia Wolfe, May 10, 2017. Economic Policy Institute. Retrieved from https://www.epi .org/files/pdf/147514.pdf.

Notes: AAPI stands for Asian American/Pacific Islander. Data for 2000 and 2018 use an average of January 1998–December 2000 and March 2015–February 2018, respectively.

■ **FIGURE 7.7** Wealth Gap by Race/Ethnicity 1983–2013

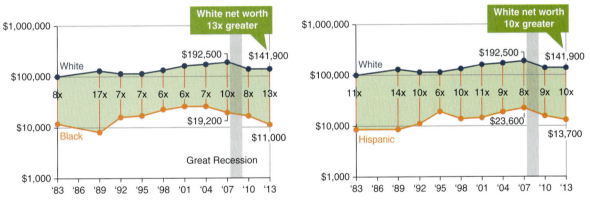

Source: "Wealth inequality has widened along racial, ethnic lines since end of Great Recession." Pew Research Center, Washington, DC (December 2014). http://www.pewresearch.org/fact-tank/2014/12/12/racial-wealth-gaps-great-recession/.

Notes: Blacks and Whites include only non-Hispanics. Hispanics are of any race. Chart scale is logarithmic; each gridline is ten times greater than the gridline below it. Great Recession began Dec. 2007 and ended June 2009.

important gauge of how U.S. families are doing relative to one another in terms of security, opportunity, and prospects.

Today, more Americans than ever have money invested in the stock market—many through 401(k) and other retirement accounts. Does that mean wealth is more evenly spread across the population than before? No, it does not—in fact, the distribution of wealth is even more unequal than the distribution of income. If we exclude the ownership of cars and homes—which, as we noted, are not normally sources of wealth that people can use to pay regular bills or get richer—the difference in wealth between high-income families and everyone else is particularly pronounced. Figure 7.8 shows the growing concentration of wealth at

the very top of the U.S. economic ladder (Saez & Zucman, 2014). Data suggest that in the last 30 years, the share of household wealth held by the top 0.1% has risen to about 22%; significantly, this share is nearly equal to that held by the bottom 90% of households, whose worth has been eroded by declining wages, a fall in home values, and an increase in debt (Monaghan, 2014).

Minority groups hold far fewer net financial assets than Whites. The wealth held by minority households has historically lagged; for instance, in 1990, Black households held about 1% of total U.S. wealth (Conley, 1999). This percentage rose markedly in the economic boom years of the 1990s and continued to expand into the 2000s. Black household wealth reached an average of just over $12,000 in 2005. This climb, however, was reversed by the housing crisis and the Great Recession, which saw a fall in household wealth among minorities. In 2013, the U.S. median net worth of a household was just over $81,400 and differences by race and ethnicity were stark: Although White median net worth was $134,000, Black household wealth was just $11,000 and Hispanic household wealth was about $14,000 (Kochhar & Fry, 2014; Jones, 2017). Mean (rather than median) wealth differences are even more stark (Urban Institute, 2017; Figure 7.7).

Many U.S. families have zero or negative net worth, a condition worsened when household wealth was eroded by the recent recession. Consider a Pew Research Center finding that in 2009, nearly one third of Hispanic households had zero or negative net worth, a figure that put them between White households (15% had zero or negative net worth) and Black households (35% had zero or negative net worth; Kochhar et al., 2011). A recent report on U.S. wealth examined the distribution of wealth by quintile: the findings show that about 90% of wealth is held by the top quintile; the bottom two quintiles hold zero or negative wealth (Wolff, 2017). When broken out like a pie with 100 slices, the distribution can be visualized as in the figure below (Figure 7.8).

Other Gaps: Inequalities in Health Care, Health, and Access to Consumer Goods

Along with the gap in income and wealth, there is a critical gap in employer benefits, including health insurance. From the 1980s to the 1990s, health care coverage for workers in the bottom quintile of earners fell more dramatically than for any other segment of workers: From a rate of 41% coverage, it dropped to 32% in the late 1990s (Reich, 2001). In

Many city neighborhoods lack access to large, well-stocked supermarkets with competitive prices. Residents must often choose between overpriced (and often poor-quality) goods and a long trip to a suburban market. The low rates of private vehicle ownership among the urban poor can make shopping for healthy food a burden.

2011, about 25% of those living in households earning less than $25,000 a year were uninsured, along with more than 21% of those in households earning $25,000–$49,999 (U.S. Census Bureau, 2012a). Altogether, more than 15% (48.6 million) of the U.S. population was without health insurance, including 7 million children younger than 18 years of age (U.S. Census Bureau, 2012a).

Many of the jobs created in the 1980s and 1990s were positions in the service sector, which includes retail sales and food service. Although the *quantity* of jobs created in this period helped push down the unemployment rate, the *quality* of jobs created for those with less education was not on par with the quality of many of the jobs lost as U.S. manufacturing became automated or moved overseas. Many service sector jobs pay wages at or just above minimum wage and have been increasingly unlikely to offer employer benefits.

One goal of President Obama's Patient Protection and Affordable Care Act (known simply as the Affordable Care

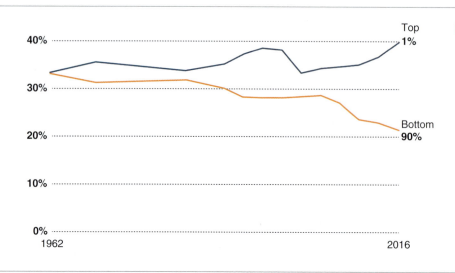

■ **FIGURE 7.8** Share of American Wealth Owned by Top 1 Percent versus Bottom 90 Percent

Source: Adapted from "Household Wealth Trends in the United States, 1962–2016: Has Middle Class Wealth Recovered? By Edward N. Wolff, working Paper 24085, National Bureau of Economic Research.

Act or ACA), signed into law in 2010, was to expand insurance coverage for the working poor. In the first year the law was in effect, more than 8 million people signed up for health insurance plans under the Affordable Care Act, and 57% of those people had been uninsured before enrolling in ACA-compliant plans. Moreover, those who enrolled in ACA-compliant plans reported slightly worse health than nonenrollers, and most said that they would not have sought insurance if the law had not taken effect (Hamel et al., 2014).

The rolls of insured Americans have grown with expanded access through Medicaid, a government health insurance program that primarily serves the poor, many of whom do not have employer-provided insurance and cannot afford to purchase insurance. At this time, 34 states provide poor residents with Medicaid enrollment opportunities through the ACA (Kaiser Family Foundation, 2018). The most recent state to expand Medicaid access is Virginia, which passed a measure that potentially provides insurance to 400,000 uninsured residents (Vozzella & Schneider, 2018).

The Republican-dominated Congress elected in November 2017 has acted to weaken key provisions of the ACA, including mandates that all Americans purchase insurance. The provision that insurance companies may not discriminate against applicants for insurance who have preexisting health conditions is also under threat. At this time, no replacement plan for the ACA has been enacted. The degree to which political and policy changes will affect access to care and coverage is as yet uncertain.

Perhaps predictably, data show a powerful relationship between health and class status. Empirical data show that those with greater income and education are less likely than their less-well-off peers to have and die of heart disease, diabetes, and many types of cancer. Just as income is distributed unevenly in the population, so is good health. Notably, modern medical advances have disproportionately provided benefits for those at the top of the income spectrum (Scott, 2005). In fact, a recent study found that greater income is associated with greater longevity. The gap in life expectancy between the richest and poorest Americans is about 15 years for men and 10 years for women (Chetty, Stepner, & Abraham, 2016).

Children in disadvantaged families are more likely than their better-off peers to have poor physical and mental health. According to the Kaiser Family Foundation (2008), the rate of hospitalization for asthma for Black children, who are more likely than their peers to be poor, is four to five times higher than that for White children. The problem is not only the lack of health insurance in families—although this factor is important—but also the lack of physical activity that may result when children don't have safe places to play and exercise and when their families are unable to provide healthy foods because both money and access to such foods

are limited. No less importantly, poverty can take a toll on mental health and mental capacity in the young: A recent study found that children who grow up poor are at risk of reduced short-term spatial memory as well as persistent feelings of powerlessness and are more likely to exhibit antisocial behaviors such as bullying (Dallas, 2017). Significantly, research suggests that families living in poverty have higher levels of the stress hormone, cortisol, and lower levels of the happiness hormone, serotonin (Johnston, 2016).

The problem of poor health may be related to another disadvantage experienced by those on the lower economic rungs: Many poor urban neighborhoods lack access to high-quality goods at competitive prices. Most middle-class shoppers purchase food at large chain grocery stores that stock items like fresh fruit and vegetables and meat at competitive prices. In contrast, inhabitants of poor neighborhoods are likely to shop at small stores that have less stock and higher prices because large grocery chains choose not to locate in poor areas. If they want to shop at big grocery stores, poor residents may need to travel great distances, a substantial challenge for those who do not own cars and a costlier proposition for those who do. As one study noted, "lower-income shoppers must travel further and/or have fewer shopping options than do higher-income shoppers" (Hatzenbuehler, Gillespie, & O'Neil, 2012, p. 54).

Some researchers refer to *areas (often urban neighborhoods or rural towns) characterized by poor access to healthy and affordable food*, as **food deserts** (DeChoudhury, Sharma, & Kiciman, 2016). A *USA Today* article describes the situation of Louisville retiree Jessie Caldwell, who regularly makes an hour-long bus trip to get fresh vegetables or meat:

> For her and many others, it's often tempting to go to a more convenient mini-market or grab some fast food. "The corner stores just sell a lot of potato chips, pop and ice cream," she said. "But people are going to eat what's available." (Kenning & Halladay, 2008, para. 8)

Although we do not always think of access to stores with competitive prices and fresh goods as an issue of class inequality, lack of such access affects people's quality of life, conferring advantage on the already advantaged and disadvantage on those who struggle to make ends meet. Writer Barbara Ehrenreich (2001) highlights this point:

> There are no secret economies that nourish the poor; on the contrary, there are a host of special costs. If you can't put up the two months' rent you need to secure an apartment, you end up paying through the nose for a room by the week. If you have only a room, with a hot plate at best,

---

Food deserts: Areas (often urban neighborhoods or rural towns) characterized by poor access to healthy and affordable food.

Social Life, Social Media

FOOD DESERTS IN THE UNITED STATES

©iStockphoto.com/ansonmiao

©iStockphoto.com/LauriPatterson

As we saw in the main text, *food deserts* are "urban neighborhoods or rural towns characterized by poor access to healthy and affordable food" (DeChoudhury et al., 2016), and they are a topic of interest to sociologists who study health and inequality (Schafft, Jensen, & Hinrichs, 2009; Whelan, Wrigley, Warm, & Cannings, 2002). One of the ways in which sociologists identify food deserts is by examining the distance residents of a neighborhood have to travel to get to a well-stocked, affordable grocery store. The alternative is often a convenience store with a worse selection of fresh foods and less competitive prices. Nevertheless, as a recent news article points out, "What's harder to measure is what the residents of these areas are actually eating day to day" (Beck, 2016, para. 1).

A key reason that food deserts are of concern to researchers and policy makers is that access to healthy and fresh food is an important component of good health. Research has linked living in a food desert to higher rates of heart disease, being overweight or obese, and diabetes. Notably as well, "Food deserts may contribute to social disparities, whereby area-level deprivation compounds individual disadvantage" (p. 1): By one U.S. government estimate, about 23.5 million people live in food deserts (DeChoudhury et al., 2016).

Recently, scientists from Georgia Tech and Microsoft Research experimented with a new way to study food deserts in the United States—examining what people around the country are eating using Instagram. This popular social media platform is used by many diners to share with friends and the world what they are eating. The researchers, who define what they are doing as *social computing*, used a computer program to mine 3 million publicly available Instagram posts that were tagged with food-related words and geotagged by location. Using U.S. government data, they categorized areas as food deserts and non-food deserts and compared each desert to a non-food desert in the same region with comparable demographics. Among others, the researchers "observed that posts from food deserts depict consumption of food higher in fat, sugar and cholesterol by 5–17% over the same measured in posts from 'matching' . . . non-food desert areas" (DeChoudhury et al., 2016, p. 2). Posts were also less likely to depict fresh fruits and vegetables as part of a meal. About 80% of the time, the scientists were able to use a computer model to predict whether an Instagram post originated in a food desert (DeChoudhury et al., 2016).

There are, of course, important limitations to this data. Although it can help to show what people in different geographic locations are eating, it cannot tell researchers how much they are eating or how often they eat the photographed food. As well, it cannot determine whether certain types of food happen to be photographed more often in particular locations. At the same time, the researchers suggest that their social computing can improve the detection of food deserts, noting that "Instagram may lend valuable empirical insights into food and nutritional choices in areas challenged by healthy food access" (DeChoudhury et al., 2016, p. 13).

Think It Through

- This box explores the use of the social media platform Instagram to examine the phenomenon of food deserts in the United States. Can you think of other sociological research questions that could be studied using social media platforms such as Instagram, Twitter, or Facebook, among others?

Follow us on Twitter to keep up with current sociological stories and research! We're at **@DiscoverSoc1.**

Share your own ideas at **#DiscoverSociology**

you can't save by cooking up huge lentil stews that can be frozen for the week ahead. You eat fast food and hot dogs and Styrofoam cups of soup that can be microwaved in a convenience store. (p. 27)

Why Has Inequality Grown?

There is a significant split between the fortunes of those who are well educated and those who do not or cannot attend college. The demand for labor over the past several decades has been differentiated on the basis of education and skills—workers with more education are more highly valued, while those with little education are becoming less valuable. These effects are among the results of the transition to a postindustrial economy in the U.S.

The nation's earlier industrial economy was founded heavily on manufacturing. U.S. factories produced a substantial proportion of the goods Americans used—cars, washing machines, textiles, and the like—and a big part of the economy depended on this production for its prosperity. This is no longer the case. In the postindustrial economy of today, the United States manufactures a smaller proportion of the goods Americans consume and fewer goods overall. Many manufacturing jobs have either been automated or gone abroad, drawn to the low-cost labor in developing countries. New manufacturing jobs created in the United States offer lower wages overall than did their predecessors in the unionized factories of the industrial Midwest (we discuss this issue in greater detail in Chapter 11). The modern U.S. economy has produced larger numbers of jobs in the production of knowledge and information and the provision of services.

One group that has grown is made up of professionals who engage in what former secretary of labor Robert Reich (1991) has called *symbolic analysis*, or "problem-solving, problem-identifying, and strategic-brokering activities" (p. 111). These occupational categories—law, engineering, business, technology, and the like—typically pay well and offer some job security, but they also require a high level of skill and at least a college education. Even well-educated middle-class workers, however, have been touched by automation and outsourcing. As well, a rising proportion of middle-level jobs have converted from relatively stable and secure long-term positions to contractual work.

The fastest-growing sector of the postindustrial economy beginning in the 1980s was the service sector, which includes jobs in food service, retail sales, health care (for instance, home health aides and nurse's aides), janitorial and housecleaning services, and security. By providing jobs to those with less education, the service sector has, in a sense, moved into the void left by the manufacturing sector of the industrial economy over the past few decades. The service

sector, which offers lower pay scales and fewer benefits, does not typically provide the kinds of jobs that offer a solid road to the middle class. Another difference is that manufacturing, especially in the auto making and steel industries, was overwhelmingly a male bastion, while service jobs favor women. The "advantage" enjoyed by less educated women over their male counterparts does not, however, translate into substantial economic gains for women or their families. Wage gains for women overall have been more fully driven by gains made by college-educated women.

In the period following the official end of the Great Recession, the bulk of new jobs created by the economy were low-wage positions, many of them service sector positions in areas such as hospitality, tourism, and retail (National Employment Law Project, 2014). By 2014, however, the economy was on track to create more high-wage jobs and the job market of "good jobs"—those with above-median wages, insurance, and retirement benefits—was growing. Notably, however, the "good jobs" being created were almost exclusively available only to those with higher education (Figure 7.9; Carnevale, Jayasundera, & Gulish, 2015).

The stratification of the U.S. labor force into a low-wage service sector, heavily tilted toward jobs in hospitality, retail, and security, and a well-paid knowledge and technology sector with clear orientation toward the highly educated appears to be continuing unabated. The narrative of a "disappearing middle class" has become a common theme in both social science and mainstream political discourse. Do you see such a trend in your own community? How does this narrative coexist with Americans' long-existing tendency to self-identify as middle-class, almost regardless of income?

TABLE 7.1   Poverty Rates of Selected U.S. Subgroups, 2017

CATEGORY	PERCENTAGE
All people	12.3%
Whites	10.7%
Blacks	21.2%
Hispanics	18.3%
Asians	10%
Under 18 years of age	17.5%
65 years of age and older	9.2%

Source: Fontenot, Semenga, & Kollar. 2018. Income and poverty in the United States. https://www.census.gov/content/dam/Census/library/publications/2018/demo/p60–263.pdf.

■ **FIGURE 7.9** Employment Change in High-Wage Occupations, 2010–2014

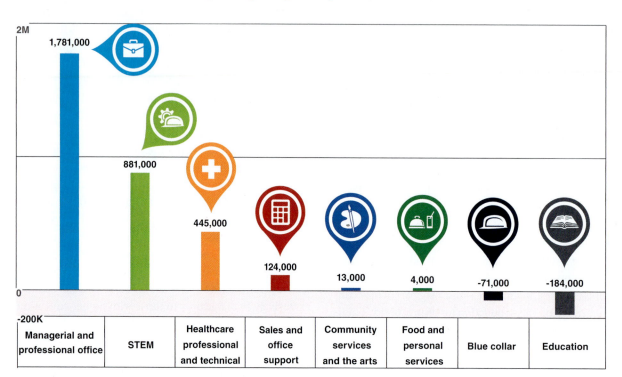

Source: Georgetown University Center on Education and the Workforce, "Good Jobs Are Back: College Graduates Are First in Line." Reprinted with permission.

DISCOVER INTERSECTIONS

Labor Markets, Gender, and Wages

In the section above, you learned about some key shifts in the U.S. labor market and how those may affect the economic fortunes of men and women in different ways. In the chapter on gender and society (Chapter 10), we will be discussing the gender wage gap and the reasons why men as a group continue to earn more than women as a group, though the gap in wages is shrinking. How might these shifts in the labor market, which are linked to a rise in income inequality in the U.S., also help to explain why the gender wage gap is shrinking?

At the Bottom of the Ladder: Poverty in the United States

There is a familiar America. It is celebrated in speeches and advertised on television and in the magazines. It has the highest mass standard of living the world has ever known.

In the 1950s, this America worried about itself, yet even its anxieties were products of abundance. . . . There was introspection about Madison Avenue and tail fins; there was discussion of the emotional suffering taking place in the suburbs. In all this, there was an implicit assumption that the basic grinding economic problems had been solved in the United States. . . .

While this discussion was being carried on, there existed another America. In it dwelt between 40,000,000 and 50,000,000 citizens of this land. They were poor. They still are.

To be sure, the other America is not impoverished in the same sense as those poor nations where millions cling to hunger as a defense against starvation. This country has escaped such extremes. That does not change the fact that tens of millions of Americans are, at this very moment, maimed in body and spirit, existing at levels beneath those necessary for human decency. If these people are not starving, they are hungry, and sometimes fat with hunger, for that is what cheap foods do. They are without adequate housing and education and medical care. (Harrington, 1963, pp. 1–2)

■ **FIGURE 7.10** Poverty Levels in the United States, 1959–2017

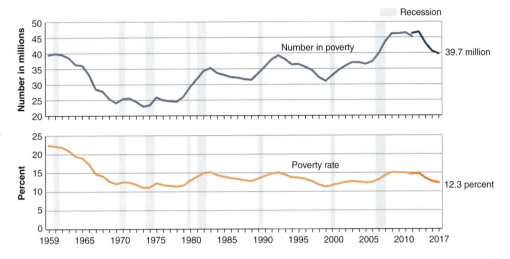

Source: Semega, Jessica L., Kayla R. Fontenot, and Melissa A. Kollar, U.S. Census Bureau, Current Population Reports, P60–259, Income and Poverty in the United States: 2016, U.S. Government Printing Office, Washington, DC, 2017; Fontenot, Kayla, Jessica Semega, and Melissa Kollar, U.S. Census Bureau, Current Population Reports, P60–263, *Income and Poverty in the United States: 2017*, U.S. Government Printing Office, Washington, DC, 2018.

These words, first published in 1963, helped to open the eyes of many to the plight of the U.S. poor, who were virtually invisible to a postwar middle class comfortably ensconced in suburbia. Michael Harrington's classic book, *The Other America: Poverty in the United States*, also caught the interest of President John F. Kennedy's administration and, later, the Johnson administration, which inaugurated the War on Poverty in 1964.

When President Lyndon B. Johnson began his War on Poverty, around 36 million U.S. citizens lived in poverty. Within a decade, the number had dropped sharply, to around 23 million. But then, beginning in the early 1970s, poverty again began to climb, reaching a high of 39 million people in 1993 before receding. Poverty climbed again in the period of economic crisis, but it has begun to decline slowly in its aftermath (Figure 7.10).

We pause on the topic of "official poverty" because it is important for us to be critical consumers of information. We are surrounded by statistics, subject to a barrage of information about the proportion of the population who support the president or reject the health care initiatives of a political party, about the numbers of teen pregnancies and births, about the percentages who are unemployed or in poverty. These statistics illuminate the social world around us and offer us a sense of what we as a nation are thinking or earning or debating. On the other hand, statistics—including social indicators such as the poverty numbers (Table 7.1)—may also obscure some important issues. To use indicators such

as the poverty numbers wisely, we should know where they come from and what their limitations are.

What is poverty from the perspective of the U.S. government? How were these numbers generated? The **official poverty line** is *the dollar amount set by the government as the minimum necessary to meet the basic needs of a family.* In 2017, the U.S. government used the following thresholds:

- One person, younger than age 65: $12,752
- One person, 65 or older: $11,756
- Three persons (one adult, two children): $19,173
- Four persons (two adults, two children): $25,283
- Five persons (two adults, three children): $30,490

From the federal government's perspective, those whose pretax income falls beneath the threshold are officially poor; those whose pretax income is above the line (whether by $10 or $10 million) are nonpoor. How are these thresholds generated? The *Behind the Numbers* box on page 186 explains.

Notably, official poverty numbers and the data we see in Table 7.1 offer us a picture of what the Census Bureau calls the *annual poverty rate*. This figure captures the number of households whose total income over the

Official poverty line: The dollar amount set by the government as the minimum necessary to meet the basic needs of a family.

■ FIGURE 7.11 Neighborhood Poverty Maps

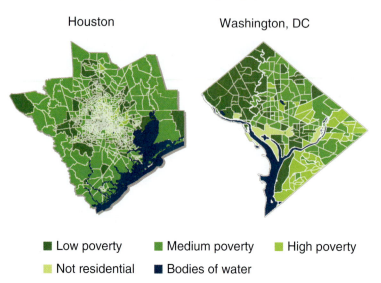

Houston   Washington, DC

■ Low poverty   ■ Medium poverty   ■ High poverty

■ Not residential   ■ Bodies of water

Source: "Neighborhood Poverty and Household Financial Security," The PEW Charitable Trusts, January 28, 2016 (www.pewtrusts.org/en/research-and-analysis/issue-briefs/2016/01/neighborhood-poverty-and-household-financial-security).

12 months of the year fell below the poverty threshold, but it does not illuminate how many families may have dropped into or climbed out of poverty and how many dwell there over a longer period. A recent Census Bureau report points out that even though the official poverty figure is around 12.7% in the period 2009 to 2011, about one third of U.S. households fell below the poverty threshold for at least two months. At the same time, only 3.5% remained poor for the full three-year period under study (Edwards, 2014). Although few households languish at the very bottom of the economic ladder for years, it is significant that nearly 10 times more households experienced periods of poverty (Figure 7.11).

Inequality and poverty in the United States are serious issues that demand both analysis and attention. Even though

Behind the Numbers

CALCULATING U.S. POVERTY

How does the U.S. government measure poverty? In the early 1960s, an economist at the Social Security Administration, Mollie Orshansky, used a 1955 U.S. Department of Agriculture study to establish a poverty line. She learned from the study that about one third of household income went to food, so she calculated the cost of a "thrifty food basket" and tripled it to take into account other family needs such as transportation and housing. Then she adjusted the figure again to take into account the size and composition of the family and the age of the head of household. The result was the poverty threshold, which is illustrated in Figure 7.12.

Orshansky's formula represented the first systematic federal attempt to count the poor, and it has been in use for more than half a century. But its age makes it a problematic indicator for the 21st century. Some critics argue that it may underestimate the number

■ FIGURE 7.12 The Poverty Threshold Calculation

3 x Crisis Food Basket
Adjusted for family size and age of head of household

Source: U.S. Census Bureau. (2010). Poverty: 2008 and 2009. American community survey briefs. Washington, DC: A. Bishaw & S. Macartney.

of those struggling with material deprivation. Consider the following points:

- The multiplier of three was used because food was estimated to constitute one third of a family budget in the 1960s. Food is a smaller part of budgets today (about one fifth), and housing and transport are much bigger ones. Using a higher multiplier would raise the official poverty line and, consequently, increase the number of households classified as poor.

- The formula makes no adjustment for where people live, even though costs of living vary tremendously by region. Although a family of three may be able to make ends meet on a pre-tax income of about $19,000 in South Dakota or Nebraska, it is doubtful that the housing costs of such areas as Boston, San Francisco, New York City, and Washington, DC, would permit our hypothetical family to survive in basic decency.

On the other hand, some critics have suggested that the poverty rate overestimates the problem because it does not account for noncash benefits that some poor families receive, including food stamps and public housing vouchers. Adding the value of those (although they cannot be converted into cash) would increase the income of some families, possibly raising them above the poverty line.

We might thus conclude that even though the official poverty statistics give us some sense of the problem of poverty and poverty trends over time, they must be read with a critical eye.

Think It Through

- Taking into consideration forms of inequality and issues of poverty discussed in this chapter, how would you create an instrument to measure poverty in the United States? The current measurement focuses on a "crisis food basket." What variables would you include?

inequality is part of any modern capitalist state, the steep rise of inequality in recent decades presents a challenge to societal mobility and perhaps, ultimately, stability.

The Problem of Neighborhood Poverty

In this section, we discuss the issue of concentrated poverty, looking specifically at measures, causes, and consequences of high levels of neighborhood (or area) poverty. We thus distinguish between *household poverty*, which an individual

Living in an impoverished neighborhood has significant consequences for both poor and nonpoor households. Diminished opportunities for work, education, consumption, and recreation affect entire neighborhoods.

or family may experience while living in a mixed-income neighborhood, and *neighborhood-level poverty*. Notably, research suggests that being poor in a poor neighborhood has more negative social, economic, and educational effects than household poverty in a more economically heterogeneous context (Wilson, 2010). Neighborhood poverty affects those households that are poor, but it also affects those in the neighborhood who are not officially poor.

A Census Bureau report shows that a growing proportion of Americans reside in *poverty areas*, defined in the report as census tracts featuring 20% or more households

in poverty (Bishaw, 2014). (Census tracts are areas with between 1,200 and 8,000 residents; most tracts fall in the 4,000 range.) In 2000, just over 18% of U.S. inhabitants lived in poverty areas; by 2010, nearly a quarter did. Poverty areas can be rural, suburban, or urban: Just over half are in central cities, another 28% are in the suburbs, and about 20% are outside metropolitan areas. Female-headed households are more likely than other family types to live in poverty areas: In 2010, more than 38% of female-headed households resided in areas with more than 20% poverty. Recent data also show a rise in residents living in *high-poverty neighborhoods*, defined as census tracts where 40% or more households fall below the poverty line. According to a 2015 report, "more than one in four of the black poor and nearly one in six of the Hispanic poor lives in a neighborhood of extreme poverty, compared to one in thirteen of the white poor" (Jargowsky, 2015, para. 3).

Sociologists study the development of poverty areas, particularly in urban neighborhoods (Wilson, 1996, 2010). The rise of the suburbs in the post–World War II period fostered the out-migration of many city residents, particularly members of the White middle class, and was accompanied by a shift of public resources to new neighborhoods outside cities. Public housing built in U.S. cities around the same period was intended to offer affordable domiciles for the poor, but it also contributed to the development of concentrated poverty, as policies foresaw income limitations that foreclosed the possibility of maintaining mixed-income neighborhoods. Racially discriminatory policies and practices, including limitations on Black access to mortgages or to homes in White neighborhoods, made Blacks far more vulnerable than their White counterparts to becoming trapped in poor neighborhoods. Even today, Black and Hispanic households are more likely to reside in poverty areas (Bishaw, 2014).

As many families moved to the suburbs in the 1950s and 1960s, jobs eventually followed, contributing to a "spatial mismatch" between jobs in the suburbs and potential workers in urban areas (Wilson, 2010). The decline of manufacturing in the 1970s and the decades following also had a profound effect on some urban areas, such as Chicago and Detroit, which were deeply reliant on heavy industry for employment.

As noted earlier, area poverty compounds the negative effects of household poverty and presents challenges to all residents of economically disadvantaged neighborhoods. Research has shown, for instance, that nonpoor Black children are more likely than their White counterparts to reside in poor neighborhoods and to experience limitations to social mobility; no less importantly, children are more likely than adults to be living in high poverty areas (Jargowsky, 2015). Poor areas are more likely than better-off or even mixed-income neighborhoods to experience high levels of crime, to have low-quality housing and education, and to offer few job opportunities to residents (Federal Reserve System & Brookings Institution, 2008; Jargowsky, 2015). Among the challenges to poor neighborhoods is that individual households that have enough resources to leave may choose to do so, contributing to even less circulating capital and an increasing withdrawal of businesses, fewer employed residents, weaker social and economic networks, and more empty buildings (Wilson, 1996). Cities such as Detroit and Cleveland have, in fact, lost thousands of residents in recent decades.

Significantly, children who live in high-poverty neighborhoods are more likely to experience food insecurity than children in low-poverty neighborhoods (Morrissey, Oellerich, Meade, Simms, & Stock, 2016). They are also less prepared for school than their peers (Wolf, Magnuson, & Kimbro, 2017). Girls who live in poverty-stricken neighborhoods are also at higher risk of experiencing sexual harassment, exploitation, pressure, and sexual violence. Poor neighborhoods may, over time, develop what the researchers have called "coercive sexual environments or CSEs," in which sexual violence becomes "normal" (Zweig, Popkin, & Bogle, 2015).

The revival of economically devastated neighborhoods is an important public policy challenge. How can the fortunes of poor—particularly very poor—neighborhoods be reversed? How does such a process begin and what does it entail? What do you think?

In the following section, we examine the issues of stratification and poverty from the functionalist and conflict

Discover & Debate

GENTRIFICATION AND U.S. CITIES

Motion: Gentrification is reviving urban neighborhoods in the United States that have suffered from poverty and crime. Gentrification is a positive development in U.S. cities.

Background: *Gentrification* is a term used to describe a process of commercial and residential rehabilitation of an economically distressed urban neighborhood. Gentrification is characterized by the movement of wealthier residents and new businesses such as shops and restaurants into a neighborhood, often leading to changes in the cost and value of housing as well as the neighborhood culture. Gentrification in some cities, including Washington, DC and New York City, has also changed the racial composition of many neighborhoods, with White residents moving in while significant numbers of Black and Hispanic residents leave. Gentrification in U.S. cities has both avid supporters and detractors.

AFFIRMATIVE ARGUMENTS	OPPOSITION ARGUMENTS
Gentrification leads to rehabilitation of old housing stock and development of new housing stock. The infrastructure in poor neighborhoods is further improved with new shops, restaurants, and other businesses moving in.	Gentrification leads to an increase in rents and home prices. This may lead to the displacement of lower-income families. Existing rental units may be replaced by luxury housing that long-time residents cannot afford.
Gentrification is associated with a reduction in violent crime in some neighborhoods.	Gentrification is associated with a rise in property crime in some neighborhoods.
Gentrification improves the tax base of a city, as it contributes to rising property values in economically flourishing neighborhoods and brings in new and more prosperous taxpayers.	Gentrification changes the character of neighborhoods, as long-term residents and their historical and cultural knowledge and institutions are overtaken by new inhabitants and their practices and preferences. Gentrification also hurts older businesses that do not match up with the tastes of new residents.

Questions for Consideration

- Can the benefits of gentrification be realized while minimizing its consequences? If so, how?

- Should local and/or state governments subsidize the gentrification of poor neighborhoods through tax credits or other policies? Should subsidies be contingent upon conditions such as the maintenance or production of low-income housing in the neighborhood?

- Can gentrification contribute to economically and racially integrated neighborhoods that have positive benefits for residents and cities?

Debate Tip

- Listen carefully to the arguments made by your teammates. Build on them, but don't repeat them.

---

perspectives. As you read, consider how these perspectives can be used as lenses for understanding phenomena such as income and wealth inequality, household and neighborhood poverty, and other issues discussed above.

Why Do Stratification and Poverty Exist and Persist in Class Societies?

We find stratification in virtually all societies, a fact that the functionalist and social conflict perspectives seek to explain. The functionalist perspective highlights the ways in which stratification is functional for society as a whole. Social conflict theorists, in contrast, argue that inequality weakens society as a whole and exists because it benefits those in the upper economic, social, and political spheres. We take a closer look at each of these theoretical perspectives next.

The Functionalist Explanation

Functionalism is rooted in part in the writings of sociologist Émile Durkheim (1893/1997), who suggested that we can best understand economic positions as performing interdependent functions for society as a whole. Using this perspective, we can think of social classes as equivalent to

the different organs in the human body: Just as the heart, lungs, and kidneys serve different yet indispensable functions for human survival, so do the different positions in the class hierarchy.

In the middle of the 20th century, Kingsley Davis and Wilbert Moore (1945) built on these foundations to offer a detailed functionalist analysis of social stratification. They argued that in all societies some positions—the most functionally important positions—require more skill, talent, and training than others. These positions are thus difficult to fill—that is, they may suffer a "scarcity of personnel." To ensure that they get filled, societies may offer valued rewards such as money, prestige, and leisure to induce the best and brightest to make sacrifices, such as getting a higher education, and to do these important jobs conscientiously and competently. According to Davis and Moore, social inequality is an "unconsciously evolved device by which societies ensure that the most important positions are conscientiously filled by the most qualified persons" (p. 243).

An implication of this perspective is that U.S. society is a **meritocracy**, *a society in which personal success is based*

Meritocracy: A society in which personal success is based on talent and individual effort.

on talent and individual effort. That means your position in the system of stratification depends primarily on your talents and efforts: Each person gets more or less what he or she deserves or has earned, and society benefits because the most functionally important positions are occupied by the most qualified individuals. Stratification is then ultimately functional for society because the differential distribution of rewards ensures that highly valued positions are filled by well-prepared and motivated people. After all, Davis and Moore might say, we all benefit when we get economic information from good economists, drive across bridges designed by well-trained engineers, and cure our ills with pharmaceuticals developed by capable medical scientists.

Clearly, the idea that the promise of higher pay and prestige motivates people to work hard has some truth. Yet, it is difficult to argue that the actual differences in rewards across positions are necessarily suitable ways of measuring the positions' relative worth to society (Tumin, 1953, 1963, 1985; Wrong, 1959). Is an NBA (National Basketball Association) point guard really worth more than a teacher or a nurse, for instance? Is a hedge fund manager that much more important than a scientist (particularly given that both positions require extensive education)?

Moreover, when people acquire socially important, higher-status positions by virtue of their skills and efforts, they are then often able to pass along their economic privilege, and the educational opportunities and social connections that go with it, to their children, even if their children are not particularly bright, motivated, or qualified. As Melvin Tumin (1953) points out in his critique of Davis and Moore, stratification may *limit* the discovery of talent in society rather than *ensure* it by creating a situation in which those who are born to privilege are given fuller opportunities and avenues to realize occupational success while others are limited by poor schooling, little money, and lack of networks upon which to call. Such a result would surely be dysfunctional for society rather than positively functional.

How would functionalism account for the fact that people are often discriminated against because of their skin color, sex, and other characteristics determined at birth that have nothing to do with their talents or motivations, resulting in an enormous waste of society's human skills and talents? Can you see other strengths or weaknesses to Davis and Moore's perspective on stratification?

In a twist on the functionalist perspective, sociologist Herbert Gans (1972) poses this provocative question: How is poverty positively functional in U.S. society? Gans begins with a bit of functionalist logic, namely, that if a social phenomenon exists and persists, it must serve a function or else it would evolve out of existence. But he does not assume that poverty is functional for everyone. So, *for whom* is it functional? Gans suggests that eliminating poverty would be

costly to the better-off. Thus, poverty is functional for the nonpoor but not functional for the poor—or even for society as a whole.

Among the "benefits" to the nonpoor of the existence of a stratum of poor people, Gans includes the following:

- Poverty ensures there will be low-wage laborers prepared—or driven by circumstances—to do society's dirty work. These are the jobs no one else wants because they are demeaning, dirty, and sometimes dangerous. A large pool of laborers desperate for jobs also pushes down wages, a benefit to employers.

- Poverty creates a spectrum of jobs for people who help the poor (social welfare workers), protect society from those poor people who transgress the boundaries of the law (prison guards), or profit from the poor (owners of welfare motels and cheap grocery shops). Even esteemed sociologist Herbert Gans has built an academic career on analyzing poverty.

- Poverty provides a market for goods and services that would otherwise go unused. Day-old bread, wilting fruits and vegetables, and old automobiles are not generally purchased by the better-off. The services of second-rate doctors and lawyers, among others, are also peddled to the poor when no one else wants them.

- Beyond economics, the poor also serve cultural functions. They provide scapegoats for society's problems and help guarantee some status for those who are not poor. They also give the upper crust of society a socially valued reason for holding and attending lavish charity events.

Gans's (1972) point is stark. He notes that the functions served by the poor have *functional alternatives*—that is, they could be fulfilled by means other than poverty. Nevertheless, he suggests, those who are better off in society are not motivated to fight poverty comprehensively because its existence is demonstrably functional for them. Although he is not arguing that anyone is in favor of poverty (which is difficult to imagine), he is suggesting that "phenomena like poverty can be eliminated only when they become dysfunctional for the affluent or powerful, or when the powerless can obtain enough power to change society" (p. 288). Do you agree with his argument? Why or why not?

The Social Conflict Explanation

Social conflict theory draws heavily from the work of Karl Marx. As we saw in the opening chapter, Marx divided society into two broad classes: workers and capitalists, or *proletarians* and *bourgeoisie*. The workers do not own the factories and machinery needed to produce wealth in capitalist societies—they possess nothing of real value except their labor power. The capitalists own the necessary equipment—the *means of production*—but require the labor power of the workers to run it.

These economic classes are unequal in their access to resources and power, and their interests are opposed. Capitalists seek to keep labor costs as low as possible to produce goods cheaply and make a profit. Workers seek to be paid ade-

Herbert Gans suggests that poverty ensures a pool of workers "unable to be unwilling" to do difficult and dirty jobs for low pay. Such jobs could also be filled in the absence of poverty through better pay and benefits. But, says Gans, this would be costly and, thus, dysfunctional to the nonpoor.

quate wages and to secure safe, decent working conditions and hours. At the same time, the two groups are interdependent: The capitalists need the labor of the workers, and the workers depend on the wages they earn (regardless of how meager) to survive.

Although more than a century has passed since Marx formulated his theory, a struggle between workers and owners (or, in our time, between workers and owners, managers, and even stockholders, who all depend on a company's profits) still exists. Conflict is often based on the irreconcilability of these competing interests. A study found that collective action lawsuits alleging wage and hour violations have skyrocketed, increasing 400% in the past 11 years. Among companies such as Bank of America,

Walmart, and Starbucks, Taco Bell has been one of the latest to be sued for allegedly forcing employees to work overtime without pay (Eichler, 2012).

The source of inequality, then, lies in the fact that the bourgeoisie own the means of production and can use their assets to make more money and secure their position in society. Most workers do not own substantial economic assets aside from their own labor power, which they use to earn a living. Although successful lawsuits for lost wages show that workers have avenues for asserting their rights against employers, the conflict perspective contrasts these small victories with the far more significant power and control exercised by large economic actors in modern society.

Inequality Matters

CHILD LABOR IN THE 21ST CENTURY

In early industrial America, some poor families sent children to work to support their households. Many employers welcomed young laborers, who were perceived to be more passive and less expensive than adult workers. Children worked in a variety of settings, including in canneries and the meatpacking industry, in the manufacture of textiles, and in agriculture; some peddled goods or shined shoes. Early in the 20th century, Congress passed two separate laws (in 1918 and 1922) seeking to regulate child labor, but the U.S. Supreme Court declared both

unconstitutional. With the support of unions and other activists, however, the Fair Labor Standards Act of 1938 set minimum ages and maximum hours for young workers. These standards remain in effect today: 16 is the minimum age for work during school hours, and 14 is the minimum for certain jobs that can be done after school hours. For designated "dangerous" jobs, 18 is the minimum age.

A report released by the nonprofit advocacy group Human Rights Watch in 2014, however, raises the

(Continued)

(Continued)

©age fotostock/Alamy Stock Photo

question of whether child labor in the United States is only a thing of the past. The introduction to the report, which focuses on child labor in the farming of tobacco, states:

Ninety percent of tobacco grown in the U.S. is cultivated in four states: North Carolina, Kentucky, Tennessee, and Virginia. Between May and October 2013, Human Rights Watch interviewed 141 child tobacco workers, ages 7 to 17, who worked in these states in 2012 or 2013. Nearly three-quarters of the children interviewed by Human Rights Watch reported the sudden onset of serious symptoms—including nausea, vomiting, loss of appetite, headaches, dizziness, skin rashes, difficulty breathing, and irritation to their eyes and mouths—while working in fields of tobacco plants and in barns with dried tobacco leaves and tobacco dust. Many of these symptoms are consistent with acute nicotine poisoning. (pp. 3–4)

The report also notes that "child tobacco workers often labor 50 or 60 hours a week in extreme heat, use dangerous tools and machinery, lift heavy loads, and climb into the rafters of barns several stories tall, risking serious injuries and falls" (p. 3) and describes their exposure to the agricultural pesticides used in tobacco farming. By one estimate, there may be as many as 300,000 to 400,000 child workers in U.S. agriculture, which includes tobacco farming (Ramchandani, 2018).

Why is it the case that more than 70 years after the passage of the Fair Labor Standards Act, young workers are toiling in American tobacco fields? One important reason is that the laws pertaining to child labor are far more lax regarding agricultural labor than they are concerning other forms of work. For example, from age 12, children can be hired for unlimited hours outside school hours with parental permission; on small farms, there is no minimum age. Of course, children have worked on family farms for centuries, helping to sow and reap crops and tend farm animals. According to Human Rights Watch, however, most of the child workers interviewed in its study are not supporting their own family farms; most are, according to a *Washington Post* editorial on the subject, "day laborers, migrants or the children of migrants; some have U.S. citizenship, others don't" ("Obama Administration," 2014).

Government interference in rural traditions surrounding the family farm has not been welcomed and efforts to prohibit child labor in tobacco fields by labelling it *hazardous*, and therefore unsuitable for those under 16, have been rejected by the industry and political supporters who see these efforts as an interference in the "rural way of life" in the U.S. (Ramchandani, 2018).

Notably, prior to the passage of child labor laws in the early 20th century, industrial and agricultural interests did not support the prohibition or regulation of child labor, which was cheap and beneficial to their production. In the early 21st century, the effort to protect children from dangerous labor is being waged—as it was a hundred years ago—by outside advocacy organizations, including Human Rights Watch and some immigrants' rights groups.

Think It Through

- If parents permit their children to work in order to supplement household income, should child labor in the tobacco fields (or other agricultural or even industrial settings) be permitted? What is the government's appropriate role in regulating child labor? Who benefits from permissive laws on child labor? Who loses?

In short, the conflict perspective suggests that significant and persistent stratification exists because those who have power use it to create economic, political, and social conditions that favor them and their children, even if these conditions are detrimental to the lower classes. Inequality thus is not functional, as Davis and Moore argued. Rather, it is dysfunctional, because it keeps power concentrated in the hands of the few rather than creating conditions of meritocracy that would give equal opportunity to all.

Similar to the functionalist perspective, the conflict perspective has analytical weaknesses. It overlooks cooperative aspects of modern capitalist businesses, some of which have begun to take a more democratic approach to management, offering workers the opportunity to participate in decision-making processes in the workplace.

Modern workplaces in the technology sector, for instance, thrive when decision making and the production of ideas come from various levels rather than only from the top down.

Like modernization theory, the dependency and world systems theoretical perspectives illuminate some aspects of the case while obscuring others. Variables such as the exploitative power of Western oil companies are a key part of understanding the failure of Nigeria to develop in a way that benefits the broader population, but conflict-oriented perspectives pay little attention to the agency of poor states and, in particular, their governing bodies in setting a solid foundation for development.

Why Study Inequality in the U.S.?

Many people today struggle to make ends meet on wages that have stagnated in recent decades. As we saw in this chapter's opening story, the downward mobility of many in the U.S. middle class is spawning new investor interest in market sectors such as low-cost trailer parks. We looked at the dimensions of both class and inequality in the United States and asked why inequality exists and persists.

The questions raised by the theoretical perspectives we have studied are not only academic: They are critical to our understanding of the world in which we live and in which (if we so choose) we will raise our children. Is it the case, as functionalists Davis and Moore asserted, that inequality is positively functional for society and that we collectively benefit from it because it ensures that the best and brightest take the most important jobs? Or, as Tumin argued, does inequality ensure the opposite, limiting the discovery of the full range of talent in society? How much should we worry about inequality and its growth? The answer may depend on whether we subscribe to the functionalist or the conflict view of socioeconomic stratification.

What about poverty? Poverty in individual cases may be the result of bad luck or poor choices, but the sheer magnitude of the problem of poverty suggests that it has structural roots as well, and a full explanation cannot be found at the individual level. Neighborhood poverty, as we have seen, is also a key public issue, although it is certainly experienced as a personal trouble, even by residents of poor neighborhoods who are not poor. Why does poverty exist and persist in a country that is arguably the wealthiest in the world? This is a question that asks us to employ our sociological imaginations.

 # What Can I Do with a Sociology Degree?

MAKING AN EVIDENCE-BASED ARGUMENT

We live in a sound-bite society where news and information are circulated in tweets and texts, and memes go viral faster than colds in a pre-K class. We regularly hear people make claims about their lives or society based on their personal experiences or things they've heard or read in passing. Ask yourself how many times you've forwarded a story without checking its validity, only to realize later that it was not true or only partially true. In a fast-moving social world, we may feel we lack the time or inclination (or even the skills) to determine whether the information we accept and share is fully reliable. Sociology invites us to become critical consumers of information, a skill that is of vital importance in both civil life and the job market.

In Chapters 1 and 2, you learned how sociology entreats us to go beyond "common wisdom" about social issues such as homelessness and the wage gap and to study society scientifically. Unlike

those conversations, in which someone makes an argument based on anecdotal evidence or a small and unrepresentative sample, sociology highlights the necessity of *evidence-based arguments*. Sociology students learn how to collect and analyze both quantitative and qualitative data, and evaluate that data for scientific rigor. In this book, you will find *Behind the Numbers* boxes that contribute to that understanding. Being able to make an evidence-based argument is an important skill in any occupation. Budget reports, employee evaluations, scientific and social scientific research, grant proposals, program and policy evaluations, and arguing a case in court all require evidence-based arguments. The ability to communicate effectively is a requirement of most jobs and necessitates showing or proving your points, not only stating your thoughts or opinions. Sociology students learn not only how to make evidence-based arguments but to evaluate the claims of others.

(Continued)

(Continued)

Jenny Xia, Data Analyst at the Institute for Women's Policy Research

University of Pennsylvania, BA in Sociology

My interest in gender equity as a sociology major led me to my current position as a data analyst at the Institute for Women's Policy Research (IWPR). At IWPR, I analyze data and compile research reports on topic areas related to women's well-being, including workplace equity and work–family policies. As IWPR's research is cited in media outlets and used to inform lawmakers, building strong evidence-based arguments is essential to my work. Before a report can be publicly disseminated, it is evaluated for the strength of its rationale and supporting evidence.

For example, we must address the limitations of our research findings and ensure that the data we use in a report have sample sizes that are large enough to contribute to meaningful analysis.

As a student of sociology, you are trained to think critically about the information you consume as well as the information put forth concerning the world around you. The ability to identify and craft strong evidence-based arguments was one of the most important skills I honed as a sociology major, as it helped me develop a critical thinking mind-set, something that is highly valuable to any occupation.

Career Data: Social Science Research Assistant

- 2017 Median Pay: $46,000 per year
- $22.12 per hour
- Typical Entry-Level Education: Bachelor's degree
- Job Growth: n/a

Source: Bureau of Labor Statistics, *Occupational Outlook Handbook*, 2017.

SUMMARY

- Class societies are more open than caste societies. In a **caste society**, a person's position in the hierarchy is determined by ascribed characteristics such as race or birth status. In a **class society**, a person's position is determined by what he or she achieves, and mobility is looked upon favorably. Nevertheless, barriers to mobility similar to those in caste societies still exist in class societies.

- **Class** refers to a person's economic role in society, associated with income, wealth, and the type of work he or she does. Class position strongly influences an individual's **life chances**—the opportunities and obstacles he or she encounters in areas such as education, social life, and work. Important components of class position are **occupation**, **income**, and **wealth**.

- We can measure inequality in the United States by looking at disparities in income, wealth, health, and access to credit and goods. All these indicators show that inequality in the United States is substantial and growing.

- Since the early 1970s, the gap between the rich and the poor has grown, as has the gap between the rich and everyone else. Some of this growth is attributable to the transformation of the U.S. economy from industrial to postindustrial, which has helped the best educated and hurt the least educated.

- Poverty is a significant problem in the United States: In 2015, 13.5% of the population was officially poor. The formula used to measure poverty gives us a sense of the problem, but it has limitations of which we should be aware.

- Researchers distinguish between household (or individual) poverty and neighborhood poverty. Studies suggest that living in a poor neighborhood amplifies the effects of poverty and also poses challenges (including limited mobility) for nonpoor residents.

- Functionalist theorists argue that inequality exists and persists because it is positively functional for society. According to this perspective, inequality is necessary to motivate the best people to assume the most important occupational positions.

- Conflict theorists argue that the privileged classes benefit from inequality and that inequality inhibits the discovery of talented people rather than fostering it. This perspective suggests that classes with differential access to power and resources are in conflict and that the interests of the well-off are most likely to be realized.

KEY TERMS

social inequality, 171

social stratification, 171

caste society, 171

class society, 171

social categories, 172

achieved status, 172

ascribed status, 172

class, 172

life chances, 172

social mobility, 172

income, 173

wealth (or net worth), 174

net financial assets, 174

occupation, 175

status, 175

political power, 176

underemployed, 177

food deserts, 181

official poverty line, 185

meritocracy, 189

DISCUSSION QUESTIONS

1. What is the difference between *wealth* and *income*? Why is it sociologically important to make a distinction between the two? Which is greater in the United States today, the income gap or the wealth gap?

2. Herbert Gans talks about the "uses of poverty" for the nonpoor. Recall some of his points presented in the chapter and then add some of your own. Would you agree with the argument Gans makes about the existence and persistence of poverty? Why or why not?

3. What is the difference between individual or household poverty and neighborhood poverty? Why is the distinction important? How does being poor in a poor neighborhood amplify the effects of economic disadvantage?

Want a better grade?

Get the tools you need to sharpen your study skills. Access practice quizzes, eFlashcards, video, and multimedia at **https://edge.sagepub.com/chambliss4e**.

Global Wealth, Poverty, and Inequality

8

WHAT DO YOU THINK?

1. Why are some countries tremendously prosperous while others are desperately poor?

2. How has the spread of modern technologies (such as mobile phones) had an impact on economic development?

3. What is the relationship between armed conflict and poverty of families and countries around the world?

LEARNING OBJECTIVES

8.1 Describe quantitative and qualitative dimensions of global wealth, poverty, and inequality.

8.2 Explain the relationship between armed conflict and poverty.

8.3 Discuss the role of technology in economic development across the globe.

8.4 Apply theoretical perspectives to analyze the existence and persistence of global inequality.

8.5 Describe characteristics of the global elite.

MIGRANTS IN LIMBO

The Greek resort island of Lesbos has long been a tranquil tourist haven in the turquoise Aegean Sea. In recent years, however, the small island has been transformed into a destination for war refugees fleeing broken homelands such as Syria and Iraq and economic migrants from Africa and Asia seeking better lives.

A recent article in the *Washington Post* describes a scene from a migrant camp in Lesbos:

> The first thing you notice is the smell: the stench from open-pit latrines mingling with the odor of thousands of unwashed bodies and the acrid tang of olive trees being burned for warmth.
>
> Then there are the sounds: Children hacking like old men. Angry shouts as people joust for food.
>
> And, finally, the sights: Thin, shivering figures drinking

©AP Photo/Manu Brabo

197

water from washed-out motor oil jugs. A brown-haired girl of no more than 3 clutching a fuzzy toy rabbit and smiling as she repeats to all who will listen, "I love you. I love you" (Witte, 2018, para. 1–3).

Several years have passed since the massive waves of migrants started arriving in Greece. The numbers have dropped off considerably since 2015 and 2016, when as many as 10,000 arrived in one day on Lesbos (Witte, 2018). But large numbers of migrants still languish in decrepit camps on Lesbos, trapped in limbo between abandoned homelands and a safe, stable future home.

Lesbos was a destination of convenience more than choice: It is a front-line port of call into Europe. While it is only five miles from the Turkish coast from which many migrants launched on smugglers' overfilled boats, problems such as poor weather conditions and boats that proved not to be seaworthy have led to hundreds of lost lives. The risks of the journey, which for many included threats of assault, kidnapping, robbery, and drowning, did not, alas, end when they reached the Greek island (Faiola, 2015).

The conditions at camps such as those situated on Lesbos are, according to aid workers, residents, and journalists, often very poor. Sanitation, food provision, medical care, and shelter are largely inadequate. By some accounts, however, the "appallingly bad conditions are no accident, but rather the result of a deliberate European strategy to keep people away" (Witte, 2018, para. 6). Indeed, the Western welcome mat has been pulled and several thousand camp residents have waited as long as two years to move forward in their journey. Many will never move forward, as most European countries, as well as the U.S., are permitting declining numbers of new migrants. Migration from poor countries in the Global South to wealthier states in the Global North is a longstanding phenomenon, but it has intensified and become more visible in recent years. Today, refugees desperately fleeing war-torn homelands mix with economic migrants in a mass movement of humanity pursuing physical safety and economic security.

Across the globe, countries, communities, and households are stratified: While some struggle to meet the most basic needs, others enjoy comfortable lives, broad opportunities, and modern amenities. We begin this chapter with a look at some of the dimensions of global inequality, examining factors such as per capita income, literacy, education, sanitation, and health in order to understand more about the hierarchy of countries in our global system. We then add in another variable that exacerbates economic struggles of countries and communities: armed conflict. Next, we consider one area—mobile technology—that may be helping to shrink economic disparities globally. This is followed by a look at theoretical perspectives that seek to understand why these deep global disparities exist and persist. We also examine the phenomenon of an increasingly wealthy global elite whose influence crosses national boundaries. We end with a brief consideration of the question of why sociologists take an interest in global inequality.

Dimensions of Global Inequality and Poverty

Many of the world's people are poor. According to a recent report from the World Bank, nearly 11% of the world's population—about 767 million people—live on the equivalent of less than $2 a day (2016). Nearly all of these economically marginal people live in the developing world, with over half living in sub-Saharan Africa. At the same time, according to a 2018 report issued by Oxfam, the wealthiest 1% of the population holds about 82% of the globe's wealth (Ratcliff, 2018).

We can look at inequality in terms of individuals or households, but we can also compare the economic positions of countries, recognizing a global class system with prosperous states, poor states, and a wide swath of countries in between. In this chapter, we look at some of the dimensions of **global inequality**, which can be defined as *the systematic disparities in income, wealth, health, education, access to technology, opportunity, and power among countries, communities, and households around the world*. While the focus is largely on differences among countries, we will see that these are only one part of a broader picture of global inequality.

We follow the World Bank in categorizing countries using four economic categories: high income, upper-middle income, lower-middle income, and low income (Figure 8.1; World Bank, 2015a). In 2018, the World Bank defined these classifications quantitatively using the following gross national income (GNI) per capita limits:

- Low-income economies: $1,005 or less

- Lower-middle-income economies: $1,006 to $3,955

- Upper-middle-income economies: $3,956 to $12,235

- High-income economies: $12,236 or more

Global inequality: The systematic disparities in income, wealth, health, education, access to technology, opportunity, and power among countries, communities, and households around the world.

Qualitatively, we can describe the *high-income countries* as those that are highly industrialized, characterized by the presence of mass education, and both urbanized and technologically advanced. Among the high-income countries, we find nations such as the United States, Canada, Japan, Germany, Norway, Estonia, and Australia. High-income countries are home to about 15% of the global population.

More than 70% of the world's population lives in *middle-income countries* (the lower- and upper-middle categories combined), which include a wide variety of nations; among them are former Soviet states such as Armenia and Belarus; South and Central American states such as Brazil and Belize; Middle Eastern countries such as Lebanon and Iran; Asian states such as Indonesia, India, and China; and African countries such as Morocco and Senegal. Many of these countries are on a path to economic diversification and development, though most also started down the road to urbanization and industrialization much later than the high-income countries and still lag in instituting mass education. Some middle-income countries, such as those in the Middle East and Africa, are home to vast natural resources, though the conversion of those resources to shared prosperity has, for reasons that theorists and observers debate, not been widespread.

Similar to high-income countries, *low-income countries* constitute a relatively small proportion of the global total.

■ **FIGURE 8.1** High-Income, Upper-Middle-Income, Lower-Middle-Income, and Low-Income Countries, 2015

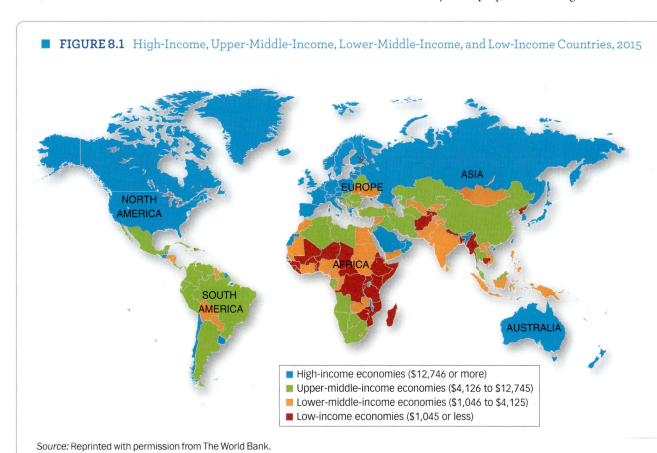

Legend:
- High-income economies ($12,746 or more)
- Upper-middle-income economies ($4,126 to $12,745)
- Lower-middle-income economies ($1,046 to $4,125)
- Low-income economies ($1,045 or less)

Source: Reprinted with permission from The World Bank.

Many are agricultural states with rapidly growing populations. While urbanization is a growing phenomenon, cities in these countries often lack the jobs and services that rural migrants seek, and both rural and urban dwellers struggle with hunger and malnutrition, economic and educational deprivation, and preventable diseases. Low-income countries may have small and wealthy groups of elites, but they lack stable middle-class populations. Low-income countries include South Asian states such as Bangladesh and Cambodia as well as Africa's poorest countries, such as Somalia and the Central African Republic.

In the remainder of this section, we describe some ways in which inequalities are manifested around the globe. Later in the chapter, we consider the key question of *why* this inequality exists and persists and examine various theoretical perspectives on the issue.

We begin with a look at **gross national income–purchasing power parity per capita (GNI-PPP)**, *a comparative economic measure that uses international dollars to indicate the amount of goods and services someone could buy in the United States with a given amount of money.* At one end of the class spectrum, we find countries with

---

Gross national income–purchasing power parity per capita (GNI-PPP): A comparative economic measure that uses international dollars to indicate the amount of goods and services someone could buy in the United States with a given amount of money.

---

very high GNI-PPP, such as the United States ($58,030), Canada ($43,420), Norway ($62,510), Germany ($49,530), and Japan ($42,870). In the middle are countries ranging from Botswana ($16,380) and Estonia ($28,920) to Turkey ($23,990) and Brazil ($14,810). At the bottom are countries whose GNI-PPP can be as low as that of Nicaragua ($5,390), Senegal ($2,480), or Gambia ($1,640; Population Reference Bureau, 2017). While GNI-PPP cannot tell us a great deal about the resources of individual families in the given countries, it gives us some insight into the economic resources available to the state and society from a macro perspective, and it offers a comparative measure for looking at stratification in the global system.

Hunger, Mortality, and Fertility in Poor Countries

As we saw in our discussion of social stratification in the United States, one important indicator of inequality is health (Table 8.1). One key aspect of good health is adequate food, in terms of both sufficient calories and basic nutrition. While the world has the capacity to produce enough food for all its inhabitants, the Food and Agriculture Organization of the United Nations (2017) estimates that 815 million people are chronically undernourished, and over 21 million children under age five are affected by *wasting*, or being too thin

TABLE 8.1   Global Inequality Indicators, 2017

	GNI-PPP	TOTAL FERTILITY RATE	INFANT MORTALITY RATE PER 1,000 LIVE BIRTHS	PERCENTAGE UNDERNOURISHED
World	$16,101	2.5	32	10.7%
By Level of Development				
More Developed:	$41,421	1.6	5	<5.0%
Less Developed:	$10,822	2.6	35	12.9%
Least Developed:	$2,566	4.3	52	24.4%
By Specific Country				
United States	$58,030	1.8	5.8	<2.5%
France	$42,380	1.9	3.5	<2.5%
Mexico	$17,740	2.2	18	4.2%
China	$15,500	1.8	10	9.6%
Jordan	$8,980	3.3	16	4.2%
Yemen	$2,490	4.1	45	28.8%
Niger	$970	7.3	61	11.3%

Source: Population Reference Bureau. (2017). *2017 World Population Data Sheet.* Source on undernourishment: Food and Agriculture Organization of the United Nations.

for one's height. At the turn of the millennium, the United Nations set as a goal the substantial reduction of hunger around the globe. In fact, data suggest that there have been marked improvements in access to adequate food supplies in many of the world's regions, most notably in those that have experienced rapid economic growth, including parts of Southeast Asia and Central and South America. At the same time, hunger has increased in other areas, including sub-Saharan Africa (Figure 8.2).

An important cause of hunger at the household level is poverty; many of those who lack sufficient food do not have the economic resources to acquire it. Subsistence farmers in developing countries, many of whom survive from season to season on their own small-scale crop yields, are vulnerable to weather events and natural disasters that can push their families into destitution and starvation. Hunger at a community level is more complex. While entire communities may suffer poverty and malnutrition, large-scale hunger is often the outcome of political decisions or armed conflicts. For example, the government of Syria under Bashar al-Assad has persistently impeded the delivery of food supplies to civilians in areas held by his opponents in the Syrian civil war that has raged since 2011. Hundreds of thousands have been killed and millions more have been displaced, fleeing Syria in search of refuge (as we saw in the opening story). Many of those left behind are the victims of hunger, which some (including the Secretary General of the United Nations, Ban Ki-Moon) claim are being used by al-Assad as a weapon of war (Melvin, Walsh, & Hume, 2016). Regardless of the causes of hunger, the costs of undernourishment are serious and often lasting: By one estimate, fully 25% of all children under age 5 are *stunted*—their growth progression is impaired by a lack of access to adequate nutrition (United Nations Educational, Scientific and Cultural Organization [UNESCO], 2014b).

In evaluating global health, we can also compare across countries the **infant mortality rate**—*the number of deaths of infants under age 1 per 1,000 live births per year.* This figure gives some insight into the health status of populations, and of women and children

in particular, because infant mortality rates are lowest in states that offer access to safe pre- and antenatal care and sanitary childbirth facilities as well as good nutrition during pregnancy. Consider the vast differences in the infant mortality rates among categories of countries: In 2017, the most-developed countries had an infant mortality rate of 5 per 1,000 live births. By contrast, the less-developed countries had an infant mortality rate of 35 per 1,000 live births, and the least-developed countries posted an infant mortality rate of 52 per 1,000 live births. Across specific countries, rates vary from lows in countries such as Sweden (2.5) and Austria (3.1) to highs such as those in Haiti (48), Pakistan (67), and Sierra Leone (92) (Population Reference Bureau, 2017).

Global health indicators such as infant and child mortality rates are linked not only to income differences *between countries* but also to income stratification *within countries.* Data suggest that those countries with a highly unequal distribution of income also experience highly variable health outcomes. For instance, in Cambodia (which is deeply stratified by income), among the top fifth of income earners, the infant mortality rate is 23 per 1,000 live births, while for those in the bottom fifth, the rate is 77 per 1,000 live births (Population Reference Bureau, 2013).

Our discussion of health may also be linked to the issue of fertility. Demographers measure **total fertility rate (TFR)**,

---

Total fertility rate (TFR): The average number of children a woman in a given country will have in her lifetime if age-specific fertility rates hold throughout her childbearing years (ages 15–49).

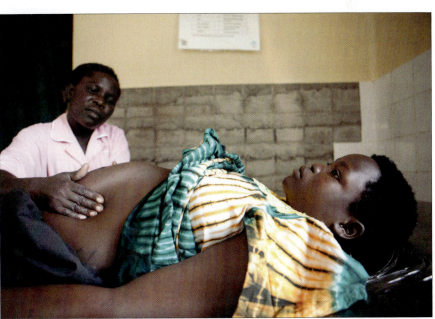

Total fertility rates have fallen across the developing world as more families gain access to information on family planning and to safe, effective contraception. In many of the countries of Western and Eastern Africa, however, there is a significant unmet need for contraception: 24% of partnered women indicate they would like to stop or delay childbearing but are not using any contraceptive method (United Nations, 2015).

Infant mortality rate: The number of deaths of infants under age 1 per 1,000 live births per year.

■ FIGURE 8.2 Number of Undernourished by Region, 1990–1992 and 2014–2016 (in Millions)

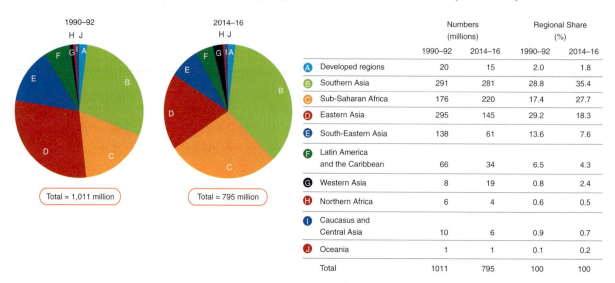

		Numbers (millions)		Regional Share (%)	
		1990–92	2014–16	1990–92	2014–16
Ⓐ	Developed regions	20	15	2.0	1.8
Ⓑ	Southern Asia	291	281	28.8	35.4
Ⓒ	Sub-Saharan Africa	176	220	17.4	27.7
Ⓓ	Eastern Asia	295	145	29.2	18.3
Ⓔ	South-Eastern Asia	138	61	13.6	7.6
Ⓕ	Latin America and the Caribbean	66	34	6.5	4.3
Ⓖ	Western Asia	8	19	0.8	2.4
Ⓗ	Northern Africa	6	4	0.6	0.5
Ⓘ	Caucasus and Central Asia	10	6	0.9	0.7
Ⓙ	Oceania	1	1	0.1	0.2
	Total	1011	795	100	100

Source: The State of Food Insecurity in the World 2015. Economic growth is necessary but not sufficient to accelerate reduction of hunger and malnutrition. Food and Agriculture Organization of the United Nations. Reproduced with permission.

Note: The areas of the pie charts are proportional to the total number of undernourished in each period. All figures are rounded.

which is *the average number of children a woman in a given country will have in her lifetime if age-specific fertility rates hold throughout her childbearing years (ages 15–49)*. We can use this measure to look at childbearing over space and time. It is notable that many of the world's poorest countries have the highest fertility rates. For example, while the TFR is 1.7 in Norway, 1.5 in Germany, 1.5 in Japan, and 1.8 in the United States, rates in the least-developed countries remain high. In 2017, some of the world's highest TFRs were found in Chad (6.4), Mozambique (5.3), Nigeria (5.5), and Afghanistan (5.3). Rates of fertility within many countries also vary by economic status; for instance, in the African country of Uganda, women in the top fifth of the income hierarchy have a TFR of 4.0, while their sisters in the lowest fifth have a TFR that is nearly double (7.9; Population Reference Bureau, 2015).

What sociological factors help explain differences in fertility? One factor is the link between infant and child mortality and fertility: In regions or countries where early child survival is threatened by disease, poverty, or other risks, families may choose to have more children in order to ensure that some survive into adulthood to contribute to the household and care for elderly parents, particularly in countries without social welfare supports for retirees. Second, it has been said that children are a poor man's riches—indeed, in many agricultural economies, many hands are needed to do work, and children are active contributors to a family's economic well-being. Economic modernization correlates historically with drops in fertility (see Chapter 17 for a fuller discussion of this topic). As well, where a lack of access to maternal and child health care

is common, there may also be little access to safe, effective contraceptives that would enable women to control their fertility. A recent United Nations (2015) report shows a significant unmet need for contraception among women: The figure reaches as high as 24% in sub-Saharan Africa and is 22% overall in the least-developed countries.

Safe Sanitation

Access to safe, hygienic sanitation facilities has emerged as an issue of public health concern for many poor communities but also as an issue of dignity and security for girls and women. Specifically, female inhabitants of communities that lack accessible, safe toilet facilities face serious vulnerabilities when they need to meet normal bodily needs. Consider the following story from June 2014: In a small Indian village in the northern state of Uttar Pradesh, two girls, ages 12 and 14, went together one evening to relieve themselves in the wild bamboo fields several minutes from their home, which has no bathroom facilities. In the darkness, the girls were brutally attacked, raped, and hanged from a mango tree, allegedly by three brothers (Banerjee, 2014).

The majority of India's 1.3 billion inhabitants do not have access to private toilets or latrines. According to the Population Reference Bureau (2013), only 60% of urban Indians and 24% of rural Indians were using "improved sanitation facilities" in 2011; while this measure focuses on the "hygienic separation of sewage from human contact" rather than safety or privacy, it points to a presence or lack of access to basic toilet facilities. In Uttar Pradesh, which is the country's largest state, about 64% of Indians have no indoor plumbing (McCarthy, 2014). Although some villages have public bathrooms, one press account notes that "many women avoid using them because they are usually in a state of disrepair and because men often hang around and harass the women." The same report quotes a local Indian police official's estimate that more than 60% of rapes occur in similar circumstances (Banerjee, 2014). A 2012 study reported that

> approximately 30% of women from the underprivileged sections of Indian society experience violent sexual assaults every year because lack of sanitation facilities forces them to go long distances to find secluded spots or public facilities to meet their bodily needs. (Bhatia, 2013)

The problem is not limited to India. Similar stories of violation and violence have been documented from Nepal to South Africa, where private toilet facilities are the exception rather than the rule (Bhatia, 2013). In Nepal, for instance, only 46% of the population has access to what the World Bank terms *improved sanitary facilities*. Figures on access vary from a full 100% in most developed countries to 59% in Gambia, 32% in Afghanistan, and 12% in Chad. Figures in rural areas are lower still: In remote areas of Chad, for instance, the figure is only 7% (World Bank, 2015b). According to the United Nations, about 2.5 billion people still lack access to basic, safe sanitation facilities, a figure linked not only (as noted above) to violence toward and degradation of women but also to high rates of diarrheal diseases among children. Reduction of that number is one of the Millennium Development Goals set by the United Nations for the improvement of global economic, environmental, and social progress and security in the 21st century.

Education Matters

In most developed countries, nearly all young people complete primary school, and most move on to high school. In less-developed states, access to education is more limited,

In 2016, about 263 million adolescents and children worldwide were out of school, and the number is rising.

In some developing countries such as Bangladesh (pictured), India, and the Ivory Coast, child labor remains a serious human rights issue. Child advocates underscore the right to care, safety, and education for all young people.

and the opportunity to go to school may be affected by a spectrum of factors. In some countries and communities, girls are discouraged or even prevented from attending school by economic or cultural factors. In others, school fees present obstacles to poor families who cannot afford to enroll their children. Sometimes schools and teachers are themselves not available because of the presence of armed conflict or the absence of communities that could sustain them.

A study by UNESCO (2016) found that in 2016, about 263 million adolescents and children worldwide were out of school. While many children do not attend school because of armed conflicts in their countries or regions, many of those not in school are, according to UNESCO, unlikely to ever attend school. School attendance is highly variable by gender, as 15 million girls of primary school age will never attend school, compared to about 10 million boys (UNESCO, 2016). Even where schools are available in poor countries, the quality of education is lacking: UNESCO (2014b) reports that about 250 million children are without basic literacy and numeracy skills, although about half of them have completed at least four years of school. Inadequate teacher preparation may combine with overcrowding (the African state of Malawi reported an average of 130 children in a Grade 1 classroom), lack of textbooks, and far distances from home to school to render efforts to educate children ineffective (Rueckert, 2018). The lack of safe transportation, running water, and toilet facilities may also discourage children, particularly girls, from attending school regularly (Rueckert, 2018).

Uneducated or poorly educated children pass into adulthood without basic skills. Literacy and numeracy skills not achieved in the years of primary school are rarely achievable in adulthood in developing countries, which have not established a tradition of adult education. UNESCO (2017) estimates that in 2016, there were 750 million fully illiterate adults worldwide, about two thirds of whom were women, though data show steady improvement across regions (Figure 8.3).

Inequality Matters

BITTERSWEET DESSERTS

©Godong/UIG via Getty Images

In the period from late 2016 to early 2017, the global price of cocoa declined dramatically, falling from about $3,000 per ton to $1,900. According to the *Cocoa Barometer* report (2018), smallholder cocoa farmers in the West African country of Ivory Coast, who already struggle to make ends meet, have seen their income drop significantly. What are the consequences of an unstable market and low prices for farmers? Some farmers are growing cocoa at a loss, and many rural growers are not earning enough to meet basic needs. Apart from the clear threat to farmers' livelihood, the fall in prices also threatens global efforts to eradicate or at least reduce child labor in the cocoa-growing industry (Terazono, 2018).

The *Cocoa Barometer* report (2018) indicates that the use of child labor has been widespread in the industry. The International Labor Organization (ILO) defines *child labor* as "work that deprives children of their childhood, potential and dignity, interferes with schooling and is harmful to their physical and mental development" (Aglionby & Atkins, n.d.). Companies that purchase cocoa for chocolate production, such as Hershey's and Mars, and governments in cocoa-growing regions have committed to combat this practice. Unfortunately, the number of children

engaging in cocoa growing in West Africa, where 70% of the world's cocoa is grown (Levaux, 2012), has actually risen from an estimated 2 million in 2013–2014 to 2.1 million in 2016–2017 (Terazono, 2018). A recent report in the *Financial Times* suggests that "the roots of child [labor] lie in poverty, with many cocoa farmers struggling to make ends meet and [being vulnerable] to wild swings in the cocoa price" (Ibid, para. 8).

What role should the chocolate candy companies that create the sweet treats enjoyed by consumers across the globe play in addressing this issue? Candy manufacturers do not want to be tarred by accusations that their products are associated with child labor. On the one hand, as a special report on the issue notes, chocolate manufacturers seeking to attain a fully child labor-free chocolate bar could choose to source exclusively from regions outside of West Africa, where child labor is not common. That would mean, however, abandoning already-poor farmers, many of whom are working to reach economic stability that would enable them to eliminate reliance on child labor (some of which comes from their own children). On the other hand, they could choose, as a small number of exclusive candy manufacturers have done, to pay more (with a set and predictable price) for cocoa, enabling farmers to stabilize their economic position (Aglionby & Atkins, n.d.). But this would mean higher prices for consumers of chocolate.

How are the interests of farmers, manufacturers, and consumers to be balanced? What do you think?

Think It Through

- Would chocolate consumers be willing to pay higher costs for candy if it ensured that child labor was not being used in cocoa production? Are consumers sensitive to the conditions under which the goods they purchase are produced?

Education improves the lives of communities and families in a multitude of ways. UNESCO (2014b) estimates that, on the global level, a year of school can equal a 10% boost in income. Education benefits both those who work for wages (by improving skills) and those who farm (by increasing access to knowledge about effective, efficient farming methods). Education also helps workers to avoid exploitation and better advocate for their interests. Apart from opening up broader avenues for economic advancement, better education is also linked to positive health outcomes. This relationship is particularly strong for women's education and child health outcomes. Research has documented a positive correlation between maternal education (even at the primary level) and decreased risk of child mortality (Glewwe, 1999; LeVine, LeVine, Schnell-Anzola, Rowe, & Dexter, 2012). For instance, a study on Nigeria found that better reading skills among mothers were linked to lower rates of child mortality (Smith-Greenaway, 2013). Other work suggests that greater maternal education translates into a greater probability that a woman's children will be educated (UNESCO, 2014b).

Significant strides have been made in many countries and regions in recent decades in educating young people (and women in particular), but much remains to be done. Even today, an estimated 102 million young people around the globe ages 15 to 24 are unable to read or write a sentence (UNESCO, 2017).

Armed Conflict and Poverty

War kills. War also destroys homes and communities, displaces populations, and strips people of the basic means to feed, clothe, and care for their families. In understanding global poverty and inequality, it is important to consider the relationship between armed conflict and the economic distress of families and countries. We look at two aspects of this relationship below. First, we consider the consequences of conflict and poverty for girls and women in the Middle Eastern country of Yemen. Second, we look at war refugees and the echoing economic effects in countries around the globe.

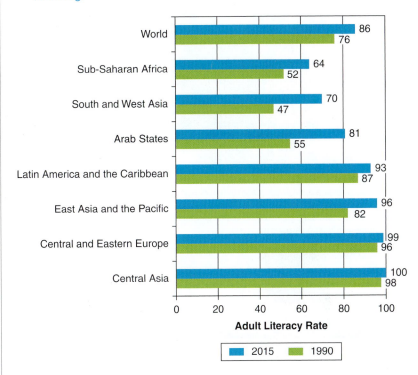

■ **FIGURE 8.3** Regions with the Highest Rates of Literacy, 1990 and 2015

Adult Literacy Rate

Legend: ■ 2015 ■ 1990

Region	2015	1990
World	86	76
Sub-Saharan Africa	64	52
South and West Asia	70	47
Arab States	81	55
Latin America and the Caribbean	93	87
East Asia and the Pacific	96	82
Central and Eastern Europe	99	96
Central Asia	100	98

Source: Data from UNESCO (2015b).

Note: North American and Europe (with the exception of Eastern Europe) are not included in the data. These regions are generally considered to have achieved full basic literacy.

Child Brides in a Time of Crisis

According to the Population Reference Bureau (2015), early marriage for girls is on the decline. While many young women in the developing world are still marrying by age 18, there are far fewer child brides than in the past. For example, between 1992 and 2012, the proportion of girls married by age 15 in the country of Niger fell from 47% to 28%. In Bangladesh, between 1993/1994 and 2011, the proportion dropped from 47% to 29%. In Ethiopia, the figure in 2011 was 16%, a small decline from the 2000 figure of 19%. Declines follow other trends in the empowerment of women and girls, including rising numbers of girls in school and greater opportunities for women to contribute to the paid workforce or to undertake entrepreneurial projects in their communities.

According to United Nations Children's Fund (UNICEF, 2018), child marriage is on the decline: Over 25 million child marriages have been prevented within the past decade, equating to a 15% decrease. Today, there are more than 650 million living women who were married as children, and 31% of young women and 4% of young men were married before their 18th birthday. It is estimated that 12 million girls under age 18 are married each year. At this rate,

it is estimated that more than 150 million additional girls under age 18 will be married by 2030.

Positive trends in empowerment of women and girls, however, are often fragile. Armed conflict is among the factors that can derail progress. In Yemen, early marriage has long been a tradition. According to a recent *Washington Post* report, however, "before the civil war began last year, international and local activists had made progress toward ending the practice. They were campaigning for a law setting 18 as the minimum age for marriage and for girls to remain in school" (Raghavan, 2016, p. A1). The war, however, has set back these efforts. Yemen is the Middle East's poorest country: The per capita GNI is only $2,490 (Population Research Bureau, 2017). The spread of armed conflict has deprived many families who had little to begin with of their homes and possessions. In this situation, some families are seeking to acquire resources and pay debts—as well as reduce family expenses—by giving young daughters in marriage for a bride price. As Yemen has no minimum age of marriage, "more girls, some as young as 8, are being married off to help their desperate families" (Raghavan, 2016).

The costs of early marriage for girls are manifold. At 270 per 100,000 births, Yemen has the highest maternal mortality rate in the region (the regional average is 54 per 100,000;

©REUTERS/Suzanne Plunkett

In 2012, Pakistani schoolgirl Malala Yousafzai was shot three times by a gunman after she publicly advocated for education in a region controlled by Taliban fighters, whose interpretation of Islam forbids the education of girls. Malala recovered and has continued her passionate fight for female education around the world.

©REUTERS/Khaled Abdullah

Yemeni women show their support for a proposed law banning marriage for girls under the age of 17. Because the country has no minimum age of marriage, girls as young as 8 may become wives before they even reach adolescence.

Population Research Bureau, 2015), a figure that can be tied to premature marriage and motherhood. Girls as young as 12 have died in childbirth in Yemen (Raghavan, 2016). Young wives are also unlikely to attend school. Yemen's ratio of school-age girls in school—only 40 of 100—is one of the lowest in the region (Population Research Bureau, 2015).

Using our sociological imaginations, we can see that personal troubles—family poverty, young girls being forced to marry—are more fully illuminated when we see them in the context of public issues such as armed conflict and mass displacement of families and communities.

Refugees and Refuges

As we saw in the opening story, millions of refugees and migrants have fled war and poverty in the Middle East, Africa, and Asia. Many have sought to make their way to Western countries such as Germany, France, and Sweden; about a million Syrian refugees currently reside there (Connor, 2018). At the same time, it is important to recognize that in most cases, refugees and migrants from war-ravaged and destitute countries are fleeing to and finding refuge in other struggling states.

Consider the war in Syria, which has pitted the sitting authoritarian ruler Bashar al-Assad against both anti-Assad rebel groups and radical Islamist groups, including the Islamic State (or ISIS), who are fighting for power. According to a Pew Research report,

> Nearly 13 million Syrians are displaced after seven years of conflict in their country—a total that amounts to about six-in-ten of Syria's pre-conflict population. . . . No nation in recent decades has had such a large percentage of its population displaced. (Connor, 2018, para. 1)

About half of the displaced Syrians remain in their own country; most of the rest reside in Turkey, Iraq, Jordan, and Lebanon. The mass influx of refugees has strained already-scarce economic resources in these countries (Figure 8.4; Ibid.)

A similar situation exists on the African continent. Armed conflicts in the Congo, Somalia, Sudan, and South Sudan have left about 15 million people displaced in sub-Saharan Africa. Most of these refugees either remain in their own countries or find shelter in neighboring states, which include some of the globe's poorest countries (Pecanha & Wallace, 2015). For instance, the country of Chad is home to an estimated 360,000

■ **FIGURE 8.4** Displaced Syrians around the World, 2018

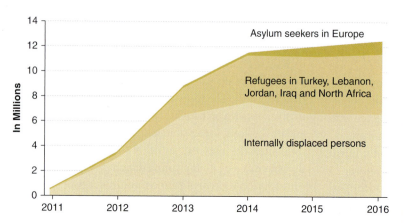

Source: "About six-in-ten Syrians are now displaced from their homes," Pew Research Center Fact Tank, Washington, DC, June 13, 2016. (http://www.pewresearch.org/fact-tank/2016/06/13/about-six-in-ten-syrians-are-now-displaced-from-their-homes/)

refugees from Sudan, many of whom have been in the country for over a decade. Chad itself is very poor: It ranks 184th of 187 countries in the United Nations Human Development Index. It also strains beneath the weight of regional tensions, including political chaos in Libya and terrorist threats from the Nigerian-based terror group Boko Haram. Chad's economic struggles are shared by both Chadian citizens and the refugees within their borders (Boyce & Hollingsworth, 2015).

As of 2016, Uganda was home to the most African refugees, with nearly half a million new arrivals, most from South Sudan, in late in 2016. As home to over 270,000 refugees, the Bidi Bidi camp in northern Uganda is the world's largest refugee camp. Refugees are drawn by Uganda's generous laws, which permit refugees to work and access public services such as education (Quartz Africa, 2017). The influx, however, has strained the resources of a country that is already among the world's poorest, with a GNI-PPP of $1,820 and its own very young population: Those 15 and under comprise fully 48% of the population (PRB World Population Data Sheet, 2017).

Discover & Debate

THE REFUGEE DILEMMA

Motion: Developed, democratic states such as the United States have an obligation to accept refugees fleeing conflict and danger.

Background: The United Nations defines a *refugee* as one who has "been forced to flee his or her country because of persecution, war, or violence." Most refugees flee war or ethnic, tribal, or religious violence; many are unable to return home, or risk persecution or death if they do so. In 1951, six years after the end of World War II, a Refugee Convention was passed that enumerated rights and protections for refugees, including the core principle that they may not be returned to countries where they face mortal danger. Refugees are distinguished from voluntary migrants,

even though some migrants (including economic migrants) may be seeking to escape dire poverty. The number of people who are displaced around the world is greater today than at any time since the World War II era: The United Nations estimates that about 22.5 million displaced persons are living outside of their country of origin, while another 40 million remain in their own country but have been forced from their homes. In the fiscal year that ended in September 2017, the United States took in about 84,995 refugees. The figures have dropped somewhat since the Trump administration reduced the admissions cap to 45,000. The question of whether the United States should take in more refugees is one that is vehemently debated.

AFFIRMATIVE ARGUMENTS	OPPOSITION ARGUMENTS
U.S. allies in Europe and the Middle East have taken in large numbers of refugees: For example, more than 2.5 million Syrian refugees reside in Turkey and hundreds of thousands of refugees from Middle Eastern and African conflicts have sought asylum in Western European countries such as Germany, Sweden, and France. The United States must contribute more fully to this effort to shelter the displaced.	An open-door policy encourages flight and may drain struggling societies of the educated and professional members they need to recover from crisis and conflict.
The Refugee Convention, to which the United States is a signatory, creates an obligation: If refugees cannot be returned to a place where they face mortal danger, then they must, by extension, be accepted for resettlement in a new country.	The United States must place limits on the number of refugees it takes in because large numbers of outsiders may be difficult to assimilate into the U.S. melting pot.
Many of today's U.S. citizens were refugees or are the descendants of refugees from World War II and other conflicts. The history of accepting people in need of safe shelter is part of the U.S. historical and cultural tradition.	The Refugee Convention obligates the United States to be part of the solution to the global refugee crisis, but that solution may not be resettlement in the United States. For example, the United States can help by supporting safe, well-resourced refugee camps in countries close to the refugees' home states.

(Continued)

Technology: The Great Equalizer?

As we have seen, global inequality is manifested today in a broad spectrum of ways, ranging from a lack of income and food to little access to good education and sanitation. At the same time, new technologies have emerged whose adoption has not been limited to the well-off. Access to the Internet is growing across the globe (Figure 8.5). Consider also the mobile phone, a technology that is bringing opportunities and change to many of the world's developing countries and their populations.

A finding of India's most recent decennial census (conducted in 2011) is that about 53% of India's estimated 1.2 billion people have mobile phones, even though only a little over 36% have toilets in their homes and an even smaller percentage have indoor sources of drinking water (Hannon, 2012). In China, one finds a similar contrast between the absence of basic household amenities and the adoption of new technologies: According to a report by the United Nations (2013b), in China, 14 million people have no access to toilets in their homes, but 980 million of China's 1.3 billion inhabitants have cell phones. Across the globe, mobile phone

■ **FIGURE 8.5** Internet Access around the World, 2015

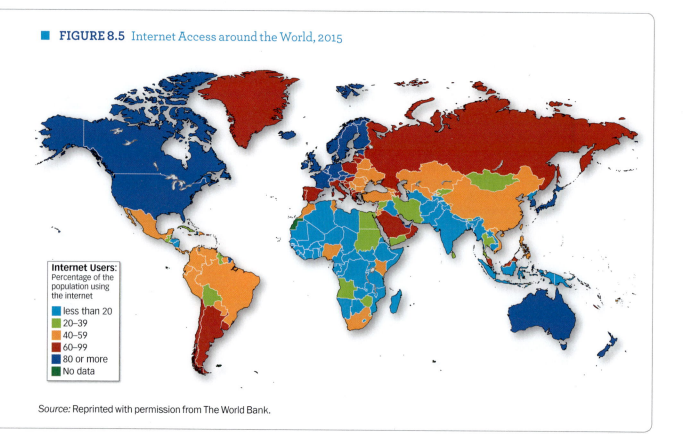

Internet Users:
Percentage of the population using the internet

- less than 20
- 20–39
- 40–59
- 60–99
- 80 or more
- No data

Source: Reprinted with permission from The World Bank.

use has surged; according to a summary of the report, "of the world's seven billion people, six billion have mobile phones" (United Nations, 2013a).

While, as noted earlier in the chapter, the absence of safe and sanitary toilet facilities is a burden and danger to communities, the mass global adoption of the mobile phone is, data suggest, an important change with the potential to affect health, education, agriculture, and social activism, among other facets of life. A recent online article posted by the *MIT Technology Review* notes that in just over a decade, Africa has transformed from a continent with little telecommunications infrastructure to a continent where about one in six inhabitants has a mobile phone; for example, "Nigeria alone has gone from a nation of just 30,000 cell subscriptions in 2000 to more than 140 million today, or roughly 87 percent penetration" (Berkley, 2013). It has been estimated that Africa will have a billion mobile phones by 2016 (Ogunlesi & Busari, 2012). This change has important implications for health care on the continent: For instance, birth registrations that parents can easily complete on their mobile phones can make government databases on live births and infant mortality more accurate. Also, mobile phone technology can improve the operation of the vaccine supply chain by allowing real-time data on vaccine availability or deficits in clinics to reach suppliers (Berkley, 2013). Scientists hope that this technology will eventually be used for diagnostic purposes, enabling even residents of remote areas to access medical advice.

Mobile phones are also having an effect on education and literacy across the globe. In South Africa, for instance, the country's most popular social media platform has partnered with a global telecommunications firm to offer an accessible math-teaching tool to users, and it is hoped that such technology can eventually be used to offer a wide variety of lessons to students (Ogunlesi & Busari, 2012). No less important, access to mobile phones is providing access to books for both new and advanced readers. As a UNESCO (2014a) report notes, "Many people from Lagos to La Paz to Lahore . . . do not read for one reason: they don't have books" (p. 13; Figure 8.6). The report goes on to observe that "a well-respected study of 16 sub-Saharan African countries found that most primary schools have few or no books, and in many countries these low levels are not improving" (Ross, 2010, cited in UNESCO, 2014a, pp. 13–14). This lack of books may compromise reading acquisition and have longer-term academic consequences. As well, mobile phone technology offers opportunities to read—whether for pleasure, formal education, reading to children, or news—to those who may lack the resources to obtain text for reading in other ways. If 6 billion of the world's 7 billion people can

■ **FIGURE 8.6** Number of Libraries per Population Ratio in the United Kingdom and Nigeria

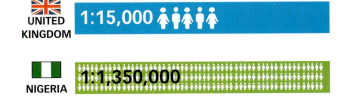

Adapted from United Nations Educational, Scientific and Cultural Organization. (2014). *Reading in the mobile era: A study of mobile reading in developing countries.* Paris: Author.

Mobile phone technology has begun to reach even the remotest parts of the globe, bringing new opportunities for contact and commerce as well as activism, education, and health care.

now access working mobile phones, a new world of literacy may be at their fingertips.

Even agriculture in the developing world, much of which is still concentrated in small family farms, is being affected by mobile technology. In countries where agriculture is still a primary sector of the economy, technology has the potential to affect both micro- and macro-level economic indicators. According to a CNN report on mobile phones in Africa, "By serving as platforms for sharing weather information, market prices, and micro-insurance schemes, mobile phones are allowing Africa's farmers to make better decisions, translating into higher-earning potentials." Farmers with cattle, for instance, can use the mobile app iCow to track cows' gestation periods and to learn additional information about breeding and nutrition (Ogunlesi & Busari, 2012).

Finally, technology has brought to the developing world a new platform for social activism. Citizen mobilization against crime, corruption, violence, and other social ills has been fostered by mobile technology that rapidly passes information across communities. Mobile phones have played important roles in many events, from Kenya in 2008, where citizens used phones to report violent incidents in the country's disputed elections, to the citizen uprisings against authoritarian regimes in North African countries such as Tunisia in 2011 to Nigeria in 2014, where the viral Twitter campaign #BringBackOurGirls brought global attention to the plight of more than 300 girls kidnapped by the radical Islamist organization Boko Haram.

Can mobile phone technology contribute to bringing greater prosperity—and equality—to the planet? How might mass adoption of mobile phones contribute to addressing some of the inequalities described in this chapter?

Theoretical Perspectives on Global Inequality

In this section, we analyze global inequality from several theoretical perspectives, raising the questions of what explains global inequality and why it exists and persists. Later, we take a critical look at the theories.

Modernization theory is *a market-oriented development theory* associated with the work of Walt Rostow (1961) and others. In contrast to many perspectives on stratification, the modernization perspective asks not why some countries are poor but why some countries are rich. In asking this question, it makes the assumption that the historical norm in states has been poverty; that is, the populations of most countries at most times have subsisted rather than prospered. The answer it proposes is that affluent states have modern institutions, markets, and worldviews; by *modern*, Rostow meant those that emulate the democratic and capitalist states of the West. He argued that economically underdeveloped states can progress if they adopt Western institutions, markets, and worldviews. Rostow used the analogy of an airplane taking flight to illustrate his key ideas about the stages of development:

- **The traditional stage:** In this pre-Newtonian (that is, prescientific) stage, societies are present- and past-time oriented, looking back into history for models of economic and political behavior rather than looking forward and seeking new models. They embrace tradition over innovation. Economic development is limited by low rates of savings and investment and by a work orientation that elevates subsistence over ambition and prosperity. The airplane is grounded and has not yet begun its journey to affluence. Today,

few such countries exist. One might look at individual communities within developing countries to find these traditional orientations.

In some developing countries, however, traditional beliefs about women's roles hinder their educational attainment and access to the labor market. Arguably, this is a cultural norm that also stifles national development, as it keeps a segment of the population that could potentially constitute half the workforce (women) from contributing its talents and skills.

- **The takeoff stage:** In this stage, societies are moving away from traditional cultural norms, practices, and institutions and are embracing economic development with a sense of purpose and increasing practices of savings and investment. The plane rises as the weight of tradition is cast overboard in favor of modernity.

Rostow, an originator of modernization theory, was an adviser to President Kennedy, whose administration was responsible for the development of the Peace Corps. The Peace Corps, which has for decades sent young U.S. workers abroad to spread innovations in agriculture and technology, to teach English, and to train leaders in developing countries in methods of modern governance, could be seen as a vehicle for moving countries from the traditional to the takeoff stage. Today, some African countries with modernity-oriented leadership, such as Liberia, might be categorized as members of the takeoff group.

- **In flight with technological progress and cultural modernity:** In this next stage, as the plane moves forward, technology is spreading to areas such as agriculture and industry, innovation is increasing, and resistance to change is declining. Many people are adopting modern cultural values, and governance increasingly reflects the rule of law. Advanced countries facilitate these processes by offering advice and money.

Progress may take the form of industrialization, which drives greater urbanization as rural dwellers leave poor agricultural areas to seek their fortunes in cities. It may also be accompanied by lower fertility, driven by the increased use of contraception as opportunities for women grow in education and the labor market. India might be considered a modern example of this stage, as it has a growing educated middle class, rising urbanization and industrialization, and (for better or worse) soaring consumer ambitions.

- **The stage of high mass consumption and high living standards:** In this stage, there is a greater em-

Modernization theory: A market-oriented development theory that envisions development as evolutionary and guided by modern institutions, practices, and cultures.

phasis on the satisfaction of consumer desires, as new affluence expands the ranks of those with disposable income. This is the stage that advanced countries such as those of Western and Northern Europe, the United States, Israel, and Japan have reached.

As these stages suggest, modernization theory assumes we can understand a given state's level of development by looking at its political, economic, and social institutions and its cultural orientation. That is, the theory uses a country's *internal variables* as key measuring sticks. In contrast, two later theories take a conflict perspective, focusing on countries' conflicting interests, unequal resources, and exploitative relationships, though they emphasize different aspects of inequality.

Just as Marx posited a fundamentally exploitative relationship between the bourgeoisie and the proletariat, so too does **dependency theory** (Emmanuel, 1972; Frank, 1966, 1979; Ghosh, 2001), which argues that *the poverty of some countries is a consequence of their exploitation by wealthy states, which control the global capitalist system.* While exploitation originated in colonial relationships, when powerful Western states such as Britain, the Netherlands, and Belgium dominated countries such as the Congo, South Africa, and India, it continues through the modern vehicle of multinational corporations that reap great profits from the cheap labor and raw materials of poor countries while local populations draw only bare subsistence from their human and natural resources.

Dependency theory draws its name from the idea that prices on the global market for human and natural resources held by poor states are intentionally kept low to benefit high-income states, so low-income states cannot fully develop industrially, technologically, or economically. Thus, these states remain in a *dependency relationship* with the well-off states that buy and exploit their labor and raw materials. Whereas modernization theory implies that high-income states want to encourage the full development of low-income countries, dependency theory suggests there is a direct relationship between the affluence of one and the poverty of the other.

World systems theory shares some of these basic ideas. Immanuel Wallerstein (1974, 1974/2011a, 1980/2011b, 1989/2011c, 2011d), one of the pioneers of the theory, argues that *the global capitalist economic system has long been shaped by a few powerful economic actors, who have constructed it in a* way that favors their class interests. He suggests that the world economy is populated by three key categories of countries:

- **Core countries:** The core countries are economically advanced, technologically sophisticated, and home to well-educated, skilled populations. They control the vast majority of the world's wealth and reap the greatest benefits from the world economic order, including trade and production practices. They include the United States, Canada, the states of Western and Northern Europe, and Japan, among others.

- **Peripheral countries:** The peripheral states have low national incomes and low levels of technological and industrial development; many still depend on agriculture. They have been exploited by the core states for their cheap labor (and, historically, slave labor) and for cheap raw materials that are exported to advanced countries and made into finished goods that bring far greater profit to core companies and consumers. Peripheral countries include parts of Central and Latin America, Asia, and many of sub-Saharan Africa's states. Some of those in Africa provide the critical mineral components of modern electronics for which consumers pay top dollar, such as smartphones and iPads, but they still suffer dire poverty.

- **Semiperipheral states:** The semiperiphery shares some characteristics with both the core and peripheral states, occupying an intermediate and sometimes stabilizing position between them. Semiperipheral states such as China, India, and Brazil may be exploited by core states, but they may in turn have the capacity to exploit the resources of peripheral states. For example, China, which has advanced industrial capacity and a growing middle class of consumers, has begun to foster economic relationships with African countries that can offer oil resources for the populous and economically growing state.

World systems theory sees the world as dynamic rather than static, with peripheral and semiperipheral states seeking to rise in the ranks and core countries attempting to hold fast to global power. The key unit of analysis in world systems theory is less about individual countries (as it is in modernization theory) than it is about relationships between countries and regions of the world. Similar to dependency theory, world systems theory sees relationships between states, such as those between core and periphery states, as fundamentally exploitative; that is, some countries benefit to the detriment of others.

Below, we use these perspectives to examine the case of Nigeria, a developing African country. Application of the perspectives will help us to assess their utility as analytical tools for understanding development and global inequality.

Dependency theory: The theory that the poverty of some countries is a consequence of their exploitation by wealthy states, which control the global capitalist system.

World systems theory: The theory that the global capitalist economic system has long been shaped by a few powerful economic actors, who have constructed it in a way that favors their class interests.

Applying the Theories: The Case of Nigerian Oil Wealth

A *National Geographic* story on the Niger Delta begins like this:

> Oil fouls everything in southern Nigeria. It spills from the pipelines, poisoning soil and water. It stains the hands of politicians and generals, who siphon off its profits. It taints the ambitions of the young, who will try anything to scoop up a share of the liquid riches—fire a gun, sabotage a pipeline, kidnap a foreigner.
>
> Nigeria had all the makings of an uplifting tale: [A] poor African nation blessed with enormous sudden wealth. . . . By the mid-1970s, Nigeria had joined OPEC (Organization of Petroleum Exporting Countries), and the government's budget bulged with petrodollars. (O'Neill, 2007)

Using the case of Nigeria and its vast oil reserves in the southern Niger Delta, we can evaluate the theories we have

described and compare how well they illuminate the case of Nigeria, a country with a per capita GNI-PPP of only $5,680 (Population Reference Bureau, 2015).

Recall that the modernization perspective highlights internal variables such as the lack of modern state, economic, and legal institutions and inadequately modern cultures to explain why some countries have lagged in development. A modernization theorist would thus point to the rampant culture of corruption and lack of rule of law that have characterized countries such as Somalia and North Korea, which Transparency International (2011), a corruption watchdog agency, has ranked as the most corrupt countries in the world. Nigeria is also near the top of the agency's list. Clearly, there are links between state corruption, the lack of an effective legal and civic structure, and the dire poverty in and around Port Harcourt. Though it is the capital of Nigeria's oil-rich Rivers state, Port Harcourt has "no electricity, no clean water, no medicine, [and] no schools" (O'Neill, 2007). But does the modernization perspective miss some key aspects of the problem of global poverty?

Critics argue that in attending almost exclusively to internal variables, the modernization perspective fails to recognize external obstacles to development and the ways in which well-off states benefit from the inferior economic position of poor states. According to *National Geographic,* in the wake of independence from colonial Britain, few observers expected that Nigeria would become a global oil source (Figure 8.7). In the decades that followed, however, five multinational oil companies—Royal Dutch Shell, Total, Italy's Agip, Exxon-Mobil, and Chevron—transformed the Rivers state. "The imprint: 4,500 miles . . . of pipelines, 159 oil fields, and 275 flow stations" (O'Neill, 2007). This massive oil infrastructure continues to leave a significant environmental footprint in the area. According to Amnesty International (2015),

> Royal Dutch Shell and the Italian multinational oil giant ENI have admitted to more than 550 oil spills in the

Port Harcourt, located in Nigeria's River State, is a key exporter of crude oil. Despite the region's valuable natural resources, many citizens in the region still face extreme hardship (including poverty) and environmental threats.

■ **FIGURE 8.7** Where the Oil Is in Africa

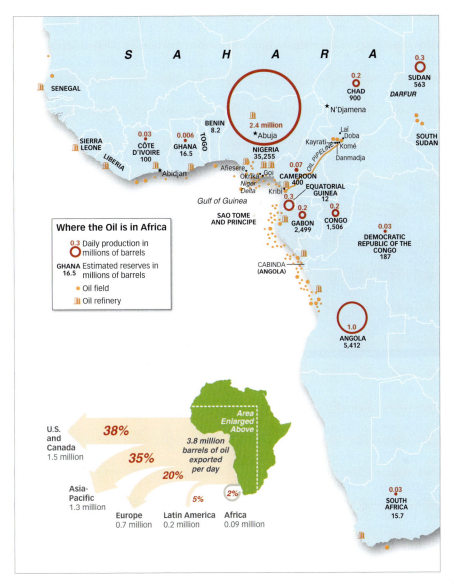

Source: Adapted from Mappery.com.

Niger Delta last year, according to an Amnesty International analysis of the companies' latest figures. By contrast, on average, there were only 10 spills a year across the whole of Europe between 1971 and 2011. (para. 1)

The United Nations Development Programme and the International Crisis Group point to decades of problematic economic strategies employed by oil companies, which have taken advantage of weak environmental controls, offered little compensation for land and few employment opportunities to local communities, engaged in corrupt deals for oil, and used private security forces to commit violence against those who resisted their efforts to control the oil fields of the Niger Delta (Brock & Cocks, 2012; O'Neill, 2007).

From the dependency and world systems perspectives, a relationship of fundamental exploitation exists between Nigeria and high-income countries, including the United States and Britain, for which Nigeria provides a critically important resource. If the United States is a core state, Nigeria appears from this perspective a peripheral state supplying oil, the basic raw building block of modern economies, without seeing the benefit of its own natural wealth. Semiperipheral states aggressively seeking to develop their own economies and wealth are also part of the picture: "China, India, and South Korea, all energy-hungry, have begun buying stakes in Nigeria's offshore [oil] blocks" (O'Neill, 2007). The dependency theory perspective suggests that developed and rapidly developing states benefit from lax government oversight of environmental pollution, low-wage pools of local labor, and corruptible officials willing to bend rules to accommodate corporate wishes.

Similar to modernization theory, the dependency and world systems theoretical perspectives illuminate some aspects of the case while obscuring others. Variables such as the exploitative power of Western oil companies are a key part of understanding the failure of Nigeria to develop in a way that benefits the broader population, but conflict-oriented perspectives pay little attention to the agency of poor states and, in particular, their governing bodies in setting a solid foundation for development.

Behind the Numbers

COUNTING THE "THREE COMMA CLUB": WHO IS A BILLIONAIRE?

©iStockphoto.com/velvetocean

In March of 2018, *Forbes* magazine released its annual report on the world's richest people. According to the report, capitalism's global conquest continues as entrepreneurs around the globe mint fortunes in everything from cryptocurrencies to telecom to bridal dresses. *Forbes* has pinned down a record 2,208 billionaires from 72 countries and territories, including the first ever from Hungary and Zimbabwe. This elite group is worth $9.1 trillion, up 18% since last year. Their average net worth is a record $4.1 billion. Americans lead the way with a record 585 billionaires, followed by mainland China with 373 (Kroll & Dolan, 2018, para. 1).

The size of the group is unprecedented, and many are newcomers to the "three comma club." The *Forbes* list is an awaited yearly ritual: It is one of the magazine's signature features. How does *Forbes* know who is—and is not—a billionaire? How is wealth calculated? What or who might be missing in the count of billionaires and their billions?

Forbes is open about its methodology and the fact that wealth (particularly wealth that is tied up in stock prices, which can fluctuate dramatically) is not necessarily stable and some members of the group "will become richer or poorer within weeks—even days—of publication" (Kroll, 2018, para. 8). The magazine examines federal financial disclosures, course records, and Securities & Exchange Commission documents, as well as

media reports. It seeks to value a spectrum of assets, including real estate, art, planes, jewelry, car collections, and stakes in public and private companies (Kroll, 2013).

Some very wealthy people do not make the list in spite of their fortunes. For example, the 2014 methodology report indicates that

> [*Forbes* does] not include royal family members or dictators who derive their fortunes entirely as a result of their position of power, nor do we include royalty who, often with large families, control the riches in trust for their nation. Over the years Forbes has valued the fortunes of these wealthy despots, dictators and royals but have listed them separately as they do not truly reflect individual, entrepreneurial wealth that could be passed down to a younger generation or truly given away. (Kroll & Dolan, 2014)

Consider the case of Russian president Vladimir Putin. According to a recent news report, "Vladimir Putin earned 38.5 million rubles (roughly $673,000) between 2011 and 2016, according to information publicly released by the Central Election Commission of the Russian Federation . . . giving the Russian president an average yearly salary of about $112,000" (Taylor, 2018, para. 1). However, the same article suggests that Putin is likely a multibillionaire and a second article asked if Putin may secretly be the richest man in the world because of his investments in highly valued Russian companies in the oil sector and ownership of one—or many—lavish palaces (Wile, 2017).

There are billionaires who do not make the list because they work hard to maintain their financial and personal privacy. After all, great wealth may invite unwanted attentions from those seeking support or donations or from those seeking to exploit or steal another's fortune. There are significant sums of global cash stashed away in countries such as Switzerland, the Cayman Islands, Belize, and the Bahamas, where they can be hidden from the gaze of national tax collectors (Shapiro, 2013). Wealth can also be held under alternative names and shell companies in complex financial arrangements that enable one to keep wealth under wraps.

There is significant interest in wealth and the wealthy. Great riches confer celebrity, and some billionaires seek attention while others avoid it. All, arguably, seek to keep as much of their money as possible. Consequently, counting the wealth of the billionaire class (and even the millionaire class) is a challenge.

Think It Through

- Is it important for the public to know how many people are billionaires and who is included in the list? How is the rise of a billionaire class sociologically significant?

Who Are the Global Elite?

Sociological perspectives on global inequality often focus on *countries* as objects of analysis. While it is recognized that countries are also stratified internally, discussions of global inequality such as those we presented earlier in this chapter compare, contrast, and analyze countries and their regions. Sociology also, however, takes an interest in the idea that there exists a **global elite**, a *transglobal class of professionals who exercise considerable economic and political power that is not limited by national borders*. Some writers suggest that an identifiable global power elite, while not an entirely new phenomenon, is a product of modernity, brought into growing significance by technological innovation and globalization. In this section, we look at the descriptive dimensions of this phenomenon. We then turn to a consideration of some key sociological ideas about the characteristics and functions of a global elite.

One important measure of membership in the global elite is wealth. In 2018, *Forbes* magazine identified 2,208 people around the world who are billionaires: Their average net worth is $4.1 billion (Kroll & Dolan, 2018). Financial writer Chrystia Freeland (2012) suggests that today's global power elite, members of which she calls "the plutocrats," is composed largely of working professionals who have made their fortunes rather than inherited them. Most have made their fortunes in business, media, or technology. According to *Forbes*, in 2018, the aggregate wealth of the world's billionaires topped $9.1 trillion (Kroll & Dolan, 2018). While many of today's multimillionaires and billionaires live in developed countries such as the United States, quite a few also live in developing countries such as China, Russia, and India, where rapid economic growth, including the privatization of previously government-held industries (for example, oil) has opened up unprecedented opportunities for establishment and expansion of personal wealth.

In the context of a growing global list of billionaires, being a millionaire looks more commonplace than extraordinary, though millionaires are certainly few in number in the context of the global population of over 7 billion. Many of those millionaires reside in the United States: In 2016, there were an estimated 4.4 million people who were considered *high-net-worth individuals*, someone with a net worth exceeding $1 million, excluding the value of one's primary residence (Knight Frank Research, 2017). While estimates vary depending on how wealth is counted, according to *The Wealth Report* (2017), the world was home to about 13.6 million millionaires in 2016. This number is expected to grow by 36% to more than 18.6 million by 2026 (Knight Frank Research, 2017). Notably, their number—and their wealth—is growing, though, according to the Boston Consulting Group (which tracks global assets), most of the wealth has grown due to a rising stock market and increases in asset prices rather than from newly created businesses (Frank, 2015).

While there is unprecedented national diversity on the current roster of the rich and the superrich, there has also been a marked rise in the gap between the world's economic elites and everyone else. According to a 2016 report by the development organization Oxfam, nearly half of the world's wealth is owned by 1% of the globe's population (Hardoon et al., 2016).

Seeking to outline a definition of the *global elite*, writer David Rothkopf (2008) suggests that

the distribution of power has clearly shifted, not just away from the United States and Europe, but away from nations. . . . Had [sociologist C. Wright] Mills been writing today, he would have turned his attention from the national elite in America to a new and more important phenomenon: the rise of a global power elite, a superclass that plays a similar role in the hierarchy of the global era to the role that the U.S. power elite played in that country's first decade as a superpower. (p. 9)

Global elite: A transglobal class of professionals who exercise considerable economic and political power that is not limited by national borders.

Rothkopf emphasizes the idea that the global elite is powerful not only because it is rich, but because it is influential in political decision making, global markets and industries, technological innovation, the production of cultural or intellectual ideas, and even world religions. The global elite and its decisions have impacts on the lives of thousands or even millions of citizens, consumers, workers, and worshippers. The global power elite, Rothkopf argues, includes corporate executives, presidents and prime ministers of powerful states, technological innovators, those who control flows of global resources such as oil, media moguls, some military elites, and a handful of well-known and active cultural and religious figures. Their power is multiplied by the fact that they are deeply networked, sharing links to other members of the elite through both personal and professional ties. Their exercise of power is not always direct, but their influence is palpable in politics, economics, and media, among other areas.

Sociologist Leslie Sklair (2002) conceptualizes the notion of a modern global elite in his writings on "transnational capitalism." His work highlights the position that nations and borders are of declining significance in capitalist globalization. He argues that important objects of analysis in a globalizing world are what he terms *transnational practices*—"practices that cross state borders but do not originate with state actors, agencies, or institutions" (p. 10). He suggests that understanding the modern economic order requires recognizing how power has become transnational rather than limited by national borders. As part of his examination of transnational practices, Sklair theorizes the rise of a *transnational capitalist class* that is composed not of capitalists (that is, the bourgeoisie) in the classical Marxian sense but of four categories of members: (1) a *corporate fraction* drawn from transnational corporations, (2) a *state fraction* composed of global political elites, (3) a *technical fraction* representing globalizing professionals, and (4) a *consumerist fraction* made up of executives of marketing and media.

While Sklair's theorized class would appear to encompass a broader swath of members than Rothkopf's (2008) global elite, his characterization of the transnational capitalist class reflects an idea shared with Rothkopf that global economic integration and the mobility of capital have fostered the birth of a transglobal class. The members of this class have the following characteristics:

- They share global (not only local) interests and perspectives as well as consumer lifestyle choices.

- They seek to exercise control or influence over key political, economic, and cultural–ideological processes on a global level.

- They hail from different national backgrounds, but they see themselves as citizens of the world rather than citizens of particular states.

Freeland (2012) echoes the last point in her journalistic account of the global elite, noting that members often feel they have more in common with their fellow elites than with their countrymen. She points out that this, however, may not be a new development: She quotes an early theorist of capitalism, Adam Smith, who wrote in 1776, "The proprietor of land is necessarily a citizen of the particular country in which his estate lies. The proprietor of stock is properly a citizen of the world, and is not necessarily attached to a particular country" (p. 67).

The transnational capitalist class is a global elite that exercises political, economic, and cultural–ideological power and acts to organize "conditions under which its interests and the interests of the global system . . . can be furthered" (Sklair, 2002, p. 99). Sklair also theorizes a particular function for the transnational capitalist class: It is a vehicle by which *transnational corporations,* modern and powerful economic entities, expand and legitimize the consumerist culture and ideology that is needed to sustain the global system of capitalist production.

In an interesting variation on the conceptualization of globalized classes, Zygmunt Bauman (1998) has written on what he describes as a *space war*. Bauman's analysis points not toward the cosmos but toward modern citizens' relationship to physical spaces and places, including countries. Bauman posits that the "winners" of globalization (and the space war) are those who are mobile, who can move through space to create value and meaning—he calls them *tourists* (though he does not mean that in the strictly conventional sense). They can move across the globe, enabled by transportation and communication technologies and their economic and professional resources. They exist, suggests Bauman, in time rather than in space because space is not constraining to them. What Bauman is describing is a globalized category of the world population whose mobility is enabled by education, economic resources, and social networks. For example, business professionals, high-level government bureaucrats and representatives, and cultural elites and celebrities have the means to seek out both personal pleasures and professional opportunities globally.

By contrast, the "losers" of modernity are those who are tied to places and spaces that have been devastated by globalization. Lacking resources, they are rooted in place and denied geographic and economic mobility. In thinking about this category, one might consider diverse groups, ranging from former automobile plant workers stripped of their livelihood by globalization and stuck in economically devastated cities to poor urban dwellers in the developing world whose lives revolve around difficult and dangerous low-wage jobs that they cannot afford to lose. Among the losers of a globalizing world are also, Bauman points out, those who are on the move, but they differ from the mobile global elite; rather, they are what he terms *vagabonds,* moving across the globe as refugees or poor economic migrants, unable to live in their own countries and unwanted elsewhere.

Bauman does not specify the precise qualities of his loosely defined global classes, but his work points to the idea that globalization has created different experiences for different groups that are not easily characterized through reference to national boundaries. This perspective may lead us to consider global inequality as a modern phenomenon that crosses borders and shapes new opportunities as well as obstacles.

As of the beginning of 2018, there were more than 2,200 billionaires in the world. The richest person in the world is Jeff Bezos, founder of Amazon.com, who is currently worth an estimated $112 billion.

Social Life, Social Media

#FIRSTWORLDPROBLEMS

If you are a user or follower of Twitter, you may be familiar with the popular hashtag #FirstWorldProblems. The site attracts a broad spectrum of contributors who engage in self-mocking about the relative insignificance of the daily tribulations of life in the modern world. The online site *Urban Dictionary* defines *first world problems* as "problems from living in a wealthy, industrialized nation that third worlders would probably roll their eyes at." The following are some samples of #firstworldproblems gathered from the site in June 2018:

- i need to shower, i want to shower but i also don't want to get out of bed

- I'm about to count down Alexa and put her in time out if she doesn't stop talking back and find my song.

- When you really want an early night but you've bid for something on Ebay that doesn't finish for another hour.

- I burned my tongue on a piece of steak

- Is there anything worse than going to make a half-time cup of tea and finding there's no f**kin milk!

- don't know where we are and I only got 3G service

- When you ask Jake to get you a Margarita and he gets you a Mojito instead

- ☹My slice of breakfast pizza was too big this morning and now I'm not hungry for taco salad lunch.

The site attracts posters from around the globe. June's sample featured posts in Finnish, Dutch, German, and Spanish, among others.

Interestingly, some have taken advantage of the hashtag's popularity to attract interest in real problems that exist in the developing world. For example, the charitable organization WATERisLIFE, which raises funds to assist communities that lack clean drinking water, posted a YouTube video featuring Haitian children and adults reading some of the #FirstWorldProblems posts (such as "I hate it when I go to the bathroom and forget my phone"). The video, arguably, both critiques and takes advantage of the hashtag to draw attention to the organization's cause. While the video drew a lot of attention to the charity, the advertising agency that made it said that WATERisLIFE hoped to eliminate a hashtag on Twitter that "showcases concerns that seem important to those living in wealthy, industrialized countries, yet are, in fact, trivial compared to the issues faced by those struggling to survive in many parts of the world." This drew an angry response from some posters who suggested that the agency failed to grasp the irony in the posts (Edwards, 2012).

The Twitter hashtag has attracted other criticism as well. While the tone of the hashtag #FirstWorldProblems is self-mocking, and posters presumably understand that the problems they are lamenting are trivial, some writers suggest that the

(Continued)

(Continued)

hashtag's purpose is not to bring recognition to the problems of the developing world but rather to act as a platform for wit and irony shared among the privileged (Madrigal, 2011). As well, as Teju Cole, a Nigerian American writer, has pointed out, people in developing countries are not beings so easily labeled as different from their first world counterparts: "Here's a First World problem: the inability to see that others are as fully complex and as keen on technology and pleasure as you are" (quoted in Madrigal, 2011).

Think It Through

- How would you characterize the sociological significance of #FirstWorldProblems? What are its functions in the first world? Would you agree more with its critics or with its defenders?

Follow us on Twitter to keep up with current sociological stories and research! We're at **@DiscoverSoc1.**

Share your own ideas at **#DiscoverSociology.**

Why Study Global Inequality from a Sociological Perspective?

Global inequality is manifested in the systematic disparities in income, wealth, health, education, and opportunities that exist between households, communities, and countries. Understanding inequality—both its dimensions and its roots—is, as you have seen in earlier chapters, one of sociology's key goals. As we have learned in this chapter, global poverty exists across different areas; it is rarely only a disparity of income that characterizes poverty. Economic disadvantage is a product but also a root of other disadvantages in areas such as health, education, and even access to safe sanitary facilities.

At the global level, we find countries arranged in a stratified hierarchy of positions, with some exercising economic, political, and cultural dominance and others lagging behind, unable to convert valued human and natural resources into national prosperity. What accounts for these differences? Sociology offers us some insights—it's up to us to study different cases and to test a variety of explanations.

Global inequality can also be studied in terms of transglobal forms of stratification, including the development of a global elite whose composition and influence transcend borders. Globalization has wrought a world system that is deeply interconnected, and both capital and people are mobile, traversing borders in pursuit of profit, power, and pleasure. Sociology considers the question of globalization's diverse effects on populations across the planet, asking about the roots, benefits, and consequences of the rapid changes of the globalizing social world.

Global inequality matters because in an ever more densely populated, interconnected, and interdependent world, the misfortunes and good fortunes of different countries and classes will not remain isolated in their effects.

 ## What Can I Do with a Sociology Degree?

ACTIVE UNDERSTANDING OF DIVERSITY

The development of an understanding of diversity is central to sociological study. As a sociology student, you will gain knowledge related to the histories, practices, and perspectives of diverse groups and will develop intercultural competence. You will also study and apply theories that lend themselves to the analysis of diversity and ways in which it can underpin societal harmony as well as conflict. The close understanding of diversity can inform important research about societal challenges and potential solutions. Active reflection on this knowledge supports the development of skills to effectively work through and with differences that

may divide communities and individuals by race, ethnicity, gender, sexuality, religion, and class, among others. A key part of developing an active understanding of diversity is learning to see the world from the perspectives of others. As a major in the social scientific discipline of sociology, you will be exposed to a breadth of theoretical and empirical work that illuminates the social world from a variety of perspectives and helps you to see how the positions of different groups in the social structure may affect perceptions, practices, and opportunities. You will be well prepared for the diverse and dynamic workplace of the present and the future.

Alex I. Yepez, Coordinator of the Migrant Student Leadership Institute at California State University, Channel Islands

California State University, Channel Islands, BA in Sociology, Minor in Chicana/o Studies and Communication

The Migrant Student Leadership Institute at California State University, Channel Islands, works with students from across California who come from migrant backgrounds to provide a college-like experience in order to motivate the students to pursue a higher education. The goal of the institute is to expose migrant children and their parents to the opportunities and benefits of a college education and STEM (science, technology, engineering, and math) learning.

In this specific population of students, many of them do not have family members who have obtained a college education, let alone gone through the educational system in the United States. Because of that, this population oftentimes does not have the cultural, social, and financial capital to succeed in college and will turn to a more vocational route. In order to understand the backgrounds of these students, it is critical to have an active understanding of diversity and to know the social barriers that prevent them from being successful in education or the workplace.

Career Data: Postsecondary Education Administrators

- 2017 Median Pay: $60,360 per year
- $29.02 per hour
- Typical Entry-Level Education: Bachelor's degree
- Job Growth, 2016–2026: 11% (Faster than average)

Source: Bureau of Labor Statistics, *Occupational Outlook Handbook,* 2017.

SUMMARY

- **Global inequality** can be described in terms of disparities in income, wealth, health, education, and access to safe, hygienic sanitation, among other things. Global gaps in equality between high-income, middle-income, and low-income countries remain substantial, even as some countries are effectively addressing problems such as malnutrition.

- There is an important relationship between armed conflict and poverty at the household, community, and country levels. Conflict exacerbates the problems of poverty and raises the risks of hunger and exploitation as well as the loss of life and property.

- While global inequalities remain substantial, access to mobile technology is improving, as nearly 6 billion of the world's 7 billion people now have access to working mobile phones.

- **Modernization theory** posits that global underdevelopment exists in states that cling to traditional cultures and fail to build modern state and market institutions.

Dependency theory and **world systems theory** highlight external variables that point out how high-income states benefit from the economic marginality of low-income states.

- Sociologists describe and analyze the phenomenon of a **global elite,** a transglobal class of professionals who exercise considerable economic and political power that is not limited by national borders. The global power elite, while not an entirely new phenomenon, is a product of modernity, brought into growing significance by technological innovation and globalization.

- Sklair theorizes a transnational capitalist class that is composed of elites with economic, political, and cultural ideological influence; he asserts that the members of this class organize the global order in a manner that realizes their own interests and contributes to the expansion and legitimation of a global consumerist ideology. Bauman looks at the development of population categories as defined by their relationships to space, in particular their mobility or lack of mobility.

KEY TERMS

global inequality, 199

gross national income–purchasing power parity per capita (GNI-PPP), 200

infant mortality rate, 201

total fertility rate (TFR), 201

modernization theory, 210

dependency theory, 211

world systems theory, 211

global elite, 215

DISCUSSION QUESTIONS

1. Why do many of the world's poorest countries have the highest fertility rates? What sociological factors can be used to explain the correlation?

2. How is armed conflict both a consequence and cause of economic scarcity?

3. Can the mass adoption of modern technologies (such as mobile phones) have an impact on poverty in developing countries? What does the chapter suggest? What other effects can you envision?

4. How do modernization theory, dependency theory, and world systems theory explain the existence and persistence of inequality between countries and regions? What are the strengths of these perspectives as analytical tools? What are their weaknesses?

5. What is meant by the term *global elite*? Who are the members of the global elite, and how do they differ from the upper-class elites described in an earlier chapter?

Want a Better Grade?

Get the tools you need to sharpen your study skills. Access practice quizzes, eFlashcards, video, and multimedia at **https://edge.sagepub.com/chambliss4e.**

©John Moore/Getty Images

Race and Ethnicity

WHAT DO YOU THINK?

1. What makes a group a *minority*? Does this term have both qualitative and quantitative dimensions?

2. Why does racial residential segregation exist and persist in many U.S. cities? What are the consequences of racial residential segregation?

3. How is the ethnic and racial composition of the U.S. changing?

LEARNING OBJECTIVES

9.1 Describe how sociologists understand race and ethnicity.

9.2 Describe different types of minority and dominant group relations in history and today.

9.3 Discuss theoretical approaches to the concepts of *ethnicity*, *racism*, and *minority status*.

9.4 Define *prejudice*, *stereotyping*, and *discrimination*.

9.5 Identify major racial and ethnic groups in the United States.

9.6 Define *genocide* and its relationship to national, ethnic, racial, or religious group membership.

VIOLENCE AND U.S. HISTORY

The violent victimization of African Americans by Whites did not end with slavery. According the National Association for the Advancement of Colored People (NAACP),

> Throughout the late 19th century racial tension grew throughout the United States.... In the south, people were blaming their financial problems on the newly freed slaves that lived around them. Lynchings were becoming a popular way of resolving some of the anger that whites had in relation to free blacks.

By one estimate, between the years 1882 and 1968, over 4,700 lynchings took place in the

©AP Photo/Emilio Morenatti

U. S. *Lynching* is the extrajudicial killing, usually premeditated, of someone suspected of a transgression, though lynchings are also used to intimidate a larger group of people. Most victims of lynching in the U.S. were Black, though some were Whites who were believed by the murderous mobs to be helping or associating with Black residents (NAACP, n.d.).

The majority of lynchings in U.S. history took place in the South. The end of slavery radically transformed the South and created strong resentments against African Americans. Sociologist E. M. Beck notes,

> The foundation of the South was white supremacy . . . when you start getting challenges to social and economic order, then you start (moving toward) things that support the old order. Black folks weren't seen as part of the community. . . . The white folks were "the community." When those boundaries began to break down, then you begin to see this violence. (quoted in Ware, n.d.)

Lynching functioned in this environment as a violent form of social control and a way for Whites to reassert their power and position over Blacks (Tolnay & Beck, 1995). Mobs involved in lynching rarely suffered legal or other consequences for their violent actions, which is one reason that they continued for decades.

While most victims of lynching were men, women were also subject to the extreme violence of lynching. Eighteen-year-old Mary Turner, a pregnant woman living in Georgia with her husband Hazel "Hayes" Turner, had the misfortune to inhabit the same town as an abusive plantation owner named Hampton Smith. Smith routinely exploited African Americans by bailing out those who had landed in jail for petty offenses and then forcing them to work off their bail on his plantation. When a confrontation with Sydney Johnson, who had not arrived to work because of illness, ended with Johnson killing Smith, a lynch mob took vengeance on 13 African Americans, all of them innocent, who lived in the area. One of those victims was Mary Turner. After Mary's husband was killed by the mob and his body hung up with shackled hands, she protested both the murder and the callous treatment of his body. "Incensed by a black woman who would dare to speak truth to power, the mob decided that Mary needed to be 'taught a lesson.'" On May 19, 1918, Mary was brutally murdered (Ware, n.d.).

In 2018, fully 100 years after Mary's lynching, the National Memorial for Peace and Justice opened in Montgomery, Alabama. The memorial, sited near the Alabama State Capitol, commemorates the victims of lynching:

At the center is a grim cloister, a walkway with 800 steel columns, all hanging from a roof. Etched on each column is the name of an American county and the people who were lynched there, most listed by name, many simply as 'unknown' . . .

> The magnitude of the killing is harrowing, all the more so when paired with the circumstances of individual lynchings. . . . Parks Banks, lynched in Mississippi in 1922 for carrying a photograph of a white woman; Caleb Gadly, hanged in Kentucky in 1894, for "walking behind the wife of his white employer;" Mary Turner, who, after denouncing her husband's lynching by a rampaging white mob, was hung upside down, burned, and then sliced open so that her unborn child fell to the ground (Robertson, 2018, para. 3–4).

The memorial recognizes the dramatic violence that took many innocent lives. It offers an unflinching look at the past, but it also offers pathways for the future:

The museum exhibit closes with a voter registration booth, information on volunteering, and guidelines for discussing lynching in U.S. history with young people.

Race and ethnicity, and their significance in society, are key issues in sociology. We begin this chapter with a discussion of the sociological definitions of race and ethnicity. We then consider some of the forms that minority–majority group relations have taken in history and today. Next, we look at theoretical perspectives on ethnicity, racism, and minority group status. This leads to a discussion of prejudice, discrimination, and stereotypes and various manifestations and consequences of these social phenomena. We then examine the experiences of different racial and ethnic groups in the United States and how group membership may shape people's political, economic, and social status. Finally, we talk about genocide as a race-based atrocity that continues to claim new victims in the 21st century.

The Social Construction of Race and Ethnicity

Sociologists W. I. Thomas and Dorothy Thomas (1928) observed that "if [people] define situations as real, they are real in their consequences" (pp. 571–572). The wisdom of their observation is powerfully demonstrated by the way societies construct definitions of race and ethnicity and then respond as though the definitions represent objective realities.

Race

One of the most dynamic areas of scientific research in recent years has been the Human Genome Project. Among its compelling findings is the discovery that genetically, all human beings are nearly identical. Less than 0.01% of the total gene pool contributes to racial differences (as manifested in physical characteristics), whereas thousands of genes contribute to traits that include intelligence, artistic and athletic talent, and social skills (Angier, 2000; Cavalli-Sforza, Menozzi, & Piazza, 1994). Based on this research, many scientists agree that "race is a *social concept,* not a *scientific* one . . . we all evolved in the last 100,000 years from the same small number of tribes that migrated out of Africa and colonized the world" (Angier, 2000, para. 6).

Sociologists define a **race** as *a group of people who share a set of characteristics (usually physical characteristics) deemed by society to be socially significant.* Notice that this definition suggests that physical characteristics are not the only—or even necessarily the most important—way of defining *races.* For many years, Catholics and Protestants in Ireland defined one another as separate races, and the

United States long considered Jews a separate racial category from Europeans, even though distinctive physical characteristics between these groups are in the eye of the beholder rather than objectively verifiable (Schaefer, 2009).

Although sociologists do not treat race as scientifically significant, it is, as we will see in this chapter, *socially significant.* Following the observation of the Thomases, we can conclude that because race is defined as real, it is real in its consequences. Racial differentiation has historically been linked to power: Racial categories have facilitated the treatment (or maltreatment) of others based on membership in given racial groups.

Notably, race is also social scientifically significant. Statistical data on phenomena ranging from obesity and poverty to crime and educational attainment are gathered and sorted by race. This book features such data throughout its pages. Even though sociologists generally agree that races cannot be objectively, biologically differentiated, they nonetheless use race to sort statistics and establish social facts about groups in society. This implicitly acknowledges that the social concept of race is profoundly real as a differentiating mechanism with historical and contemporary consequences.

Ethnicity

Although race may be a particularly significant social category in terms of consequences for people's lives, other socially defined categorizations are also important. **Ethnicity** refers to *characteristics of groups associated with national origins, languages, and cultural and religious practices.* Although ethnicity can be based on cultural self-identification (that is, one may choose to embrace one's Irish or Brazilian roots and traditions), an acknowledgment or degree of acceptance by a larger

Race: A group of people who share a set of characteristics (usually physical characteristics) deemed by society to be socially significant.

Ethnicity: Characteristics of groups associated with national origins, languages, and cultural and religious practices.

South Africa's apartheid was a system of privilege based on race. With racial identity determining social status and access to resources in society, Whites sat atop a hierarchy of power, while Black South Africans were at the bottom.

group is often necessary. For example, a third-generation Italian American may choose to self-identify as Italian. If she cannot speak Italian, however, others who identify as Italian may not see her as authentically Italian. The sociological significance of belonging to a particular racial or ethnic group is that society may treat group members differently, judging them or giving them favorable or unfavorable treatment based on membership and perceived affiliation.

Minorities

Any racial, ethnic, religious, or other group can constitute a minority in a society. **Minorities** are *less powerful groups who are dominated politically and economically by a more powerful group and, often, discriminated against on the basis of characteristics deemed by the majority to be socially significant.* Minorities are usually distinguished by physical and cultural attributes that make them recognizable to the dominant group. Minorities are generally fewer in number than the dominant population, though this is not invariably the case. In the U.S., African Americans, Latinos, and Asians are less numerous than the White majority, although the higher number of births among nonwhites, combined with immigration, will begin to change this in coming decades.

Although both the common understanding of the term and the implied numerical difference of the term itself suggest that minorities are fewer in number than the majority, an important aspect of minority group status is that the group has less access than the majority to power and resources valued by society. Thus, sociologically, women in the U.S., and in societies worldwide, may be considered a minority, despite the fact that they typically outnumber men. In South Africa before the end of apartheid rule in the early 1990s, a small number of Whites dominated the much larger minority population of what were termed *Black, colored,* and *mixed* races. Minority status is determined by access to power, status, and resources, not by the numerical size of a group.

Minority and Dominant Group Relations

Modern societies are characterized by racial and ethnic heterogeneity as well as divisions between dominant and minority groups. The coexistence of racial and ethnic groups can be a source of social conflict. Among minorities' most frequently used methods of resolving such conflict are social movements designed to challenge and change existing social relations. In extreme cases, resolution may be sought through revolution or rebellion. Dominant populations respond to such social movements with a variety of social and political policies, ranging from expulsion and segregation to assimilation of minorities and the acceptance of cultural pluralism. We discuss this spectrum of relationships between majority and minority groups below.

Expulsion

Conflicts between White settlers and Native Americans over land and resources in the United States in the 1800s often ended with the removal of Native Americans to isolated reservations. Sociologically, *the process of forcibly removing people from a particular area* is referred to as **expulsion**. Native Americans populated broad swaths of North America when the first European settlers arrived. As U.S. settlement expanded westward, Native Americans were driven under military arms to march, sometimes thousands of miles, to areas designated by the government as Native American reservations. These reservations continue to be socially and economically marginal areas.

Today, across the globe, people are being forced from their homes due to civil wars and ethnic and sectarian conflicts. According to recent figures from the United Nations High Commissioner for Refugees (UNHCR, 2017), in 2016, there were almost 66 million refugees and internally displaced people around the globe, equaling about 20 new displacements every minute or 28,300 every day.

Segregation

Segregation is *the practice of separating people spatially or socially on the basis of race or ethnicity.* In South Africa,

---

Minorities: Less powerful groups who are dominated by a more powerful group and, often, discriminated against on the basis of characteristics deemed by the majority to be socially significant.

Expulsion: The process of forcibly removing a population from a particular area.

Segregation: The practice of separating people spatially or socially on the basis of race or ethnicity.

apartheid was state policy until the beginning of the 1990s. The release from prison of anti-apartheid activist Nelson Mandela in 1990 and the end of a ban on previously forbidden political groups began the process of desegregation in that country, which has slowly evolved in the wake of the establishment of democracy in 1994. Apartheid was an extreme form of segregation that included not only prohibitions on where members of different racial and ethnic groups could live, but where they could travel and at what hours of the day they could be in different parts of particular cities. Although apartheid is no longer policy, the legacy of segregation lives on in many South African communities, where the White, Black, and colored populations still live separately and unequally.

In 1968, Black Memphis sanitation workers went on strike carrying placards stating "I Am a Man" in bold red letters. This phrase became an embodiment of the civil rights movement, as it showed that workers were not only fighting for better wages or working conditions, but for the recognition of their humanity.

©Bettmann/Bettmann/Getty Images

Before the 1960s, segregation on the basis of race was common practice and legally upheld in many parts of the United States. In some places, Whites were not permitted to rent apartments or sell homes to nonwhites, a practice upheld, for instance, through restrictive covenants. **Restrictive covenants** are *contractual agreements that restrict the use of land, ostensibly in order to preserve the value of adjacent land or a neighborhood.* Up until 1968, when the Fair Housing Act made their racially exclusive utilization illegal, these covenants could be used to prevent White homeowners from selling their home to Black buyers (Massey & Denton, 1993).

In the South, Blacks could not sit in the same restaurants as Whites. When they rode the same buses, Blacks were required by law to sit at the back, and on trains, they occupied different cars than White riders. In many parts of the country, restaurants and hotels refused to serve dark-skinned customers. Professional offices required separate waiting rooms for Blacks and Whites, and courts required different Bibles for witnesses of difference races to swear upon. Segregation infiltrated virtually every aspect of everyday living, including building entrances, water fountains, and waiting lines (Jim Crow Laws, 2018).

The civil rights movement of the 1960s succeeded in securing the passage of federal laws that outlawed segregation. Despite this success, high levels of racial residential segregation remain a reality in U.S. cities. Why is this the case in the post–civil rights era? First, it is legal and commonplace for housing markets to be segregated by income. Since racial minorities as a group have lower household incomes than Whites as a group, some cannot afford to live in predominantly White neighborhoods, where housing costs may be higher. Second, laws outlawing the consideration of race in home rental and sale practices are not always followed by real estate agents, landlords, and lenders, who may steer minorities away from predominantly White neighborhoods (Squires, 2003; Squires, Friedman, & Saidat, 2002). Third, White residents sometimes move out of neighborhoods when increasing numbers of minority residents move in (Woldoff, 2011).

Notably, many cities that are racially and ethnically diverse are, nonetheless, highly segregated. Consider Chicago: The city's population is about 33% Black, 32% White, and 29% Hispanic (Silver, 2015). At the neighborhood level, however, segregation by race and ethnicity is dramatic. For example, Chicago's south side is largely Black: Neighborhoods such as Washington Park are about 97% African American. By contrast, in the city's north, Lincoln Park neighborhoods are typically at least 80% White. To the west, the Cicero area is about 90% Hispanic (Block, Cox, & Giratiknon, 2015; Figure 9.1). Racial residential segregation remains a significant phenomenon, particularly in the larger, older cities of the Northeast and Midwest that are home to older housing stock and relatively large populations of poor minorities. Where integration has taken place, it has been limited mostly to areas with "relatively affluent and well-educated

---

Restrictive covenants: Contractual agreements that restrict the use of land, ostensibly in order to preserve the value of adjacent land or a neighborhood.

■ FIGURE 9.1 Concentration of Whites, Blacks, and Hispanics in Chicago, 2010

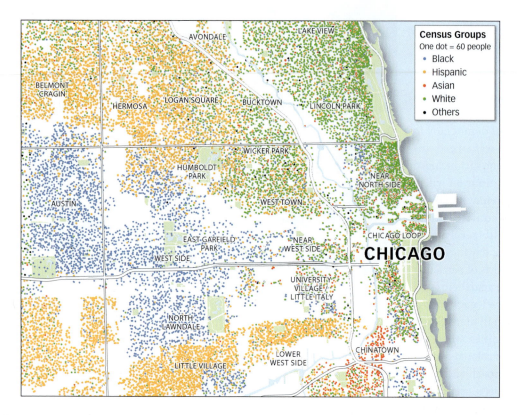

■ FIGURE 9.2 Median and Average Wealth, by Race

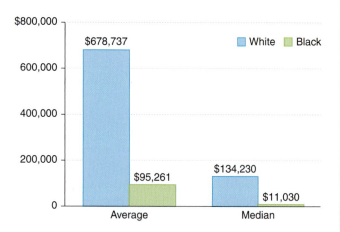

minority populations, low levels of anti-Black and anti-Latino sentiment, low rates of immigration, and permissive regimes of density zoning" (Rugh & Massey, 2014, p. 221).

Segregation has significant consequences for minority groups. Apart from denying them residential choice, it may compel them to live in poorer neighborhoods that offer less access to high-quality schools, jobs, and medical facilities (Kozol, 1995; Massey & Denton, 1993). Some of the effects of segregated neighborhoods can be seen in the racial wealth gap: In 2013, White median household net worth was just over $134,000; by contrast, Black median household wealth was around $11,000 (Figure 9.2; Jones, 2017).

As we noted in Chapter 7, the primary source of wealth for most working- and middle-class Americans is home equity. Lower average property values in minority neighborhoods translate to lower wealth in the community and in individual households.

Poor and segregated neighborhoods and regions are also more likely to be home to hazardous waste facilities and other sources of pollution, a problem that plagues minority communities from urban Los Angeles to rural Louisiana. As an article on segregation and pollutant exposure notes,

Behind the Numbers

COUNTING—AND NOT COUNTING—HATE CRIMES IN THE UNITED STATES

The U.S. Federal Bureau of Investigation (FBI) defines a *hate crime* as a "criminal offense against a person or property motivated in whole or in part by an offender's bias against a race, religion, disability, sexual orientation, ethnicity, gender, or gender identity." In 2016, the FBI reported 6,121 hate crimes in the United States, about two thirds of which were against persons and one third of which were against property. The majority of hate crimes in the report were motivated by racial or ethnic (58.5%) animosity. Most of the crimes against persons were cases of intimidation or simple assault, while most property crimes were vandalism and destruction or damage of property (Federal Bureau of Investigation, 2017; Figure 9.3).

According to a recent Associated Press report on FBI hate crimes data,

> Under FBI guidelines, an incident should be reported as a suspected hate crime if a "reasonable and prudent" person would conclude a crime was motivated by bias. Among the criteria for evaluation is whether an incident coincided with a significant holiday or date, specifically citing the King holiday. A suspect need not be identified to meet the threshold for reporting. (Cassidy, 2016, para. 12)

FIGURE 9.3 Hate Crime Breakdown

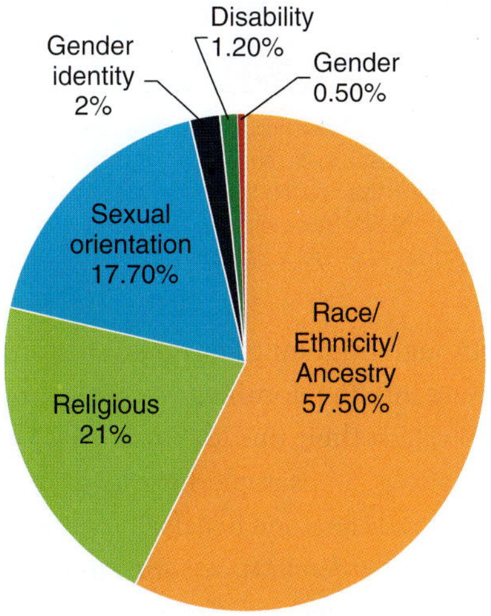

Source: Federal Bureau of Investigation, 2017a.

The filing of hate crime reports to federal authorities is voluntary, although guidelines ask that reports be submitted by local policing agencies, even if the count is zero.

FBI hate crimes reports are an important source of information for policymakers, police, and the public. They offer a means for tracking trends in hate crimes. For example, although Jews remain the most frequently targeted religious group, hate crimes against Muslims increased 19% from 2015 to 2016, and doubled in number from 2014 (Simpson & McCool, 2017).

At the same time, some research suggests that FBI statistics fail to capture the full picture of hate crimes in the United States: "[Bureau of Justice Statistics] studies have found that while the FBI has reported over the last 20 years between about 6,000 and about 11,500 total hate crimes in America each year, the real annual totals in recent years have been nearly 260,000" (Potok, 2015, para. 5). Why is there a gap between FBI figures and what the Southern Poverty Law Center report calls the "real annual totals" (Potok, 2015) of hate crimes? Several factors may explain the gap.

First, the U.S. Bureau of Justice Statistics suggests that about half of hate crimes go unreported because victims "believed the police could not or would not help" (Langton, Planty, & Sandholtz, 2013). Second, victims may be frightened of a backlash from the community if they report hate crimes. For example,

> In recent years, members of the Sikh community have been targeted by attackers who, in some cases, confused them with Muslims because of their turbans or other head coverings. But S. Gulbarg Singh Basi, chairman of the American Sikh Council, said that some in his community fear that reporting those incidents might invite even more hate crimes. (Cassidy, 2016, Section 3, para. 3)

Third, because reporting by law enforcement agencies is voluntary, some information never reaches the FBI. A recent Associated Press report points out that

> more than 2,700 city police and county sheriff's departments across the country . . . have not submitted a single hate crime report for the FBI's annual crime tally during the past six

(Continued)

(Continued)

years—about 17 percent of all city and county law enforcement agencies nationwide. (Cassidy, 2016, para. 4)

The report highlights the case of Barbara Hicks Collins, an African American woman and daughter of a prominent civil rights leader in Louisiana who was closely involved with legal efforts to desegregate area schools. When Ms. Hicks Collins's car and home were set alight on Martin Luther King Jr. Day in 2012, she reported the case to local authorities, but the incident was never counted in the federal report of hate crimes. As the Associated Press notes, "Neither the police department nor the local sheriff has filed a hate crime report with the FBI since at least 2009" (Cassidy, 2016, para. 3). Finally, a component of labeling a hate crime is determining the existence of bias: Investigators must not only look at *what* happened but also *why*

it happened, and motivation may not always be easy to discern.

Accurate documentation of hate crimes is important. Effective enforcement and policymaking depend on reliable figures. As well, full reporting of hate crimes recognizes the victims and their experiences as important. As the Associated Press story on Ms. Hicks Collins, whose home and car were burned, notes, "For Hicks Collins, the failure to count the 2012 attack as a hate crime is a painful reminder of the continuing struggle for racial progress" (Cassidy, 2016, para. 13).

Think It Through

- This essay described several factors that may stand in the way of the collection of hate crimes statistics. How might these obstacles be addressed to foster more accurate reporting?

Studies dating back to the 1970s have pointed to a consistent pattern in who lives near the kinds of hazards—toxic waste sites, landfills, congested highways—that few of us would willingly choose as neighbors. The invariable answer: poor people and communities of color. (Badger, 2014, p. 1)

In sum, racial residential segregation contributes to the concentration of economic disadvantage. Pursuing greater opportunities, members of minority groups may seek to move to more diverse neighborhoods. Unfortunately, historically and today, powerful social forces of poverty and discrimination have kept and continue to keep many from achieving this goal.

Assimilation and Cultural Pluralism

Throughout much of the 20th century, sociologists who studied minorities, race, and ethnicity assumed that the ultimate destiny of most minority groups was **assimilation**, or *absorption of a minority group into the dominant culture*. U.S. citizens have long prided themselves on being part of a vast "melting pot" in which significant differences between groups gradually disappear and the population is boiled into a single cultural soup. This view was strengthened by the experience of many immigrant groups, particularly from Northern European countries, who adopted the norms, values, and folkways of the dominant culture to increase their social acceptance as well as their economic success.

© AP Photo/LM Otero

Families living in this West Port Arthur, Texas, public housing project are routinely exposed to the pollution generated by surrounding oil refineries. One in five households has a member with a respiratory illness (Stephenson, 2014). Those with the least political voice in society are most likely to find themselves in highly polluted residential areas.

Although migrant groups have historically sought to assimilate into the dominant majority group, many also want to retain their unique identities. Some American Indian nations, for example, have long sought to keep alive their own traditions and beliefs. In **cultural pluralism**, *the coexistence of different racial and ethnic groups is characterized by the acceptance of one another's differences*. Such a society resembles a salad bowl rather than a melting pot. Cultural differences are respected for their contribution to

---

Assimilation: The absorption of a minority group into the dominant culture.

Cultural pluralism: The coexistence of different racial and ethnic groups is characterized by the acceptance of one another's differences.

the richness of society as a whole. Even though cultural pluralists criticize the forced segregation that results from prejudice and discrimination, they argue that people's continuing connections to their own ethnic communities help them to preserve their cultural heritages and, at the same time, provide networks of mutual social and economic support.

The relative merits of assimilation and cultural pluralism remain controversial, but sociologists generally agree that the debates over these issues will continue to be a fundamental part of changing racial and ethnic relations in the modern world.

Theoretical Approaches to Ethnicity, Racism, and Minority Status

Throughout this text, we seek to highlight the ways in which key theoretical perspectives in sociology can illuminate social phenomena, including socioeconomic stratification, poverty, and deviance. In this section, we look at ethnicity, racism, and minority group status using the functionalist, conflict, and symbolic interactionist lenses.

The Functionalist Perspective

One of functionalism's key assumptions is that a social phenomenon exists and persists because it serves a positive function in a community or society, contributing to order and harmony. Beginning with classical sociologists Auguste Comte and Émile Durkheim and extending to contemporary functionalist theorizing, the basic functionalist assumption is that solidarity characterizes social groupings. Durkheim believed that social groups held together by mechanical solidarity and based on homogeneity in, among other things, language and culture are more culturally durable than are those based on organic solidarity, which involves interdependence (for instance, economic interdependence). This may help us understand the cohesion of many ethnic groups in the United States. Whether they are Armenian Americans, Egyptian Americans, Cuban Americans, or some other group, people gravitate toward those who are similar to them, a process rooted in shared pasts and practices.

It is far more challenging to apply the functionalist perspective to racism as a phenomenon. Racism cannot be positively functional for a community or society because, by definition, it marginalizes some members of the group. It can, however, be positively functional for some groups while being detrimental for others. Asking "How is this functional for some groups?" takes us close to the key conflict question: "Who benefits from this phenomenon or institution—and who loses?" In the next section, we examine who benefits from racism.

The Conflict Perspective

Consider that **racism**, *the idea that one racial or ethnic group is inherently superior to another,* offers a justification for racial inequality and associated forms of stratification such as socioeconomic inequality. If a powerful group defines itself as "better" than another group, then the unequal treatment and distribution of resources can be rationalized as acceptable or even natural.

Slavery in the United States was a fundamentally racist phenomenon. It was possible for Whites in the South (and many in the North) to justify the maltreatment of Blacks because they did not see Blacks as fully human. Senator John Calhoun, who represented South Carolina and died just over a decade before the Civil War, wrote in a letter that "the African is incapable of self-care and sinks into lunacy under the burden of freedom. It is a mercy to him to give him the guardianship and protection from mental death" (quoted in Silva, 2001, p. 71). In legal terms, racism was clear in the Three-Fifths Compromise, which emerged at the Constitutional Convention in Philadelphia in 1787. Delegates from the North and South agreed that for purposes of taxation and political representation, each slave would be counted as three fifths of a person. The compromise was needed because abolitionists wanted to count only free people. Slaveholders and their supporters wanted to count slaves, whose presence would add to their states' population counts and thus their representation in Congress. Those who held slaves but did not permit them to be free or to vote still gained politically from their presence. In economic terms, slavery was of benefit to plantation owners and their families, who could reap the financial benefits of a population of workers who could be bought and sold, who could be exploited and abused, and who performed difficult and demanding work without pay.

It can be argued that capitalism and economic development in the early United States would not have been so robust without the country's reliance on an enslaved labor force, which contributed most fully to the development of a growing agricultural economy in the South. The North, too, was home to numerous beneficiaries and proponents of slavery.

After the end of slavery, racism continued to manifest in new forms, including Jim Crow laws, which followed in the decade after slavery and lasted until the middle of the 20th century. These laws legally mandated segregation of public facilities in the South and fundamentally limited Blacks' ability to exercise their rights. The schools,

---

Racism: The idea that one racial or ethnic group is inherently superior to another; often results in institutionalized relationships between dominant and minority groups that create a structure of economic, social, and political inequality based on socially constructed racial or ethnic categories.

Slaves were leased by their owners to mine sandstone from local quarries, which slaves then used to build the iconic structures of U.S. democracy—the U.S. Capitol building and the White House—in Washington, DC.

Many popular sports teams proudly use Native Americans as their mascots, a practice that has generated controversy. Opponents argue that the images are demeaning and promote negative stereotypes. Where do you stand on the use of Native Americans as sports mascots?

accommodations, and opportunities afforded to Blacks were invariably inferior to those offered to Whites. Local and state governments could therefore expend fewer funds on their Black populations, and White populations benefited from reduced competition in higher education and the labor market. Racism made Jim Crow laws both possible and widely acceptable because it offered a justification for their existence and persistence.

Although racism is clearly of no benefit to its victims and has negative effects on society as a whole, the conflict perspective entreats us to recognize the ways in which it has been functional for more powerful groups in society. These benefits help explain the existence and persistence of racism over time.

The Symbolic Interactionist Perspective

Sociologist Louis Wirth (1945) has noted that minority groups share particular traits. First, membership in a minority group is essentially involuntary—that is, someone is socially classified as a member of a group that is discriminated against and is not, in most instances, free to opt out. Second, as we discussed above, minority status is a question not of numbers (minorities may outnumber the dominant group) but rather of control of valued resources. Third, minorities do not share the full privileges of mobility or opportunity enjoyed by the dominant group. Finally, membership in the minority group conditions the treatment of group members by others in society. Specifically, Wirth states, societal minorities are "treated as members of a category, irrespective of their individual merits" (p. 349).

Wirth's definition recalls symbolic interactionist Erving Goffman's concept of a **stigma**, *an attribute that is deeply discrediting to an individual or a group because it overshadows*

other attributes and merits the individual or group may possess. Goffman (1963b) presented the unlikely scenario of a young woman born without a nose: Although the young woman has a spectrum of interesting and engaging characteristics—she is a bright student and a good dancer—she is defined by her stigma, and her treatment by others is ever defined and determined by her difference.

Goffman examined what he called **mixed contacts**—*interactions between those who are stigmatized and those who are "normal"* (by *normal,* he meant only those who are members of the dominant, nonstigmatized group—the term was not intended to denote *normality* as contrasting with *deviance*). Goffman concluded that mixed contacts are shaped by the presence of the stigma, which influences the way each social interaction unfolds. Although the stigmatized identity may not be the point of the interaction, it is inevitably a part of it. Think about your own social interactions: Have you experienced what Goffman describes? How would you expand or modify his sociological description based on those experiences?

In the next section, we turn to issues of prejudice and discrimination, considering how our judgments about someone's race or ethnicity—or about the racial or ethnic identity of an entire group—are manifested in practice.

Prejudice, Stereotyping, and Discrimination

Prejudice is *a belief about an individual or a group that is not subject to change on the basis of evidence.* Prejudices are thus inflexible attitudes toward others. Sociologist Zygmunt

---

Stigma: An attribute that is deeply discrediting to an individual or a group because it overshadows other attributes and merits the individual or group may possess.

Mixed contacts: Interactions between those who are stigmatized and those who are "normal."

Prejudice: A belief about an individual or a group that is not subject to change on the basis of evidence.

Private Lives, Public Issues

#LIVINGWHILEBLACK

One sunny day in Washington, DC, in 2018, an African American father went for a stroll in a park with his sick baby son. While walking, the pair was observed by a woman on a bicycle, who reported a "suspicious man walking the bike path with a baby" to a park security officer. The officer flagged down Donald Sherman, a local lawyer, and ascertained that there was absolutely nothing untoward taking place. Why was Mr. Sherman characterized by the biker, a White woman, as suspicious? Was it because he is a dark-skinned man and his son has lighter skin? In an account of the encounter posted on Facebook, Mr. Sherman wrote,

> If this complaint had been made to a different security officer or an actual cop, things could have gone very differently.... This is exactly why we have to talk about white privilege and why black lives matter. Because at any point, doing anything anywhere, my safety and my child's safety could [have] been in jeopardy because [of] some well-intentioned complaint. (Helm, 2018)

The sociological imagination entreats us to recognize the nexus between private lives and public issues—the relationship between biography and history. In this instance, the individual experience of Mr. Sherman cannot be fully grasped without recognizing the ubiquity of everyday, even ordinary, racism in the U.S. that is based on fear and suspicion of Black people, particularly those who are inhabiting what may be perceived by some to be White spaces. Consider a recent case of #sleepingwhileblack that occurred at Yale University. In that incident, a Black graduate student studying in her dormitory's common room late in the evening fell asleep. She was observed sleeping in the common room by a White graduate student, who indicated that she did not know the napping student and called the police. Similar to the incident in the park, the issue was resolved shortly, but not without having made a tuition-paying student with a right to the space she was occupying the object of a common thread of racial suspicion (Wootson, 2018).

In a recent incident in Rialto, California, police were called by a neighbor who had spotted three African Americans, two women and a man, leaving a nearby home. They were apparently accompanied by a White woman as well, though she was not mentioned in the call. The four were paying guests at an Airbnb lodging, but the neighbor, a White woman, grew concerned when the guests did not smile and wave at her. According to a story on the incident in *The Hill*, "As the guests were taking their luggage to their car, police appeared and ordered them to put their hands up. They were detained for roughly 20 to 45 minutes" (Greenwood, 2018, para. 7).

The incidents have sparked a social media storm that documents the shadow of suspicion that accompanies #livingwhileblack, including

> couponing while black, graduating too boisterously while black, waiting for a school bus while black, throwing a kindergarten temper tantrum while black, drinking iced tea while black, ... shopping for underwear while black, having a loud conversation while black, golfing too slowly while black, buying clothes at Barney's while black, or Macy's, or Nordstrom Rack, getting locked out of your own home while black, going to the gym while black, asking for the Waffle House corporate number while black and reading C.S. Lewis while black. (Wootson, 2018, para. 7)

Think It Through

- The sociological imagination provides a lens through which to view individual incidents of #livingwhileblack as part of a larger societal phenomenon that casts suspicion on African Americans solely because of their race. Does the sociological imagination offer ways of imagining an alternative future in which prejudice does not drive actions?

Bauman (2001), writing about the Holocaust, eloquently captures this idea: "Man *is* before he *acts*; nothing he does may change what he is. That is, roughly, the philosophical essence of racism" (p. 60). Recall Wirth's point about the characteristics of a social minority: Membership in the disadvantaged group matters more than individual merit.

When prejudices are strongly held, no amount of evidence is likely to change the belief. Among neo-Nazis, for example, prejudice against Jews runs deep. Some neo-Nazis even deny the occurrence of the Holocaust, despite clearly authentic firsthand accounts, films, and photographs of Nazi Germany's concentration camps, where millions of Jews, Roma, Soviet prisoners of war, and other victims were killed during World War II. Why do prejudicial beliefs trump evidence in cases such as Holocaust denial? Why is prejudice difficult to overcome, even with facts? We may gain some insight into these issues by looking at another social phenomenon linked to prejudice—stereotyping.

Stereotyping is *the generalization of a set of characteristics to all members of a group.* Ethnic and racial stereotypes are often produced and reproduced in popular films: Think about images in U.S. action movies of scheming Italian Mafiosi, tough African American street gangs, and violent Asian gangsters or martial artists. Or consider the ways that we may attribute characteristics—intelligence, entrepreneurship, sloth, or slyness—to entire groups based on experiences with or information from others about only a few members of that group. Stereotyping offers a way for human beings to organize and categorize the social world—but the attributions we make may be deeply flawed.

From a sociological perspective, we may argue that even though stereotypes are often flawed, they are also functional for some groups—although dysfunctional for others. Consider that one of the social forces contributing to racism is the desire of one group to exploit another. Research on early contacts between Europeans and Africans suggests that negative stereotypes of Africans developed *after* Europeans discovered the economic value of exploiting African labor and the natural resources of the African continent. That is, White Europeans stereotyped Black Africans as inferior when such images suited the Europeans' need to justify enslavement and economic exploitation of this population.

Discrimination is *the unequal treatment of individuals on the basis of their membership in a group.* Discrimination is often targeted and intentional, but it may also be unintentional—in either case, it denies groups and individuals equal opportunities and blocks access to valued resources.

Sociologists distinguish between individual and institutional discrimination. **Individual discrimination** is *overt and intentional unequal treatment, often based on prejudicial beliefs.* If the manager of an apartment complex refuses to rent a place to someone on the basis of his or her skin color or an employer chooses not to hire a qualified applicant because he or she is foreign-born, that is individual discrimination. **Institutionalized discrimination** is *discrimination enshrined in law, public policy, or common practice—it is unequal treatment that has become part of the routine operation of such major social institutions as businesses, schools, hospitals, and the government.* Institutionalized discrimination

is particularly pernicious because, although it may be clearly targeted and intentional, it may also be the outcome of customary practices and bureaucratic decisions that result in discriminatory outcomes.

Discrimination against African Americans and women was initially institutionalized in the Constitution of the United States, which excluded members of both groups from voting and holding public office. In 1866, Congress passed the first civil rights act, giving Black men the right to vote, hold public office, use public accommodations, and serve on juries. In 1883, however, the U.S. Supreme Court declared the 1866 law unconstitutional, and states passed laws restricting where minorities could live, go to school, receive accommodations, and such. These laws were upheld by the U.S. Supreme Court in the case of *Plessy v. Ferguson* in 1896. It took more than 75 years for the court to reverse itself.

In the 1960s, the Supreme Court held that laws institutionalizing discrimination were unconstitutional. Open forms of discrimination, such as signs and advertisements that said "Whites only" or "Jews need not apply," were deemed illegal. Research and experience suggest, however, that discrimination often continues in more subtle and complex forms. Consider, once again, the case of housing and discrimination. Institutionalized discrimination affects opportunities for housing and, by extension, opportunities for building individual and community wealth through home ownership. We noted earlier in the chapter that African Americans often still live in segregated neighborhoods. Discrimination is part of the reason; for example, Blacks have been historically less likely to secure mortgages. Paired testing studies in which researchers have sent Black and White applicants with nearly identical financial profiles to apply for mortgages have determined that Whites as a group continue to be advantaged in their treatment by lending institutions (Silverman, 2005). Among other benefits, Whites enjoy higher rates of approval and better loan conditions (Turner, Popkin, & Rawlings, 2009).

The turn of the millennium, however, ushered in a shift in mortgage lending. Banks had plenty of money to lend for home purchases, and among those targeted by banks eager to make mortgage loans were minorities, even those with low incomes and poor credit. The lending bonanza was no boon for these groups, however, because many of the loans made were subprime (subprime loans carry a higher risk that the borrower will default, and the terms are more stringent to compensate for this risk). Subprime loans were five times more common in predominantly Black neighborhoods than in White ones (Pettit & Reuben, 2010), and many borrowers did not fully understand the terms of their loans, such as "balloon" interest rates that rise dramatically over the life of a loan. One consequence was a massive wave of foreclosures beginning in 2008. Although minority and

---

Stereotyping: The generalization of a set of characteristics to all members of a group.

Discrimination: The unequal treatment of individuals on the basis of their membership in a group.

Individual discrimination: Overt and intentional unequal treatment, often based on prejudicial beliefs.

Institutionalized discrimination: Discrimination enshrined in law, public policy, or common practice; it is unequal treatment that has become a part of the routine operation of such major social institutions as businesses, schools, hospitals, and the government.

poor communities were not the only ones affected by the subprime loan fiasco, they were disproportionately harmed and have been slow to regain economic ground. According to a recent investigation,

> Nationwide, home values in predominantly African American neighborhoods have been the least likely to recover. . . . Across the 300 largest U.S. metropolitan areas, homes in 4 out of 10 zip codes where blacks are the largest population group are worth less than they were in 2004. That's twice the rate for mostly white zip codes across the country. (Badger, 2016, para. 6)

In the sections that follow, we discuss other contemporary manifestations and consequences of individual and institutionalized discrimination in the United States, highlighting the criminal justice system, women's and children's health, and the Internet housing market.

Prison, Politics, and Power

One of the key rights of U.S. citizenship is the right to vote—that is, the right to have a voice in the country's political process. Some citizens, however, are denied this right. Many of those who cannot vote have been legally disenfranchised because of state laws that prohibit ex-felons who have served their prison sentences from voting. Statistically speaking, this translates into over 5.3 million disenfranchised individuals, including roughly 1.4 million Black men. A staggering 13% of the Black population cannot legally vote as a direct result of these laws (Sentencing Project, 2011).

In the mid-20th century, more than 70% of those incarcerated in the United States were White; by the end of the 20th century those numbers had reversed, and most prisoners were nonwhite (Wacquant, 2002; Western & Pettit, 2010). This shift has had a profound effect on African Americans' political voice: 48 states prohibit inmates from voting while they are incarcerated; 14 states and the District of Columbia restore voting rights after incarceration; four states restore it after incarceration and parole; and 20 states restore it after incarceration, parole, and probation have been completed. Alabama, Arizona, Delaware, Florida, Iowa, Kentucky, Mississippi, Nevada, Tennessee, and Wyoming foresee the possibility of a lifetime voting ban on anyone who has been convicted of a felony (Uggen, Larsen, & Shannon, 2016).

Among those disenfranchised African Americans is Jarvious Cotton. Law professor Michelle Alexander writes about Cotton in *The New Jim Crow: Mass Incarceration in the Age of Colorblindness* (2010):

> Like his father, grandfather, great-grandfather, and great-great-grandfather, [Jarvious Cotton] has been denied the right to participate in our electoral democracy. . . . Cotton's great-great-grandfather could not vote as a slave. His great-grandfather was beaten to death by the Ku Klux Klan for attempting to vote. His grandfather was prevented from voting by Klan intimidation. His father was barred from voting by poll taxes and literacy tests. Today, Jarvious Cotton cannot vote because he, like many black men in the United States, has been labeled a felon and is currently on parole. . . .
>
> Once you're labeled a felon, the old forms of discrimination—employment discrimination, housing discrimination, denial of the right to vote, denial of educational opportunity, denial of food stamps and other public benefits, and exclusion from jury service—are suddenly legal. . . . We have not ended racial caste in America; we have merely redesigned it. (pp. 1–2)

Alexander (2010) argues that the U.S. criminal justice system effectively functions as a modern incarnation of the Jim Crow laws. Today, she suggests, the expansion of the prison population to include nonviolent offenders, particularly people of color (a topic discussed in Chapter 6 of this book), has contributed to the development of a population denied opportunities to have a political voice as well as education, work, and housing.

Consequences of Prejudice and Discrimination: Race and Health

Sociologists studying discrimination take an interest in the health of minority populations. For example, some researchers argue that racism and other disadvantages suffered by Black women in the United States contribute to the much higher level of negative birth outcomes, including low birth weight and infant mortality (Colen, Geronimus, Bound, & James, 2006). Consider the following statistics:

DISCOVER INTERSECTIONS

Mass Incarceration and Its Consequences in Communities of Color

As Michelle Alexander notes in the section above, mass incarceration has had a disproportionate impact on communities of color. It has had an effect on political voice, educational and job options, and opportunities to secure safe shelter and food. In the chapter on deviance and social control (Chapter 6), you learned about some of the roots of mass incarceration in the U.S. How can an understanding of the roots of this phenomenon help us to imagine an alternative set of policies and practices that could reduce mass incarceration and mitigate the negative effects it has had on families and communities?

Black women are 60% more likely than White women to experience premature births, and Black babies are about 230% more likely than White babies to die before the age of 1 (Norris, 2011; Figures 9.4 and 9.5). Black women are also more than twice as likely to give birth to very-low-weight infants than their White or Latina sisters (Ventura, Curtin, Abma, & Henshaw, 2012).

These data suggest that race trumps other identified predictors of health, including age, income, and educational attainment (Norris, 2011). Although health outcomes are predictably favorable among White women as they gain economic status and give birth in their 20s and early 30s (rather than their teens), Black women's birth outcomes do not appear to follow this pattern (Colen et al., 2006).

■ **FIGURE 9.4** Preterm Births, by Gestational Age and Race and Hispanic Origin, 2014

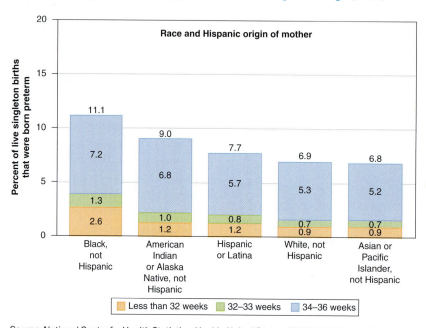

Source: National Center for Health Statistics. Health, United States, 2015: With Special Feature on Racial and Ethnic Health Disparities. Hyattsville, MD. 2016.

■ **FIGURE 9.5** Infant Mortality Rates, by Race and Hispanic Origin, 1999–2013

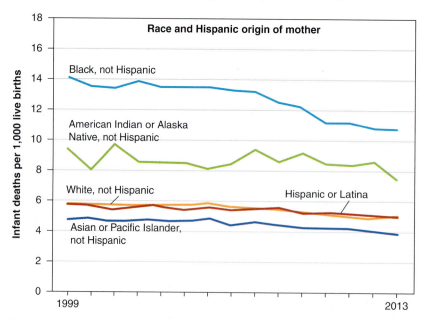

Source: National Center for Health Statistics. Health, United States, 2015: With Special Feature on Racial and Ethnic Health Disparities. Hyattsville, MD. 2016.

Why is race such a powerful predictor of birth outcomes? Answers to this question are varied and complex. Access to prenatal care may be one factor: Data show that nearly 10% of Black women receive late or no prenatal care. By comparison, about 4% of White women and 6% of Latina women get late or no prenatal care (ChildTrends, 2018). Notably, however, public health researcher Arline Geronimus (1992) argues that the racial disparity in birth outcomes—and its stubborn resistance to improvement, even as Black women make educational and economic gains—can be attributed to a phenomenon she terms *weathering*. Geronimus describes weathering as an amalgamation of racism and stressors ranging from environmental pollutants to crime to poor health care. These lead, she argues, to a demonstrable deterioration of health, including poor birth outcomes, advanced aging, and even early death.

Geronimus's argument was met with skepticism when she proposed it two decades ago, but it has increasingly gained acceptance. Even in their 20s and 30s, Geronimus says, African American women are

> suffering from hypertension at two or three times the rate of whites their own age. African Americans at age 35 have the rates of disability of white Americans who are 55, and we haven't seen much traction over 20 to 30 years of trying to reduce and eliminate these disparities. (quoted in Norris, 2011, "'Enormous Stressors Take A Toll on Black Women," para. 13)

To see such medical statistics through the prism of social science is a goal of **social epidemiology**, which is *the study of communities and their social statuses, practices, and problems with the aim of understanding patterns of health and disease.*

It is challenging to draw a direct connection between race-related social stressors and negative health outcomes; critics have questioned the link, and more work remains to be done. Nevertheless, the work of Geronimus demonstrates how sociology can highlight connections between private troubles—such as the birth of a low-weight or preterm infant—and public issues, including lack of access to care and the wearing effects of racism.

Technologies of Discrimination

Today, most people who are seeking housing go to the Internet first. According to a joint study from the National Association of Realtors and Google, 90% of homebuyers searched online during their home buying process (National Association of Realtors, 2012). Sites such as

Social epidemiology: The study of communities and their social statuses, practices, and problems with the aim of understanding patterns of health and disease.

In 2016, the hip-hop musical *Hamilton*, written and scored by Lin-Manuel Miranda (front), won 11 awards at the Tony Awards, including Best Musical. The unique take on U.S. history, populated by a talented and multicultural cast, has been wildly popular on Broadway.

©Theo Wargo/Getty Images for Tony Awards Productions

Craigslist cater to those seeking temporary or long-term rentals. Enforcement of the Fair Housing Act, the primary purpose of which is to keep discriminatory practices in check, has not kept pace with the explosive growth of the online home buying and rental markets. From blatant "Whites only" statements to more veiled implications that people of color will not be accepted, the Internet is rife with the potential for housing discrimination.

Research shows that some housing providers and sellers are selecting interested parties who have "White-sounding" names over those whose names sound "ethnic." For example, one study used Craigslist to analyze responses of potential housing providers to home seekers giving their names as Neil, Tyrone, and Jorge (Friedman, Squires, & Galvan, 2010). The researchers found that respondents with "White-sounding" names (for example, Neil) were most likely to get multiple responses, be put in touch with the housing provider, be offered the opportunity to look at the house, and be told the property is available. Although racial and ethnic discrimination are not legal in modern America, new forms of digitally enabled discrimination are challenging integration efforts and reinforcing long-existing patterns of segregation in U.S. communities.

We conclude this section on prejudice, discrimination, and stereotypes with a look at the underrepresentation of minority actors and actresses in Hollywood—and a discussion of some promising new paths to diversifying popular culture on both the stage and the big screen.

Race and Ethnicity in Hollywood and on Broadway

Who are the actors and actresses most likely to be recognized for their cultural achievements in the United States? It is notable that out of more than 2,900 Oscars awarded since the founding of the Academy Awards,

©PA Images / Alamy Stock Photo

Actor Daniel Kaluuya was nominated for an Oscar for his role as Chris Washington in the 2017 horror film *Get Out*, which explored various aspects of racism in the United States.

Communication and Journalism at the University of Southern California found that in 600 popular films from 2007 to 2013, White actors populated about 75% of speaking roles. Nearly a fifth of films had no Black speaking characters at all (Smith, Choueiti, & Pieper, 2014).

Recent press accounts (Simons, 2016) have also documented the long-standing practice in Hollywood of casting White actors to play minority characters. For instance, in the 2017 film, *Ghost in the Shell*, Scarlett Johansson played a Japanese woman, and Ben Affleck played the role of Tony Mendez, a Hispanic character, in the 2012 film, *Argo*. In most cases, White actors have taken prominent film roles as Asian or Hispanic characters, though Robert Downey, Jr., earned an Oscar nomination for playing a Black soldier in *Tropic Thunder* (2008). In the 2013 film, *The Lone Ranger*, actor Johnny Depp was cast as the Lone Ranger's American Indian sidekick, Tonto.

In response to the marginalization of actors of color in Hollywood, some celebrities (such as Will Smith and Jada Pinkett Smith) boycotted the 2016 Oscars. The Academy released a statement recognizing inequities and committing to increase diversity by doubling the number of women and people of color in its membership by 2020 (Wagner, 2016). Indeed, as the *Los Angeles Times* reported in July of 2016,

> The motion picture academy, responding to the outcry over an absence of minorities in its ranks—and consequently its nominees—invited nearly 700 film professionals to become members. It's by far the academy's biggest new class, with more than 40% of the invitees [being] people of color. (Zeitchik, 2016, para. 2)

which recognize achievements in film, only 38 have gone to African Americans (Sangweni, 2017). Until 2017, there were no Asian, Hispanic, or American Indian Best Actor winners, and only one African American—Halle Berry in 2001—had won Best Actress. In 2017, however, actress Viola Davis won the Best Supporting Actress award. In 2018, there were quite a few African American nominees on the roster, including Jordan Peele, who was nominated for producing, directing, and writing *Get Out*, and Daniel Kaluuya, who was nominated for Best Actor for his role in that film. As well, Octavia Spencer was nominated for Best Supporting Actress for her role in the widely lauded film, *The Shape of Water* and Mary J. Blige received nominations in the categories of Best Supporting Actress and Best Original Song for *Mudbound*. Peele won the award for Best Original Screenplay.

Actor George Clooney has suggested that the problem is not primarily who the Academy is choosing to nominate but rather "how many options are available to minorities in film, particularly in quality films" (Setoodeh, 2016, para. 2). Indeed, we often see African Americans in stereotypical roles such as gangsters, single parents, singers, dancers, maids, or slaves. Their characters are more likely than others to be violent, hypersexualized, or poor; fewer are presented as leaders, intellectuals, or professionals. This lack of diversity in available roles extends as well to Asian American, Native American, and Hispanic actors, who are frequently slotted into stereotypical film roles. No less notably, minority characters are less likely to be prominent in films: A study done at the Annenberg School for

While Hollywood has been slow to change, a wildly popular Broadway musical has brought drama and diversity to thousands of theatergoers. The musical hit *Hamilton*, based on a biography of Alexander Hamilton by Ron Chernow and written and scored by Lin-Manuel Miranda, who was also part of the original cast, has taken New York City by storm. *Hamilton* is a historical tale rendered through hip-hop lyrics; its key historical figures, including Alexander Hamilton, George Washington, Thomas Jefferson, and Aaron Burr, are played by Black or Hispanic actors. At the 2016 Tony Awards, which recognize achievements in musicals, the show won 11 awards, including Best Musical,

Best Actor, Best Supporting Actor and Actress, and Best Choreography (Marks, 2016).

Will big screen films follow the example of *Hamilton*, offering unexpected but celebrated new roles to minority actors and actresses? Why are visibility and diverse roles in popular culture important? What do you think?

In the next section, we look at some of the major groups that make up the U.S. population and see how their numbers are contributing to the changing composition of the country.

Racial and Ethnic Groups in the United States

The area now called the United States was once occupied by hundreds of Native American nations. Later came Europeans, most of whom were English, although early settlers also included the French, Dutch, and Spanish, among others. Beginning in 1619, Africans were brought as slaves and added a substantial minority to the European population. Hundreds of thousands of Europeans continued to arrive from Norway, Sweden, Germany, and Russia to start farms and work in the factories of early industrial America. In the mid-1800s, Chinese immigrants were brought in to provide the heavy labor for building railroads and mining gold and silver. Between 1890 and 1930, nearly 28 million people immigrated to the United States. After the 1950s, immigrants came mostly from Latin America and Asia.

The U.S. population is growing increasingly diverse (see Figure 9.6). According to one recent source, in 2016, Whites comprised about 61% of the population; Blacks about 12%; Hispanics nearly 18%; Asians 6%; American Indians and Alaska Natives about 0.2%; and people self-identifying as mixed race about 2% (Henry J. Kaiser Family Foundation, 2017). If current trends hold, nonwhites will constitute a numeric majority nationwide by about 2040.

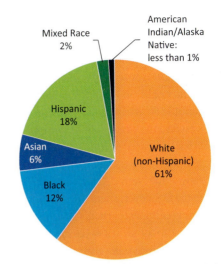

■ **FIGURE 9.6** Racial/Ethnic Composition of the U.S. Population, 2016

Source: Henry J. Kaiser Family Foundation. (2017). Population Distribution by Race/Ethnicity. Retrieved from https://www.kff.org/other/state-indicator/distribution-by-raceethnicity/?currentTimeframe=0&sortModel=%7B%22colId%22:%22Location%22,%22sort%22:%22asc%22%7D.

The rapid growth of minority populations reflects growth from both new births and migration. Migration is the primary engine of population growth in the United States. In fact, demographers estimate that by the middle of the 21st century, fully one fifth of the U.S. population will be immigrants. In a population estimated to reach more than 438 million by 2050, 67 million will be immigrants, and about 50 million will be the children and grandchildren of immigrants (Pew Research Center, 2008). Overall, the trend toward a more racially and ethnically diverse country is clear: At the time of the 2010 census, the majority of children under two years old were nonwhite.

In the following sections, we look in more depth at the racial and ethnic groups that have come together to constitute U.S. culture and society today.

American Indians

There is no agreement on how many people were living in North America when the Europeans arrived around the beginning of the 16th century, but anthropologists' best guess is about 20 million. Thousands of thriving societies existed throughout North and South America in this period. Encounter between European explorers and Native Americans soon became conquest, and despite major resistance, the indigenous populations were eventually defeated and their lands confiscated by European settlers. It is believed that between 1500 and 1800, the North American Indian population was reduced from more than 20 million to fewer than 600,000 (Haggerty, 1991). American Indians, like

American Indians lived in the territorial United States long before the political state was established. They suffered the loss of territory and population as a result of U.S. government policies. Even today, American Indian communities face unique challenges.

© National Geographic Image Collection / Alamy Stock Photo

conquered and oppressed peoples everywhere, did not passively accept the European invasion. The "Indian Wars" are among the bloodiest in U.S. history, but resistance was not enough. First, White settlers had access to superior weaponry that Native Americans could not effectively counter. Second, Whites' control of political, economic, and environmental policies gave them a powerful advantage. Consider, for instance, the U.S. government's decision to permit the unregulated slaughter of bison (buffalo) in the post–Civil War era. From about 1866, when millions of bison roamed the American West and the Great Plains, to the 1890s, this key Native American resource was decimated until only a few thousand remained (Moloney, 2012; Smits, 1994).

Since the 1960s, some Native Americans have focused on efforts to force the U.S. government to honor treaties and improve their living conditions, particularly on reservations. In 1969, the group Indians of All Tribes (IAT), citing the 1868 Treaty of Fort Laramie, which states that all unused or abandoned federal land must be returned to the Indians, seized the abandoned island of Alcatraz, a former prison island in the San Francisco Bay, and issued a proclamation that contained the following (deliberately ironic) declarations:

> We, the native Americans, re-claim the land known as Alcatraz Island in the name of all American Indians by right of discovery.... We feel that this so-called Alcatraz Island is more than suitable for an Indian Reservation, as determined by the white man's own standards.

The IAT went on to note the island's "suitability" by pointing out that, among other things, it had no fresh running water, no industries to provide employment, no health care facilities, and no oil or mineral rights for inhabitants. This comparison was intended to point to the devastating conditions on most reservations.

The IAT occupied Alcatraz for more than 18 months. The occupation ended when some IAT members left due to poor living conditions, as the federal government shut off all power and water to the island, and others were removed when the government took control of the island in June 1971.

Despite centuries of struggle, more than 60% of the 4.9 million American Indians in the United States today live in urban areas and are among the poorest people in the nation: More than half of all Native American children are born into poverty, three times the rate for White children. About 1.9 million Native Americans live on reservations, where unemployment rates run as high as 50%. With limited economic opportunities, Native Americans also have relatively low educational attainment: Only 13% have earned bachelor's degrees (Ogunwole, Drewery, & Rios-Vargas, 2012).

The *Inequality Matters* box on page 241 raises another issue pertinent to the status of Native Americans in the United States: Who has the power to name this population?

African Americans

In 1903, W.E.B. Du Bois penned the following words: "The problem of the Twentieth Century is the problem of the color line" (1903/2008, p. 9). By that, he meant that grappling with the legacy of 250 years of slavery would be one of the great problems of the 20th century. Indeed, as this chapter shows, Du Bois was right, although he did not foresee that the "color line" would incorporate not only African Americans but Hispanics, Asians, American Indians, and other minorities as well.

Slavery forcibly brought more than 9 million people, mostly from West Africa, to North and South America as well as the islands of the Caribbean. Passage across the ocean was brutal: In many instances, half or fewer of the Africans who were forced onboard slave ships made it to their destination. The treatment of those who survived was no less horrific. In 1808, a federal law ended the importation of enslaved people to the U.S. As a result, the internal slave trade grew, and more enslaved people were torn from their families and sold to work the plantations that were expanding westward (National Museum of African American Culture and History). Slave revolts were frequent throughout the South. More than 250 Black uprisings against slavery were recorded from 1700 to 1865, and many others were not recorded (Greenberg, 1996; Williams-Meyers, 1996).

Immediately following the end of slavery, during the Reconstruction period, African Americans sought to establish political and economic equality. The exploitation of African Americans did not end with slavery: The sharecropping system, under which Blacks farmed someone else's land and paid the owner with a fraction of the crop, kept former slaves tied to landowners who often charged excessive sums for rent, seed, and tools. This meant that sharecroppers, rather than earning money, ended up owing money to the landowner. Some progress was made, however, and former slaves (men only) gained the right to vote, and in some jurisdictions, they constituted the majority of registered voters. Black legislators were elected in every southern state. Between 1870 and 1901, 22 Blacks served in the U.S. Congress, while hundreds of others served in state legislatures, on city councils, and as elected and appointed officials throughout the South (Holt, 1977). Their success was short-lived. White southern legislators, still a majority, passed Jim Crow laws, which excluded Blacks from voting and using public transportation. In time, every aspect of life was constrained for Blacks, including access to hospitals, schools, restaurants, churches, jobs, recreation sites, and cemeteries. By 1901, because literacy was required to vote and most Blacks had been effectively denied even a basic education, the registration of Black voters had dwindled to a mere handful (Morrison, 1987).

The North's higher degree of industrialization offered a promise of economic opportunity, even though social and political discrimination existed there as well. Between 1940 and 1970, more than 5 million African Americans left the rural South for what they hoped would be a better life in the North (Lemann, 1991). Whether they stayed in the South or moved to the North, however, many Blacks were still being denied fundamental rights nearly 100 years after slavery was abolished.

By the 1950s, the social landscape was changing—having fought against a racist regime in Nazi Germany in the 1940s, the United States found it far more difficult to justify continued discrimination against its own minority populations. Legal mandates for equality, however, did not easily translate to actual practices, and the 1960s saw a wave of protest from African Americans eager to claim greater rights and opportunities. The civil rights movement was committed to nonviolent forms of protest. Participants in

 Inequality Matters

WHO HAS THE POWER TO NAME?

"A language is a dialect that has an army and a navy," said sociolinguist Max Weinreich. Before White Europeans came to North America, one of the largest Indian nations was the *Dineh*, a name that means "the People of the Earth." No one knows exactly why, but the Spaniards renamed them *Navajo*, the designation by which Americans have referred to them ever since. Although Native Americans were being outgunned and oppressed by the wave of White European settlers, their language was also subject to marginalization, as was their power to name themselves.

Sociologist Pierre Bourdieu (1991) has pointed out that language is a medium of power, a vehicle that may confer status or function as a means of devaluation and exclusion. Historically, minority groups have been denied opportunities to name themselves. What is the appropriate name for the people who lived for thousands of years in what today is known as North and South America? They are commonly referred to in the United States as *Indians, Native Americans, indigenous peoples*, or simply *Natives*. These are not the only terms used to label this group. U.S. sports teams from the professional to the high school level use a variety of monikers: In football, we find the Washington *Redskins* and Kansas City *Chiefs*; in baseball, the Atlanta *Braves;* at the high school level, there are a variety of *Warriors, Big Reds, Redmen, Scouts*, and *Savages*. Particularly at the professional level, these names have evoked controversy, with some American Indian groups arguing that they are demeaning.

Two prominent organizations—the National Congress of American Indians and the American Indian Movement—use *American Indian* to describe themselves. Yet others object to the term because, like the word *Navajo*, it was given to them by European settlers and their descendants. Those who object to *American Indian* feel the alternative, *Native American,* captures the fact that they alone among ethnic groups are native to this continent, but this name also was given by European settlers. Others argue that nothing short of the correct name for each nation (such as Sioux, Pawnee, Cheyenne, Dineh, or Cherokee) is acceptable. Nevertheless, referring to each separate nation is problematic when one speaks of the collective. After years of controversy, their leaders agreed to accept *American Indian* to refer to themselves collectively (Scott, Tehranian, & Mathias, 2002).

The name for a particular racial or ethnic group may be highly contested, since it carries with it information about the group's social history. The effort by many groups to name themselves reflects their belief that to passively accept the name given by society's dominant group is to potentially accept being silenced. American Indian activists Laura Waterman Wittstock and Elaine J. Salinas (1998) suggest in their history of the American Indian Movement that

in the 30 years of its formal history, the American Indian Movement (AIM) has given witness to a great many changes. We say formal history, because the movement existed for 500 years without a name. The leaders and members of today's AIM never fail to remember all of those who have traveled on before, having given their talent and their lives for the survival of the people.

Think It Through

- Bourdieu highlights the power to name as one that is more likely to be held and exercised by dominant groups in society. Can you name another situation in which the power to name gives a group an advantage over another group?

Follow us on Twitter to keep up with current sociological stories and research! We're at **@DiscoverSoc1**.

Share your own ideas at **#DiscoverSociology**

the movement used strikes, boycotts, voter registration drives, sit-ins, and freedom rides in their efforts to achieve racial equality. In 1964, following what was at the time the largest civil rights demonstration in the nation's history (a march on Washington, DC), the federal government passed the first in a series of civil rights laws that made it illegal to discriminate on the basis of race, sex, religion, physical disability, or ethnic origin.

All African Americans have not benefited from legislation aimed at abolishing discrimination (Wilson, 2010). In particular, the poorest Blacks—those living in disadvantaged urban and rural areas—lack the opportunities that could make a difference in their lives. Many poor Black Americans suffer from having little cultural and social capital; inadequate schools, lack of skills and training, and poor local job opportunities raise the risk of persistent poverty. Today, nearly half of African American workers are employed in unskilled or semiskilled service jobs—as health care aides, janitors, and food service workers, for example—compared with only a quarter of Whites. Few of these occupations offer the opportunity to earn a living wage.

Over time, many African Americans have been broadly successful in improving their economic circumstances, particularly as they have gained access to education. The economic gains of African Americans, however, have been more tenuous than those of most other groups. As we saw earlier in the chapter, the Great Recession that began in 2007 substantially eroded Black wealth and income in America, and many communities are still struggling to recover.

Although African Americans have had mixed success in gaining economic power, as a group, they have seen important gains in political power. In the early 1960s, there were only 103 African Americans holding public office in the United States. By 1970, about 715 Blacks held elected office at the city and county levels. By the 1990s, however, the figure had surpassed 5,000, and in recent decades, major cities—including New York, Los Angeles, Chicago, and Washington—have elected Black mayors, and Black representation on city and town councils and state bodies has grown dramatically. At the federal level, there have been fewer gains, although, clearly, President Obama's election in November 2008 and reelection in 2012 represented a profound political breakthrough for Blacks. As of 2017, the House of Representatives had 47 Black members, but only three African Americans serve in the Senate.

Latinos/Latinas

The category of Latino/a (or *Hispanic*, the term used by the U.S. Census Bureau) includes people whose heritages lie in the many different cultures of Latin America. According to a recent Pew Research Center estimate, about 57 million Hispanics reside in the U.S., making them the largest minority group. Latinos are increasing in numbers more rapidly than any other minority group, because of both high immigration rates and high birthrates.

Many Latinos trace their ancestry to a time when the southwestern states were part of Mexico. During the mid-19th century, the United States sought to purchase from Mexico what is now Texas and California. Mexico refused to sell, leading to the 1846–1848 U.S.–Mexican War. Following its victory, the U.S. government forced Mexico to sell two fifths of its territory, enabling the United States to acquire all the land that now makes up the southwestern states, including California, Texas, New Mexico, and Arizona. Along with this vast territory came the people who inhabited it, including tens of thousands of Mexicans who were forced by White settlers to forfeit their property and who suffered discrimination at the hands of the Whites (Valenzuela, 1992).

Latinos have experienced some of the same obstacles of prejudice and discrimination in the United States as have African Americans. They continue to be discriminated against and live below the standards of the dominant population. At the same time, the very category of *Latino* is problematic for sociologists because it encompasses several different ethnic groups with very different experiences of immigration. Latinos are often referred to in a way that implies uniformity across members of this group, when in reality, Latinos constitute a diverse ethnic population with roots in a range of countries in Central America, South America, and the Caribbean. Today, about half of Hispanic adults were born in the U.S. and about half are foreign-born (Figure 9.7). We discuss two of the most prominent Latino groups below.

Mexican Americans

Mexicans are the largest group of Latinos in the United States. A large proportion of the Mexican American population lives in California, New Mexico, Texas, and Arizona, although migration to the American South has grown substantially. The immigration of Mexican Americans has long reflected the immediate labor needs of the U.S. economy (Barrera, 1979; Muller & Espenshade, 1985). During the 1930s, state and local governments forcibly sent hundreds of thousands of Mexican immigrants back to Mexico, but when the United States experienced a labor shortage during World War II, immigration was again encouraged. After the war, the *bracero* (manual laborer) program enabled 4 million Mexicans to work as temporary farm laborers in the United States, often under exploitative conditions. The program was ended in 1964, but by the 1980s, immigration was on the upsurge, with millions of people fleeing poverty and political turmoil in Latin America by illegally entering the United States.

The debate over how to deal with illegal immigrants seeking U.S. jobs has been a subject of heated debate in American politics, although the numbers of such immigrants appear to be falling. In fact, data suggest that a host of factors—including the dangers of crossing the U.S.–Mexico border due to drug violence on the Mexican side, harsher immigration laws in states from Georgia to Arizona, and the dearth of employment in the wake of the recession—have pushed illegal immigration down (Massey, 2011).

Most ethnic Mexicans in the United States are legal residents, and the number of those rising into the middle class has grown considerably, although the number living in poverty rose after the economy crisis that began in 2008.

Cuban Americans

When Fidel Castro came to power in Cuba in 1959, Cubans who opposed his communist regime sought to emigrate to the United States. These included some of Castro's political opponents, but most were middle-class Cubans whose standard of living was declining under Castro's economic policies and the U.S. economic embargo of Cuba. About half a million entered the United States, mostly through Florida, which is only 90 miles away from Cuba.

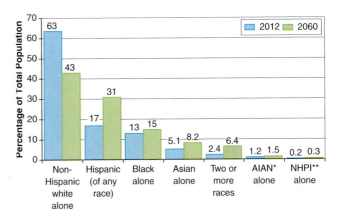

■ **FIGURE 9.7** U.S. Population by Race and Hispanic Origin, 2012 and 2060 (projected)

Source: U.S. Census Bureau. (2012f). USA QuickFacts.

*AIAN: American Indian and Alaska Native

**NHPI: Native Hawaiian and other Pacific Islander

Beginning in 1942, the U.S. government relocated an estimated 110,000 Japanese Americans living on the West Coast to internment camps. The government feared disloyalty after the Japanese attack on Pearl Harbor, in spite of the fact that more than 60% of those interned were U.S. citizens.

The Cuban community has enjoyed both economic and, perhaps as a result, political success in Florida (Ferment, 1989; Stepick & Grenier, 1993). In contrast to many immigrants, who tend to come from the poorer strata of their native countries, Cuban immigrants were often highly educated professionals and businesspeople before they fled to the United States. They brought with them a considerable reserve of training, skill, and sometimes wealth.

The anticommunist stance of the new migrants was also a good fit with U.S. foreign policy and the effort to crush communist politics in the Western Hemisphere. The U.S. government provided financial assistance such as small business loans to Cuban immigrants. It also offered a spectrum of language classes, job training programs, and recertification classes for physicians, architects, nurses, teachers, and lawyers who sought to reestablish their professional credentials in the United States. About three-quarters of all Cubans arriving before 1974 received some form of government benefits, the highest rate of any minority community.

Although Cuban migrants have tended to have higher levels of education than Mexican immigrants do, their status in the United States has also been strongly influenced by the political and economic (that is, the structural) needs of the U.S. government. U.S. economic needs have determined whether the government encouraged or discouraged the migration of manual labor power from Mexico, while political considerations have fostered a support network for migrants endorsing the U.S. government's effort to end the communist Castro regime in Cuba.

Asian Americans

Asian immigrants were instrumental in the development of industrialization in the United States. In the mid-1800s, construction began on the transcontinental railroad that would link California with the industrializing East. At the same time, gold and silver were discovered in the American West. Labor was desperately needed to mine these natural resources and to work on building the railroad. At the time, China was suffering a severe drought. American entrepreneurs seeking labor quickly saw the potential fit of supply and demand, and hundreds of thousands of Chinese were brought to the United States as inexpensive manual labor. Most came voluntarily, but some were kidnapped by U.S. ship captains and brought to the West Coast.

About 4% of Americans today trace their origins to Asian countries such as India, China, Japan, Korea, and Vietnam. The number of Asian Americans is growing, primarily because of immigration (Asian American birthrates, following the pattern in Asian countries, are low). Similar to Latinos, Asian Americans constitute a population of great ethnic diversity; the wide-ranging characteristics of this population cannot be fully captured by the term *Asian American* (Figure 9.8).

Asian Americans, similar to members of other minority groups, have experienced prejudice and discrimination. For example, during World War II, many Japanese Americans were forcibly placed in internment camps, and their property was confiscated (Harth, 2001). The U.S. government feared their allegiances were with Japan—an enemy in World War II—rather than the United States.

Although the teaching of German was banned in some schools, drastic measures were not taken against German or Italian Americans, although Germany and Italy were allied with Japan during the war.

In spite of obstacles, the Asian American population has been successful in making economic gains. Asian Americans as a whole have the highest median household income of any minority group, as well as the lowest rates of divorce, teenage pregnancy, and unemployment. Their economic success reflects the fact that, similar to Cuban Americans, recent Asian immigrants have come from higher socioeconomic backgrounds, bringing greater financial resources and more human capital (Zhou, 2009). Family networks and kinship obligations also play an important role. In many Asian American communities, informal community-based lending organizations provide capital for businesses, families and friends support one another as customers and employees, and profits are reinvested in the community (Ferment, 1989; Gilbertson & Gurak, 1993; Kasarda, 1993).

At the same time, there are substantial differences within the Asian American population. Nearly half of all Asian Indian Americans, for example, are professionals, compared with less than a quarter of Korean Americans, who are much more likely to run small businesses and factories. Poverty and hardship are more prevalent among those from Southeast Asia, particularly immigrants from Cambodia and Laos, which are deeply impoverished countries with less-educated populations.

Arab Americans

Immigrants from Arab countries began coming to the United States in the 1880s. The last major wave of Arab migration occurred in the decade following World War II (PBS, 2011). Contrary to popular perceptions, most members of today's Arab American population were born in the United States. The majority trace their roots back to Lebanon, Syria, Palestine, Egypt, and Iraq (Arab American Institute, 2012).

Arab Americans face a unique set of challenges and obstacles. Immediately following the September 11, 2001 terrorist attacks, Arab Americans as a group suffered stigma, and acts of discrimination against them increased sharply. The terror attacks provided an avenue for legitimating the views of racists and xenophobes (Salaita, 2005), but institutionalized prejudice was also obvious in the increase in "random" screenings and searches that targeted Arab Americans.

At the same time, Arab Americans represent a *model minority*—a racial or ethnic group with higher levels of achievement than the general population

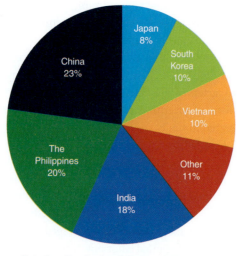

■ **FIGURE 9.8** Countries of Origin of the Asian Population in the United States, 2010

Japan 8%
South Korea 10%
China 23%
Vietnam 10%
The Philippines 20%
Other 11%
India 18%

Source: Data from Pew Research Center. 2012. *The rise of Asian Americans.* Pew Social & Demographic Trends. (http://www.pewsocialtrends.org/2012/06/19/the-rise-of-asian-americans/)

in areas such as education and income. Similar to Asian Americans, Arab Americans as a demographic group have been notably successful in these two areas: 45% have at least a bachelor's degree or higher (compared to 28% for the general population), and in 2008, their mean individual income was 27% higher than the national average (Arab American Institute Foundation, 2011).

White Ethnic Americans

White people have always made up a high percentage of the foreign-born population in the United States. The stereotype of minorities as people of color leaves out significant pockets of White ethnic minorities. In the early days of mass migration to the United States, the dominant group was White Protestants from Europe. Whites from Europe who were not Protestant—particularly Catholics and Jews—were defined as ethnic minorities, and their status was clearly marginal in U.S. society.

In mid–19th-century Boston, for example, Irish Catholics made up a large portion of the city's poor and were stereotyped as drunken, criminal, and generally immoral (Handlin, 1991). The term *paddy wagon,* used to describe a police van that picks up the drunk and disorderly, came from the notion that the Irish were such vans' most common occupants. (*Paddy* was a derogatory term for an Irishman.) Over time, however, White ethnic groups assimilated with relative ease because, for the most part, they looked much like the dominant population (Prell, 1999). To further their assimilation, some families changed their names and encouraged their children to speak English only. Today, most of these White ethnic groups—Irish, Italians, Russians, and others—have integrated fully into U.S. society (Figure 9.9). They are, on the whole, born wealthier, have more social capital, and encounter fewer barriers to mobility than other racial and ethnic groups.

If dark skin has historically been an obstacle in U.S. society, light skin has been an advantage. That advantage, however, may go unrecognized. As Peggy McIntosh writes in her thought-provoking article "White Privilege: Unpacking the Invisible Knapsack" (1990),

> As a white person, I realized I had been taught about racism as something that puts others at a disadvantage, but had been taught not to see one of its corollary aspects, white privilege, which puts me at an advantage. . . . I have come to see white privilege as an invisible package of unearned assets that I can count on cashing in each day, but about which I was "meant" to remain oblivious. (p. 31)

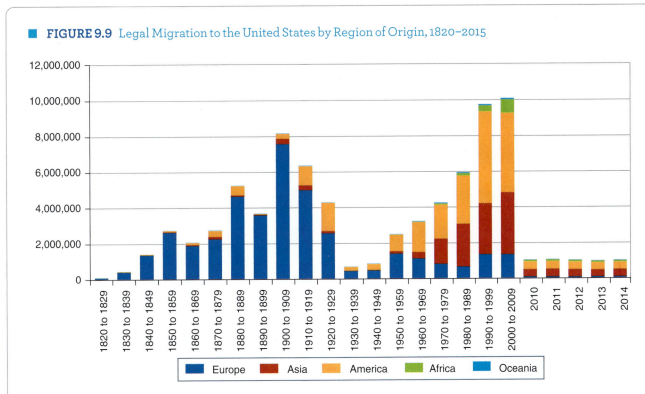

■ **FIGURE 9.9** Legal Migration to the United States by Region of Origin, 1820–2015

Source: Yearbook of Immigration Statistics: 2015 Legal Permanent Residents. U.S. Department of Homeland Security.

McIntosh goes on to outline these "assets," including the following: When Whites are told about their national heritage or the origins of civilization, they are shown that White people shaped it. Posters, picture books, greeting cards, toys, and dolls all overwhelmingly feature White images. As a White person, she need not worry that her coworkers at an affirmative action employer will suspect she got her job only because of her race. If she needed any medical or legal help, her race alone would not be considered a risk factor or hindrance in obtaining such services. These are only a few among the 50 unearned privileges of White skin that McIntosh identifies. Her argument is essentially that obliviousness to the advantages of White skin "maintain[s] the myth of meritocracy, the myth that democratic choice is equally available to all" (1990, p. 36). Recognition of skin privilege, in contrast, would be a challenge to the structure of power, which prefers to ignore whatever does not support the story of achievement as an outcome of merit.

Is the recognition of racial or ethnic advantages as important as the recognition of racial or ethnic disadvantages? Can this help to level the field of opportunity for all Americans? What do you think?

Multiracial Americans

As we note in the *Inequality Matters* box on page 241, naming is an important sociological action. It may be an exercise of power or an act of recognition. In 2000, the U.S. Census Bureau's questionnaire permitted respondents to select more than one race in describing themselves for the first time (Figure 9.10). In 2000, about 2.4% of Americans, or 6.8 million people, identified themselves as multiracial. In the 2010 census that figure grew to 9 million people (2.9% of Americans). Interestingly, the self-reported multiracial population grew much more dramatically than the single-race population: The former rose by 32%, while the latter rose by just over 9% (Jones & Bullock, 2012).

The rise in the numbers of U.S. residents describing themselves as belonging to more than one race should perhaps not come as any surprise. On one hand, more children

■ FIGURE 9.10 Race, Ethnicity, and Hispanic Origin Questions, U.S. Bureau of the Census Form, 2010

6. **What is this person's race?** *Mark X one or more boxes.*

☐ White
☐ Black, African Am., or Negro
☐ American Indian or Alaska Native — *Print name of enrolled or principal tribe.*

☐ Asian Indian   ☐ Japanese   ☐ Native Hawaiian
☐ Chinese   ☐ Korean   ☐ Guamanian or Chamorro
☐ Filipino   ☐ Vietnamese   ☐ Samoan
☐ Other Asian — *Print race, for example, Hmong, Laotian, Thai, Pakistani, Cambodian, and so on.*   ☐ Other Pacific Islander — *Print race, for example, Fijian, Tongan, and so on.*

☐ Some other race – *Print race.*

Source: "The Two or More Races Population: 2010. 2010 Census Briefs, September 2012. U.S. Bureau of the Census.

are being born into interracial partnerships: In 2010, 10% of heterosexual married couples (5.4 million) were interracial, and the figure is even higher among unmarried couples (Lofquist, Lugaila, O'Connell, & Feliz, 2012). On the other hand, because this is a self-reported status, more people may be choosing to identify themselves as multiracial as the availability of the category becomes more widely known and as multiracial status becomes more broadly accepted.

Notably, being biracial or multiracial is not a new phenomenon. It is, in some respects, a newly named phenomenon that is also of growing interest to researchers. The politics of multiracialism can be complicated, with competing interests at play. For example, leading up to the 2000 census, many mixed-race individuals and advocacy groups favored the addition of an entirely separate *multiple race* option on the census questionnaire, as opposed to allowing respondents to check multiple boxes from among the established racial categories. They argued that the addition of such an option would allow for fluidity in the way that individuals identify themselves, freeing them from the constraints of categories imposed on them by the state. Others, including some prominent civil rights leaders, countered that identification according to the established racial categories is necessary to ensure that civil rights legislation is enforced and that inequalities in housing, income, education, and so on are documented accurately (Roquemore & Brunsma, 2008). On one hand, the lived experience of multiracial Americans and their right to self-identify must be respected; on the other hand, the Census Bureau must fulfill its obligation to provide legislators with accurate information on inequality. Social science research tells us that individuals' racial identification plays an important role in how others interact with them, their social networks, and even their life chances (Khanna, 2011). Thus, the question of how a person self-identifies, and how others perceive him or her, has real consequences in that individual's everyday life.

Race and Ethnicity from a Global Perspective

Although our focus to this point has been on the United States, issues of racial and ethnic identities and inequalities are global in scope. Around the world, unstable minority and majority relationships, fears of rising migration from developing countries, and even ethnic and racial hatreds that explode into brutal violence highlight again how important it is for us to understand the causes and dynamics of categories that, while socially constructed, are powerfully real in their consequences.

European countries such as France, Germany, and Denmark have struggled in recent years to deal with challenges of immigration, discrimination, and prejudice.

Migration to Northern and Western Europe from developing states, particularly those in North Africa and the Middle East, has risen, driven by a combination of *push factors* (social forces such as dire economic conditions and inadequate educational opportunities that encourage migrants to leave their home countries) and *pull factors* (forces that draw migrants to a given country, such as labor shortages that can be filled by low- or high-skilled migrants or an existing ethnic network that can offer new migrants support). In a short period of time, the large numbers of job seekers from developing countries in search of better lives have transformed the populations of many European countries from largely ethnically homogeneous to multicultural—a change that has caused some political and social tensions.

Tensions in Europe revolve at least in part around the fact that a substantial proportion of migrants from developing states are Muslim, and some have brought with them religious practices, such as veiling, that are not perceived to be a good fit with largely secular European societies. By some estimates, Muslims will account for about a fifth of the population of the European Union by 2050 (Mudde, 2011). In 2011, France, in which about 10% of the population is Muslim, became the first country in Europe to ban the full-face veil, also known as the *burqa*, which is the customary dress for some Muslim women. Similar legislation has been introduced, but not passed, in Belgium and the Netherlands. Earlier, when France banned all overt religious symbols from schools in 2004, civil defiance and violence followed. The Parisian suburbs burned as young French Muslims rioted, demanding opportunity and acceptance in a society that has traditionally narrowly defined who is "French."

In some cases, ethnic and racial tensions have had even more explosive effects. Earlier in this chapter, we talked about four forms that majority–minority relations can take: expulsion, segregation, assimilation, and cultural pluralism. Here we add a fifth form: genocide.

Genocide: The Mass Destruction of Societies

Genocide can be defined as *the mass, systematic destruction of a people or a nation.* According to the Convention on the Prevention and Punishment of the Crime of Genocide, adopted by the United Nations General Assembly in 1948, when genocide was declared a crime under international law, it includes "any of the following acts committed with intent to destroy, in whole or in part, a national, ethnical, racial or religious group, as such:

a. Killing members of the group;

b. Causing serious bodily or mental harm to members of the group;

Genocide: The mass, systematic destruction of a people or a nation.

c. Deliberately inflicting on the group conditions of life calculated to bring about its physical destruction in whole or in part;

d. Imposing measures intended to prevent births within the group;

e. Forcibly transferring children of the group to another group."

The mass killing of people because of their membership in a particular group is ages old. Hans Van Wees (2010) notes that ancient Christian and Hebrew religious texts contain evidence of early religiously motivated mass killings. Roger W. Smith (2002) points out that the Assyrians, Greeks, Romans, and Mongols, among others, engaged in genocide, but their perspective on mass killing was shaped by their time. He notes that rulers boasted about the thousands they killed and the peoples they eliminated. Genocide as both a term and a defined crime is much more recent.

The word *genocide* was coined in the 1940s by Polish émigré Raphael Lemkin, who left his native country in the late 1930s, several years before Adolf Hitler's Nazi army overran it. A lawyer and an academic, Lemkin was also a crusader for human rights, and, aware of Nazi atrocities in Europe, he sought to inspire U.S. decision makers to act against the mass killing of Jews and other targeted groups. In a 1941 radio broadcast, British prime minister Winston Churchill decried the "barbaric fury" of the Nazis and declared, "We are in the presence of a crime without a name." Lemkin, who heard the broadcast, undertook to name the crime and, through this naming, to bring an end to it (Power, 2002).

Sociologist Pierre Bourdieu (1991) points to the significance of language in structuring the perception that social agents (such as governments or populations) have of the world around them. The very act of naming a phenomenon confers on it a social reality. Lemkin sought to use the act of naming as a vehicle for action against Nazi atrocities and against future threats to the physical, political, cultural, and economic existence of collectivities (Shaw, 2010). Lemkin settled on *genocide,* a hybrid of the Greek *geno,* meaning *tribe* or *race,* and the Latin *cide* (from *caedere*), or *killing.*

The 1948 U.N. Convention on the Prevention and Punishment of the Crime of Genocide created a potentially powerful new political reality, although it narrowed the definition from the broad articulation championed by Lemkin (Shaw, 2010). Theoretically, state sovereignty could no longer shield a country from the consequences of committing genocide, because the nations that signed the U.N. convention were bound by it to prevent, suppress, and punish such crimes. At the same time, the notion of an obligation to intervene is loose and open to interpretation, as history has shown. Humanitarian organizations such as Genocide Watch and institutions such as the U.S. Holocaust Memorial Museum have sounded the alarm on recent atrocities, often labeling them genocide even as many governments have resisted using the term.

Genocides in the second half of the 20th century include slaughters carried out by the Khmer Rouge in Cambodia in the 1970s, Saddam Hussein's 1987–1988 campaign against ethnic Kurds in Iraq, and Serb atrocities in the former Yugoslav states of Bosnia-Herzegovina and Kosovo in the late 1990s (Figure 9.11). The 21st century has already seen the genocidal destruction of Black Africans, including the Darfuris, Abyei, and Nuba, by Arab militias linked to the government in Sudan.

One of the most discussed cases of genocide in the late 20th century took place in Rwanda, where, in 1994, no fewer than 800,000 ethnic Tutsis were killed by ethnic Hutus in the space of 100 days. Many killings were done by machete, and women and girls were targeted for sexual violence. By most accounts, Tutsis and Hutus are not so different from one another; they are members of the same ethnic group, live in the same areas, and share a common language. One cultural difference of considerable importance, however, is that for the Tutsis, the cow is sacred and cannot be killed or used for food. The Hutus, who have a long tradition of farming, were forced to leave large areas of land open for cattle grazing, thus limiting the fertile ground available for farming. As the cattle herds multiplied, so did tensions and conflict. Notably, for many years, the Tutsis, while fewer in number (representing approximately 14% of the population), dominated the Hutus politically and economically (Kapuscinski, 2001).

Rwanda was long a colony of Belgium, but in the 1950s, Tutsis began to demand independence, as did many other colonized peoples in Africa. The Belgians incited the Hutus to rebel against the Tutsi ruling class. The rebellion was unsuccessful, but the seeds for genocide were planted in fertile soil, and sporadic ethnic violence erupted in the decades that followed. Belgium finally relinquished power and granted Rwanda independence in 1962. From the early 1970s, the government was headed by a moderate Hutu leader, Major General Juvénal Habyarimana (BBC, 2008). In the early 1990s, General Habyarimana agreed to a power-sharing arrangement with Tutsis in Rwanda, angering some nationalist Hutus, who did not want to see a division of power. In 1994, the general was assassinated (his private jet was shot down), and radical Hutus took the opportunity to turn on both Tutsi countrymen and moderate Hutus, murdering at least 800,000 people in a few short months.

In the section below, we consider the question of how genocide—such as the mass killing of Rwanda's Tutsi population in 1994—looks through a sociological lens.

■ FIGURE 9.11 Select Genocides around the World, 1914–Present

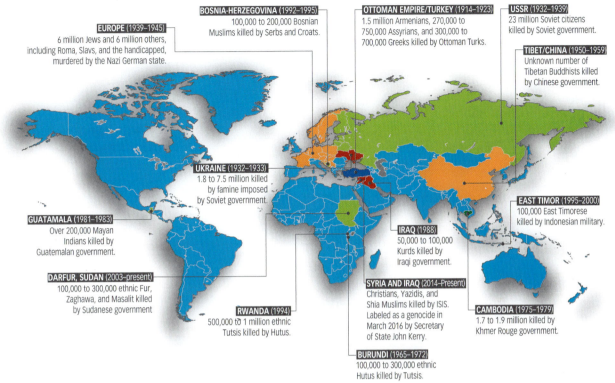

EUROPE (1939–1945)
6 million Jews and 6 million others, including Roma, Slavs, and the handicapped, murdered by the Nazi German state.

BOSNIA-HERZEGOVINA (1992–1995)
100,000 to 200,000 Bosnian Muslims killed by Serbs and Croats.

OTTOMAN EMPIRE/TURKEY (1914–1923)
1.5 million Armenians, 270,000 to 750,000 Assyrians, and 300,000 to 700,000 Greeks killed by Ottoman Turks.

USSR (1932–1939)
23 million Soviet citizens killed by Soviet government.

TIBET/CHINA (1950–1959)
Unknown number of Tibetan Buddhists killed by Chinese government.

UKRAINE (1932–1933)
1.8 to 7.5 million killed by famine imposed by Soviet government.

GUATAMALA (1981–1983)
Over 200,000 Mayan Indians killed by Guatemalan government.

EAST TIMOR (1995–2000)
100,000 East Timorese killed by Indonesian military.

IRAQ (1988)
50,000 to 100,000 Kurds killed by Iraqi government.

DARFUR, SUDAN (2003–present)
100,000 to 300,000 ethnic Fur, Zaghawa, and Masalit killed by Sudanese government

SYRIA AND IRAQ (2014–Present)
Christians, Yazidis, and Shia Muslims killed by ISIS. Labeled as a genocide in March 2016 by Secretary of State John Kerry.

CAMBODIA (1975–1979)
1.7 to 1.9 million killed by Khmer Rouge government.

RWANDA (1994)
500,000 to 1 million ethnic Tutsis killed by Hutus.

BURUNDI (1965–1972)
100,000 to 300,000 ethnic Hutus killed by Tutsis.

Source: Adapted from Online Resources from The Choices Program, Brown University.

Note: The term *genocide* has not been legally applied to all mass killings listed above. The number of victims has also been disputed for each of these killings.

What Explains Genocide?

Taking a sociological perspective, we might ask, "Who benefits from genocide?" Why do countries or leaders make a choice to pursue or allow genocidal actions? Genocide is the product of conscious decisions made by those who stand to benefit from it and who anticipate minimal costs for their actions.

Chalk and Jonassohn (1990) suggest that those who pursue genocide do so to eliminate a real or perceived threat, to spread fear among enemies, to eliminate a real or potential threat to another group, to gain wealth or power for a dominant group, and/or to realize an ideological goal. Shaw (2010) has noted that "genocide is a crime of social classification, in which power-holders target particular populations for social and often physical destruction" (p. 142).

Anton Weiss-Wendt (2010) points out that to the degree that genocide "requires premeditation" (p. 81), governments are generally implicated in the crime. Among the necessary parts is also the creation of a "genocidal mentality"

In the 1994 genocide in Rwanda, nearly a million ethnic Tutsis were systematically killed by ethnic Hutus in fewer than 100 days.

not only among the leadership but also among a sufficient number of individuals to ensure the participation, or at least the support or indifference, of a large proportion of the population (Goldhagen, 1997; Markusen, 2002). Part of creating a genocidal mentality is dehumanizing the victims. By emphasizing their *otherness*, or the idea that the group to be victimized is less than fully human, agents of genocide stamp out sympathy for their targets, replacing it with a sense of threat or disgust. Modern media have made the process of disseminating the propaganda of dehumanization increasingly easy. Radio broadcasts to a Hutu audience in Rwanda in the time leading up to the genocide implored Hutus to "kill [Tutsi] cockroaches" (Gourevitch, 1999).

Another mechanism is the "establishment of genocidal institutions and organizations," which construct propaganda to justify institutions or other means to carry out the genocide. Finally, the recruitment and training of perpetrators is important, as is the establishment of methods of group destruction (Markusen, 2002). In Rwanda, it is notable that some Hutu Power groups had, in the early 1990s, begun to arm civilians with hand weapons such as machetes, ostensibly as self-defense against Tutsi rebels. Many of these were later used in the genocide. As Hutus and Tutsis lived side by side in many cities and rural areas, identification of victims was rapid and easy.

Choosing genocide as a policy incurs costs as well as benefits. Clearly, outside forces can impose costs on a genocidal regime; we have seen that signatories to the 1948 U.N. convention are theoretically obligated to intervene. But historically, intervention has often been too little and too late. Why, in the face of overwhelming evidence of genocide (as in Rwanda or Bosnia-Herzegovina or Sudan), does the

Discover & Debate

THE U.S. CENSUS AND CITIZENSHIP

Motion: Unlike recent iterations of the U.S. Census, the 2020 Census will include a question asking whether or not respondents are citizens (see Figure 9.12). The inclusion of a citizenship question is a good addition.

Background: The first U.S. Census took place in 1790. The Census is foreseen by the Constitution and must be conducted every 10 years. It is the only time the government undertakes to count every single person who resides in the United States. Census questions tend to be standard, though some also reflect contemporary concerns: For instance, around the middle of the 19th century, respondents were asked to indicate where they were born, as the government was interested in learning about internal migration, which was growing as the United States expanded its territories. A question on citizenship has not been used on the U.S. Census since 1950, though it was included for a smaller population sample in 1965 and is currently included in the American Community Survey, which collects data based on a population sample on an annual basis. In 2018, the U.S. Department of Justice asked the Census Bureau to add a question on citizenship to the 2020 Census and the request was approved.

■ **FIGURE 9.12** 2020 U.S. Census Citizenship Question

Is this person a citizen of the United States?

☐ Yes, born in the United States

☐ Yes, born in Puerto Rico, Guam, the U.S. Virgin Islands, or Northern Marianas

☐ Yes, born abroad of U.S. citizen parent or parents

☐ Yes, U.S. citizen by naturalization – *Print year of naturilization.* ↙

☐☐☐☐

☐ No, not a U.S. citizen

Source: U.S. Census Bureau.

Questions for Consideration

- What is the sociological significance of obtaining a full count of the U.S. population in the decennial census? Why does this matter? To whom does it matter?

- What are key challenges to gathering comprehensive information about populations and communities?

- Does trust in institutions affect decisions people make about responding to the Census or to political or other types of surveys?

Debate Tip

- Try not to let yourself get overwhelmed with emotion. It can be particularly difficult to debate a stance that runs counter to your own personal beliefs, but remember that the ability to develop evidence-based arguments on both sides of a debate will serve you well, both in school and beyond.

AFFIRMATIVE ARGUMENTS	OPPOSITION ARGUMENTS
The U.S. Census is intended to gather important information about the U.S. population. Asking about citizenship is one way to learn more about the composition of the U.S. population.	The question may be unconstitutional. Specifically, if it depresses response rates, it may violate the Constitution's entreaty to the Census Bureau to count "the whole number of persons in each state."
The annual American Community Survey has long included a question battery on citizenship status. The American Community Survey, which is based on sampling rather than a full population count, has successfully gathered reliable population information.	The question may affect response rates for the Census. If noncitizens and their families fear consequences for revealing information about their status, they will be less likely to complete the Census.
A reliable count of voting-age citizens in a locality or state is useful in order to ensure the integrity of voting.	An inaccurate count may have political and economic consequences. Because the Census is used to allocate Congressional seats and federal resources, an undercount could have a particularly pernicious effect on states and cities with large migrant populations that are not fully counted.

international community not step in? One answer is that these states also make choices based on perceived costs and benefits. Intervention in the affairs of another state can be costly, and many leaders avoid it. In a historical overview of U.S. responses to genocide, for instance, Samantha Power (2002) argues that "American leaders did not act because they did not want to. They believed that genocide was wrong, but they were not prepared to invest the military, financial, diplomatic, or domestic political capital needed to stop it" (p. 508).

Genocide is an extreme and brutal manifestation of majority–minority relations. It is the effort to destroy indiscriminately an entire racial or ethnic group. Does genocide continue to be a viable option for states or regimes wishing to destroy groups labeled by powerful leaders as inferior or dangerous? How should outside states—and concerned individuals—respond when conflict and intolerance evolve into genocide? What do you think?

Why Study Race and Ethnicity from a Sociological Perspective?

Living in the United States, we are surrounded by serious and casual discussions and comments about race, ethnic jokes, and anecdotes, stories, and studies about race and ethnicity. Rarely do we stop to ask ourselves what racial and ethnic categories really mean and why they are significant. Who decided they should be significant, and why? What institutions in society reinforce this belief? What institutions challenge it? As a society, we have simply accepted such categories as *Black* and *White* as real. Sociologists, however, argue that they are socially constructed—what is real is not race but rather the consequences of racism, with its accompanying prejudice and discrimination.

Sociologically defined concepts such as *race*—as well as *prejudice, discrimination, assimilation,* and the like—help us see domestic and international conflicts in a different light. We may begin to understand that socially constructed categories marginalize and even dehumanize certain groups and that we must recognize these symbolic acts as well as the violent acts—from hate crimes to genocides—that may accompany them.

We benefit in our personal lives, too, from recognizing the socially constructed nature of categories such as race. We ought to pause and ask ourselves: Why is treatment of individuals often conditioned on skin color? Why has our society opted to define this marker as significant? What must we do culturally, socially, politically, educationally, and economically to pull down the artificial barriers imposed by socially constructed categories?

What Can I Do with a Sociology Degree?

ADVOCATING FOR SOCIAL JUSTICE

As you learned in Chapter 1, sociology emerged in the midst of the large-scale social changes of the 19th century. While many early sociologists such as Comte, Marx, and Durkheim sought to understand, predict, and even manage social change, others, including Park, Du Bois, Martineau and Addams, were not only social theorists and researchers but also social activists. They were outraged by social inequality and used their sociological knowledge to advocate for social justice. For Mills, social responsibility was an integral part of sociology.

Many of us have a desire for a more just society and world. The capacity to actively advocate for social justice, whether personally or professionally (as a career), requires knowledge and skills that can be gained by studying sociology. First and foremost, it requires that we understand the complex nature of injustice. We live in an individualistic culture, where success and failure are often seen as proportional to one's effort and talent. While *agency* (the power to exercise free will and affect change) is an important concept in sociology, as a field, sociology seeks to provide a more multifaceted understanding of social life. By examining how the unequal distribution of opportunities, resources, and power shapes life chances, sociology students gain a more sophisticated understanding of the nature of social inequality. They learn the critical difference between individual discrimination and discrimination that is built into the policies and practices of social institutions such as education and the criminal justice systems. Despite the centrality of social structure, sociology does not discount agency. Sociology students gain a framework for understanding the nature of social movements and examine forces that may foster or impede social change.

Many sociology students have opportunities to not only study social justice but also to engage in social justice work through group organizations on campus and service-learning, internships, and other experiential learning opportunities in off-campus community agencies. Anyone can work for social justice on an individual level by being aware of their own prejudices and privileges and by taking action in their personal and professional lives—for example, by confronting acts of prejudice and discrimination, being an advocate and ally for oppressed groups, and voting for candidates and causes that support a social justice mission. You can practice your own career in a way that contributes to

social justice (for example, by doing pro bono work and using the power you may have to hire people) or you may choose to follow a career that has an explicit focus on social justice. Some colleges and universities now offer graduate degrees in social justice fields (such as social justice education). Many of the other career skills outlined in this book, including those concerning interpersonal skills (Chapter 4), diversity (Chapter 8), team work (Chapter 5), ethical decision making (Chapter 10), community resources and services (Chapter 13), and social change (Chapter 18), are necessary in social justice work.

Kelsey Edwards, Program Assistant at Equal Justice Works

The George Washington University, BA in Sociology and Human Services & Social Justice, Minor in Sustainability

Through my sociology degree, I was able to study and research societal issues and problems affecting our population and develop solutions on how to address those issues to combat injustice. My sociology major has helped me understand the world around me, including the institutional structures and barriers that make it harder for people to succeed and cause an unleveled playing field. As a sociology major, I focused mainly on how the intersection of race, gender, and class affects one's ability to succeed in our society. Knowing the structural and institutional barriers in our society gives me a different perspective when meeting new people and hearing their background and testimonies.

After graduating from The George Washington University with a degree in sociology, I started working as a program assistant at Equal Justice Works. In my role, I work with lawyers and law students to seek social justice for clients in need, including veterans, the elderly, those experiencing homelessness, survivors of natural disasters, and those who are unemployed and underemployed. We provide resources and opportunities to individuals who are from underprivileged and marginalized backgrounds. I gained many practical skills as a sociology major, including research, writing, and critical thinking that has helped me grow as a working professional. When applying for grants and funding, we use research-based evidence, including quantitative and qualitative research, to show foundations and grant makers how our current and proposed programs can make a difference in the lives of the people we serve. Additionally, the major has given me a deeper understanding of the complex systems that are contributing to individual experiences of the clients our organization serves as well as all individuals experiencing injustice within our society.

My future aspirations are to work in race-based policy making to ensure that your race/ethnicity and where you live do not determine whether you live.

Source: Bureau of Labor Statistics, *Occupational Outlook Handbook,* 2017.

Regardless of one's ethnicity, socioeconomic status, or level of education, we all deserve equal access to opportunities and resources. With my background in sociology, I have the right skills, tools, and understanding of historical context, which allows me to successfully advocate for systemic change.

Career Data: Paralegals/Legal Assistants

- 2017 Median Pay: $50,410 per year
- $24.24 per hour
- Typical Entry-Level Education: Associate degree
- Job Outlook, 2016–2026: 15% (Much faster than average)

SUMMARY

- **Race** is not a biological category but a social construct. Its societal significance derives from the fact that people in a particular culture believe, falsely, that there are biologically distinguishable races and then act on the basis of this belief. The perceived differences among races are often distorted and lead to **prejudice** and **discrimination**.

- Many societies include different ethnic groups with varied histories, cultures, and practices.

- **Minorities**, typically because of their race or **ethnicity**, may experience prejudice and discrimination. Different types of minority–dominant group relations include **expulsion**, **assimilation**, **segregation**, and **cultural pluralism**.

- Prejudice usually relies on **stereotyping** and scapegoating. During difficult economic times, prejudice may increase as people seek someone to blame for their predicament.

- The civil rights struggles that began in the United States more than 60 years ago led to passage of civil rights and affirmative action legislation that has reduced, but not eliminated, the effects of prejudice and discrimination against minorities.

- Although discrimination is against the law in the United States, it is still widely practiced. **Institutionalized discrimination** in particular results in the unequal treatment of minorities in employment, housing, education, and other areas.

- The United States is a multiethnic, multiracial society. Minority groups—including American Indians, African Americans, Latinos, Asian Americans, and Arab Americans—make up close to 40% of the population. This figure will continue to rise as a result of new births and immigration, changing the demographic face of the country.

- Historically, the vast majority of immigrants to the United States have come from Europe, but in recent years, the pattern has changed; currently, most immigrants come from Latin America and Asia.

- With a few exceptions, minority groups are disadvantaged in the United States relative to the majority-White population in terms of income, numbers living in poverty, and the quality of education and health care, as well as political voice. Although the disadvantages of dark skin are recognized, the privileges of light skin have not been widely acknowledged.

- **Genocide** is the mass and systematic destruction of a people or a nation. The 1948 United Nations Convention on the Prevention and Punishment of the Crime of Genocide obligates signatories to act against genocide.

KEY TERMS

race, 225

ethnicity, 225

minorities, 226

expulsion, 226

segregation, 226

restrictive covenants, 227

assimilation, 230

cultural pluralism, 230

racism, 231

stigma, 232

mixed contacts, 232

prejudice, 232

stereotyping, 234

discrimination, 234

individual discrimination, 234

institutionalized discrimination, 234

social epidemiology, 237

genocide, 247

DISCUSSION QUESTIONS

1. If genetic differences between people who have different physical characteristics (such as skin color) are minor, why do we as a society continue to use race as a socially significant category?

2. As noted in the chapter, racial residential segregation remains a key problem in the United States. What sociological factors explain its persistence in an era when housing discrimination is illegal?

3. What links have researchers identified between race and health outcomes in the United States? What sociological factors explain relatively poorer health among minorities than among Whites? How might public policy be used to address this problem?

4. Do you think immigration will continue to grow in coming decades in the United States? What kinds of factors might influence immigration trends?

5. What factors make communities vulnerable to genocide? How should other countries respond when genocide seems imminent or is already under way?

Want a better grade?

Get the tools you need to sharpen your study skills. Access practice quizzes, eFlashcards, video, and multimedia at **https://edge.sagepub.com/chambliss4e**.

©John Moore/Getty Images

Gender and Society

10

WHAT DO YOU THINK?

1. Why are women today more likely to enroll in and complete college than their male peers?

2. Why do men as a group continue to earn more money than women as a group?

3. What are key issues of feminism in the United States in the 21st century? Who is a feminist today?

LEARNING OBJECTIVES

10.1 Distinguish among *sex*, *gender*, and *sexuality*.

10.2 Identify key agents of gender socialization.

10.3 Describe gender inequality in society.

10.4 Explain the sociological roots of the gender wage gap.

10.5 Discuss different types of feminist thought in the United States.

10.6 Describe manifestations of inequality faced by women around the globe.

I AM A WOMAN AND I AM FAST

How fast can a woman run? A rule reinstated in 2017 by the International Association of Athletics Federations (IAAF) engages with this question, albeit, not by questioning how fast a female athlete can potentially round the track but rather by asking who is legitimately a woman. The rule establishes that female athletes with naturally elevated testosterone levels cannot race in 400-meter to one-mile (1,600-meter) races unless they undergo treatment to bring down their testosterone levels to a standard acceptable to the

©AP Photo/Tim Ireland

257

IAAF. Apart from having hormone therapy or surgery, athletes subject to the rule may also choose to run distances greater than one mile, may compete against men, or may enter competitions designated for intersex athletes, if those are offered (Macur, 2017). The IAAF, says one athlete who is subject to the rule, have set a hormone level that comports with their "perceived notions of femininity" and permits discrimination against runners who do not meet the standard (Longman, 2018).

By one estimate, about 7 of every 1,000 elite female track and field athletes have elevated levels of testosterone. Most of these athletes compete in high-speed and endurance sports such as the 400-meter sprint. Among these athletes is India's Dutee Chand. Chand is a sprinter who, because of high testosterone levels, was subjected to gender testing at the age of 17 and has been excluded from competitions because of her elevated testosterone. In 2015, Chand

> challenged a rule made by track's international governing body that barred her from competing against other women because her natural level of testosterone was too high. She said no way would she take hormone-suppressing drugs to lower that testosterone level. No chance that she—a healthy, strong 18-year-old—would have surgery to limit how much testosterone her body produced.

> On Monday, the Court of Arbitration for Sport, sport's highest court, announced that it had ruled in her favor. It was hard not to celebrate Chand's victory, given that all she wanted to do was compete with the body she was born with. (Macur, 2015, para. 2–3)

The victory for Chand and other female athletes with elevated levels of testosterone, however, was short-lived: Two years later, the IAFF returned with a reinforced case showing performance advantages of 5% to 6% for women athletes with hormonal anomalies such as Chand's (Ibid.).

Another elite runner, South Africa's Caster Semenya, is taking legal action against the rule, challenging the IAAF's mandate that female athletes with elevated testosterone levels cannot race in women's competitions unless they undergo treatment. In the absence of such treatment, the rule implies, the athlete cannot be a *woman* athlete. She and her attorneys argue that the new rules extend "the offensive practice of intrusive surveillance and judging of women's bodies which has historically haunted women's sports" (Longman, 2018, para. 6). Semenya rejects the IAAF's position. In her own words, "I am Mokgadi Caster Semenya. I am a woman and I am fast" (Longman, 2018, para. 8).

The question of how to address the advantages on the track of women runners with elevated testosterone levels is by no means simple. Dr. Myron Genel, a consultant to the International Olympic Committee's medical commission, however, has recommended that "athletes with what is known as a disorder of sex development—a biological anomaly that might result in atypically high testosterone production—should compete as females if they were raised as females." Genel offers the analogy of other elite athletes, such as runner Usain Bolt and swimmer Michael Phelps, who have genetic advantages of, respectively, an "uncommonly long stride" and "flipper-size feet" (Macur, 2015, para. 19–20).

What makes someone a woman athlete—or a woman? Is it hormones? Self-identification? The recognition of others of her gender? These are questions that challenge society and sociologists to think deeply and critically about who has the power to label others and what it means when the labels offered by outside agents do not match those embraced by an individual.

We begin with a discussion of key concepts of sex and gender and how those are used in sociological study. We then address the construction of gendered selves, looking at agents of socialization—including the family, media, and schools—and examining the idea that gender is as much a process as an identity. This leads us to a wide-ranging discussion of gender and society. We focus on gender and family life, higher education, the wage gap, and sexual harassment to understand how gender norms, roles, and expectations shape the experiences of men and women in key societal institutions. Next, we turn to both the classical canon and contemporary feminist thinking about gender, ending with a section on women's global concerns, including maternal mortality, sex trafficking, and rape in war. We examine the marginality of women and the steps being taken to empower them to change their own lives and communities.

Concepts of Sex, Gender, and Sexuality

Sociologists acknowledge that complex interactions between biology and culture shape behavioral differences associated with gender. They seek to take both forces into account, though most believe culture and society play more important roles in structuring gender and **gender roles**, *the attitudes and behaviors considered appropriately masculine or feminine in a particular culture.* Sociologists thus argue that gender-specific behaviors are not reducible to biological differences; rather, biology, culture, and social learning all interact to shape human behaviors.

To highlight the distinction between biological and social factors, sociologists use the term *sex* to refer to biological identity and the term *gender* to refer to the masculine or feminine roles associated with sex. **Sex** encompasses the *anatomical and other biological differences between males and females that originate in human genes.* Many of these biologically based sex differences, such as differences in genitalia, are usually present at birth. Others, triggered by male or female hormones, develop later—for example, female menstruation and differences in muscle mass, facial hair, height, and vocal characteristics.

Gender encompasses *the norms, roles, and behavioral characteristics associated in a given society with being male or female.* Gender is less about being biologically male or

female than about conforming to mainstream notions of masculinity and femininity, though the characteristics we associate with gender vary across time and space. Biologically based sex differences are not unimportant in shaping social norms of gender. The fact that only biological women can bear and nurse children, for example, has enormous implications for women's roles in all societies (Huber, 2006), but this does not mean that, as Sigmund Freud asserted, biology is destiny.

Sexuality is a term used in a variety of ways. Sociologically, we can think of it as *encompassing sexual identity, attraction, and relationships.* Sexuality may or may not align conventionally with one's sex and gender. Sociologists use the term *heteronormative* to designate the beliefs and practices that align with heterosexuality; that is, in modern Western societies, social institutions and norms embrace and elevate heterosexual relationships between biological males and females. This has often led to the marginalization of other sexualities, including homosexuality, bisexuality, and asexuality.

Sociologists generally consider sex and gender to be dynamic concepts. Although it is clear that *gender,* which is associated with norms, roles, and behaviors that shift over time, is socially constructed and thus subject to transformations, a growing number of researchers have suggested that *sex* is also socially constructed rather than solely biological (Preves, 2003). They cite cases of infants born with ambiguous sex characteristics and/or an abnormal chromosomal makeup. Doctors, parents, or society rarely tolerate uncertainties in sex categorization. As a result, these children are usually subjected to surgeries and medications intended to render them categorizable in societally normative terms.

Gender roles: The attitudes and behaviors that are considered appropriately masculine or feminine in a particular culture.

Sex: The anatomical and other biological characteristics that differ between males and females and that originate in human genes.

Gender: The norms, roles, and behavioral characteristics associated in a given society with being male or female.

Sexuality: A term used to encompass sexual identity, attraction, and relationships.

Transgender is *an umbrella term used to describe those whose gender identity, expression, or behavior differs from their assigned sex at birth or is outside the gender binary.* A person who was female assigned at birth (FAAB) but identifies as a man (FTM) may be described as *transgender* (or *trans*), as may a person who was male assigned at birth (MAAB) but identifies as a woman (MTF). Transgender also includes but is not limited to other categories and identities, such as transsexual, cross-dresser, androgynous, genderqueer, bigender, third gender, and gender non-conforming. **Transsexual** usually refers to *people who use surgery and hormones to change their sex to match their preferred gender.* Transgender people may have heterosexual, lesbian, gay, or bisexual sexual orientation.

The issue of the transgender community and its visibility and rights have garnered attention in the media recently. In a revolutionary interview with Diane Sawyer (ABC News, 2015) and iconic *Vanity Fair* photo spread in the spring of 2015, U.S. Olympic gold medalist and television celebrity Bruce Jenner introduced the world to Caitlyn, sharing her decision to embrace a feminine identity after years of uncertainty about who she was or how her decision would be received. "For all intents and purposes, I'm a woman," Jenner explained to journalist Diane Sawyer. She told the interviewer that she has not and will not undergo surgery to remove her male genitalia (ABC News, 2015), though she underwent "facial feminization surgery" (Bissinger, 2015). In terms of sexuality, Caitlyn Jenner labels herself as heterosexual. She also identifies as a woman, and her gender display is clearly feminine.

The size of the transgender community in the United States is difficult to ascertain, as many people still live under the radar. A study from the Williams Institute at the University of California, Los Angeles, suggests a figure of 700,000 (Gates, 2011). In 2016, a fight continued in several U.S. states, including North Carolina, over bills to require people to use the restroom of the "sex they were assigned at birth," regardless of their gender identity or outward presentation of self. North Carolina's "bathroom bill" spurred some notable backlash: The National Basketball Association (NBA) pulled the 2017 league's all-star game out of Charlotte, citing "the issue of legal protections for the LGBT [lesbian, gay, bisexual, and transsexual] community" (Helin, 2016). Some institutions have reacted to this issue by embracing nongendered restrooms: The Cooper Union, a college in New York, announced that it

is removing gender identification from restrooms on campus and opening single-occupancy toilets for anyone's use. "We have always been ahead of our time and we must continue being leaders on issues of social justice," Bill Mea, acting president, wrote in an e-mail to the campus (Sutter, 2016). Other significant societal institutions have also taken steps against discrimination: In July of 2016, the U.S. military reversed a ban on transgender service members, allowing transgender members of the military forces to serve openly.

Is sex at birth an immutable category? Should individuals have the freedom to define themselves, pushing boundaries of sex, gender, and sexuality to find the space in which they feel at home? How should institutions respond? What do you think?

Constructing Gendered Selves

Across the diverse cultures of our world, males are generally expected to behave in culturally defined "masculine" ways and females in "feminine" ways. Few people fully conform to these stereotypes—most exhibit a blend of characteristics. Still, in many cultures, people believe male and female stereotypes represent fundamental and real sex differences, and although some blending is acceptable, there are social consequences for diverging too far from the social scripts of gender.

What is considered masculine and feminine differs across cultures, and gender displays can vary dramatically. Among the Canela of Brazil, for example, large, colorful disks called *kui* are inserted into holes pierced into a boy's ears. Repeated piercings and insertions stretch the holes to a large size in order to enable the ears to eventually accommodate disks that are several inches across. This painful process is performed to enable the boy to better hear the wisdom of his elders as well as to make him attractive to women (Crocker, 1986, 1990, 1994). This practice would not be considered masculine in U.S. culture, although earrings, once considered a mark of femininity, are now commonplace symbols of masculinity in some U.S. subcultures.

Pressures to conform to conventional gender roles exist in all cultures. At the same time, norms and characteristics are dynamic: Men and women both shape and are shaped by these expectations. We can think of gender roles as being continuously learned and relearned through social interaction (Fenstermaker & West, 2002). That is, they are neither biologically determined nor passively acquired from others. Rather, each of us plays an active role in learning what it means to be a boy or a girl and a man or a woman in a particular culture. In becoming accomplished actors in our roles, we often forget we are playing parts and become closely identified with the roles themselves. Yet, because we

---

Transgender: An umbrella term used to describe those whose gender identity, expression, or behavior differs from their assigned sex at birth or is outside the gender binary.

Transsexual: A term used to refer to people who use surgery and hormones to change their sex to match their preferred gender.

watching less television than in the past, research also suggests that many teens are frequent consumers of Netflix and YouTube (McAlone, 2017).

Although much has changed in U.S. society in terms of gender roles, media images often appear frozen in time, persistently producing domestic or highly sexualized images of women—or highlighting cattiness and personal deceit, traits that appear frequently on reality TV programs such as the various *Real Housewives* shows and *Dance Moms* as well as on fictional shows like *Pretty Little Liars*. Television images of men are rarely diverse: They are still likely to be portrayed as more aggressive and analytical than women; they also disproportionately occupy fictional positions of leadership, whether in business, politics, or the media (think of programs such as *Mad Men* and *House of Cards*).

Cartoons also convey gendered images. One study found that male cartoon characters outnumber female characters four to one—the same ratio as 25 years before. Moreover, male cartoon characters tend to be powerful, dominant, smart, and aggressive; female characters are more likely to lack personalities altogether (Spicher & Hudak, 1997; Thompson & Scantlin, 2007). Other research has found that male cartoon characters use more physical aggression, while females are more likely to display behaviors that are fearful, polite and supportive, or romantic (Gokcearslan, 2010; Leaper, Breed, Hoffman, & Perlman, 2002). Researchers draw attention not only to how characters look and what they do, but also what they say. A recent linguistic analysis of several decades of Disney princess films uncovered a striking finding: In Disney's older "classic" princess films, female characters were more likely to speak than female characters in newer Disney films. For example, in *Cinderella* (1950), women spoke about 60% of lines. In *The Little Mermaid* (1989), female characters spoke 32% of the time, and in *Mulan* (1998), 23% of the time. In the hit film *Frozen* (2013), two young princesses take center stage, but female characters have 41% of spoken lines (Guo, 2016).

In another study, researchers examined accounts of heterosexuality in media for children by analyzing G-rated films grossing $100 million dollars or more between 1990 and 2005. The study found that, first, heterosexuality is constructed through hetero-romantic love relationships as exceptional, magical, and transformative. Second, heterosexuality outside of relationships is constructed through portrayals of men gazing desirously at women's bodies. Male characters are usually clothed, while the female characters are shown with deep cleavage, visible stomachs, and lean bodies (Martin & Kazyak, 2009). Nevertheless, newer Disney movies may be challenging how female characters are portrayed on screen: *Moana* (2016) did not involve a love interest, but a journey of a young girl trying to save her island.

Data suggest that the popular music industry is rife with gender stereotypes. Wallis (2011) and Turner (2011) found that popular music videos tend to portray women as sex objects who are submissive in relationships with men. Indeed, as Aubrey and Frisby (2011) point out, "although sexual objectification is commonplace in media culture, music videos provide the most potent examples of it" (p. 475). Caputi (2014) notes the sexism inherent in the way that young female pop stars are branded, with the media hypersexualizing them and subjecting their romantic relationships to intense scrutiny. Although research finds the objectification of women in the music industry to be strongest in hip-hop and pop music, it can be observed across genres (Aubrey & Frisby, 2011). Moreover, because music videos today are often viewed online and on mobile devices in addition to the more traditional outlets of television channels such as MTV, these gendered images reach a wider audience than they might have even a decade ago.

Video games offer a rich area for research on media and socialization. By some estimates, fully 91% of children ages 2 to 17 play video games. The majority of gamers are male, though the proportion of girls has been growing, and the percentage of players among the very young has also risen, particularly as more gaming has moved to mobile devices (NPD Group, 2011). This is significant because content studies suggest that popular video games consistently convey stereotypical gender images. Downs and Smith (2010), in an analysis of 60 video games with a total of 489 characters, determined that women were likely to be presented in hypersexualized ways that included being partially nude or wearing revealing attire. Reflecting common findings that men are *action* figures while women are largely *passive*, Haninger and Thompson (2004) discovered that in the 81 teen-rated games they sampled, fully 72 had playable male characters, while only 42 had playable female characters. Interestingly, among adults who play video games, the perception of gender representation is mixed: A recent study

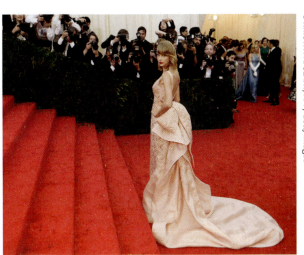

The media takes an intense interest in the love life of singer Taylor Swift. Are the personal lives of male celebrities subject to the same scrutiny as those of female celebrities such as Swift?

©TIMOTHY A. CLARY/AFP/Getty Images

found that 26% of all players and 35% of frequent players (those who labeled themselves *gamers*) do not think women are portrayed poorly in most games. Another 16% of players and 24% of gamers agreed that women are portrayed poorly in most games (Duggan, 2015).

In an age of growing media influence, when stories and images and ideas reach us not only through television, films, and games but also through computers, smartphones, and other devices, it is important to consider what kinds of gender images are conveyed. Do new media sources offer more diverse images? Are old stereotypes still pervasive? What do you think?

Gender in the Classroom: Schools and Socialization

According to some researchers, in addition to providing instruction in basic subjects, schools are an important site of a "hidden curriculum," the unspoken socialization to norms, values, and roles—including gender roles (Basow, 2004; Margolis, 2001). For example, there is evidence that from an early age, shyness is discouraged in boys at school because it is viewed as violating the masculine norm of assertiveness (Doey, Coplan, & Kingsbury, 2013). The roles of teachers, administrators, and other adults in the school provide some early lessons to students about their future career prospects. Pre-K and elementary teaching is still largely female dominated, and in many elementary schools, the only men are administrators, physical education teachers or coaches, and janitors (Figure 10.1).

Classroom materials reflect gender power and position, too. Books on history, for instance, are still heavily populated by male characters, the great heroes and villains of the global and local past. Until very recently, when books began to present a more diverse cast of historical characters,

women were not viewed as an integral part of the historical record. The vast majority remained silent and invisible, their history subsumed under general descriptions of men's lives. . . . Extraordinary figures like the queens of sixteenth-century Europe or the nineteenth-century reformers in the United States, active agents in their own right, fared no better. Though [they were] sometimes praised for having successfully assumed male roles, traditional, patronizing phrases and denigrating stereotypes abstracted and diminished even their exceptional personalities and experiences. (Zinsser, 1993, p. 3)

Even today, where women and, often, racial and ethnic minorities, appear in history textbooks, they are often shown in special features outside the main text that are more likely to be overlooked. In their book, *Failing at Fairness*

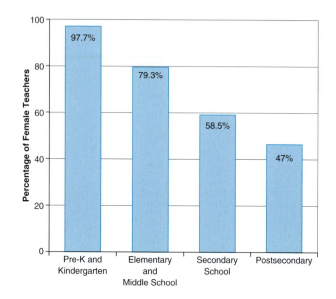

FIGURE 10.1 Percentage of Female Teachers in Educational Occupations, 2017

Source: U.S. Bureau of Labor Statistics. (2017). Retrieved from https://www.bls.gov/cps/cpsaat11.htm.

(1997), David Sadker and Myra Sadker argue that in most history texts, students see few women. Their study of one 819-page text yielded less than a full page of references devoted to women. Another book contained four pictures of men for every one of women, and about 3% of the text was allotted to telling about women.

The authors write about challenging high school seniors to name 20 famous U.S. women, past or present (not including sports or entertainment figures). In the allotted five minutes, most students were able to come up with only a handful, but they had little trouble naming famous men (Sadker & Sadker, 1997). Important changes have taken place in the teaching of history since Sadker and Sadker's work. For instance, the advanced placement U.S. history curriculum devotes considerable space to women's rights movements. Have these changes altered the gender landscape in U.S. history teaching and learning? How would you perform in a quiz similar to that administered by the Sadkers to students in 1997, and what sociological factors would you cite to explain your performance?

History is not the only discipline in which women's images and voices are underrepresented. A recent study found that only 23% of people mentioned in introductory economic books, real or fictional, were female (Stevenson & Zlotnick, 2018). Even the most female-friendly textbook in the study only had a 25% share of female representation. The study also found that even when females were mentioned, they were more likely to be involved in food, fashion, and household tasks. This phenomenon of women being seldom portrayed in textbooks is a global issue, according to sociologist Rae Blumberg, who has studied textbooks from around the world and has found that the women who are mentioned in textbooks are placed into stereotypical, sub-servient roles (typically domestic) or are not mentioned at all. By contrast, boys are portrayed as strong and intelligent workers (Singh, 2015).

Doing Gender

Sociologists commonly define *gender* as a product of agents of socialization, the combined influences of which create gendered selves. The implication is that gender is an internal-ized identity, not natural, but still a fundamental aspect of the social self. Another sociological perspective, described below, suggests that gender is less an identity than an activity.

As we saw in Chapter 4, sociologist Erving Goffman (1959) argued that the social self is the *product* of a social interaction. Thus, the individual engages in impression management to tailor his or her presentation of self in a way most favorable to the given situation. Goffman argued that the individual (or a group) is concerned with defining the situation and ensuring a believable performance.

Goffman's work does not have gender at its center, though some of his examples of impression management are telling. For instance, he illustrated *idealization,* in which we present ourselves in ways that exemplify the values and norms of society, with a young woman choosing not to appear smarter than her male date. Although her decision to play dumb may have gone the way of the 1950s (when Goffman's book was written), it demonstrates how indi-viduals seek to perform gender in accordance with societal expectations. Can you think of contemporary examples of gender performance that we might use to illustrate this idea?

Building on some of Goffman's ideas, Candace West and Don Zimmerman's (1987) article "Doing Gender" suggests that gender is an activity we *do* rather than a fixed identity. West and Zimmerman posit that *sex* is a set of biological cat-egories for classifying people as male or female; a person's **sex category** is the *socially required identification display that confirms his or her membership in a given category,* including displaying and enacting gender as social norms and expec-tations determine. Thus, *gender* is an activity that creates differences between men and women that, although not biological, appear natural because they are so consistently enacted. Membership in a sex category also brings differen-tial access to power and resources, affecting interpersonal relationships and social status.

How do you see the future division of labor in your family? If you are already a spouse or parent, think about your level of satisfaction with how household work is divided in your family. What might you want to change and why?

Gender and Society

Anthropological studies have found that inequalities in almost all known societies, past and present, favor men over women (Huber, 2006). Women are occasionally equal to men economically, politically, or socially, but in no known society do they have greater control over economic and political resources, exercise greater power and authority, or enjoy more prestige than men (Chafetz, 1984). Many sociol-ogists explain this inequality by noting that women alone can give birth to and (particularly important before modern bottle-feeding) nurse infants, two activities essential to a soci-ety's continuation but usually lacking in social status. Given that a major source of power, wealth, and status is the ability to earn money or acquire other material goods of value, any limitations on women's ability to pursue these rewards affects their social position.

In hunting and gathering and early horticultural soci-eties, women produced nearly as much food as men and were more equal in power and prestige, though wealth differences were minimal in such subsistence economies (Huber, 1990, 1993; Mukhopadhyay & Higgins, 1988). With the emergence of agricultural societies and the devel-opment of metallurgy, trade and warfare became much more central features of social organization. Because women spent large portions of their active years pregnant or nursing infants, they were less likely to become mer-chants or warriors. Strong states emerged to manage war-fare and trade, and these were controlled by men. Research suggests that women's status suffered accordingly (Friedl, 1975; Grant, 1991).

In modern industrial societies, the requirements of physical survival, reproduction, and economic organization

Sex category: The socially required identification display that confirms someone's membership in a given category.

no longer exert the same sorts of constraints. The advent of reliable birth control, along with the invention of bottle-feeding around 1910, freed women from long periods of pregnancy and nursing. Mass education, established in most industrial nations by the end of the 19th century, encouraged women to seek knowledge and eventually careers outside the home.

Today, gender stratification persists, but in a rapidly changing and dynamic social environment. Two areas in which we can explore both stasis and change are the family and education.

Gender and Family Life

Domestic tasks—child care, cooking, cleaning, and shopping for necessities of living—can entail long hours of work. In the United States, women still do the disproportionate share of housework and child care. Men are more likely to engage in nonroutine domestic tasks, such as making home repairs, preparing a barbeque, or taking the children on outings.

Attitudes and practices change, although slowly. Just over a generation ago, a study found that fewer than 5% of husbands did as much housework as their wives (Coltrane & Ishii-Kuntz, 1992). In a 15-year study that tracked thousands of men and women born after World War II, Goldscheider and Waite (1991) found that, in two-parent families with teenage boys and girls, girls were assigned five times as many household chores as their brothers.

A 2007 *Time* magazine survey found that 84% of respondents (men and women) agreed that husbands and wives "negotiate the rules, relationships and responsibilities more than those earlier generations did" (Gibbs, 2009). A study by the University of Michigan found that the total amount of housework done by women has fallen since 1976 from an average of 26 hours per week to about 17, while the amount done by men has grown from 6 hours to 13 hours (Achen & Stafford, 2005; Reaney & Goldsmith, 2008).

Clearly, there has been some convergence. Labor-saving devices (such as the microwave oven) have contributed to changes, as has the ability of more dual-earner households to pass the burden of domestic work to housekeepers, gardeners, and the like. At the same time, women are still primarily responsible for domestic work in most two-parent heterosexual households (Davis, Greenstein, & Marks, 2007), a phenomenon Arlie Hochschild (2012) calls the **second shift**—*the unpaid housework women typically do after they come home from their paid employment.* Interestingly, recent research suggests that place of residence—in this case, the state where couples live—has an influence on the household division of labor. Ruppanner and Maume (2016) found that in states where women have more labor market power (measured by, among others, the number of women who are in the paid labor force, are college educated, and work in management), married men are spending more time on domestic tasks. Mothers in these

Second shift: The unpaid housework that women typically do after they come home from their paid employment.

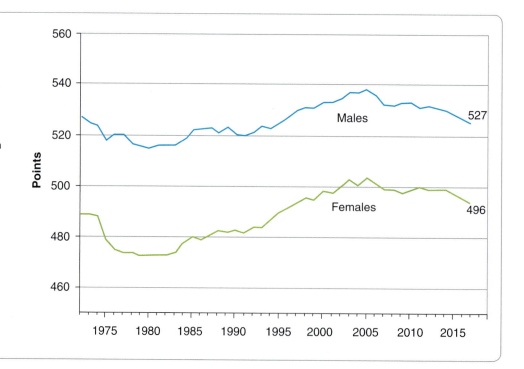

FIGURE 10.2
Average SAT Mathematics Scores for Males and Females, 1972–2017

Source: Reprinted with permission from The American Enterprise Institute.

states, whether or not they work, are spending less time on housework. Conversely, in states with lower female labor market power and greater cultural traditionalism (measured by, for instance, higher church attendance and higher marriage and fertility rates), married men spent less time on housework and mothers devoted more hours to home chores.

Some data show that unmarried women who live with men spend less time on housework than do married women—even when numbers of children and hours of paid work are taken into account (Davis et al., 2007). The division of household labor is also more likely to be equal among lesbian and gay couples (Kurdek, 2007). What might explain these differences? One study with about 17,000 respondents in 28 countries suggests that marriage has a traditionalizing effect on couples, even those who describe themselves and their practices in egalitarian terms (Davis et al., 2007).

Gender and Standardized Tests: Why Do Boys Outscore Girls on the SAT?

Girls outperform boys on many academic measures: earning high grades, enrolling in many of the advanced placement (AP) courses, achieving academic honors, finishing in the top 10% of their class, and graduating, to name a few. One measure where boys have consistently outpaced their female peers, however, is the SAT (originally the Scholastic Aptitude Test, later renamed the Scholastic Assessment Test, and now officially known by the initials SAT). In 2016, the average score for boys on the mathematics section of the SAT was 527 out of 800; girls scored an average of 496. Although both boys' and girls' scores have risen over time (though there has been a decline in recent years), the gap has remained steady (Figure 10.2). Even though boys' advantage on the verbal section of the SAT is smaller, it has also persisted, though girls tend to earn markedly better average grades in courses such as English.

What explains the difference? Some researchers have suggested that the gap points to a gender bias in the test (Sadker & Sadker, 1997; Sadker & Zittleman, 2009). Why, they ask, do boys continue to outscore girls if girls do better in school and continue doing better in college? After all, the SAT is intended to measure college readiness. In a study published in 1989, Rosser argued that girls did better than boys on questions focused on relationships, aesthetics, and the humanities, while boys performed better when questions involved sports, the natural sciences, or business. Rosser's study followed an earlier report by Carol Dwyer of the Educational Testing Service (ETS). Dwyer (1976) concluded that gender differences could be altered through selective use of test items. In an effort to balance the test,

Think back to our discussion of agents of gender socialization. Are there any clues in these materials about why boys outscore girls on standardized math tests such as the SAT?

©Rui Vieira/PA Wire URN:7145753 (Press Association via AP Images)

she reported, ETS added more test items highlighting politics, sports, and business—areas on which boys did better. Questions about whether the test favors boys continue to be raised 40 years later (Sadker & Zittleman, 2009).

Some researchers argue that girls may underperform on math tests because they have been socialized to believe that boys are better at math. This is an example of what researchers call **stereotype threat**, *a situation in which an individual is at risk of confirming a negative stereotype about his or her social group* (Steele & Aronson, 1995). This concept highlights the assertion that a person's performance on a task may be negatively affected by anxiety related to perceived low expectations of the individual's group—such as the expectation that girls are not good at math. One experimental study showed that informing female test takers of stereotype threat before a test improved their performance (Johns, Schmader, & Martens, 2005).

On the other hand, some observers suggest that boys' higher scores on the math section of the SAT are a result of a different phenomenon. Christina Hoff Sommers (2000) argues that more girls—and girls representing more varying levels of achievement and ability—take the test, explaining their lower average score. Boys' higher average score, suggests Hoff, is the product of a limited pool of test takers representing the best-prepared young men.

Is the SAT gender biased because it shows boys outperforming girls, even though girls end up earning better grades and dropping out of college less frequently? Or is it evidence of girls' advantages, because girls are more likely to take college entrance exams and go to college? What other factors may be at play here?

Stereotype threat: A situation in which an individual is at risk of confirming a negative stereotype about his or her social group.

■ **FIGURE 10.3** Percentage of the Population 25 and Older with a Bachelor's Degree or Higher by Sex and Age Group, 2014

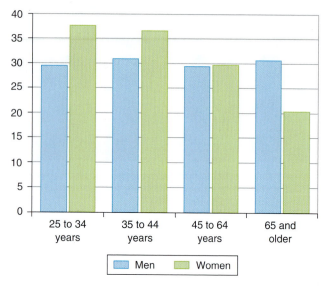

Source: Bauman, K. & C. Ryan. (2015).

Gender and Higher Education

If you attend college on a coed campus and suspect that there are fewer men than women in many of your courses, it's not your imagination. A *New York Times* article about campus life at one school begins as follows:

Another ladies' night, not by choice.

After midnight on a rainy night last week in Chapel Hill, N.C., a large group of sorority women at the University of North Carolina squeezed into the corner booth of a gritty basement bar. Bathed in a neon glow, they splashed beer from pitchers, traded jokes, and belted out lyrics to a Taylor Swift heartache anthem thundering overhead. As a night out, it had everything—except guys.

"This is so typical, like all nights, 10 out of 10," said Kate Andrew, a senior from Albemarle, N.C. The experience has grown tiresome: they slip on tight-fitting tops, hair sculpted, makeup just so, all for the benefit of one another, Ms. Andrew said, "because there are no guys."

North Carolina, with a student body that is nearly 60 percent female, is just one of many large universities that at times feels eerily like a women's college. Women have represented about 57 percent of enrollments at American colleges since at least 2000, according to a report by the American Council on Education. Researchers there cite several reasons: women tend to have higher grades; men tend to drop out in disproportionate numbers; and female enrollment skews higher among older students, low-income students, and Black and Hispanic students. (Williams, 2010, para. 1–4)

Data show the dimensions of the shift toward greater college enrollment among women than men, a trend that holds true, albeit to different degrees, across all major demographic groups: For instance, in 1975, 29% of males and about 24% of females ages 18 to 24 were enrolled in a degree-granting post-secondary institution. Among Whites, the gap in enrollment favored men by about 6 points. Among Black students, it favored women by 1 point and among Hispanics, it favored men by 2 points. In 2015, more women were enrolled (43%) than men (38%). Among White students, there was a 5-point gap in enrollment between females and males; among Black students, a 1-point gap; and among Hispanic students, an 8-point gap (National Center for Education Statistics, 2016a).

Today, more women than men also hold bachelor's degrees. The difference in the population as a whole is small: 29.9% of men and 30.2% of women have completed a bachelor's degree. The gap in younger age groups (24–34) has grown: over 37% of women hold bachelor's degrees compared to just under 30% of men (Figure 10.3; Bauman & Ryan, 2015).

In decades and centuries past, women were actively discouraged from pursuing higher education. In the late 19th century, powerful social barriers stood in the way, such as beliefs about women's capacity to succeed at *both* education and reproduction. Some believed that the "ovaries—not the brain—were the most important organ in a woman's body" (Brumberg, 1997). Author Joan Brumberg (1997) writes,

The most persuasive spokesperson for this point of view was Dr. Edward Clarke, a highly regarded professor at Harvard Medical School, whose popular book *Sex in Education; Or, A Fair Chance for the Girls* (1873) was a powerful statement of the ideology of "ovarian determinism." In a series of case studies drawn from his clinical practice, Clarke described adolescent women whose menstrual cycles, reproductive capacity, and general health were all ruined, in his opinion, by inattention to their special monthly demands [menstruation]. . . . Clarke argued against higher education because he believed women's bodies were more complicated than men's; this difference meant that young girls needed time and ease to develop, free from the drain of intellectual activity. (p. 8)

Although the idea of a "brain–womb conflict" faded as the United States entered the 20th century, other beliefs persisted. Ordinary families with resources to support college study were more likely to invest them in their sons, who were expected to be their future families' primary breadwinners. Families that did seek education for their daughters ran into structural barriers. For example, until the passage of Title IX in 1972, some U.S. colleges and universities, particularly at the graduate and professional school level, limited or prohibited female enrollment. Title IX is often associated with increasing equity in women's access to collegiate athletic opportunities. It is, however, a much broader mandate, as it foresees gender equity for men and women in every educational program receiving federal funding.

Women's representation among bachelor's graduates has soared in recent decades. It has risen considerably as well in professional degrees (Figure 10.4). In 1972, women earned only 7% of law degrees and 9% of medical degrees in the United States (National Organization for Women, n.d.). According to the American Bar Association (2014), in 2013, women earned 47% of the law degrees conferred. In 2017, women were 48% of medical school graduates in the United States (Kaiser Family Foundation).

The *proportion* of women enrolled in college has been greater than the proportion of men since 1991, though the actual *numbers* of women have been greater since the early 1980s, since women make up a larger share of the population. Women's climb to equality in educational opportunity has been long, but their gains in higher education since Title IX have been dramatic. At the same time, men's higher education gains have slowed.

Researchers suggest several reasons for the growing college enrollment gap. First, a high school degree is a prerequisite to college, and significantly more men than women leave high school without diplomas. In high school, as well as college, struggles have been attributed in some instances not to differences in "cognitive abilities," which are comparable in boys and girls, but rather to differences in "'non-cognitive skills' among boys, including the inability to pay attention in class, to work with others, to organize and keep track of homework or class materials and to seek help from others" (Jacob, 2002, p. 4). Boys are also more likely than girls to have behavioral or disciplinary problems that lead to dropping out before completion of high school (Stearns & Glennie, 2006).

■ **FIGURE 10.4** Percentage of male and female high school graduates enrolling in college, 1994 and 2012

Share of recent high school completers enrolled in college the following October

Hispanic	Women	Men	% point gap, women/men
1994	52%	52%	0
2012	76	62	+13 women
Black			
1994	48	56	+9 men
2012	69	57	+12 women
White			
1994	66	62	+4 women
2012	72	62	+10 women
Asian			
1994	81	82	+1 men
2012	86	83	+3 women

Source: Ryan, Camille L. and Kurt Bauman. "Educational Attainment in the United States: 2015." United States Census Bureau, March, 2016.

Second, and related in some respects to the noncognitive factors noted above, young women as a group have higher grades than young men, a factor that is predictive of college matriculation and success: A large-scale study found that the mean high school grade point average for female students was 3.1 of a possible 4.0, while for male students it was 2.9 (National Center for Education Statistics, 2009).

Third, women perceive college as bringing greater returns. A Pew Research Center survey found that women are more likely than men to say college was "very useful" in increasing their knowledge and helping them grow intellectually (81% compared to 67%) as well as helping them grow and mature as a person (73% compared to 64%). Perceptions about the necessity of a college education for getting ahead in life were also split by gender: 77% of respondents indicated this was true for women, while 68% felt it was true for men (Wang & Parker, 2011).

Indeed, the benefits of a college education have grown for women (Goldin, Katz, & Kuziemko, 2006),

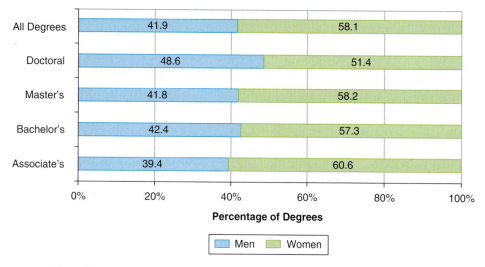

■ **FIGURE 10.5** U.S. College Degree Gap in Favor of Women, 2016

	Men	Women
All Degrees	41.9	58.1
Doctoral	48.6	51.4
Master's	41.8	58.2
Bachelor's	42.4	57.3
Associate's	39.4	60.6

Source: "Digest of Education Statistics." National Center for Education Statistics, U.S. Department of Education.

and they may be more motivated to use college as a stepping-stone to a desired job. A recent study (Olivieri, 2014) makes this argument based on the observation that in the last half century, women have made significant inroads into historically male-dominated occupations: According to the author's calculations, of all White women who were either staying home or employed in 1960, only 8% were in male-dominated occupations. In 2010, fully 29% worked in these occupations, which include physicians, lawyers, managers, and scientists. By contrast, the proportion of men in female-dominated occupations such as teaching and nursing has remained low. Olivieri concludes that sexism is at the foundation of this phenomenon: Even though women are occupying a greater share of historically male jobs that require a college education, sexist notions about masculinity and women's jobs are keeping men from pursuing other occupations—including in growing fields such as nursing—that need a college credential. Rather, men may be choosing other historically masculine fields such as construction and manufacturing, even though those sectors have seen declines in recent decades.

Finally, men are more likely than women to leave college without finishing a degree (Figure 10.5). One study points to the pivotal role of student debt in this process. For most American college students, the ability to secure loans has become a prerequisite to entering college. For some, mounting debt during their undergraduate years leads to a rethinking of the benefit of the degree versus dropping out to enter the workforce. Data suggest that men may be more averse than women to accruing debt: Men drop out with lower levels of debt than women do, but they are also more likely to leave before graduating (Dwyer, Hodson, & McCloud, 2013).

As we have noted above, there are identifiable factors that help us understand the growing gap between men and women in college attendance and completion. Notably, however, the picture becomes more complex when we look not only at gender but also sexuality.

Recent U.S. Department of Education data show that women have a lower probability of acceptance to many private elite colleges than their male peers. Because private institutions are exempt from Title IX prohibitions against discrimination on the basis of gender, some schools may choose to "balance" their admitted classes between men and women, even when more qualified women apply.

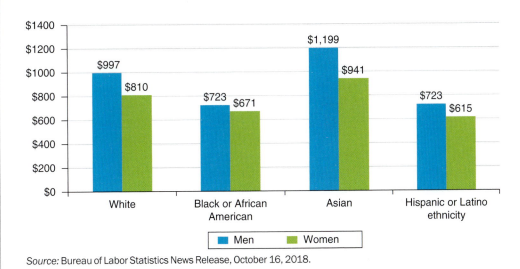

■ **FIGURE 10.6** Median Weekly Earnings of Full-Time Workers, by Race/Ethnicity and Gender, First Quarter of 2018

Source: Bureau of Labor Statistics News Release, October 16, 2018.

Recent research suggests that the probability of college completion is reversed when we look at gay men and lesbian women: Gay men are more likely to finish college than their heterosexual male and female peers, and lesbian women are less likely to complete their higher education than either gay men or heterosexual men and women. One study found that homosexual men had a 44% probability of completing a college degree by age 30, while heterosexual men had a 28% probability of doing the same. Among women, however, heterosexual women had a 34% probability of completion by age 30, while homosexual women's probability was only 24% (Fine, 2012). How might sociologists study these differences? How might they go about explaining them?

Gender and Economics: Men, Women, and the Gender Wage Gap

Given their rising achievements in education, are women enjoying earnings that equal or surpass those of men? Women have made tremendous gains in the workplace, but in the United States and across the globe, they continue to lag behind men in earnings in most occupational categories. The **gender wage gap** is *the difference between*

the earnings of women who work full-time year-round as a group and those of men who work full-time year-round as a group. It exists across all men as a group and all women as a group and also within racial and ethnic groups (Figure 10.6). Why does it persist?

At the end of the 19th century, only one in five women age 16 or older was paid for her work; most paid female employees were young, unmarried, or poor (often all three) and held very-low-wage jobs. By 1950, five years after the end of World War II, the proportion of American women working outside the home for pay rose to one third. The enormous economic expansion that continued through the 1970s drew even more women into the paid workforce, attracted by higher pay and supported by the passage of laws such as the Equal Pay Act of 1963, which made unequal pay for doing the same job illegal. Women's educational gains also opened up more professional and well-paid positions to them. By 1980, more than half of U.S. women were in the paid workforce.

At the beginning of the 20th century, median earnings for women working in full-time, year-round jobs were only half as much as those for men. In 1963, they were still only about three fifths as much, but by 1999, the gap had narrowed and women earned just over 72% of the median male wage. These gains were partly the result of postwar "baby boom" women, many of them educated and skilled, entering the workforce and moving into higher-paying jobs as they gained experience.

Gender wage gap: The difference between the earnings of women who work full-time year-round as a group and those of men who work full-time year-round as a group.

An important aspect of the gender wage gap is the fact that *men and women are still* (and more than we might think) *concentrated in different occupations.* Researchers label this phenomenon **occupational segregation by gender**. When we identify the 20 most common occupations for women and for men, only three appear on both lists: "first-line supervisors of retail sales workers; managers, all other; and retail salespersons" (Institute for Women's Policy Research, 2015). Nearly 40% of women are employed in traditionally female occupations, and about 44% of men work in traditionally male occupations (Hegewisch & Liepmann, 2012).

Why does gender occupational segregation exist and persist? To answer this question, we borrow some terms from economics. For the purposes of our analysis, **labor supply factors** *highlight reasons that women or men may prefer particular occupations,* preparing for, pursuing, and accepting these positions in the labor force. **Labor demand factors** *highlight the needs and preferences of the employer.*

Labor supply factors draw our attention to the agency we exercise in choosing a career path and the decisions we make about how and when to be a part of the paid labor force. Several decades ago, many high school– or college-educated working women were likely to work in one of three occupational categories: secretarial work, nursing, and teaching (below the college level). Why were women opting for these occupations? One factor was socialization; women were encouraged to choose feminine occupations, and many did. Another factor was choices women made based on their families' needs: For instance, a schoolteacher's daytime hours and summers off were a good fit with her children's schedules. Today, women are far less limited by either imagination or structural obstacles, as we have seen in the educational and occupational statistics. At the same time, the top 10 jobs most commonly occupied by women today still include several heavily and traditionally feminine jobs done by women since they entered the workforce in large numbers starting in the 1960s and 1970s (see Table 10.1).

We can also use labor supply factors to talk about men's preferences in the workforce. Men are more broadly spread throughout the U.S. Census Bureau's occupational categories than are women, though in many categories, such as engineer and pilot, they make up a substantial share of all workers. Imagine a young man interested in health and medicine. Would he be encouraged to pursue a career as a nurse? There is still a powerful sense in our society that nursing is a female occupation. A study of five popular U.S. medical television shows, including *Grey's Anatomy, Nurse Jackie,* and *Mercy,* found that

common stereotypes that the shows reinforced include the nurse who is mistaken for a doctor and the gay or emasculated male nurse. Male nurses and midwives in the shows tend to suffer condescension from their colleagues and patients and are the object of comedy. (Goodier, 2013)

We even use the term *male nurse* when referring to men in the nursing profession because our default understanding of *nurse* is a woman. Perhaps it is not surprising, then, that men still make up only a small fraction of nurses, though the occupation is growing and offers a wide variety of professional opportunities and specialties.

Labor demand factors highlight what employers need and prefer—employees with **human capital**, *the skills, knowledge, and credentials a person possesses that make him or her valuable in a particular workplace.* A landscaper seeking a partner will want to hire someone with skills in landscaping, an office manager will seek an administrative assistant who is tech savvy and organized, an accounting firm will want a well-trained certified accountant, and a legal firm a well-trained lawyer who has passed the bar. These preferences are not gendered but instead focus on skills, knowledge, and credentials. It is, however, notable that a pay gap exists at every educational level; in a sense, women cannot educate themselves out of the gap (Figure 10.7).

Nevertheless, other labor supply factors may introduce gender more explicitly into employer preferences. For example, some employers believe they will incur higher indirect labor costs by hiring females. **Indirect labor costs** include *the time, training, or money spent when an employee takes time off to care for sick family members, opts for parental leave, arrives at work late, or leaves after receiving employer-provided training.* Because women are

Occupational segregation by gender: The concentration of men and women in different occupations.

Labor supply factors: Factors that highlight reasons that women or men may prefer particular occupations.

Labor demand factors: Factors that highlight the needs and preferences of the employer.

Human capital: The skills, knowledge, and credentials a person possesses that make him or her valuable in a particular workplace.

Indirect labor costs: The time, training, or money spent when an employee takes time off to care for sick family members, opts for parental leave, arrives at work late, or leaves a position after receiving employer-provided training.

TABLE 10.1   Most Common Occupations for U.S. Women and Men (Full-Time), 2015

RANK	MOST COMMON OCCUPATIONS FOR WOMEN	MOST COMMON OCCUPATIONS FOR MEN
1	Secretaries and administrative assistants	First-line supervisors/production and operating
2	Elementary and middle school teachers	Production workers (all others)
3	Registered nurses	Electricians
4	Nursing, psychiatric, and home health aides	General and operations managers
5	First-line supervisors/managers of retail sales workers	Accountants and auditors
6	Customer service representatives	Customer service representatives
7	Managers, all other	Assemblers and fabricators
8	Cashiers	Marketing and sale managers
9	Accountants and auditors	Police and sheriff's patrol officers
10	First-line supervisors/office and admin support workers	First-line supervisors/non-retail sales workers

Source: U.S. Department of Labor. (2015). Most Common Occupations for Women. Retrieved from https://www.dol.gov/wb/stats/most_common_occupations_for_women.htm.

■ **FIGURE 10.7** Average Hourly Wages, by Gender and Education, 2016

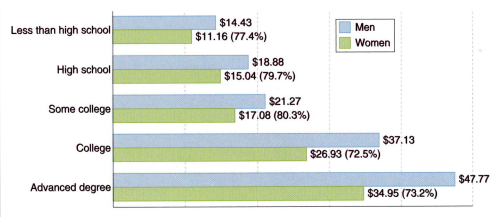

Source: "Women can't educate their way out of the gender wage gap," by Elise Gould and Teresa Kroeger, March 6, 2017. "On average, women are paid less than men at every education level." Washington, DC: Economic Policy Institute. Reprinted with permission.

still associated with the roles of wife and mother, employers may assume they are more likely than men to be costly employees.

Stereotypes may also condition employers' views, especially when jobs are perceived as feminine or masculine. Just as a preschool or child-care center might be wary of hiring a man to work with small children or infants (because women are perceived to be more nurturing), a construction firm might hesitate to hire a woman to head a team of workers (because men are widely perceived to be more comfortable under male leadership).

Looking at labor supply and labor demand factors can help us to sort out how men and women have become concentrated in different occupations. Gender occupational segregation is significant because jobs dominated by men have historically paid more than jobs dominated by women.

That is, those jobs have higher pay scales, which means that men's earnings tend to start higher and end higher than women's earnings.

Even *within* occupational categories, however, men commonly earn more than their female counterparts. Consider a recent study of earnings among doctors in academia, in this case, physicians who teach at U.S. public medical schools. Research on over 10,000 faculty members (65% male, 35% female) at 24 schools found a gender earnings gap: Without accounting for rank and other differences such as specialty and years of residency, male doctors were found to average $257,000 annual salary, while women averaged $206,000. Importantly, even controlling for factors such as rank, age, specialty, publications, years of residency, and research funding, the researchers found a gap of close to $20,000 (Anupam, Olenski, & Blumenthal, 2016). Differences exist across the occupational spectrum. Data show that, for example, in retail sales, a robust field of employment for both men and women, women earn about 70% of what men earn. Among managers and wait staff, women earn about 82% of men's earnings. Even in fields where women make up a significant share of all employees, men outearn their female peers: For instance, among registered nurses, women earn 90% of men's earnings (Institute for Women's Policy Research, 2015).

What explains these differences within occupations? First, although the Equal Pay Act of 1963 made it illegal to pay men and women different wages for the same work, differences have been documented in fields from journalism to construction to academia. For example, a recent study of several major media outlets, including the *Wall Street Journal* and *Barron's*, which are owned by Dow Jones, found that, "'male reporters' at the company typically make 11 percent more than female reporters. . . . Male 'senior special writers,' a high-level distinction, also outearn their female counterparts by 11 percent" (Paquette, 2016, para. 15). As we note in the *Social Life, Social Media* box in this chapter, many employees do not know what their colleagues earn and are hesitant to ask, raising the risk that differences could persist unbeknownst to workers.

Second, in some occupations, men and women concentrate in different specialties, with men tending to occupy the most lucrative sectors. For instance, male physicians are more likely than females to specialize in cardiology, which pays better than areas where women tend to concentrate, such as pediatrics and obstetrics. Similarly, women real estate agents are more likely to sell residential properties, while men are more likely to sell commercial properties, which bring in higher profits and commissions. Even among restaurant servers, men tend to concentrate in high-end restaurants, while women dominate in diners and chain restaurants.

Third, economist Claudia Goldin (2014) suggests that a key factor in understanding the wage gap both within occupations and more broadly is *temporal flexibility*. She argues that the persistence of the wage gap lies in how jobs are structured and remunerated: Many women are economically disadvantaged by their need or desire for flexibility in work hours. Women may work a comparable number of hours to men, but they are less likely to work odd hours or be willing or able to be available at any hour. Some writers have described this as a "caregiving penalty" (Slaughter, 2015), as the lack of women workers' flexibility is usually linked to their obligations to children or aging parents. Goldin suggests that "the gender gap in pay would be considerably reduced and might vanish altogether if firms did not have an incentive to disproportionately reward individuals who labored long hours and worked particular hours" (Goldin, 2014, p. 1091)

Finally, sociologist Christine Williams's (1995) work points to ways in which men who work in traditionally women's fields, such as librarianship, social work, nursing, and elementary school teaching, benefit from a **glass escalator**, a *nearly invisible promotional boost that men gain in female-dominated occupations*. Williams found that bosses often presumed that the men in her study wanted to move up—for example, a teacher is assumed to want an administrative position or a nurse is assumed to want to be a head nurse. Many of the men were put on promotional tracks even when they were ambivalent about leaving positions in which they felt satisfied. Nevertheless, it should be noted that men experience the glass escalator effect differently based on their race. Wingfield (2008), for example, found that African American male nurses did not benefit from their gender in the same way that White male nurses did.

The concept of the glass escalator recalls one final concept that may illuminate gender disparities in the workplace: the glass ceiling. When it comes to the positions with the highest status and pay, data suggest that qualified women may still encounter a **glass ceiling**, *an artificial boundary that allows women to see the next occupational or salary level even as structural obstacles keep them from reaching it*. A study of 1,200 executives in eight countries, including the United States, Austria, and Australia, found that a substantial proportion of women (70%) and

---

Glass escalator: The nearly invisible promotional boost that men gain in female-dominated occupations.

Glass ceiling: An artificial boundary that allows women to see the next occupational or salary level even as structural obstacles keep them from reaching it.

Inequality Matters

THE QUEEN AND HER PRINCE: A STORY OF THE GENDER WAGE GAP

In the spring of 2018, it was reported in the press that the queen was earning a smaller paycheck than her fair prince. As the popular Netflix series, *The Crown*, a dramatized historical story of England's Queen Elizabeth, enjoyed a second successful season, a scandal arose over the revelation that the program's lead actress, Claire Foy, who plays the queen, was being paid less than actor Matt Smith, who plays her husband, Prince Phillip. Foy was, according to reports, earning $13,760 less than her co-star. The producers explained that Matt Smith, formerly associated with the program *Doctor Who*, was

©Pictorial Press Ltd / Alamy Stock Photo

better known than his co-star. At the same time, Foy has had markedly more screen time in the series than her co-star (Zhou, 2018). The producers made a decision after the revelation that they would pay Foy the difference, which added up to $275,000. In the words of one of the producers, "Going forward, no one gets paid more than the Queen" (Singer, 2018, para. 2).

The story of the queen and her prince, however, is consistent with the wage gap that characterizes Hollywood, and few women outearn their male co-stars. As a recent *Vanity Fair* article points out,

> Hollywood has proven that it is an industry marked by an extraordinary gender wage gap. Just look at the disparity between the top-earning actresses and actors on *Forbes*'s annual highest-paid lists: last year, Mark Wahlberg was at No. 1 on the actors' list with $68 million, while the highest-earning actress, Emma Stone, made a comparatively paltry $26 million (Desta, 2018, para. 1). Stone's pay, in fact, is closest to that of the male actor who is 15th on the best-paid actors list. (Rothman & Korn, 2017)

What explains the sometimes-dramatic discrepancies in pay between female and male co-stars? In some instances, one of the actors is significantly better-known than the other and may be considered

the primary box-office or TV screen draw for an audience. Another factor is that there are fewer roles for women in the big-budget action films that tend to showcase male leads, though a recent exception to that was Jennifer Lawrence, whose earnings rose considerably after the release of the first *Hunger Games* film (Rothman & Korn, 2017). In some instances, it appears to be the case that women have been paid less because the entertainment industry has made it possible to pay them less. That is, there have not been major consequences in terms of talent recruitment or poor publicity to end the practice. Importantly as well, female actresses have not felt empowered to speak out about pay inequality, lest they be labelled as uncooperative, difficulty, or bitchy. This may, however, be changing: As actress Claire Foy commented after the pay gap between the queen and the prince on *The Crown* was revealed, the episode taught her "to feel you can be your own advocate, and you can make a point, and you can say something without it being you being 'difficult'" (Singer, 2018, para. 3).

Think It Through

- How do societal labels or expectations affect women's ability to negotiate higher pay, whether in the entertainment industry or other occupational sectors? How, in light of this, can fair pay be achieved?

Gender, Race, Ethnicity, and the Wage Gap

In the section above, you learned about the gender wage gap and some of the key sociological roots of this phenomenon. Data, as you saw, show that this difference varies by race and ethnicity: For instance, Asian American women as a group earn about 93% of White men's earnings; White women earn about 82% of the White male wage; Black women earn about 68% of the White male wage; and Hispanic women earn about 62% of the White male wage (Hegewisch & Williams-Baron, 2018). Can you use what you learned in this chapter and our earlier chapter on race and ethnicity (Chapter 9) to hypothesize differences not only between women and men, but between women of different racial and ethnic groups?

a majority of men (57%) agreed that a glass ceiling prevents women from moving ahead in the business hierarchy (Clark, 2006). They may be correct; women occupied only 23 chief executive officer positions in the *Fortune* 500 companies in 2015 (Bellstrom, 2015).

In this section, we have reviewed some key aspects of the gender wage gap. Although it is a persistent problem in the United States, women have made tremendous strides toward closing the gap: Legal protection against discrimination and high rates of women's college completion are among the factors that have contributed to improvements in women's economic status. Notably, however, a part of the declining gap can also be attributed to men's worsening labor market position, a topic we will cover in greater detail in Chapter 15. Wages of men without a college education have been on the decline in recent decades, as well-paying jobs in sectors such as manufacturing have been automated or moved to lower-wage areas abroad. A decreasing pay gap, then, is attributable to improvements for women—but also diminished economic prospects for some men.

Classical Theories, Feminist Thought, and the Sociology of Masculinities

Until the middle of the 20th century, most sociological theories assumed that existing sex roles and norms were natural and, by extension, positively functional for society.

Contemporary scholarship, particularly by feminist sociologists, challenges this perspective, taking a critical look at both the genesis and consequences of rigid gender rules and roles.

Classical Sociological Approaches to Gender

For the founding fathers of sociology, whom we met in Chapter 1, gender stratification was all but invisible. Although Friedrich Engels addressed women's experience of inequalities, a common theme was that men and women were organically suited to the (unequal) gender roles in European society. Auguste Comte and Émile Durkheim drew on earlier philosophers, including Jean-Jacques Rousseau, to argue that women were best suited to private family roles such as nurturance and child rearing and were naturally subordinate to men. Men were seen as possessing inherent advantages in such spheres as science, industry, and government (Comte, 1975; Durkheim, 1895/1964).

To a significant degree, these perspectives were rooted in now-dated understandings of human physiology. In one popular theory, women were reported to have smaller brain capacity than men based on their relative skull sizes. (By this standard, elephants should be more intelligent than humans, because their skulls are larger.) Because of ostensible differences in brain size, men were assumed to be biologically more rational, with an advantage in pursuits that required reasoning and logic, such as business and governance. Women were seen as inherently more emotional and better at pursuits requiring emotional skills, such as nurturing.

Few women's voices were present in early sociology. Charlotte Perkins Gilman (1898/2006) was one of the first female and feminist sociologists. Gilman viewed heterosexual marriage between males and females as a *sexuoeconomic relation*: Women were expected to be financially dependent on men, and in turn, to serve as caregivers for their husbands and children. Women's gender socialization included significant pressure to find husbands, who in turn felt obligated to support their wives. Thus, the sexual relationship between men and women also became an economic one, with negative effects for the relationship as well as women's autonomy.

Until the middle of the 20th century, some sociologists argued that sex-role differences—whether biological or social in origin—were positively functional for social harmony, order, and stability. For example, functionalist sociologist Talcott Parsons offered a theory of sex roles in the U.S. kinship system that sought to explain them in terms of their functionality for family and society (Parsons, 1954; Parsons & Bales, 1955). Parsons argued that in a modern capitalist society, women make their contribution by raising children and maintaining the family unit; men do so by earning the family income through outside labor. Parsons did not attribute this role specialization to biology; rather, he argued, women were socialized in the family to acquire expressive qualities needed in the private sphere of the home, such as sympathy and emotionality. Men were socialized into instrumental qualities, such as rationality and competitiveness, which were needed for the capitalist workplace. Competition for standing in the family was avoided with a division of roles, and the family's status in society was clear because it derived from the man's position in the workforce. Sex roles, suggested Parsons, functioned positively on both the micro (family) and macro (society) levels.

Feminist theorists rejected Parsons's theory. Although he recognized sex roles as the product of socialization rather than of nature, his perspective appeared to justify what many feminists saw as fundamentally unequal positions in society. In a capitalist society, power derives from the ability to earn independently, and the role Parsons foresaw for women was one of economic and social dependence.

Contemporary U.S. Feminist Thinking on Gender

If you were a woman . . . 40 years ago, the odds were good that your husband provided the money to buy [this magazine]. That you voted the same way he did. That if you got breast cancer, he might be asked to sign the form authorizing a mastectomy. That your son was heading to college but not your daughter. That your boss, if you had a job, could explain that he was paying you less because, after all, you were probably working just for pocket money. (Gibbs, 2009, para. 1)

The fact that the world looks fundamentally different today is, to a large degree, thanks to the feminist movements of both the distant and the recent past.

Feminism is *the belief that social equality should exist between the sexes*; the term also refers to *social movements aimed at achieving that goal*. Feminism is directly tied to both analysis and action. It seeks to explain, expose, and eliminate **sexism**, *the belief that one sex is innately superior to the other and is therefore justified in having a dominant social position*. In the United States and most other societies,

sexism takes the form of men's dominance over women. Feminists seek to analyze why it exists and how it can be eliminated.

Feminism emerged in the United States in connection with *abolitionism*, the campaign to end slavery in the 1830s; this movement gave birth to the struggle by women to achieve basic rights, including the right to vote and own land. The first wave of feminism began in 1848, when Elizabeth Cady Stanton and Lucretia Mott organized a convention in Seneca Falls, New York, to pursue women's expanded rights. Although their efforts were a landmark in women's history, the results they sought were achieved only much later (women did not gain the vote in the United States until 1920). Feminist activism was limited to a small group of women and their male supporters in an environment that saw sex differences as natural.

The 1963 publication of Betty Friedan's *The Feminine Mystique,* which argued that rigid stereotypes of femininity distorted women's real-life experiences and contributed to their unhappiness, helped initiate the second wave of the women's movement, with social theorizing and activism that was much broader in scope (Bernard, 1981, 1982; Friedan, 1963, 1981). Women's experiences in the civil rights and anti–Vietnam War social movements also helped shape a growing feminist consciousness.

The second wave, like the first, called for the equal treatment of women. Women and men were to be viewed not as fundamentally different but as similar; given equal opportunity, women would show themselves the equals of men in all respects. This revival of feminist thinking strongly appealed to the growing number of well-educated, professional women drawn to work and public life during the 1960s (Buechler, 1990), and an explosion of feminist thinking and activism followed.

Women in their 20s, 30s, and 40s today came of age after the feminist social movement had already made great strides and are less likely to have experienced the same degree of discrimination as their predecessors. At the same time, although only about a quarter of U.S. women describe themselves as *feminist*, more than two thirds believe the women's movement has made their lives better—including 75% of women under age 35. Furthermore, 82% believe that the status of women has

---

Feminism: The belief that social equality should exist between the sexes; also, the social movements aimed at achieving that goal.

Sexism: The belief that one sex is innately superior to the other and is therefore justified in having a dominant social position.

improved over the past 25 years, and about half of all younger women believe there is still a need for a strong women's movement (Alfano, 2009).

Several broad streams of feminist thinking agree on the importance of basic economic, social, and political equality for women—equal pay for equal work and the sharing of housework. They differ in their analyses of the causes of inequality, however, and in the solutions they propose. Below, we provide a brief overview of feminism's varied manifestations.

Liberal feminism, reflected in the work of Betty Friedan and those who followed her lead, holds that *women's inequality is primarily the result of imperfect institutions, which can be corrected by reforms that do not fundamentally alter society itself*. To eliminate this inequality, liberal feminists have fought to elect women to the U.S. House and Senate, to enact legislation to ensure equal pay for equal work, and to protect women's rights to make choices about their fertility and their family lives.

As its name implies, **socialist feminism** is rooted in the socialist tradition. It is deeply critical of capitalist institutions and practices and regards *women's inequality as the result of the combination of capitalistic economic relations and male domination (patriarchy), arguing that both must be fundamentally transformed before women can achieve equality* (Chafetz, 1997). This viewpoint originated in the writings of Marx and Engels, who argued that inequality, including that of women, is an inevitable feature of capitalism. Engels (1884/1942), for example, sought to demonstrate that the family unit was historically based on the exploitation and male "ownership" of women (the practice of a father "giving away" his daughter in marriage is rooted in the symbolic "giving" of a young woman from one keeper to a new one). Socialist feminism in the United States emerged in the 1960s, when liberal feminists became frustrated by the pace of social reform and sought to address more fundamental sources of women's oppression (Hartmann, 1984; Jaggar, 1983; MacKinnon, 1982; Rowbotham, 1973).

Some feminists also grew frustrated with the civil rights and antiwar organizations of the 1960s and 1970s, which were headed by male leaders who often treated women as second-class citizens. Mindful that full equality for women has yet to be achieved in any existing political or economic system, **radical feminism** argues that *women's inequality underlies all other forms of inequality*. Radical feminists point to gender inequality in the economy, religion, and other institutions to argue that relations between the sexes must be radically transformed before women can hope to achieve true equality. Radical feminists thus focus their attention on the nature of **patriarchy**, *any set of social relationships in which men dominate women*, pointing to male dominance in economics and politics as chief examples.

Radical feminists argue that if patriarchal norms and values go unchallenged, many women will accept them as normal, even natural. Thus, although men should also work to end male domination, it is only by joining with other women that women can empower themselves. Radical feminists advocate all-women efforts to provide shelters for battered women, rape crisis intervention, and other issues that affect women directly (Barry, 1979; Dworkin, 1981, 1987, 1989; Faludi, 1991; Firestone, 1971; Griffin, 1978, 1979, 1981; Millett, 1970).

Multicultural feminism aims to *understand and end inequality for all women, regardless of race, class, nationality, age, sexual orientation, physical ability, or other characteristics* (B. Smith, 1990). Multicultural feminists seek to build coalitions among women, creating international and global organizations, networks, and programs to achieve women's equality. They acknowledge that much of the contemporary women's movement originated among heterosexual, White, and middle- or upper-class women in Europe and North America and that, as a result, its central ideas reflect these women's perspectives. These perspectives are being challenged and changed by feminists of color from Africa, Asia, and Latin America, as well as homosexual, bisexual, queer, and trans women, contributing to an enriched multicultural feminist understanding (Andersen & Collins, 1992; Anzaldúa, 1990; Chafetz, 1997; Narayan & Harding, 2000; Zinn, Weber, Higginbotham, & Dill, 1986).

Third-wave feminism emerged in the early 1990s as a response to some of the perceived shortcomings of second-wave feminism but also as a product of changing societal norms and opportunities—and the Internet. Although

---

Liberal feminism: The belief that women's inequality is primarily the result of imperfect institutions, which can be corrected by reforms that do not fundamentally alter society itself.

Socialist feminism: The belief that women's inequality results from the combination of capitalistic economic relations and male domination (patriarchy), arguing that both must be fundamentally transformed before women can achieve equality.

Radical feminism: The belief that women's inequality underlies all other forms of inequality, including economic inequality.

Patriarchy: Any set of social relationships in which men dominate women.

Multicultural feminism: The belief that inequality must be understood—and ended—for all women, regardless of race, class, nationality, age, sexual orientation, physical ability, or other characteristics.

third-wave feminists have paid significant attention to issues such as gendered violence and reproductive rights, they also argue that any issue a feminist finds important can and should be talked about. Choice is a central tenet; whether a woman wants to wear makeup, dress in feminine clothing, and be a stay-at-home mother or whether she wants to cut her hair short, wear gender-ambiguous clothing, and work in a male-dominated field—any choice is valid. A journalistic exploration of "new wave feminism" suggests that

> this feminism looks different, in many ways, than that of earlier generations. . . . [It] is shaped less by a shared struggle against oppression than by a collective embrace of individual freedoms, concerned less with targeting narrowly defined enemies than with broadening feminism's reach through inclusiveness, and held together not by a handful of national organizations and charismatic leaders but by the invisible bonds of the Internet and social media. (Sheinin, Thompson, McDonald, & Clement, 2016, p. A1)

Interestingly, a recent poll suggests that in the last 20 years, more women are calling themselves *feminists*, though nearly 40% do not identify as feminists at all or call themselves *anti-feminists* (Figure 10.8). Among millennial women, about 63% call themselves *feminists*, a figure higher than that of Generation X women but below the proportion of baby boomer women calling themselves *feminists* (68%; this generation of women is most likely to have been part of the second wave feminist movement).

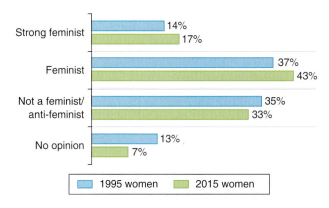

■ FIGURE 10.8 Percentage of People Who Identify as Feminist, 1995 and 2015

Strong feminist: 14% (1995), 17% (2015)
Feminist: 37% (1995), 43% (2015)
Not a feminist/anti-feminist: 35% (1995), 33% (2015)
No opinion: 13% (1995), 7% (2015)

Legend: 1995 women, 2015 women

Source: Sheinin, D., K. Thompson, S.N. McDonald, & S. Clement. (2016). New Wave Feminism. *The Washington Post,* January 31: A1, A17.

Note: 1995 results based on Feminist Majority Foundation poll. Percentages may not add up to 100% due to rounding.

There is also an emphasis on *intersectionality* in the new wave, which recognizes the intersecting identities and oppressions of race, class, gender, sexuality, and so on. "Like much of American society, the feminist agenda has migrated to the Internet, making it at once less centered and communal, but more accessible and democratized" (Sheinin et al., 2016, p. A17).

Do you identify with any of the types of feminism mentioned above? What would you identify as important feminist issues today?

Activists have long sought to bring attention to conditions of female oppression and male dominance. Although mid-20th-century activists (including Bella Abzug) highlighted problems such as limited roles for women outside of motherhood, 21st-century activists have come out against restrictions on women's control of their reproduction and sexual harassment of women in the workplace.

Feminist Perspectives on Doing Sociology

Sociologists Dorothy Smith and Patricia Hill Collins offer valuable perspectives on what it means to do sociology from a feminist perspective, explicitly recognizing women as both subjects and creators of new knowledge. Dorothy Smith (1987, 1990, 2005) is an important contributor to **standpoint theory**, which suggests that *the knowledge we create is conditioned by where we stand or by our subjective social position.* Our sociological picture of the world has emerged from a variety of standpoints, but until recently, they were largely the perspectives of educated and often economically privileged White males. Smith thus suggests that our base of knowledge is incomplete because much of what we know—or think we know—about the social world has come from a limited number of perspectives.

Standpoint theory offers a challenge to the sociological (and general scientific) idea that researchers can be, in Max Weber's words, "value-free." Smith argues that standpoint does matter, since we do not so much *discover* knowledge as we *create* it from data we gather and interpret from our own standpoint. Recall Victorian doctor Edward Clarke's influential book about the brain–womb conflict, positing that higher education could damage young women's reproductive capacity. Could such "knowledge" have emerged from the research of a female physician of that time? Would the theorizing of Karl Marx or Talcott Parsons look the same from a woman's perspective? What do you think?

Patricia Hill Collins (1990) has integrated elements of this idea into her articulation of "Black feminist thought." She offers **standpoint epistemology**, *a philosophical perspective that argues that what we can know is affected by the position we occupy in society.* Epistemology is the study of how we know what we know and how we discern what we believe to be valid knowledge. Collins argues that Black women have long been denied status as agents of knowledge—creators of knowledge about their own lives and experiences. Other groups have used their power to define Black women, creating a picture that is incomplete and disempowering. Collins calls for recognition of Black women as agents of knowledge and the use of Black feminist thought as a tool for resisting oppression.

Collins points to factors that fundamentally affect status and standpoint, including gender, race, class, and sexual orientation. The concept of a **matrix of domination**, *a system of social positions in which any individual may concurrently* *occupy a status (for example, gender, race, class, or sexual orientation) as a member of a dominated group and a status as a member of a dominating group,* highlights this point. Collins (1990) writes that "all groups possess varying amounts of penalty and privilege in one historically created system. . . . Depending on the context, an individual may be an oppressor, a member of an oppressed group, or simultaneously oppressor and oppressed" (p. 225).

Black women's experience of multiple oppressions makes them wary of dominant frames of knowledge, few of which have emerged from their own experience. Thus, Collins argues, comprehensive knowledge is born of a multitude of standpoints, and creation of knowledge is a form of power that should extend across social groups.

The Sociology of Masculinities

Integrating women's voices into contemporary sociology is an important goal and one that is being achieved. At the same time, as sociologist Michael Kimmel (1986) argues, because men still dominate sociology—as well as society—it is also necessary to develop a *sociology of masculinities.* Raewyn Connell (2010) notes that *masculinities* are not the same as *men*, adding that masculinities concern in particular the position of men in the gender order. Among men, status and power are not evenly distributed and may diverge along lines of class, race, and sexuality, among others. Hence, the focus is not on recognizing and analyzing *masculinity* (in the singular) so much as it is on examining the variety of cultural, social, and institutional influences that "make men."

At the same time, there may be a dominant strand of masculinity. Kimmel (1996) follows David and Brannon's (1976) idea that in U.S. culture there are four "basic rules of manhood":

- No "sissy stuff"—avoid any hint of femininity.
- Be a "big deal"—acquire wealth, power, and status.
- Be a "sturdy oak"—never show your emotions.
- "Give 'em hell"—exude a sense of daring and aggressiveness.

These "rules" reflect the concept of *hegemonic masculinity,* the culturally normative idea of male behavior, which often emphasizes strength, control, and aggression (Connell & Messerschmidt, 2005). This is a variety of masculinity that we may recognize in men's sports, such as football. In a

---

Standpoint theory: A perspective that says the knowledge we create is conditioned by where we stand or by our subjective social position.

Standpoint epistemology: A philosophical perspective that argues that what we can know is affected by the position we occupy in society.

Matrix of domination: A system of social positions in which any individual may concurrently occupy a status (for example, gender, race, class, or sexual orientation) as a member of a dominated group and a status as a member of a dominating group.

recent investigative book on brain injuries among football players and the reticence of the National Football League—as well as many players—to acknowledge the risks and injuries to athletes, the authors profile a player, Gary Plummer, who tells them that

> I had been playing football since I was eight years old, and there is nothing more revered in football than being a tough guy. . . . The coaches have euphemisms. They'll say: "You know, that guy has to learn the difference between pain and injury." . . . What he's saying is the guy's a pussy and he needs to get tough or he's not going to be on the team." (quoted in Fainaru-Wada & Fainaru, 2014, pp. 79–80)

Kimmel (1996, 2013) argues that some notions of masculinity are so deeply ingrained in culture that when we discuss social problems such as teen violence (particularly shootings) in U.S. schools, we forget that we are talking almost entirely about the behavior of men. Consider the issue of mass shootings in the United States more generally: A *Washington Post* investigation of "mass shootings" (defined as shootings in which four or more people were killed by a lone shooter, though in three instances, there were two shooters) in the United States over the past 50 years found

that of the 129 shooters, most were ages 20 to 49 and all but three were male (Berkowitz, Gamio, Lu, Uhrmacher, & Lindeman, 2016). As journalist James Hamblin (2016) wrote in the aftermath of the killing of 49 victims at a gay nightclub in Orlando, Florida, in June 2016, "That makes masculinity a more common feature than any of the elements that tend to dominate discourse—religion, race, nationality, political affiliation, or any history of mental illness" (para. 3). What explains this commonalty? Why are men more likely to be mass shooters—or to commit homicide (which is a crime committed by men over 90% of the time; D. Ford, 2015)? Educator Jackson Katz points to the rarity, and importance, of this question by offering a hypothetical scenario: "Imagine if 61 out of 62 mass killings were done by women? Would that be seen as merely incidental and relegated to the margins of discourse? . . . No. It would be the first thing people talked about" (quoted in Murphy, 2012, para. 18).

Some writers suggest that "men's studies"—the study of masculinities—should become as much a part of the college curriculum as "women's studies." In many respects, men are already well integrated into the curriculum: As Kimmel writes, "Every course that isn't in 'women's studies' is de facto a course in men's studies. Except we call it history, political science, literature, chemistry" (2000, pp. 5–6). At the same time, this fails to give scholars and students insight into ways in which masculinities shape boys, men, institutions, and societies. In a recent interview with the *New York Times*, Kimmel suggested that studying masculinity would entail a cross-disciplinary examination of

> what makes men men, and how are we teaching boys to fill those roles? It would look at the effects of race and sexuality on masculine identity and the influence of the media and pop culture. It would also allow scholars to take seemingly unrelated phenomena—male suicide and the fact that men are less likely to talk about their feelings, say, or the financial collapse and the male tendency for risk-taking—and try to connect the dots. (Bennett, 2015, para. 25)

Only by studying the social construction of masculinity can we understand that men are made and not born. And that, sociologists of masculinity believe, is an important step toward achieving gender equality in both attitudes and practices.

Women's Lives in a Global Perspective

Being born a woman is a risk. If you are reading these words in the United States, you might feel that statement is an exaggeration. Certainly, women in the United States are at greater risk than their male counterparts of falling victim

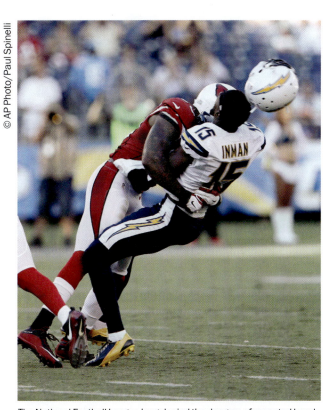

© AP Photo/Paul Spinelli

The National Football League long denied the dangers of repeated head trauma to players' long-term health. A masculine ethic of toughness in the face of injury helped to maintain this position among coaches and players.

to crimes such as sexual assault or rape, of experiencing discrimination in the workplace, or of being subjected to sexual harassment on the street, at work, or in school. U.S. women are also more likely to be poor or uninsured than their female counterparts in other advanced states, including Denmark, France, and Canada. At the same time, as we have seen in this chapter, women have made dramatic gains in areas such as education, which have brought them independence, earning power, and greater workplace opportunities. Women are assuming positions of power in politics, the economy, culture, and education.

In many places across the globe, if you are reading these words, you are likely a male; millions of women are denied education and cannot read. They are at greater risk of being denied medical care, trafficked into the sex trade, and refused the right to own or inherit property. They are less likely than their male counterparts to go to school, to earn wages equivalent to their work, and to eat or get medical care when family resources are scarce. In this section, we highlight issues of gender and equality from a global perspective.

Mothers and Children: The Threat of Maternal Mortality

In a small hospital in Yokadouma, Cameroon, 24-year-old Prudence died in childbirth. Here is a small piece of her story:

> Prudence had been living with her family in a village seventy-five miles away [from the hospital], and she had received no prenatal care. She went into labor at full term, assisted by a traditional birth attendant who had no training. But Prudence's cervix was blocked, and the baby couldn't come out. After three days of labor, the birth attendant sat on Prudence's stomach and jumped up and down. That ruptured Prudence's uterus. The family paid a man with a motorcycle to take Prudence to the hospital. The hospital's doctor . . . realized that she needed an emergency cesarean. But he wanted $100 for the surgery, and Prudence's husband and parents said that they could raise only $20. . . . If she had been a man, the family probably would have sold enough possessions to raise $100. (Kristof & WuDunn, 2009, pp. 109–110)

The dangers of childbirth have been nearly alleviated in industrialized countries, and maternal mortality is a rarity. In many developing countries, however, women have little control over their fertility and childbirth is a persistent risk (Table 10.2). Kristof and WuDunn (2009) write that Prudence died due to a massive infection, but her death can also be linked more broadly to problems such as the lack of schooling, lack of rural health care capacity, and cultural disregard for women.

Women and Education

Educated, literate women are healthier women; there is a strong correlation between education and health that manifests in a variety of ways. For instance, a global study found a conclusive link between greater education of mothers and lower child mortality, as more educated mothers are more likely to understand and practice good hygiene and health practices (Brown, 2010). Declining child mortality in a society further correlates with fewer pregnancies and smaller families; according to the *child survival hypothesis* (Taylor, Newman, & Kelly, 1976), if women feel confident their children will survive, they are less inclined to feel the need for "extra" children to ensure that some reach adulthood.

Education may foster healthier mothering and better care of mothers. A better-educated birth attendant can treat her patient more effectively; she is clearly less likely to sit on a patient's stomach and risk rupturing her uterus. A United Nations Population Fund report on midwifery (2014) suggests that "implementing quality midwifery services could prevent about two thirds of women's and infants' deaths globally," but those states most in need have the fewest trained midwives, nurses, and physicians.

Lack of Rural Health Systems

Kristof and WuDunn (2009) write that

> if Cameroon had a better health care structure, the hospital would have operated on Prudence as soon as she arrived. It would have had powerful antibiotics to treat her infection. It would have trained rural birth attendants in the area, equipped with cell phones to summon an ambulance. Any one of these factors might have saved Prudence. (p. 114)

"Brain drain" is also an obstacle to the development of rural health care systems: Nurses and physicians from developing states are welcomed by wealthier countries experiencing shortages of health care providers, further diminishing access in poorer countries and communities. Consider the dramatic differences in the ratio of physicians to population across the globe, with wealthy countries far more likely to have a significant number of doctors per 1,000 population than poor states (see Table 10.3).

Societal Disregard for Women

Countries where women are marginalized have higher rates of maternal mortality. Indeed, where women have little social, cultural, economic, or political voice, their lives have less significance than those of men, and scarce resources may be directed elsewhere (Hausmann, Tyson, & Zahidi, 2011). In 21st-century China, "39,000 girls die annually . . . because parents don't give them the same medical care and attention that boys receive—and that is just in the first year of life" (Kristof & WuDunn, 2009, p. xiv). The All-India National Family Health Survey recently found that, for instance, about 72% of boys were brought for treatment of acute respiratory infections versus 66% of girls, and boys suffering from diarrhea were 7% more likely to be taken to a health facility than girls with the same problem. Oxfam India reports that the head of pediatrics at a government medical college confirmed this bias, noting, "More boys are vaccinated than girls, even though it is free. Because unlike the Pulse Polio programme, where a health worker goes from home to home to administer the drops, the children have to be brought to a medical facility for these shots. Parents are willing to make the effort for their sons, but not their daughters" (Trivedy, 2015, para. 14).

In spite of the power of some women on the global stage (among others, Democratic presidential nominee Hillary Clinton, recent U.S. secretaries of state Condoleezza Rice and Madeleine Albright, as well as German chancellor Angela Merkel and influential International Monetary Fund head Christine Lagarde of France), women's global voice is still limited. Inadequate funding of "women's concerns," including maternal health initiatives—and perhaps even their definition as *women's concerns* rather than *family* or *national concerns*—speak to the priority they hold.

"Unclean" Women

In many societies, being a girl or a woman is itself a source of social stigma, though the manifestation of that stigma varies across traditions and communities. Consider the following story from rural western Nepal:

> In this corner of Nepal, deep in the Himalayas, women are banished from their homes every month when they get their period. They are considered polluted, even toxic, and an oppressive regime has evolved around this taboo, including the construction of a separate hut for menstruating women to sleep in. Some of the spaces are as tiny as a closet, walls made of mud or rock, basically menstruation foxholes. (Gettleman, 2018, para. 4)

Unmarried women are forced to stay in the huts for six days. Their sisters who have a son and daughter stay for five days, while women who have only daughters are compelled to stay for seven days (Bhattaral, 2018).

The practice of forcing women from their homes during menstruation has been linked to the deaths of girls and women who are exposed to myriad risks. According to one report,

> As they are compelled to sleep in poorly constructed and dirty huts, these women face health problems and other risks. Woman who live in the huts are always at risk of diarrhea, pneumonia, and respiratory diseases. While living in the isolated huts, they also face the danger of attack by wild animals, or even abuse and rape by their fellow villagers (Bhattaral, 2018).

A *New York Times* account of the practice of *chhaupadi* points out that some women have been smothered by smoke in their tiny huts as they tried to stay warm in the bitter Himalayan winter months (Gettleman, 2018).

The dangers of *chhaupadi* have recently evoked action in the country's legislature: Forcing a woman into seclusion during her menstrual period will henceforth be a crime punishable by three months in jail. The ritual banishment, however, is rooted in hundreds of years of history, as well as some fundament Hindi beliefs about purity and pollution (Gettleman, 2018.) It is practiced by

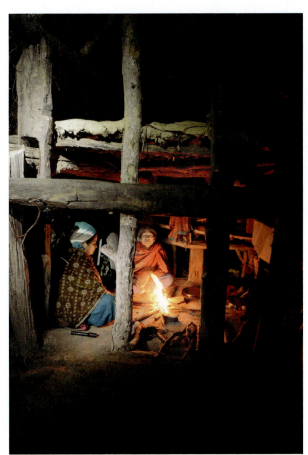

©PRAKASH MATHEMA/AFP/Getty Images

Two Nepalese women attempt to stay warm in a chhaupadi hut.

more than 90% of women in the western regions of Nepal (Bhattaral, 2018). Whether the mandated punishment, which follows on the Nepali Supreme Court's prohibition of the practice in 2005, will improve women's lives remains to be seen.

The Price of (Being) a Girl

On the illicit global market, available goods include weapons, drugs, pirated software and films, and women and girls. Impoverished girls from the developing world are particularly vulnerable to sexual exploitation and trafficking. According to the annual *Trafficking in Persons Report* published by the U.S. Department of State (2012), it is difficult to pin down the extent of this "modern-day slavery." The International Labour Organization, however, estimates that almost 21 million people are victims of forced labor: about 11.4 million women and girls and 9.5 million men and boys (International Labour Organization, n.d.). Of those exploited by individuals or enterprises, 4.5 million are victims of forced sexual exploitation (International Labour Organization, n.d.).

In India, the sex trade and sex trafficking are pervasive (Kara, 2009). A British Broadcasting Corporation (Patel, 2013) examination of Indian brothels told the story of one woman:

> Guddi was only 11 years old when her family was persuaded by a neighbour to send her to the city of Mumbai hundreds of miles away from her poverty-stricken village in the eastern state of West Bengal.
>
> They promised her a well-paid job as a housemaid to help feed her family.
>
> Instead, she ended up at one of Asia's largest red-light districts to become a sex worker.
>
> Trafficked by her neighbour, she arrived at a brothel. She was raped by a customer and spent the next three months in hospital.
>
> Guddi's sad and harrowing story is similar to many of the estimated 20,000 sex workers in Kamathipura, established over 150 years ago during colonial rule as one of Mumbai's "comfort zones" for British soldiers. (para. 1–5)

Kristof and WuDunn (2009) estimate that there are 2 to 3 million prostitutes in India.

TABLE 10.2   Maternal Mortality Rate for Selected Countries, 2015

COUNTRY	MATERNAL DEATHS PER 100,000 LIVE BIRTHS
Cameroon	596
Afghanistan	396
Bangladesh	176
India	174
Brazil	44
China	27
United States	14
Turkey	16
Canada	7
Denmark	6

Source: World Health Organization. (2015). Maternal mortality country profiles. Global Health Observatory (GHO).

TABLE 10.3   Physician Density Rate in Selected Countries, 2011

COUNTRY	PHYSICIANS PER 1,000 POPULATION
Germany	3.50 (2008)
Denmark	3.40 (2007)
Austria	2.99 (2009)
Egypt	2.80 (2009)
United States	2.60 (2004)
Brazil	1.70 (2007)
India	0.59 (2005)
Cameroon	0.19 (2004)
Mali	0.04 (2008)
Afghanistan	0.02 (2009)

Source: World Health Organization. (2011). Health workforce—Aggregated data, density per 1,000. *Data Repository: World Health Statistics.*

Global Issues

FIGHTING SEXTORTION AROUND THE WORLD

The International Association of Women Judges (IAWJ) defines *sextortion* as follows:

When people in positions of authority—whether government officials, judges, educators, law enforcement personnel, or employers—seek to extort sexual favors in exchange for something within their power to grant or withhold. In effect, sextortion is a form of corruption in which sex, rather than money, is the currency of the bribe. (IAWJ, n.d., para. 1)

Although nearly anyone could potentially fall victim to this practice, poor women around the world, according to the United Nations Development Project, are particularly vulnerable

because they may be more dependent on public officials for access to such services as health care, water, or education, and, with lower literacy levels, they may have less awareness of their entitlements to public programs, making them more susceptible to extortion. (as quoted in Bigio, 2016, para. 4).

Although men may also fall victim to this practice, evidence suggests that women are the most likely targets.

Sextortion may take the form of an immigration official demanding sex in exchange for approval of a refugee application or a border crossing, or a United Nations peacekeeper trading relief supplies to desperate women or children in return for sexual favors (Bigio, 2016). A recent Reuters news article reported that the African country of Tanzania was undertaking efforts to combat sextortion after

9 out of 10 women working in the public sector reported sexual harassment, including superiors using positions of power to coerce women into sex (Makoye, 2015).

Sextortion, according to the IAWJ (n.d.), is fundamentally a form of corruption because officers, officials, or others with authority are using their power "for personal benefit rather than with integrity, fairness, and impartiality expected of their position." Notably, sextortion is a form of corruption that is widely recognized anecdotally but poorly tracked in official measures. As Jamille Bigio (2016, para. 3) points out, "Regional and global instruments also don't capture sextortion: none of the most common tools used to measure corruption include sex-disaggregated data, and so do not track how men and women are affected differently by corruption."

What can be done about sextortion? How can the victimization of vulnerable populations be stopped? Bigio (2016) suggests the following: First, there is a need for strong data collection to systematically document the problem. Second, countries can pass stronger anti-corruption laws and policies. Third, the stigma of victimization should be addressed, and victims should be encouraged to speak out.

Think It Through

- How could sociologists take a role in combating sextortion? What skills do sociologists possess that would enable them to participate in addressing this problem?

The size of the sex trade in some developing states is rooted in several factors. First, in conservative societies such as India, Pakistan, and other regional states, societal norms dictate that young couples wait until marriage to consummate a relationship. "Respectable" middle-class girls are expected to save their virginity for their husbands. For young men, then, access to prostitutes offers a penalty-free way to gain sexual pleasure and experience before marriage. Second, the girls and young women in the brothels are usually poor, illiterate villagers with no power or voice and few advocates or protectors (Kara, 2009). Police are not only unlikely to help them but may participate in their exploitation as well.

The diminished status conferred by deep poverty and being female imposes a profound double burden on girls and women. It is no coincidence that in a global environment that so often marginalizes women and girls, the trade in their bodies and lives is vast, widespread, and often ignored by authorities.

Discover & Debate

EQUAL GENDER REPRESENTATION

Motion: Equal gender representation should be a priority in the U.S. president's cabinet appointments. One way to ensure fair gender representation is through a quota system.

Background: The cabinet, an important part of the U.S. government, acts as an advisory board to the president. It comprises the vice president, the heads of 15 executive departments, and several additional cabinet-level appointments. Cabinet members are nominated by the president and subject to approval by the U.S. Senate. Gender representation in the first-term cabinets of recent presidents has been mixed. As of mid-2018, Donald Trump's cabinet includes 22 members: 5 women and 17 men. President Barack Obama had 7 female cabinet members out of 23 total members; President George W. Bush had 5 female members out of 22 members; and President Bill Clinton had 6 female members out of 22 members. Some counties where voluntary quotas have been adopted by political parties include the United Kingdom, France, the Czech Republic, Argentina, Australia, Canada, and Germany.

Questions for Consideration

- If the government introduces a mandatory gender quota, is it also obligated to create quotas based on race, ethnicity, sexual orientation, religion, and other categories?

- What have been the experiences of democratic countries that have a gender-based quota system? What can these experiences and public reaction to the quota system tell us about the necessity or desirability of a quota system?

- Are quotas in a free, open political system consistent with democratic norms?

Debate Tip

- Be open during the research process to finding evidence that runs counter to your debate stance. This will allow you to prepare in advance for possible arguments the other team may present.

AFFIRMATIVE ARGUMENTS	OPPOSITION ARGUMENTS
The president's cabinet should be reflective of the general population. A male-dominated cabinet fails to represent the gender balance of the country, which in turn affects the inclusion of a spectrum of interests in policy making.	Cabinet members should be selected based on their knowledge and experience. Having a mandatory minimum gender representation threatens to undermine a merit-based selection process that ensures the most qualified candidates occupy cabinet jobs.
Countries such as Canada and Norway showcase gender equality in their executive cabinets. Having a quota, as these countries do, reduces structural obstacles that prevent women from breaking the glass ceiling.	Quotas do not advance the cause of gender equality because women may be perceived as only having a position on the basis of gender rather than of qualifications.
Having a significant proportion of women in the cabinet minimizes the pressure a female member assuming the role of the "token" woman.	There is a strong case for diversity in the U.S. cabinet, such as public perception of the cabinet by citizens as well as foreign nationals, and research data showing benefits of diversity. This provides an incentive to increase gender diversity even without a mandated quota.

Change Happens: Women's Empowerment

It is possible to empower women across the globe. The non-profit organization Oxfam America (http://www.oxfamamerica.org), for example, features a program called Saving for Change, which emphasizes "savings-led microfinance." Participating groups of women save and pool their money, agree on guidelines for investing or lending in their communities, and organize their resources to serve local needs. The groups enhance not only the women's economic capital

©Rebecca Blackwell/Oxfam America

According to the nonprofit organization Oxfam, more than 700,000 women around the world had participated in Saving for Change by 2015. The women in the groups make small weekly deposits into a common fund and lend to one another from the fund at a 10% monthly interest rate. More women today are using cellphones to save and track money, which has led to greater savings.

but also their social capital, building ties that support them in times of economic or other crises. Although Oxfam funds coaches who help the women get started, Saving for Change groups are not financed or managed from the outside; they are fully autonomous and run by the women themselves.

According to the Population Reference Bureau (2015), only 40 girls are in school for every 100 boys enrolled in secondary school. Mali has high rates of early marriage and few legal protections for women. But Mali, a site where the Saving for Change program is in operation, also has a growing practice of savings-led microfinance, empowering women to save, earn, lend, and invest. According to Oxfam, "households in villages [in Mali] with savings groups experienced an 8 percent increase in food security and saved 31 percent more on average" (Kramer, 2013). With coaching, women gain financial literacy and empowerment, despite their lack of schooling. More mature savings groups are serving the global market for local commodities such as shea butter, a popular cosmetic ingredient. Other countries where women are participating in savings-led microfinance programs include Senegal, Cambodia, and El Salvador (Oxfam, 2015).

Some fear that women's empowerment can foster backlash, manifested as violence or social repercussions. Some patriarchal, conservative societies may not be ready to see women take the initiative to address sexual exploitation, bring attention to crimes against women, or grow economically independent of men, and the victimization of women who step out of traditionally subjugated roles is a risk.

On the other hand, greater independence—social or economic—may allow women to leave violent relationships or challenge norms that marginalize them. The effects of women's economic empowerment can also go beyond their own lives, improving prospects for their children and communities. Studies suggest that when women earn and control economic resources, family money is more likely to go toward needs such as food, medicine, and housing (Kristof & WuDunn, 2009). Maternal and child mortality are reduced with women's empowerment, as are the poverty, marginality, and illiteracy that may lead desperate girls and women to the global sex trade. Mobilization of human and intellectual capital is a critical part of domestic development for a country. It is not a coincidence that countries offering opportunity and mobility to women prosper economically; where fully half the population is deprived of rights, education, and access to the labor market, the consequences are ultimately borne by the whole society and state.

Why Study Gender from a Sociological Perspective?

Gender matters. Whether we are talking about the toys a child may receive on a birthday, encouragement to study different academic subjects, or pay and promotions on the job, gender can make a difference in someone's experience. It can determine whether someone has the opportunity to visit a health clinic, attend school, or work in a paid job. Historically, and often today, it still gives men the power to choose whom women will marry, what women can own, and whether women can assert control over their own lives, fertility, economic independence, and physical safety.

When we study gender roles, we have the opportunity to recognize the power of sex and gender as categories that offer opportunities and construct obstacles. Girls and women have made tremendous strides in schools, families, and workplaces, and for many, equality seems achievable. For many others, marginality is still the hallmark of societal experiences. But women have agency, and even women in deprived circumstances can develop economic and political and social voice. Public interest and political will can open doors to better lives for millions of girls and women.

Boys and men are a key part of this picture, too. Women's growing roles challenge men to reconsider long-held ideas about sex and gender and to imagine, along with women, a world in which gender equality improves not only individual lives but also families, communities, and countries.

What Can I Do with a Sociology Degree?

ETHICAL DECISION MAKING

As you learned in Chapter 6, ideas of right and wrong are socially constructed. Ethical standards are socially, culturally, and even historically specific as societies struggle to adopt new ethical standards that keep pace with the speed of discovery and technological innovation. While many occupations have written codes of ethics to guide employees, such as the Hippocratic Oath that instructs medical professionals to do no harm, most of us are on our own to make personal and professional decisions. Ethical decision-making requires understanding the impact of those outcomes on others, be they individuals, groups, communities, society, or even the world.

Sociology can help you develop the skills to make decisions that are both effective and ethical. Sociology demands a more complex understanding of social life and tries to get at the root of social issues, for example, by examining the links between housing discrimination and educational segregation or the limited effects of social control policies in the criminal justice system. Sociology also looks at the ways in which access and outcomes are affected by social categories of class, race, gender, sexual orientation, age, and religion. Sociology also asks us to think about our own theoretical perspectives and social locations. It illuminates how different assumptions about how society operates lead to very different explanations for the causes and therefore solutions to social problems. By understanding these differences, you can unmask your own and other's potential biases and better understand the impact of decisions. To make ethical decisions, you have to understand how different groups of people will be impacted and you need to understand root causes. Both are at the core of sociology.

Leah Hubbard, Associate at Estolano LeSar Perez Advisors

Loyola Marymount University, BA in Sociology and Music

University of Southern California, Master's of Public Affairs

Source: Bureau of Labor Statistics, *Occupational Outlook Handbook,* 2017.

ELP Advisors is a mission-driven consulting firm that exists to build better communities through strategic vision. We work with public agencies, foundations, businesses, nonprofits, and other stakeholders to provide innovative approaches to complex policy issues.

When taking on a new project or providing strategic guidance to a client, we must understand and dissect the broad, complex issues of community and economic development, including markets, local and national policy, and social inequalities as well as consider the impact of potential outcomes on various groups of stakeholders. This helps us effectively address client challenges with integrity and equity.

Sociology provides the perfect opportunity to get a first look at these complex social systems at work. My theoretical classes gave me the ability to think critically through policy and planning recommendations and to consider their unintended consequences. On the other hand, my quantitative courses gave me the skills to translate data into narratives that can be used to inform and generate solutions. Consulting requires that I be a problem solver who is not only a creative thinker but an ethical decision maker who understands the roots of inequality and biases.

Career Data: Urban and Regional Planners

- 2017 Median Pay: $71,490 per year
- $34.37 per hour
- Typical Entry-Level Education: Master's degree
- Job Outlook, 2016–2026: 13% (Faster than average)

SUMMARY

- **Gender roles** are the attitudes and behaviors considered appropriately masculine or feminine in a particular culture. In understanding such roles, sociologists use the term **sex** to refer to biological differences between males and females and **gender** to refer to differences between males and females that are socially learned.

- Children begin to learn culturally appropriate masculine and feminine gender identities as soon as they are born, and these roles are reinforced and renegotiated throughout life.

- Gender roles are learned through social interaction with others. Early family influences, peer pressure, the mass media, and the "hidden curriculum" in schools are especially important sources of gender socialization.

- Gender stratification is found in virtually all known societies, largely because, until the advent of modern industrial production, the requirements of childbearing and nursing constrained women to roles less likely to provide major sources of food. In modern societies, technological changes have removed such barriers to full equality, although stratification continues to persist.

- Women do more housework than men in all industrial societies, even when they engage in full-time paid employment outside the home.

- Women typically work in lower-paying occupations than men and are paid less than men are for similar jobs. They have made gains but are still less likely to be promoted in most positions than are their male peers.

- **Liberal feminism** argues that women's inequality is primarily the result of imperfect institutions. **Socialist feminism** argues that women's inequality results from the combination of capitalistic economic relations and male domination. **Radical feminism** focuses on **patriarchy** as the source of domination. Finally, **multicultural feminism** emphasizes ending inequality for all women, regardless of race, class, nationality, age, sexual orientation, or other characteristics. Third-wave feminism is a nascent movement highlighting women's agency. A key vehicle of its dissemination is the Internet.

- Some sociologists advocate for the creation of a study of masculinities to understand more fully the sociological influences on the perceptions and practices of men and boys.

- Globally, being born female is still a risk. Women are disadvantaged in access to power, health care, and safety. At the same time, women are taking the initiative in many developing areas to improve their own lives and those of their communities and families.

KEY TERMS

gender roles, 259
sex, 259
gender, 259
sexuality, 259
transgender, 260
transsexual, 260
sex category, 265
second shift, 266
stereotype threat, 267
gender wage gap, 271

occupational segregation by gender, 272
labor supply factors, 272
labor demand factors, 272
human capital, 272
indirect labor costs, 272
glass escalator, 274
glass ceiling, 274
feminism, 277
sexism, 277

liberal feminism, 278
socialist feminism, 278
radical feminism, 278
patriarchy, 278
multicultural feminism, 278
standpoint theory, 280
standpoint epistemology, 280
matrix of domination, 280

DISCUSSION QUESTIONS

1. How does one "become" a boy/man or a girl/woman? Explain how an individual is socialized into the gender he or she identifies with at the following life stages: early childhood, preteen years, adolescence, young adulthood, and parenthood. Now consider the other gender. How is this socialization different?

2. Throughout the chapter, we learned about gender inequalities in institutions including the family, education, and the workplace. Think about another institution, such as religion, politics, or criminal justice. What kinds of research questions could we create to study gender inequality in those institutions?

3. There have been several waves of feminism, and women have gained a spectrum of legal rights and new opportunities. Is feminism as an ideology still needed in our society? What would be the key characteristics of a feminism that meets today's societal challenges?

4. In this chapter, we discussed the overwhelming proportion of men among those who commit both individual homicides and mass shootings in the United States. Can any aspects of gender norms, roles, expectations, or practices in this country help us to understand the overrepresentation of men among perpetrators?

5. Why is maternal mortality much higher in some developing countries than in more economically advanced countries? How might countries with high rates of maternal mortality address this problem effectively? How can the international community contribute to reducing the incidence of maternal mortality?

Want a Better Grade?

Get the tools you need to sharpen your study skills. Access practice quizzes, eFlashcards, video, and multimedia at **https://edge.sagepub.com/chambliss4e.**

©ozgurdonmaz/E+/Getty Images

Families and Society

WHAT DO YOU THINK?

1. Why are U.S. young adults today less likely to marry than previous generations of young adults?

2. What have been some of the consequences of the massive opioid epidemic for U.S. families?

3. Do styles and priorities of parenting differ across the socioeconomic class spectrum?

LEARNING OBJECTIVES

11.1 Explain key concepts sociologists use to study families.

11.2 Apply theoretical perspectives to the study of marriage and the family.

11.3 Describe trends in family formation and family life in the U.S., including marriage, divorce, child care arrangements, and domestic violence, and describe family patterns in immigrant, Native American, and deaf families.

11.4 Explain what sociological research suggests about ways in which social class influences family formation and parenting practices.

11.5 Understand the relationship between globalization and family life, particularly for U.S. families and women from less-developed countries.

MILLENNIALS AND MARRIAGE

A May 2015 blog in the *Washington Post* begins as follows:

> Millennials are poised to become the nation's largest living generation this year. As they grow as a percentage of the population, more of them will reach the age at which Americans historically have gotten married. And many baby-boomer parents are probably eagerly anticipating the big day when their son or daughter walks down the aisle (and the grand-kids that will follow).
>
> But, according to new research, millennials are not showing many signs of interest in getting hitched as they get older, and, as a result, the marriage rate is expected to fall by [2016] to its lowest level to date....

©Cultura Creative (RF) / Alamy Stock Photo

"Millennials are such a big generation, we're going to have more people of prime marriage age in the next five years than we've had at any time in U.S. history. For that alone, we'd expect an uptick in marriage rates," said Sam Sturgeon, president of Demographic Intelligence. "That's not happening." ...

In 1867, the first year for which national marriage statistics were recorded, the marriage rate was 9.6 per 1,000 Americans. It peaked in 1946 at 16.4 per 1,000 as men were returning from World War II, and it bounced around from 8.5 in 1960 to a high of 10.8 in the mid-1980s. Starting in the 1990s, it began a long and ... precipitous drop. (Schulte, 2015, para. 1–4)

Indeed, of the roughly 73 million men and women who comprise the millennial generation, only 27% are married. By comparison, about 65% of the baby boomer generation was married at the same point in their lives (Vasquez, 2018).

Marriage is only one way in which young people create families today. According to a Pew Research Center analysis, about a quarter of never-married young adults (25–34) are living with a partner (Wang & Parker, 2014). Parenthood has also become increasingly separated from marriage, and a contemporary family may well consist of a never-married mother (or, less commonly, a father) raising a child or children. Today, more than 50% of single mothers have never been married (the rest are divorced or widowed); by contrast, that figure in 1960 was 4% (U.S. Census Bureau, 2017).

At the same time, most young adults do not reject marriage as an institution. According to Pew, "only 4% of never-married adults ages 25 to 34 say they don't want to get married. A majority of them either want to marry (61%) or are not sure (34%)," although the collective attitude to marriage is far less traditional than that of older generations: Only about a third of those in the 18 to 29 age group agreed that it was "very important" that a couple marries if they plan to spend their lives together, while about half of those 50 to 64 agreed, and fully 65% of those 65 and over agreed (Wang & Parker, 2014).

What factors are shaping young adults' opportunities for marriage and decisions about marriage? How have changes in norms, educational attainment, and the economy, among others, affected marriage trends in the United States? Further along, we examine these questions, look at practices of family formation, and explore modern challenges to family life.

In this chapter, we focus on the U.S. family in the past and today. We begin by introducing key concepts used in the sociological study of families and discuss the idea of the *family* as an institution. Then we review functionalist and feminist perspectives on families and, in particular, on traditional sex roles in marital relationships. We devote a broad section of the chapter to an overview of modern U.S. families, looking at trends in marriage and divorce as well as family life in a sampling of subcultures—immigrant, Native American, and deaf families. Sociologists take a strong interest in issues of social class and its roots and effects, so next, we explore practices of child rearing and differences across class, the decline of marriage in the poor and working classes, and work and family life in the middle class. Finally, we explore the relationship between globalization and family in the United States and beyond.

How Do Sociologists Study the Family?

Families come in a broad spectrum of forms, but they share important qualities. A **family**, at the most basic level, is *two or more individuals who identify themselves as being related to one another, usually by blood, marriage, or adoption, and who share intimate relationships and dependency*. The family is a key social institution. Although families and their structures vary, the family as an institution is an organized system of social relationships that both reflects societal norms and expectations and meets important societal needs. It plays a role in society as a site for the reproduction of community and citizenry, socialization and transmission of culture, and the care of the young and old. Families, as micro units in the social order, also serve as sites for the allocation of social roles, such as *breadwinner* and *caregiver*, and contribute to the economy as consumers.

Many families are formed through marriage. Sociologists define **marriage** as *a culturally normative relationship, usually between two individuals, that provides a framework for economic cooperation, emotional intimacy, and sexual relations*. Marriages may be legitimated by legal or religious authorities or, in some instances, by the norms of the prevailing culture. Although marriage has historically united partners of different sexes, same-sex marriages have become increasingly common in the United States and other modern countries, although their legal recognition is still incomplete.

Most societies have clear and widely accepted norms regarding the institution and practice of marriage that have varied across time and space. Two common patterns are **monogamy**, *a form of marriage in which a person may have only one spouse at a time,* and **polygamy**, *a form of marriage in which a person may have more than one spouse at a time.* Within the latter category are **polygyny**, *a form of marriage in which a man may have multiple wives,* and **polyandry**, *a form of marriage in which a woman may have multiple husbands.* In feudal Europe and Asia, monogamy prevailed, although in some parts of Asia, wealthy men supported concubines (similar to mistresses; Goody, 1983). George Peter Murdock's (1949) classic anthropological study of 862 preindustrial societies found that 16% had norms supportive of monogamy, 80% had norms that underpinned the practice of polygyny, and 4% permitted polyandry.

The polygynist practice of a man taking multiple wives is unusual (and not legally recognized) in the United States, but according to researchers at Brigham Young University, an estimated 30,000 to 50,000 U.S.

◼ FIGURE 11.1 Historical Trends in Living Arrangements of Families with Children

% of children living with . . .

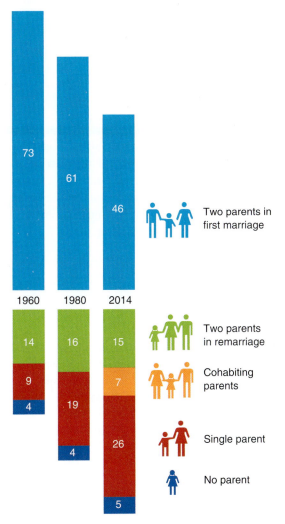

Source: "The American family today," Pew Research Center, Washington, DC (December 2015) http://www.pewsocialtrends.org/2015/12/17/1-the-american-family-today/.

Note: Based on children younger than 18. Data regarding cohabitation are not available for 1960 and 1980; in those years, children with cohabiting parents are included in "one parent." For 2014, the total share of children living with two married parents is 62% after rounding. Figures do not add up to 100% due to rounding.

Family: Two or more individuals who identify themselves as being related to one another, usually by blood, marriage, or adoption, and who share intimate relationships and dependency.

Marriage: A culturally approved relationship, usually between two individuals, that provides a framework for economic cooperation, emotional intimacy, and sexual relations.

Monogamy: A form of marriage in which a person may have only one spouse at a time.

Polygamy: A form of marriage in which a person may have more than one spouse at a time.

Polygyny: A form of marriage in which a man may have multiple wives.

Polyandry: A form of marriage in which a woman may have multiple husbands.

■ **FIGURE 11.2** Since 1967, a Steady Increase in U.S. Intermarriage

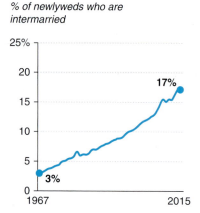

% of newlyweds who are intermarried

Source: "Since 1967, a steady increase in U.S. intermarriage," Pew Research Center, Washington, DC, May 15, 2017. (http://www.pewsocialtrends.org/2017/05/18/intermarriage-in-the-u-s-50-years-after-loving-v-virginia/)

■ **FIGURE 11.3** Racial and Ethnic Intermarriage in the U.S.

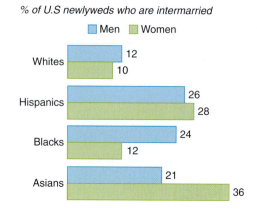

% of U.S newlyweds who are intermarried

Source: Livingston & Brown, 2017.

residents practice polygamy. Many are members of breakaway sects of the Mormon church.

Some sociologists have suggested that, because divorce and remarriage are so common in postindustrial countries such as the U.S., our marriage pattern might be labeled **serial monogamy**, *the practice of having more than one wife or husband, but only one at a time.* Most modern societies are strongly committed to monogamy, and the selection of a lifelong mate—at least in principle, if not always in practice. Later in this chapter, we will explore a trend noted in our opener: More women and men in the U.S., as well as other countries across the globe, are foregoing marriage altogether, turning the tables on an institution that has long been considered normative in the life course—and the social order.

In many societies, marriages tend to be **endogamous**—*limited to partners who are members of the same social group or caste.* Sexual or marital partnerships outside the group may be cause for a range of sanctions, from family disapproval to social ostracism to legal consequences. Consider that in the United States, **anti-miscegenation laws**—*laws prohibiting interracial sexual relations and marriage*—were ruled unconstitutional only in 1967. Until then, some states defined miscegenation as a felony, prohibiting residents from marrying outside their racial groups. Today, such laws are history. In fact, a rising number of new marriages are between spouses

of different races or ethnicities: In 1967, intermarriages constituted only 3% of new marriages; today, the figure is 17% (Figure 11.2). Interestingly, the rate of intermarriage is dramatically different across U.S. racial and ethnic groups: As Figure 11.3 shows, Asian Americans and Hispanics are far more likely to marry outside of the group than are White or Black Americans (Livingston & Brown, 2017).

Serial monogamy: The practice of having more than one wife or husband, but only one at a time.

Endogamous: A characteristic of marriages in which partners are limited to members of the same social group or caste.

Anti-miscegenation laws: Laws prohibiting interracial sexual relations and marriage.

DISCOVER INTERSECTIONS

Racial and Ethnic Group Membership and Marriage

As we see in this section, racial and ethnic intermarriage has increased significantly. At the same time, most people who marry still do so within their own racial or ethnic group. We learned in the chapter on groups, organizations, and bureaucracies (Chapter 5) about the importance of primary and secondary groups in the formation of our social selves and our social lives. How might these groups also influence our exposure to the pool of potential marital partners? How might they influence preferences and norms that guide our decisions about a potential partner? Think about the married couples you know: Would you say that most match up on the basis of membership in groups based on ascribed characteristics such as race or ethnicity? What about achieved characteristics such as educational attainment? Can what you've learned in other chapters help to explain the change—and stasis—we see in intermarriage rates among newlyweds in the U.S.?

Families and the Work of Raising Children

The role of parent or primary caregiver in the U.S. and much of Europe has traditionally been assumed by biological parents (and occasionally stepparents), but this is one of many possible family formations in which adults have raised children in different times and places. Consider the Baganda tribe of Central Africa, in which the biological father's brother was traditionally responsible for raising the children (Queen, Habenstein, & Adams, 1961). The Nayars of southern India offer another variation, assigning responsibility to the mother's eldest brother (Renjini, 2000; Schneider & Gough, 1974). In Trinidad and other Caribbean communities, extended family members have often assumed the care of children whose parents have migrated north to seek work (in the United States, in most instances; Ho, 1993).

A substantial minority of children in the United States also live in **extended families**, *social groups consisting of one or more parents, children, and other kin, often spanning several generations, living in the same household*. An extended family may include grandparents, aunts and uncles, cousins, and other close relatives. In Northern and Western Europe, Canada, the United States, and Australia, most children live in **nuclear families**—*families characterized by one or parents living with their biological, dependent children in a household with no other kin*—while extended families are more common in Eastern and Southern Europe, Africa, Asia, and Central and Latin America. In the United States, the extended family form is most common among those with lower income, in rural areas, and among recent migrants and minorities.

For close and extended family members to function as caregivers is neither new nor unusual. In fact, a growing number of children in the United States live with one or a pair of grandparents, although the proportion who live with neither parent is still only 4%. In 2015, 69% of children lived with two parents, and just under 23% lived with only their mothers, while just over 4% resided with only their father and 2% lived with grandparents or a grandparent (U.S. Census Bureau, 2016).

Theoretical Perspectives on Families

When sociologists study families, their perspectives are shaped by their overall theoretical orientations toward society. Thus, as in the study of other institutions, it is helpful to distinguish between the functionalist and conflict perspectives, although, as we will see, there are some important variations and additions to these classic categories.

The Functionalist Perspective

Recall that functionalism asks the following question: What positive functions does a given institution or phenomenon serve in society? Based on the foundational assumption that if something exists and persists, it must serve a function, functionalist theory has highlighted in particular the economic, social, and cultural functions of the family. Arguably, the shift from an agricultural to industrial to postindustrial economy in the U.S. has made the family's economic purpose less central than its reproductive and socializing functions, although micro-level consumption decisions made by families continue to drive a national economy that is deeply dependent on consumer activity.

In his work on sex roles in the U.S. kinship system, sociologist Talcott Parsons (1954) theorized that men and women play different but complementary roles in families. In the "factory of personalities"—in other words, the family—socialization produces males and females prepared to pursue and fulfill different roles in the family and society. Parsons posited that women were socially prepared for the *expressive* role of mothers and wives, while men were prepared for *instrumental* roles in the public sphere, working and earning money to support the family. These complementary roles, he suggested, were positively functional, as they ensured cooperation rather than competition for status or position. Distinct sex roles also clarified the social status of the family, which was derived from the male's social position.

Aside from his belief that the family served the function of primary socialization—that is, the process of learning and internalizing social roles and norms (such as those relating to gender)—Parsons suggested that the nuclear family of his time functioned to support adult family members emotionally, a phenomenon he called *personality stabilization* (Parsons & Bales, 1955). In industrial societies, in which the nuclear family unit was often disconnected from the extended kin networks that characterized earlier eras, this stabilization function was particularly vital.

Writing in the 1950s, Parsons worried that disruption of the roles he observed in families could cause dysfunctions for the family and society. Indeed, there is some correlation between women's assumption of autonomous roles outside the home and the rise of divorce. Correlation is, of course, not causation. Possible explanations for the link include the advent of no-fault divorce laws, decline in the normative stigma related to divorce, and women's greater economic independence, which has enabled them to leave unhappy marriages that might earlier have been sustained by their dependence on spouses' wages.

Extended families: Social groups consisting of one or more parents, children, and other kin, often spanning several generations, living in the same household.

Nuclear families: Families characterized by one or two parents living with their biological, dependent children in a household with no other kin.

Critics see Parsons's work as reinforcing and legitimating traditional roles. The functionalist perspective—and Parsons's application of it—has been criticized for neglecting power differentials inherent in a relationship where one party (the wife) is economically dependent on the other (the husband). In a capitalist system, power tends to accrue to those who hold economic resources. Functionalists also neglect family dysfunctions, including ways in which the nuclear family—central to modern society yet, in many respects, isolated from support systems such as kin networks—may perpetuate gender inequality and even violence.

The Feminist Approach: A Conflict Perspective . . . and Beyond

You can probably anticipate that in looking at the family, the conflict perspective will ask how it might produce and reproduce inequality. Feminist theories about the family have reflected a conflict orientation in its efforts to understand the family as a potential site of both positive support and unequal power. From the 1970s, a period following intense activity in the women's movement and a rise in the number of women taking jobs outside the home, feminist perspectives became central to sociological debates on the family.

Although early theorizing about the family highlighted its structure and roles as well as its evolution from the agricultural to the industrial era, feminist theorizing in the late 20th century turned its attention to women's experiences of domestic life and their status in the family and social world. Feminists endeavored to critique the **sexual division of labor in modern societies**, *the phenomenon of dividing production functions by gender* (men produce, women reproduce) *and designating different spheres of activity: the "private" to women and the "public" to men.* Even though theorists, including Parsons, saw this division as fundamentally functional, feminists challenged a social order that gave males privileged access to the sphere offering capitalism's most prized rewards, including social status, opportunities for advancement, and economic independence.

His and Her Marriage

An important sociological analysis that captures some of liberal feminism's key concerns is Jessie Bernard's *The Future of Marriage* (1982). (See Chapter 10 for a fuller discussion of varieties of modern feminism, including liberal feminism.) Bernard confronts the issue of equality in marriage, positing that a husband and wife experience different marriages. In her analysis of marriage as a cultural system comprising beliefs and ideals, an institutional arrangement of norms and roles, and a complicated individual-level interactional

and intimate experience, Bernard identifies *his* and *her* marriage experiences:

- *His* marriage is one in which he may define himself as burdened and constrained (following societal norms that indicate this is what he *should* be experiencing) while at the same time experiencing authority, independence, and a right to the sexual, domestic, and emotional services of his wife.

- *Her* marriage is one in which she may seek to define herself as fulfilled through her achievement of marriage (following societal norms that indicate this is what she *should* be experiencing) while at the same time experiencing associated female dependence and subjugation.

Bernard understood these gender-differentiated experiences as rooted in the cultural and institutional foundations of marriage in the era she studied. Marriage functioned, from this perspective, to allocate social roles and expectations—but not to women's advantage. In a good example of the sociological imagination, Bernard saw a connection between the personal experiences of individual men and women and the norms, roles, and expectations that create the context in which their relationship is lived.

Bernard's analysis pointed to data showing that married women, ostensibly fulfilled by marriage and family life, and unmarried men, ostensibly privileged by freedom, scored highest on stress indicators, while their unmarried female and married male counterparts scored lowest. Although this was true when Bernard was writing several decades ago, recent social indicators show a mix of patterns. Some are similar to those she identified. For instance, a 2010 article in the *Harvard Men's Health Watch Newsletter* reported,

> A major survey of 127,545 American adults found that married men are healthier than men who were never married or whose marriages ended in divorce or widowhood. Men who have marital partners also live longer than men without spouses; men who marry after age 25 get more protection than those who tie the knot at a younger age, and the longer a man stays married, the greater his survival advantage over his unmarried peers. (Harvard Medical School, 2010, "Men, marriage, and mortality," para. 1)

Other studies paint a different picture. For instance, an examination of a spectrum of marriage studies determined that married women were less likely to experience depression than their unmarried counterparts. Researchers controlled for such factors as the possibility that less depressed people were more likely to get married (which would confound results) and found that self-selection was not an issue.

Sexual division of labor in modern societies: The phenomenon of dividing production functions by gender and designating different spheres of activity, the "private" to women and the "public" to men.

©Lambert/Getty Images

According to the Census Bureau, about one fifth of U.S. households are composed of married couples with children. In 1950, about 43% of households fit this description. Some contemporary television shows both parody and reproduce traditional family images and gender roles.

That is, marriage did seem to have positive health effects for women (Wood, Goesling, & Avellar, 2007).

In fact, the issue is more complex than either Bernard's work or recent studies can embrace in a single narrative. Consider other variables at play here. For example, men do seem to have *more* health benefits than women from marriage, even if women have some. Yet marriage as an institution does not appear to confer health benefits; rather, it is the *quality* of marriage that matters. According to a recent study, people in happy marriages rate their health better as they age (Proulx & Snider-Rivas, 2013). Solid and low-conflict marriages are healthy, and unstable, high-conflict marriages are not. The never married are better off than those in high-conflict marriages (Parker-Pope, 2010).

Bernard's work gives us an opportunity to look at marriage as a *gendered institution*—that is, one in which gender fundamentally affects the experience of marriage. Although her analysis, which is nearly four decades old, cannot fully capture the reality of today's marriages, her recognition that men and women may experience marriage in different ways remains an important insight.

The feminist perspective and other conflict-oriented perspectives offer a valuable addition to functionalist theorizing. Nevertheless, their focus on the divisive and unequal aspects of family forms and norms may overlook the valuable functions of caring, socializing, and organizing that families have long performed and continue to perform in society. Indeed, both these macro-level approaches may have difficulty capturing the complexities of any family's

lived experiences, particularly as they evolve and change over the years. Nonetheless, they offer a useful way of thinking about families and family members, their place in the larger social world, and the way they influence and are influenced by societal institutions and cultures.

The Psychodynamic Feminist Perspective

Sociologist Nancy Chodorow (1999) asks, "Why do women mother?" She suggests that to explain women's choice to *mother*, a verb that describes a commitment to the care and nurturing of children, and men's choice to *not mother* (that is, to assume a more distant role from child rearing), we must look at personality development and relational psychology. Although mothering is rooted in biology, Chodorow argues that biology cannot fully explain mothering, because fathers or other kin can perform key mothering functions as well.

Drawing from Sigmund Freud's object relations perspective, Chodorow argues that an infant of either sex forms his or her initial bond with the mother, who satisfies all the infant's basic needs. Later, the mother pushes a son away emotionally, whereas she maintains the bond with a daughter. Through such early socialization, daughters come to identify more fully with their mothers than with their fathers; boys, on the other hand, develop masculine personalities, but those draw from societal models of masculinity (or, sometimes, hypermasculinity) rather than predominantly from their fathers, who take a far less prominent role in child rearing than do mothers. Chodorow suggests that masculinity in boys may thus develop in part as a negation and marginalization of qualities associated with femininity, which is rejected for both social and psychological reasons.

Women, reared by mothers who nurture close and critical bonds, are rendered "relational" through this process, seeking close bonds and defining themselves through relationships (Anna's mom, Joe's wife, and so on). Men, by contrast, define themselves more autonomously and have a harder time forming close bonds. Again, the roots of this difficulty are social (society defines men as autonomous and independent) and psychological (the pain of an early break in the mother–son bond results in fear or avoidance of these deep bonds). So why do women mother? Because men in heterosexual relationships are not socially or psychologically

©Yasser Chalid/Moment/Getty Images

While fathers are more involved with the day-to-day care of their children than in generations past, mothers continue to play the role of primary caregiver in most families. Do you expect that division of roles to remain static in coming generations? Why or why not?

well prepared for close relational bonding, women choose to mother to reproduce this intimate connection with a child.

Although these processes play out primarily on the micro level of the family and relationships, Chodorow also recognizes macro-level effects. She suggests that because of a lack of available male role models at home, the masculine personality develops in part as a negation of the feminine personality. Chodorow argues that the higher valuation of traits associated with masculinity in areas such as politics, business, and the labor market (which men still dominate) is, at least in part, linked to the devaluation of the feminine that men carry with them from their early childhood experiences.

Chodorow's work on sex roles and socialization in the family offers a unique marriage of Freud and feminism that is both challenging and compelling, asking us to consider the effects that psychological processes in early childhood have on social institutions from the family to politics and the economy.

U.S. Families Yesterday and Today

The traditional nuclear family often appears in popular media and political debates as a nostalgic embodiment of values and practices to which U.S. families should return. Historian Stephanie Coontz (2000, 2005), who has written about the history of U.S. families, points out that the highly venerated traditional nuclear family model is, in fact, a fairly recent development.

Consider that in the preindustrial era, when the U.S. economy was primarily agricultural, families were key social and economic units. Households often included multiple generations and sometimes boarders or farmworkers. Families were typically large, and children were valued for their contributions to a family's economic viability, participating along with the other members in productive activities. Marriages tended to endure; divorce was neither

normative nor especially easy to secure. At the same time, average life expectancy was about 45 years (Rubin, 1996). As life spans increased, divorce also became more common, replacing death as the factor most likely to end a marriage.

The period of early industrialization shifted these patterns somewhat, not least because it was accompanied by urbanization, which brought workers and their families to cities for work. The family's economic function declined; some children worked in factories, but the passage of child labor laws and the rise of mass public schooling made this increasingly uncommon (although, according to one source, at the end of the 19th century, a quarter of textile workers in the American South were children, whose cheap labor was a boon to employers; Wertheimer, 1977). Over time, children became more of an economic cost than a wage-earning benefit; in a related development, families became smaller and began to evolve toward the nuclear family model.

The basic nuclear family model, with a mother working in the private sphere of the home while focused on child rearing and a father working in the public sphere for pay, evolved among middle-class families in the late 19th century. It was far less common among the working class at this time; working-class women, in fact, often toiled in the homes of the new middle class as housekeepers and nursemaids.

Coontz (2000) points out that, as the popular imagination suggests, the mother-as-homemaker and father-as-breadwinner model of the nuclear family is most characteristic of the widely idealized era of the 1950s. The post–World War II era witnessed a range of interconnected social phenomena, including suburbanization supported by federal government initiatives to build a network of highways and encourage home ownership, a boom in economic growth and wages that brought greater consumption power along with technologies that made the home more comfortable and convenient, and a "baby boom," as a wave of pregnancies delayed by the years of war came to term.

Although prosperity and technology brought new opportunities to many, mass suburbanization largely left behind minorities, including Black Americans, who were not given full access to the government's subsidized mortgages (including mortgages subsidized through the G.I. Bill, which was theoretically available to all returning veterans of World War II) and were often left behind in segregated, devalued neighborhoods. As the jobs followed White workers to the suburbs, the economic condition of many Black families and their neighborhoods deteriorated.

Furthermore, it is not clear that all was well in the prosperous suburbs either. As we noted in the section on feminist theoretical perspectives, some sociological observers detected a streak of discontent that ran through the idealized nuclear family. Betty Friedan's book *The Feminine*

Mystique (1963) highlighted "the problem that has no name," a broad discontent born of women's exclusion from or marginalization in the workplace and the disconnect between their low status and opportunities and society's expectation that marriage and children were the ultimate feminine fulfillment. Coontz (2000) points out that tranquilizers, one of many medical innovations of the era, were largely consumed by women, and in considerable quantities—at least 1.15 million pounds in 1959 alone.

Marriage and Divorce in the U.S.

The traditional nuclear family with the man as breadwinner and the woman as caregiver is still in existence, although it has changed in many respects since the 1950s and today represents only about 7% of U.S. households. At the same time, even though commentators often lament the "decline of the family," most children in the United States still live in two-parent households, and as we saw above, all but about 5% live with at least one parent (U.S. Census Bureau, 2016; see Figure 11.1). More children are living with single parents than in the past, but more adults are also living in nonfamily households, consisting of either a single householder or unrelated individuals. Today, about a quarter of adults live alone.

One reason for the growth of single-person households is the rising median age at first marriage, which in 2017 was 29.5 for men and 27.4 for women (Figure 11.7). Consider the fact that for men, the median age at first marriage was 22.8 in 1960, 26.1 in 1980, and 26.8 in 2000; for women, it was 20.3 in 1960, 23.9 in 1980, and 25.1 in 2000 (U.S. Census Bureau, 2017). The steep rise in the median age at first marriage suggests that many people are not marrying until their 30s—or even later. Most U.S. adults indicate a desire to marry, and most will at some point in their lives; more than 2.2 million married in 2016, and the U.S. marriage rate of 6.9 per 1,000 population exceeds that of many other economically advanced countries, including the states of Western and Northern Europe (Centers for Disease Control and Prevention, 2017).

At the same time, rates of marriage in the U.S. have declined, and far fewer adults today are married than in generations past (Figure 11.8). We opened this chapter with a story about decline of marriage in the millennial generation and asked what factors are driving this drop. Below, we examine several key issues.

First, there is a relationship between attitudes and practices. Data appear to show a declining sense that marriage is a necessary part of the adult life course. Consider data from a Pew Research Center study that shows a shift that has taken place across merely one generation (Figure 11.4): In 1997, 42% of 18- to 29-year-olds (Generation X)

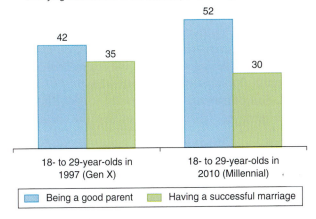

■ FIGURE 11.4 The Importance of Marriage and Parenthood for Millennials and Gen Xers

% saying each is one of the most important things in their life

18- to 29-year-olds in 1997 (Gen X): 42, 35
18- to 29-year-olds in 2010 (Millennial): 52, 30

Being a good parent   Having a successful marriage

Source: "For Millennials, Parenthood Trumps Marriage," Pew Research Center, Washington, DC (March 2011). http://www.pewsocialtrends.org/2011/03/09/for-millennials-parenthood-trumps-marriage/.

indicated that being a good parent was "one of the most important things" in their lives, and 35% said that having a successful marriage was "one of the most important things in their lives." In 2010, young adults in the same age group (millennials) were more likely to value parenthood but less likely to value marriage: Although 52% said that being a good parent was important to them, only 30% said the same about having a successful marriage. Even though most millennials said that they would like to get married, this traditional milestone is no longer the vital component of adulthood that it once was (Pew Research Center, 2011): Recall that in our opening story, we learned that only 27% of millennials today are married, while 65% of baby boomers were married at the same phase of their lives.

Second, there are more viable and normatively acceptable alternatives to marriage available. **Cohabitation** and **common-law marriage**, *in which partners live as if married but without the formal legal framework of traditional marriage,* are options that have gained popularity in recent decades. An estimated quarter of never-married young adults (25–34) live with a partner (Wang & Parker, 2014). The decision to forego marriage in favor of short- or long-term cohabitation is not one limited to today's young adults: More older adults are choosing to build households without traditional marriage as well.

Third, economic circumstances, including the rising burden of student debt, are having an influence on decisions

Cohabitation: Living together as a couple without being legally married.

Common-law marriage: A type of relationship in which partners live as if married but without the formal legal framework of traditional marriage.

about family formation. Research shows some correlation between debt and the ability or willingness of young adults to start families (Smock, Manning, & Porter, 2005). Students graduating from higher education in the past decade are the first U.S. generation to finance so much of their education with interest-bearing loans. A 2002 survey from Nellie Mae (a nonprofit corporation and, until recently, the largest private source of student loans) offers some early insights into the relationship between debt and delayed family formation: In the survey, 14% of borrowers indicated that "loans delayed marriage," a rise from 9% in 1987, when the debt burden was smaller. More than one fifth responded

that they had "delayed having children because of student loan debt," an increase from 12% in 1987. More recently, an IHS Global Insight report highlighted the fact that even though other types of debt have declined, student loan debt continues to rise—and it correlates with a discernible trend among young adults of delaying marriage and childbearing (Dwoskin, 2012). In fact, financial concerns more generally appear to have an effect on young adults' decisions about marriage: In a Pew Research Center (2014a) survey, a third of young adults indicated that economic reasons were a key obstacle to getting married (Figure 11.5).

Fourth, the marriage market has shifted. If it is the case that nearly a third of young adults indicate that they have not met someone they would like to marry yet, some of that can be explained with the application of the sociological imagination. That is, rather than looking at this on an individual level, we may want to ask what sociological factors may underpin difficulty in meeting a suitable partner. For instance, even though there are more unmarried young adult men than unmarried young adult women (implying a robust pool of partners), a closer look at the marital pool shows that there are fewer *employed* unmarried men than women. Figure 11.6 shows the number of men per 100 women among never-married adults aged 25 to 34. In the figure, we see that there are 126 never-married men aged 25 to 34 for every 100 never-married women aged 25 to 34. Notably, however, the number of *employed* never-married men aged 25 to 34 per 100 never-married women in the same age group is only 91. To the degree that being employed is a variable that makes a man "marriageable," the

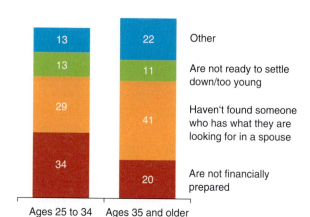

Source: Robert Alexander/Archive Photos Getty Images

Marriages between partners of a different race or ethnicity are on the rise in the United States. About 10% of all marriages are intermarriages, and in 2015, fully 17% of newlyweds married a partner of a different race or ethnicity (Livingston & Brown, 2017).

■ **FIGURE 11.5** Reasons Adults in the United States Give for Not Being Married

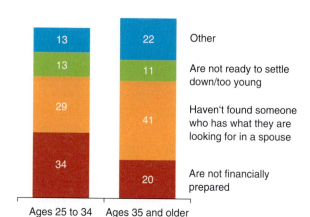

Ages 25 to 34 | Ages 35 and older |
Other: 13 | 22
Are not ready to settle down/too young: 13 | 11
Haven't found someone who has what they are looking for in a spouse: 29 | 41
Are not financially prepared: 34 | 20

Source: Record Share of Americans Have Never Been Married, September 24, 2014.

Note: Based on never-married adults ages 25 and older who want to marry or are not sure (n = 208). "In school" and "engaged to be married" not shown.

■ **FIGURE 11.6** Number of Men per Women among Never-Married Adults, Ages 25–34

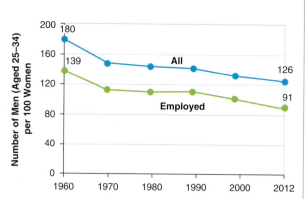

Source: Pew Research Center analysis of the 1960–2000 decennial censuses and 2010–2012 American Community Survey, Integrated Public Use Microdata Series (IPUMS).

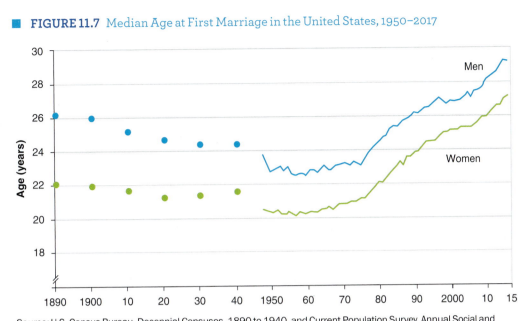

FIGURE 11.7 Median Age at First Marriage in the United States, 1950–2017

Source: U.S. Census Bureau, Decennial Censuses, 1890 to 1940, and Current Population Survey, Annual Social and Economic Supplements, 1947 to 2017.

data suggest that the marriage market may be weaker than it appears (Pew Research Center, 2014b).

Interestingly, as younger generations of heterosexual adults have drifted away from marriage as a normative part of the life course, many of their gay and lesbian peers have been fighting for the opportunity to marry. Just a few years ago—2014—33 states prohibited same-sex marriage while only 17 states and the District of Columbia permitted it (Ahuja, Barnes, Chow, & Rivero, 2014). States that rejected same-sex marriage tended to cite the same language as the federal law prohibiting same-sex marriage, the Defense of Marriage Act (DOMA): "The word 'marriage' means only a legal union between one man and one woman as husband and wife." DOMA was signed into law by President Bill Clinton in 1996. It also included the provision that states were not obligated to recognize same-sex marriages conducted in states or cities that permit them.

A dramatic shift took place in June of 2015, when the U.S. Supreme Court held in *Obergefell v. Hodges* that states must allow same-sex couples to marry and that they must recognize same-sex marriages from other states. The 5-to-4 decision indicated that a fundamental right to marry is guaranteed to same-sex couples by the Due Process Clause and the Equal Protection Clause of the Fourteenth Amendment to the Constitution. According to

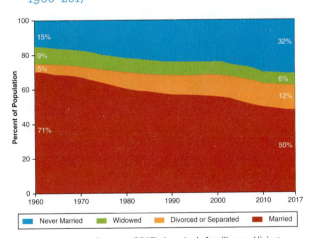

FIGURE 11.8 Marital Status in the United States, 1960–2017

Source: U.S. Census Bureau. (2017). America's families and living arrangements: 2017: Adults (A table series): Table A1.

a Gallup poll reported in the *Washington Post* prior to the Obergefell decision, about 390,000 married same-sex couples resided in the United States. Another 1.2 million adults were living in same-sex domestic partnerships (Schwarz, 2015). Whether the newly gained right to marry will have any significant effect on the falling rate of marriage in the United States remains to be seen, but recent data show that two years after the *Obergefell* decision, just over 10%

of lesbian, gay, bisexual, and transsexual (LGBT) adults are married to a same-sex partner. The figure prior to the Court's decision was 7.9% (Jones, 2017).

With the decline of marriage, the United States has also experienced a decline in divorce. After rising through the 1960s and 1970s, the rate of divorce has leveled off (Figure 11.9). There is a relationship between these two phenomena, since a smaller number of marriages reduces the pool of people who can divorce. The rate overall is still high, however, and the United States has one of the highest divorce rates in the world, with the rate for second and later marriages exceeding that for first marriages.

Why is the U.S. divorce rate, while declining, persistently high? Historian Stephanie Coontz (2005) argues that divorce is, in part, driven by our powerful attachment to the belief that marriage is the outcome of romantic love. Although historically, many societies accepted marriage primarily as part of an economic or social contract—and some still do—modern U.S. adults are smitten with love. Yet the powerful early feelings and passion that characterize many relationships are destined to wane over time. In a social context that elevates romantic love and passion in films, music, and books, we may have less tolerance for the more measured emotions inherent in most long-term marriages. Could our strong focus on romantic love be a driver of both marriage *and* divorce? What do you think?

Families are surely in the process of changing—and not only in the United States. See the *Global Issues* box on page 319 for a look at how dating and mating are changing in Japan.

Who's Minding the Children?

In a reversal of a longtime (nearly four-decade) trend in the United States, increasing numbers of mothers are staying home to care for children: In 2012, 29% of mothers reported that they did not work outside the home (Figure 11.10). About two thirds of today's stay-at-home mothers are part of "traditional" families; that is, they care for children in the home while their husbands work for pay. The rest include single and cohabiting women as well as women whose husbands are unemployed. The shift toward fewer mothers working outside the home is driven by a variety of social, cultural, and economic factors. Among these are the growing percentage of immigrant women who are mothers and stagnating wages that have led some women to conclude that the costs of outside child care outweigh the benefits of working for pay (Cohn, Livingston, & Wang, 2014).

At the same time, in the slow growth of another trend, more fathers are assuming the primary child-care role in the home. According to one study, about 16% of stay-at-home parents today are fathers, up from 10% in 1989. Interestingly, this trend appears to be driven by labor market and health issues more than by changes in social or cultural norms that support more active fathering. Data show that even though about three quarters of mothers are motivated by a desire to care for the family, only one fifth of men offer the same explanation: Almost 60% of stay-at-home fathers indicate that they are at home because they are either ill or disabled or because they are unemployed (Livingston, 2014). Notably, public attitudes about men as primary caregivers are, in spite of myriad changes in family life, still only nominally supportive. Livingston (2014) reports on a Pew Research Center poll in which about 76% of respondents said that they believed children are "just as well off" if their father works, but only 34% said that children are "just as well off" if their mother works, and 51% said that children are "better off" if the mother stays home; only 8% responded that the children are "better off" with the father at home.

Although the number of stay-at-home fathers is rising, 63% of fathers say that they do not spend enough time with their children. By contrast, about

The proportion of LGBT adults married to a same-sex partner is slowly growing in the United States after the Supreme Court's legalization of same-sex marriage in the 2015 *Obergefell v. Hodges* decision.

©Hinterhaus Productions/DigitalVision/Getty Images

■ FIGURE 11.9 U.S. Divorce Rate, 1950–2016

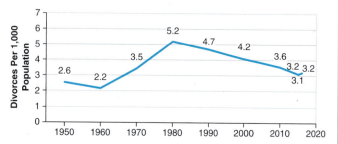

Source: National Center for Health Statistics. (2017). *Aggregate data 1950–2016.* Atlanta, GA: Centers for Disease Control and Prevention.

■ **FIGURE 11.10** Percentage of Stay-at-Home Mothers in the United States

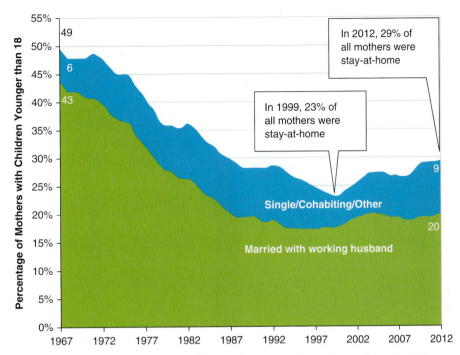

Source: 7 Key Findings About Stay-at-Home Moms, D'Vera Cohn and Andrea Caumont, April 8, 2014.

Note: Based on mothers ages 18–69 with their own child(ren) younger than 18 in the household. Mothers are categorized based on employment status in the year prior to the survey. "Other" stay-at-home mothers are those who are married with a nonworking or absent husband.

35% of mothers say the same. While education is a factor in determining how fathers self-report their time spent with their children, it is not a factor for mothers: 69% of fathers who do not have a bachelor's degree say they spend too little time with their children, while 50% of fathers with a bachelor's degree say the same. Employment is a better determining factor for mothers: Only 28% who are unemployed or work part time say they spend too little time with their children, while 43% of full-time working mothers say the same. Parents of both sexes share the sentiment that time spent at work is the biggest obstacle to spending time with children. This is particularly salient in a time when a growing share of women are primary or co-breadwinners in the family (Figure 11.11).

Notably, the second leading reason that parents give for spending too little time with children differs by sex, with mothers saying the reason is because they have other family or household obligations and fathers responding that it is because their children do not live with them. Of all fathers, 17% live apart from all their children, a percentage that varies based on education and race. Only 8% of fathers with a bachelor's degree or more live apart from their children, while 28% of those without a bachelor's degree say the same. As for race, more Black fathers reported living apart from some or all of their children (47%), while

■ **FIGURE 11.11** Share of All Mothers Who Are Breadwinners or Co-Breadwinners

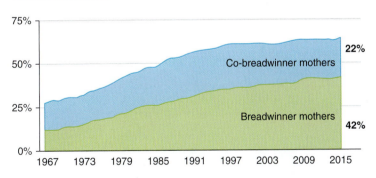

Source: "Breadwinning Mothers Are Increasingly the U.S. Norm," Sarah Jane Glynn, December 19, 2016, Center for American Progr.

FIGURE 11.12 Top 10 Largest U.S. Immigration Groups, 2016

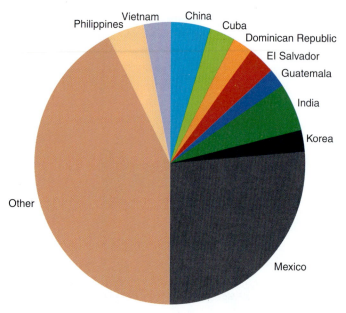

Source: Migration Policy Institute. (2017). Largest U.S. Immigrant Groups over Time, 1960–Present. Retrieved from http://www.migrationpolicy.org/programs/data-hub/charts/largest-immigrant-groups-over-time.

26% of Hispanic and 17% of white fathers say the same (Livingston, 2018).

Although mothers and fathers of young children are in the labor force, child care has remained largely in the domain of the family. Data show that about half of children age 4 and younger whose mothers work for pay are cared for by relatives. A quarter get their primary care in child-care centers or preschools, and around 13% are looked

In nearly half of two-parent households, both parents work full time. About 60% of mothers and 52% of fathers say it is difficult to find a balance between family and work demands (Pew Research Center, 2015a).

after in home-care arrangements or by a nanny or other nonrelative (ChildStats, 2013).

Choosing who will care for a young child is a highly personal decision for a family, but there are some discernible patterns in child-care arrangements by socioeconomic status. For example, poorer fathers are more likely to be stay-at-home parents than are their better-off male peers (Livingston, 2014). As well, working mothers who hold college degrees are most likely to use center-based child care, which is often costly (ChildStats, 2013). How would you explain these patterns? What other patterns of child care could you hypothesize? Below, we turn to an examination of family patterns in immigrant, Native American, and deaf families in the United States.

Immigration and Family Patterns

The United States has more foreign-born residents than any other country in the world. Given its low fertility rate, a substantial proportion of the country's population growth is the result of immigration (Table 11.1 and Figure 11.12). With the proportion of foreign-born residents at about 13%, it is not surprising that immigrants and the cultures they carry with them have important effects on family patterns in the U.S.

Predictably, more recent immigration correlates with a group's stronger ties to its homeland culture (Moore & Pinderhughes, 2001). Many scholars are now focusing on the *transnational* nature of immigrant families. Embodying transnationalism may mean living, working, worshipping, and being politically active in one nation while still maintaining strong political, social, religious, and/or cultural ties to other nations (Levitt, 2004). Family members may send money to relatives in their countries of origin, keep in nearly constant contact with those they left behind through modern communication technologies, and travel back and forth between countries frequently to maintain close emotional ties.

Many immigrant parents also prefer their children to marry within the group. According to research by the Center for Immigration Studies, in some devout Muslim communities, parents' traditional values exist in a tense relationship with new norms embraced by their children:

Just when Muslim girls traditionally would be separated from boys, taken out of school, and perhaps start wearing a head covering, their American counterparts begin to discover and experiment with their sexuality. To prevent such experimentation, Muslim parents seek to enforce the traditional rules . . . sometimes even cloistering their daughters. [Nevertheless,] . . . by law, girls must go to school until 16 or so; and at 18, they acquire additional rights. . . .

To encourage the young to marry within the faith, American Muslims are developing several novel solutions, including summer camps, socials for singles, and marriage advertisements. But even these Muslim institutions have a difficult time keeping boys and girls apart. (Pipes & Durán, 2002, pp. 5–6)

Interestingly, reflecting the influence of home cultures on migrants, first-generation migrants often have birthrates above those of the native-born U.S. population. One study found that among some groups, immigrant women in the United States were having more children on average (2.9) than women in their home countries (2.3; Camarota, 2005). In the second generation, however, the rate typically declines to the average U.S. rate—that is, approximately 2.1 children per woman (Hill & Johnson, 2002). Nevertheless, some studies have found that the trend toward decreasing fertility in first- and second-generation immigrant women may actually be reversed in the third generation for some groups (Parrado & Morgan, 2008). Historically, fertility rates have decreased for immigrant families the longer they reside in the United States. It is important, however, to note that factors such as country of origin, education, religion, and cultural attitudes add to the complexity of understanding these trends.

Below, we narrow our focus to a pair of specific examples of family subcultures in the United States—those of Native Americans and deaf families.

America's First Nations: Native American Families

Family patterns among Native Americans are highly diverse. There are nearly 500 different nations, although more than half of all American Indians identify as coming from six of these (U.S. Census Bureau, 2011). American Indians often live in extended family households that include uncles, aunts, cousins, and grandparents. According to Harriett Light and Ruth Martin (1986), writing in the *Journal of American Indian Education,*

The central unit of Indian society is the family. . . . Indian families do not have the rigid structure of relationships found in Western white culture. Instead, Indians relate to people outside the immediate family in supportive and caring ways. (Levine & Laurie, 1974)

An example of family involvement in child rearing outside the immediate parents is found in Sioux families. This involvement begins early in a child's life, when a second set of parents are selected for the newborn (Sandoz, 1961). Therefore, the total family involved in child rearing and support includes unrelated members of the Indian community (Ryan, 1981). This community support and protection can be viewed as responsibility for others' actions (Light & Martin, 1986).

More recent studies have shown that Native American family ties extend across generations. Native American grandparents have shown high levels of involvement in the care of their grandchildren (Mutchler, Baker, & Lee, 2007). Native Americans also report high levels of caregiving to their elderly relatives (McGuire, Okoro, Goins, & Anderson, 2008). Indeed, Native American culture and families traditionally emphasize sensitivity toward kin, tribe, and land and value the collective over the individual, in contrast to the mainstream U.S. emphasis on individual fulfillment and achievement (Light & Martin, 1986; Newcomb, 2008). Research on Native Americans of the Southwest suggests that many members of these groups see their children as belonging to the entire American Indian nation: to the land, the sky, the tribe, and its history, customs, and traditions (Nicholas, 2009).

Some controversies over family life taking place within Native American communities mirror those taking place in U.S. society more generally. For instance, beginning in 2008, some tribes began to permit same-sex marriage; in that year, the Coquille tribe of Oregon was the first to pass a law defining marriage or domestic partnership as a "formal and express civil contract entered into by two persons, regardless of their sex." The sovereign Navajo Nation, together with tribes such as the Kickapoo and Chicksaw, has resisted this step, even after the legalization of same-sex marriage by

©Lawrence Migdale/Science Source

The 2010 U.S. Census counted just over half a million (557, 185) American Indian and Alaska Native families in the United States. About 57% were reported to be married-couple families.

TABLE 11.1 Top 10 Feeder Countries for Migration to the United States, 2016

COUNTRY OF BIRTH	POPULATION	PERCENTAGE OF U.S. MIGRANTS BY COUNTRY OF ORIGIN
Mexico	11,541,444	27
India	2,216,455	6
China	1,929,738	5
Philippines	1,912,397	4
El Salvador	1,295,462	3
Vietnam	1,293,961	3
Cuba	1,180,543	3
Dominican Republic	1,012,296	3
Korea	1,061,290	2
Guatemala	902,969	2

Source: U.S. Census Bureau. (2017). *Place of birth for the foreign-born population.* Washington, DC: U.S. Government Printing Office.

the U.S. Supreme Court in 2015: According to the Navajo nation's marriage law, "Marriage between persons of the same sex is void and prohibited." These sovereign tribes' laws are not affected by the Supreme Court ruling because the tribes were never parties to the U.S. Constitution (Drew, 2015). Interestingly, some research shows that gay partnerships were historically accepted in many tribal cultures, where the term *two spirits* was used to categorize LGBT members (Kronk, 2013).

Deaf Culture and Family Life

Census Bureau data show that about one fifth of the U.S. population has some kind of disability. How does disability affect family life? In this subsection, we examine the case of deaf people and the choices and challenges that family life brings for them. According to Gallaudet University (2012) figures, in 2012, approximately 13% of the U.S. population had hearing problems that may range from being fully deaf to being hard of hearing. Fewer than 1 in 1,000 were deaf before the age of 18; more than half became deaf at some point after childhood (Gallaudet Research Institute, 2005). Family life poses unique challenges for many deaf people, and, as a consequence, some prefer to practice endogamy, marrying others who are deaf and therefore share a common experience.

There has been a movement within the deaf community to redefine the meaning of deafness to denote not a form of disability but a positive culture. Some deaf people see themselves as similar to an ethnic group: sharing a common language (American Sign Language, or ASL), possessing

a strong sense of cultural identity, and taking pride in their heritage. Identifying as an ethnic group rather than as a disability group, some deaf people believe that cochlear implant surgery, a procedure through which some deaf people can become hearing, is problematic, especially when it is performed on children who cannot consent. Often, deaf people who undergo this surgery are still unable to attain mastery of any oral language (Lane, 2005). The National Association of the Deaf (2000) takes a cautionary stance on cochlear implants, advising hearing parents of deaf children to conduct thorough research, create a support system, and, most important, communicate with their children before undertaking the transition. Julie Mitchiner takes pride in being deaf. She writes,

> Growing up with deaf parents and attending deaf schools, I have a strong sense of pride of being deaf and being part of the Deaf community. I do not look at myself as disabled. I often say if I were given a choice to hear or stay deaf, I'd choose to stay deaf. It is who I am. My family, my friends, and my community have taught me that being deaf is part of our culture and is a way of life. (Mitchiner & Sass-Lehrer, 2011, p. 3)

Many deaf people succeed in the hearing world, but they may confront daunting problems (Heppner, 1992). Often, they are not able to speak in a way that hearing people fully understand, and most hearing people do not know ASL. It is not surprising that an estimated 85% of deaf people choose to marry others who share their own language and culture (Cichowski & Nance, 2004) or that many deaf parents

Gallaudet University in Washington, DC, is unique in serving specifically people who are deaf and hearing-impaired by offering bilingual instruction in English and ASL. The rising proportion of students who are hearing or come from mainstream schools and do not know ASL has led to debates over the centrality of deaf culture at the school.

are wary when their deaf children form relationships with hearing people. When a deaf couple has a hearing child, the family must make difficult choices as they negotiate not only the ordinary challenges of child rearing but also the raising of a child who may be "functionally hearing" but "culturally deaf" (Bishop & Hicks, 2009; Preston, 1994).

Families typically confer their own cultural status on their children, but this may not be true for 9 of 10 deaf children born to hearing parents. On one hand, hearing parents want the same sorts of things for their deaf children as any parents want for their children: happiness, fulfillment, and successful lives as adults. Many would like their children to mainstream into the hearing world as well as possible, in spite of the challenges. On the other hand, some in the deaf community argue that the deaf children of hearing parents can never fully belong to the hearing world. Many in the deaf community believe hearing parents should send their deaf children to residential schools for the deaf, where they will be fully accepted, learn deaf culture, and be with people who share their experience of deafness (Dolnick, 1993; Lane, 1992; Sparrow, 2005).

The situations of deaf parents raising a hearing child and hearing parents raising a deaf child raise interesting and fundamental questions about what happens when family members are also members of different cultures and how the obstacles of difference within a micro unit such as the family are negotiated.

Families in Crisis

Domestic (or family) violence is *physical or sexual abuse committed by one family member against another.* It may be perpetrated by adults against their children, by one spouse against another, by one sibling against another, or by adult children against their elderly parents. As little as three to four decades ago, domestic violence was rarely studied. Many people regarded violence in the home as a private matter, an attitude that was reflected in lawmaking as well, which provided few sanctions for violence that did not reach the level of severe injury or death. Today, domestic violence is understood to be a serious public issue, as researchers have come to realize that it is sadly commonplace.

Accurate data on family violence are difficult to obtain for a variety of reasons. Abused partners or children are reluctant to call attention to the fact that they are abused. Police do not want to mediate or make arrests in family conflicts, and even today, the courts are hesitant to intervene in what are often perceived as family matters (Tolan, Gorman-Smith, & Henry, 2005). Some good estimates of the prevalence of this crime are available, however. According to the U.S. Bureau of Justice Statistics, between 2003 and 2013, domestic violence made up about a fifth of all violent crime in the United States. The most common form of domestic violence is *intimate partner violence* (IPV), that is, violence that involves current or former spouses or nonmarried partners (Truman & Morgan, 2014).

The National Intimate Partner and Sexual Violence Survey, an ongoing survey developed and administered by the Centers for Disease Control and Prevention (CDC), found in 2010 that one in three women and one in four men surveyed had been victims of IPV in their lifetimes. As defined by the CDC, IPV includes physical violence, rape, and stalking by a former or current partner or spouse. About one in four women and one in seven men surveyed had experienced severe physical violence at the hands of their partners. Although these data are for experiences over the life course, even the data from a single year reveal a serious epidemic of IPV. According to the survey, more than 12 million people experienced IPV in 2010 (Centers for Disease Control and Prevention, 2018).

Child abuse—sexual and/or physical assaults on children by adult members of their families—is also common in our society. According to the U.S. Department of Health and Human Services (2010), approximately 3.3 million child abuse reports and allegations were made in 2009 involving about 6 million children. On any given day, no fewer than five children die as the result of abuse (U.S. Government Accountability Office, 2011), although the main form of abuse is neglect (U.S. Department of Health and Human Services, 2010). Boys and girls are equally likely to be physically abused, but girls are more likely to be sexually abused as well. According to Childhelp (2010), an

Domestic (or family) violence: Physical or sexual abuse committed by one family member against another.

organization dedicated to the prevention of child abuse, the cycle of abuse is difficult to break; one study suggests that about 30% of abused and neglected children will later abuse their own children.

Elder abuse is the victimization of elderly persons by family members or other caregivers. In a National Institute of Justice study, 11% of elderly U.S. adults (those 65 or older) surveyed reported experiencing either emotional, physical, or sexual abuse or potential neglect (Acierno, Hernandez-Tejada, Muzzy, & Steve, 2009). Similar to child abuse, elder abuse is likely underreported, because victims are often in a subordinate position in the family and unable to access help outside the home. Elder abuse also shares with child abuse some of its forms, including neglect—the failure of caregivers to provide for basic needs such as nutritious food and hygienic conditions—and physical abuse. Some aspects of elder abuse differ from abuse of other kinds of victims, however. For example, elder abuse may take the form of financial exploitation or outright theft of property. Those who care for elderly relatives may feel entitled to the resources the seniors possess—or they may simply take advantage of the older persons' vulnerabilities.

As sociologists examining a problem that is both a private trouble and a public issue, we need to ask, "Why does domestic violence exist and persist in family life?" The acceptance of a husband's "right" to subject his wife to physical discipline has roots in Anglo-American culture. British common law permitted a man to strike his wife and children with a stick as a form of punishment, provided the stick was no thicker than his thumb; the phrase *rule of thumb* originates in this practice. Through the end of the 19th century in the United States, men could legally beat their wives (Renzetti & Curran, 1992). Research has found that domestic violence is most likely to be prevalent in societies in which family relationships are characterized by high emotional intensity and attachment, there is a pattern of male dominance and sexual inequality, a high value is placed on the privacy of family life, and violence is common in other institutional spheres, such as entertainment or popular culture (Straus & Gelles, 1990; Straus, Gelles, & Steinmetz, 1988).

People have become more aware of child and spousal abuse and its spectrum of consequences in recent years, largely because of efforts by the women's movement to bring them into the open. Shelters for battered women and children enable victims to be protected from violence. Although still limited in number, such refuges have enabled women to get counseling while terminating abusive relationships in relative safety (Haj-yahia & Cohen, 2009). Family violence is clearly a dysfunctional

social phenomenon. It is both a personal trouble and a public issue. A fuller understanding of its roots and consequences can contribute to both a better-informed national conversation about the problem and more robust efforts to address it.

Domestic violence is a persistent source of family crisis in society. A more recent phenomenon is the dramatic rise in opioid addiction in some U.S. regions and the effect this is having on families. According to recent data, on any given day in 2016, about 437,500 children were in foster care and in the same year, over 273,000 entered foster care for the first time. **Foster care** is *a situation in which a child is cared for by people who are not his or her parents for either a brief or extended period of time.* Foster care may be used when a parent is determined by authorities to no longer be capable of safely caring for the child. A foster parent may be a relative but may also be a nonrelative who has been vetted by authorities. While not all children enter foster care because of a parent's drug addiction, the opioid crisis has been a catalyst in the rise of children needing foster homes. A judge in Indiana (which, together with other parts of the Midwest, has been hard-hit by the opioid crisis) recently noted that the intake of children into foster care has more than doubled in the past two years in his area (Simon 2017). A recent *New York Times* report notes, "In Montana, the number of children in foster care has doubled since 2010. In Georgia, it has increased by 80 percent, and in West Virginia, by 45 percent." It continues,

The data points to drug abuse as a primary reason, and experts have identified opioids in particular. Neglect remains the main reason children enter foster care. But

A five-year-old participates in the Hope Not Heroin march and rally held in Norwalk, Ohio on July 15, 2017. Both of the boy's parents are heroin addicts.

©Spencer Platt/Getty Images News/Getty Images

Foster care: A situation in which a child is cared for by people who are not his or her parents for either a brief or extended period of time.

from 2015 to 2016, the increase in the number of children who came into foster care as a result of parental drug abuse was far greater than the increases in the 14 other categories, like housing instability, according to data from the federal Adoption and Foster Care Analysis and Reporting System. (Lachman 2017, para. 2–3)

Authorities in areas ravaged by the opioid crisis are struggling to find enough foster homes to care for children removed from threatening situations (Lachman 2017; Figure 11.13). Widespread opioid addiction, born of prescription drugs such as Oxycontin and Vicodin, given by health care providers for pain, has birthed a crisis of heroin and fentanyl use and abuse that has devastated families in many communities not only through death and injury, but through the dissolution of families (Quinones 2015).

■ **FIGURE 11.13** The Opioid Epidemic

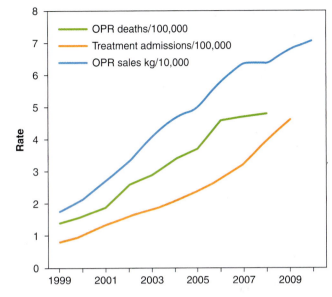

Source: Morbidity and Mortality Weekly Report, November 4, 2011, Center for Disease Control and Prevention.

💬 Social Life, Social Media

CLICK HERE: DATING AND DIVORCE IN THE AGE OF THE INTERNET

The initiation and dissolution of relationships have become increasingly rationalized and efficient in the digital age. It may take only a few taps on one's computer keyboard or a handful of swipes on a phone to meet someone, and it *may* take only a few hours and uploaded files to end it all.

A growing number of U.S. adults of all ages are meeting potential dates and mates online. According to a Pew Research Center survey, in 2015, about 15% of U.S. adults used online dating sites or mobile dating apps. There is some variation by generation in these figures: For instance, mobile dating apps appear to be rapidly pushing up the proportion of young adults who seek to meet someone online. In 2013, only 5% of those in this age group reported using mobile dating apps; by 2015, this had risen to 22%. Significant proportions of respondents also indicate that they know someone who engages in online dating (41%) or who has met a long-term partner online (29%; Geiger & Livingston, 2018).

Online dating tools are variable. Some Internet services such as Match and eHarmony offer users the opportunity to find a suitable match based on shared interests or characteristics. Others,

such as the wildly popular dating app Tinder, are based largely on where one finds oneself: They use a phone's geolocation system to determine the presence of potential partners who are proximate to the user. With the Tinder app, for instance, users swipe right on profiles that appeal to them and swipe left on profiles that are not of interest. Tinder claims that it hosts about 1.6 billion swipes a day that take place across at least 196 countries (Purvis, 2017). Though Tinder has gotten a reputation as a platform oriented toward short-term relationships, at least one qualitative study has found that more users say they are interested in long-term love than hookups (Sumter, Vandenbosch, & Ligtenberg, 2016.

While meeting someone online may have been a source of trepidation or mild embarrassment in the past, today, it is widely accepted: 59% of respondents in a Pew Research Center poll indicated that is a good way to meet people and just under half agreed that it is "easier and more efficient" than alternative ways of meeting people (Geiger & Livingston, 2018).

If meeting dates and mates is easier and more efficient in the Internet era, then so is the

(Continued)

(Continued)

process of shaking loose from the legal ties of a relationship. Led by a new website entitled "It's Over Easy," divorce is also now available for online purchase. The site offers various package levels that are priced from $750 and up, depending on the services desired by the user. Invited to comment on her motivation for the site, the lawyer who initiated "It's Over Easy," notes that "couples today date online and bank online. . . . They're do-it-yourselfers. If they can buy an espresso maker

online, they can get divorced online" (Sohn, 2018, para. 7).

Think It Through

- Who benefits and who loses from the rationalization of initiating and ending intimate relationships? How is efficiency in the form of dating and divorce apps a benefit to modern relationships? How is it a cost?

Socioeconomic Class and Family in the United States

An array of family differences are linked to social class differences. In this section, we consider research showing that social class may have an effect on child-rearing practices as well as on family formation through marriage.

Social Class and Child Rearing

Parents are often caught in a dilemma: They must instill some degree of conformity in their children as they attempt to socialize them into the norms and values that will be socially appropriate for adult behavior, but at the same time, they must foster a degree of independence—after all, children must eventually leave the nest and survive in the adult world. Given the tension between protecting children and instilling independence, it should not be surprising that in most families, neither is fully achieved. Parents may understand that they need to help build their children's independence yet still be unwilling to trust their children's judgment, especially during adolescence. They may hang on to their children, prolonging dependence past the point in which children are ready to make decisions on their own. Growing up includes some degree of conflict no matter what approach parents use.

Some studies suggest that parental attitudes toward children's independence may differ by social class. In the United States, middle- and upper-class families tend to value self-direction and individual initiative in their children. Working-class parents, by contrast, have been observed by some researchers to value respect for authority, obedience, and a higher degree of conformity and to rely on punishment when these norms are violated. Sociologist Melvin Kohn (1989), who spent many years studying class differences in child rearing, attributes these differences to the parents' work experiences: Middle- and upper-class jobs often require individual initiative and innovation, while working-class jobs tend to emphasize conformity.

Annette Lareau (2002) goes beyond Kohn's focus on work experiences to argue that social class (which we experience in a multitude of ways) has an impact on family life, in particular on the styles of child rearing in which parents engage. In reporting her study, in which 88 White and Black American families were interviewed and 12 were closely observed at home, Lareau writes,

> It is the interweaving of life experiences and resources, including parents' economic resources, occupational conditions, and educational backgrounds, that appears to be most important in leading middle-class parents to engage in concerted cultivation and working-class and poor parents to engage in the accomplishment of natural growth. (pp. 771–772)

These two concepts—concerted cultivation and accomplishment of natural growth—form a key foundation for Lareau's argument. She defines *concerted cultivation* as a style of parenting associated most fully with the middle class and characterized by an emphasis on negotiation, discussion, questioning of authority, and cultivation of talents and skills through, among other things, participation in organized activities. Lareau explains the *accomplishment of natural growth* as a parenting style associated with working-class and poor families. Directives rather than negotiation and explanation, a focus on obedience, and an inclination to care for children's basic needs characterize this style, in which parents leave children to play and grow in a largely unstructured environment. Notably, Lareau identifies a tension between obedience and trust in this style, suggesting it is characterized by something close to distrustful consent born of frustration with authority and dominant institutions but a sense of powerlessness in their presence. From this, she suggests, children take away an emerging sense of constraint. Consider the following observation by Kathryn Edin and Maria Kefalas (2005):

Discover & Debate

MARRIAGE AND MODERNITY

Motion: Marriage is a fundamental part of a healthy society and a healthy family. States and the federal government should adopt policies that encourage and support marriage.

Background: Traditional marriage has long been a part of the religious, cultural, and social fabric of the United States, but some important changes have taken place. According to the Pew Research Center, fewer Americans are married today than in the past: Although in 1960, 72% of adults were married, by 2000, the figure had fallen to 57%. Today, about half of adults are in a marital relationship. Marriage rates among young adults are far lower than they were in previous generations: Only about a quarter of millennials are married. By comparison, when they were the same age as millennials are now, about 36% of Gen Xers, 48% of baby boomers, and 65% of those in the Silent Generation were married.

Questions for Consideration

- How does the debate over same-sex marriage, legalized by the U.S. Supreme Court in 2015, fit into the debate over the state's role in marriage?

- A recent study (Kalmijn, 2017) suggests that even though marriage has a small positive effect on life satisfaction, the negative effect of divorce on satisfaction is pronounced. What does this suggest about the desirability of policies that incentivize marriage?

- What should be the role of the government in related issues such as childbearing, child care, and divorce?

Debate Tip

- Anecdotal evidence ("I know someone who . . .") is something upon which we rely in conversations about issues. In a debate, however, anecdotal evidence may be of limited value because the experience of one person or small group of people cannot be generalized. Look for strong empirical evidence to support your arguments.

AFFIRMATIVE ARGUMENTS	OPPOSITION ARGUMENTS
Families are a fundamental cornerstone of society, and the government should encourage and support family formation with policies such as tax benefits for married couples.	Financial incentives to marriage such as tax benefits unfairly penalize those who, whether by choice or circumstance, are unmarried.
There is evidence that marriage has positive psychological and health benefits for couples.	Marriage is a private decision, and the state should neither encourage nor discourage it. The government should accept and adopt policies that support a wide variety of family forms without prioritizing one over another.
Marriage has positive benefits for children, including a lower risk of poverty in married-couple families.	The psychological and health benefits of marriage are mixed and heavily dependent on the level of conflict in a relationship.

While poor mothers see keeping a child housed, fed, clothed, and safe as noteworthy accomplishments, their middle-class counterparts often feel they must earn their parenting stripes by faithfully cheering at soccer league games, chaperoning boy scout camping trips and attending ballet recitals or martial arts competitions. (p. 141)

What are the effects of these differing styles of child rearing, which Lareau argues are associated with class status? Examining the outcomes for children in her study as they approached adulthood, Lareau (2002) concludes that the accomplishment of natural growth style not only tends to cultivate early independence but also leads young people toward jobs that require respect for authority and obedience to directives, such as those associated with the working class. In contrast, the concerted cultivation approach to child raising tended to lead young people both to hold a sense of entitlement and to pursue careers that require a broad vocabulary and ease in negotiating with people in authority. Following up with the families she studied, Lareau found that all the middle-class children had completed high school and that most were attending college. Many of the children of low-income families had left high school and few were in college. "In sum," she writes, "differences in family life lie not only in the advantages parents obtain for their children, but also in the skills they transmit to children for negotiating their own life paths" (p. 749).

These studies strongly suggest that family life, and practices of child rearing in particular, contribute to the reproduction of class status. Although structural factors, including obstacles related to educational and economic resources, are an important part of the picture, Lareau suggests that the orientations and skills developed in childhood, which become part of a young adult's human capital as he or she negotiates the path through school and toward a job, are also relevant to understanding socioeconomic outcomes and the reproduction of class status.

Economy, Culture, and Family Formation

Class status is linked with changing patterns of family life in another important way. Some sociologists believe that macro-level economic changes, in particular the rise of a postindustrial economy and associated labor market, have had a powerful effect on micro-level practices of family formation (Edin & Kefalas, 2005; Wilson, 1996, 2010). In this section, we examine the sociological roots of the decline of marriage and the rise of nonmarital births in poor and working-class Black, White, and Latino communities.

In 1965, Daniel Patrick Moynihan, a former professor of sociology who was then the assistant U.S. secretary of labor and would later become a U.S. senator from New York, published a controversial study of the African American family titled *The Negro Family: The Case for National Action,* which later came to be called *the Moynihan Report.* In it, Moynihan argued that lower-class Black family life was often dysfunctional, as reflected in high rates of family dissolution, single parenting, and the dominance of female-headed families.

Moynihan saw the breakdown of Black families, together with continued racial inequality, as leading to a new crisis in race relations. He identified the legacy of slavery, which intentionally broke up Black families, as one of the roots of the problem. He also argued that many rural Blacks had failed to adapt adequately to urban environments. Moynihan concluded that these patterns in family life were, at least in part, responsible for the failure of many low-income Black Americans to make it into the economic mainstream in the United States. He saw Black poverty and inner-city violence, which exploded in the urban riots of the 1960s, as partly the result of Black family breakdown.

The Moynihan Report was widely criticized as racist and sexist, and Moynihan was accused of blaming the victims of racism and poverty (primarily Black female heads of household) for their disadvantages. Many critics ignored Moynihan's attention to structural as well as cultural factors in his analysis, however. Although he wrote that "at the center of the tangle of pathology is the weakness of the

family structure," he also implicated social phenomena such as unemployment, poverty, and racial segregation in the decline of families and the rise of dysfunctions. Still, critics focused largely on his cultural analysis, and Moynihan's findings were disregarded while sociologists avoided examining the connections among race, family characteristics, and poverty for at least two decades.

In 1987, sociologist William Julius Wilson published *The Truly Disadvantaged: The Inner City, the Underclass, and Public Policy,* in which he revisited the issues Moynihan had raised in the 1965 report. In the two intervening decades, much had changed—and much had stayed the same. The family patterns that Moynihan had identified as problematic, including nonmarital births and high levels of family dissolution, had become more pronounced among poor and working-class Black Americans. At the same time, social problems such as joblessness in the inner city had grown more acute, as deindustrialization and the movement of jobs to the suburbs dramatically reduced the number of positions available for less-educated and low-skilled workers. These changes, Wilson noted, had important consequences for family formation.

Almost 10 years later, Wilson (1996) argued that falling rates of marriage and rising numbers of nonmarital births were, at least in part, rooted in the declining numbers of "marriageable men" in inner-city neighborhoods. He posited that the ratio of unmarried Black women to single and "marriageable" Black men of similar age was skewed by male joblessness, high rates of incarceration, and high death rates for young Black men. The loss of jobs in the inner city had a powerfully negative effect on male employment opportunities. The consequences were felt not only in the economic fortunes of communities but also, and no less importantly, in families, where women were choosing motherhood but options for marriage were diminished by the uneven ratio of single women to marriageable men. Although rates of nonmarital births had previously been high in Black communities, where extended families have traditionally been available to support mothers and children (Gerstel & Gallagher, 1994), Wilson saw new urban circumstances as central to the rise of nonmarital births among Black Americans from one quarter in 1965 (when Moynihan published his report) to about 70% by the middle 1990s, where it remains today (Figure 11.14). By then, about half of Black American families were headed by a woman (Wilson, 2010).

When Wilson revisited this issue in 2010, he found that research on the relationship between male employment and rates of marriage and single parenthood offered mixed findings:

Joblessness among black men is a significant factor in their delayed entry into marriage and in the decreasing

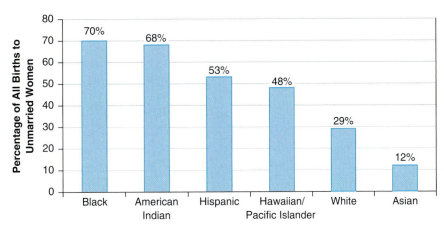

■ **FIGURE 11.14** Nonmarital Birthrate by Race/Ethnicity in the United States, 2016

Source: National Vital Statistics Report. Vol. 67, No 1. p. 31. Table 9. (January 31, 2018). Retrieved from https://www.cdc.gov/nchs/data/nvsr/nvsr67/nvsr67_01.pdf.

rates of marriage after a child has been born, and this relationship has been exacerbated by sharp increases in incarceration that in turn lead to continued joblessness. Nevertheless, much of the decline in marriages in the inner city, including marriages that occur after a child has been born, remains unexplained when only structural factors are examined. (p. 108)

Wilson (2010) also cited cultural factors in the fragmentation of the poor Black family. Although sociologists have been reluctant to use culture as an explanation, not least due to fear of the backlash generated by the Moynihan Report, Wilson writes that structure and culture interact to create normative contexts for behavior. He points out, for instance, that

> both inner-city black males and females believe that since most marriages will eventually break up and no longer represent meaningful relationships, it is better to avoid the entanglements of wedlock altogether. . . . Single mothers who perceive the fathers of their children as unreliable or as having limited financial means will often—rationally—choose single parenthood. (p. 125)

In this social context, the stigma of unmarried parenthood is minimal, and behaviors rooted in structure become culturally normative.

Examining the phenomenon of low marriage rates and high nonmarital births in some communities, sociologists Kathryn Edin and Maria Kefalas (2005) looked at data on low-income White, Black, and Puerto Rican single mothers in Camden, New Jersey, and Philadelphia, Pennsylvania. Black communities have historically had higher nonmarital birthrates and lower rates of marriage than White and Latino communities, but in low-income White and Latino communities, comparable trends have taken root.

Edin and Kefalas found that the women in their study placed a high value on both motherhood and marriage. They saw motherhood as a key role and central achievement in their lives, and few made serious efforts to delay motherhood. If anything, they saw early motherhood as something that had forced them to mature and kept them from getting into trouble. At the same time, they held a utopian view of marriage that may, ironically, have put it out of their reach. Many dreamed of achieving financial security and owning a home before marrying—but their poverty made this a challenge. More problematic, perhaps, was that they did not consider the men in their lives—often the fathers of their children—to be good partners, their marriageability undermined by low education, joblessness, poor economic prospects, criminal records, violence, drug and alcohol abuse, and infidelity.

Notably, then, even though they highly valued marriage, the women had few realistic opportunities to achieve stability and independence first, and little hope of finding stable partners. Motherhood, however, was an achievable dream, an opportunity to occupy an important social role and to achieve success as a parent, where other paths of opportunity were often blocked by poor structural circumstances.

Statistics show that children in single-mother homes are among those most likely to be born and to grow up impoverished. They are also more likely than their better-off peers to repeat the patterns of their parents and to remain in poverty. Here, some interesting sociological questions emerge: Is single parenthood a cause (not the only one) of poverty, or is living in poverty a sociological root of single parenthood? Or perhaps both are true? What are the implications of the answers to these questions for the design of public policies that address poverty?

The relationships among class, poverty, and family patterns are complex, but Wilson and Edin and Kefalas offer sociological lenses for understanding some of the structural and cultural roots of low marriage rates and high nonmarital birthrates in many poor U.S. communities. As Wilson notes in his book *More Than Just Race: Being Black and Poor in the Inner City*, "How families are formed among America's poorest citizens is an area that cries out for further research" (p. 129). What other factors should sociologists examine? How would you conduct such a study? What kinds of questions would you ask?

Family Life in the Middle Class

Today, parents in the U.S. middle class, particularly its upper fraction, devote an unprecedented amount of resources to child rearing. Although some of the rising financial outlays are for basic needs and child care, parents are also committing time and money to enrichment activities intended to give their offspring advantages in competition, education, and the future labor market. According to a 2013 study, the growing U.S. income gap is reflected in a gap in spending on children that opened up in the period from the 1990s to the 2000s, with families in the top half of the income distribution spending more on their progeny while families in the bottom spend less (Kornrich & Furstenberg, 2013). More economically advantaged parents are actively engaged in building what Hilary Levey Friedman (2013) calls "competitive kid capital." Friedman's study of 95 families with elementary school–age children who were involved in competitive after-school activities such as chess, dance, and soccer found that many parents

> saw their kids' participation in competitive afterschool activities as a way to develop certain values and skills: the importance of winning; the ability to bounce back from a loss to win in the future; to succeed in stressful situations; and to perform under the gaze of others. (p. 31)

Interestingly, Friedman points out that parents of upper-middle-class girls are more likely to enroll their girls in soccer or chess than in dance, pursuing an "aggressive femininity" that they perceive to offer their daughters a future labor market advantage.

Middle-class family life is often characterized by a strong commitment to constructive and active child rearing (as we saw in Lareau's study and the research described above) and to the parents' pursuit of careers. These competing commitments often leave parents without the time to do everything or to do it well and feeling rushed and stressed instead of satisfied.

Sociologist Arlie Russell Hochschild (2001b) has come to some interesting and perhaps surprising conclusions about this modern dilemma. Hochschild conducted a series of interviews with employees at a well-known *Fortune* 500 firm that had gone to some lengths to be family friendly, offering flextime, the option of part-time work, parental leave, job sharing, and even a course titled "Work–Life Balance for Two-Career Couples." But she noticed that the family-friendly measures didn't make much of a difference. Most employees said they put "family first," but they also felt strained to the limit, and almost none cut back on work time. Few took advantage of parental leave or the option of part-time employment.

Why do people say they want to strike a better balance between work and the rest of their lives and yet do nothing about it when they have the opportunity? Some reasons are practical; several employees in Hochschild's study feared that taking advantage of liberal work policies would count against them in their careers, while others simply needed the money—they couldn't afford to work less. Yet Hochschild identified a more surprising reason many people worked long hours: They liked being at work better than being at home. Previous research had shown that many men regard work as a haven, and Hochschild found that a notable number of working women now feel the same way. Despite the stress of long hours and guilt about being away from their families, they are reluctant to cut back on their commitment to paid work.

Hochschild found that both men and women often derive support, companionship, security, pride, and a sense of being valued when they are working. In the absence of family time and kin and community support at home, some parents sought and found—and sometimes preferred—a sense of competence and achievement in the workplace. In about a fifth of the families Hochschild studied, work (rather than home) was the site at which the parents derived the most satisfaction.

Many studies since have found that workplaces with more family-friendly policies have higher levels of workplace satisfaction and productivity as well as lower levels of stress (Bilal, Zia-ur-Rehman, & Raza, 2010; Frye & Breaugh, 2004). Still, Hochschild's (2001b) research suggests that many people derive satisfaction from being workaholics. As she concludes, "Working families are both prisoners and architects of the time bind in which they find themselves" (p. 249).

Private Lives, Public Issues

PARENTING IN POVERTY

©REUTERS/Shannon Stapleton

Parents across the economic spectrum seek to raise healthy and happy children and to meet the many challenges of shepherding boys and girls from infancy to adulthood. But parenting in poverty presents a range of obstacles and fears that well-off families are far less likely to face.

For one thing, parenting in poverty is expensive. As a blog post in the *Washington Post* noted, for parenting families in the middle quintile of the household income spectrum, diapers consume just under 3% of their income; for those in the upper two quintiles, the figure is closer to 1 to 2%. By contrast, nearly 14% of the household income of the poorest quintile goes to diapers (Badger & Eilperin, 2016). What explains this dramatic difference? Consider the fact that today many middle- or upper-income families buy their disposable diapers in bulk from shopping clubs such as Sam's Club or through the mail from Amazon, which offers free shipping for subscribed members. This can considerably reduce the cost and increase the convenience of buying a good that has become a basic necessity of modern life.

For low-income families, these avenues are often foreclosed. Poor parents may not be able to afford a costly membership to a shopper's club—or even a car to travel to a distant warehouse shop where these items could be bought. They may not have space at home to store bulk purchases of diapers or other household goods. Those with little money may not be able to purchase the larger bags of diapers that offer a better value; instead, they are forced by economic circumstances to buy in small quantities. As the authors of the blog write,

> Cheap diapers are hard to come by for the families that have the least to spend on them. Mora, 27, scans coupons and travels for bargains. She tells her children "no" at the grocery store, when she has to choose

between the kiwis they want and the diapers 2-year-old Nathan needs. Then, sometimes, when she finds a good deal, it comes in the wrong sizes. "Sometimes you have to decide between 'Okay, this box has 120 diapers, and this is the size that he doesn't use. But if I get the size that he's using, it's just 70 diapers, and I have 50 diapers more. So what should I do?'" she says, knowing that a too-small size might chafe her son's skin. "You just have to make things happen." (Badger & Eilperin, 2016, para. 3)

The challenges do not end at the doorstep of an individual household. Parenting in poverty often means raising children in economically disadvantaged neighborhoods, which present a further set of challenges. A recent Pew Research Center report titled "Parenting in America" reports that "higher-income parents are nearly twice as likely as lower-income parents to rate their neighborhood as an 'excellent' or 'very good' place to raise kids (78% to 42%)." Fully 38% of families with incomes under $30,000 described their neighborhood as only a "fair or poor" place to raise children. Among families with incomes over $75,000, the figure was only 7%. The differences do not stop there: Nearly half of the poorest families expressed a fear that their child could get shot, and over half worried that their child could get beat up or attacked. Although these concerns were also expressed by better-off families, 22% of whom worried about shooting and 38% of whom were concerned about other physical violence, the figures suggest a lower perceived degree of threat (Pew Research Center, 2015a).

There are, to be sure, commonalities that many parents share, regardless of income. Comparable numbers of parents expressed fears of a son or daughter struggling with anxiety or depression or having problems with drugs or alcohol (Pew Research Center, 2015a). At the same time, families with greater economic means are likely to have fuller access to resources to address these problems, again highlighting some of the challenges to poor parents seeking, like their better-off peers, to make a good life for their children.

Think It Through

- How does this essay on parenting in poverty highlight the intersection between private troubles and public issues? What are the private troubles and the public issues to which the essay draws our attention?

Globalization and Families

The impact of globalization on families depends to a substantial degree on social class and country or region of residence. In this section, we look at ways in which different families experience globalization and its myriad costs and benefits.

Consider the economic and labor market impact of globalization on U.S. families. On the one hand, globalization has contributed to an increase in many employers' demands for men and women with high degrees of skill and formal training, particularly in technical fields. On the other hand, low-skilled U.S. workers have been priced out of many sectors of the global job market by the fact that lower-wage labor is readily available elsewhere around the globe. Globalization can produce national economic gains even as it diminishes the prospects of some categories of workers.

About 70% of the individuals who make up the U.S. labor force do not hold four-year college degrees. As we see elsewhere in this text, these are the workers who have been hit hardest by global economic change. Writing about domestic manufacturing industries, journalist Louis Uchitelle (2007) observes:

> As customers defected, sales plummeted and failed to bounce back. Nowhere was that more apparent than in the auto industry's struggle with [lower-cost] Japanese imports. But nearly every manufacturer was hit, and the steep recession in 1981 and 1982 compounded the damage. The old world has never returned. (p. 8)

Many working-class families have found themselves confronting flat or declining incomes as a result of competition with a global workforce. Household incomes at the bottom of the economic spectrum have declined most dramatically since the 1970s, when globalization began to transform the domestic economy. This decline has had a multitude of effects on U.S. families. Recall our discussion in this chapter of the diminished pool of "marriageable" males. Here, we see some of the effects of declining job opportunities and wages in manufacturing, which used to offer gainful employment to less-educated men.

The need for a family to have two incomes to make ends meet is one of the reasons for the dramatic increase in the number of women working outside the home. The movement of women into the paid workforce has, in turn, provided some women with a degree of economic independence and an opportunity to rethink the meaning of marriage. As women join the paid workforce, some postpone marriage until they are older. Couples choose cohabiting as an alternative to marriage, and when they do decide to have children, their families are likely to be smaller. Some may never marry; as we learned earlier, marriage is continuing to decline among young adults.

Globalization means greater mobility for families and more fluid ways of organizing work and life. The benefits of globalization enjoyed by some U.S. families, however, are accompanied by the losses suffered by others.

International Families and the Global Woman

Macro-level processes of globalization affect U.S. families in a variety of ways. In this section, we examine the dual phenomena of *international families* and the *global woman* to emphasize some of the micro-level effects of globalization on women, particularly women from the developing world.

Anthropologist Christine Ho (1993) has examined what she terms **international families**—*families that result from globalization.* Focusing on mothers who emigrate from the Caribbean to the United States, Ho documents how they often rely on child

©George Wilhelm/Los Angeles Times via Getty Images

The effects of economic globalization on families have been uneven, with negative consequences borne disproportionately by those with less education. Can you identify any current trends that suggest the circumstances of households headed by adults with a high school education or less will improve or worsen in coming decades?

International families: Families that result from globalization.

Global Issues

DATING, MATING, AND TECHNOLOGY IN JAPAN

The popularity of establishing and maintaining a relationship with a member of the opposite sex appears to be on the decline in Japan. A decreased interest in dating, mating, and marriage among young men and women is apparent in sociological studies. One survey of Japanese people ages 18 to 34, for instance, found that almost 70% of unmarried men and 60% of unmarried women were not in relationships (Aoki 2016).

Japan has experienced a dramatic decline in young adults' interest in dating and marriage in the past decade due, at least in part, to diverging paths of women and men. A growing number of women are pursuing advanced education and professional careers and showing less interest in traditional women's roles, particularly since there is a common societal expectation that childbearing and child raising, done primarily by the wife, will shortly follow marriage. At the same time, many women seek men who are financially secure, but with more men in part-time or temporary jobs or struggling to establish financial security, neither men nor women are rushing into relationships (*The Economist*, 2016).

While the formation of dating or marital relationships is on the decline, some young adults in Japan are engaging in "dating sim" games that let a player craft a partner to his or her preferences and then maintain a relationship with the virtual partner as if it were real life. The players are able to adjust the moods and personalities of their partners and even give gifts and send romantic e-mails (Glascock 2015). A recent article in *The Guardian* on the phenomenon of "stranded singles" in Japan notes that a recent survey found that about 30% of single women and 15% of single men aged between 20 and 29 admitted to having fallen in love with a meme or character in a game—higher than the 24% of those women and 11% of men who admitted to falling in love with a pop star or actor (McVeigh, 2016, para. 4).

While dating sim games may be an amusing distraction for some players, in other cases, relationships with virtual partners may be replacing the pursuit of human relationships. The same survey determined that over 37% "had no interest in a romantic partner, and most of them cited 'bothersome' as their biggest reason for shunning relationships" (Glascock, 2015, para. 2).

The emotional bond established with a virtual person is referred to as *moe*. According to one source, the phenomenon originated in the 1990s as a subculture. It made its way into more mainstream culture through the 2000s (*The Day*, 2016). While *moe* has been heavily associated with men, journalists writing on the phenomenon suggest that a growing proportion of women are enjoying virtual romance with *otome*, romance-centered games that "are targeted towards single women who want to have the perfect relationship" (*Japan Info*, 2017, para. 2).

Young adults in Japan, which has a historically conservative culture, continue to meet, marry, and start families. At the same time, a growing number are shunning traditional milestones of adulthood, and some are finding satisfaction in virtual relationships.

Think It Through

- Would you expect that relationships with virtual persons, whether romantic or practical, will become commonplace or even normative in the future? Why or why not?

minding, an arrangement in which extended family members and even friends cooperate in raising the women's children while they pursue work elsewhere, often thousands of miles away. This practice adds a global dimension to cooperative child-rearing practices that are a long-standing feature of Caribbean culture.

Ho suggests in her profiles of these female global citizens—most of whom work in lower-wage sectors of the economy, including clerical work and child care—that such global family arrangements enable Caribbean immigrants to avoid becoming fully Americanized: International families and child minding provide a strong sense of continuity with their Caribbean homeland culture. Ho predicts that Caribbean immigrants will retain their native culture by regularly receiving what she characterizes as "bicultural booster shots" through the shuttling of family members between the United States and the Caribbean. At the same time, Ho notes, this process contributes to the

Americanization of the Caribbean region, which may eventually give rise to an ever more global culture.

Barbara Ehrenreich and Arlie Russell Hochschild (2002) have turned their attention to what they call the "global woman." Like Ho, they examine the female migrant leaving home and family to seek work in the wealthy first world. Unlike Ho, however, they take a pointedly critical view of this phenomenon, suggesting that these female workers, many of them employed as nannies or housekeepers (or even prostitutes), are filling a "care deficit" in the wealthier countries, where many female professionals have pursued opportunities outside the home. In doing so, the migrants create a new deficit at home, leaving their own children and communities behind:

> Third World migrant women achieve their success only by assuming the cast-off domestic roles of middle- and high-income women in the First World—roles that have been previously rejected, of course, by men. And their "commute" entails a cost we have yet to fully comprehend. (Ehrenreich & Hochschild, 2002, p. 3)

Ehrenreich and Hochschild (2002) argue that Western global power, previously manifested in the extraction of natural resources and agricultural goods, has evolved to embrace an extraction of women's labor and love, which is transferred to the well-off at a cost to poorer countries, communities, and—most acutely perhaps—families:

> The lifestyles of the First World are made possible by a global transfer of the services associated with a wife's traditional role—child care, homemaking, and sex—from poor countries to rich ones. To generalize and perhaps oversimplify: in an earlier phase of imperialism, northern countries extracted natural resources and agricultural products . . . from lands they conquered and colonized. Today, while still relying on Third World countries for agricultural and industrial labor, the wealthy countries also seek to extract something harder to measure and quantify, something that can look very much like love. (p. 4)

Although the women from the developing world are, for the most part, agents in their own choice to migrate to countries of the developed world in search of work (unless they are trafficked or tricked into migration), Ehrenreich and Hochschild point to powerful social forces that figure into this choice. On one hand, many women encounter the *push* factor of poverty: the choice of facing destitution at home or leaving families behind to earn what are, for them, substantial wages abroad. On the other hand, there is the *pull* factor of opportunities abroad: Their services are welcomed and needed, and they may gain human as well as economic capital. Even though these women make choices, their decisions may be driven by strong economic pressures and carry substantial noneconomic costs.

Why Study Family through a Sociological Lens?

In the United States today, there are many possible ways of understanding what constitutes a family. They range from the narrower definitions embraced by the U.S. government and socially conservative communities to the broader options a growing number of groups are recognizing. A sociological perspective helps us to understand the roots of both stasis and change in family life and family formation. The decline of marriage, the rise of divorce beginning in the latter part of the 20th century, and the dramatic increase in nonmarital births are, as Émile Durkheim might have suggested, "social facts," and *social facts can be explained only by other social facts.* These are not changes that appear randomly; rather, they are the results of complex sociological phenomena with identifiable and interesting social, cultural, and economic antecedents.

Theoretical perspectives on the family and associated sex roles add another layer of analysis to the picture. Functionalist theory looks at the family's functions for societal stability, emphasizing reproduction, the nurturance and socialization of children, and the allocation of family members into complementary roles that ensure harmony and order. The more conflict-oriented feminist theory looks at the way the family reproduces gender inequality, ignoring the differential experiences and resources of men and women in relationships. The psychodynamic feminist perspective

©Terese Loeb Kreuzer/Alamy Stock Photo

Arlie Hochschild defines the nanny chain thus: "An older daughter from a poor family in a third world country cares for her siblings, while her mother works as a nanny caring for the children of a nanny migrating to a first world country, who, in turn, cares for the child of a family in a rich country" (Hochschild, 2001a, para. 3).

What Can I Do with a Sociology Degree?

PROBLEM SOLVING

Problem solving is a fundamental skill in social scientific disciplines such as sociology and in a wide variety of contemporary occupational fields. Managing and addressing complex problems by identifying their dimensions, researching their roots, and using the knowledge to craft well-reasoned responses is a skill set that is developed through careful study, training in research and analysis, and practice. Problem solving is, in many respects, comprised of other key skills we discuss in this feature, including data and information literacy, critical thinking, quantitative and qualitative research competency, and understanding of diversity. At the same time, it is a skill that has its own characteristics as a product of sociological training. Sociological research data, which form the foundation of what sociologists do and teach, cannot solve problems; rather, research data contribute to the informed understanding of the dimensions of a problem. Data are also used to hypothesize the roots of a problem. Once the roots of a problem are identified, they can be addressed through, for instance, policy or community interventions. Research can be used to follow up on whether and how solutions worked and to rework hypotheses based on new information.

Researching the roots of a problem can involve a spectrum of different approaches, and a sociologist often needs to try more than one approach to generate a comprehensive picture of the problem. Social life is complex, and most serious social problems are not amenable to simple solutions. At the same time, the probability of successfully addressing a problem is appreciably greater when one has used careful research to understand its causes.

The problems encountered in different occupational fields vary, but the need for people who are skilled in breaking down a problem, defining it, analyzing it, crafting solutions based on good data, and effectively communicating identified paths of action is common across many areas.

Skyler Larrimore, Executive Assistant for the Metropolitan Planning Council

Macalester College, BA in Sociology and Geography with a Concentration in Urban Studies

As a professional community organizer, my job is to enable people to identify problems, envision solutions, and use tactics for neighborhood- and policy-level change. I've held many different roles in this capacity, from a resident connections coordinator at an affordable housing organization to a community organizer in public schools to an assistant at a public policy nonprofit. Sociological research in these roles looks like talking with people, such as renters in their homes and parents outside of schools, to deeply examine the detriments to community well-being.

After grounded research on a social problem, much of my work involves communicating the need for change through tools like door knocking, community meetings, lobbying, rallies, policy research, blogs, and social media. My typical day entails coordinating meetings to brief civic leaders on topics, identifying relevant news updates for our work, and writing grants to build the case for our efforts. Sociology provides you with the analytical skills necessary to advance policy change that will impact the most pressing social and environmental issues of our time.

Career Data: Social and Community Service Managers

- 2017 Median Pay: $64,100 per year
- $30.82 per hour
- Typical Entry-Level Education: Bachelor's degree
- Job Growth, 2016–2026: 18% (Much faster than average)

Source: Bureau of Labor Statistics, *Occupational Outlook Handbook*, 2017.

blends psychology and sociology to draw together the experiences of early childhood with relationship choices of adulthood and structural obstacles and opportunities. Although these perspectives have strengths and weaknesses, they offer us a range of possible lenses through which we can consider why families and roles are constituted as they are. The field remains open for new theoretical perspectives, and the family remains a fruitful area of research for sociologists.

Sociologists are concerned with commonalities and differences across families and explanations for these differences. Class, race, immigration status, health status—all of these may influence the ways that family formation, roles, cultures, and practices are manifested. Macro-level societal changes also have powerful impacts on families; globalization, deindustrialization, and the massive growth of student debt in an era of rapidly rising college costs are all seemingly "nonfamily" phenomena that may, in fact, have important impacts on families across the globe. Sociology helps us to make these connections.

SUMMARY

- The meaning of **family** is socially constructed within a particular culture. In the United States, as in other modern societies, the meaning and practices of family life have been changing.

- **Marriage**, found in some form in all societies, can take several different forms, from the most common—**monogamy**—to many variations of **polygamy**, in which a person has multiple spouses simultaneously.

- The functionalist perspective highlights the family's functionality in terms of social stability and order, emphasizing such activities as sex-role allocation and child socialization.

- Feminist perspectives on the family are more conflict oriented, highlighting the **sexual division of labor** in society and its stratifying effects. Feminist perspectives also examine the different experiences of men and women in marriage and the way social expectations and roles affect those experiences. The psychodynamic feminist perspective takes a sociopsychological approach, emphasizing the impact of early mothering on the later assumption of gender roles.

- In U.S. society today, the composition of families and the roles within families are shifting. The age at first marriage has risen across the board, and rates of marriage have declined, particularly among the less educated. Same-sex marriage was recognized as legal in the entire United States in 2015. Young adults are less likely than prior generations to marry, although most still value parenthood. Nonmarital births account for more than 40% of all births. Divorce rates have leveled off but remain at a high level.

- Socioeconomic class status affects child-rearing practices and family formation patterns. Lower rates of marriage and high rates of nonmarital births are present in the working class and among the poor. Middle-class family life is often structured around the needs of children.

- In the United States, the effects of globalization include changes in household income and employment opportunities. Women from developing countries often leave their homes and children to work for families in the developing world.

KEY TERMS

family, 295	endogamous, 296	common-law marriage, 301
marriage, 295	anti-miscegenation laws, 296	domestic (or family)
monogamy, 295	extended families, 297	violence, 309
polygamy, 295	nuclear families, 297	foster care, 310
polygyny, 295	sexual division of labor in	international families, 318
polyandry, 295	modern societies, 298	
serial monogamy, 296	cohabitation, 301	

DISCUSSION QUESTIONS

1. Why do people get married? Why do people *not* marry? Think about individual and sociological reasons. Link your answers to the discussion of marriage trends and the experience of marriage discussed in this chapter.

2. Recent data show some changes in the child-care practices of U.S. families. What do trends show? How do sociological factors help to explain the changes?

3. How does the case of deaf families with hearing children show the opportunities and challenges of family life characterized by different cultures? Can this case be compared to immigrant families with children? What similarities and differences can you identify?

4. Lareau's research suggests that middle- and working-class families have different child-rearing styles.

How does she describe these styles? Why might the differences be sociologically significant? Does the essay on parenting in poverty help to shed light on differences?

5. Who is the "global woman"? What are the costs and benefits to women and families of a global labor market for care work?

Want a Better Grade?

Get the tools you need to sharpen your study skills. Access practice quizzes, eFlashcards, video, and multimedia at **https://edge.sagepub.com/chambliss4e**

Education and Society

12

WHAT DO YOU THINK?

1. What is the relationship between family socioeconomic status and educational attainment? What explains this relationship?
2. Why does racial segregation exist and persist in many U.S. public schools?
3. Why do significant numbers of students drop out of college before completing a degree?

LEARNING OBJECTIVES

12.1 Describe the historical and contemporary roles of education in society.

12.2 Apply conflict, functionalist, and symbolic interactionist theoretical perspectives to the institution of education.

12.3 Explain how education may function to both reduce and reproduce social inequalities.

12.4 Discuss key issues in U.S. higher education, including the relationship between education and income potential, the debate over college internships, and the college dropout phenomenon.

12.5 Learn about the importance of higher education globally and the growth of U.S. student contact with other students from around the world.

FOOD INSECURITY IN U.S. COLLEGES AND UNIVERSITIES

How many U.S. college students are hungry? That is a question that was posed in a nationwide study on food insecurity among students who study at two- and four-year schools (Broton & Goldrick-Rab, 2017). The U.S. Department of Agriculture defines **food insecurity** as *a lack of consistent access to enough food for an active, healthy life*. For students who suffer from food insecurity, it may mean skipping meals to save money, trying to grab

©David L. Moore - CA / Alamy Stock Photo

Food insecurity: A lack of consistent access to enough food for an active, healthy life.

325

extra food at the cafeteria so they will have another meal for the day or the weekend, or experiencing the fatigue and anxiety that accompany pangs of hunger.

Sociologists Katharine M. Broton and Sarah Goldrick-Rab (2017) have found that significant proportions of college students at two-year and four-year schools struggle with food insecurity associated with disrupted eating patterns and/or hunger at least some of the time. A recent study by researchers at the City University of New York, for instance, determined that about 30% of community college students and 22% of four-year college students had experienced food insecurity (Goldrick-Rab, 2018).

What explains this phenomenon? Why are so many students confronting the challenges of school while also facing the threat of hunger? Food insecurity has become part of the landscape of U.S. higher education for a variety of reasons. First, more first-generation college students than ever are matriculating. As a significant proportion of students from this group come from lower-income families, they may not be able to fall back on family resources when they run short of money or meals. Even where students have meal plans, they are not necessarily structured in a way that meets the needs of those who are food insecure. For example, college cafeterias often have limited hours, which may not correspond to the schedules of students who are busy with school and work. As well, many schools do not permit students to roll over unused funds or meals to a future semester. Recently, a group of students at Spelman and Morehouse Colleges in Georgia went on a hunger strike to protest school policy that prevents students from sharing unused meal vouchers with classmates who might need them (Mitchell, 2017). After less than a week of the hunger strike, both institutions made commitments to offer 14,000 meals per year for students facing food insecurity (Carter, 2017).

Second, college costs continue to rise: Tuition is only one of a spectrum of costs that students face. School service fees, lab fees, books, housing, and food may add up to more than students' savings, loans, and scholarships can cover. Research suggests that students of color, LGBT students, and young people coming out of foster care into college are at particular risk of food insecurity (Goldrick-Rab, 2018).

The consequences of food insecurity for students pursuing higher education can be significant. Research shows a correlation between food insecurity and both lower grade point averages (Maroto, 2015) and lower graduation rates (Goldrick-Rab, 2018). For students seeking to earn a college degree that will help to propel them to a more economically secure future, food insecurity can be a significant obstacle, as it is associated with consequences such as a lower grade point average and higher risk of dropping out (Yavorski, 2017).

Student-led campaigns such as Swipe Out Hunger, which advocates for policies that would permit students to donate their meal "swipes" to students facing food insecurity, and the growing number of schools opening food pantries to assist students are helping to address this largely hidden problem, but more remains to be done. U.S. higher education has much to offer students and society, but it also faces considerable contemporary challenges.

In this chapter, we discuss sociological issues in education, including key challenges that schools at all levels are facing today. We begin the chapter with a discussion of the roots of mass public education in the United States and the development of the "credential society" that is driving rising enrollments in higher education today. We continue with a critical look at education, using the functionalist, conflict, and symbolic interactionist perspectives to think about the roles played by the education system in modern society. We then turn to the issue of education and inequality, examining education as a key to understanding how inequality is both reduced and reproduced in society. We also consider the relationship between higher education and income and the problem of college dropouts. Finally, we look at education in a global perspective, considering how the U.S. educational system and its graduates compare to other those of peer countries.

Education, Industrialization, and the "Credential Society"

As societies change, so too does the role of **education**, *the transmission of society's norms, values, and knowledge base by means of direct instruction.* For much of human history, education occurred informally, within the family or the immediate community. Children often learned by doing—by working alongside their parents, siblings, and other relatives in the home, in the field, or on the hunt.

With the emergence of industrial society, **formal education**, *education that occurs within academic institutions such as schools*, became increasingly common. As schooling became important in industrial societies, it came to be seen as the birthright of all society members. **Mass education**, *the extension of formal schooling to wide segments of the population*, is the norm today. Not only is mass education consistent with the democratic ideals held in most modern and economically advanced or advancing societies, but it is also the principal means by which people acquire the skills they need to participate effectively as workers and citizens in the midst of technological, cultural, and economic change of dramatic proportions.

Modern society requires its members to master a large number of complex skills. People must know how to read and write and do basic math, but that is rarely enough. Societies need people to organize production, invent new products, and program computers; others engage in creating art or literature, curing diseases, resolving human conflicts, and addressing scientific challenges such as climate change. Building an educated population requires more than the on-the-job training of apprentices or helpers. It requires the transmission of more knowledge than most families are willing or able to pass on from one generation to the next.

The first educational institutions in the U.S. were created in the 17th century by the religious leaders of the New England Puritan communities. Their intent was to provide religious education; children were taught to read so that they could study Scripture (Monroe, 1940; Vinovskis, 1995).

Education: The transmission of society's norms, values, and knowledge base by means of direct instruction.

Formal education: Education that occurs within academic institutions such as schools.

Mass education: The extension of formal schooling to wide segments of the population.

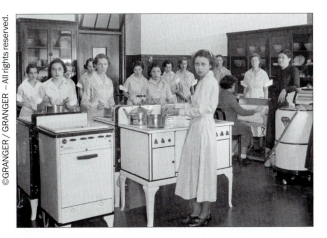

In the United States, girls and boys used to be educated separately and unequally in many public schools. Far fewer young women had the opportunity to go to college and their high school education was more likely to emphasize domestic skills, such as meal preparation.

In 1647, the Massachusetts Bay Colony passed a law requiring every community of 50 or more people to establish a town school. The law, named Ye Old Deluder Satan Act, was intended to protect New England's youth from acquiescing to the temptations of the devil.

By the 18th century, the goal of education had shifted from religious training to cultivating practical and productive skills (Vinovskis, 1995). The emergence of industrial societies not only increased the need for people to be literate—**literacy** is defined as *the ability to read and write at a basic level*—but it also required that they learn skills, work habits, and discipline that would prepare them for jobs as industrial laborers, accountants, inventors, designers, merchandisers, lawyers, operators of complex machinery, and more (Bergen, 1996).

From the outset, schools in the United States were divided along social class lines. The sons of the middle and upper classes went to private schools that trained them for business and the professions. There were initially few public schools, and those that existed provided working- and lower-class children with the minimal education necessary for them to acquire the skills and obedience for factory work or farming (Bowles & Gintis, 1976; Wyman, 1997).

When workers began forming labor unions in the 19th century, one of their demands was for free **public education** for their children, *a universal education system provided by the government and funded by tax revenues rather than student fees* (fees served to exclude economically disadvantaged students from the classroom; Horan & Hargis, 1991). Political activists, philanthropic organizations, and newspapers joined the unions in their demand. By the late 19th century, public elementary schools had been established in most of the industrial centers of the United States, and mass public schooling soon spread throughout the country, though segregated by gender and race. In some places, no schooling was provided for girls or African Americans. In other places, girls and boys were educated separately and unequally, with girls receiving training in cooking and homemaking skills and boys studying academic subjects such as literature and mathematics (Riordan, 1990; Tyack & Hansot, 1982). Schools for African Americans were segregated by law in the southern states until the U.S. Supreme Court ruled the practice unconstitutional in 1954; elsewhere in the country, Blacks and Whites attended different schools that offered unequal opportunities in education because they lived in different neighborhoods and schools were locally funded (Aviel, 1997; Bergen, 1996).

In some states, school attendance was compulsory for at least the first six years. The concept of public education was soon expanded to include high schools, and by the end of the 19th century, the average U.S. student achieved eight years of schooling, while 10% completed high school and 2% completed college or university (Bettelheim, 1982; Vinovskis, 1992; Walters & James, 1992).

With the creation of mass public education, the United States increasingly became a **credential society**, one in which access to desirable jobs and social status depends on the possession of a certificate or diploma certifying the completion of formal education (Collins, 1979; Vinovskis, 1995). A socially validated credential such as a bachelor's degree or professional degree thus serves as a filter, determining the kinds of jobs and promotions for which a person is eligible. People with only high school diplomas have a difficult time competing in the job market with those who have college degrees, even if they possess a keen intellect and good skills. If a position announcement indicates that a college degree is required, the candidate with only a high school diploma is unlikely to be considered at all. Since a person's job is a major determinant of income and social class, educational credentials play a major role in shaping opportunities for social and economic mobility.

Next, we look at some key theoretical perspectives on education and its functions in modern society.

Theoretical Perspectives on Education

What is the role of the educational system in society? Although functionalist theorists highlight the ways in which the educational system is positively functional for society, conflict theorists point to its role in reinforcing and reproducing social stratification. Symbolic interactionist theories help to illuminate how relational processes in the classroom may contribute to educational success—or failure.

The Functionalist Perspective

Émile Durkheim (1922/1956, 1922/1973b), whose work forms a foundation for functionalist theorizing in sociology, wrote about the importance of education in modern societies. According to Durkheim, modern societies are complex, with specialized yet interdependent institutions. This complexity creates a special problem for *social solidarity*—the bonds that unite the members of a social group. Modern society is no longer characterized by communities with high degrees of cultural, religious, or social homogeneity, so social ties have weakened. One function of mass education is to address this problem by socializing

---

Literacy: The ability to read and write at a basic level.

Public education: A universal education system provided by the government and funded by tax revenues rather than student fees.

Credential society: A society in which access to desirable work and social status depends on the possession of a certificate or diploma certifying the completion of formal education.

©Hero Images Inc. / Alamy Stock Photo

School is an important agent of socialization. Among the lessons young children learn in school are obedience to authority and conformity to schedules, imperatives that some sociologists say are rooted in early capitalism's need for compliant workers.

members of a society into the norms and values necessary to produce and maintain social solidarity. Durkheim talked about this function in terms of *moral education*, meaning that educational institutions not only provide the knowledge and training necessary for members to fulfill their economic roles in modern society but also function to socialize individuals, building solidarity in the group.

Contemporary functionalist theories echo Durkheim's concerns about social solidarity, emphasizing the function of formal education in socializing people into the norms, values, and skills necessary for society to survive and thrive (Parsons & Mayhew, 1982). Functionalist theory also proposes that education has both manifest and latent functions (Bourdieu & Coleman, 1991; Merton, 1968). What are these functions?

The *manifest* (intended) functions of education include the transmission of general knowledge and specific skills needed in society and the economy, such as literacy and numeracy. The *latent* (unintended) functions include the propagation of societal norms and values that Durkheim argued should be explicit concerns of moral education. For example, beginning with kindergarten, children learn to organize their lives according to schedules, to sit at desks, to follow rules, and to show respect for authority. Sociologist Harry Gracey (1991) has argued that "the unique job of the kindergarten seems . . . to be teaching children the student role. The student role is the repertoire of behavior and attitudes regarded by educators as appropriate to children in school" (p. 448). Having "mastered" the student role, children internalize the external social norms and rules that govern the school day and their academic lives.

Consider other latent functions of the system of mass public education in the United States. For example, in keeping children occupied from about 8:00 a.m. until 3:00 p.m., schools serve as supervisors for a large population of children whose parents work to contribute to both the micro-level economies of their homes and the productivity of the macro-level economy. Schools are also sources of peer

socialization, offering an environment in which conventional gender roles are enacted and enforced. Although some young people challenge expected roles through dress, for example, many conform to avoid conflict or ostracism. Can you think of other latent functions of mass education that are social, cultural, economic, or political?

What are the weaknesses of the functionalist perspective in furthering our understanding of the system of education? Critics suggest that it ignores ways in which schools may also function to reproduce social inequality. Functionalist theory assumes, for instance, that the educational system educates people in accordance with their abilities and potential, giving credentials to those who deserve them and who can contribute most to society while withholding credentials from those incapable of doing the most demanding work. Critics, however, say schools function to reproduce the existing class system, favoring those who are already the most advantaged and putting obstacles in the paths of those who are disadvantaged. They point to substantial differences in educational attainment across socioeconomic groups (a topic we take up later in this chapter) as evidence that socioeconomic class status is as important as intellectual capability in influencing educational attainment within the institution of education (Bowles & Gintis, 1976).

Notably as well, although education may socialize students into society's norms and values, it also potentially undermines societal authority by promoting a critical approach to dominant ideas. Education contributes to the development of a capacity for self-direction (Miller, Kohn, & Schooler, 1986), and students often develop inquiring, critical spirits because they are exposed to views and ways of thinking that challenge their previously held ideas. For example, Phelan and McLaughlin (1995) found that people with higher levels of education are more sympathetic to and less likely to blame homeless people for their condition than are people with lower levels of education.

The Conflict Perspective

Conflict theorists agree that education trains people in the dominant norms and values of society and the work skills and habits demanded by the economic system. Nevertheless, they reject the functionalist notion that the system of education channels individuals into the positions for which they are best suited in terms of ambition, skills, and talents. Instead, they believe, it reproduces rather than reduces social stratification and, rather than ensuring that the best people train for and conscientiously perform the most socially important jobs (Davis & Moore, 1945), it ensures that the discovery of talent will be limited (Tumin, 1953).

According to conflict theory, poor and working-class children have fewer opportunities to demonstrate their talents and abilities because they lack equal access to educational opportunities. Moreover, part of the "hidden curriculum" of the classroom is to socialize members of the working class to accept their class position (Bowles & Gintis, 1976). Children are taught at an early age to define their academic ambitions and abilities in keeping with the social class of their parents. Conflict theorists argue that lowered educational ambitions are reinforced through inferior educational opportunities as well as labeling and discrimination in the classroom (Bowles & Gintis, 1976; Glazer, 1992; Kozol, 1991; Oakes, 1985; Willis, 1990). In the United States, this inequality has racial as well as economic dimensions.

Consider the experience of Malcolm X, a prominent champion of the rights of African Americans, who was assassinated in 1965. In his autobiography, Malcolm X recounts how, despite being a top student, he was discouraged by his high school English teacher from becoming a lawyer:

> Mr. Ostrowski looked surprised, I remember. . . . He kind of half-smiled and said, "Malcolm, one of life's first needs is for us to be realistic. Don't misunderstand me, now. We all like you, you know that. . . . A lawyer—that's no realistic goal for a [Black man]. You need to think about something you can be. You're good with your hands—making things. . . . Why don't you plan on carpentry? People like you as a person—you'd get all kinds of work." (Haley & Malcolm X, 1964, p. 41)

Author Jonathan Kozol (2000) writes that more than a half century later, poor and minority children continue to experience lower educational expectations and opportunities:

> Many people in Mott Haven [an impoverished neighborhood in the South Bronx] do a lot of work to make sure they are well-informed about the conditions in their children's public schools. Some also know a great deal more about the schools that serve the children of the privileged than many of the privileged themselves may recognize. They know that "business math" is not the same as calculus and that "job-readiness instruction" is not European history or English literature. They know that children of rich people do not often spend semesters of their teenage years in classes where they learn to type an application for an entry-level clerical position; they know that these wealthy children are too busy learning composition skills and polishing their French pronunciation and receiving preparation for the SATs. They come to understand the process by which a texture of enlightenment is stitched together for some children while it is denied to others. They also understand that, as the years go by, some of these children will appear to have deserved one kind of role in life, and some another. (pp. 100–101)

Today, there continue to be disparities in education. Consider the issue of student access to Advanced Placement (AP) courses, which help prepare students for college-level work and offer a chance to earn college credit even before matriculation. Although thousands of students across the country enroll in AP courses every year, not all students have equal access to these accelerated and challenging classes: A Pro Publica study determined, for instance, that in New York, "many of the state's affluent school districts offer far more AP classes than do economically disadvantaged schools with high percentages of minority students" (Glorioso, 2011, para. 3). Researchers found that equity in AP offerings varied dramatically by state, with some states (such as Florida) providing broad access to AP courses and others (including Kansas, Oklahoma, and Maryland) providing fewer opportunities in schools serving poorer families (Coutts & LaFleur, 2011). The Pro Publica study highlighted socioeconomic class as a determining variable in access, but racial and ethnic minorities are often enrolled in lower-income schools, suggesting that the effects of limited access to AP courses are experienced most acutely by Black and Hispanic students. According to the Education Commission of the States (2006), requiring that all high schools offer AP courses helps decrease the achievement gap between advantaged and disadvantaged schools by offering equality of opportunity. Today, 20 states require that all high schools or school districts offer at least one AP course (or another advanced opportunity course, such as International Baccalaureate [IB] or dual enrollment); in 2007, this was mandated by only 12 states (Education Commission of the States, 2016).

Among the most prominent conflict theorists in the sociology of education are Samuel Bowles and Herbert Gintis, whose 1976 book, *Schooling in Capitalist America*, posited three key arguments. First, the authors argued that schools not only impart cognitive skills but also "prepare people to function well and without complaint in the hierarchical structure of the modern corporation" (p. ix). Second, Bowles and Gintis used statistical data to support the argument that parental economic status is passed on to children, at least in part, through unequal educational opportunity, though the advantages conferred on children of higher-social-status families are not limited to their educational preparation. Finally, the authors suggested that the modern school system was not the product of the evolutionary perfection of democratic pedagogy but rather primarily a reflection of the interests of raising profits for capitalist enterprises such as factories.

■ **FIGURE 12.1**

Relationship between U.S. Family Income and Years of Schooling for White Males Ages 35–44, 1962

Source: Bowles, Samuel, and Herbert Gintis. *Schooling in Capitalist America: Educational Reform and the Contradictions of Economic Life.* Copyright © 1976 Bowles, Samuel; Gintis, Herbert M. Reprinted by permission of Basic Books, a member of the Perseus Books Group.

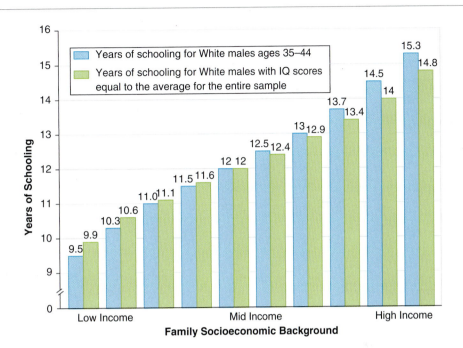

■ **FIGURE 12.2** Percentage of Spring 2002 High School Sophomores Who Earned a Bachelor's Degree or Higher by 2012, by Socioeconomic Status and Mathematics Achievement Quartile in 2002

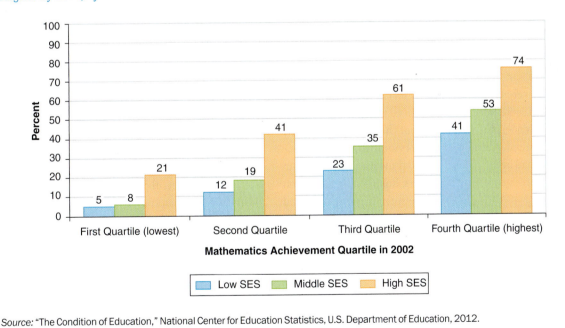

Source: "The Condition of Education," National Center for Education Statistics, U.S. Department of Education, 2012.

Frequently cited results of Bowles and Gintis's early work include a graph showing the powerful correlation between socioeconomic status (as measured by income) and educational attainment. The data, from a sample of men with similar childhood IQ scores, demonstrate an unmistakable relationship between the socioeconomic backgrounds of the subjects and the average number of years of education they completed (Figure 12.1). Although a precise update of Bowles and Gintis's data is not available, other data on the correlations among family income category, demonstrated academic potential, and educational attainment show that the same relationship identified by the theorists is relevant decades later. For example, Figure 12.2 shows bachelor's degree completion rates by both family income (socioeconomic status) and math achievement early in high school. Note that among the highest scoring students (fourth quartile), 74% of high-income students had graduated from college a decade later, whereas only 41% of low-income students had completed a degree. The graduation gap is consistent across score categories: In every category, students in the middle and top income categories were more likely to graduate than their lower-income counterparts.

Critics of conflict theories of education point out that education, even in highly stratified societies, offers an important way for poor and working-class people to improve their circumstances, and it remains the primary means of upward mobility. Education has been a crucial path by which generations of U.S. immigrants have escaped poverty. Thus, although it may contribute to the reproduction of an unequal socioeconomic structure, the educational system also provides meaningful opportunities for mobility and change.

The Symbolic Interactionist Perspective

Symbolic interactionists study what occurs in the classroom, alerting us to subtle and not-so-subtle ways in which schools affect students' interactions and self-images. By looking at how students are labeled, for instance, symbolic interactionists shed light on the way schools help to reinforce and perpetuate differences among students.

In a classic study, Rosenthal and Jacobson (1968) conducted an intriguing experiment in which elementary school teachers were intentionally misinformed about the intelligence test scores of selected students. The teachers were told, in confidence, that certain students had scored unusually high on standardized tests the previous year. In fact, these students had been randomly selected and were no different in known intelligence from their peers. Rosenthal and Jacobson then observed the interactions between these students and their teachers and monitored the students' academic performance. The students labeled *exceptional* soon outperformed their peers, a difference that persisted for several years.

The teachers described the labeled students as more curious or more interested and communicated their heightened expectations of these learners through their voices, facial expressions, and use of praise. Enacting a self-fulfilling prophecy, the students came to see themselves through their teachers' eyes and began performing as if they were, in fact, more intelligent than their peers, earning still more positive attention from teachers. Younger students, whose self-images were more flexible, exhibited the greatest improvements in performance. Rosenthal and Jacobson concluded that the teachers behaved differently toward some students because the students had been labeled *exceptional*.

The findings of other studies suggest similar conclusions. A study of student–teacher interaction in a largely African American kindergarten found that such labels as *fast* and *slow*, which the teacher assigned by the eighth day of class, tended to stay with the labeled students throughout the year (Rist, 1970). Further research has confirmed the harmful effects of teachers' stereotyped beliefs about minority students' competence on students' performance (Garcia & Guerra, 2004). One study found that female and Asian American students frequently received classroom grades higher than their actual test scores, while Latino, Black, and White males received lower grades (Farkas, Grobe, Sheehan, & Shuan, 1990; Farkas, Sheehan, & Grobe, 1990). The differences were explained by the teachers' perceptions of their students' attitudes. Those who appeared to be attentive and cooperative were judged to be hard workers and good students and were graded up; those who appeared to be indifferent or hostile were graded down (Rosenbloom & Way, 2004).

A recent study found that both nonblack and Black teachers had lower expectations for Black students when it came to going to college, especially Black male students. However, Black teachers' expectations were 30%–40% higher than nonblack teachers' expectations (Gershenson, Holt, & Papageorge, 2015). An analysis of data from the Education Longitudinal Study, which followed tenth graders for a decade beginning in 2002 and ending in 2012, found that even after accounting for other factors, teachers' expectations and students' college-going outcomes had a significant relationship, and teacher expectations were predictive of college completion rates. In fact, after controlling for student demographics, teacher expectations were more predictive of college success than many major factors, including student motivation and student effort. These findings build on other research that suggests teacher expectations are powerful predictors of future success (Boser, Wilhelm, & Hanna, 2014, para. 2).

The labeling of students also affects disciplinary actions taken when students misbehave. Even as early as preschool, Black students are four times as likely to be suspended as White students and twice as likely to be expelled (Young, 2016). A recent study also found that Black students receive harsher punishments when compared White students (Harriot, 2017). When examining fights between one Black student and one White student, the study found that Black students received longer suspensions (Harriot, 2017).

Classroom labeling has been studied in other countries as well. In one influential study, Paul Willis (1990) found that British boys from working-class families were systematically labeled as low academic achievers and socialized to think of themselves as capable of doing only working-class jobs. The boys understood quite well that this labeling process worked against them, and they resisted it by the use of

DISCOVER INTERSECTIONS

Race, Ethnicity, and Classroom Labelling

In the section above, you read about the practice of classroom labeling and the effects of labeling on student performance, academic marks, and disciplinary actions. In our chapter on race and ethnicity (Chapter 9), you learned about individual discrimination and institutional discrimination. Can you link the discussion of discrimination back to the practice of classroom labeling? How could you describe the relationship? Is the practice of labeling, documented in research that spans several decades, an example of individual or institutional discrimination? Would the category in which you place it affect how it should be addressed?

humor and other challenges to authority. These behaviors reinforced their teachers' perception that the boys would never make it and would eventually drop out of school and assume their "rightful position" in the working class. The boys thus accepted their teachers' labeling, creating a self-fulfilling prophecy in which they wound up in working-class jobs.

Symbolic interactionism is well suited to studying the ways in which teachers and administrators consciously or unintentionally affect their students, but a critic might note that because it focuses on social interaction, it cannot give us a picture of the role of the educational system in society as a whole or help us recognize and analyze structural problems such as unequal funding of schools across poor, middle-class, and wealthy areas.

Education, Opportunity, and Inequality

Functionalists argue that education is a vehicle for mobility and for filling the positions necessary for society to survive and thrive. Conflict theorists posit that the educational system reinforces existing inequalities by unequally according opportunities based on class, race, or gender. In fact, the U.S. educational system may operate to open avenues to

Inequality Matters
AMERICAN INDIAN SCHOOLS

The 183 schools sited on American Indian reservations across 23 states are among the most decrepit and worst performing in the United States. Consider a description of one school offered in a journalistic investigation:

> Tucked into the desert hills on a Navajo reservation 150 miles east of the Grand Canyon, Crystal [Boarding School] has cracks running several feet down the walls, leaky pipes in the floors and asbestos in the basement. Students come from extremely troubled backgrounds, but there is no full-time counselor. Last year, a new reading coach took one look at the rundown cinder block housing and left the next day. Science and social studies have been cut to put more attention on the abysmal reading and math scores, but even so, in 2013 only 5 percent of students were considered to have grade-level math skills. (Severns, 2015, para. 4)

Few of these schools have after-school programs for children to support academic learning or to provide opportunities to do sports or art. In 2014, only 67% of American Indian students graduated from high school, compared to the national average of 80%. Graduation rates among Native youth who attend schools run by the Bureau of Indian Education (BIE) are even worse: only 53% (Camera, 2015). The National Congress of American Indians (2017), an advocacy organization, reports that fewer than half of native students graduate from high school in the seven states with the highest percentage of American Indian and Alaska Native students.

A 1928 report described the education provided to Native Americans (which had attempted to forcibly assimilate schoolchildren by, among others, changing their Native names and banning them from speaking their Native languages) as "grossly inadequate." Nearly a century later, forcible assimilation has ended, but the public education offered to American Indian children has scarcely improved. In 2015, President Barack Obama's Secretary of Education, Arne Duncan, described the

(Continued)

(Continued)

American Indian school system as the poorest in the country: "It's just the epitome of broken . . . just utterly bankrupt" (Severns, 2015, para. 2).

Many residents of American Indian reservations have been fighting to make their schools good places of learning, but bureaucratic and financial obstacles have made significant change difficult:

> While one office (which would later be called the Bureau of Indian Education) handled educational matters, other offices within the larger Bureau of Indian Affairs had say over school construction and maintenance, personnel and technology, all of which are major parts of school operations. The tribes also have some power and, particularly in the Southwest, so do school boards, which further diffuses the authority—and the accountability over the schools' failures—across the country (Severns, 2015, section 2, para. 8).

"We have the worst of the worst statistics," said Aaron Payment, chairperson of the Sault Ste. Marie Tribe of Chippewa Indians in Michigan, speaking not only about graduation rates but also rates of suicide, domestic violence, and drug use. "The first Americans have become the last Americans," he said (Camera, 2015). Many Indian schools exist in impoverished

©Visions of America/Universal Images Group/ Getty Images

communities with almost no tax base to support even basic improvements (Mongeau, 2016).

Think It Through

- The U.S. government created American Indian reservations and has overseen the schools on reservations for most or all of their existence. Does the federal government have a responsibility to ensure an adequate and equal education for American Indian children? How can the state, society, and community ensure that this is taking place?

mobility for all students *and* to create obstacles to achievement among the less privileged. That is, it may both reduce and reproduce inequality. In the following sections, we look at issues of education and inequality, focusing on questions about childhood and adult literacy, school segregation by race and income, and the college dropout phenomenon. We conclude the section with a look at the relationship between education and income in the United States.

Word Poverty and Adult Illiteracy

Researcher Louisa Cook Moats uses the term *word poverty* to characterize the impoverished language environments in which some children grow up. Word poverty is a particular problem in economically disadvantaged homes: Research on a community in California found that by age 5, children in impoverished language environments had heard 32 million fewer words spoken to them than the average middle-class child. Perhaps not surprisingly, the fewer words that were spoken to children, the fewer they could actively use themselves: In a study of how many words children could produce at age 3, "children from

impoverished environments used less than half the number of words already spoken by their more advantaged peers" (Wolf, 2008, pp. 102–103).

Word poverty is also linked to a deficit of books in the homes of many children. Research conducted in three Los Angeles communities found that in the most economically impoverished community in the study, it was common to find no children's books in the home. In low- to middle-income homes, an average of three books could be found. By contrast, in the most affluent families, there was an average of 200 books in each home (Wolf, 2008). According to a global study, the deficit or wealth of books in a home is of significance in children's later schooling: Being raised in a home without books is as likely to affect children's educational attainment as having parents with very low educational attainment. The researchers conclude that "growing up in a home with 500 books would propel a child 3.2 years further in education, on average" (Evans, Kelley, Sikora, & Treiman, 2010, p. 179). In the United States, the advantage to having an expansive library is equal to an average of more than two years of education. Commenting on the study, an article on the website ScienceDaily noted,

The researchers were struck by the strong effect having books in the home had on children's educational attainment even above and beyond such factors as education level of the parents, the country's GDP [gross domestic product], the father's occupation or the political system of the country. (University of Nevada, Reno, 2010, para. 10)

Why is word poverty significant? The answer is that it is linked to low literacy. A fundamental necessity for any country in the modern world is a population that is functionally literate. No less important, literacy is necessary for individual success in education and the job market. The Program for the International Assessment of Adult Competencies (PIAAC) defines *literacy* as "understanding, evaluating, using and engaging with written text to participate in society, to achieve one's goals and to develop one's knowledge and potential" (Rampey et al., 2016, p. 2). PIAAC identifies six categories of literacy using a numerical scale (Figure 12.3). The PIAAC study, which was based on a sample of 8,670 people (even though the number in the cited figure is slightly smaller, as it excludes those over the age of 65) found the following:

- About 17% of adults were at (13%) or below Level 1 (4%) on the literacy test. At Level 1, respondents performed simple tasks such as locating

information in a text. At this level, "knowledge and skill in recognizing basic vocabulary, determining the meaning of sentences, and reading paragraphs of text is expected."

- Another 33% of respondents reached Level 2 on the test. "Tasks at this level require respondents to make matches between the text and information, and may require paraphrasing or low-level inferences."

- About 36% of respondents were at Level 3. At this level, readers were expected to read "dense or lengthy" texts and to interpret, evaluate, and infer information. "Competing information is often present, but it is not more prominent than the correct information."

- Finally, about 13% of respondents were at Levels 4 and 5. At these levels, readers were examining, taking account of subtle rhetorical clues, evaluating evidence-based arguments, applying abstract ideas. (Rampey et al., 2016, p. B-3)

Wolf (2008) suggests that a strong foundation in literacy is a key to later educational success. Students who enter high school with shaky foundations in literacy have a higher probability of school failure than do their peers who grew up in homes with books and parents who read to them at an early age. At the same time, failure to complete high school is likely to affect someone's ability to complete literacy activities successfully. If you were to research the correlation between literacy and high school completion, how would you proceed? What variables would you choose to study and why? What kind of relationship would you hypothesize?

School Segregation

School segregation, *the education of racial minorities in schools that are geographically, economically, and/or socially separated from those attended by the racial majority* (usually Whites), is a long-standing pattern that is worsening today, despite more than four decades of civil rights legislation intended to alleviate it and reduce its devastating effects. School segregation has long been linked to educational inequality in the United States.

Before slavery was abolished in the United States, it was a crime to teach slaves to read and write; formal education was reserved solely for Whites. Following the abolition of slavery and the end of the Civil War, Black students could be educated, but Jim Crow laws soon initiated a century

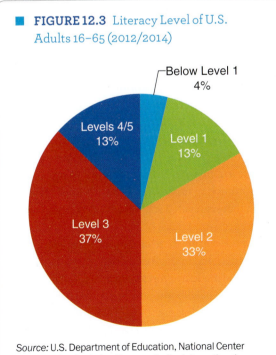

FIGURE 12.3 Literacy Level of U.S. Adults 16–65 (2012/2014)

Below Level 1
4%

Levels 4/5
13%

Level 1
13%

Level 3
37%

Level 2
33%

Source: U.S. Department of Education, National Center for Education Statistics, Program for the International Assessment of Adult Competencies (PIAAC), U.S. PIAAC 2012/2014; Organization for Economic Cooperation and Development, PIAAC 2012.

School segregation: The education of racial minorities in schools that are geographically, economically, and/or socially separated from those attended by the racial majority.

of discrimination against Black Americans in the South. These laws determined, among other things, where Black Americans could live, where they could eat and shop, and where they would be educated. In the North, there were no laws segregating schools by race, but segregated schooling occurred nonetheless as a consequence of racial residential segregation.

Laws, customs, and discrimination created schools segregated by race in the United States until the 1950s (Jordan, 1992). Black activists challenged the constitutionality of segregation, but U.S. courts repeatedly found it did not violate the U.S. Constitution. For example, in its 1896 *Plessy v. Ferguson* decision, the U.S. Supreme Court upheld the states' rights to segregate public accommodations as long as they followed the principle of "separate but equal." In 1954, however, the Supreme Court reversed itself. Relying in part on social science research showing that segregated schools were not in fact equal, the Court ruled in *Brown v. Board of Education of Topeka* that laws segregating public schools were unconstitutional (Miller, 1995).

This decision met with considerable resistance, especially in the South, where schools were segregated by law. Governor George Wallace of Alabama personally blocked the entrance to the University of Alabama in an effort to stop Black students from enrolling, and a Black college student named James Meredith went to prison for trying to enroll and attend classes at the University of Mississippi. Black and White students who tried to integrate schools were beaten by police and fellow citizens (Branch, 1988; Chong, 1991; McCartney, 1992).

Court challenges, civil protests, and mass civil disobedience ultimately broke down barriers, and some racial integration of schools took place across the country. Although the Supreme Court decision in *Brown v. Board of Education* had prohibited purposeful discrimination on the basis of race, it did not provide for specific methods to achieve school integration. The fact that racial and ethnic groups were residentially segregated meant that most Blacks would continue to attend schools that were predominantly Black, while Whites would continue to attend mostly White schools.

Subsequent court decisions provided one method of achieving integration: school busing, a court-ordered program of transporting public school students to schools outside their neighborhoods. Mandated busing proved highly controversial, provoking criticism among some academics and hostility among many parents and policy makers. Controversy erupted in 1974 when Black students were bused into poor Irish neighborhoods in South Boston, whose schools were among the worst in the state. Instead of providing equal educational opportunity, busing worsened racial conflict in some of Boston's most economically disadvantaged neighborhoods. Violence resulted, and over the next 10 years, public school enrollment in the city plummeted (Frum, 2000).

Today, despite decades of civil rights activism and laws aimed at promoting integration, racial segregation persists in U.S. schools, and in some places, it has even worsened. An article on schools in Louisville, Kentucky, which have gained attention for their desegregation efforts, points out that

> nationwide, in 1954, zero percent of black students attended majority-white schools. By 1972, that number was 36.4 percent. . . . School integration reached its peak in 1988, when 43.5 percent of black students attended majority-white schools, but that number has declined since then, and in 2011, stood at just 23.2 percent. (Semuels, 2015, para. 64)

How is this possible? First, the movement over time of middle- and upper-class Whites into largely White school districts in suburban or outlying areas has left mostly poor minorities in U.S. inner-city schools, many of which are highly segregated (Coleman, Hoffer, & Kilgore, 1982; Kozol, 2005; Orfield & Eaton, 1996). Because they are often located in low-income neighborhoods, highly segregated schools also tend to be the most poorly funded. There are variations in state formulas for funding schools, but the source on which most U.S. school districts still depend most heavily is local property tax revenue. Although this system ensures that those who live in areas with high property values will generally accrue adequate—or even excellent— funds for the academic programs and physical maintenance of their schools, it also puts those who live in lower-income rural and urban areas at a distinct disadvantage, since even high property tax rates cannot bring in the level of resources that schools in middle- to upper-class areas enjoy (Ball, Bowe, & Gewirtz, 1995; Kozol, 2005).

Second, U.S. Supreme Court decisions such as *Board of Education of Oklahoma City v. Dowell*, *Freeman v. Pitts*, and *Missouri v. Jenkins* have limited the scope of previous laws aimed at promoting racial integration of schools. The Court has ruled that segregated schools resulting from "residential preferences" are a result of people making choices about where to reside and are therefore beyond the scope of the law. The Court declared in these cases that school districts that previously had made an effort to integrate schools could send students back to neighborhood schools even if those schools were segregated and inferior (Orfield & Eaton, 1996).

Latino and Black students are more likely to be in segregated schools today than in earlier decades (Figure 12.4). In Chicago in 2012, for instance, 44% of students enrolled in public schools were Hispanic, 43% were Black, and only 9% were White. In Washington, DC, public school enrollment was 79% African American and 13% Hispanic.

■ **FIGURE 12.4** Racial Composition of U.S. Public Schools in Selected Cities, 2012

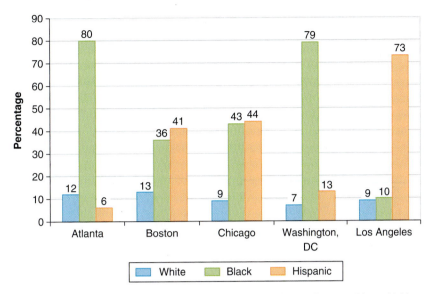

Source: Data from Federal Education Budget Project, "Comparative Analysis of Funding, Student Demographics and Achievement Data," New America Foundation, 2012.

Behind the Numbers

MINORITY STUDENTS AND COLLEGE ATTENDANCE

Data show that the percentage of U.S. college students who are members of minority groups has been on the rise, both in terms of absolute numbers and proportions. From 1976 to 2015, for instance, the percentage of Hispanic students rose from 4% to 17% of all U.S. residents enrolled in degree-granting postsecondary institutions, and the percentage of Black students grew from 10% in 1976 to 14% in 2015, though the 2015 percentage reflects a small decrease since 2011, when Black students made up 15% of enrolled U.S. residents. The proportion of Asian American students enrolled in higher education has also risen (U.S. Department of Education, 2018).

During this period, however, the proportion of Black students enrolled at elite U.S. institutions of higher education has declined; in fact, it is lower today than it was 35 years ago. Black students comprise 15% of college-age Americans, but they make up only 6% of Black freshmen attending elite schools. These elite schools include campuses of the University of California, liberal arts colleges such as Amherst and Vassar, universities such as Duke and Emory, and Ivy League schools such as Harvard and Yale, where

only 9% of freshmen are Black. The University of California system banned affirmative action in 1998 and saw a decline in the number of Black and Hispanic freshmen immediately afterward. As for Hispanic students, though the number of college-age students and the number of Hispanic freshmen has increased at elite schools, the gap between the two has widened since 1980 (Ashkenas, Park, & Pearce, 2017).

Why is the proportion of Black and Hispanic students at elite schools on the decline? Minority underrepresentation in college stems from equity issues that begin in primary and secondary education, particularly in racially segregated schools. These schools are less likely to have opportunities that foster a college-going culture. For example, high-minority enrollment schools are likely to have fewer experienced teachers, a smaller selection of advanced courses, and inadequate facilities compared to peer schools in more economically advantaged areas where White students are in the majority (Ashkenas, Park, & Pearce, 2017). Significantly as well, some minority students do not feel or witness a sense of inclusion, which, in turn, makes them question if they want

(Continued)

(Continued)

to attend institutions where there are few Black or Hispanic students enrolled (McGill, 2015).

The admission practices of elite schools may also help explain why the proportion is low, as certain aspects of the selection criteria put minority students at a disadvantage, such as the use of standardized tests such as the SAT or ACT. Because of the strict criteria for admissions, counselors may be more likely to steer minority students to less selective schools (McGill, 2015). Finally, *undermatching* also contributes to the underrepresentation of minorities. Undermatching occurs when students who are disadvantaged but high achieving do not apply to elite institutions, even though they are admissible. Minority and low-income students are most likely to experience undermatching, and as a result, they are not offered the same opportunities as their White and Asian American counterparts to compete for places. Undermatching occurs for many reasons, including lack of awareness by students of opportunities, a dearth of guidance and guidance counselors, and students being overlooked by college recruiters,

who tend to recruit high-achieving students from schools with reputations for rigor (Harris, 2018).

Affirmative action has aided in the increase of Black and Hispanic students at many colleges and universities, yet underrepresentation of these students still occurs, especially at elite institutions (Ashkenas, Park, & Pearce, 2017). Because underrepresentation is still so prevalent—and because it is linked to the perpetuation of educational and economic inequality—understanding why African American and Hispanic students are underrepresented is critical.

Think It Through

- How might elite education institutions increase the number of African American and Hispanic students? Will equal representation decrease opportunities for White and Asian American students? Is it possible to have equal representation without decreasing opportunities for others? What are solutions to having equal representation and equal opportunity?

In Los Angeles, fully three quarters of students were Hispanic and about 9% were White, while 10% were Black (New America Foundation, 2012). Many schools that operate under **de facto segregation** (*school segregation based largely on residential patterns*) face daunting problems, including

> low levels of competition and expectation, less qualified teachers who leave as soon as they get seniority, more limited curricula, peer pressure against academic achievement and supportive of crime and substance abuse, high levels of teen pregnancy, few connections with colleges and employers who can assist students, less serious academic counseling and preparation for college, and powerless parents who themselves failed in school and do not know how to evaluate or change schools. (Orfield & Eaton, 1996, p. 54)

By contrast, most Asian American students are integrated into schools with Whites. Asian American communities such as "Chinatowns" and "Little Saigons," which are populated with recent immigrants from China, Vietnam, Korea, and other Asian countries, are an exception, even though

integration becomes more common in later generations (Chen, 1992; Loo, 1991; Zhou, 2009).

American Indians on reservations are the most segregated of all minorities. The various tribes are recognized by treaty as separate nations whose rights are governed by agreements between them and the U.S. government. Their schools are run by the Bureau of Indian Affairs, which employs teachers and sets the curriculum. Treaties between the U.S. government and Indian nations have sought to ensure education that recognizes the value of American Indian culture and tradition. Yet the teachers employed by the Bureau of Indian Affairs are ordinarily expected to cover the standard subjects of U.S. school curricula—and in English. Problems within the tribal communities have resulted, since Native Americans often see such instruction as failing to respect their linguistic and cultural differences.

Issues in U.S. Higher Education

In the United States today, nearly three quarters of high school graduates continue on to higher education. The importance of higher education in the modern world and economy are common themes in educational and political discourse. Below, we look at the relationship between education, employment, and earnings. We continue with an examination of the college internship, a

De facto segregation: School segregation based largely on residential patterns, which persists even though legal segregation is now outlawed in the United States.

growing phenomenon that has invited both praise and critique. We end with a discussion the college dropout phenomenon, its dimensions, and its probable causes and possible cures.

Education, Employment, and Earnings

There is a strong relationship between educational attainment and the labor force participation rate, which shows the proportion of those of working age (usually 16–64) who are either employed or unemployed and actively seeking work. It does not include those who are institutionalized (in prison, for instance) or those who are serving in the armed forces; other groups who are not participating in the labor force include many full-time students and homemakers. In mid-2017, labor force participation rates of adults varied significantly by education: The labor force participation rate for those with less than a high school education was 46%; for those with a high school education, it climbed to 58%; and for those with some college or an associate degree,

it was 66%. For adults with a bachelor's degree or higher, it rose to 74% (Brundage, 2017).

In Figures 12.5 and 12.6, we also see a strong correlation between educational attainment and income and between educational attainment and vulnerability to unemployment. We have seen in other chapters that educational attainment has grown in importance in the postindustrial era, as the living wage jobs of the industrial era in sectors such as automobile manufacturing, steel, and textiles have fallen victim to outsourcing and automation. What remains as the foundation of the U.S. economy are advanced professional occupations (which require higher education and often even graduate degrees) and service jobs (which are often part-time, low-pay, and low-benefit positions in sectors such as child and elder care, retail, and hospitality). Although some manufacturing has continued to be sited in the United States, new manufacturing jobs are far less likely to be unionized, are more likely to involve short-term contracts, and are characterized by a lower pay scale than similar jobs in the past. Several new manufacturing jobs demand

■ **FIGURE 12.5** Real Average Hourly Wages of Young Workers with a Bachelor's Degree, 1989–2018

Source: "The Class of 2018" by Elise Gould, Zane Mokhiber, and Julia Wolfe, May 10, 2018. Figure H. Washington, DC: Economic Policy Institute. Reprinted with permission.

Note: The wage series is based on a 12-month moving average. The most recent data point is the average of March 2017 through February 2018. Dollar amounts are adjusted for inflation to 2017 dollars.

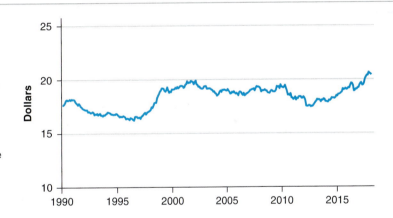

■ **FIGURE 12.6** Rates of Unemployment for Young College Graduates (Ages 21–24) with a Bachelor's Degree by Gender and Race/Ethnicity, 2000 and 2018

Source: "The Class of 2018" by Elise Gould, Zane Mokhiber, and Julia Wolfe, May 10, 2018. Figure F. Washington, DC: Economic Policy Institute. Reprinted with Permission.

Note: AAPI stands for Asian American/Pacific Islander. Data for 2000 and 2018 use an average of January 1998–December 2000 and March 2015–February 2018, respectively.

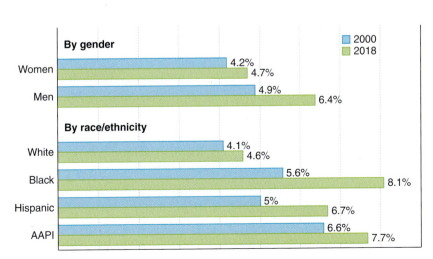

proficiency with high-technology equipment, which may require either college education or other advanced training beyond high school.

In the wake of the Great Recession, which ended in 2009, many students still struggle to find post-graduation employment, but their prospects have improved with strong job growth. Some experts caution, however, that the poorer employment prospects of graduates in the years 2009 to 2014 created a backlog of college completers seeking employment, which may have raised competition for the entry-level jobs to which many new graduates aspire. The wages of young graduates (21–24) have recovered somewhat in the postrecession period, even though they continue to be volatile (Figure 12.5). Significantly, some entry-level jobs have evolved into unpaid internships, rendering the first step on the career ladder more tenuous for new graduates.

Although more recent graduates appear to be finding jobs in a stronger labor market, many are also burdened by student loan debt. According to the Federal Reserve Bank of New York, between 2004 and 2014, there was a 92% increase in the number of student loan borrowers and a 74% rise in average loan balances (Davis, Kimball, & Gould, 2015). Notably, borrowing differs by race and ethnicity: An estimated 80% of Black students take on debt compared to about 63% of White students. Among Hispanic students, the rate is similar to that of Whites attending public universities, though they borrow more heavily when attending private schools (Huelsman, 2015). One key reason why this difference is significant is the fact that Black and Hispanic college graduates have higher rates of unemployment than their White peers: In the period between early 2015 and early 2018, the unemployment rate for young graduates (21–24 years of age) who were White was 4.6%. For Black graduates, it was 8.8%; for Hispanic graduates, it was 6.7%; and for Asian American/Pacific Islander graduates, it was 7.7% (Gould, Mokhiber, & Wolfe, 2018).

At the same time, the assertion that higher education opens doors to employment and higher lifetime earnings remains essentially correct. According to the Center on Education and the Workforce at Georgetown University, "By 2020, 65 percent of all jobs in the economy will require postsecondary education and training beyond high school." Significantly as well, "The United States is more educated than ever: In 1973, workers with postsecondary education held only 28 percent of jobs; by comparison, they held 59 percent of jobs in 2010 and will hold 65 percent of jobs in 2020" (Carnevale, Smith, & Strohl, 2014, pp. 2–3)

Although slow wage growth and the rise of student debt are critical concerns for students, their families, and the economy as a whole, educational attainment will continue to grow in importance as a pathway to professional careers and higher earning potential.

Internships and Higher Education

Thousands of U.S. college students build their résumés and job experience with unpaid internships, which have become a staple of summer or a part of the regular academic year for students living in cities such as Washington, DC, and New York, where opportunities are abundant to work in politics, the fashion industry, public relations, and other fields. A 2014 survey of 43,000 graduating seniors at about 700 universities found that 61% had an internship or co-op experience during college; most of those internships (over 53%) were unpaid (Venator & Reeves, 2015). Many universities require students to complete an internship to earn credit toward a major or graduation. More students than ever are also working in unpaid internships *after* graduation, having been unable to secure paid entry-level positions, even with their degrees. Critics, however, are raising questions about the legality and morality of employing young people, sometimes full-time, without paying them wages or salaries. While some internships, particularly in business, engineering, and financial services, offer stipends or pay, most do not.

What are some of the benefits to students of participating in unpaid internships? Both students and their universities often believe internships are a vital component of building human capital in preparation for the world of paid and professional work. Indeed, a 2012 survey of about 50,000 U.S. employers found that internship experience was a significant factor in hiring a new employee (Figure 12.7). Universities have an interest in helping students work outside campus on activities that can build their knowledge base, and students have an interest in developing skills and social networks that will help them find good jobs after graduation. Many look forward with excitement to the possibility of working with a representative in Congress, a lawyer, a public relations specialist, a fashion designer, or a nonprofit. For many students, the internship experience is a positive one.

The U.S. Department of Labor's Wage and Hour Division (2010) recognizes legal internships as a means for preparing interns for work and has established a set of six criteria that most public and private institutions must meet:

- The internship, even though it includes actual operation of the facilities of the employer, is similar to training that would be given in an educational environment.

- The internship experience is for the benefit of the intern.

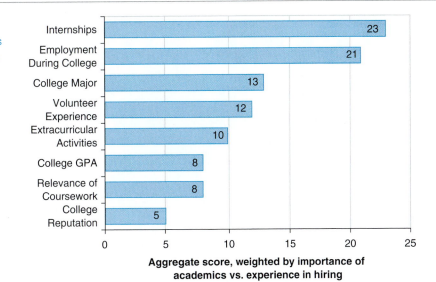

■ **FIGURE 12.7** Relative Importance of Attributes in Evaluating Graduates for Hire

Source: "Unpaid internships: Support beams for the glass floor." Venator, J, & Reeves, R. (2015).

Aggregate score, weighted by importance of academics vs. experience in hiring

Q: How much weight do you give each of the following educational credentials when you evaluate a recent college graduate's resume? How much weight do you give each of the following types of experience when you evaluate a recent college graduate's resume?

- The intern does not displace regular employees but works under close supervision of existing staff.

- The employer that provides the training derives no immediate advantage from the activities of the intern, and on occasion, its operations may actually be impeded.

- The intern is not necessarily entitled to a job at the conclusion of the internship.

- The employer and the intern understand that the intern is not entitled to wages for the time spent in the internship.

There is room for interpretation of these criteria on multiple points. For instance, can we clearly determine whether an employer derives no immediate advantage from the activities of the intern? Or that no regular employees have been displaced?

Another way of looking at internships is to ask how an arrangement intended by law to benefit students and other prospective workers may benefit other entities—perhaps even to the detriment of the intern, as writer Ross Perlin (2011) points out. Among the points Perlin raises are the following: Universities benefit from mandating student internships for credit, because students are thereby required to pay tuition dollars for an experience that—unlike the classroom experience—costs the university comparably little. And employers are effectively provided with the services of often well-educated and enthusiastic workers—for no pay. Perlin argues that a range of institutions and employers thus exploit the services of young workers for their own economic advantage in the fashion and finance industries, in politics, and in the nonprofit world.

Who loses in this equation? Perlin (2012) and Eisenbrey (2012) suggest that lower-income students are losers in the internship game. That is, while students from better-off families can afford (at least for a while) to work without pay in order to secure human and social capital, poor and working-class students need to work for pay, even if it's in a field unrelated to their area of career interest. Perlin (2012) argues that "lucrative and influential professions—politics, media and entertainment, to name a few—now virtually require a period of unpaid work, effectively barring young people from less privileged backgrounds." All students, however, are potentially disadvantaged where jobs that once were or might otherwise have been entry-level jobs are reinvented as unpaid internships, a shift that removes an economically and professionally important stepping-stone for students leaving school with degrees. A recent article on unpaid internships in Washington, DC, where thousands of students arrive every summer to work on Capitol Hill with advocacy organizations and in other political or cultural institutions notes

As an undergraduate student, you may have the opportunity to do an unpaid internship. Interns provide public and private organizations with important yet unpaid labor, while students benefit from getting work experience.

Such interns may cost their employers nothing, but some economists worry such programs do carry a cost. Free labor could be depressing wages in Washington while turning the federal government and Capitol Hill into arenas where only wealthy students can afford to work. In turn, children of privilege get another leg up on their less fortunate classmates. (Shepherd, 2016, para. 6)

Perlin (2011, 2012) asserts that the internship boom constricts social and professional mobility, contributes to growing inequality, and supports an economy in which those in the top tier are becoming less and less diverse. Even more seriously, a fundamental ethic in American life is under threat: the idea that a hard day's work demands a fair wage.

What, then, are we to conclude about internships, a growing and pervasive phenomenon that will be part of the experience of thousands of students this year and in years to come? It is clear that students benefit from spending time in a professional market that values both formal educational credentials and hands-on work experience. Universities benefit from giving their students opportunities to link classroom learning to experiential learning. And employers benefit from the creativity, skills, and enthusiasm of young workers. On the other hand, it remains important that benefits should not accrue disproportionately to the parties with the most power—universities and employers—to the detriment of students. How can students, their schools, and the law ensure opportunity for all and contribute to making internships meaningful work experiences that provide foundations for careers? What do you think?

Dropping in, Dropping out: Why Are College Dropout Rates So High?

Most high school graduates in the United States today go to college. According to data from the National Center for Education Statistics (2016a), in 2014, 68% of high school completers enrolled in college. This figure has grown over time: In 1960, it was 45% and in 1990, 60%. Students of all racial and ethnic backgrounds are enrolling at high rates: Fully 85% of Asian American students, 68% of White students, 63% of Black students, and 62% of Hispanic students enrolled in college immediately after completing high school (National Center for Education Statistics, 2016a). Data suggest that education is more critical than ever for raising earning potential and strengthening competitiveness in the job market. In light of this, it is not surprising that most students are seeking to continue their education beyond high school.

Some observers, however, point out that all is not well in U.S. higher education. In fact, they suggest, the high rate of enrollment obscures a troubling reality: Many students leave college with debt—and no degree. Journalist David Leonhardt (2009, para. 3) writes that "in terms of its core mission—turning teenagers into educated college graduates—much of the system is simply failing." Leonhardt argues that while the United States does an excellent job getting high school graduates to enroll in higher education, colleges have been far less successful in fostering timely graduation of students—or graduating them at all. Statistics suggest that many who enroll in college never finish with degrees, even though many end their college careers with substantial debt.

College attainment levels have remained flat for generations (Lewin, 2011a). About 59% of students enrolled in four-year institutions go on to graduate, but there are some significant differences in six-year completion rates by race and ethnicity. For example, for the class enrolled in a four-year college in the year 2006, there were notable differences in graduation rates four, five, and six years after enrollment (see Figure 12.9). There were also notable differences by institution: For example, although the six-year completion rate at the country's most selective schools (those that accept 25% or fewer applicants) is about 89%, this falls to about 62% for somewhat selective schools (those accepting 50% to 74% of applicants), and drops to 36% for open-admission schools

(National Center for Education Statistics, 2016b). Dropouts are costly, both to the nation as a whole, which loses potentially educated and productive workers, and to individuals, whose earning potential is diminished by their failure to obtain degrees and whose financial security may be compromised when they leave college with debt but no degree.

So, what is behind the college dropout phenomenon? Several factors contribute. First, high college costs drive many students out of higher education. The cost of a four-year private college has outpaced inflation as well as wage growth, and student borrowing has risen (Figure 12.8). Costs are a particularly acute issue for lower-income students, who are more likely than their better-off peers to drop out before completing a degree. The financial burden of a college education falls more heavily on those with fewer resources, even when support (such as federal Pell Grants) defray some tuition costs.

Second, the rigors of college work lead some students to drop out. This factor is complex. With an increasing proportion of high school graduates enrolling in college, there may be more new students who are unready for the workload or the level of work. Half of students in associate degree programs and about a fifth of those in bachelor's programs are required by their institutions to enroll in remedial classes to address academic shortcomings. Some of these courses do not confer college credit, raising the cost of an education, lengthening the time needed to earn a degree, and increasing the likelihood that a student will leave without completing college. Advocates for students suggest that colleges can do more to help students stay and

■ **FIGURE 12.8** Federal Student Loan Portfolio by Borrower Debt Size

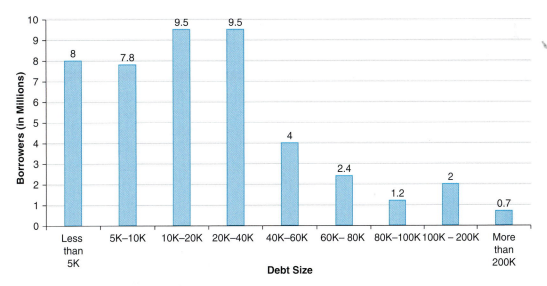

Source: U.S. Department of Education. Federal Student Loan Portfolio. Retrieved from https://studentaid.ed.gov/sa/about/data-center/student/portfolio.

■ **FIGURE 12.9** Six-Year College Completion by Race/Ethnicity for First-Time Students Starting in 2007 (Four-Year Schools)

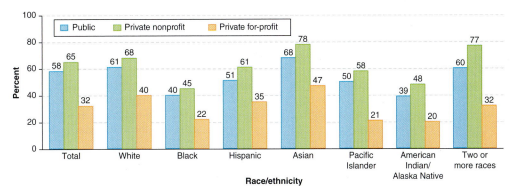

Source: U.S. Department of Education (2017). Status and Trends in the Education of Racial and Ethnic Groups 2016. Retrieved from https://nces.ed.gov/pubs2016/2016007.pdf.

Across the country, unequal funding of public schools and the resulting inequalities in resources are problems that perpetuate disparities in education and upward mobility.

succeed with coaching, scheduling that meets the needs of working students, and accelerated programs that speed the time to degree with rigorous work offered in concentrated time periods (Lewin, 2011a). At the same time, budget cuts, particularly at state institutions, have reduced rather than expanded opportunities to provide targeted services to struggling students.

Third, part-time attendance raises the probability of non-completion. Many students find it challenging to balance the rigors of school and work. According to Complete College America (2011), the majority of community college students work more than 20 hours per week, and a substantial proportion also take care of their families. The costs, as noted above, may also compel some students to choose part-time study. Alas, while attending college part-time seems like a viable solution, it substantially lowers the chance that a student will ever earn a degree: According to one study, only 13% of part-time students seeking a bachelor's degree had earned one in an eight-year time span. Only about a quarter of students today fit the stereotypical model of full-time, on-campus students, suggesting that the scope of the problem is bigger than it appears (Complete College America, 2011).

Discover & Debate

FREE COLLEGE

Motion: States in the United States should establish programs that provide in-state students the opportunity to get free college tuition.

Background: In 2017, the state of New York passed legislation that offers New York residents with household incomes below a set threshold the opportunity to attend public universities and colleges tuition-free. This development was widely welcomed by families concerned by the rising cost of higher education. Indeed, the price of a degree has risen dramatically in recent decades, outpacing wage and cost of living increases in society. According to the College Board, the average cost of a four-year degree at a public institution is $74,000; the average cost of the same degree at a private institution is $179,000. The growth of college costs has been accompanied by a mass proliferation of student debt: Over 44 million Americans have student loan debt, totaling an estimated $1.48 trillion.

Questions for Consideration

- Many countries around the world offer free or very low-cost tuition. What can we learn about this debate from studying their experiences?

- Are there creative ways that states could pay for free (or very low-cost) college tuition?

- What will happen to private universities and colleges if states make public higher education free to some or all state residents?

Debate Tip

- Though it's important to avoid anecdotal evidence in favor of empirical evidence, remember to include examples. Relevant examples will bring your argument to life, illustrating your point for your audience.

AFFIRMATIVE ARGUMENTS	OPPOSITION ARGUMENTS
If tuition were free, students would be able to minimize the amount of debt acquired through student loans, allowing them to save money for future adult milestones such as buying a home or starting a family	The money for free college is not free, and ultimately, funding for the program would have to come from higher taxes and/or reduced benefits in other areas.
With collegiate institutions being free, more students would have the opportunity to complete higher education. There are increasing numbers of jobs that require college degrees, and free college would enable students to get better jobs in the future.	Are there creative ways that states could pay for free (or very low-cost) college tuition?
Statistics show that those with a college degree are less likely to fall into poverty. With little or no debt from college loans and greater access to professional jobs with solid pay and health and retirement benefits, graduates could expect a good standard of living.	With college becoming accessible to everyone, the college degree will become devalued, becoming similar to a second high school degree.

According to the Organisation for Economic Co-operation and Development (Weston, 2014), the United States ranks 19th in college degree attainment among 28 wealthy democratic countries. At one time, it was near the top of the list. Although everyone may not desire or even need a college degree, the competitive global economic environment has put a premium value on higher education, which offers greater security from unemployment and greater earning potential than a high school credential alone. Understanding why students drop out is the first step to addressing this problem effectively.

Education in a Global Perspective

Education brings gains to individuals, communities, and countries. Today, more people than ever are literate, attending institutions of higher education and completing degrees, and sharing knowledge globally across new communication platforms. It is not unusual for a U.S. classroom to have a partner in another country so students can meet other students through the Internet to share interests and ideas. Nor is it unusual to meet U.S. students abroad who are studying for credit and seeing places they might only have read about in books. Education has the potential to bring people and cultures together to foster greater understanding, innovation, and prosperity. Below, we take a look at how the United States lines up with its global peers in areas related to education and at what some American students are doing in their studies across the planet.

Higher Education and Job Opportunities

When the OECD was formed in 1960, its members were 18 European nations, the United States, and Canada.

Today, the OECD has 35 member states across the globe, including countries as geographically, culturally, and economically diverse as Mexico and Turkey. Its goal is to both foster and track economic and policy development and changes in member states. The OECD collects data on the relationship between higher education and employment. From these data, we can get a basic picture of where the United States falls in relation to other member states in the achievement of educational credentials and the fortunes of college graduates (Table 12.1).

TABLE 12.1 Percentage of Young Adults Expected to Graduate from College in Selected OECD Countries, 2015

COUNTRY	PERCENTAGE
Australia	60%
New Zealand	57%
Denmark	53%
Canada	40%
United States	39%
Germany	32%
Turkey	27%
Hungary	27%
Mexico	24%

Source: OECD (2017), Education at a Glance 2017: OECD Indicators, OECD Publishing. Retrieved from https://www.oecd-ilibrary.org/education/education-at-a-glance-2017_eag-2017-en.

■ FIGURE 12.10 Earnings and Unemployment Rates by Educational Attainment in the United States, 2017

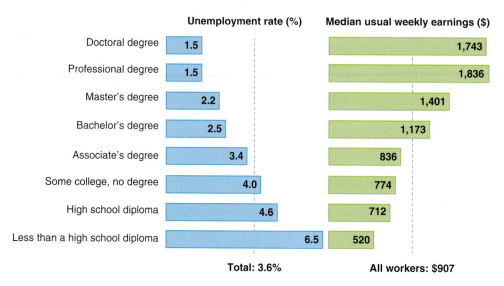

Source: Bureau of Labor Statistics.

Note: Data are for persons age 25 and over. Earnings are for full-time wage and salary workers.

In the OECD states, though they include both highly developed states such as the United States and Germany and developing countries such as Mexico and Chile, the correlations we have observed among educational attainment, income, and labor market prospects hold true. The global economic crisis that began in 2008 hit many member countries hard, and unemployment rates grew in each one. The most heavily affected workers were adults without post–high school education, whose unemployment rates rose overall from nearly 9% to more than 11% (Figure 12.10). For those with higher education, however, unemployment rates grew only one percentage point between 2008 and 2009 and stayed below 5% in most countries through 2009 (Spain and Turkey were the most notable exceptions). No less important, those with higher education continued to enjoy substantially higher wages than their peers with less education. Clearly, then, education matters across the globe.

U.S. Students Meet the World

For many U.S. students, the world beckons. Seized by curiosity to see and experience the world outside home, campus, and work, they are taking advantage of a small but growing number of college study-abroad programs (Table 12.2). In the past ten years, the number of U.S. students going to other countries to study has increased by almost 46% to 325,300. While this figure has grown, it is interesting to note that the number of students coming from foreign countries to study in the U.S. has also grown, reaching about 1,079,000 in

TABLE 12.2   Top Destinations for U.S. Students Studying Abroad

RANK	COUNTRY
1	United Kingdom
2	Italy
3	Spain
4	France
5	Germany
6	China
7	Ireland
8	Australia
9	Costa Rica
10	Japan
11	South Africa
12	Mexico
13	Denmark
14	Czech Republic
15	India

Source: Data from Institute of International Education. 2017. "Open Doors." *Fast Facts.*

2016–2017, an 85% rise within the past decade (Institute of International Education, 2017).

The top destinations for U.S. students have remained largely steady over time and include the United Kingdom, France, Spain, and Italy. Other destinations that are growing in popularity are China, India, Israel, Brazil, and New Zealand (Institute of International Education, 2010).

Any study-abroad experience holds the potential for culture shock, especially when it involves venturing to a new destination with a culture quite divergent from that of the mainstream United States. Clearly, however, many students are excited to embrace this possibility. More U.S. students are spending their junior years abroad in places about which they knew little before they entered college, such as the American University in Cairo and Ibadan University in Nigeria: "These students visit places most Americans know only through news reports—the West Bank, Ethiopia and even northern Iraq" (Conlin, 2010).

Part of the growth of academic interest in the Middle East, in particular, is driven by the availability of new

---

Global Issues

SOUTH KOREAN SCHOOLS: ACHIEVEMENT—AND PRESSURE

On international educational tests such as the Program of International Student Assessment (PISA), South Korea's students consistently rank among the highest in the world. In the 2012 test of 15-year-olds in 65 countries, South Korea ranked fifth in math (after Shanghai in China, Singapore, Hong Kong, and Taiwan) and fifth in reading (after Shanghai, Hong Kong, Singapore, and Japan). The United States ranked in the middle of the list: 24th in reading and 36th in math (BBC, 2015).

South Korea is a country that places a high value on education. It has a longer school year and a longer school day than many other countries around the world. Notably, for about three quarters of the country's students, education does not end when the school day comes to a close. Rather, students continue their studies through the evening at one of South Korea's many *hagwons* ("cram schools") at which students study English, math, and other subjects and work to prepare for a high-stakes exam that can determine whether a student succeeds in gaining admission to one of the country's top-ranked schools of higher education (Ripley, 2013): The exam, called the *suneung*, is taken in November. According to one account, "It's so

critical that planes are grounded on test day for fear of disturbing the kids" (Hu, 2015).

South Korea's ascent to the global peak of educational achievement has been rapid. As a *Wall Street Journal* article notes,

> Thanks in part to such tutoring services [*hagwons*], South Korea has dramatically improved its education system over the past several decades and now routinely outperforms the U.S. Sixty years ago, most South Koreans were illiterate; [in 2009,] South Korean 15-year-olds rank No. 2 in the world in reading, behind Shanghai. The country now has a 93% high school graduation rate, compared with 77% in the U.S. (Ripley, 2013)

The strong valuation of education translates into high earnings for many private tutors who teach in *hagwons*. Public school teachers earn modest salaries, though most are about 25% higher than those in the United States (Lynch, n.d.). In 2012, South Korean parents spent an estimated $17 billion in the private education market. "Rock star teachers" in this highly competitive sphere can earn in the millions of dollars (Ripley, 2013).

What are the origins of South Korea's determined pursuit of educational excellence? Answers to this question vary, but among the explanations are the country's economic needs and cultural orientation. South Korea has experienced rapid growth in the last half century, moving from a poor and little-developed country to an advanced and competitive player in the global economy. But as a researcher at the Korea Institute for Health and Social Affairs points out, "We don't have enough natural resources; the only resources we have [are] human resources" (quoted in Hu, 2015). Macroeconomic

©Chung Sung-Jun/Getty Images

(Continued)

(Continued)

goals are consistent with micro-level goals of families: In a country with one of the lowest total fertility rates in the world, parents are driven to invest significant resources in their child or children to ensure success (Koo, 2014). A reported 8 of 10 parents say that they feel the financial pressure created by *hagwon* tuition costs, but they are determined to ensure economic success for their children and status for the family (Lynch, n.d.; Ripley, 2013). These are not, however, the only costs of the consuming drive for achievement.

Surveys of young people in the states of the OECD find relatively lower levels of youth happiness (Koo, 2014) and higher levels of stress, even among students as young as 11 in South Korea (Hu, 2015). Significantly, the country has a notable rate of suicide among the young: According to the English-language *Korea Herald,*

> The number of suicides per 100,000 people aged 10 to 19 rose 57.2 percent to 5.58 in 2011 from 3.19 in 2001, according to the data by the state-run Korea Health Promotion Foundation (KHPF) on

the occasion of World Suicide Prevention Day, which falls on Sept. 10. ("Youth Suicides," 2013)

Most consequences are less dire: Some observers point out, for instance, that while South Korea's students are very strong test takers, they lag in areas of creative thinking (Lynch, n.d.).

South Korea has made enormous economic strides since the 1960s. Much of the success of the country and its population has been driven by a relentless pursuit of educational excellence. While this has put the country atop many global rankings, it has come with some serious costs.

Think It Through

- South Korean education has sometimes been cited as a model for the United States, which scores in the middle range in international educational tests. What are the challenges of building practices of educational excellence while maintaining a healthy balance in the lives of young people? Can these challenges be met?

Critical Language Scholarships, created in 2006 by the U.S. Department of State to facilitate the study of languages such as Arabic, Pashto, Dari, Azerbaijani, and Punjabi—languages not typically offered for study in U.S. high schools or colleges. Some students desire to be part of the political discourse, study public diplomacy, and witness the potential for change in a tumultuous region of the world. Others want to work in nongovernmental organizations or with the American Foreign Service (Conlin, 2010).

Whether the study-abroad experience takes them to London, Beijing, Beirut, Rio de Janeiro, or Cairo, many students say their worldviews are forever transformed by the opportunity to live in places they might otherwise know only from books or television. As one student said, "I will never again look at a story about the Middle East with such a one-sided perspective." Another added, "I genuinely enjoyed watching the bottom fall out of every one of my preconceived ideas about the Muslim world" (quoted in Conlin, 2010).

Why Study Education from a Sociological Perspective?

Education opens up the world to us. Through education, we gain new perspectives and build skills and knowledge to understand the world around us and to address key issues

and problems. In an increasingly interdependent and inter-connected world, education gives us advantages in navigating new challenges. Opportunities are not, however, equally distributed, and factors including socioeconomic status and place of residence can profoundly affect access to a good education. That matters because undeveloped potential cannot improve the lives or prospects of individuals, communities, and the country.

The significance of education in determining one's prospects is growing as the economy and labor market are changing. Whether you were born in the 1960s, the 1970s, the 1980s, the 1990s, or later, the U.S. economy has experienced dramatic changes in your lifetime. In the 1960s, more than one third of the U.S. nonagricultural workforce was engaged in manufacturing. At the same time, more Americans were pursuing higher education and demand for skilled professionals was high. In the latter years of the 1970s, the United States experienced a steep rise in imports—U.S.–made goods and U.S. workers were forced to compete with lower-priced goods and lower-priced labor. From this period forward, the share of goods made in the United States and the number of workers making them fell (Uchitelle, 2007). Starting in the early 1980s, wages, which had increased for decades, stagnated. Manufacturing jobs continued to shrink, but the service sector expanded; demand for educated workers remained robust. By the 1990s, advances in computer technologies brought a new wave of outsourcing, not of manufacturing jobs (many of which had already moved offshore) but of information technology and, increasingly, customer service jobs (Erber & Sayed-Ahmed, 2005). Countries such as India, with large populations of educated and English-speaking workers, benefited from American firms' pursuit of lower-cost labor not only in manufacturing but in service as well.

The shape of our economy and our economic fortunes has changed in myriad ways and continues to do so in the new millennium. Some of the early contours of a digitally networked economy are apparent in the United States: As noted early in the chapter, advanced technology is

---

What Can I Do with a Sociology Degree?

CONSIDERING GRADUATE AND PROFESSIONAL EDUCATION

Chapter 12 discusses the nature of our "credential society," where, in the contemporary world of work, your credentials—specifically, the higher education degree or degrees you earn—will have a big impact on your path to a career. While it is true that education pays with increased income opportunities and decreased risk of unemployment, the choice of whether to pursue advanced study is a very individual decision.

There are several types of graduate degrees. The Master of Arts (MA) and Master of Science (MS) academic degrees focus on intellectual development and the mastery of a core of knowledge in a particular discipline. Professional master's degrees include the Master of Business Administration (MBA) and the Master of Social Work (MSW), which are designed to advance careers or professions in their respective fields. The Doctor of Medicine (MD) and Juris Doctorate (JD) degrees focus on the acquisition of advanced skills and knowledge in the areas of medical practice and law, respectively. The Doctor of Philosophy degree (PhD), or *doctorate*, focuses on the broad mastery of disciplinary knowledge, the development of areas of specialization in the discipline, and rigorous, original research that contributes to the discipline and, perhaps, to policy and general societal knowledge of important topics.

A degree in sociology provides a strong foundation for graduate and professional education in any field. The core knowledge and diverse skills that you acquire as a sociology major prepare you for the rigors of graduate or professional school by helping you develop competencies in research, writing, communication, and critical thinking. The three main exams that are requirements for graduate admissions—the GRE (graduate school), MCAT (medical school), and LSAT (law school)—are designed to measure skills considered essential for success in those programs. These are skills inherent in sociology and have been described in the various career boxes throughout this book, including

synthesizing information, problem solving using data analysis, making evidence-based arguments, and communicating complex ideas effectively in writing.

Andrew Barondess, JD Candidate, Class of 2020 at UCLA School of Law

The George Washington University, BA in Sociology

Obtaining a sociology degree enabled me to have a seamless transition into graduate school. Studying sociology affords one the opportunity to develop and hone a broad set of skills. While pursuing my degree, I gained invaluable experience not only in writing and researching but also in critical analysis of societal issues such as poverty and crime. Furthermore, my degree gave me a leg up in law school over others who may not have had firsthand experience researching, writing, and thinking critically. A sociology degree offers a better understanding of society and why people act the way they do. This is particularly important for tackling the complex legal problems faced in law school and afterword as a practicing attorney. Lastly, while I chose to pursue a legal education after undergrad, a sociology degree provides the building blocks for success in any graduate program.

Career Data: Lawyers

- 2017 Media Pay: $119,250 per year
- $57.33 per hour
- Typical Entry-Level Education: Doctoral or professional degree
- Job Outlook, 2016–2026: 8% (As fast as average)

Source: Bureau of Labor Statistics, *Occupational Outlook Handbook*, 2017.

shifting its role from that of assisting workers to replacing them. This is already taking place in manufacturing, and it is seeping into the service sector. Even occupational sectors requiring advanced education are not immune to these dramatic changes. Will technology, particularly in the form of automation, robotics, and artificial intelligence, contribute to the creation of new jobs and opportunities? Will it diminish or destroy existing economic sectors? These questions remain to be answered.

Understanding the relationship between the skills and knowledge gained through education and the demands of the economy and labor market is critical to gaining a perspective on how we as individuals and as a country can both prepare for and shape our future.

SUMMARY

- **Education** is the transmission of society's norms, values, and knowledge base by means of direct instruction.

- **Mass education** spread with industrialization and the need for widespread **literacy**. Today, the need is not only for literacy but for specialized training as well. All industrial societies today, including the United States, have systems of **public education** that continue through the high school level and frequently the university level as well. Such societies are sometimes termed **credential societies**, in that access to desirable jobs and social status depends on the possession of a certificate or diploma.

- Functionalist theories of education emphasize the role of the school in serving the needs of society by socializing students and filling positions in the social order, while conflict theories emphasize education's role in reproducing rather than reducing social inequality.

- Symbolic interactionist theory, by focusing on the classroom itself, reveals how teachers' perceptions of students—as well as students' self-perceptions—are important in shaping students' performance.

- Early literacy and later educational attainment are powerfully correlated. Access to books and early reading experiences are among the strongest predictors of basic literacy at an early age. Researchers measure multiple levels of literacy.

- U.S. public schools are highly segregated by race and ethnicity. Before the 1954 U.S. Supreme Court decision in *Brown v. Board of Education,* segregation was legal. Since that time, schools have continued to show **de facto segregation** because segregated residential patterns still exist, because many White parents decide to send their children to private schools, and because the courts have recently limited the scope of previous laws aimed at promoting full integration.

- Differences in school funding by race, ethnicity, and class reinforce existing patterns of social inequality. In general, the higher someone's social class, the more likely he or she is to complete high school and college. Low-income people, in contrast, are often trapped in a cycle of low educational attainment and poverty.

- There are strong demonstrable relationships between educational attainment and employment prospects and between educational attainment and income. There is also a correlation between the socioeconomic status of a family and the probability of its members' further educational attainment.

- Artificial intelligence has the potential to transform the labor market, as machines shift from the role of being an instrument for human workers to being workers. This change may affect jobs for both less-educated and highly educated employees.

KEY TERMS

food insecurity, 325
education, 327
formal education, 327

mass education, 327
literacy, 328
public education, 328

credential society, 328
school segregation, 335
de facto segregation, 338

DISCUSSION QUESTIONS

1. What are some of the key reasons students drop out of college? How can identifying the sociological roots of the problem help us to develop effective policies to address it?

2. What do contemporary data show us about the relationship between family income and academic achievement, as measured by variables such as educational attainment or SAT scores? How do sociologists explain the relationship? What are the strengths and weaknesses of their arguments?

3. What is the current state of racial segregation in U.S. public schools? How has it changed since the civil rights era of the 1960s? What sociological factors help explain high levels of racial segregation in schools? How can the United States address high levels of racial segregation in our schools?

4. How is unemployment in the United States measured? What aspects of this phenomenon does the unemployment rate measure and what aspects does it fail to capture?

5. What effects might the expansion of automation and artificial intelligence have on the U.S. and global workforce? What evidence of the effect is available today? What sectors of the labor market may be affected in the future?

Want a better grade?

Get the tools you need to sharpen your study skills. Access practice quizzes, eFlashcards, video, and multimedia at **https://edge.sagepub.com/chambliss4e**.

Religion and Society

13

13

WHAT DO YOU THINK?

1. What sociological functions does religion have in modern societies?

2. Why are young adults in the United States more likely than previous generations to profess no religious affiliation?

3. Is religion a source of stability or a source of conflict on a global scale? Might it be both?

LEARNING OBJECTIVES

13.1 Explain how sociologists approach the study of religion.

13.2 Apply classical and contemporary sociological perspectives to analyze the place of religion in human societies.

13.3 Describe different types of religious organizations.

13.4 Identify key characteristics of the four major global religions.

13.5 Discuss the status and role of women in religion.

13.6 Discuss religion in the United States, including trends in affiliation and disestablishment, and the practice of civil religion.

13.7 Discuss globalization's effects on relations between religious groups.

A NEW RELIGION RISES: THE JEDI FAITHFUL

One of the most successful movie franchises in history is also the foundation of a small but growing religion. The original *Star Wars* film, which debuted in 1977, and the nine prequels and sequels that followed have spawned not only consumer goods such as toys, books, and video games but also spiritual beliefs and values that have caught the attention of the film's legions of fans.

Jediism is the religion of adherents who embrace "a belief that collective thought can influence

©dpa picture alliance / Alamy Stock Photo

353

external change," a variation on the Force that forms a central theme in the *Star Wars* films (Rowen, 2018, para. 5). Among its component parts are entreaties to followers to engage in meditation, self-improvement, and service (Rowen, 2018). As one adherent noted in an interview, "We are absolutely looking to achieve the outcomes of any other religion. . . . A better life, and a better death." (Shea, 2017, para. 7).

The Jedi religion emerged, according to a recent article on the phenomenon, out of early role-playing games based on the films, which offered the outlines of a moral code, including the ideas that "There is no emotion; there is peace" and "There is no ignorance; there is knowledge" (Rowen, 2018, para. 10). The role-playing games had a strong following, which may explain the moderate success of an e-mail circulated in 2001 that entreated those without a dominant religion to identify themselves as *Jedi*. The U.S. does not have a question about religion on the national census, but among those in countries that use the question, including the United Kingdom and Australia, over 550,000 people marked their religion as Jedi. According to the article, "in the United Kingdom, more people listed their religion as Jedi than Jewish or Buddhist" (Ibid., para. 11).

While some people provided the answer in jest, an article from the British Broadcasting Corporation suggests that at least some of the self-reported Jedi are earnest in their commitment. It notes,

> Beth Singler, a researcher in the Divinity Faculty of Cambridge University, estimates that there are about 2,000 people in the UK who are "very genuine" about being Jedi. That's roughly the same number as the Church of Scientology, she says. Jediism is not a joke for them but an inspiration. (DeCastella, 2014, para. 5)

Estimates of U.S. followers range from 5,000 to 10,000 (Rowen, 2018).

In 2015, the Temple of the Jedi Order, which operates in the U.S., successfully petitioned the Internal Revenue Service for status as a tax-exempt ministry. This success has not been realized, however, in the United Kingdom, Australia, or New Zealand, where Jedi adherents have failed to gain official recognition as a religion. This raises some interesting sociological questions: What makes a religion? Who has the power to decide what belief systems do or do not constitute a religion?

Rowen (2018) writes,

> One common argument against the validity of Jediism is that, unlike traditional religions, it recognizes a canon it understands to be fictional. But throughout the 20th century, scientific advances that directly contradicted religious texts led to a demythologizing of Judeo-Christian religious books too. Many, including church leaders, came to understand the Bible's cosmology and myths not as literal, but as fable. . . . Once traditional religion takes some of its stories as fictional, its parallels to pop-culture inspired religions, like Jediism, become quite pronounced: Belief in the moral force of stories about saints is similar to belief in the moral force of stories about superheroes and masters of telekinesis. (para. 28)

So, is Jediism a religion? Does it fulfill the same functions as acknowledged religions? What makes it more or less real than sister religions from which it draws, including the Judeo-Christian and Buddhist traditions? What do you think?

In this chapter, we examine the relationship between religion and society, beginning with a consideration of what religion is and what functions it has in communities and societies. We explore classical and contemporary theoretical perspectives on religion and society and examine the place of religion in people's private and public lives. We look at different types of religious organizations as well as the great world religions. We then explore issues of religion in the United States, including changing religious affiliations and the phenomenon of civil religion. We conclude by looking at expanding global contacts and relationships between religious groups.

How Do Sociologists Study Religion?

From a sociological perspective, we define a **religion** as *a system of common beliefs and rituals centered on sacred things that unites believers and provides a sense of meaning and purpose* (Durkheim, 1912/2008). We often think of **theism**, *a belief in one or more supernatural deities*, as basic to religion (the term originates from the Greek word for god, *theos*), but there is no clear conceptual distinction between worship of a spiritual being and worship of an entity such as a nation. Indeed, we could see nationalism as a form of civic religion.

Sociologists look at religion in the context of society, asking about its role and function and identifying its basic social elements. First, religion is a form of culture. Recall from Chapter 3 that culture is composed of *the beliefs, norms, behaviors, and products common to the members of a particular group.* Religion embodies these characteristics, as it is constituted by a common worldview that draws together those who identify with it.

Second, religion includes the ritualization and routinization of beliefs. All religions have a behavioral aspect: Adherents engage in practices that identify them as members of the group and create or affirm group bonds. Sociologist Émile Durkheim (1912/2008) argued that religious rituals create and reinforce social cohesion. Robert Merton (1968) added to this idea, suggesting that while rituals have a manifest (or obvious) function, they also have the latent (secondary or unintentional) function of reinforcing group solidarity. The manifest function of the Hopi rain dance was to bring rain; its latent function was to strengthen community ties.

Third, religion provides a sense of purpose and meaning. Religions commonly tell coherent and compelling stories about the forces that transcend everyday life, in ways that other aspects of culture such as a belief in democracy typically cannot (Geertz, 1973; Wuthnow, 1988). Where we cannot find empirical answers to fundamental questions about life, death, and fate, faith may stand in.

When sociologists study religion, they do so as sociologists, not as believers or atheists. From the sociological perspective, religion is an important social institution. How, then, do sociologists approach the study of religion in society?

Religion: A system of common beliefs and rituals centered on sacred things that unites believers and provides a sense of meaning and purpose.

Theism: A belief in one or more supernatural deities.

A daily prayer ritual, also known as *Salah,* is one of the five pillars of Islam. It is performed five times a day by Muslim worshippers facing the direction of the Kaaba in Mecca (in Saudi Arabia).

©Robertus Pudyanto/Getty Images

In Hinduism, cows symbolize wealth, strength, abundance, and a full earthly life. They roam freely in many Indian villages and cities.

©iStockphoto.com/flocu

First, they do not study whether religious beliefs are true or false. They regard religious beliefs not as truths decreed by deities but as the social constructions of human beings. Throughout history, humans have told stories about the world in which they live. Before the coming of Christianity to Northern Europe, for instance, people told stories about gods of nature or divinities who brought good fortune or ill fate to explain the tension between good and evil in human existence. Communities have always sought to construct logical frameworks to explain the world around them, and organized religion is only one way they engage in the quest for understanding and control.

Second, sociologists are interested in the social organization of religion. Within Christianity and Judaism, for example, religious practice often occurs in formal organizations, such as churches or synagogues. Yet this is not necessarily true of Hinduism and Buddhism, whose rituals may be practiced in the home or in natural settings. In Islamic societies such as Saudi Arabia and Iran, religious beliefs and practices are incorporated into daily life and guide political, cultural, and even economic practices.

Third, sociologists examine the function of religion as a source of solidarity within a group or society. Émile Durkheim (1912/2008) described religion as a "unified system of beliefs and practices related to sacred things" that are held in awe and elevated above the "profane" elements of daily existence and that unite believers in a moral community (p. 47). According to Durkheim, the "god of the clan"—the object of worship—is "nothing else than the clan itself, personified and represented to the imagination" (p. 206). This view highlights the importance of the group in constructing and worshipping, through the objects of devotion, an image of itself.

If a single religion dominates a society, it may function as a source of social stability. If several religions compete for resources and power in a shared space, differences between religions or sects may lead to sectarian conflicts. Examples of destabilizing religious conflicts include struggles among Sikhs, Hindus, and Muslims in India; between Muslims and Christians in Bosnia and Kosovo; and between Sunni and Shiite Muslims in Iraq and Pakistan. The recent influx of refugees from the Middle East and North Africa, many of whom are Muslim, into predominantly secular European states such as France and Germany has also led to social tension, though the term *sectarian struggle* cannot precisely characterize the tension, which stems from perceived and real differences in cultures and religious orientations.

Finally, sociologists study the ways in which social forces, rather than individual spiritual experiences, affect people's commitment to religion. Religious beliefs are deeply personal for many, creating a profound sense of connection with forces that transcend everyday reality. Sociologists do not question the depth of such feelings, but they do not limit themselves to spiritual explanations of religious devotion. They examine ways that "getting religion" coincides with community or individual experiences of loss, grief, poverty, or disaster. This perspective has deep historical roots: As far back as the first century bc, the Latin poet Lucretius saw religion as originating in human fears and needs. He believed

men had dreamed of gods, to whom they attributed omnipotence and immortality. Unable to account for natural phenomena, especially in its more terrifying aspects, men had gone on to ascribe all such things to the gods, whom they consequently feared and sought to propitiate. (Brandon, 1973, p. 93)

Theoretical Perspectives on Religion and Society

In this section, we examine classical sociological perspectives on the role of religion in society, but we begin by considering the birth of religion and early human society through the lens of a sister discipline, anthropology. **Anthropology** is *the study of human cultures and societies and their development.* Similar to sociology, it offers different perspectives on questions, including the relationships among religion, human civilization, and agriculture—it gives us different theoretical "glasses" we can use to see the development of our common human past.

Our story begins in what is now southern Turkey, near the border with Syria. As long as 11,600 years ago, pillars measuring 18 feet and weighing up to 16 tons were raised at Göbekli Tepe, the home of what archaeologists believe to be the world's oldest temple (Mann, 2011). Carved into the temple are animal totems, figures that may represent guardian spirits. Göbekli Tepe has challenged a long-held anthropological belief that organized religion arose as a way for humans to establish social bonds when hunter–gatherers evolved from living in nomadic bands into forming village communities. Instead, says archaeologist Klaus Schmidt, the massive temple shows that organized religion may predate the rise of agriculture and other key aspects of civilization. Lacking evidence of human settlement, Göbekli Tepe may have been a gathering place for foragers living within a hundred-mile radius. Settled agricultural activity may have arisen from a need to ensure adequate food for those drawn to the temple. We may then understand religion—in this instance, "the human impulse to gather for sacred rituals [that] arose as humans shifted from seeing themselves as part of the natural world to seeking mastery over it" (Mann, 2011)—as a critical precursor to agriculture and village settlements.

Anthropology: The study of human cultures and societies and their development.

Did organized religion arise in response to a need for cohesion in early human societies, or did religion come first, fostering a shift from nomadic hunting and gathering to settled agricultural communities? These questions shed light on the concerns of both anthropologists and sociologists of religion.

The Classical View: Religion, Society, and Secularization

Classical sociological theorizing on religion focuses on the relationship between religion and society and includes the work of Émile Durkheim, Karl Marx, and Max Weber. Next, we discuss each of these key perspectives.

Durkheim

The Functions of Religion. Émile Durkheim's *The Elementary Forms of the Religious Life* (1912/2008) sets forth one of the most influential and enduring theories in the sociology of religion. Durkheim based his theories on studies of Australian Aborigines, small hunting and gathering tribes who had lived in much the same way for thousands of years. Aborigines divided their world into two parts: the **profane**, *a sphere of routine, everyday life,* and the **sacred**, *that which is set apart from the ordinary; the sphere endowed with spiritual meaning.* The sacred sphere included many ordinary objects, which Durkheim called **totems**, *ordinary objects believed to have acquired transcendent or magical qualities connecting humans with the divine.* Durkheim posited that *totemism* was the most primitive form of religion. Similar to the ancient worshippers at Göbekli Tepe, early Native Americans elevated elements of the natural world to sacred status, giving particular pride of place to the bison. Contemporary examples of totems include the wafer and wine used in a Catholic Mass, which the devout believe are ritually transformed into the body and blood of Christ.

Sacred activities for the Australian Aborigines included rituals and ceremonies that provided a heightened emotional awareness and a spiritual connection with divine forces and other members of the community. During such rituals, Durkheim suggested, people lost their sense of individuality and merged with the larger group. His key theoretical conclusion was that the realm of the sacred serves an important social function—it brings the community together, reaffirms its norms and values, and strengthens its social bonds. According to Durkheim,

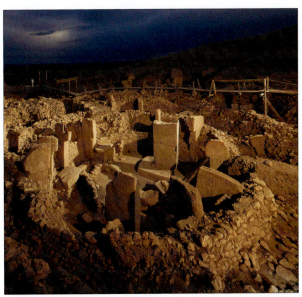

Göbekli Tepe is an ancient sanctuary erected at the top of a mountain ridge in the Southeastern Anatolia region of Turkey. It is the oldest known human-made religious structure. Archeologists estimate that the temple was built by hunter–gatherers in the 10th millennium BCE.

©National Geographic Creative/Alamy Stock Photo

the realm of the sacred is society's projection of itself onto divine objects or beings, a view with roots in early history. Xenophanes, a philosopher who lived around 570 bc, wrote that humans have created gods in their own image. The sacred *is* the group, endowed with divine powers and purpose. By worshipping the sacred, society worships itself, becoming stronger and more cohesive as a result.

Durkheim believed the sacred was disappearing from modern industrial society, with the realm of the profane extending over wider areas of life. However, while societies were likely to eventually reject the religiosity of earlier communities, Durkheim believed they could create *secular* forms of religion with the same function but a different form. In the United States, for instance, we can identify rituals, both religious and civic, that function to create or reinforce a collective conscience or group solidarity, such as rooting for American athletes in the Olympic Games, reciting the Pledge of Allegiance, and singing the national anthem. The U.S. flag carries a symbolic meaning because it stands for the collective nation; in "worshipping" the flag by affording it pride of place in venues from classrooms to ballparks, the community venerates itself and its values, beliefs, and practices.

Durkheim's work suggests that one of religion's key functions in society is to create and reinforce the collective bond. Sociologist Herbert Blumer (1986) notes that the meaning of a thing for a person grows out of the ways in which others respond to the object and the person's actions toward it. A flag, as a physical object, is only a piece of colored fabric, but citizens of a country endow it with a meaning that elevates it to a sacred symbol. A wafer is only a wafer unless it is blessed in a Christian religious ceremony, when it

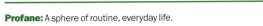

Profane: A sphere of routine, everyday life.

Sacred: That which is set apart from the ordinary; the sphere endowed with spiritual meaning.

Totems: Within the sacred sphere, ordinary objects believed to have acquired transcendent or magical qualities connecting humans with the divine.

becomes a representation of the body of Christ and its consumption becomes an act of worship.

Marx

Religion and Inequality. Karl Marx's writings about religion examine its role in society and the capitalist class hierarchy. In Marx's view, religion serves the interests of the ruling class by providing an outlet for human misery that obscures the true source of suffering among the subordinate classes—their exploitation by the ruling class.

Marx (1844/2000) wrote that "religion is the sigh of the oppressed creature, the feeling of a heartless world, and the soul of soulless circumstances. It is the opium of the people" (p. 72). In other words, by promising spiritual solutions—such as a better afterlife—as the answer to human suffering, religion discourages oppressed people from understanding the nature of their oppression in the present life and serves the interests of the powerful, who then have an easier time maintaining passivity among the economically deprived masses. After all, if there are rewards in the afterlife, then striving for betterment in the present life is not only unnecessary but also possibly counterproductive.

Marx also believed that once capitalism was overthrown, religion would no longer be necessary, since the stratification and dire economic disadvantage he saw as inevitable in the capitalist system would no longer exist. Similar to Durkheim, Marx believed secularization was inevitable. **Secularization** is *the rise in worldly thinking, particularly as seen in the rise of science, technology, and rational thought, and a simultaneous decline in the influence of religion.* While Durkheim was concerned about the fraying of social bonds that he believed would accompany secularization, Marx viewed secularization as a progressive trend, since the social solidarity and harmony promoted by religion were contrary to the interests of the masses and prevented their recognition of their own exploitation.

Weber

Religious Values as Sources of Social Change. Religion was a key subject for sociologist Max Weber, who wanted to explain, in particular, why the culture of modern capitalism had emerged first in England, France, and Germany rather than in India or China—which had once been more advanced than Northern and Western Europe in science, culture, and commerce. Weber concluded that capitalism first appeared where the Protestant Reformation had taken hold and that the driving force behind its development was Protestantism's religious tenets and the economic behaviors they fostered.

Secularization: The rise in worldly thinking, particularly as seen in the rise of science, technology, and rational thought, and a simultaneous decline in the influence of religion.

Weber (1904–1905/2002) found that the beliefs of early Protestantism provided fertile ground for capitalism's development. First was the idea that God places each person on earth to fulfill a particular calling. Whether someone would be saved was predestined by God, but people could find evidence of God's plan in a life dedicated to hard work because economic success was an indicator of salvation. Second, since Protestantism held that consumption-centered lifestyles were sinful, believers were expected to live simple lives, work hard, and save and reinvest their earnings rather than enjoy the immediate gratifications of idleness or acquisition. A hardworking, frugal, sober population reinvesting its earnings in new economic activities was, suggested Weber, a fundamental foundation for economic growth and, significantly, for early capitalism.

Yet Weber also wrote that once capitalism took hold, it became institutionalized and shed the religious ethic that fueled its development. Capitalism, scientific ways of thinking, and bureaucratic forms of organization, he said, would marginalize religion in the drive for productivity and profit. Weber was concerned about the disenchantment he believed would result from secularization and bureaucratization. Modern society, in his well-known metaphor, would become an "iron cage," imprisoning people in rationalized but irrational bureaucratic structures, rote work, and lives bereft of spirituality or creativity.

Synthesizing the Classical Theories. Durkheim's observations that sacred rituals and objects function to strengthen community solidarity and embody the community itself were among his most important contributions to the sociology of religion. However, his perspective seems most applicable to highly homogeneous and cohesive societies such as the small Australian tribes that provided inspiration for his ideas. In modern, complex societies, which are racially, socially, and ethnically diverse, religion no longer serves such a clear purpose. Durkheim recognized a relationship between modernization and secularization and wrote of the potential for alienation in secular societies, but he also saw that religion, perhaps in another form, might foster social solidarity.

Marx's insight that religion may divert people from the immediate problems of daily life is illuminating, particularly where the same elite circles hold both religious and political power. Yet his central idea that religion is purely a mystification enabling the ruling class to deceive the masses is problematic for at least two reasons. First, while religions have supported ruling groups in many historical instances, they have also challenged such groups. Catholicism, along with the labor movement, was a powerful driving force in the social movements that overthrew the Polish communist state through nonviolent mass mobilization, replacing it with a democratic government in 1989.

Private Lives, Public Issues

I PLEDGE ALLEGIANCE . . . OR NOT

©Dennis MacDonald / Alamy Stock Photo

Here are words that nearly all children who have attended school in the U.S. have said: "I pledge allegiance to the flag of the United States of America, and to the Republic for which it stands, one nation, under God, indivisible, with liberty and justice for all." But not all students in the U.S. have chosen to stand and pledge: These individual decisions have been part of a broader examination of the role religion plays in public life.

In 2004, the U.S. Supreme Court reversed an appeals court ruling that requiring students in classrooms to recite the Pledge of Allegiance, with the words "under God," was unconstitutional because it violated the separation of church and state enshrined in the Constitution. The First Amendment to the U.S. Constitution includes what is known as the **Establishment Clause**: *"Congress shall make no law respecting an establishment of religion, or prohibiting the free exercise thereof."* The basis of the Supreme Court's ruling, however, was specifically related to the case at hand: The court argued that the petitioner, a California atheist, did not have standing to sue on behalf of his school-age daughter. The implication was that his daughter could have sued, but he could not sue for her (Pew Forum on Religion and Public Life, 2004).

In 2013, an anonymous family in the state of Massachusetts brought the issue back to the courts, claiming that the phrase "under God" is in violation of that state's equal rights laws. Rather than challenging the constitutionality of the words, the petitioners argued that the phrase discriminates against atheists. Attorney David Niose, representing the plaintiffs, argued in his opening statement that the repeated use of the Pledge of Allegiance in public schools is "indoctrinating and alienating" to atheists (Rosenbaum, 2013). In May of 2014, the court returned the finding in the *Doe v. Acton-Boxborough Regional School District* case that inclusion of "under God" in the pledge is constitutional and, further, that there is no "differing treatment of any class or classes of students based on their sex, race, color, creed, or national origin. All students are treated alike." The court suggested that students may freely participate or abstain; hence, there is no discrimination (Volokh, 2014).

The Pledge of Allegiance has been used in American public life for more than a century, but the phrase "under God" was added by Congress only in 1954, two years after President Harry Truman declared May 7 the National Day of Prayer, a day when presidents proclaim that "the people of the United States may turn to God in prayer and meditation at churches, in groups, and as individuals" (Lipka, 2015a). Both of these decisions were taken, in part, to underscore the contrast between the United States and the atheistic Soviet Union at a time when the rival countries were locked in a tense political relationship. Notably, however, the solicitor general of the United States has argued before the Supreme Court that "under God" is "descriptive" and "ceremonial" rather than a prayer or "religious invocation" (Pew Forum on Religion and Public Life, 2004), suggesting that it embodies a civic rather than an overtly religious value.

Think It Through

- What do you think is the function of the phrase "under God" in the Pledge of Allegiance? Should we interpret it as civic or religious?

Second, for many people, religious beliefs fill a need that has little to do with political or economic power—a function Marx ignored. When communist countries such as Cuba and the former Soviet Union sought to follow Marx's ideas and marginalize religion, they were remarkably unsuccessful. Religious beliefs flourished underground, and in countries such as Poland, Ukraine, and Uzbekistan, they experienced a resurgence after the fall of communism.

Finally, while Weber's idea that a religious ethic of hard work and thrift contributes to economic growth has been

Establishment Clause: The passage in the First Amendment to the U.S. Constitution that states, "Congress shall make no law respecting an establishment of religion, or prohibiting the free exercise thereof."

The Soviet Union was an atheistic communist state in which religious life was discouraged and sometimes actively persecuted. This Soviet poster from the 1920s makes a link between imperialism, capitalism, and the "poison drug of religion."

Protestant theologians rather than on the actual practices of Protestants. During the colonial period he cited as the birthplace of the U.S. capitalist ethic, "Boston's taverns were probably fuller on Saturday night than were its churches on Sunday morning" (Finke & Stark, 1992, p. 23). Second, some scholars argue that capitalism developed among Jews and Catholics—and, for that matter, among Hindus, Muslims, and Confucians—as well as among Protestants (Collins, 1980; Hunter, 1987).

No single theoretical perspective can capture the full sociological picture of religion. Together, however, these perspectives may help us understand why religion exists and persists and how it functions in human societies. Next, we look at contemporary theorizing on religion, which draws from modern perspectives on economic exchange.

The "Religious Economy" Perspective

One recent and influential approach to the sociology of religion is tailored to modern societies, including the United States, which are home to a wide variety of religious faiths. Taking their cue from economic theory, sociologists developed the **religious economy** approach, which *suggests that religions can be fruitfully understood as organizations in competition with one another for followers* (Finke & Stark, 1988, 1992, 2005; Hammond, 1992; Moore, 1994; Stark & Bainbridge, 1987/1996; Warner, 1993). In this view, competition is preferable to monopoly for ensuring religious vitality. Compare this view to that of the classical theorists Durkheim, Marx, and Weber, who assumed religion weakens when challenged by competing religious or secular viewpoints.

The religious economy perspective suggests that competition leads to increased engagement in religious organizations for two reasons. First, competition compels each religious group to exert more effort to win followers, reaching out to the masses in

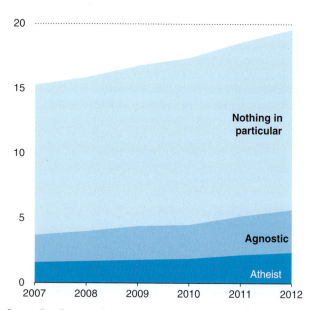

■ **FIGURE 13.1** Growth of the Religiously Unaffiliated

Source: Pew Forum on Religion in Public Life. (2012) 'Nones' on the Rise. http://www.pewforum.org/2012/10/09/nones-on-the-rise/.

used to explain examples of economic success around the world (Berger, 1986; Berger & Hsiao, 1988; Morishima, 1982), it has also been criticized on a number of grounds. First, his conclusions were based on the writings of

Religious economy: An approach to the sociology of religion that suggests that religions can be fruitfully understood as organizations in competition with one another for followers.

a variety of ways in order to capture their attention. Second, the presence of a multitude of religions means there is likely to be something for just about everyone. In a culturally diverse society such as the United States, a single religion will probably appeal to only a limited range of followers, but the presence of Indian gurus, fundamentalist preachers, and mainline churches may encourage broad religious participation.

The religious economy analysis is adapted from the business world, in which competition (in theory) encourages the emergence of specialized products that appeal to specific markets. Sociologists who embrace this perspective even borrow the language of business. According to Finke and Stark (1992), a successful religious group must be well organized for competition, have eloquent preachers who are engaging "sales reps" in spreading the word, offer beliefs and rituals packaged as an appealing product, and develop effective marketing techniques. Religion, in this view, is a business much like any other. Television evangelists, for example, have been effective purveyors of religious "products."

While people's motivations are not easy to pinpoint, a study conducted by the Pew Forum on Religion and Public Life (2010) found that about 28% of U.S. adults change their religious affiliations over the course of their lives. If we count those who change their affiliations *within* religious traditions (for instance, from Baptist to Lutheran, both Protestant religions), the figure rises to 44%. While people's motivations are not easy to pinpoint, a study conducted by the Pew Forum on Religion and Public Life (2015) found that religious switching among U.S. Christians is not uncommon. At the same time, some respondents were leaving the religious group in which they were raised but were not joining a new group. In fact, the proportion of the U.S. population claiming no religious affiliation has risen significantly in recent decades (Figure 13.1). One study found that while in 1991, only 6% of Americans claimed no religious affiliation, by 2012, the figure had reached 20%. In 2016, 25% professed no religious affiliation (Cooper, Cox, Lienesch & Jones, 2016).

The religious economy approach is, of course, subject to critique. It likely overestimates the extent to which people rationally pick and choose among different religions, as if they were shopping for a new car or a pair of shoes. Among deeply committed believers, particularly in societies or communities that lack religious pluralism, it is not obvious that religion is a matter of rational choice. Even when people are allowed to choose among different religions, most are likely to practice their childhood religions without considering alternatives (Roof, 1993). Further, as the most common shift in affiliation is from a religious group to the nonaffiliated group, it is not clear that U.S. believers are trading one set of beliefs for another set that is better marketed or more enticing. They would, in fact, seem to be leaving organized religion behind. Can the religious economy perspective account for this large and growing shift?

Types of Religious Organizations

Sociologist Thomas O'Dea (1966) captures an important distinction when he writes that in traditional societies, "the same social groups provide satisfaction for both expressive and adaptive needs; in modern societies, organizations which meet adaptive needs tend to be separated out from those which provide an outlet for expressive needs" (p. 36). That is, in modern societies, religion may soothe people's fears about death or the future, inject meaning into the routine of daily life, and comfort the sick or grieving, but rarely is it an exclusive channel for education and medical services (though some students may attend religious schools from prekindergarten to college, and many private hospitals are affiliated with religious groups).

In modern societies, religion is typically institutionalized. Max Weber (1921/1963) wrote that after the loss of the charismatic figure from whose life a religion was born, there is a crisis among followers, but there can also be a subsequent "routinization of charisma," which institutionalizes the religion and beliefs into an organizational structure. Early theorists such as Weber, Ernst Troeltsch (1931), and Richard Niebuhr (1929) described religious organizations as falling along a continuum based on the degree to which they are well established and conventional: Churches, for instance, reside at one end (they are conventional and well established), *cults* are at the other (they are neither), and *sects* fall somewhere between. These distinctions were based on the study of European and U.S. religions, and there is some debate over how well they apply to the non-Christian world. Also, because the terms *sect* and *cult* have negative connotations today, sociologists sometimes use the phrase *new religious movements* to characterize novel religious organizations that lack mainstream credibility (Hadden, 1993; Hexham & Poewe, 1997). Next, we look at the different forms religious organizations take.

Church

A **church** is *a well-established religious organization that exists in a fairly harmonious relationship with the larger society* (Finke & Stark, 1992). In everyday terms, churches are respectable, mainstream organizations that reflect their

---

Church: A well-established religious organization that exists in a fairly harmonious relationship with the larger society.

religious communities' prevailing values and beliefs. They are likely to be formally and bureaucratically organized, with fairly conventional practices. In the United States, examples include the Presbyterian, United Methodist, Greek Orthodox, and Roman Catholic churches.

A church can take one of two forms. An **ecclesia** is *a church that is formally allied with the state and is the official religion of the society.* As such, it is likely to enjoy special rights and privileges that other churches lack. In Greece, for instance, while the practice of other religions is not prohibited or punished, the constitution holds that the Greek Orthodox Church is the prevailing religion of the country. A **denomination**, in contrast, is *a church that is not formally allied with the state.* Since there is no established church (or ecclesia) in the United States, all U.S. churches are by definition denominations. The existence of denominations allows for freedom of religious choice, so different denominations may compete with one another for membership, and none enjoys the special favor of the state.

Sect

Unlike a church, which exists in relative harmony with the larger society, a **sect** is *a religious organization that has splintered off from an established church in an effort to restore perceived true beliefs and practices believed to have been lost by the established religious organization.* Protestant fundamentalist and evangelical religious groups are typically sects.

Sects often tend to hold religious beliefs consistent with the dominant ones in society. Yet because they are splinter groups, they also may exist in tension with more established religious organizations. While churches tend to intellectualize religious practice, sects may emotionalize it, emphasizing heightened personal experience and religious conversion (Finke & Stark, 1992; Stark & Bainbridge, 1987/1996). Sects often appeal more to marginalized individuals than to people in the mainstream, drawing followers from among lower-income households, racial and ethnic minorities, and the rural poor.

Yet sects provide new sources of religious ideas and vitality outside mainstream faiths. When they are successful, they may grow in size and evolve into churches, becoming bureaucratized and losing their emotional appeal (Niebuhr, 1929). A new sect may then break off, seeking to return to its religious roots. This occurred within both

U.S. Protestantism and Japanese Buddhism in the late 20th century. Disturbed by the increasingly intellectualized and liberal direction taken by mainstream Protestant churches, numerous sects broke off, seeking to return to what they viewed as the biblical roots of the Protestant faith (Finke & Stark, 1992). Similarly, Buddhist sects in Japan sought a return to original Buddhist beliefs in response to what they regarded as the social isolation and irrelevance of mainstream Buddhist groups (Davis, 1991).

Cult

A **cult** is *a religious organization that is thoroughly unconventional with regard to the larger society* (Finke & Stark, 1992; Richardson, 2009). While sects often originate as offshoots of well-established religious organizations, cults tend to be new, with unique beliefs and practices that typically originate outside the religious mainstream. They may be led by charismatic figures who draw on a wide range of teachings to develop their novel ideas (Stark & Bainbridge, 1987/1996). The presence of a powerful personality can thus define a cult, and the loss of the leader can spell its end.

Cults may have relationships with the larger society that are characterized by strife and distrust. In recent years, "doomsday cults" that prophesy the end of the world have proliferated. The Church Universal and Triumphant (CUT), led by the charismatic leader Elizabeth Clare Prophet, is an example. The CUT's doctrine amalgamated bits of major religions such as Christianity and Buddhism along with mysticism, astrology, Western philosophy (Melton, 1996), and a belief in reincarnation (rebirth). Prophet herself, who led the cult after the death of her husband, Mark Prophet, claimed to have lived past lives as Marie Antoinette, Queen Guinevere of King Arthur's court, and the biblical figure Martha.

In 1990, Prophet predicted that the world would end, and hundreds of her followers fled to bomb shelters near Yellowstone National Park where the CUT had created a self-reliant community. Apparently, the group was also stockpiling weapons in its underground bunkers, and several members were later prosecuted on weapons charges. While the CUT lost members after the failed doomsday prediction, it continued to operate and grew in later years, though Elizabeth Clare Prophet passed away in 2009.

Similar to sects, cults flourish when there is a breakdown in well-established societal belief systems or when segments of the population feel alienated from the mainstream and seek meaning elsewhere. Cults may originate within or outside a society. Interestingly, what is perceived

---

Ecclesia: A church that is formally allied with the state and is the official religion of the society.

Denomination: A church that is not formally allied with the state.

Sect: A religious organization that has splintered off from an established church in an effort to restore perceived true beliefs and practices believed to have been lost by the established religious organization.

Cult: A religious organization that is thoroughly unconventional with regard to the larger society.

as a cult in one country may be accepted as established religious practice in another. Christianity began as an indigenous cult in ancient Jerusalem, and in many Asian countries today, evangelical Protestantism is regarded as a cult imported from the United States.

The youth culture of the 1960s and 1970s was fertile ground for the flowering of religious cults, leading sociologists of religion to adopt a more neutral term to describe them: **new religious movements (NRMs)**, *new spiritual groups or communities that occupy a peripheral place in a country's dominant religious landscape.* Such movements may be small and based on the charisma of a single leader, evolving out of existence with the leader's death or departure. The growth of NRMs presented an ideal situation for sociological research into the development of new religions, helping to shed light on how the world's great religions came into being. There are many NRMs—by one estimate, between 1,500 and 2,000 in North America and perhaps 10,000 in Africa—but few are enduring and most exist outside their countries' religious mainstreams (Hadden, 2006). NRMs may, however, evolve into sustained religious movements.

One such well-known religious movement is Scientology. The Church of Scientology began in the 1950s

New religious movements (NRMs): New spiritual groups or communities that occupy a peripheral place in a country's dominant religious landscape.

largely as a self-help movement. Today, it is a religious movement with members across the globe, and it benefits from the endorsement of a number of Hollywood figures such as Tom Cruise and John Travolta. As it has grown, Scientology has also courted its fair share of controversy. Its founder, L. Ron Hubbard, was a charismatic leader revered by adherents and reviled by detractors. Scientologists believe that Hubbard's ideology provides a path to greater self-awareness and spiritual enlightenment, while critics counter that the secretive religion is a cult that brainwashes its members and convinces them to pay exorbitant sums of money to access the esoteric knowledge central to their faith. While the controversy shows no signs of abating, Scientology's high-profile followers and considerable financial resources make it likely that this religious movement is here to stay (Urban, 2011).

The Great World Religions

From humankind's beginnings, the spiritual search for meaning and the function of religion as an organizing principle in communities have brought us to a point where thousands of different religions are followed across the world (Figure 13.4). However, three—Christianity, Islam, and Hinduism—are practiced by about 70% of the people on earth (Figure 13.2). We look at these below, as well as at Judaism, Buddhism, and Confucianism, all of which have had powerful influence on global religious, political, and social practices.

Christianity

With an estimated 2.2 billion followers—nearly a third of the world's population—Christianity encompasses a broad spectrum of denominations, sects, and even new religious movements (Pew Research Center, 2015). Common to all these is the belief that Jesus of Nazareth was the Messiah or savior foretold in the Hebrew Bible. While doctrinal differences separate the Christian faiths, almost all teach that at the beginning of time, humans fell from God's grace through their sinful acts and that acceptance of Christ and his teachings provides the key to salvation. Most Christians also believe in the New Testament account of the Resurrection, according to which Jesus rose from the dead on the third day after his crucifixion and then ascended to heaven. Christianity is a form of **monotheism**—*belief in a single all-knowing, all-powerful God*—although in most Christian faiths God is also regarded as a trinity made up of a Heavenly Father, His Son the Savior, and His sustaining Holy Spirit.

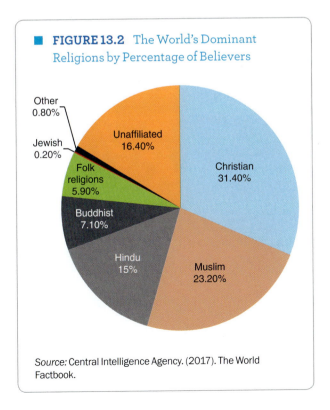

■ **FIGURE 13.2** The World's Dominant Religions by Percentage of Believers

Other 0.80%
Jewish 0.20%
Unaffiliated 16.40%
Folk religions 5.90%
Buddhist 7.10%
Hindu 15%
Muslim 23.20%
Christian 31.40%

Source: Central Intelligence Agency. (2017). The World Factbook.

Monotheism: Belief in a single all-knowing, all-powerful God.

Pope Francis, the head of the Catholic Church, visits Nairobi, Kenya, in November 2015, where nearly a quarter of the population identifies as Catholic.

When Christianity emerged in Palestine some 2,000 years ago, it was a persecuted sect outside the mainstream of Jewish and Roman religious practices. Within four centuries, it had become an ecclesia (official religion) of the Roman Empire. In the 11th century, it divided into the Eastern Orthodox Church (based in Turkey) and the Catholic Church (based in Rome). A second great split occurred within the Catholic branch when the 16th-century Protestant Reformation gave rise to numerous Protestant denominations, sects, and cults. Protestants tend to emphasize a direct relationship between the individual and God. Catholics, by contrast, emphasize the importance of the church hierarchy as intermediary between the individual and God, with the pope in Rome being the final earthly authority.

Christianity continues to gain adherents and grow around the world. Growth is particularly robust in parts of Africa: For instance, the number of Catholic converts is high in the Democratic Republic of Congo, Uganda, Nigeria, and Kenya (Rocca, Hong, & Ulick, n.d.). A recent study estimates that by 2050, there will be about 2.9 billion Christians, though their share of religious adherents will hold steady at about 31% because of the predicted rapid rise of the number of Muslims around the world (Pew Research Center, 2015).

Islam

With 1.6 billion believers, Islam is the second largest and the fastest-growing religion in the world today. By one estimate, the number of Muslims will roughly equal the number of Christians in the world by 2050

■ FIGURE 13.3 Muslims as Percentage of Country Population, 2009

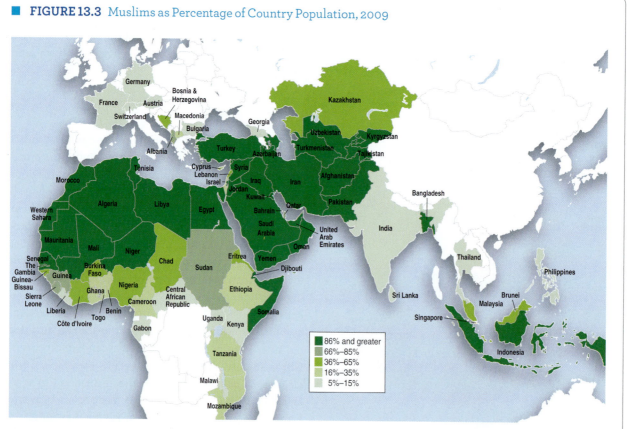

Source: Data from "Mapping the Global Muslim Population," Pew Forum on Religion and Public Life, Washington, DC, October, 2009. (http://www.pewforum.org/2009/10/07/mapping-the-global-muslim-population/)

(Pew Research Center, 2015). *Muslim* is the term for those who practice *al-Islam,* an Arabic word meaning submission without reservation to God's will. About 60% of Muslims live in the Asia Pacific region, and about 20% in the Middle East and North Africa. Sub-Saharan Africa, Europe, and the Americas have growing Muslim populations as well (Figure 13.3; Pew Forum on Religion and Public Life, 2011a).

Although modern Islam dates to the seventh-century Arab prophet Muhammad, Muslims trace their religion to the ancient Hebrew prophet Abraham, also the founder of Judaism. The precepts of Islam as revealed to Muhammad are contained in a sacred book dictated to his followers and called the *Koran* (or *Qur'an*), which means "recitation." Muhammad's ideas were not initially accepted in his birthplace of Mecca, so in the year 622, he and his followers moved to Medina (both cities are in today's Saudi Arabia). This migration, called the *hijra,* marks the beginning of Islam, which later spread across Arabia. Muhammad is not worshipped by Muslims, who believe in positive devotion to Allah (God). Nor is Muhammad a messiah; rather, he is a teacher and prophet, the last in a line that includes Abraham, Noah, Moses, and Jesus.

Islam's sacred *sharia* (or "way") includes prescriptions for worship, daily life, ethics, and even government. Muslim life is governed by the Five Pillars of Islam, which are (1) accepting Allah as God and Muhammad as Allah's messenger; (2) worshipping according to rituals, including facing toward Mecca and bowing in prayer at five set times each day; (3) observing Ramadan, a month of prayer and fasting during the daylight hours; (4) giving *alms* (donations) to those who are poor or in need; and (5) making a holy pilgrimage to Mecca at least once in a lifetime (Weeks, 1988). The Koran also invokes *jihad* as a spiritual, personal struggle

for enlightenment. Terrorist groups, such as the Islamic State (or ISIS), interpret *jihad* as armed struggle against the West and Western values, but this violent, intolerant interpretation is rejected by the vast majority of the Muslim community. Muslims around the world are divided into Sunnis and Shiites. Though they share much in common, there are also tensions between the communities in some countries; Iraq, for instance, is Shiite dominated but has a strong Sunni minority. Globally, there are more Sunnis than Shiites: It is estimated that Sunnis comprise between 85% and 90% of all Muslims (Pew Research Center, 2011b).

Judaism

With about 13 million followers worldwide, Judaism is the *smallest* of the world's major religions. Most Jews live in two countries—Israel (home to about 42% of the global Jewish population) and the United States (39%)—with small populations in many other countries (DellaPergola, 2010). Judaism has exerted a strong influence on the world, first as a key foundation of Islam and Christianity. Second, in European and U.S. culture, Jews have played a role disproportionate to their numbers in such diverse fields as music, literature, science, education, and business. Third, the existence of Israel as a Jewish state since 1948 has given the Jewish people and faith international prominence.

Judaism was one of the first religions to teach monotheism. Similar to many other religions, it teaches that its followers are God's chosen people, but unlike other religions, it does not teach that followers have a duty to convert others to their faith. The primary religious writing for the Jews is the *Torah* (or "law"), a scroll on which are inscribed the first five books of the Bible. Biblical tradition holds that Jewish law was given by God to Moses when he led the Jews out of slavery in Egypt about 3,500 years ago, and since then, it has

In the last month of the Muslim year, thousands of Muslims make an annual pilgrimage (a *hajj*) to a holy shrine called the Kaaba in Mecca. This site is believed to be the original location of a place of worship that God commanded Abraham and Ishmael to build over 4,000 years ago.

The Bar Mitzvah (for boys) and Bat Mitzvah (for girls) rituals are an important rite of passage for Jewish youth.

been elaborated upon by *rabbis*, or teachers. Today, it is codified in books called the *Mishnah* and the *Talmud*.

Three principal divisions in Judaism reflect differing perspectives on the nature of biblical law. Orthodox Judaism believes that the Bible derives from God and that its teachings are absolutely binding, while Reform Judaism views the Bible as a historical document containing important ethical precepts, but it is not literally the word of God. Conservative Judaism occupies a middle ground, maintaining many traditional practices while adapting others to modern society.

Jews have often suffered persecution, and anti-Semitism has a long global history. From the 12th century on, European and Russian Jews were often forced to live in special districts termed *ghettos*, where they lacked full rights as citizens and were sometimes targets of harassment and violence. Partly in reaction to these conditions, and partly because the Torah identifies Jerusalem as the center of the Jewish homeland, some Jews embraced **Zionism**, *a movement calling for the return of Jews to Palestine and the creation of a Jewish state.* (Zion is a biblical name for the ancient city of Jerusalem.)

Zionists established settlements in Palestine early in the 20th century, living for the most part peacefully with their Arab and Palestinian neighbors. Following World War II and the Nazi extermination of 6 million Jews, the state of Israel was created as a homeland for the survivors, an action that both gave refuge to Jews and ignited territorial tensions in the region that continue to this day.

Hinduism

Hinduism, about 2,000 years older than Christianity, is one of the oldest religions in the world and the source of Buddhism and Sikhism. It is not based on the teachings of any single individual, and its followers do not trace their origins to a single deity. It is a broadly defined religion that calls for an ideal way of life. By one estimate, there are just over 1 billion Hindus throughout the world, primarily in India, where they make up the majority of the population. The population of Hindus is expected to rise apace with global population, growing to about 1.4 billion by 2050 (Pew Research Center, 2015).

Indian social structure is characterized by a caste system, officially abolished in 1949 but still powerful, in which people are believed to be born to a certain status that they must occupy for life. This system has its origins in the Hindu belief that one achieves an ideal life in part by performing the duties appropriate to one's caste. Hindus, similar to Buddhists, believe in *samsara*, the reincarnation of the soul according to a person's *karma*, or actions on earth. Whether

someone is reborn into a higher or lower caste depends on the degree to which the person is committed to *dharma*, or the ideal way of life. Although orthodox Hinduism requires observance of caste duties, for the past 500 years, religious societies have organized around gurus who break with caste conventions, emphasizing devotional love as the central spiritual act. This tradition influenced Mahatma Gandhi, the leader of India's independence movement, and others who have viewed Hinduism as a vehicle for social reform (Juergensmeyer, 1995).

Perhaps because Hinduism does not have a central organization or leader, its philosophy and practice are particularly diverse. Religious teachings touch all aspects of life, from the enjoyment of sensual pleasures to stark renunciation of earthly pursuits. Hindus believe in the God-like unity of all things, yet their religion also has aspects of **polytheism**, *the belief that there are different gods representing various categories of natural forces.* For example, Hindus worship different gods representing aspects of the whole, such as the divine dimension of a spiritual teacher (Basham, 1989).

Buddhism

Buddhism was founded in India by Siddhartha Gautama five centuries before Christ. According to legend, the young Siddhartha renounced an upper-caste life of material splendor in search of a more meaningful existence. A lifetime of wandering, occasional poverty, and different spiritual practices eventually taught him the way to achieve enlightenment, and he became the *Buddha*, the awakened or enlightened one. Buddhism is an example of a **nontheistic religion**, in that it involves *belief in the existence of divine spiritual forces rather than a god or gods.* It is more a set of rules for righteous living than a doctrine of belief in a particular god.

Gautama Buddha's philosophy is contained in the Four Noble Truths. First, all beings—gods, humans, and animals—are caught up in an endless round of suffering and rebirth, the result of their karma or actions. Second, suffering results from desire or attachment. To the extent that we depend on wealth or friends or family or even religious beliefs for satisfaction, we are condemned to suffer unending frustration and loss. Third, suffering can be overcome if we break the endless cycle of karma and rebirth and achieve nirvana—a blissful state of emptiness. Fourth, the means of achieving nirvana are contained in the Eightfold Path, which advocates ethical behavior, a simple lifestyle, renunciation of material pleasures, meditation, and (eventually) enlightenment.

Zionism: A movement calling for the return of Jews to Palestine and the creation of a Jewish state.

Polytheism: The belief that there are different gods representing various categories of natural forces.

Nontheistic religion: Belief in the existence of divine spiritual forces rather than a god or gods.

■ FIGURE 13.4 The World's Dominant Religions by Region

Majority of population composed of

- Roman Catholics
- Protestants
- Christians from various churches
- Orthodox Christians
- Churches of Eastern Christianity
- Mormons
- Muslims (Sunnis)
- Muslims (Shiites)
- Jews
- Buddhists
- Japanese Shintoists and Buddhists
- Hindus
- Sikhs
- Indigenous religions
- no dominant religion/nonreligious
- unpopulated

Source: "Faith on the Move - The Religious Affiliation of International Migrants." Pew Research Center. Washington, DC (March, 2012). Retrieved from http://www.pewforum.org/2012/03/08/religious-migration-exec/.

Many people practice certain precepts of Buddhism without calling themselves Buddhists, so it is difficult to estimate accurately the number of Buddhists in the world today. Estimates put the figure at about 490 million, a figure that is, interestingly, not expected to grow considerably in coming decades (Pew Research Center, 2015). Theravada Buddhism, the "Way of the Elders" or the "Lesser Vehicle," predominates in Myanmar, Thailand, Laos, Cambodia, and Sri Lanka. It is strongly identified with local cultures, and traditional rulers in Thailand and Sri Lanka are religious figures as well. Mahayana Buddhism, the "Greater Vehicle," is practiced in China, Korea, and Japan, where it is not the official religion but mixes with other cultural strands. In China, Buddhism is intertwined with Taoist folk religion and Confucian codes of ethical practice. In Japan, Shinto Buddhism combines emperor worship with elements of **animism**, *the belief,* common to many religions, *that naturally occurring phenomena, such as mountains and animals, are possessed of indwelling spirits with supernatural powers.*

Animism: The belief that naturally occurring phenomena, such as mountains and animals, are possessed of indwelling spirits with supernatural powers.

Buddhism's meditative lifestyle may strike some people as incompatible with life in a modern industrial society, which emphasizes work, consumption, achievement, and all forms of karma that Buddhists regard as barriers to enlightenment and happiness. On the other hand, it is primarily Buddhist monks rather than ordinary practicing Buddhists who devote extended periods to meditation. Perhaps because of its emphasis on contemplation and meditation, Buddhism continues to attract followers in Western countries, including celebrities such as actor Orlando Bloom, singer Tina Turner, and the late Steve Jobs of Apple (Lampman, 2006; MacLeod, 2011).

Confucianism

Confucianism, the name of which comes from the English pronunciation of the name of its founder, K'ung-Fu-tzu (551–479 bc), is more of a philosophical system for ethical living on earth than a religion honoring a transcendental god (Fingarette, 1972). K'ung-Fu-tzu never wrote down his teachings, but his followers compiled many in a book called *The Analects* that became the foundation of official ethics and politics for some 2,000 years in China, until Confucianism was banned after the communist revolution in 1949. Though there are only about 6 million practitioners of Confucianism—almost all in Asia—this religion has had enormous influence in China, neighboring countries such as Korea and Vietnam, and Japan (Barrett, 2001).

Confucianism emphasizes harmony in social relations; respect for authority, hierarchy, and tradition; and the honoring of elders. Rulers are expected to be morally virtuous, setting an example for others to imitate. The group is more important than the individual. The key element in Confucian ethics is *jen,* meaning "love" or "goodness" and calling for faithfulness and altruism; we should never do anything to another person we would not want done to ourselves. Contemporary Confucianism, sometimes called "neo-Confucianism," has mystical elements as well as moral ones, including belief in the *Tao* (pronounced *dow*), or "way of being," determined by the natural harmony of the universe.

Confucianism teaches that opposites are not necessarily antagonistic; together, they make up a harmonious whole that is constantly in a creative state of tension or change. The two major principles in the universe, *yin* (the female principle) and *yang* (the male principle), are found in all things, and their dynamic interaction accounts for both harmony and change. The *I Ching* (Book of Changes) contains philosophical teachings based on this view and a technique for determining a wise course of action.

Today, many scholars argue that Confucian values such as respect for authority and a highly disciplined work ethic partly explain the current rapid economic growth in Singapore, Taiwan, China, and other Asian countries (Berger, 1986; Berger & Hsiao, 1988; MacFarquhar, 1980). On one hand, this perspective supports Weber's argument that actions rooted in religious beliefs are linked to economic development. On the other hand, it challenges Weber's exclusive emphasis on Western religion, and Protestantism in particular, as the source of this development.

Women and Religion

Although both men and women embrace the major religions of the world, the principal deities, prophets, and leaders of religions have historically been male. God is depicted as male, beliefs typically emphasize male religious and political superiority, and women are often excluded from positions of theological power. The sociological explanation is straightforward: These religions were initially developed by men within patriarchal societies and therefore reflect patriarchal norms and values. As we noted earlier, sociologists see religions as social creations reflecting the norms, roles, and values embraced by communities and societies.

According to the Jewish and Christian Bible, Eve, the first woman, violated God's command and tempted Adam to eat fruit from the Tree of Knowledge, leading to the pair's loss of innocence and expulsion from the Garden of Eden, or Paradise. Consequently, all human suffering can be traced to Eve's deception (Genesis 3). The book of Proverbs instructs the good wife to oversee the servants, to care for her family, and to be kind, fertile, obedient, and submissive to her husband. Even today, Orthodox Jewish males recite a daily prayer thanking God "that thou hast not created me a Gentile [non-Jew], a Slave, or a Woman." For Christians, Saint Paul's teachings instructed wives

> to submit yourselves to your husbands as to the Lord. For the husband is the head of the wife, even as Christ is the head of the church. . . . So also wives should submit to their husbands in everything. (Ephesians 5:23–24)

Women have long played an important but unheralded role in religion. For example, Ann Lee (1736–1784), the leader of the "Shaking Quakers" in England, led a group to the United States and founded the first Shaker settlement in 1776. Alma White (1862–1946) was not only the first female evangelist ordained a bishop in the United States but also a pioneer in the use of an electronic medium, the radio, to spread beliefs (Stanley, 1993). Aimee Semple McPherson (1890–1944) founded the International Church of the Foursquare Gospel, which today claims some 26,000 churches in 74 countries (Epstein, 1993). Mary Baker Eddy (1821–1910) founded Christian Science, along with the newspaper, *The Christian Science Monitor.* Her influence was felt not only in religion but also in the early women's movement. Eddy was a strong feminist who argued passionately for women's equality:

> In natural law and in religion, the right of women to fill the highest measure of enlightened understanding and the highest places in government is inalienable. . . . This is women's hour, with all its sweet amenities and its moral and religious reforms. (Eddy, 1887/1999, p. 45)

In recent years, there has been an upsurge of feminist spirituality, especially within the United States. Some women have turned to religious traditions that predate Judaism and Christianity, including the celebration of goddess-based religions. The goddess acts not only as a literal divine entity

DISCOVER INTERSECTIONS:

Religion and Gender Norms and Practices

As noted above, the world's major religions are constructed largely around real and mythical figures who are male. Women's roles in the dominant stories and rituals of world religions have been marginal. We learned in the chapter on socialization and social interaction (Chapter 4) that religion is a key agent of socialization. What is the relationship between religious norms and practices and gender roles as they are taught and enacted in the U.S. or in other countries? Do changes in organized religion foster changes in gender socialization or do changes in gender socialization lead to initiatives to change norms and practices in organized religion? What do you think?

but also as a symbol of the historical significance and celebration of the feminine ideal.

Some feminist activists have sought reform within mainstream religions, fighting for the reimagination of God as ungendered, calling for nonsexist language in Scripture and services, and redesigning traditions and rituals along nonsexist lines (Eller, 2000; Wallace, 1992; Weidman, 1984). Almost all Protestant denominations now have female clergy, and even some Catholic churches offer women the opportunity to act as lay clergy, although the mainstream Catholic Church continues to oppose the practice (Wallace, 1992).

Religion in the United States

Compared to citizens of other modern industrial nations, Americans are unusually religious. While secularization has weakened the power of religious institutions, religious adherence and beliefs remain strong in the United States, where most adults profess an affiliation with a religious group: Just under 71% self-identify as Christian, with smaller numbers identifying as Jewish (1.9%), Muslim (0.9%), and Buddhist (0.7%). Americans practice their religions in public forums, including houses of worship and virtually, with about a fifth saying that they regularly share their faith online and half noting that they have seen someone else share their faith online (Pew Forum on Religion and Public Life, 2014). Many also practice it in private: 55% indicate that they pray daily (Lipka, 2015a).

At the same time, about 23% of U.S. adults describe themselves as unaffiliated with a religion, a figure that has continued to grow (Pew Forum on Religion and Public Life, 2015).

Trends in Religious Affiliation

The United States is more religious than other economically developed countries. One reason for the continuing high levels of religious group membership among Americans is that churches, synagogues, and mosques are important sources of social ties and friendship networks, connecting people with others who share the same beliefs and values. Another reason is simply that there is an enormous number of such organizations to belong to—supporting the religious economy perspective we examined earlier. The United States is the most religiously diverse country in the world, with an estimated 1,500 distinct religions (Melton, 1996; T. W. Smith, 2002), though many of those are tiny and most American adherents belong to the world's major religions.

While Americans are more likely to profess affinity to religious faiths and to practice religion at home and in places of worship, it is also the case that religious affiliation has taken a dramatic downward turn in recent decades. The proportion of the U.S. population that describes itself as *unaffiliated* is rising. This change has been driven most fully by younger generations, who are more likely than young adults of earlier generations to indicate no religious affiliation (Figure 13.5; Lipka, 2015b); in studies done in the 1970s and 1980s, about half as many young adults identified themselves as unaffiliated with a religion. The Pew Forum on Religion and Public Life (2010) suggests that this change is "a result, in part, of the decision by many young people to leave the religion of their upbringing without becoming involved with a new faith" (p. 4). Data show that the unaffiliated are more likely than the affiliated to say that religious organizations are overly concerned with money and power, too focused on rules, and too closely involved in politics (Pew Forum on Religion and Public Life, 2012). Robert Wuthnow (2007) has argued that declining affiliation correlates with other demographic changes, including declining rates of marriage and parenthood among young adults. Research also suggests a link between the decline of religious affiliation and the decline of social capital as defined by Robert Putnam (2000), who writes that Americans are increasingly likely to live separate lives and disengage from community activities, a phenomenon he famously termed "bowling alone."

Recall the religious economy perspective discussed earlier. Can it help us understand the growing numbers of

■ **FIGURE 13.5** Changing Religious Affiliations of U.S. Adults by Generation, 2014

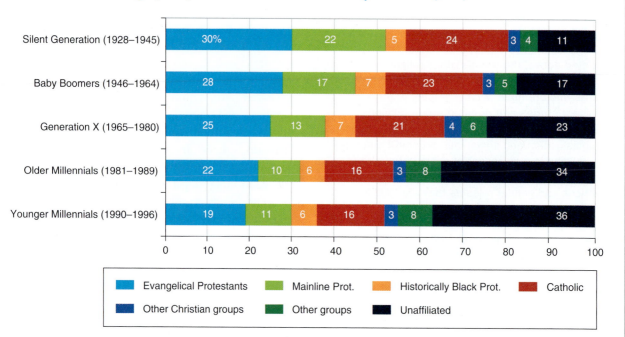

Silent Generation (1928–1945)	30%	22	5	24	3 4	11
Baby Boomers (1946–1964)	28	17	7	23	3 5	17
Generation X (1965–1980)	25	13	7	21	4 6	23
Older Millennials (1981–1989)	22	10	6	16	3 8	34
Younger Millennials (1990–1996)	19	11	6	16	3 8	36

Legend:
- ■ Evangelical Protestants
- ■ Mainline Prot.
- ■ Historically Black Prot.
- ■ Catholic
- ■ Other Christian groups
- ■ Other groups
- ■ Unaffiliated

2014 Religious Landscape Study, conducted June 4–Sept. 30, Figures may not add to 100% because of rounding. Don't know/refused answers not shown. "Other Christian groups" includes Mormons, Orthodox Christians, Jehovah's Witnesses, and a number of smaller Christian groups.

Source: "Millennials increasingly are driving growth of 'nones'" Pew Research Center, Washington, DC (May 2015) http://www.pewresearch.org/fact-tank/2015/05/12/millennials-increasingly-are-driving-growth-of-nones/.

Some evangelical Christian groups have access to extensive resources for recruitment and worship. The facility here used to be home to the Houston Rockets and was converted to an evangelical church that took about $75 million to renovate.

young people who do not affiliate with a religion? Does it suggest that religious organizations are failing to market themselves effectively? Or does it mean that other sources of spiritual or personal fulfillment are available to young adults and act as what Robert Merton called "functional equivalents," fulfilling the functions of religion but assuming a different form?

Religion and Politics

The conservative strand of U.S. Protestantism has been growing in both membership and influence in recent years. Conservative Protestants emphasize a literal interpretation of the Bible, Christian morality in daily life as well as public politics, and conversion of others through evangelizing. Liberal Protestants generally adopt a more flexible, humanistic approach to their religious practices, and moderate Protestants are somewhere in between. While all groups grew from the 1920s through the 1960s, both liberal and moderate churches have since experienced a decline in membership, while the number of conservative Protestants has grown (Pew Forum on Religion and Public Life, 2008).

A key aspect of this growth is the rise of **evangelicalism**, *a belief in spiritual rebirth (conventionally denoted as being "born again")*. This often includes the admission of personal sin and salvation through acceptance of Christ, a literal interpretation of the Bible, an emphasis on highly emotional and personal spiritual piety, and a commitment to spreading "the Word" to others (Balmer, 1989). (The word *evangel* comes from the Greek for "bringing good news.") We can

Evangelicalism: A belief in spiritual rebirth (conventionally denoted as being "born again").

interpret the rise of evangelicalism as a response to growing U.S. secularism, religious diversity, and, in general, the decline of once-core Protestant values in U.S. life (Wuthnow, 1988).

Conservative Protestants have been an active force in U.S. politics, and their growing numbers may be linked to a recent rise in their political influence, particularly within the Republican Party. They have, in fact, become a key constituency for Republicans. Data from the past decade confirm the emergence of a "worship attendance gap" in presidential politics; specifically,

> the more observant members of religious communities tend to vote Republican while their less observant co-religionists tend to vote Democratic. This attendance gap has been largest among the white Christian traditions, but has appeared in a more modest form within nearly all religious affiliations. (Dionne & Green, 2008, p. 5)

Not only are strongly religious voters more likely to vote Republican, but they also seem increasingly more likely to vote at all. That is, they are active in politics to a degree that some other groups are not.

Many U.S. voters' political beliefs and actions are shaped by religious faith. Not surprisingly, then, some voters expect their political leaders to share their faith: A 2016 survey showed that 51% of respondents would be less likely to support a presidential candidate who "does not believe in God." At the same time, some belief systems do not confer an advantage: 42% of respondents indicated they would not vote for a Muslim candidate and 23% would reject a Mormon candidate. The influence of religion on presidential politics may, however, be on the wane: The same study showed that a growing proportion of Americans would not be influenced by a candidate's professed atheism (Figure 13.6; Pew Research Center, 2016b).

Religion and Disestablishment

According to Phillip Hammond (1992), religion in the United States has three times undergone **disestablishment**, *a period during which the political influence of established religions is successfully challenged.* One occurred with the 1791 ratification of the first 10 amendments to the U.S. Constitution (the Bill of Rights), the first of which calls for a firm separation of church and state. Some sociologists see this separation as part of a larger trend in industrial societies, in which different institutions specialize in different

■ **FIGURE 13.6** American Support for an Atheist Presidential Candidate, 2016

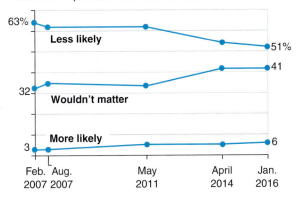

% of U.S. adults who would be more/less likely to support a candidate for president who does not believe in God

Source: "10 facts about atheists" Pew Research Center, Washington, DC (June 2016) http://www.pewresearch.org/fact-tank/2016/06/01/10-facts-about-atheists/.

functions—from economics to medicine, from education to politics. Religion is no exception (Alexander & Thompson, 2008; Chaves, 1993, 1994; Parsons, 1951, 1960, 1966). Recall Thomas O'Dea's (1966) suggestion, noted earlier, that in traditional societies, "the same social groups provide satisfaction for both expressive and adaptive needs," whereas modern societies separate these two functions (p. 36).

The second period of disestablishment occurred between the 1890s and the 1920s, fed by an influx of about 17 million immigrants, mainly European and many Catholic. For the first time, the notion of a predominantly Protestant United States was challenged, and the mainstream Protestant churches never regained their influence in politics or in defining national values. The third period occurred during the 1960s and the 1970s, when core religious beliefs and values were further eroded by the anti–Vietnam War movement, the fight for racial equality, and experimentation with alternative lifestyles. Fundamental challenges came in the form of increased openness about sexuality and lifestyle preferences, the women's movement, and changes in attitudes and laws about birth control (Glock & Bellah, 1976; Hammond, 1992; Roof & McKinney, 1990; Wuthnow, 1976, 1978).

Disestablishment of religion reduces its political influence but does not make it less important to individuals. In fact, if religious groups compete with one another for followers, religious practices are more likely to be tailored to public tastes (Moore, 1994); this result fits the perspective of religious economy that we discussed earlier.

Discover & Debate

PUBLIC FUNDS AND RELIGIOUS SCHOOLS

Motion: Public funds should be available for voucher students seeking to enroll in a religiously affiliated school.

Background: A growing number of U.S. cities are experimenting with the use of vouchers. In the U.S., more than 15 states have adopted voucher programs that use public funds for private school tuition. School vouchers are government-issued certificates that parents can apply toward school tuition. From the policy perspective, school vouchers are intended to expand educational opportunities for students who come from lower socioeconomic backgrounds. However, a debate has arisen about whether or not vouchers, which draw from the same taxpayer-generated funds as public schools, should be usable at religiously affiliated private schools.

Questions for Consideration

- Should the decision to permit or not permit use of vouchers for religiously affiliated schools be determined by the academic success of voucher students in those schools?

- If the government provides a family with a school voucher, and the family chooses a religiously affiliated private school, is it the family or the government that is supporting a religious education?

- Because most parents pay taxes that support education that then pay for school vouchers in their district, should these parents not be allowed to choose where their children attend school?

Debate Tip

- Avoid making hasty generalizations. When drawing a conclusion based on statistics, make sure the sample size is large enough, for example, to justify your conclusion.

AFFIRMATIVE ARGUMENTS	OPPOSITION ARGUMENTS
Inclusion of religiously affiliated schools in the range of options increases educational choices for families with vouchers. Religiously affiliated schools may offer advantages in proximity, safety, teacher experience, and academic opportunities.	The use of public money for education at religiously affiliated schools, which may evangelize to impressionable students, is a violation of the Constitutional separation of church and state. (Note: In 2002, the U.S. Supreme Court ruled that providing school vouchers, which can be used at religious schools, is not a violation of the separation of church and state, leaving the issue to individual states to decide.)
Research has shown that public schools in close proximity to private schools that accept vouchers have improved overall due to the competition brought about by school vouchers.	Public schools are largely compelled to accept all students that seek an education. Private schools, by contrast, may exclude some students on the basis of religion, academic achievement, or disciplinary history. Public money should not be used to support schools that are exclusive rather than inclusive.
School vouchers may foster more racially and economically integrated schools as students from more diverse backgrounds gain access to private education in both secular and religiously affiliated schools.	Research has shown that the use of school vouchers at private schools does not necessarily improve student performance. In some cases, students' academic achievement remains the same and in other cases, students fare worse.

"Civil Religion" in the United States

Some sociologists have argued that the United States has a **civil religion**, *a set of sacred beliefs and practices that become part of how a society sees itself* (Alexander & Thompson, 2008; Bellah, 1968, 1975; Mathisen, 1989). Civil religion usually involves the use of "god language" in reference to the

Civil religion: A set of sacred beliefs and practices that become part of how a society sees itself.

Behind the Numbers

RELIGIOSITY AND EDUCATION IN THE U.S.: WHAT IS THE RELATIONSHIP?

■ **FIGURE 13.7** Education and Religiosity in the United States

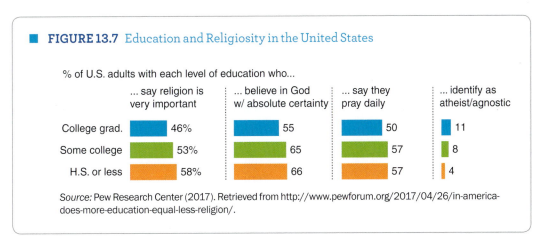

% of U.S. adults with each level of education who...

	... say religion is very important	... believe in God w/ absolute certainty	... say they pray daily	... identify as atheist/agnostic
College grad.	46%	55	50	11
Some college	53%	65	57	8
H.S. or less	58%	66	57	4

Source: Pew Research Center (2017). Retrieved from http://www.pewforum.org/2017/04/26/in-america-does-more-education-equal-less-religion/.

Secularization theory posits that religiosity declines as societies modernize (Berger, 1967; Weber, 1963). Religiosity, by extension, is also widely held to correlate negatively with educational attainment. That is, that more highly educated people are less likely to profess or practice a commitment to organized religion. Data, including a recent Pew Research Center study (2017), also seem to point to that conclusion: Among those with a high school education or less, fully 58% indicate that religion is "very important" to them, whereas about 46% of college graduates say the same. An "absolute certainty" about the existence of God is also more widely shared among those with some college or a high school education or less than among those with a college degree, and the more highly educated are far more likely to profess no religion (Figure 13.7).

At the same time, data also show considerable variation in this relationship based on membership in particular religions and generations. Consider the following: Among those who identify with the Christian religion, the college-educated are as likely or even more likely to indicate that they are religiously observant as are less-educated members of their religion. For instance, about 52% of college-educated Christians indicated that they attend church services weekly compared to 45% of those with some college education and 46% of those with a high school degree or less. On the broader index of "religious commitment," which encompasses attendance at religious services, frequency of prayer, belief in God, and the self-reported importance of religion in one's life, the difference

between those with a completed college education (70%), some college (73%), and no college (71%) was small. By contrast, among Jews, there is considerably more variation, with just over half of Jews with some or no college saying that they believe in God with "absolute certainty" (54%), while only about 28% of college graduates saying the same (Pew Research Center: Religion & Public Life, 2013, 2017).

Another recent study points to changes in the relationship between education and religiosity that have occurred across generations. Sociologist Philip Schwadel (2014) argues that "increases in higher education have led to a decline in the individual-level effect of college education on religious non-affiliation." That is, as a greater proportion of each generation has gained access to higher education, the effect has dissipated. For instance, people born in the late 1920s and 1930s who graduated from college were two times as likely to drop out of religion than noncollege graduates. For those born in the 1960s, however, there was no appreciable difference in dropping out of religion. Notably as well, for those born in the 1970s, those without a college education are more likely to leave religion.

Think It Through

- Secularization has long been understood as a phenomenon that more fully affects the highly educated. Does this appear to be changing? What factors may be driving greater religiosity among the college-educated and declining religiosity among the less-educated?

nation, including historical myths about the society's divine origins, beliefs about its sacred historical purpose, and, occasionally, religious restrictions on societal membership (Wuthnow, 1988).

The infusion of divine meaning into historical events is visible in President Abraham Lincoln's (1809–1865) oratory on the Civil War. In the Gettysburg Address, Lincoln, who was not highly religious himself, drew on religious imagery to attach meaning to the brutal destruction and enormous human cost of the war. He labeled his fellow citizens the "almost chosen people" and called the United States "the last, best hope on earth." You might have noticed that even today, the president and other politicians often end their speeches with the words "God bless America." It is not only political events, however, that are carriers of civil religion. In the United States, there is widespread societal veneration of sports and winning athletes. Popular sporting events such as the Olympic Games, the Super Bowl, and the World Series are also infused with patriotic rituals that reinforce national pride and emphasize a sense of American exceptionalism.

The phrase "under God" was added to the Pledge of Allegiance by Congress in 1954, amid fears of the Cold War and "godless communism." The words are consistent with the construction of a civil religion and a nation worshipping itself and envisioning itself as fulfilling a divine destiny. Even though the First Amendment to the U.S. Constitution clearly calls for a separation of church and state, this profession of allegiance to "one nation, under God" came to be seen as central to U.S. citizenship. What do you think about the content of the Pledge of Allegiance? Does it endorse religion, or is it a civil rather than a religious declaration?

Why do you think different people read this legal question differently?

Religion and Global Societies

Thanks in part to the Internet, globalization has transformed religion into a more fluid form that easily crosses boundaries and mixes traditions from different areas. While religions have always evolved, today's sustained and regular contact among people of varying religious traditions is unprecedented. The exchange of new ideas may create understanding, or it may create tension and even violence.

The global emergence of a scientific/technological culture that colors people's views and behaviors presents a powerful challenge to the world's traditional religions. It means that fewer people employ religious explanations for natural or social phenomena, as increasing numbers probe beyond explanations that refer to a divine plan. Religion may still enrich personal lives, but its role in public life—at least in the most economically advanced countries—has declined.

A second challenge of globalization is the growing contact between large religions with mass followings that claim to possess exclusive accounts of history and the nature of reality. This contact is both a potential and an actual source of conflict, which can fuel "culture wars" as well as real wars that leaders cast as battles between religions and values or even between good and evil. In fact, rather than leading to a merging of religions (in the manner of a global culture of consumption or popular music), globalization may be fostering a backlash against blending that reveals itself as fundamentalism. Fundamentalism is also associated with the rise of religious nationalism.

Religious nationalism is *the linkage of religious convictions with beliefs about a nation's or ethnic group's social and political destiny*. It is on the rise in countries around the world where religious nationalist movements have revived traditional religious beliefs and rejected the separation of religion and the state (Beyer, 1994; Kinnvall, 2004). While the trend is most pronounced among Islamic fundamentalists in some Middle Eastern and North African countries, the United States has

The Olympic Games might be considered a component of civil religion. The games, as well as ads that are shown during the Olympics, are suffused with patriotic content, and winning may reinforce a widespread sense of national pride.

©XIN LI/Getty Images Sport/Getty Images

Religious nationalism: The linkage of religious convictions with beliefs about a nation's or ethnic group's social and political destiny.

Global Issues

RELIGION AND THE ENVIRONMENT

©Dinodia Photos/Alamy Stock Photo

Journalist Cameron Conaway (2015a), who has documented the beauty and distress of India's massive Ganges River, writes

> It's a few hours before sunrise and already the banks of the Ganges river in Varanasi are lined with meditators, yogis and people offering prayers. For many, this opportunity to pay respect to the Ganges—Ganga in Hindi—is a morning ritual. For others, this is the end of a long pilgrimage, a cherished time to be with the holy waters. Others are here because a loved one's corpse will soon be burned at nearby Manikarnika Ghat; they are asking the Ganga to wash away sins and take care of the deceased. (para. 1)

The Ganges River is a massive waterway situated in the Indian State of Uttar Pradesh. In the Hindu

vtradition, the Ganges—also referred to as *Ma Ganga (Mother Ganga)*—is more than a river. The Ganges is believed to have sacred powers: Specifically, Hindus believe that if their ashes are spread on the river or their bodies washed down the river after death, they can break the cycle of birth and rebirth (*samsara*) and achieve eternal liberation (*moksha*). In Varanasi, on the banks of the Ganges, bodies burn 24 hours a day: According to a worker at a cremation site, "The same fire has been going for 3,000 years.... We average anywhere from 30 to 100 bodies per day" (quoted in Conaway, 2015b, para. 3).

In a country of over a billion people, many of them Hindu, the Ganges is a uniting force, a widely shared symbol of culture and country, as well as a centerpiece of a religious belief system. It is a lifeline: By one estimate, the Ganges supports about 10% of the world's population. Its waters are used for drinking, fishing, crops, and bathing (Conaway, 2015b). Cities around pilgrimage sites such as the Ganges also expand economically to cater to tourism, which has grown with the expansion of modern transportation (Shinde, 2007): The city of Varanasi is host to hotels that serve tourists as well as those who come to the banks of the river to await death (Conaway, 2015b).

The Ganges is the final resting place of bodies and cremated remains. It is also a destination of millions of Hindu pilgrims who come to the river to pray and to bathe themselves. In West Bengal,

---

■ FIGURE 13.8 Percentage of Countries with Restrictions on Religion and Religious Hostilities, 2015

% of **198 countries** with high or very high levels of . . .

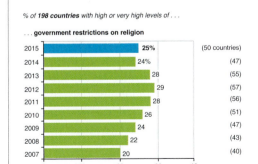

. . . **government restrictions on religion**

Year	%	(countries)
2015	25%	(50 countries)
2014	24%	(47)
2013	28	(55)
2012	29	(57)
2011	28	(56)
2010	26	(51)
2009	24	(47)
2008	22	(43)
2007	20	(40)

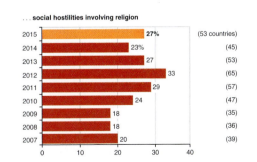

. . . **social hostilities involving religion**

Year	%	(countries)
2015	27%	(53 countries)
2014	23%	(45)
2013	27	(53)
2012	33	(65)
2011	29	(57)
2010	24	(47)
2009	18	(35)
2008	18	(36)
2007	20	(39)

Source: "Global Restrictions on Religion Rise Modestly in 2015, Reversing Downward Trend" Pew Research Center, Washington, DC (April 2017) http://www.pewforum.org/2017/04/11/=global-restrictions-on-religion-rise-modestly-in-2015-reversing-downward-trend/.

(Continued)

(Continued)

near the point where the Ganges drains into the Bay of Bengal, Hindus celebrate Ganga's mythical descent from heaven at the Gangasagar Mela, an annual gathering at which an estimated half-million believers dip into the water to purify their souls. The mass utilization of the river, however, brings with it serious pollution (Conaway, 2015b). In a country with a growing population, the river that is the object of worship and life can also be a source of distress and disease.

Religious pilgrimages are a fundamental part of the community experience for many Indians. Shinde (2007) writes that "a majority of pilgrim centres in India are closely associated with nature" (p. 235) and are often close to riverbanks

or high mountains. The devotional functions fulfilled by pilgrimage sites such as the Ganges, however, are also contributing to dramatic environmental degradation. How can traditional religious rituals and environmentally fragile sites successfully coexist? How can the spiritual needs of communities and the practical needs of the natural world be reconciled?

Think It Over

- Who should be responsible for addressing the problem of pollution at pilgrimage sites such as the Ganges River? Is the religious community responsible? Is the state responsible? What about local communities?

---

experienced the rising political influence of evangelical Protestantism.

The conservative Christian lobby in the United States has been particularly vocal—and often influential—on domestic issues such as abortion and gay marriage, both of which it opposes. It has also had some impact on global policy making. For example, Christian evangelicals have lobbied for U.S. recognition of violence against Christians in Iraq and Syria by the Islamic State group as genocide. In March of 2016, the U.S. House of Representatives unanimously passed a resolution categorizing the actions of the Islamic State as *genocide*, a term that the United States has been hesitant to use in global conflicts, lest it create the perception of an obligation to intervene.

Christian and Islamic religious nationalist movements accept modern technology, politics, and economics; many use the Internet and social media to disseminate information and ideas. At the same time, they interpret religious values strictly and reject secularization, drawing selectively on traditions and past events that serve their current beliefs and interests. Benedict Anderson (1991) writes about "imagined communities," suggesting that nations are real but not natural—that is, they are unified by both real and invented traditions and heroes that legitimate their claims about territories, the past, and the present. Part of the Israeli and Palestinian conflict over land, for instance, is rooted in different narratives of history that tell diverging stories about who has true dominion over the territory.

Religious affiliations can bring communities together or tear them apart. India is the world's largest democracy, one

of the world's largest countries in terms of population (more than 1 billion), and home to Hindus, Muslims, Christians, and believers in dozens of other religions. Diversity and democracy sometimes appear to be on shaky ground there, however, particularly when the extreme nationalist ideology of *Hindutva* (or "Hinduness") comes into contact with Muslim extremism. In the northern Indian town of Ayodhya, a mosque was built in the early 16th century on the site where Hindus believe Lord Ram, a sacred deity in Hinduism, was born. Since the 19th century, clashes between Hindus and Muslims have taken place on the site. In 1992, Hindu nationalists attacked the mosque, sparking riots across the country that killed more than 2,000 people. The site continues to be the object of contention, though the conflict appears to have shifted to the Indian courts: In 2010, a high court ruled that the site should be split among Muslims, Hindus, and a local sect (BBC, 2012).

Millions around the world are subject to state restrictions and social hostilities based on religion. The Pew Forum on Religion and Public Life (2015) found that in 2013, over a quarter of countries had government restrictions on religious practices that ranged from discriminatory policies and practices to outright religious bans. Three quarters of the world's population lived in countries with high or very high levels of social hostilities involving religion, which "run the gamut from vandalism of religious property and desecration of sacred texts to violent assaults resulting in deaths and injuries" (Figure 13.8).

Most of the world's religions actively embrace the values of peace, humanity, and charity. Many believe religion is the basis of morality. On the other hand, religion in various forms, including religious nationalism, has been associated with intolerance, discrimination, and violence. How are we to reconcile these two sides of religion as a local, national, and global institution? Is religion as an institution a force for positive change or a rationale for conflict? Might it be both? What do you think?

Why Study the Sociology of Religion?

Studying religion from a sociological perspective does not mean embracing or rejecting religious values; it means examining and analyzing an institution that is central to humans on an individual, societal, and global level. In the United States today, the sociology of religion may be

---

 ## What Can I Do with a Sociology Degree?
COMMUNITY RESOURCE AND SERVICE SKILLS

Community resource competencies link knowledge of nonprofit, government, and private community resources with the skills to access appropriate services and funding to best serve clients, organizations, and communities. Resources in communities take multiple forms, including individual donors, volunteers, politicians, business owners, religious leaders, schools, libraries and community centers, and public and private service agencies. Service skills may be developed through the study of and active participation in community organizations that engage with local populations and issues.

As a sociology major, you will develop important intercultural competencies and understandings of diversity. You will also learn important occupational professional skills, such as the ability to gather and summarize data in order to characterize community needs effectively, and develop the habits of mind to be resourceful in addressing problems in ways that take different perspectives into account. Many educational institutions offer opportunities for service learning or volunteering that enable students to become familiar with the particular needs and resources of their own communities and to gain experience listening to and learning from both service providers and the people they serve.

Hunter Scott, Senior Outreach Specialist with Pathways to Housing DC

The George Washington University, BA in Sociology

As part of my senior thesis for my sociology degree, I used participant observation techniques among those

experiencing homelessness in Washington, DC. In my conversations with those individuals, they often mentioned how they worked with the Pathways to Housing DC street outreach team to succeed in their goals. That snowballed to an interview with the director of the team, which eventually led to a job in which I now work with many of the same individuals. My role is to develop relationships with people living on the street with the goal of connecting them to services like mental and physical health care, Social Security income, and eventually, housing. I describe myself to my clients as "human red-tape scissors" for people that have consistently fallen through the cracks of the social services system and now live out of sight right in front of the White House.

In my work, I have found that I take advantage of all the same skills that I did in my sociological research. In order to build relationships with my clients, many of whom have paranoid schizophrenia, I have to utilize participant observation techniques: essentially "hanging out" until they trust me to start working toward better health care with them. I have had to develop an expertise in the many parts of the social service system as a whole in order to connect my different clients (who all have very different obstacles and needs) to the appropriate resources. This ability to understand the system as a whole and make strategic connections between points in the system came from my training in sociology.

I also often write summaries of a client's history and current functioning from records I have collected, arguing why he or she needs a certain type of service. This is just another form of a research paper. Finally, our team logs notes on every engagement with clients and service we provide, which we compile into broader statistics to track our progress.

Because of my statistical training and sociological imagination, I am able to help my team use this data to increase our effectiveness and find larger

(Continued)

(Continued)

trends in the population we serve, such as increased housing placements or decreased psychiatric responses.

Career Data: Social and Community Service Managers

- 2017 Median Pay: $64,100 per year

- $30.82 per hour

Source: Bureau of Labor Statistics, *Occupational Outlook Handbook,* 2017.

- Typical Entry-Level Education: Bachelor's degree

- Job Growth, 2016–2026: 18% (Much faster than average)

especially relevant. First, the question of whether disestablishment is proceeding or receding is an important one. Though the country's political foundations call for the separation of church and state, religious organizations seek to influence politics and public policy. Can religious devotion mix comfortably with domestic and foreign policy, or are the two a volatile brew to be avoided? These are questions of both intellectual and political significance.

Second, on a global level, the "war on terror" initiated by President George W. Bush in 2001 in the wake of the terrorist attacks of 9/11 brought questions about religion and politics to the forefront across the globe. For instance, the United States was faulted for failing to recognize why calling the "war on terror" a *crusade* would offend Muslim sensibilities. Tensions between the West and the Muslim world provoked questions about whether there is a "clash of civilizations" that makes conflict difficult to avoid. Some in the United States worry about the "Islamization" of the Middle East and other regions, while others question the power and political influence of religion in their own U.S. government. Debates about religion and its place in communities, societies, and the world will continue to challenge sociologists in the decades to come.

SUMMARY

- **Religion** is a system of common beliefs and rituals centered on sacred things that unites believers and provides a sense of meaning and purpose. Religion may serve many functions in society, lending groups a common worldview, helping to ritualize or routinize behaviors or beliefs, and providing people with a sense of purpose.

- Sociologists who study religion are interested in how religion helps to organize and structure societies and group behavior, along with the functions religion serves for producing and maintaining group solidarity (or, conversely, creating instability in certain circumstances), and how religion becomes a force in society and within the lives of individuals.

- Classical theorists have differing interpretations of religion's sociological function. Marx emphasized the role of religion in pacifying the oppressed masses; Weber highlighted the role of Protestantism in the development of capitalism; Durkheim looked at the role of religion in reinforcing social solidarity.

- The modern **religious economy** perspective emphasizes the role of competition between groups as religions seek followers and potential adherents seek affiliations.

- Religions manifest themselves in more than shared beliefs. They take the form of institutions. Types of religious organizations can be conceptually placed on a spectrum of conventionality in larger society. A **church** would be on the far end of conventionality, and a **cult** would fit on the opposite end of the spectrum. A **sect** would be somewhere between the two.

- **New religious movements (NRMs)** represent a break from existing religious organizations and a push toward new religious practices.

- Christianity, Islam, and Hinduism are the three largest and most practiced religions on earth, but Judaism, Buddhism, and Confucianism are also influential.

- Women have been historically marginalized in major world religions. Today, some activists seek to introduce nonsexist language into Scripture and services and to expand women's roles and representation in religious beliefs and practices.

- Youth and young adults in the United States today are less likely than older adults to claim a religious affiliation. At the same time, religious faith continues to exercise influence in U.S. life, including in politics.

- **Disestablishment** refers to periods in which the political influence of religion is significantly challenged.

- **Civil religion** involves the elevation of a nation as an object of worship; it involves a set of sacred beliefs and practices that become part of how a society sees itself.

- Globalization has provided both challenges and opportunities to religions of the world. Religions may function to bring both peace and conflict at the global level.

KEY TERMS

religion, 355
theism, 355
anthropology, 356
profane, 357
sacred, 357
totems, 357
secularization, 358
Establishment Clause, 359
religious economy, 360

church, 361
ecclesia, 362
denomination, 362
sect, 362
cult, 362
new religious movements
   (NRMs), 363
monotheism, 363
Zionism, 366

polytheism, 366
nontheistic religion, 366
animism, 367
evangelicalism, 370
disestablishment, 371
civil religion, 372
religious nationalism, 374

DISCUSSION QUESTIONS

1. How do classical sociologists theorize the role of religion in society? Compare and contrast the views of Durkheim and Marx.

2. If religion serves as a source of stability, as functionalists claim, does that mean that a nation of atheists would be less stable than a nation of religious believers? Make a sociological case to support your position.

3. Consider the opening story on Jediism. Would you agree or disagree with the proposition that Jediism is a real religion? Use information from the chapter to support your position.

4. What are the key characteristics of the current generational shift in religious affiliation in the United States? How might sociologists explain this shift? Do you believe it will continue? Explain your reasoning.

5. Describe the role of religion in U.S. politics today. Has the role of religion in politics changed in recent years or decades? Considering trends in religious affiliation, might we expect it to change in the near future?

Want a better grade?

Get the tools you need to sharpen your study skills. Access practice quizzes, eFlashcards, video, and multimedia at **https://edge.sagepub.com/chambliss4e**.

The State, War, and Terror

14

WHAT DO YOU THINK?

1. What means do states have to exercise control over their populations? What means do citizens have to exercise control over their own governance?

2. Why do states go to war? What are the functions and dysfunctions of war? Is war inevitable?

3. It is sometimes said that "one person's terrorist is another person's freedom fighter." What does this statement mean? Do you agree with this statement?

LEARNING OBJECTIVES

14.1 Describe the ideal-typical characteristics of the modern state.

14.2 Explain theories of state power.

14.3 Identify forms of authority and how they function.

14.4 Describe the major forms of state governance in the modern world.

14.5 Describe key characteristics of the U.S. political system.

14.6 Apply sociological perspectives to understand war and its historical and contemporary functions.

14.7 Take a sociological perspective on terrorists and terrorism in the modern world.

THE BIRTH AND DEATH OF COUNTRIES

How is a country born? Countries come into being in a variety of ways. They may be established through armed conflict, diplomatic negotiation, or public referendums. They may be the products of indigenous ethnic groups striving for their own states or the results of colonial powers drawing borders that suit their political and economic interests. The 195 recognized countries in the world today are the products of a spectrum of historical times and events.

The world's newest recognized country is South Sudan, which came into being less than a decade ago. In 2011, after a decades-long civil war with the state from which it separated (Sudan), South Sudan declared its independence and was recognized by the global community as a sovereign state. In 2008, only a few years earlier, another new country was born

©ALBERT GONZALEZ FARRAN/AFP/Getty Images

out of brutal civil conflict, as Kosovo declared its independence from the Southern European country of Serbia. In 2003, Eritrea came into being after fighting for three decades for independence from the Eastern African country of Ethiopia. Other states around the world have much longer histories: Both Japan and China claim origins that date back more than 2,000 years. China marks 221 BC as its founding year. European states such as France, Austria, Denmark, and Hungary are more than five centuries old. The United States is, by comparison, a fairly young state. The United States as a political entity came into being only in the 18th century after separating from its colonial parent, Great Britain. It, too, has experienced tribulations: During the civil war in the 1860s, it nearly broke into two separate entities, as the Southern states sought to seceded in order to preserve slavery as a legal practice.

Just as countries are born out of the circumstances and interests of their times, they may also die, torn apart by political turmoil, economic collapse, or armed conflict. In 1991, the Soviet Union, a country that officially came into being in 1922 as the successor state to a fallen Russian Empire, split into 15 different countries. While there was some violence in the last months of the Soviet Union's existence as those with a stake in its future fought for the continuation of the communist state, the split was largely peaceful, and the enormous country (it covered 11 time zones) was dissolved with signatures on paper rather than lethal weapons.

In 2018, several states around the globe were embroiled in brutal and destabilizing civil conflicts that threatened to tear their states apart. Among them are the world's newest state, South Sudan, where over 50,000 civilians have been killed and over 1.3 million displaced since the start of the conflict in 2013, which has broken largely along ethnic lines, with ethnic Dinka pitted against the Nuer community. The country of Libya is also in a state of chaos: After the country's authoritarian leader Colonel Muammar al-Qaddafi was deposed in October 2011, various factions sought to establish power, but the country has no central government recognized as legitimate by the country's various ethnic and political groups. Crime, including large-scale smuggling of African and Middle Eastern refugees to Europe, is endemic in many parts of the country and services for the population, including health care and education, are scarce.

Iraq, a country in which the United States has had a presence since President George W. Bush dispatched troops there in 2003 to overthrow the dictatorial regime of Saddam Hussein, has also become destabilized by over a decade of war, sectarian conflict between the Shiite and Sunni Muslim communities, and attacks by terrorist groups such as the Islamic State (ISIS). Iraq as a recognized state came into existence in 1920, after the collapse of the Ottoman Empire. It was, similar to many states of its time, created by a colonial power (Britain), which drew Iraq's boundaries based on political expediency rather than along ethnic, religious, or tribal community lines. Britain continued to administer the country until it gained independence in 1932.

From 1979, Iraq was ruled by Saddam Hussein, a brutal dictatorial leader whose Baath Party favored the interests of Sunni Muslims over the more numerous Shiite Muslims and minority Kurds. In 1990, Saddam's Iraqi forces invaded the neighboring country of Kuwait, a U.S. ally. A large-scale U.S.–led effort, now known as the First Gulf War, commenced to liberate Kuwait, and Iraqi forces were compelled to withdraw in February 1991. Relations between the United States and Iraq continued to be tense, and U.S. forces invaded Iraq in 2003 after President George W. Bush accused the country of possessing weapons of mass destruction (which were not subsequently found and the existence of which has not been definitively shown). The U.S. occupation of Iraq followed shortly after U.S. forces invaded Afghanistan and deposed the Taliban rulers who were believed to harbor terrorist Osama bin Laden. The military action against Iraq was commonly understood to be part of the "global war on terror" that the United

States began after the terrorist attacks of September 11, 2001, on the World Trade Center and the Pentagon. The large-scale U.S. military presence in Iraq ended in 2011. Iraq remains politically unstable and is currently ranked 11th out of 178 countries in the Fragile States Index (Fund for Peace, 2018). Whether it will survive the tribulations of continued sectarian violence, terrorism, and poverty and in what form it will survive remains to be seen.

The world has seen the births and deaths of hundreds of states. Some have endured for centuries or even millennia—others have lasted only a few decades. Countries are core parts of the modern world, and they represent key vehicles for the exercise of power domestically and globally. They are also human-created entities and are subject to dramatic and dynamic change, which makes them a topic of interest to sociologists.

We begin this chapter with a discussion of power and the modern nation-state and an examination of citizenship rights and their provision. We then look at theoretical perspectives on state power, its exercise, and its beneficiaries. A consideration of the types of authority and forms of governance in the modern world provides the background for an examination of the U.S. political system. We then turn to a discussion of war and society and an analysis of war from the functionalist and conflict perspectives. This is followed by a critical look at the issue of terrorism as well as the question of defining who is a terrorist. We conclude with a consideration of the question of why we study state power and its manifestations in phenomena that range from elections to making war.

The Modern State

For most of human history, people lived in small and homogeneous communities within which they shared languages, cultures, and customs. Today, however, the world's more than 7 billion people are distributed across 195 countries (the number of countries recognized by the United States, though other entities exist that claim statehood, including Palestine and Kurdistan). On the world stage, countries are key actors: They are responsible for war and peace, the economic and social welfare of their citizens, and the quality of our shared global environment and security.

Social scientists commonly characterize the modern country as a **nation-state**—that is, *a single people (a* nation*) governed by a political authority (a* state*)* (Gellner, 1983). Very few countries neatly fit this model, however. Most are made up of many different peoples brought together through warfare, conquest, immigration, or boundaries drawn by colonial authorities without respect to ethnic or religious differences of the time. For instance, many Native Americans think of themselves as belonging to the Navajo, Lakota, Pawnee, or Iroquois nation rather than only to the United States. In Nigeria, most people identify primarily with others who are Yoruba, Ibo, or Hausa rather than with a country called Nigeria. In Iraq, a shared Iraqi identity is less common than allegiance to the Sunni or Shiite Muslim or the Kurdish community. Because most political entities are not characterized by the homogeneity implied by the definition of nation-state, we will use the more familiar terms *country* and *state* rather than *nation-state*.

While not all countries possess them in equal measure, the characteristics we list below represent what Max Weber would term an *ideal-typical model*, a picture that

©REUTERS/David Ryder

Obtaining citizenship is a dream for many immigrants to the U.S. Every year, thousands take the Naturalization Oath of Allegiance. Immigration has been a key building block of U.S. society and its cultural, economic, and political life.

Nation-state: A single people (a *nation*) governed by a political authority (a *state*); similar to the modern notion of *country*.

approximates but does not perfectly represent reality. Modern countries emerged along with contemporary capitalism, which benefited from strong central governments and legal systems that regulated commerce and trade both within and across borders (Mann, 1986; Wallerstein, 1974; Weber, 1921/1979). This history accounts for several unique features of modern countries that distinguish them from earlier forms of political organization:

- Underlying the social organization of the modern country is a system of **law**, the *codified rules of behavior that regulate the actions of people pertaining to a given jurisdiction* (Chambliss & Seidman, 1982). The rule of law is a critical aspect of democratic governance.

- The governments of modern countries claim complete and final authority over the people who reside within the countries' borders (Hinsley, 1986).

- People living within a country's borders are divided between **citizens**, *legally recognized individuals who are part of a political community in which they are granted certain rights and privileges and, at the same time, have specified responsibilities*, and **noncitizens**, *individuals who reside in a given jurisdiction but do not possess the same rights and privileges as citizens* (Held, 1989). (Noncitizens are *sometimes referred to as residents, temporary workers, or aliens*.)

Citizenship rights may take several forms. *Civil rights,* which protect citizens from injury by individuals and institutions, include the right to equal treatment in places such as the school or workplace regardless of race, gender, sexual orientation, or disabilities. *Political rights* ensure that citizens can participate in governance, whether by voting, running for office, or openly expressing political opinions. *Social rights,* which call for the governmental provision of various forms of economic and social security, include such things as retirement pensions and guaranteed income after losing a job or becoming disabled. Citizens are afforded legal protections from arbitrary rule and in turn are expected to pay taxes, to engage in their own governance through voting or other activities, and to perform military service (with specific expectations of such service varying by country). In reality, the extent to which all people enjoy the full rights of citizenship in any given country varies. Below, we discuss two specific aspects of citizenship rights—the first relates to the evolution of state provisions for ensuring social rights, the second to the degree to which citizens enjoy freedom in the form of political rights and civil liberties.

The Welfare State

In most modern countries, political and civil rights evolved and were institutionalized before social rights were realized. The category of *social rights* is broad and encompasses entitlements that include health care insurance, old-age pensions, unemployment benefits, a minimum wage floor for workers, and a spectrum of other benefits intended to ensure social and economic security for the citizenry. Social rights have largely been won by groups of citizens mobilizing (on the basis of the civil and political rights they enjoy) to realize their interests.

Social rights are often embodied in what is termed the **welfare state**, *a government or country's system of providing for the financial and social well-being of its citizens, typically through government programs that provide funding or other resources to individuals who meet certain criteria.* The welfare state has been a part of Western systems of governance in the post–World War II period. Social Security, a social welfare program that ensures a stable income for retired workers, and Medicare, which provides for at least basic health care for the elderly, are examples of the U.S. welfare state. Social Security was created through the Social Security Act of 1935, signed by President Franklin D. Roosevelt, which established a social insurance program to provide continuing income for retired workers at age 65 or older (Social Security Administration, 2013). Although the provision of basic health care coverage was the vision of President Harry S. Truman, Medicare and Medicaid did not get signed into law until a few decades later, when they were endorsed by President Lyndon B. Johnson. The welfare state has long been a hallmark of advanced and wealthy countries; most developing states have much thinner social safety nets, and few have had the resources to provide for retirees or even, often, for the unemployed or ill.

While it has come to represent a culmination of the three key rights of citizenship in modern countries, the welfare state is shrinking rather than expanding. Factors such as global wage competition, the economic pressure of aging populations, and large budget deficits have hampered the expansion of social rights in many Western countries. While it is difficult to reduce benefits to already existing constituencies—for example, in the U. S., discussion of reducing Social Security payments or raising the age of eligibility evokes protest from many retirees and soon-to-be retirees—the economic crises of recent years have led to attempts by lawmakers to curb benefits to less powerful constituencies, including the poor and immigrants.

Law: A system of binding and recognized codified rules of behavior that regulate the actions of people pertaining to a given jurisdiction.

Citizens: Legally recognized individuals who are part of a political community in which they are granted certain rights and privileges and, at the same time, have specified responsibilities.

Noncitizens: Individuals who reside in a given jurisdiction but do not possess the same rights and privileges as citizens; sometimes referred to as *residents, temporary workers,* or *aliens.*

Welfare state: A government or country's system of providing for the financial and social well-being of its citizens, typically through government programs that provide funding or other resources to individuals who meet certain criteria.

The law bringing Social Security into being was signed in 1935 by President Franklin D. Roosevelt. Social security benefits have contributed to the reduction of poverty among seniors in the United States.

Political Rights and Civil Liberties

Every year, Freedom House, an organization dedicated to monitoring and promoting democratic change and human rights, publishes an evaluation of "freedom" in 195 countries, as well as 14 related and disputed territories (Figure 14.1). The report includes ratings that measure political rights (based on the electoral process, political pluralism, and participation) and civil liberties (based on freedom of expression and belief, rights of association and organization, rule of law, and individual rights).

Even in the United States, which earns top scores in Freedom House's survey, problems with voting procedures have raised the question of whether some voters, especially minorities, have been denied a political voice in elections. Nationwide, 6.1 million Americans were disenfranchised due to a felony conviction, including 77% who are not in prison. Disenfranchisement is vastly disproportionate by race, as 1 of every 13 African Americans has been disenfranchised compared to 1 of every 56 nonblack voters (The Sentencing Project, 2016). Disenfranchisement is also disproportionate by region, as Southeastern states have higher rates compared to Northeastern and Midwestern states. For example, Florida has the highest rate of total felony disenfranchisement at 10.4% and one of the highest rates of disenfranchisement of African Americans at 21.4% (the highest rate is in Kentucky at 26%). By contrast, states such as Massachusetts, Maryland, and Utah have fewer than 0.5% (Uggen, Larson, & Shannon, 2016).

Recently, some U.S. state legislatures have sought to implement voter identification laws, which require voters to show identification when they vote in person. As of 2017,

■ **FIGURE 14.1** Freedom Status Worldwide, 2018

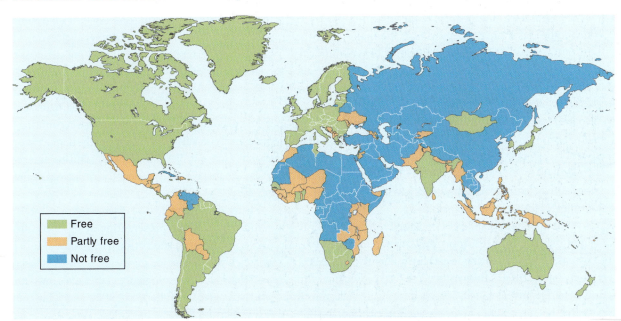

Free
Partly free
Not free

Source: Freedom House. (2018). 2018 Freedom in the World.

■ **FIGURE 14.2** Voter Identification Laws in the United States, June 2018

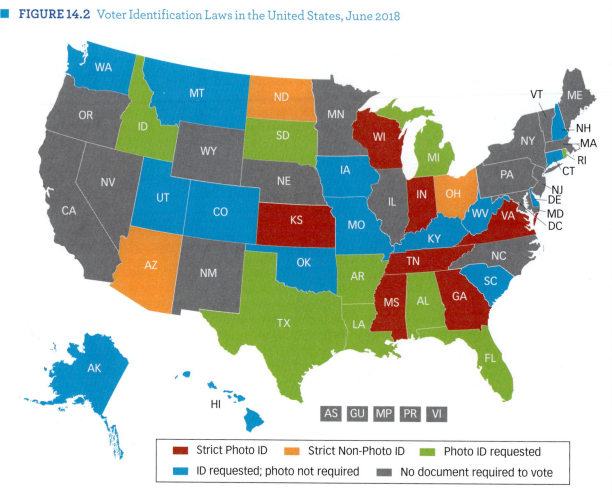

Source: Voter identification requirements: Voter ID laws. *Legislature & Elections*. Copyright © 2018 National Conference of State Legislatures. Reprinted with permission.

ten states had strict photo ID laws, while others had a variety of other laws ranging from required non-photo ID to no required documents (Figure 14.2; Brennan Center for Justice, 2017). Critics point out that members of minority groups (in particular, those who are elderly or poor) are among those least likely to have photo identification in the form of a driver's license or passport. The practical effect of voter ID laws, they say, is not to combat voter fraud (which has been very infrequently documented in the U.S.: There were fewer than 31 credible voting fraud cases identified from 2000 to 2014 and only four in the 2016 election) but rather to disenfranchise minorities and the poor (Brennan Center for Justice, 2017; Cohen, 2012).

The 2016 presidential election also brought to the fore the vulnerability of U.S. voting systems to hacking and the potential for foreign states to exercise influence on U.S. elections. At the time of this writing, a special prosecutor with the U.S. Department of Justice was investigating allegations of Russian interference in the presidential election. As well,

investigations by various security agencies in the U.S. of risks to the integrity of the voting process itself are continuing: By some accounts, states that record voter choices only electronically are at greater risk of inaccurately registering voter preferences than states that use both electronic count and provide a paper receipt for the ballot. This is because some voting systems have been shown to be vulnerable to hackers whose goal is to compromise them. A precise accounting of voter preferences is vital to the integrity of the democratic political system. How do you think U.S. states and localities could act to ensure that elections reflect the expressed desires of the citizenry?

Later in this chapter, we discuss more fully the issue of *political voice* (the representation of a group's interests in bodies such as state and national legislatures) and the ways in which political voice may vary. In the next section, we turn to broader sociological perspectives on state power, which can give us a fuller context for analyzing contemporary debates on power and politics.

Theories of State Power

Sociologists have developed different approaches to explaining how authority is exercised in modern states. Below, we highlight two theoretical approaches, which disagree about how expansively power is shared. These theories are based largely on governance in the United States today, although we can also apply them to other modern societies.

The Functionalist Perspective and Pluralist Theory

Classical sociologist Émile Durkheim (1922/1956, 1922/1973b) saw government as an institution that translates broadly shared values and interests into fair-minded laws and effective policies. Contemporary functionalist theorists recognize that modern societies are socially and culturally heterogeneous and likely to have a greater diversity of needs and perspectives. The government, they suggest, is a neutral umpire, balancing the conflicting values, norms, and interests of a variety of competing groups in its laws and actions.

In the United States, most people agree on such general values as liberty, democratic governance, and equality of opportunity, but there is vigorous public debate over issues such as abortion, the death penalty, the government's role in ensuring access to health care, and the degree to which the United States should take a leading role in global affairs. Recognizing the pluralistic—that is, diverse—nature of contemporary societies, sociologists and political scientists have developed theories of government that highlight state power and how it is exercised.

Pluralist theory tries to answer the question, "Given that modern societies are pluralistic, how do they resolve the inevitable conflicts?" To answer this question, Robert Dahl (1961, 1982, 1989) studied decision making in New Haven, Connecticut. Dahl (1961) concluded that power is exercised through the political process, which is dominated by different groups of leaders, each having access to a different amalgamation of political resources. Dahl argues that, in their efforts to exert political influence, individuals come together in **interest groups**—*groups made up of people who share the same concerns on particular issues who use their organizational and social resources to influence legislation and the functioning of social institutions.* An interest group may be short-lived, such as a local citizens' group that bands together to have a road repaved or a school built, or long-lasting, such as a labor union or a manufacturers' association.

Interest groups: Groups made up of people who share the same concerns on particular issues who use their organizational and social resources to influence legislation and the functioning of social institutions.

DISCOVER INTERSECTIONS

Political Voice, Race, and Education

Critics contend that even if laws are passed to protect the values and interests of people who are not economically powerful, the laws may not be actively and forcefully implemented or their reach may be limited. For example, de facto racial segregation continues to exist in public education even though school segregation has been outlawed in the U.S. since 1954. Can you draw together what you have learned about political power and influence in this chapter with what you read earlier in our chapter on *Race and Ethnicity* (Chapter 9) about forces that have fostered and maintained racial segregation in neighborhoods and schools? How can an understanding of political forces and social and economic forces help us to more fully grasp why educational segregation exists and persists?

Dahl's theory asserts that interest groups serve the function of ensuring that everyone's perspectives (that is, their values, norms, and interests) are represented in the government. The influence of one group is offset by the power of another. For instance, if a group of investors bands together to seek government approval to clear-cut a forest to build homes, a group of citizens concerned about the environment may coalesce into an interest group to oppose the investors' plan. The ideal result, according to Dahl, would be a compromise: Perhaps cutting would be limited or some particularly sensitive areas would be preserved. Similarly, from this perspective, big businesses and organized labor may routinely face off over issues of pay, benefits, and worker voice in decision making, but neither exercises disproportionate influence on the political process.

When powerful interests oppose one another, pluralists see compromise as the likely and optimal outcome, and the role of the government is to broker solutions that benefit as many interest groups as possible. In this view, power is dynamic, passing from one stakeholder to another over time rather than becoming concentrated in the hands of a powerful few. Competition and the fluidity of power contribute to democratic governance and society.

A critical view of the pluralist characterization of political power points out that government is unlikely to represent or recognize all interests (Chambliss & Seidman, 1982; Domhoff, 2006). Critics also dispute the assumption that government is a neutral mediator between competing interests. They argue that laws may favor some groups over others. For example, when the U.S. Constitution was framed by White male

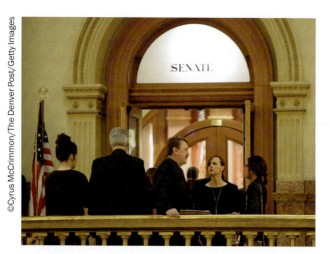

Lobbying for special interests that range from multinational corporations and fossil fuel companies to workers' unions and immigrant rights organizations is common in the U.S. political system. What factors affect the influence that special interests can exercise in the legislative and executive branches? Do some have more influence than others?

property owners, only White male property owners could vote: People without property, women, Blacks, and American Indians were excluded from the political process.

Indeed, political practices demonstrate that some interest groups are more powerful than others. And governments do not apply the rules neutrally, as the theory claims. Rather, political leaders interpret (or even bend) the rules to favor the most powerful groups in society, including big business and other moneyed interests that finance increasingly costly political campaigns for those who favor them (Domhoff, 2006, 2009; Friedman, 1975, 1990).

The Conflict Perspective and Class Dominance Theory

Conflict theory highlights power differences between social groups. This perspective recognizes that modern societies are pluralistic, but it argues that the interests of social groups are often incompatible with one another. Further, conflict theory posits that some groups are more powerful than others and are therefore more likely to see their interests and values reflected in government policymaking. Groups with greater resources use their power to create systems of law, economy, politics, and education that favor them, their children, and other group members.

Unlike pluralistic theory, which views competing interests as having relatively comparable and shifting opportunities and access to power, conflict theory sees power as being concentrated in the hands of a few privileged groups and individuals. The gains of the elite, conflict theorists suggest, come at the expense of those who have fewer resources, including economic, cultural, and social capital.

Conflict theory is rooted in the ideas of Karl Marx. You may recall from previous chapters that Marx believed the most important sources of social conflict are economic, and that, as a consequence, class conflict is fundamental to all other forms of conflict. Within a capitalist society, government represents and serves the interests of the capitalist class or *bourgeoisie*, the ruling class that exerts disproportionate influence on the government. Still, a well-organized working class may effectively press government for such economic reforms as a shorter working day or the end of child labor.

Contemporary conflict theory extends Marx's concept of the *bourgeoisie* (those who own the means of production) to include other groups that wield considerable power. **Class dominance theory** argues *that power is concentrated in the hands of a small group of elite or upper-class people who dominate and influence societal institutions* (Domhoff, 1983, 1990, 2002; Mills, 1956/2000a). These individuals have often attended the same elite schools, belong to the same social organizations, and cycle in and out of top positions in government, business, and the military (the so-called *revolving door*). Class dominance theory complements Marx's original ideas with a focus on the elite social networks themselves rather than only on capitalism as a political economic system.

G. William Domhoff (2002, 2006, 2009) posits that we can show the existence of a dominant class by examining the answers to several basic questions, which he calls *power indicators*: Who benefits? Who governs? Who wins?

- In terms of "Who benefits?" Domhoff asks us to consider who gets the most of what is valued in society. Who gets money and material goods? What about leisure and travel or status and prestige? Domhoff (2006) asserts that "those who have the most of what people want are, by inference, the powerful" (p. 13).

- In terms of "Who governs?" he asks who is positioned to make the important political and economic and legal decisions in the country or community. Are all demographic groups relatively well represented? Are some disproportionately powerful? Domhoff (2006) suggests, "If a group or class is highly overrepresented or underrepresented in relation to its proportion of the population, it can be inferred that the group or class is relatively powerful or powerless, as the case may be" (p. 14).

- Asking "Who wins?" entails inquiring about which group or groups have their interests realized most often. Domhoff concedes that movements with fewer resources, including, for instance, environmental groups, may win desired legislation sometimes. However, we need to look at who has their desires

---

Class dominance theory: The theory that power is concentrated in the hands of a small group of elite or upper-class people who dominate and influence societal institutions; a variation of conflict theory.

realized most consistently and often. Is it small interest groups representing civil rights, environmental activists, or same-sex marriage advocates? Is it large corporate interests with friends in high places and the ability to write big campaign donation checks?

After examining the power indicators in his book, *Who Rules America?*, Domhoff concludes that it is the upper class, particularly the owners and managers of large for-profit enterprises, that benefits, governs, and wins. This, he suggests, challenges the premise of pluralist theories that power is dynamic, passing between a variety of interests and groups. Domhoff argues that there exists a small but significant **power elite**, which is *a group of people with a disproportionately high level of influence and resources who utilize their status to influence the functioning of societal institutions*. Though the corporations, organizations, and individuals who make up the power elite may be divided on some issues, Domhoff contends that cooperation is stronger than competition among them: The members of the power elite are united by a common set of interests (including a probusiness and antiregulation environment) and common enemies (including environmentalists and labor and consumer activists).

From a critical perspective, class dominance theory may overemphasize the unified nature of the ruling class. For instance, Domhoff highlights the fact that many members of the power elite share similar social backgrounds. Often, they attend the same private high schools and colleges, spend their vacations in the same exclusive resorts, and marry into one another's families. They share a strong belief in the importance and value of capitalism and, as Domhoff argues, are steeped in a similar set of worldviews. However, it is difficult to show that they necessarily share the same political beliefs or even economic orientations (Chambliss & Seidman, 1982; Chambliss & Zatz, 1994).

Further, government decisions sometimes appear to be in direct opposition to the expressed interests of powerful groups. For example, when faced with major conflicts between labor and management during the Depression years of the 1930s, the U.S. government passed laws legalizing trade unions and giving workers the right to bargain collectively with their corporate employers, even though both laws were strongly opposed by corporation executives and owners (Chambliss & Zatz, 1994; Skocpol, 1979; Tilly, 1975). Mark Smith (2000) found that when businesses act to influence public policy to support or oppose a given issue, they may experience backlash as labor and public interest groups organize in opposition to the perceived power seizure.

Does a power elite exercise disproportionate influence in the political sphere of the U.S.? Domhoff and other conflict theorists would answer in the affirmative. A pluralist perspective might see corporations, the upper class, and policy organizations as some among many players who compete in the political power game, balanced by other groups such as unions and environmentalists, and answer in the negative. What do you think?

Power and Authority

In the section above, we looked at different perspectives on how state power functions and who it serves. We now turn to the question of how countries exercise their power in practice, asking, "How do governments maintain control over their populations?"

One way that states exercise power is through outright **coercion**—*the threat or use of physical force to ensure compliance*. Relying solely on coercion, however, is costly and difficult because it requires surveillance and sometimes suppression of the population, particularly those segments that might be inclined to dissent. Governments that ground their authority in coercion are vulnerable to instability, as they generally fail to earn the allegiance of their people. It is more efficient, and in the long run more enduring, if a government can establish legitimate authority, which, as you recall from Chapter 5, is *power that is recognized as deserved or earned.*

One of sociology's founders, Max Weber (1864–1920), was also one of the first social scientists to analyze the nature of legitimate authority, and his ideas have influenced our understanding of power and authority in the modern world. Weber sought to answer the question, "Why do people consent to give up power, allowing others to dominate them?" His examination of this question, which was based on detailed studies of societies throughout history, identified three key forms of legitimate authority: traditional, rational-legal, and charismatic.

Traditional Authority

For most of human history, state power relied on **traditional authority**, *power based on a belief in the sanctity of long-standing traditions and the legitimate right of rulers to exercise authority in accordance with these traditions* (Weber, 1921/1979). Traditional rulers claim power on the basis of age-old norms, beliefs, and practices. When the people being governed accept the legitimacy of traditional

Power elite: A group of people with a disproportionately high level of influence and resources who utilize their status to influence the functioning of societal institutions.

Coercion: The threat or use of physical force to ensure compliance.

Traditional authority: Power based on a belief in the sanctity of long-standing traditions and the legitimate right of rulers to exercise authority in accordance with those traditions.

©Express Newspapers via AP Images

In the United Kingdom, traditional authority peacefully and functionally coexists with rational-legal authority. In this photo, Prime Minister Theresa May, who is the head of government, shakes hands with Queen Elizabeth II, who is the constitutional monarch.

authority, it tends to be relatively stable over time. The monarchies of Europe, for example, ruled for hundreds of years based on traditional authority. Their people were considered the king's or queen's subjects, whose loyalty derived from their recognition of the fundamental legitimacy of monarchical rule, with its long-standing hierarchy and distribution of power on the basis of blood and birth. In modern Europe, however, monarchies such as those in Denmark and Sweden have little more than symbolic power—they have been largely stripped of political power. Traditional authority, in these instances, coexists with the rational-legal authority exercised by modern elected bodies, which we discuss below.

Traditional authority supports the exercise of power at both the macro and micro levels: Just as reverence for traditional norms and practices may give legitimacy to a state, a religion, or other government, it may also drive the decisions and actions of families. If a family marks a particular holiday or date with an obligatory ritual, then even if an individual questions the need for that ritual, the reasoning "We've *always* done that" is a micro-level exercise of traditional authority that ensures compliance and discourages challenges by any member of the group.

Rational-Legal Authority

Traditional authority, in Weber's view, was incompatible with the rise of modern capitalist states. Capitalism is based on forms of social organization that favor rational, rule-governed calculation rather than practices grounded in tradition. As capitalism evolved, traditional authority gave way to **rational-legal authority**, *power based on a belief in the lawfulness of enacted rules (laws) and the legitimate right of leaders to exercise authority under such rules* (Weber, 1921/1979). The legitimacy of rational-legal authority derives from a belief in the rule of law. We do something not simply because it has always been done that way but because it conforms to established rules and procedures.

In a system based on rational-legal authority, leaders are regarded as legitimate as long as they act according to law. Laws, in turn, are enacted and enforced through formal, bureaucratic procedures rather than reflecting custom and tradition or the whims of a ruler. Weber argued that rational-legal authority is compatible with modern economies, which are based on rational calculation of costs and benefits, profits, and other economic decisions. Rational-legal authority is commonly exercised in the ideal-typical modern state described earlier in this chapter. In practice, we could take the United States, Canada, Japan, or the countries of the European Union as specific examples of states governed by rational-legal authority.

Charismatic Authority

Weber's third form of authority can threaten both traditional and rational-legal authority. **Charismatic authority** is *power based on devotion inspired in followers by the personal qualities of a leader* (Weber, 1921/1979). It derives from widespread belief in a given community that an individual has a gift of great—even divine—powers, so it rests most significantly on an individual personality rather than on that individual's claim to authority on the basis of tradition, legal election, or appointment. Charismatic authority may also be the product of a *cult of personality*, an image of a leader that is carefully manipulated by the leader and other elites. In North Korea's long-standing dictatorship, power has passed through several generations of the same family, as has the government's careful construction of a cult of personality around each leader that elevates him as supremely intelligent, patriotic, and worthy of unquestioning loyalty.

Prominent charismatic leaders in religious history include Moses, Jesus Christ, the Prophet Muhammad, and Buddha. Some military and political rulers whose power was based in large part on charisma are Julius

Rational-legal authority: Power based on a belief in the lawfulness of enacted rules (laws) and the legitimate right of leaders to exercise authority under such rules.

Charismatic authority: Power based on devotion inspired in followers by the personal qualities of a leader.

Caesar, Napoleon Bonaparte, Vladimir Lenin, and Adolf Hitler (clearly, not all charismatic leaders are charitable, ethical, or good).

Charismatic leaders have also emerged to lead communities and countries toward democratic development. Václav Havel, a dissident playwright in what was then communist Czechoslovakia, challenged the authority of a government that was not elected and that citizens despised; he spent years in prison and doing menial jobs because he was not permitted to work in his artistic field. Later, he helped lead the 1989 opposition movement against the government and, with its fall, was elected president of the newly democratic state. (Czechoslovakia no longer exists; its Czech and Slovak populations wanted to establish their own nation-states, and in 1993, they peacefully formed two separate republics.) Similarly, Nelson Mandela, despite spending 27 years in prison, was a key figure in the opposition movement against the racist policies of apartheid in South Africa. Mandela became South Africa's first democratically elected president in 1994, four years after his release from prison. His death in 2013 marked the passing of a significant era in South African politics.

Notably, Weber also pointed to a phenomenon he termed the *routinization of charisma*. That is, with the decline, departure, or death of a charismatic leader, his or her authority may be transformed into legal-rational or even traditional authority. While those who follow may govern in the charismatic leader's name, the authority of successive leaders rests either on emulation (traditionalized authority) or on power that has been routinized and institutionalized (rationalized authority).

Authority exists in a larger context, and political authority is often sited in a government. Governance takes place in a variety of forms, which we discuss below.

Forms of Governance in the Modern World

In the modern world, the three principal forms of governance are authoritarianism, totalitarianism, and democracy. Below, we discuss each type, offering ideal-typical definitions as well as illustrative examples. Two modern global trends in governance are the growth of rational-legal authority and the spread of representative democracy.

Authoritarianism

Under **authoritarianism**, *ordinary members of society are denied the right to participate in government, and political power is exercised by and for the benefit of a small political elite*. At the same time, authoritarianism is distinguished from totalitarianism (which we will discuss shortly) by the

fact that at least some social, cultural, and economic institutions exist that are not under the control of the state. Two prominent types of authoritarianism are monarchies and dictatorships.

Monarchy is *a form of governance in which power resides in an individual or a family and is passed from one generation to the next through hereditary lines*. Monarchies, which derive their legitimacy from traditional authority, were historically the primary form of governance in many parts of the world and in Europe until the 18th century. Today, the formerly powerful royal families of Europe have been either dethroned or relegated to peripheral and ceremonial roles. For example, the queens of England, Denmark, and the Netherlands and the kings of Sweden and Spain do not have any significant political power or formal authority to govern. A few countries in the modern world are still ruled by monarchies, including Saudi Arabia, Jordan, Qatar, and Kuwait. Even the monarchs of these nations, however, govern with the consent of powerful religious and social or economic groups.

In the territory of Saudi Arabia, for instance, the royal family, also known as the House of Saud, has ruled for centuries, though the country of Saudi Arabia itself was established only in 1932. The Basic Law of 1992 declared Saudi Arabia to be a monarchy ruled by the sons and grandsons of King Abdul Aziz al-Saud, making the country the only one in the world named after a family. The constitution of the country is the Koran, and, consequently, sharia law (which is based on Islamic traditions and beliefs) is in effect. The country does not hold national elections, nor is the formation of independent political parties permitted. However, the royal rulers govern within the bounds of the constitution, tradition, and the consent of religious leaders, the *ulema*.

A more modern form of authoritarianism is **dictatorship**, *a form of governance in which power rests in a single individual*. An example of an authoritarian dictatorship is the government of Iraqi president Saddam Hussein, who ruled his country from 1979 to 2003, when he was deposed. As this case shows, the individual in power in a dictatorship is actually closely intertwined with an inner circle of governing elites. In Iraq, Saddam was linked to the inner circle of the Báath Party. Further, because of the complexity of modern society, even the most heavy-handed authoritarian

---

Authoritarianism: A form of governance in which ordinary members of society are denied the right to participate in government, and political power is exercised by and for the benefit of a small political elite.

Monarchy: A form of governance in which power resides in an individual or a family and is passed from one generation to the next through hereditary lines.

Dictatorship: A form of governance in which power rests in a single individual.

dictator requires some degree of support from military leaders and an intelligence apparatus. No less important to the dictator's power is the compliance of the masses, whether it is gained through coercion or consent.

We might argue that today, it would be difficult for a single individual or even a handful of individuals to run a modern country effectively for any length of time. In recent years, many dictators have been deposed by foes or ousted in popular revolutions. Some have even allowed themselves to be turned out of office by relatively peaceful democratic movements, as happened in the former Soviet Union and the formerly communist states of Eastern Europe, such as Czechoslovakia and Hungary. China, which has become progressively more capitalistic while retaining an authoritarian communist government, remains an exception to this pattern.

Totalitarianism

When authoritarian dictatorships persist and become entrenched, the end result may be a totalitarian form of government. **Totalitarianism** *denies popular political participation in government and also seeks to regulate and control all aspects of the public and private lives of citizens.* In totalitarianism, there are no limits to the exercise of state power. All opposition is outlawed, access to information not provided by the state is stringently controlled, and citizens are required to demonstrate a high level of commitment and loyalty to the system. A totalitarian government depends more on coercion than on legitimacy in exercising power.

Totalitarianism: A form of governance that denies popular political participation in government and also seeks to regulate and control all aspects of the public and private lives of citizens.

Here, North Korean totalitarian leader Kim Jong-un visits the Korean People's Army. According to a United Nations report, North Korea's human rights violations include "violations of the freedoms of expression; discrimination; freedom of movement; right to food and right to life; arbitrary detention, torture, and execution; abductions and enforced disappearances from other countries" (OHCHR, 2014).

It thus requires a large intelligence apparatus to monitor the citizenry for antigovernment activities and to punish those who fail to conform. Members of the society are urged to inform on any of their fellow members who break the rules or criticize the leadership.

One characteristic shared by totalitarian regimes of the 20th century was a ruthless commitment to power and coercion over the rule of law. Soviet leader Vladimir Lenin has been quoted as stating that "the dictatorship—and take this into account once and for all—means unrestricted power based on force, not on law" (Amis, 2002, p. 33). Another characteristic of these regimes was a willingness to destroy the opposition by any means necessary. Joseph Stalin's regime in the Soviet Union, which lasted from 1922 to 1953, purged millions of perceived, potential, or imagined enemies; Stalin's Great Terror tore apart the ranks of even the Soviet military apparatus. Martin Amis (2002) cites the following statistics in characterizing Stalin's war on his own military: From the late 1930s to about 1941, Stalin purged 3 of 5 marshals, 13 of 15 army commanders, 154 of 186 divisional commanders, and at least 43,000 officers lower down the chain of command (p. 175). An often-told story about

Nazi Germany, the Soviet Union under the leadership of Lenin and later Stalin, Chile under Augusto Pinochet, and the Spain of Francisco Franco are historical examples of totalitarian regimes. This image of "Big Brother," a symbol of totalitarianism's penetration of private as well as public life, comes from the film version of George Orwell's classic book, *1984*.

©KNS/AFP/Getty Images

©AF archive / Alamy Stock Photo

Stalin cites him telling his political inner circle that each should find two replacements for himself.

Perhaps more than any other political system, totalitarianism is built on terror and the threat of terror—including genocide, imposed famine, purges, deportation, imprisonment, torture, and murder. Fear keeps the masses docile and the dictator in power. Torture has a long, brutal history in the dictatorships of the world, and, in trying to uncover its function, Amis (2002) makes the compelling observation that "torture, among its other applications, was part of Stalin's war against truth. He tortured, not to force you to reveal a fact, but to force you to collude in a fiction" (p. 61).

Today, few totalitarian states exist. Certainly, in the age of the Internet, control of information is an enormous challenge to states that seek full control of their populations. North Korea remains one of the last totalitarian regimes on the planet, where the citizenry is isolated from the rest of the world and few North Koreans outside the elite have Internet connections, smartphones, and computers—or even regular electricity and access to nutritious food.

Democracy

Democracy literally means "the rule of the people." (The word comes from the Greek *demos,* "the people," and *kratos,* "rule.") The concept of democracy originated in the Greek city-state of Athens during the fifth century bc, where it took the form of **direct democracy**, *in which all citizens fully participate in their own governance.* This full participation was possible because Athens was a small community by today's standards and because the vast majority of its residents (including women and slaves, on whose labor the economy relied) were excluded from citizenship (Sagan, 1992).

Direct democracy is rarely possible today because of the sheer size of most countries and the complexity of their political affairs. One exception is the referendum process that exists in some U.S. states, including California and Oregon. In Oregon, for instance, the signatures of a specified percentage of registered voters can bring a referendum to the ballot. In 2014, for instance, Oregonians approved an effort to permit adults to purchase marijuana for recreational use, though the quantity is limited and the drug may not be used in public.

Democracy in the modern world more typically takes the form of **representative democracy**, *a political system in which citizens elect representatives to govern them.* In a representative democracy, elected officials are expected to make decisions that reflect the interests of their constituents. Representative democracy first took hold in the industrial capitalist countries of Europe. It is now the principal form of governance throughout the world, although some parts of the populations in democratic states may be disenfranchised. For instance, only in recent years have women been legally granted the right to vote in many countries (Figure 14.3). Some countries, such as China, the largest remaining authoritarian society, claim to have free elections for many government positions, but eligibility is limited to members of the Communist Party. Thus, even though voting is the hallmark of representative democracy, the mere option of voting does not ensure the existence of a true democracy.

The U.S. Political System

Politics in democratic societies is *the art or science of influencing public policy*; it is structured around competing political parties whose purpose is to gain control of the government by winning elections. Political parties serve this purpose by defining alternative policies and programs, building their membership, raising funds for their candidates, and helping to organize political campaigns. Not only must candidates win elections and retain their offices, but they must also, once in office, make decisions with far-reaching financial and social effects. These decisions ideally reflect the needs and desires of their constituents as well as the interests of their parties and the entities that contribute to their campaigns. Some politicians argue that their constituents' issues take priority; other observers suggest that politicians are beholden to party or donor interests.

In the section below, we discuss electoral politics in the United States. Sociologists take an interest in electoral politics because it is an important site at which power in modern countries is exercised. Thus, key questions that sociologists ask—How is this functional for society? Who benefits from the existing social order? How do perceptions structure behaviors in the electoral process?—can be applied to electoral politics.

Electoral Politics and the Two-Party System

Most modern democracies are based on a parliamentary system, in which the chief of state (called a *prime minister*) is the head of the party that has the largest number of seats in the national legislature (typically called a *parliament*). Britain, for example, has a parliamentary system. This arrangement can give a significant degree of influence to minority parties (those that have relatively few

---

Direct democracy: A political system in which all citizens fully participate in their own governance.

Representative democracy: A political system in which citizens elect representatives to govern them.

Politics: The art or science of influencing public policy.

representatives in parliament), since the majority party often requires minority party support to pass legislation or even to elect a prime minister.

In the United States, the president is chosen by voters—although, as happened in the 2000 and 2016 presidential elections, a candidate who wins the popular vote (in these cases, Al Gore and Hillary Clinton, respectively) cannot become president without also winning the requisite number of Electoral College votes.

The separate election of the president and Congress (rather than having the legislature choose a national leader, as is common in parliamentary democracies) is intended to help ensure a separation of powers between the executive and legislative branches of the government. At the same time, it weakens the power of minority or third parties, since—unlike in parliamentary systems—they are unlikely to have much impact on who will be selected chief of state. In Britain or Germany, by contrast, if a minority party stops voting with the majority party in parliament, its members can force a national election, which might result in a new prime minister. This gives minority parties potential power in parliament to broker deals that serve their interests. No such system exists in the U.S. and, as a consequence, third parties play only a minor role in national politics. No third-party candidate has won a presidential election since Abraham Lincoln was elected in 1860.

The domination of national elections and elected positions by the Republican and Democratic Parties is virtually ensured by the current political order. Parties representing well-defined interests are ordinarily eliminated from the national political process, since there are few avenues by which they can exert significant political power. Unlike in many other democracies, there are no political parties in the United States that effectively represent the exclusive interests of labor, environmentalists, or other constituencies at the national level. On the contrary, there is a strong incentive for political groups to support one of the two major political parties rather than to "waste" their votes on third parties that have no chance at all of winning the presidency; at most, such votes are generally offered as "protest" votes.

Third parties can occasionally play an important—even decisive—role in national politics, particularly when voters are unhappy with the two dominating parties. The presidential campaign of H. Ross Perot of the Reform Party in 1992 was probably significant in taking votes away from Republican George Bush and helping Democrat Bill Clinton to win the presidential election. Perot, running at the head of his own party organization, won nearly 19% of the popular vote. In 2000, the situation favored Republicans, as Democrat Al Gore probably lost votes to Green Party candidate Ralph Nader; in some states, George W. Bush had fewer votes than Gore and Nader combined, but more than Gore alone. Bush won the electoral votes of those states. Another candidate from the Green Party, Jill Stein, was also active in the 2016 presidential race, though she did not earn a significant number of votes (1.1%) and functioned primarily as an option for voters who were disaffected with both parties. Many voters who feel that the choices they

■ FIGURE 14.3 When Women Won the Right to Vote in Selected Countries

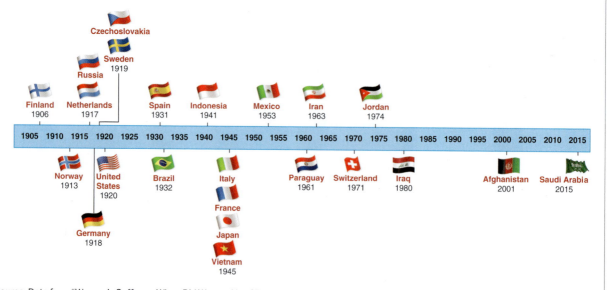

Source: Data from "Women's Suffrage: When Did Women Vote?" Interactive Map. Scholastic.com.

have do not match up with their interests opt out of voting entirely, however. The issue of apathy in U.S. politics is one that we take up in the next section.

Voter Activism and Apathy in U.S. Politics

One consequence of the lack of political choices in the entrenched two-party system in the U.S. may be a degree of political apathy, reflected in voter turnouts that are among the lowest in the industrialized world. Among democracies, the United States scores in the bottom fifth when it comes to voter participation. Whereas many European countries typically have voter turnouts between 70% and 90% of eligible voters, in 2000, about 55% of the voting-eligible U.S. population participated in the presidential election. The percentage has risen in subsequent presidential election years: Estimates put turnouts for 2008 at more than 62% and 2012 around 59%. In 2016, a similar proportion of voting-eligible citizens participated (60%), though there were considerable variations by state: About 75% of Minnesota voters turned out, while only 43% of Hawaii opted to vote (Pillsbury & Johannesen, 2016; U.S. Elections Project, 2013).

Historically, the proportion of eligible voters turning out for elections in the United States has varied by education (Figure 14.5), race and ethnicity (Figure 14.6), and age (Figure 14.7). Voters who are White, older, and more educated have historically had greater influence than other demographic groups on the election of officials and, consequently, on government policies. Interestingly, however, data suggest that President Obama's 2012 reelection was driven in part by the votes of young people (60% of voters

18–29 cast a vote for Obama) and minorities (for example, about 70% of ethnic Latino voters cast a ballot for Obama; Pew Research Center for the People and the Press, 2012).

Though the votes of young people and minorities had a notable effect on the outcome of the 2012 presidential election, the lower proportions of these groups among voters prompt us to ask why people who are poor or working class, minority, and/or young are less likely to be active voters. One thesis is that voters do not turn out if they do not perceive that the political parties represent their interests (Delli Carpini & Keeter, 1996). Some of Europe's political parties represent relatively narrow and specific interests. If lower- to middle-class workers can choose a workers' party (for instance, the Labour Party in Britain or the Social Democratic Party in Germany) or environmentalists a Green Party (several European states, including Germany, have active Green Parties),or minority ethnic groups a party of their ethnic kin (in the non-Russian former Soviet states that are now democracies, Russians often have their own political parties), they may be more likely to participate in the process of voting. This is particularly likely if membership in the legislative body—say, a parliament—is proportionally allocated, in contrast to a winner-takes-all contest such as that in the United States.

In the United States, the legislative candidate with the greater number of votes wins the seat; the loser gets nothing. In several European countries, including Germany, parties offer lists of candidates, and the total proportion of votes received by each party determines how many members of the list are awarded seats in parliament. In *proportional voting*, small parties that can break a minimum barrier (in

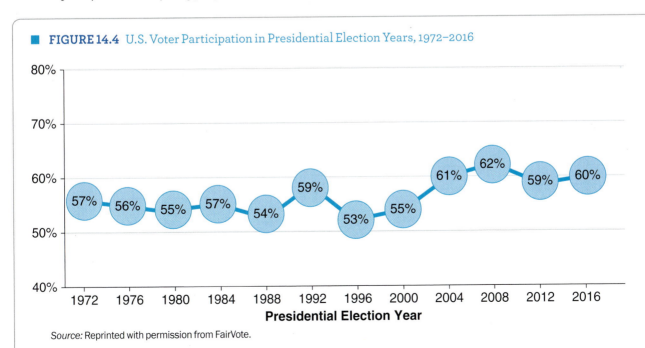

■ **FIGURE 14.4** U.S. Voter Participation in Presidential Election Years, 1972–2016

Source: Reprinted with permission from FairVote.

Germany, it is 5% of the total vote) are able to garner at least a small number of seats and enjoy a political voice through coalition building or by positioning themselves in the opposition.

Consider the winner-takes-all system and the proportional division of electoral votes. Is one more representative of the will of the people than the other? What do you think?

Some other reasons for low voter turnout among some demographic groups might be practical; low-wage workers may work two or more jobs and may not be able to visit polling places on the designated day of voting (for federal elections in the United States, the first Tuesday following the

©Hero Images Inc./Alamy Stock Photo

The participation of young adults (18–29) in voting is consistently lower than for other age groups. What might motivate more young adults to register and vote?

first Monday of November, usually between about 6:00–8:00 a.m. and 6:00–8:00 p.m.). In many European states, Election Day is a national holiday, and workers are given the day off to participate in the voting process. Recently, more U.S. states have offered early voting, extending the opportunity to vote by several days or even weeks at designated polling places. Oregon has allowed voting by mail since 1998, and other states have also begun to offer this alternative. Data suggest that these initiatives increase voter participation. However, in advance of the 2012 election, five states either passed or attempted to pass legislation that would shorten the time for early voting, a trend that continued in 2016.

What about young people? In 1971, the Twenty-Sixth Amendment to the U.S. Constitution lowered the voting age from 21 to 18, giving 18- to 20-year-olds the right to vote. This age group has taken advantage of suffrage in relatively small numbers, however: 18- to 24-year-olds are less than half as likely as older citizens to cast ballots. In the 2016 presidential election, about 50% of young adults (18–29) voted, a figure higher than the 45% who voted in 2012, despite many having negative views of both major party candidates (Figure 14.4). Under 20% of young adults turned out to vote in the 2014 midterm elections (Center for Information & Research on Civic Learning and Engagement [CIRCLE], 2016).

Research suggests that young people are generally not apathetic about civic involvement; in fact, many volunteer and are eager to give back to their communities

■ **FIGURE 14.5** Reported Voting Rates by Educational Attainment: 1980–2016 (Percentage)

	1980	1984	1988	1992	1996	2000	2004	2008	2012	2016
Bachelor's degree or more	79.9	79.1	77.6	81	72.6	72	74.2	73.3	71.7	71
Some college or associate's degree	67.2	67.5	64.5	68.7	60.5	60.3	66.1	65	61.5	60.5
High school graduate or GED	58.9	58.7	54.7	57.5	49.1	49.4	52.4	50.9	48.7	47.4
9th to 12th grade, no diploma	45.6	44.4	41.3	41.2	33.8	33.6	34.6	33.7	32.2	29.3
Less than 9th grade	42.6	42.9	36.7	35.1	29.9	26.8	23.6	23.4	21.6	18.3

— Less than 9th grade
— 9th to 12th grade, no diploma
— High school graduate or GED
— Some college or associate's degree
— Bachelor's degree or more

Source: U.S. Census Bureau. "Table A-2. Reported Voting and Registration by Region, Educational Attainment, and Labor Force: November 1964 to 2016." Retrieved from https://www.census.gov/data/tables/time-series/demo/voting-and-registration/voting-historical-time-series.html

■ FIGURE 14.6 Reported Voting Rates by Race and Hispanic Origin: 1980–2016 (Percentage)

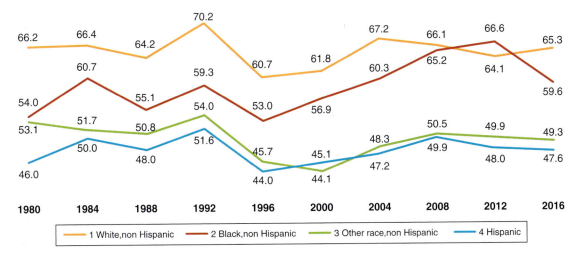

Source: U.S., Census Bureau. "Figure 2. Reported Voting Rates by Race and Hispanic Origin: 1980–2016." Retrieved from https://www.census.gov/newsroom/blogs/random-samplings/2017/05/voting_in_america.html.

■ FIGURE 14.7 Reported Voting Rates by Age: 1980–2016 (Percentage)

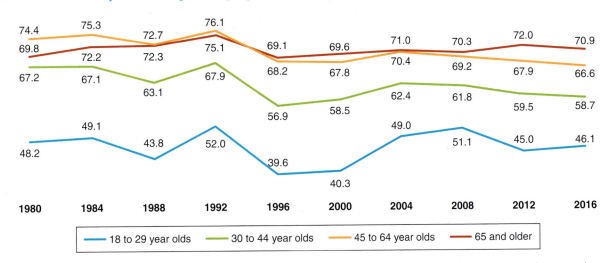

Source: U.S. Census Bureau. "Figure 4. Reported Voting Rates by Age; 1980–2016." Retrieved from https://www.census.gov/newsroom/blogs/random-samplings/2017/05/voting_in_america.html.

(The Atlantic, 2014). Voting, however, does not appear to inspire the same commitment. The young are less likely to be courted by the parties and candidates, who tailor messages to attract the interests of groups such as the elderly, who vote in larger numbers, and other groups who are historically more likely to turn out at the polls or make campaign donations. Perhaps because of a perception that the candidates and parties do not seem to speak to or for them, younger voters have reciprocated with limited participation in the voting process.

Other factors have also been identified as relevant in influencing the youth vote, including contact from organizations or campaigns and the accessibility of information about how, where, and when to vote. Data show that young people who are registered to vote turn out in high numbers: In 2008, 84% of young people (18–29) who were registered to vote cast a ballot (CIRCLE, n.d.).

The U.S. electorate is changing. Over the past few decades, Republicans and Democrats seem increasingly divided, though the changes we see are not only ideological. While, as we discuss in this chapter, young people are less likely to vote than older generations, their numbers make them a potentially powerful political force. Consider that, as of 2016, an estimated 69 million millennials are of voting age, a number nearly equal to that of the politically influential baby boomer generation (70 million; Fry, 2016), and

The March for Our Lives protests organized in March 2018 by student victims of the mass shooting at Marjorie Stoneman Douglas High School in Parkland, Florida, highlighted issues of school safety and gun control. Young people, who have tended to vote in smaller numbers than older generations, were also encouraged to register to vote.

in 2015, there were more 24-year-olds in the United States than any other age category (Gao, 2016). The U.S. electorate in 2016 is also the country's most racially and ethnically diverse in history. Almost one third of eligible voters (31%) are Hispanic, Black, Asian American, or another racial or ethnic minority (Krogstad, 2016). How a changing electorate will exercise its political voice, who it will support, and how and whether it will choose to be part of the voting process remains to be seen.

Before we move on to the next section, which discusses the issue of political influence, let's pause to consider the following questions: How might our elected government and its policies be altered if people turned out to vote in greater numbers? Would higher turnouts among the poor, minorities, and young people make issues particularly pertinent to them higher priorities for decision makers? What do you think?

Power and Politics

While parts of the general public may show apathy about elections and politics, wealthy and powerful individuals, corporations, labor unions, and interest groups have a great deal at stake. Legislators have the power to make decisions about government contracts and regulations, taxes, federal labor and environmental and health standards, national security budgets and

practices, and a spectrum of other important policies that affect profits, influence, and the division of power among those competing to have a voice in legislation.

The shortest route to political influence is through campaign contributions. The cost of campaigning has gone up dramatically in recent years, and candidates for public office must spend vast sums of money on getting elected. Donald Trump's campaign spent about $398 million, less than that spent by his rival for the presidency, thanks in large part to free media coverage (equating to an estimated $5.9 billion). Hillary Clinton's campaign, on the other hand, spent nearly $768 million, 62% of total campaign expenditures (Ingraham, 2017; Sultan, 2017).

A substantial proportion of the money candidates and parties raise comes from corporate donors and well-funded interest groups. In many instances, companies and well-resourced interest groups donate money to candidates of both parties in order to ensure that they will have a voice and a hand in decision making, regardless of the electoral outcome. Clearly, while most politicians would deny that there is an explicit *quid pro quo* (a term that means "something for something") with big donors, most would also admit that money can buy the time and interest of a successful candidate and determine which issues are most likely to be heard. Small interest groups and grassroots organizations lacking financial means may not be able to purchase passes into the halls of power.

Young adults in the United States are less likely to participate in elections than older generations. They have significant potential to influence elections: In 2015, there were more 24-year-olds than people of any other age in the United States!

Global Issues

BRITAIN HEADS FOR THE BREXIT

At the beginning of 2016, the European Union was composed of 28 members, ranging geographically from Britain in the north of Europe to the Baltic countries of Latvia, Lithuania, and Estonia on the eastern rim; to France, Germany, and the Netherlands to the west; and to Greece, Spain, and Italy in the European south. On June 23, 2016, however, a small majority of British voters chose to head for the Brexit: The term *Brexit* was coined as shorthand for "British exit," a campaign embraced by some politicians and constituents to quit the European Union. In a referendum asking voters, "Should the United Kingdom remain a member of the European Union or leave the European Union?" (Taub, 2016), about 52% opted to leave while 48% voted to stay.

What issues drove the decision by a majority of one of the European Union's anchor states to leave? Data suggest that those in support of Brexit viewed the withdrawal from the European Union as a way to ensure the country's sovereignty in political and economic decision-making. It was also a way to make a statement against high levels of immigration, which are perceived by some as undermining the economic status of Britons, particularly those of the working class, because migrants are believed to be willing to work for lower wages. Citizens voting against exiting the European Union wanted to remain in order to take advantage of the economic benefits of a shared space of trade (Europe is the country's biggest export market) and the benefits of geographic mobility in working or studying in other member states; they suggested that concerns about migration did not outweigh the consequences of exit (Taub, 2016).

The Brexit vote was sharply divided along lines of socioeconomic class. It was characterized by one British academic as "a vessel for anti-establishment and anti-elite feelings directed at the leaders of the mainstream British political parties as much as at Europe" (quoted in Taub, 2016). Residents with less education and those living in lower-income areas were more likely to vote for Brexit. Areas in which residents had higher education and more income, including the capital city of London, skewed toward remaining in the union (Speed, 2016).

Strikingly, the demographic variable with the most significant impact was age. While 60% of

senior citizens voted to leave the European Union, about three quarters of those 18 to 24 voted to stay, as did about two thirds of those 25 to 34 years of age. Turnout among the young, however, was low (Figure 14.8). One commentator pointed out that

> the Brexit vote . . . posed a paradox. Those who have to live the longest with the decision's ramifications are also ones least likely to vote. There is almost a mismatch between having stakes in an election and participating in it. (Bearak, 2016, para. 1)

By one estimate, only 36% of those in the 18–24 age group voted (Rhodes, 2016). Had young adult turnout at the referendum matched that of older generations, it is very likely that Britain would have voted to remain in the European Union.

In the wake of the vote, thousands of young people marched on the streets of London to protest the vote. Others took to social media to express their frustration and anger, using hashtags such as #whathavewedone and #notinmyname. An online petition, which quickly garnered over 4 million signatures, was also created (Stone, 2016), as was a petition on Change.org for London to secede from the United Kingdom and apply to join the European Union (BBC Trending, 2016).

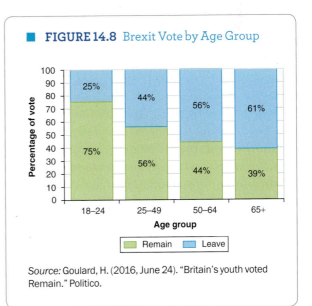

■ **FIGURE 14.8** Brexit Vote by Age Group

Source: Goulard, H. (2016, June 24). "Britain's youth voted Remain." Politico.

(Continued)

(Continued)

In spite of these late efforts, in July of 2016, it appeared that Britain, headed by a new Prime Minister (Theresa May, who replaced the pro-European Union David Cameron) was indeed headed for the Brexit.

Think It Through

- What does the Brexit experience say about the significance of the youth vote? Why do you think young adults in countries such as the United

Kingdom and the United States vote in relatively small numbers, particularly in contrast to older generations? How might young adults be encouraged to participate in greater numbers?

Follow us on Twitter to keep up with current sociological stories and research! We're at **@DiscoverSoc1**.

Share your own ideas at **#DiscoverSociology**.

©Gerardo Mora/Getty Images

In November 2016, Republican Donald Trump was elected to the U.S. presidency. While Democratic candidate Hillary Clinton won the popular vote, Trump defeated Clinton by winning the Electoral College.

The 2012 election had ushered a new player—the super PAC—into electoral politics (as noted above in our description of spending in the 2012 election). **Political action committees (PACs)** are *organizations created by groups such as corporations, unions, environmentalists, and other interest groups for the purpose of gathering money and contributing to political candidates who favor the groups' interests.* In 2010, the U.S. Supreme Court ruled in *Citizens United v. Federal Election Commission* that the government cannot restrict the monetary expenditures of such organizations in political campaigns, citing the First Amendment. This effectively means that these entities can contribute unlimited amounts of money to PACs. The term *super PAC* is used to describe the numerous well-funded PACs that have sprung up since the *Citizens United* decision.

While super PACs cannot contribute directly to specific campaigns or parties, they can demonstrate support for particular candidates through, for instance, television advertising. Many critics of the *Citizens United* decision have been disturbed by the implications of unlimited corporate spending in politics. The primary drivers of this new political spending have been extremely wealthy individuals and (often) anonymous donors. According to the Center for Responsive Politics, the top 100 individual donors to super PACs make up less than 4% of contributors but have been responsible for more than 80% of donations made (Riley, 2012).

Efforts to influence legislation are not limited to direct or indirect campaign contributions. Special interest groups often hire **lobbyists**, *paid professionals whose job it is to influence legislation.* Lobbyists commonly maintain offices in Washington, DC, or in state capitals, and the most powerful lobbies are staffed by full-time employees. Many of the best-funded lobbies represent foreign governments. Lobbying is especially intense when an industry or other interest group stands to gain or lose a great deal if proposed legislation is enacted. Oil companies, for instance, take special interest in legislation that would allow or limit drilling on U.S. territories, as do environmental groups. In an instance such as this, lobbyists from green groups and the oil and gas industry generally stand opposed to one another and seek to influence political decision makers to side with them.

Many lobbyists are former politicians or high-level government officials. Since lobbyists are often experts on matters that affect their organizations' interests, they may help in writing the laws that elected officials will introduce as legislation. Consider the example described below.

In an article titled "A Stealth Way a Bill Becomes a Law," the magazine *Bloomberg Businessweek* pointed out that several state-level bills rejecting cap-and-trade legislation

Political action committees (PACs): Organizations created by groups such as corporations, unions, environmentalists, and other interest groups for the purpose of gathering money and contributing to political candidates who favor the groups' interests.

Lobbyists: Paid professionals whose job it is to influence legislation.

(which is intended to reduce carbon dioxide emissions, believed by most scientists to contribute to climate change) used identical wording: "There has been no credible economic analysis of the costs associated with carbon mandates" (Fitzgerald, 2011). What was the source of this wording? It was supplied by the American Legislative Exchange Council, an organization supported by companies such as Walmart, Visa, Bayer, ExxonMobil, and Pfizer. In exchange for a large membership fee, a corporation can buy itself a seat on the bill-writing task force, which prepares model legislation, primarily for Republican political decision makers. The group boasts that it gets about 200 state laws passed each year.

Is the interaction of private sector corporations and public sector legislators an example of fruitful and appropriate cooperation on matters of mutual interest? When, if ever, is the writing of laws by corporate sponsors appropriate? When is it inappropriate?

Social Movements, Citizens, and Politics

Well-organized, popularly based social movements can also be important in shaping public policy. Among the most important social movements of the 19th and 20th centuries was the drive for women's suffrage, which invested half a century of activism to win U.S. women the right to vote. The movement's leaders fought to overcome the ideas that women ought not vote because their votes were represented by their husbands, because the muddy world of politics would besmirch feminine purity, and because women, like adolescents and lunatics, were not fit to vote.

The women's suffrage movement was born in the United States in 1869, when Susan B. Anthony and Elizabeth Cady Stanton founded the American Woman Suffrage Association. It worked for decades to realize its goal: In 1920, the Nineteenth Amendment to the Constitution was ratified and women were granted the right to vote on a national level (some states had granted this right earlier).

The second wave of the women's movements, which began in the 1960s, boasted other important achievements, including the passage of laws prohibiting gender-based job discrimination and rules easing women's ability to obtain credit independent of their husbands.

The temperance movement, symbolized by Carry Nation's pickax attacks on saloons in the early 1900s, sought to outlaw the use and sale of alcoholic beverages. This movement eventually resulted in the 1919 ratification of the Eighteenth Amendment to the Constitution, which made it a crime to sell or distribute alcoholic beverages. The Twenty-First Amendment eventually repealed Prohibition in 1933.

The labor movement grew throughout the first half of the 20th century, providing a powerful counterweight to the influence of business in U.S. politics. Labor unions were critical in getting federal and state laws passed to protect the rights of workers, including minimum wage guarantees, unemployment compensation, the right to strike, and the right to engage in collective bargaining. By midcentury, at the height of the unions' power, roughly 25% of all U.S. workers belonged to labor unions. Today, globalization and the flight of U.S. factories to low-wage areas have contributed to a decline in union membership, and just under 12% of workers belong to unions (U.S. Bureau of Labor Statistics, 2013e). At the same time, large unions (including the American Federation of Labor and Congress of Industrial Organizations [AFL-CIO]) have retained a good deal of political power, and candidates (particularly Democrats) vie for the unions' endorsements, which bring with them the virtual guarantee of large blocs of votes.

On one hand, social movements provide a counterbalance to the power and influence in politics of large corporate donors, which we discussed above. These movements offer a political voice to grassroots groups representing interests contrary to those of big business, such as labor rights and environmental protection. On the other hand, if we return to Domhoff's (2002) question, "Who wins?" we see that these groups rarely have more influence than large corporations and donors.

Constituents. Wealthy individuals, interest groups, PACs, and lobbyists exert considerable political influence through their campaign contributions. Still, these factors alone are not sufficient to explain political decisions. If they hope to be reelected, elected representatives must also serve their constituents. That is why politicians and their aides poll constituents, read their mail and e-mail, and look closely at the last election results.

One way politicians seek to win their constituents' support is by securing government spending on projects that provide jobs for or otherwise help their communities and constituents. If a new prison is to be built, for instance, legislators vie to have it placed in their district. Although a prison may seem like an undesirable neighbor, it can represent an economic windfall for a state or region. Among other things, prisons provide jobs to individuals who may not have the education or training to work in professional sectors of the economy and would otherwise be unemployed or working in the poorly paid service sector.

Projects that legislators push to bring to their home districts are sometimes labeled "pork." Pork may be superfluous or unnecessary for the macro-level economy but good for the legislator's home district. On the other hand, when a government commission proposes closing military bases, cost-conscious members of Congress will support the recommendation—*unless* any of the bases marked for closure are in their districts.

Politicians spend substantial amounts of time in their home districts. Over the course of the calendar year, the U.S. Congress is in session for an average of 103 days (Library of Congress, 2012). Congressional representatives spend much of their off-session time in their home districts because they are interested in hearing the views of their constituents—as well as in raising money and getting reelected.

Contradictions in Modern Politics: Democracy and Capitalism

Leaders in modern democratic capitalist societies such as the United States are caught between potentially contradictory demands. They seek widespread popular support, yet they must satisfy the demands of the elites whose financial backing is essential for electoral success. On one hand, voters are likely to look to their political leaders to back benefits such as retirement income (in the form of Social Security, for instance), housing supports (affordable housing for low-income families or mortgage tax breaks for wealthier ones), and environmental protection. On the other hand, such programs are costly to implement and entail economic costs to corporations, developers, and other members of

the elite. Some theorists argue that modern governments thus are caught in a conflict between their need to realize the interests of the capitalist class and their desire to win the support and loyalty of other classes (Held, 1989; Offe, 1984; Wolfe, 1977).

Jürgen Habermas (1976), a contemporary theorist with a conflict orientation, argues that modern countries have integrated their economic and political systems, reducing the likelihood of economic crisis while increasing the chances of a political crisis. He terms this the *legitimation crisis.* Governments have intervened in the market and, to some degree, solved the most acute contradictions of capitalism—including extreme income inequalities and tumultuous economic cycles—that Marx argued could be addressed only in a proletarian revolution. Governments often act to keep inflation and deflation in check, to regulate interest rates, and to provide social assistance to those who have lost jobs. Thus, economics is politicized, and the citizenry may come to expect that economic troubles will be solved through state structures and social welfare.

To understand Habermas's argument more fully, imagine a postindustrial U.S. city. The loss of jobs and industries manifests itself as a crisis—thousands of jobs in auto and other manufacturing industries move abroad, local businesses suffer as the amount of disposable income held by

■ **FIGURE 14.9**　Estimated Military and Civilian Casualties of Some 20th- and 21st-Century Wars

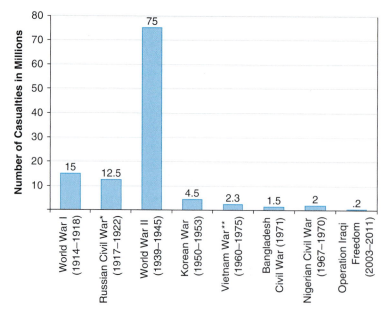

Source: Leitenberg, Milton. 2006. "Deaths in Wars and Conflicts in the 20th Century." Cornell University Peace Studies Program, Occasional Paper #29, 3rd edition; Fischer, Hannah. 2010. "Iraq Casualties: U.S. Military Forces and Iraqi Civilians, Police, and Security Forces." Congressional Research Service.

*Including Soviet–Polish conflict.

**Including North Vietnam versus South Vietnam.

Discover & Debate

THE ELECTORAL COLLEGE AND U.S. PRESIDENTIAL ELECTIONS

Motion: The United States should elect the president by popular vote. The Electoral College should be abolished.

Background: The Electoral College system was written into the U.S. Constitution more than 200 years ago by our country's founders, who feared that direct popular vote for the presidency might lead to (unruly) rule by the masses, even though at the time only about 6% of the population could legally vote. Under the current electoral system, when you vote for president, you are actually voting for your state's electors. Each state has the same number of electors as it has members in its Congressional delegation. California, the most populous state, has the most electors (54). Small states including Delaware, Montana, and Vermont have only 3. In nearly all U.S. states, the election is winner-take-all, so a presidential candidate who gets only one vote more than his or her opponent in a given state gets all of that state's electoral votes.

Historically, triumphant presidential candidates have won both the popular vote and the Electoral College. However, since 2000, presidential elections have twice been determined by the Electoral College only: The declared winner (George W. Bush in 2000 and Donald J. Trump in 2016) did not win the popular vote.

Questions for Consideration

- What would be the key challenges to abolishing the Electoral College?

- The Electoral College system seems to promote the reproduction of a two-party system in the United States. How does it do that? Is the two-party system beneficial to good governance?

- How do other developed democratic states elect their leaders? What might we learn from studying the practices of, for instance, multiparty states in Europe such as France or Belgium?

Debate Tip

- Don't attack your opponents. Point out the inconsistencies and irrationalities of your opponent's argument using appropriate language and gestures.

AFFIRMATIVE ARGUMENTS	OPPOSITION ARGUMENTS
The electoral college system was initially put into place by the founding fathers to ensure that the uninformed masses were not making an uneducated vote. Today, there is enough information available about the candidates that the electorate can make an informed decision on who should be president.	With a popular vote for the presidency, the voices of less populous states would potentially be underrepresented, as they could be overpowered by densely populated regions. The Electoral College protects the interest of smaller, more rural, and less populated areas.
With the electoral college system in place, states considered "swing states" get most of the candidates' attention. States that are strongly Republican or Democratic do not get much attention from the candidates on the campaign trail because their electors are broadly perceived as falling into one or the other party's electoral vote tally.	The Electoral College was created by the founders with the intention of having decisions about the presidency made by an informed group of individuals. There is mixed evidence about how well-informed the U.S. electorate is about candidates.
There is no guarantee that a state's electors will vote for the candidate chosen by their state's voters: This is the phenomenon of the "faithless elector." In general, electors tend to be true to their state population's preference, but there is no guarantee of this.	The Electoral College helps maintain the federalism of the United States, as voting practices in a given state are determined by that state's own laws. For instance, some states may choose to permit early voting or same-day registration, whereas others may not.

local people plummets, and economic pain is acute. How, in modern society, does our hypothetical city (which has hundreds of authentic counterparts in the United States) respond? Does it erupt in revolutionary fervor, with displaced laborers calling for class struggle? Or do people look to their local, state, and federal governments to provide relief in the form of tax cuts or credits, unemployment benefits, and plans for attracting new industries?

The citizenry of modern capitalism, says Habermas, does not widely question the legitimacy of capitalism. If there is a crisis, it is political, and it is solved with policies that may smooth capitalism's bumpy ride. In a sense, the state becomes the focus of discontent—in a democracy, political decision makers can be changed and a crisis averted. The economic system that brings many of these crises into being, however, remains in shadow, its legitimacy rarely questioned.

In the next part of the chapter, we look into some of the other challenges confronted by states and their populations, including war and terrorism. States are key players in modern warfare, and military conflict is an important domestic political issue and global concern. Terrorism has also become increasingly entwined with war today, as recent wars undertaken by the United States, for instance, have been part of an effort to combat the threat of terrorism.

War, State, and Society

Conflict between ethnic or religious groups, states, and other social entities has a long history. War has been part of human societies, cultures, and practices in some form for millennia. In the 5th century BC, the ancient Greeks created a game called *petteia,* the first board game known to have been modeled on war. In the 6th century AD, chess, another game of strategic battle, was born in northern India; it developed into its modern form by the 15th century. Military training in ancient Greece also gave birth to the first Olympic Games. In the 20th century, war games took on far more advanced forms, ranging from battlefield exercises used to prepare for defensive or offensive war to sophisticated computer simulations used for both popular entertainment and military readiness training (Homans, 2011).

Today, the countries of the world spend trillions of dollars preparing for war or fighting in wars. At the same time, armed conflict and associated casualties have declined (Figures 14.9 and 14.10). Goldstein (2011) suggests that the nature of armed conflict has changed, shifting from larger wars in which powerful state actors confronted one another directly (such as World War II or the Korean War of the 1950s) to asymmetrical guerrilla wars, such as those the U. S. has fought in Iraq and Afghanistan in the past decade. He notes,

> Worldwide, deaths caused directly by war-related violence in the new century have averaged about 55,000 per year, just over half of what they were in the 1990s (100,000 a year), a third of what they were during the Cold War (180,000 a year from 1950 to 1989), and a hundredth of what they were in World War II. (p. 53)

Whatever the forms war has taken, it has been a key part of the human experience throughout history. What explains its existence and persistence? Recall from earlier chapters that

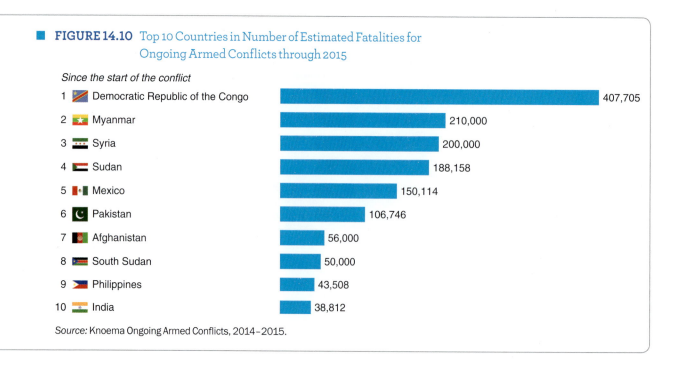

■ **FIGURE 14.10** Top 10 Countries in Number of Estimated Fatalities for Ongoing Armed Conflicts through 2015

Since the start of the conflict

	Country	Fatalities
1	Democratic Republic of the Congo	407,705
2	Myanmar	210,000
3	Syria	200,000
4	Sudan	188,158
5	Mexico	150,114
6	Pakistan	106,746
7	Afghanistan	56,000
8	South Sudan	50,000
9	Philippines	43,508
10	India	38,812

Source: Knoema Ongoing Armed Conflicts, 2014–2015.

manifest functions are intended and obvious, while *latent functions* are hidden, unexpected, or "nonpurposive" (in Robert Merton's words). Functionalists look at a phenomenon or an institution that exists in society, assert that its existence presupposes a function, and ask what that function is. If something did not serve a function, it would cease to exist. Does war have a function? We begin with a functionalist perspective on war, considering its role and consequences at the macro and micro societal levels.

A Functionalist Perspective on War

What are the manifest functions of war? Historically, one function has been to gain territory. The Roman Empire (27 BC–476 AD) waged war on surrounding territories, acquiring a substantial swath of the Middle East, including Cleopatra's Egypt, and then holding it with its massive armies. Another manifest function of war is to gain control of the natural resources of another state, while a third is to prevent the disintegration of a territorial unit. The American Civil War (1861–1865) sought to avert the secession of the South, which still favored slavery, from the North, which sought to abolish slavery.

What about the latent functions of war? First, war has historically operated as a stimulus to the economy: The term **war economy** refers to *the phenomenon of war boosting economic productivity and employment, particularly in capital- and labor-intensive sectors such as industrial production.* Notably, however, the wars in which the United States took part in the 20th century were fought outside its borders, and the benefits to the U.S. economy, especially in the World War II era, were not necessarily repeated elsewhere. The Soviet Union, France, Belgium, Poland, and many other European countries on whose territory World War II was waged emerged with shattered economies.

As well, the first wars in which the United States has engaged in the 21st century—the conflict in Afghanistan that began in October 2001 and the military occupation of Iraq, which began in March 2003—have arguably had negative effects on the U.S. economy and have failed to benefit all but a few large corporations in the defense and energy sectors.

A second latent function of war is the fostering of patriotism and national pride. In times of war, governments implore their citizens to rally around the national cause, and citizens may display their patriotism with flags or demonstrations. Even those who oppose military action may shy away from open opposition in a climate of war-inspired patriotism: During the early years of the conflict in Iraq, officials of President George W. Bush's administration several times chastised those who expressed criticism of the president and his actions "in a time of war," raising the question of whether dissent was unpatriotic.

A third latent function of war is its effect on family life and demographics. In the post–World War II years, the United States (and a number of other countries that had participated in the conflict) experienced a "baby boom," partially the product of the return of men who had been away at war and of childbearing postponed in the war years.

Of course, family life and individual lives are also prone to the deep dysfunctional consequences of war. With the long absence or loss of a father, husband, or son (or mother, wife, or daughter), families may be drawn closer together or they may break apart. They may experience economic deprivation with the loss of an income. A spouse who has not previously worked outside the home may be compelled by circumstances to join the labor force. War may also have disproportionate effects on different socioeconomic classes, as history shows that it has often been members of the working class who bear the greatest burden in war fighting. Clearly, war has a spectrum of manifest and latent functions as well as dysfunctions.

A Conflict Perspective on War

The conflict perspective suggests that some groups benefit from a given social order or phenomenon at the expense of others. We can turn a conflict-oriented lens on war to ask, "Who benefits from war? Who loses?"

While we might be inclined to answer that the war's victor wins and the defeated state or social group loses, the conflict perspective offers us the opportunity to construct a more nuanced picture. Consider the conflict in Iraq that began with the U.S. occupation of that country in March 2003: The war commenced as an effort to topple the dictatorial regime of Saddam Hussein, which was believed by President George W. Bush and some of his political allies to possess weapons of mass destruction (though none were subsequently found in the country). While most troops were withdrawn in 2011, a small number reengaged in 2014 as the United States sought to support Iraq's fight for stability and battles against ISIS militants who had launched deadly terror attacks against soldiers and civilians. Who benefited from the war in Iraq that commenced in 2003?

Beneficiaries of any conflict include those who are freed from oppressive state policies or structures or from ongoing persecution by the defeat of a regime. Among the beneficiaries in Iraq, we might count the minority Kurdish population, who were victims of Saddam Hussein's genocidal

---

War economy: The phenomenon of war boosting economic productivity and employment, particularly in capital- and labor-intensive sectors such as industrial production.

attacks in 1987 and 1988 and were threatened by the Iraqi dictator's presence. Were the rest of the people of Iraq beneficiaries? To the degree that Saddam was an oppressive political tyrant, the answer may be yes; Saddam's ruling Báath Party, composed primarily of Sunni Muslims, persecuted the majority Shiite Muslim population of the country, particularly after some Shiites sought to foment an uprising at the end of the First Gulf War (1990–1991). Ordinary Sunni Muslims as well had no voice in the single-party state that Saddam ruled with a strong hand. At the same time, the long war has led to thousands of civilian and military casualties, fundamentally destabilized the country, and left it with a badly damaged economy and infrastructure. Today, Iraq continues to be plagued by *sectarian violence*—that is, violence between religious groups—that presents, together with ISIS violence, an existential threat to the country itself.

Other beneficiaries of the nearly decade-long Iraq War were corporations (mostly U.S.–based) that profited from lucrative government contracts to supply weapons and other military supplies. War generates casualties and destruction—it also generates profits. In assessing who benefits from war, we cannot overlook capitalist enterprises for which war is a business and investment opportunity. Among those who benefit directly from war and conflict are private military corporations (PMCs), which provide military services such as training, transportation, and the protection of human resources and infrastructure. The use of private contractors in war has a long history. The new U.S. government, fighting against the British in the American Revolution, paid private merchant ships to sink enemy ships and steal their cargo. The modern military term *company,* which refers to an organized formation of 200 soldiers, comes from the private "companies" of mercenaries who were hired to fight in conflicts during the Middle Ages in Europe.

At the same time, until recently, wars in the modern world were largely fought by the citizens of the nation-states involved. Sociologist Katherine McCoy (2009) writes,

> Scholars have long thought of fighting wars as something nation-states did through their citizens. Max Weber famously defined the modern state as holding a monopoly over the legitimate use of violence, meaning that only state agents—usually soldiers or police—were allowed to wield force. (p. 15)

In today's conflicts, governments, including the U.S. government, increasingly rely on PMCs to provide a vast array of services that used to be functions of the governments or their militaries. This situation raises critical questions about the accountability and control of these private armies, which are motivated by profit rather than patriotism (McCoy, 2009). The rise of PMCs has been driven by reductions in the size of armies since the end of the Cold War, the availability of smaller advanced weaponry, and a political-ideological trend toward the privatization and outsourcing of activities previously conducted by governments (Singer, 2003).

The conflict perspective on war also asks, "Who loses?" Losers, of course, include those on both sides of a conflict who lose their lives, limbs, or livelihoods in war. Increasingly, according to some reports, they have been civilians, not soldiers. By one estimate, in World War I, about 5% of casualties were civilians (Swiss & Giller, 1993). In World War II, the figure has been estimated at 50% (Gutman & Rieff, 1999). While some researchers argue that the figure is much higher (Swiss & Giller, 1993), Goldstein (2011) suggests that the ratio of civilian to military casualties has remained at about 50:50 into the 21st century. Specific casualty figures also vary widely, often depending on the

A terrorist attack on the United States on September 11, 2001, brought down the World Trade Center Towers in New York City. A memorial has been built on the site that honors the victims of the terror attack, which included the airplane passengers, occupants of the towers, and many first responders.

methodologies and motivations of the organizations or governments doing the counting.

What about the less-apparent losers? Who else pays the costs of war? Modern military action has substantial financial costs, which are largely borne by taxpayers. In the decade between 2001, when the United States was the victim of terrorist attacks, and 2011, when the Iraq War ended and the war in Afghanistan began to wind down, the country spent an estimated $7.6 trillion on defense and homeland security. Even since the end of active U.S. engagement in Iraq and Afghanistan, the United States has continued to devote a substantial part of its federal budget to the Departments of Defense and Homeland Security. At the same time, many U.S. domestic programs in areas such as education, job training, and environmental conservation have lost funding as budgets have shrunk. Growth in the defense and security allocations of the federal budget has not been without costs.

In the next section, we consider the phenomena of terrorists and terrorism, which have been drivers—and consequences—of some of the world's most recent armed conflicts.

Terrorists and Terrorism

The "global war on terror" was initiated in 2001 after the September 11 attacks on the United States, which claimed 2,996 victims, as four commercial airliners were hijacked by Al-Qaeda terrorists. Two of the planes were crashed by the hijackers into New York City's World Trade Center towers, one into the Pentagon in Washington, DC, and one by desperate and heroic passengers into the ground in western Pennsylvania to thwart a fourth attack. The unprecedented events of September 2001 brought terrorism and terrorists more fully than ever into the U.S. experience and consciousness. The political response was to refocus domestic priorities on the war on terror and homeland security, drawing resources and attention from other areas such as education and immigration reform. Terrorism became a key theme of U.S. politics, policies, and spending priorities and a subject of concern and discussion among diplomats, decision makers, and ordinary citizens.

The terms *terrorist* and *terrorism,* however, are broad and may not be defined or understood in the same ways across groups or countries. Acts of violence labeled by one group as terrorism may be embraced as heroic by another. The label of terrorist may be inconsistently applied depending on the ethnicity, religion, actions, and motivations of an individual or a group. Below, we examine these concepts and consider their usage with a critical eye.

Who Is a Terrorist?

Close your eyes and picture a terrorist. Why do you think that particular image appeared to you? The images we generate are culturally conditioned by the political environment, the mass media, and the experiences we have, and they differ across communities, countries, and cultures. The idea of a terrorist is not the same across communities because, as we will see below, violent acts condemned by one community may be embraced by another as necessary sacrifices in the pursuit of political ends.

It has been said that one person's terrorist is another person's freedom fighter. Michael Collins was born in West Cork, Ireland, in 1890. Before he turned 20, he had sworn allegiance to the Irish Republican Brotherhood, a group of revolutionaries struggling for Irish independence from three centuries of British rule, and he worked and fought with them throughout the first decades of the 20th century. In Ireland and Northern Ireland today, Collins is widely regarded as a hero (Coogan, 2002). The 1996 film *Michael Collins,* starring Liam Neeson and Julia Roberts, cast him in a generally positive light: The film's tagline declared, "Ireland, 1916. His dreams inspired hope. His words inspired passion. His courage forged a nation's destiny."

In Britain, however, many consider Collins to be a terrorist. In 1920, while he was director of intelligence for the Irish Republican Army (IRA), his secret service squad assassinated 14 British officers (Coogan, 2002). The British responded to the IRA with violence as well. Notably, the Continuity Irish Republican Army continues to be on the U.S. Department of State's (2012a) global list of terrorist groups.

Was Michael Collins a terrorist or a hero? How do we judge Britain's violent military response? The label of *terrorist* is a subjective one, conditioned by whether one rejects or sympathizes with the motives and actions under discussion. As an expert on terrorism notes, "If one party can successfully attach the label *terrorist* to its opponent, then it has indirectly persuaded others to adopt its moral viewpoint" (Hoffman, 2006, p. 23).

The issue is, arguably, more complex when it involves acts of mass violence perpetrated by domestic terrorists, for example, incidents in the United States committed by U.S. citizens or residents. On April 20, 1995, 168 people perished in the bombing of a federal building in Oklahoma City, Oklahoma. While initial media suspicion pointed to foreign perpetrators, further investigation determined that American Timothy McVeigh, with the cooperation of a small group of antigovernment compatriots, was responsible for the crime. In the wake of the incident, the U.S. government increased its scrutiny of domestic threats. The terrorist incidents of September 11, 2001, which were perpetrated by Islamic radicals, shifted attention to the Middle East, including Afghanistan and, later, Iraq and Pakistan, among others.

Recent incidents of mass shootings in the United States have refocused attention on domestic threats to peace and security. Among a spate of incidents in recent years are the following: In June of 2015, Dylan Roof murdered nine African American churchgoers during a prayer service in North Carolina. Roof later indicated that he had hoped to ignite a "race war." In June of 2016, Omar Mateen killed 49 people at a gay nightclub in Florida. During a call to 911, Mateen pledged allegiance to the Middle Eastern terror group, ISIS. In July of 2016, Micah Xavier Johnson shot to death five Dallas police officers who were working at a peaceful rally by Black Lives Matter activists. Johnson's online activities suggest he sought to target White officers in particular because he was angry about the killings of Black men by law enforcement. In October of 2017, Stephen Paddock opened fire in a crowd of 22,000 in Las Vegas, killing 58. After the shooting, Paddock was found dead in his hotel room from a self-inflicted gunshot wound. In February of 2018, a former student, Nikolas Cruz, opened fire in a Florida high school, killing 17. Cruz was expelled from the school the year prior for disciplinary problems. In May of 2018, Dimitrios Pagourtzis Jr. entered his Texas high school with a shotgun and pistol, opened fire, and killed 10. According to a police report, Pagourtzis stated that he did not shoot the students he liked so that his story could be told (Martin, Berman, Achenbach, & Wang, 2018).

In 2014, the U.S. Department of Justice relaunched the work of a group focused on domestic threats. As a Council on Foreign Relations publication points out, however, there is inconsistency in understandings and legal approaches to what terrorism is and whether domestic and international incidents of violence both fall under that term (Masters, 2011). Are individuals or small groups in the United States who target government buildings, public events, or other groups for violence *terrorists*? What is the significance of using that term rather than *criminal* or even *violent extremist*?

What Is Terrorism?

There is no single definition of **terrorism**. The U.S. Department of Defense (2011) defines it as "*the unlawful use of violence or threat of violence to instill fear and coerce governments or societies. Terrorism is often motivated by religious, political, or other ideological beliefs and committed in the pursuit of goals that are usually political.*" The years following the terror attacks of September 11, 2001, have seen a rise in the number of victims of terror attacks. Recently, several high-profile attacks having taken place in Europe, including the May 2017 explosion of a homemade bomb at an Ariana Grande concert in Manchester, England, where 22 people (including children) were killed. In August of 2017, in Barcelona, Spain, terrorists used a van to attack pedestrians, leaving 13 people dead and more than 100 injured. Most deaths from mass terror incidents, however, take place in countries outside of Europe and the West generally: by one estimate, in 2016, 75% of terror deaths were concentrated in ten countries, including Iraq, Afghanistan, Pakistan, Syria, Yemen, and Nigeria (Chou, 2017).

The Federal Bureau of Investigation (FBI) definition of terrorism adds another layer to the phenomenon. The FBI highlights *terrorism* as "the unlawful use of force or violence against persons or property to intimidate or coerce a government, the civilian population, or any segment thereof, in furtherance of political or social objectives" (National Institute of Justice, 2011). While the FBI definition echoes the definitions used by other sectors of the U.S. government in its attention to terrorism's function as an instrument of intimidation and coercion, its attention to the destruction of property, particularly critical infrastructure, may signal the agency's interest in a contemporary manifestation of terrorism, **cyberterrorism**, which entails "*hacking into government and private computer systems and crippling the military, financial, and service sectors of advanced economies*" (Weimann, 2004). For example, banks in some countries have been targeted: In 2011, "South Korean officials said that 30 million customers of the Nonghyup agricultural bank were unable to use ATMs or online services for several days and that key data were destroyed" when North Korea launched a cyberattack on its neighbor (Harlan & Nakashima, 2011). South Korean banks have also been subject to viruses that wipe hard drives of information, rendering the data permanently irretrievable. In 2013, a group calling itself the Syrian Electronic Army launched a denial-of-service attack against media organizations, including the *Washington Post* and the *New York Times*, temporarily rendering the sites unreachable by readers. Critical infrastructure such as

---

Terrorism: "the unlawful use of violence or threat of violence to instill fear and coerce governments or societies. Terrorism is often motivated by religious, political, or other ideological beliefs and committed in the pursuit of goals that are usually political" (U.S. Department of Defense, 2011).

Cyberterrorism: "Hacking into government and private computer systems and crippling the military, financial, and service sectors of advanced economies" (Weimann, 2004).

In 2017 and 2018, large-scale terror acts committed by attackers affiliated with or sympathetic to ISIS claimed many lives. The Ariana Grande concert in Manchester, England (left), and Kabul, Afghanistan (right), were among the scenes of terror.

power grids is also widely considered to be vulnerable to cyberterrorism (Gregg, 2014).

According to the National Institute of Justice (2011), Title 22 of the U.S. Code, Section 2656f(d) defines *terrorism* as "premeditated, politically motivated violence perpetrated against noncombatant targets by subnational groups or clandestine agents, usually intended to influence an audience." Note the attention in this definition to the presence of an audience. This definition points more deliberately to terrorism as an instrument of horrific political theater whose direct victims are props on the stage of a larger political or ideological play. While such "media-oriented terrorism" does not, by one analysis, make up the majority of the terror acts of the past half century, it is widespread and has historical roots in the acts of 19th-century anarchists, who pioneered the concept of "propaganda of the deed" (Surette, Hansen, & Noble, 2009).

In some sense, the media offers a stage for acts of atrocity, not only functioning as reporters of terror events but also conditioning terrorist groups' selection of targets and actions (see the *Social Life, Social Media* box in this chapter). Media attention, which has expanded from the print media and television to include the Internet, the "Twitterverse," and other new media, has a powerful multiplier effect on modern terrorism, offering a broad platform of publicity even for small and relatively weak groups or "lone wolf" terrorists whose combat and political capabilities are otherwise very limited (Surette et al., 2009). Indeed, according to one report, "lone wolf" attackers were responsible for 70% of the terror deaths in Western countries between 2005 and 2015 (Institute for Economics and Peace, 2015).

Notably, the success of some nations in building strong, centralized militaries may have contributed to terrorism's spread in both developed and developing states. As an effective form of asymmetric conflict, terrorism is one of the few avenues open to those who want power, attention, or change yet lack the military means to challenge dominant global powers directly. Robert Pape (2005) has pointed to terrorism as a weapon of the weak. Based on his analysis of 315 incidences of suicide terrorism between 1980 and 2003, he concluded that a consistent causal logic of these events was the attempt to exercise coercive power against a stronger state perceived as a homeland occupier.

As of this writing, the United Nations Comprehensive Convention on International Terrorism remains in draft form, subject to debate and negotiation, particularly over language that highlights terrorism's roots in the motive to "intimidate a population, or to compel a Government or an international organization to do or abstain from doing any act." At issue here, among other things, is what constitutes the line between an act of terrorism and an act of war. Is an act of war by a state an act of "politically motivated violence" and therefore subject to the convention's regulation? Leaders also debate whether to include in the definition of terrorist groups national "liberation movements," examples of which could be the Irish Republican Army, Palestinian movements such as Hamas, and Kurdish militants in Turkey. Those who support the aims of such groups say no. In light of the fact that perceptions of a given act may differ widely across groups and countries, is a global definition of terrorism even possible? Is it necessary in order to address the threat of violence to states and civilian populations with global action? What do you think?

Social Life, Social Media

THE TERROR SHOW

Social media has become a fundamental part of contemporary terrorism. If, as Timothy Furnish (2005) writes, "the purpose of terrorism is to strike fear into the hearts of opponents in order to win political concession," then social media has multiplied the effects of acts of terror, expanding the audience for horrific violence and transforming atrocities into media shows that can be played over and over again.

The terror group called the Islamic State (also known as ISIS [the Islamic State of Iraq and Syria] and ISIL [the Islamic State of Iraq and the Levant]) has used Twitter, Facebook, YouTube, and other sites to disseminate images of the killing of soldiers and civilians and the destruction of communities across their Middle Eastern battlegrounds. ISIS, according to reports, is an offshoot of Al-Qaeda, the terror group that claimed responsibility for the attacks in the United States on September 11, 2001. While both Al-Qaeda and ISIS are adherents of an extreme brand of Sunni Islam, the two groups apparently broke over ISIS's unfettered willingness to slaughter Muslim civilians. A writer on the *Vox Media* news website, writing of ISIS's use of images depicting atrocities against Iraqi soldiers, has pointed out that the multitude of graphic images is not merely

ISIS bragging about their murderousness. ISIS has a well-developed social media presence, which they're using deliberately in this campaign to do two things: intimidate Iraqis who might oppose them and win supporters in their battle with Al-Qaeda for influence over

This Facebook page is just one of thousands of ISIS social media accounts. When social media sites shut down accounts, new ones quickly spring up in their place.

the international Islamist extremist movement. (Beauchamp, 2014)

Indeed, dissemination of fear is not the only function of ISIS's use of social media and the Internet. It has been widely used to entice new recruits, particularly in Western countries. ISIS employs slickly produced videos glamorizing violence and touting its military successes; most videos, in an effort to appeal to foreign recruits, are produced in English, German, or French (NBC News, 2015). As documented by the *Washington Post*, "Social-media sites used by Islamic State fighters . . . have included numerous accounts of the buying and selling of sex slaves," women whom ISIS captured as they grabbed territory in Syria and Iraq (Warrick, 2016). Previously, ISIS has used its online magazine, *Dabiq*, to offer up foreign hostages it has captured for ransom (Clarion Project, 2014).

ISIS's use of social media appears carefully managed. On Twitter, for example, it involves tweeting at regular intervals and choosing hashtags that will reach the audiences it seeks (Beauchamp, 2014). A study by the Brookings Institution of ISIS's use of Twitter notes that "in October through November 2014, at least 46,000 Twitter accounts were used by ISIS supporters." The social media platform has become active in responding to its use by terror groups and supporters, however. "Thousands of accounts have been suspended by Twitter since October 2014, measurably degrading ISIS's ability to project its propaganda to wider audiences." While new accounts are created as existing feeds are suspended, those appear to lag in terms of replacing the accounts deleted by Twitter (Berger, 2015). Facebook has also been active in suspending pages associated with ISIS; images of the female sex slaves being offered for sale were quickly deleted by the company (Warrick, 2016). In response, ISIS and its supporters have turned to other less-regulated platforms such as the Russia-based Telegram Messenger, on which users can broadcast messages via "channels" (Berger & Perez, 2016). Interestingly, ISIS may be turning away from its prodigious earlier use of social media: In May 2017, the group issued a ban on individual social media posts by its "soldiers," noting that for security reasons, the group's official propaganda wing would manage its online activities (Price & Al-Ubaydi, 2017).

Clearly, it is horrifying when social media platforms, most of which have codes of conduct, are used to disseminate violent and disturbing images. At the same time, it has been suggested that shocking images can impel the international community toward action in some cases (Chandler, 2014). They may also offer the documentation that countries and the international community need to prosecute killers for the crimes they have chosen to glorify.

While fundamentalist terror groups such as ISIS embrace an archaic, violent, and deeply conservative interpretation of Islam, their means of sharing their bloody battles, extremist ideology, and brutalized victims are thoroughly modern.

Think It Through

- Images of and calls for extreme violence have been targeted by social media companies for deletion, but what about the social media presence of other groups, including those in the United States, that disseminate hate and call in subtle or not-so-subtle language for violence? How should social media companies distinguish between acceptable and unacceptable content?

Follow us on Twitter to keep up with current sociological stories and research! We're at **@DiscoverSoc1.**

Share your own ideas at **#DiscoverSociology.**

Why Study the State and Warfare through a Sociological Lens?

In the modern world, politics and the state directly affect the lives of everyone. Understanding how politics and the state work is essential to our lives as informed, active local and global citizens. In this chapter, we have inquired into the processes that directly affect the functioning of the state and politics and into state decision making, including the decision to go to war. In the face of the apparently overwhelming power of the state and the seeming distance of political decision-making from the lives of most people, it is easy for us to shrug our shoulders and feel powerless. Yet one of the lessons we learn from the sociological analysis of the state and politics is that both are subject to influence by ordinary citizens, especially when people are mobilized into social movements and interest groups, politically aware, and able to evaluate politics and policies critically. Public ignorance and apathy benefit those who use politics to ensure their own or their social groups' well-being; active citizenship is an authentic instrument of power, even where it faces significant obstacles.

Understanding issues of state and politics also helps us understand the roots and consequences of armed conflict. Wars are the products of choices made by leaders—usually the civilian or military leaders of countries or empires. Wars do not just happen. In understanding war, we benefit from recognizing the ways in which it confers benefits and incurs costs. Those with power make calculations and choices. Those without power—women and children and sometimes citizens and soldiers—do not make such choices, though they may pay the cost. While war is a reality in our world, we need to move beyond a simple understanding of war as an inevitable part of the human experience to recognize its more complex and less obvious sociological elements. Perhaps with a better understanding of war and its motivations and consequences, we can help to clear a path to greater civility and peace in the world.

Robert Merton (1968) posited the idea of functional alternatives. If we recognize that war has functions (as we have seen in this chapter), we might also begin to imagine *functional alternatives*—that is, other means of realizing those functions. For instance, if war has a manifest function of acquiring access to needed or desired natural resources such as oil or water, perhaps greater conservation of the resources would diminish the need for aggressive action to secure access. If war acts as a way of resolving territorial disputes, perhaps creative diplomatic thinking can begin to carry us toward more nonmilitary alternatives. If war is also functional in fostering patriotism, perhaps a country could construct national pride and patriotism on a foundation other than the battlefield of glory and sacrifice, as so many countries do.

Social change demands imagination—a changed world must be imagined before it can be realized. While a future without war seems unimaginable, our expanded understanding of this phenomenon may give us some of the tools we need to make it less probable and less costly to civilians and soldiers alike.

What Can I Do with a Sociology Degree?

WRITTEN COMMUNICATION SKILLS

Written communication is an essential skill for a broad spectrum of 21st-century careers. Sociology students have many opportunities to practice and sharpen written communication skills. Among others, sociologists learn to write *theoretically*, applying classical and contemporary theories to construct an analysis of social issues and phenomena, and to write *empirically*, preparing and communicating evidence-based arguments about the social world. Sociology majors write papers in a variety of forms and for a variety of audiences; these may include reaction papers, book reviews, theoretical analyses, research papers, quantitative analysis reports, field note write-ups, letters to decision makers or newspaper editors, and reflections on sociological activities or experiences. Excellent written communication is fundamental in many occupational fields, including politics, business and entrepreneurship, communications and marketing, law and criminal justice, community organizing and advocacy, journalism, higher education, law, and public relations.

Michelle Berger, Research Associate

The George Washington University, BA in Sociology, Minor in Classical and Near Eastern Studies

The goal of Higher Education Services is to provide educational institutions with research, best practices, and peer examples to inform important decisions. As a research associate, I compile this information into digestible, data-driven scripting for our account management team to send to administrators and other key education stakeholders. Every day, I draw from my working knowledge of the company's library of studies and resources in order to craft responses to specific questions or initiatives from our member institutions (colleges, universities, state university systems, and K–12 school districts).

One of the most important traits for someone to have in order to be a successful research associate is to be detail oriented. For example, noticing the unique characteristics of an educational institution might guide me to a specific resource that would be perfect to send to them. Or I might remember a small but relevant detail from a study I read weeks ago, and that will form the foundation of my entire response to a question from an administrator. Luckily, I am part of a great team of fellow research associates and research managers who are all here to help one another write detailed, accurate deliverables.

If you want to be a research associate, hone your writing skills. It is not always obvious how our existing research applies to emerging situations and questions in the education sector. So, a big part of my job is writing up our findings in a way that "connects the dots" for people like provosts and deans without too much time on their hands. I am constantly thinking in terms of trends, so that I can match up different education institutions with the resources that will be most relevant for them. I am expected to use my best judgement about what to include and how to write about it. My ability to synthesize empirical and conceptual information into comprehensible written advice forms the basis of my job.

The best part about my job is that I get to learn every day! Whether it is about the best type of meal plan to offer at a mid-sized state school or the most effective advising structure to use in order to reach first-generation college students at risk of dropping out, I am always learning. Then, through written communication, I pass this information along to people who can truly make a difference in the lives of students.

Career Data: Operations Research Analysts

- 2017 Median Pay: $81,390 per year
- $39.13 per hour
- Typical Entry-Level Education: Bachelor's degree
- Job Outlook, 2016–2026: 27% (Much faster than usual)

Source: Bureau of Labor Statistics, *Occupational Outlook Handbook,* 2017.

SUMMARY

- The world today is politically divided into 195 **nation-states**. Most countries are made up of many different peoples, brought together through warfare, conquest, or boundaries drawn by colonial authorities without respect to preexisting ethnic or religious differences.

- Modern countries are characterized by governments that claim complete and final authority over their **citizens**, systems of **law**, and notions of citizenship that contain obligations as well as civil, social, and political rights.

- State power is typically based on one of three kinds of legitimate authority: **traditional authority**, based on custom and tradition; **rational-legal authority**, based on a belief in the law; or **charismatic authority**, based on the perceived inspirational qualities of a leader.

- Functionalist theories of power argue that the role of the government is to mediate neutrally between competing interests; they assert that the influence of one group is usually offset by that of another group with an opposing view. Conflict theories of state power draw the opposite conclusion: The state serves the interests of the most powerful economic and political groups in society. Different versions of social conflict theories emphasize the importance of a **power elite**, structural contradictions, and the relative autonomy of state power from the economic elites.

- Governance in the modern world takes a number of forms, including **authoritarianism** (including **monarchies** and **dictatorships**), **totalitarianism**, and democracy.

- Democracy is one of the primary forms of governance in the world today, and most countries claim to be democratic in theory (if not in practice). Most democratic countries practice **representative democracy** rather than **direct democracy**.

- The U.S. political system is characterized by low voter turnouts. Voter participation varies, however, on the basis of demographic variables such as age and education.

- In the United States, elected officials depend heavily on financial support to get elected and to remain in office. Fund-raising is a major part of **politics**, and individuals and organizations that contribute heavily do so in hopes of influencing politicians. Special interests use **lobbyists** to exercise influence in U.S. politics. Politicians still depend on their constituents' votes to get elected, and so they must satisfy voters as well as special interests.

- We can examine war from various sociological perspectives. The functionalist perspective asks about the manifest (obvious) and latent (hidden) functions of war and conflict in society. The conflict perspective asks who benefits from war and conflict and who loses.

- The "global war on terror" was initiated in 2001 after the September 11 terrorist attacks on U.S. soil. The United States and its allies are fighting terror threats domestically, globally, and online.

- No single image of a terrorist is shared across communities and countries and cultures. Irishman Michael Collins is an example of someone regarded as a hero by some and a terrorist by others. **Terrorism** is a calculated use of violence to coerce or to inspire fear. It is also "theater"—intended to send a powerful message to a distinct or a global audience. A newer form of terrorism that targets critical infrastructure rather than populations directly is **cyberterrorism**.

KEY TERMS

nation-state, 383	traditional authority, 389	politics, 393
law, 384	rational-legal authority, 390	political action committees
citizens, 384	charismatic authority, 390	(PACs), 400
noncitizens, 384	authoritarianism, 391	lobbyists, 400
welfare state, 384	monarchy, 391	war economy, 405
interest groups, 387	dictatorship, 391	terrorism, 408
class dominance theory, 388	totalitarianism, 392	cyberterrorism, 408
power elite, 389	direct democracy, 393	
coercion, 389	representative democracy, 393	

DISCUSSION QUESTIONS

1. In this chapter, you learned about theories of state power. Would you say that U.S. governance today is characterized more by pluralism or by the concentration of power in the hands of an elite? Cite evidence supporting your belief.

2. What is authoritarianism? What potential roles do modern technology and social media play in either supporting or challenging authoritarian governments around the world?

3. The chapter raised the issue of low voting rates for young people. Recall the reasons given in the chapter and then think about whether you can add others. Do most of the young people you know participate in elections? What kinds of factors might explain their participation or nonparticipation?

4. What are the manifest and latent functions and dysfunctions of war? Review the points made in the chapter. Can you add some of your own?

5. What is terrorism? How should this term be defined and by whom? When should domestic incidents of mass violence be labeled terrorism? Explain your reasoning.

Want a better grade?

Get the tools you need to sharpen your study skills. Access practice quizzes, eFlashcards, videos, and multimedia at **https://edge.sagepub.com/chambliss4e**.

©Artyom Geodakyan\TASS via Getty Images

Work, Consumption, and the Economy

15

WHAT DO YOU THINK?

1. What will be the role of robots and artificial intelligence in the future economy? Will these technologies replace human workers? Or will they contribute to the creation of new jobs?

2. What kinds of jobs comprise the informal (or shadow) economy? Who works in the informal economy and why?

3. Why has average household debt grown in recent decades?

LEARNING OBJECTIVES

15.1 Describe the three major economic revolutions that have shaped the contemporary world.

15.2 Discuss current and potential effects of automation and artificial intelligence on the labor market.

15.3 Compare the economic characteristics of capitalism and communism.

15.4 Distinguish between the formal and informal economy.

15.5 Describe historical and contemporary trends in U.S. consumption and consumer debt.

15.6 Discuss the relationship between globalization and the U.S. economy.

ROBOTS AND JOBS

A recent article on the automation of restaurant labor in Japan begins as follows:

Visitors to Henn-na, a restaurant outside Nagasaki, Japan, are greeted by a peculiar sight: their food being prepared by a row of humanoid robots that bear a passing resemblance to the Terminator. The "head chef," incongruously named Andrew, specializes in *okonomiyaki*, a Japanese pancake. Using his two long arms, he stirs batter in a metal bowl, then pours it onto a hot grill. While he waits for the batter to cook, he talks cheerily in Japanese about how much he

©Zhong Zhenbin/Anadolu Agency/Getty Images

enjoys his job. His robot colleagues, meanwhile, fry donuts, layer soft-serve ice cream into cones, and mix drinks. (Semuels, 2018, para. 1)

The author notes that in Japan, with its aging population and barely growing workforce, robots appear to fill a void in the labor market. But what about in the U.S.? The article points out that a broad spectrum of restaurants, including Wendy's, Panera, and McDonald's, are shifting to kiosk-based ordering. Some well-known chains such as Olive Garden and Red Robin are also bringing out tablet ordering that will reduce or eliminate the need for wait staff and cashiers (Semuels, 2018). As in Japan, changes are also afoot in the kitchen: Economist Martin Ford (2015) quotes the co-founder of a robotics company that produced a machine that shapes burgers from ground meat and grills them precisely to order as saying, "Our device isn't meant to make employees more efficient … it's meant to completely obviate them" (12). By one estimate, over half of the tasks workers do in U.S. hotels and restaurants could be automated using only the technologies that are already available (Semuels, 2018).

While some restaurant owners claim that their goal is to improve the customer experience by moving employees out from the kitchen and from behind cash registers (Semuels, 2018), living workers are a significant cost to employers: About 30% of business costs in the industry are comprised by labor (DePillis, 2015). While robots are also costly, the chief executive officer (CEO) of the company that owns Henn-na points out that "since you can work them 24 hours a day, and they don't need a vacation, eventually it's more cost-efficient to use the robot" (Semuels, 2018, para. 3).

The restaurant industry is, however, a vital part of the U.S. employment picture and its significance has grown in the wake of manufacturing's decline. Indeed, by one estimate, food-service and accommodation jobs in the U.S. employ about 13.7 million workers (Semuels, 2018). These are jobs that have functioned for generations as stepping stones for young workers seeking a first job as well as the primary occupations of breadwinners who have not completed high school or college.

The road to robotic restaurants and hotels does not promise to be a smooth one, and there is little danger of an imminent decline in this employment sector. Recent reports indicate that several restaurants in China that were attempting to use robots as waitstaff had to "fire" them for a spectrum of customer service failures, including an inability to carry soup (Kraft, 2016). At the same time, automation and robotics, which have had a transformative effect on manufacturing in recent decades, promise to bring significant changes to the service sector, which includes hospitality and retail jobs, among others. But it will not stop there: Professional sectors from journalism to medicine to the law have the potential to be transformed by fast-moving technological innovations.

In this chapter, we discuss key issues in economic sociology and examine the implications of a new globalized economy—postindustrial, technologically sophisticated, and consumption oriented—for the world and for U.S. society in particular. We begin with a brief historical overview of the three great economic revolutions that have transformed human society. We then examine the characteristics and potential sociological implications of our evolving high-technology economy, focusing (as we did in the opening story) on the automation of jobs, robotics, artificial intelligence, and the future of work. We look at capitalism and communism, the two principal types of economic systems that dominated the

20th century and continue to influence the 21st century. Next, we turn to a discussion of work in the formal and informal economies. We also discuss social and economic issues of consumption, hyperconsumption, and debt. The chapter concludes with a discussion of the changes and challenges globalization has brought to our economic system and prospects.

The Economy in Historical Perspective

The **economy** is *the social institution that organizes the ways in which a society produces, distributes, and consumes goods and services.* By **goods**, we mean *objects that have an economic value to others, whether they are the basic necessities for survival* (a safe place to live, nutritious food to eat, weather-appropriate clothing) *or things that people simply want* (designer clothing, an iPhone, popcorn at the movies). **Services** are *economically productive activities that do not result directly in physical products; they can be relatively simple* (shining shoes, working a cash register, waiting tables at a restaurant) *or quite complex* (repairing an airplane engine or computer, conducting a medical procedure).

In human history, three technological revolutions have brought radically new forms of economic organization. The first led to the growth of agriculture several millennia ago, and the second led to modern industry some 250 years ago. We are now in the throes of the third revolution, which has carried us into a digital and postindustrial age.

The Agricultural Revolution and Agricultural Society

The agricultural revolution vastly increased human productivity over that of earlier hunting, gathering, and pastoral societies. This achievement was spurred by the development of innovations such as irrigation and crop rotation methods as well as by expanding knowledge about animal husbandry and the use of animals in agriculture. For example, the plow, which came into use about 5,000 years ago, had a transformational effect on agriculture when it was harnessed to a working animal. Greater productivity led to economic surplus. While the majority of people in agricultural societies still engaged in subsistence farming, an increasing number could produce surplus crops, which they could then barter or sell.

Eventually, specialized economic roles evolved. Some people were farmers; others were landowners who profited from farmers' labor. A number of families specialized in the making of handicrafts, working independently on items of their own design. This work gave rise to *cottage industries—* so called because the work was usually done at home.

The production of agricultural surpluses, as well as handicrafts, created an opportunity for yet another economic role to emerge—that of merchants, who specialized in trading surplus crops and crafted goods. Trading routes developed and permanent cities grew up along them, and the number and complexity of economic activities increased. By about the 15th century, early markets arose to

Economy: The social institution that organizes the ways in which a society produces, distributes, and consumes goods and services.

Goods: Objects that have an economic value to others, whether they are the basic necessities for survival or things that people simply want.

Services: Economically productive activities that do not result directly in physical products; they may be relatively simple or quite complex.

Karl Marx saw industrial workers as instruments of labor tethered to an exploitive system. One 19th-century British mother described her seven-year-old to a government commission: "He used to work 16 hours a day. . . . I have often knelt down to feed him, as he stood by the machine, for he could not leave it or stop" (quoted in Hochschild, 2003, p. 3).

©Public Domain—Library of Congress

serve as sites for the exchange of goods and services. Prices in markets were set (as they are in free markets today) at the point where *supply* (available goods and services) was balanced by *demand* (the degree to which those goods and services are wanted).

The Industrial Revolution and Industrial Society

The Industrial Revolution, which began in England with the harnessing of water and steam power to run machines such as looms, increased productivity still further. Cottage industries were replaced by factories—the hallmark of industrial society—and urban areas became centers of economic activity, attracting rural laborers seeking work and creating growing momentum for urbanization. Industrialization spread through Europe and the United States and then to the rest of the world. The change was massive. In 1810, about 84% of the U.S. workforce worked in agriculture and only 3% in manufacturing; by 1960, only 8% of all U.S. workers labored in agriculture and fully a quarter of the total workforce was engaged in manufacturing (Blinder, 2006).

Industrial society is characterized by the increased use of machinery and mass production, the centrality of the modern industrial laborer, and the development of a class society rooted in the modern division of labor.

Increased Use of Machinery and Mass Production

Machines increase the productive capacity of individual laborers by enabling them to efficiently produce more goods at lower cost. New machines have historically required new sources of energy as well: Waterwheels gave way to steam engines, then the internal combustion engine, and eventually, electricity and other modern forms of power.

In 1913, automobile mogul Henry Ford introduced a new system of manufacturing in his factories. **Mass production** is *the large-scale, highly standardized manufacturing of identical commodities on a mechanical assembly line.* Under Ford's new system, a continuous conveyor belt moved unfinished automobiles past individual workers, each of whom performed a specific operation on each automobile: One worker would attach the door, another the windshield, another the wheels. (The term *Fordism* is sometimes used to describe this system.) Mass production resulted in the development of large numbers of identical components and products that could be produced efficiently at lower cost. This linked system of production became a foundation for the evolution and expansion of productive industries that went far beyond auto manufacturing.

The Birth of the Industrial Laborer

With the birth of industry came the rise of the industrial labor force, comprising mostly migrants from poorer rural areas or abroad seeking their fortunes in growing cities. Often the number of would-be workers competing for available jobs created a surplus of labor. Karl Marx described this as a **reserve army of labor**, *a pool of job seekers whose numbers outpace the available positions and thus contribute to keeping wages low and conditions of work tenuous* (those who do not like the conditions of work are easy to replace with those seeking work).

If it is possible to create an assembly line on which each worker performs a single, repetitive task, why not design those tasks to be as efficient as possible? This was the goal of **scientific management**, *a practice that sought to use principles of engineering to reduce the physical movements of workers.* Frederick Winslow Taylor's *Principles of Scientific Management,* published in 1911, gave factory managers the information they needed to greatly increase their control over the labor process by giving explicit instructions to workers regarding how they would perform their well-defined tasks. While Taylor was focused on the goal of efficiency, "Taylorism" also had the consequence of further deskilling work. Deskilling rendered workers more vulnerable to layoffs, since they—like the components they were making—were standardized and therefore easily replaced (Braverman, 1974/1988).

Classes in Industrial Capitalism

New economic classes developed along with the rise of industrial capitalist society. One important new class was composed of industrialists who owned what Marx called the *means of production*—for example, factories. Another was made up of wage laborers—workers who did not own land, property, or tools. They had only their labor power to sell at the factory gate. Work in early industrial capitalism was demanding, highly regimented, and even hazardous. Workers labored at tedious tasks for 14 to 16 hours a day, six or seven days a week, and were at risk of losing their jobs if economic conditions turned unfavorable or if they raised too many objections (recall the concept of the *reserve army of labor*). The pool of exploitable labor was expanded by migrant workers from rural areas and abroad, and even children of poor families were sometimes forced to labor for wages.

Influenced by the poor conditions they saw in 19th-century English factories, Karl Marx and Friedrich Engels posited that these two classes—the *bourgeoisie*

Mass production: The large-scale, highly standardized manufacturing of identical commodities on a mechanical assembly line.

Reserve army of labor: A pool of job seekers whose numbers outpace the available positions and thus contribute to keeping wages low and conditions of work tenuous.

Scientific management: A practice that sought to use principles of engineering to reduce the physical movements of workers.

(capitalists) and the *proletariat* (working class)—would come into conflict. They argued in the *Manifesto of the Communist Party* (1848) that the bourgeoisie exploited the proletariat by appropriating the surplus value of their labor. That is, capitalists paid workers the minimum they could get away with and kept the remainder of the value generated by the finished products for themselves as profit or as a means to gather more productive capital in their own hands. The exploitation of wage labor by capitalists would, they believed, end in revolution and the end of private ownership of the means of production.

While some observers of early capitalism, including Marx and Engels, offered scathing critiques of the social and economic conditions of factory laborers, the early and middle decades of the 20th century (with the exception of the period of the Great Depression) witnessed improved conditions and opportunities for the blue-collar workforce in the United States. In the early 20th century, Henry Ford, the patriarch of Fordist production, took the audacious step of paying workers on his Model T assembly line in Michigan fully $5 for an 8-hour day, nearly three times the wage of a factory employee in 1914. Ford reasoned that workers who earned a solid wage would become consumers of products such as his Model T. Indeed, his workers bought, his profits grew, and industrial laborers (and, eventually, the workers of the unionized U.S. car industry) set off on a slow but steady path to the middle class (Reich, 2010).

The class structure that emerged from advanced industrial capitalism in the United States, Europe, Japan, Canada, and other modern states boasted substantial middle classes composed of workers who ranged from well-educated teachers and managers to industrial workers and mechanics with a high school or technical education. The fortunes of blue-collar and semiprofessional workers were boosted by a number of factors. Among these were extended periods of low unemployment in which workers had greater leverage in negotiating job conditions (Uchitelle, 2007). Unions supported autoworkers, railroad workers, and workers in many other industries in the negotiation of contracts that ensured living wages, job security, and benefits. Unionization surged following the Great Depression and the 1935 passage of the Wagner Act, which "guaranteed the rights of workers to join unions and bargain collectively" (VanGiezen & Schwenk, 2001), growing to more than 27% of the labor force by 1940. At their peak in 1979, U.S. unions claimed 21 million members (Mayer, 2004).

Changes in the U.S. economy have shaken the relatively stable middle class that emerged around the middle of the 20th century. Since the 1970s, mass layoffs have grown across industries, though manufacturing has been hardest (Uchitelle, 2007). As a result, today, the industrial laborer is less likely to belong to a union, less likely to have appreciable job security, and more likely to have experienced a decline in wages and benefits. Income gains have slipped, and, for many, membership in the U.S. middle class has become tenuous (Table 15.1).

The Information Revolution and Postindustrial Society

During the past quarter century, the "information revolution," which began with Intel's invention of the microchip in 1971, has altered economic life, accelerating changes in the organization of work that were already under way. Pressured by global competition that intensified by the end of the 1970s, U.S. firms began to move away from the inflexible Fordist system of mass production, seeking ways to accommodate rapid changes in products and production processes and to reduce high labor costs that were making U.S. products less competitive. Postindustrial economic organization

TABLE 15.1   Selected Characteristics of Industrial and Postindustrial Societies

CHARACTERISTIC	INDUSTRIAL SOCIETY	POSTINDUSTRIAL SOCIETY
Principal technology	Industrial machinery	Advanced technologies including computers, automation of tasks
Key types of labor categories	Industrial workers and professionals	"Knowledge workers" and service workers
Type of production	Mass production	Flexible production
Labor control	"Scientific management"	Outsourcing (threatened and real), technological control of work
Selected social stratification characteristics	Development of a modern class society with a dominant economic class, an expanding middle class that may integrate workers, and an economic underclass	Segmentation of the middle class by educational attainment, concentration of wealth and income at the top, and an expanding stratum of working poor

is complex, so the sections below focus on only some of the key aspects, including the growth of automation and flexible production, reliance on outsourcing and offshoring, and the growth of the service economy.

Automation and Flexible Production

Postindustrial production relies on ever-expanding **automation**, *the replacement of human labor by machines in the production process.* Today, robots can perform tedious and dangerous work that once required the labor of hundreds of workers. While automation increases efficiency, it has also eliminated jobs.

Computer-driven assembly lines can be quickly reprogrammed, allowing manufacturers to shift to new products and designs rapidly and to shorten the time from factory to buyer. "Just-in-time" delivery systems also minimize the need for businesses to maintain warehouses full of parts and supplies; instead, parts suppliers ship components to factories on an as-needed basis so they move right to the production floor and into the products. Such reliance on more flexible, less standardized forms of production is sometimes termed *post-Fordism.*

Notably, while to this point, automation has had its most visible impact on manufacturing jobs, it is becoming significant (as we saw in the opening story) in the large U.S. service industry as well. Consider, for instance, the mass expansion of self-checkout lines at supermarkets, drug stores, and home improvement stores, among many others. In many cities, one can easily go into a retail store, find the items one needs, and check out—without ever speaking to another human being. While offering lower labor costs to employers and some convenience to consumers, self-ordering and self-checkout technologies are reducing the numbers of jobs available at dining and retail establishments. Further along in the chapter, we look at the potentially dramatic shifts in the future labor market as automation and artificial intelligence reach into other sectors of the labor market.

Reliance on Outsourcing and Offshoring

Businesses can perform activities associated with producing and marketing a product in house or they can contract some of the work to outside firms, which in turn can do their own subcontracting to other firms. The term *outsourcing* often describes the use of low-cost foreign labor, but it can also mean contracting U.S. workers to do a job, typically for less pay than a company employee would earn.

According to a recent *Forbes* magazine article on the decline of union influence, between 20% and 40% of autoworkers at foreign-owned factories in the United States, most of which are in the South, are temporary hires (Muller, 2014). The emergence of outsourcing across a wide spectrum of industries is striking. For example, United Airlines used to rely on its own mechanics to service the company's planes. The mechanics were well paid and enjoyed benefits negotiated by their union. By the late 1990s, however, United increasingly turned to nonunionized mechanics operating from lower-cost, lower-wage hangars in the South. The terrorist attacks of September 11, 2001, which temporarily halted air travel, exacerbated the financial difficulties of airlines. In spite of billions in government aid and loans, airlines have continued to struggle. Major carriers have become even more reliant on outsourcing to cut costs (Uchitelle, 2007).

The phenomenon of contracted work—that is, temporary work that minimizes the commitment of employer and employee to a long-term economic relationship—is not limited to the blue-collar workforce. Computer giant Microsoft's use of "permatemps," initiated in the 1990s, is a striking example. During this time, 1,500 permatemps worked with the 17,000 regular domestic employees of the company. While they performed comparable tasks, the permatemps (some of whom had been in their jobs for five years or more) not only were denied the same vacation, health, and retirement benefits as other workers but also were denied discounts at the Microsoft store, opportunities for further job training, and even use of the company basketball court. A class-action suit was filed against Microsoft, and the company agreed to an out-of-court settlement of $97 million (FACE Intel, 2000).

Offshoring refers more specifically to the practice among U.S. companies of contracting with businesses outside the country to perform services that would otherwise be done by U.S. workers. The movement of manufacturing jobs overseas to lower-wage countries, as noted earlier, has been taking place since the 1970s and 1980s. More recently, however, workers and policy makers have expressed concern about the offshoring of professional jobs, such as those in information technology. According to a recent Congressional Research Service paper on the topic, this trend has been fostered by the widespread adoption of technologies enabling rapid transmission of voice and data across the globe, economic crises in the United States that have created greater pressure to achieve economic efficiencies (such as lower labor costs), and the availability of a growing pool of well-educated and often English-speaking labor abroad (Levine, 2012).

Automation: The replacement of human labor by machines in the production process.

Transformation of the Occupational and Class Structure

Among the most highly compensated workers in the modern economy are those who invent or design new products, engineer new technologies, and solve problems. They are creative people who "make things happen," organizers who bring people together, administrators who make firms run efficiently, legal and financial experts who help firms to be profitable, and computer scientists who are driving digital networking innovations (Bell, 1973; Reich, 2010). Workers in this category are sometimes called *symbolic analysts* (Reich, 1991) or *knowledge workers*. Most symbolic analysts are highly educated professionals who engage in mental labor and, in some way, the manipulation of symbols (numbers, computer codes, words). They include engineers, university professors, physicians, scientists, lawyers, and financiers and bankers, among others.

While the ranks of symbolic analysts have grown overall in recent decades and the ranks of routine production workers in manufacturing have been declining, most job growth over this period has been concentrated in the service sector. Services constitute a diverse sector of the labor market. As of 2014, the service sector employed more than 120 million U.S. workers and accounted for almost 80% of the U.S. workforce (U.S. Bureau of Labor Statistics, 2015c). Service occupations include a number of jobs that require higher education, including financial and private educational services, but also include retail sales, home health and nurses' aides, food service, and security services.

Many service positions do not require extensive education or training, and a growing fraction are

Some manufacturing jobs have returned to the U.S. after the decline of this job sector beginning in the late 1970s and early 1980s. Many of today's industrial jobs, however, pay less and are temporary contract positions rather than permanent jobs.

DISCOVER INTERSECTIONS

Labor Market Shifts and Their Economic and Social Consequences

In the sections above, we discussed the decline of employment opportunities in manufacturing in the U.S., which has been driven primarily by a combination of automation and the offshoring of jobs. Many of these jobs, as we noted, were held in the past by men with less than a college education. Among those men were also a substantial proportion of minority workers. Think back to our earlier chapters on race and ethnicity (Chapter 9), gender and society (Chapter 10), and families and society (Chapter 11). How does the story of the postindustrial economy and its loss of manufacturing jobs fit with other contemporary sociological phenomena, such as the struggle of African Americans and Hispanic workers to accrue wealth and the dramatic decline in marriage among the U.S. working class?

part-time rather than full-time, are nonunionized, and have few or no benefits. Quite a few of these jobs require people skills that are stereotypically associated with females and are often viewed as "women's jobs" (but by no means invariably, since private security guards, a growing occupation, tend to be men). By contrast, many routine production jobs in the past were manufacturing jobs that commonly employed men. The decline in manufacturing employment opportunities, along with declines in educational attainment among men (a topic we examined in Chapter 12), has made unemployment and underemployment particularly acute for some demographic groups, including minority males (Autor, 2010).

Together, these diverse labor market trends point to significant shifts in the U.S. class structure. Economist David Autor (2010) argues that a polarization of job opportunities has taken place, particularly in the past two decades. Autor sees a modern economy characterized by "expanding opportunities in both high-skill, high-wage occupations and low-skill, low-wage occupations, coupled with contracting opportunities in middle-wage, middle-skill, white-collar and blue-collar jobs." He views this as the basis of a split in the middle class, with those whose membership in that group bolstered by good manufacturing jobs now losing ground and those who occupy

©David Butow/Corbis via Getty Images

Behind the Numbers

UNEMPLOYMENT, EMPLOYMENT, AND UNDEREMPLOYMENT IN THE UNITED STATES

According to the U.S. Bureau of Labor Statistics (BLS, 2018), in May of 2018, the U.S. labor force participation rate was 62.7%, and over 155 million U.S. residents were employed. At the same time, about 3.8% of U.S. workers were counted by the BLS as unemployed. What do these numbers tell us? What do they illuminate, and what do they obscure?

Consider some of the most frequently cited BLS figures—unemployment in the United States. According to BLS, the **unemployed** are *people who are jobless, have actively looked for work in the prior four weeks, and are available for work.* The BLS figures are based on the monthly Current Population Survey, which uses a representative sample of 60,000 households and has been conducted every month since 1940. While the BLS cannot count every U.S. household, the size of the sample and its configuration are believed to ensure a statistically accurate representation of the U.S. labor force.

Unemployed: People who are jobless, have actively looked for work in the prior four weeks, and are available for work.

Official unemployment figures (Figure 15.1), however, do not include those who, after a brief or extended period of joblessness, have given up looking for work or whose job seeking is *passive*—for instance, limited to scanning newspaper or online classified ads. Those persons are categorized as **not in the labor force**, because they are *neither officially employed nor officially unemployed. Persons who would like to work and have searched actively for a job in the past 12 months (but not in the prior four weeks)* are categorized as **marginally attached to the labor force:** In May of 2018, there were about 1.5 million such individuals. BLS also identifies a category they call **discouraged workers**, which includes *those who would like to work but have given up searching, believing that*

Not in the labor force: Persons who are neither officially employed nor officially unemployed.

Marginally attached to the labor force: Persons who would like to work and have searched actively for a job in the past 12 months (but not in the prior four weeks).

Discouraged workers: Those who would like to work but have given up searching, believing that no jobs are available for them.

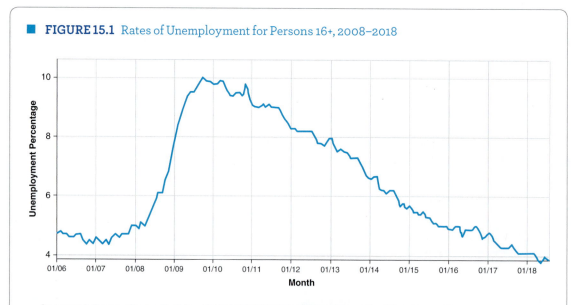

■ **FIGURE 15.1** Rates of Unemployment for Persons 16+, 2008–2018

Source: U.S. Bureau of Labor Statistics, 2016, LNS14000000, Retrieved from http://data.bls.gov/timeseries/LNS14000000.

no jobs are available for them: Recent data puts this figure at about 378,000. Widely cited official unemployment statistics omit these categories and may thus underestimate the numbers of those who need and want to work.

Who, then, according to BLS calculations, is **employed**? In BLS statistics, *employed persons are those who are 16 years of age or older in the civilian, noninstitutional population (that is, not in the military or in mental or penal institutions) who did any paid work—even as little as one hour—in the reference week or worked in their own businesses or farms.* This figure is a useful overview of economic activity and is valuable for examining labor market conditions over time, but it fails to capture the problem of underemployment. Also significant is the labor force participation rate. As noted above, in May 2018, the labor force participation rate was just under 63%. This rate shows us the number of officially employed *and* unemployed persons as a percentage of the population 16 years of age or older. As such, it gives an indication of the percentage of people who work or actively want to work. Notably, the labor force participation rate has been falling for several years, particularly among men.

Employed: Employed persons are those who are 16 years of age or older in the civilian, noninstitutional population who did any paid work—even as little as one hour—in the reference week or worked in their own businesses or farms.

Underemployment manifests in two key ways. First, the underemployed include workers forced to work part-time when they would like to work full-time. According to BLS, in May 2018, there were about 4.9 million involuntary part-time workers in the United States; these are workers who are in part-time positions because their hours have been reduced or they are unable to find a full-time job. Second, workers in jobs that are below their skill or credential level can also be considered underemployed. According to a recent Economic Policy Institute report, the underemployment rate, when calculated using this measure, is considerably higher, particularly for recent college graduates (Gould, Mokhiber, & Wolfe, 2018).

Unemployment and employment figures are important measures that help to track trends over time and enable comparisons between demographic groups. At the same time, while they illuminate some aspects of the complex labor market, they obscure others.

Think It Through

- As we saw, underemployment is an economic phenomenon that does not appear in mainstream unemployment numbers. Why is it economically significant? Why is it sociologically significant?

---

the upper, professional rungs of the middle class maintaining their status amid growing opportunities.

However, not all economists agree with this assessment. Economist Alan Blinder (2006) argues that

> many people blithely assume that the critical labor-market distinction is, and will remain, between highly educated (or highly skilled) people and less-educated (or less-skilled) people—doctors versus call-center operators, for example. The supposed remedy for the rich countries, accordingly, is more education and a general "upskilling" of the work force. But this view may be mistaken. (p. 118)

Blinder suggests that the more critical social division in the future may not be between jobs that require high levels of education and those that do not but rather between work that can be wirelessly outsourced and work that cannot. Consider the growth of online university education. Whereas a college professor may be able to accommodate 100 or even 500 students in a massive lecture hall, an online instructor can have thousands of students and teach them at a considerable cost savings to the institution—and, in some instances, to the students. Some universities, such as the Massachusetts Institute of Technology (MIT), are offering free college course lectures online (though these are not normally available for credit). While this is not outsourcing as we typically define it, trends suggest that even many highly educated workers will be vulnerable to technological changes in the decades ahead, a topic we take up in more detail further along.

The Service Economy and Emotional Labor

As discussed above, recent decades have seen the expansion of the service sector of the U.S. economy. Many service jobs today require a substantial amount of emotional labor. According to sociologist Arlie Russell Hochschild

(2003), **emotional labor** is *the commodification of emotions, including "the management of feeling to create a publicly observable facial and bodily display"* (p. 7). Like physical labor, the symbol of the industrial economy, emotional labor is also "sold for a wage and . . . has exchange value" (p. 7).

Hochschild (2003) uses the example of flight attendants, who do emotional labor in the management of airline passengers' comfort, good feelings, and sense of safety, but we could also use as examples customer service workers, retail sales associates, and restaurant servers. While these workers may enjoy their jobs, they are also forced to feign positive feelings even when such feelings are absent and to work relentlessly to evoke positive feelings in their customers. In addition to producing emotions, workers in these jobs may also be called upon to suppress feelings, particularly when poor behavior on the part of a customer or client evokes frustration or anger. The emotional laborer is, in a sense, compelled to "sell" his or her smile in exchange for a wage, just as the industrial laborer sells his or her physical labor. The emotional laborer's actions are programmed for profit and efficiency, as he or she is asked to perform emotions that maximize both.

Consider, for instance, the common use of scripts for employees in sales jobs or restaurants that closely instruct workers on how to maintain a message and close a sale, even if it causes the employee (or the consumer) distress or discomfort. The strain between real and performed feelings, notes Hochschild, leads to an emotive dissonance—a disconnect—between what the worker really feels and the emotions to be shown or suppressed. Hochschild posits that just as Marx's proletarian laboring in a mill was alienated from the work and from himself or herself, so too, is the emotional laborer alienated from work and his or her emotional life.

In the next section of the chapter, we discuss some evolving aspects of the economy, returning to a theme introduced in our opening story: the current and potential future effects of automation and artificial intelligence on work and the workplace.

The Technological Revolution and the Future of Work

In the previous section, we discussed key characteristics of the postindustrial economy of recent decades and today. In

Emotional labor entails creating or suppressing feelings (whether positive or negative) in return for a wage. Have you ever worked as an emotional laborer? In what ways does Hochschild's concept capture or fail to capture your experience?

this section, we consider possible paths of economic development in the years ahead, focusing in particular on ways in which expanded automation and the rise of artificial intelligence may reshape the future labor market in the U.S. and the world.

Technological change has historically wrought both prosperity and pain in the economy and labor market. For example, while innovations such as the mechanization of agriculture in the 19th century dramatically improved productivity and enabled some landowners and farmers to grow a surplus that could be sold at a profit, it also created significant disruptions for agricultural laborers. At the same time, new technological innovations in production created a mass of new jobs in urban industry, spurring rural to urban migration and a new economic order heavily rooted in manufacturing. Put simply, in the past, technological innovations and accompanying economic shifts have put workers out of jobs, but in the words of economist Martin Ford (2015), "it never became systematic or permanent. New jobs were created and dispossessed workers found new opportunities" (p. x).

Today, we are experiencing a new era of change and, potentially, disruption as technology is changing how work and the workplace are structured. What are evolving trends in the economy and labor market? Below we discuss two key points.

Big Names, Few Workers: Digital Networking Companies in the Contemporary Economy

The most visible and well-known companies in the United States today do not employ large numbers of workers.

Emotional labor: "The commodification of emotions, including the management of feeling to create a publicly observable facial and bodily display" (Hochschild, 2003).

Consider an observation made by computer scientist Jaron Lanier (2013):

> At the height of its power, the photography company Kodak employed more than 140,000 people and was worth $28 billion. They even invented the first digital camera. But today Kodak is bankrupt, and the new face of digital photography has become Instagram. When Instagram was sold to Facebook for a billion dollars in 2012, it employed only thirteen people. (p. 2)

Lanier's example points to a significant contemporary trend: We are seeing the dramatic rise of companies whose fortunes are tied to digital networking—Instagram, Facebook, WhatsApp, and Snapchat are only a few. Companies engaged in digital networking are among the most financially valuable firms operating in the global economy. At the same time, the number of jobs they directly contribute to the labor market is relatively low. For example, in 2015, Snapchat had a valuation of $55 billion; at that time, it had 330 employees. When Facebook recently purchased WhatsApp at a cost of $22 billion, the company had a total of 55 employees. Figure 15.2 offers a visual representation of the highest valuation per employee. That is, it helps us see that some companies have both high valuations and few employees: Snapchat's valuation per employee is $48 million. As one article noted, "Ultimately, software has proven

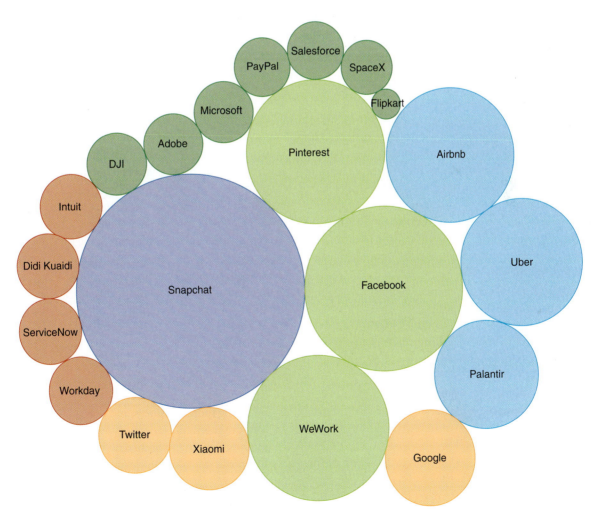

■ **FIGURE 15.2** Visualization of Value of Tech Companies per Employee

Source: Data from "The Most Valuable Employees: Snapchat Doubles Facebook," Liyan Chen, Forbes, August 11, 2015.

to be one of the most headcount-efficient businesses in the world" (Chen, 2015, para. 6).

While headcount efficiency is a boon for companies and shareholders, it is less beneficial for jobseekers. In the heyday of U.S. manufacturing, prominent and technologically modern companies were providers of significant numbers of jobs: In 1955, for instance, General Motors had a workforce of over 576,000; U.S. Steel employed about 268,000 workers; and Chrysler had over 167,000 employees ("America's 5 Biggest Employers," 2010). The digitally networked economy is producing new, well-paying, and interesting jobs, but will there be enough of them to employ the workforce of the future?

Rise of the Robots?

Economist Martin Ford (2015) writes that we are in a moment when the role of technology in the workplace is changing. Ford notes that

> [this] shift will ultimately challenge one of our basic assumptions about technology: that machines are tools that increase the productivity of workers. Instead machines themselves are turning into workers, and the line between the capability of labor and capital is blurring as never before. (p. xii)

Ford (2015) suggests that the change is underpinned by "the relentless acceleration of computer technology" (p. xii). When Ford writes that "machines themselves are turning into workers," he is recognizing the myriad ways in which technology has the potential to disrupt the contemporary labor market—and, by extension, society—in ways that are still difficult to fully grasp.

For example, consider the seemingly imminent introduction of self-driving cars on our roads. An article in the *Washington Post* looks at one company's efforts to bring this goal to fruition in the city of Pittsburgh:

> Uber is about to build a vast, high-tech playground in one of this city's poorest areas.
>
> The ride-hailing giant wants a protected place to test driverless Ubers, part of its effort to replace costly human drivers.
>
> So on the site of an abandoned steel mill south of the Hot Metal Bridge, the company will carve out a 20-plus-square block, Pac-Man-like maze lined with trapezoidal obstacles. It is the same place where thousands of workers once streamed in to take punishing jobs at the

Self-driving trucks are coming to a highway near you. What will be the benefits of self-driving trucks to society and economy? What might be the costs?

beehive-shaped ovens for baking coal and the furnaces that were fueled by it. (Laris, 2016, p. 1)

As self-driving cars become part of our world, "costly human drivers" may indeed be replaced. A key question, then, is what is what will those human drivers do? According to the U.S. Bureau of Labor Statistics (2015b), in 2014, the country had about 1.4 million truck drivers and 800,000 delivery drivers. These are only two of the many occupations that are based on driving, including taxi and Uber drivers.

Significantly, the advent of artificial intelligence is also changing the labor market for those with advanced education. Consider the case of journalists. The effect of the Internet on journalism has been widely discussed. On the one hand, as more people get their news for free on the Internet, paid subscriptions to newspapers and magazines have fallen and the availability of jobs for reporters has contracted. On the other hand, the Internet has seen the birth of new online news sites that have opened opportunities for writers. The effects of artificial intelligence on journalism, however, are still nascent and may be even more disruptive. New technology is permitting media outlets to produce narrative without employing reporters. According to Ford (2015),

> Narrative Science's technology is used by top media outlets . . . to produce automated articles in a variety of areas, including sports, business, and politics. The company's software generates a news story every thirty seconds, and many of these are published on widely known websites that prefer not to acknowledge the use of their services. (pp. 84–85)

In 2015, the Associated Press, a major producer of news content, revealed that it has used a fully automated program for the production of some content since 2014: The "robot reporter" writes about 1,000 articles a month (Gleyo, 2015). When asked by a reporter to predict how many news articles would be written algorithmically within 15 years, the cofounder of Narrative Science estimated the proportion to be over 90% (Ford, 2015).

Significantly, some observers of artificial intelligence trends suggest that while human input is still needed in decision making, robots are *better* at many tasks than humans. A recent article on robot surgeons noted that "in experiments on pigs, surgical stitches made by autonomous robots were as good or better than stitches made by skilled surgeons" (Seaman, 2016). The author of the study is quoted as saying, "No matter how steady a surgeon's hands are, there is always some tremor." Hence, "Using autonomous robots in some

of the 44.5 million soft tissue surgeries in the United States each year might reduce human errors and improve efficiency, surgical time and access to quality surgeons." Human physicians and surgeons will remain a central part of patient care and care decisions for the foreseeable future, but medicine is only one of many fields in which change is coming.

As artificial intelligence becomes capable of taking on both routine tasks (as it has been doing already) and more complex analytical and technological tasks (as it is beginning to do), it is worth asking how decision makers and society will respond. Will advances in artificial intelligence create new jobs and new job sectors that enable society and the economy to flourish? Or will computer intelligence push "costly" human workers out of jobs permanently? What do you think?

Private Lives, Public Issues

IS THAT REALLY A JOB?

When you graduate from college, you may go on to get further education or you may venture into the job market to look for work. What job will you be doing? The answer to that question depends on a variety of factors: Of course, it will depend on your skills and interests, which will guide your search. It will also depend on the general health of the labor market, both nationally and in your local area. As we noted earlier in our chapter on gender and society (Chapter 10), the job one gets is, in many respects, an outcome of labor supply factors (what a prospective employee wants and brings to a job) and labor demand factors (what a prospective employer seeks).

There is, however, another significant variable to consider: Some jobs that currently exist, may evolve out of existence, while other jobs—which we have perhaps yet to imagine—will come into being. Consider some of the jobs that are done by thousands of workers today that did not exist (at least in their present form) a decade ago:

- Uber, Lyft, and other on-demand car service drivers: While drivers do jobs that are similar to those done for decades by taxi drivers, services such as Uber do not employ drivers and the company does not have a responsibility to provide benefits or jobs security. Rather, drivers use their personal vehicles and rely on the platform to link them up with customers, for which they pay a fee to the company. In 2015,

Uber doubled the number of drivers worldwide who are registered with the company (Moore, 2017; World Economic Forum, 2016).

- Driverless car engineers: This even-newer job category, which demands advanced technical knowledge, could possibly render the previous one obsolete in the future (World Economic Forum, 2016).

- YouTube content creators: Early bloggers were around a decade ago, but today, vloggers (who post content on sites such as YouTube) can make considerable sums of money if they find sufficient followers. Related to this job is the podcast producer: Today, podcasts draw wide audiences who enjoy podcasts that appeal to mass audiences as well as more specific demographics, such as turkey hunters, banjo players, and comic book collectors.

- Drone operators: While still in its infancy, this job could take off as large retailers such as Amazon gain permission in local markets to do drone deliveries of goods. Across the globe, the number of unmanned aerial vehicles has risen dramatically. Piloting those drones in the interest of commerce and security, among others, presents new opportunities (World Economic Forum, 2017).

- Social media manager: This job is among the older jobs on our list. Social media managers work for the companies that dominate the social

(Continued)

(Continued)

media market, such as Instagram, Twitter, and Facebook, but they are also increasingly in demand at smaller firms that seek to shape their online image and to reach out to customers using these platforms. According to GlassDoor, a platform that matches employees and employers, "It's a booming career field, with an average salary of $57,802 and over [18,000] job openings" (Moore, 2017).

- Social media influencer: According to a recent article in *Adweek*, "In a new report from #Hashoff, an influencer discovery and content marketing platform, found that 28 percent of creators they surveyed consider being an influencer their main job. Six months ago, just 12 percent of respondents said it was their full-time job" (Main, 2017). Social media influencers use platforms such as Instagram to tag brands with the goal of enticing their followers to buy the fashion or other item they are showing. In return, they are paid by the companies. While in the past, this role was fulfilled by traditional advertising agencies and marketing campaigns, today, social media influencers are a key vehicle for disseminating marketing messages to potential consumers.

As we have discussed in this chapter, technological changes will likely bring dramatic shifts to the U.S. and global labor markets. Some jobs will disappear. Other new ones will be born. What characteristics do the new jobs listed above share? Do they provide any clues about other future jobs and job sectors and who may occupy those—and who may be left behind?

Think It Through

- Make a list of future occupations that you can imagine. Make a list of jobs that may evolve out of existence. On what basis did you make your lists?

Types of Economic Systems

Two principal types of economic systems dominated the 20th century: capitalism and socialism. Industrialization occurred in capitalist economic systems in North America, Western Europe, Japan, and South Korea, among others, and under socialism in the Soviet Union, Eastern Europe, China, Vietnam, and Cuba. After 1989, the collapse of socialism in Eastern Europe and the (former) Soviet Union fostered the expansion of capitalist market systems. Orthodox socialism appears to be in decline elsewhere as well, notably in China, which remains politically tied to the Communist Party but is increasingly entrepreneurial and capitalist in its economic practices. Even Cuba, which remains steadfast in its socialist rhetoric, recently introduced some capitalist-style reforms.

Even though capitalism and socialism as ideologies share a common commitment to economic growth and increased living standards, they differ profoundly in their ideas about how the economy should be organized to achieve these goals and the degree to which the fruits of economic labor should be shared by everyone in a community. The following descriptions are of ideal-typical (that is, model) capitalist and socialist systems. Real economies often include some elements of both.

Capitalism

Capitalism is *an economic order characterized by the market allocation of goods and services, production for private profit, and private ownership of the means of producing wealth.* Workers sell their labor to the owners of capital in exchange for a wage, and capitalists are then free to make a profit on the goods and services their workers produce. Capitalism emphasizes free, unregulated (or minimally regulated) markets and private (rather than government) economic decision-making about the goods and services that should be produced.

At the same time, governments in capitalist economies often play a key role in shaping economic life, even in countries such as the U.S. that have historically tended to keep the government's role to a minimum (which is sometimes referred to as *laissez-faire* capitalism—literally, *hands-off* capitalism). In a capitalist country, the labor market is comprised of both **public sector** jobs

---

Capitalism: An economic order characterized by the market allocation of goods and services, production for private profit, and private ownership of the means of producing wealth.

Public sector: The sector of the labor market in which jobs are linked to the government (whether national, state, or local) and encompass production or allocation of goods and services for the benefit of the government and its citizens.

and **private sector** jobs. The public sector is *linked to the government (whether national, state, or local) and encompasses production or allocation of goods and services for the benefit of the government and its citizens.* The private sector also *provides goods and services to the economy and consumers, but its primary motive is gaining profit.*

Because capitalists compete with one another for customers, they experience persistent pressure to keep costs and therefore prices down. They can gain a competitive edge by adopting innovative processes such as mass production (think of early Fordism), reducing expensive inventories, and developing new products that either meet existing demands or create new demands (which sociologists call *manufactured needs*). One important process of innovation is minimizing the cost of labor, which capitalists have historically done by adopting technologies that increase productivity and keep wages low. Automation has enabled a reduction in production costs, and technological advances such as artificial intelligence promise to further push down costs, though this has the potential to entail a significant loss of jobs in some sectors.

On one hand, capitalism can create uneven development, inequality, and conflict between workers and employers, whose interests may be at odds. On the other hand, it has been successful in producing diverse and desirable products and services, encouraging invention and creativity by entrepreneurs who are willing to take risks in return for potential profit, and raising living standards in many countries across the globe.

The role of government varies widely among different capitalist economies. In the United States and England, for example, there is greater skepticism about government's role in the private sector and greater emphasis on the private sector as the means for allocating goods and services (though Britain, unlike the United States, has nationalized health care). In contrast, in many European economies, the government takes a strong role in individual lives. Sweden and France offer "cradle to grave" social supports, with paid parental leave, child allowances, national health insurance, and generous unemployment benefits. Japan, on the other hand, does not expect government to take such a major role but does expect businesses to assume almost family-like responsibility for the welfare of their employees.

Private sector: The sector of the labor market that provides goods and services to the economy and consumers with the primary motive of gaining profit.

A Case of Capitalism in Practice:
A Critical Perspective

Profit is the driving motive of capitalist systems. While the desire for profit spawns creativity and productivity, it may also give rise to greed, corruption, and exploitation. Industries cut costs in order to increase profits; there is economic logic in such a decision. Cutting costs, however, can also compromise the health and safety of workers and consumers.

What do such compromises look like? A case study of profit over people in the meat industry in the U.S. offers one example. In the first decade of the 20th century, Upton Sinclair's novel *The Jungle* offered a powerful and frightening fictionalized account of the real-life problems of the meat industry. The novel chronicles the struggles of a Lithuanian immigrant family working and struggling in "Packingtown," Chicago's meat district. The excerpt below offers a snapshot of one family member's workplace experience in Packingtown:

> It was only when the whole ham was spoiled that it came into the department of Elzbieta. Cut up by the two-thousand-revolutions-a-minute flyers, and mixed with half a ton of other meat, no odor that ever was in a ham could make any difference. There was never the least attention paid to what was cut up for sausage. . . . There would be meat stored in great piles in rooms, and the water from leaky roofs would drip over it, and thousands of rats would race about on it. . . .

> Such were the new surroundings in which Elzbieta was placed, and such was the work she was compelled to do. It was stupefying, brutalizing work; it left her no time to think, no strength for anything. She was part of the machine she tended, and every faculty that was not needed for the machine was doomed to be crushed out of existence. (Sinclair, 1906/1995, pp. 143–145)

Sinclair was critical of capitalism and the profit motive, which he felt underpinned the suffering of the workers and the stomach-turning products churned out in the filthy packinghouses. His work was a stirring piece of social criticism dressed as fiction, and it spurred change. President Theodore Roosevelt's inquiry into the conditions described by Sinclair brought about legislation requiring federal inspection of meat sold through interstate commerce and the accurate labeling of meat products and ingredients (Schlosser, 2002). The novel had little effect, however, on the conditions experienced by industrial laborers, to which Sinclair had sought to draw attention. As he later wryly

Concerns have been raised about the use of chemicals in the poultry processing industry today. The chemicals may present a danger to both workers and consumers.

remarked, "I aimed for the public's heart . . . and by accident I hit it in the stomach."

In the years since Sinclair's novel was published, capitalism has evolved (as has regulation), though profit and the need to cut costs have remained basic characteristics. What does cost cutting look like in today's more closely regulated meat industry? In *Fast Food Nation* (2002), writer Eric Schlosser describes his experience in a 21st-century meat processing plant:

A man turns and smiles at me. He wears safety goggles and a hardhat. His face is splattered with gray matter and blood. He is the "knocker," the man who welcomes cattle to the building. Cattle walk down a narrow chute and pause in front of him, blocked by a gate, and then he shoots them in the head with a captive bolt stunner. . . . For eight and a half hours, he just shoots. . . .

When a sanitation crew arrives at a meatpacking plant, usually around midnight, it faces a mess of monumental proportions. . . . Workers climb ladders with hoses and spray the catwalks. They get under tables and conveyor belts, climbing right into the bloody muck, cleaning out grease, fat, manure, leftover scraps of meat. (pp. 170–171, 177)

The work is not only brutal; it is also dangerous. More recently, concerns have been raised about the use of chemicals in the poultry processing industry. U.S. demand for chicken and turkey is high and growing. In response, companies have sought to increase efficiency by allowing more chemical decontamination of bird carcasses on the production line:

To keep speeds up, the new regulations "would allow visibly contaminated poultry carcasses to remain online for treatment"—rather than being discarded or removed for offline cleaning . . . . The heightened use of chemicals would follow a pattern that has already emerged in poultry plants. In a private report to the House Appropriations Committee, the USDA [United States Department of Agriculture] said that [in] plants that have already accelerated line speeds, workers have been exposed to larger amounts of cleaning agents.

Exposure to chemicals has affected line workers, but also USDA and industry inspectors, who describe a variety of ailments ranging from respiratory problems and skin rashes to irritated eyes and nasal ulcers. (Kindy, 2013, para. 6–7)

Critics of capitalism would suggest that conditions in the meat industry—past and present—illuminate a fundamental problem of capitalism: Capital accumulation and profit are based on driving down the costs of production. The case of the meat industry shows that capitalists sometimes drive down the costs by compromising worker and consumer safety. The potentially high human cost of industrial profits is a central point of the critique of capitalism.

Socialism and Communism

Modern ideas about communism and socialism originated in the theories of 19th-century philosophers and social scientists, especially those of Karl Marx. **Communism**, in its ideal-typical form, is *a type of economic system without private ownership of the means of production and, theoretically, without economic classes or economic inequality*. In an ideal-typical communist society, the capitalist class has been eliminated, leaving only workers, who manage their economic affairs cooperatively and distribute the fruits of their labor "to each according to his needs, from each according to his abilities." Since Marx believed that governments exist primarily to protect the interests of capitalists, he concluded that once the capitalist class and private property were eliminated, there would be no need for the state, which would, in his words, "wither away."

Communism: A type of economic system without private ownership of the means of production and, theoretically, without economic classes or economic inequality.

Marx recognized that there would most likely have to be a transitional form of economic organization between capitalism and communism, which he termed **socialism**. In a socialist system, *theoretically, the government manages the economy in the interests of the workers; it owns the businesses, factories, farms, hospitals, housing, and other means of producing wealth and redistributes that wealth to the population through wages and services.* The laborer works for a state-run industrial enterprise, the farmer works for a state-run farm, and the bureaucrat works in a state agency. Profit is not a driving economic imperative because there is no private property and no private profit.

Socialism: A type of economic system in which, theoretically, the government manages the economy in the interests of the workers; it owns the businesses, factories, farms, hospitals, housing, and other means of producing wealth and redistributes that wealth to the population through wages and services.

In the socialist period in the Soviet Union and allied countries of Eastern Europe, the state controlled all production, essentially eliminating competition in the marketplace for goods and services. Instead of advertisements in public spaces, political posters and propaganda elevated the achievements and builders of socialism and denigrated the capitalist way of life.

Before the collapse of the Soviet Union and its socialist allies in Eastern Europe, nearly a third of the world's population lived in socialist countries. Far from withering away as Marx predicted, these socialist governments remained firmly in place until 1989 (1991 in the Soviet Union), when popular revolutions ushered in transformations—not to the classless communist economies Marx envisioned, but to new capitalist states. The largest remaining socialist country in the world—China—has transitioned over the past 20 years into a market economy of a size and scale to nearly rival that of the United States, though the state still exercises control over large industries.

These transformations occurred in part because socialism proved too inflexible to manage a modern economy. Having the central government operate tens of thousands of factories, farms, and other enterprises was a deterrent to economic growth. Further, though the capitalist class was eliminated, a new class emerged—the government bureaucrats and communist officials who managed the economy and who were often inefficient, corrupt, and more interested in self-enrichment than in public service (Djilas, 1957). Moreover, most socialist governments were intolerant of dissent, often persecuting, imprisoning, and exiling those who disagreed with their policies. At the same time, socialist governments were often successful in eliminating extreme poverty and providing their populations with housing, universal education, health care, and basic social services. Inequality was typically much lower in socialist states than in capitalist economies—although the overall standard of living was lower as well.

The dramatic rise in economic inequality and poverty in the newly capitalist states of the former Soviet Union and Eastern Europe has created some nostalgia for the socialist past, particularly among the elderly, who have a threadbare social safety net in many states. While few miss the authoritarian political governments, there is some longing for the basic economic and social security that socialism offered.

A Case of Socialism in Practice: A Critical Perspective

In theory, a driving motive of socialist systems is achievement of a high degree of economic equality. This is realized in part through the creation of full-employment economies. In the Soviet Union, full employment gave all citizens the opportunity to earn a basic living, but it also brought about some socially undesirable results. For instance, inefficiency and waste flourished in enterprises that were rewarded for how much raw material they consumed rather than how much output they produced (Hanson, 2003). Human productivity was only partially utilized when work sites had to fill required numbers of positions but did not have meaningful work for all who occupied them. Disaffection and anger grew in workplaces where promotions were as likely to be based on political reliability, connections, and Communist Party membership as on merit. A system that theoretically ensured the use of resources for the good and equality of all workers was undermined by the realities of Soviet-style communism.

In practice, socialist systems such as that of postwar Hungary were characterized by both low wages and low productivity: A popular saying among workers was that "we pretend to work and the state pretends to pay us." Lacking a competitive labor market, workers may not have felt compelled to work particularly hard; unemployment was rare. At the same time, public sector (government) jobs, which made up the bulk of the labor market, were poorly paid; many workers sought supplementary pay in the informal economy (Ledeneva, 1998). Further, in the absence of a profit motive, there was limited entrepreneurial activity and the consumer market offered goods and services that were largely mediocre and often difficult to get.

Socialism in practice, according to sociologists Michael Burawoy and Janos Lukács (1992), was in part a performance:

> Painting over the sordid realities of socialism is simultaneously the painting of an appearance of brightness, efficiency, and justice. Socialism becomes an elaborate game of pretense which everyone sees through but which everyone is compelled to play. . . . The pretense becomes a basis against which to assess reality. If we have to paint a world of efficiency and equality—as we do in our [factory] production meetings, our brigade competitions, our elections—we become more sensitive to and outraged by inefficiency and inequality. (p. 129)

In the book he coauthored with Lukács, *The Radiant Past: Ideology and Reality in Hungary's Road to Capitalism* (1992), Burawoy, a U.S. sociologist who spent time working in socialist enterprises in Poland and Hungary as part of his study of socialist economies, recounts an instance of such a "painting ritual" when the Hungarian prime minister makes a visit to the Lenin Steel Works. Areas of the factory to be visited are literally painted over in bright hues, debris is swept up, and workers halt their productive tasks to create an appearance of productivity, for the prime minister "had to be convinced that the Lenin Steel Works was at the forefront of building socialism" (p. 127). For critics of socialism, the case of Hungarian steel in the socialist period highlights a fundamental problem of the system as it was practiced: Its weaknesses were made more rather than less apparent by the "painting rituals" that asked workers to pretend socialism was fundamentally efficient and equal when their own experience showed it was not. This was among the flaws that led to the collapse of socialism in Eastern Europe and the Soviet Union.

Working on and off the Books

Work consists of *any human effort that adds something of value to the goods and services that are available to others.* By this definition, work includes paid labor in the factory or office, unpaid labor at home, and volunteer work in the community. Workers include rock stars and street musicians, corporate executives and prostitutes, nurses and babysitters. Almost the only activities excluded from this definition of work are those that individuals conduct purely for their own pleasure or benefit, such as pursuing a hobby or playing a musical instrument for fun.

The concept of work as consisting exclusively of labor that is sold for a wage is a relatively recent development of modern industrial society. Throughout most of human history, work was not done for a wage. In agricultural societies, subsistence farming was common: Families often worked their own plots of land and participated with others in the community in a **barter economy**, *an economy based on the exchange of goods and services rather than money.* With the advent of industrial society, however, work shifted largely to the economic setting of a formal, paid, and regulated job.

Day laborers often work for low pay in unregulated conditions. Some of them are illegal migrants. Their status and language barriers make it challenging for them to report dangerous or abusive conditions of work.

©REUTERS/Lucas Jackson

Work: Any human effort that adds something of value to the goods and services that are available to others.

Barter economy: An economy based on the exchange of goods and services rather than money.

The term *underground economy* may evoke images of drugs, weapons, and stolen passports, but this type of economy also involves more mundane products, such as food. Los Angeles and other major cities have unlicensed and unregistered vendors providing food and services for residents, which has a mixture of positive and negative effects.

Today, work for pay occurs in two markets: the formal economy and the informal (or underground) economy. We look at each of these next.

The Formal Economy

The **formal economy** consists of *all work-related activities that provide income and are regulated by government agencies.* It includes work for wages and salaries as well as self-employment; it is what people ordinarily have in mind when they refer to *work.* It has grown in importance since the Industrial Revolution. Indeed, one of the chief functions of government in industrial society is regulation of the formal economy, which contributes to the shape and character of the labor market (Sassen, 1991; Tilly & Tilly, 1994).

In the United States, as in most countries of the world, private businesses are supposed to register with governmental entities ranging from tax bureaus (the Internal Revenue Service) to state and local licensing agencies. Whether they work in the private or the public sector, U.S. workers must pay income, Medicare, and Social Security taxes on their earnings, and employers are expected to withhold such taxes on their behalf and report employee earnings to the government. Numerous agencies regulate wages and working conditions, occupational health and safety, the environmental effects of business activities, product quality, and relationships among firms.

When statistical indicators such as employment and unemployment are tabulated by government entities such as the BLS, they rely on data from the formal economy. Work is also done—and value produced—in the informal economy, but this is not included in BLS numbers.

The Informal (or Underground) Economy

A notable amount of income-generating work avoids formal regulation and is not organized around officially recognized jobs. This part of the economy is termed the **informal (or underground) economy;** it includes *all income-generating activities that are not regulated by the governmental institutions that ordinarily regulate similar activities.* Some of these sources of income are illegal, such as selling guns or pirated DVDs, drug dealing, and sex trafficking. Other work activities are not illegal but still operate under the government radar. These include selling goods at garage sales and on Internet auction sites such as eBay; housecleaning, gardening, and babysitting for employers who pay without reporting the transactions to the government; and informal catering of neighborhood events for unreported pay. In one way or another, most of us participate in the informal economy at some point in our lives.

Workers' reasons for participating in the informal economy are varied. A worker with a regular job may take up a second job "off the books" to make up a deficit in his or her budget, or someone may be compelled to work outside the legal economy because of his or her undocumented immigration status. Others may find the shadow economy more profitable (Schneider & Enste, 2002). Many of the underground economy's workers occupy the lowest economic rungs of society and are likely to be pursuing basic survival rather than untold riches. They are disproportionately low income, female, and immigrant, and the jobs they do lack the protections that come with many jobs in the formal economy, such as health care benefits, unemployment insurance, and job security. While "off the books" jobs enable more people to make a living, the work they do cannot typically be cited on a resume, and "colleagues" in activities such as fixing cars or making and selling food informally cannot be used as references; hence, parlaying experience in the informal economy into a job in the formal economy is rarely tenable (Venkatesh, 2008).

Among the employers in the illegal U.S. underground economy are unlicensed "sweatshop" factories that make clothing, furniture, and other consumer goods (Castells & Portes, 1989; Sassen, 1991). Factories in the United States

---

Formal economy: All work-related activities that provide income and are regulated by government agencies.

Informal (or underground) economy: Those income-generating economic activities that are not regulated by the governmental institutions that ordinarily regulate similar activities.

are competing with factories around the world where workers are paid a fraction of U.S. wages. To remain competitive (or to raise profits), U.S. firms sometimes subcontract their labor to low-cost sweatshop firms in the informal sector. Requirements to comply with environmental laws, meet health and safety standards, make contributions to Social Security and other social benefit programs, and pay taxes lead some businesses to seek to establish themselves off the books. Small businesses may operate without licenses, and large firms may illegally subcontract out some of their labor to smaller, unlicensed ones.

Shadow economies exist around the globe, though their size varies dramatically. According to one report, of 12 developed nations, the biggest shadow economies were to be found in Greece (21%), Italy (20%), and Spain (17%), while the smallest were in the Netherlands (8%), Switzerland (6%), and the United States (5%; McCarthy, 2017). According to International Monetary Fund estimates, the largest shadow economies are found in developing states around the globe: For instance, shadow economies comprise about 65% of the gross domestic product (GDP) in Georgia, 62% in Bolivia, and 61% in Zimbabwe. Altogether, the average size of the shadow economies of all the countries is about 32% of the GDP (Medina & Schneider, 2018).

Consumers, Consumption, and the U.S. Economy

As we have seen in this chapter, production has been an important part of the rise of modern capitalist economies. In modern industrial countries, including the United States, however, production has receded in importance. The economies of advanced capitalist states today rely heavily on consumption to fuel their continued growth. Today, an estimated 70% of the U.S. economy is linked to consumption. In this section, we examine consumption and its relationship to the economy as well as to our lives as consumers.

Theorizing the Means of Consumption

Karl Marx is well known for his concept of the *means of production* (defined in Chapter 1), which forms a basis for his theorizing on capitalism, exploitation, and class. While the early industrial era in which Marx wrote influenced his focus on production, he also sought to understand consumption in 19th-century capitalism. Marx defined the term *means of consumption* as "commodities that possess a form in which they enter individual consumption of the capitalist and working class" (quoted in Ritzer, 1999, p. 56). Marx distinguished between the levels of consumption of different classes, suggesting that *subsistence consumption* ("necessary means of consumption") characterizes the working class, whereas *luxury consumption* is the privilege

One of Disney World's long-standing attractions is the Jungle Cruise, described on the website of the park as an adventure cruise of the most "exotic and 'dangerous' rivers in Asia, Africa, and South America," although it is a virtually danger-free boat trip on a man-made waterway populated by plastic figures. Modern consumers, sociologist George Ritzer suggests, are buying the fantasy rather than the reality of such experiences.

"Cathedrals of Consumption," such as the casinos and hotels of Las Vegas, entice consumers to spend with bright, fun, and fantastical venues. The Luxor Hotel simulates the splendor of Ancient Egypt, featuring replicas of the Great Sphinx and Great Pyramid of Giza.

of the exploiting capitalist class. In sum, Marx's definition focused on the consumption of the end products of the exploitative production process.

Sociologist George Ritzer has expanded Marx's concept. He distinguishes between the end product (that is, a consumer good such as a pair of stylish dress shoes, a new car, or a gambling opportunity) and the means of consumption that allow us to obtain the good (for instance, the shopping mall, the car dealership, or the Las Vegas casino). For Ritzer (1999), the **means of consumption** are *"those things that make it possible for people to acquire goods and services and for the same people to be controlled and exploited as consumers"* (p. 57). For example, a venue such as a mall offers the consumer buying options and opportunities, but it is also part of a system of consumer control through which consumers are seduced into buying what they do not need, thinking they need what they merely want, and spending beyond their means.

Ritzer's concept of the means of consumption also integrates German sociologist Max Weber's ideas about rationalization, enchantment, and disenchantment. Briefly, the Weberian perspective holds that premodern societies were more "enchanted" than modern societies. That is, societies or communities, which were often small and homogeneous, were grounded in ideas that he characterized as magical and mystical. Individuals and groups defined and pursued goals based on abstract teachings such as the ideals and ideas of a religion rather than on detailed, specific rules and regulations. Even early capitalism was linked to an enchanted world. Weber theorized that early Protestantism (and Calvinism in particular) embraced values of thrift, efficiency, and hard work and viewed economic success as an indicator of divine salvation. This so-called *Protestant ethic,* which he identified as characteristic in Northern Europe, laid foundations for the rise of capitalism, though capitalism eventually shed its religious aspects (Weber, 1904–1905/2002).

Modern capitalism lacks authentic enchantment: It is a highly rationalized system characterized by efficiency, predictability, and the pursuit of profit (rather than divine salvation!). This heavily bureaucratized and regulation-reliant environment is virtually devoid of spontaneity, spirituality, or surprise. Ritzer argues, however, that enchantment is important for controlling consumers, because consumption is, at least in part, a response to a fantasy about the item or service being consumed. Consequently, disenchanted structures must be "reenchanted" through spectacle and simulation (Baudrillard, 1981), which draw in consumers. For instance, Disney simulates a kind of childhood dreamworld

(think of the Magic Kingdom), Niketown is a sports fantasy, and Las Vegas aims to bring to a single city the dazzle of Egyptian pyramids, New York's towering urban structures, and Paris's Eiffel Tower. In such a context, the consumer is not merely buying sneakers (say, at Niketown) but embracing a broader fantasy about athletic achievement. In sum, from Ritzer's perspective, the means of consumption are a modern instrument of control not of the *worker* but of the *consumer,* who is enchanted, led to believe that he or she needs certain goods, and given optimal—sometimes nearly inescapable—avenues for acquisition, such as malls with long hallways and few exits to maximize the number of shops a consumer must pass before exiting.

A Historical Perspective on Consumption

Consumer society is a political, social, and economic creation. Consider, for instance, that during World War II, the U.S. government asked its citizen-consumers to serve the greater good by reducing consumption. In contrast, in the wake of the terror attacks on the United States in 2001 and the wars that followed, citizen-consumers were encouraged to spend more money to stimulate the economy. Former secretary of labor Robert Reich termed this appeal for consumption *market patriotism.* Taking a broader perspective, economist Juliet Schor (1998) argues that consumption patterns and the dramatic growth of consumption in the U.S. are heavily driven by Americans' reliance on reference groups. That is, consumers compare themselves and their consumption to the reference groups in their social environments. Significantly, says Schor, those reference groups have changed. In the 1950s, suburban middle-class consumers knew and emulated their neighbors. The substantial number of women outside the paid workforce meant that neighbors were more aware of what others were doing, wearing, and driving. By the 1970s, more women were moving into the workforce; consequently, fewer people knew their neighbors, and the workplace became an important source of reference groups. In contrast to the economically homogeneous neighborhood, however, the workplace is heterogeneous. Low five-figure wages coexist in the same space as high six-figure salaries, and coworkers may aspire upward and far beyond their means.

The 1980s, 1990s, and 2000s brought further upscaling of ambitions and spending, as television sold a powerful picture of consumer decadence masked as normal life. In the 1990s, young consumers embraced media referents such as the television sitcom *Friends,* about a group of young professionals living in lavish New York City apartments, wearing ever-changing stylish wardrobes, and casually consuming the pleasures around them. Lavish consumption came to seem normal rather than unreachable for people of average incomes (Schor, 1998). A new generation is now exposed to

Means of consumption: "Those things that make it possible for people to acquire goods and services and for the same people to be controlled and exploited as consumers" (Ritzer, 1999).

reality TV shows, including *The Real Housewives of Potomac* (and other locales), *Keeping Up with the Kardashians, Platinum Weddings,* and *Million Dollar Rooms,* which emphasize the benefits of conspicuous consumption among celebrities and ordinary people alike.

A somewhat different perspective on how the U.S. consumer economy has been built and sustained is offered by Robert Reich (2010), who believes the consumption-driven economy originated in a "basic bargain" between workers and employers that offered good pay in sectors such as manufacturing, creating a consumer class that could afford to spend (recall Henry Ford's decision to pay above-average wages so his autoworkers could buy cars). Reich notes that, until about 1970, pay rose more quickly in the middle- and lower-income segments of the U.S. labor pool than it did at the top. Consumption grew with the standard of living. The real value of workers' pay stagnated in the 1970s, however, profoundly affected by forces that included globalization and automation. While income rose at the very top of the economic ladder, in the middle and lower strata, it stalled. Consumption continued to rise, however, driven not by gains in income but by the growing credit markets, which offered new ways to spend with or without cash on hand. Next, we review the consequences of that shift to credit-driven spending.

Credit: Debt and More Debt

Do you have a credit card? Do you carry debt? If you answered yes to either or both these questions, you are not alone. In 2017, the credit card debt of Americans reached a record high of over $1 trillion. Credit card debt can be substantial: By one estimate, the average American has a credit card debt of $6,354. Student loan debt adds up to about $34,144 for the individual and $1.4 trillion collectively. The average mortgage debt of Americans in 2017 was $201,811, a 3% increase from 2016 (Sullivan, 2018).

In the early years of the 21st century, "Americans were more likely to go bankrupt than to get divorced" (Quiggin, 2010, p. 26). Consumption (or overconsumption) was not the direct cause of bankruptcies (most of which were precipitated by the loss of a job or unexpected health care costs), but the "culture of indebtedness," the widespread tendency to owe a great deal of money, left people less able to bear any added financial stress. While financial reforms passed into law in 2005 made the declaration of bankruptcy more onerous and less common, the financial crisis that began in 2007 saw another rise in bankruptcies: More than 1.5 million bankruptcy filings were made in 2010 (Administrative Office of the United States Courts, 2011). The number of filings has gone down since then, with bankruptcy filings in the United States falling to 766,698 for the 2017 calendar year (ACA International, 2018).

Humorist Will Rogers commented during the Great Depression that the United States was the first country to drive to the poorhouse in an automobile (cited in Sullivan, Warren, & Westbrook, 2000, p. 3). Car debt was a particularly notable burden during the late 1990s and early 2000s, when many U.S. drivers opted to purchase high-end cars, especially aggressively advertised sport utility vehicles. Rising gasoline prices through the 2000s, coupled with the economic recession that struck in 2007, reversed the trend, and consumers began opting for more fuel-efficient sedans, hybrid vehicles, and smaller crossover vehicles that combine features of cars and SUVs. Since the first hybrid cars came on the U.S. scene in late 1999, Americans have purchased over 4 million of these fuel savers (Cobb, 2016), though larger and less fuel-efficient vehicles continue to be popular in the United States: In 2017, sports utility vehicles (SUVs) and crossovers or cross/utility vehicles (CUVs) accounted for 64% of the auto market, compared to the 36% share comprised by passenger cars (Korn, 2017). U.S. consumers continue to spend considerable sums to put a car (or several cars) in the driveway: In 2017, a record 107 million Americans held car loans, averaging about $25,000, resulting in a total auto loan market of about $1.2 trillion (Sullivan, 2018).

Discover & Debate

THE MINIMUM WAGE

Motion: Politicians and the public should support a $15 minimum wage.

Background: The minimum wage is the lowest wage that can legally be paid to workers, even though some exceptions exist, such as tipped workers and young or disabled workers. In the United States, the minimum wage was first set in 1938 by federal law (the Fair Labor Standards Act). The first minimum wage was $0.25 cents per hour. It has been raised 22 times since 1938, most recently in 2009, when it was raised to $7.25. Some states have their own minimum wage laws: As of January 2018, 29 states and the District of Columbia had minimum wage floors higher than the federal minimum wage. There is a vigorous debate about the minimum wage and who may benefit or lose from a higher minimum wage.

Questions for Consideration

- What are the characteristics of minimum wage workers in the United States today? What are the characteristics of industries paying the minimum wage in the United States today? How does this information help us to evaluate the necessity of a higher minimum wage?

- What do the experiences of states and cities with lower or higher minimum wages suggest about the strength of the affirmative and opposition arguments?

- Will increasing automation in industries such as fast food and retail affect the minimum wage? Will the minimum wage affect the pace of automation in these industries?

Debate Tip

- Practice your arguments. Prepare cue cards for guidance if needed, but don't read your arguments.

AFFIRMATIVE ARGUMENTS	OPPOSITION ARGUMENTS
A higher minimum wage increases earnings, reducing workers' poverty and lowering their reliance on government benefits such as food stamps.	A higher minimum wage increases prices as employers pass on higher labor costs to consumers.
A higher minimum wage increases demand for goods, as poorer households spend a larger proportion of their income than do richer households. Greater demand can act as an economic stimulus, increasing hiring and profits.	A higher minimum wage reduces employment, as employers hire fewer workers or offer fewer hours to current workers.
A higher minimum wage reduces employee turnover, which is costly to businesses.	A higher minimum wage reduces business profits.

Globalization and the New Economic Order

The U.S. economic order today has been powerfully affected by the emergence of a unified global economic system. In fact, some writers have argued that it no longer makes sense to think of the United States—or any other country—as an isolated economic society at all: In many respects, we can regard the world as a single economic unit (Friedman, 2005). We conclude this chapter by examining how global economic interdependence and the global labor market have affected work and economic life in the United States.

Global Economic Interdependence

The U.S. economy is interwoven with the economies of other countries. Many goods made in the United States are sold in foreign markets, while many goods bought by U.S. consumers are made by foreign workers. Economic integration is multidimensional and can be shallow or deep (Dicken, 1998). Shallow integration is more characteristic of the globalization of several decades past, when a single product (say, a German automobile) was made in a single country and that country's government would regulate its export as well as the import of other goods into the country. Countries did business with one another, but their ties were looser and less interdependent.

Deep integration is characteristic of the modern global economy in which corporations are often multinational rather than national, products are made of raw materials or parts from a spectrum of countries (Figure 15.3), and a corporation's management or engineering may be head-quartered in one country while the sales force or customer service contingent may reside anywhere from Denver to Delhi. Familiar companies such as Nike, Apple, and Ford are among the many with globalized labor forces.

A Global Market for Labor

As a result of economic globalization, a growing number of U.S. workers are competing with workers all over the world. This trend may affect the job prospects of all workers,

■ **FIGURE 15.3** Global Origins of Boeing 787 Parts

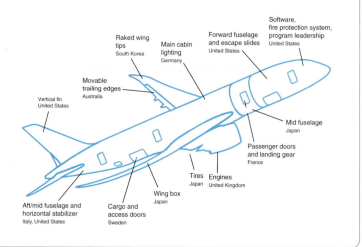

whether they hold high school diplomas or advanced degrees. There are substantial wage differences between countries. While the United States is intermediate among industrial countries, its wages are considerably higher than those in developing countries (Table 15.3).

Jobs will increasingly go wherever on the planet suitable workers can be found. Low labor costs, the decline or absence of labor unions, and governments that enforce worker compliance through repressive measures are all factors influencing the globalization of labor. Some sociologists call this trend a *race to the bottom* (Bonacich & Appelbaum, 2000), in which companies seeking to maximize profits chase opportunities to locate wherever conditions are most likely to result in the lowest costs. This has been the case in, for example, apparel manufacturing; much of the clothing we buy and wear today, including brands sold at popular shops such as H&M and Zara, is made by young workers abroad who labor for very low wages under poor working conditions. China, Bangladesh, Vietnam, and India are the world's leaders in garment manufacturing. China accounts for 21%; followed by Bangladesh and India, both at 14%; and Vietnam at 12%. Most garment companies look to locations with low labor costs to manufacture their goods, which makes Bangladesh, which has a monthly minimum wage of only $65, a popular site. This minimum wage is about $50 less than that of India and Vietnam, and $85 less than China (Knack, 2017).

The current minimum wage in Bangladesh was established in 2013 when a government-appointed panel voted to raise the minimum wage for garment workers; under the plan, it was scheduled to rise from a monthly minimum of about $38 to $66. However, recently Bangladesh unions and workers organized a conference to demand an increase in

the monthly minimum wage to $192, due to the rising cost of living (BDnews24, 2018). Whether this will result in better conditions for workers or an abandonment of the country by low-wage-seeking manufacturers remains to be seen.

We have seen above that the emergence of an increasingly global labor market has resulted in job losses and declining wages in many U.S. industries, including auto and apparel manufacturing. We may be witnessing the emergence of a *global wage,* equivalent to the lowest worldwide cost of obtaining comparable labor for a particular task once the costs of operating at a distance are taken into account. For virtually any job, this wage is far lower than U.S. workers are accustomed to receiving.

The global labor market is not limited to manufacturing. A global market is emerging for a wide range of professional and technical occupations as well. In fact, some of the "knowledge worker" jobs touted as the jobs of the future may be among the most vulnerable to globalization. Unlike cars or clothing, engineering

TABLE 15.3 Average Wages in Select Countries

COUNTRY	AVERAGE WAGES
1. Luxemburg	$63,062
2. United States	$60,558
3. Norway	$51,212
4. Australia	$49,126
5. Canada	$47,622
6. Germany	$47,585
7. United Kingdom	$43,732
8. Japan	$40,863
9. Spain	$38,507
10. Korea	$35,191
11. Greece	$26,064
12. Portugal	$25,367
13. Lithuania	$24,287
14. Hungary	$22,576
15. Mexico	$15,314

Source: Organization for Economic Co-operation and Development. (2017). Average wages. Retrieved from https://data.oecd.org/earnwage/average-wages.htm.

designs and computer programs can move around the globe electronically at no cost, and transportation time is, for all practical purposes, nonexistent. Electronic engineering, computer programming, data entry, accounting, insurance claims processing, and other specialized services, such as medical image reading, can now be inexpensively purchased in such low-wage countries as India, Malaysia, South Korea, China, and the Philippines, where workers communicate digitally with employers in the United States.

Also among those selling their labor on the new global market are highly educated professionals from postsocialist countries such as Estonia and Hungary, both of which have full literacy, educated populations, and many individuals fluent in English and other world languages. While we often associate cheap labor with the low-wage factories of developing countries, these post-Soviet European states also advertise their educated workers (on their investment-promoting websites, for instance) as cheap labor. Indeed,

much global labor is low in cost. As of 2016, the average monthly wage in well-educated Estonia was $1,269. By contrast, in the United Kingdom, it was $3,843; in the United States, it was $5,013 (United Nations Economic Commission for Europe, n.d.).

While globalization has had some negative effects on earnings for American workers in the lower- to middle-income ranges, corporate executive salaries have skyrocketed. Even in the midst of a plummeting economy (2007–2009), as the federal government was distributing billions of bailout dollars to corporations, banks, and investment firms to prevent them from failing, CEOs in the United States were bringing home multiple millions of dollars in compensation. While median CEO pay declined somewhat during the recession period, it has rebounded in the post-crisis period (Table 15.4). According to a 2017 EPI report, CEOs in America's largest firms made on average $15.6 million annually in 2016—271 times the annual average pay of their workers. This 271-to-1 ratio is down from the 299-to-1 ratio from 2014, but extremely far from the 59-to-1 ratio from 1989 (Mishel & Schieder, 2017).

TABLE 15.4 Annual Compensation of Selected CEOs, 2017

CORPORATION	CEO	COMPENSATION
CBS Corporation	Leslie Moonves	$69,332,723
TripAdvisor	Stephen Kaufer	$47,933,462
Oracle Corporation	Mark V. Hurd	$40,832,279
Walt Disney Company	Robert A. Iger	$36,283,680
Weight Watchers International	Mindy Grossman	$33,372,283
Time Warner	Jeffrey L. Bewkes	$32,614,304
PepsiCo	Indra K. Nooyi	$31,082,648
American Express	Ken I. Chenault	$18,611,373
Nike	Mark G. Parker	$13,851,499
Starbucks Corporation	Kevin Johnson	$11,480,364

Source: Adapted from "100 Highest Paid CEOs," AFL-CIO.
Note: Annual compensation includes the value of executives' base salary, value of stock and option awards, and other financial compensation vehicles.

Why Study Economic Systems and Trends?

Whether you were born in the 1960s, the 1970s, the 1980s, the 1990s, or later, the U.S. economy has experienced some dramatic changes in your lifetime. In 1953, for instance, manufacturing accounted for 30% of the U.S. gross domestic product (Blinder, 2006), and about a third of the workforce was unionized (Reich, 2010). By the mid-2000s, that share of jobs in manufacturing had declined to about 13%, and the proportion of unionized workers had fallen to 12.3%, or 15.3 million people, down from 20% or 17 million people in 1980, the first year for which comparable data are available (U.S. Bureau of Labor Statistics, 2013c).

In the 1960s, more than one third of the U.S. nonagricultural workforce was engaged in manufacturing, and about two thirds of American workers were in the service sector. Since that time, the service sector's share of jobs has grown by nearly 20%, a massive change that has brought both new opportunities and new challenges, particularly to those workers without higher education.

In the latter years of the 1970s, the United States experienced a steep rise in imports—U.S.-made goods and U.S. workers were increasingly forced to compete with lower-priced goods and lower-priced labor. From this period forward, the share of goods made in the United States and the number of workers making them fell (Uchitelle, 2007).

Inequality Matters

THE DIGITAL SWEATSHOP

The exploitation of labor is a fundamental characteristic of industrial capitalism, according to Karl Marx. While few industrial sites like those he and Upton Sinclair described exist in developed countries today, factories with strikingly poor conditions and large pools of low-wage labor flourish in other countries, including Bangladesh, China, and Vietnam. Workers in developing countries bear many of the costs of the high technology we enjoy in the form of smartphones, laptops, and other electronic necessities and amenities.

In January 2012, the *New York Times* published an investigative article about Foxconn, one of Apple's key suppliers in China. The article points out that while

Apple and other global companies have been under scrutiny for the hazardous working conditions in some offshore factories. Some workers have responded with strikes. A small number have committed suicide on factory grounds.

> Apple and its high-technology peers—as well as dozens of other American industries—have achieved a pace of innovation nearly unmatched in modern history . . . the workers assembling iPhones, iPads and other devices often labor in harsh conditions, according to employees inside those plants, worker advocates and documents published by companies themselves. (Duhigg & Barboza, 2012)

Among documented issues noted by workers and their advocates were excessive employee overtime, difficult work conditions that include standing for long hours, and work injuries resulting from poisonous chemicals used in the manufacture and cleaning of products such as iPads. The article noted that "underage workers have helped build Apple's products, and the company's suppliers have improperly disposed of hazardous waste and falsified records." Since the article's publication, Apple has sought to more closely scrutinize its supplier's conduct (Sin, 2016; Apple, 2018), though it has not been alone in its efforts to continue to push down costs, often at the cost of human and environmental exploitation.

In 2017, Samsung production facilities in Vietnam were also investigated for their harsh working conditions. The investigation was based on interviews with 45 workers, 80% of whom were women. Almost all of the workers reported experiencing fatigue and dizziness, both signs of toxic exposure and overwork. Some of the female workers reported having miscarriages, which was noted to be a common occurrence among the factory workers. The company

has also been sued by the family of a former worker who died of a brain tumor caused ostensibly by exposure to toxic substances in the factory (Chen, 2018). According to the lawyer representing the family, brain tumors are the second most common disease, behind leukemia, among former Samsung workers (CBS News, 2017).

Similar to any modern capitalist enterprise, Apple and Samsung operate in a deeply competitive economic environment, and holding costs down is a path to greater profit. Tightly controlled and rapid manufacturing is also key to maintaining the innovations that drive the technology marketplace.

According to *Fortune* magazine, Apple continues to sit atop the list of the world's most admired companies (Samsung did not make the list; Fortune, 2018). Interestingly, this list is the product of a survey of thousands of executives and experts in the business field. Clearly, the focus of these admirers is on products and profit, not on the conditions of labor. Without pressure for change from consumers or companies themselves, the voices of laborers are unlikely to be heard and their interests unlikely to be realized. As an Apple executive interviewed for the *New York Times's* story noted,

> You can either manufacture in comfortable, worker-friendly factories, or you can reinvent the product every year, and make it better and faster and cheaper, which requires factories that seem harsh by American standards. . . . And right now, customers care more about a new iPhone than

working conditions in China (quoted in Duhigg & Barboza, 2012).

Think It Through

- Consider the interests that come into play in this environment: Apple, Samsung, and other manufacturers are interested in low labor costs, efficient and effective production, and high profits. Consumers are interested in new gadgets and technologies to increase their productivity and pleasure. Workers are interested in safe working conditions and good pay. Can all these interests be realized? What do you think?

Starting in the early 1980s, U.S. wages, which had increased for decades, stagnated. Former secretary of labor Robert Reich (2010) writes that

> contrary to popular mythology, trade and technology have not really reduced the number of jobs available to Americans. . . . The real problem [is] that the new [jobs] they got often didn't pay as well as the ones they lost. (pp. 53–54)

Today, wages in the middle and lower segments of the economic hierarchy remain flat.

By the 1990s, advances in computer technologies brought a new wave of outsourcing, not of manufacturing jobs, many of which had already moved offshore, but of information technology and, increasingly, customer service jobs (Erber & Sayed-Ahmed, 2005). Countries such as India, with large populations of educated and English-speaking workers, benefited from American firms' pursuit of lower-cost labor not only in manufacturing but also in service. This movement of technology jobs and other jobs that, as economist David Autor (2010) points out, can be done "over the wires" (digitally) continues unabated today.

The shape of our economy and our economic fortunes has changed in myriad ways and continues to do so. Some of the early contours of a digitally networked economy are becoming apparent in the United States: As noted early in the chapter, advanced technology is shifting its role from that of assisting workers to replacing them. This is already taking place in manufacturing, and it is slowly seeping into the service sector. Even occupational sectors requiring advanced education are not immune to these dramatic changes. Will technology, particularly in the form of robotics and artificial intelligence, contribute to the creation of new jobs and opportunities? Will it diminish or destroy existing economic sectors? These questions remain to be answered. Understanding economic patterns and trends of the past and present is critical to gaining a perspective on how we as individuals and as a country can both prepare for and shape our economic future.

 # What Can I Do with a Sociology Degree?

DATA AND INFORMATION LITERACY

Paradoxically, in the modern world, we are surrounded by information, but we are not always truly well informed. The abilities to distinguish between credible and questionable data, to seek out solid and reliable sources of information, and to use those sources wisely are critical skills in our information society and in today's job market. *Data and information literacy* encompasses the skills to identify the information needed to understand an issue or problem, to seek out credible and accurate sources of information, to recognize what a body of data illuminates and what it obscures, and to apply the information to a description and analysis of the issue at hand.

As a student, you need the skills of data and information literacy to complete tasks such as writing research papers and preparing class presentations. As a consumer, you employ these skills to guide your decisions about the purchase of a home or a vehicle. As a citizen, you need the tools of data and information literacy to make informed political choices about which candidates or causes to support. Data and information literacy is no less significant in the world of work.

As a sociology major, you will be asked to do research on social issues and problems. You are likely to encounter and utilize diverse information

(Continued)

(Continued)

sources, such as databases of the U.S. government (for example, the U.S. Bureau of Labor Statistics or the U.S. Census Bureau) and international organizations (like the World Bank or the United Nations), academic books and research journals, and the mass media. You will have the opportunity to develop data and information literacy skills that enable you to be a solid researcher and a critical consumer of information.

Jessica LeBlanc, Assistant Study Director at the Center for Survey Research, University of Massachusetts Boston

University of New Hampshire, BA in Sociology & International Affairs (Concentration in Spanish Language/Culture)

University of Massachusetts Boston, MA in Applied Sociology

Jessica LeBlanc majored in sociology at the University of New Hampshire, but she didn't really know what kind of career it would lead to. Then she took an undergraduate statistics course and found she really enjoyed it. She took additional methods courses—survey research and an individual research project course—and really liked those also.

By the time she graduated, LeBlanc knew she wanted a job in social research. She looked online for research positions in marketing, health care, and other areas. She noticed an opening at the Center for Survey Research (CSR) at the University of Massachusetts in Boston and thought their work sounded fascinating. The job description said "MA preferred," but within a week, she had an interview and then was hired.

LeBlanc liked CSR because it was academic, had a wide range of projects, and had many that were focused on her primary interests in health.

LeBlanc designed survey questions, transcribed focus group audiotapes, programmed web surveys, and managed incoming data. She also conducted focus groups and interviews and programmed computer-assisted telephone surveys.

The knowledge that LeBlanc gained in her methods courses about research designs, statistics, question construction, and survey procedures prepared her well for her position at CSR. She has found that it's important to understand validity and reliability and the basics of statistical software. Her advice to aspiring researchers: Pay attention in your first methods class!

LeBlanc has also benefited from on-the-job training. In her first year, she learned the ins and outs of the center and social research, she completed an online course in human subjects protections, and she learned how to conduct cognitive interviews and moderate focus groups. She's also learned how to use Microsoft Access and Excel and how to program surveys delivered through computers. Overall, LeBlanc enjoys the nitty-gritty and hands-on, day-to-day management tasks.

Career Data: Survey Researchers

- 2017 Median Pay: $54,270 per year
- $26.09 per hour
- Typical Entry-Level Education: Master's degree
- Job Outlook, 2016–2026: 2% (Slower than average)

Source: Bureau of Labor Statistics, *Occupational Outlook Handbook,* 2017.

SUMMARY

- The **economy**—the social institution that organizes the ways in which a society produces, distributes, and consumes **goods** and services—is one of the most important institutions in society.

- Three major technological revolutions in human history have brought radically new forms of economic organization. The first led to agriculture, the second to modern industry, and the third to the postindustrial society that characterizes the modern United States.

- Industrial society is characterized by **automation**, the modern factory, **mass production, scientific management**, and modern social classes. Postindustrial society is characterized by the use of computers, the increased importance of higher education for well-paying jobs, flexible forms of production, increased reliance on out-sourcing, and the growth of the service economy.

- Although postindustrial society holds the promise of prosperity for people who work with ideas and information, automation and globalization have also allowed for new forms of exploitation of the global workforce and job loss and declining wages for some workers in manufacturing and other sectors.

- Artificial intelligence has the potential to transform the labor market, as machines shift from the role of being an instrument for human workers to being workers themselves. This change may affect jobs for both less-educated and highly educated employees.

- **Capitalism** and **socialism** are the two principal types of political economic systems that emerged with industrial society. While both are committed to higher standards of living through economic growth, they differ on the desirability of private property ownership and the appropriate role of government. Both systems have theoretical and practical strengths and weaknesses.

- **Work** consists of any human effort that adds something of value to goods and services that are available to others. Economists consider three broad categories of work: the **formal economy**, the **informal (or underground) economy**, and unpaid labor.

- The informal economy is an important part of the U.S. economy even though it does not appear in official labor statistics. Although in industrial societies, the informal economy tends to diminish in importance, in recent years, this process has reversed itself.

- In the modern economy, consumption replaces production as the most important economic process. The means of consumption, as defined by sociologist George Ritzer (1999), are "those things that make it possible for people to acquire goods and services and for the same people to be controlled and exploited as consumers" (p. 57). A mall offers consumers buying options, but it also is part of a system of consumer control, as consumers are seduced into buying what they do not need.

- We acquire goods in part based on our consideration of reference groups. As consumption reference groups have changed in the past decades, U.S. consumers have increased spending and taken on a much larger debt load.

- Economic globalization is the result of many factors: technological advances that greatly increased the speed of communication and transportation while lowering their costs, increased educational attainment in low- and middle-income countries, and the opening of many national economies to the world capitalist market. Globalization has had profound effects on the U.S. economy.

KEY TERMS

economy, 419	marginally attached to the labor force, 424	socialism, 432
goods, 419	discouraged workers, 424	work, 434
services, 419	employed, 425	barter economy, 434
mass production, 420	emotional labor, 426	formal economy, 435
reserve army of labor, 420	capitalism, 430	informal (or underground) economy, 435
scientific management, 420	public sector, 430	means of consumption, 437
automation, 422	private sector, 431	
unemployed, 424	communism, 432	
not in the labor force, 424		

DISCUSSION QUESTIONS

1. How is unemployment in the United States measured? What aspects of this phenomenon does the unemployment rate measure and what aspects does it fail to capture?

2. What effects might the expansion of robotics and artificial intelligence have on the U.S. and global workforce?

What evidence of the effect is available today? What sectors of the labor market may be affected in the future?

3. What are the main differences between the formal economy and the informal economy? What are the similarities? What sociological factors explain the existence of the informal economy in the United States?

4. What are the main characteristics of a socialist economic system? Where have such systems been found in recent history? What are their strengths and weaknesses?

5. What sociological factors explain the dramatic rise of consumer debt in the United States over the past three to four decades? Why should this be of concern to society and to policy makers?

Want a Better Grade?

Get the tools you need to sharpen your study skills. Access practice quizzes, eFlashcards, video, and multimedia at **https://edge.sagepub.com/chambliss4e**

WELD QUEEN

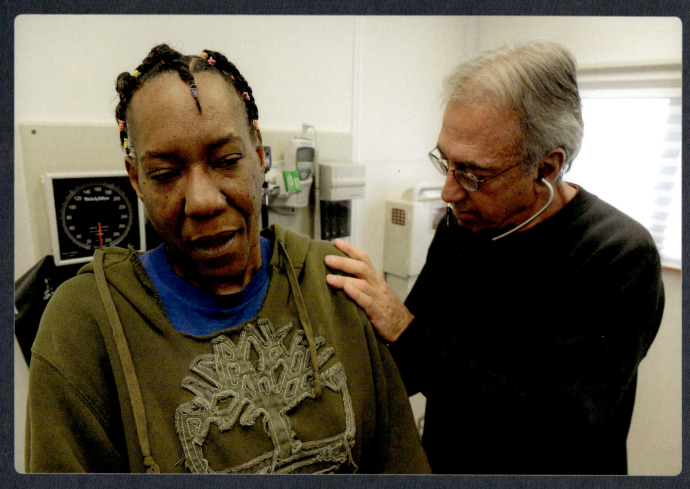
© Andy Cross/The Denver Post via Getty Images

Health and Medicine

16

WHAT DO YOU THINK?

1. What sociological factors help explain the rise of opioid use and abuse in U.S. communities?

2. Do you think that use of the Internet—similar to the use of tobacco, drugs, or alcohol—can become an addiction? If so, how should society respond?

3. Why are the poor more likely than their middle-class counterparts to be overweight or obese? What sociological factors might researchers look at to understand this correlation?

LEARNING OBJECTIVES

16.1 Explain cultural definitions of health and illness.

16.2 Describe key issues in health care in the United States.

16.3 Define public health and identify important public health problems in the United States. Analyze public health issues through the lens of sociological theory.

16.4 Recognize HIV/AIDS as a sociological concern.

16.5 Identify sociological aspects of global health issues.

THE SCOURGE OF ADDICTION

Opioid addiction is having a dramatic and devastating effect on U.S. communities and families. According to the U.S. Department of Health and Human Services, in 2016, 11.5 million people misused prescription opioids. Another 948,000 used heroin, an illegal opioid. In the same year, over 42,000 people died from an opioid overdose, an average of 116 each day (U.S. Department of Health and Human Services, 2018). The problem has continued to grow: The number of opioid overdose deaths has grown five-fold since 1999 and statistically significant increases in overdose death rates were recorded in 26 U.S. states (Figure 16.1; U.S. Centers for Disease Control and Prevention 2017).

According to recent research (Cicero, Ellis, Surratt, & Kurtz, 2014), while the epidemic of addiction is widespread, heroin use involves "primarily white men and women in their late 20s living outside of large urban areas." Notably, a segment of these users "graduated" to heroin after becoming addicted to prescription opioids, in particular, painkillers such as OxyContin and Vicodin: The authors point out that "the

©REUTERS/Brian Snyder

■ **FIGURE 16.1** Statistically Significant Drug Overdose Death Increase, 2015–2016

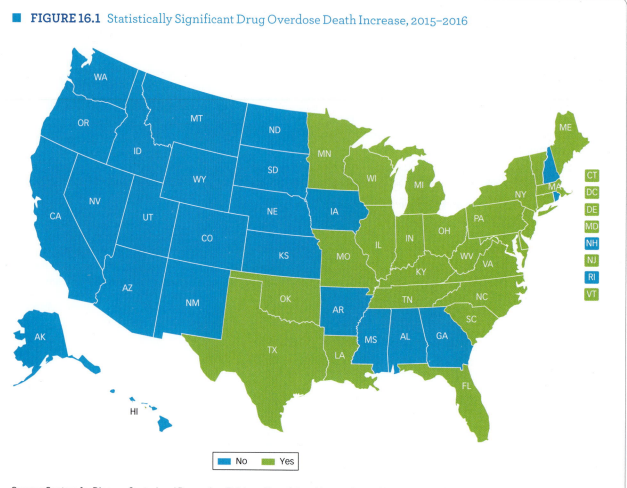

Source: Centers for Disease Control and Prevention. Retrieved from https://www.cdc.gov/drugoverdose/data/statedeaths.html.

factors driving this shift may be related to the fact that heroin is cheaper and more accessible than prescription opioids, and there seems to be widespread acceptance of heroin use among those who abuse opioid products."

Among the areas hit hard by this epidemic are the cities and towns of Ohio. In 2016, the state had 3,613 opioid overdose deaths. Ohio's rate of overdose deaths was 32.9 per 100,000; by comparison, the national rate was 13.3 per 100,000 (National Institute on Drug Abuse, 2018). Stunningly, from 2000 to 2015, the number of fatal drug overdoses overall in Ohio grew by 642%. In terms of opioid overdose deaths, Ohio trails only the state of West Virginia (Hamilton, 2017). At the root of this phenomenon is the deceptive marketing of opioid painkillers by drug companies as nonaddictive and opioid painkillers being overprescribed by healthcare providers (Quinones, 2015). In fact, the state of Ohio is suing five drug manufacturers, alleging that the companies made misleading claims about the addictive potential of the drugs (Hamilton, 2017).

The ongoing opioid epidemic in the U.S. requires examination and action. Efforts are being made by families, public officials, law enforcement, and health professionals to address the problem in Ohio and across the country, though the problem is still acute. Interestingly, many (though certainly not all) of those efforts have focused on treatment—which implies the recognition of drug addiction, including heroin abuse, as a health problem—rather than criminalization. Observing this response, journalist Andrew Cohen (2015) raises some interesting sociological questions:

> Are policymakers going easier today on heroin users (white and often affluent) than their elected predecessors did a generation ago when confronted with crack addicts who were largely black, disenfranchised, and economically bereft? Can we explain the disparate response to the "black" heroin epidemic of the 1960s, in which its use and violent crime were commingled in the public consciousness, and the white heroin "epidemic" today, in which its use is considered a disease to be treated or cured, without using race as part of our explanation? (para. 5)

Research has shown that people of every age group benefit from regular exercise. In this photo, older women in South Africa participate in local soccer matches. Soccer is wildly popular in the country and it is played by members of every age group.

©REUTERS/Siphiwe Sibeko

Cohen's questions help us to see how issues of health and illness may be intimately intertwined with contemporary issues of race, class, and political power. The medicalization or criminalization of addiction, which we discuss further along in the chapter, can have a significant effect on how users are viewed and treated.

At one time, sociology and the study of human health and illness went their separate ways. In the past half century, however, this situation has changed significantly (Cockerham & Glasser, 2000; Weitz, 2012). Today, it is widely accepted that sociology can contribute to our understanding of mental and physical health and illness, social group disparities in health, and public health issues such as smoking, gun violence, obesity, and opioid abuse and treatment. In this chapter, we look at health and medicine from a sociological perspective. We focus on the important role that social forces play in health and health care in the United States, and we address issues at the crossroads of medicine, health, public policy, and sociology. We begin by distinguishing *health* from *medicine*. We then turn to an examination of the ways in which ideas about health and illness are socially constructed in culture. We look at health and safety as well as the relationship between class status and health care and outcomes in the United States, delving into the important issue of health care access and reform in the United States. Further, we highlight sociological issues related to public health, including tobacco use, obesity, and opioid addiction. We also discuss the sociology of HIV/AIDS, a global health challenge that continues to threaten lives, livelihoods, and entire communities and countries. We end with a consideration of global issues of health and their sociological roots.

Cultural Definitions of Health and Illness

Although health and medicine are closely related, sociologists find it useful to distinguish between them. **Health** is *the extent to which a person experiences a state of mental,*

Health: The extent to which a person experiences a state of mental, physical, and social well-being.

physical, and social well-being. It encompasses not merely the absence of illness but a positive sense of soundness as well. This definition, put forth by the World Health Organization (WHO, 2005), draws attention to the interplay of psychological, physiological, and sociological factors in a person's sense of well-being. It makes clear that excellent health cannot be achieved in purely physical terms. Health cannot be realized if the body is disease-free but the mind is troubled or the social environment is harmful.

Medicine is *an institutionalized system for the scientific diagnosis, treatment, and prevention of illness.* It focuses on identifying and treating physiological and psychological conditions that prevent a person from achieving a state of normal health. In this effort, medicine typically applies scientific knowledge derived from physical sciences such as chemistry, biology, and physics as well as psychology. In the United States, we usually view medicine in terms of the failure of health: When people become ill, they seek medical advice to address the problem. Yet, as the above definition suggests, medicine and health can go hand in hand. The field of **preventive medicine**—*medicine that emphasizes a healthy lifestyle that will prevent poor health before it occurs*—is of key interest to health professionals, patients, and policy makers.

Sociologist Talcott Parsons introduced the concept of the *sick role*, which offers sociologists the opportunity to think about the condition of being ill as not only a physical condition but also a social status with particular characteristics and expectations.

The Sick Role

Cultural definitions of sickness and health and their causes vary widely (Sagan, 1987). There are sick roles in every society. **Sick roles** are *rooted in cultural definitions of the appropriate behavior of and response to people labeled as sick* and are thus sociologically determined (Cockerham & Glasser, 2000; Parsons, 1951, 1975). The sick role of being mentally ill, for instance, varies enormously across time and space (Foucault, 1988). In some societies, mentally ill people have been seen as having unique spiritual qualities, while in others, they have been labeled as victims of demonic possession. In modern societies, mental illness is characterized sometimes as a disease with physiological antecedents and, at other times, as a sign of character weakness.

One of the pioneers in the sociology of medicine, Talcott Parsons (1975), observed that, in the United States, the role of *sick person* includes the right to be excused from social responsibilities and other normal social roles. Parsons, whose theories reflect a functionalist perspective on social

life, suggested that illness is medically and socially defined, because a normal state of functioning includes both physiological equilibrium and the capacity to enact expected social roles and behaviors.

Even if illness results from a lifestyle that puts a person at risk, society does not usually hold him or her accountable. On the other hand, the sick person has a societal obligation to try to get well and to seek competent medical help in order to do so. Failure to seek help can lead others to refuse to confer on the suffering individual the benefits of the sick role.

The notion that a sick person is enacting a social role may remind us of Erving Goffman's (1959) ideas about humans as actors on a social stage. Goffman suggested that life is like a dramatic play, with front and back stages, scripts for certain settings, costumes, and props. In order to define situations in ways that are favorable to ourselves, he argued, we all play roles on the "front stage" that conform to what is expected and that will show us in the best light and contribute to a smooth social interaction.

Imagine a doctor's office as a stage: The doctor arrives wearing a "costume" (often a white lab coat and stethoscope). The patient also wears a "costume" (a cloth or paper gown rather than street clothing). The doctor is expected to greet the patient, ask questions about the illness, examine the patient, and offer advice. The patient is expected to assume a more passive role, submitting to an examination, accepting the diagnosis, and taking advice rather than dispensing it. Now imagine a scenario in which the doctor arrives dressed in evening attire, and the patient gives the doctor medical counsel or refuses to lie on the

---

Medicine: An institutionalized system for the scientific diagnosis, treatment, and prevention of illness.

Preventive medicine: Medicine that emphasizes a healthy lifestyle that will prevent poor health before it occurs.

Sick roles: Social roles rooted in cultural definitions of the appropriate behavior of and response to people labeled as sick.

examining table, choosing instead to sit in the doctor's chair. The result would be failed expectations about the encounter as well as an unsuccessful social and medical interaction. As Parsons pointed out, the sick person has an expected role, as so do doctors, nurses, and others who are part of the "sick play."

The Social Construction of Illness

Parsons's model underscores the fact that the sick role is culturally determined. Illnesses that are culturally defined as legitimate, such as cancer and heart disease, entitle those diagnosed with them to adopt the role of sick person. The afflicted are forgiven for missing time at work, spending days in bed, and asking others for consideration and assistance. A seriously ill person who persists in leading a normal life is given credit for an extraordinary exertion of effort.

Changes in U.S. society's response to alcoholism highlight the importance of cultural definitions of illness. In the middle of the 20th century, people addicted to alcohol were widely seen as weak and of questionable character. In 1956, however, the American Medical Association (2013) declared alcoholism an illness. With the broad acceptance of this medical model of alcoholism, alcoholics often expect and receive sympathy from family members for their illness, employers may offer programs to help them fight the disease, and the government funds research in an effort to combat the problem.

While there also exists a disease model of drug addiction (Le Moal & Koob, 2007), someone addicted to illegal drugs is more likely than an alcoholic to be denied the sick role. Cocaine, heroin, and methamphetamine addicts, for example, face the possibility of being sent to prison if they are found in possession of the drugs, and they may or may not be referred for treatment of their addiction. In 24 states and the District of Columbia, substance use during pregnancy is considered to be child abuse; another three states categorize it as grounds for civil commitment. Of particular note is the South Carolina Supreme Court's holding that a viable fetus is a "person" under the state's criminal child-endangerment statute: thus, "maternal acts endangering or likely to endanger the life, comfort, or health of a viable fetus" are criminal acts of child abuse (quoted in Guttmacher Institute 2018). This is significant because, according to a recent study on the issue of criminal charges for child harm in pregnancy, "the judicial decision depended on the disposition of the question of whether . . . a fetus is a child. The balance in the courts in favor of treating substance use during pregnancy depends on the definition of a child for the purposes of criminal statutes" (Angelotta & Appelbaum 2017, p. 193).

While there are clear reasons to be concerned about the welfare of infants born to addicted mothers, it is less clear that there are significant benefits to criminally charging new mothers and separating them from their children than to supporting their recovery in treatment programs.

As we saw in the opening story, some drug addiction is widely understood as *illness* while some is labeled as *deviance*, transforming the status of the individual who carries the label (Goffman, 1963b). What explains the difference? Do you think these differing definitions are justified?

Health Care and Public Health in the United States

Health care can be defined as *all those activities intended to sustain, promote, and enhance health.* An adequate health care system includes more than the provision of medical services for those who need them—it also encompasses policies that minimize violence and the chance of accidents, whether on the highways, at work, or at home; policies that promote a clean, nontoxic environment; ecological protection; and the availability of clean water, fresh air, and sanitary living conditions.

Health and Public Safety Issues

By the standards noted above, few societies come close to providing excellent health care for their citizens. Some, however, do much better than others. The record of the United States in this regard is mixed.

On one hand, the U.S. government spends vast sums of money in its efforts to construct safe highways, provide clean drinking water, and eliminate or reduce air and ground pollution. Laws are in place to regulate working conditions with the aim of promoting healthy and safe workplace environments: The federal Occupational Safety and Health Administration is responsible for enforcing regulations intended to guard the lives and health of U.S. workers. Local health inspectors visit the premises of restaurants and grocery stores to check that food is handled in a sanitary manner, and agricultural inspectors check the quality of U.S. and imported food products. States require drivers to use seat belts, motorcyclists to wear helmets, and children to be strapped into car seats, all of which have been shown to reduce injuries and fatalities in road accidents. While these efforts do not guarantee the safety of life, work, food, or transport, they contribute to public safety in important ways.

Health care: All those activities intended to sustain, promote, and enhance health.

On the other hand, compared to most other modern countries, the U.S. is more violent, a factor that compromises safety, in particular for some high-risk groups. Gun violence is a serious problem (Figure 16.2) as are gun accidents and suicides (Figure 16.3). The U.S. has the 31st highest rate of gun violence in the world, and incidences of homicides due to gun violence are 25 times higher in the U.S. than in 22 other developed countries (Aizenman, 2018; Grinshteyn & Hemenway, 2016). Homicide is a leading cause of death among young African American males, and the majority of this violence is perpetrated using guns: in fact, Black men are 13 times more likely to be killed by gun violence than White men (Kaiser Family Foundation, 2006; Violence Policy Center, 2010; Gun Violence by the Numbers, n.d.). Significantly as well, of the over 40,000

Americans who die by suicide each year, just over half are killed by a firearm (National Institute of Mental Health, 2018).

Domestic violence puts thousands of women at risk: At least 85% of victims of domestic violence are women, and an average of three women are murdered by a husband or boyfriend every day in the United States. In 2010, 38% of all female murder victims in the United States were killed by a husband or boyfriend (National Center for Victims of Crime, 2012). The abuse may start young: In one study, one in three adolescent females reported being physically and/or sexually abused by a dating partner (Davis, 2008). Additionally, 9% of high school students report purposeful physical abuse by a partner within the past 12 months (National Center for Injury Prevention and Control, 2014). This occurs in spite of the fact that

■ **FIGURE 16.2** Rate of Violent Gun Deaths per 100,000 Population for Selected Countries, 2016

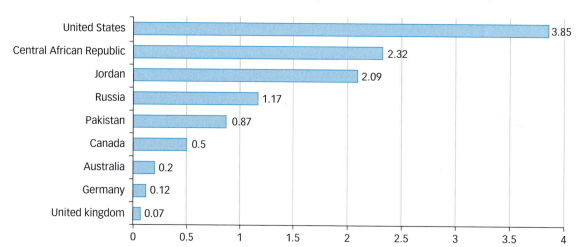

Source: Data from Institute for Health Metrics and Evaluation (IHME). GBD Compare. Seattle, WA: IHME, University of Washington, 2018.

■ **FIGURE 16.3** Number of Firearm Suicides by Age Group and Sex, 2016

Source: CDC. "Suicide Rates in the United States Continue to Increase." Retrieved from https://www.cdc.gov/nchs/products/databriefs/db309.htm.

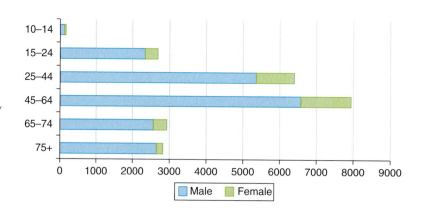

there are myriad laws against abuse, mechanisms for securing restraining orders against would-be attackers, and shelters for battered women. Efforts to protect victims and potential victims of domestic violence may fall short because batterers are often given a pass by those hesitant to

interfere and because victims lack resources to leave their abusers or fear reprisals.

Different social groups experience different degrees of violence and safety. Black Americans are far more likely than Whites to be victims of homicide, and women are more

Social Life, Social Media
ADDICTION AND THE INTERNET

An advertisement for a leading telecommunications company opens with a young boy and his mother happily staring into a tablet screen while the gentleman seated next to them on the train struggles to get a signal on his smartphone. The ad declares that "if you're losing the connection with everything you love, stop searching" and entreats viewers to sign up for the ostensibly more reliable network. The things loved by the viewer are presumed to be that which is available on the Internet: In fact, the average person has twice as many social media accounts today as in 2012 (Mander, 2017). But is this really "everything" we love today? Is something also being lost when we spend a growing proportion of each day interacting with our electronic devices? In a time when, according to a 2015 Common Sense Media report, teens spend an average of nine hours per day engaged in using media for enjoyment (Wallace, 2015), it may make sense to ask whether this love comes at a cost.

Scientific studies point to a growing epidemic of technological dependency, even addiction. A *Newsweek* article on the issue notes, "In less than the span of a single childhood, Americans have merged with their machines, staring at a screen for

at least eight hours a day, more time than we spend on any other activity including sleeping" (Dokoupil, 2012a). Some Internet users neglect sleep, family, and health in favor of the virtual world: In one extreme case, a British widow and mother of three was arrested after she reportedly stopped buying food for her children and allowed her two dogs to starve because she was obsessed with playing a video game called "Small Worlds" (Freeman, 2012). At least 10 cases have been documented of Internet surfers getting fatal blood clots from prolonged sitting at the computer. While most cases are not so acute in their consequences, the American Psychiatric Association has included "Internet addiction disorder" in the fifth edition of the *Diagnostic and Statistical Manual of Mental Disorders* (*DSM-5*) as a condition for further study (Dokoupil, 2012a). A publication by psychiatric researchers in Asia, which has very high rates of heavy Internet use, particularly by gamers, points out, "A functional magnetic resonance imaging (MRI) study found that a cue-induced online gaming urge among individuals with Internet gaming abuse activated brain areas similar to those involved in craving in people with drug addiction" (Yen, Yen, & Ko, 2010). Observers suggest that while questions remain about whether brain changes lead to addictive behavior or heavy Internet use fosters brain changes, it is becoming increasingly clear that technology is linked in some way to problems that include addictive behavior, declining attention spans, increasing impulsiveness, anxiety, and depression.

©iStockphoto.com/THEPALMER

How many hours each day do members of your family spend online? What about your friends and you? What are the costs and benefits of our increasing dependence on electronic gadgets and social media?

Think It Through

- Do you think that heavy Internet use is a problem? If so, is it an individual problem or a social problem?

Follow us on Twitter to keep up with current sociological stories and research! We're at **@DiscoverSoc1.**

Share your own ideas at **#DiscoverSociology.**

likely than men to be killed by intimate partners. Why are some groups in society more vulnerable to violence? Is there a link between physical safety and the power a group has (or does not have) in society? What do you think?

Social Inequalities in Health and Medicine

By nearly every measure, health follows the social class curve: Poor people are more likely than their better-off counterparts to suffer chronic illnesses and die earlier. Among children, poverty affects health, food security, housing stability, and maltreatment, with the former two factors playing a significant role in the likelihood of developing chronic illnesses and other negative outcomes such as malnutrition, stunted growth, and suppressed immunity (Henry, 2010). Recessions and economic slumps also hurt families, straining their ability to afford quality food, housing, and health care.

Lower-income people are more likely to live in areas that have high levels of air pollution, which raises their risks of asthma, heart disease, and cancer (Calderón-Garcidueñas & Torres-Jardón, 2012). The poor have a considerably higher risk of exposure to dangerous levels of lead from paint in older homes or aging public infrastructure, including lead pipes (see the *Private Lives, Public Issues* box in this chapter for a discussion of the recent crisis of lead in the water in Flint, Michigan). Low-income Americans have a greater probability of exposure to violence and the mental and physical health problems that entails. Their work is also more likely to involve physical and health risks than is the work of middle- and upper-class people (Commission to Build a Healthier America, 2009).

The poor often have less-healthy diets than do their higher-income counterparts: Inexpensive foods may be highly processed, fatty, and high in sugar. Fresh fruits and vegetables and lean meats may be out of financial reach for those who struggle to make ends meet, and time pressures can limit a working-man's or workingwoman's opportunities to shop for and prepare healthy foods. Children in poor communities may also lack access to safe places for active outdoor play and exercise, contributing to higher rates of obesity and being overweight. Another factor that affects the health of the poorer classes is that they are less likely to perceive the symptoms of illness as requiring attention from a physician (Keeley, Wright, & Condit, 2009).

Inequalities start even before birth, since poor mothers are less likely to have access to prenatal care. A report prepared for the Annie E. Casey Foundation suggests

that "at any age, and at any income, education or socioeconomic level, an African American mother is more than twice as likely to lose her infant as a white woman" (Shore & Shore, 2009, p. 6). Indeed, 2015 data show the rate of infant mortality to be 4.82 per 1,000 live births for White mothers and 11.73 per 1,000 live births for Black mothers in the United States. Black mothers are also significantly more likely than nonblack mothers to give birth to infants with low birth weight (13.68%) or very low birth weight (3%): By comparison, only 7% of infants of White or Hispanic mothers have low birth weight and 1% are of very low birth weight (Martin et al., 2018).

Race and class closely intersect in the U.S. and data show that racial minorities, on average, suffer from worse health than Whites, which is reflected in differences in life expectancy (see Figure 16.4). In 2015, the overall life expectancy at birth in the United States was 78.8 years. White women's life expectancy was highest at 81.1, while Black women's was lower at 78.1. White men had a life expectancy of 76.3 years, but their Black counterparts had a life expectancy of 71.8 years (Murphy, Xu, Kochanek, Curtin, & Arias , 2017). The differences are linked to, among other factors, higher rates of death among Blacks due to high blood pressure, heart disease, cancer, diabetes, and homicide. Self-reported health status figures underscore disparities: Between 2013 and 2016, about 15.7% of Whites reported that their health status was "fair or poor," while 20.5% of Blacks indicated the same (Kaiser Family Foundation, 2016).

It is notable that Hispanic women and men have longer average life expectancy than their White and Black

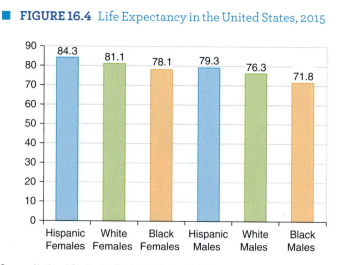

FIGURE 16.4 Life Expectancy in the United States, 2015

Source: National Center for Health Statistics. Health, United States, 2017. Life expectancy at birth, by race and Hispanic origin, and sex: United States, 1940, 1950, 1960, 1970, 1980, 1990, and 2000–2015.

peers. Given that Hispanic families and communities are more likely to be poor than White ones and that Hispanics also suffer negative effects from prejudice and discrimination, how can this be explained? Among the hypotheses advanced to explain this are the healthy migrant effect, which suggests that immigrants are less likely to be drawn from the fraction of a population that is in ill health or of advanced age. As well, researchers cite "salmon bias," which posts that immigrant Hispanic residents in the U.S. may return to their home country when ill, particularly if they lack access to good health care options in the U.S. (Murphy et al., 2017; Scommenga, 2017). Some research also shows that Hispanic immigrants are less likely to be smokers than their nonimmigrant counterparts (Scommenga, 2017).

Inequality Matters

RACE, MEDICAL SCIENCE, AND EXPLOITATION

For much of its history, the medical establishment in the U.S. exploited poor minorities to advance the frontiers of science. In the infamous Tuskegee study, which ran from the 1930s to the 1970s, Black males who had contracted syphilis were intentionally left untreated so that researchers could study the progress of the disease (Brandt, 1983; Washington, 2007). The U.S. Public Health Service in collaboration with Tuskegee University, a historically black college, carried out the study between 1932 and 1972. Over that period, 399 African American men who were predominantly poor and illiterate sharecroppers were never told of the disease they were suffering from or of its serious consequences. Rather, doctors informed them that they were being treated for "bad blood." The doctors and scientists performing the study, however, had no intention of curing them, as experimental data was to be collected from the autopsies of the men.

During the Cold War years following World War II, U.S. government agencies funded and conducted hundreds of research tests on unwitting citizens to assess the effects of radiation and other by-products of war (Budiansky, Goode, & Gest, 1994). These tests were usually conducted on the poor and disproportionately on minorities (Washington, 2007).

A 2010 book by Rebecca Skloot, *The Immortal Life of Henrietta Lacks*, tells the compelling story of a woman who has become a significant symbol of the ethical dilemmas—and lapses—of medical science. Henrietta Lacks was a 31-year-old wife and mother of five when she was diagnosed with virulent cervical cancer, which would kill her in 1951. She was a poor Black woman treated in the colored ward of a Baltimore, Maryland, hospital. Without her knowledge, the cells removed during her cancer biopsy were cultured in a lab and discovered to have unique properties that enabled them to reproduce in the lab. These *HeLa* cells (named with the first two letters of her first and last names), according to one account, have "helped build thousands of careers,

©GL Archive / Alamy Stock Photo

not to mention more than 60,000 scientific studies, with nearly 10 more being published every day, revealing the secrets of everything from aging to cancer to mosquito mating" (Margonelli, 2010, para. 2).

Shockingly, as Skloot recounts, the family did not know about the HeLa cells and their contributions, both financial and scientific, until many years after Henrietta Lacks's death Skloot (2010). In the book, one of Henrietta's daughters, Deborah, points poignantly to the paradox of the family's position:

> Truth be told, I can't get mad at science, because it helped people live, and I'd be a mess without it. I'm a walking drugstore. . . . But I won't lie, I would like some health insurance so I don't got to pay all that money every month for drugs my mother cells probably helped make. (quoted in Margonelli, 2010, para. 7)

Henrietta Lacks's cells were cultured in a lab at Johns Hopkins University Hospital without her or her family's permission. They have been a boon to medical science and to researchers across the globe. What is owed to her and to her family for their contribution to these discoveries? What do you think?

Think It Through

- When significant scientific discoveries about diseases or their treatment and prevention are made by medical science using unethical means, how should society use those discoveries? Should they use them at all?

While only part of the U.S. Hispanic population is comprised of immigrants, the factors cited by researchers highlight some of the sociological roots of Hispanic longevity in the U.S.

Access to Health Care

One important reason the poor—as well as some families in the working and middle classes—in the United States are less likely to experience good health is that a notable proportion are unable to access regular care for prevention and treatment of disease. In the fall of 2010, three years after the start of the Great Recession and shortly before the Patient Protection and Affordable Care Act (which we discuss below) was signed into law, the U.S. Census Bureau reported that more than 16% of people in the United States were without health insurance, the highest figure in 23 years (Kaiser Family Foundation, 2010a). Key sources of this decline were the economic crisis and the associated rise in unemployment; most U.S. adults get health insurance coverage from their employers. Workplace coverage is variable, however, and ranges from full benefits requiring little or no financial contribution from the employee to partial benefits paid for through shared employer and employee contributions. Cost-saving measures in U.S. workplaces in recent decades have shifted a greater share of the cost of these benefits from employers to employees.

As the economic picture has improved since 2010, many people have gone back to work, but millions of employees are still uninsured or underinsured. This problem has been worsened by a changing labor market and economic structure that favors part-time or contractual employment, with

Private Lives, Public Issues
DANGER IN THE WATER

In February 2015, Lee Anne Walters, a resident of Flint, Michigan, learned some startling news: According to Michigan Radio, the water flowing from Walters's tap turned up with "a lead content of 104 parts per billion. Fifteen parts per billion is the [Environmental Protection Agency's] limit for lead in drinking water." In April, Walters reported that her child had been diagnosed with lead poisoning (Kennedy, 2016), a condition that can lead to impaired cognition, behavioral disorders, and delayed puberty, among other health consequences (CNN, 2016). By June, a team of researchers from Virginia Tech had tested the water at Walters's home and determined that some of the tap water had a lead level as high as 13,200 parts per billion; by comparison, water contaminated with 5,000 parts per billion is classified by the EPA as hazardous waste (Kennedy, 2016).

Lee Anne Walters and her child were not, as subsequent investigation has revealed, alone in their exposure to Flint's toxic water cocktail. A substantial proportion of Flint's 99,000 residents, most of whom are Black and over 40% of whom live below the poverty line, had also been drinking and bathing in the same water and many were ill, experiencing a range of symptoms that included skin rashes and hair loss. About a year earlier, in an effort to save money, Flint officials, together with state-level authorities, had opted to switch Flint's water source from Detroit's water system to the Flint River, which was less costly to access (Kennedy, 2016). According to a later study by Virginia Tech researchers, Flint's "river water was found to be 19 times more corrosive than water from Detroit" (CNN, 2016).

The case of Flint is one that entreats us to apply our sociological imagination. While a single case or a handful of cases of lead poisoning—which may also be the result of peeling lead paint in older homes—might be seen as a personal trouble to be addressed with home repairs and health measures for children (similar to a healthy diet and robust educational programs), the mass exposure to lead that occurred through Flint's water supply beginning in 2014 is surely a public issue. What, then, are the issues from a sociological perspective? Among others, we might consider the following. First, Flint, a former industrial city that built its early prosperity as home to the country's largest General Motors plant, is an example of a postindustrial city that, in the wake of the mass deindustrialization that began in the United States in the 1970s, has seen its economic fortunes collapse into widespread poverty and joblessness. The cost of this has been borne by individual households as well as the city itself, which has long been in dire economic crisis. It was, at least in part, the city's poor financial condition that led to the decision to switch away from the clean water supply coming from Detroit.

Second, as noted above, Flint's population is largely African American and poor. *The New York Times* writes that "residents and advocates have expressed outrage over the government's failure to protect Flint's children, something many of them say would not have happened if the city were largely white" (Goodnough, 2016). Some use the term *environmental racism*, coined in the 1980s, to describe what has transpired in Flint over the last several years, suggesting that Flint is one in a long line of sites at which Black residents have been disproportionately exposed to "some of the most industrialized and dilapidated environments," which also include a southwest pocket of Detroit that is 84% Black and has been identified as the most polluted ZIP code in the state (Eligon, 2016).

Modern industry has generated wealth, convenience, and comfort. It has also wrought consequences that include waste and pollution. Are the former concentrated more fully at the top of the socioeconomic ladder and enjoyed by White residents? Are the latter more likely to be visited upon minorities and poor? These are questions that sociologists explore.

Think It Through

- Why are the poor and minorities in the U.S. more likely to be exposed to pollution and its health consequences than others? How should decision makers and communities respond to these pervasive inequalities?

---

fewer benefits such as the employer-based health insurance coverage that has traditionally applied to full-time employees.

A substantial number of Americans have access to health care through government-funded programs such as Medicare, an elder insurance program that covers most of those ages 65 and over (about 47.8 million in 2016) and some younger residents with disabilities (about 9.0 million in the same year; NCPSSM, 2018). Medicaid, a shared federal and state insurance program that provides coverage for many poor adults and children, reached an enrollment of 67.5 million in February 2018 (Medicaid.gov, 2018). Medicare was created in 1965 to serve as a federal health insurance program for people age 65 and older, regardless of income or medical history. It covers very diverse populations, because most people over the age of 65 and those with permanent disabilities are entitled to coverage (Kaiser Family Foundation, 2014a). Medicaid, on the other hand, is the country's major health insurance program designed to assist low-income people of all ages with their health care needs, but it is not available to everyone who needs long-term services; to be eligible for Medicaid, individuals must meet stringent financial qualifications (Kaiser Family Foundation, 2012a).

A contemporary issue related to Medicare is the fact that members of the post–World War II baby-boomer generation (those born between about 1946 and 1964) are now entering the 65+-year-old cohort. As the "boomers" reach eligibility age, their massive numbers will have an effect on the nation's need for health care dollars and resources. The U.S. Census Bureau reports that between 2000 and 2010, the 65+-age cohort grew at a faster rate than the total population; the total population of the United States increased by less than 10%, while the population of those 65 and older grew by more than 15% (Werner, 2011). The increase in eligible Medicare recipients, medical advancements that extend the lives of the elderly, and a relatively smaller tax base are the ingredients of a debate over care and government spending that will grow more acute in the years to come (Antos, 2011).

At the opposite end of the age spectrum, the State Children's Health Insurance Program (SCHIP) was created in the late 1990s in an effort to cover more uninsured children. Because individual states administer SCHIP in partnership with the federal government, state governments largely dictate its implementation, so the comprehensiveness of coverage and eligibility standards varies from state to state. As of the start of 2018, however, there were about 6.4 million children enrolled in SCHIP programs (Medicaid.gov, 2018).

While the care that the poorest U.S. adults can access through Medicaid is limited, it is often the working poor and other low-income employees who are shut out of insurance coverage altogether. They are most likely to be working in economic sectors such as the service industry (fast-food restaurants, retail establishments, and the like) that provide few or no insurance benefits to employees—employees earn too little to afford self-coverage but too much to qualify for government health coverage. The fact, as noted above, that low-income people are more likely to have health problems has also affected their ability to get insurance coverage in the past, because insurers were allowed to exclude those with preexisting conditions such as diabetes, high blood pressure, and other illnesses and disabilities.

The Patient Protection and Affordable Care Act (known simply as the Affordable Care Act or ACA), signed into law by President Barack Obama in 2010, was created to expand insurance coverage to more people in the U.S. at a time when the numbers of the uninsured had been rising. The goal of this massive health insurance overhaul was to bring more people into the insurance fold by making coverage more broadly accessible and affordable, in part by requiring that everyone buy insurance and that private insurance companies offer coverage under new terms that extend benefits to those who may have had difficulty purchasing insurance in the past, such as those with preexisting conditions. Among the ACA provisions was also the requirement that insurance companies permit young people up to age 26 to remain on their parents' health insurance policies if they do not have other coverage. Recent changes to the ACA by the Republican-dominated Congress have done away with some provisions of the law, including the individual mandate. While the ACA remains in force at the time of this writing, the effects of changes made in the last year are not yet clear.

Since its passage, the ACA has been the source of heated political debate. President Obama and other supporters of the act have argued that the law has expanded insurance coverage to a broader swath of people, many of whom had been locked out of the insurance market due to preexisting conditions or unaffordability of individual insurance policies. They suggest that the law has supported this expansion of coverage through the operation of new state-level insurance markets (or exchanges) that keep prices down by enabling purchasers to buy insurance as part of a group. Those with low incomes are eligible for federal subsidies to support their insurance purchases. Supporters also note that greater coverage means that more people can seek primary and preventive care, which helps to keep patients out of emergency rooms and hospitals, where care is far more costly.

Opponents have argued that the U.S. government overstepped its limits in requiring that people purchase health insurance or pay a penalty tax for failing to do so; thus, the individual mandate was eliminated by Congress in 2017. The effect of this change, however, may be to increase the cost of insurance, as those who are sicker opt to stay insured, while those who are in good health leave the marketplace. There have also been attempts to portray the ACA as a path to socialized medicine, though most people will receive their insurance through private insurance companies rather than through the government.

Both supporters and opponents of the ACA have expressed concerns about the costs of health care in the U.S. Indeed, the country spends more per capita on health care than most economically developed states (Figure 16.5), though many of its health indicators compare poorly to those of its peers. Opponents of health care reform have argued that the ACA drives up costs by requiring insurers to

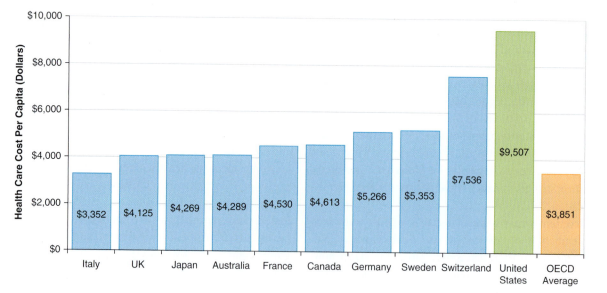

■ **FIGURE 16.5** Per Capita Health Care Spending for Selected Developed Countries, 2015

Source: Peter G. Peterson Foundation. (2018). Per Capita Healthcare Costs International Comparison. Retrieved from https://www.pgpfg.org/chart-archive/0006_health-care-oecd.

Note: Data are for 2015 or latest available. Chart uses purchasing power parities to convert data into U.S. dollars.

Communications researcher Jean Kilbourne (1999) says female-targeted cigarette ads often contain subtexts about female thinness, using *thin*, *slim*, or *light* in the product name. Ads also imply that smoking can help women lose weight; in the past, Lucky cigarettes urged, "Reach for a Lucky instead of a sweet."

cover those who have costly health conditions. Supporters of the law point out that having a large pool of uninsured contributes to higher costs when they fail to get preventive care and must resort to far more expensive emergency room care or hospitalization. Certainly, an aging U.S. population will likely need more, not fewer, health care services in the future. How the U.S. government and states will address these needs in the future remains to be seen.

Can Technology Expand Health Care Access?

Would you like to have a doctor on demand? Technological innovations are bringing health care into people's homes, opening the door for greater access to medical care as well as a potential reduction in unneeded doctor's office visits. As a *Time* magazine article on the technological expansion of access to medical care points out, such technology was "previously reserved mostly for luxe private practices or rural communities that lack access to health care" (Sifferlin, 2014). Today, it is available on a downloadable app.

New technological innovations such as Doctor on Demand, American Well, and AskMD offer a range of services, from the opportunity to ask physicians medical questions by text and receive free responses to online appointments that require payment for consultations. Employers are increasingly making telehealth options available to employees: According to *Money* magazine, both outside investors and large employers have shown a strong interest in telehealth (Pinsker, 2015). Potential beneficiaries of these technologies include entrepreneurs and investors (who seek to profit from this new health care vehicle), patients (who have new avenues to reach medical professionals), and doctors (as online consultations can help them build their public profiles and earn some extra income).

Are there potential pitfalls to the use of these technologies as well? Are there potential losers? Those patients who have acute or urgent needs are still best served by personal visits to a healthcare provider. As well, those who do not

own computers or smartphones or cannot pay the fees for online consultations may still be locked out of these opportunities. Telehealth technology may, however, offer a potential vehicle for bringing medical advice to both advantaged and underserved communities. Can you think of other ways that technological innovations could be used to address medical needs across the income spectrum?

Sociology and Issues of Public Health in the United States

Public health is *the science and practice of health protection and maintenance at a community level.* Public health officials try to control hazards and habits that may harm the health and well-being of the population. They have long sought to educate the public about the hazards of tobacco use, for example, and to prevent young people from taking up smoking. More recently, public health officials have warned that obesity is becoming an ever more serious problem for young and old alike. The issue of teen pregnancy has also garnered attention, though rates of pregnancy among teenagers have fluctuated.

Smoking

One of the largest and most profitable industries in the United States is the manufacture and sale of tobacco products, estimated to be a $47.1 billion industry. At the same time, tobacco is the number one cause of preventable disease and death in the U.S., accounting for about 480,000 deaths each year, 41,000 of which are due to secondhand smoke exposure (CDC, 2017b). Fully 9 in 10 lung cancers are due to smoking, and mortality among smokers is three times higher than among nonsmokers. Notably, however, the smoking rate continues to drop, falling to about 15.5% today (CDC, 2018).

While statistics on **morbidity**, *the rate of illness in a particular population,* and **mortality**, *the rate of death in a particular population,* highlight important medical aspects of cigarette smoking, we can also use sociological analysis to illuminate this public health issue. Why do so many people continue to smoke (see Figure 16.6) and so many young people take up smoking despite the evidence of its ill effects? Why do more men than women smoke? Why are young women the fastest-growing population of new smokers? Why does the government not regulate the production

---

Public health: The science and practice of health protection and maintenance at a community level.

Morbidity: The rate of illness in a particular population.

Mortality: The rate of death in a particular population.

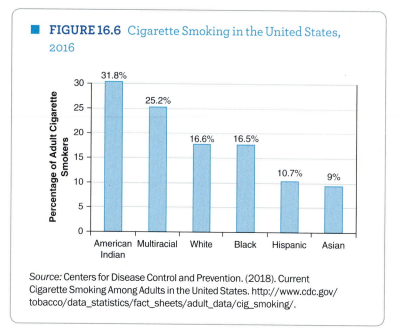

■ **FIGURE 16.6** Cigarette Smoking in the United States, 2016

Source: Centers for Disease Control and Prevention. (2018). Current Cigarette Smoking Among Adults in the United States. http://www.cdc.gov/tobacco/data_statistics/fact_sheets/adult_data/cig_smoking/.

and sale of such an addictive and dangerous product more stringently?

Sociology offers us some insight into these questions. Among other things, cigarette advertising both constructs and reinforces gender stereotypes (Kilbourne, 1999). Male smoking has been associated with independence, ruggedness, and machismo (think of the Marlboro Man, an iconic figure in U.S. advertising). On the other hand, female smoking has been associated with images that are elegant, chic, and playful or carefree. A symbolic interactionist might highlight the way in which a cigarette is more than tobacco rolled in paper. To a young teen, it might be a symbol of maturity; to an older teen, it might represent being cool or rebellious. In what other ways do cigarettes function as symbols of self in our society?

Two Theoretical Perspectives on Public Health: The Case of Cigarettes

The conflict perspective offers some insight into why cigarettes are not regulated more stringently despite their addictive properties: Who benefits from the existence of a large population of smokers? Who loses?

Smoking may give pleasure to smokers, but its benefits are largely outweighed by its consequences, which include poorer health and a thinner wallet. Smoking does, however, bring profit to the tobacco companies, which have tenaciously defended their product for decades. Tobacco companies are generous contributors to candidates for political office. They are advantaged by wealth and access to the halls of government, where their voices are heard. While the smoker gets a mixed bag of benefits (pleasure) and consequences (addiction, disease, financial cost) from smoking,

cigarette companies clearly benefit from purchases of their goods and the recruitment of new smokers—men and boys, women and girls—to replace those who die or quit.

Is the easy availability of cigarettes also functional? A functionalist might suggest that, in fact, it is positively functional in its creation of jobs, which range from tobacco farming to marketing and lobbying, and in its contribution to rural economies that depend on income from farming tobacco. The highly coveted plant has been subject to human cultivation and use for hundreds of years. Consider its historical functions: Tobacco became a major influence in the development of the economy of early America. During the Revolutionary War, profits from the tobacco trade helped the Revolution by serving as collateral for loans provided to Americans by France (Randall, 1999). According to the Center for Responsive Politics (2016), OpenSecrets blog (which tracks lobbying) in mid-2016, about 152 lobbyists were actively working for 24 clients. By this point in the year, over $4 million had already been spent on these efforts.

Viewing cigarette smoking through a theoretical lens lets us see it as more than an individual choice or action. Rather, cigarettes and smoking are social symbols and phenomena with profound effects on public health as well as sources of profit for some and pain for others.

Obesity

The CDC identifies obesity in the United States as a national health problem: It is a major cause of mortality, second only to smoking. According to the Kaiser Family Foundation (n.d.), about 65% of adults in the United States between the ages of 20 and 74 are overweight or obese (Figure 16.7). The rate of obesity in American children has risen even faster and is twice what it was in the late 1970s: Today, 1 in 6 children and adolescents are obese (CDC, 2016). Children who are much bigger than their peers sometimes experience social ostracism. Further, they may suffer serious health effects, including high blood pressure, joint problems, high cholesterol, and fatty liver disease. Very obese children have been observed to suffer health problems once believed to affect only older adults, including heart attacks and type 2 diabetes. With the popularity of sedentary activities such as video games, participation in social media, and television viewing, society will likely see this problem increase.

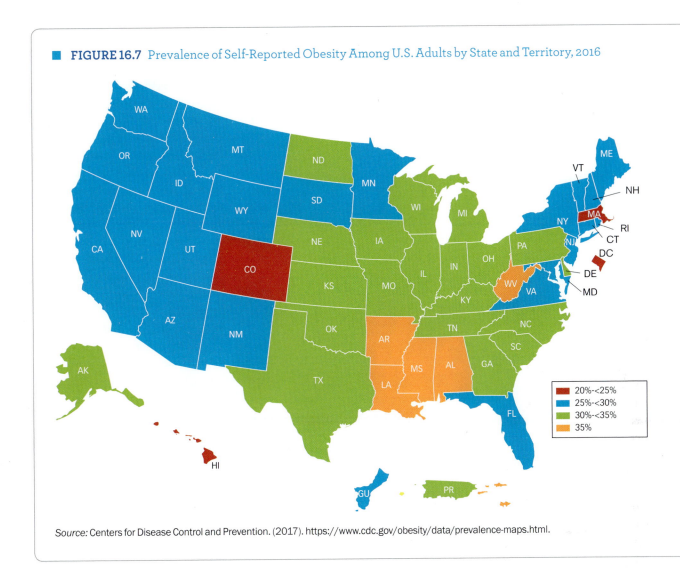

FIGURE 16.7 Prevalence of Self-Reported Obesity Among U.S. Adults by State and Territory, 2016

Legend:
- 20%–<25%
- 25%–<30%
- 30%–<35%
- 35%

Source: Centers for Disease Control and Prevention. (2017). https://www.cdc.gov/obesity/data/prevalence-maps.html.

Among the factors to which the rise in size has been attributed is that families in the United States eat more meals outside the home than in the past, and many of these meals are consumed at fast-food establishments. As well, the portions diners are offered in restaurants are growing because many ingredients have become very inexpensive. In *Fast Food Nation,* Eric Schlosser (2012) notes that "commodity prices have fallen so low that the fast food industry has greatly increased its portion sizes, without reducing profits, in order to attract customers" (p. 243), a point supported by mathematician and physicist Carson C. Chow, who argues that the obesity epidemic in the United States is an outcome of the overproduction of food since the 1970s (cited in Dreifus, 2012). Federal subsidies for food production favor meat and dairy, which soak up almost three quarters of these funds. Just over 10% support the production of sugar, oils, starches, and alcohol, and less than a third of 1% support the growing of vegetables and fruits. These data show that the U.S. Congress has opted to subsidize the production of foods that contribute to obesity rather than those, including fruits and vegetables, recommended in the government's own nutrition guidelines (Rampell, 2010).

Physician and scientist Deborah A. Cohen (2014) argues in her book, *A Big Fat Crisis*, that "obesity is primarily the result of exposure to an obesogenic environment" (p. 191), and she points to three key components of that environment. First, she notes (consistent with Chow) that factors such as agricultural advances have led to an abundance of cheap food. Second, she suggests that the availability of food, particularly junk food, has grown: More than 41% of retail stores, including hardware stores, furniture stores, and drugstores, offer food. Third, food advertising has vastly expanded. Cohen notes that grocery stores today earn more from companies paying for prime display locations than from consumers buying groceries.

■ **FIGURE 16.8** Overweight and Obesity Rates in the United States by Race and Ethnicity, 2016

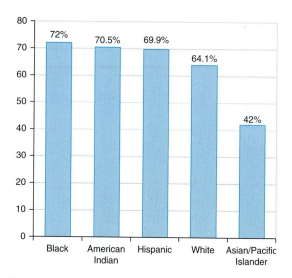

Source: Kaiser Family Foundation. (2016b).

Carroll, Kit, & Flegal, 2012), including majorities in some communities, this is a public issue and one that, to paraphrase C. Wright Mills, we may not hope to explain by focusing only on individual cases. Rather, we need to seek out its sociological roots.

Consider how this issue might look through the conflict lens. Who benefits, and who loses? While "losers" in this instance are surely those whose health is compromised by excessive weight, there are also macro-level effects such as lost productivity when employees miss work due to obesity-linked illnesses (such as diabetes). In fact, the CDC has estimated that the medical care costs associated with obesity in the United States total about $209 billion annually (Cawley & Meyerhoefer, 2012).

Who benefits? The food industry, particularly fast food companies, arguably benefits when consumers prioritize quantity over quality. By offering bigger portions (which cost only a bit more to provide), restaurants draw bigger crowds and bigger profits. The massive U.S. weight-loss industry also benefits, since the rise in obesity exists in the presence of widespread societal obsession with thinness. Often, the same companies that market high-fat, unhealthy foods also peddle "lite" versions (Lemonnier, 2008).

Obesity is also linked to social class. Poor access to nutritious food in the U.S. is more likely to be manifested in obesity than emaciation. Consider, for example, that some of the country's poorest states have the highest obesity rates (see Figure 16.8). In West Virginia and Mississippi, a little over 37% of adults are obese; in Louisiana and Alabama, 36% are obese (CDC, 2017c). Among the demographic groups most likely to be poor are also those most at risk of obesity; over half of African American women are obese (55%), as are 51% of Hispanic women (Hales, Carroll, Fryar, & Ogden, 2017). Those without a high school education are more likely to be obese (35.5%) than those who complete high school (over 32%) or college (just under 22%; CDC, 2017c). According to the *Handbook on Obesity*, "In heterogeneous and affluent societies like the United States, there is a strong inverse correlation of social class and obesity" (quoted in Critser, 2003, p. 117).

Clearly, obesity is a complex phenomenon driven by a variety of factors—biological, genetic, environmental, social, and economic. As you will see below, poverty is also an important factor in the prevalence of obesity. From a sociological perspective, we consider the connection between the personal trouble and the public issue of obesity and being overweight. That is, if one individual or a handful in a community are obese, that may be a personal trouble, attributable to genetics, illness, eating habits, or any other set of factors. However, when more than one third of the U.S. population is obese (Ogden,

DISCOVER INTERSECTIONS:

Household Poverty, Neighborhood Disadvantages, and Health

In this chapter, you learned about the correlation between obesity and poverty in the U.S. Think back to our chapter on social class and inequality in the United States (Chapter 7). In that chapter, we recognized the significance of neighborhoods for people experiencing poverty. While a poor household in a nonpoor neighborhood might still have access to important resources such as quality schools and amenities such as grocery stores and parks, impoverished households in economically struggling neighborhoods are less likely to be able to avail themselves of such amenities. How might the quality of a neighborhood affect the risk of obesity for the poor? How might that help us understand the relationship between poverty and obesity in a more complex and nuanced way?

Teen Pregnancy and Birth

In 2016, there were just under 209,800 births to mothers ages 15 to 19. Most of the young mothers (about 89%) were unmarried when they gave birth (U.S. Department of Health and Human Services, 2018). Figure 16.9 shows changes in the birthrate among teens across recent decades. While it continues to be high, the rate has dropped continuously and considerably in recent decades.

Pregnancy and births among teenagers are public health issues because young women who conceive or give birth before their bodies are fully developed put themselves and their babies at risk. Compared to older mothers, teen mothers have worse health, more pregnancy complications, and more stillborn, low-weight, or medically fragile infants. But teen pregnancy and birth are of more than medical concern. They are also associated with another public health problem: poverty.

Giving birth early and outside marriage compounds the risk that young women and their children will become or remain poor; over 30% of female-headed households in the U.S. live below the poverty line, compared with about 6% of married-couple families (U.S. Census Bureau, 2015). Parenthood is a leading cause of dropping out of school among teenage women; teen mothers are at greater risk than their peers of not completing high school—only 50% of teenage mothers earn a high school diploma before age 22, and fewer than 2% earn a college degree by age 30 (CDC, 2017c; National Campaign to Prevent Teen Pregnancy, 2010).

The relationship between teen pregnancy and birth and poverty is complicated. On one hand, as noted, early and unwed motherhood compounds the risk of poverty. On the other hand, poverty is itself a risk factor for teenage motherhood: An estimated 80% of teen mothers grew up in low-income households (Shore & Shore, 2009), and poor teens have a higher incidence of early sexual activity, pregnancy, and birth than their better-off peers (National Campaign to Prevent Teen Pregnancy, 2010).

In her book, *Dubious Conceptions: The Politics of Teenage Pregnancy* (1996), sociologist Kristin Luker suggests that poverty is a *cause* as well as a *consequence* of teen pregnancy and birth. She argues that poor young women's probability of early motherhood is powerfully affected by "disadvantage and discouragement" (p. 111). By *disadvantage* she means the social effects of poverty, which reduce opportunities for a solid education and the realization of professional aspirations. Consider, for instance, a high school senior from an affluent household: She may spend her 18th birthday contemplating whether to begin college immediately or take a year off for travel abroad. A young woman who hails from a poor household in rural Louisiana or the Bronx's depressed Mott Haven neighborhood may have received an inferior education in her underfunded school and, having little money, has no hope for college. Travel beyond her own state or even city is unthinkable. Local jobs in the service industry are an option, as is motherhood. *Discouragement,* according to Luker, is the effect of poverty that may prevent poor young women from exercising agency in confronting obstacles. In an impoverished situation, the *opportunity costs* of early

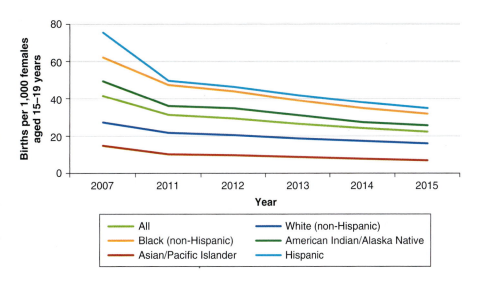

■ **FIGURE 16.9** Birth Rates (Live Births) per 1,000 Females Aged 15–19 Years, by Race and Ethnicity, 2007–2015

Source: Centers for Disease Control and Prevention. (2017). Birth rates (Live Births) per 1,000 Females Aged 15–19 Years, by Race and Ethnicity, 2015–2017. https://www.cdc.gov/teenpregnancy/about/alt-text/birth-rates-chart-2007-2015-text.htm.

motherhood—that is, the educational or other opportunities lost—may seem relatively low.

Notably, a study by Kathryn Edin and Maria Kefalas (2005) found that many poor young women embrace early motherhood as an honorable and even desirable choice. Some of the women the researchers interviewed also saw it as something that saved them from trouble with drugs or the law and matured them. Most of the women Edin and Kefalas interviewed expressed a desire to marry and embark on a career in the future. At the same time, discouraged by what they perceived as a limited pool of stable partners, whose marriageability was compromised by poor employment prospects and problems such as alcohol and drug use, the women did not put marriage ahead of motherhood, though many retained hopes for marriage at a point when they felt financially independent. In neighborhoods where early motherhood was the norm, many expressed a preference to have their children while young, a preference shared by the young men with whom they had relationships. While few of these young women's pregnancies were planned, many couples took no steps to avoid pregnancy.

Though rates of teen motherhood remain higher in the United States than in many other economically advanced countries, they have declined in some groups. Among other factors, the use of condoms has increased markedly (U.S. Department of Health and Human Services, 2013), perhaps due to a desire to protect against both pregnancy and sexually transmitted infections. There have also been small drops in the numbers of

Early parenthood is a leading reason that teen women drop out of school. About a third cite this reason for leaving high school. Staying in school, however, is key to job prospects that enable families to stay out of poverty. What might schools do to encourage young mothers to graduate?

teenagers approving of and engaging in premarital sexual activity, and the rate of births among teenage women has dropped compared to the rate in earlier decades (Ventura & Hamilton, 2011).

Teen pregnancies and births are *social facts*, or phenomena that, as Émile Durkheim put it, we can explain only by using other social facts. That is, to understand sociologically both the rise and the fall of the rates of teen pregnancies and births, we must recognize that these are not only personal troubles or individual issues, but that they are fundamentally tied to other economic, social, and cultural issues in society.

○ DISCOVER & DEBATE

STUDY DRUGS ON CAMPUS

Motion: The off-prescription use of "study drugs" is a form of academic dishonesty. Universities and colleges should implement zero-tolerance policies toward the use of study drugs by students.

Background: In 2011, Duke University expanded its list of behaviors that constitute academic dishonesty: It now included "the unauthorized use of prescription medication to enhance academic performance." Duke's policy, which so far has not been widely adopted, represents an attempt to address student use and abuse of so-called "study drugs," prescription

medications intended to alleviate conditions such as attention deficit hyperactivity disorder (ADHD). Sales of prescription stimulants such as Ritalin and Adderall have surged in recent years; between 2006 and 2010, they increased from $4 billion to over $7 billion. According to the Higher Education Research Institute, about 5% of incoming freshmen in 2011 had diagnosed ADHD (Johnson, 2011). But the number of students using the drugs off-prescription is much higher. By one estimate, up to a quarter of students on some campuses had used the drugs in the previous year (Trudeau, 2009).

One way that schools can address this growing problem is with zero-tolerance policies toward study drug abuse. Zero-tolerance policies are defined as institutional policies that set predetermined punishments for particular infractions and punish the same way no matter the severity or context of the behavior.

Questions for Consideration

- How is the use of study drugs similar to and different from more traditional and recognized forms of academic dishonesty such as copying someone else's test answers, downloading a paper written by someone else from the Internet, or getting a copy of a test or quiz from a classmate who already took it?

- How is the use of study drugs similar to and different from recognized means of cheating in athletics, such as doping, which is the use of performance-enhancing drugs?

- Should students be encouraged to report other students who use study drugs? Would reports by fellow students be adequate evidence of an infraction?

Debate Tip

- Use the full time allotted to you. If you're concerned that you don't have enough to say, go back and do further research to bolster your argument.

AFFIRMATIVE ARGUMENTS	OPPOSITION ARGUMENTS
When students matriculate at a university or college, they implicitly agree to abide by an academic code of conduct that includes academic integrity. It is in the interest of school administrations to ensure that the code of conduct is recognized and realized in practice.	Zero-tolerance policies for disciplinary infractions at universities and colleges are not appropriate because they do not take into account mitigating factors related to the behavior. The punishments cannot be modified based on recommendations from students, teachers, and administrators.
Zero-tolerance policies for conduct that violates school rules ensure that all infractions of the policy are treated equally and without consideration of particular circumstances or characteristics of a student.	The policy may not achieve the intended goal of deterring the use of study drugs because the effects of the drugs are difficult to discern. Students are likely to be caught only if their actions are linked to a related infraction, such as selling study drugs to peers.
Zero-tolerance policies for infractions such as study drug abuse have a deterrent effect because with a predictable punishment, the deviant behavior will be discouraged.	Using study drugs does not do harm to others. It should not be punished at all.

The Sociology of HIV/AIDS

The case of acquired immunodeficiency syndrome (AIDS) and the virus that causes it, human immunodeficiency virus (HIV), is another example of the importance of understanding the social construction of illness. Perceptions of HIV/AIDS and those who contract HIV have varied across time, depending on who the most visible victims have been. As well, this global pandemic demands a sociological approach because it is closely intertwined with a host of sociological issues, including gender inequality, poverty, violence and conflict, and the pursuit of both medical breakthroughs and profits in a globalizing world.

In 2016, about 36 million people around the globe were living with HIV (Figures 16.10 and 16.11). While this is a substantial figure—and there were at least 1.8 million new infections that year—there has been a decrease in new infections as a result of HIV/AIDS prevention efforts: According to UNAIDS, there has been an 11% decrease in new infections globally since 2010 and, since their peak in 2005, AIDS-related deaths have dropped by 48%. The situation, however, varies by region, and HIV/AIDS continues to present substantial medical and societal challenges. For instance, while the number of new infections in Eastern and Southern Africa declined, in the region of East and Central Europe and Central Asia, as well as the Middle East and North Africa, new infections and AIDS-related deaths increased (UNAIDS, 2017).

Gender, Sexuality, and HIV/AIDS

We can better understand the spread of sexually transmitted diseases, including HIV/AIDS, if we examine how these diseases are related to gender and inequality. Globally, the

■ **FIGURE 16.10** HIV Diagnoses in the United States for the Most-Affected Subpopulations, 2016

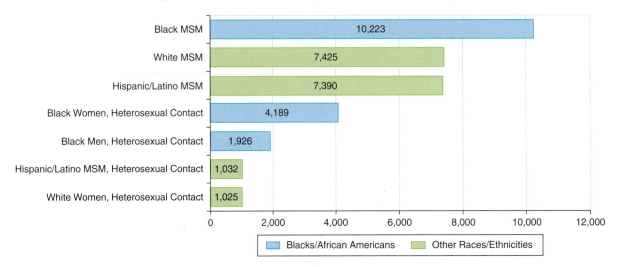

Source: Centers for Disease Control and Prevention. (2016). Diagnoses of HIV Infection in the United States and Dependent Areas. Retrieved from https://www.cdc.gov/hiv/pdf/library/reports/surveillance/cdc-hiv-surveillance-report-2016-vol-28.pdf.

Note: MSM stands for "Men who have sex with men."

■ **FIGURE 16.11** HIV Prevalence Worldwide, 2016

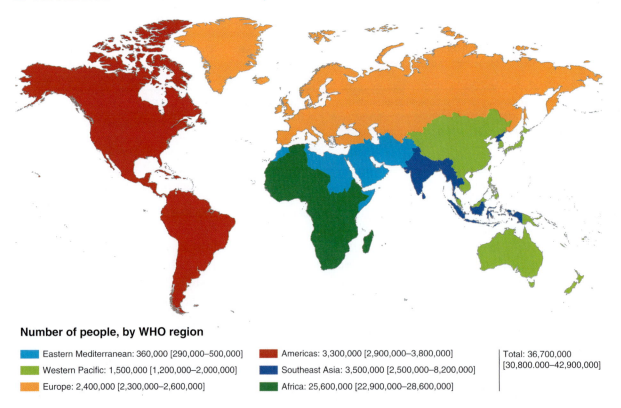

Number of people, by WHO region

- Eastern Mediterranean: 360,000 [290,000–500,000]
- Western Pacific: 1,500,000 [1,200,000–2,000,000]
- Europe: 2,400,000 [2,300,000–2,600,000]
- Americas: 3,300,000 [2,900,000–3,800,000]
- Southeast Asia: 3,500,000 [2,500,000–8,200,000]
- Africa: 25,600,000 [22,900,000–28,600,000]

Total: 36,700,000 [30,800.000–42,900,000]

Source: World Health Organization. (2016). Global Health Observatory data: HIV/AIDS. http://www.who.int/gho/hiv/epidemic_status/cases_all/en/.

number of women with HIV/AIDS has risen: Fully half of new infections are now diagnosed among women. In some regions, women's infection rates outpace men's: In 2014, in sub-Saharan Africa, two and a half times as many adolescent girls were newly infected with HIV than boys between the ages of 15 and 19 (UNICEF, 2016).

Norms and traditions in many regions reinforce women's lower status in society. In some traditional communities in Africa, for example, it is socially acceptable—or even desirable—for men to have multiple sexual partners both before and after marriage. In this case, marriage itself becomes a risk factor for women. Many women also still lack accurate knowledge regarding sexually transmitted diseases, a problem made more acute by widespread female illiteracy in poor regions. Women who are uninfected may not know how to protect themselves, and women who are infected may not know how to protect their partners.

Gender stereotypes and vulnerability to HIV/AIDS are also pertinent. In a *New York Times Magazine* article examining the phenomenon of Black men who present themselves to the outside world as heterosexual but engage in homosexual activity on the down low, Benoit Denizet-Lewis (2003) writes about a culture of Black masculinity in which Black male bisexuality and homosexuality are little discussed and little accepted. Hence, Black males who want to have sexual relationships with males are often compelled to put on a facade for their families and society. In the words of one man on the down low,

> If you're white, you can come out as an openly gay skier or actor or whatever. It might hurt you some, but it's not like if you're black and gay, because it's like you've let down the whole black community, black women, black history, black pride. (quoted in Denizet-Lewis, 2003)

An important consequence is that some men who are having sex with other men are also having sex with women—wives and girlfriends. Notably, CDC (2018) data show that Blacks made up 44% of those found to have HIV in 2016, though they only made up 12% of the U.S. population. The CDC partly attributes the greater prevalence of HIV diagnoses in the Black community to the fact that African Americans tend to have sexual partners of the same race, may experience higher rates of other sexually transmitted diseases, and have limited access to quality health care (2018).

Poverty and HIV/AIDS

Across the globe, there is a powerful relationship between the risk of HIV/AIDS and poverty. China, for instance, has experienced a rise in new cases in the past decade. A serious epidemic was detected in central China's Henan Province, where tens of thousands of rural villagers have been infected in the past decade through selling their blood for money under unsafe and unsterile conditions. In China as a whole, it is estimated that at the end of 2005 there were 55,000 commercial blood and plasma donors infected with HIV ("AIDS in China," 2007). In developing countries, economic insecurity and the lack of gainful employment sometimes drive workers (particularly men) to seek work far from home. For example, migrant workers from surrounding countries toil in the mines of South Africa. Away from their families and communities, some of these men seek out the services of prostitutes, who may be infected (UNAIDS, 2010).

The sex workers themselves are often victims of dire and desperate economic circumstances. Women in the sex trade, some of whom have been trafficked and enslaved, are highly vulnerable to HIV/AIDS. They have little protection from robbery or rape and limited power to negotiate safe sex with paying customers, though some countries, such as Thailand, have sought to empower sex workers to demand condom use (Avert, 2017).

Poor states, as well as poor individuals, are vulnerable to the ravages of disease. Consider the cases of these southern African states: HIV prevalence among young women ages 15–24 is about 10% in Botswana, 14% in Lesotho, and 18% in Swaziland (PRB, 2017). The high rates of infection and death among young and middle-aged adults also mean that countries are left with diminished workforces. Without productive citizens, the state of a country's economy declines, further reducing the resources that might be put into HIV/AIDS prevention or treatment. While HIV/AIDS is far from limited to poor victims or poor countries, poverty clearly increases the risk of disease at both the individual and the national level.

Violence and HIV/AIDS

Women's risk of contracting HIV/AIDS is increased by situations of domestic violence. Data gathered by the United Nations suggest that up to half the women in the world may experience violence from a domestic partner at some point; this includes forced sex, which is not likely to take place with a condom (UNAIDS et al., 2004). According to UNAIDS, women who have experienced violence are up to three times more likely to be infected with HIV than those who have not. Statistics show that younger women in Africa are more likely to experience physical or sexual violence than older women, generally from an intimate partner (UNAIDS, 2010).

Much progress has been made in developing medicine that helps keep HIV/AIDS under control and maintains one's quality of life, and even better advancements have been made in prevention, awareness, and education on how to avoid contracting HIV. Nevertheless, it continues to be a global epidemic that claims millions of lives. In this photo, a woman infected with HIV who has been ostracized from her village sits outside her small hut.

The rape of men by other males, not uncommon in prison settings, can also be implicated in the spread of the infection. In many countries, the incidence of HIV/AIDS in prisons is significantly higher than the incidence of the disease in the noninstitutionalized population. Part of this phenomenon is linked to the sharing of needles among drug-injecting prisoners, tattooing with unsterile equipment, or consensual male sexual activity, but part is also linked to the underreported sexual violence behind bars (Avert, 2017).

HIV/AIDS is a medical issue. It is also a sociological issue. Vulnerability to infection is compounded by factors such as gender stereotypes and poverty. At a time when hope of new treatments and prevention strategies has materialized but the pandemic continues to ravage communities and countries, a sociological perspective can help us to identify the social roots of HIV/AIDS and to seek the most fruitful paths for combating its spread.

Global Issues in Health and Medicine

Ever since human beings first began to migrate from their African origins, taking their illnesses with them, the spread of disease has known no global boundaries. Plagues and epidemics have traveled from populations that have developed some degree of biological immunity to others that have not. During the 14th century, the bubonic plague, known as the Black Death, arrived in Europe by way of Asia and eliminated a third of the European population in only 20 years. The European conquerors of the Americas brought smallpox and other diseases with them that virtually eliminated the indigenous population in many areas (Thornton, 1987).

U.S. soldiers returning from Europe at the end of World War I carried previously unknown influenza strains that killed an estimated 20 million people worldwide. Today, tuberculosis, once all but eliminated from the industrialized nations, is making a comeback, with new treatment-resistant strains brought by immigrants from poor nations.

In 2010, the United States publicly apologized to the nation of Guatemala when it was discovered that in the 1940s, U.S. government researchers deliberately infected hundreds of Guatemalan mental patients with gonorrhea and syphilis for observational purposes and encouraged them to transfer their infections to others (Bazell, 2010). Such unethical experiments endanger larger populations by introducing diseases that can erupt in outbreaks.

Overall, however, the 20th century witnessed a striking global triumph over many diseases, as sanitation, clean water, sewage systems, knowledge about the importance of diet, and other public health and medical practices and treatments spread throughout the world. For example, in only a few years, the WHO's plan for "Health for All by the Year 2000" succeeded in immunizing half the world's children against measles, polio, and four other diseases (Steinbrook, 1988). Successes have continued into the 21st century. In 2004, the Bill and Melinda Gates Foundation, working with the Global Alliance for Vaccines and Immunization, was able to vaccinate an estimated 78% of children in the world against diphtheria, tetanus, and whooping cough (Bill and Melinda Gates Foundation, 2006). Today, the Bill and Melinda Gates Foundation (2013) reports that it is 99% of the way toward eradicating polio and that a new vaccine will save the lives of an additional 400,000 children per year on a global scale. Successes such as these have produced a sharp decline in death rates in most of the world's countries (Andre et al., 2008).

The AIDS epidemic is the most recent example of the global spread of a fatal disease. What makes it unique is the rapidity with which it spread around the world to industrialized and less-developed nations alike. HIV/AIDS is also a global issue in terms of treatment and prevention. Globalization is both functional and dysfunctional for real and potential victims of the infection. On one hand, HIV/AIDS was global in its path of spread, and it appears likely that its defeat will also be global, as it was for other once-deadly and widespread diseases such as smallpox, polio, and malaria (Steinbrook, 1988). There is a concerted global effort to combat the disease. Doctors across the globe work together to share information and knowledge on HIV/AIDS and their efforts to stop it. International organizations including the United Nations are also instrumental in leading information and empowerment campaigns.

On the other hand, globalization has thrown obstacles in the path of those who seek to expand the reach of therapeutic drugs that lengthen health and life for those with the infection. The global market in HIV/AIDS treatment has been dominated by Western pharmaceutical companies, most of which have jealously guarded their patent rights on the drug therapies shown to be most effective for treatment. Their fierce desire to protect patents and profits has made it more difficult for drug makers in developing states to manufacture cheaper generic versions that could save more lives in poor countries.

Together with HIV/AIDS, one of the most threatening diseases in developing countries is malaria: According to some estimates, malaria is a threat to no less than half the global population. It kills more than 445,000 people every year. The most vulnerable populations are children and pregnant women in Africa, which has the most malaria deaths (CDC, 2018b).

The toll taken by malaria is felt at the individual, community, and national levels. For individual families, malaria is costly in terms of drugs, travel to clinics, lost time at work or school, and burial, among other expenses. For governments, malaria means the potential loss of tourism and productive members of society and the cost of public health interventions, including treatments and mosquito nets, which many individuals are unable to pay for themselves (CDC, 2012b). Malaria, together with HIV/AIDS and tuberculosis, has attracted a substantial proportion of available funding from international and national donors and governments seeking to improve the health of populations in the developing world.

Critics of international health spending priorities point to a growing threat in the developing world that has not received substantial funding or attention: chronic disease. Heart disease, stroke, and cancer have long been chronic maladies associated with the habits of the populations of developed countries, such as overeating, lack of exercise, and smoking. One scientist notes that while 80% of global deaths from chronic diseases take place in low- and middle-income countries, those illnesses receive the smallest fraction of donor assistance for health. Of the nearly $26 billion allocated for health in 2009, only 1% targeted chronic disease (Lomborg, 2012).

Chronic disease, however, is a growing threat in the developing world, driven by a dramatic rise in both obesity and smoking. According to the World Health Organization, global obesity rates doubled between 1980 and 2008. The WHO estimates that about half the adult populations of Brazil, Russia, and South Africa are overweight. In Africa, around 8% of adults are obese. While these figures are low compared to those in the United States, where two thirds of adults are estimated to be overweight and one third are obese, the numbers are rising. A variety of factors contribute to this phenomenon, including growing incomes in many parts of the developing world, which enable more consumption, economic changes that shift work from physical labor to indoor and sedentary labor, and the movement of fast-food restaurants into new regions where people can now afford to splurge on burgers and soda (Kenny, 2012).

While smoking has decreased in many developed countries in recent decades, it has grown dramatically in some parts of the developing world. Today, about 80% of smokers live in the developing world (Qian et al., 2010). By some estimates, China has 350 million smokers (which is more people than live in the United States), and about 60% of Chinese men smoke. Tobacco use has grown fourfold in China since the 1970s and has become a key component of the nation's growing prosperity. Cigarettes, particularly expensive brands of cigarettes, are given as gifts to friends and family; red cigarettes are special presents for weddings, bringing "double happiness." China also has its own tobacco manufacturing industry, which is run by the government. This creates a conflict of interest, since the same entity that regulates tobacco and might be interested in promoting better public health is profiting from the large number of tobacco users (PBS, 2010). Since 2001, when China joined the World Trade Organization and its markets opened to new goods, Western cigarette makers have also been aggressively marketing their products there, targeting relatively untapped consumer categories such as women, who are otherwise less likely than men to smoke (Qian et al., 2010).

Growing income and improvements in the standards of living in developing countries represent important changes. For the most part, these changes are positive and include growing opportunities for education, health care, and access to technology, among others. At the same time, the chronic diseases long associated with the developed world threaten populations in new ways. Whether and how the international community, national governments, and local institutions react to these problems today will have an enormous impact on the health of populations in the decades to come.

Why Should Sociologists Study Health?

Even as our medical and technological knowledge grows, threats to the goal of a healthy society and world continue to expand. In a globalizing world, no one is isolated from diseases spawned in distant places; we are all part of the same community, linked by communications, travel, and commerce. Neither are we isolated from the far-reaching consequences of health dangers that threaten to destabilize regions far from our own. In a world where the very poor exist together with the very wealthy and billions are seeking to scramble up the ladder of prosperity, the acute illnesses

of poverty can be found alongside the chronic maladies of affluence. Sociology offers us the tools to examine the sociological antecedents of a spectrum of public health problems.

By using a sociological perspective, we can recognize the ways that medical issues such as HIV/AIDS intersect with social phenomena such as gender inequality, gender stereotypes, violence, and poverty. We can examine the global obesity epidemic through new eyes when we see that individuals' choices about food and fitness are made in social and economic environments that profoundly affect those choices. While medicine and technology clearly have an enormous amount to contribute to reducing the consequences of serious health issues, including HIV/AIDS, obesity, and tobacco-related illnesses, sociology also has a role to play in discovering the social roots of and imagining creative, constructive responses to health problems that threaten many lives and livelihoods.

 ## What Can I Do with a Sociology Degree?

QUALITATIVE RESEARCH SKILLS

Sociologists use qualitative research skills to gather rigorous, in-depth information on social behaviors, phenomena, and institutions. Qualitative research highlights data that cannot be *quantified* (that is, cannot be converted into numbers). It relies on the gathering of data through methods such as focus groups, participant and nonparticipant observation, interviews, and archival research. Generally, population samples are small in qualitative research because the aim of the research is to gain deep understanding.

Throughout this book, you will encounter qualitative research studies, and you will see how they contribute to our knowledge of the social world. As you advance in your sociological studies, you will have the opportunity to learn how to do qualitative sociology. For example, you may learn to prepare interview questions that will allow you to accurately assess respondents' attitudes toward a particular social trend, or you may learn to take detailed field notes on observations you make of a practice or population you seek to study.

Knowledge of qualitative research methods is a beneficial skill in today's job market. Learning to collect data through observation, interviews, and

focus groups, for instance, prepares you to do a wide variety of job tasks, including survey development, questionnaire design, data collection and reporting, and market research. Further, qualitative research experience fosters communication competencies through the processes of small-group management and rapport building as well as negotiation with study participants.

Elizabeth Bogumil, Professional Expert at Mt. San Antonio

California State University, Northridge, MA in Sociology

I work in the Research and Institutional Effectiveness Office of a community college. My office supports the mission of the college by collecting, analyzing, and summarizing accurate, timely, and reliable data. We work with various departments, centers, and projects across the college campus to determine and document the effectiveness of programs and services. Our office focuses on both qualitative and quantitative research and stresses the collaborative nature of every stage of the research process. One does not often hear about institutional research in higher education; however, every university and community college has institutional researchers providing insight, data, and support to the administrative services, the instructional services, the student services, human resources, and the office of the college or university president.

Although our office uses both quantitative and qualitative research, my project focus is on qualitative research. When studying sociology, one of the most important skills I learned was how to perform systematic and rigorous qualitative research rooted in theory. I am typically provided a research question and a set of parameters (often student demographics) from which I have to conceive an appropriate form of qualitative inquiry (typically interviews, focus groups, or open-ended question surveys) to explore or answer the research question. After collecting the data, during

the analysis process, it is important to make sure that the themes or conclusions being derived from the data make sense within the project's theory. Finally, as qualitative research yields large amounts of descriptive data, it is important to clearly and concisely refine the resulting key themes in a report that are accessible and useful to the department, center, or individual coordinating the project and who helped formulate the original research question. It is because of my sociology training that I have the ability to effectively engage in qualitative research, in a timely manner, and the knowledge of how to distill the pertinent results into a clear and understandable report.

Career Data: Operations Research Analysts

- 2017 Median Pay: $81,390 per year
- $39.13 per hour
- Typical Entry-Level Education: Bachelor's degree
- Projected Job Growth by 2016–2026: 27% (Much faster than average)

Source: Bureau of Labor Statistics, *Occupational Outlook Handbook*, 2017.

SUMMARY

- **Health** is the degree to which a person experiences a generalized state of wellness, while medicine is an institutionalized approach to the prevention of illness. Although the two are clearly related, they are not the same thing.

- Notions of illness are socially constructed, as are the social roles that correspond to them. The sociological concept of the **sick role** is important to an understanding of societal expectations and perceptions of the ill individual.

- Not all forms of addiction are treated the same in society. Some (including alcoholism) are medicalized, while others (including drug use) are criminalized.

- The U.S. health care system does not serve all segments of the population equally. Good health and good **health care** are still often privileges of class and race.

- **Public health** issues such as smoking, obesity, and teen pregnancy can be examined through a sociological lens.

- The sociological imagination gives us the opportunity to see the relationship between private troubles (such as being addicted to tobacco, being obese, or becoming a teen mother) and public issues ranging from the relentless drive for profits in a capitalist country to the persistent poverty of generations.

- The global pandemic of HIV/AIDS demands a sociological approach as well as a medical approach. The mass spread of the infection is closely intertwined with sociological issues. Gender inequality makes women vulnerable to infection. Poverty renders both individuals and countries more vulnerable to the disease. Violence and war are pathways for the spread of HIV/AIDS.

- Rising standards of living in many parts of the developing world have had many positive effects, but the accompanying sedentary lifestyles and access to fast food and tobacco have also contributed to an increase in chronic diseases associated with obesity and smoking.

KEY TERMS

health, 451

medicine, 452

preventive medicine, 452

sick roles, 452

health care, 453

public health, 461

morbidity, 461

mortality, 461

DISCUSSION QUESTIONS

1. What is the *sick role* as defined by sociologist Erving Goffman? What are our expectations of the ill in contemporary U.S. society? Do the responsibilities of the sick role vary by community or culture?

2. The chapter opened with a story on the rise of opioid addiction in the United States. We also noted that some addictions are medicalized while others are criminalized. What is the difference? How might we explain why different addictions are labeled and approached in varying ways?

3. African Americans and Latinos in the United States experience worse health and higher mortality rates than their White and Asian American counterparts. What sociological factors help to explain this health gap?

4. The chapter looked at cigarettes and smoking through a sociological lens. Recall how we applied the functionalist and conflict perspectives to this topic, and try applying those perspectives to junk food, such as soda, candy, and fast food.

5. How is HIV/AIDS a sociological issue as well as a medical one? What are key sociological roots of the spread of this disease in communities and countries?

Want a better grade?

Get the tools you need to sharpen your study skills. Access practice quizzes, eFlashcards, videos, and multimedia at **https://edge.sagepub.com/chambliss4e**.

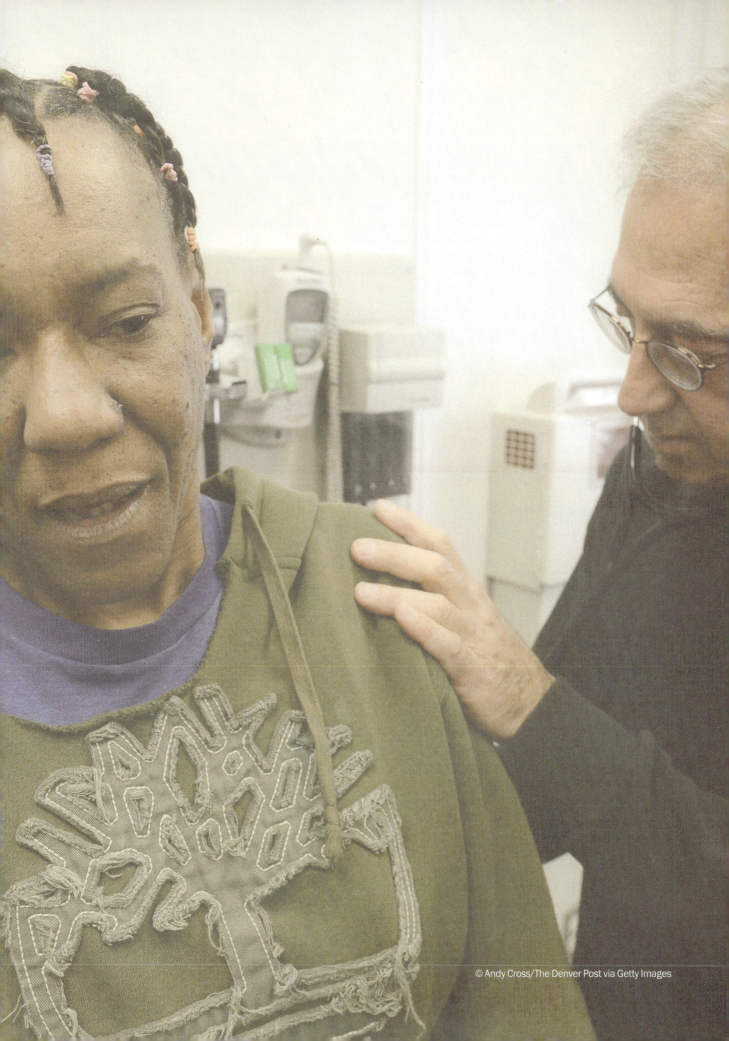

Population, Urbanization, and the Environment

17

WHAT DO YOU THINK?

1. Should we be concerned about global population growth? What are the benefits and costs of a growing population?
2. How should cities revitalize poor neighborhoods?
3. Is it possible to balance the imperatives of economic growth and environmental protection?

LEARNING OBJECTIVES

17.1 Identify key global population trends, including regional differences and birth, death, and growth rates.

17.2 Understand the debate over population growth and consumption.

17.3 Describe U.S. historical and contemporary trends in urbanization and the rise of global cities.

17.4 Take a sociological perspective on issues of environmental protection and destruction.

WHERE THE BOYS ARE . . . AND THE GIRLS ARE NOT

A recent article in *The Economist* describing the state of marriage in some regions of China in 2017 begins as follows:

> In Pi Village, on the outskirts of Beijing, a man in his late 50s who gives his name as Ren is mixing cement for a new apartment building. As he shovels, he gives an account of bride-price inflation. When he married, his parents gave his wife 800 yuan, which seemed like a lot. Twelve years ago, one of Mr. Ren's sons married. His bride got 8,000 yuan. Recently another son married, and Mr. Ren had to stump up 100,000 yuan ($15,000). He is likely to be mixing cement well into his 60s.
>
> Like India, most of China is patrilocal: in theory, at least, a married woman moves into her husband's home and looks after his parents. Also like India, China has a deep cultural preference for boys. But whereas India has dowries, China has bride prices. The groom's parents, not the bride's, are expected to pay

©China Photos/Getty Images News/Getty Images

for the wedding and give money and property to the couple. These bride prices have shot up, bending the country's society and economy out of shape ("A distorted sex ratio is playing havoc with marriage in China", 2017, para. 1–2).

According to a United Nations Population Fund (UNFPA) report, "If China had had a normal sex ratio at birth ... it would have had [721 million] girls and women in 2010. In fact, it had only [655 million]—a difference of [66 million], or 10% of the female population." In India, "had [the ratio] been normal, the country would have had [43 million] more women, or 7% more, than it actually did" ("Bare Branches, Redundant Males," 2015). Today, the "missing women" of the region are at the heart of a dramatic new phenomenon: a skewed sex ratio and a dearth of brides for a generation coming of age in countries where traditional marriage is part of the expected life course.

The missing women are the result of systematic gender discrimination manifested as son preference. Globally, the natural ratio of male births to female births varies from 104:100 to 106:100. In some Asian countries, however, male births dramatically outpace female births. In China, between 2010 and 2015, the sex ratio at birth was 116 boys to 100 girls. In India over this period, the ratio was 111 boys to 100 girls. While the skewed ratios have declined in recent years, their effects promise to be felt for years to come ("Bare Branches, Redundant Males," 2015).

In China and India, among other regional states, there has been widespread use of prenatal sex selection: That is, parents learn the sex of their fetus prior to birth and are more likely to opt for an abortion if it is female, particularly if the family already has a girl child (UNFPA, 2012). While sex-selective abortion is illegal, enforcement of the prohibition has been difficult and lax.

Reasons for son preference are complex. In India, preference is driven by a widespread belief that boys have greater economic, social, and religious value for the family. Where a bride's parents are required to pay dowry to the groom's family, the costs to a poor (or even middle-class) family can be great; consequently, girls are often seen as economic liabilities (Mutharayappa, Choe, Arnold, & Roy, 1997; Seager, 2003). Even among families who can afford dowries for their daughters (though dowry sizes have decreased as brides have become scarcer), boys are more highly valued because they pass on the family line, provide old-age security to parents, and are responsible for fulfilling religious traditions such as lighting the pyres at parents' funerals (International Development Research Centre, n.d.; Mutharayappa et al., 1997). Interestingly, sex selection is more prevalent among affluent urban dwellers in India than their rural counterparts, though traditional norms are more likely to be associated with the latter. Urban residents have greater access to medical technologies such as prenatal sex screening. As well, they typically want and have fewer children than do rural dwellers, so the perceived urgency of having a son in the first two or three births is more acute (Hvistendahl, 2011).

Personal decisions based on economic considerations as well as societal and cultural norms are made in individual families, but they have macro-level consequences. Among other consequences, Guilmoto (2011) has hypothesized a "marriage squeeze" in China and India (Figure 17.1). He estimates that between 2020 and 2055, unmarried men will outnumber unmarried women in China by as much as 60%, and in India, unmarried men will outnumber unmarried women by a similar proportion between 2040 and 2060. In addition, the fall in fertility rates in both countries (though China is experiencing a small uptick) has the potential to further diminish the pool of potential brides:

■ **FIGURE 17.1** The Marriage Squeeze and Sex Ratio at Birth

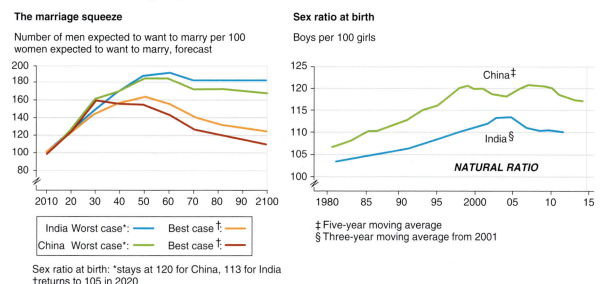

The marriage squeeze

Number of men expected to want to marry per 100
women expected to want to marry, forecast

Sex ratio at birth

Boys per 100 girls

India Worst case*: ——   Best case †: ——
China Worst case*: ——   Best case †: ——

Sex ratio at birth: *stays at 120 for China, 113 for India
†returns to 105 in 2020

‡ Five-year moving average
§ Three-year moving average from 2001

Source: Bare branches, redundant males. (2015, April 18). *The Economist.* https://www.economist.com/asia/2015/04/18/bare-branches-redundant-males.

Fertility is important, because men tend to marry women a few years younger than themselves. In India, the average age of marriage for men is 26; for women, it is 22. This means that when a country's fertility is falling, the cohort of women in their early 20s will be slightly smaller (or will be rising more slowly) than the cohort of men they are most likely to marry—those in their late 20s. ("Bare Branches, Redundant Males," 2015, para. 7)

China and India are the globe's biggest countries. They remain bastions of traditionalism in many respects, and marriage has long been an expected part of the life course. Demographic realities, however, are already beginning to have an effect on family formation.

This chapter takes on a variety of critical contemporary issues. First, we discuss issues of global population growth and look at the debate on rising populations. Next, we examine issues of urbanization, gentrification, and the growth of megacities around the world. Finally, we turn to the global environment and address some of the ways in which the dual pressures of population growth and urbanization are affecting our planet. While the three key topics in this chapter are diverse, they share a common thread: *Individual choices add up to phenomena that can have powerful wider impacts.* An individual family may choose to have six children rather than one, just as an individual family may opt to leave the suburbs or a rural village to move to a city or may decide to buy a large sport utility vehicle rather than a fuel-efficient automobile. What appears at the micro level as an individual decision with direct effects only on a particular family can add up to macro-level phenomena with national or global effects and consequences, as we saw in our opening story.

Global Population Growth

The world's population is growing at a rapid rate, expanding as much since 1950 as it did in the preceding 4 million years. By 1850, the global population reached 1 billion; by 1950, it was 2.3 billion. As of 2012, it had reached more than 7 billion; and in 2017, there were an estimated 7.3 billion inhabitants on our planet. Based on 2017 data, the Population Research Bureau estimates that global population will reach 9.9 billion by 2050 (Population Reference Bureau, 2018, p. 1). The study of population, including the rise in number of earth's inhabitants, is called *demography*. **Demography** is the *science of population size, distribution, and composition* (Keyfitz, 1993).

Population growth is highly uneven around the world, with the greatest expansion taking place in developing countries. Consider that about half of the increase in global population between 2010 and 2050 is projected to take place in nine countries, all but one of which are in the developing world: India, Pakistan, Nigeria, Ethiopia, the United States, the Democratic Republic of Congo, Tanzania, China, and Bangladesh (Figure 17.2). In the United States, most population growth will take place as a result of immigration; elsewhere, it will be the product of *natural population increase*—that is, it will result from births outpacing deaths.

While the global total fertility rate (TFR)—the average number of births per woman, as noted in Chapter 8—was 2.5 in 2017, TFR differed substantially across countries and regions. In reporting TFR, the Population Reference Bureau distinguishes among *more developed countries*, *less developed countries*, and *least developed countries*. In the more developed countries in 2017, the TFR was 1.6; in less developed countries, it was 2.6 (2.9 when China is excluded); and in the least developed countries, it was 4.3 (Population Reference Bureau, 2017). *Replacement rate fertility*—the rate at which two parents are only replacing themselves—is

©iStockphoto.com/Yamtono_Sardi

Jakarta, the capital of Indonesia, is one of Asia's rapidly growing cities. While urbanization is a key characteristic of modernity, it also brings new health, cultural, political, and economic challenges.

Demography: The science of population size, distribution, and composition.

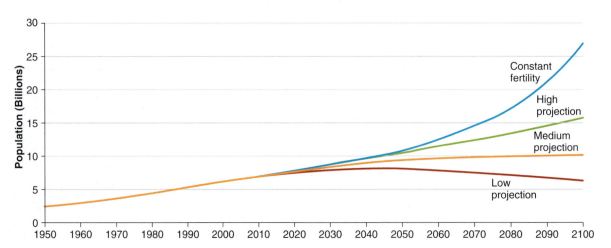

■ **FIGURE 17.2** Estimated World Population Growth, 1950–2100

Source: United Nations, Department of Economic and Social Affairs, Population Division. (2011). *World population prospects: The 2010 revision, highlights and advance tables* (Working Paper ESA/P/WP.220). New York: Author.

represented by a TFR of 2.1 (with an allowance of risk for mortality in the fraction above 2.0). Below this rate, populations decline; above it, they grow.

Central Africa, which comprises mainly less developed and least developed countries, is the fastest-growing region in the world. Its population is expected to grow 129% between 2010 and 2050, whereas South America's population is estimated to rise 23% in the same period, and Western Europe's will grow by only 0.5%. Other regions will lose population, including Eastern Europe, where the population is expected to decrease 14% by 2050, due in large part to below-replacement-level fertility rates (Population Reference Bureau, 2010; Table 17.1).

China and India, the world's most populous countries, present interesting cases for a discussion of population growth. China and India both have more than 1 billion inhabitants and high **population momentum**, which is *the tendency of population growth to continue beyond the point when replacement rate fertility has been achieved because of the high concentration of people of childbearing age.* China

---

Population momentum: The tendency of population growth to continue beyond the point when replacement rate fertility has been achieved because of the high concentration of people of childbearing age.

---

long sought to check its population growth with a one-child policy, which slowed its rate of growth and put its total fertility rate below replacement rate (1.8), though a recent easing of the policy has led to a small rise in the TFR. India's population growth has declined markedly over time (today, the TFR is 2.3), but the nation's population momentum remains high and its current population of 1.3 billion is expected to grow to about 1.5 billion by 2030 and 1.6 billion by 2050 (Table 17.2; Population Reference Bureau, 2017).

To the east of China is Japan, which, like its close neighbor Russia and distant neighbors in Eastern and Western Europe, is also experiencing population decline: It has a population of about 126 million people and a TFR of 1.4; by current projections, its population will fall to 97 million by 2050. Russia, currently one of the world's most populous countries with 144 million inhabitants, has a TFR of 1.8 and is also expected to lose population by midcentury, declining to about 134 million people (Population Reference Bureau, 2015).

While some developing countries struggle with rapid population growth because it puts a strain on basic services such as sanitation and education, as well as on the conservation of natural resources, many modern industrialized countries are lamenting a "birth dearth" that leaves aging populations dependent for their social welfare (in the form of public retirement benefits, for instance) on the financial contributions of fewer young workers.

Demography and Demographic Analysis

Demographers have developed statistical techniques for predicting future population levels on the basis of current characteristics. Annual population growth or decline in a

TABLE 17.1 Total Fertility Rates for Selected Countries, 2017

COUNTRY	TOTAL FERTILITY RATE
South Korea	1.2
Spain	1.3
Germany	1.5
Russia	1.7
United States	1.8
Turkey	2.1
Mexico	2.2
Israel	3.1
Egypt	3.3
Senegal	4.9
Mozambique	5.3
Niger	7.8

Source: Population Reference Bureau (2017). *2017 world population data sheet.* Washington, DC: Author. Retrieved from https://www.prb.org/wp-content/uploads/2017/08/2017_World_Population.pdf.

©Reuters/Sebastien Pirlet

Imagine a pond with a single water lily that doubles in size each day. On the 30th day, it covers the entire pond. On what day does it cover half the pond? The answer gives us a way of thinking about how population momentum drives rising population sizes, even given a constant growth rate. The answer can be found at the end of the chapter on page 509 (Edward O. Wilson, "Is Humanity Suicidal?" *New York Times Magazine*, May 30, 1993).

TABLE 17.2   Current and Projected Population Growth for Global Regions, 2030 and 2050

REGION	2017 POPULATION (MILLIONS)	MID-2030 PROJECTED POPULATION (MILLIONS)	MID-2050 PROJECTED POPULATION (MILLIONS)	BIRTHS PER 1,000 POPULATION
World	7,536	8,563	9,846	20
Sub-Saharan Africa	1,021	1,419	2,193	37
Northern Africa	230	287	381	28
Western Africa	371	517	809	39
Eastern Africa	422	586	886	36
Middle Africa	163	243	410	42
Southern Africa	65	74	88	22
Northern America	362	399	444	12
Central America	177	205	232	20
Caribbean	43	46	47	17
South America	423	467	504	16
Western Asia	269	325	390	21
South Central Asia	1,956	2,238	2,510	22
Central Asia	71	85	104	24
South Asia	1,885	2,153	2,406	22
Southeast Asia	644	722	789	18
East Asia	1,625	1,653	1,557	12
Northern Europe	104	112	121	12
Western Europe	195	202	207	10
Eastern Europe	293	286	267	11
Southern Europe	153	150	141	9
Oceania	42	51	63	16

Source: Population Reference Bureau. (2017). *2017 world population data sheet.* Washington, DC: Author. Retrieved from https://www.prb.org/wp-content/uploads/2017/08/2017_World_Population.pdf.

country is the result of four factors: (1) the number of people born in the country during the year, (2) the number who die, (3) the number who immigrate into the country, and (4) the number who emigrate out. In the language of demographers, population changes are based on **fertility** (*the number of live births in a given population*), mortality (*the number of deaths in a given population*), and **net migration** (*in-migration minus out-migration*).

Let's look at fertility first. Demographers estimate future fertility on the basis of past fertility patterns of women of childbearing age. Although it is possible to make a rough estimate of population growth on the basis of

Fertility: The number of live births in a given population.

Net migration: In-migration minus out-migration.

crude birthrate—*the number of births each year per 1,000 women*—a far more accurate measure is **age-specific fertility rate**, *the number of births typical for women of a specific age in a particular population*. Demographers divide women into five-year cohorts—for example, women ages 15 to 19, 20 to 24, 25 to 29, and so on. If the current average number of live births per 1,000 women is known for each of these age groups, it is relatively easy to project future fertility. Five years from now, for example, today's 15- to 19-year-old women will be 20 to 24, which means that the fertility rates of today's 20- to 24-year-old women can be applied to them. In this way, each successive cohort of women can be "aged" at five-year intervals, and the result is an estimate of total live births. Since fertility rates in most cultures peak during women's late teens and 20s, the largest number of babies will be born to women in these age groups; thereafter, as the cohort ages into the 30s and 40s, the total number of babies born to the group will decline, dropping to zero as the cohort ages out of childbearing altogether.

The second source of population change is mortality. Again, although **crude death rate**—*the number of deaths each year per 1,000 people*—yields a rough measure, demographers prefer to rely on **age-specific mortality rate**, or *an estimate of the number of deaths typical in men and women of specific ages in a particular population*. Similar to age-specific fertility rates, these rates are then applied to successive cohorts of men and women as they age. As you might guess, female mortality rates also affect the number of babies born, since as a cohort of females ages, some of its members will die, leaving fewer women of childbearing age. While in economically advanced regions (such as Western Europe), most women live well beyond their childbearing years, female mortality rates in younger cohorts may have notable effects on birthrates in regions with higher rates of early mortality such as Southern Africa (which includes countries such as South Africa, Botswana, and Namibia), in which an estimated 10.5% of women ages 18 to 24 are infected with HIV/AIDS (Population Reference Bureau, 2017).

One measure of the overall mortality of a society is its **life expectancy**, *the average number of years a newborn is expected to live based on existing health conditions in the country*. In almost all societies, the life expectancy at birth is higher for females than for males. In the United States in

2017, for example, the average life expectancy for females was 81 years, while it was 76 for males. In Eastern Europe, the gap between male and female life expectancy averages 10 years (Population Reference Bureau, 2017). Some of this gap is attributable to the fact that males are more likely than females to die in early childhood, to die from accidents or violence in young adulthood, and to experience early death from poor health in middle to later life.

Life expectancy varies significantly among countries of the world. It also varies by gender (Table 17.3). Women in San Marino rank at the top in terms of life expectancy (89 years), followed by women in Hong Kong and Japan (both at 87). However, men in Central Africa Republic rank very low, with a life expectancy at birth of only 50 (Population Reference Bureau, 2017). By region, life expectancy is lowest for men and women (55 and 57, respectively) in Western Africa and is highest in Western and Southern Europe, with life expectancies for men at 79 and women at 84.

It is difficult to make predictions about population growth with precision because predictions depend on assumptions about human behavior. If a government

---

Crude birthrate: The number of births each year per 1,000 women.

Age-specific fertility rate: The number of births typical for women of a specific age in a particular population.

Crude death rate: The number of deaths each year per 1,000 people.

Age-specific mortality rate: An estimate of the number of deaths typical in men and women of specific ages in a particular population.

Life expectancy: The average number of years a newborn is expected to live based on existing health conditions in the country.

TABLE 17.3 Life Expectancy at Birth by Gender for Selected Countries, 2017

COUNTRY	LIFE EXPECTANCY AT BIRTH	
	MALES	FEMALES
Democratic Republic of the Congo	58	61
Nigeria	52	54
South Africa	61	67
India	67	70
Pakistan	65	67
Senegal	65	69
Egypt	71	73
China	75	78
Mexico	75	79
United States	76	81
Denmark	79	83
Israel	80	84

Source: Population Reference Bureau. (2017). *2017 world population data sheet.* Washington, DC: Author. Retrieved from https://www.prb.org/wp-content/uploads/2017/08/2017_World_Population.pdf.

effectively implements family planning programs, for example, the fertility of the population may differ substantially after a decade or two. An unforeseen epidemic (on a scale such as that of HIV/AIDS) may increase mortality; conversely, the development of new drugs (such as new antibiotics or a cure for AIDS) could greatly reduce it. For this reason, demographers typically offer a range of estimates of future populations: a low estimate that assumes high mortality and low fertility; a high estimate that assumes low mortality and high fertility; and an intermediate estimate that represents an informed figure somewhere in between.

About a third of India's 1.3 billion people are under 15, representing momentum for future population growth, even if family planning leads to smaller cohorts in the future. But son preference skews sex ratios at birth in some regions, which may affect the number of future mothers

Population forecasting also depends on fertility, but, again, momentum is critical. In 1979, China decided to limit fertility by rewarding one-child families with additional income and preferential treatment in terms of jobs, housing, health care, and education, while threatening punishment for those who refused to keep their families small. This policy reduced China's TFR well below replacement rate fertility. Yet this reduction does not mean China's population will decline markedly from the 1.38 billion people it reached in 2017. With about 17% of its population under the age of 15—nearing childbearing years—China has substantial population momentum. According to the Population Reference Bureau (2017), its population will grow to about 1.4 billion in 2030 before falling back to 1.3 billion by 2050.

Theory of the First Demographic Transition

Extrapolating from the Western model of population change, demographers have argued that many societies go through roughly the same stages of population transition. They suggest that societies begin with an extended stage of low or no growth resulting from high fertility and equally high mortality, pass through a transitional stage of explosive growth resulting from high fertility and low mortality, and end up in a final stage of slow or no growth resulting from low fertility and low mortality (Figure 17.3). This perspective on population change is called the *theory of the first demographic transition*. We outline this transition in more detail below.

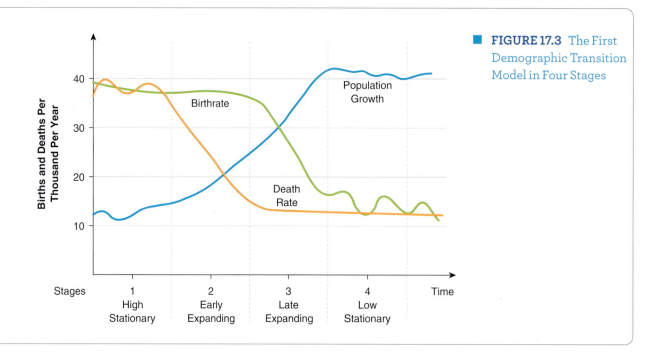

FIGURE 17.3 The First Demographic Transition Model in Four Stages

Early agricultural societies had high fertility and mortality rates that generally counterbalanced one another. Consequently, the population was either stable or grew very slowly. Crude death rates as high as 50 per 1,000 were caused by harsh living conditions, unstable food supplies, poor medical care, and lack of disease control. Epidemics, famines, and wars produced high rates of death, periodically reducing the population even more dramatically. Such societies had to develop strong norms and institutions in support of high fertility to prevent a decline in population. Children were valued for a variety of cultural and economic reasons, particularly where they made contributions to hunting, farming, herding, weaving, and the other work necessary in a household-based economy (Simon, 1981).

As societies modernized (that is, became more urban and industrial), their birthrates initially remained high. At the same time, mortality rates plummeted due to improved food supplies brought about by growing trade links, sanitation control that accompanied greater public health knowledge and prosperity, and, eventually, modern medicine. Consider, for instance, the discovery that hand washing is important for doctors attending women giving birth. While this does not sound revolutionary today, it had a critical impact on maternal and child survival. In the 19th century, women in Europe and the United States had stunning rates of maternal mortality: Up to 25% of women delivering babies at hospitals died from puerperal sepsis, also known as *childbed fever*. Dr. Ignaz Semmelweis, a Viennese physician practicing in the 1840s, observed this phenomenon and recommended that attending physicians wash their hands with a chlorinated solution before assisting in childbirth. Semmelweis and his findings were harshly criticized, and he was ostracized for speaking out; his medical colleagues, nearly all of whom hailed from the upper classes, did not believe that gentlemen (even those attending a birth after dissecting a cadaver) could have dirty hands. As support for germ theory spread, however, Semmelweis's discovery proved to be critically important for the reduction of maternal mortality (Nuland, 2003).

Because people did not initially change their fertility behavior—specifically, they did not stop having many children—as death rates dropped, the result was rapid population growth. Eventually, however, expanding industrialization and urbanization brought about a fall in fertility. Although during the early stages of industrialization, children often worked in factories and contributed to family income, the hardships of child labor eventually led to its legal prohibition. Rather than being an economic necessity, then, children became an expense. Urban living was also less amenable to large families than rural life had been. Population growth stabilized as low mortality came to be matched by falling fertility. At this point, the first demographic transition in the industrialized societies of the West was complete.

The theory of the first demographic transition offers a useful perspective based on a pattern observed in Western countries. We can critique it, however, for the same reason; that is, it describes the historical experience of today's modern Western societies. It does not describe nearly as well the experience of the developing world, which accounts for most global population growth today. In newly industrializing low-income countries, families do not always drastically reduce their fertility. And many low-income nations have not industrialized, yet their mortality rates have declined because populations have access to food, medicine (particularly antibiotics), agricultural and sanitation technologies, and pesticides, which contribute to better health and longer lives. Drops in mortality, however, have not been accompanied by drops in fertility as in modern industrialized states, where decreased fertility stemmed from economic growth, urbanization, industrialization, and expanded educational opportunities.

High fertility combined with low (or relatively low) mortality underlies much of the population explosion in the developing world. Fertility remains high in poor countries for a number of reasons, including health and culture. For instance, families in regions that still experience high child mortality are more likely to have "extra" children to ensure that some survive, and notions about the ideal size of families are culturally variable.

Economic factors also shape fertility decisions. Consider the relationship between economic rationality and childbearing. The saying "Children are a poor man's riches" highlights the fact that in agricultural societies in particular, children (specifically male children) are a value more than a cost. In rich and industrialized countries, children, while

©Bettmann/Getty Images

Dr. Ignaz Semmelweis observed higher maternal mortality in Clinic 1 of his hospital, staffed by male obstetricians who performed autopsies, than in Clinic 2, staffed by female midwives who did not. Chlorine washing of male birth attendants' hands reduced maternal mortality until 1850, when Semmelweis left the hospital and old practices resumed.

emotionally valued, are economically costly and contribute little or nothing to the household in terms of economic value. Economic rationality, then, is present in both the decision of a poor household in the developing world to have many children and the decision of a rich household in the developed world to have few.

One of the most important factors contributing to both reduced fertility and improved child survival is the education of women (Figure 17.4). According to one study, for every one-year increase in the average education of women in their childbearing years, a country experienced a 9.5% fall in child mortality (Gakidou, Cowling, Lozano, & Murray, 2010). Strikingly, a child born to a literate woman is 50% more likely to survive to age 5 than a child born to a woman who cannot read (United Nations Educational, Scientific and Cultural Organization, 2010).

Women who are more educated are more likely to be familiar with family planning methods and more likely to use them. Better-educated women are also more likely to have jobs in the formal labor force and, consequently, to limit their fertility in order to bring in economic resources. Finally, women with some economic resources also tend to have more decision-making power in the family, allowing them to participate in making choices about birth control and family size (Pradhan, 2015; United Nations, 1995).

Better health services for children and declining infant and child mortality also have important effects on fertility decisions. When women have reason to believe that all or most of their offspring will survive into adulthood, they are less likely to have "extra" children to ensure that a few survive (Kibirige, 1997).

■ FIGURE 17.4 Relationship between Fertility and Female Education: Total Fertility Rate by Years of Schooling

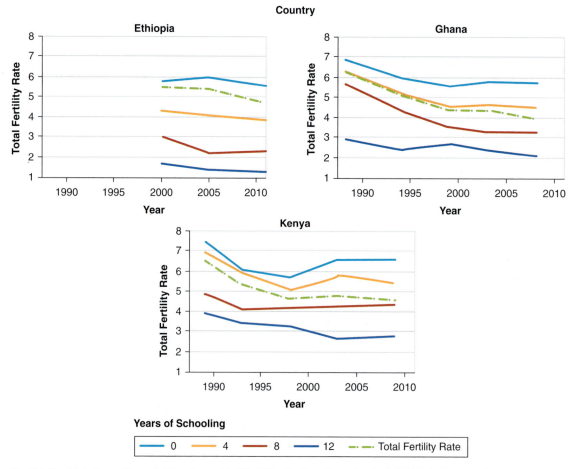

Source: "The Relationship between Women's Education and Fertility," Elina Pradhan, November 27, 2015, World Economic Forum.

Developed countries and the governments of some high-fertility countries have helped finance family planning programs in order to educate people about birth control. In addition, they have provided residents with condoms, birth control pills, and other means of reducing fertility. While such programs have met with some success, they often run up against deep-seated religious and other cultural values, some of which are found in the developed states as well. For instance, during Ronald Reagan's presidency and the presidencies of both George H. W. Bush and George W. Bush, U.S. governmental funding of family planning programs abroad was cut significantly because birth control (and especially abortion) violated the beliefs of conservative supporters of those administrations. It is clear that global efforts in family planning are fraught with problems. It remains to be seen whether they will ultimately succeed in reducing fertility (and hence global population growth).

Is a Second Demographic Transition Occurring in the West?

In the theory of the first demographic transition, population reaches a point of stabilization in Stage 4. What happens after that? Some demographers argue that at least in the most developed countries, stabilization has been followed by a *second demographic transition* (Lesthaeghe, 1995; McNicoll, 2001) characterized by broad changes in family patterns. Countries experiencing a second demographic transition may be characterized by increased rates of divorce and cohabitation, for instance, as well as decreased rates of marriage and fertility and a rise of nonmarital births as a

proportion of all births. According to some demographers, Germany, France, and Sweden are among the countries experiencing a second demographic transition. Because changes in family patterns are associated with smaller families, the second demographic transition often includes a decline in the population's **rate of natural increase (RNI)**—that is, *the crude birthrate minus the crude death rate.*

If a country has a negative RNI, this can lead to population declines. Russia, for example, is experiencing relatively rapid loss of population: People are dying at a faster rate than they are being born, and Russia can expect to see a population loss of about 10% through the middle of the century (Population Reference Bureau, 2010). The result is an inverted age pyramid, wider at the top and narrower at the bottom (Figure 17.5). Some countries with a negative RNI, however, still experience growing populations as a result of immigration. By contrast, countries with above-replacement-level fertility rates and growing populations have normal pyramids, such as that for Kenya shown in Figure 17.5.

What accounts for the second demographic transition? Demographer Ron Lesthaeghe (1995) argues that "the motivations underlying the 'second transition' are clearly different from those supporting the 'first transition,' with individual autonomy and female emancipation more central to the second than to the first" (p. 18). According to this perspective, more people associate personal satisfaction with consumption and personal fulfillment and are not as likely to seek fulfillment through family relationships. Female emancipation has also been broadened by the medical evolution of the "perfectly contracepting society" (Westoff & Ryder, 1977), such that women have unprecedented control over their fertility, and many have chosen smaller families or have opted not to have children.

Critics suggest that the second transition describes only a fraction of the world's population. However, the number of countries experiencing below-replacement birthrates is rising, and a sociological and demographic perspective such as the theory of the second transition offers sociologists analytical tools for understanding these key trends in advanced industrial states.

©REUTERS/Joe Penney

In the West African country of Mali, women with a secondary education or more bear an average of three children, while women without education have an average of seven children. Global demographic data shows a strong correlation between women's educational attainment and fertility.

Rate of natural increase (RNI): The crude birthrate minus the crude death rate.

■ **FIGURE 17.5** Population Pyramids for Canada and Kenya, 2016

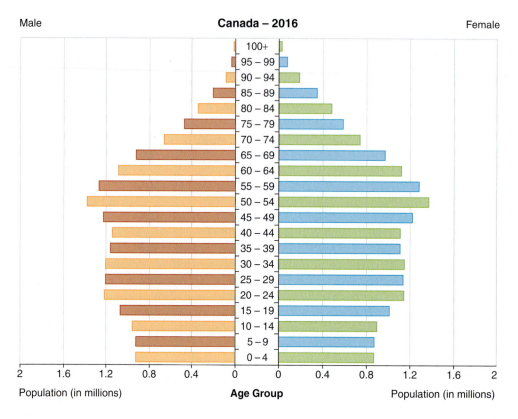

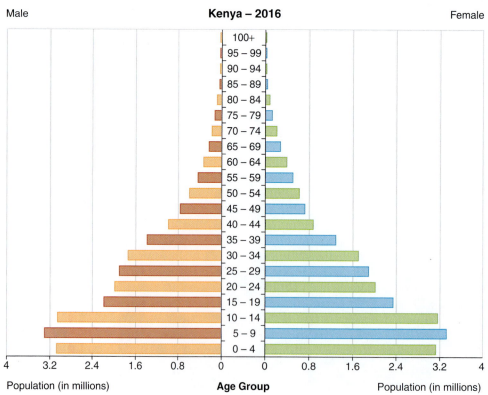

Source: Central Intelligence Agency, *The World Fact Book*.

Private Lives, Public Issues

WHY ARE FEWER PEOPLE IN DEVELOPED COUNTRIES CHOOSING TO HAVE CHILDREN?

©Yamaguchi Haruyoshi/Corbis via Getty Images

In economically developed countries such as England, Germany, and Japan, growing proportions of young adults are choosing to forgo having children. According to a recent article on the topic,

> Just 9% of English and Welsh women born in 1946 had no children. For the cohort born in 1970—who, barring a few late surprises, can be assumed to be done with babies—the proportion is 17%. In Germany, 22% of women reach their early 40s without children; in Hamburg, 32% do. ("The rise of childlessness," 2017, para. 2)

Declines in childbearing are being felt in demographic indicators:

> Since Japan began counting its newborns more than a century ago, more than a million infants have been added to its population each year. . . . No longer, in the latest discomforting milestone for a country facing a steep population decline. Last year, the number of births in Japan dropped below one million for the first time. (Soble, 2017, para. 1–2).

What explains the rise in childlessness among young adults? The sociological roots of this growing phenomenon are complex. In this essay, we consider a few explanations.

In Japan, where there has been a significant fall in marriage as well, some researchers cite economic reasons for rising childlessness. Specifically, as Japan's labor market has shifted toward jobs that are more likely to be part-time or insecure temporary positions, young adults have shown less inclination to take on the traditional responsibilities of family life:

Japan's birth rate may be falling because there are fewer good opportunities for young people, and especially men, in the country's economy. In a country where men are still widely expected to be breadwinners and support families, a lack of good jobs may be creating a class of men who don't marry and have children because they—and their potential partners—know they can't afford to. (Semuels, 2017, para. 2)

At the same time, women in Japan and elsewhere are enjoying expanded educational and professional opportunities that they are eager to embrace. Shifts in cultural attitudes about gender and, particularly among women themselves, whether motherhood is an essential part of a woman's life are also part of the story. According to one account, in Japan, some women "shun marriage and children because Japan's old-fashioned corporate culture, together with a dire shortage of child care, forces them to give up their careers if they have children" ("Why the Japanese Are Having So Few Babies," 2014, para. 3).

In Germany, there has been public discussion about how to reconcile long-standing societal expectations that women with children remain at home to raise the children rather than returning to the workforce with the country's concern about rising childlessness. Women who wish to have children but also to continue their careers have faced challenges in Germany (Nicholson, 2013).

Interestingly, German demographer Michaela Kreyenfeld points to the possibility of some explanatory variation for childlessness by gender:

> Women often have no children because they have prioritised education or work in their 20s and 30s. Men are more likely to remain childless because women do not view them as good boyfriend material—let alone good husband or father material. "They have a problem finding partners." ("The rise of childlessness," 2017, para. 15)

Decisions about having a child or children are highly personal. At the same time, they are made in normative, economic, and social contexts that influence the decisions of young adults. The sociological imagination helps us to see how

(Continued)

(Continued)

individual choices add up to societal-level outcomes and how societal conditions structure those choices.

Think It Through

- What are other sociological factors that may explain why fewer young adults in many developed countries are choosing to have children? Can what you learned in previous chapters on, for instance, family, education, or work and the economy offer some insights into this question?

Malthus and Marx: How Many People Are Too Many?

High rates of population growth in some parts of the world may seem daunting, even alarming to some, but numbers alone do not tell the entire story. There is still a great deal of sparsely settled land in the world, and if the planet's 7.3 billion people were all somehow transplanted to the territory of the United States, the resulting crowding would be no greater than currently exists in the country of Taiwan.

Is the world overpopulated? This question is the subject of debate. On one side are those who predict catastrophe if population growth is not slowed or stopped altogether. Activists who fear that a population doomsday is just around the corner often conclude that drastic measures are required, including stringent public policies that promote small families. On the other side are those who argue that while population growth should be slowed, extreme measures are unwarranted. They tend to favor expanded female education, voluntary family planning programs (though some groups object to contraception as well as abortion), and economic policies that raise living standards, making smaller families a more rational economic choice.

Malthus: Overpopulation and Natural Limits

The argument that the world is overpopulated was first made two centuries ago by British social philosopher Thomas Malthus (1766–1834). Malthus (1798/1926) developed the theory of exponential population growth: the belief that, similar to compound interest, a constant rate of population growth produces a population that grows by an increasing amount with each passing year. **Exponential population growth**, thus, refers to *a constant growth rate that is applied to a base that is continuously growing in size, producing a population that grows by an increasing amount with each passing year.* Malthus also posited that although population grows exponentially, the food supply does not; the earth's resources are finite. Consequently, though the

population may continue to double, the amount of food is more likely to grow at a constant rate. The result, according to Malthus's dire warning, is a growing mismatch between population and food resources. Unless we take steps to control our population growth, Malthus predicted, nature will do it for us: Wars fought over scarce resources, epidemics, and famine will keep population in check. Back when only a billion people occupied the entire planet, Malthus believed doomsday was already on the horizon.

How accurate was Malthus's prediction? Although war, epidemic, and famine have in fact been sadly evident throughout human history, and population has continued to grow exponentially, the food supply has grown along with it. Malthus failed to recognize that modern technology can also be applied to agriculture, yielding an exponential growth in food supplies—at least for a time. A report by the Food and Agriculture Organization of the United Nations (2009) concludes that although the world's population may reach over 9 billion by 2050, "the required increase in food production can be achieved if the necessary investment is undertaken and policies conducive to agricultural production are put in place," along with "policies to enhance access by fighting poverty, especially in rural areas, as well as effective safety net programmes" (p. 2).

Although Malthus's predictions of global catastrophe have not been borne out, there may be a limit to the carrying capacity of the planet. World population cannot continue rapid growth indefinitely without consequences. Yet to point out that population growth presents serious challenges is not the same as concluding that the limits have been reached. Despite Malthus's pessimistic prophecies and Paul Ehrlich's dire warnings in *The Population Bomb* (1968), the long-predicted population doomsday has yet to arrive. In fact, the connection between population growth and human misery appears to be more complicated than many analyses have suggested. The issue is not simply how much additional food will be required to feed more mouths, but also whether the food that is produced will reach those who need it. Mass hunger in many countries is as much a product of politics as of true lack of food; in civil conflicts, for instance, hunger may be used as a weapon, with opposing forces blocking food shipments to enemy areas.

Exponential population growth: A constant rate of population growth applied to a base that is continuously growing in size, producing a population that grows by an increasing amount with each passing year.

Simon: A Modern Critic Takes on Malthus

Economist Julian Simon (1977, 2000) became well known for his pointedly anti-Malthusian perspective on population. Simon not only rejected the notion that unchecked population growth would lead humanity down a path to hunger, deprivation, and poverty but also posited precisely the opposite. He argued that population growth has positive economic effects. In his most recent work, published posthumously, Simon (2000) suggested that *sudden modern progress* (SMP)—the rapid rise in living standards and technology—is the result of population growth and density. Put another way, the great population growth of the modern period was a causal factor of "the great breakthrough" (which is also the title of his book)—that is, population growth brings about technological progress. More people means more minds and more innovation, so human-generated resources, Simon argued, can overcome limitations on natural resources. Unlike Malthus, Simon was encouraged rather than daunted by the prospect of rising populations.

Indeed, the question of whether more minds can balance the pressure caused by more bodies is an engaging and imperative one. Can population growth be both problematic and powerful? What do you think?

Marx: Overpopulation or Maldistribution of Wealth?

Malthus forecast misery and inevitable overpopulation under conditions of growth. Simon saw population growth and density as necessary conditions for economic progress. Karl Marx focused on the unequal distribution of resources across populations.

Marx was concerned about the dominance of an economic system that enables the wealthy few to consume the world's resources at the expense of the impoverished masses.

Only India and China have reached the 1 billion population mark. While its large population strains the country's resources, India has also experienced steady economic growth and gains in education and innovation. One of the results is a growing middle class with rising incomes.

He was critical of Malthus for claiming that overpopulation is the central cause of human starvation and misery. In Marx's (1867/1992a) view, the central problem is not a mismatch between population size and resource availability but rather the unequal distribution of resources; in most societies, as well as in the world as a whole, he argued, the members of a small elite enjoy the lion's share of the wealth and resources while the majority are left to take up the crumbs that fall from the richly endowed tables of the few.

Parente (2008) notes that even after adjustments are made for differences in relative prices and gross domestic product per capita, the living standards in the wealthiest industrial countries are about 50 to 60 times greater than those in the world's poorest countries. Most of the world's resources and goods are consumed by the West: Western Europe and North America, with 12% of the world's population, account for 60% of private consumption expenditures. The United States alone, home to about 5% of the world's population, burns about a quarter of the globe's coal, oil, and natural gas. In contrast, sub-Saharan Africa and South Asia, which together are home to more than one third of humanity, account for just over 3% of private consumer expenditures. At the beginning of the new millennium, about two fifths of the earth's inhabitants lived on less than $2 per day (Worldwatch Institute, 2011). Marx argued that such maldistribution is the result of a capitalist economic system that divides people into unequal social classes.

Both Malthus and Marx were writing when the world's population was only around 1 billion people. Marx's criticism of Malthus has stood the test of time, since world population has doubled and more than doubled again since Malthus's predictions were made, but global resources have not run dry. Looking critically at Marx's ideas, we might note that although the maldistribution of wealth is an important factor in understanding poverty and human misery, Marx underestimated the importance of population growth itself as a variable.

Malthus, Marx, and Modernity

Consider this question: What is the greater threat to the health and survival of our global environment—the rapid growth of the populations of the developing world or the overconsumption of resources by the small stratum of the wealthy? While some policy makers in the West express concern about the threats posed by unchecked population growth or the use of "dirty" technologies in developing states or the decimation of rain forests in the Amazon and elsewhere, there is little vigorous mainstream debate over the global threat presented by the recklessly wasteful consumption of resources by Western consumers. To cite only one example of the way Western consumption is masked by a focus on the global poor: Broad media attention has been given to the millions of acres of rain forest lost to clear-cutting in poor states, not least because of the immense biodiversity that has been sacrificed. Many in the United States have donated money to campaigns aimed at saving these precious resources. At the same time, heedless U.S. consumers of steaks, burgers, and other beef products may not recognize that some of the clear-cutting is done by ranchers seeking land on which to farm cattle, the meat from which will be sent to our supermarkets, restaurants, and dinner tables.

The question of whether overpopulation or overconsumption is the greater threat is a provocative one. Neither phenomenon is without consequences. Malthus feared that population would outpace food production; Marx posited that elites would consume far more than their share. A modern take on this debate points us to the conflict between underdevelopment in some states and "overdevelopment" in others.

As we shall see later in this chapter, environmental stresses have grown substantially since Malthus's and Marx's time, and some scientists believe we are approaching a point of no return in inflicting environmental damage on the planet. While overconsumption presents threats to our future, the consequences of the population explosion must also be faced. Since much of the world's population increase is currently concentrated in urban areas, we will next examine the impact of urbanization on modern life before turning to the environmental effects of urbanization and population growth combined.

Urbanization

What is a *city*? Do you find it easy or difficult to come up with a definition? Early urban sociologist Louis Wirth (1938) wrote that "a sociologically significant definition of the city seeks to select those elements of urbanism which mark it as a distinctive mode of human group life" (p. 4). For sociological purposes, and thus for ours too, Wirth's definition is useful: A **city** is *"a relatively large, dense, and permanent settlement of socially heterogeneous individuals"* (p. 8).

City: A relatively large, dense, and permanent settlement of socially heterogeneous individuals.

Like many cities, the capital of the Philippines, Manila, is a study in contrasts, with a nascent professional middle class and a persistent problem of poverty. In this photo, a homeless child sleeps beneath a bustling city bridge.

©REUTERS/Romeo Ranoco

In the eyes of some literary writers, cities are grim places of human degradation and misery. In the 19th-century poem "The City of Dreadful Night," James Thomson (1874) describes such a place:

That city's atmosphere is dark and dense,

Although not many exiles wander there,

With many a potent evil influence,

Each adding poison to the poisoned air;

Infections of unalterable sadness,

Infections of incalculable madness,

Infections of incurable despair.

Other writers have praised the modernity, power, and culture of the city, while still others have recognized the contradictions of cities, their beautiful madness, their inhabitants' paradoxical excitement and indifference, and their ability to both attract and repel. Honoré de Balzac wrote of the inhabitants of Paris in 1833:

By dint of taking in everything, the Parisian ends by being interested in nothing. No emotion dominating his face, which friction has rubbed away, it turns gray like the faces of those houses upon which all kinds of dust and smoke have blown. . . . [The Parisian] grumbles at everything, consoles himself for everything, jests at everything, forgets, desires, and tastes everything, seizes all with passion, quits all with indifference—his kings, his conquests, his glory, his idols of bronze or glass—as he throws away his stockings, his hats, and his fortune. In Paris, no sentiment can withstand the drift of things.

The city is a place of kings and presidents, as it is a place of thugs and beggars. It is lovely and disgusting, wealthy and poor, rewarding and despairing. Cities have become part of our lives and lore, but they were not always so. Cities have a long history, but until the Industrial Revolution, most people were rural dwellers. Today, most of the world's people live in cities and embody the beauties, miseries, and contradictions of those places. Below, we turn a sociological lens on the cities of the United States and the world.

The Rise of Industry and Early Cities

Preindustrial cities, based on both agriculture and trade, first appeared 10,000 to 12,000 years ago. The development of settled agricultural areas enabled farmers to produce an **agricultural surplus**, *food beyond the amount required for immediate survival.* This surplus in turn made it possible for cities to sustain populations in which residents were not engaged primarily in farming. The first known cities were small, their populations seldom exceeding a few thousand, since the surplus production of 10 or more farmers was required to support a single nonfarming city dweller. The need for access to transportation routes and rich soil for farming figured prominently in the siting of the earliest cities along major river systems (Hosken, 1993). Early city residents included government officials, priests, handicraft workers, and others specializing in nonagricultural occupations, although many city dwellers engaged in some farming as well. Until modern times, very few cities in the world surpassed 100,000 people. More than 2,000 years ago, Rome was considered an enormous metropolis with 800,000 people; today, it would be comparable in population to a U.S. city such as San Francisco (Mumford, 1961).

The Industrial Revolution of the 18th century radically changed the nature of cities. While cities of the past had served primarily as centers of trade, industrial cities now emerged as centers of manufacturing. Although some of the earliest English factories were in smaller cities, by the 19th century, industrialization was moving hand in hand with **urbanization**, *the concentration of people in urban areas.* At the beginning of the 19th century, there were barely 100 places in England with more than 5,000 inhabitants; by the end of the century, there were more than 600 that, together, contained more than 20 million people. The city of London grew from 1.1 million to 7.3 million people between 1800 and 1910 (Hosken, 1993), becoming a center of industry as well as an ever more important hub of commerce and culture. In the United States as well, the explosion of cities coincided with the onset of industrialization at the end of the 19th century. By the early 20th century, most U.S. citizens could be classified as urban, and today, as in Britain and other Western European industrial states, the vast majority live in metropolitan areas.

Sociologists and the City

The early industrial cities were grimy places in which people lived in shanties and shacks, often in the shadows of the factories where they spent more than a dozen working hours each day. In the absence of proper sanitation and sewage systems, illness and epidemics were common, and many people died of typhoid, cholera, dysentery, and tuberculosis. Writers such as Charles Dickens captured the miseries of early urban industrial life, where men, women, and children toiled in dank, squalid conditions and lived lives of deprivation and degradation. Early sociologists also turned their lenses on the city, some viewing urban life as bordering on the pathological. At the same time, most recognized that cities provided opportunities for individuality and creativity.

During the rapid urbanization of the 19th century, some of the earliest sociologists worried about the differences between a presumably serene country life and the "death and decay" of city life (Toennies, 1887/1963). The rural community (*Gemeinschaft* in the original German) was contrasted with urban society (*Gesellschaft*), much to the disadvantage of the latter. Rural community life was said to be characterized by intimate relationships, a strong sense of family, powerful folkways and mores, and stabilizing religious foundations. Urban life, by contrast, was believed to be characterized by impersonal and materially based relationships, family breakdown, and the erosion of traditional beliefs and religious values. The behavior of city dwellers was viewed as governed no longer by long-standing folkways and mores, but by cold cost-benefit calculations, individual preferences rather than group norms, and ever-changing public opinion.

While alienation was assumed to be a product of this grimly efficient urban world, Émile Durkheim put forth the notion that the *mechanical solidarity* of traditional community life (based on homogeneity) could be replaced by the *organic solidarity* of modern societies, with complex divisions of labor in which people were heterogeneous but interdependent for survival and prosperity.

During the 1920s and 1930s, researchers at the University of Chicago turned their city into a vast laboratory for urban studies, pioneering urban sociology as a field. Early 20th-century U.S. sociology centered on the study of "social problems"

Agricultural surplus: Food beyond the amount required for immediate survival.

Urbanization: The concentration of people in urban areas.

Inequality Matters

THE GEOMETRY OF THE CITY

Among the important early urban sociologists at the University of Chicago was Ernest Burgess (1886–1966). Burgess (1925) developed the *concentric zone hypothesis* in part to explain how different social groups come to be distributed across urban spaces. It suggests that sociological factors, including socioeconomic class, are relevant to understanding the competition for favorable locations in an urban area.

Burgess believed a key city pattern could be represented by five concentric circles (Figure 17.6). The small inner circle represents the *central business district,* a relatively affluent zone characterized by government buildings, financial institutions, and major retailers. The next ring is a *zone in transition,* with low-rent areas occupied by poor and minority residents and some manufacturing. The third ring from the center is the *workingman's zone,* with housing typified by small individual units and apartments. The fourth ring is the *middle-class residential district,* with more upscale housing options. The outer ring is the *commuters' zone or suburban zone,* with larger housing units and upper-income residences. Burgess noted that as we move from the inner zone to the outer circle, we find decreased population density and increased class status, higher rates of home ownership, lower rates of crime, and smaller families. The patterns could be explained, he

argued, by the amount people and businesses were willing to pay for land, with valued commercial space in the center (which has the greatest access to customers) and valued residential space in outer areas.

Burgess's model has been criticized for, among other flaws, hypothesizing a cityscape that has characterized many U.S. cities but cannot capture the patterns of global cities, many of which exhibit the opposite pattern of class composition, with the wealthiest in the center and suburban districts of poverty at the city's edges. Contemporary gentrification in some U.S. cities has also brought high-rent residences and pricey condominiums to previously poor and neglected urban neighborhoods.

At the same time, Burgess's work is important because it seeks to cast a sociological eye on the U.S. city and to recognize sociological factors that help explain social group distribution across the urban landscape.

Think It Through

- Can you create a sociological map of your city or town? What kinds of patterns of commercial activity or residence can you identify, and how would you explain them sociologically?

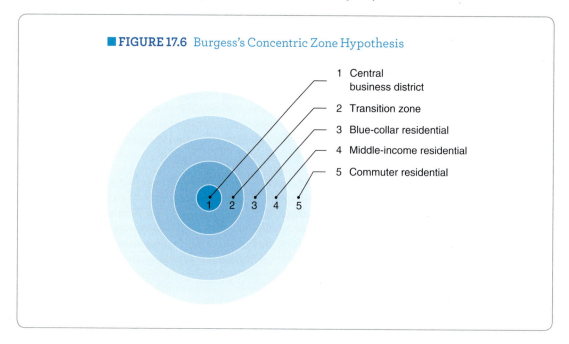

■ **FIGURE 17.6** Burgess's Concentric Zone Hypothesis

1 Central business district
2 Transition zone
3 Blue-collar residential
4 Middle-income residential
5 Commuter residential

such as hoboes, the mentally ill, juvenile delinquents, criminals, prostitutes, and others who were seen as casualties of urban living. Urbanism was believed to be a specific way of life that resulted from the geographic concentration of large numbers of socially diverse people (see the *Inequality Matters* box on page 494). Sociologists believed that one feature of this life was a good deal of mutual mistrust, leading city residents to segregate themselves on the basis of race, ethnicity, class, and even lifestyle into neighborhoods of like-minded people (Wirth, 1938). Of course, as we saw in our discussion of race in Chapter 9, self-segregation should be distinguished from imposed segregation that is the result of individual or institutional racism.

Although early sociologists often linked city life with pathology, even in supposedly impersonal cities, people maintain intense social networks and close personal ties. Numerous sociological studies have found that significant community relationships persist within even the largest cities (Duneier, 1992; Fischer, 1982, 1984; Gans, 1962a, 1962b; Liebow, 1967; Whyte, 1943; Wirth, 1928). Physical characteristics such as size and density do not by themselves account for urban problems. What is important is the way a particular society organizes itself in cities. Below, we look at the case of cities in the United States.

Cities in the United States

Transportation and communication technologies have played important roles in helping to shape U.S. cities. The automobile and urban rail and subway systems enabled cities to expand outward by allowing people to travel greater distances between home and work. Similarly, modern construction technologies permitted cities to expand skyward, with massive skyscrapers that take up little land space but create living or working space for thousands.

The Social Dynamics of U.S. Cities and Suburbs

Political and economic forces are also key to shaping modern cities. Sociologists John Logan and Harvey Molotch (1987; Molotch, 1976; Warner, Molotch, & Lategola, 1992) have argued that cities are shaped by what they call the **urban growth machine**, *those persons and institutions that have a stake in an increase in the value of urban land and that constitute a power elite in most cities.* These people and institutions are said to include downtown businesses, real estate owners (particularly those who own commercial and rental property), land developers and builders, newspapers

Urban growth machine: Those persons and institutions that have a stake in an increase in the value of urban land and that constitute a power elite in cities.

(whose advertising revenues are often tied to the size of the local population), and the lawyers, accountants, architects, real estate agents, construction workers, and others whose income is tied to serving those who own land. Logan and Molotch view the urban growth machine as dominating local politics in most U.S. cities, with the result that cities often compete with one another to house factories, office buildings, shopping malls, and other economic activities that will increase the value of the land owned by the members of the growth machine.

G. William Domhoff (2002) expands this notion with his concept of *growth coalitions,* groups "whose members share a common interest in intensifying land use in their geographic locale" (p. 39). Growth coalitions are a powerful force in local politics, though they encounter conflicts in their pursuit of growth and profit. Domhoff notes that

> neighborhoods are something to be used and enjoyed in the eyes of those who live in them, but they are often seen as sites for further development by growth coalitions, who justify new developments with a doctrine claiming the highest and best use for land. (p. 40)

Consider Domhoff's conflict-oriented analysis of U.S. politics and decision making, which we examined in Chapter 14. Recall that Domhoff asks us to ponder the questions *Who benefits? Who governs? Who wins?* Looking at growth politics—the increasing development of already crowded suburbs or the gentrification of urban neighborhoods at the expense of older neighborhoods—we may ask who has the power and the resources to realize their interests. Are those who favor *use value* (the enjoyment of the neighborhood) or those who favor *exchange value* (the economic development of an area) more powerful? Is the shape of modern cities and suburbs a product primarily of those who inhabit them or those who profit from them?

The post–World War II development of U.S. cities and suburbs illustrates how the growth machine operates at the national level. The rapid growth of suburbs during the 1950s and the 1960s is often attributed to people's preference for suburban living, but it was also a product of economic forces and government policies designed to stimulate the postwar economy (Jackson, 1985; Mollenkopf, 1977). The government influence is illustrated by the 1956 National Interstate and Defense Highways Act, which established a highway trust fund paid for by a federal tax on gasoline. This legislation ensured a self-renewing source of funding to construct high-speed freeways connecting cities and suburbs across the country. The legislation eventually financed nearly 100,000 miles of highway, characterized by President

The great highway building projects of the postwar period literally paved the roads to America's suburbanized future. Robert Fishman suggests that "every true suburb is the outcome of two opposing forces, an attraction toward the opportunities of the great city and a simultaneous repulsion against urban life" (quoted in Gainsborough, 2001, p. 33). Is this an accurate characterization? Why or why not?

Dwight Eisenhower at the time as "the greatest public works program in history" and enough to build a "Great Wall" around the world 50 feet wide and 9 feet high. The law originated in the planning efforts of a powerful consortium of bankers, corporations, and unions connected with the automobile, petroleum, and construction industries (Mollenkopf, 1977).

The Highways Act, in combination with other government programs, spurred the growth of the U.S. economy, both by improving transportation and by promoting the automobile and construction industries. The existence of freeways encouraged people to buy more cars and to drive additional miles, generating still more gasoline tax revenues for additional highway construction. Large numbers of people bought houses in the suburbs with federally insured and subsidized loans, commuted on federally financed highways to work in federally subsidized downtown office buildings, and even shopped in suburban shopping centers built in part with federal dollars. All this development ushered in a quarter century of growth and relative prosperity for working- and middle-class residents of the suburbs.

In fact, the rapid growth of suburbs in this period represents one of the most dramatic population shifts in U.S. history. In 1950, cities contained 33% of the U.S. population, considerably more than their surrounding suburbs (23%). During the 1960s the suburbs overtook the cities, and by 1990, the suburban population had reached 46%, while the city population had declined slightly to 31% (Frey & Speare, 1991). In 2000, 46% lived in the suburbs, while the proportion in central cities dropped slightly to 30% (Hobbs & Stoops, 2002). In 2010, more than 80% of the U.S. population inhabited metropolitan areas, but the 2010 census also showed a shift back toward urban growth (Mackun & Wilson, 2011).

The emergence of postindustrial society has encouraged further development beyond the economic activity of the urban core. Modern information technology has made it easier for corporations to locate high-tech factories and office parks in once-remote suburban or even rural locations, where they find relatively inexpensive land, modern industrial facilities, fewer environmental problems, and incentive packages that can improve their profitability (Maidenberg, 2016). Since 1980, more than two thirds of employment growth in the United States has taken place outside central cities, and even manufacturing, while in decline nationally, has found a home in the suburbs; today, more than 70% of manufacturing is suburban (Wilson, 2010). According to *Crain's Chicago Business*, for example,

> Overall industrial employment . . . fell 21 percent between 2003 and 2013, as companies became more productive, and some firms shuttered while others moved factory work elsewhere. But the suburbs' decline was lighter than the city's: from 2003–2013, suburban manufacturing jobs fell 18 percent to about 292,000 positions, according to data provided by CMAP. By contrast, Chicago lost 33 percent of its manufacturing jobs, ending 2013 with 64,439 positions. (Maidenberg, 2016, para. 6)

While those who benefit from such relocations tend to be well-educated managerial, technical, and professional specialists, the suburbs are also home to a substantial proportion of entry-level positions. This is significant because it contributes to the loss of employment opportunities in central cities. Sociologist William Julius Wilson (2010) writes of the *spatial mismatch* between urban job seekers and suburban jobs, noting that "opportunities for employment are geographically disconnected from the people who need the jobs" (p. 41). He offers the example of Cleveland, where, "although entry-level workers are concentrated in inner-city neighborhoods, 80 percent of the entry-level jobs are located in the suburbs" (p. 41).

The migration of middle- and upper-income families from the cities begun in the post–World War II era evolved into a critical socioeconomic disparity between the suburbs and central cities. Analyzing the concentrated poverty of urban core areas such as South Chicago, Wilson (2010) points out that political forces created a new urban poverty that plagues inner-city neighborhoods deeply segregated by both race and class. These forces included government support for highway building, a postwar mortgage lending boom that benefited predominantly White veterans and their families, and the decline of the industrial base that long provided economic sustenance to U.S. cities and less educated workers.

Gentrification and U.S. Cities

The decline of U.S. cities, most visible in the economically distressed urban cores of cities, including Chicago, Washington, DC, and Baltimore, has fostered efforts toward **urban renewal**, *the transformation of old neighborhoods with new buildings, businesses, and residences.* Urban renewal is linked to **gentrification**, a process characterized by *change in the socioeconomic composition of older and poorer neighborhoods with the remodeling of old structures and building of new residences and shops to attract new middle- and high-income residents.* Gentrification may have a variety of demographic effects, reducing the number of racial and ethnic minority residents and lowering the average household size, as families are replaced by young singles and couples with more robust stores of disposable income (Beauregard, 1986).

Gentrification may transform struggling neighborhoods into flourishing and economically viable urban spaces that offer cultural and business opportunities to residents and visitors. Gentrification may also have the effect of reducing crime, as previously bereft or abandoned buildings return to active use and the number of residents in a neighborhood rebounds: One study correlated a rise in urban coffee shops in gentrifying neighborhoods to a decline in homicides. Interestingly, the effect on robberies was mixed: While they declined in predominantly White and Latino neighborhoods, they rose in predominantly Black neighborhoods (Papachristos, Smith, Scherer, & Fugiero, 2011). Cities also benefit from gentrification as the process

rebuilds a middle-class and upper-middle-class base of residents who pay city taxes and pushes up the value of taxable property and, consequently, revenues for city governments. Some of this is the result of the building of new luxury housing units and some derives from the transformation of rental units into higher-priced condominiums.

Gentrification heralds a rise in rents and other costs of living, which may push out longtime low-income residents who cannot afford to be part of the boom in condominiums or the luxury amenities intended to make gentrified spaces inviting to upwardly mobile new residents. For older residents, gentrification may entail the loss of local cultural spaces and longtime businesses. In 2015, the *Washington Post* reported on the closing of a small hair salon in the newly gentrified Bloomingdale neighborhood in the District of Columbia:

> [Latosha] Jackson-Martin's father, William Jackson, opened Jak & Co. Hairdressers downtown 50 years ago, and moved it to now-trendy Bloomingdale in 1988. For much of its past quarter-century, the store has been surrounded by a laundromat, a uniform business and liquor stores with Plexiglass windows.
>
> Now, it's nestled between a pub with an extensive whiskey and scotch menu, a gourmet bakery and a Mexican restaurant that sells cucumber margaritas.
>
> "I want people in the community to know, especially young people, that the community is filled with people who have and people who don't have," Jackson-Martin said. "I want people to know that we put up a fight to stay where we are, but we are in the 'has not' . . . I can't afford to pay double the rent like the other folks." (Stein, 2015)

Jackson-Martin's experience mirrors that of a spectrum of older businesses that not only cannot afford rising retail rents but may also be facing a loss of their traditional customer base as new residents move in and demand grows for different shops and restaurants. Her experience also highlights some of the social tensions that underlie gentrification, as the interests of old and new residents come into conflict.

What, then, are we to conclude about gentrification? How can urban renewal and efforts to bring upwardly mobile residents back to U.S. city centers and to revitalize economically distressed neighborhoods be balanced with the needs and aspirations of low-income residents and long-term businesses at risk of displacement as the cost of living in the gentrified neighborhood climbs?

Urban renewal: The transformation of old neighborhoods with new buildings, businesses, and residences.

Gentrification: The change in the socioeconomic composition of older and poorer neighborhoods with the remodeling of old structures and building of new residences and shops to attract new middle- and high-income residents.

Segregation and Gentrification in the U.S.

In the section above, you learned about gentrification in U.S. cities such as Washington, DC. Consider the examination of racial residential segregation in our chapter on race and ethnicity (Chapter 9). What is the relationship between racial residential segregation, which is a long-existing phenomenon in the U.S., and the newer phenomenon of gentrification? Can gentrification be part of a process of desegregation? Or would one expect it to exacerbate the problem of racial residential segregation in U.S. cities? What do you think?

The Emergence of Global Cities

We live in an age of urban dominance. Today, more than half the world's population resides in cities, many of which are massive global centers such as London (population 10.3 million), New York (18.6 million), and Tokyo (38 million; World Atlas, 2018). **Global cities** are *metropolitan areas that are highly interconnected with one another in their role*

Global cities: Metropolitan areas that are highly interconnected with one another in their role as centers of global political and economic decision making, finance, and culture.

as centers of global political and economic decision making, finance, and culture (Sassen, 1991). Their economic role is defined as much by the large role they play in the global economy as by their influence in their immediate geographic regions.

Saskia Sassen (1991) identifies four principal functions of global cities. First, they are command posts in the organization of the world economy. Second, they serve as key locations for businesses related to finance, accounting, marketing, design, and other highly specialized (and profitable) services that are replacing manufacturing as the leading economic sectors. Third, they are the most important sites of innovation and new product development. Finally, they serve as the principal markets for global businesses. Sassen (2000) also notes that "whether at the global or regional level, these cities must inevitably engage each other in fulfilling their functions. . . . There is no such entity as a single global city" (p. 4).

In global cities, multinational corporations and international bankers maintain their headquarters and oversee the operation of diverse production and management operations that are spread across the globe. Global cities are sites for the creation and concentration of enormous economic wealth: By one estimate, 100 cities account for 30% of the world's economy (Khanna, 2010). New York city's $1.5 trillion gross domestic product (GDP) ranks it among the 20 largest economies in the world. Dominant global cities are on par economically with many countries (Florida, 2017; Figure 17.7).

■ **FIGURE 17.7** Top 10 Metros by GDP with Comparable Nations (PPP-Adjusted $Billions)

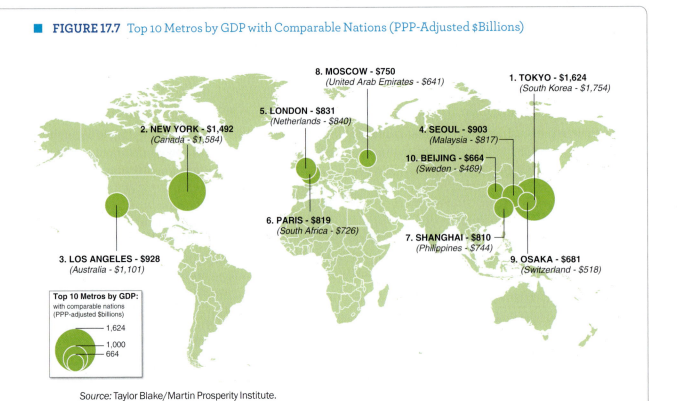

Source: Taylor Blake/Martin Prosperity Institute.

At the same time, cities have long been magnets for those who cannot make an adequate living elsewhere, whether in other countries or in the impoverished rural areas or small towns of the cities' own countries. Low-wage services, low-skill factory production, and sweatshops coexist with the most profitable activities of international businesses in global cities; we find dire poverty and spectacular wealth side by side. In Los Angeles, for example, hundreds of thousands of immigrants from Mexico and Central America work in the shadows of the downtown skyscrapers that house the world's largest banks and corporations. These immigrants labor as janitors, domestics, or workers in small clothing factories that sew apparel for global garment manufacturers (Milkman, 2006; Singer, 2012). Cities are places of intense contrasts and contradictions: The inequalities that permeate relationships, institutions, and countries are on vivid display in the global cities of the world.

World Urbanization Today

Some of the most highly urbanized countries in the world today are those that, only a century ago, were almost entirely rural. As recently as 1950, only 18% of the inhabitants of developing countries lived in urban areas. In 2012, 51% did. For the first time in history, there are more people living in urban areas than in rural areas throughout the world (Population Reference Bureau, 2012). Today, more than 30% of the world's poor inhabit cities—some in the developed countries, most in developing countries. A 2012 UNICEF report identifies urban poverty as a critical and growing problem, particularly for children, noting that

in fact, hundreds of millions of children today live in urban slums, many without access to basic services. They are vulnerable to dangers ranging from violence and exploitation to the injuries, illnesses and death that result

TABLE 17.4   The World's 15 Largest Megacities, 2016 and 2030 (Estimate)

RANK	CITY, COUNTRY	POPULATION IN 2016 (THOUSANDS)	CITY, COUNTRY	POPULATION IN 2030 (THOUSANDS)
1	Tokyo, Japan	38,140	Tokyo, Japan	37,190
2	Delhi, India	26,454	Delhi, India	36,060
3	Shanghai, China	24,484	Shanghai, China	30,751
4	Mumbai (Bombay), India	21,357	Mumbai (Bombay), India	27,797
5	São Paulo, Brazil	21,297	Beijing, China	27,706
6	Beijing, China	21,240	Dhaka, Bangladesh	27,374
7	Ciudad de México (Mexico City), Mexico	21,157	Karachi, Pakistan	24,838
8	Kinki M.M.A. (Osaka), Japan	20,337	Al-Qahirah (Cairo), Egypt	24,502
9	Al-Qahirah (Cairo), Egypt	19,128	Lagos, Nigeria	24,239
10	New York-Newark, USA	18,604	Ciudad de México (Mexico City), Mexico	23,865
11	Dhaka, Bangladesh	18,237	São Paulo, Brazil	23,444
12	Karachi, Pakistan	17,121	Kinshasa, Democratic Republic of the Congo	19,996
13	Buenos Aires, Argentina	15,334	Kinki M.M.A. (Osaka), Japan	19,976
14	Kolkata (Calcutta), India	14,980	New York-Newark, USA	19,885
15	Istanbul, Turkey	14,365	Kolkata (Calcutta), India	19,092

Source: United Nations. (2017). *The World's Cities in 2016.* New York: Author. Retrieved from http://www.un.org/en/development/desa/population/publications/pdf/urbanization/the_worlds_cities_in_2016_data_booklet.pdf.

from living in crowded settlements atop hazardous rubbish dumps or alongside railroad tracks. (p. v)

According to the United Nations, as of 2016, there were 31 **megacities**, defined as *metropolitan areas or cities with a total population of 10 million or more.* About 6.8% of people worldwide currently reside in a megacity, and projections indicate that about 8.7% of people will reside in a city of more than 10 million by 2030 (Table 17.4; United Nations, 2017). Khanna (2010) suggests that

> we need to get used to the idea of nearly 100 million people clustered around Mumbai [in India] or Shanghai [in China]. Across India, more than 275 million people are projected to move into the country's teeming cities over the next two decades, a population nearly equivalent to that of the United States. (p. 123)

Cities are dynamic places and the centerpiece of modern life in many countries, sites of innovation, creativity, education, and positive social change. They are also often wasteful producers of garbage, pollution, and greenhouse gases. In the next section, we explore the environmental challenges that cities and modern societies present for our planet.

The Local and Global Environment

According to the National Oceanic and Atmospheric Administration (NOAA), "Earth's globally averaged temperature for 2017 made it the third warmest year in NOAA's 138-year climate record, behind 2016 (warmest) and 2015 (second warmest)" (2018, para. 2). Across the globe, a spectrum of devastating weather events took place. The U.S. government's National Climatic Data Center, part of NOAA, has reported the following:

- Thaws have brought ice levels in the Arctic to record lows. As average global temperatures rise, Arctic ice is melting with increasing rapidity. Warming has reduced the thickness of the ice, which also fosters faster melting: 2017 was the fourth consecutive year of unusually low ice levels.

- Chile's Atacama Desert is one of the world's driest places (picking up a mere 0.07 inches of rain a year). In late March of 2015, it got 0.96 inches of rain in 24 hours; without soil and plant cover to help absorb rainfall, torrents of water were created and proved to be deadly, taking nine lives as it flooded the Copiapo River.

- Earth's globally averaged temperature decreased slightly in 2017, making it the third warmest year on record, behind 2015, the second, and 2016, the warmest. The five warmest years on record have occurred since 2010.

- In 2017, Hurricanes Harvey, Irma, Maria, and Nate caused extensive damage in the U.S. and Caribbean, resulting in the first three named storms being ranked in the top costliest storms in U.S. history.

- Global carbon dioxide levels in 2016 were higher than any point in the past 800,000 years. Excess carbon dioxide negatively affects the greenhouse effect, which helps keep the Earth at its normal temperature.

- In Cape Town, South Africa, a multiyear drought has led to water use restrictions and a prediction of "Day Zero," a day when most of the city's taps will be turned off and active water rationings will commence.

- France experienced floods at the second highest level since 1982, due to one of the rainiest winters and the flood of the Seine River, which flows through downtown Paris.

The events of recent years follow on the heels of other occurrences of extreme weather, including Hurricane Sandy in 2012, which became the largest Atlantic hurricane ever recorded, causing $20 billion worth of damage; the U.S. tornado outbreak of 2011; the 2009 heat waves in Argentina; numerous tropical storms and cyclones throughout South

©RODGER BOSCH/AFP/Getty Images

Cape Town, South Africa's second-largest city, may be the first major city in the developed world to run out of water. The region is experiencing a dramatic and long-running drought, which experts say has been exacerbated by rapid population expansion in the city as well as climate change.

Megacities: Metropolitan areas or cities with a total population of 10 million or more.

■ **FIGURE 17.8** How Much Americans Worry About Global Warming

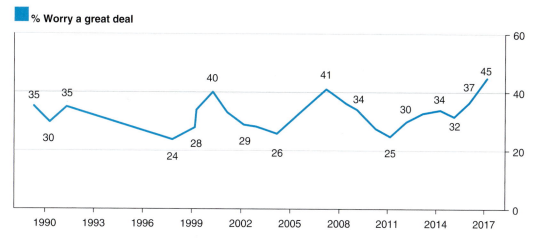

■ **% Worry a great deal**

Source: Gallup, "Global Warming Concern at Three Decades High in U.S." March 14, 2017. Retrieved from http://news
.gallup.com/poll/206030/global-warming-concern-three-decade-high.aspx.

Asia in 2008; the 2005 Hurricanes Katrina and Rita, which devastated the U.S. Gulf Coast; and the 2004 Indian Ocean tsunami that laid waste to parts of Thailand, Myanmar (Burma), Bangladesh, and Southern India (Figure 17.9).

What is behind the increase in extreme weather events across the globe? Many scientists suspect it is global warming, also referred to as *climate change*, since not all its effects are manifested in the form of rising temperatures. Global warming is widely understood to occur because so-called greenhouse gases, by-products of industrialization such as carbon dioxide (CO_2) and methane gas, become trapped in the earth's atmosphere and hold heat at the surface. While part of this process is naturally occurring and is related to a climate cycle that keeps the earth at a habitable temperature, the industrial era has seen a growing concentration of greenhouse gases in the atmosphere. The resulting "greenhouse effect" is believed to be causing an unprecedented rise in air temperatures, melting the world's ice caps and glaciers and raising ocean temperatures and sea levels. Warm air also retains more water vapor than cold air, a condition that scientists warn will be linked to greater downpours and a higher probability of floods (McKibben, 2011).

The acceleration of climate change and the growing reach of its effects are on the research agendas of climate scientists, biologists, and other physical scientists. Sociologists have also taken an interest. Among their concerns is the way in which this phenomenon, which most climate scientists accept as a credible threat to our planet and its inhabitants, has been framed in the mainstream social and political

discourse as a societal problem. Some sociologists have argued that public attention to problems such as climate change depends in part on the presence of a "social scare" (Ungar, 1992)—that is, an event (such as extreme weather) that draws attention to a phenomenon by allowing it to "piggyback on dramatic real-world events" (Ungar, 1992, p. 483).

Recent extreme weather events may be having an effect on public concern in the United States. A recent Gallup survey found heightened levels of worry about climate change, noting that self-reported concern is at an eight-year high, with 64% of Americans indicating that they worry "a great deal" or a "fair amount" about global warming (Saad & Jones, 2016).

The figure above (Figure 17.8) shows Americans' concern about the threat of global warming, a worry that has fluctuated over time. What accounts for changes in levels of concern? Research suggests that the creeping nature of climate change—the fact that effects are not constantly apparent and are perceived by some to be far in the future—leads some people to discount it as a potential problem (Moser & Dilling, 2004). Some sociologists also point to the **treadmill of production**, *the constant and aggressive growth needed to sustain the modern economy* (Schnaiberg & Gould, 1994). On the political and economic agenda, this growth takes precedence over environmental concerns.

Treadmill of production: The constant and aggressive growth needed to sustain the modern economy.

■ **FIGURE 17.9**   Natural Disasters Worldwide in 2017

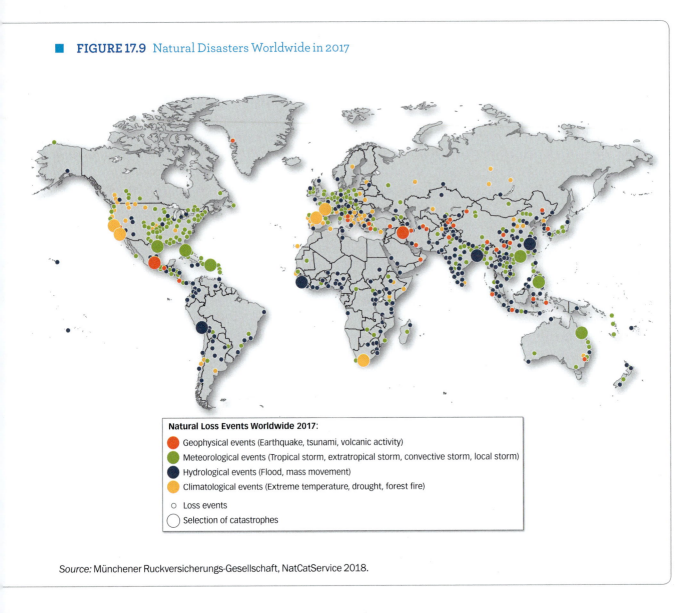

Natural Loss Events Worldwide 2017:

● Geophysical events (Earthquake, tsunami, volcanic activity)

● Meteorological events (Tropical storm, extratropical storm, convective storm, local storm)

● Hydrological events (Flood, mass movement)

● Climatological events (Extreme temperature, drought, forest fire)

○ Loss events

◯ Selection of catastrophes

Source: Münchener Ruckversicherungs-Gesellschaft, NatCatService 2018.

Climate change is leading to ice melt at the poles that could raise sea level significantly. The photo shows the disintegration of an ice shelf in Antarctica.

Governments—as well as companies that drill for oil, mine coal, manufacture products, or engage in other energy-intensive endeavors—are concerned about maintaining profitability in the private sector, which may lead them to ignore, minimize, or even deny the problem.

Are these two imperatives—the need for a vigorous economy and the need for a clean and sustainable environment—irreconcilable? How can we build an economy that can both grow and be green?

Population Growth, Modernization, and the Environment

Industrialization and urbanization, combined with rapid population growth, have taken a toll on the global environment and its resources. Threats to the environment exist in both underdevelopment and overdevelopment. On one hand, the world's population, surpassing 7 billion people, needs basic resources: water, food, shelter, and energy. As humans seek to meet these needs, they tax the earth by impinging on the natural habitats of unique animal and plant species to make room for human habitation. More important, perhaps, the rise of the **global consumer class**—*those who actively use technology, purchase consumer goods, and embrace the culture of consumption*—has meant that more individuals are using more resources per person than ever before.

By some ewstimates, a quarter of the world's population falls within the global consumer class. A large percentage of the members of this class live in developed countries; according to the Worldwatch Institute, the United States and Canada, home to just over 5% of the world's population, account for about 31% of private consumption expenditures and Western Europe, with around 6% of the globe's people, accounts for more than 28% of expenditures. However, the consumer class is expanding. More than half its members now live in areas of advancing prosperity in the developing world, such as China and India. In 2009, China passed the United States to become the biggest market for automobiles on the planet (Langfitt, 2013), and half of the world's new shopping malls are being built in China, where luxury consumption is growing particularly rapidly ("Chinese Consumers," 2014). The future consumer markets of the world are in developing countries rather than developed countries, which are characterized by sagging population growth and already high consumption rates.

In many respects, urbanization and industrialization are important achievements in the developing world, where more people have the opportunity to meet their needs and realize their dreams, leaving behind the travails of deprivation. Though the gulf between rich and poor remains wide, prosperity has advanced around the globe. Development's darker underbelly, however, becomes visible when we look at the problems presented by the consumer class and its growing ranks. Arguably, among the most critical problems of development is overconsumption.

Global consumer class: Those who actively use technology, purchase consumer goods, and embrace the culture of consumption.

Overconsumption may be understood as a recklessly wasteful use of resources, from fuel to food and consumer goods. Overconsumption is a symptom of development. Among its health consequences are *obesity* (having a body mass index [BMI] of 30 or higher) and *being overweight* (having a BMI between 25 and 29.9); a healthy BMI is between 18.5 and 24.9, according to the Centers for Disease Control and Prevention. More than two thirds of U.S. adults are overweight or obese, conditions that can lead to heart disease and other dangerous maladies (Centers for Disease Control and Prevention, 2015). Globally, more than 1 billion people are overweight, and at least 300 million of these are obese. While these problems used to be problems of Western prosperity, more people in developing countries are joining the ranks of the overweight and obese as they move from more traditional diets to modern foods (Popkin, Adair, & Ng, 2012). High-fat and high-sugar foods are widely consumed: These foods are aggressively advertised, cheap, and popular, especially among young people.

Rising consumption also threatens the environment, as more people buy, use, and toss away ever more "stuff." The global fleet of passenger cars is more than 531 million and growing; in the United States, there are more cars than licensed drivers. Many modern consumers also value size as a sign of material success: SUVs and trucks continue to be the most popular vehicles among U.S. consumers, and new home sizes continue to expand. In 1993, the average house size was about 2,095 square feet; by 2014, the size was 2,598 (Christie, 2014; Worldwatch Institute, 2004, 2010). The average U.S. home size today is twice as big as the average European or Japanese dwelling and 26 times bigger than the typical living space in Africa (Worldwatch Institute, 2010).

Consider as well the environmental effect of our ubiquitous electronic devices: Discarded computers, mobile phones, and the like are creating a growing toxic waste problem in all countries. A report by the United Nations Environment Programme (2009) suggests that the volume of e-waste generated by computers alone could rise by

Global Issues

WHAT'S ON THE MENU? ENVIRONMENT AND SOCIAL JUSTICE

Among Americans' favorite dinner treats are dishes made with shrimp. Italian restaurants serve shrimp scampi; Chinese and Thai restaurants offer a wide variety of spicy, saucy shrimp dishes; and shrimp cocktail has long been a popular appetizer. More than 1.3 billion pounds of shrimp are consumed in the U.S. each year (Mason, McDowell, Mendoza, & Htusan, 2015). Where exactly does all that shrimp come from?

A great deal comes from shrimp farms in developing countries. Some governments and wealthy donor nations have encouraged shrimp farming, arguing that it contributes to economic development in poor states and promotes a so-called blue revolution to increase the production of seafood without depleting natural marine stocks.

(Continued)

(Continued)

Community activists, farmers, and environmentalists, however, have questioned the benefits of shrimp farms (Gatsiounis, 2008; Trent, Williams, Thornton, & Shanahan, 2004; Worldwatch Institute, 2004). From a conflict perspective, we might ask who benefits and who loses from the expansion of shrimp farming in developing states.

Major beneficiaries include consumers in the United States, Europe, and Japan, who purchase and eat most of the shrimp produced. Thailand, for instance, is home to a $7 billion seafood export industry, half of which focuses on the U.S. market (Mason et al., 2015). Other beneficiaries are the governments of exporting countries (since shrimp exports can bring in substantial revenue) and the private owners of shrimp farms (who are often foreign nationals).

According to some researchers and activists, losers in the blue revolution of shrimp farming are local communities and the marine environment. Common problems include the loss of agricultural land, which is flooded with saline water to create shrimp ponds, and the reduced availability of crabs and fish for consumption and exchange in the local economy (Gatsiounis, 2008; Trent et al., 2004). The salinization process can also pollute supplies of drinking and washing water. In Thailand,

> as local fishermen have pulled back from shrimp farming, large-scale conglomerates have filled the void. Behind the small concrete houses . . . backhoes are digging out shrimp

If people know that a particular food is sourced unsustainably, or even unethically, will that alter their choice to purchase the product? What would you predict, and why?

ponds as far as the eye can see. Villagers say there will be 100 ponds in total, owned by industrial conglomerates based in Bangkok, and operated mainly by imported labor. (Gatsiounis, 2008)

Shrimp peelers working in Thai factories also absorb the costs, laboring for exploitative wages and under the threat of violence or job loss for taking time off. Many are underage or migrant workers forced into debt slavery to pay off loans to smugglers (Motlagh, 2012). A recent investigation by the Associated Press (Mason et al., 2015) also documented the use of trafficked labor in some peeling factories in Thailand:

> Every morning at 2 a.m., they heard a kick on the door and a threat: Get up or get beaten. For the next 16 hours, No. 31 and his wife stood in the factory that owned them with their aching hands in ice water. They ripped the guts, heads, tails and shells off shrimp bound for overseas markets, including grocery stores and all-you-can-eat buffets across the United States.

> After being sold to the Gig Peeling Factory, they were at the mercy of their Thai bosses, trapped with nearly 100 other Burmese migrants. Children worked alongside them, including a girl so tiny she had to stand on a stool to reach the peeling table. Some had been there for months, even years, getting little or no pay. (p. 1)

The investigation found that some of this shrimp made it to U.S. tables, served in popular restaurants and marketed at well-known grocery stores.

Think It Through

- Where did the shrimp in your supermarket or favorite restaurant originate? Should you care? Should other consumers of shrimp care? Can we balance our culinary desires with concern for the environment and social justice?

Follow us on Twitter to keep up with current sociological stories and research! We're at **@DiscoverSoc1**.

Share your own ideas at **#DiscoverSociology**.

200% to 400% of the 2007 levels in China and South Africa over the coming decade. In India, the report predicts, the increase in computer e-waste could reach 500% of the 2007 level. Although e-waste makes up only 1% to 2% of total waste in the United States, it accounts for 70% of toxic waste (Environmental Protection Agency, 2011).

As more people across the globe strive, understandably, for prosperity and modernity, it may be wise for us to ask: Can such consumption be sustained? Those who live in the prosperous countries might also ask: Is it hypocritical to raise concerns about the global destruction wrought by overconsumption when the West has been the primary consumer of the world's resources for the past century? To give you the opportunity to consider these important questions, we discuss the environmental impacts of population growth in developing states and of consumption growth in developed states and newly prosperous areas.

Massive ships used by developed countries for the transportation of goods and oil end their useful lives on the shores of developing states such as India and Pakistan. Workers at shipbreaking yards deconstruct the giant and complex vessels, a process that releases dangerous toxins into the environment and into their bodies.

Underdevelopment and Overdevelopment in the Modern World

Environmental problems that appear in one part of the globe often result from actions taken elsewhere and may have far-reaching effects for all of the planet's inhabitants. They are indeed global. However, many immediate environmental effects are local.

The most degraded local environments tend to be those inhabited by the poorest people. Air pollution is far worse in Bangkok, Mexico City, and Beijing than in the most polluted U.S. cities such as Los Angeles. China's rapid development has brought new prosperity to many Chinese, but the rising number of factories, power stations, and cars has also brought serious pollution. A 2012 World Health Organization study suggests that more than 7 million people die each year globally from causes associated with air pollution (Khullar, 2014).

Disease runs rampant in the large cities of India, where the infrastructure (including sewage systems, which should carry away waste and ensure the flow of potable water) cannot meet the needs of growing populations. In some coastal areas of India, toxic pollution streams flow from shipbreaking yards, where laborers take apart ships no longer fit to sail the seas. Local environmental problems have also arisen from deforestation in the tropical rain forests of Central America and the destruction of mangrove ponds and wetlands in Asia, as these areas are transformed into agricultural production sites for growing numbers of farmers.

Population pressures in developing countries are important contributors to these problems. However, the world's developed states are also implicated. Consider, for instance, deforestation and wetlands destruction. Some of the rainforest land in the Amazon has been cleared to make room for cattle ranching that produces beef to be consumed not locally but in the United States and other developed nations. Similarly, the wetlands of some coastal areas of Asia are being transformed into shrimp farms to grow the delicacy enjoyed in wealthy countries. The ships in India's coastal shipbreaking yards are largely the corpses of Western fleets. The consequences of the developed world's consumption are, indeed, felt in the furthest corners of the developing world, highlighting the fact that we cannot understand threats to the earth exclusively in terms of population explosion. We should also recognize environmental dangers as the products of choices made by a small wealthy elite of countries and consumers (Eglitis, 2010).

Industrialization in both the developed and developing worlds is also a critical aspect of the environmental equation. On one hand, some developing countries, such as China, are aggressively pursuing industrialization and multisector economic growth. Because of its enormous size and rapid move toward industrialization, China is fast becoming the world's major contributor to greenhouse gases. Coal, a highly polluting source of energy, provides the country with three quarters of its energy, creating so much pollution in some urban areas that residents must wear surgical masks for protection. In the southern and eastern parts of China, where urbanization and industrialization are proceeding at historically unprecedented rates, the environmental damage has been considerable. On the other hand, just as it did in the West, industrialization is bringing greater prosperity and prospects to many Chinese. This raises the question of whether we must choose between a good life and a good earth. What would it mean to achieve a balance between the needs and desires of people around the world and the needs of the planet? The *Private Lives, Public Issues* box on page 503 looks at the problem of the desires of humans and needs of the planet through the prism of what we choose to eat.

Discover & Debate

DEVELOPING COUNTRIES AND THE GLOBAL ENVIRONMENT

Motion: Developing countries should be held to the same environmental protection standards as more economically advanced states.

Background: Climate change poses a vital threat to the planet, including all the places, species, and life that it supports. Due to increased carbon pollution, sea levels are rising, the Arctic is melting, and weather events are becoming more sporadic across the world. The Paris Agreement brings together nations into a common cause and makes efforts to combat global climate change. In the long term, 195 countries have agreed to mitigate pollution via the accord. Though the Paris Agreement is a legally binding agreement, it leaves room for nations to set their own emissions targets, so long as each target is more ambitious than the last. The relative responsibility of nations to adopt strict environmental protection measures is hotly contested.

Questions for Consideration

- Is the idea that states must choose between economic growth and environmental protection a false choice? Can the two be reconciled? If so, how?

- Are state policies the best vehicle for pursuing environmental protection? What are the responsibilities of private corporations and other businesses? What are the responsibilities of individuals?

Debate Tip

- While the strength of your verbal communication is central to the debate, nonverbal communication is important, too. Remember to consider eye contact, facial expressions, and posture, as these nonverbal cues all contribute to your ability to make a compelling argument.

AFFIRMATIVE ARGUMENTS	OPPOSITION ARGUMENTS
Many of the developing countries are experiencing rapid population growth, so the development of clean technologies and progressive environmental practices is particularly important to the global environment, which will suffer if fast-growing countries adopt the consumer and production practices of developed states.	Poorer states aspire to modernize just as developed states have done. It is unfair to penalize them for using the same older and less environmentally friendly technologies that developed states used to accomplish this goal.
Higher standards may spur innovations in clean energy and other environmental practices that help the global environment and offer new avenues for economic growth for scientifically savvy states. Clean technology development and implementation is an economic opportunity rather than a burden.	Developed states have the economic means to develop ecologically clean technologies and to implement them and they should be held to higher environmental protection standards than developing states.
Many developing states, such as those in coastal areas, are particularly vulnerable to consequences of climate change, such as rising sea levels. Therefore, it is in their interest to adopt high environmental protection standards.	The economic growth of developing countries may be hampered by environmental protection standards that impede industrial or consumer activities.

Why Study Population, Urbanization, and the Environment from a Sociological Perspective?

Gentrification is a process of change that has physical, social, cultural, and economic components. As we have seen in this book, change comes with costs and benefits that may accrue to different groups. The sociological imagination helps us to see how a private trouble, such as an individual struggling to pay rising rent, can be more fully understood in terms of public issues, such as the decisions made by public officials and developers about urban renewal.

We opened the chapter by learning about son preference. The preference for a son and decisions about how to ensure the birth of a son are individual, but the effect, as we saw in the discussion about marriage markets, is societal. Demographics are both statistics and lived realities. Whether we live in fast-growth states whose resources may be increasingly taxed by rapidly rising populations or in no-growth states that may experience economic troubles as workers age without being replaced, our lives will be affected in some way by demographic forces.

We make individual choices about consumption and disposal. When we purchase a new car or truck, order a meal in a restaurant, toss out bags of old clothes at spring cleaning, or decide to replace an outdated computer, we are part of a mass of other global consumers making similar choices, and our choices—like theirs—affect the economies and environments of countries around the world. Just as there is no "single global city" (in Saskia Sassen's words), there are no single choices about consumption or disposal that do not cumulatively have global effects.

By understanding the social forces that affect personal choices and struggles as well as the way personal choices affect phenomena such as population growth or decline, rising urban prosperity and poverty, and environmental health or degradation, we become better equipped to recognize and confront some of the paramount global challenges of this century.

 ## What Can I Do with a Sociology Degree?

THE GLOBAL PERSPECTIVE

The study of sociology helps you develop a broad understanding of the social world, which includes relationships between cultures and countries over time and space and the ability to see the world from a variety of perspectives. A global perspective encompasses knowledge and skills. A global perspective evolves through study and experiences that lead to a strong understanding and appreciation of the significance and effects of global cultural, economic, political, and social connections on individuals, communities, and countries. It also encompasses the development of skills for working effectively in intercultural environments.

Understanding different cultures, recognizing a diverse spectrum of legitimate political and economic interests, and having the ability to see issues from multiple perspectives are key to global efforts to deal cooperatively with environmental and other threats to the planet. As a sociology student, you will have the opportunity to develop the kind of thoughtful global perspective that will enable you to make critical connections between decisions about, for instance, economic consumption or production, which are made at the individual or community or country level, and effects that are experienced globally.

Voltaire Xodus, Social Entrepreneur and Founder of ReUp

DePaul University, BA in Sociology

When I graduated from DePaul University in 2007 with a background in sociology, I never thought about all the possibilities and ways I could apply my discipline to generate global solutions and personal opportunities. Currently, I'm a social entrepreneur

who runs a tech startup (ReUp) in Amsterdam, the Netherlands. Being 10 years removed from my graduation, I'm very pleased to have found the growing field of social enterprise. In short, social enterprises/social entrepreneurs are individuals who create businesses that have a core value base philosophy of people first, financial profit second. This alternative value-based system empowers students majoring in the liberal arts (i.e., sociology, poly sci, anthropology, and philosophy) with a platform to innovate and create sustainable ideas that solve many of the economic, environmental, and global social justice issues of our time. If you're looking for examples of social enterprises, check out the work TOMS Shoes is doing for children around the world without shoes. Or the social and economic impact Radha Agrawal is having on women with her THINX underwear invention.

Social entrepreneurship allowed me to put my social justice values to work by combining sociology with entrepreneurship. Moreover, it helped me think and become global. Over the past two years, I've done behavioral research in 17 countries and 40 cities on people's passion, purpose, and goal achievement. My work led me to produce an app game called ReUp that measures people's willpower toward their goals in life. Because ReUp can measure individuals and groups, it can measure the productivity of cities and countries in real time. The big data generated from people playing the game helps users see how their small choices have value. For example, if 50,000 people in New Delhi don't smoke, we can see how that impacts the health care system in India. Or if 80,000 people in Los Angeles take their bike to work for 30 days, we'd be able to show how that impacts CO_2 admissions. Global issues such as these are problems that must be solved, and I'm a firm believer that social entrepreneurs will be the heroes of the 21st century that solve our big problems.

SUMMARY

- The world's population is growing at a rapid rate, having increased as much since 1950 as it did in the preceding 4 million years. Growth is highly uneven around the world, with most taking place in developing countries. Other regions, including most in Europe, are losing population.

- Annual population growth or decline in a country is the result of four factors: (1) the number of people born in the country during the year, (2) the number who die, (3) the number who immigrate into the country, and (4) the number who emigrate out. In the language of demographers, population changes are based on **fertility**, mortality, and **net migration**.

- The theory of the first demographic transition proposes that many societies go through roughly the same stages of population growth: low growth resulting from high fertility and equally high mortality, a transitional stage of explosive growth resulting from high fertility and low mortality, and a final stage of slow or no growth resulting from low fertility and low mortality.

- Advanced industrial states may be undergoing a second demographic transition, seen as changes in family patterns that affect population. For instance, in the world's industrialized states, divorce has increased, cohabitation has increased, marriage has declined, fertility has fallen, and nonmarital births as a proportion of all births have increased.

- Thomas Malthus developed the theory of **exponential population growth**: the belief that, similar to compound interest, a constant rate of population growth produces a population that grows by an increasing amount with each passing year. Malthus claimed that while population grows exponentially, the food supply does not; the earth's resources are finite. Others, such as economist Julian Simon, have suggested that population growth increases humanity's potential for uncovering talent and innovation.

- Karl Marx was critical of Malthus and felt the central problem was not a mismatch between population size and resource availability but rather the inequitable distribution of resources between the wealthy and the disadvantaged.

- Sociologist Louis Wirth (1938) defined the *city* as a relatively large, densely populated, and permanent settlement that brought together heterogeneous populations. While cities of the past served primarily as centers of trade, in the 18th century, industrial cities emerged as centers of manufacturing. By the 19th century, industrialization was advancing hand in hand with **urbanization**.

- Some of the most highly urbanized countries in the world today are those that, only a century ago, were almost entirely rural. As recently as 1950, only 18% of the inhabitants of developing countries lived in urban areas. Today, more than half do. For the first time in history, there are more people living in urban areas than in rural areas throughout the world (Population Reference Bureau, 2012). More than 30% of the world's poor inhabit cities—some in the developed countries, most in developing countries.

- With the emergence of postindustrial society, **global cities** have appeared. These metropolitan areas are highly interconnected with one another and serve as centers of global political and economic decision making, finance, and culture. Examples include New York, London, Tokyo, Hong Kong, Los Angeles, Mexico City, and Singapore.

- The combination of rapid population growth and modernization, in the form of industrialization and urbanization, takes a toll on the global environment and its resources. Both underdevelopment and overdevelopment threaten the environment.

- The study of **demography** and population growth helps us gain a fuller understanding of the ways that micro-level events, such as childbearing decisions in a family, are linked to macro-level issues, such as population growth or decline, threats of mortality, and challenges to the sustainability of resources and development.

KEY TERMS

demography, 480	age-specific mortality rate, 483	urban growth machine, 495
population momentum, 481	life expectancy, 483	urban renewal, 497
fertility, 482	rate of natural increase (RNI), 487	gentrification, 497
net migration, 482	exponential population growth, 490	global cities, 498
crude birthrate, 483	city, 492	megacities, 500
age-specific fertility rate, 483	agricultural surplus, 493	treadmill of production, 501
crude death rate, 483	urbanization, 493	global consumer class, 503

DISCUSSION QUESTIONS

1. What factors have contributed to the decline of population growth in many modern countries? What are the benefits and consequences of fertility declines?

2. Do populations stop growing when fertility declines to replacement rate fertility (a total fertility rate of 2.1)? Explain your answer.

3. As you saw in the chapter, urbanization continues to increase across the globe. What draws populations to cities? What sociological factors point to this trend continuing?

4. What is gentrification? What are some of the key costs and benefits of gentrification in U.S. cities?

5. Are economic growth and environmental protection irreconcilable values? Consider what you have read both in earlier chapters about economic growth and employment and in this chapter about environmental challenges such as climate change, and respond thoughtfully to the question.

Answer to question on page 481: on the 29th day.

Want a Better Grade?

Sharpen your skills with SAGE edge at **edge.sagepub.com/chambliss4e**, which provides you with a personalized approach to help you accomplish your course work goals in an easy-to-use learning environment.

Social Movements and Social Change

18

WHAT DO YOU THINK?

1. Are students on college campuses today socially or politically active? What are the issues driving campus activism today?

2. Do people behave differently in crowds than they do individually or in small groups? What sociological factors explain crowd behavior?

3. Does social media contribute to activism—or does it function to distract and pacify people? Might it do both?

LEARNING OBJECTIVES

18.1 Apply sociological perspectives to understand characteristics and paths of social change.

18.2 Describe key sources of social change in society.

18.3 Identify different types of social movements.

ACTIVIST AMERICA?

A recent poll conducted by the *Washington Post* and the Kaiser Family Foundation finds that a growing number of Americans are engaged in social and political activism. According to the survey, "One in 5 Americans have protested in the streets or participated in political rallies since the beginning of 2016. Of those, 19 percent said they had never before joined a march or a political gathering" (Jordan & Clement, 2018, p. A1). This activation of U.S. political and social movements may represent a new development in this decade: Consider the fact that a 2014 publication, citing a study on participation in civic activities such as voting, volunteering, calling elected officials, donating to a campaign or cause, or attending political meetings, among others, lamented that, "Forty-one percent of Americans do not participate very often in any of 10 bedrock activities of American civic and political life" and just 1% could be classified as very politically active ("Only one percent of Americans are really politically active," 2014, para. 1).

Who is engaging in this new wave of political activism? The data, collected from a random representative sample of 1,850 adults 18 years of age and older, suggest that about a fifth of Americans attended a political

©John Lamparski/WireImage

rally of some kind in the past two years. Of those who attended a rally, most categorized themselves as Democrats (40%) or independents (36%). Another 20% reported that they were Republicans. Rally-goers were also broken down by educational attainment: About 21% reported having a high school education or less, while 29% reported some college, and 50% reported having a college degree of some kind. Many of those who attended rallies—about 70%—indicated that they do not approve of President Donald Trump and his administration's policies (Jordan & Clement, 2018). Indeed, a significant number of political protests, including the Women's March in January 2017, the March for Science in April 2017, and pro-immigrant marches in states from New York to Texas to California, have highlighted resistance to administration positions and policies.

Significantly, however, this statistical portrait of protest may be missing a robust and rising new wave of activism among those who fall outside of the 18 and over respondent pool. That is, the past year has seen a dramatic shift in public activism by young people, particularly high school students. Among the most high-profile activists have been survivors of the mass shooting at Marjorie Stoneman Douglas High School in Parkland, Florida, on February 14, 2018. Just over a month later, a group of students who had lost 17 of their classmates emerged to lead a massive rally in Washington, DC. March for Our Lives, which highlighted issues of school safety and gun control, drew an estimated 800,000 demonstrators to Washington's streets. Rallies were also held in dozens of other cities and towns around the country (Shabad, Baily, & McCausland, 2018). Students from Marjorie Stoneman Douglas High School have taken their activism to other well-off suburban schools similar to their own as well as to urban schools and neighborhoods that have long been threatened by deadly violence (Zornick, 2018).

Many student activists have pledged to speak out at events and on mass media and social media, to reach out to decision makers in Congress and statehouses, and, when they turn 18, to vote and even campaign for office. Data show that few young adults vote and, while many engage in community activities such as volunteering, they do not engage closely in political life (Dalton, 2016). Does March for Our Lives, and the interest it has generated, signal a change in young people's activism not only on the issue of guns and school violence, but on other issues of concern to this generation? What do you think?

We begin this chapter with an overview of sociological theorizing on social change. We continue with an examination of key sources of social change, focusing in particular on collective behavior and resources. Next, we provide an overview of forms that social movements take, and we conclude with some reflections on the nature of social change going forward in a rapidly changing and globalized world.

Sociological Perspectives on Social Change

The concept of *social change* is all-encompassing. It refers to small-group changes, such as a social club changing a long-standing policy against admitting women or minorities, and to global-level and national-level transformations, such as the outsourcing of jobs to low-wage countries and the rise of social movements that seek to address the threat of climate change.

When sociologists speak of social change, they are generally referring to changes that occur throughout the social structure of an entire society. *Societies* are understood sociologically as entities comprising those people who share a common culture and common institutions. *Social change* may refer to changes within small, relatively isolated communities such as those of the Amish or the small, culturally homogeneous tribes that dot the Amazon basin; changes across complex and modern societies such as the United States, Japan, or Germany; or changes common across similar societies, such as the economically advanced states of the West or the Arab countries of North Africa and the Middle East.

Three key types of social change theories in sociology are functionalist theories, conflict theories, and cyclical theories. Sociological perspectives on social change begin with particular assumptions about both the social world and basic processes of change. Below, we briefly consider each theoretical perspective and discuss its utility for helping us understand the nature of social change in the world today.

The Functionalist Perspective

Functionalist theories of social change assume that as societies develop, they become more complex and interdependent. Herbert Spencer (1892) argued that what distinguishes modern societies is **differentiation**—*the development of increasing societal complexity through the creation of specialized social roles and institutions.* Spencer was referring to what Émile Durkheim conceptualized as the division of labor, which is characterized by the sorting of people into interdependent occupational and task categories (and, by extension, class categories). Think of medieval England, when craftsmen working at home made tools and shoes that they exchanged for food or clothing, using a broad range of skills to act relatively independently of one another. Compare this to modern society, where factory workers each produce parts of an automobile, managers sell completed cars to dealerships, and salespeople sell them to customers. Today, people master a narrow range of tasks within a large number of highly specialized (differentiated) institutional roles and thus are highly interdependent. (Note the similarity here to Durkheim's notion that societies evolve over time from *mechanical* to *organic solidarity*—the former being characteristic of traditional, homogeneous societies and the latter characteristic of diverse, modern societies.)

The earliest functionalist theories of social change were *evolutionary theories,* which assumed that all societies begin as simple or primitive and eventually develop into more complicated and civilized forms along a single, unidirectional evolutionary path. During the 20th century, however, this notion of unilinear development became increasingly

shaky, as anthropologists came to believe that societies evolve in many different ways. More recent evolutionary theories (sometimes termed *multilinear*) argue that multiple paths to social change exist, depending on the particular circumstances of the society (Moore, 2004; Sahlins & Service, 1960). Technology, environment, population size, and social organization are among the factors that play roles in determining the path a society takes.

Some evolutionary theorists viewed societies as eventually reaching an equilibrium state in which no further change would occur unless an external force set it in motion. For example, Durkheim believed that primitive or less developed societies were largely unchanging unless population growth resulted in such a differentiation of social relationships that organic solidarity replaced mechanical solidarity. Talcott Parsons (1951) viewed societies as equilibrium systems that constantly seek to maintain balance—the status quo—unless something external disrupts equilibrium, such as changes in technology or economic relationships with other societies. Parsons later came to argue, however, that societies do change by becoming more complicated systems that are better adapted to their external environments (Parsons & Shils, 2001).

Although no one can deny that modern societies contain many more specialized roles and institutions than earlier ones, evolutionary theories also assume that social changes are progressive and that modern (European) societies are more evolved than earlier primitive ones. Such beliefs appealed to countries whose soldiers, missionaries, and merchants were conquering or colonizing much of the rest of the world, since these beliefs helped justify those imperialist actions as part of the "civilizing" mission of a more advanced people. Anthropologists and sociologists eventually rejected these ideas (Nolan & Lenski, 2009).

Up to the early 20th century, it was commonly believed that women should not vote and should not be involved in politics. Women such as Elizabeth Cady Stanton and Susan B. Anthony challenged both public beliefs and legal practices that prevented women from casting ballots.

©FPG/Archive Photos/Getty Images

Differentiation: The development of increasing societal complexity through the creation of specialized social roles and institutions.

On a more micro level, consider dedifferentiation in the mainstream marital relationship. Traditionally, the man was the head of the household and often ruled over his wife and children with an iron fist. Both the norm and the reality of marriage today are characterized by a dedifferentiation of roles in which men take on domestic responsibilities and, increasingly, the wife is a major income producer for the family.

Since different parts of society undergo the processes of differentiation and dedifferentiation to varying degrees and at different times, considerable conflict may arise between them (Alexander, 1998; Alexander & Colomy, 1990; Colomy, 1986, 1990). It is, however, the conflict perspective that assumes conflict as the foundation for social change. We look at that perspective below.

The Conflict Perspective

Conflict theories suggest that conflict is the product of divergent and perhaps irreconcilable social group interests and contradictory goals of social relationships. Even if a population or technology is in a state of stasis rather than change, conflict theorists see social change as inevitable, as people create ways of dealing with the conflicts and contradictions inherent in social life. Responding to the conflicts and contradictions can potentially bring a society to the brink of sharp and sometimes violent breaks with the past.

Unlike their functionalist peers in sociology, conflict theorists do not see social stability as the ultimate goal of social organization. They recognize conflict as a vital, transformative part of social life.

Karl Marx focused his research on the contradictions and conflicts built into capitalist societies, where the world is divided between owners of the means of production and workers who own only their own labor power and must sell it under conditions not of their own making. In Marx's view, the revolutionary transformation of a society into a new type—from feudalism to capitalism or from capitalism to socialism, for example—would occur when the consciousness of the people or the concentration of power in one social class was sufficient to create a social movement able to transform political and economic institutions into new sets of social relationships. As we have seen throughout this text, Marx's conflict theory adhered to its own evolutionary view of social change, in which all societies would advance to the same final destination: a classless, stateless society. We have earlier noted several weaknesses in this theory. Of particular importance is Marx's tendency to overemphasize economic conflict while underestimating cultural conflict and other noneconomic factors, such as gender, ethnicity, race, and nationalism, which have become increasingly important in the world today.

Later conflict theorists have addressed key questions about processes of social change, such as how groups come to want and pursue social change. Italian Marxist Antonio Gramsci (1971), for instance, highlighted the importance of ideas in maintaining order and oppression in society. He observed that the ruling class is often able to create *ideological hegemony,* a generally accepted view of what is of value and how people should relate to their economic and social status in society. Ideological hegemony may lead people to consent to their own domination by, for instance, socializing them to believe that the existing hierarchy of power is the best or only way to organize society. Consider, for example, that in the past, women were socialized by schools, families, and religious institutions to believe they should not have jobs outside the home or vote. The idea that women should not hold positions outside the home could be considered a *hegemonic idea* of this period.

Gramsci also spoke of *organic intellectuals*—those who emerge from oppressed groups to create counterhegemonies that challenge dominant (and dominating) ideas. In the mid-19th century, women's suffrage activists—including Lucretia Mott, Susan B. Anthony, and Elizabeth Cady Stanton—were organic intellectuals, challenging powerful beliefs that women should be excluded from politics. Over time and through the efforts of activists, the counterhegemonic idea that women should have a voice in politics became the hegemonic, or dominant, belief in Western society.

In the 1950s, in response to the dominant functionalist paradigm, sociologist Ralf Dahrendorf published an influential article titled "Out of Utopia" (1958). Dahrendorf argued that functionalist theory, with its emphasis on how social institutions exist to maintain the status quo, overlooks critically important characteristics of society that lead to social conflict, such as the role of power, social change, and the unequal distribution of resources. The distribution of authority in society, said Dahrendorf, is a means of determining the probability of conflict. Where hierarchical structures such as states, private economic entities such as manufacturing firms, and even religious organizations are all dominated by the same elite, the potential for conflict is higher than in societies where authority is more dispersed. Put another way, if Group A dominates all or most key hierarchical authority structures and Group B is nearly always subordinate, conflict will be likely because Group B has little stake in the existing social order. Nevertheless, if Group B has authority in some hierarchical structures and Group A has authority in others, neither group has great incentive to challenge the status quo.

Marx emphasized control of the means of production as a source of power and conflict; Gramsci highlighted control of dominant ideas in society as an important source of power and change; and Dahrendorf put authority and its concentration or distribution at the center of his work. Conflict theorists differ in their beliefs about what sources are most likely to underlie social conflict and social change, but all agree that social conflict and social change are both inevitable and desirable components of society and progress.

Rise-and-Fall Theories of Social Change

Rise-and-fall theories of social change deny that there is any particular forward direction to social change; rather, they *argue that social change reflects a cycle of growth and decline.* Rise-and-fall or cyclical theories are common in the religious myths of many cultures, which view social life as a reflection of the life cycle of living creatures or the seasons of the year, with the end representing some form of return to the beginning. Sociology, emerging in an era that equated scientific and technological advancement with progress, at first tended to reject such cyclical metaphors in favor of more evolutionary or revolutionary ones that emphasized the forward motion of progress.

There have been several significant exceptions, however, among historically oriented social theorists. Pitirim Sorokin (1957/1970, 1962), a historical sociologist of the mid-20th century, argued that societies alternate among three different kinds of mentalities: those that give primacy to the senses, those that emphasize religiosity, and those that celebrate logic and reason. Societies that value hedonism and the satisfaction of immediate pleasures more highly than the achievement of long-term goals give primacy to the senses; religiosity occurs in societies that value following the tenets of a religion over enjoying the senses or solving problems through logic and reason. We tend to think of modern societies as defined largely by the emphasis on logic and reason.

Societies everywhere have contained a mixture of religiosity, an emphasis on the senses, and the celebration of logic and reason. Sorokin's ideal types may nonetheless be useful for describing the *relative* emphasis of each of these modes of adaptation in different societies. For example, we might say that the modern Western world puts greater emphasis on logic and reason than on religion or giving primacy to the senses; it would be a mistake, however, to say that there is no emphasis on the senses or religion, because these traits also play important roles in shaping the modern Western world.

In *The Rise and Fall of the Great Powers* (1987), historian Paul Kennedy traces the conditions associated with national power and decline during the past five centuries. As nations grow in economic power, he argues, they often seek to become world military powers as well, a goal that proves to be their undoing in the long run. Wielding global military power eventually weakens a nation's domestic economy, undermining the prosperity that once fueled it. Kennedy forecasts that this might well be the fate of the United States. More recently, writer Cullen Murphy (2007) has pointed to parallels between the Roman Empire and the United States, noting that Rome was also characterized by an overburdened and costly military, a deep sense of exceptionalism, and a tendency to denigrate and misunderstand other cultures. He also notes the Roman pattern of shifting the onus for providing services to citizens away from the public sector to the private sector, seeing this as a form of enrichment for the few but a disadvantage for the many. A key point in rise-and-fall narratives is that social change can be both progressive and regressive—power does not invariably beget more power; it may also beget decline.

The most renowned sociologist considered by some to be a cyclical theorist is Max Weber. Although he took an evolutionary view of society as increasingly moving toward a politically and economically legal-rational society governed by rules and regulations, Weber (1919/1946) also emphasized the role of irrational elements in shaping human behavior. For example, although he wrote about the growing formal rationality of the modern world, he also recognized the possibility that a society's path could be altered by the appearance of a charismatic figure whose singular personal authority transcended institutionalized authority structures. Leaders who drastically changed a nation's trajectory include Haile Selassie, who governed Ethiopia

©CNP/Hulton Archive/Getty Images

Rise-and-fall theories of social change: Theories that argue that social change reflects a cycle of growth and decline.

Dr. Martin Luther King Jr. had a transformational dream. His words and deeds inspired and continue to inspire social change. The actions of a single person can be truly significant.

Inequality Matters

SPORTS AND SOCIAL CHANGE

The U.S. is a country that loves sports and idolizes its greatest athletes. Some of those talented athletes are among those who have used their status and visibility to drive social change and, more specifically, draw attention to racial inequality.

Jackie Robinson was the first African American baseball player in the major leagues, joining the Brooklyn Dodgers at first base in 1947. Robinson was a player of exceptional talent, which helped him gain acceptance in the ranks of White-dominated Major League Baseball (MLB), although he was still subject to racism. Robinson was a tireless advocate for racial equality. When Robinson retired and took a senior position at the Chock Full O'Nuts company, he used his power to advocate for fair wages for Black workers in the company. At his final public appearance in 1972, Robinson declared in an award acceptance speech at the World Series that he would be even more proud of Major League Baseball if he looked over toward third base and saw an African American coach: The first Black MLB manager, Frank Robinson, took that position in 1975. Although Jackie Robinson was one of the first prominent Black athletes to use his status to take a stand against racial inequality, he would not be the last.

After medaling in the 200-meter race at the 1968 Olympic Games in Mexico City, U.S. team members Tommie Smith and John Carlos famously raised their fists in a Black power salute to protest the treatment of African Americans (Cosgrove, 2014). They stood on the podium as the U.S. national anthem played with their fists raised and shoeless, wearing black socks to symbolize the struggle of Black poverty. In response to what was construed as a political action, the International Olympic Committee expelled Smith and Carlos from the games. Smith later reflected on the moment, saying that

> if I win, I am American, not a black American. But if I did something bad, then they would say "a Negro." We are black and we are proud of being black. Black America will understand what we did tonight. (BBC, 2005)

Contemporary athletes have also used their visibility to bring attention to issues of concern to minority communities. In 2010, for instance, the Phoenix Suns, a National Basketball Association (NBA) team, wore "Los Suns" jerseys to draw attention to Arizona's new

©Photo File/MLB Photos via Getty Images

Baseball player Jackie Robinson was the first African American to play on a Major League Baseball team. He was recruited by the Brooklyn Dodgers and played for the team for the first time in 1947. In 1997, his uniform number, 42, was retired across major league baseball.

immigration law (SB 1070), which permitted police to use "reasonable suspicion" as a basis for detaining people. Advocates for the Latino/a community argued that the law promoted and justified racial profiling. In December 2014, Cleveland Cavaliers basketball players LeBron James and Kyrie Irving entered the team warm-up against the Brooklyn Nets wearing T-shirts emblazoned with the words "I can't breathe." Four players from the opposing team wore them as well. The words were the last ones uttered by Eric Garner, a Staten Island man who died in July of that year in a confrontation with a New York City police officer. Eric Garner was the fourth unarmed African American man to die in a confrontation with police in July 2014 (Harkinson, 2014). James told reporters, "As a society we have to do better. We have to be better for one another no matter what race you are" (Strauss & Scott, 2014, para. 14).

From the time Jackie Robinson integrated the MLB to the time NBA players launched their protest actions on the court, there has been important progress, including better access to education,

for half a century, Adolf Hitler in Germany, Mao Zedong in China, and Fidel Castro in Cuba. In the United States, Martin Luther King Jr. led the civil rights movement in the 1960s and fundamentally changed race relations.

Cyclical theories have not enjoyed great popularity among sociologists. Even Weber's theory is not truly cyclical; his idea of charismatic authority is a sort of wild card, providing an unpredictable twist in an otherwise predictable march of social change from one form of authority to another. The more far-reaching versions of cyclical theory, such as Sorokin's theory that society swings among three different worldviews, are framed in such broad terms that it is challenging to prove them right or wrong.

Sources of Social Change

Social change ultimately results from human action. Sociologists studying how change occurs often analyze the mass action of large numbers of people and the institutionalized behaviors of organizations. In this section, we examine social change within the context of mass action by groups of people, focusing on theories of collective behavior and the role played by social movements.

Collective Behavior

Collective behavior is *voluntary, goal-oriented action that occurs in relatively disorganized situations in which society's predominant social norms and values cease to govern individual behavior* (Oberschall, 1973; Turner & Killian, 1987). Although collective behavior is usually associated with disorganized aggregates of people, it may also occur in highly regimented social contexts when order and discipline break down.

Beginning with the writings of the 19th-century French sociologist Gustave Le Bon (1896/1960), the sociological study of collective behavior has been particularly concerned

with the behavior of people in **crowds**—*temporary gatherings of closely interacting people with a common focus.* People in crowds were traditionally seen as prone to being swept up in group emotions, losing their ability to make rational decisions as individuals. The "group mind" of the crowd has long been viewed as an irrational and dangerous aspect of modern societies, with crowds believed to consist of rootless, isolated individuals prone to herdlike behavior (Arendt, 1951; Fromm, 1941; Gaskell & Smith, 1981; Kornhauser, 1959).

More recently, however, it has become clear that there can be a fair degree of social organization in crowds. For example, the Occupy Wall Street movement of 2011–2012 and the Arab Spring revolutions, which began in late 2010, although representing spontaneous beginnings, quickly developed a degree of predictability and organization, and in turn became social movements. It is important to note that crowds alone do not constitute social movements, but they are a critical ingredient in most cases. In a social media age, however, sociologists may need to rethink the very notion of *spontaneity*, as collective action today is often rooted in activist social media that contributes to informing and organizing collective behavior.

Sociologists seek to explain the conditions that may lead a group of people to engage in collective behavior, whether violent or peaceful. Below, we examine three principal sociological approaches: contagion theories, which emphasize nonsocial factors such as instincts; emergent norm theories, which seek out some kind of underlying social organization that leads a group to generate norms governing collective action; and value-added theories, which combine elements of personal, organizational, and social conditions to explain collective behavior.

Contagion Theories

Contagion theories assume that human beings can revert to herdlike behavior when they come together in large crowds. Herbert Blumer (1951), drawing on symbolic interactionism, emphasized the role of raw imitation,

Collective behavior: Voluntary, goal-oriented action that occurs in relatively disorganized situations in which society's predominant social norms and values cease to govern individual behavior.

Crowds: Temporary gatherings of closely interacting people with a common focus.

which leads people in crowds to mill about much like a group of animals, stimulating and goading one another into movement actions, whether peaceful or violent. Individual acts, therefore, become contagious; they are unconsciously copied until they eventually explode into collective action. A skilled leader can effectively manipulate such behavior, working the crowd until it reaches a fever pitch.

Sociologists have used the contagion theory perspective to study the panic flights of crowds, epidemics of bizarre collective behaviors such as uncontrollable dancing or fainting, and reports of satanic child abuse. In 1983, a local panic erupted in a small California city after a parent of a preschool child accused teachers at her child's school of raping and sodomizing dozens of students. The trial in the case stretched on for years, but no wrongdoing was ever proved and no defendant convicted. Accusations in the case, which drew on allegations from children and parents, included stories about teachers chopping up animals at the school, clubbing to death a horse, and sacrificing a baby. Public accounts of the trial unleashed a national panic about abuse and satanism in child-care facilities, even though there was no serious documentation of such activities (Haberman, 2014). Some sociologists believe that a few well-publicized cases of deviant behavior—including wild accusations such as those described above—can trigger imitative behavior until a virtual epidemic emerges that then feeds on itself (Goode, 2009).

Contagion has been linked in some research to the risk of suicide. For instance, data suggests that high levels of media coverage of celebrity suicides are followed by increased incidences of death by suicide and suicidal ideation, particularly among those who are demographically similar to the person who died. A controversy emerged in 2017 over the Netflix adaptation of a popular young adult novel, *13 Reasons Why*, which tells the story of a young women who kills herself and leaves behind 13 tapes meant for each of the people she believes led her to the decision to take her own life (Devitt, 2017). Research suggests that suicide can occur in clusters. That is, multiple suicides can occur in close temporal and geographic proximity: "It happens on average in at least five communities a year in this country. . . . Up to 5 percent of suicides among adolescents occur close to others, a higher rate than found in adults" (Carey, 2018, para. 7–8). More recently, the deaths by suicide of celebrity chef Anthony Bourdain and designer Kate Spade led to a debate over how much media coverage is appropriate and how much may be harmful to those who might be at risk of contagion (Ibid.).

Although copycat behavior may occur in a group, community, or society, an explanation limited to this factor is unlikely to account fully for collective behavior.

Furthermore, such explanations are sometimes used to discredit particular instances of collective behavior as resulting from an irrational (and therefore dangerous) tendency of people to jump on the bandwagon. In the 1960s, some people dismissed antiwar and civil rights protesters as misled "flower children" rather than recognizing them as people concerned about injustice and war. Sociologists, however, seek ways to determine *why* collective behavior occurs and to understand the rational and organizational basis for its emergence (Chafetz & Dworkin, 1983; Wright, 1993). We look next at what some other theories suggest.

Emergent Norm Theories

Most sociologists prefer to look for norms and values that shape conscious human behavior rather than rely on the idea that instincts govern unconscious processes. Some have suggested that emergent norms offer an explanation for collective behavior. We can define **emergent norms** as *norms that are situationally created to support a collective action*. For example, Ralph H. Turner and Lewis M. Killian (1987) argue that even when crowd behavior appears chaotic and disorganized, norms emerge that explain the crowd's actions. Crowd members take stock of what is going on around them, are mindful of their personal motivations, and in general, collectively define the situation in which they find themselves. In this respect, crowd behavior is not very different from ordinary behavior; there is no need to fall back on instincts or contagion to explain it. For instance, some attendees in a crowd at a political rally may not agree with a candidate's position on, for instance, immigration, but the influence of the candidate and the crowd can function to create an environment where disagreeable positions on immigration come to seem rational, normative, and desirable. Hence, a cheering crowd of political supporters willing to work to elect a candidate can emerge even where there was not initially widespread embrace of a candidate's position on a given issue.

The emergent norm approach offers only a partial explanation of collective behavior. First, all crowds do not develop norms that govern their actions; crowds often emerge out of shared sets of norms among the participants. Second, purely spontaneous emotional outbursts may also occur as people act on their immediate impulses. Furthermore, when norms governing crowd behavior do emerge, they are unlikely by themselves to account fully for collective behavior. When crowds gathered in Baltimore to protest after Freddie Gray, a Black man, died in police custody, they were responding to fear of and frustration with police violence against minorities, but their demonstrations

---

Emergent norms: Norms that are situationally created to support a collective action.

were not merely a result of emergent norms, even though some actions were spontaneous. The grievances being expressed were rooted in long-standing disaffection with the treatment of poor minority communities in the city.

Value-Added Theory

Both contagion and emergent norm theories focus primarily on the micro level of individual action and thought, largely ignoring macro-level factors—poverty, unemployment, governmental abuses of authority, and so on—that may explain the emergence of collective behavior. More than 50 years ago, Neil Smelser (1962) sought to develop what he termed a *value-added approach* to understanding collective behavior. He identified several micro- and macro-level factors that each contribute something of value to the outcome and that form a foundation for collective behavior. Think about a revolution or social movement discussed in this chapter or that you have learned about elsewhere—can you identify the factors below in that context?

1. *Structural conduciveness* exists when the existing social structure favors the emergence of collective behavior.

2. *Structural strain* occurs when the social system breaks down.

3. *Generalized beliefs* are shared explanations of the conditions that are troubling people. People must define the problem, identify its causes, and—to use C. Wright Mills's phrase—come to see their personal troubles as public issues.

4. *Precipitating factors* are dramatic events that confirm the generalized beliefs of the group, thereby triggering action.

5. *Mobilization for action* occurs when leaders arise who encourage action.

6. *The failure of social control* leaves those charged with maintaining law and order unable to do so in the face of mounting pressures for collective action.

Smelser's approach has been used to analyze collective behavior in a variety of settings, including self-help groups (D. H. Smith & Pillemer, 1983), social welfare organizations (M. J. Smith & Moses, 1980), and nuclear-weapons-freeze activism (Tygart, 1987). The theory's strength is that it combines societal-, organizational-, and individual-level factors into one comprehensive theory. Yet it has also been criticized for emphasizing the part that people's *reactions* play in collective behavior more than the fact that people themselves are conscious agents creating the conditions that can bring about significant social change.

How Do Crowds Act?

We have all participated in some form of collective behavior in our social lives. Collective behavior comes in a spectrum of different forms, including riots, fads and fashions, panics and crazes, and rumors. We discuss each of these forms of collective behavior below.

Riots

A **riot** is *an illegal, prolonged outbreak of violent behavior by a sizable group of people directed against individuals or property.* Riots represent a form of crowd behavior; often, they are spontaneous, although sometimes they are motivated by a conscious set of concerns. Prison and urban riots are common examples. During a riot, conventional norms, including respect for the private property of others, are suspended and replaced with other norms developed within the group. For example, inmates may destroy property to force prison officials to adopt more humane practices, and the theft of property during an urban riot may reflect the participants' desire for a more equitable distribution of resources.

The very use of the term *riot* to characterize a particular action is often highly political. In 1773, a crowd of Bostonians protesting British taxation of the American colonies seized a shipment of tea from a British vessel and dumped it into Boston Harbor. Although the British Crown roundly condemned this action as the illegal act of a rioting mob, U.S. history books celebrate the Boston Tea Party as the noble act of inspired patriots and an opening salvo in the Revolutionary War.

Fads and Fashions

The desire to join others in being different (itself perhaps something of an irony) continually feeds the rise of new looks and sounds. **Fads**—*temporary, highly imitated outbreaks of mildly unconventional behavior*—are particularly common responses to popular entertainment such as music, movies, and books and require social networks (electronic or otherwise) to spread (Iribarren & Moro, 2007). The fads of piercing body parts to wear ornaments and extensive body tattooing have captured several generations and seem to be continuing today. Other fads have included wearing blue jeans with holes in the knees, staging "panty raids" on sorority houses, and adopting the hipster style popularized by young people united by a common interest in alternative music and Pabst Blue Ribbon beer.

Riot: An illegal, prolonged outbreak of violent behavior by a sizable group of people directed against individuals or property.

Fads: Temporary, highly imitated outbreaks of mildly unconventional behavior.

As fads become popular, they sometimes cease being fads and instead become **fashions**, that is, *somewhat long-lasting styles of imitative behavior or appearance.* Georg Simmel (1904/1971) first examined the sociological implications of fashions more than a century ago. He pointed out that fashions reflect a tension between people's desire to be different and their desire to conform. By adopting a fashion, a person initially appears to stand out from the group, yet the fashion itself reflects group norms. As the fashion catches on, more and more people adopt it, and it eventually ceases to express any degree of individuality. Its very success undermines its attractiveness, so the eventual fate of all fashions is to become unfashionable.

Simmel's observations offer another insight into fashions: Unlike fads, they often grow out of the continuous and well-organized efforts of those who work in design, manufacturing technology, marketing, and media to define what is in style. As grunge music became popular in the 1990s, it spawned a profitable clothing industry, and highly paid fashion designers created clothing that was grungy in everything but price. Today, there are a variety of fashion trends that resonate with different audiences and subcultures. Whether it is the look of skinny or torn jeans, oversize sunglasses or owl-like reading spectacles, or brand-name yoga pants or basketball sneakers, manufacturers and marketers will spend millions of dollars attempting to convince youthful consumers that they must buy particular products to be fashionable and popular.

Panics and Crazes

A **panic** is *a massive flight from something feared.* The most celebrated example was created by an infamous radio

---

Fashions: Somewhat long-lasting styles of imitative behavior or appearance.

Panic: A massive flight from something that is feared.

Contemporary consumer fads and fashions are often driven by social media influencers such as the Kardashians, who use platforms like Instagram to showcase products and practices that are then taken up by followers.

broadcast on the night before Halloween in 1938: Orson Welles's Mercury Theatre rendition of H. G. Wells's science fiction novel *War of the Worlds.* The broadcast managed to convince thousands that Martians had landed in Grover's Mill, New Jersey, and were wreaking havoc with deadly laser beams. People panicked, flooded the telephone lines with calls, and fled to "safer" ground.

Panics are often ignited by the belief that something is awry in the corporate world or in consumer technology. As the year 2000 approached, panic over the Y2K problem, also known as the "millennium bug," gripped many people who believed reports that computer systems worldwide would crash when the year 2000 began (supposedly computers would be unable to distinguish the year 2000 from 1900, because they used only two digits to designate the year). A recent example of a panic involved the Mayan calendar, which was projected to end during our calendar equivalent of December 2012. The fact that the structure of the Mayan calendar and the Mayan system of counting and noting dates did not pass December 2012 led many to believe that the Mayans had predicted the end of the world.

Some panics, similar to that involving Y2K, reflect the fear that, in modern industrial society, we are highly dependent on products and technological processes about which we have little knowledge and over which we have no control.

A **craze** is *an intense attraction to an object, a person, or an activity.* Crazes are similar to fads but are more intense. Body disfigurement has been a periodic craze, ranging from nose piercing to putting rings through nipples, belly buttons, lips, and tongues. The fact that these practices instill horror in some people probably accounts in part for the attraction they hold for others. In many cultures, body disfigurement is considered a necessary condition of beauty or attractiveness. Although such practices would be regarded as crazes in the West, they are normal enhancements of beauty in other cultures (Brown, Edwards, & Moore, 1988).

Rumors

Rumors are *unverified forms of information that are transmitted informally, usually originating in unknown sources.* The classic study on rumors was conducted more than 65 years ago by Gordon W. Allport and Leo Postman (1947). In one version of this research, a White student was asked to study a photograph depicting an urban scene: two men on a subway car, one menacing the other. The student was then

---

Craze: An intense attraction to an object, a person, or an activity.

Rumors: Unverified forms of information that are transmitted informally, usually originating in unknown sources.

asked to describe the picture to a second White student, who in turn was asked to pass the information along to a third, and so on. Eventually, after numerous retellings, the information changed completely to reflect the students' previously held beliefs. For example, as the "rumor" in the study took shape, the person engaging in the menacing act was described as Black and the victim as White—even though in the actual photograph the reverse was true.

Allport and Postman's (1947) research revealed several features unique to rumors. The information they contain is continually reorganized according to the belief systems of those who are passing them along. Some information is forgotten, and some is altered to fit into more familiar frameworks, such as racist preconceptions in the example above. Furthermore, the degree of alteration varies according to the nature of the rumor; it is greatest for rumors that trigger strong emotions or that pass through large numbers of people.

For a rumor to have an effect, it must tap into collectively held beliefs, fears, or hopes. For some, the rumor that the world will be ending imminently is a hopeful message;

Political activism swept the country in the 1960s and 1970s with widespread demonstrations focused on civil rights, women's rights, and the Vietnam War. The dramatic protests and social transformations of this period helped fuel the reformulation of theories on social change.

for others, it is a source of great fear. Rumors often reinforce subcultural beliefs. The rumor that the Central Intelligence Agency and the National Security Agency are planting listening devices in everyone's homes feeds into the belief that the government is out to control us. Political campaigns are infamous for starting and perpetuating rumors: In the 2016 presidential campaign, the Internet was rife with rumors about the health of candidate Hillary Clinton, who was said to be hiding a serious illness. While an abundance of evidence was available to contradict the rumors, they continued to be widely embraced, particularly on the far right of the political spectrum.

Social Movements

Theories of collective behavior generally emphasize the passive, reactive side of human behavior. Social movement theory, in contrast, regards human beings as agents of their own history—actors who have visions and goals, analyze existing conditions, weigh alternative courses of action, and organize themselves as best they can to achieve success.

A **social movement** is *a large number of people who come together in a continuing and organized effort to bring about (or resist) social change and who rely at least partially on noninstitutionalized forms of political action*. Social movements thus have one foot outside the political establishment, and this is what distinguishes them from other efforts aimed at bringing about social change. Their political activities are not limited to such routine efforts as lobbying or campaigning; they include noninstitutionalized political actions such as boycotts, marches, and other demonstrations and civil disobedience.

Social movements often include some degree of formal organization oriented toward achieving longer-term goals, along with supporting sets of beliefs and opinions, but their strength often derives from their ability to disrupt the status quo by means of spontaneous, relatively unorganized political actions. As part of its support for the civil rights movement in the 1960s, the National Association for the Advancement of Colored People (NAACP) advocated the disruption of normal business activities, such as boycotting buses and restaurants, to force integration. The people who participate in social movements typically are outside the existing set of power relationships in society; such movements provide one of the few forms of political voice available to the relatively powerless (McAdam, McCarthy, & Zald, 1988; Tarrow, 1994). A recent example is the Dreamer movement, which has supported passage of the Dream Act.

Social movement: A large number of people who come together in a continuing and organized effort to bring about (or resist) social change and who rely at least partially on noninstitutionalized forms of political action.

Discover & Debate

#ACTIVISM

Motion: Online social activism is an effective way to foster social change.

Background: A common form of social activism today is what has been termed *hashtag activism* (Dewey, 2014). This kind of activism can be understood as a movement to spread awareness online about social issues. It is practiced by well-known public figures and organizations as well as by ordinary individuals. Hashtag activism is prominent on Twitter, but similar online campaigns are spread on social media platforms such as Facebook and Instagram.

Questions for Consideration

- How do we measure the effectiveness of an online social issues campaign? How should we define *success*?

- What is the relationship between online issue activism and in-person activism, such as participation in a march?

- Do motivations for online activism differ from those of in-person activism?

Debate Tip

- Be aware of your audience, and take care to articulate your argument in a way that will be understood by your listeners. Avoid academic jargon and slang words. Use clear, straightforward language.

AFFIRMATIVE ARGUMENTS	OPPOSITION ARGUMENTS
Social media is an effective way to spread information about important social issues, particularly among young people who are very connected to social media and less likely to read a newspaper or listen to television or radio news.	Online activism makes concerned citizens feel better, but there are more effective ways of fostering change—calling elected representatives, donating money to social causes, or participating in marches, for example.
Social media is a powerful platform for fostering change in countries with media censorship. For example, social media activism led to the #UmbrellaMovement in Hong Kong, a territory of China with a high level of censorship. Although mainstream media did not cover the protests, potential participants learned about protest activities through social media.	Although it is easy to gather support for many issues on social media platforms, there is often a lack of organizational support to follow up on the demands made by online activists.
Online activism is effective because it expands the number of people who can participate. For example, online activism is accessible to people with disabilities, as well as to others who cannot participate in in-person activism due to financial, health, or other constraints that limit mobility.	Some research (Kristofferson, White, & Peloza, 2013) suggests that participation in symbolic public activism (such as joining a Facebook group) may reduce the chance that an issue enthusiast takes further steps to foster social change: "once our need to act has been satisfied, we may not be motivated to do more" (Feldman, 2017, p. 40).

This immigration reform legislation allows undocumented young people who migrated to the United States with their families when they were children to have access to higher education and, over time, permanent residency or citizenship. An executive order signed by President Obama in 2012 allows the Dreamers to apply for deferred action permits and avoid deportation under certain conditions.

The body of research on social movements in the United States is partially the result of movements that began in the late 1950s and gained attention and support in the 1960s and

TABLE 18.1   Principal Types of Social Movements

TYPE	PRINCIPAL AIMS	EXAMPLES
Reformist	To bring about change within the existing economic and political system	• U.S. civil rights movement • March for Our Lives, the student-led gun control movement • Climate change activism • Teacher activism seeking better pay and funding for education
Revolutionary	To fundamentally change the existing social, political, and/or economic system in light of an alternative vision	• 1776 U.S. Revolutionary War • 1905 and 1917 Russian Revolutions • 1991 South African antiapartheid movement • 2010 Arab Spring
Rebellious	To fundamentally alter the existing political and/or economic system without a detailed alternative vision	• Nat Turner slave rebellion • Urban riots following the assassination of Martin Luther King Jr.
Reactionary	To restore an earlier social system—often based on a mythical past	• White supremacist organizations in the U.S. • European skinheads and neofascist movements
Utopian	To withdraw from society and create a utopian community	• Religious communities such as the Quakers, Mennonites, and Mormons • 1960s communes in the U.S.
New social movements	To make fundamental changes in values, culture, and private life	• Gay, lesbian, bisexual, and transgender rights movements • Fat acceptance movement • Mindfulness movements

early 1970s. Theories of collective behavior, with their emphasis on the seemingly irrational actions of unorganized crowds, were ill equipped to explain the rise of well-organized efforts by hundreds of thousands of people to change government policies toward the Vietnam War and civil rights for African Americans. As these two social movements spawned others, including the second-wave feminist movement, which saw women demanding greater rights and opportunities in the workplace, sociologists had to rethink their basic assumptions and develop new theoretical perspectives. Below, we examine different types of social movements, looking especially at sociological theories about why they arise.

Types of Social Movements

Social movements are typically classified according to the direction and degree of change they seek. For purposes of our discussion, we will distinguish five different kinds: reformist, revolutionary, rebellious, reactionary, and utopian (Table 18.1). In fact, these distinctions are not clear-cut, and the categories are not mutually exclusive. Rather, they represent ideal types. In the final section of the chapter, we

will also consider some examples of a new sixth category: new social movements that aim to change values and beliefs.

Reformist Movements

Reformist social movements *seek to bring about social change within the existing economic and political system* and usually address institutions such as the courts and lawmaking bodies and/or public officials. They are most often found in societies where democratic institutions make it possible to achieve social change within the established political processes. Yet even reformist social movements can include factions that advocate more sweeping, revolutionary social changes. Sometimes the government fails to respond, or it responds very slowly, raising frustrations. At other times, the government may actively repress a movement, arresting its leaders, breaking up its demonstrations, and even outlawing its activities.

The American Woman Suffrage Association, formed in 1869 by Susan B. Anthony and Elizabeth Cady Stanton, was

Reformist social movements: Movements seeking to bring about social change within the existing economic and political system.

a reformist organization that resulted in significant social changes. During the latter part of the 19th century, it became one of the most powerful political forces in the United States, seeking to liberate women from oppression and ensure them the right to vote (Vellacott, 1993), precipitating the first wave of the women's movement. In 1872, Victoria Woodhull helped to organize the Equal Rights Party, which nominated her for the U.S. presidency (even though, by law, no woman could vote for her); she campaigned on the issues of voting rights for women, the right of women to earn and control their own money, and free love (Underhill, 1995). After a half century of struggle by numerous social movement activists, women finally won the right to vote with the ratification of the Nineteenth Amendment to the U.S. Constitution in 1920.

The civil rights movement of the late 1950s and the 1960s called for social changes that would enforce the constitutionally mandated civil rights of African Americans; it often included nonviolent civil disobedience directed at breaking unjust laws. The ultimate aim of the civil rights movement was to change those laws, rather than to change society as a whole. Thus, for example, when Rosa Parks violated the laws of Montgomery, Alabama, by refusing to give up her seat on a city bus to a White person, she was challenging the city ordinance, not the government itself.

Much early civil rights activism was oriented toward registering southern Blacks to vote, so that by exercising their legal franchise, they could achieve a measure of political power. Within the civil rights movement, however, there were activists who concluded that the rights of Black Americans would never be achieved through reformist activities alone. Like many social movements, the civil rights movement was marked by internal struggles and debates regarding the degree to which purely reformist activities were adequate to the movement's objectives (Branch, 1988). The Black Panther Party, for example, argued for far more radical changes in U.S. society, advocating for "Black power" instead of merely fighting for an end to racial segregation. The Black Panthers often engaged in reformist activities, such as establishing community centers and calling for the establishment and support of more Black-owned businesses. At the same time, they also engaged in revolutionary activities, such as arming themselves against what they viewed to be a hostile police presence within Black neighborhoods.

The experience of U.S. labor unions, another example of a reformist social movement, shows the limits of the reformist approach to social change. Organized labor's principal demands have been for fewer hours, higher wages and benefits, job security, and safer working conditions. (In Europe, similar demands have been made, although workers there have sought political power as well.) Labor unions

In April 2018, thousands of teachers in Kentucky marched to the state capital building in Frankfort to protest cuts in education budgets and changes to their pensions. Their protest followed teacher protests in other states, including West Virginia, that were seeking better pay and better funding for public education.

©Charles Bertram/Lexington Herald-Leader/ TNS via Getty Images

within the United States seldom appeal to a broad constituency beyond the workers themselves, and as a result, their success has depended largely on workers' economic power. U.S. workers have lost much of that power since the early 1970s, as economic globalization has meant the loss of many jobs to low-wage areas. Threats of strikes are no longer quite as menacing, as corporations can close factories down and reopen them elsewhere in the world.

Revolutionary Movements

Revolutionary social movements *seek to fundamentally alter the existing social, political, and economic system in keeping with a vision of a new social order.* They frequently result from the belief that reformist approaches are unlikely to succeed because the political or economic system is too resistant. In fact, whether a social movement becomes predominantly reformist or revolutionary may well hinge on the degree to which its objectives can be achieved within the system.

Revolutionary movements call for basic changes in economics, politics, norms, and values, offering a blueprint for a new social order that can be achieved only through mass action, usually by fostering conflict between those who favor change and those who favor the status quo. They are directed at clearly identifiable targets, such as a system of government believed to be unjust or an economy believed to be based on exploitation. Yet even the most revolutionary of social movements is likely to have reformist elements, members or factions who believe some change is possible within

Revolutionary social movements: Movements seeking to fundamentally alter the existing social, political, and economic system in keeping with a vision of a new social order.

the established institutions. In most social movements, members debate the relative importance of reformist and revolutionary activities. Although the rhetoric may favor revolution, most day-to-day activities are likely to support reform. Only when a social movement is suppressed and avenues to reform are closed off will its methods call for outright revolution.

Revolutionary social movements sometimes, although by no means always, include violence. In South Africa, for example, the movements that were most successful in bringing about an end to apartheid were largely nonviolent. Those that defeated socialism in the former Soviet Union and Eastern Europe did so with a minimal amount of bloodshed. Nevertheless, revolutionary movements associated with the Arab Spring, which began in 2010 in countries such as Egypt, Tunisia, and Libya, resulted in considerable violence, most often perpetrated against the protesters by those already in power or their allies. It is unclear, however, whether the Arab Spring movements were truly revolutionary; most new governments are not radically more democratic than their predecessors. It takes time for political and economic conditions to change within any given country, however, and although some dictators have been removed from power, it remains to be seen whether these changes in political office will result in the changes desired by constituents.

Rebellions

Rebellions *seek to overthrow the existing social, political, and economic systems but lack detailed plans for a new social order.* They are particularly common in societies where effective mobilization against existing structures is difficult or impossible because of the structures' repressive nature. The histories of European feudalism and U.S. slavery are punctuated by examples of rebellions. Nat Turner, a Black American slave, led other slaves in an 1831 uprising against their White owners in the state of Virginia. Before the uprising was suppressed, 55 Whites were killed, and subsequently, Turner and 16 of his followers were hanged (Greenberg, 2003).

Reactionary Movements

Reactionary social movements *seek to restore an earlier social system—often based on a mythical past—along with the traditional norms and values that once presumably accompanied it.* These movements are termed *reactionary* because they arise in reaction to recent social changes that threaten or have replaced the old order. They are also

sometimes referred to as *countermovements* or *resistance movements* for the same reason.

For these groups, a mythical past is often the starting point for pursuing goals aimed at transforming the present. The Ku Klux Klan (KKK), the White Aryan Resistance, and other White supremacist organizations have long sought to return to a United States where Whites held exclusive political and economic power. Their methods have ranged from spreading discredited social and biological theories that expound the superiority of the "White race" to acts of violence against Black Americans, Asians, Latinos, Jews, gays and lesbians, and others deemed to be inferior or otherwise a threat to the "American way of life" (Gerhardt, 1989; Moore, 1991).

Whether a social movement is viewed as reactionary or revolutionary depends to some extent on the observer's perspective. In Iran, for example, a social movement led by the Ayatollah Khomeini overthrew the nation's pro-U.S. leader in 1979 and created an Islamic republic that quickly reestablished traditional Muslim laws. In the pronouncements of U.S. policy makers and the mass media, the new Iranian regime was reactionary: It required women to be veiled, turned its back on democratic institutions, and levied death sentences on those who violated key Islamic values or otherwise threatened the Islamic state. Yet from the point of view of the clerics who led the upheaval, the movement overthrew a corrupt and brutal dictator who had enriched his family at the expense of the Iranian people and had fostered an alien way of life offensive to traditional Iranian values. From this standpoint, the movement claimed to be revolutionary, promising to provide a better life for Iranians.

As globalization threatens traditional ways of life around the world, we might expect to see an increase in reactionary social movements. This is especially likely to be the case if threats to long-standing traditional values are

---

Rebellions: Movements seeking to overthrow the existing social, political, and economic systems but lacking detailed plans for a new social order.

Reactionary social movements: Movements seeking to restore an earlier social system—often based on a mythical past—along with the traditional norms and values that once presumably accompanied it.

In August 2017, about 500 White nationalist demonstrators marched in Charlottesville, Virginia. Their rally, which featured symbols of the Confederacy, the KKK, and Nazism, was met with vigorous protests.

©AP Photo/Steve Helber

Reactionary Social Movements and the Rise of Women and the Minorities

In the section above, you read about reactionary movements, which are driven in part by a nostalgia for a real or imagined past. Reactionary movements include White supremacist and neo-Nazi movements, which have in recent years become more active in the U.S. Members of these movements, the majority of whom are male, often see racial, ethnic, and religious minorities and women as threats to their status. Consider what you learned earlier in the chapters on race and ethnicity (Chapter 9) and gender and society (Chapter 10) about demographic changes in the U.S. and trends in women's educational attainment. Should we expect the ranks of reactionary movements to grow in coming years? If reactionary movements grow, how should society respond?

accompanied by declines in standards of living. In Germany, for example, a decline in living standards for many working-class people has spawned a small but significant resurgence of Nazi ideology, and racial supremacist groups blame foreign immigrants for their economic woes. The result has been a vocal campaign by skinhead groups against immigrants, particularly in the states that made up the former East Germany, which have seen greater economic upheavals than other parts of the country.

Utopian Movements

Utopian social movements *seek to withdraw from the dominant society by creating their own ideal communities.* The youth movements of the 1960s had a strong utopian impulse; many young (and a few older) people "dropped out" of conventional society and formed their own communities, starting alternative newspapers, health clinics, and schools and in general seeking to live according to their own value systems outside the established social institutions. Some sought to live communally as well, pooling their resources and sharing tasks and responsibilities. They saw these efforts to create intentional communities, based on cooperation rather than competition, as the seeds of a revolutionary new society.

Although religious utopian movements have proved to be somewhat enduring, those based on social philosophy have not. Some utopian socialist communities were founded in the United States during the 19th century; some provided models for the socialist collectives of the 1960s. Few lasted for any length of time. The old ways of thinking and acting proved remarkably tenacious, and the presence of the larger society—which remained basically unchanged by the experimentation—was a constant temptation. Alternative institutions such as communally run newspapers and health clinics found they had to contend with well-funded mainstream competitors. Most folded or reverted to mainstream forms (Fairfield, 1972; Nordhoff, 1875/1975; Rothschild & Whitt, 1987).

Utopian social movements: Movements seeking to withdraw from the dominant society by creating their own ideal communities.

 # Behind the Numbers

THERE WERE MILLIONS . . . OR NOT

How many demonstrators attended a protest action on a given day in a particular place? This can be a surprisingly contentious issue. For example, how many people attended the Million Man March, a massive 1995 grassroots gathering intended to highlight issues of concern to Black men and their families and communities? As Ira Flatow noted on the National Public Radio (2010) program *Science Friday,*

> It depends on whom you ask. According to the U.S. Park Police, about 400,000. But the organizers of the march took issue with that number and asked for a recount. And using

©Visions of America/UIG via Getty Images

different images . . . a crowd counting expert at Boston University estimated the crowd to be closer to 800,000—almost twice the number that the Park Service had.

Once you become familiar with research methods in the social sciences, you realize that the *method* of obtaining information may be as important as the information itself. When a statistic, fact, or figure is produced, it is vital to consider the process behind its production. We often hear media accounts that report numbers of demonstrators in given units of space or time (for instance, there were 200 protesters in front of the mayor's office in Buffalo, or 20,000 demonstrators on the streets of Baltimore). Where do these numbers come from?

In taking a look behind the numbers, we find that the National Park Service does not conduct official head counts of demonstrators in public spaces such as the National Mall in Washington, DC, which has long been a popular venue for large gatherings. Journalists often rely on best-guess estimates for crowds. Satellite pictures have been common sources of information on crowds, even though each such photo captures only a few moments in time (National Public Radio, 2010).

Technology is bringing us closer to being able to get an accurate count of participants in a collective action. Whereas it may, until recently, have taken days to ascertain even a basic estimate of a crowd, researchers at the University of Central Florida have introduced the world's first mass crowd-counting program. In September 2015, the software was used to count the number of demonstrators in Barcelona calling for the independence of the region of

Catalonia. The computer program scanned 67 aerial images of the demonstrators, whose protest action stretched for 3.2 miles. The data, which was ready in only 30 minutes, led researchers to conclude that just over half a million people were in attendance, a figure significantly below that offered by the protest organizers (Science Daily, 2015).

Social media is also enabling new means of counting marchers through crowdsourcing. The Women's March took place on January 21, 2017, in cities across the U.S. and the globe. How many people marched? The Washington, DC, march, together with marches in other U.S. cities, may have gathered from 3 to 4 million people, figures assembled in part through a Google spreadsheet tweeted by a political science professor. The public was invited to share information and sources to the spreadsheet: According to an account of the effort,

> The spreadsheet currently has entries for nearly 550 cities and towns in the U.S., from the march in DC (470,000 to 680,000 participants) to a protest in Show Low, Arizona (one participant). The spreadsheet also tallies attendance at rallies in more than 100 cities around the world. (Waddell, 2017)

Clearly, counting participants is an important and improving process but still an inexact science.

Think It Through

- Why are counts of participants at public demonstrations and events potentially controversial and contested? What makes them significant?

Why Do Social Movements Arise?

Although social movements have existed throughout history, modern society has created conditions in which they thrive and multiply. The rise of the modern democratic nation-state, along with the development of capitalism, has fueled their growth. Democratic forms of governance, which emphasize social equality and rights of political participation, legitimate the belief that people should organize themselves politically to achieve their goals. Democratic nation-states give rise to social movements—and often protect them as well. Capitalism, which raises universal economic expectations while producing some inequality, further spurs the formation of such movements.

Given these general historical circumstances, sociologists have advanced several theories to explain why people sometimes come together to create or resist social change. Some focus on the micro level, looking at the characteristics

and motivations of the people who join social movements. Some focus on the organizational level, looking at the characteristics that result in successful social movement organizations. Some focus on the macro level, examining the societal conditions that give rise to social movements. More recently, theories have emphasized cultural dimensions of social movements, stressing the extent to which social movements reflect—as well as shape—larger cultural understandings. An ideal theory would bridge all these levels, and some efforts have been made to develop one.

Micro-Level Approaches

Much research has focused on what motivates individuals to become active members of social movements. Psychological factors turn out to be poor predictors. Neither personality nor personal alienation adequately accounts for activist leanings. Rather, participation seems motivated more by psychological identification with others who are similarly afflicted (Marwell & Oliver, 1993; McAdam, 1982).

Sociology generally explains activism in such terms as having had prior contact with movement members, belonging to social networks that support movement activity, and having a history of activism (McAdam, 1986; Snow, Zurcher, & Ekland-Olson, 1980). Coming from a family background of social activism may also be important. One study, for example, found that many White male activists during the early 1960s social movements had parents who themselves had been activists 30 years earlier (Flacks, 1971). A lack of personal constraints may also be a partial explanation; it is obviously easier for individuals to engage in political activity if work or family circumstances afford them the necessary time and resources (McCarthy & Zald, 1973). Finally, a sense of moral rightness may provide a powerful motivation to become active, even when the work is difficult and the monetary rewards are small or nonexistent (Jenkins, 1983).

Social movements always suffer from the **free rider problem**, however—that is, *many people avoid the costs of social movement activism (such as time, energy, and other personal resources) and still benefit from its success* (Marwell & Oliver, 1993). Why not let others join the social movement and do the hard work, since if the movement succeeds then everyone will benefit, regardless of degree of participation? Clearly, it takes a great deal of motivation and commitment as well as a conviction that their efforts may make a difference for people to devote their time to mailing leaflets or organizing marches; building such motivation and commitment is a major challenge faced by all social movements.

Organizational-Level Approaches

Some recent research has been devoted to understanding how social movements are consciously and deliberately organized to create social change. This research focuses on **social movement organizations (SMOs)**, *formal organizations that seek to achieve social change through noninstitutionalized forms of political action*. The study of SMOs represents a major sociological step away from regarding social change as resulting from unorganized individuals and crowds. Instead, it places the study of social change within the framework of the sociology of organizations.

Because SMOs constitute a type of formal organization, sociologists use the same concepts and tools to study civil rights organizations and revolutionary groups as they do to study business firms and government bureaucracies. Researchers conceptualize SMOs' actions as rational, their goals as more or less clearly defined, and their organizational structures as bureaucratically oriented toward specific measurable goals (Jenkins, 1983; McCarthy & Zald, 1977).

SMOs range from informal volunteer groups to professional organizations with full-time leadership and staff. A single social movement may sustain numerous such organizations: A partial list associated with the 1960s civil rights movement includes the NAACP, the Student Nonviolent Coordinating Committee (SNCC), the Congress of Racial Equality (CORE), the Southern Christian Leadership Conference (SCLC), Students for a Democratic Society (SDS), and the Black Panther Party. As social movements grow, so too do the number of SMOs associated with them, each vying for members, financial support, and media attention.

One influential approach to the study of SMOs is **resource mobilization theory**, *a theory that focuses on the ability of social movement organizations to generate money, membership, and political support to achieve their objectives*. This approach argues that since discontent and social strain are always present among some members of any society, these factors cannot explain the rise or the relative success of social movements. Rather, what matters are differences in the resources available to different groups and how effectively they use them. The task for sociologists, then, is to explain why some SMOs are better able to deploy scarce resources than others (Jenkins, 1983; McAdam, 1988). Among the most important resources are tangible assets such as money, facilities, and means of communication, as well as such intangibles as a central core of dedicated, skilled, hardworking members (Jenkins, 1983).

Much like businesses, then, SMOs rise or fall on their ability to be competitive in a resource-scarce environment. Some scholars have even written of social movement "industries," with competing organizations engaging in "social marketing" to promote their particular "brands" of social change (Jenkins, 1983; Zald & McCarthy, 1980).

Governmental policies are important determinants of the success or failure of SMOs. The government may repress an organization, driving it underground so that it has difficulty in operating. Or the government may favor more moderate organizations (for example, Martin Luther King Jr.'s SCLC) over other, more radical ones (such as the Black Panther Party). Other ways in which the government affects

---

Free rider problem: The problem that many people avoid the costs of social movement activism (such as time, energy, and other personal resources) and still benefit from its success.

Social movement organizations (SMOs): Formal organizations that seek to achieve social change through noninstitutionalized forms of political action.

Resource mobilization theory: A theory that focuses on the ability of social movement organizations to generate money, membership, and political support to achieve their objectives.

SMOs are through regulating them, providing favorable tax treatment for those that qualify, and refraining from excessive surveillance or harassment (McAdam et al., 1988).

The success or failure of SMOs also depends on their ability to influence the mass media. During the 1960s, the anti–Vietnam War organizations became very effective in commanding the television spotlight, although this effectiveness proved a mixed blessing: Media coverage frequently sensationalized demonstrations rather than presenting the underlying issues, thus contributing to rivalries and tensions within the antiwar movement (Gitlin, 1980). Today, arguably, social media exercises even greater influence on movement success.

Although some scholars have argued that larger, more bureaucratic SMOs are likely to be successful in the long run (Gamson, 1975), others have claimed that mass defiance, rather than formal organization, is the key to success (Piven & Cloward, 1977). Paradoxically, too much success may undermine social movements, since their strength derives partly from their being outside society's power structures as they make highly visible demands for social change. Once a group's demands are met, the participants are often drawn inside the very power structures they once sought to change. Movement leaders become bureaucrats, their fights are conducted by lawyers and government officials, and rank-and-file members disappear; the militant thrust of the organization is then blunted (Piven & Cloward, 1977).

A related problem is goal displacement, which occurs when a SMO's original goals become redirected toward enhancing the organization and its leadership (McCarthy & Zald, 1973). The U.S. labor movement is an example: Once labor unions became successful, many of them became large and prosperous bureaucracies that were perceived as distanced from the needs of their rank-and-file members.

In the end, SMOs have to motivate people to support their causes, often with dollars as well as votes. Many groups engage in **grassroots organizing**, *attempts to mobilize support among the ordinary members of a community*. This organizing may range from door-to-door canvassing to leafleting to get people to attend massive demonstrations. Most social movements emerge from a group that has some grievance, and their active members consist largely of people who will directly benefit from any social change that occurs.

Some SMOs also depend on **conscience constituents**, *people who provide resources for a social movement organization but who are not themselves members of the aggrieved group that the organization champions* (McCarthy & Zald, 1973). Such supporters are motivated by strong ethical convictions rather than by direct self-interest in achieving the social movement's goals. The National Coalition for the Homeless, for example, consists primarily of public interest lawyers, shelter operators, and others who advocate on behalf of homeless people; only a relatively small number of homeless people are directly involved in the organization. Homeless advocacy groups raise money from numerous sources, including media celebrities and direct mailings to ordinary citizens (Blau, 1992).

Macro-Level Approaches

Regardless of the efforts particular SMOs make, large-scale economic, political, and cultural conditions ultimately determine a movement's success or failure. For a social movement to arise and succeed, conditions must be such that people feel it is necessary and are willing to support it. Therefore, social movements emerge and flourish in times of other social change, particularly if people experience that change as disruptive of their daily lives (McAdam et al., 1988; Tilly, 1978). For example, the labor movement arose with the emergence of industrial capitalism, which brought harsh conditions to the lives of many people, and the women's movement reemerged in the 1960s, when expanded educational opportunities for women left many female college graduates feeling marginalized and alienated as full-time homemakers and workplace discrimination threw obstacles in the way of their workplace aspirations.

Some political systems encourage social movements, while others repress them (Gale, 1986). When a government is in crisis, it may respond by becoming more repressive, or it may create a space for social movements to flourish. The former action occurred in China in 1989, when thousands of students and workers, frustrated by deteriorating economic conditions and rigid government controls, took to the streets to demand greater economic and political freedom. The brutal crackdown at Beijing's Tiananmen Square, televised live to a global audience, ended the nascent social movement for democracy. Likewise, government crackdowns on demonstrators and social movement participants have been widespread throughout the Middle East and North Africa as the Arab Spring movements have progressed—Syria's protest movement has, as of this writing, deteriorated into a civil war between the authoritarian government and those who seek its replacement.

Just as economic and political collapse may facilitate the rise of social movements, so too may prosperity. Resources for social activism are more abundant, mass media and

---

Grassroots organizing: Attempts to mobilize support among the ordinary members of a community.

Conscience constituents: People who provide resources for a social movement organization but who are not themselves members of the aggrieved group that the organization champions.

This iconic image shows one man standing in opposition to four tanks in Tiananmen Square, China, on June 5, 1989. Thousands of pro-democracy demonstrators sought political and economic changes in a weeks-long occupation of the square. Many were injured or killed in a government crackdown.

other means of communication are more likely to be readily available, and activists are more likely to have independent means of supporting themselves. Prosperous societies are also more likely to have large classes of well-educated people, a group that has historically provided the leadership in many social movements (McAdam et al., 1988; McCarthy & Zald, 1973; Zald & McCarthy, 1980).

Finally, even the spatial organization of society may have an impact on social movements. Dense, concentrated neighborhoods or workplaces facilitate social interaction and spur the growth of social movements. A century and a half ago, Karl Marx recognized that cities and factories were powerful breeding grounds for revolutionary insurgency against capitalism, since they brought previously isolated workers together in single locations. Subsequent research has sustained his conclusion (Marx & Engels, 1848/1998; Tilly, 1975). The concentration of students on college campuses contributed to the rise of student activism in the 1960s (Lofland, 1985). As we saw in our opening story, it may be having a comparable effect on activism today.

Cultural-Level Studies and Frame Alignment

Much of the research we have discussed emphasizes the political, economic, and organizational conditions that either help or hinder the rise of social movements. Sociologists have often regarded social movements as by-products of favorable social circumstances rather than as the active accomplishments of their members. Today, however, instead of stressing how important it is for conditions to be ripe for social movements to thrive, many sociologists are thinking about how SMOs themselves are continually interpreting events so as to align themselves better with the cultural understanding of the wider society. The Tea Party

movement is a good example. Although it has a long list of political goals it wants to achieve, it has succeeded in rallying people around the idea that "big government" and taxation are a threat to freedom and liberty. These are ideas that resonate with those who have some suspicion of intrusive government. The movement seeks to create a good fit between itself and the people who are its likely constituents.

Sociologists think of that fit in terms of **frame alignment**, *the process by which the interests, understandings, and values of a social movement organization are shaped to match those in the wider society*. If their members' understandings align with the understandings of others in a community or society, social movements are likely to be successful; otherwise, they are likely to fail. SMOs achieve frame alignment in a variety of ways, ranging from modifying the beliefs of members to attempting to change the beliefs of the entire society (Snow, Rochford, Worden, & Benford, 1986).

In one common situation, people already share the social movement's concerns and understandings but lack the means to bring about the desired changes. In this case, there is no need for the SMO to get people to change their thinking about the problem; rather, the task is to get people to support the movement's efforts to do something about it. The SMO must get the word out, whether through informal networks, social media, direct-mail campaigns, or (more recently) social media.

The #MeToo movement in the United States is an awareness campaign against sexual harassment and assault, first started in 2006. In 2017, following the surfacing of sexual violence accusations of prominent film producer Harvey Weinstein, actress Alyssa Milano took to Twitter encouraging survivors of sexual violence to spread the hashtag #MeToo, to give the world "a sense of the magnitude of the problem" (Gilbert, 2017). Since then, #MeToo has become an international movement, bringing awareness to the fact that millions of women (and men) have been victims of sexual assault and/or harassment in many spheres (Me Too, n.d.). The movement calls for action against perpetrators and has shown survivors that they have an entire community to turn to for support. The #MeToo movement has manifested as both online activism and live protest actions.

Finally, a SMO may seek to build support by attempting to change the way people think entirely. Revolutionary SMOs, for example, urge people to stop thinking of themselves as victims of bad luck, focusing attention instead on the faults of the political or economic system, which presumably requires a drastic overhaul.

Frame alignment: The process by which the interests, understandings, and values of a social movement organization are shaped to match those in the wider society.

The #MeToo movement unleashed a wave of activism in 2017 and 2018 after some prominent survivors of sexual assault came forward to share their stories and to encourage other women to share theirs as well.

To sum up, SMOs are competing for the hearts and minds of their constituents, with whom they must somehow bring their own beliefs and analyses into alignment if they are to succeed.

New Social Movements

Social movements have often served as a means to an end: People come together to achieve specific objectives, such as improving the conditions of workers, gaining equality for the disadvantaged, or protesting a war. In the past, participation in such social movements was often separate from members' personal lives. Since the 1960s, however, many social movements have sought to break the boundary between politics and personal life. In addition to being a means for changing the world, the SMO has come to be seen as a vehicle for personal change and growth (Giugni & Passy, 1998).

In a sense, this progression reflects the *sociological imagination,* which calls for us to understand the relationship between our personal experiences and larger social forces. Social movements that have embraced this perspective have been labeled **new social movements**. Although they often address political and economic issues, they *are fundamentally concerned with the quality of private life, often advocating large-scale cultural changes in the way people think and act.*

New social movements may be formally organized, with clearly defined roles (leadership, recruiting, and so on), or they may be informal and loosely organized,

preferring spontaneous and confrontational methods to more bureaucratic approaches. Part of the purpose of new social movements in protesting, in fact, is not to force a distinction between "them" and "us" but to draw attention to the movement's own right to exist as equals with other groups in society (Gamson, 1991; Omvedt, 1992; Tucker, 1991).

The new social movements aim to improve life in a wide range of areas subject to governmental, business, or other large-scale institutional control, from the workplace to sexuality, health, education, and interpersonal relationships. Four characteristics set these movements apart from earlier ones (Melucci, 1989):

1. The new social movements focus not only on the distribution of material goods but also on the control of symbols and information—an appropriate goal for an "information society" in which the production and ownership of knowledge are increasingly valuable.

2. People join new SMOs not purely to achieve specific goals but also because they value participation for its own sake. For instance, LGBT (lesbian, gay, bisexual, and transgender) movements have provided safe havens for members in addition to pursuing social change.

3. Rather than large, bureaucratically run, top-down organizations, the new social movements are often networks of people engaged in routine daily activities. For example, a small online movement was begun by a woman who objected to an unannounced $5 charge on her credit card bill; her protest was joined by thousands of others, and the bank rescinded the charge. Groups trying to raise awareness of climate change and threats to the environment often are loosely organized and register their concerns online and through other media such as newspapers and television talk shows.

4. The new social movements strongly emphasize the interconnectedness of planetary life and may see their actions as tied to a vision of the planet as a whole, rather than centering on narrow self-interest. "Think globally, act locally" is the watchword and includes but is not limited to an awareness of environmental issues.

New social movements: Movements that have arisen since the 1960s and are fundamentally concerned with the quality of private life, often advocating large-scale cultural changes in how people think and act.

Social Life, Social Media

TECHNOLOGY, DYSTOPIA, AND SOCIAL CHANGE

The chapter opened with a story showing that more Americans today are engaging in political activism. Furthermore, as this and other chapters have shown, social activism has fostered significant social change across time and place. Fearless protest of injustice, fierce resistance to tyranny, and sustained challenges to oppression and inequality have often borne fruit.

At the same time, the opening story also shows that a significant proportion of Americans are *not* participating in political or social activism. As well, relatively few Americans vote. This chapter has sought to explain activism. Sociology, however, also needs to explain passivity and disengagement. Below, we consider one possible answer.

In George Orwell's classic dystopian novel, *1984*, published in 1949, the author describes a future in which people are controlled by an authoritarian state that Orwell calls "Big Brother." Big Brother uses propaganda to mislead and frighten, as well as devices such as telescreens to distract citizens into submission. In a memorable line from *1984*, a character who works for the government dismisses the prospects for resistance to tyranny, stating, "The people will not revolt. They will not look up from their screens long enough to notice what's happening" (Orwell, 1949). Notably, scientific studies today point to a growing epidemic of technological dependency, even addiction. A *Newsweek* article on the issue notes, "In less than the span of a single childhood, Americans have merged with their machines, staring at a screen for at least eight hours a day, more time than we spend on any other activity including sleeping" (Dokoupil, 2012a, para. 9).

Significantly, people around the world appear to be spending increasing amounts of time pursuing entertainment. For instance, according to a 2015 Common Sense Media report, teens spend an average of nine hours per day engaged in using media for enjoyment (Wallace, 2015). Author Jane McGonigal (2011) writes that worldwide, at least half a billion people are playing computer games for at least an hour a day. Remarkably, she suggests that the average young person has spent as much as 10,000 hours of his or her life gaming by the age of 21. About 5 million players in the United States spend 40 hours per week or more engaged in games, a time commitment equivalent to a full-time job, even though McGonigal takes a largely positive rather than critical perspective on the global gaming rage.

Well before the advent of the Internet and the ever-growing spectrum of entertainment options it brings us, another author of dystopian fiction, Aldous Huxley, penned *Brave New World* (1932/2006), a novel that describes a future in which "soma," a fictitious drug of pleasure, pacifies the masses and hedonistic pleasures are a driving societal motivation. In his "negative utopia," political oppression and a stark social hierarchy are sustained by distraction and disinterest, as citizens trade freedom for amusement. As Huxley writes in Chapter 12 of his book, "most men and women will grow up to love their servitude and will never dream of revolution."

Modern technology is a paradox: It can inform and engage, and it can provide pleasures that pacify and distract. Did writers such as Orwell and Huxley, writing in the middle of the 20th century, correctly foretell a dire future of domination through technology, or did they misunderstand the emancipatory potential of modern innovations? What do you think?

Think It Through

- What might Orwell and Huxley say about today's technologies? How would you characterize their effects on social activism?

Follow us on Twitter to keep up with current sociological stories and research! We're at **@DiscoverSoc1**.

Why Study Social Change?

Human beings make their own history, but they do not make it out of thin air. Every generation inherits certain *constraints*, characteristics of the society that limit their vision and their choices, and *resources*, characteristics of the society that they can mobilize in new and creative ways. People are constrained by existing institutions and social relationships. Social structures provide the resources for human action, even as the actions themselves are oriented toward changing those structures (Giddens, 1985).

The sociologically significant processes of globalization and technological change provide both resources and constraints for people everywhere. Social movements themselves may become increasingly internationalized (Marx & McAdam, 1994). Economic globalization, similar to most social processes, has both positive and negative effects. On one hand, it opens up the possibility of a vast increase in global productive capacity, technological advances, global cooperation, and an increase in the standard of living for people around the world. On the other hand, globalization may also lead to lowered wages and to job losses in high-wage industrial countries as well as to exploitative labor conditions in the low-wage countries of the world. Concerns about such problems have given rise to labor and environmental groups that operate across national borders (Barry & Sims, 1994).

We live at a moment in history that contains enormous possibilities as well as daunting problems. Without an understanding of these social forces, we will be unable to act intelligently to bring about the kind of world we most desire. Your understanding of the forces shaping social change today will enable you and tomorrow's citizens to act more effectively to shape your social world.

 # What Can I Do with a Sociology Degree?

UNDERSTANDING AND FOSTERING SOCIAL CHANGE

Social change comes about as a result of shifts in the social order of society. Although changes may be evolutionary or revolutionary in pace, change is inevitable. Understanding social change and the factors that underlie its dynamics is key to bringing about positive change, whether at the micro or the macro level. Sociologists study factors that bring about large-scale social change—for instance, shifts in population growth or health, technological innovations, economic and labor market changes, the mobilization of civil society, or the rise of a charismatic leader—and seek to understand barriers to normative or structural change. They are also interested in factors that affect change or resistance to change in smaller groups and communities. Skills in the areas of leadership, communications, strategic thinking, motivation and mobilization, and advocacy can evolve from knowledge gained in the study of social change. Students interested in social change may also take advantage of internships or practicums in community or political organizations involved in fostering positive change. Supervised practice and the opportunity for reflection on your work nurture skills in the area of social change.

Careers in social change may focus on specific areas, including the environment, labor, human rights, free speech, legal reform, social justice, conflict resolution, poverty, health care, gender equity, economic justice, and corporate ethics. They may be careers in public service (such as in federal, state, or local government) or in the private sector (with advocacy organizations or in research-focused organizations, for instance).

An understanding of social change and the development of skills associated with fostering positive social change are important in a wide variety of occupational fields.

Holly Millet, Social Media Coordinator at Capstrat

James Madison University, BA in Sociology, Minors in Women's and Gender Studies and Communication Studies

In my last year of college, I faced the classic question, "What do you hope to do with your life?" countless times. My response had always been, "I hope to change the world." While ambitious, this goal was very much true, and it was the defining factor of my career search. In college, learning about the social issues that we face in society was enlightening, frustrating, and most of all, motivating. As I considered career options, one thing was for certain: I knew that my choice must allow me to make a positive difference. In many of my courses, I studied the impact that the media has on our culture. From our norms to our gender roles to our beauty standards, the media greatly influences our daily life. A career in this field would allow me to become an agent of change.

This career is a nontraditional one, and it is empowering. I write social media posts and website

(Continued)

SUMMARY

- Sociologists disagree about whether social change is gradual or abrupt, and about whether all societies are changing in roughly the same direction. The evolutionary, revolutionary, and **rise-and-fall theories of social change** are three approaches to these questions.

- Some early sociologists viewed **collective behavior** as a form of group contagion in which the veneer of civilization gave way to more instinctive, herdlike forms of behavior.

- A more sociological approach, **emergent norm** theory, examines the ways in which **crowds** and other forms of collective behavior develop their own rules and shared understandings.

- The most comprehensive theory of collective behavior—value-added theory—attempts to take into account the necessary conditions for collective behavior at the individual, organizational, and even societal levels.

- Social movements have been important historical vehicles for bringing about social change. They are usually achieved through **social movement organizations (SMOs)**, which we study using the tools and understandings of organizational sociology.

- We can classify social movements as **reformist**, **revolutionary**, **rebellious**, **reactionary**, or **utopian**, depending on their vision of social change.

- **Resource mobilization theory** argues that we can explain the success or failure of SMOs not by the degree of social strain that may explain their origins but by their organizational ability to marshal the financial and personal resources they need.

- In recent years, sociologists have sought to explain how **social movements** align their own beliefs and values with those of their potential constituents in the wider society. **Frame alignment** activities range from modifying the beliefs of the SMO to attempting to change the beliefs of the entire society.

- Many social movements depend heavily on **conscience constituents** for their support. Micro-mobilization contexts are also important incubators of social movements.

- Globalization has created an opportunity for the formation of global social movements, since many of the problems in the world today are global and require global solutions.

- **New social movements**, organized around issues of personal identity and values, differ from earlier social movements in that they focus on symbols and information as well as material issues, participation is frequently seen as an end in itself, the movements are organized as networks rather than bureaucratically, and they emphasize the interconnectedness of social groups and larger social entities.

KEY TERMS

differentiation, 513

rise-and-fall theories of social
    change, 515

collective behavior, 517

crowds, 517

emergent norms, 518

riot, 519

fads, 519

fashions, 520

panic, 520

craze, 520

rumors, 520

social movement, 521

reformist social movements, 523

revolutionary social movements, 524

rebellions, 525

reactionary social movements, 525

utopian social movements, 526

free rider problem, 528

social movement organizations
    (SMOs), 528

resource mobilization theory, 528

grassroots organizing, 529

conscience constituents, 529

frame alignment, 530

new social movements, 531

DISCUSSION QUESTIONS

1. Consider what you have learned about social movements and social change in this chapter. How is the global expansion of social media likely to change how people pursue social change? How has it done so already?

2. Under what kinds of societal conditions do movements for social change emerge? Describe a societal context that has brought about or could bring about the development of such a movement.

3. How do fads differ from fashions? Offer some examples of each, and consider whether and how setting

phenomena in these different categories can shed light on their roots and functions.

4. What are the different types of social movements identified by sociologists? Does the growing influence of social media require the expansion of these categories?

5. Design a social movement. What problem or issue would you want to address? How would you disseminate information and engage other participants? How would you overcome the problems of social movements that were identified in this chapter?

Want a better grade?

Get the tools you need to sharpen your study skills. Access practice quizzes, eFlashcards, video, and multimedia at **https://edge.sagepub.com/chambliss4e**.

Glossary

Achieved status: Social position linked to an individual's acquisition of socially valued credentials or skills.

Agency: The ability of individuals and groups to exercise free will and to make social changes on a small or large scale.

Age-specific fertility rate: The number of births typical for women of a specific age in a particular population.

Age-specific mortality rate: An estimate of the number of deaths typical in men and women of specific ages in a particular population.

Agricultural surplus: Food beyond the amount required for immediate survival.

Alliance (or coalition): A subgroup that forms between group members, enabling them to dominate the group in their own interest.

Animism: The belief that naturally occurring phenomena, such as mountains and animals, are possessed of indwelling spirits with supernatural powers.

Anomie: A state of normlessness that occurs when people lose touch with the shared rules and values that give order and meaning to their lives.

Anthropology: The study of human cultures and societies and their development.

Anticipatory socialization: Adoption of the behaviors or standards of a group one emulates or hopes to join.

Anti-miscegenation laws: Laws prohibiting interracial sexual relations and marriage.

Ascribed status: Social position linked to characteristics that are socially significant but cannot generally be altered (such as race or gender).

Assimilation: The absorption of a minority group into the dominant culture.

Atavisms: Throwbacks to primitive early humans.

Authoritarianism: A form of governance in which ordinary members of society are denied the right to participate in government, and political power is exercised by and for the benefit of a small political elite.

Automation: The replacement of human labor by machines in the production process.

Barter economy: An economy based on the exchange of goods and services rather than money.

Behaviorism: A psychological perspective that emphasizes the effect of rewards and punishments on human behavior.

Beliefs: Particular ideas that people accept as true.

Bias: A characteristic of results that systematically misrepresent the true nature of what is being studied.

Bourgeoisie: The capitalist (or property-owning) class.

Bureaucracies: Formal organizations characterized by written rules, hierarchical authority, and paid staff, intended to promote organizational efficiency.

Capital crime: A crime, such as murder, which is severe enough to merit the death penalty (see capital offenses).

Capital offenses: Crimes punishable by death.

Capitalism: An economic order characterized by the market allocation of goods and services, production for private profit, and private ownership of the means of producing wealth.

Caste society: A system in which social positions are closed, so that all individuals remain at the social level of their birth throughout life.

Causal relationship: A relationship between two variables in which one variable is the cause of the other.

Charismatic authority: Power based on devotion inspired in followers by the personal qualities of a leader.

Church: A well-established religious organization that exists in a fairly harmonious relationship with the larger society.

Citizens: Legally recognized inhabitants who are part of a political community in which they are granted certain rights and privileges and, at the same time, have specified responsibilities.

City: A relatively large, dense, and permanent settlement of socially heterogeneous individuals.

Civil religion: A set of sacred beliefs and practices that become part of how a society sees itself.

Class conflict: Competition between social classes over the distribution of wealth, power, and other valued resources in society.

Class dominance theory: The theory that a small and concentrated group of elite or upper-class people dominate and influence societal institutions; a variation of conflict theory.

Class society: The theory that power is concentrated in the hands of a small and concentrated group of elite or upper-class people who dominate and influence societal institutions; a variation of conflict theory.

Class: A person's economic position in society, which is usually associated with income, wealth, and occupation (and sometimes associated with political voice).

Class-dominant theories: Theories that propose that what is labeled deviant or criminal—and therefore who gets punished—is determined by the interests of the dominant class.

Coercion: The threat or use of physical force to ensure compliance.

Coercive organizations: Organizations in which people are forced to give unquestioned obedience to authority.

Cognitive development: The theory, developed by Jean Piaget, that an individual's ability to make logical decisions increases as the person grows older.

Cohabitation: Living together as a couple without being legally married.

Collective behavior: Voluntary, goal-oriented action that occurs in relatively disorganized situations in which society's predominant social norms and values cease to govern individual behavior.

Collective conscience: The common beliefs and values that bind a society together.

Common-law marriage: A type of relationship in which partners live as if married but without the formal legal framework of traditional marriage.

Communism: A type of economic system without private ownership of the means of production and, theoretically, without economic classes or economic inequality.

Concepts: Ideas that summarize a set of phenomena.

Conscience constituents: People who provide resources for a social movement organization but who are not themselves members of the aggrieved group that the organization champions.

Control theory: The theory that explains that the probability of delinquency or deviance among children and teenagers is rooted in social control.

Conversation analysis: The study of how participants in social interaction recognize and produce coherent conversation.

Correlation: The degree to which two or more variables are associated with one another.

Craze: An intense attraction to an object, a person, or an activity.

Credential society: A society in which access to desirable work and social status depends on the possession of a certificate or diploma certifying the completion of formal education.

Crime: Any act defined in the law as punishable by fines, imprisonment, or both.

Critical thinking: The ability to evaluate claims about truth by using reason and evidence.

Crowds: Temporary gatherings of closely interacting people with a common focus.

Crude birthrate: The number of births each year per 1,000 women.

Crude death rate: The number of deaths each year per 1,000 people.

Cult: A religious organization that is thoroughly unconventional with regard to the larger society.

Cultural capital: Wealth in the form of knowledge, ideas, verbal skills, and ways of thinking and behaving.

Cultural inconsistency: A contradiction between the goals of ideal culture and the practices of real culture.

Cultural pluralism: The coexistence of different racial and ethnic groups, which is characterized by the acceptance of one another's differences.

Cultural relativism: A worldview whereby the practices of a society are understood sociologically in terms of that society's norms and values, and not the norms and values of another society.

Culture: The beliefs, norms, behaviors, and products common to the members of a particular group.

Cyberterrorism: "Hacking into government and private computer systems and crippling the military, financial, and service sectors of advanced economies" (Weimann, 2004).

De facto segregation: School segregation based largely on residential patterns, which persists even though legal segregation is now outlawed in the United States.

Deductive reasoning: Starts from broad theories about the social world but proceeds to break them down into more specific and testable hypotheses.

Demography: The science of population size, distribution, and composition.

Denomination: A church that is not formally allied with the state.

Dependency theory: The theory that the poverty of some countries is a consequence of their exploitation by wealthy states, which control the global capitalist system.

Dependent variables: Variables that change as a result of changes in other variables.

Deviance: Any attitude, behavior, or condition that violates cultural norms or societal laws and results in disapproval, hostility, or sanction if it becomes known.

Dictatorship: A form of governance in which power rests in a single individual.

Differential association theory: The theory that deviant and criminal behavior results from regular exposure to attitudes favorable to acting in ways that are deviant or criminal.

Differentiation: The development of increasing societal complexity through the creation of specialized social roles and institutions.

Direct democracy: A political system in which all citizens fully participate in their own governance.

Discouraged workers: Those who would like to work but have given up searching, believing that no jobs are available for them.

Discrimination: The unequal treatment of individuals on the basis of their membership in a group.

Disestablishment: A period during which the political influence of established religions is successfully challenged.

Document analysis: The examination of written materials or cultural products: previous studies, newspaper reports, court records, campaign posters, digital reports, films, pamphlets, and other forms of text or images produced by individuals, government agencies, private organizations, or others.

Domestic (or family) violence: Physical or sexual abuse committed by one family member against another.

Double consciousness: Among African Americans, an awareness of themselves as both American and Black, never free of racial stigma.

Doxic: Taken for granted as natural or normal in society.

Dramaturgical approach: Developed by Erving Goffman, the study of social interaction as if it were governed by the norms of theatrical performance.

Dyad: A group consisting of two persons.

Ecclesia: A church that is formally allied with the state and is the official religion of the society.

Economic capital: Money and material that can be used to access valued goods and services.

Economy: The social institution that organizes the ways in which a society produces, distributes, and consumes goods and services.

Education: The transmission of society's norms, values, and knowledge base by means of direct instruction.

Ego: According to Sigmund Freud, the part of the mind that is the "self," the core of what is regarded as a person's unique personality.

Egocentric: Experiencing the world as if it were centered entirely on oneself.

Emergent norms: Norms that are situationally created to support a collective action.

Emic perspective: The perspective of the insider, the one belonging to the cultural group in question.

Emotional labor: The commodification of emotions, including the management of feeling to create a publicly observable facial and bodily display in return for a wage.

Employed: Employed persons are those who are 16 years of age or older in the civilian, noninstitutional population who did any paid work—even as little as one hour—in the reference week or worked in their own businesses or farms.

Endogamous: A characteristic of marriages in which partners are limited to members of the same social group or caste.

Establishment Clause: The passage in the First Amendment to the U.S. Constitution that states, "Congress shall make no law respecting an establishment of religion, or prohibiting the free exercise thereof."

Ethnicity: Characteristics of groups associated with national origins, languages, and cultural and religious practices.

Ethnocentrism: A worldview whereby one judges other cultures by the standards of one's own culture and regards one's own way of life as normal and better than others.

Ethnomethodology: A sociological method used to study the body of commonsense knowledge and procedures by which ordinary members of a society make sense of their social circumstances and interaction.

Etic perspective: The perspective of the outside observer.

Evangelicalism: A belief in spiritual rebirth (conventionally denoted as being "born again").

Experiments: Research techniques for investigating cause and effect under controlled conditions.

Exponential population growth: A constant rate of population growth applied to a base that is continuously growing in size, producing a population that grows by an increasing amount with each passing year.

Expulsion: The process of forcibly removing a population from a particular area.

Extended families: Social groups consisting of one or more parents, children, and other kin, often spanning several generations, living in the same household.

Fads: Temporary, highly imitated outbreaks of mildly unconventional behavior.

Family: Two or more individuals who identify themselves as being related to one another, usually by blood, marriage, or adoption, and who share intimate relationships and dependency.

Fashions: Somewhat long-lasting styles of imitative behavior or appearance.

Feminism: The belief that social equality should exist between the sexes; also, the social movements aimed at achieving that goal.

Feminist perspective on deviance: A perspective that suggests that studies of deviance have been biased because almost all the research has been done by, and about, males, largely ignoring female perspectives on deviant behavior as well as analyses of differences in the types and causes of female deviance.

Fertility: The number of live births in a given population.

Fieldwork: A research method that relies on in-depth and often extended study to describe and analyze a group or community; also called *ethnography*.

Folkways: Fairly weak norms that are passed down from the past, the violation of which is generally not considered serious within a particular culture.

Food deserts: Areas (often urban neighborhoods or rural towns) characterized by poor access to healthy and affordable food.

Food insecurity: A lack of consistent access to enough food for an active, healthy life.

Formal economy: All work-related activities that provide income and are regulated by government agencies.

Formal education: Education that occurs within academic institutions such as schools.

Formal organization: An organization that is rationally designed to achieve its objectives, often by means of explicit rules, regulations, and procedures.

Formal rationality: A context in which people's pursuit of goals is shaped by rules, regulations, and larger social structures.

Formal social control: Official attempts to discourage certain behaviors and visibly punish others; most often exercised by the state.

Foster care: A situation in which a child is cared for by people who are not his or her parents for either a brief or extended period of time.

Frame alignment: The process by which the interests, understandings, and values of a social movement organization are shaped to match those in the wider society.

Free rider problem: The problem that many people avoid the costs of social movement activism (such as time, energy, and other personal resources) and still benefit from its success.

Gender roles: The attitudes and behaviors that are considered appropriately masculine or feminine in a particular culture.

Gender wage gap: The difference between the earnings of women who work full-time year-round as a group and those of men who work full-time year-round as a group.

Gender: The norms, roles, and behavioral characteristics associated in a given society with being male or female.

Generalized other: The abstract sense of society's norms and values by which people evaluate themselves.

Genocide: The mass, systematic destruction of a people or a nation.

Gentrification: The change in the socioeconomic composition of older and poorer neighborhoods with the remodeling of old structures and building of new residences and shops to attract new middle- and high-income residents.

Glass ceiling: An artificial boundary that allows women to see the next occupational or salary level even as structural obstacles keep them from reaching it.

Glass escalator: The nearly invisible promotional boost that men gain in female-dominated occupations.

Global cities: Metropolitan areas that are highly interconnected with one another in their role as centers of global political and economic decision making, finance, and culture.

Global consumer class: Those who actively use technology, purchase consumer goods, and embrace the culture of consumption.

Global culture: A type of culture—some would say U.S. culture—that has spread across the world in the form of Hollywood films, fast-food restaurants, and popular music heard in virtually every country.

Global elite: A transglobal class of professionals who exercise considerable economic and political power that is not limited by national borders.

Global inequality: The systematic disparities in income, wealth, health, education, access to technology, opportunity, and power among countries, communities, and households around the world.

Globalization: The process by which people all over the planet become increasingly interconnected economically, politically, culturally, and environmentally.

Goods: Objects that have an economic value to others, whether they are the basic necessities for survival or things that people simply want.

Grassroots organizing: Attempts to mobilize support among the ordinary members of a community.

Gross national income–purchasing power parity per capita (GNI-PPP): A comparative economic measure that uses international dollars to indicate the amount of goods and services someone could buy in the United States with a given amount of money.

Groupthink: A process by which the members of a group ignore ways of thinking and plans of action that go against the group consensus.

Habitus: The internalization of objective probabilities and subsequent expression of those probabilities as choice.

Health: The extent to which a person experiences a state of mental, physical, and social well-being.

Health care: All those activities intended to sustain, promote, and enhance health.

Hidden curriculum: The unspoken classroom socialization into the norms, values, and roles of a society that schools provide along with the "official" curriculum.

High culture: Music, theater, literature, and other cultural products that are held in particularly high esteem in society.

Human capital: The skills, knowledge, and credentials a person possesses that make him or her valuable in a particular workplace.

Hypotheses: Ideas about the world, derived from theories, that describe possible relationships between social phenomena.

I: According to George Herbert Mead, the part of the self that is the impulse to act; it is creative, innovative, unthinking, and largely unpredictable.

Id: According to Sigmund Freud, the part of the mind that is the repository of basic biological drives and needs.

Ideal culture: The values, norms, and behaviors that people in a given society profess to embrace.

Income: The amount of money a person or household earns in a given period of time.

Independent or experimental variables: Variables the researcher changes intentionally.

Indirect labor costs: The time, training, or money spent when an employee takes time off to care for sick family members, opts for parental leave, arrives at work late, or leaves a position after receiving employer-provided training.

Individual discrimination: Overt and intentional unequal treatment, often based on prejudicial beliefs.

Inductive reasoning: Starts from specific data, such as interviews, observations, or field notes, that may focus on a single community or event and endeavors to identify larger patterns from which to derive more general theories.

Inequality: Differences in wealth, power, political voice, educational opportunities, and other valued resources.

Infant mortality rate: The number of deaths of infants under age 1 per 1,000 live births per year.

Informal (or underground) economy: Those income-generating economic activities that are not regulated by the governmental institutions that ordinarily regulate similar activities.

Informal social control: The unofficial means through which deviance and deviant behaviors are discouraged in society; most often occurs among ordinary people during their everyday interactions.

Institutionalized discrimination: Discrimination enshrined in law, public policy, or common practice; it is unequal treatment that has become a part of the routine operation of such major social institutions as businesses, schools, hospitals, and the government.

Interest groups: Groups made up of people who share the same concerns on particular issues who use their organizational and social resources to influence legislation and the functioning of social institutions.

International families: Families that result from globalization.

International governmental organization (IGO): An international organization established by treaties between governments to facilitate and regulate trade between the member countries, promote national security, protect social welfare and human rights, or ensure environmental protection.

International nongovernmental organization (INGO): An international organization established by agreements between the individuals or private organizations making up the membership and existing to fulfill an explicit mission.

Interview: A detailed conversation designed to obtain in-depth information about a person and his or her activities.

Iron law of oligarchy: Robert Michels's theory that there is an inevitable tendency for a large-scale bureaucratic organization to become ruled undemocratically by a handful of people.

Labeling theory (or societal reaction theory): A symbolic interactionist approach holding that deviant behavior is a product of the labels people attach to certain types of behavior.

Labor demand factors: Factors that highlight the needs and preferences of the employer.

Labor supply factors: Factors that highlight reasons that women or men may prefer particular occupations.

Language: A symbolic system composed of verbal, nonverbal, and written representations that are vehicles for conveying meaning.

Latent functions: Functions of a phenomenon or institution that are not recognized or expected.

Law: A system of binding and recognized codified rules of behavior that regulate the actions of people pertaining to a given jurisdiction.

Laws: Codified norms or rules of behavior.

Leading questions: Questions that tend to elicit particular responses.

Legitimate authority: A type of power that is recognized as deserved or earned.

Liberal feminism: The belief that women's inequality is primarily the result of imperfect institutions, which can be corrected by reforms that do not fundamentally alter society itself.

Life chances: The opportunities and obstacles a person encounters in education, social life, work, and other areas critical to social mobility.

Life expectancy: The average number of years a newborn is expected to live based on existing health conditions in the country.

Literacy: The ability to read and write at a basic level.

Lobbyists: Paid professionals whose job it is to influence legislation.

Looking-glass self: The concept developed by Charles Horton Cooley that our self-image results from how we interpret other people's views of us.

Macro-level paradigms: Theories of the social world that are concerned with large-scale patterns and institutions.

Mandatory minimum sentences: Legislation stipulating that a person found guilty of a particular crime must be sentenced to set minimum numbers of years in prison.

Manifest functions: The obvious and intended functions of a phenomenon or institution.

Marginally attached to the labor force: Persons who would like to work and have searched actively for a job in the past 12 months (but not in the prior four weeks).

Marriage: A culturally approved relationship, usually between two individuals, that provides a degree of economic cooperation, emotional intimacy, and sexual relations.

Mass education: The extension of formal schooling to wide segments of the population.

Mass media: Media of public communication intended to reach and influence a mass audience.

Mass production: The large-scale, highly standardized manufacturing of identical commodities on a mechanical assembly line.

Material culture: The physical objects that are created, embraced, or consumed by society that help shape people's lives.

Matrix of domination: A system of social positions in which any individual may concurrently occupy a status (for example, gender, race, class, or sexual orientation) as a member of a dominated group and a status as a member of a dominating group.

Me: According to George Herbert Mead, the part of the self through which we see ourselves as others see us.

Means of consumption: "Those things that make it possible for people to acquire goods and services and for the same people to be controlled and exploited as consumers" (quoted in Ritzer, 1999).

Means of production: The sites and technology that produce the goods we need and use.

Medicine: An institutionalized system for the scientific diagnosis, treatment, and prevention of illness.

Megacities: Metropolitan areas or cities with total population of 10 million or more.

Meritocracy: A society in which personal success is based on talent and individual effort.

Micro-level paradigm: A theory of the social world that is concerned with small-group social relations and interactions.

Minorities: Less powerful groups who are dominated by a more powerful group and, often, discriminated against on the basis of characteristics deemed by the majority to be socially significant.

Mixed contacts: Interactions between those who are stigmatized and those who are "normal."

Modernization theory: A market-oriented development theory that envisions development as evolutionary and guided by modern institutions, practices, and cultures.

Monarchy: A form of governance in which power resides in an individual or a family and is passed from one generation to the next through hereditary lines.

Monogamy: A form of marriage in which a person may have only one spouse at a time.

Monotheism: Belief in a single all-knowing, all-powerful God.

Morbidity: The rate of illness in a particular population.

Mores: Strongly held norms, the violation of which seriously offends the standards of acceptable conduct of most people within a particular culture.

Mortality: The rate of death in a particular population.

Multicultural feminism: The belief that inequality must be understood—and ended—for all women, regardless of race, class, nationality, age, sexual orientation, physical ability, or other characteristics.

Multiculturalism: A commitment to respecting cultural differences rather than trying to submerge them into a larger, dominant culture.

Nation-state: A single people (a *nation*) governed by a political authority (a *state*); similar to the modern notion of *country*.

Negative correlation: A relationship showing that as one variable increases, the other decreases.

Net financial assets: A measure of wealth that excludes illiquid personal assets such as the home and vehicles.

Net migration: In-migration minus out-migration.

New religious movements (NRMs): New spiritual groups or communities that occupy a peripheral place in a country's dominant religious landscape.

New social movements: Movements that have arisen since the 1960s and are fundamentally concerned with the quality of private life, often advocating large-scale cultural changes in how people think and act.

Noncitizens: Individuals who reside in a given jurisdiction but do not possess the same rights and privileges as the citizens who are recognized inhabitants; sometimes referred to as *residents, temporary workers,* or *aliens.*

Nonmaterial culture: The abstract creations of human cultures, including ideas about behavior, language, and social practices.

Nontheistic religion: Belief in the existence of divine spiritual forces rather than a god or gods.

Normative organizations (or voluntary associations): Organizations that people join of their own will to pursue morally worthwhile goals without expectation of material reward.

Norms: Accepted social behaviors and beliefs.

Not in the labor force: Persons who are neither officially employed nor officially unemployed.

Nuclear families: Families characterized by one or two parents living with their biological, dependent children in a household with no other kin.

Objectivity: The ability to represent the object of study accurately.

Occupation: A person's main vocation or paid employment.

Occupational segregation by gender: The concentration of men and women in different occupations.

Official poverty line: The dollar amount set by the government as the minimum necessary to meet the basic needs of a family.

Operational definition: Describes the concept in such a way that it can be observed and measured.

Opportunity theory: The theory that people differ not only in their motivations to engage in deviant acts but also in their opportunities to do so.

Organization: A group with an identifiable membership that engages in concerted collective actions to achieve a common purpose.

Organized crime: Crime committed by criminal groups that provide illegal goods and services.

Panic: A massive flight from something that is feared.

Patriarchy: Any set of social relationships in which men dominate women.

Personal power: Power that depends on the ability to persuade rather than the ability to command.

Phrenology: A theory that the skull configurations of deviant individuals differ from those of nondeviants.

Pluralistic societies: Societies made up of many diverse groups with different norms and values.

Political action committees (PACs): Organizations created by groups such as corporations, unions, environmentalists, and other interest groups for the purpose of gathering money and contributing to political candidates who favor the groups' interests.

Political power: The ability to exercise influence on political institutions and/or political actors in order to realize personal or group interests.

Politics: The art or science of influencing public policy.

Polyandry: A form of marriage in which a woman may have multiple husbands.

Polygamy: A form of marriage in which a person may have more than one spouse at a time.

Polygyny: A form of marriage in which a man may have multiple wives.

Polytheism: The belief that there are different gods representing various categories of natural forces.

Popular culture: The entertainment, culinary, and athletic tastes shared by the masses.

Population: The whole group of people studied.

Population momentum: The tendency of population growth to continue beyond the point when replacement rate fertility has been achieved because of the high concentration of people of childbearing age.

Positional power: Power depends on the leader's role in the group.

Positive correlation: A relationship showing that as one variable rises or falls, the other does as well.

Positivist: Science that is based on facts alone.

Power: The ability to mobilize resources and achieve goals despite the resistance of others.

Power elite: A group of people with a disproportionately high level of influence and resources who utilize their status to influence the functioning of societal institutions.

Prejudice: A belief about an individual or a group that is not subject to change on the basis of evidence.

Presentation of self: The creation of impressions in the minds of others to define and control social situations.

Preventive medicine: Medicine that emphasizes a healthy lifestyle that will prevent poor health before it occurs.

Primary deviance: A term developed by Edwin Lemert; the first step in the labeling of deviance, it occurs at the moment an activity is labeled deviant (see also secondary deviance).

Primary groups: Small groups characterized by intense emotional ties, face-to-face interaction, intimacy, and a strong, enduring sense of commitment.

Principle of falsification (or falsifiability): The principle, advanced by philosopher Karl Popper, that a scientific theory must lead to testable hypotheses that can be disproved if they are wrong.

Private sector: The sector of the labor market that provides goods and services to the economy and consumers with the primary motive of gaining profit.

Profane: A sphere of routine, everyday life.

Proletariat: The working class; wage workers.

Property crimes: Crimes that involve the violation of individuals' ownership rights, including burglary, larceny/theft, motor vehicle theft, and arson.

Psychoanalysis: A psychological perspective that emphasizes the complex reasoning processes of the conscious and unconscious mind.

Public education: A universal education system provided by the government and funded by tax revenues rather than student fees.

Public health: The science and practice of health protection and maintenance at a community level.

Public sector: The sector of the labor market in which jobs are linked to the government (whether national, state, or local) and encompass production or allocation of goods and services for the benefit of the government and its citizens.

Qualitative research: Research that is characterized by data that cannot be quantified (or converted into numbers), focusing instead on generating in-depth knowledge of social life, institutions, and processes.

Qualitative variables: Variables that express qualities and do not have numerical values.

Quantitative research: Research that gathers data that can be quantified and offers insight into broad patterns of social behavior and social attitudes.

Quantitative variables: Factors that can be counted.

Race: A group of people who share a set of characteristics (usually physical characteristics) deemed by society to be socially significant.

Racism: The idea that one racial group is inherently superior to another; often results in institutionalized relationships between dominant and minority groups that create a structure of economic, social, and political inequality based on socially constructed racial or ethnic categories.

Radical feminism: The belief that women's inequality underlies all other forms of inequality, including economic inequality.

Random sampling: Sampling in which everyone in the population of interest has an equal chance of being chosen for the study.

Rape culture: A social culture that provides an environment conducive to rape.

Rate of natural increase (RNI): The crude birthrate minus the crude death rate.

Rational-legal authority: Power based on a belief in the lawfulness of enacted rules (laws) and the legitimate right of leaders to exercise authority under such rules.

Reactionary social movements: Movements seeking to restore an earlier social system—often based on a mythical past—along with the traditional norms and values that once presumably accompanied it.

Real culture: The values, norms, and behaviors that people in a given society actually embrace and exhibit.

Rebellions: Movements seeking to overthrow the existing social, political, and economic systems but lacking detailed plans for a new social order.

Reference groups: Groups that provide standards for judging our attitudes or behaviors.

Reformist social movements: Movements seeking to bring about social change within the existing economic and political system.

Reliability: The extent to which researchers' findings are consistent with the findings of different studies of the same thing or with the findings of the same study over time.

Religion: A system of common beliefs and rituals centered on sacred things that unites believers and provides a sense of meaning and purpose.

Religious economy: An approach to the sociology of religion that suggests that religions can be fruitfully understood as organizations in competition with one another for followers.

Religious nationalism: The linkage of religious convictions with beliefs about a nation's or ethnic group's social and political destiny.

Replication: The repetition of a previous study using a different sample or population to verify or refute the original findings.

Representative democracy: A political system in which citizens elect representatives to govern them.

Research methods: Specific techniques for systematically gathering data.

Reserve army of labor: A pool of job seekers whose numbers outpace the available positions and thus contribute to keeping wages low and conditions of work tenuous.

Resocialization: The process of altering an individual's behavior through control of his or her environment, for example, within a total institution.

Resource mobilization theory: A theory that focuses on the ability of social movement organizations to generate money, membership, and political support to achieve their objectives.

Restrictive covenants: Contractual agreements that restrict the use of land, ostensibly in order to preserve the value of adjacent land or a neighborhood.

Revolutionary social movements: Movements seeking to fundamentally alter the existing social, political, and economic system in keeping with a vision of a new social order.

Riot: An illegal, prolonged outbreak of violent behavior by a sizable group of people directed against individuals or property.

Rise-and-fall theories of social change: Theories that argue that social change reflects a cycle of growth and decline.

Role-taking: The ability to take the roles of others in interaction.

Rumors: Unverified forms of information that are transmitted informally, usually originating in unknown sources.

Sacred: That which is set apart from the ordinary; the sphere endowed with spiritual meaning.

Sample: A small number of people; a portion of the larger population selected to represent the whole.

School segregation: The education of racial minorities in schools that are geographically, economically, and/or socially separated from those attended by the racial majority.

School-to-prison pipeline: The policies and practices that push students, particularly at-risk youth, out of schools and into the juvenile and criminal justice system.

Scientific: A way of learning about the world that combines logically constructed theory and systematic observation.

Scientific management: A practice that sought to use principles of engineering to reduce the physical movements of workers.

Scientific method: A process of gathering empirical (scientific and specific) data, creating theories, and rigorously testing theories.

Scientific theories: Explanations of how and why scientific observations are as they are.

Second shift: The unpaid housework that women typically do after they come home from their paid employment.

Secondary deviance: A term developed by Edwin Lemert; the second step in the labeling of deviance, it occurs when a person labeled deviant accepts the label as part of his or her identity and, as a result, begins to act in conformity with the label (see also primary deviance).

Secondary groups: Groups that are impersonal and characterized by functional or fleeting relationships.

Sect: A religious organization that has splintered off from an established church in an effort to restore perceived true beliefs and practices believed to have been lost by the established religious organization.

Secularization: The rise in worldly thinking, particularly as seen in the rise of science, technology, and rational thought, and a simultaneous decline in the influence of religion.

Segregation: The practice of separating people spatially or socially on the basis of race or ethnicity.

Serial monogamy: The practice of having more than one wife or husband, but only one at a time.

Services: Economically productive activities that do not result directly in physical products; may be relatively simple or quite complex.

Sex category: The socially required identification display that confirms someone's membership in a given category.

Sex: The anatomical and other biological characteristics that differ between males and females and that originate in human genes.

Sexism: The belief that one sex is innately superior to the other and is therefore justified in having a dominant social position.

Sexual division of labor in modern societies: The phenomenon of dividing production functions by gender and designating different spheres of activity, the "private" to women and the "public" to men.

Sexuality: A term used to encompass sexual identity, attraction, and relationships.

Sick roles: Social roles rooted in cultural definitions of the appropriate behavior of and response to people labeled as sick.

Significant others: According to George Herbert Mead, the specific people who are important in children's lives and whose views have the greatest impact on the children's self-evaluations.

Social bonds: Individuals' connections to others (see also control theory).

Social capital: The personal connections and networks that enable people to accomplish their goals and extend their influence.

Social categories: Categories of people who share common characteristics without necessarily interacting or identifying with one another.

Social class reproduction: The way in which class status is reproduced from generation to generation, with parents passing on a class position to their offspring.

Social closure: The ability of a group to strategically and consciously exclude outsiders or those deemed "undesirable" from participating in the group or enjoying the group's resources.

Social conflict paradigm: A theory that seeks to explain social organization and change in terms of the conflict that is built into social relations; also known as *conflict theory*.

Social control: The attempts by certain people or groups in society to control the behaviors of other individuals and groups to increase the likelihood that they will conform to established norms or laws.

Social desirability bias: A response bias based on the tendency of respondents to answer a question in a way that they perceive will be favorably received.

Social diversity: The social and cultural mixture of different groups in society and the societal recognition of difference as significant.

Social dynamics: The laws that govern social change.

Social embeddedness: The idea that economic, political, and other forms of human behavior are fundamentally shaped by social relations.

Social epidemiology: The study of communities and their social statuses, practices, and problems with the aim of understanding patterns of health and disease.

Social facts: Qualities of groups that are external to individual members yet constrain their thinking and behavior.

Social inequality: A high degree of disparity in income, wealth, power, prestige, and other resources.

Social learning: The way people adapt their behavior in response to social rewards and punishments.

Social mobility: The upward or downward status movement of individuals or groups over time.

Social movement organizations (SMOs): Formal organizations that seek to achieve social change through noninstitutionalized forms of political action.

Social movement: A large number of people who come together in a continuing and organized effort to bring about (or resist) social change and who rely at least partially on noninstitutionalized forms of political action.

Social power: The ability to exercise social control.

Social solidarity: The bonds that unite the members of a social group.

Social statics: The way society is held together.

Social stratification: The systematic ranking of different groups of people in a hierarchy of inequality.

Socialism: A type of economic system in which, theoretically, the government manages the economy in the interests of the workers; it owns the businesses, factories, farms, hospitals, housing, and other means of producing wealth and redistributes that wealth to the population through wages and services.

Socialist feminism: The belief that women's inequality results from the combination of capitalistic economic relations and male domination (patriarchy), arguing that both must be transformed fundamentally before women can achieve equality.

Socialization: The process by which people learn the culture of their society.

Sociological imagination: The ability to grasp the relationship between individual lives and the larger social forces that help to shape them.

Sociological theories: Logical, rigorous frameworks for the interpretation of social life that make particular assumptions and ask particular questions about the social world.

Sociology: The scientific study of human social relations, groups, and societies.

Spurious relationship: A correlation between two or more variables caused by another factor that is not being measured rather than a causal link between the variables themselves.

Standpoint epistemology: A philosophical perspective that argues that what we can know is affected by the position we occupy in society.

Standpoint theory: A perspective that says the knowledge we create is conditioned by where we stand or our subjective social position.

State crimes: Consist of criminal or other harmful acts of commission or omission perpetrated by state officials in the pursuit of their jobs as representatives of the government.

Statistical data: Quantitative information obtained from government agencies, businesses, research studies, and other entities that collect data for their own or others' use.

Status: The prestige associated with a social position.

Stereotype threat: A situation in which an individual is at risk of confirming a negative stereotype about his or her social group.

Stereotyping: The generalization of a set of characteristics to all members of a group.

Stigma: An attribute that is deeply discrediting to an individual or a group because it overshadows other attributes and merits the individual or group may possess.

Stigmatization: The branding of behavior as highly disgraceful (see also labeling theory).

Strain theory: The theory that when there is a discrepancy between the cultural goals for success and the means available to achieve those goals, rates of deviance will be high.

Stratified sampling: Dividing a population into a series of subgroups and taking random samples from within each group.

Structural contradiction theory: The theory that conflicts generated by fundamental contradictions in the structure of society produce laws defining certain acts as deviant or criminal.

Structural functionalism: A theory that seeks to explain social organization and change in terms of the roles performed by different social structures, phenomena, and institutions; also known as *functionalism*.

Structural strain: The theory that when there is a discrepancy between the cultural goals for success and the means available to achieve those goals, rates of deviance will be high.

Structuralism: The idea that an overarching structure exists within which culture and other aspects of society must be understood.

Structure: Patterned social arrangements that have effects on agency and are, in turn, affected by agency.

Subcultural theories: Theories that explain deviance in terms of the conflicting interests of different segments of a population.

Subcultures: Cultures that exist together with a dominant culture but differ from it in some important respects.

Superego: According to Sigmund Freud, the part of the mind that consists of the values and norms of society insofar as they are internalized, or taken in, by the individual.

Survey: A research method that uses a questionnaire or interviews administered to a group of people in person or by telephone or e-mail to determine their characteristics, opinions, and behaviors.

Symbolic interactionism: A microsociological perspective that posits that both the individual self and society as a whole are the products of social interactions based on language and other symbols.

Symbols: Representations of things that are not immediately present to our senses.

Taboos: Powerful mores, the violation of which is considered serious and even unthinkable within a particular culture.

Terrorism: "the unlawful use of violence or threat of violence to instill fear and coerce governments or societies. Terrorism is often motivated by religious, political, or other ideological beliefs and committed in the pursuit of goals that are usually political" (U.S. Department of Defense, 2011).

Theism: A belief in one or more supernatural deities.

"Three strikes" laws: State and federal laws that sentence an individual to life in prison who has been found guilty of committing three felonies or serious crimes punishable by a minimum of a year in prison.

Total fertility rate (TFR): The average number of children a woman in a given country will have in her lifetime if age-specific fertility rates hold throughout her childbearing years (15–49).

Total institutions: Institutions that isolate individuals from the rest of society in order to achieve administrative control over most aspects of their lives.

Totalitarianism: A form of governance that denies popular political participation in government and also seeks to regulate and control all aspects of the public and private lives of citizens.

Totems: Within the sacred sphere, ordinary objects believed to have acquired transcendent or magical qualities connecting humans with the divine.

Traditional authority: Power based on a belief in the sanctity of long-standing traditions and the legitimate right of rulers to exercise authority in accordance with those traditions.

Transactional leader: A leader who is concerned with accomplishing the group's tasks, getting group members to do their jobs, and making certain that the group achieves its goals.

Transformational leader: A leader who is able to instill in group members a sense of mission or higher purpose, thereby changing (transforming) the nature of the group itself.

Transgender: An umbrella term used to describe those whose gender identity, expression, or behavior differs from their assigned sex at birth or is outside the gender binary.

Transsexual: A term used to refer to people who use surgery and hormones to change their sex to match their preferred gender.

Treadmill of production: The constant and aggressive growth needed to sustain the modern economy.

Triad: A group consisting of three persons.

Underemployed: Working in jobs that do not make full use of one's skills or working part time when one would like to be working full time.

Unemployed: Persons who are jobless, actively looked for work in the prior four weeks, and are available for work.

Urban growth machine: Those persons and institutions that have a stake in an increase in the value of urban land and that constitute a power elite in cities.

Urban renewal: The transformation of old neighborhoods with new buildings, businesses, and residences.

Urbanization: The concentration of people in urban areas.

Utilitarian organizations: Organizations that people join primarily because of some material benefit they expect to receive in return for membership.

Utopian social movements: Movements seeking to withdraw from the dominant society by creating their own ideal communities.

Validity: The degree to which concepts and their measurements accurately represent what they claim to represent.

Value neutrality: The characteristic of being free of personal beliefs and opinions that would influence the course of research.

Values: The abstract and general standards in society that define ideal principles, such as those governing notions of right and wrong.

Variable: A concept or its empirical measure that can take on two or more possible values.

Verstehen: The German word for interpretive understanding; Weber's proposed methodology for explaining social relationships by having the sociologist imagine how subjects might perceive a situation.

Violent crimes: Crimes that involve force or threat of force, including murder and negligent manslaughter, rape, robbery, and aggravated assault.

War economy: The phenomenon of war boosting economic productivity and employment, particularly in capital- and labor-intensive sectors such as industrial production.

"War on drugs": Actions taken by U.S. state and federal governments to curb the illegal drug trade and reduce drug use by punishing drug possession, use, and trafficking more harshly.

Wealth (or net worth): The value of everything a person owns minus the value of everything he or she owes.

Welfare state: A government or country's system of providing for the financial and social well-being of its citizens, typically through government programs that provide funding or other resources to individuals who meet certain criteria.

White-collar crime: Crime committed by people of high social status in connection with their work.

Work: Any human effort that adds something of value to the goods and services that are available to others.

World systems theory: The theory that the global capitalist economic system has long been shaped by a few powerful economic actors, who have ordered it in a way that favors their interests.

Zero tolerance policies: School or district policy that sets predetermined punishments for certain misbehaviors and punishes the same way, no matter the severity or the context of the behavior.

Zionism: A movement calling for the return of Jews to Palestine and the creation of a Jewish state.

References

ABC News. (2015, April 24). The twelve biggest moments from Bruce Jenner: The interview. Retrieved from http://abcnews.go.com/Entertainment/12-biggest-moments-bruce-jenner-interview/story?id=30572364

Achen, A. C., & Stafford, F. P. (2005). *Data quality of housework hours in the Panel Study of Income Dynamics: Who really does the dishes?* (PSID Technical Series Paper 05-04). Ann Arbor: Institute for Social Research, University of Michigan. Retrieved from http://psidonline.isr.umich.edu/Publications/Papers/tsp/2005-04_Data_Qual_of_Household_Hours-_Dishes.pdf

Acierno, R., Hernandez-Tejada, M., Muzzy, W., & Steve, K. (2009). *Final report: The National Elder Mistreatment Study.* Report submitted to the U.S. Department of Justice, National Institute of Justice. Retrieved from https://www.ncjrs.gov/pdffiles1/nij/grants/226456.pdf

Ackbar, S. (2011). *Constructions and socialization of gender and sexuality in lesbian-/gay-headed families* (Doctoral dissertation, University of Windsor). Retrieved from ProQuest (NR77959).

Adachi, P. J. C., & Willoughby, T. (2011). The effect of video game competition and violence on aggressive behavior: Which characteristic has the greatest influence? *Psychology of Violence, 1,* 259–274.

Administrative Office of the United States Courts. (2011). *Report of statistics required by the Bankruptcy Abuse Prevention and Consumer Protection Act of 2005.* Washington, DC: Government Printing Office. Retrieved from http://www.uscourts.gov/uscourts/Statistics/BankruptcyStatistics/BAPCPA/2010/2010BAPCPA.pdf

Adorno, T. (1975). The culture industry reconsidered. *New German Critique, 6*(Fall), 12–19.

Ahola, A. S., Christianson, S., & Hellstrom, A. (2009). Justice needs a blindfold: Effects of gender and attractiveness on prison sentences and attributions of personal characteristics in a judicial process. *Psychiatry, Psychology, and Law, 16,* S90–S100.

Ahuja, M., Barnes, R., Chow, E., & Rivero, C. (2014, September 4). The changing landscape on same-sex marriage. *Washington Post.* Retrieved from http://www.washingtonpost.com/wp-srv/special/politics/same-sex-marriage

AIDS in China: Blood debts. (2007, January 18). *The Economist.* Retrieved from http://www.economist.com/node/8554778

Albanese, J. S. (1989). *Organized crime in America.* New York: Anderson.

Aldrich, H. E., & Marsden, P. V. (1988). Environments and organizations. In N. J. Smelser (Ed.), *Handbook of sociology* (pp. 361–392). Newbury Park, CA: Sage.

Alexander, J. C., & Thompson, K. (2008). *A contemporary introduction to sociology: Culture and society in transition.* Boulder, CO: Paradigm.

Alexander, M. (2010). *The new Jim Crow: Mass incarceration in the age of colorblindness.* New York: New Press.

Alfano, S. (2009, February 11). Poll: Women's movement worthwhile. CBS News. Retrieved from http://www.cbsnews.com/2100-500160_162-965224.html

Allen, V. L., & Levine, J. M. (1968). Social support, dissent and conformity. *Sociometry, 31,* 138–149.

American Association of University Women. (2016, Spring). *The simple truth about the gender pay gap.* Washington, DC: Author. Retrieved from http://www.aauw.org/research/the-simple-truth-about-the-gender-pay-gap/

American Medical Association. (2013). AMA history timeline 1941–1960. Retrieved from http://www.ama-assn.org/ama/pub/about-ama/our-history/ama-history-timeline.page

Amis, M. (2002). *Koba the dread.* New York: Miramax.

Amnesty International. (2015, March 19). Nigeria: Hundreds of oil spills continue to blight Niger delta. Retrieved from https://www.amnesty.org/en/latest/news/2015/03/hundreds-of-oil-spills-continue-to-blight-niger-delta/

Andersen, M. L., & Collins, P. H. (Eds.). (1992). *Race, class, and gender: An anthology.* Stamford, CT: Wadsworth.

Anderson, B. (1991). *Imagined communities: Reflections on the origin and spread of nationalism.* London: Verso.

Anderson, N. (1940). *Men on the move.* Chicago: University of Chicago Press.

Anderson, T. D. (2000). Sex-role orientation and care-oriented moral reasoning: An online test of Carol Gilligan's theory. *Dissertation Abstracts International, 61,* 1618-A. Retrieved from http://search.proquest.com.proxygw.wrlc.org/socabs/docview/60390650/13C8E238511536831E/1?accountid=11243

Andre, F. E., Boy, R., Bock, H. L., Clemens, J., Datta, S. K., John, T. J., . . . Schmitt, H. J. (2008). Vaccination greatly reduces disease, disability, death and inequity worldwide. *Bulletin of the World Health*

Organization, 86. Retrieved from http://www.who .int/bulletin/volumes/86/2/07-040089/en

Angier, N. (2000, August 22). Do races differ? Not really, genes show. *New York Times.* Retrieved from http:// www.nytimes.com/2000/08/22/science/do-races- differ-not-really-genes-show.html?pagewanted= all&src=pm

Antos, J. (2011). Medicare reform and fiscal reality. *Journal of Policy Analysis and Management, 30,* 934–942.

Anzaldúa, G. (Ed.). (1990). *Making face, making soul: Haciendo caras.* San Francisco: Aunt Lute Foundation.

Appelo, T. (2012). THR poll: 'Glee' and 'Modern Family' drive voters to favor gay marriage—even many Romney voters. *The Hollywood Reporter.* Retrieved from http://www.hollywoodreporter.com/news/ thr-poll-glee-modern-family-386225

Armstrong, L., Phillips, J. G., & Saling, L. L. (2000). Potential determinants of heavier Internet use. *International Journal of Human-Computer Studies, 53,* 537–550.

Asch, S. (1952). *Social psychology.* Englewood Cliffs, NJ: Prentice-Hall.

Aubrey, J. S., & Frisby, C. M. (2011). Sexual objectification in music videos: A content analysis comparing gen- der and genre. *Mass Communication and Society, 14,* 475–501.

Aubrey, J. S., & Harrison, K. (2004). The gender-role con- tent of children's favorite television programs and its links to their gender-related perceptions. *Media Psychology, 6,* 111–146.

Autor, D. (2010, April). *The polarization of job oppor- tunities in the U.S. labor market: Implications for employment and earnings.* Washington, DC: Center for American Progress and the Hamilton Project. Retrieved from http://www.scribd.com/doc/52779456/ The-Polarization-of-Job-Opportunities-in-the-U-S- Labor-Market

Aviel, D. (1997). Issues in education: A closer examina- tion of American education. *Childhood Education, 73,* 130–132.

The Atlantic. (2014). When It Comes to Politics, Do Millennials Care about Anything? Retrieved from https://www.theatlantic.com/sponsored/allstate/ when-it-comes-to-politics-do-millennials-care- about-anything/255/

Babbie, E. R. (1998). *The practice of social research.* Belmont, CA: Wadsworth.

Babcock, P., & Marks, M. (2010, August). Leisure col- lege, USA: The decline in student study time (Research Education Outlook No. 7). Washington, DC: American Enterprise Institute for Public Policy. Retrieved from http://www.aei.org/ files/2010/08/05/07-EduO-Aug-2010-g-new.pdf

Badger, E. (2014, April 15). Pollution is segregated too. Retrieved from https://www.washingtonpost.com/ news/wonk/wp/2014/04/15/pollution-is-substantially- worse-in-minority-neighborhoods-across-the-u-s/

Badger, E. (2016, May 22). This Can't Happen by Accident. *The Washington Post.* Retrieved from https://www .washingtonpost.com/graphics/business/wonk/ housing/atlanta/

Badger, E., & Eilperin J. (2016, March 14). The cruelest thing about buying diapers. Retrieved from https://www .washingtonpost.com/news/wonk/wp/2016/03/14/ the-cruelest-thing-about-buying-diapers/

Bailey, K., West, R., & Anderson, C. A. (2011). The influence of video games on social, cognitive, and affective infor- mation processing. *Handbook of social neuroscience,* 1001–1011.

Baldwin, J. D., & Baldwin, J. I. (1986). *Behavior principles in everyday life.* Englewood Cliffs, NJ: Prentice Hall.

Baldwin, J. D., & Baldwin, J. I. (1988). Factors affecting AIDS-related sexual risk-taking behavior among col- lege students. *Journal of Sex Research, 25,* 181–196.

Ball, S. J., Bowe, R., & Gewirtz, S. (1995). Circuits of schooling: A sociological exploration of parental choice of school in social class contexts. *Sociological Review, 43,* 52–77.

Balmer, Z. (1989). *Mine eyes have seen the glory: A journey into the evangelical subculture in America.* New York: Oxford University Press.

Bandura, A. (1977). *Social learning theory.* Englewood Cliffs, NJ: Prentice Hall.

Bandura, A., & Walters, R. H. (1963). *Social learning and personality development.* New York: Holt, Rinehart & Winston.

Banerjee, B. (2014, June 3). Indian gang rape case highlights lack of toilets. *Associated Press.* Retrieved from http://big story.ap.org/article/ india-gang-rape-case- highlights-lack-toilets

Barber, B. K. (1992). Family, personality, and adolescent problem behaviors. *Journal of Marriage and the Family, 54,* 69–79.

Bare Branches, Redundant Males. (2015, April 18). *The Economist.* Retrieved from http://www.economist .com/news/asia/21648715-distorted-sex-ratios-birth- gen eration-ago-are-changing-marriage-and- dam- aging-societies-asias

Barner, M. (1999). Sex-role stereotyping in FCC- mandated children's educational television. *Journal of Broadcasting & Electronic Media, 43,* 551–564.

Barrett, D. B. (2001). *World Christian encyclopedia.* New York: Oxford University Press.

Barry, K. (1979). *Female sexual slavery.* Englewood Cliffs, NJ: Prentice Hall.

Barthel, M. (2016). "How to Stop Cheating in College." *The Atlantic Monthly,* April 20. Retrieved from https:// www.theatlantic.com/education/archive/2016/04/ how-to-stop-cheating-in-college/479037/

Basham, A. L. (1989). *The origins and development of clas- sical Hinduism.* New York: Oxford University Press.

Basow, S. (2004). The hidden curriculum: Gender in the classroom. In M. Paludi (Ed.), *Praeger guide to the psychology of gender* (pp. 117–132). Westport, CT: Praeger.

Baudrillard, J. (1981). *Simulacra and simulation* (S. F. Glaser, Trans.). Ann Arbor: University of Michigan Press.

Bauman, K., & Ryan, C. (2015, October 7). Women now at the head of the class, lead men in college attainment [Web log post]. Retrieved from http://blogs.census.gov/2015/10/07/women-now-at-the-head-of-the-class-lead-men-in-college-attainment/?cid=RS23

Bauman, Z. (1998). *Globalization: The human consequences.* New York: Columbia University Press.

Bauman, Z. (2001). *Modernity and the Holocaust.* Ithaca, NY: Cornell University Press.

Bazell, R. (2010, October 1). U.S. apologizes for Guatemala STD experiments. NBC News. Retrieved from http://www.msnbc.msn.com/id/39456324/ns/health-sexual_health/t/us-apologizes-guatemala-std-experiments/#.ULbLqe-igkI

BBC. (2012, December 6). Timeline: Ayodhya holy site crisis. Retrieved from http://www.bbc.com/news/world-south-asia-11436552

BBC. (2014a, February 17). Former Barclays employees named in Libor criminal case. Retrieved from http://www.bbc.co.uk/news/business-26228635

BBC. (2015, October 14). PISA tests: Top 40 for maths and reading. Retrieved from http://www.bbc.com/news/business-26249042

Bearak, M. (2016, June 27). Young Brits are angry about older people deciding their future, but most didn't vote. Retrieved from https://www.washingtonpost.com/news/worldviews/wp/2016/06/27/young-brits-are-angry-about-older-people-deciding-their-future-but-most-didnt-vote/

Beauchamp, Z. (2014, June 16). What ISIS has to gain from tweeting these photos of a massacre. Vox Media. Retrieved from http://www.vox.com/2014/6/16/5814900/isis-photos-horrifying-iraq

Beauregard, R. (1986). The chaos and complexity of gentrification. In N. Smith & P. Williams (Eds.), *Gentrification of the City.* London: Unwin Hyman.

Beaver, K. M., Wright, J. P., DeLisi, M., & Vaughn, M. G. (2008). Genetic influences on the stability of low self-control: Results from a longitudinal sample of twins. *Journal of Criminal Justice, 36,* 478–485.

Beck, J. (2016, March 1). The Instagrams of food deserts. Retrieved from http://www.theatlantic.com/health/archive/2016/03/the-instagrams-of-food-deserts/471540/

Bell, D. (1973). *The coming of post-industrial society: A venture in social forecasting.* New York: Basic Books.

Bellah, R. N. (1968). Meaning and modernization. *Religious Studies, 4,* 37–45.

Bellah, R. N. (1975). *The broken covenant: American civil religion in time of trial.* New York: Seabury Press.

Bellstrom, K. (2015, June 29). GM's Mary Barra sets a *Fortune* 500 record for female CEOs. Retrieved from http://fortune.com/2015/06/29/female-ceos-fortune-500-bar ra/? iid=sr-link9

Bennett, J. (2015, August 8). A master's degree in . . . masculinity? Retrieved from http://www.nytimes.com/2015/08/09/fashion/masculinities-studies-stonybrook-michael-kimmel.html

Bergen, T. J., Jr. (1996). The social philosophy of public education. *School Business Affairs, 62,* 22–27.

Berger, J. M. (2015, March 6). The ISIS Twitter census: Making sense of ISIS's use of Twitter. Retrieved from http://www.brookings.edu/blogs/order-from-chaos/posts/2015/03/06-isis-twitter-census- berger

Berger, P. L. (1986). *The capitalist revolutions: Fifty propositions about prosperity, equality, and liberty.* New York: Basic Books.

Berger, P. L., & Hsiao, H.-H. M. (Eds.). (1988). *In search of an East Asian development model.* Piscataway, NJ: Transaction Books.

Berkley, S. (2013, September 12). How cell phones are transforming health care in Africa. *MIT Technology Review,* guest blog. Retrieved from http://www.technology review.com/view/519041/how-cell-phones-are-transforming-health-care-in-africa

Berkowitz, B., Gamio, L., Lu, D., Uhrmacher, K., & Lindeman, T. (2016, July 27). The math of mass shootings. Retrieved from https://www.washingtonpost.com/graphics/national/mass-shootings-in-america/

Bernard, J. (1981). *The female world.* New York: Free Press.

Bernard, J. (1982). *The future of marriage.* New Haven, CT: Yale University Press.

Berns, R. (1989). *Child, family, community: Socialization and support.* New York: Holt, Rinehart & Winston.

Bettelheim, B. (1979). *Surviving, and other essays.* New York: Knopf.

Bettelheim. B. (1982). Difficulties between parents and children: Their causes and how to prevent them. In N. Stinnett et al. (Eds.), *Family strengths 4: Positive support systems* (pp. 5–14). Lincoln: University of Nebraska Press.

Beyer, P. (1994). *Religion and globalization.* London: Sage.

Bhatia, S. (2013, February 3). Women, rape, and lack of toilets. Feminist Wire. Retrieved from http://www.thefeminist wire.com/2013/02/op-ed-women-rape-and-lack-of-toilets

Bilal, M., Zia-ur-Rehman, M., & Raza, I. (2010). Impact of family friendly policies on employees' job satisfaction and turnover intention (A study on work–life balance at workplace). *Interdisciplinary Journal of Contemporary Research in Business, 2,* 378–395.

Bill and Melinda Gates Foundation. (2006). Ensuring the world's poorest children benefit from lifesaving vaccines. Retrieved from http://www.gatesfounda-tion.org/learning/Documents/GAVI.pdf

Bill and Melinda Gates Foundation. (2013). What we do: Vaccine delivery strategy. Retrieved from http://www.gatesfoundation.org/vaccines/Documents/vaccines-fact-sheet.pdf

Bishaw, A. (2014). *Changes in areas with concentrated poverty: 2000 to 2010 (American Community Survey Report 27)*. Washington, DC: U.S. Census Bureau. Retrieved from http://www.census.gov/content/dam/Cen sus/library/publications/2014/acs/acs-27.pdf

Bishop, C. J., Kiss, M., Morrison, T. G., Rushe, D. M., & Specht, J. (2014). The association between gay men's stereotypic beliefs about drag queens and their endorsement of hypermasculinity. *Journal of Homosexuality, 62,* 554–567.

Bishop, K. (2009). Dead man still walking: Explaining the zombie renaissance. *Journal of Popular Film and Television, 33,* 196–205.

Bishop, K. (2010). *American zombie gothic: The rise and fall (and rise) of the walking dead in popular culture.* Jefferson, NC: McFarland.

Bishop, M., & Hicks, S. L. (Eds.). (2009). *Hearing, mother father deaf.* Washington, DC: Gallaudet University Press.

Bissinger, B. (2015, July). Caitlyn Jenner: The full story. Retrieved from http://www.vanityfair.com/hollywood/2015/06/caitlyn-jenner-bruce-cover-annie-leibovitz

Blalock, H. (1967). *Toward a theory of minority group rela-tions.* New York: Wiley.

Blau, P. M. (1964). *Exchange and power in social life.* New York: Wiley.

Blau, P. M. (1977). *Inequality and heterogeneity: A primitive theory of social structure.* New York: Free Press.

Blau, P. M., & Meyer, M. (1987). *Bureaucracy in modern society* (3rd ed.). New York: Random House.

Blinder, A. S. (2006). Offshoring: The next industrial rev-olution? *Foreign Affairs, 85,* 113–128.

Block, A., & Chambliss, W. J. (1981). *Organizing crime.* New York: Elsevier.

Block, A., & Weaver, A. (2004). *All is clouded by desire: Global banking, money laundering, and international organized crime.* Westport, CT: Praeger.

Block, M., Cox, A., & Giratiknon, T. (2015, July 8). Mapping segregation. Retrieved from http://www.nytimes.com/interactive/2015/07/08/us/census-race-map.html

Blumberg, J. (2007, October 23). A brief history of the Salem witch trials. Smithsonian. Retrieved from http://www.smithsonianmag.com/history-archaeology/brief-salem.html

Blumer, H. (1986). *Symbolic interactionism: Perspective and method.* Univ of California Press.

Blumer, H. (1970). *Movies and conduct.* New York: Arno Press.

Bohnert, D., & Ross, W. H. (2010). The influence of social networking Web sites on the evaluation of job candidates. *Cyberpsychology, Behavior, and Social Networking, 13,* 341–347.

Bonacich, E., & Appelbaum, R. P. (2000). *Behind the label: Inequality in the Los Angeles apparel industry.* Berkeley: University of California Press.

Booker, M. K. (2001). *Monsters, mushroom clouds, and the Cold War: American science fiction and the roots of post-modernism, 1946–1964.* Westport, CT: Greenwood.

Bos, H., & Sandfort, T. G. M. (2010). Children's gender identity in lesbian and heterosexual two-parent families. *Sex Roles, 62,* 114–126.

Boser, U., Wilhelm, M., & Hanna R. (2014, October 6). The power of the Pygmalion effect: Teacher expectations strongly predict college outcomes. Retrieved from https://www.americanprogress.org/issues/education/report/2014/10/06/96806/the-power-of-the-pygmalion-effect/

Bourdieu, P. (1977). *Outline of a theory of practice.* New York: Cambridge University Press.

Bourdieu, P. (1984). *Distinction: A social critique of the judgment of taste.* Cambridge, MA: Harvard University Press.

Bourdieu, P., & Coleman, J. S. (1991). *Social theory for a changing society.* Boulder, CO: Westview Press.

Bowles, S., & Gintis, H. (1976). *Schooling in capitalist America: Educational reform and the contradictions of economic life.* New York: Basic Books.

Boyce, M., & Hollingsworth, A. (2015). Sudanese refu-gees in Chad: Passing the baton to no one. Retrieved from http://www.refu geesinternational.org/reports/2015/9/29/sudanese-refugees-in-chad-passing-the-baton-to-no-one

Braga, A. A., & Dusseault, D. (2018). Can homicide detec-tives improve homicide clearance rates? *Crime & Delinquency, 64*(3), 283–315.

Branch, T. (1988). *Parting the waters: America in the King years, 1954–1963.* New York: Simon & Schuster.

Brandon, S. G. (1973). *Ancient empires.* New York: Newsweek Books.

Brandt, A. M. (1983). Racism and research: The case of the Tuskegee syphilis study. In J. W. Leavitt & R. L. Numbers (Eds.), *Sickness and health in America* (pp. 392–404). Madison: University of Wisconsin Press.

Branson, C. E., & Cornell, D. G. (2009). A comparison of self and peer reports in the assessment of middle school bullying. *Journal of Applied School Psychology, 25*(1), pp. 5–27.

Braverman, H. (1988). *Labor and monopoly capital: The degradation of work in the 20th century.* New York: Monthly Review Press. (Original work published 1974)

Bremer, C. (2012, March). Economic commentary (T. Vaughn, managing director). Retrieved from http://www.tom-vaughn.com/Economic-Commentary-March-2012.c3472.htm

Bremer, J., & Rauch, P. K. (1998). Children and computers: Risks and benefits. *Journal of the American Academy of Child and Adolescent Psychiatry, 37*, 559–560.

Brenner, P. S., & DeLamater, J. D. (2014). Social desirability bias in self-reports of physical activity: is an exercise identity the culprit? *Social Indicators Research, 117*(2), pp. 489–504.

Brock, J., & Cocks, T. (2012, March 8). Insight: Nigeria oil corruption highlighted by audits. Reuters. Retrieved from http://www.reuters.com/article/2012/03/08/us-nigeria-corruption-oil-idUSBRE8270GF20120308

Brown, D. (2010, September 16). A mother's education has a huge effect on a child's health. *Washington Post.* Retrieved from http://www.washingtonpost.com/wp-dyn/content/article/2010/09/16/AR2010091 606384.html

Brumberg, J. J. (1997). The body project: An intimate history of American girls. New York: Vintage Books.

Brundage, V. (2017, August). Profile of the labor force by educational attainment. Bureau of Labor Statistics. Retrieved from https://www.bls.gov/spotlight/2017/educational-attainment-of-the-labor-force/home.htm

Budiansky, S., Goode, E. E., & Gest, T. (1994, January 16). The Cold War experiments. *U.S. News & World Report.* Retrieved from http://www.usnews.com/usnews/news/articles/940124/archive_012286.htm

Buechler, S. M. (1990). Women's movements in the United States: Women's suffrage, equal rights, and beyond. New Brunswick, NJ: Rutgers University Press.

Burawoy, M., & Lukács, J. (1992). *The radiant past: Ideology and reality in Hungary's road to capitalism.* Chicago: University of Chicago Press.

Bureau of Labor Statistics. (2017). Unemployment rates and earnings by educational attainment. *Employment projections.* Washington, DC: U.S. Government Printing Office. Retrieved from https://www.bls.gov/emp/chart-unemployment-earnings-education.htm

Burgess, E. W. (1925). The growth of the city. In R. E. Park, E. W. Burgess, & R. McKenzie (Eds.), *The city.* Chicago: University of Chicago Press.

Burgess, R. L., & Akers, R. L. (1966). A differential association-reinforcement theory of criminal behavior. *Social problems, 14*(2), 128–147.

Burns, J. M. (1978). *Leadership.* New York: Harper & Row.

Cabeza, M. F., Johnson, J. B., & Tyner, L. J. (2011). Glass ceiling and maternity leave as important contributors to the gender wage gap. *Southern Journal of Business and Ethics, 3*, 73–85.

Calderón-Garcidueñas, L., & Torres-Jardón, R. (2012). Air pollution, socioeconomic status and children's cognition in megacities: The Mexico City scenario. *Frontiers in Developmental Psychology, 3.* Retrieved from http://www.frontiersin.org/Developmental_Psychology/10.3389/fpsyg.2012.00217/full

Camarota, S. (2005). *Birth rates among immigrants in America: Comparing fertility in the U.S. and home countries.* Washington, DC: Center for Immigration Studies. Retrieved from http://www.cis.org/articles/2005/back1105.pdf

Camera, L. (2015, November 6). Native American students left behind. *U.S. News & World Report.* Retrieved from http://www.usnews.com/news/articles/2015/11/06/native-american-students-left-behind

Campbell, A., & Muncer, S. (Eds.). (1998). *The social child.* East Sussex, England: Psychology Press.

CareerBuilder. (2015). Employers reveal biggest resume blunders in annual CareerBuilder survey. Retrieved from http://www.careerbuilder.com/share/aboutus/pressre leasesdetail.aspx? sd=8/13/2015&id=pr909&ed=12/31/2015

Carson, E. & Golinelli, D. (2014, September). Prisoners in 2012. Washington, DC: Bureau of Justice Statistics. Retrieved from https://www.bjs.gov/content/pub/pdf/p12tar9112.pdf

Carson, E. A. (2015). *Prisoners in 2014.* Washington, DC: U.S. Department of Justice, Bureau of Justice Statistics. Retrieved from http://www.bjs.gov/content/pub/pdf/p14.pdf

Carson, E. A., & Anderson, E. (2016, December). Prisoners in 2015. Washington, DC: Bureau of Justice Statistics. Retrieved from https://www.bjs.gov/content/pub/pdf/p15.pdf

Cassidy, C. (2016, June 5). *Patchy reporting undercuts national hate crimes count.* Associated Press. Retrieved from http://bigstory.ap.org/article/8247a1d2f76b4baea2a121186dedf768/ap-patchy-reporting-undercuts-national-hate-crimes-count

Cassidy, L., & Hurrell, R. M. (1995). The influence of victim's attire on adolescents' judgments of date rape. *Adolescence, 30*(118), 319.

Castells, M., & Portes, A. (1989). World underneath: The origins, dynamics, and effects of the informal economy. In A. Portes, M. Castells, & L. A. Benton (Eds.), *The informal economy: Studies in advanced and less developed countries* (pp. 11–37). Baltimore: Johns Hopkins University Press.

Cavalli-Sforza, L. L., Menozzi, P., & Piazza, A. (1994). *The history and geography of human genes.* Princeton, NJ: Princeton University Press.

Cawley, J. (2001). The impact of obesity on wages. *Journal of Human Resources, 39*, 451–474.

Center for Responsive Politics. (2016). Tobacco industry profile: Summary, 2016. Retrieved from https://www.opensecrets.org/lobby/indusclient.php? id=A02

Centers for Disease Control and Prevention. (2014). HIV surveillance report: Diagnoses of HIV infection in the

United States and dependent areas, 2014. Retrieved from http://www.cdc.gov/hiv/pdf/library/reports/surveillance/cdc-hiv-surveillance-report- us.pdf

Centers for Disease Control and Prevention. (2015). Adult obesity facts. Retrieved https://www.cdc.gov/obesity/data/adult.html

Centers for Disease Control and Prevention. (2017a). Marriage and Divorce. Retrieved from https://www.cdc.gov/nchs/fastats/marriage-divorce.htm

Centers for Disease Control and Prevention. (2017b). Tobacco Use: Extinguishing the Epidemic. Retrieved from https://www.cdc.gov/chronicdisease/resources/publications/aag/pdf/2017/tobacco-aag-H.pdf

Centers for Disease Control and Prevention. (2017c). Adult Obesity Prevalence Maps. Retrieved from https://www.cdc.gov/obesity/data/prevalence-maps.html

Centers for Disease Control and Prevention. (2018a). National Intimate Partner and Sexual Violence Survey. Retrieved from https://www.cdc.gov/violenceprevention/nisvs/index.html

Centers for Disease Control and Prevention. (2018b). Malaria's Impact Worldwide. Retrieved from https://www.cdc.gov/malaria/malaria_worldwide/impact.html

Chafetz, J. S. (1997). Feminist theory and sociology: Underutilized contributions for mainstream theory. *Annual Review of Sociology, 23,* 97–120.

Chaffey, D. (2015, April 27). Social network popularity by country. Retrieved from http://www.smartinsights.com/social-media-marketing/social-media-strategy/new-global-social-media-research/attachment/2015-social-network-popularity-by-country/

Chaffey, D. (2016). Global social media research summary 2016. Retrieved from http://www.smartinsights.com/social-media-marketing/social-media-strategy/new-global-social-media-research/

Chambliss, W. J. (1973). The Saints and the Roughnecks. *Society 11,* 24–31.

Chambliss, W. J. (1988a). *Exploring criminology.* New York: Macmillan.

Chambliss, W. J. (1988b). *On the take: From petty crooks to presidents.* Bloomington: Indiana University Press.

Chambliss, W. J. (2001). *Power, politics, and crime.* Boulder, CO: Westview Press.

Chambliss, W. J., & Hass, A. (2011). *Criminology: Connecting theory, research, and practice.* New York: McGraw-Hill.

Chambliss, W. J., & King, H. (1984). *Boxman: A professional thief's journey.* New York: Macmillan.

Chambliss, W. J., & Seidman, R. B. (1982). *Law, order, and power.* Reading, MA: Addison-Wesley.

Chambliss, W. J., & Zatz, M. S. (1994). *Making law: The state, the law, and structural contradictions.* Bloomington: Indiana University Press.

Chambliss, W. J., Michalowski, R., & Kramer, R. C. (Eds.). (2010). *State crime in the global age.* London: Willan.

Chandler, A. (2014, June 15). Should Twitter have suspended the violent ISIS Twitter account? The Wire. Retrieved from http://www.thewire.com/global/2014/06/should-twitter-have-suspended-the-violent-isis-twitter-account/372805

Charity Navigator. (2016). Islamic Relief USA. Retrieved from http://www.charitynavigator.org/index.cfm?bay=search.summary&orgid=3908#.Vryv7jbYXEw

Chaves, M. (1993). Denominations as dual structures: An organizational analysis. *Sociology of Religion, 54,* 147–169.

Chaves, M. (1994). Secularization as declining religious authority. *Social Forces, 72,* 749–774.

Chen, H. S. (1992). *Chinatown no more: Taiwan immigrants in contemporary New York.* Ithaca, NY: Cornell University Press.

Chen, L. (2015, August 15). The most valuable employees: Snapchat doubles Facebook. Retrieved from http://www.forbes.com/sites/liyanchen/2015/08/11/the-most-valuable-employees-snapchat-doubles-facebook/#1ba06be3f754

Chia, R. C., Allred, L. J., Grossnickle, W. F., & Lee, G. W. (1998). Effects of attractiveness and gender on the perception of achievement-related variables. *Journal of Social Psychology, 138,* 471–477.

Chiang, S. (2009). Personal power and positional power in a power-full "I": A discourse analysis of doctoral dissertation supervision. *Discourse and Communication, 3,* 255–271.

Childhelp. (2010). National child abuse statistics: Child abuse in America. Retrieved from http://www.childhelp.org/pages/statistics#gen-stats

ChildTrends. (2018). Late or No Prenatal Care. Retrieved from https://www.childtrends.org/indicators/late-or-no-prenatal-care

ChildStats. (2013). America's children: Key national indicators of well-being, 2013. Retrieved from http://www.childstats.gov/americaschildren/famsoc3.asp

Chodorow, N. (1999). *The reproduction of mothering: Psychoanalysis and the sociology of gender.* Berkeley: University of California Press.

Chong, D. (1991). *Collective action and the civil rights movement.* Chicago: University of Chicago Press.

Christiansen, K. O. (1977). Preliminary study of criminality among twins. In S. A. Mednick & K. O. Christiansen (Eds.), *Biosocial bases of criminal behavior.* New York: Gardner Press.

Christie, L. (2014, June 5). America's homes are bigger than ever. Retrieved from http://money.cnn.com/2014/06/04/real_estate/american-home-size/index.html

Cicero, T. J., Ellis, M. S., Surratt, H. L., & Kurtz, S. P. (2014). The changing face of heroin use in the United States. *JAMA Psychiatry, 71,* 821–826. doi:10.1001/jamapsychiatry.2014.366

Cichowski, L., & Nance, W. E. (2004). More marriages among the deaf may have led to doubling of common form of genetic deafness in the U.S. Virginia Commonwealth University News Center. Retrieved from http://www.news.vcu.edu/news/More_mar riages_among_the_deaf_may_have_led_to_dou bling_of_common

Clarion Project. (2014, September 10). The Islamic State's magazine. Retrieved from http://www.clarionproject.org/news/islamic-state-isis-isil-propaganda-maga zine-dabiq

Cline, E. L. (2013). *Overdressed: The shockingly high cost of cheap fashion.* New York, NY: Portfolio.

Cloward, R. A., & Ohlin, L. E. (1960). *Delinquency and opportunity: A theory of delinquent gangs.* Glencoe, IL: Free Press.

CNN. (2016, May 5). Flint water crisis fast facts. Retrieved from http://www.cnn.com/2016/03/04/us/flint-water-crisis-fast-facts/

Cobb, J. (2016). Americans buy their four-millionth hybrid car. Retrieved from http://www.hybridcars.com/americans-buy-their-four-millionth-hybrid-car/

Cockerham, W. C., & Glasser, M. (2000). *Readings in medical sociology* (2nd ed.). Englewood Cliffs, NJ: Prentice Hall.

Cohen, A. (2012, March 16). How voter ID laws are being used to disenfranchise minorities and the poor. *Atlantic.* Retrieved from http://www.theatlantic.com/politics/archive/2012/03/how-voter-id-laws-are-being-used-to-disenfranchise-minorities-and-the-poor/254572

Cohen, A. (2015, August 12). When heroin hits the white suburbs. The Marshall Project. Retrieved from https://www.themarshallproject.org/2015/08/12/when-heroin-hits-the-white-suburbs#.wdS3vHv63

Cohen, A. K. (1955). *Delinquent boys: The culture of the gang.* Glencoe, IL: Free Press.

Cohen, D. A. (2014). *A big fat crisis: The hidden forces behind the obesity crisis—and how we can end it.* New York: Nation Books.

Cohn, D., Livingston, G., & Wang, W. (2014). *After decades of decline, a rise in stay-at-home mothers.* Washington, DC: Pew Research Center. Retrieved from http://www.pewsocialtrends.org/2014/04/08/after-decades-of-decline-a-rise-in-stay-at-home-mothers

Coleman, J. M., & Hong, Y.-Y. (2008). Beyond nature and nurture: The influence of lay gender theories on self-stereotyping. *Self and Identity, 7,* 34–53.

Coleman, J. S. (1990). *The foundations of social theory.* Cambridge, MA: Harvard University Press.

Coleman, J. S., Hoffer, T., & Kilgore, S. (1982). *High school achievement: Public, Catholic, and private schools compared.* New York: Basic Books.

Colen, C. G., Geronimus, A. T., Bound, J., & James, S. A. (2006). Maternal upward socioeconomic mobility and Black–White disparities in infant birthweight. *American Journal of Public Health, 96,* 2032–2039.

Collins, P. H. (1990). *Black feminist thought: Knowledge, consciousness and the politics of empowerment.* New York: Routledge.

Collins, R. (1979). *The credential society: An historical sociology of education and stratification.* New York: Academic Press.

Collins, R. (1980). Weber's last theory of capitalism: A systematization. *American Sociological Review, 45,* 925–942.

Coltrane, S., & Ishii-Kuntz, M. (1992). Remarriage, step-parenting, and household labor. *Journal of Family Issues, 13,* 215–233.

Common Sense Media. (2015). The Common Sense Census: Media Use by Tweens and Teens. Retrieved from https://www.commonsensemedia.org/research/the-common-sense-census-media-use-by-tweens-and-teens

Commission to Build a Healthier America. (2009, April). *Race and socioeconomic factors affect opportunities for better health* (Issue brief 5). Princeton, NJ: Robert Wood Johnson Foundation. Retrieved from http://www.commissiononhealth.org/PDF/506edea1-f160-4728-9539-aba23 57047e3/Issue%20Brief%205%20April%2009%20-%20Race%20and%20Socioeco nomic%20Factors.pdf

Complete College America. (2011, September). Time Is The Enemy. Retrieved from https://www.luminafoundation.org/files/resources/time-is-the-enemy.pdf

Conaway, Cameron. (2015a, June 18). *Rejuvenating the Ganges: Bridging the gap between religion and conservation.* Washington, DC: Pulitzer Center on Crisis Reporting. Accessed at http://pulitzercenter.org/reporting/india-asia-ganges-river-environment-conservation-religion

Conaway, Cameron. (2015b, September 23). The Ganges is dying under the weight of modern India. Retrieved from http://www.newsweek.com/2015/10/02/gan ges-river-dying-under-weight-modern-india-375347.html

Condron, D. J. (2009). Social class, school and non-school environments, and Black/White inequalities in children's learning. *American Sociological Review, 74,* 685–708.

Condry, J. C. (1989). *The psychology of television.* Hillsdale, NJ: Erlbaum.

Conley, D. (1999). *Being Black, living in the red: Race, wealth, and social policy in America.* Berkeley: University of California Press.

Conlin, J. (2010, August 6). For American students, life lessons in the Mideast. *New York Times.* Retrieved from http://www.nytimes.com/2010/08/08/fash ion/08Abroad.html?pagewanted=all

Connell, R. W. (2005). Change among the gatekeepers: Men, masculinities, and gender equality in the global arena. *Signs, 30,* 1801–1826.

Connell, R. W., & Messerschmidt, J. W. (2005). Hegemonic masculinity: Rethinking the concept. *Gender & Society, 19,* 829–859.

Consumer Financial Protection Bureau. (2015). CFPB orders Citibank to pay $700 million in consumer relief for illegal credit card practices. Retrieved from http://www.consumerfinance.gov/about-us/newsroom/cfpb-orders-citibank-to-pay-700-million-in-consumer-relief-for-illegal-credit-card-practices/

Coogan, T. P. (2002). *Michael Collins: The man who made Ireland.* New York: Palgrave Macmillan.

Cooley, C. H. (1909). *Social organization: A study of the larger mind.* New York: Charles Scribner's Sons.

Cooley, C. H. (1964). *Human nature and the social order.* New York: Schocken Books. (Original work published 1902)

Coontz, S. (2000). Historical perspectives on family studies. *Journal of Marriage and the Family, 62,* 283–297.

Coontz, S. (2005). *Marriage, a history: From obedience to intimacy, or how love conquered marriage.* New York: Penguin Books.

Cooper, B., Cox, D., Liensch, R., & Jones, R. P. (2016). Exodus: Why Americans Are Leaving Religion—And Are Unlikely to Come Back. *PRRI.* Retrieved from https://www.prri.org/research/prri-rns-poll-nones-atheist-leaving-religion/

Coutts, S., & LaFleur J. (2011). Some states still leave low-income students behind; others make surprising gains. Retrieved from https://www.propublica.org/article/opportunity-gap-schools-data

Critser, G. (2003). *Fatland: How Americans became the fattest people in the world.* New York: Houghton Mifflin.

Crocker, W. H. (1986). Canela body painting. *Review: Latin American Literature and Arts, 36,* 24–26.

Crocker, W. H. (1990). The Canela (Eastern Timbira), I: An ethnographic introduction. *Smithsonian Contributions to Anthropology, 33.* Washington, DC: Smithsonian Institution Press.

Crocker, W. H. (1994). The Canela: Bonding through kinship, ritual, and sex (Case studies in cultural anthropology). Fort Worth, TX: Harcourt Brace College.

Culhane, D. (2010, July 11). Five myths about America's homeless. *The Washington Post.* Retrieved from http://www.washingtonpost.com/wp-dyn/content/article/2010/07/09/AR2010070902357.html

Curtiss, S. (1977). *Genie: A psycholinguistic study of a modern-day "wild child."* Boston: Academic Press.

Cutright, P., & Fernquist, R. M. (2000). Effects of societal integration, period, region, and culture of suicide on male age-specific suicide rates: Twenty developed countries, 1955–1989. *Social Science Research, 29,* 148–172.

Dahl, R. A. (1961). *Who governs?* New Haven, CT: Yale University Press.

Dahl, R. A. (1982). *Dilemmas of a pluralist democracy: Autonomy vs. control.* New Haven, CT: Yale University Press.

Dahl, R. A. (1989). *Democracy and its critics.* New Haven, CT: Yale University Press.

Davis, A. (2008, September). Interpersonal and physical dating violence among teens. *Focus: Views From the National Council on Crime and Delinquency.* Retrieved from http://nccdglobal.org/sites/default/files/publication_pdf/focus-dating-violence.pdf

Davis, A., Kimball, W., & Gould, E. (2015, May 27). The class of 2015. Retrieved from http://www.epi.org/publication/the-class-of-2015/

Davis, K., & Moore, W. (1945). Some principles of stratification. *American Sociological Review,* 10, 242–249.

Davis, S. N., Greenstein, T. N., & Marks, J. P. (2007). Effects of union type on division of household labor: Do cohabiting men really perform more housework? *Journal of Family Issues, 28,* 1246–1272.

Davis, W. (1991). *Fundamentalism in Japan: Religious and political.* Chicago: University of Chicago Press.

de Vise, D. (2012, May 21). Is college too easy? As study time falls, debate rises. Washington Post. Retrieved from http://www.washingtonpost.com/local/education/is-college-too-easy-as-study-time-falls-debate-rises/2012/05/21/gIQAp7uUgU_story.html

Death Penalty Information Center. (n.d.). Execution of Juveniles in the U.S. and Other Countries. Retrieved from https://deathpenaltyinfo.org/execution-juveniles-us-and-other-countries

Death Penalty Information Center. (2016). States with and without the death penalty. Retrieved from https://deathpenaltyinfo.org/states-and-without-death-penalty

Death Penalty Information Center. (2018) Facts about the Death Penalty. Retrieved from https://deathpenalty-info.org/documents/FactSheet.pdf

DeBeaumont, R. (2009). Occupational differences in the wage penalty for obese women. *Journal of Socio-Economics, 38,* 344–349.

DeChoudhury, M., Sharma, S., & Kiciman, E. (2016, February). Characterizing dietary choices, nutrition, and language in food deserts via social media. Paper presented at Computer-Supported Cooperative Work and Social Computing 2016, San Francisco, California. doi: http://dx.doi.org/10.1145/2818048.2819956

DellaPergola, S. (2010). *World Jewish population 2010* (Current Jewish Population Reports 2). New York: Berman Jewish DataBank. Retrieved from http://www.jewishdatabank.org/Reports/World_Jewish_Population_2010.pdf

Delli Carpini, M. X., & Keeter, S. (1996). *What Americans know about politics and why it matters.* New Haven, CT: Yale University Press.

DeNavas-Walt, C., & Proctor, B. D. (2014). Income and poverty in the United States: 2013 (Current Population Reports P60-249). Washington, DC: U.S.

Census Bureau. Retrieved from http://www.census .gov/con tent/dam/Census/library/publications/2014/ demo/p60-249.pdf

Denizet-Lewis, B. (2003, August 3). Double lives on the down low. *New York Times Magazine.* Retrieved from http://www.nytimes.com/2003/08/03/ magazine/double-lives-on-the-down-low.html?page wanted=all&src=pm

Denno, B. W. (1990). *Biology and violence from birth to adulthood.* Cambridge: Cambridge University Press.

DePillis, L. (2015). Minimum-wage offensive could speed arrival of robot-powered restaurants. Retrieved from https://www.washingtonpost.com/business/ capitalbusi ness/minimum-wage-offensive-could-spe ed-arrival-of-robot-powered-restaurants/2015/08/16/ 35f284ea-3f6f-11e5-8d45- d815146f81fa_story.html? wprss=rss_homepage

DeSantis, A., & Kayson, W. A. (1997). Defendants' characteristics of attractiveness, race, sex and sentencing decisions. *Psychological Reports, 81,* 679–683.

Desmond, M. (2015, March). *Unaffordable America: Poverty, housing, and eviction.* Fast Forward, No. 22. Madison: University of Wisconsin, Institute for Research on Poverty. Retrieved from http://www.irp .wisc.edu/publications/fastfocus/pdfs/FF22-2015.pdf

Desmond, M. (2016a). *Evicted: Poverty and profit in the American city.* New York, NY: Crown.

Desmond, M. (2016b, June 9). *Evicted: Housing, poverty, and policy.* Presentation at Georgetown Law School, Washington, DC.

DeWitt, A. L., Cready, C. M., & Seward, R. R. (2013). Parental role portrayal in twentieth century children's picture books: More egalitarian or ongoing stereotyping? *Sex Roles, 69,* 89–106.

Diaz, J. D. (1999). *Suicide in the Las Vegas homeless population: Applying Durkheim's theory of suicide* (Doctoral dissertation, University of Nevada, Las Vegas).

Dicken, P. (1998). *The global shift: Transforming the world economy* (3rd ed.). New York: Guilford Press.

Dilmac, B. (2009). Psychological needs as a predictor of cyberbullying: A preliminary report on college students. *Educational Sciences: Theory and Practice, 9,* 1308–1325.

DiMaggio, P. J., & Powell, W. (1983). The iron cage revisited: Institutional isomorphism and collective rationality in organizational fields. *American Sociological Review, 48,* 147–160.

Dion, K., Berscheid, E., & Walster, E. (1972). What is beautiful is good. *Journal of Personality and Social Psychology, 24,* 285–290.

Dionne, E. J., Jr., & Green, J. C. (2008). *Religion and American politics: More secular, more evangelical . . . or both?* Washington, DC: Brookings Institution. Retrieved from http://www.brookings.edu/~/media/ res earch/files/papers/2008/2/religion%20gre en%20 dionne/02_religion_green_dionne.pdf

Dishion, T. J., McCord, J., & Poulin, F. (1999). When interventions harm: Peer groups and problem behavior. *American Psychologist, 54,* 755–764.

Djilas, M. (1957). *The new class: An analysis of the communist system.* New York: Harvest Books.

Doey, L., Coplan, R. J., & Kingsbury, M. (2013). Bashful boys and coy girls: A review of gender differences in childhood shyness. *Sex Roles, 70,* 255–266.

Dokoupil, T. (2012a, July 9). Is the Web driving us mad? *Newsweek.* Retrieved from http://www.thedailybeast .com/newsweek/2012/07/08/is-the-internet-making-us-crazy-what-the-new-research-says.html

Dokoupil, T. (2012b, July 16). Tweets, texts, email, posts: Is the onslaught making us crazy? *Newsweek,* pp. 24–30.

Dollard, J. (1957). *Caste and class in a Southern town* (3rd ed.). New York: Anchor Books.

Dolnick, E. (1993, September). Deafness as culture. *Atlantic Monthly,* pp. 37–53.

Domhoff, G. W. (1983). *Who rules America now?* New York: Simon and Schuster.

Domhoff, G. W. (1990). *The power elite and the state: How policy is made in America.* New York: Aldine de Gruyter.

Domhoff, G. W. (2002). *Who rules America? Power and politics* (4th ed.). New York: McGraw-Hill.

Domhoff, G. W. (2006). *Who rules America? Power, politics, and social change* (5th ed.). New York: McGraw-Hill.

Domhoff, G. W. (2009). *Who rules America? Challenges to corporate and class dominance* (6th ed.). New York: McGraw-Hill.

Dominus, S. (2017, May 11). Is An Open Marriage A Happier Marriage? *New York Times Magazine.* Retrieved from https://www.nytimes .com/2017/05/11/magazine/is-an-open-marriage-a-happier-marriage.html

Douglas, D. (2013, March 6). Attorney general says big banks' size may inhibit prosecution. *Washington Post,* p. A12.

Drake, B. (2014, January 7). *Number of older Americans in the workforce is on the rise.* Washington, DC: Pew Research Center. Retrieved from http://www.pew research.org/fact-tank/2014/01/07/number-of-older-americans-in-the-workforce-is-on-the- rise/

Dreifus, C. (2012, May 14). A mathematical challenge to obesity. *New York Times.* Retrieved from http:// www.nytimes.com/2012/05/15/science/a-mathematical-chal lenge-to-obesity.html

Drew, J. (2015, April 6). A list of tribal laws prohibiting gay marriage. Retrieved from https://www.yahoo .com/news/list-tribal-laws-prohibiting-gay-marriage-162248831.html? ref=gs

Du Bois, W. E. B. (2008). *The souls of Black folk.* Rockville, MD: Arc Manor. (Original work published 1903)

Duggan, M. (2015, December 15). Who plays video games and identifies as a "gamer." *Internet &*

Technology. Pew Research Center. Retrieved from http://www.pewinternet.org/2015/12/15/who-plays-video-games-and-identifies-as-a-gamer/

Duggan, M., Ellison, N. B., Lampe, C., Lenhart, A., & Madden, M. (2015, January 9). *Social media update 2014.* Washington, DC: Pew Research Center. Retrieved from http://www.pewinternet.org/2015/01/09/social-media-update-2014/

Duhigg, C., & Barboza, D. (2012, January 25). In China, human costs are built into an iPad. *New York Times.* Retrieved from http://www.nytimes.com/2012/01/26/business/ieconomy-apples-ipad-and-the-human-costs-for-workers-in-china.html?_r=2&pagewanted=print

Duneier, M. (1992). *Slim's table: Race, respectability, and masculinity.* Chicago: University of Chicago Press.

Dunner, D. L., Gershon, E. S., & Barrett, J. S. (1988). *Relatives at risk for mental disorder.* New York: Ravens Press.

Durkheim, É. (1951). *Suicide.* New York: Free Press. (Original work published 1897)

Durkheim, É. (1956). *Education and sociology* (S. L. Fox, Trans.). New York: Free Press. (Original work published 1922)

Durkheim, É. (1973a). *Émile Durkheim on morality and society.* Chicago: University of Chicago Press. (Original work published 1922)

Durkheim, É. (1973b). *Moral education: A study in the theory and application of the sociology of education.* New York: Free Press. (Original work published 1922)

Durkheim, É. (1997). *The division of labor in society.* New York: Free Press. (Original work published 1893)

Durkheim, É. (2008). *The elementary forms of the religious life.* New York: Dover. (Original work published 1912)

Dworkin, A. (1981). *Pornography: Men possessing women.* New York: Pedigree.

Dworkin, A. (1987). *Intercourse.* New York: Free Press.

Dworkin, A. (1989). *Letters from the war zone: Writings, 1976–1987.* New York: Dutton.

Dwoskin, E. (2012, March 28). Will you marry me (after I pay off my student loans)? *Bloomberg Businessweek.* Retrieved from http://www.businessweek.com/articles/2012-03-28/will-you-marry-me-after-i-pay-off-my-student-loans

Eccles, J. S., & Barber, B. L. (1999). Student council, volunteering, basketball, or marching band: What kind of extracurricular involvement matters? *Journal of Adolescent Research, 14,* 10–43.

Eddy, M. B. (1999). *Christian science: No and yes.* Boston: Author. (Original work published 1887)

Edin, K., & Kefalas, M. (2005). *Promises I can keep: Why poor women put motherhood before marriage.* Berkeley: University of California Press.

Edwards, J. (2012, October 7). This video of Haitians reading "#FirstWorldProblems" from Twitter is making people really angry. *BusinessInsider.* Retrieved from http://www.businessinsider.com/anger-over-haitians-reading-firstworldproblems-from-twitter-2012-10#ixzz33sB1IhdT

Edwards, K. E. (2007). *"Putting my man face on": A grounded theory of college men's gender identity development* (Doctoral dissertation, University of Maryland-College Park). Retrieved from ProQuest (3260431).

Effinger, A., & Burton, K. (2014, April 9). Trailer parks lure Wall Street investors looking for double-wide returns. Bloomberg. Retrieved from http://www.bloomberg.com/news/2014-04-10/trailer-parks-lure-investors-pursuing-double-wide-returns.html

Eglitis, D. S. (2010). The uses of global poverty: How economic inequality benefits the West. In J. J. Macionis & N. V. Benokraitis (Eds.), *Seeing ourselves: Classic, contemporary, and cross-cultural readings in sociology* (8th ed., pp. 199–206). New York: Pearson.

Ehrenreich, B. (2001). *Nickel and dimed: On (not) getting by in America.* New York: Metropolitan Books.

Ehrenreich, B., & Hochschild, A. R. (2002). Introduction. In B. Ehrenreich & A. R. Hochschild (Eds.), *Global woman: Nannies, maids, and sex workers in the new economy* (pp. 1–14). New York: Metropolitan Books.

Eichler, A. (2012, May 30). *Unpaid overtime: Wage and hour lawsuits have skyrocketed in the last decade.* Huffington Post. Retrieved from http://www.huffingtonpost.com/2012/05/30/wage-hour-lawsuits_n_1556484.html

Eisenbrey, R. (2012, March 2). Pushing back against illegal unpaid internships. Economic Policy Institute Blog. Retrieved from http://www.epi.org/blog/pushing-back-illegal-unpaid-internships

Eligon, J. A. (2016, January 21). Question of environmental racism in Flint. Retrieved from http://www.nytimes.com/2016/01/22/us/a-question-of-environmental-racism-in-flint.html

Eliot, L. (2009). *Pink brain, blue brain: How small differences grow into troublesome gaps—and what we can do about it.* New York: Houghton Mifflin Harcourt.

Eller, C. (2000). *The myth of matriarchal prehistory: Why an inventive past won't give women a future.* Boston: Beacon Press.

Emerson, R. M. (1962). Power-dependence relations. *American Sociological Review, 27,* 31–41.

Emmanuel, A. (1972). *Unequal exchange: A study of the imperialism of trade.* New York: Monthly Review Press.

Environmental Protection Agency. (2011). *Electronics waste management in the United States through 2009.* Washington, DC: Author.

Epstein, D. M. (1993). *Sister Aimee: The life of Aimee Semple McPherson.* New York: Harcourt Brace Jovanovich.

Erber, G., & Sayed-Ahmed, A. (2005). Offshore outsourcing: A global shift in the present IT industry. *Intereconomics, 40,* 100–112.

Erikson, E. H. (1950). *Childhood and society.* New York: Norton.

Etter, G. (1998). Common characteristics of gangs: Examining the cultures of the new urban tribes. *Journal of Gang Research, 5*, 19–33.

Etzioni, A. (1975). *A comparative analysis of complex organizations: On power, involvement, and their correlates.* New York: Free Press.

Evans, M. D. R., Kelley, J., Sikora, J., & Treiman, D. J. (2010). Family scholarly culture and educational success: Books and schooling in 27 nations. *Research in Social Stratification and Mobility, 28*, 171–197.

FACE Intel (Former and Current Employees of Intel). (2000). Related class action lawsuits: A huge victory for the worker. Retrieved from http://www.faceintel .com/relatedclass actions.htm

Fainaru-Wada, M., & Fainaru, S. (2014). *League of denial: The NFL, concussions, and the battle for truth.* New York: Three Rivers Press.

Faiola, A. (2015, April 21). A global surge of refugees leaves Europe struggling to cope. *Washington Post.* Retrieved from https://www.washingtonpost.com/ world/europe/new-migration-crisis-overwhelms- european-refugee-system/2015/04/21/3ab83470- e45c-11e4-ae0f-f8c46aa8c3a4_story.html

Faiths unite for day of dignity to help homeless. (2015, October 18). Retrieved from http://news3lv.com/archive/ faiths-unite-for-day-of-dignity-to-help-homeless

Faludi, S. (1991). *Backlash: The undeclared war against American women.* New York: Crown.

Farkas, G., Grobe, R. P., Sheehan, D., & Shuan, Y. (1990). Cultural resources and school success: Gender, ethnicity, and poverty groups within an urban school district. *American Sociological Review, 55,* 127–142.

Farkas, G., Sheehan, D., & Grobe, R. P. (1990). Coursework mastery and school success: Gender, ethnicity, and poverty groups within an urban school district. *American Educational Research Journal, 27,* 807–827.

Federal Bureau of Investigation. (2017a). Violent crime. In *Crime in the United States 2017* (Uniform Crime Reports). Washington, DC: Author. Retrieved from https://ucr.fbi.gov/crime-in-the-u.s/2017/ crime-in-the-u.s.-2017/topic-pages/violent-crime

Federal Bureau of Investigation. (2017b). Property crime. In *Crime in the United States 2017* (Uniform Crime Reports). Washington, DC: Author. Retrieved from https://ucr.fbi.gov/crime-in-the-u.s/2017/ crime-in-the-u.s.-2017/topic-pages/property-crime

Federal Reserve Bank of New York. (2018, July). The Labor Market for Recent College Graduates. Retrieved from https://www.newyorkfed.org/research/college-la- bor-market/college-labor-market_underemploy- ment_rates.html

Federal Reserve System & Brookings Institution. (2008). *The enduring challenge of concentrated poverty in America: Case studies from communities across the U.S.* Washington, DC: Authors. Retrieved from http://www.frbsf.org/community-develop ment/files/ cp_fullreport.pdf

Fenstermaker Berk, S. (1985). *The gender factory: The apportionment of work in American households.* New York: Plenum Press.

Fenstermaker, S., & West, C. (2002). *Doing gender, doing difference: Inequality, power, and institutional change.* New York: Routledge.

Financial Crimes Enforcement Network. (2014). JPMorgan admits violation of the Bank Secrecy Act (press release). Retrieved from http://www.fincen .gov/news_room/nr/pdf/20140107.pdf

Finckenauer, J. O., & Waring, E. (1996). Russian emigre crime in the U.S.: Organized crime or crime that is organized? *Transnational Organized Crime, 2,* 139–155.

Fine, L. (2012). Sexual identity and postsecondary education: Outcomes, institutional factors, and narratives (Electronic thesis or dissertation). Ohio State University, Ohio.

Fingarette, H. (1972). *Confucius: The secular as sacred.* Long Grove, IL: Waveland Press.

Finke, R., & Stark, R. (1988). Religious economies and sacred canopies: Religious mobilization in American cities, 1906. *American Sociological Review, 53,* 41–49.

Finke, R., & Stark, R. (1992). *The churching of America, 1776–1980: Winners and losers in our religious economy.* New Brunswick, NY: Rutgers University Press.

Finke, R., & Stark, R. (2005). *The churching of America, 1776–2005: Winners and losers in our religious economy.* New Brunswick, NY: Rutgers University Press.

Firestone, S. (1971). *The dialectic of sex.* London: Paladin.

Fischer, C. (1982). *To dwell among friends: Personal networks in town and city.* Chicago: University of Chicago Press.

Fischer, C. (1984). *The urban experience* (2nd ed.). New York: Harcourt Brace Jovanovich.

Fitzgerald, A. (2011, July 28). A stealth way a bill becomes a law. *Bloomberg Businessweek.* Retrieved from http:// www.business week.com/magazine/a-stealth-way-a- bill-becomes-a-law- 07282011.html

Food and Agriculture Organization of the United Nations. (2009). *How to feed the world in 2050.* Rome: Author. Retrieved from http://www.fao.org/fileadmin/ templates/wsfs/docs/expert_paper/How_to_Feed_ the_World_in_2050.pdf

Ford, D. (2015, July 24). Who commits mass shootings? Retrieved from http://www.cnn.com/2015/06/27/us/ mass-shootings/

Foucault, M. (1988). *Madness and civilization: A history of insanity in the age of reason.* New York: Vintage Books.

Frank, A. G. (1966). The development of underdevelopment. *Monthly Review, 18*(4):, 17–31.

Frank, A. G. (1979). *Dependent accumulation and under-development.* London: Macmillan.

Frank, R. (2015, June 15). Millionaires control 41% of world's wealth, expected to take more. Retrieved from http://www.cnbc.com/2015/06/15/millionaires- con trol-41-of-worlds-wealth.html

Freeland, C. (2012). *Plutocrats: The rise of the new global super-rich and the fall of everyone else*. New York: Penguin Books.

Freeman, D. W. (2012, January 12). Video game-obsessed mom neglects kids, starves dogs. Retrieved from http://www.cbsnews.com/news/video-game-obsessed-mom-neglects-kids-starves-dogs/

Freire, P. (1972). *Pedagogy of the oppressed*. New York: Herder & Herder.

Freud, S. (1905). Three essays on sexuality. In *Standard Edition* (Vol. 7). London: Hogarth.

Freud, S. (1929). Civilization and its discontents. In *Standard Edition* (Vol. 21). London: Hogarth.

Freud, S. (1933). *New introductory lectures on psychoanalysis*. New York: Norton.

Frey, W. H., & Speare, A. (1991). *U.S. metropolitan area population growth, 1960–1990: Census trends and explanations* (Population Studies Center Research Report No. 91-212). Ann Arbor: Institute for Social Research, University of Michigan.

Friedan, B. (1963). *The feminine mystique*. New York: Norton.

Friedan, B. (1981). *The second stage*. New York: Summit.

Friedl, E. (1975). *Women and men: An anthropologist's view*. New York: Holt, Rinehart & Winston.

Friedman, H. L. (2013). Tiger girls on the soccer field. *Contexts, 12*, 30–35.

Friedman, L. M. (1975). *The legal system: A social science perspective*. New York: Russell Sage Foundation.

Friedman, L. M. (1990). *The republic of choice: Law, authority, and culture*. Cambridge, MA: Harvard University Press.

Friedman, S., Squires, G. D., & Galvan, C. (2010). *Cybersegregation in Dallas and Boston: Is Neil a more desirable tenant than Tyrone or Jorge?* Paper presented at the annual meeting of the Population Association of America, Dallas, TX.

Friedman, T. L. (2005). *The world is flat: A brief history of the twenty-first century*. New York: Farrar, Straus and Giroux.

Frum, D. (2000). *How we got here: The '70s*. New York: Basic Books.

Fry, R. (2016). *Millennials match baby boomers as largest generation in U.S. electorate, but will they vote?* Washington, DC: Pew Research Center. Retrieved from http://www.pewresearch.org/fact-tank/2016/05/16/millennials-match-baby-boomers-as-larg est-generation-in-u-s-electorate-but-will-they-vote/

Frye, N. K., & Breaugh, J. A. (2004). Family-friendly policies, supervisor support, work–family conflict, family–work conflict, and satisfaction: A test of a conceptual model. *Journal of Business and Psychology, 19*, 197–220.

Furnish, T. (2005). Beheading in the name of Islam. *Middle East Quarterly, 12*, 51–55. Retrieved from http://www.meforum.org/713/beheading-in-the-name-of-islam

Gainsborough, J. F. (2001). *Fenced off: The suburbanization of American politics*. Washington, DC: Georgetown University Press.

Gakidou, E., Cowling, K., Lozano, R., & Murray, C. J. L. (2010). Increased educational attainment and its impact on child mortality in 175 countries between 1970 and 2009: A systematic analysis. *The Lancet, 376*, 959–974.

Gallaudet Research Institute. (2005). A brief summary of estimates for the size of the deaf population in the USA based on available federal data and published research. Retrieved from http://research.gallaudet.edu/Demographics/deaf-US.php

Gallaudet University. (2012). Local and regional deaf populations. Retrieved from http://libguides.gallaudet.edu/content.php? pid=119476&sid=1029190

Gamble, J. L., & Hess, J. J. (2012). Temperature and violent crime in Dallas, Texas: Relationships and implications of climate change. *Western Journal of Emergency Medicine, 13*, 239–246.

Gans, H. J. (1962a). Urbanism and suburbanism as ways of life. In A. Rose (Ed.), *Human behavior and social processes*. Boston: Houghton Mifflin.

Gans, H. J. (1962b). *The urban villagers: Group and class in the life of Italian-Americans*. New York: Free Press.

Gans, H. J. (1972). The positive functions of poverty. *American Journal of Sociology, 78*, 275–289.

Gao, G. (2016, July 7). *Biggest share of whites in U.S. are Boomers, but for minority groups it's Millennials or younger*. Washington, DC: Pew Research. Retrieved from http://www.pewresearch.org/fact-tank/2016/07/07/biggest-share-of-whites-in-u-s-are-boomers-but-for-minority-groups-its-millennials-or-younger/

Garcia, S. B., & Guerra, P. L. (2004). Deconstructing deficit thinking: Working with educators to create more equitable learning environments. *Education and Urban Society, 36*, 150–168.

Garfinkel, H. (1963). A conception of, and experiments with, "trust" as a condition of stable concerted actions. In O. J. Harvey (Ed.), *Motivation and social interaction* (pp. 187–238). New York: Ronald Press.

Garfinkel, H. (1985). *Studies in ethnomethodology*. New York: Blackwell.

Gates, G. J. (2011). *How many people are lesbian, gay, bisexual, and transgender?* Los Angeles, CA: The Williams Institute, University of California-Los Angeles. Retrieved from http://williamsinstitute.law.ucla.edu/wp-content/uploads/Gates-How-Many-People-LGBT-Apr-2011.pdf

Gatsiounis, I. (2008, March 20). In Thailand, pollution from shrimp farms threatens a fragile environment. *New York Times*. Retrieved from http://www.nytimes.com/2008/03/20/business/worldbusiness/20iht-rbogcoast.1.11278833.html?_r=0

Gauntlett, D. (2008). *Media, gender, and identity: An introduction* (2nd ed.). New York: Taylor & Francis.

Geertz, C. (1973). *The interpretation of cultures.* New York: Basic Books.

Gellner, E. (1983). *Nations and nationalism.* Ithaca, NY: Cornell University Press.

Gerding, A., & Signorielli, N. (2014). Gender roles in tween television programming: A content analysis of two genres. *Sex Roles, 70,* 43–56.

Geronimus, A. (1992). The weathering hypothesis and the health of African-American women and infants: Evidence and speculations. *Ethnicity and Disease, 2,* 207–221.

Gershoff, E. T., & Grogan-Kaylor, A. (2016, June). Spanking and child outcomes: Old controversies and new meta-analyses. *Journal of Family Psychology, 30,* 453–469 http://dx.doi.org/10.1037/fam0000191

Gerstel, N., & Gallagher, S. (1994). Caring for kith and kin: Gender, employment, and the privatization of care. *Social Problems, 41,* 519–539.

Ghosh, B. N. (2001). *Dependency theory revisited.* London: Ashgate.

Gibbs, N. (2009, October 14). The state of the American woman: What women want now. *Time.* Retrieved from http://www.time.com/time/specials/packages/article/0,28804,1930277_1930145_ 1930309,00.html

Giedd, J. N. (2004). Structural magnetic resonance imaging of the adolescent brain. *Annals of the New York Academy of Sciences, 1021,* 77–85.

Gilbert, D. L. (2011). *The American class structure in an age of growing inequality* (8th ed.). Thousand Oaks, CA: Pine Forge.

Gilbert, S. (2017). The Movement of #metoo. *The Atlantic Monthly.* Retrieved from https://www.theatlantic.com/entertainment/archive/2017/10/the-movement-of-metoo/542979/

Gilligan, C. (1982). *In a different voice: Psychological theory and women's development.* Cambridge, MA: Harvard University Press.

Gilligan, C., Ward, J. V., & Taylor, J. M. (Eds.). (1989). *Mapping the moral domain: A contribution of women's thinking to psychological theory and education.* Cambridge, MA: Harvard University Press.

Gilman, C. P. (2006). *Women and economics: A study of the economic relation between men and women as a factor in social evolution.* New York, NY: Cosimo. (Original work published 1898)

Glassdoor. (2015). Here's how much more CEOs earn than their employees. Retrieved from https://www.glassdoor.com/blog/heres-ceos-earn-employee/

Glazer, N. (1992). The real world of education. *The Public Interest* (Winter), 57–75.

Glazer, N. (1997). *We are all multiculturalists now.* Cambridge, MA: Harvard University Press.

Glenny, M. (2009). *McMafia: A journey through the global criminal underworld.* New York: Knopf.

Glewwe, P. (1999). Why does mother's schooling raise child health in developing countries? Evidence from Morocco. *Journal of Human Resources, 34,* 124–159.

Gleyo, F. (2015, October 10). AP has a robot journalist that writes a thousand articles per month. Retrieved from http://www.techtimes.com/articles/93473/20151010/ap-has-a-robot-journalist-that-writes-a-thousand-articles-per-month.htm

Glock, C. Y., & Bellah, R. N. (1976). *The new religious consciousness.* Berkeley: University of California Press.

Glorioso, C. (2011, September 27). AP opportunity gap: NY's poor students enroll in fewer college-prep courses. Retrieved from http://www.nbcnewyork.com/news/local/Advanced-Placement-AP-Classes-College-Prep-New-York-State-130672323.html

Goffman, E. (1959). *The presentation of self in everyday life.* New York: Doubleday.

Goffman, E. (1961). *Asylums: Essays on the social situation of mental patients and other inmates.* Garden City, NY: Anchor Books.

Goffman, E. (1963a). *Behavior in public place.* New York: Free Press.

Goffman, E. (1963b). *Stigma: Notes on the management of spoiled identity.* Englewood Cliffs, NJ: Prentice Hall.

Goffman, E. (1967). *Interaction ritual: Essays on face to face behavior.* Garden City, NY: Anchor.

Goffman, E. (1972). *Relations in public: Microstudies of the public order.* New York: Harper & Row.

Gokcearslan, A. (2010). The effect of cartoon movies on children's gender development. *Procedia: Social and Behavior Sciences, 2,* 5202–5207.

Goldin, C. (2014). A grand gender convergence: Its last chapter. *American Economic Review, 104,* 1091–1119.

Goldin, C., Katz, M. F., & Kuziemko, I. (2006). *The homecoming of American college women: The reversal of the college gender gap* (Working Paper 12130). Cambridge, MA: National Bureau of Economic Research. Retrieved from http://faculty.smu.edu/millimet/classes/eco7321/papers/goldin%20et%20al.pdf

Goldscheider, F. K., & Waite, L. J. (1991). *New families, no families? The transformation of the American home.* Berkeley: University of California Press.

Goldstein, J. S. (2011, September/October). World peace could be closer than you think. *Foreign Policy,* pp. 53–56.

Goldstone, J. A. (2001). Towards a fourth generation of revolutionary theory. *Annual Review of Political Science, 4,* 139–187.

Gooden, A. M., & Gooden, M. A. (2001). Gender representation in notable children's picture books: 1995–1999. *Sex roles, 45,* 89–101.

Goodier, R. (2013, September 17). TV may reinforce stereotypes about men in nursing. Retrieved from http://www.reuters.com/article/us-tv-nurses-idUS-BRE98G 18G20130917

Goodnough, A. (2016, January 29). Flint weighs scope of harm to children caused by lead in water. Retrieved from http://www.nytimes.com/2016/01/30/us/flint-weighs-scope-of-harm-to-children-caused-by-lead-in-water.html

Goody, J. (1983). *The development of the family and marriage in Europe.* Cambridge: Cambridge University Press.

Gottfredson, M. R., & Hirschi, T. (2004). *A general theory of crime.* Stanford, CA: Stanford University Press. (Original work published 1990)

Gould, E., Mokhiber, Z., & Wolfe, J. (2017). "The Class of 2018." *Economic Policy Institute.* Retrieved from https://www.epi.org/files/pdf/147514.pdf

GovTrack. (2018). "A bill would make English the official language." GovTrack, August 16, 2018. Retrieved from https://govtrackinsider.com/a-bill-would-make-english-the-official-language-975fa22ea0f2

Gracey, H. L. (1991). Learning the student role: Kindergarten as academic boot camp. In J. M. Henslin (Ed.), *Down to earth sociology: Introductory readings* (6th ed.). New York: Free Press.

Grant, R. (1991). The sources of gender bias in international relations theory. In R. Grant & K. Newland (Eds.), *Gender and international relations* (pp. 8–26). Bloomington: Indiana University Press.

Great Nonprofits. (2016). Islamic Relief USA. Retrieved from http://greatnonprofits.org/org/islamic-relief-usa

Greenberg, A. (2015, June 2). The dark web drug lords who got away. Retrieved from https://www.wired.com/2015/06/dark-web-drug-lords-got-away/

Gregg, M. (2014, September 25). Five ways cyberterrorists could target the U.S. Retrieved from http://www.huffingtonpost.com/michael-gregg/five-ways-cyber terrorists_b_5874860.html

Griffin, S. (1978). *Woman and nature: The roaring inside her.* New York: Harper & Row.

Griffin, S. (1979). *Rape, the power of consciousness.* New York: Harper & Row.

Griffin, S. (1981). *Pornography as silence: Culture's revenge against nature.* New York: Harper & Row.

Grusky, O., Bonacich, P., & Webster, C. (1995). The coalition structure of the four person family. *Current Research in Social Psychology, 2,* 16–28.

Guilmoto, C. Z. (2011). *Skewed sex ratios at birth and future marriage squeeze in China and India, 2005–2100* (Working Paper 15). Paris: Centre Population & Développement.

Gump, L. S., Baker, R. C., & Roll, S. (2000). Cultural and gender differences in moral judgment: A study of Mexican Americans and Anglo-Americans. *Hispanic Journal of Behavioral Sciences, 22,* 78–93.

Gunnell, J. J., & Ceci, S. J. (2010). When emotionality trumps reason: A study of individual processing style and juror bias. *Behavioral Sciences & the Law, 28,* 850–877.

Gunnoe, M. L. (1997). Toward a developmental contextual model of the effects of parental spanking on children's aggression. *Archives of Pediatrics and Adolescence, 151,* 768–775.

Guo, J. (2016, January 25). Researchers have found a major problem with 'The Little Mermaid' and other Disney movies. *Washington Post.* Retrieved from https://www.washingtonpost.com/news/wonk/wp/2016/01/25/researchers-have-discovered-a-major-problem-with-the-little-mermaid-and-other-disney-movies/

Gutman, R., & Rieff, D. (1999). *Crimes of war: What the public should know.* New York: Norton.

Habermas, J. (1976). *Legitimation crisis.* London: Heinemann.

Hadden, J. K. (1993). *Religion and the social order: The handbook on cults and sects in America.* Bingley, England: Emerald Group.

Hadden, J. K. (2006). New religious movements. Hartford Institute for Religion Research. Retrieved from http://hirr.hart sem.edu/denom/new_religious_move ments.html

Haj-yahia, M. M., & Cohen, H. C. (2009). On the lived experience of battered women residing in shelters. *Journal of Family Violence, 24,* 95–109.

Haley, A., & Malcolm X. (1964). *The autobiography of Malcolm X.* New York: Ballantine Books.

Hall, E. (1973). *The silent language.* New York: Doubleday.

Hall, P. M. (2003). Interactionism, social organization, and social processes: Looking back there, reflecting now here, and moving ahead then. *Symbolic Interaction, 26,* 33–55.

Hamblin, J. (2016, June 16). Toxic masculinity and murder. *The Atlantic.* Retrieved from http://www.theatlantic.com/health/archive/2016/06/toxic-masculinity-and-mass-murder/486983/

Hamel, L., Rao, M., Levitt, L., Claxton, G., Cox, C., Pollitz, K., & Brodie, M. (2014). *Survey of non-group health insurance enrollees: A first look at people buying their own health insurance following implementation of the Affordable Care Act.* Menlo Park, CA: Kaiser Family Foundation. Retrieved from http://kaiserfamilyfoundation.files .wordpress.com/2014/06/survey-of-non-group-health-insurance-enrollees-findings-final1.pdf

Hamermesh, D. S. (2011). *Beauty pays: Why attractive people are more successful.* Princeton, NJ: Princeton University Press.

Hamermesh, D. S., & Parker, A. (2005). Beauty in the classroom: Professorial pulchritude and putative pedagogical productivity. *Economics of Education Review, 24,* 369–376.

Hammond, P. E. (1992). *Religion and personal autonomy: The third disestablishment in America.* Columbia: University of South Carolina Press.

Haney, C., Banks, W. C., & Zimbardo, P. G. (1973). Interpersonal dynamics in a simulated prison.

International Journal of Criminology and Penology, 1, 69–97.

Hannon, E. (2012, April 8). India's census: Lots of cellphones, too few toilets. *Weekend Edition,* NPR. Retrieved from http://www.npr.org/2012/04/08/150133880/indias-census-lots-of-cellphones-too-few-toilets

Hanson, P. (2003). *An economic history of the USSR, 1945–1991.* New York: Longman.

Hardoon, D., Fuentes-Nieva, R., & Ayele, S. (2016, January 18). *An economy for the 1%: How privilege and power in the economy drive extreme inequality and how this can be stopped.* Oxfam International. Retrieved from http://policy-practice.oxfam.org.uk/publications/an-eco nomy-for-the-1-how-privilege-and-power-in-the-economy-drive-extreme-inequ- 592643

Harlan, C., & Nakashima, E. (2011, August 29). Suspected North Korean cyber attack on a bank raises fears for S. Korea, allies. Retrieved from https://www.washington-post.com/world/national-security/suspected-north-korean-cyber-attack-on-a-bank-raises-fears-for-s-korea-allies/2011/08/07/gIQAvWwIoJ_story.html

Harper, B. (2000). Beauty, stature and the labour market: A British cohort study. *Oxford Bulletin of Economics and Statistics, 62,* 771–800.

Harring, H. A., Montgomery, K., & Hardin, J. (2011). Perceptions of body weight, weight, weight management strategies, and depressive symptoms among US college students. *Journal of American College Health, 59,* 43–50.

Harrington, M. (1963). *The other America: Poverty in the United States.* New York: Simon & Schuster.

Harris, J. R. (2009). *The nurture assumption: Why children turn out the way they do* (2nd ed.). New York: Free Press.

Hartmann, H. (1984). The unhappy union of Marxism and feminism: Toward a more progressive union. In A. M. Jaggar & P. S. Rothenberg (Eds.), *Feminist frameworks: Alternative theoretical accounts of the relations between women and men* (2nd ed., pp. 172–188). New York: McGraw- Hill.

Harvard Medical School. (2010, July). Marriage and men's health. *Harvard Men's Health Watch Newsletter.* Retrieved from http://www.health.harvard.edu/newsletters/Harvard_Mens_Health_Watch/2010/July/marriage-and-mens-health

Hattery, A. J. (2001). *Families in crisis: Men and women's perceptions of violence in partner relationships.* Blacksburg, VA: Southern Sociological Society.

Hatzenbuehler, P. L., Gillespie, J. M., & O'Neil, C. E. (2012, April). Does healthy food cost more in poor neighborhoods? An analysis of retail food cost and spatial competition. *Agricultural and Resource Economics Review, 41,* 43–56.

Hausmann, R., Tyson, L. D., & Zahidi, S. (2011). *The global gender gap report 2011.* Geneva, Switzerland: The World Economic Forum.

Hedwig, L. (2011). Inequality as an explanation for obesity in the United States. *Sociology Compass, 5,* 215–232.

Hegewisch, A., & Liepmann, H. (2012). *Fact sheet: The gender wage gap by occupation.* Washington, DC: Institute for Women's Policy Research. Retrieved from http://www.iwpr.org/publications/pubs/the-gender-wage-gap-by-occupation

Held, D. (1989). *Political theory and the modern state.* Stanford, CA: Stanford University Press.

Helin, K. (2016, July 21). NBA makes it official: 2017 All-Star Game pulled from Charlotte due to 'Bathroom Law.' Retrieved from http://nba.nbcsports.com/2016/07/21/nba-makes-it-official-2017-all-star-game-pulled-from-charlotte-due-to-bathroom-law/

Henry J. Kaiser Family Foundation. (2018). 33 States and DC Have Adopted Medicaid Expansion as of May 2018. Retrieved from https://www.kff.org/medicaid/slide/33-states-and-dc-have-adopted-medicaid-ex-pansion-as-of-may-2018/

Henry, T. (2010, November 15). Even short-term poverty can hurt kids' health. *CNNHealth.* Retrieved from http://thechart.blogs.cnn.com/2010/11/15/even-short-term-poverty-can-hurt-kids-health

Heppner, C. M. (1992). *Seeds of disquiet: One deaf woman's experience.* Washington, DC: Gallaudet University Press.

Heritage, J., & Greatbatch, D. (1991). On the institutional character of institutional talk: The case of news interviews. In D. H. Zimmerman & D. Boden (Eds.), *Talk and social structure* (pp. 93–137). Cambridge: Polity Press.

Hersey, P., Blanchard, K., & Natemeyer, W. (1987). *Situational leadership, perception, and the use of power.* Escondido, CA: Leadership Studies.

Hess, H. (1973). *Mafia and mafiosi: The structure of power.* Farnborough, England: Saxon House.

Hesse-Biber, S. (1997). *Am I thin enough yet? The cult of thinness and the commercialization of identity.* New York: Oxford University Press.

Hexham, I., & Poewe, K. (1997). *New religions as global cultures: Making the human sacred.* Boulder, CO: Westview Press.

Hill, L. E., & Johnson, H. P. (2002). *How fertility changes across immigrant generations.* San Francisco: Public Policy Institute of California. Retrieved from http://www.ppic.org/content/pubs/rb/RB_402LHRB.pdf

Hillin, T. (2016, May 24). Facebook apologized after fat-shaming a model—but the damage was already done. Retrieved from http://fusion.net/story/306275/facebook-apolo gized-after-fat-shaming-model-tess-holli day/

Hine, T. (2000). *The rise and fall of the American teenager.* New York: Bard/Avon.

Hinsley, F. H. (1986). *Sovereignty* (2nd ed.). Cambridge: Cambridge University Press.

Hirschi, T. (1969). *Causes of delinquency*. Berkeley: University of California Press.

Hirschi, T. (2004). Self-control and crime. In R. F. Baumeister & K. D. Vohs (Eds.), *Handbook of self-regulation: Research, theory, and applications* (pp. 537–552). New York: Guilford.

Ho, C. (1993). The internationalization of kinship and the feminization of Caribbean migration: The case of Afro-Trinidadian immigrants in Los Angeles. *Human Organization, 52*, 32–40.

Hobbs, F., & Stoops, N. (2002). *Demographic trends in the 20th century* (Census 2000 Special Report CENSR-4). Washington, DC: U.S. Census Bureau. Retrieved from http://www.census.gov/prod/2002pubs/censr-4.pdf

Hochschild, A. (2001a). *The Nanny Chain. The American Prospect*. Retrieved from http://prospect.org/article/nanny-chain.

Hochschild, A. (2001b). *The Time Bind: When Work Becomes Home and Home Becomes Work*. New York: Holt.

Hochschild, A. R. (2003). *The managed heart: Commercialization of human feeling*. Berkeley: University of California Press.

Hoffman, B. (2006). *Inside terrorism*. New York: Columbia University Press.

Holbrook, A. L., & Krosnick, J. A., (2009). Social desirability bias in voter turnout reports: Tests using the item count technique. *Public Opinion Quarterly, 74*(1), pp. 37–67.

Homans, C. (2011, September/October). Anthropology of an idea: War games. *Foreign Policy*, pp. 30–31.

Hong, S. (2016). Representative bureaucracy, organizational integrity, and citizen coproduction: Does an increase in police ethnic representativeness reduce crime? *Journal of Policy Analysis and Management, 35*(1), 11–33.

Hooton, E. A. (1939). *The American criminal: An anthropological study*. Cambridge, MA: Harvard University Press.

Hopkins, D. J. (2009). No more Wilder effect, never a Whitman effect: When and why polls mislead about black and female candidates. *Journal of Politics, 71*, 769–781.

Hopper, R. (1991). Hold the phone. In D. H. Zimmerman & D. Boden (Eds.), *Talk and social structure* (pp. 217–231). Cambridge: Polity Press.

Horan, P. M., & Hargis, P. G. (1991). Children's work and schooling in the late nineteenth century family economy. *American Sociological Review, 56*, 583–596.

Horkheimer, M. (1947). *The eclipse of reason*. Oxford: Oxford University Press.

Hosken, F. (1993). City. In *Academic American encyclopedia*. Danbury, CT: Grolier.

Houghton, S., Hunter, S. C., Rosenberg, M., Wood, L., Zadow, C., Martin, K., & Shilton, T. (2015). *Virtually impossible: Limiting Australian children and adolescents daily screen based media use*. BMC Public Health. doi: 10.1186/1471-2458-15-5

Hu, E. (2015, April 15). The all-work, no-play culture of South Korean education. Retrieved from http://www.npr.org/sections/parallels/2015/04/15/393939759/the-all-work-no-play-culture-of-south-korean-education

Huber, J. (1990). Macro-micro links in gender stratification: 1989 presidential address. *American Sociological Review, 55*, 1–10.

Huber, J. (1993). Gender role change in families: A macrosociological view. In T. Brubaker (Ed.), *Family relations: Challenges for the future*. Newbury Park, CA: Sage.

Huber, J. (2006). Comparative gender stratification. In J. S. Chafetz (Ed.), *Handbook of the sociology of gender* (pp. 65–80). New York: Springer.

Huelsman, M. (2015, May 19). The debt divide: The racial and class bias behind the "new normal" of student borrowing. Retrieved from http://www.demos.org/publication/debt-divide-racial-and-class-bias-behind-new-normal-student-borrowing

Huffman, M. L., & Torres, L. (2002). It's not only "who you know" that matters: Gender, personal contacts, and job lead quality. *Gender & Society, 16*, 793–813.

Hunter, J. D. (1987). *Evangelicalism: The coming generation*. Hutchinson, KS: de Wit Books.

Hutcheon, D. (1999). *Building character and structure*. Westport, CT: Praeger.

Hutchinson, A. (2016, March 18). Here's why Twitter is so important, to everyone. Retrieved from http://www.socialmedia today.com/social-networks/heres-why-twitter-so-important-everyone

Hvistendahl, M. (2011). *Unnatural selection: Choosing boys over girls, and the consequences of a world full of men*. New York: Public Affairs.

Hyman, H. H. (1942). The psychology of status. *Archives of Psychology, 38*, 147–165.

Immerwahr, D. (2007). Caste or colony? Indianizing race in the United States. *Modern Intellectual History, 4*, 275–301.

Ingraham, C. (1999). *White weddings: Romancing heterosexuality in popular culture*. New York: Routledge.

Institute for Economics and Peace. (2015). *Global terrorism index*. Retrieved from http://static.visionof humanity.org/sites/default/files/2015%20Global%20Terror ism%20Index%20Report_2.pdf

Institute of International Education. (2010, November). Study abroad by U.S. students slowed in 2008/09 with more students going to less traditional destinations (press release). Retrieved from http://www.iie.org/Who-We-Are/News-and-Events/Press-Center/

Press-Releases/2010/2010-11-15-Open-Doors-US-Study-Abroad

Institute of International Education. (2017). International Students. Retrieved from https://www.iie.org/Research-and-Insights/Open-Doors/Data/International-Students.

Isidore, C. (2012, September 6). 3 answers to the auto bailout debate. CNNMoney. Retrieved from http://money.cnn.com/2012/09/06/autos/auto-bailout

Jackson, K. T. (1985). *Crabgrass frontier: The suburbanization of America.* New York: Oxford University Press.

Jaffee, S., & Hyde, J. (2000). Gender differences in moral orientation: A meta analysis. *Psychological Bulletin, 126,* 703–726.

Jaggar, A. M. (1983). *Feminist politics and human nature.* Totowa, NJ: Rowman & Allanheld.

Janis, I. L. (1972). *Victims of groupthink.* Boston: Houghton Mifflin.

Janis, I. L. (1989). *Crucial decisions: Leadership in policy making and crisis management.* New York: Free Press.

Janis, I. L., & Mann, L. (1977). *Decision making: A psychological analysis of conflict, choice, and commitment.* New York: Free Press.

Jargowsky, P. (2015, August 7). Architecture of segregation: Civil unrest, the concentration of poverty, and public policy. Retrieved from https://tcf.org/content/report/architecture- of-segregation/

Johns, M., Schmader, T., & Martens, A. (2005). Knowing is half the battle: Teaching stereotype threat as a means of improving women's math performance. *Psychological Science, 16*(3), 175–179.

Johnson, J. (2011, November 27). College administrators worry that use of prescription stimulants is increasing. *Washington Post.* Retrieved from http://articles.washingtonpost.com/2011-11-27/local/35281941_1_prescription-drugs-study-drugs-prescription-stimulants

Johnson, J. M., & Ferraro, K. J. (1984). The victimized self: The case of battered women. In J. A. Kotarba & A. Fontana (Eds.), *The existential self in society* (pp. 119–130). Chicago: University of Chicago Press.

Johnson, M. (2013, January 23). The history of Twitter. Retrieved from http://socialnomics.net/2013/01/23/the-history-of-twitter/

Jones, R. P., & Cox D. (2015). *How race and religion shape millennial attitudes on sexuality and reproductive health.* Washington, DC: Public Religion Research Institute. Retrieved from http://www.prri.org/wp-content/uploads/2015/03/PRRI-Millennials-Web-FINAL.pdf

Jordan, M. (1992, January 9). Big city schools become more segregated in the 1980s, a study says. *Washington Post,* p. A3.

Josephson Institute Center for Youth Ethics. (2012). Report card on the ethics of American youth. Retrieved from http://charac tercounts.org/programs/reportcard/2012/index.html

Josephson Institute of Ethics. (2009). *A study of values and behavior concerning integrity: The impact of age, cynicism and high school character.* Los Angeles: Author.

Juergensmeyer, M. (1995). The social significance of Radhasoami. In D. Lorenzen (Ed.), *Bhakti religion in North India: Community identity and political action* (pp. 67–89). Albany: State University of New York Press.

Junco, R. (2012). Too much face and not enough books: The relationship between multiple indices of Facebook use and academic performance. *Computers in Human Behavior, 28,* 187–198.

Kaeble, D. & Cowhig, M. (2018, April). Correctional Populations in the United States, 2016. Washington, DC: Bureau of Justice Statistics. Retrieved from https://www.bjs.gov/index.cfm?ty=pbdetail&iid=6226

Kagay, M. R. (1994, July 8). Poll on doubt of Holocaust is corrected: Roper says 91% are sure it occurred. *New York Times.*

Kahlenberg, S. G., & Hein, M. M. (2010). Progression on Nickelodeon? Gender-role stereotypes in toy commercials. *Sex Roles, 62,* 830–847.

Kaiser Family Foundation. (2006, July). *Race, ethnicity, and health care: Fact sheet.* Menlo Park, CA: Author. Retrieved from http://kaiserfamilyfoundation.files.wordpress.com/2013/01/7541.pdf

Kaiser Family Foundation. (2010a, September 17). Census Bureau: Recession fuels record number of uninsured Americans. Kaiser Health News. Retrieved from http://www.kaiserhealthnews.org/daily-reports/2010/september/16/uninsured-census-statistics.aspx

Kaiser Family Foundation. (2012a). Medicaid and long-term care services and supports. Retrieved from http://www.kff.org/medic aid/upload/2186-09.pdf

Kaiser Family Foundation. (2014a). Medicare at a glance. Retrieved from http://kff.org/medicare/fact-sheet/medicare-at-a-glance- fact-sheet

Kaiser Family Foundation. (2016a). Percent of adults reporting fair or poor health statuses. Retrieved from https://www.kff.org/other/state-indicator/percent-of-adults-reporting-fair-or-poor-health-status-by-raceethnicity/?currentTimeframe=1&sortModel=%7B%22colId%22:%22Location%22,%22sort%22:%22asc%22%7D

Kaiser Family Foundation. (2016b). Overweight and Obesity Rates. Retrieved from https://www.kff.org/other/state-indicator/adult-overweightobesity-rate-by-re/?currentTimeframe=1&sortModel=%7B%22colId%22:%22Location%22,%22sort%22:%22asc%22%7D

Kaiser Family Foundation. (2017). Distribution of Medical School Graduates by Gender. Retrieved from https://www.kff.org/other/state-indicator/medical-school-graduates-by-gender/?dataView=1&currentTimeframe=0&sortModel=%7B%22colId%22:%22Location%22,%22sort%22:%22asc%22%7D

Kanazawa, S., & Still, M. C. (2000). Parental investment as a game of chicken. *Politics and the Life Sciences, 19,* 17–26.

Kandal, T. R. (1988). *The woman question in classical sociological theory.* Gainesville: University of Florida Press.

Kanter, R. M. (1983). *The change masters: Innovation for productivity in the American corporation.* New York: Simon & Schuster.

Kara, S. (2009). *Sex trafficking: Inside the business of modern slavery.* New York: Columbia University Press.

Karpinski, A. C., & Duberstein, A. (2009). A description of Facebook use and academic performance among undergraduate and graduate students. Columbus: Ohio State University, College of Education and Human Ecology. Retrieved from http://researchnews.osu.edu/archive/facebook2009.jpg

Katz, J., & Chambliss, W. J. (1995). Biology and crime. In J. F. Sheley (Ed.), *Criminology: A contemporary handbook* (2nd ed.). Belmont, CA: Wadsworth.

Kaufman, J. M. (2009). Gendered responses to serious strain: The argument for a general strain of deviance. *Justice Quarterly, 26,* 410–444.

Kavner, L. (2012, August 15). Compliance, a low budget indie, might be the most disturbing movie ever made. *Huffington Post.* Retrieved from http://www.huffingtonpost.com/2012/08/15/compliance-movie-film_n_1779123.html

Keeley, B., Wright, L., & Condit, C. M. (2009). Functions of health fatalism: Fatalistic talk as face saving, uncertainty management, stress relief and sense making. *Sociology of Health and Illness, 31,* 734–747.

Kelley, B., & Carchia, C. (2013, July 11). "Hey, data data—swing!": The hidden demographics of youth sports. *ESPN The Magazine.* Retrieved from http://espn.go.com/espn/story/_/id/9469252/hidden-demographics-youth-sports-espn-magazine

Kelly, M. (2012, June 13). Hollywood's problem with senior citizen sex. *The Atlantic.* Retrieved from http://www.theatlantic.com/entertainment/archive/2012/06/hollywoods-problem-with-senior-citizen-sex/258444/

Kennedy, M. (2016, April 20). Lead-laced water in Flint: A step-by-step look at the makings of a crisis. Retrieved from http://www.npr.org/sections/thetwo-way/2016/04/20/465545378/lead-laced-water-in-flint-a-step-by-step-look-at-the-makings-of-a-crisis

Kenning, C., & Halladay, J. (2008, January 25). Cities study dearth of healthy food. *USA Today.* Retrieved from http://usatoday30.usatoday.com/news/health/2008-01-24-fooddesert_N.htm

Kenny, C. (2012, June 4). The global obesity bomb. *Bloomberg Businessweek.* Retrieved from http://www.businessweek.com/articles/2012-06-04/the-global-obesity-bomb

Kessler, E.-M., Racoczy, K., & Staudinger, U. (2004). The portrayal of older people in prime time television series: The match with gerontological evidence. *Ageing and Society, 24,* 531–552.

Keyfitz, N. (1993). Thirty years of demography and *Demography. Demography, 30,* 533–549.

Khanna, P. (2010, August 16). Beyond city limits: The age of nations is over. The new urban era has begun. *Foreign Policy.* Retrieved from http://www.foreignpolicy.com/articles/2010/08/16/beyond_city_limits?page=full

Khullar, A. (2014, March 25). WHO: Air pollution caused one in eight deaths. Retrieved from http://www.cnn.com/2014/03/25/health/who-air-pollution-deaths/

Kibirige, J. S. (1997). Population growth, poverty, and health. *Social Science & Medicine, 45,* 247–259.

Kilbourne, J. (1999). *Deadly persuasion: Why women and girls must fight the addictive power of advertising.* New York: Free Press.

Kimmel, M. S. (1996). *Manhood in America: A cultural history.* New York: Free Press.

Kimmel, M. S. (2013). *Angry white men: Masculinity in America at the end of an era.* New York: Nation Books.

Kindy, K. (2013, April 25). At chicken plants, chemicals blamed for health ailments are poised to proliferate. Retrieved from https://www.washingtonpost.com/politics/at-chicken-plants-chemicals-blamed-for-health-ailments-are-poised-to-proliferate/2013/04/25/d2a65ec8-97b1-11e2-97cd-3d8c1afe4f0f_story.html

King, H., & Chambliss, W. J. (1984). *Harry King: A professional thief's journey.* New York: Macmillan.

Kinnvall, C. (2004). Globalization and religious nationalism: Self, identity, and the search for ontological security. *Political Psychology, 25,* 741–767.

Kluckhohn, F. R., & Strodtbeck, F. L. (1961). *Variations in value orientations.* Evanston, IL: Row, Peterson.

Kochhar, R., & Fry, R. (2014, December 12). *Wealth inequality has widened along racial, ethnic lines since end of Great Recession.* Washington, DC: Pew Research Center. Retrieved from http://www.pewresearch.org/fact-tank/2014/12/12/racial-wealth-gaps-great-recession/

Kochhar, R., Fry, R., & Taylor, P. (2011). *Wealth gaps rise to record highs between Whites, Blacks, Hispanics.* Washington, DC: Pew Research Center. Retrieved from http://www.pewsocialtrends.org/files/2011/07/SDT-Wealth-Report_7-26-11_FINAL.pdf

Kohlberg, L. (1969). Stage and sequence: The cognitive-developmental approach to socialization. In

A. Goslin (Ed.), *Handbook of socialization theory and research* (pp. 347–480). Chicago: Rand McNally.

Kohlberg, L. (1983). *The philosophy of moral development.* New York: Harper & Row.

Kohlberg, L. (1984). *The psychology of moral development.* New York: Harper & Row.

Kohn, M. L. (1989). *Class and conformity: A study in values* (2nd ed.). Chicago: University of Chicago Press.

Kolowich, S. (2011, August 22). What students don't know. Inside Higher Ed. Retrieved from http://www.insidehighered.com/news/2011/08/22/erial_study_of_student_research_habits_at_illinois_university_libraries_reveals_alarmingly_poor_information_literacy_and_skills

Koo, S. (2014, August 1). An assault upon our children: South Korea's education system hurts students. New York Times. Retrieved from http://www.nytimes.com/2014/08/02/opinion/sunday/south-koreas-education-system-hurts-students.html?_r=0

Kornrich, S., & Furstenberg, F. (2013). Investing in children: Changes in parental spending on children, 1972–2007. *Demography, 50,* 1–23.

Koss, M. D. (2015). Diversity in contemporary picturebooks: A content analysis. *Journal of Children's Literature, 41*(1), 32.

Kozol, J. (1991). *Savage inequalities: Children in American schools.* New York: HarperCollins.

Kozol, J. (1995). *Amazing grace: Lives of our children and the conscience of a nation.* New York: Crown.

Kozol, J. (2000). *Ordinary resurrections: Children in the years of hope.* New York: Crown.

Kozol, J. (2005). *The shame of the nation: The restoration of apartheid schooling in America.* New York: Three Rivers Press.

Kraft, A. (2016, April 18). Chinese restaurant fires subpar robot waiters. Retrieved from http://www.cbsnews.com/news/chinese-restaurant-fires-subpar-robot-waiters/

Kramer, A. (2013, May 13). How are savings groups changing lives? Oxfam America. Retrieved from http://firstperson.oxfamamerica.org/2013/05/how-are-savings-groups-changing-lives/

Kraut, R., Patterson, M., Lundmark, V., Kiesler, S., Mukopadhayay, T., & Scherlis, W. (1998). Internet paradox: A social technology that reduces social involvement and psychological well-being? *American Psychologist, 53,* 1017–1032.

Kristof, N., & WuDunn, S. (2009). *Half the sky: Turning oppression into opportunity for women worldwide.* New York: Knopf.

Kristofferson, K., White, K., & Peloza, J. (2013). The nature of slacktivism: How the social observability of an initial act of token support affects subsequent prosocial action. *Journal of Consumer Research, 40*(6), 1149–1166.

Kroeger, T., & Gould, E. (2017) "The Class of 2017." *Economic Policy Institute.* Retrieved from http://www.edpi.org/publication/the-class-of-2017/

Krogstad, J. (2016). *2016 electorate will be the most diverse in U.S. history.* Washington, DC: Pew Research Center. Retrieved from http://www.pewresearch.org/fact-tank/2016/02/03/2016-electorate-will-be-the-most-diverse-in-u-s-history/

Kronk, E. A. (2013, April 16). One statute for two spirits: Same-sex marriage in Indian country. Jurist Forum. Retrieved from http://jurist.org/forum/2013/04/elizabeth-kronk-two-spritis.php

Kubrin, C. E. (2005). Gangstas, thugs, and hustlas: Identity and the code of the street in rap music. *Social Problems, 52,* 360–378.

Lampman, J. (2006, September 14). American Buddhism on the rise. *Christian Science Monitor.* Retrieved from http://www.csmon itor.com/2006/0914/p14s01-lire.html

Lane, H. (1992). *The mask of benevolence: Disabling the deaf.* New York: Random House.

Lane, H. (2005). Ethnicity, ethics, and the deaf world. *Journal of Deaf Studies and Deaf Education, 10,* 291–310.

Langfitt, F. (2013, April 29). *As the car market moves east, an extravaganza in Shanghai.* National Public Radio. Retrieved from http://www.npr.org/blogs/thetwo-way/2013/04/27/179025891/as-the-car-market-moves-east-an-extravaganza-in-shanghai

Langton, L., Planty, M., & Sandholtz, N. (2013). *Hate crime victimization, 2003–2011* (NCJ 241291). Washington, DC: U.S. Department of Justice, Bureau of Justice Statistics. Retrieved from http://www.bjs.gov/index.cfm? ty=pbdetail&iid=4614

Lanier, J. (2013). *Who owns the future?* New York: Simon & Schuster.

Lareau, A. (2002). Invisible inequality: Social class and childrearing in Black families and White families. *American Sociological Review, 67,* 747–776.

Laris, M. (2016, June 9). This government competition could completely change the American city. Retrieved from https://www.washingtonpost.com/local/trafficandcommuting/can-a-wonked-out-reality-competition-help-save-the-american-city/2016/06/08/f5f0b3d8-112f-11e6-8967-7ac733c56f12_story.html

Lauzen, M., Dozier, D., & Horan, N. (2008). Constructing gender stereotypes through social roles in prime-time television. *Journal of Broadcasting & Electronic Media, 52,* 200–214.

Lawson, K. M., Crouter A. C., & McHale. S. M. (2015, October). Links between family gender socialization experiences in childhood and gendered occupational attainment in young adulthood. *Journal of Vocational Behavior, 90,* 26–35.

Le Moal, M., & Koob, G. F. (2007). Drug addiction: Pathways to the disease and pathophysiological perspectives. *European Neuropsychopharmacology, 17,* 377–393.

Leaper, C., Breed, L., Hoffman, L., & Perlman, C. A. (2002). Variations in the gender-stereotyped content of children's television cartoons across genres. *Journal of Applied Social Psychology, 32,* 1653–1662.

Ledeneva, A. V. (1998). *Russia's economy of favours: Blat, networking, and informal exchange.* Cambridge: Cambridge University Press.

Lee, M. M., Carpenter, B., & Meyers, L. S. (2007). Representations of older adults in television advertisements. *Journal of Aging Studies, 21,* 23–30.

Lemonnier, J. (2008, February 18). Big players in diet industry shift focus to online presences. Consumer Lab. Retrieved from http://consumerlab.wordpress.com/2008/02/18/big-players-in-diet-industry-shift-focus-to-online-presences

Lempert, D. (2007). Women's increasing wage penalties from being overweight and obese. Washington, DC: U.S. Bureau of Labor Statistics. Retrieved from http://www.bls.gov/osmr/abstract/ec/ec070130.htm

Leonhardt, D. (2009, September 8). Colleges are failing in graduation rates. *New York Times.* Retrieved from http://www.nytimes.com/2009/09/09/business/economy/09leonhardt.html

Lester, D. (Ed.). (2000). *Suicide prevention: Resources for the millennium.* Philadelphia: Brunner-Routledge.

Lesthaeghe, R. (1995). The second demographic transition in Western countries: An interpretation. In K. O. Mason & A. Jensen (Eds.), *Gender and family change in industrialized countries* (pp. 17–62). Oxford: Clarendon Press.

Levine, L. (2012, December 17). *Offshoring (or offshore outsourcing) and job loss among U.S. workers* (CRS 7-5700; RL32292). Washington, DC: Congressional Research Service. Retrieved from http://fas.org/sgp/crs/misc/RL32292.pdf

Levine, M., & Crowther, S. (2008). The responsive bystander: How social group membership and group size can encourage as well as inhibit bystander intervention. *Journal of Interpersonal Psychology, 95,* 1429–1439.

LeVine, R. A., LeVine, S., Schnell-Anzola, B., Rowe, M. L., & Dexter, E. (2012). *Literacy and mothering: How women's schooling changes the lives of the world's children.* New York: Oxford University Press.

Levine, S., & Laurie, N. O. (Eds.). (1974). *The American Indian today.* Baltimore: Penguin Books.

Levitt, P. (2004, October 1). *Transnational migrants: When "home" means more than one country.* Migration Policy Institute. Retrieved from http://www.migrationpolicy.org/article/transnational-migrants-when-home-means-more-one-country

Lewin, T. (2011a, September 27). College graduation rates are stagnant even as enrollment rises, a study finds. *New York Times.* Retrieved from http://www.nytimes.com/2011/09/27/education/27remediation.html

Lewin, T. (2011b, October 25). Screen time higher than ever for children. *New York Times.* Retrieved from http://www.nytimes.com/2011/10/25/us/screen-time-higher-than-ever-for-children-study-finds.html

Library of Congress. (2012). Days in session calendars: 112th Congress 2nd session. Retrieved from http://thomas.loc.gov/home/ds/h1122.html

Liebow, E. (1967). *Talley's corner: A study of Negro street-corner men.* Boston: Little, Brown.

Lienert, P., & Thompson, M. (2014, April 2). GM avoided defective switch redesign in 2005 to save a dollar each. Reuters. Retrieved from http://www.reuters.com/article/2014/04/02/us-gm-recall-delphi-idUSBREA3105R20140402

Light, H. K., & Martin, R. E. (1986). American Indian families. *Journal of American Indian Education,* 1–5.

Lipka, Michael. (2015a, May 6). 5 facts about prayer. Washington, DC: Pew Research Center. Retrieved from http://www.pewresearch.org/fact-tank/2015/05/06/5-facts-about-prayer/

Lipka, Michael. (2015b). Millennials increasingly are driving growth of 'nones.' Pew Research Center, Fact Tank. Retrieved from http://www.pewresearch.org/fact-tank/2015/05/12/millennials-increasingly-are-driving-growth-of-nones/

Lips, H. (2008). *Sex and gender: An introduction* (6th ed.). Boston: McGraw-Hill.

Livingston, G. (2014). *Growing number of dads home with the kids.* Washington, DC: Pew Research Center. Retrieved from http://www.pewsocialtrends.org/2014/06/05/growing-number-of-dads-home-with-the-kids

Livingstone, S., & Brake, D. R. (2010). On the rapid rise of social networking sites: New findings and policy implications. *Children and Society, 24,* 75–83.

Logan, J. R., & Molotch, H. L. (1987). *Urban fortunes: The political economy of place.* Berkeley: University of California Press.

Logan, J. R., Minca, E., & Adar, S. (2012). The geography of inequality: Why separate means unequal in American public schools. *Sociology of Education, 85,* 287–301.

Lomborg, B. (2012, April 30). The high cost of heart disease and cancer. Slate. Retrieved from http://www.slate.com/articles/technol ogy/copenhagen_consensus_2012/2012/04/copenhagen_consensus_ideas_for_reduc ing_cancer_and_heart_disease.html

Lombroso, C. (1896). *L'homme criminel.* Paris: F. Alcan.

Lonsdorf, K. (2017). From Rolls-Royce to Grey Poupon, A Look at Brand Mentions in Chart-Topping Songs. *NPR,* August 22. Retrieved from https://www.npr.org/2017/08/22/545314024/rolls-royce-tops-list-as-musics-most-popular-brand

Loo, C. M. (1991). *Chinatown: Most time, hard time.* New York: Praeger.

Lucas, J. W., & Lovaglia, M. J. (1998). Leadership status, group size, and emotion in face-to-face groups. *Sociological Perspectives, 41,* 617–637.

Lynch, D. J. (n.d.). U.S. could learn from South Korean schools. Retrieved from http://abcnews.go.com/Business/story? id= 6293334&page=1

MacFarquhar, R. (1980, February 9). The post-Confucian challenge. *The Economist,* pp. 67–72.

MacKinnon, C. A. (1982). Feminism, Marxism, method and the state: An agenda for theory. *Signs, 7,* 515–544.

Mackun, P., & Wilson, S. (2011). *Population distribution and change: 2000 to 2010* (Census Brief CS2020BR-01). Washington, DC: U.S. Census Bureau. Retrieved from http://www.census.gov/prod/cen2010/briefs/c2010br-01.pdf

MacLeod, C. (2011, November 2). In China, tensions rising over Buddhism's quiet resurgence. *USA Today.* Retrieved from http://www.usatoday.com/news/religion/story/2011-11-01/tibetan-buddhism-china-communist-tension/51034604/1

Madlock, P. E., & Westerman, D. (2011). Hurtful cyber-teasing and violence: Who's laughing out loud? *Journal of Interpersonal Violence, 26,* 3542–3560.

Madrigal, A. (2011, November). What's wrong with #FirstWorldProblems? *Atlantic Monthly.* Retrieved from http://www.theatlantic.com/technology/archive/2011/11/whats-wrong-with-firstworldproblems/248829

Maher, J. K., Herbst, K. C., Childs, N. M., & Finn, S. (2008). Racial stereotypes in children's television commercials. *Journal of Advertising Research, 48,* 80–93.

Maher, L. (1997). *Sexed work: Gender, race, and resistance in a Brooklyn drug market.* New York: Oxford University Press.

Maidenberg, M. (2016, April 29). Where do Chicago manufacturing, transportation employees live and work? Retrieved from http://www.chicagobusiness.com/article/20160429/NEWS05/160429806/where-do-chicago-manufacturing-transportation-employees-live-and-work

Malacrida, C. (2005). Discipline and dehumanization in a total institution: Institutional survivors' descriptions of time-out rooms. *Disability & Society, 20,* 523–537.

Malinauskas, B. M., Raedeke, T. D., Aeby, V. G., Smith, J. L., & Dallas, M. B. (2006). Dieting practices, weight perceptions, and body composition: A comparison of normal weight, overweight, and obese college females. *Nutrition Journal, 5.*

Malthus, T. (1926). *First essay on population.* London: Macmillan. (Original work published 1798)

Mann, C. C. (2011, June). The birth of religion. *National Geographic,* pp. 34–59.

Mann, M. (1986). *The sources of social power: Vol. 1. A history of power from beginning until 1760.* New York: Cambridge University Press.

Margolis, E. (2001). *The hidden curriculum in higher education.* New York: Routledge.

Margonelli, L. (2010, February 7). Eternal Life. *New York Times.* Retrieved from https://www.nytimes.com/2010/02/07/books/review/Margonelli-t.html

Marini, M. M. (1990). Sex and gender: What do we know? *Sociological Forum, 5,* 95–120.

Markert, J. (2010). The changing face of racial discrimination: Hispanics as the dominant minority in the United States—A new application of power-threat theory. *Critical Sociology, 36,* 307–327.

Marlowe, C. M., Schneider, S. L., & Nelson, C. E. (1996). Gender and attractiveness biases in hiring decisions: Are more experienced managers less biased? *Journal of Applied Psychology, 81,* 11–21.

Maroto, M. E., Snelling, A., & Linck, H. (2015). Food insecurity among community college students: Prevalence and association with grade point average. *Community College Journal of Research and Practice, 39*(6), 515–526.

Martin, C. L., & Fabes, R. A. (2001). The stability and consequences of young children's same-sex peer interactions. *Developmental Psychology, 37,* 431–446.

Martin, D. S. (2012, March 1). Vets feel abandoned after secret drug experiments. CNN. Retrieved from http://edition.cnn.com/2012/03/01/health/human-test-subjects

Martineau, H. (1837). *Society in America.* New York: Saunders & Otley.

Marx, K. (1992a). *Capital: A critique of political economy* (Vol. 1). New York: Penguin Classics. (Original work published 1867)

Marx, K. (1992b). *Capital: A critique of political economy* (Vol. 2). New York: Penguin Classics. (Original work published 1885)

Marx, K. (1992c). *Capital: A critique of political economy* (Vol. 3). New York: Penguin Classics. (Original work published 1894)

Marx, K. (2000). Towards a critique of Hegel's *Philosophy of right*: Introduction. In D. McLellan (Ed.), *Karl Marx: Selected writings* (rev. ed.). New York: Classic Books International. (Original work published 1844)

Marx, K., & Engels, F. (1998). *The communist manifesto.* New York: Verso. (Original work published 1848)

Mason, M., McDowell, R., Mendoza, M., & Htusan, E. (2015, December 14). Global supermarkets selling shrimp peeled by slaves. Associated Press. Retrieved from http://bigstory.ap.org/article/8f64fb25931242a985bc30e3f5a9a0b2/ap-global-supermarkets-selling-shrimp-peeled-slaves

Massey, D. S. (2011). Epilogue: The past and future of Mexico–U.S. migration. In O.-V. Mark (Ed.), *Beyond la frontera: The history of Mexico–U.S. migration* (pp. 241–265). New York: Oxford University Press.

Massey, D. S., & Denton, N. A. (1993). *American apartheid: Segregation and the making of the underclass.* Boston: Harvard University Press.

Masters, J. (2011, February 7). Militant extremists in the United States. Council on Foreign Relations. Retrieved from http://www.cfr.org/terrorist-organizations-and-networks/militant-extremists-united-states/p9236

Mathisen, J. A. (1989). Twenty years after Bellah: Whatever happened to American civil religion? *Sociological Analysis, 50,* 129–146.

Mayer, G. (2004). *Union membership trends in the United States.* Washington, DC: Congressional Research Service. Retrieved from http://digitalcommons.ilr.cornell.edu/cgi/viewcontent.cgi?article=1176&context=key_workplace

Mazur, E., & Richards, L. (2011). Adolescents' and emerging adults' social networking online: Homophily or diversity? *Journal of Applied Developmental Psychology, 32,* 180–188.

Mazzella, R., & Feingold, A. (1994). The effects of physical attractiveness, race, socioeconomic status, and gender of defendant and victims on judgments of mock jurors: A meta-analysis. *Journal of Applied Social Psychology, 24,* 1315–1344.

McAdam, D., McCarthy, J. D., & Zald, M. N. (1988). Social movements. In N. J. Smelser (Ed.), Handbook of sociology (pp. 695–737). Newbury Park, CA: Sage.

McCarthy, J. (2014, June 2). Double rape, lynching in India exposes caste fault lines. *National Public Radio.* Retrieved from http://www.npr.org/blogs/parallels/2014/06/02/318259419/double-rape-lynching-in-india-exposes-caste-fault-lines

McCartney, J. T. (1992). *Black power ideologies: An essay in African American political thought.* Philadelphia: Temple University Press.

McCoy, A. W. (1991). *The politics of heroin: CIA complicity in the global drug trade.* New York: Lawrence Hill.

McCoy, K. (2009). Uncle Sam wants them. *Contexts, 8,* pp. 14–19.

McDonald, S., & Day, J. C. (2010). Race, gender, and the invisible hand of social capital. *Sociology Compass, 4,* 532–543.

McDonald, S., & Mair, C. A. (2010). Social capital across the life course: Age and gendered patterns of network resources. *Sociological Forum, 25,* 335–359.

McDonald, S., Lin, N., & Ao, D. (2009). Networks of opportunity: Gender, race, and job leads. *Social Problems, 56,* 385–402.

McGregor, J. (2014, January 3). Zappos says goodbye to bosses. *Washington Post.* Retrieved from http://www.washingtonpost.com/blogs/on-leadership/wp/2014/01/03/zappos-gets-rid-of-all-managers

McGuire, L. C., Okoro, C. A., Goins, R. T., & Anderson, L. A. (2008). Characteristics of American Indian and Alaska native adult caregivers: Behavioral Risk Factor Surveillance System, 2000. *Ethnicity & Disease, 18,* 520.

McKenna, K. Y. A., & Bargh, J. A. (1998). Coming out in the age of the Internet: Identity "demarginalization" through virtual group participation. *Journal of Personality and Social Psychology, 75,* 681–694.

McKibben, B. (2011, April 7). Resisting climate reality. *New York Review of Books.* Retrieved from http://www.nybooks.com/articles/archives/2011/apr/07/resisting-climate-reality/? pagination=false

McLean, B., & Elkind, P. (2003). *The smartest guys in the room: The amazing rise and scandalous fall of Enron.* New York: Penguin/Portfolio.

McLean, B., & Nocera, J. (2010). *All the devils are here: The hidden history of the financial crisis.* New York: Penguin/Portfolio.

McLoyd, V. C., & Smith, J. (2002). Physical discipline and behavior problems in African American, European American, and Hispanic children: Emotional support as a moderator. *Journal of Marriage and Family, 64,* 40–53.

McNeely, C. L. (1995). *Constructing the nation-state: International organization and prescriptive action.* Westport, CT: Greenwood.

McNicoll, G. (2001). Government and fertility in transitional and post-transitional societies. *Population and Development Review, 27,* 129–159.

Mead, G. H. (1934). *Mind, self, and society.* Chicago: University of Chicago Press.

Mead, G. H. (1938). *The philosophy of the act.* Chicago: University of Chicago Press.

Mednick, S. A., Gabrielli, W. F., Jr., & Hutchings, B. (1987). Genetic factors in the etiology of criminal behavior. In S. A. Mednick, T. E. Moffitt, & S. A. Stack (Eds.), *The causes of crime: New biological approaches.* Cambridge: Cambridge University Press.

Mehra, A., Dixon, A. L., Brass, D. J., & Robertson, B. (2006). The social network ties of group leaders: Implications for group performance and leader reputation. *Organization Science, 17,* 64–79.

Melton, J. G. (Ed.). (1996). *Encyclopedia of American religions* (5th ed.). New York: Gale Research.

Melvin, D., Walsh, N. P., & Hume, T. (2016, January 15). Starvation in Syria a 'War Crime,' U.N. chief says. Retrieved from http://www.cnn.com/2016/01/15/middleeast/syria-madaya-starvation/

Mendelson, S. (2017). "Box Office: 'Fate of the Furious' Joins 'Furious 7' in the $1B Club." *Forbes,* April 30. Retrieved from https://www.forbes.com/sites/

scottmendelson/2017/04/30/box-office-fate-of-the-furious-joins-furious-7-in-the-1-billion-club/#7514f82f2f54

Merton, R. K. (1938). Social structure and anomie. *American Sociological Review, 3,* 672–682.

Merton, R. K. (1968). *Social theory and social structure.* New York: Free Press.

Merton, R. K. (1996). *On social structure and science.* Chicago: University of Chicago Press.

Michalowski, R., & Dubisch, J. (2001). *Run for the wall: Remembering Vietnam on a motorcycle pilgrimage.* New Brunswick, NJ: Rutgers University Press.

Milgram, S. (1963). Behavioral studies in obedience. *Journal of Abnormal Psychology, 67,* 371–378.

Milkman, R. (2006). *L.A. story: Immigrant workers and the future of the U.S. labor movement.* New York: Russell Sage Foundation.

Miller, K. A., Kohn, M. A., & Schooler, C. (1986). Educational self-direction and personality. *American Sociological Review, 5,* 372–390.

Miller, K. E., Melnick, M. J., Barnes, G. M., Farrell, M. P., & Sabo, D. F. (2005). Untangling the links among athletic involvement, gender, race, and adolescent academic outcomes. *Sociology of Sport Journal, 22,* 178–193.

Miller, L. P. (1995). Tracking the progress of *Brown. Teachers College Record, 96,* 609–613.

Millett, K. (1970). *Sexual politics.* Garden City, NY: Doubleday.

Mills, C. M. (2000b). *The sociological imagination* (40th anniversary ed.). New York: Oxford University Press. (Original work published 1959)

Mills, C. W. (2000a). *The power elite.* New York: Oxford University Press. (Original work published 1956)

Miner, H. (1956). Body ritual among the Nacirema. *American Anthropologist, 58,* 503–507.

Mitchiner, J., & Sass-Lehrer, M. (2011). My child can have more choices: Reflections of deaf mothers on cochlear implants for their children. In R. Paludneviciene & I. W. Leigh (Eds.), *Cochlear implants: Evolving perspectives.* Washington, DC: Gallaudet University Press.

Mizruchi, M. S., & Potts, B. B. (1998). Centrality and power revisited: Actor success in group decision making. *Social Networks, 20,* 353–387.

Mollenkopf, J. (1977). The postwar politics of urban development. In J. Walton & D. E. Carns (Eds.), *Cities in change* (2nd ed., pp. 549–579). Boston: Allyn & Bacon.

Molotch, H. L. (1976). The city as a growth machine. *American Journal of Sociology, 82,* 309–333.

Monaghan, A. (2014, November 13). US wealth inequality—top 0.1% worth as much as the bottom 90%. Retrieved from https://www.theguardian.com/business/2014/nov/13/us-wealth-inequality-top-01-worth-as-much-as-the-bottom-90

Mongeau, L. (2016). Pulling reservation schools back from the brink. Retrieved from http://hechingerreport.org/pulling-reservation-schools-back-brink/

Monroe, P. (1940). *Founding of the American public school system.* New York: Macmillan.

Moore, J., & Pinderhughes, R. (2001). The Latino population: The importance of economic restructuring. In M. L. Andersen & P. H. Collins (Eds.), *Race, class, and gender: An anthology* (4th ed., pp. 251–258). Belmont, CA: Wadsworth.

Moore, L. R. (1994). *Selling God: American religion in the marketplace culture.* New York: Oxford University Press.

Morgan, R. E., & Kena, G. (2017, December). Crime Victimization, 2016. Washington, DC: Bureau of Justice Statistics. Retrieved from https://www.bjs.gov/content/pub/pdf/cv16.pdf

Morishima, M. (1982). *Why has Japan "succeeded"? Western technology and the Japanese ethos.* New York: Cambridge University Press.

Moser, S., & Dilling, L. (2004). Making climate hot: Communicating the urgency and challenge of global climate change. *Environment, 46,* 32–46.

Motlagh, J. (2012, September 19). In a world hungry for cheap shrimp, migrants labor overtime in Thai sheds. *Washington Post.* Retrieved from http://www.washingtonpost.com/world/asia_pacific/in-a-world-hungry-for-cheap-shrimp-migrants-labor-overtime-in-thai-sheds/2012/09/19/3435a90e-01a4-11e2-b257-e1c2b3548a4a_story.html

Mukhopadhyay, C. C., & Higgins, P. (1988). Anthropological studies of women's status revisited: 1977–87. *Annual Review of Anthropology, 17,* 461–495.

Muller, J. (2014, February 15). UAW's loss and what it means for your paycheck. *Forbes.* Retrieved from http://www.forbes.com/sites/joannmuller/2014/02/15/uaws-loss-and-what-it-means-for-your-paycheck

Mumford, L. (1961). *The city in history: Its origins, its transformations, and its prospects.* New York: Harcourt.

Muncer, S. J., & Campbell, A. (2000). Comments on "Sex differences in beliefs about aggression: Opponent's sex and the form of aggression" by J. Archer and A. Haigh. *British Journal of Social Psychology, 39,* 309–311.

Münchener, Rückversicherungs-Gesellschaft. 2016. "Natural Loss Events Worldwide 2015." Retrieved from www.munichre.com/site/wrap/get/documents_E1656163460/mram/assetpool.munichreamerica.wrap/PDF/07Press/2015_World_map_of_nat_cats.pdf

Murdock, G. P. (1949). *Social structure.* New York: Macmillan.

Murphy, M. (2012, December 18). But what about the men? Masculinity and mass shootings. Retrieved from http://www.feministcurrent.com/2012/12/18/but-what-about-the-men-on-masculinity-and-mass-shootings/

Murphy, R. (1988). *Social closure: The theory of monopolization and exclusion.* Oxford: Clarendon.

Mutchler, J. E., Baker, L. E., & Lee, S. (2007). Grandparents responsible for grandchildren in Native-American families. *Social Science Quarterly, 88,* 990–1009.

Mutharayappa, R., Choe, M. K., Arnold, F., & Roy, T. K. (1997, March). *Son preference and its effect on fertility in India* (National Family Survey Subject Reports No. 3). Honolulu: East-West Center Program on Population. Retrieved from http://scholarspace.manoa.hawaii.edu/bitstream/handle/10125/3475/NFHSsubjrpt003.pdf? sequence=1

Myrdal, G. (1963). *Challenge to affluence.* New York: Random House.

Narayan, U., & Harding, S. (2000). *Decentering the center: Philosophy for a multicultural, postcolonial, and feminist world.* Bloomington: Indiana University Press.

National Association of Realtors. (2012). The digital house hunt: Consumer and market trends in real estate. Retrieved from http://www.realtor.org/sites/default/files/Study-Digital-House-Hunt-2013-01_1.pdf

National Association of the Deaf. (2000). NAD position statement on cochlear implants. Retrieved from http://www.nad.org/issues/technology/assistive-listening/cochlear-implants

National Campaign to Prevent Teen Pregnancy. (2010). Why it matters: Teen pregnancy, poverty, and income disparity. Retrieved from http://www.thenationalcampaign.org

National Center for Education Statistics. (2016a, May). Immediate college enrollment rate. Retrieved from http://nces.ed.gov/programs/coe/indicator_cpa.asp

National Center for Education Statistics. (2016b). Annual earnings of young adults. Retrieved from http://nces.ed.gov/programs/coe/indicator_cba.asp

National Center for Injury Prevention and Control. (2014). *Understanding teen dating violence: Fact sheet.* Washington, DC: Centers for Disease Control and Prevention. Retrieved from http://www.cdc.gov/violence prevention/pdf/teen-dating-violence-2014-a.pdf

National Center for Victims of Crime. (2012). Intimate partner violence. Retrieved from http://www.victimsofcrime.org/library/crime-information-and-statistics/intimate-partner-violence

National Employment Law Project. (2014, April). *The low-wage recovery: Industry employment and wages four years into the recovery (Data Brief).* New York: Author. Retrieved from http://www.nelp.org/page/-/reports/low-wage-recovery-industry-employment-wages-2014-report.pdf? nocdn=1

National Institute of Justice. (2011, September 13). Terrorism. Retrieved from http://www.nij.gov/topics/crime/terrorism/welcome.htm

National Public Radio. (2010, November 5). Counting crowds: Results may very. *Science Friday.* Retrieved from http://www.npr.org/templates/story/story.php?storyId= 131099075

National Survey of Student Engagement. (2012). Fostering student engagement campuswide: Annual results 2012. Bloomington: Indiana University Center for Postsecondary Research. Retrieved from http://nsse.iub.edu/html/annual_results.cfm

Naylor, N. T. (2002). *Wages of crime: Black markets, illegal finance, and the underworld economy.* Ithaca, NY: Cornell University Press.

NBC News. (2015, April 22). ISIS using social media and violence to recruit [Video]. Retrieved from http://www.nbcnews.com/watch/long-story-short/isis-using-social-media-and-violence-to-recruit-432161347692

NCPSSN. (2018). Medicare Fast Facts. Retrieved from https://www.ncpssm.org/our-issues/medicare/medicare-fast-facts/

Neate, R. (2015, May 3). America's trailer parks: The residents may be poor but the owners are getting rich. Retrieved from http://www.theguardian.com/life andstyle/2015/may/03/owning-trailer-parks-mobile-home-univer sity-investment

Neuman, W. L. (2000). *Social research methods: Qualitative and quantitative approaches.* Toronto: Allyn & Bacon.

New America Foundation. (2012). Federal education budget project. Retrieved from http://febp.newamerica.net/k12

Newcomb, T. C. (2008). *Parameters of parenting in Native American families* (Doctoral dissertation, Oklahoma State University). Retrieved from ProQuest (3320882).

Neyazi, T. A. (2010). Cultural imperialism or vernacular modernity? Hindi newspapers in a globalizing India. *Media, Culture & Society, 32,* 907–924.

Nicholas, S. E. (2009). "I live Hopi, I just don't speak it": The critical intersection of language, culture and identity in the lives of contemporary Hopi youth. *Journal of Language, Identity & Education, 8,* 321–334.

Niebuhr, H. R. (1929). *The social sources of denominationalism.* New York: Meridian Books.

Nielsen. (2017). The Nielsen total audience report: Q2 2017. Retrieved from http://www.nielsen.com/us/en/insights/reports/2017/the-nielsen-total-audience-q2-2017.html http://www.nielsen.com/us/en/insights/reports/2017/the-nielsen-total-audience-q2-2017.html.

Nisbet, R. (1970). *The social bond: An introduction to the study of society.* New York: Knopf.

Norris, M. (2011, July 8). Why Black women, infants lag in birth outcomes. *National Public Radio.* Retrieved from http://www.npr.org/2011/07/08/137652226/-the-race-gap

Nuland, S. B. (2003). *The doctors' plague: Germs, childbed fever, and the strange story of Ignac Semmelweis.* New York: Norton.

O'Dea. T. (1966). *The sociology of religion.* Upper Saddle River, NJ: Prentice Hall.

Oakes, J. (1985). *Keeping track: How schools structure inequality.* New Haven, CT: Yale University Press.

Obama administration must do more to protect children harvesting tobacco. (2014, May 18). *Washington Post.* Retrieved from http://www.washingtonpost.com/opinions/obama-administration-must-do-more-to-protect-children-harvesting-tobacco/2014/05/18/23b8a7c4-dd36-11e3-b745-87d39690c5c0_story.html

Offe, C. (1984). *Contradictions of the welfare state.* Cambridge: MIT Press.

Ogden, C. L., Carroll, M. D., Kit, B. K., & Flegal, K. M. (2012). *Prevalence of obesity in the United States, 2009–2010* (NCHS Data Brief 82). Hyattsville, MD: National Center for Health Statistics. Retrieved from http://www.cdc.gov/nchs/data/databriefs/db82.pdf

Ogunlesi, T., & Busari, S. (2012, September 14). Seven ways mobile phones have changed lives in Africa. CNN. Retrieved from http://www.cnn.com/2012/09/13/world/africa/mobile-phones-change-africa

Okun, A. (2013, October 9). Some terrible people on Twitter have decided that it's "Fat Shaming Week." Retrieved from https://www.buzzfeed.com/alannaokun/some-terrible-people-on-twitter-have-decided-that-its-fat-sh? utm_term=.cxw62AABWz#.ogZvdDDLjw

Olivieri, E. (2014). *Occupational choice and the college gender gap* [Working Paper]. Retrieved from https://docs.google.com/viewer?a=v&pid=sites&srcid=ZGVmYXVsdGRvbWFpbnxlbGlzYW9saXZpZXJpfGd4Ojh kNmI5NTg2NTgyOTYYx

Orfield, G., & Eaton, S. E. (1996). *Dismantling desegregation: The quiet reversal of* Brown v. Board of Education. New York: Norton.

Organisation for Economic Co-operation and Development. (2011). Chart A1.1. Percentage of population that has attained tertiary education, by age group (2009). In *Education at a glance.* Paris: Author. Retrieved from http://www.oecd.org/education/highereducationandadultlearning/48630299.pdf

Orwell, G. (1949). *1984.* London: Secker and Warburg.

Oxfam. (2015). A decade of saving for change [Brochure]. Retrieved from https://www.oxfamamerica.org/static/media/files/SFCtimeline-final-AA.pdf

Paoli, L. (2003). *Mafia brotherhoods: Organized crime Italian style.* Oxford: Oxford University Press.

Papachristos, A. V., Smith, C. M., Scherer, M. L., & Fugiero, M. A. (2011). More coffee, less crime? The relationship between gentrification and neighborhood crime rates in Chicago, 1991 to 2005. *City & Community, 10,* 215–240.

Pape, R. (2005). *Dying to win: The strategic logic of suicide terrorism.* New York: Random House.

Parente, S. L. (2008). Narrowing the economic gap in the 21st century. In K. R. Holmes, E. J. Feulner, & M. A. O'Grady (Eds.), *2008 index of economic freedom.* Washington, DC: Heritage Foundation.

Parker, K. (2012). Where the Public Stands on Government Assistance, Taxes, and Presidential Candidates. Pew Research, September 20. Retrieved from http://www.pewsocialtrends.org/2012/09/20/where-the-public-stands-on-government-assistance-taxes-and-the-presidential-candidates/

Parker-Pope, T. (2010, April 14). Is marriage good for your health? *New York Times Magazine.* Retrieved from http://www.nytimes.com/2010/04/18/magazine/18marriage-t.html? pagewanted=all

Parkin, F. (1979). Social closure and class formation. In A. Giddens & D. Held (Eds.), *Classes, power, and conflict* (pp. 175–184). Los Angeles: University of California Press.

Parrado, E. A., & Morgan, S. P. (2008). Intergeneration fertility among Hispanic women: New evidence of immigrant assimilation. *Demography, 45,* 651–671.

Parsons, T. (1951). *The social system.* New York: Free Press.

Parsons, T. (1954). The kinship system of the contemporary United States. In *Essays in sociological theory* (pp. 189–194). New York: Free Press.

Parsons, T. (1960). Some principle characteristics of industrial societies. In T. Parson (Ed.), *Structure and process in modern societies* (pp. 132–168). New York: Free Press.

Parsons, T. (1966). *Societies: Evolutionary and comparative perspectives.* Upper Saddle River, NJ: Prentice Hall.

Parsons, T. (1967). *The structure of social action.* New York: Free Press.

Parsons, T. (1975). The sick role and the role of the physician reconsidered. *Milbank Memorial Fund Quarterly, Health and Society, 53,* 257–278.

Parsons, T. (2007). *Social structure and personality.* New York: Free Press. (Original work published 1964)

Parsons, T., & Bales, R. F. (1955). *Family, socialization and interaction process.* Glencoe, IL: Free Press.

Parsons, T., & Mayhew, H. D. (1982). *On institutions and social evolution: Selected writings.* Chicago: University of Chicago Press.

Parsons, T., & Smelser, N. J. (1956). *Economy and society.* New York: Free Press.

Pascoe, C. J. (2007). *Dude, you're a fag: Masculinity and sexuality in high school.* Berkeley: University of California Press.

Patterson, D. (1989). *Power in law enforcement: Subordinate preference and actual use of power base in special weapons teams (SWAT)* (Doctoral dissertation, Fielding Institute, Santa Barbara, CA).

PBS. (2010, May 31). China faces growing health threat from prevalent tobacco use. *NewsHour.* Retrieved from http://www.pbs.org/newshour/bb/health/jan-june10/tobacco_05–31.html

Pearlstein, S. (2010, October 6). The costs of rising economic inequality. *Washington Post*. Retrieved from http://www.washingtonpost.com/wp-dyn/content/article/2010/10/05/AR2010100505535.html

Pecanha, S., & Wallace, T. (2015, June 20). The flight of refugees around the globe. *New York Times*. Retrieved from http://www.nytimes.com/interactive/2015/06/21/world/map-flow-desperate-migration-refugee-crisis.html?_r=1

Peek, K. L. (1999). *The good, the bad, and the "misunderstood": A study of the cognitive moral development theory and ethics in the public sector*. Fort Lauderdale, FL: Nova Southeastern University.

Perlin, R. (2011). *Intern nation: How to earn nothing and learn little in the brave new economy*. New York: Verso.

Perlin, R. (2012, February 6). These are not your father's internships. *New York Times*. Retrieved from http://www.nytimes.com/roomfordebate/2012/02/04/do-unpaid-internships-exploit-college-students/todays-internships-are-a-racket-not-an-opportunity

Pettit, K. L. S., & Reuben, K. (2010). Investor-owners in the boom and bust. Urban Institute. Retrieved from http://metrotrends.org/mortgagelending.html

Pew Forum on Religion and Public Life. (2004, June 14). Supreme Court upholds "under God" in Pledge of Allegiance: Court overturns lower court ruling on legal technicality. Retrieved from http://www.pewforum.org/Press-Room/Press-Releases/Supreme-Court-Upholds-Under-God-in-Pledge-of-Allegiance.aspx

Pew Forum on Religion and Public Life. (2008). *Summary of key findings: U.S. Religious Landscape Survey*. Washington, DC: Pew Research Center.

Pew Forum on Religion and Public Life. (2009). *Mapping the global Muslim population: A report on the size and distribution of the world's Muslim population*. Washington, DC: Pew Research Center. Retrieved from http://www.pewforum.org/2009/10/07/mapping-the-global-muslim-population/

Pew Forum on Religion and Public Life. (2010). *Religion among the millennials*. Washington, DC: Pew Research Center. Retrieved from http://www.pewforum.org/files/2010/02/millennials-report.pdf

Pew Forum on Religion and Public Life. (2012). 'Nones' on the Rise. Retrieved from http://www.pewforum.org/2012/10/09/nones-on-the-rise/

Pew Forum on Religion and Public Life. (2011a). *The future of the global Muslim population: Projections for 2010–2030*. Washington, DC: Pew Research Center. Retrieved from http://www.pewforum.org/files/2011/01/FutureGlobalMuslimPopulation-WebPDF-Feb10.pdf

Pew Forum on Religion and Public Life. (2014). Religious Landscape Study. Retrieved from http://www.pewforum.org/religious-landscape-study/

Pew Forum on Religion and Public Life. (2015). *America's changing religious landscape*. Washington, DC: Pew Research Center. Retrieved from http://www.pewforum.org/2015/05/12/americas-changing-religious-landscape/

Pew Research Center for the People and the Press. (2012, November 26). Young voters supported Obama less, but may have mattered more. Retrieved from http://www.people-press.org/2012/11/26/young-voters-supported-obama-less-but-may-have-mattered-more

Pew Research Center. (2011a). *Republican candidates stir little enthusiasm*. Washington, DC: Author. Retrieved from http://www.people-press.org/files/legacy-pdf/06-02-11%202012%20Campaign%20Release.pdf

Pew Research Center. (2011b). Sunni and Shia Muslims. Retrieved from http://www.pewforum.org/2011/01/27/future-of-the-global-muslim-population-sunni-and-shia/

Pew Research Center. (2012, March). "Faith on the Move – The Religious Affiliation of International Migrants." Washington, DC. Retrieved from http://www.pewforum.org/2012/03/08/religious-migration-exec/

Pew Research Center. (2014a, January 27). Climate change: Key data points from Pew Research. Retrieved from http://www.pewresearch.org/key-data-points/climate-change-key-data-points-from-pew-research

Pew Research Center. (2014b). *Older adults and technology use*. Washington, DC: Author. Retrieved from http://www.pewinternet.org/files/2014/04/PIP_Seniors-and-Tech-Use_040314.pdf

Pew Research Center. (2015a). *Latest trends in religious restrictions and hostilities*. Retrieved from http://www.pewforum.org/2015/02/26/religious-hostilities

Pew Research Center. (2015b). "Parenting in America." Washington, DC. Retrieved from http://www.pewsocialtrends.org/2015/12/17/parenting-in-america/

Pew Research Center. (2016b). *Faith and the 2016 campaign*. Retrieved from http://www.pewforum.org/2016/01/27/faith-and-the-2016-campaign/

Pew Research Center. (2018, February 5). Social Media Fact Sheet. Retrieved from http://www.pewinternet.org/fact-sheet/social-media/

Phelan, A. M., & McLaughlin, H. J. (1995). Educational discoveries: The nature of the child and practices of new teachers. *Journal of Teacher Education, 46*, 165–174.

Piaget, J. (1926). *The language and thought of the child*. New York: Harcourt, Brace.

Piaget, J. (1928). *Judgment and reasoning in the child*. New York: Harcourt, Brace.

Piaget, J. (1930). *The child's conception of physical causality*. New York: Harcourt, Brace.

Piaget, J. (1932). *The moral judgment of the child*. New York: Harcourt, Brace.

Pinsker, B. (2015, August 12). Online doctor visits are set to surge. Retrieved from http://time.com/money/3994614/online-doctor-visit-increase/

Pipes, D., & Durán, K. (2002, August). *Muslim immigrants in the United States*. Washington, DC: Center for Immigration Studies. Retrieved from http://www.cis.org/sites/cis.org/files/articles/2002/back802.pdf

Podsakoff, P., & Schriesheim, C. (1985). Field studies of French and Raven's bases of power: Critique, reanalysis, and suggestions for future research. *Psychological Bulletin, 97,* 387–411.

Ponton, L. (2000). *The sex lives of teenagers.* New York: Dutton.

Popkin, B. M., Adair, L. S., & Ng, S. W. (2012). Global nutrition transition and the pandemic of obesity in developing countries. *Nutrition Reviews, 70,* 3–21.

Popper, K. (1959). *The logic of scientific discovery.* New York: Basic Books.

Population Reference Bureau. (2010). *2010 world population data sheet.* Washington, DC: Author. Retrieved from http://www.prb.org/pdf10/10wpds_eng.pdf

Population Reference Bureau. (2012). *2012 world population data sheet.* Washington, DC: Author. Retrieved from http://www.prb.org/pdf12/2012-population-data-sheet_eng.pdf

Population Reference Bureau. (2015). *2015 world population data sheet.* Washington, DC: Author. Retrieved from http://www.prb.org/pdf15/2015-world-population-data-sheet_eng.pdf

Population Reference Bureau. (2018). World Population Data Sheet. Retrieved from https://www.prb.org/2018-world-population-data-sheet-with-focus-on-changing-age-structures/

Poteet, G. A. (2007). Perceptions of pretty people: An experimental study of interpersonal attractiveness (Master's thesis, Washington State University). Retrieved from http://www.dissertations.wsu.edu/Thesis/Spring2007/a_poteet_050307.pdf

Potok, M. (2015, November 16). FBI: Reported hate crimes down nationality except against Muslims. Retrieved from https://www.splcenter.org/hatewatch/2015/11/16/fbi-reported-hate-crimes-down-nationally-except-against-muslims

Powell, R. (2013). Social desirability bias in polling on same-sex marriage ballot initiatives. *American Politics Research, 41,* 1052–1070.

Pradhan, E. (2015, November 27). The relationship between women's education and fertility. Retrieved from https://www.weforum.org/agenda/2015/11/the-relationship-between-womens-education-and-fertility/

Presser, S. (1990). Can changes in context reduce vote overreporting in surveys? *Public Opinion Quarterly, 54,* 586–593.

Preston, P. (1994). *Mother father deaf: Living between sound and silence.* Cambridge, MA: Harvard University Press.

Preves, S. E. (2003). *Intersex and identity: The contested self.* New Brunswick, NJ: Rutgers University Press.

Proulx C. M., & Snyder-Rivas, L. A. (2013). The longitudinal associations between marital happiness, problems, and self-rated health. *Journal of Family Psychology, 27,* 194–202. http://dx.doi.org/10.1037/a0031877

Putnam, R. (2000). *Bowling alone: The collapse and revival of American community.* New York: Simon & Schuster.

Qian, J., Cai, M., Gao, J., Tang, S., Xu, L., & Critchley, J. A. (2010). Trends in smoking and quitting in China from 1993 to 2003: National Health Service survey data. *Bulletin of the World Health Organization, 88.* Retrieved from http://www.who.int/bulletin/volumes/88/10/09-064709/en/index.tml

Queen, S. A., Habenstein, R. W., & Adams, J. B. (1961). *The family in various cultures* (2nd ed.). Philadelphia: J. B. Lippincott.

Quiggin, J. (2010). *Zombie economics: How dead ideas still walk among us.* Princeton, NJ: Princeton University Press.

Quinones, S. (2015). *Dreamland: The true tale of America's opiate epidemic.* New York: Bloomsbury Publishing.

Raghavan, S. (2016, July 7). In Yemen, child brides are part of the ravages of civil war. *Washington Post,* pp. A1, A14.

Rampell, C. (2010, March 9). Why a Big Mac costs less than a salad. *New York Times.* Retrieved from http://economix.blogs.nytimes.com/2010/03/09/why-a-big-mac-costs-less-than-a-salad

Rampey, B. D., Finnegan, R., Goodman, M., Mohadjer, L., Krenzke, T., Hogan, J., . . . Xie, H. (2016, March). Skills of U.S. unemployed, young, and older adults in sharper focus: Results from the Program for the International Assessment of Adult Competencies (PIAAC) 2012/2014: First Look. Washington, DC: National Center for Education Statistics. Retrieved from http://nces.ed.gov/pubsearch/pubsinfo.asp? pubid= 2016039

Randall, V. R. (1999). History of tobacco. Boston University Medical Center. Retrieved from http://academic.udayton.edu/health/syllabi/tobacco/history.htm#industry

Raven, B., & Kruglianski, W. (1975). Conflict and power. In P. Swingle (Ed.), *Structure of conflict* (pp. 177–219). New York: Academic Press.

Reaney, P., & Goldsmith, B. (2008, April 4). Husbands create 7 hours of extra housework a week: Study. Reuters. Retrieved from http://www.reuters.com/article/2008/04/04/us-housework-husbands-idUSN0441782 220080404

Reich, R. (1991). *The work of nations: Preparing ourselves for 21st century capitalism.* New York: First Vintage Books.

Reich, R. (2001, April 9). The case (once again) for universal health insurance. *American Prospect.* Retrieved from http://prospect.org/article/case-once-again-universal-health-insurance

Reich, R. (2010). *Aftershock: The next economy and America's future.* New York: Knopf.

Reingold, J. (2016). How a radical shift left Zappos reeling. *Fortune.* Retrieved from http://fortune.com/zappos-tony-hsieh-holacracy/

Renjini, D. (2000). *Nayar women today: Disintegration of matrilineal system and the status of Nayar women in Kerala.* India: India Classical.

Renzetti, C. M., & Curran, D. J. (1992). *Women, men, and society* (2nd ed.). Boston: Allyn & Bacon.

Reskin, B., & Padavic, I. (2002). *Women and men at work* (2nd ed.). Thousand Oaks, CA: Sage.

Rhodes, A. (2016, June 28). Young people—if you're so upset by the outcome of the EU referendum, then why didn't you get out and vote? Retrieved from http://www.independent.co.uk/voices/eu-referendum-brexit-young-people-upset-by-the-outcome-of-the-eu-referendum-why-didnt-you-vote-a7105396.html

Richards, C. (2012). Playing under surveillance: Gender performance and the conduct of the self in a primary school playground. *British Journal of Sociology of Education, 33,* 373–390.

Richardson, J. (2009). Satanism in America: An update. *Social Compass, 56,* 552–563.

Ridgeway, C. L., & Correll, S. J. (2004). Unpacking the gender system: A theoretical perspective on gender beliefs and social relations. *Gender & Society, 18,* 510–531.

Ridgeway, C. L., & Smith-Lovin, L. (1999). The gender system and interaction. *Annual Review of Sociology, 25,* 191–217.

Ridley, M. (1998). *The origins of virtue: Human instincts and the evolution of cooperation.* New York: Viking Press.

Riley, C. (2012, March 26). Can 46 rich dudes buy an election? *CNNMoney.* Retrieved from http://money.cnn.com/2012/03/26/news/economy/super-pac-donors/index.htm

Riordan, C. (1990). *Girls and boys in school: Together or separate?* New York: Teachers College Press.

Ripley, A. (2013, August 3). The $4 million dollar teacher. Retrieved from http://www.wsj.com/articles/SB10001424127887324635904578639780253571520

Rist, R. S. (1970). Student, social class, and teacher expectations: The self-fulfilling prophecy in ghetto education. *Harvard Educational Review, 40,* 411–451.

Ritzer, G. (1999). *Enchanting a disenchanted world: Revolutionizing the means of consumption.* Thousand Oaks, CA: Pine Forge.

Rodenhizer, K., and & Edwards, K. (2017). The Impacts of sexual media exposure on adolescent and emerging adults' dating and sexual violence attitudes and behaviors: A critical review of the literature. Retrieved from http://journals.sagepub.com/doi/abs/10.1177/1524838017717745http://journals.sagepub.com/doi/abs/10.1177/1524838017717745.

Romer, D., Jamieson, P. E., & Jamieson, K. H. (2017). The continuing rise of gun violence in PG-13 movies, 1985 to 2015. *Pediatrics,* January. Retrieved from http://pediatrics.aappublications.org/content/early/2017/01/09/peds.2016-2891

Roof, W. C. (1993). *A generation of seekers: Spiritual journeys of the baby boom generation.* San Francisco: HarperSanFrancisco.

Roof, W. C., & McKinney, W. (1990). *American mainline religion: Its changing shape and future.* New Brunswick, NJ: Rutgers University Press.

Roschelle, A. R., & Kaufman, P. (2004). Fitting in and fighting back: Stigma management strategies among homeless kids. *Symbolic Interaction, 27,* 23–46. Retrieved from http://onlinelibrary.wiley.com/doi/10.1525/si.2004.27.1.23/abstract

Rosen, J. (2014, September 5). Animal Traffic. *New York Times.* Retrieved from https://www.nytimes.com/2014/09/05/t-magazine/animal-trafficking-black-market.html

Rosenbaum, S. (2013, September 4). Pledge of Allegiance challenged in Massachusetts Supreme Court. NBC News. Retrieved from http://www.nbcnews.com/news/us-news/pledge-allegiance-challenged-massachusetts-supreme-court-v20327848

Rosenbloom, S. R., & Way, N. (2004). Experiences of discrimination among African American, Asian American, and Latino adolescents in an urban high school. *Youth & Society, 35,* 420–451.

Rosenfeld, M. J., & Thomas, R. J. (2012). Searching for a mate: The rise of the Internet as a social intermediary. *American Sociological Review, 77*(4), pp. 523–547.

Rosenthal, R., & Jacobson, L. (1968). *Pygmalion in the classroom.* New York: Holt, Rinehart & Winston.

Rosenwald, M. S. (2016, May 17). Youth sports participation is up slightly, but many kids are still left behind. *The Washington Post.* Retrieved from https://www.washingtonpost.com/news/local/wp/2016/05/17/youth-sports-participation-is-up-slightly-but-many-kids-are-still-left-behind/?utm_term=.d9bca4eae1cb

Rosoff, S., Pontell, H., & Tillman, R. (2010). *Profit without honor: White-collar crime and the looting of America.* Upper Saddle River, NJ: Prentice Hall.

Rostow, W. W. (1961). *The stages of economic growth.* Cambridge: Cambridge University Press.

Rothkopf, D. (2008). *Superclass: The global power elite and the world they are making.* New York: Farrar, Straus and Giroux.

Rothschild-Whitt, J. (1979). The collectivist organization: An alternative to rational-bureaucratic models. *American Sociological Review, 44,* 509–527.

Rowbotham, S. (1973). *Woman's consciousness, man's world.* Middlesex, England: Pelican.

Rowen, B. (2018, March 16). The Jedi Faithful. *Pacific Standard.* Retrieved from https://psmag.com/economics/the-jedi-faithful

Rubin, B. (1996). *Shifts in the social contract: Understanding change in American society.* Thousand Oaks, CA: Pine Forge.

Rubin, L. B. (2006). What am I going to do with the rest of my life? *Dissent, 53,* 88–94.

Rugh, J. S., & Massey, D. S. (2014). Segregation in post-civil rights America: Stalled integration or the end of the segregated century? *Du Bois Review: Social Science Research on Race, 11,* 205–232.

Ryan, R. A. (1981). Strengths of the American Indian family: State of the art. In F. Hoffman (Ed.), *The American Indian family: Strengths and stresses.* Isleta, NM: American Indian Social Research and Development Associates.

Rymer, R. (1993). *Genie: A scientific tragedy.* New York: HarperCollins.

Rymer, R. (2012, July). Vanishing voices. *National Geographic,* pp. 60–93.

Saad, L., & Jones, J. M. (2016, March 16). U.S. concern about global warming at eight-year high. Retieved from http://www.gallup.com/poll/190010/concern-global-warming-eight-year-high.aspx

Sabo, D. F., Miller, K. E., Farrell, M. P., Melnick, M. J., & Barnes, G. M. (1999). High school athletic participation, sexual behavior, and adolescent pregnancy: A regional study. *Journal of Adolescent Health, 25,* 597–613.

Sadker, D. M., & Sadker, M. P. (1997). *Failing at fairness: How our schools cheat girls.* New York: Scribner.

Sadker, D. M., & Zittleman, K. (2009). *Still failing at fairness: How gender bias cheats girls and boys in school and what we can do about it.* New York: Scribner.

Sadker, D. M., Zittleman, K., & Sadker, M. P. (2003). *Teachers, schools, and society.* New York: McGraw-Hill.

Saez, E. (2010). Striking it richer: The evolution of top incomes in the United States (updated with 2008 estimates). Retrieved from http://elsa.berkeley.edu/~saez/saez-UStopincomes-2008.pdf

Saez, E., & Zucman, G. (2014). *Wealth inequality in the United States since 1913: Evidence from capitalized income tax data* (NBER Working Paper 201625). Cambridge, MA: National Bureau of Economic Research. Retrieved from http://gabriel-zucman.eu/files/SaezZucman2014.pdf

Sagan, E. (1992). *The honey and the hemlock: Democracy and paranoia in ancient Athens and modern America.* New York: Basic Books.

Sagan, L. L. (1987). *The health of nations: True causes of sickness and well-being.* New York: Basic Book.

Sandoz, M. (1961). *These were the Sioux.* New York: Dell.

Sangweni, Y. (2017, February 17). The Way-too-short List of Black Oscar Winners. *Essence Magazine.* Retrieved from https://www.essence.com/celebrity/way-too-short-list-black-oscar-winners/

Sassen, S. (1991). *The global city: New York, London, Tokyo.* Princeton, NJ: Princeton University Press.

Sassen, S. (2000). *Cities in a world economy* (2nd ed.). Thousand Oaks, CA: Pine Forge.

Schaefer, D. R. (2011). Resource characteristics in social exchange networks: Implications for positional advantage. *Social Networks, 33,* 143–151.

Schaefer, R. T. (2009). *Race and ethnicity in the United States* (5th ed.). Upper Saddle River, NJ: Pearson Prentice Hall.

Schafft, K. A., Jensen, E. B., & Hinrichs, C. C. (2009). Food deserts and overweight schoolchildren: Evidence from Pennsylvania. *Rural Sociology, 74,* 153–177.

Scheff, T. J. (1988). Shame and conformity: The deference/emotion system. *American Sociological Review, 53,* 395–406.

Schegloff, E. (1990). On the organization of sequences as a source of "coherence" in talk-in-interaction. In B. Dorval (Ed.), *Conversational organization its development* (pp. 55–77). Norwood, NJ: Ablex.

Schegloff, E. (1991). Reflections on talk and social structure. In D. H. Zimmerman & D. Boden (Eds.), *Talk and social structure* (pp. 44–70). Cambridge: Polity Press.

Schlosser, E. (2012). *Fast food nation: The dark side of the all-American meal.* Boston: Houghton Mifflin Harcourt.

Schmidt, S. (2017). "The Wedding Industry in 2017 and Beyond." Marketresearch.com, May 16. Retrieved from https://blog.marketresearch.com/the-wedding-industry-in-2017-and-beyond

Schnaiberg, A., & Gould, K. A. (1994). *Environment and society: The enduring conflict.* New York: St. Martin's Press.

Schneider, D. M., & Gough, K. (1974). *Matrilineal kinship.* Berkeley: University of California Press.

Schneider, F., & Enste, D. (2002, March). Hiding in the shadows: The growth of the underground economy. *Journal of Economic Issues, 30.* Retrieved from http://www.imf.org/external/pubs/ft/issues/issues30/index.htm

Schneider, G. S., & Vozzella, L. (2018, June 4). How a reshaped Virginia legislature learned to love medicaid. *The Washington Post.* Retrieved from https://www.washingtonpost.com/local/virginia-politics/how-a-reshaped-virginia-legislature-learned-to-love-medicaid-expansion/2018/06/04/aeac0f50-65b9-11e8-99d2-0d678ec08c2f_story.html?utm_term=.d7e59e52d0dc

Schor, J. B. (1998). *The overspent American: Why we want what we don't need.* New York: Harper Perennial.

Schulte, B. (2015). Why parents should stop hoping their kids will get married. Retrieved from https://www.washingtonpost.com/news/wonk/wp/2015/05/17/why-parents-should-stop-expecting-their-kids-to-get-married/

Schuman, H., & Presser, S. (1981). *Questions and answers in attitude surveys: Experiments on question form, wording, and context.* New York: Academic Press.

Schwarz, H. (2015, April 28). There are 390,000 gay marriages in the U.S. The Supreme Court could quickly make it half a million. Retrieved from https://www.washing tonpost.com/news/the-fix/wp/2015/04/28/heres-how-many-gay-marriages-the-supreme-court-could-make-way-for/

Scott, J. (2005, May 16). Life at the top in America isn't just better, it's longer. *New York Times*. Retrieved from http://www.nytimes.com/2005/05/16/national/class/HEALTH-FINAL.html? pagewanted=all

Scott, W. R., & Meyer, J. W. (1994). *Institutional environments and organizations: Structural complexity and individualism*. Thousand Oaks, CA: Sage.

Seager, J. (2003). *The Penguin atlas of women in the world*. New York: Penguin Books.

Seaman, A. M. (2016, June 14). Robots may push surgeons to the sidelines – but not soon. *Washington Post*, p. E6.

Sebald, H. (2000). *Adolescence: A social psychological approach* (4th ed.). Englewood Cliffs, NJ: Prentice Hall.

Sellin, T. (1938). *Culture, conflict and crime*. New York: Social Science Research Council.

Semuels, A. (2015, March 27). The city that believed in desegregation. Retrieved from http://www.theatlantic.com/business/archive/2015/03/the-city-that-believed-in-desegregation/388532/

Senior, J. (2016, February 21). Review: In 'Evicted,' home is an elusive goal for America's poor. New York Times. Retrieved from http://www.nytimes.com/2016/02/22/books/evicted-book-review-mat-thew-desmond.html

Sennett, R. (1998). *The corrosion of character: The personal consequences of work in the new capitalism*. New York: Norton.

Sentencing Project. (2011). Felony disenfranchisement. Retrieved from http://www.sentencingproject.org/template/page.cfm? id=133

The Sentencing Project. (n.d.) Criminal Justice Facts. Retrieved from https://www.sentencingproject.org/criminal-justice-facts/

Severns, M. (2015, November 25). How Washington created some of the worst schools in America. Retrieved from http://www.politico.com/story/2015/11/how-washing ton-created-the-worst-schools-in-amer ica-215774

Shahani-Denning, C. (2003). Physical attractiveness bias in hiring: What is beautiful is good. Hempstead, NY: Hofstra University Office for Research and Sponsored Programs. Retrieved from http://www.hofstra.edu/pdf/orsp_shahani-denning_spring03.pdf

Shamir, R. (2011). Mind the gap: The commodification of corporate social responsibility. *Symbolic Interaction, 28*, 229–253. Retrieved from http://onlinelibrary.wiley.com/doi/10.1525/si.2005.28.2.229/abstract

Shattuck, R. (1980). *The forbidden experiment*. New York: Farrar, Straus and Giroux.

Sheinin, D., Thompson, K., McDonald, S. N., & Clement, S. (2016, January 31). New wave feminism. *Washington Post*, pp. A1, A17.

Sheldon, W. H. (1949). *Varieties of delinquent youth: An introduction to constitutional psychiatry*. New York: Harper.

Shepherd, K. (2016, July 5). Part time jobs and thrift: How unpaid interns in DC get by. Retrieved from http://www.nytimes.com/2016/07/06/us/part-time-jobs-and-thrift-how-unpaid-interns-in-dc-get-by.html?_r=0

Shinde, Kiran. (2007). Pilgrimage and the environment: Challenges in a pilgrimage centre. *Current Issues in Tourism, 10*. doi: 10.2167/cit259

Shipler, D. K. (2005). *The working poor: Invisible in America*. New York: Vintage Books.

Shore, R., & Shore B. (2009). *Reducing infant mortality* (KIDS COUNT Indicator Brief). Baltimore: Annie E. Casey Foundation. Retrieved from http://www.aecf.org/m/resourcedoc/AECF-KCReducingInfantMor tality-2009.pdf

Sifferlin, A. (2014, January 13). The doctor will Skype you now: Telemedicine apps aim to replace nonemergency visits. *Time*, p. 12.

Silva, E. B. (2001). *White supremacy and racism in the post–civil rights era*. Boulder, CO: Lynne Rienner.

Silver, N. (2015, May 1). The most diverse cities are often the most segregated. Retrieved from http://fivethir tyeight.com/features/the-most-diverse-cities-are-often-the-most-segregated/

Silverman, R. M. (2005). Community socioeconomic status and disparities in mortgage lending: An analysis of metropolitan Detroit. *Social Science Journal, 42*, 479–486.

Simmel, G. (1955). *Conflict and the web of group affiliations* (K. Wolf, Trans.). Glencoe, IL: Free Press.

Simon, J. L. (1977). *The economics of population growth*. Princeton, NJ: Princeton University Press.

Simon, J. L. (1981). *The ultimate resource*. Princeton, NJ: Princeton University Press.

Simon, J. L. (2000). *The great breakthrough and its cause*. Ann Arbor: University of Michigan Press.

Simpson, M. E., & Conklin, G. H. (1989). Socioeconomic development, suicide, and religion: A test of Durkheim's theory of religion and suicide. *Social Forces, 67*, 945–964.

Sinclair, U. (1995). *The jungle*. New York: Doubleday, Page. (Original work published 1906)

Singer, A. (2012). *Immigrant workers in the U.S. labor force*. Washington, DC: Brookings Institution. Retrieved from http://www.brookings.edu/research/papers/2012/03/15-immigrant-workers-singer#8

Singer, P. W. (2003). *Corporate warriors: The rise of the privatized military industry*. Ithaca, NY: Cornell University Press.

Sipes, L. A., Jr. (2012, February 6). Statistics on women offenders. Corrections.com. Retrieved from http://www.corrections.com/news/article/30166-statistics-on-women-offenders

Skinner, B. F. (1938). *The behavior of organisms.* Cambridge, MA: B. F. Skinner Foundation.

Skinner, B. F. (1953). *Science and human behavior.* Cambridge, MA: B. F. Skinner Foundation.

Sklair, L. (2002). *Globalization: Capitalism and its alternatives.* Oxford: Oxford University Press.

Skloot, R. (2017). *The immortal life of Henrietta Lacks.* New York: Broadway Books.

Skocpol, T. (1979). *States and social revolutions.* New York: Cambridge University Press.

Slaughter, A. M. (2015). *Unfinished business: Women men work family.* New York: Random House.

Slovak, K., & Singer, J. B. (2011). School social workers' perceptions of cyberbullying. *Children & Schools, 33,* 1–16.

Smelser, N. J. (1962). *The theory of collective behavior.* New York: Free Press.

Smith, B. (1990). Racism and women's studies. In G. Anzaldúa (Ed.), *Making face, making soul: Haciendo caras.* San Francisco: Aunt Lute Foundation.

Smith, D. (1987). *The everyday world as problematic: A feminist sociology.* Boston: Northeastern University Press.

Smith, D. (1990). *The conceptual practices of power: A feminist sociology of knowledge.* Boston: Northeastern University Press.

Smith, D. (2005). *Institutional ethnography: A sociology for people.* Walnut Creek, CA: AltaMira Press.

Smith, M. (2000). *American business and political power: Public opinions, elections, and democracy.* Chicago: University of Chicago.

Smith, P. K. (2009). *Obesity among poor Americans: Is public assistance the problem?* Nashville, TN: Vanderbilt University Press.

Smith, P. K., Mahdavi, J., Carvalho, M., Fisher, S., Russell, S., & Tippett, N. (2008). Cyberbullying: Its nature and its impact in secondary school pupils. *Journal of Child Psychology and Psychiatry, 49,* 376–385.

Smith, R. W. (2002). As old as history. In C. Rittner, J. K. Roth, & J. M. Smith (Eds.), *Will genocide ever end?* (pp. 31–34). St. Paul, MN: Paragon House.

Smith, S. (2001). *Allah's mountains: The battle for Chechnya.* London: I. B. Tauris.

Smith, S. C., Choueiti, M., & Pieper, K. (2014). *Race/Ethnicity in 600 popular films: Examination of on screen portrayals and behind the camera diversity.* Los Angeles, CA: Annenberg School for Communication and Journalism, University of Southern California. Retrieved from http://annenberg.usc.edu/pages/~/media/MDSCI/Racial%20Inequality%20in%20Film%202007-2013%20Final.ashx

Smith, T. W. (2002). Religious diversity in America: The emergence of Muslims, Buddhists, Hindus, and others. *Journal for the Scientific Study of Religion, 41,* 577–585.

Smith-Greenaway, E. (2013). Maternal reading skills and child mortality in Nigeria: A reassessment of why education matters. *Demography, 50,* 1551–1561.

Smock, P. J., Manning, W. D., & Porter, M. (2005). "Everything's there except money": How money shapes decisions to marry among cohabiting adults. *Journal of Marriage and Family, 67,* 680–696.

Social Security Administration. (2013). Social Security history. Retrieved from http://www.ssa.gov/history

Sorokowska, A., Sorokowski, P., Hilpert, P., Cantarero, K., Frackowiak, T., Ahmadi, K . . . John D. P, Jr. et al. (2017). Preferred Interpersonal Distances: A Global Comparison. *Journal of Cross-Cultural Psychology,* Vol. 48: 4, page(s): 577–592. Retrieved from https://doi.org/10.1177/0022022117698039https://doi.org/10.1177/0022022117698039.

Sparrow, R. (2005). Defending deaf culture: The case of cochlear implants. *Journal of Political Philosophy, 13,* 135–152.

Speed, B. (2016, June). How did different demographic groups vote in the EU referendum? Retrieved from http://www.new statesman.com/politics/staggers/2016/06/how-did-different-demographic-groups-vote-eu-referendum

Spicher, C. H., & Hudak, M. A. (1997, August). *Gender role portrayal on Saturday morning cartoons: An update.* Paper presented at the annual meeting of the American Psychological Association, Chicago.

Squires, G. D. (2003). Racial profiling, insurance style: Insurance redlining and the uneven development of metropolitan America. *Journal of Urban Affairs, 24,* 391–410.

Squires, G. D., Friedman S., & Saidat, C. E. (2002). Experiencing residential segregation: A contemporary study of Washington, DC. *Urban Affairs Review, 38,* 155–183.

Stark, R., & Bainbridge, W. S. (1996). *A theory of religion.* New York: Peter Lang. (Original work published 1987)

Steele, C. M., & Aronson, J. (1995). Stereotype threat and the intellectual test performance of African Americans. *Journal of Personality and Social Psychology, 69,* 797–811.

Stein, P. (2015, April 10). After 50 years, a D.C. store will close 'due to gentrification.' Retrieved from https://www.washingtonpost.com/news/local/wp/2015/04/10/after-50-years-a-d-c-store-will-close-due-to-gentrification/? tid=pm_local_pop_b

Steinbrook, R. (1988, January 29). AIDS summit delegates adopt a unanimous call for action. *Los Angeles Times.* Retrieved from http://articles.latimes.com/1988-01-29/news/mn-26467_1_aids-control

Stephens, T., Kamimura, A., Yamawaki, N., Bhattacharya, H., Mo, W., Birkholz, R., Makomenaw, A., & Olson, L. M. (2016). Rape myth acceptance among college students in the United States, Japan, and India. *SAGE Open, 6*(4), https://doi.org/10.1177/2158244016675015.

Stephenson, W. (2014, June 3). Welcome to West Port Arthur, Texas, ground zero in the fight for climate justice. Retrieved from https://www.thenation.com/article/wel come-west-port-arthur-texas-ground-zero-fight-climate-justice/

Stevenson, B. (2010). Beyond the classroom: Using Title IX to measure the return to high school sports. *Review of Economics & Statistics, 92,* 284–301.

Stiglitz, J. E. (2012). *The price of inequality: How today's divided society endangers our future.* New York: Norton.

Stokes, R., & Chevan, A. (1996). Female-headed families: Social and economic context of racial differences. *Journal of Urban Affairs, 8,* 245–268.

Stolle, D. (1998). Why do bowling and singing matter? Group characteristics, membership, and generalized trust. *Political Psychology, 19,* 497–525.

Stone, J. (2016). Brexit protest: Thousands march against Leave vote in London. Retrieved http://www.independent.co.uk/news/uk/politics/brexit-eu-referendum-protest-march-london-saturday-2-july-anti-result-live-a7111581.html

Straus, M. A., & Gelles, R. J. (Eds.). (1990). *Physical violence in American families: Risk factors and adaptations to violence in 8,145 families.* New Brunswick, NJ: Transaction.

Straus, M. A., Gelles, R. J., & Steinmetz, S. K. (1988). *Behind closed doors: Violence in the American family.* Newbury Park, CA: Sage.

Straus, M. A., Sugarman, D. B., & Giles-Sims, J. (1997). Spanking by parents and subsequent antisocial behavior of children. *Archives of Pediatrics and Adolescence, 151,* 761–767.

Straus, M. A., Sugarman, D. B., & Giles-Sims, J. (1997). Spanking by parents and subsequent antisocial behavior of children. *Archives of Pediatrics and Adolescence, 151,* 761–767.

Subrahmanyam, K., & Lin, G. (2007). Adolescents on the net: Internet use and well-being. *Adolescence, 42,* 659–677.

Sullivan, T. A., Warren, E., & Westbrook, J. (2000). *The fragile middle class: Americans in debt.* Binghamton, NY: Vail-Ballou Press.

Sumter, S. R., Vandenbosch, L., & Ligtenberg, L. (2017). Love me Tinder: Untangling emerging adults' motivations for using the dating application Tinder. *Telematics and Informatics, 34*(1), 67–78.

Supple, A. J., Ghazarian, S. R., Frabutt, J. M., Plunkett, S. W., & Sands, T. (2006). Contextual influences on Latino adolescent ethnic identity and academic outcomes. *Child Development, 77*(5), 1427–1433

Surette, R., Hansen, K., & Noble, G. (2009). Measuring media oriented terrorism. *Journal of Criminal Justice, 37,* 360–370.

Sutherland, E. H. (1983). *White collar crime: The uncut version.* New Haven, CT: Yale University Press. (Original work published 1949)

Sutter, J. (2016). We need a restroom revolution. Retrieved from http://www.cnn.com/2016/05/09/opinions/sutter-gender- neutral-restrooms/

Swiss, S., & Giller, J. E. (1993). Rape as a crime of war. *Journal of the American Medical Association, 270,* 619–622.

Tankersley, J. (2016, January 6). What top researchers discovered when they re-ran the numbers of income inequality. *Washington Post.* Retrieved from https://www.washingtonpost.com/news/wonk/wp/2016/01/06/what-top-researchers-discovered-when-they-re-ran-the-numbers-of-income-inequality/

Tarrow, S. G. (1994). *Power in movement: Social movements, collective action, and politics.* New York: Cambridge University Press.

Taub, A. (2016, June 21). Brexit, explained: 7 questions about what it means and why it matters. Retrieved from http://www.nytimes.com/2016/06/21/world/europe/brexit-britain-eu-explained.html?_r=0

Taylor, P., & Lopez, M. H. (2013, May 8). Six take-aways from the Census Bureau's voting report. Washington, DC: Pew Research Center. Retrieved from http://www.pewresearch.org/fact-tank/2013/05/08/six-take-aways-from-the-census-bureaus-voting-report/

Taylor, S., & Butcher, M. (2007). *Extra-legal defendant characteristics and mock juror ethnicity re-examined.* Paper presented at the annual conference of the British Psychological Society, York Conference Park, York, England.

Tews, M. J., Stafford, K., & Zhu, J. (2009). Beauty revisited: The impact of attractiveness, ability, and personality in the assessment of employment suitability. *International Journal of Selection and Assessment, 17,* 92–100.

Thomas, G. M., Meyer, J. W., Ramirez, F. O., & Boli, J. (1987). *Institutional structure: Constituting state, society, and the individual.* Newbury Park, CA: Sage.

Thomas, W. I., & Thomas, D. S. (1928). *The child in America: Behavior problems and programs.* New York: Knopf.

Thompson, T. L., & Scantlin, R. M. (2007). Gender representation in cartoons. In J. J. Arnett (Ed.), *Encyclopedia of children, adolescents, and the media* (pp. 141–144). Thousand Oaks, CA: Sage.

Thomson, J. (1874). The city of dreadful night. *National Reformer.*

Thorne, B. (1993). *Gender play: Girls and boys in school.* New Brunswick, NJ: Rutgers University Press.

Thornton, R. (1987). *American Indian holocaust and survival: A population history since 1492.* Norman: University of Oklahoma Press.

Tilly, C. (1975). *The formation of national states in Europe.* Princeton, NJ: Princeton University Press.

Tilly, C., & Tilly, L. (1994). Capitalist work and labor markets. In N. J. Smelser & R. Swedberg (Eds.), *The handbook of economic sociology.* Princeton, NJ: Princeton University Press.

Toennies, F. (1963). *Gemeinschaft and Gesellschaft.* New York: Harper & Row. (Original work published 1887)

Tolan, P., Gorman-Smith, D., & Henry, D. (2005). Family violence. *Annual Review of Psychology, 57,* 557–583.

Transparency International. (2011). Corruption perceptions index 2011. Retrieved from http://cpi.transparency.org/cpi2011/results

Trent, S., Williams, J., Thornton, C., & Shanahan, M. (2004). *Farming the sea, costing the earth: Why we must green the blue revolution.* London: Environmental Justice Foundation. Retrieved from http://www.ejfoundation.org/pdf/farming_the_sea_costing_the_earth.pdf

Trimble, L. B., & Kmec, J. A. (2011). The role of social networks in the job attainment process. *Sociology Compass, 5,* 165–178.

Troeltsch, E. (1931). *The social teaching of the Christian churches* (Vol. 1). New York: Macmillan.

Trudeau, M. (2009, February 5). More students turning illegally to "smart" drugs. National Public Radio. Retrieved from http://www.npr.org/templates/story/story.php? storyId=100254163

Truman, J. L., & Morgan, R. E. (2014, April). *Nonfatal domestic violence, 2003–2012.* U.S. Department of Justice, Office of Justice Programs, Bureau of Justice Statistics. Retrieved from http://www.bjs.gov/content/pub/pdf/ndv0312.pdf

Tumin, M. M. (1953). Some principles of stratification: A critical analysis. *American Sociological Review,* 18, 387–393.

Tumin, M. M. (1963). On inequality. *American Sociological Review,* 28, 19–26.

Tumin, M. M. (1985). *Social stratification: The forms and functions of inequality* (2nd ed.). Englewood Cliffs, NJ: Prentice Hall.

Turner, M. A., Popkin, S. J., & Rawlings, L. (2009). *Public housing and the legacy of segregation.* Washington, DC: Urban Institute Press.

Tyack, D., & Hansot, E. (1982). *Managers of virtue: Public school leadership in America, 1820–1980.* New York: Basic Books.

Tyman, K., Saylor, C., Taylor, L. A., & Comeaux, C. (2010). Comparing children and adolescents engaged in cyberbullying with matched peers. *Cyberpsychology, Behavior, and Social Networking, 13,* 195–199.

Uggen, C., Larsen, R., & Shannon, S. (2016). State-level Estimates of Felony Disenfranchisement, 2016. *The Sentencing Project.* Retrieved from https://www.sentencingproject.org/publications/6-million-lost-voters-state-level-estimates-felony-disenfranchisement-2016/

UNAIDS. (2017). UNAIDS Data 2017. Retrieved from http://www.unaids.org/sites/default/files/media_asset/20170720_Data_book_2017_en.pdf

Urban Institute. (2017). Nine Charts about Wealth Inequality in America. Retrieved from http://apps.urban.org/features/wealth-inequality-charts/

U.S. Bureau of Labor Statistics. (2013c, March 8). Table A-1. Employment status of the civilian population by sex and age. Retrieved from http://www.bls.gov/news.release/empsit.t01.htm

U.S. Bureau of Labor Statistics. (2013e). *Union members—2012* (USDL-13-0105). Washington, DC: U.S. Department of Labor. Retrieved from http://www.bls.gov/news.release/pdf/union2.pdf

U.S. Bureau of Labor Statistics. (2015b). May 2015 national occupational employment and wage estimates. Retrieved from http://www.bls.gov/oes/current/oes_nat.htm

U.S. Bureau of Labor Statistics. (2015c, December 15). Employment by major industry sector. Retrieved from http://www.bls.gov/emp/ep_table_201.htm

U.S. Census Bureau. (2011). American Indian and Alaska Native Heritage Month: November 2011. Retrieved from https://www.census.gov/newsroom/releases/archives/facts_for_features_special_editions/cb11-ff22.html

U.S. Census Bureau. (2012a). Characteristics of same-sex couple households: 2012. Retrieved from http://www.census.gov/hhes/samesex

U.S. Census Bureau. (2015). Families in poverty by type of family: 2013 and 2014. Retrieved from http://www.census.gov/library/publi cations/2015/demo/p60-252.html

U.S. Census Bureau. (2016, November 17). The Majority of Children Live with Two Parents, Census Bureau Reports. Retrieved from https://www.census.gov/newsroom/press-releases/2016/cb16-192.html

U.S. Department of Commerce, Economics and Statistics Administration. (2010, January). Middle class in America (prepared for the Office of the Vice President of the United States Middle Class Task Force). Washington, DC: Author. Retrieved from http://www.commerce.gov/sites/default/files/documents/migrated/Middle%20Class%20Report.pdf

U.S. Department of Defense. (2011). Dictionary of military terms. Retrieved from http://www.dtic.mil/doctrine/dod_dictionary

U.S. Department of Health and Human Services. (2010). Statistics and research: Child maltreatment 2010. Retrieved from http://www.acf.hhs.gov/programs/cb/research-data-technology/statistics-research/child-maltreatment

U.S. Department of Health and Human Services. (2013). *Healthy people 2020.* Washington, DC: Government Printing Office. Retrieved from http://healthypeople.gov/2020

U.S. Department of Labor, Wage and Hour Division. (2010). *Internship programs under the Fair Labor Standards Act.* Washington, DC: Author. Retrieved from http://www.dol.gov/whd/regs/compliance/whdfs71.pdf

U.S. Department of State. (2012a, September 28). Foreign terrorist organizations. Retrieved from http://www.state.gov/j/ct/rls/other/des/123085.htm

U.S. Elections Project. (2013, February 9). 2012 general election turnout rates. Retrieved from http://elections.gmu.edu/Turnout_2012G.html

U.S. Government Accountability Office. (2011). *Child maltreatment: Strengthening national data on child fatalities could aid in prevention* (GAO-11-599). Washington, DC: Government Printing Office. Retrieved from http://www.gao.gov/new.items/d11599.pdf

U.S. Government Accountability Office. (2016). K–12 Education: Better use of information could help agencies identify disparities and address racial discrimination (GAO-16-345). Washington, DC: Government Printing Office. Retrieved from http://www.gao.gov/products/GAO-16-345

U.S. Securities and Exchange Commission. (2015). SEC adopts rule for pay ratio disclosure. Washington, DC: Author. Retrieved from http://www.sec.gov/news/pressrelease/2015-160.html

Uchitelle, L. (2007). *The disposable American: Layoffs and their consequences.* New York: Vintage Books.

UNAIDS. (2010). *Women, girls and HIV fact sheet.* Geneva: Author.

UNAIDS, UNFPA, & UNIFEM. (2004). *Women and HIV/AIDS: Confronting the crisis.* New York: UNFPA. Retrieved from http://www.unfpa.org/hiv/women/docs/women_aids.pdf

United Nations Population Fund (UNFPA). (2012). Sex imbalances at birth: Current trends, consequences, and policy implications. Retrieved from https://www.unfpa.org/publications/sex-imbalances-birth

Ungar, S. (1992). The rise and (relative) decline of global warming as a social problem. *Sociological Quarterly, 33,* 483–501.

UNICEF. (2016, March). The AIDS epidemic continues to take a staggering toll, especially in sub-Saharan Africa. Retrieved from http://data.unicef.org/hiv-aids/global-trends.html

Union of International Associations. (2011). Historical overview of number of international organizations by type, 1909–2011. In *Yearbook of international organizations, 2011/2012 edition.* Herndon, VA: Brill.

United Nations. (1995). *Women's education and fertility behavior: Recent evidence from the demographic and health surveys.* New York: Author.

United Nations Educational, Scientific and Cultural Organization. (2010). *Education counts: Towards the millennium development goals.* Paris: Author. Retrieved from http://unesdoc.unesco.org/images/0019/001902/190214e.pdf

United Nations Environment Programme. (2009). *Recycling: From e-waste to resources.* Berlin: Author. Retrieved from http://www.unep.org/PDF/PressReleases/E-Waste_publication_screen_FINALVERSION-sml.pdf

University of Nevada, Reno. (2010, May 21). Books in home as important as parents' education in determining children's education level. *ScienceDaily.* Retrieved from http://www.sciencedaily.com/releases/2010/05/100520213116.htm

Urban, H. B. (2011). *The Church of Scientology: A history of a new religion.* Princeton, NJ: Princeton University Press.

U.S. Department of Justice Office of Public Affairs. (2017). Volkswagen AG Agrees to Plead Guilty and Pay $4.3 Billion in Criminal and Civil Penalties. Retrieved from https://www.justice.gov/opa/pr/volkswagen-ag-agrees-plead-guilty-and-pay-43-billion-criminal-and-civil-penalties-six

Valentine, G. (2006). Globalizing intimacy: The role of information and communication technologies in maintaining and creating relationships. *Women's Studies Quarterly, 34,* 365–393.

Van DeBosch, H., & Van Cleemput, K. (2008). Defining cyberbullying: A qualitative research into the perceptions of youngsters. *CyberPsychology & Behavior, 11,* 499–503.

VanGiezen, R., & Schwenk, A. E. (2001, Fall). Compensation before World War I through the Great Depression. *Compensation and Working Conditions* (U.S. Department of Labor, Bureau of Labor Statistics). Retrieved from http://www.bls.gov/opub/mlr/cwc/compensation-from-before-world-war-i-through-the-great-depression.pdf

Vasel, K. (2017). Couples are spending a record amount to get married. *CNN,* February 2. Retrieved from https://money.cnn.com/2017/02/02/pf/cost-of-wedding-budget-2016-the-knot/index.html

Vatz, S. (2013, May 24). Why America stopped making its own clothes. Retrieved from http://ww2.kqed.org/lowdown/2013/05/24/madeinamerica/

Veblen, T. (1899). *The theory of the leisure class.* New York: Macmillan.

Venator, J., & Reeves, R. V. (2015, July 7). *Unpaid internships: Support beams for the glass floor.* Washington, DC: Brookings Institution. Retrieved from http://www.brook ings.edu/blogs/social-mobility-memos/posts/2015/07/07-unpaid-internships-reeves

Venkatesh, S. A. (2008). *Off the books.* Cambridge, MA: Harvard University Press.

Ventura, S. J., & Hamilton, B. E. (2011). *U.S. teenage birth rate resumes decline* (NCHS Data Brief 58). Hyattsville, MD: National Center for Health Statistics. Retrieved from http://www.cdc.gov/nchs/data/databriefs/db58.pdf

Ventura, S. J., Curtin, S. C., Abma, J. C., & Henshaw S. K. (2012). Estimated pregnancy rates and rates of pregnancy outcomes for the United States, 1990–2008. *National Vital Statistics Reports, 60.* Retrieved from http://www.cdc.gov/nchs/data/nvsr60/nvsr60_07.pdf

Vinovskis, M. A. (1992). Schooling and poor children in 19th-century America. *American Behavioral Scientist, 35,* 313–331.

Vinovskis, M. A. (1995). *Education, society, and economic opportunity: A historical perspective on persistent problems.* New Haven, CT: Yale University Press.

Violence Policy Center. (2010). *Black homicide victimization in the United States: An analysis of 2007 homicide data.* Washington, DC: Author. Retrieved from http://www.vpc.org/studies/blackhomicide10.pdf

Volokh, E. (2014, May 9). 'Under God' in Pledge of Allegiance is constitutional, says Massachusetts's highest court. Retrieved from https://www.washingtonpost.com/news/volokh-conspiracy/wp/2014/05/09/under-god-in-pledge-of-allegiance-is-constitutional-says-massachusettss-highest-court/?utm_term=.e8d2e62509b1

Wacquant, L. (2002). From slavery to mass incarceration. *New Left Review, 13,* 40–61.

Waddell, K. (2017, January 23). *The Atlantic Monthly.* The Exhausting Work of Tallying America's Largest Protest. Retrieved from https://www.theatlantic.com/technology/archive/2017/01/womens-march-protest-count/514166/

Wade, C., & Tavris, C. (1997). *Psychology.* New York: Longman.

Wald, M. L. (2014, March 30). U.S. agency knew about G.M. flaw but did not act. *New York Times.* Retrieved from http://www.nytimes.com/2014/03/31/business/us-regulators-declined-full-inquiry-into-gm-ignition-flaws-memo-shows.html?_r=0

Wallace, K. (2015). Teens spend a 'mind-boggling' 9 hours a day using media, report says. Retrieved from http://www.cnn.com/2015/11/03/health/teens-tweens-media-screen-use-report/

Wallace, R. (1992). *They call him pastor: Married men in charge of Catholic parishes.* Mahwah, NJ: Paulist Press.

Wallenstein, A. (2014, February 10). How *The Walking Dead* breaks every rule we know about TV hits. *Variety.* Retrieved from http://variety.com/2014/tv/news/how-the-walking-dead-breaks-every-rule-we-know-about-tv-hits-1201089433

Wallerstein, I. (1974). *The modern world-system.* New York: Academic Press.

Wallerstein, I. (2011a). *The modern world-system I: Capitalist agriculture and the origins of the European world-economy in the sixteenth century.* Berkeley: University of California Press. (Original work published 1974)

Wallerstein, I. (2011b). *The modern world-system II: Mercantilism and the consolidation of the European world-economy, 1600–1750.* Berkeley: University of California Press. (Original work published 1980)

Wallerstein, I. (2011c). *The modern world-system III: The second era of great expansion of the capitalist world-economy, 1730–1840s.* Berkeley: University of California Press. (Original work published 1989)

Wallerstein, I. (2011d). *The modern world system IV: Centrist liberalism triumphant, 1789–1914.* Berkeley: University of California Press.

Walters, P. B., & James, R. J. (1992). Schooling for some: Child labor and school enrollment of Black and White children in the early 20th century South. *American Sociological Review, 57,* 635–650.

Wang, W., & Parker, K. (2011). *Women see value and benefits of college: Men lag on both fronts, survey finds.* Washington, DC: Pew Research Center. Retrieved from http://www.pewsocialtrends.org/files/2011/08/Gender-and-higher-ed-FNL-RPT.pdf

Wang, W., & Parker K. (2014, September 24). *Record number of Americans have never married.* Washington, DC: Pew Research Center. Retrieved from http://www.pewso cialtrends.org/2014/09/24/record-share-of-americans-have-never-married/

Ward, L. M. (2016). Media and sexualization: State of empirical research, 1995–2015. Retrieved from https://www.tandfonline.com/doi/abs/10.1080/00224499.2016.1142496https://www.tandfonline.com/doi/abs/10.1080/00224499.2016.1142496.

Warner, K., Molotch, H. L., & Lategola, A. (1992). *Growth of control: Inner workings and external effects.* Berkeley: University of California Press.

Warner, R. S. (1993). A work in progress toward a new paradigm for the sociological study of religion in the United States. *American Journal of Sociology, 98,* 1044–1093.

Warrick, J. (2016, May 28). ISIS fighters seem to be trying to sell sex slaves online. Retrieved from https://www.washingtonpost.com/world/national-security/isis-fighters-appear-to-be-trying-to-sell-their-sex-slaves-on-the-internet/2016/05/28/b3d1edea-24fe-11e6-9e7f-57890b612299_story.html

Washington, H. (2007). *Medical apartheid: The dark history of medical experimentation on Black Americans from colonial times to the present.* New York: Doubleday.

Wasserman, I. M. (1999). *African Americans and the criminal justice system: An explanation for changing patterns of Black male suicide.* Paper presented at the annual conference of the Midwest Sociological Society, Minneapolis.

Watson, J. B. (1924). *Behaviorism.* New York: People's Institute.

Weber, M. (1946). *From Max Weber: Essays in sociology* (H. Gerth & C. W. Mills, Eds. and Trans.). New York: Oxford University Press. (Original work published 1919)

Weber, M. (1963). *The sociology of religion.* Boston: Beacon Press. (Original work published 1921)

Weber, M. (1979). *Economy and society: An outline of interpretive sociology* (2 vols.). Berkeley: University of California Press. (Original work published 1921)

Weber, M. (2002). *The Protestant ethic and the spirit of capitalism, and other writings.* New York: Penguin Books. (Original work published 1904–1905)

Weber, M. (2012). *The theory of social and economic organization.* Eastford, CT: Martino Fine Books. (Original work published 1921)

Webster, H. (2014, July 14). What parents and kids should know about selfies. *U.S. News & World Report.* Retrieved from http://health.usnews.com/health-news/health-wellness/articles/2014/07/14/what-parents-and-kids-should-know-about-selfies

Weeks, J. R. (1988). The demography of Islamic nations. *Population Bulletin, 43,* 5–54.

Weidman, J. L. (Ed.). (1984). *Christian feminism: Visions of a new humanity.* New York: Harper & Row.

Weimann, G. (2004). *Cyberterrorism? How real is the threat?* Washington, DC: United States Institute of Peace. Retrieved from https://www.usip.org/sites/default/files/sr119.pdf

Weitz, R. (2012). *The sociology of health, illness, and health care: A critical approach* (6th ed.). Boston: Wadsworth Cengage Learning.

Weitzer, R., & Kubrin, C. E. (2009). Misogyny in rap music: A content analysis of prevalence and meanings. *Men and Masculinities, 12,* 3–29.

Wellman, B., & Hampton, K. (1999). Living networked on and offline. *Contemporary Sociology, 28,* 648–654.

Welsh, R. (1998). Severe parental punishment and aggression: The link between corporal punishment and delinquency. In I. A. Hyman & J. H. Wise (Eds.), *Corporal punishment in American education: Readings in history, practice and alternatives* (pp. 126–142). Philadelphia: Temple University Press.

Werdigier, J. (2010, June 4). J. P. Morgan penalized by regulator in Britain. *New York Times,* p. B3.

Werner, C. A. (2011). *The older population: 2010* (Census Brief C2010BR-09). Washington, DC: U.S. Census Bureau. Retrieved from http://www.census.gov/prod/cen2010/briefs/c2010br-09.pdf

Wertheimer, B. (1977). *We were there: The story of working women in America.* New York: Pantheon.

Western, B., & Pettit, B. (2010). Incarceration and social inequality. *Daedalus, 139,* 8–19.

Westoff, C. F., & Ryder, N. B. (1977). *The contraceptive revolution.* Princeton, NJ: Princeton University Press.

Weston, L. (2014, September 9). OECD: The U.S. Has Fallen Behind Other Countries in College Completion. *Business Insider.* Retrieved from https://www.businessinsider.com/r-us-falls-behind-in-college-completion-oecd-2014-9

Whalen, J., & Zimmerman, D. H. (1987). Sequential and institutional contexts in calls for help. *Social Psychology Quarterly, 50,* 172–185.

Whalen, J., & Zimmerman, D. H. (1990). Describing trouble: Epistemology in citizen calls to the police. *Language in Society, 19,* 465–492.

Whalen, J., Zimmerman, D. H., & Whalen, M. R. (1990). When words fail: A single case analysis. *Social Problems, 35,* 335–362.

Whelan, A., Wrigley, N., Warm, D., & Cannings, E. (2002). Life in a 'food desert.' *Urban Studies, 39,* 2083–2100.

Whyte, W. F. (1943). *Street corner society: The social structure of an Italian slum.* Chicago: University of Chicago Press.

Whyte, W. F. (1991). *Participatory action research.* Newbury Park, CA: Sage.

Williams, J. P., & Kirschner, D. (2012). Coordinated action in the massively multiplayer online game *World of Warcraft. Symbolic Interaction.* Advance online publication. Retrieved from http://onlinelibrary.wiley.com/doi/10.1002/j.1533-8665.2012.00022.x/abstract

Williams, R. M., Jr. (1970). *American society: A sociological interpretation* (3rd ed.). New York: Knopf.

Willis, P. (1990). *Common culture: Symbolic work at play in the everyday cultures of the young.* Boulder, CO: Westview Press.

Willoughby, T., Adachi, P. J. C., & Good, M. (2012). A longitudinal study of the association between violent video game play and aggression among adolescents. *Developmental Psychology, 48,* 1044–1057.

Wilson, B. J. (2008). Media and children's aggression, fear, and altruism. *The future of children,* 87–118.

Wilson, D. C., Moore, D. W., McKay, P. F., & Avery, D. R. (2008). Affirmative action programs for women and minorities: Expressed support affected by question order. *Public Opinion Quarterly, 72,* 514–522.

Wilson, T. P. (1991). Social structure and the sequential organization of interaction. In D. H. Zimmerman & D. Boden (Eds.), *Talk and social structure* (pp. 22–43). Cambridge: Polity Press.

Wilson, W. J. (1978). *The declining significance of race: Blacks and changing American institutions.* Chicago: University of Chicago Press.

Wilson, W. J. (1996). *When work disappears: The world of the new urban poor.* New York: Vintage Books.

Wilson, W. J. (2010). *More than just race: Being Black and poor in the inner city.* New York: Norton.

Wirth, L. (1928). *The ghetto.* Chicago: University of Chicago Press.

Wirth, L. (1938). Urbanism as a way of life. *American Journal of Sociology, 44,* 1–24.

Wirth, L. (1945). The problem of minority groups. In R. Linton (Ed.), *The science of man in the world crisis* (pp. 347–372). New York: Columbia University Press.

Woldoff, R. A. (2011). *White flight/Black flight: The dynamics of racial change in an American neighborhood.* Ithaca, NY: Cornell University Press.

Wolf, M. (2008). *Proust and the squid: The story and science of the reading brain.* New York: Harper Perennial.

Wolfe, A. (1977). *The limits of legitimacy.* New York: Free Press.

Wolff, E. N. (2017). *Household Wealth Trends in the United States, 1962 to 2016: Has Middle Class Wealth Recovered?* (No. w24085). National Bureau of Economic Research.

Wolfson, A. (2005, October 9). A hoax most cruel: Caller coaxed McDonald's managers into strip-searching a worker. *Courier Journal.* Retrieved from http://www.courier-journal.com/apps/pbcs.dll/article?AID=/20051009/NEWS01/510090392&loc=interstitialskip&nclick_check=1

Wonacott, M. E. (2002). Gold-collar workers (Eric Digest EDO-CE-02-234). Retrieved from http://www.calpro-online.org/ERIC/docs/dig234.pdf

Wood, G. S. (1993). *The radicalism of the American Revolution.* New York: Vintage Books.

Wood, R. G., Goesling, B., & Avellar, S. (2007). *The effects of marriage on health: A synthesis of recent research evidence.* Princeton, NJ: Mathematica Policy Research. Retrieved from http://www.mathematicampr.com/publi cations/PDFs/marriagehealth.pdf

Woodiwiss, M. (2000). Organized crime: The dumbing of discourse. In G. Mair & R. Tarling (Eds.), *British Criminology Conference: Selected proceedings* (Vol. 3). London: British Society of Criminology. Retrieved from http://www.britsoccrim.org/volume1/017.pdf

World Bank. (2015a). WDI 2016 maps. Retrieved from http://data.worldbank.org/products/wdi-maps

World Bank. (2015b). Improved sanitation facilities (% of population with access). Retrieved from http://data.worldbank.org/indicator/SH.STA.ACSN

World Economic Forum. (2017). More efficient and safer: How drones are changing the workforce. Retrieved from https://www.weforum.org/agenda/2017/06/more-efficient-and-safer-how-drones-are-changing-the-workplace/

World Health Organization. (2005). Widespread misunderstandings about chronic disease—and the reality. Retrieved from http://www.who.int/chp/chronic_disease_report/media/Factsheet2.pdf

Worldwatch Institute. (2004). *State of the world: Consumption by the numbers.* Washington, DC: Author.

Worldwatch Institute. (2010). *State of the world: Transforming cultures from consumerism to sustainability.* Washington, DC: Author.

Worldwatch Institute. (2011). *State of the world: Innovations that nourish the planet.* Washington, DC: Author.

Wright, E. O. (1994). *Interrogating inequality: Essays on class analysis, socialism and Marxism.* New York: Verso.

Wright, E. O. (1998). *Classes* (2nd ed.). New York: Verso.

Wright, J. P., Tibbetts, S. G., & Daigle, L. E. (2008). *Criminals in the making: Criminality across the life course.* Thousand Oaks, CA: Sage.

Wrong, D. H. (1959). The functional theory of stratification: Some neglected considerations. *American Sociological Review, 24,* 772–782.

Wuthnow, R. (1976). *The consciousness reformation.* Berkeley: University of California Press.

Wuthnow, R. (1978). *Experimentation in American religion: The new mysticisms and their implications for churches.* Berkeley: University of California Press.

Wuthnow, R. (1988). *The restructuring of American religion: Society and faith since World War II,* Princeton, NJ: Princeton University Press.

Wuthnow, R. (1989). *Communities of discourse: Ideology and social structure in the Reformation, the Enlightenment, and European socialism.* Cambridge, MA: Harvard University Press.

Wuthnow, R. (2007). *After the baby boomers.* Princeton, NJ: Princeton University.

Wyman, A. (1997). *Rural women teachers in the United States: A sourcebook.* Lanham, MD: Scarecrow Press.

Wyss, S. (2007). "This was my hell": The violence experienced by gender non-conforming youth in US high schools. *International Journal of Qualitative Studies in Education, 17,* 709–730.

Ybarra, M., Strasburger, V., and & Mitchell, K. (2014). Sexual media exposure, sexual behavior, and sexual violence victimization in adolescence. Retrieved from http://journals.sagepub.com/doi/abs/10.1177/0009922814538700http://journals.sagepub.com/doi/abs/10.1177/0009922814538700.

Yen, C.-F., Yen, J.-Y., & Ko, C.-H. (2010). Internet addiction: Ongoing research in Asia. *World Psychiatry, 9,* 97. Retrieved from http://www.ncbi.nlm.nih.gov/pmc/articles/PMC2911088

Young, S., & Martin, D. S. (2012, March 9). CNN readers share stories about secret army drug testing program. CNN. Retrieved from http://edition.cnn.com/2012/03/09/health/soldier-guinea-pigs/index.html

Zhou, C. (2018, April 30). 'The Crown' star Claire Foy gets $275,000 in back pay after gender wage gap dispute. *Newsweek.* Retrieved from https://www.newsweek.com/crowns-claire-foy-gets-275000-back-pay-after-gender-pay-gap-dispute-906045

Zhou, M. (2009). *Contemporary Chinese America: Immigration, ethnicity, and community transformation.* Philadelphia: Temple University Press.

Zimbardo, P. G. (1974). On "obedience to authority." *American Psychologist, 29,* 566–567.

Zimmerman, D. H. (1984). Talk and its occasion: The case of calling the police. In D. Schiffrin (Ed.), *Meaning, form, and use in context: Linguistic applications* (pp. 210–228). Washington, DC: Georgetown University Press.

Zimmerman, D. H. (1992). The interactional organization of calls for emergency assistance. In P. Drew & J. Heritage (Eds.), *Talk at work: Interaction in institutional settings* (pp. 418–469). New York: Cambridge University Press.

Zinn, M. B., Weber, L., Higginbotham, E., & Dill, B. T. (1986). The costs of exclusionary practices in women's studies. *Signs, 11,* 290–303.

Index